Fixed Income, Derivatives, Alternative Investments and Portfolio Management

CFA PROGRAM CURRICULUM • VOLUME IV

LEVEL I
2006

CFA
INSTITUTE

PEARSON

Custom
Publishing

Printed in the United States of America

10 9 8 7 6 5 4 3 2

ISBN 0-536-91634-9

2004160641

BK/JS

Please visit our web site at *www.pearsoncustom.com*

PEARSON CUSTOM PUBLISHING
75 Arlington Street, Suite 300, Boston, MA 02116
A Pearson Education Company

CONTENTS

ANALYSIS OF FIXED INCOME INVESTMENTS

The candidate should be able to demonstrate a working knowledge of the analysis of debt investments, including basic characteristics of bonds in alternative sectors, valuation tools, and factors that influence bond yields.

STUDY SESSION 14
FIXED INCOME INVESTMENTS: BASIC CONCEPTS

LEARNING OUTCOMES

Reading 62: Features of Debt Securities

The candidate should be able to:

a. explain the purposes of a bond's indenture, and describe affirmative and negative covenants;

b. describe the basic features of a bond (e.g., maturity, par value, coupon rate, provisions for redeeming bonds, currency denomination, options granted to the issuer or investor) the various coupon rate structures (e.g., zero-coupon bonds, step-up notes, deferred coupon bonds, floating-rate securities), the structure of floating-rate securities (i.e., the coupon formula, caps and floors), and define accrued interest, full price, and clean price;

c. explain the provisions for early retirement of debt, including call and refunding provisions, prepayment options, and sinking fund provisions, differentiate between a regular redemption price and a special redemption price, explain the importance of options embedded in a bond issue, and indicate whether such options benefit the issuer or the bondholder;

d. describe methods used by institutional investors in the bond market to finance the purchase of a security (i.e., margin buying and repurchase agreements).

Reading 63: Risks Associated with Investing in Bonds

The candidate should be able to:

a. explain the risks associated with investing in bonds (e.g., interest rate risk, yield curve risk, call and prepayment risk, reinvestment risk, credit risk, liquidity risk, exchange-rate risk, inflation risk, volatility risk, and event risk);

Note:
Candidates are responsible for the questions at the end of the readings.

3

b. identify the relationship among a bond's coupon rate, the yield required by the market, and the bond's price relative to par value (i.e., discount, premium, or equal to par);

c. explain how features of a bond (e.g., maturity, coupon, and embedded options) affect the bond's interest rate risk;

d. identify the relationship among the price of a callable bond, the price of an option-free bond, and the price of the embedded call option;

e. explain the interest rate risk of a floating-rate security and why such a security's price may differ from par value;

f. compute and interpret the duration of a bond, given the bond's change in price when interest rates change, the approximate percentage price change of a bond, given the bond's duration, the approximate new price of a bond, given the bond's duration and new yield level, explain why duration does not account for yield curve risk for a portfolio of bonds, and explain how the yield level impacts the interest rate risk of a bond;

g. explain the disadvantages of a callable or prepayable security to an investor;

h. identify the factors that affect the reinvestment risk of a security and explain why prepayable amortizing securities expose investors to greater reinvestment risk than nonamortizing securities;

i. describe the various forms of credit risk (i.e., default risk, credit spread risk, downgrade risk), and describe the meaning and role of credit ratings;

j. explain why liquidity risk might be important to investors even if they expect to hold a security to the maturity date;

k. describe the exchange rate risk an investor faces when a bond makes payments in a foreign currency;

l. describe inflation risk and explain why it exists;

m. explain how yield volatility affects the price of a bond with an embedded option and how changes in volatility affect the value of a callable bond and a putable bond;

n. describe the various forms of event risk (e.g., natural catastrophe, corporate takeover/restructuring, and regulatory risk) and the components of sovereign risk.

Reading 64: Overview of Bond Sectors and Instruments

The candidate should be able to:

a. describe the different types of international bonds (e.g., Eurobonds, global bonds, sovereign debt);

b. describe the types of securities issued by the U.S. Department of the Treasury (e.g. bills, notes, bonds, and inflation protection securities), differentiate between on-the-run and off-the-run Treasury securities, discuss how stripped Treasury securities are created, and distinguish between coupon strips and principal strips;

c. describe a mortgage-backed security, and explain the cash flows for a mortgage-backed security, define prepayments, and explain prepayment risk;

d. describe the types and characteristics of securities issued by federal agencies (including mortgage passthroughs and collateralized mortgage obligations);

e. state the motivation for creating a collateralized mortgage obligation, describe the types of securities issued by municipalities in the United States, and distinguish between tax-backed debt and revenue bonds;

f. describe insured bonds and prefunded bonds;

g. summarize the bankruptcy process and bondholder rights, explain the factors considered by rating agencies in assigning a credit rating to a corporate debt instrument, and describe secured debt, unsecured debt, and credit enhancements for corporate bonds;

h. distinguish between a corporate bond and a medium-term note;

i. describe a structured note, explain the motivation for their issuance by corporations, describe commercial paper, and distinguish between directly-placed paper and dealer-placed paper, and describe the salient features, uses and limitations of bank obligations (negotiable CDs and bankers acceptances);

j. define an asset-backed security, describe the role of a special purpose vehicle in an asset-backed securities transaction, state the motivation for a corporation to issue an asset-backed security, and describe the types of external credit enhancements for asset-backed securities;

k. describe collateralized debt obligations;

l. contrast the structures of the primary and secondary markets in bonds

Reading 65: Understanding Yield Spreads

The candidate should be able to:

a. identify the interest rate policy tools available to a central bank (such as the U.S. Federal Reserve or European Central Bank);

b. describe a yield curve and the different yield curve shapes observed and explain the basic theories of the term structure of interest rates (i.e., pure expectations theory, liquidity preference theory, and market segmentation theory) and describe the implications of each theory for the shape of the yield curve; explain the different types of yield spread measures (e.g., absolute yield spread, relative yield spread, yield ratio), and compute yield spread measures given the yields for two securities;

c. explain why investors may find a relative yield spread to be a better measure of yield spread than the absolute yield spread, distinguish between an intermarket and intramarket sector spread, and describe a credit spread and discuss the suggested relationship between credit spreads and the economic well being of the economy;

d. identify how embedded options affect yield spreads;

e. explain how the liquidity of an issue affects its yield spread relative to Treasury securities and relative to other issues that are comparable in all other ways except for liquidity and describe the relationships that are argued to exist among the size of an issue, liquidity, and yield spread;

f. compute the after-tax yield of a taxable security and the tax-equivalent yield of a tax-exempt security;

g. define LIBOR and why it is an important measure to funded investors who borrow short-term.

FEATURES OF DEBT SECURITIES

READING

62

LEARNING OUTCOMES

The candidate should be able to:

a. explain the purposes of a bond's indenture, and describe affirmative and negative covenants;

b. describe the basic features of a bond (e.g., maturity, par value, coupon rate, provisions for redeeming bonds, currency denomination, options granted to the issuer or investor) the various coupon rate structures (e.g., zero-coupon bonds, step-up notes, deferred coupon bonds, floating-rate securities), the structure of floating-rate securities (i.e., the coupon formula, caps and floors), and define accrued interest, full price, and clean price;

c. explain the provisions for early retirement of debt, including call and refunding provisions, prepayment options, and sinking fund provisions, differentiate between a regular redemption price and a special redemption price, explain the importance of options embedded in a bond issue, and indicate whether such options benefit the issuer or the bondholder;

d. describe methods used by institutional investors in the bond market to finance the purchase of a security (i.e., margin buying and repurchase agreements).

INTRODUCTION 1

In investment management, the most important decision made is the allocation of funds among asset classes. The two major asset classes are equities and fixed income securities. Other asset classes such as real estate, private equity, hedge funds, and commodities are referred to as "alternative asset classes." Our focus in this book is on one of the two major asset classes: fixed income securities.

While many people are intrigued by the exciting stories sometimes found with equities—who has not heard of someone who invested in the common

Fixed Income Analysis for the Chartered Financial Analyst® Program, Second Edition, by Frank J. Fabozzi. Reprinted with permission.

stock of a small company and earned enough to retire at a young age?—we will find in our study of fixed income securities that the multitude of possible structures opens a fascinating field of study. While frequently overshadowed by the media prominence of the equity market, fixed income securities play a critical role in the portfolios of individual and institutional investors.

In its simplest form, a fixed income security is a financial obligation of an entity that promises to pay a specified sum of money at specified future dates. The entity that promises to make the payment is called the **issuer** of the security. Some examples of issuers are central governments such as the U.S. government and the French government, government-related agencies of a central government such as Fannie Mae and Freddie Mac in the United States, a municipal government such as the state of New York in the United States and the city of Rio de Janeiro in Brazil, a corporation such as Coca Cola in the United States and Yorkshire Water in the United Kingdom, and supranational governments such as the World Bank.

Fixed income securities fall into two general categories: debt obligations and preferred stock. In the case of a debt obligation, the issuer is called the **borrower.** The investor who purchases such a fixed income security is said to be the **lender** or **creditor.** The promised payments that the issuer agrees to make at the specified dates consist of two components: interest and principal (principal represents repayment of funds borrowed) payments. Fixed income securities that are debt obligations include **bonds, mortgage-backed securities, asset-backed securities,** and **bank loans.**

In contrast to a fixed income security that represents a debt obligation, **preferred stock** represents an ownership interest in a corporation. Dividend payments are made to the preferred stockholder and represent a distribution of the corporation's profit. Unlike investors who own a corporation's common stock, investors who own the preferred stock can only realize a contractually fixed dividend payment. Moreover, the payments that must be made to preferred stockholders have priority over the payments that a corporation pays to common stockholders. In the case of the bankruptcy of a corporation, preferred stockholders are given preference over common stockholders. Consequently, preferred stock is a form of equity that has characteristics similar to bonds.

Prior to the 1980s, fixed income securities were simple investment products. Holding aside default by the issuer, the investor knew how long interest would be received and when the amount borrowed would be repaid. Moreover, most investors purchased these securities with the intent of holding them to their maturity date. Beginning in the 1980s, the fixed income world changed. First, fixed income securities became more complex. There are features in many fixed income securities that make it difficult to determine when the amount borrowed will be repaid and for how long interest will be received. For some securities it is difficult to determine the amount of interest that will be received. Second, the hold-to-maturity investor has been replaced by institutional investors who actively trade fixed income securities.

We will frequently use the terms "fixed income securities" and "bonds" interchangeably. In addition, we will use the term bonds generically at times to refer collectively to mortgage-backed securities, asset-backed securities, and bank loans.

In this reading we will look at the various features of fixed income securities and in the next reading we explain how those features affect the risks associated with investing in fixed income securities. The majority of our illustrations throughout this book use fixed income securities issued in the United States. While the U.S. fixed income market is the largest fixed income market in the world with a diversity of issuers and features, in recent years there has been significant growth in the fixed income markets of other countries as borrowers have shifted from funding via bank loans to the issuance of fixed income securities. This is a trend that is expected to continue.

INDENTURE AND COVENANTS 2

The promises of the issuer and the rights of the bondholders are set forth in great detail in a bond's **indenture.** Bondholders would have great difficulty in determining from time to time whether the issuer was keeping all the promises made in the indenture. This problem is resolved for the most part by bringing in a trustee as a third party to the bond or debt contract. The indenture identifies the trustee as a representative of the interests of the bondholders.

As part of the indenture, there are **affirmative covenants** and **negative covenants.** Affirmative covenants set forth activities that the borrower promises to do. The most common affirmative covenants are (1) to pay interest and principal on a timely basis, (2) to pay all taxes and other claims when due, (3) to maintain all properties used and useful in the borrower's business in good condition and working order, and (4) to submit periodic reports to a trustee stating that the borrower is in compliance with the loan agreement. Negative covenants set forth certain limitations and restrictions on the borrower's activities. The more common restrictive covenants are those that impose limitations on the borrower's ability to incur additional debt unless certain tests are satisfied.

MATURITY 3

The **term to maturity** of a bond is the number of years the debt is outstanding or the number of years remaining prior to final principal payment. The **maturity date** of a bond refers to the date that the debt will cease to exist, at which time the issuer will redeem the bond by paying the outstanding balance. The maturity date of a bond is always identified when describing a bond. For example, a description of a bond might state "due 12/1/2020."

The practice in the bond market is to refer to the "term to maturity" of a bond as simply its "maturity" or "term." As we explain below, there may be provisions in the indenture that allow either the issuer or bondholder to alter a bond's term to maturity.

Some market participants view bonds with a maturity between 1 and 5 years as "short-term." Bonds with a maturity between 5 and 12 years are viewed as "intermediate-term," and "long-term" bonds are those with a maturity of more than 12 years.

There are bonds of every maturity. Typically, the longest maturity is 30 years. However, Walt Disney Co. issued bonds in July 1993 with a maturity date of 7/15/2093, making them 100-year bonds at the time of issuance. In December 1993, the Tennessee Valley Authority issued bonds that mature on 12/15/2043, making them 50-year bonds at the time of issuance.

There are three reasons why the term to maturity of a bond is important:

Reason 1: Term to maturity indicates the time period over which the bondholder can expect to receive interest payments and the number of years before the principal will be paid in full.

Reason 2: The yield offered on a bond depends on the term to maturity. The relationship between the yield on a bond and maturity is called the **yield curve** and will be discussed in Reading 65.

Reason 3: The price of a bond will fluctuate over its life as interest rates in the market change. The price volatility of a bond is a function of its maturity (among other variables). More specifically, as explained in Reading 68, all other factors constant, the longer the maturity of a bond, the greater the price volatility resulting from a change in interest rates.

4 PAR VALUE

The **par value** of a bond is the amount that the issuer agrees to repay the bondholder at or by the maturity date. This amount is also referred to as the **principal value, face value, redemption value,** and **maturity value.** Bonds can have any par value.

Because bonds can have a different par value, the practice is to quote the price of a bond as a percentage of its par value. A value of "100" means 100% of par value. So, for example, if a bond has a par value of $1,000 and the issue is selling for $900, this bond would be said to be selling at 90. If a bond with a par value of $5,000 is selling for $5,500, the bond is said to be selling for 110.

When computing the dollar price of a bond in the United States, the bond must first be converted into a price per US$1 of par value. Then the price per $1 of par value is multiplied by the par value to get the dollar price. Here are examples of what the dollar price of a bond is, given the price quoted for the bond in the market, and the par amount involved in the transaction:[1]

Quoted price	Price per $1 of par value (rounded)	Par value	Dollar price
90½	0.9050	$1,000	905.00
102¾	1.0275	$5,000	5,137.50
70⅝	0.7063	$10,000	7,062.50
113¹¹⁄₃₂	1.1334	$100,000	113,343.75

[1] You may not be able to precisely reproduce some of the results in these readings. Rounding practices vary depending on the spreadsheet or calculator, and differences may be particularly noticeable in examples involving several interim calculations.

Notice that a bond may trade below or above its par value. When a bond trades below its par value, it is said to be **trading at a discount.** When a bond trades above its par value, it is said to be **trading at a premium.** The reason why a bond sells above or below its par value will be explained in Reading 63.

Practice Question 1

Given the information in the first and third columns for a U.S. investor, complete the information in the second and fourth columns:

Quoted price	Price per $1 of par value	Par value	Dollar price
103 1/4		$1,000	
70 1/8		$5,000	
87 5/16		$10,000	
117 3/32		$100,000	

COUPON RATE   5

The **coupon rate,** also called the **nominal rate,** is the interest rate that the issuer agrees to pay each year. The annual amount of the interest payment made to bondholders during the term of the bond is called the **coupon.** The coupon is determined by multiplying the coupon rate by the par value of the bond. That is,

coupon = coupon rate × par value

For example, a bond with an 8% coupon rate and a par value of $1,000 will pay annual interest of $80 (= $1,000 × 0.08).

When describing a bond of an issuer, the coupon rate is indicated along with the maturity date. For example, the expression "6s of 12/1/2020" means a bond with a 6% coupon rate maturing on 12/1/2020. The "s" after the coupon rate indicates "coupon series." In our example, it means the "6% coupon series."

In the United States, the usual practice is for the issuer to pay the coupon in two semiannual installments. Mortgage-backed securities and asset-backed securities typically pay interest monthly. For bonds issued in some markets outside the United States, coupon payments are made only once per year.

The coupon rate also affects the bond's price sensitivity to changes in market interest rates. As illustrated in Reading 63, all other factors constant, the higher the coupon rate, the less the price will change in response to a change in market interest rates.

5.1 Zero-Coupon Bonds

Not all bonds make periodic coupon payments. Bonds that are not contracted to make periodic coupon payments are called **zero-coupon bonds.** The holder of a zero-coupon bond realizes interest by buying the bond substantially below its par value (i.e., buying the bond at a discount). Interest is then paid at the maturity date, with the interest being the difference between the par value and the price paid for the bond. So, for example, if an investor purchases a zero-coupon bond for 70, the interest is 30. This is the difference between the par value (100) and the price paid (70). The reason behind the issuance of zero-coupon bonds is explained in Reading 63.

5.2 Step-Up Notes

There are securities that have a coupon rate that increases over time. These securities are called **step-up notes** because the coupon rate "steps up" over time. For example, a 5-year step-up note might have a coupon rate that is 5% for the first two years and 6% for the last three years. Or, the step-up note could call for a 5% coupon rate for the first two years, 5.5% for the third and fourth years, and 6% for the fifth year. When there is only one change (or step up), as in our first example, the issue is referred to as a **single step-up note.** When there is more than one change, as in our second example, the issue is referred to as a **multiple step-up note.**

An example of an actual multiple step-up note is a 5-year issue of the Student Loan Marketing Association (Sallie Mae) issued in May 1994. The coupon schedule is as follows:

6.05%	from	5/3/94	to	5/2/95
6.50%	from	5/3/95	to	5/2/96
7.00%	from	5/3/96	to	5/2/97
7.75%	from	5/3/97	to	5/2/98
8.50%	from	5/3/98	to	5/2/99

5.3 Deferred Coupon Bonds

There are bonds whose interest payments are deferred for a specified number of years. That is, there are no interest payments during for the deferred period. At the end of the deferred period, the issuer makes periodic interest payments until the bond matures. The interest payments that are made after the deferred period are higher than the interest payments that would have been made if the issuer had paid interest from the time the bond was issued. The higher interest payments after the deferred period are to compensate the bondholder for the lack of interest payments during the deferred period. These bonds are called **deferred coupon bonds.**

5.4 Floating-Rate Securities

The coupon rate on a bond need not be fixed over the bond's life. **Floating-rate securities,** sometimes called **variable-rate securities,** have coupon payments that reset periodically according to some reference rate. The typical formula (called the **coupon formula**) on certain determination dates when the coupon rate is reset is as follows:

coupon rate = reference rate × quoted margin

The **quoted margin** is the additional amount that the issuer agrees to pay above the reference rate. For example, suppose that the reference rate is the 1-month London interbank offered rate (LIBOR).[2] Suppose that the quoted margin is 100 basis points.[3] Then the coupon formula is:

coupon rate = 1-month LIBOR + 100 basis points

---

[2] LIBOR is the interest rate which major international banks offer each other on Eurodollar certificates of deposit.

[3] In the fixed income market, market participants refer to changes in interest rates or differences in interest rates in terms of basis points. A basis point is defined as 0.0001, or equivalently, 0.01%. Consequently, 100 basis points are equal to 1%. (In our example the coupon formula can be expressed as 1-month LIBOR + 1%.) A change in interest rates from, say, 5.0% to 6.2% means that there is a 1.2% change in rates or 120 basis points.

So, if 1-month LIBOR on the coupon reset date is 5%, the coupon rate is reset for that period at 6% (5% plus 100 basis points).

The quoted margin need not be a positive value. The quoted margin could be subtracted from the reference rate. For example, the reference rate could be the yield on a 5-year Treasury security and the coupon rate could reset every six months based on the following coupon formula:

coupon rate = 5-year Treasury yield − 90 basis points

So, if the 5-year Treasury yield is 7% on the coupon reset date, the coupon rate is 6.1% (7% minus 90 basis points).

It is important to understand the mechanics for the payment and the setting of the coupon rate. Suppose that a floater pays interest semiannually and further assume that the coupon reset date is today. Then, the coupon rate is determined via the coupon formula and this is the interest rate that the issuer agrees to pay at the next interest payment date six months from now.

A floater may have a restriction on the maximum coupon rate that will be paid at any reset date. The maximum coupon rate is called a **cap.** For example, suppose for a floater whose coupon formula is the 3-month Treasury bill rate plus 50 basis points, there is a cap of 9%. If the 3-month Treasury bill rate is 9% at a coupon reset date, then the coupon formula would give a coupon rate of 9.5%. However, the cap restricts the coupon rate to 9%. Thus, for our hypothetical floater, once the 3-month Treasury bill rate exceeds 8.5%, the coupon rate is capped at 9%. Because a cap restricts the coupon rate from increasing, a cap is an unattractive feature for the investor. In contrast, there could be a minimum coupon rate specified for a floater. The minimum coupon rate is called a **floor.** If the coupon formula produces a coupon rate that is below the floor, the floor rate is paid instead. Thus, a floor is an attractive feature for the investor. As we explain in Section 10, caps and floors are effectively embedded options.

Practice Question 2

A floating-rate issue has the following coupon formula:

6-month Treasury rate + 50 basis points with a cap of 7%

The coupon rate is set every six months. Suppose that at the reset date the 6-month Treasury rate is as shown below. Compute the coupon rate for the next 6-month period:

	6-month Treasury rate	Coupon rate
First reset date	5.5%	?
Second reset date	5.8%	?
Third reset date	6.3%	?
Fourth reset date	6.8%	?
Fifth reset date	7.3%	?
Sixth reset date	6.1%	?

While the reference rate for most floaters is an interest rate or an interest rate index, a wide variety of reference rates appear in coupon formulas. The coupon for a floater could be indexed to movements in foreign exchange rates, the price of a commodity (e.g., crude oil), the return on an equity index (e.g., the S&P 500), or movements in a bond index. In fact, through financial engineering, issuers have been able to structure floaters with almost any reference rate. In several countries, there are government bonds whose coupon formula is tied to an inflation index.

The U.S. Department of the Treasury in January 1997 began issuing inflation-adjusted securities. These issues are referred to as **Treasury Inflation Protection Securities** (TIPS). The reference rate for the coupon formula is the rate of inflation as measured by the Consumer Price Index for All Urban Consumers (i.e., CPI-U). (The mechanics of the payment of the coupon will be explained in Reading 64 where these securities are discussed.) Corporations and agencies in the United States issue **inflation-linked** (or **inflation-indexed**) **bonds.** For example, in February 1997, J.P. Morgan & Company issued a 15-year bond that pays the CPI plus 400 basis points. In the same month, the Federal Home Loan Bank issued a 5-year bond with a coupon rate equal to the CPI plus 315 basis points and a 10-year bond with a coupon rate equal to the CPI plus 337 basis points.

Typically, the coupon formula for a floater is such that the coupon rate increases when the reference rate increases, and decreases when the reference rate decreases. There are issues whose coupon rate moves in the opposite direction from the change in the reference rate. Such issues are called **inverse floaters** or **reverse floaters**.[4] It is not too difficult to understand why an investor would be interested in an inverse floater. It gives an investor who believes interest rates will decline the opportunity to obtain a higher coupon interest rate. The issuer isn't necessarily taking the opposite view because it can hedge the risk that interest rates will decline.[5]

The coupon formula for an inverse floater is:

$$\text{coupon rate} = K - L \times (\text{reference rate})$$

where K and L are values specified in the prospectus for the issue.

For example, suppose that for a particular inverse floater, K is 20% and L is 2. Then the coupon reset formula would be:

$$\text{coupon rate} = 20\% - 2 \times (\text{reference rate})$$

Suppose that the reference rate is the 3-month Treasury bill rate, then the coupon formula would be

$$\text{coupon rate} = 20\% - 2 \times (\text{3-month Treasury bill rate})$$

If at the coupon reset date the 3-month Treasury bill rate is 6%, the coupon rate for the next period is:

$$\text{coupon rate} = 20\% - 2 \times 6\% = 8\%$$

If at the next reset date the 3-month Treasury bill rate declines to 5%, the coupon rate increases to:

$$\text{coupon rate} = 20\% - 2 \times 5\% = 10\%$$

---

[4] In the agency, corporate, and municipal markets, inverse floaters are created as structured notes. We discuss structured notes in Reading 64. Inverse floaters in the mortgage-backed securities market are common and are created through a process that will be discussed at Level II (Chapter 10).

[5] The issuer hedges by using financial instruments known as derivatives, which we cover at Level II.

Notice that if the 3-month Treasury bill rate exceeds 10%, then the coupon formula would produce a negative coupon rate. To prevent this, there is a floor imposed on the coupon rate. There is also a cap on the inverse floater. This occurs if the 3-month Treasury bill rate is zero. In that unlikely event, the maximum coupon rate is 20% for our hypothetical inverse floater.

There is a wide range of coupon formulas that we will encounter in our study of fixed income securities.[6] These are discussed below. The reason why issuers have been able to create floating-rate securities with offbeat coupon formulas is due to derivative instruments. It is too early in our study of fixed income analysis and portfolio management to appreciate why some of these offbeat coupon formulas exist in the bond market. Suffice it to say that some of these offbeat coupon formulas allow the investor to take a view on either the movement of some interest rate (i.e., for speculating on an interest rate movement) or to reduce exposure to the risk of some interest rate movement (i.e., for interest rate risk management). The advantage to the issuer is that it can lower its cost of borrowing by creating offbeat coupon formulas for investors.[7] While it may seem that the issuer is taking the opposite position to the investor, this is not the case. What in fact happens is that the issuer can hedge its risk exposure by using derivative instruments so as to obtain the type of financing it seeks (i.e., fixed rate borrowing or floating rate borrowing). These offbeat coupon formulas are typically found in "structured notes," a form of medium-term note that will be discussed in Reading 64.

Practice Question 3

Identify the following types of bonds based on their coupon structures:

A. Coupon formula:

$$\text{coupon rate} = 32\% - 2 \times (\text{5-year Treasury rate})$$

B. Coupon structure:

Years 1-3	5.1%
Years 4-9	5.7%
Years 10-20	6.2%

C. Coupon formula:

$$\text{coupon rate} = \text{change in the consumer price index} + 3.1\%$$

5.5 Accrued Interest

Bond issuers do not disburse coupon interest payments every day. Instead, typically in the United States coupon interest is paid every six months. In some countries, interest is paid annually. For mortgage-backed and asset-backed securities, interest is usually paid monthly. The coupon payment is made to the bondholder

---

[6] In Reading 64, we will describe other types of floating-rate securities.

[7] These offbeat coupon bond formulas are actually created as a result of inquiries from clients of dealer firms. That is, a salesperson will be approached by fixed income portfolio managers requesting a structure be created that provides the exposure sought. The dealer firm will then notify the investment banking group of the dealer firm to contact potential issuers.

of record. Thus, if an investor sells a bond between coupon payments and the buyer holds it until the next coupon payment, then the entire coupon interest earned for the period will be paid to the buyer of the bond since the buyer will be the holder of record. The seller of the bond gives up the interest from the time of the last coupon payment to the time until the bond is sold. The amount of interest over this period that will be received by the buyer even though it was earned by the seller is called accrued interest. We will see how to calculate **accrued interest** in Reading 66.

In the United States and in many countries, the bond buyer must pay the bond seller the accrued interest. The amount that the buyer pays the seller is the agreed upon price for the bond plus accrued interest. This amount is called the **full price.** (Some market participants refer to this as the **dirty price.**) The agreed upon bond price without accrued interest is simply referred to as the **price.** (Some refer to it as the **clean price.**)

A bond in which the buyer must pay the seller accrued interest is said to be trading *cum-coupon* ("with coupon"). If the buyer forgoes the next coupon payment, the bond is said to be trading *ex-coupon* ("without coupon"). In the United States, bonds are always traded *cum-coupon.* There are bond markets outside the United States where bonds are traded *ex-coupon* for a certain period before the coupon payment date.

There are exceptions to the rule that the bond buyer must pay the bond seller accrued interest. The most important exception is when the issuer has not fulfilled its promise to make the periodic interest payments. In this case, the issuer is said to be in default. In such instances, the bond is sold without accrued interest and is said to be **traded flat.**

6 PROVISIONS FOR PAYING OFF BONDS

The issuer of a bond agrees to pay the principal by the stated maturity date. The issuer can agree to pay the entire amount borrowed in one lump sum payment at the maturity date. That is, the issuer is not required to make any principal repayments prior to the maturity date. Such bonds are said to have a **bullet maturity.** The bullet maturity structure has become the most common structure in the United States and Europe for both corporate and government issuers.

Fixed income securities backed by pools of loans (mortgage-backed securities and asset-backed securities) often have a schedule of partial principal payments. Such fixed income securities are said to be **amortizing securities.** For many loans, the payments are structured so that when the last loan payment is made, the entire amount owed is fully paid.

Another example of an amortizing feature is a bond that has a **sinking fund provision.** This provision for repayment of a bond may be designed to pay all of an issue by the maturity date, or it may be arranged to repay only a part of the total by the maturity date. We discuss this provision later in this section.

An issue may have a **call provision** granting the issuer an option to retire all or part of the issue prior to the stated maturity date. Some issues specify that the issuer must retire a predetermined amount of the issue periodically. Various types of call provisions are discussed below.

6.1 Call and Refunding Provisions

An issuer generally wants the right to retire a bond issue prior to the stated maturity date. The issuer recognizes that at some time in the future interest rates may fall sufficiently below the issue's coupon rate so that redeeming the issue and replacing it with another lower coupon rate issue would be economically beneficial. This right is a disadvantage to the bondholder since proceeds received must be reinvested in the lower interest rate issue. As a result, an issuer who wants to include this right as part of a bond offering must compensate the bondholder when the issue is sold by offering a higher coupon rate, or equivalently, accepting a lower price than if the right is not included.

The right of the issuer to retire the issue prior to the stated maturity date is referred to as a **call provision.** If an issuer exercises this right, the issuer is said to "call the bond." The price which the issuer must pay to retire the issue is referred to as the **call price** or **redemption price.**

When a bond is issued, typically the issuer may not call the bond for a number of years. That is, the issue is said to have a **deferred call.** The date at which the bond may first be called is referred to as the **first call date.** The first call date for the Walt Disney 7.55s due 7/15/2093 (the 100-year bonds) is 7/15/2023. For the 50-year Tennessee Valley Authority 6$\frac{7}{8}$s due 12/15/2043, the first call date is 12/15/2003.

Bonds can be called in whole (the entire issue) or in part (only a portion). When less than the entire issue is called, the certificates to be called are either selected randomly or on a **pro rata basis.** When bonds are selected randomly, a computer program is used to select the serial number of the bond certificates called. The serial numbers are then published in *The Wall Street Journal* and major metropolitan dailies. Pro rata redemption means that all bondholders of the issue will have the same percentage of their holdings redeemed (subject to the restrictions imposed on minimum denominations). Pro rata redemption is rare for publicly issued debt but is common for debt issues directly or privately placed with borrowers.

A bond issue that permits the issuer to call an issue prior to the stated maturity date is referred to as a **callable bond.** At one time, the callable bond structure was common for corporate bonds issued in the United States. However, since the mid-1990s, there has been significantly less issuance of callable bonds by corporate issuers of high credit quality. Instead, as noted above, the most popular structure is the bullet bond. In contrast, corporate issuers of low credit quality continue to issue callable bonds.[8] In Europe, historically the callable bond structure has not been as popular as in the United States.

6.1.1 Call (Redemption) Price

When the issuer exercises an option to call an issue, the call price can be either (1) fixed regardless of the call date, (2) based on a price specified in the call schedule, or (3) based on a make-whole premium provision. We will use various debt issues of Anheuser-Busch Companies to illustrate these three ways by which the call price is specified.

6.1.1.1 Single Call Price Regardless of Call Date

On 6/10/97, Anheuser-Busch Companies issued $250 million of notes with a coupon rate of 7.1% due June 15, 2007. The prospectus stated that:

> . . . The Notes will be redeemable at the option of the Company at any time on or after June 15, 2004, as set forth herein.

---

[8] As explained in Reading 63, high credit quality issuers are referred to as "investment grade" issuers and low credit quality issuers are referred to as "non-investment grade" issuers. The reason why high credit quality issuers have reduced their issuance of callable bonds while it is still the more popular structure for low credit quality issuers is explained at Level III.

The Notes will be redeemable at the option of the Company at any time on or after June 15, 2004, in whole or in part, upon not fewer than 30 days' nor more than 60 days' notice, at a Redemption Price equal to 100% of the principal amount thereof, together with accrued interest to the date fixed for redemption.

This issue had a deferred call of seven years at issuance and a first call date of June 15, 2004. Regardless of the call date, the call price is par plus accrued interest.

6.1.1.2 Call Price Based on Call Schedule

With a **call schedule,** the call price depends on when the issuer calls the issue. As an example of an issue with a call schedule, in July 1997 Anheuser-Busch Companies issued $250 million of debentures with a coupon rate of $7\frac{1}{8}$ due July 1, 2017. (We will see what a debt instrument referred to as a "debenture" is in Reading 64.) The provision dealing with the call feature of this issue states:

The Debentures will be redeemable at the option of the Company at any time on or after July 1, 2007, in whole or in part, upon not fewer than 30 days' nor more than 60 days' notice, at Redemption Prices equal to the percentages set forth below of the principal amount to be redeemed for the respective 12-month periods beginning July 1 of the years indicated, together in each case with accrued interest to the Redemption Date:

12 Months Beginning July 1	Redemption Price	12 Months Beginning July 1	Redemption Price
2007	103.026%	2012	101.513%
2008	102.723%	2013	101.210%
2009	102.421%	2014	100.908%
2010	102.118%	2015	100.605%
2011	101.816%	2016	100.303%

This issue had a deferred call of 10 years from the date of issuance, and the call price begins at a premium above par value and declines over time toward par value. Notice that regardless of when the issue is called, the issuer pays a premium above par value.

A second example of a call schedule is provided by the $150 million Anheuser-Busch Companies $8\frac{5}{8}$s due 12/1/2016 issued November 20, 1986. This issue had a 10-year deferred call (the first call date was December 1, 1996) and the following call schedule:

If redeemed during the 12 months beginning December 1:	Call price	If redeemed during the 12 months beginning December 1:	Call price
1996	104.313	2002	101.725
1997	103.881	2003	101.294
1998	103.450	2004	100.863
1999	103.019	2005	100.431
2000	102.588	2006 and thereafter	100.000
2001	102.156		

Notice that for this issue the call price begins at a premium but after 2006 the call price declines to par value. The first date at which an issue can be called at par value is the **first par call date.**

6.1.1.3 Call Price Based on Make-Whole Premium

A **make-whole premium provision,** also called a **yield-maintenance premium provision,** provides a formula for determining the premium that an issuer must pay to call an issue. The purpose of the make-whole premium is to protect the yield of those investors who purchased the issue at issuance. A make-whole premium does so by setting an amount for the premium, such that when added to the principal amount and reinvested at the redemption date in U.S. Treasury securities having the same remaining life, it would provide a yield equal to the original issue's yield. The premium plus the principal at which the issue is called is referred to as the **make-whole redemption price.**

We can use an Anheuser-Busch Companies issue to illustrate a make-whole premium provision—the $250 million 6% debentures due 11/1/2041 issued on 1/5/2001. The prospectus for this issue states:

> We may redeem the Debentures, in whole or in part, at our option at any time at a redemption price equal to the greater of (i) 100% of the principal amount of such Debentures and (ii) as determined by a Quotation Agent (as defined below), the sum of the present values of the remaining scheduled payments of principal and interest thereon (not including any portion of such payments of interest accrued as of the date of redemption) discounted to the date of redemption on a semi-annual basis (assuming a 360-day year consisting of twelve 30-day months) at the Adjusted Treasury Rate (as defined below) plus 25 basis points plus, in each case, accrued interest thereon to the date of redemption.

The prospectus defined what is meant by a "Quotation Agent" and the "Adjusted Treasury Rate." For our purposes here, it is not necessary to go into the definitions, only that there is some mechanism for determining a call price that reflects current market conditions as measured by the yield on Treasury securities. (Treasury securities are explained in Reading 64.)

6.1.2 Noncallable versus Nonrefundable Bonds

If a bond issue does not have any protection against early call, then it is said to be a **currently callable** issue. But most new bond issues, even if currently callable, usually have some restrictions against certain types of early redemption. The most common restriction is that of prohibiting the refunding of the bonds for a certain number of years or for the issue's life. Bonds that are noncallable for the issue's life are more common than bonds which are nonrefundable for life but otherwise callable.

Many investors are confused by the terms **noncallable** and **nonrefundable.** Call protection is much more robust than refunding protection. While there may be certain exceptions to absolute or complete call protection in some cases (such as sinking funds and the redemption of debt under certain mandatory provisions discussed later), call protection still provides greater assurance against premature and unwanted redemption than refunding protection. Refunding protection merely prevents redemption from certain sources, namely the proceeds of other debt issues sold at a lower cost of money. The holder is protected only if interest rates decline and the borrower can obtain lower-cost money to pay off the debt.

For example, Anheuser-Busch Companies issued on 6/23/88 10% coupon bonds due 7/1/2018. The issue was immediately callable. However, the prospectus specified in the call schedule that

> prior to July 1, 1998, the Company may not redeem any of the Debentures pursuant to such option, directly or indirectly, from or in anticipation of the proceeds of the issuance of any indebtedness for money borrowed having an interest cost of less than 10% per annum.

Thus, this Anheuser Busch bond issue could not be redeemed prior to July 2, 1998 if the company raised the money from a new issue with an interest cost lower than 10%. There is nothing to prevent the company from calling the bonds within the 10-year refunding protected period from debt sold at a higher rate (although the company normally wouldn't do so) or from money obtained through other means. And that is exactly what Anheuser Busch did. Between December 1993 and June 1994, it called $68.8 million of these relatively high-coupon bonds at 107.5% of par value (the call price) with funds from its general operations. This was permitted because funds from the company's general operations are viewed as more expensive than the interest cost of indebtedness. Thus, Anheuser-Busch was allowed to call this issue prior to July 1, 1998.

6.1.3 Regular versus Special Redemption Prices

The call prices for the various issues cited above are called the **regular redemption prices** or **general redemption prices.** Notice that the regular redemption prices are above par until the first par call date. There are also **special redemption prices** for bonds redeemed through the sinking fund and through other provisions, and the proceeds from the confiscation of property through the right of eminent domain or the forced sale or transfer of assets due to deregulation. The special redemption price is usually par value. Thus, there is an advantage to the issuer of being able to redeem an issue prior to the first par call date at the special redemption price (usually par) rather than at the regular redemption price.

A concern of an investor is that an issuer will use all means possible to maneuver a call so that the special redemption price applies. This is referred to as the **par call problem.** There have been ample examples, and subsequent litigation, where corporations have used the special redemption price and bondholders have challenged the use by the issuer.

6.2 Prepayments

For amortizing securities that are backed by loans that have a schedule of principal payments, individual borrowers typically have the option to pay off all or part of their loan prior to a scheduled principal payment date. Any principal payment prior to a scheduled principal payment date is called a **prepayment.** The right of borrowers to prepay principal is called a **prepayment option.**

Basically, the prepayment option is the same as a call option. However, unlike a call option, there is not a call price that depends on when the borrower pays off the issue. Typically, the price at which a loan is prepaid is par value. Prepayments will be discussed when mortgage-backed and asset-backed securities are discussed at Level II.

6.3 Sinking Fund Provision

An indenture may require the issuer to retire a specified portion of the issue each year. This is referred to as a **sinking fund requirement.** The alleged purpose of the sinking fund provision is to reduce credit risk (discussed in the next reading). This kind of provision for debt payment may be designed to retire all of a bond issue by the maturity date, or it may be designed to pay only a portion of the total indebtedness by the end of the term. If only a portion is paid, the remaining principal is called a **balloon maturity.**

An example of an issue with a sinking fund requirement that pays the entire principal by the maturity date is the $150 million Ingersoll Rand 7.20s issue due 6/1/2025. This bond, issued on 6/5/1995, has a sinking fund schedule that begins on 6/1/2006. Each year the issuer must retire $7.5 million.

Generally, the issuer may satisfy the sinking fund requirement by either (1) making a cash payment to the trustee equal to the par value of the bonds to be retired; the trustee then calls the bonds for redemption using a lottery, or (2) delivering to the trustee bonds purchased in the open market that have a total par value equal to the amount to be retired. If the bonds are retired using the first method, interest payments stop at the redemption date.

Usually, the periodic payments required for a sinking fund requirement are the same for each period. Selected issues may permit variable periodic payments, where payments change according to certain prescribed conditions set forth in the indenture. Many bond issue indentures include a provision that grants the issuer the option to retire more than the sinking fund requirement. This is referred to as an **accelerated sinking fund provision.** For example, the Anheuser Busch 8⅝s due 12/1/2016, whose call schedule was presented earlier, has a sinking fund requirement of $7.5 million each year beginning on 12/01/1997. The issuer is permitted to retire up to $15 million each year.

Usually the sinking fund call price is the par value if the bonds were originally sold at par. When issued at a premium, the call price generally starts at the issuance price and scales down to par as the issue approaches maturity.

CONVERSION PRIVILEGE   7

A **convertible bond** is an issue that grants the bondholder the right to convert the bond for a specified number of shares of common stock. Such a feature allows the bondholder to take advantage of favorable movements in the price of the issuer's common stock. An **exchangeable bond** allows the bondholder to exchange the issue for a specified number of shares of common stock of a corporation different from the issuer of the bond. These bonds are discussed at Level II where a framework for analyzing them is also provided.

PUT PROVISION   8

An issue with a **put provision** included in the indenture grants the bondholder the right to sell the issue back to the issuer at a specified price on designated dates. The specified price is called the **put price.** Typically, a bond is putable at par if it is issued at or close to par value. For a zero-coupon bond, the put price is below par.

The advantage of a put provision to the bondholder is that if, after the issuance date, market rates rise above the issue's coupon rate, the bondholder can force the issuer to redeem the bond at the put price and then reinvest the put bond proceeds at the prevailing higher rate.

9   CURRENCY DENOMINATION

The payments that the issuer makes to the bondholder can be in any currency. For bonds issued in the United States, the issuer typically makes coupon payments and principal repayments in U.S. dollars. However, there is nothing that forces the issuer to make payments in U.S. dollars. The indenture can specify that the issuer may make payments in some other specified currency.

An issue in which payments to bondholders are in U.S. dollars is called a **dollar-denominated issue.** A **nondollar-denominated issue** is one in which payments are not denominated in U.S. dollars. There are some issues whose coupon payments are in one currency and whose principal payment is in another currency. An issue with this characteristic is called a **dual-currency issue.**

10   EMBEDDED OPTIONS

As we have seen, it is common for a bond issue to include a provision in the indenture that gives the issuer and/or the bondholder an option to take some action against the other party. These options are referred to as **embedded options** to distinguish them from stand alone options (i.e., options that can be purchased on an exchange or in the over-the-counter market). They are referred to as embedded options because the option is embedded in the issue. In fact, there may be more than one embedded option in an issue.

10.1 Embedded Options Granted to Issuers

The most common embedded options that are granted to issuers or borrowers discussed in the previous section include:

▷ the right to call the issue
▷ the right of the underlying borrowers in a pool of loans to prepay principal above the scheduled principal payment
▷ the accelerated sinking fund provision
▷ the cap on a floater

The accelerated sinking fund provision is an embedded option because the issuer can call more than is necessary to meet the sinking fund requirement. An issuer usually takes this action when interest rates decline below the issue's coupon rate even if there are other restrictions in the issue that prevent the issue from being called.

The cap of a floater can be thought of as an option requiring no action by the issuer to take advantage of a rise in interest rates. Effectively, the bondholder has granted to the issuer the right not to pay more than the cap.

Notice that whether or not the first three options are exercised by the issuer or borrower depends on the level of interest rates prevailing in the market relative to the issue's coupon rate or the borrowing rate of the underlying loans (in the case of mortgage-backed and asset-backed securities). These options become more valuable when interest rates fall. The cap of a floater also depends on the prevailing level of rates. But here the option becomes more valuable when interest rates rise.

10.2 Embedded Options Granted to Bondholders

The most common embedded options granted to bondholders are:

- conversion privilege
- the right to put the issue
- floor on a floater

The value of the conversion privilege depends on the market price of the stock relative to the embedded purchase price held by the bondholder when exercising the conversion option. The put privilege benefits the bondholder if interest rates rise above the issue's coupon rate. While a cap on a floater benefits the issuer if interest rates rise, a floor benefits the bondholder if interest rates fall since it fixes a minimum coupon rate payable.

10.3 Importance of Understanding Embedded Options

At the outset of this reading, we stated that fixed income securities have become more complex. One reason for this increased complexity is that embedded options make it more difficult to project the cash flows of a security. The cash flow for a fixed income security is defined as its interest and the principal payments.

To value a fixed income security with embedded options, it is necessary to:

1. model the factors that determine whether or not an embedded option will be exercised over the life of the security, and
2. in the case of options granted to the issuer/borrower, model the behavior of issuers and borrowers to determine the conditions necessary for them to exercise an embedded option.

For example, consider a callable bond issued by a corporation. Projecting the cash flow requires (1) modeling interest rates (over the life of the security) at which the issuer can refund an issue and (2) developing a rule for determining the economic conditions necessary for the issuer to benefit from calling the issue. In the case of mortgage-backed or asset-backed securities, again it is necessary to model how interest rates will influence borrowers to refinance their loan over the life of the security. Models for valuing bonds with embedded options will be covered at Level II.

It cannot be overemphasized that embedded options affect not only the value of a bond but also the total return of a bond. In the next reading, the risks associated with the presence of an embedded option will be explained. What is critical to understand is that due to the presence of embedded options it is necessary to develop models of interest rate movements and rules for exercising embedded options. Any analysis of securities with embedded options exposes an investor to **modeling risk.** Modeling risk is the risk that the model analyzing embedded options produces the wrong value because the assumptions are not correct or the assumptions were not realized. This risk will become clearer at Level II when we describe models for valuing bonds with embedded options.

BORROWING FUNDS TO PURCHASE BONDS   11

At Level II, we will discuss investment strategies an investor uses to borrow funds to purchase securities. The expectation of the investor is that the return earned by investing in the securities purchased with the borrowed funds will exceed the borrowing cost. There are several sources of funds available to an investor when borrowing funds. When securities are purchased with borrowed funds, the most common practice is to use the securities as collateral for the loan. In such instances, the transaction is referred to as a **collateralized loan.** Two collateralized borrowing arrangements are used by investors—margin buying and repurchase agreements.

11.1 Margin Buying

In a **margin buying arrangement,** the funds borrowed to buy the securities are provided by the broker and the broker gets the money from a bank. The interest rate banks charge brokers for these transactions is called the call money rate (or broker loan rate). The broker charges the investor the call money rate plus a service charge. The broker is not free to lend as much as it wishes to the investor to buy securities. In the United States, the Securities and Exchange Act of 1934 prohibits brokers from lending more than a specified percentage of the market value of the securities. The 1934 Act gives the Board of Governors of the Federal Reserve the responsibility to set initial margin requirements, which it does under Regulations T and U. While margin buying is the most common collateralized borrowing arrangement for common stock investors (both retail investors and institutional investors) and retail bond investors (i.e., individual investors), it is not the common for institutional bond investors.

11.2 Repurchase Agreement

The collateralized borrowing arrangement used by institutional investors in the bond market is the repurchase agreement. We will discuss this arrangement in more detail at Level III. However, it is important to understand the basics of the repurchase agreement because it affects how some bonds in the market are valued.

A **repurchase agreement** is the sale of a security with a commitment by the seller to buy the same security back from the purchaser at a specified price at a designated future date. The **repurchase price** is the price at which the seller and the buyer agree that the seller will repurchase the security on a specified future date called the repurchase date. The difference between the repurchase price and the sale price is the dollar interest cost of the loan; based on the dollar interest cost, the sales price, and the length of the repurchase agreement, an implied interest rate can be computed. This implied interest rate is called the **repo rate.** The advantage to the investor of using this borrowing arrangement is that the interest rate is less than the cost of bank financing. When the term of the loan is one day, it is called an **overnight repo** (or overnight RP); a loan for more than one day is called a **term repo** (or term RP). As will be explained at Level III, there is not one repo rate. The rate varies from transaction to transaction depending on a variety of factors.

SUMMARY   12

- A fixed income security is a financial obligation of an entity (the issuer) who promises to pay a specified sum of money at specified future dates.

- Fixed income securities fall into two general categories: debt obligations and preferred stock.

- The promises of the issuer and the rights of the bondholders are set forth in the indenture.

- The par value (principal, face value, redemption value, or maturity value) of a bond is the amount that the issuer agrees to repay the bondholder at or by the maturity date.

- Bond prices are quoted as a percentage of par value, with par value equal to 100.

- The interest rate that the issuer agrees to pay each year is called the coupon rate; the coupon is the annual amount of the interest payment and is found by multiplying the par value by the coupon rate.

- Zero-coupon bonds do not make periodic coupon payments; the bondholder realizes interest at the maturity date equal to the difference between the maturity value and the price paid for the bond.

- A floating-rate security is an issue whose coupon rate resets periodically based on some formula; the typical coupon formula is some reference rate plus a quoted margin.

- A floating-rate security may have a cap, which sets the maximum coupon rate that will be paid, and/or a floor, which sets the minimum coupon rate that will be paid.

- A cap is a disadvantage to the bondholder while a floor is an advantage to the bondholder.

- A step-up note is a security whose coupon rate increases over time.

- Accrued interest is the amount of interest accrued since the last coupon payment; in the United States (as well as in many countries), the bond buyer must pay the bond seller the accrued interest.

- The full price (or dirty price) of a security is the agreed upon price plus accrued interest; the price (or clean price) is the agreed upon price without accrued interest.

- An amortizing security is a security for which there is a schedule for the repayment of principal.

- Many issues have a call provision granting the issuer an option to retire all or part of the issue prior to the stated maturity date.

- A call provision is an advantage to the issuer and a disadvantage to the bondholder.

- When a callable bond is issued, if the issuer cannot call the bond for a number of years, the bond is said to have a deferred call.

- The call or redemption price can be either fixed regardless of the call date or based on a call schedule or based on a make-whole premium provision.

- With a call schedule, the call price depends on when the issuer calls the issue.

- A make-whole premium provision sets forth a formula for determining the premium that the issuer must pay to call an issue, with the premium designed to protect the yield of those investors who purchased the issue.

- The call prices are regular or general redemption prices; there are special redemption prices for debt redeemed through the sinking fund and through other provisions.

- A currently callable bond is an issue that does not have any protection against early call.

- Most new bond issues, even if currently callable, usually have some restrictions against refunding.

- Call protection is much more absolute than refunding protection.

- For an amortizing security backed by a pool of loans, the underlying borrowers typically have the right to prepay the outstanding principal balance in whole or in part prior to the scheduled principal payment dates; this provision is called a prepayment option.

- A sinking fund provision requires that the issuer retire a specified portion of an issue each year.

- An accelerated sinking fund provision allows the issuer to retire more than the amount stipulated to satisfy the periodic sinking fund requirement.

- A putable bond is one in which the bondholder has the right to sell the issue back to the issuer at a specified price on designated dates.

- A convertible bond is an issue giving the bondholder the right to exchange the bond for a specified number of shares of common stock at a specified price.

- The presence of embedded options makes the valuation of fixed income securities complex and requires the modeling of interest rates and issuer/borrower behavior in order to project cash flows.

- An investor can borrow funds to purchase a security by using the security itself as collateral.

- There are two types of collateralized borrowing arrangements for purchasing securities: margin buying and repurchase agreements.

- Typically, institutional investors in the bond market do not finance the purchase of a security by buying on margin; rather, they use repurchase agreements.

- A repurchase agreement is the sale of a security with a commitment by the seller to repurchase the security from the buyer at the repurchase price on the repurchase date.

- The borrowing rate for a repurchase agreement is called the repo rate and while this rate is less than the cost of bank borrowing, it varies from transaction to transaction based on several factors.

PROBLEMS

1. Consider the following two bond issues.

Bond A: 5% 15-year bond
Bond B: 5% 30-year bond
Neither bond has an embedded option. Both bonds are trading in the market at the same yield.

Which bond will fluctuate *more* in price when interest rates change? Why?

2. Given the information in the first and third columns, complete the table in the second and fourth columns:

Quoted price	Price per $1 of par value	Par value	Dollar price
96¼		$1,000	
102⅞		$5,000	
109⁹⁄₁₆		$10,000	
68¹¹⁄₃₂		$100,000	

3. A floating-rate issue has the following coupon formula:

1-year Treasury rate + 30 basis points with a cap of 7% and a floor of 4.5%

The coupon rate is reset every year. Suppose that at the reset date the 1-year Treasury rate is as shown below. Compute the coupon rate for the next year:

	1-year Treasury rate	Coupon rate
First reset date	6.1%	?
Second reset date	6.5%	?
Third reset date	6.9%	?
Fourth reset date	6.8%	?
Fifth reset date	5.7%	?
Sixth reset date	5.0%	?
Seventh reset date	4.1%	?
Eighth reset date	3.9%	?
Ninth reset date	3.2%	?
Tenth reset date	4.4%	?

4. An excerpt from the prospectus of a $200 million issue by Becton, Dickinson and Company 7.15% Notes due October 1, 2009:

> *OPTIONAL REDEMPTION* We may, at our option, redeem all or any part of the notes. If we choose to do so, we will mail a notice of redemption to you not less than 30 days and not more than 60 days before this redemption occurs. The redemption price will be equal to the greater of: (1) 100% of the principal amount of the notes to be redeemed; and (2) the sum of the present values of the Remaining

Scheduled Payments on the notes, discounted to the redemption date on a semiannual basis, assuming a 360-day year consisting of twelve 30-day months, at the Treasury Rate plus 15 basis points.

A. What type of call provision is this?

B. What is the purpose of this type of call provision?

5. An excerpt from Cincinnati Gas & Electric Company's prospectus for the 10⅛% First Mortgage Bonds due in 2020 states,

> The Offered Bonds are redeemable (though CG&E does not contemplate doing so) prior to May 1, 1995 through the use of earnings, proceeds from the sale of equity securities and cash accumulations other than those resulting from a refunding operation such as hereinafter described. The Offered Bonds are not redeemable prior to May 1, 1995 as a part of, or in anticipation of, any refunding operation involving the incurring of indebtedness by CG&E having an effective interest cost (calculated to the second decimal place in accordance with generally accepted financial practice) of less than the effective interest cost of the Offered Bonds (similarly calculated) or through the operation of the Maintenance and Replacement Fund.

What does this excerpt tell the investor about provisions of this issuer to pay off this issue prior to the stated maturity date?

6. An assistant portfolio manager reviewed the prospectus of a bond that will be issued next week on January 1 of 2000. The call schedule for this $200 million, 7.75% coupon 20-year issue specifies the following:

> The Bonds will be redeemable at the option of the Company at any time in whole or in part, upon not fewer than 30 nor more than 60 days' notice, at the following redemption prices (which are expressed in percentages of principal amount) in each case together with accrued interest to the date fixed for redemption:
> If redeemed during the 12 months beginning January 1,

2000 through 2005	104.00%
2006 through 2010	103.00%
2011 through 2012	101.00%
from 2013 on	100.00%

> provided, however, that prior to January 1, 2006, the Company may not redeem any of the Bonds pursuant to such option, directly or indirectly, from or in anticipation of the proceeds of the issuance of any indebtedness for money borrowed having an interest cost of less than 7.75% per annum.

The prospectus further specifies that

> The Company will provide for the retirement by redemption of $10 million of the principal amount of the Bonds each of the years 2010 to and including 2019 at the principal amount thereof, together with accrued interest to the date of redemption. The Company may also provide for the redemption of up to an additional $10 million principal amount . . . annually, . . . such optional right being non-cumulative.

The assistant portfolio manager made the following statements to a client after reviewing this bond issue. Comment on each statement. *(When answering this question, remember that the assistant portfolio manager is responding to statements just before the bond is issued in 2000.)*

A. "My major concern is that if rates decline significantly in the next few years, this issue will be called by the Company in order to replace it with a bond issue with a coupon rate less than 7.75%."

B. "One major advantage of this issue is that if the Company redeems it *for any reason* in the first five years, investors are guaranteed receiving a price of 104, a premium over the initial offering price of 100."

C. "A beneficial feature of this issue is that it has a sinking fund provision that reduces the risk that the Company won't have enough funds to pay off the issue at the maturity date."

D. "A further attractive feature of this issue is that the Company can accelerate the payoff of the issue via the sinking fund provision, reducing the risk that funds will not be available at the maturity date."

E. In response to a client question about what will be the interest and principal that the client can depend on if $5 million par value of the issue is purchased, the assistant portfolio manager responded: "I can construct a schedule that shows every six months for the next 20 years the dollar amount of the interest and the principal repayment. It is quite simple to compute—basically it is just multiplying two numbers."

7. There are some securities that are backed by a pool of loans. These loans have a schedule of interest and principal payments every month and give each borrower whose loan is in the pool the right to payoff their respective loan at any time at par. Suppose that a portfolio manager purchased one of these securities. Can the portfolio manager rely on the schedule of interest and principal payments in determining the cash flow that will be generated by such securities (assuming no borrowers default)? Why or why not?

8. A. What is an accelerated sinking fund provision?

   B. Why can an accelerated sinking fund provision be viewed as an embedded call option granted to the issuer?

9. The importance of knowing the terms of bond issues, especially those relating to redemption, cannot be emphasized. Yet there have appeared numerous instances of investors, professional and others, who acknowledge that they don't read the documentation. For example, in an Augusts 14, 1983 article published in *The New York Times* titled "The Lessons of a Bond Failure," the following statements were attributed to some stockbrokers: "But brokers in the field say they often don't spend much time reading these [official] statements," "I can be honest and say I never look at the prospectus . . . . Generally, you don't have time to do that," and "There are some clients who really don't know what they buy . . . . They just say, 'That's a good interest rate.'"

Why it is important to understand the redemption features of a bond issue?

10. What is meant by an embedded option?

11. A. What is the typical arrangement used by institutional investors in the bond market: bank financing, margin buying, or repurchase agreement?

   B. What is the difference between a term repo and an overnight repo?

RISKS ASSOCIATED WITH INVESTING IN BONDS

LEARNING OUTCOMES

The candidate should be able to:

a. explain the risks associated with investing in bonds (e.g., interest rate risk, yield curve risk, call and prepayment risk, reinvestment risk, credit risk, liquidity risk, exchange-rate risk, inflation risk, volatility risk, and event risk);

b. identify the relationship among a bond's coupon rate, the yield required by the market, and the bond's price relative to par value (i.e., discount, premium, or equal to par);

c. explain how features of a bond (e.g., maturity, coupon, and embedded options) affect the bond's interest rate risk;

d. identify the relationship among the price of a callable bond, the price of an option-free bond, and the price of the embedded call option;

e. explain the interest rate risk of a floating-rate security and why such a security's price may differ from par value;

f. compute and interpret the duration of a bond, given the bond's change in price when interest rates change, the approximate percentage price change of a bond, given the bond's duration, the approximate new price of a bond, given the bond's duration and new yield level, explain why duration does not account for yield curve risk for a portfolio of bonds, and explain how the yield level impacts the interest rate risk of a bond;

g. explain the disadvantages of a callable or prepayable security to an investor;

h. identify the factors that affect the reinvestment risk of a security and explain why prepayable amortizing securities expose investors to greater reinvestment risk than nonamortizing securities;

i. describe the various forms of credit risk (i.e., default risk, credit spread risk, downgrade risk, and describe the meaning and role of credit ratings;

j. explain why liquidity risk might be important to investors even if they expect to hold a security to the maturity date;

k. describe the exchange rate risk an investor faces when a bond makes payments in a foreign currency;

l. describe inflation risk and explain why it exists;

Fixed Income Analysis for the Chartered Financial Analyst® Program, Second Edition, by Frank J. Fabozzi. Reprinted with permission.

m. explain how yield volatility affects the price of a bond with an embedded option and how changes in volatility affect the value of a callable bond and a putable bond;

n. describe the various forms of event risk (e.g., natural catastrophe, corporate takeover/restructuring, and regulatory risk) and the components of sovereign risk.

1 INTRODUCTION

Armed with an understanding of the basic features of bonds, we now turn to the risks associated with investing in bonds. These risks include:

- interest rate risk
- call and prepayment risk
- yield curve risk
- reinvestment risk
- credit risk
- liquidity risk
- exchange-rate risk
- volatility risk
- inflation or purchasing power risk
- event risk
- sovereign risk

We will see how features of a bond that we described in Reading 62—coupon rate, maturity, embedded options, and currency denomination—affect several of these risks.

2 INTEREST RATE RISK

As we will demonstrate in Reading 66, the price of a typical bond will change in the opposite direction to the change in interest rates or yields.[1] That is, when interest rates rise, a bond's price will fall; when interest rates fall, a bond's price will rise. For example, consider a 6% 20-year bond. If the yield investors require to buy this bond is 6%, the price of this bond would be $100. However, if the required yield increased to 6.5%, the price of this bond would decline to $94.4479. Thus, for a 50 basis point increase in yield, the bond's price declines by 5.55%. If, instead, the yield declines from 6% to 5.5%, the bond's price will rise by 6.02% to $106.0195.

Since the price of a bond fluctuates with market interest rates, the risk that an investor faces is that the price of a bond held in a portfolio will decline if market interest rates rise. This risk is referred to as **interest rate risk** and is the major risk faced by investors in the bond market.

---

[1] At this stage, we will use the terms interest rate and yield interchangeably. We'll see in Reading 67 how to compute a bond's yield.

2.1 Reason for the Inverse Relationship between Changes in Interest Rates and Price

The reason for this inverse relationship between a bond's price change and the change in interest rates (or change in market yields) is as follows. Suppose investor X purchases our hypothetical 6% coupon 20-year bond at a price equal to par (100). As explained in Reading 67, the yield for this bond is 6%. Suppose that immediately after the purchase of this bond two things happen. First, market interest rates rise to 6.50% so that if a bond issuer wishes to sell a bond priced at par, it will require a 6.50% coupon rate to attract investors to purchase the bond. Second, suppose investor X wants to sell the bond with a 6% coupon rate. In attempting to sell the bond, investor X would not find an investor who would be willing to pay par value for a bond with a coupon rate of 6%. The reason is that any investor who wanted to purchase this bond could obtain a similar 20-year bond with a coupon rate 50 basis points higher, 6.5%.

What can the investor do? The investor cannot force the issuer to change the coupon rate to 6.5%. Nor can the investor force the issuer to shorten the maturity of the bond to a point where a new investor might be willing to accept a 6% coupon rate. The only thing that the investor can do is adjust the price of the bond to a new price where a buyer would realize a yield of 6.5%. This means that the price would have to be adjusted down to a price below par. It turns out, the new price must be 94.4479.[2] While we assumed in our illustration an initial price of par value, the principle holds for any purchase price. Regardless of the price that an investor pays for a bond, an instantaneous increase in market interest rates will result in a decline in a bond's price.

Suppose that instead of a rise in market interest rates to 6.5%, interest rates decline to 5.5%. Investors would be more than happy to purchase the 6% coupon 20-year bond at par. However, investor X realizes that the market is only offering investors the opportunity to buy a similar bond at par with a coupon rate of 5.5%. Consequently, investor X will increase the price of the bond until it offers a yield of 5.5%. That price turns out to be 106.0195.

Let's summarize the important relationships suggested by our example.

1. A bond will trade at a price equal to par when the coupon rate is equal to the yield required by market. That is,[3]

   coupon rate = yield required by market → price = par value

2. A bond will trade at a price below par (sell at a discount) or above par (sell at a premium) if the coupon rate is different from the yield required by the market. Specifically,

   coupon rate < yield required by market → price < par value (discount)
   coupon rate > yield required by market → price > par value (premium)

3. The price of a bond changes in the opposite direction to the change in interest rates. So, for an instantaneous change in interest rates the following relationship holds:

   if interest rates increase → price of a bond decreases
   if interest rates decrease → price of a bond increases

---

[2] We'll see how to compute the price of a bond in Reading 67.

[3] The arrow symbol in the expressions means "therefore."

Practice Question 1

The following information is reported in the business section of a newspaper:

Issue	Coupon	Maturity	Yield required by market	Price
A	7⅜%	16 years	6.00%	114.02
B	6¾%	4 years	7.00%	99.14
C	0%	10 years	5.00%	102.10
D	5½%	20 years	5.90%	104.15
E	8½%	18 years	8.50%	100.00
F	4½%	6 years	4.00%	96.50
G	6¼%	25 years	6.25%	103.45

Which issues have an error in their reported price? (No calculations are required.)

2.2 Bond Features that Affect Interest Rate Risk

A bond's price sensitivity to changes in market interest rates (i.e., a bond's interest rate risk) depends on various features of the issue, such as maturity, coupon rate, and embedded options.[4] While we discuss these features in more detail in Reading 68, we provide a brief discussion below.

2.2.1 The Impact of Maturity

All other factors constant, *the longer the bond's maturity, the greater the bond's price sensitivity to changes in interest rates*. For example, we know that for a 6% 20-year bond selling to yield 6%, a rise in the yield required by investors to 6.5% will cause the bond's price to decline from 100 to 94.4479, a 5.55% price decline. Similarly for a 6% 5-year bond selling to yield 6%, the price is 100. A rise in the yield required by investors from 6% to 6.5% would decrease the price to 97.8944. The decline in the bond's price is only 2.11%.

2.2.2 The Impact of Coupon Rate

A property of a bond is that all other factors constant, *the lower the coupon rate, the greater the bond's price sensitivity to changes in interest rates*. For example, consider a 9% 20-year bond selling to yield 6%. The price of this bond would be 134.6722. If the yield required by investors increases by 50 basis points to 6.5%, the price of this bond would fall by 5.13% to 127.7605. This decline is less than the 5.55% decline for the 6% 20-year bond selling to yield 6% discussed above.

An implication is that zero-coupon bonds have greater price sensitivity to interest rate changes than same-maturity bonds bearing a coupon rate and trading at the same yield.

---

[4] Recall from Reading 62 that an embedded option is the feature in a bond issue that grants either the issuer or the investor an option. Examples include call option, put option, and conversion option.

2.2.3 The Impact of Embedded Options

In Reading 62, we discussed the various embedded options that may be included in a bond issue. As we continue our study of fixed income analysis, we will see that the value of a bond with embedded options will change depending on how the value of the embedded options changes when interest rates change. For example, we will see that as interest rates decline, the price of a callable bond may not increase as much as an otherwise option-free bond (that is, a bond with no embedded options).

For now, to understand why, let's decompose the price of a callable bond into two components, as shown below:

price of callable bond = price of option-free bond − price of embedded call option

The reason for subtracting the price of the embedded call option from the price of the option-free bond is that the call option is a benefit to the issuer and a disadvantage to the bondholder. This reduces the price of a callable bond relative to an option-free bond.

Now, when interest rates decline, the price of an option-free bond increases. However, the price of the embedded call option in a callable bond also increases because the call option becomes more valuable to the issuer. So, when interest rates decline both price components increase in value, *but* the change in the price of the callable bond depends on the relative price change between the two components. Typically, a decline in interest rates will result in an increase in the price of the callable bond but not by as much as the price change of an otherwise comparable option-free bond.

Similarly, when interest rates rise, the price of a callable bond will not fall as much as an otherwise option-free bond. The reason is that the price of the embedded call option declines. So, when interest rates rise, the price of the option-free bond declines but this is partially offset by the decrease in the price of the embedded call option component.

Practice Question 2

All of the issues below are option-free bonds and the yield required by the market for each bond is the same. Which issue has the greatest interest rate risk and which has the least interest rate risk?

Issue	Coupon rate	Maturity
1	5¼%	15 years
2	6½%	12 years
3	4¾%	20 years
4	8½%	10 years

(No calculations are required.)

2.3 The Impact of the Yield Level

Because of credit risk (discussed later), different bonds trade at different yields, even if they have the same coupon rate, maturity, and embedded options. How, then, holding other factors constant, does the level of interest rates affect a bond's price sensitivity to changes in interest rates? As it turns out, the higher a bond's yield, the lower the price sensitivity.

To see this, we compare a 6% 20-year bond initially selling at a yield of 6%, and a 6% 20-year bond initially selling at a yield of 10%. The former is initially at a price of 100, and the latter 65.68. Now, if the yield for both bonds increases by 100 basis points, the first bond trades down by 10.68 points (10.68%) to a price of 89.32. The second bond will trade down to a price of 59.88, for a price decline of only 5.80 points (or 8.83%). Thus, we see that the bond that trades at a lower yield is more volatile in both percentage price change and absolute price change, as long as the other bond characteristics are the same. An implication of this is that, for a given change in interest rates, price sensitivity is lower when the level of interest rates in the market is high, and price sensitivity is higher when the level of interest rates is low.

Practice Question 3

The following four issues are all option-free bonds; which has the greatest interest rate risk?

Issue	Coupon rate	Maturity	Required yield by the market
4	6½%	12 years	7.00%
5	7¼%	12 years	7.40%
6	6½%	12 years	7.20%
7	7½%	11 years	8.00%

(No calculations are required.)

2.4 Interest Rate Risk for Floating-Rate Securities

The change in the price of a fixed-rate coupon bond when market interest rates change is due to the fact that the bond's coupon rate differs from the prevailing market interest rate. For a floating-rate security, the coupon rate is reset periodically based on the prevailing market interest rate used as the reference rate plus a quoted margin. The quoted margin is set for the life of the security. The price of a floating-rate security will fluctuate depending on three factors.

First, the longer the time to the next coupon reset date, the greater the potential price fluctuation.[5] For example, consider a floating-rate security whose coupon resets every six months and suppose the coupon formula is the 6-month Treasury rate plus 20 basis points. Suppose that on the coupon reset date the 6-month Treasury rate is 5.8%. If on the day after the coupon reset date, the 6-month Treasury rate rises to 6.1%, this security is paying a 6-month coupon rate that is less than the prevailing 6-month rate for the next six months. The price of the security must decline to reflect this lower coupon rate. Suppose instead that the coupon resets every month at the 1-month Treasury rate and that this rate rises immediately after the coupon rate is reset. In this case, while the investor would be realizing a sub-market 1-month coupon rate, it is only for one month. The one month coupon bond's price decline will be less than the six month coupon bond's price decline.

The second reason why a floating-rate security's price will fluctuate is that the required margin that investors demand in the market changes. For example, consider once again the security whose coupon formula is the 6-month Treasury

---

[5] As explained in Reading 62, the coupon reset formula is set at the reset date at the beginning of the period but is not paid until the end of the period.

rate plus 20 basis points. If market conditions change such that investors want a margin of 30 basis points rather than 20 basis points, this security would be offering a coupon rate that is 10 basis points below the market rate. As a result, the security's price will decline.

Finally, a floating-rate security will typically have a cap. Once the coupon rate as specified by the coupon reset formula rises above the cap rate, the coupon will be set at the cap rate and the security will then offer a below-market coupon rate and its price will decline. In fact, once the cap is reached, the security's price will react much the same way to changes in market interest rates as that of a fixed-rate coupon security. This risk for a floating-rate security is called **cap risk.**

Practice Question 4

A floating-rate issue of NotReal.com has the following coupon formula that is reset every six months:

> coupon rate = 6-month Treasury rate + 120 basis points with a cap of 8.5%

A. Assume that subsequent to the issuance of this floater, the market wants a higher margin than 120 basis points for purchasing a similar issue to NotReal.com. What will happen to the price of this issue?

B. Assume that the 6-month Treasury rate was 4% when this issue was purchased by an investor but today the 6-month Treasury rate is 7%. What risk has increased since the time the NotReal.com issue was purchased?

2.5 Measuring Interest Rate Risk

Investors are interested in estimating the price sensitivity of a bond to changes in market interest rates. We will spend a good deal of time looking at how to quantify a bond's interest rate risk in Reading 68, as well as other readings. For now, let's see how we can get a rough idea of how to quantify the interest rate risk of a bond.

What we are interested in is a first approximation of how a bond's price will change when interest rates change. We can look at the price change in terms of (1) the percentage price change from the initial price or (2) the dollar price change from the initial price.

2.5.1 Approximate Percentage Price Change

The most straightforward way to calculate the percentage price change is to average the percentage price change resulting from an increase and a decrease in interest rates of the same number of basis points. For example, suppose that we are trying to estimate the sensitivity of the price of bond ABC that is currently selling for 90 to yield 6%. Now, suppose that interest rates increase by 25 basis points from 6% to 6.25%. The change in yield of 25 basis points is referred to as the "rate shock." The question is, how much will the price of bond ABC change due to this rate shock? To determine what the new price will be if the yield increases to 6.25%, *it is necessary to have a valuation model.* A valuation model provides an estimate of what the value of a bond will be for a given yield level. We will discuss the various models for valuing simple bonds and complex bonds with embedded options in later readings.

For now, we will assume that the valuation model tells us that the price of bond ABC will be 88 if the yield is 6.25%. This means that the price will decline by 2 points or 2.22% of the initial price of 90. If we divide the 2.22% by 25 basis points, the resulting number tells us that the price will decline by 0.0889% per 1 basis point change in yield.

Now suppose that the valuation model tells us that if yields decline from 6% to 5.75%, the price will increase to 92.7. This means that the price increases by 2.7 points or 3.00% of the initial price of 90. Dividing the 3.00% by 25 basis points indicates that the price will change by 0.1200% per 1 basis point change in yield.

We can average the two percentage price changes for a 1 basis point change in yield up and down. The average percentage price change is 0.1044% [= (0.0889% + 0.1200%)/2]. This means that for a 100 basis point change in yield, the average percentage price change is 10.44% (100 times 0.1044%).

A formula for estimating the *approximate percentage price change for a 100 basis point change in yield is:*

$$\frac{\text{price if yields decline} - \text{price if yields rise}}{2 \times (\text{initial price}) \times (\text{change in yield in decimal})}$$

In our illustration,

> price if yields decline by 25 basis points = 92.7
> price if yields rise by 25 basis points = 88.0
> initial price = 90
> change in yield in decimal = 0.0025

Substituting these values into the formula we obtain the approximate percentage price change for a 100 basis point change in yield to be:

$$\frac{92.7 - 88.0}{2 \times (90) \times (0.0025)} = 10.44$$

There is a special name given to this estimate of the percentage price change for a 100 basis point change in yield. It is called **duration.** As can be seen, duration is a measure of the price sensitivity of a bond to a change in yield. So, for example, if the duration of a bond is 10.44, this means that the approximate percentage price change if yields change by 100 basis points is 10.44%. For a 50 basis point change in yields, the approximate percentage price change is 5.22% (10.44% divided by 2). For a 25 basis point change in yield, the approximate percentage price change is 2.61% (10.44% divided by 4).

Notice that the approximate percentage is assumed to be the same for a rise and decline in yield. When we discuss the properties of the price volatility of a bond to changes in yield in Reading 68, we will see that the percentage price change is not symmetric and we will discuss the implication for using duration as a measure of interest rate risk. *It is important to note that the computed duration of a bond is only as good as the valuation model used to get the prices when the yield is shocked up and down. If the valuation model is unreliable, then the duration is a poor measure of the bond's price sensitivity to changes in yield.*

2.5.2 Approximating the Dollar Price Change

It is simple to move from duration, which measures the approximate percentage price change, to the approximate dollar price change of a position in a bond given the market value of the position and its duration. For example, consider again bond ABC with a duration of 10.44. Suppose that the market value of this bond is $5 million. Then for a 100 basis point change in yield, the approximate dollar price change is equal to 10.44% times $5 million, or $522,000. For a 50 basis point change in yield, the approximate dollar price change is $261,000; for a 25 basis point change in yield the approximate dollar price change is $130,500.

The approximate dollar price change for a 100 basis point change in yield is sometimes referred to as the **dollar duration.**

Practice Question 5

A. A portfolio manager wants to estimate the interest rate risk of a bond using duration. The current price of the bond is 106. A valuation model employed by the manager found that if interest rates decline by 25 basis points, the price will increase to 108.5 and if interest rates increase by the same number of basis points, the price will decline to 104. What is the duration of this bond?

B. If the portfolio manager purchased $10 million in market value of this bond, using duration to estimate the percentage price change, how much will the value of the bond change if interest rates change by 50 basis points?

YIELD CURVE RISK   3

We know that if interest rates or yields in the market change, the price of a bond will change. One of the factors that will affect how sensitive a bond's price is to changes in yield is the bond's maturity. A portfolio of bonds is a collection of bond issues typically with different maturities. So, when interest rates change, the price of each bond issue in the portfolio will change and the portfolio's value will change.

As you will see in Reading 65, there is not one interest rate or yield in the economy. There is a structure of interest rates. One important structure is the relationship between yield and maturity. The graphical depiction of this relationship is called the **yield curve.** As we will see in Reading 65, when interest rates change, they typically do not change by an equal number of basis points for all maturities.

For example, suppose that a $65 million portfolio contains the four bonds shown in Exhibit 63-1. All bonds are trading at a price equal to par value.

If we want to know how much the value of the portfolio changes if interest rates change, typically it is assumed that all yields change by the same number of basis points. Thus, if we wanted to know how sensitive the portfolio's value is to a 25 basis point change in yields, we would increase the yield of the four bond issues by 25 basis points, determine the new price of each bond, the market value of each bond, and the new value of the portfolio. Panel (a) of Exhibit 63-2 illustrates the 25 basis point increase in yield. For our hypothetical portfolio, the value of each bond issue changes as shown in panel (a) of Exhibit 63-1. The portfolio's value decreases by $1,759,003 from $65 million to $63,240,997.

Suppose that, instead of an equal basis point change in the yield for all maturities, the 20-year yield changes by 25 basis points, but the yields for the other maturities change as follows: (1) 2-year maturity changes by 10 basis points (from 5% to 5.1%), (2) 5-year maturity changes by 20 basis points (from 5.25% to 5.45%), and (3) 30-year maturity changes by 45 basis points (from 5.75% to 6.2%). Panel (b) of Exhibit 63-2 illustrates these yield changes. We will see at Level II that this type of movement (or shift) in the yield curve is referred to as a "steepening of the yield curve." For this type of yield curve shift, the portfolio's value is shown in panel (b) of Exhibit 63-1. The decline in the portfolio's value is $2,514,375 (from $65 million to $62,485,625).

EXHIBIT 63-1 Illustration of Yield Curve Risk Composition of the Portfolio

Bond	Coupon (%)	Maturity (years)	Yield (%)	Par value ($)
A	5.00	2	5.00	5,000,000
B	5.25	5	5.25	10,000,000
C	5.50	20	5.50	20,000,000
D	5.75	30	5.75	30,000,000
Total				65,000,000

A. Parallel Shift in Yield Curve of +25 Basis Points

Bond	Coupon (%)	Maturity (years)	Original Yield (%)	Par value ($)	New yield (%)	New bond price	Value
A	5.00	2	5.00	5,000,000	5.25	99.5312	4,976,558
B	5.25	5	5.25	10,000,000	5.50	98.9200	9,891,999
C	5.50	20	5.50	20,000,000	5.75	97.0514	19,410,274
D	5.75	30	5.75	30,000,000	6.00	96.5406	28,962,166
Total				65,000,000			63,240,997

B. Nonparallel Shift of the Yield Curve

Bond	Coupon (%)	Maturity (years)	Original Yield (%)	Par value ($)	New yield (%)	New bond price	Value
A	5.00	2	5.00	5,000,000	5.10	99.8121	4,990,606
B	5.25	5	5.25	10,000,000	5.45	99.1349	9,913,488
C	5.50	20	5.50	20,000,000	5.75	97.0514	19,410,274
D	5.75	30	5.75	30,000,000	6.20	93.9042	28,171,257
Total				65,000,000			62,485,625

C. Nonparallel Shift of the Yield Curve

Bond	Coupon (%)	Maturity (years)	Original Yield (%)	Par value ($)	New yield (%)	New bond price	Value
A	5.00	2	5.00	5,000,000	5.05	99.9060	4,995,300
B	5.25	5	5.25	10,000,000	5.40	99.3503	9,935,033
C	5.50	20	5.50	20,000,000	5.75	97.0514	19,410,274
D	5.75	30	5.75	30,000,000	6.10	95.2082	28,562,467
Total				65,000,000			62,903,074

Suppose, instead, that if the 20-year yield changes by 25 basis points, the yields for the other three maturities change as follows: (1) 2-year maturity changes by 5 basis points (from 5% to 5.05%), (2) 5-year maturity changes by 15 basis points (from 5.25% to 5.40%), and (3) 30-year maturity changes by 35 basis points (from 5.75%

to 6.1%). Panel (c) of Exhibit 63-2 illustrates this shift in yields. The new value for the portfolio based on this yield curve shift is shown in panel (c) of Exhibit 63-1. The decline in the portfolio's value is $2,096,926 (from $65 million to $62,903,074). The yield curve shift in the third illustration does not steepen as much as in the second, when the yield curve steepens considerably.

The point here is that portfolios have different exposures to how the yield curve shifts. This risk exposure is called **yield curve risk.** The implication is that any measure of interest rate risk that assumes that the interest rates changes by an equal number of basis points for all maturities (referred to as a "parallel yield curve shift") is only an approximation.

This applies to the duration concept that we discussed above. We stated that the duration for an individual bond is the approximate percentage change in price for a 100 basis point change in yield. A duration for a portfolio has the same meaning: it is the approximate percentage change in the portfolio's value for a 100 basis point change in the yield *for all maturities.*

EXHIBIT 63-2 A. Parallel Shift in Yield Curve of +25 Basis Points

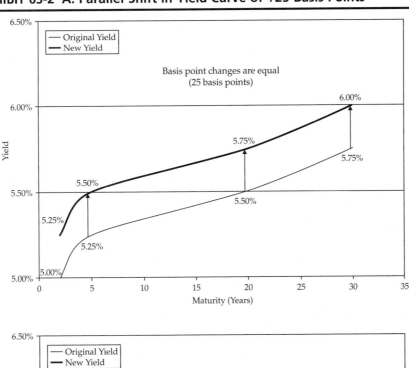

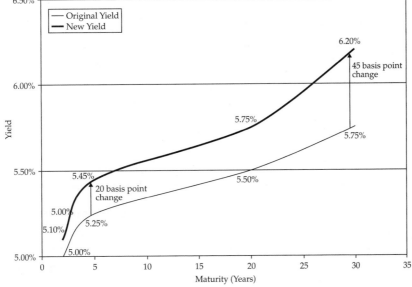

C. Another Nonparallel Shift of the Yield Curve

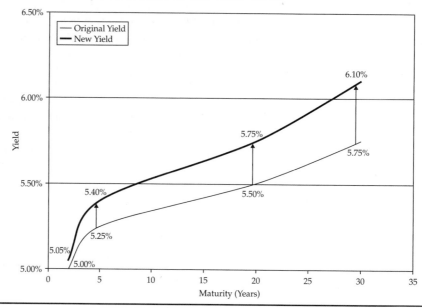

Because of the importance of yield curve risk, a good number of measures have been formulated to try to estimate the exposure of a portfolio to a non-parallel shift in the yield curve. We defer a discussion of these measures until Reading 68. However, we introduce one basic but popular approach here. In the next reading, we will see that the yield curve is a series of yields, one for each maturity. It is possible to determine the percentage change in the value of a portfolio if only one maturity's yield changes while the yield for all other maturities is unchanged. This is a form of duration called **rate duration,** where the word "rate" means the interest rate of a particular maturity. So, for example, suppose a portfolio consists of 40 bonds with different maturities. A "5-year rate duration" of 2 would mean that the portfolio's value will change by approximately 2% for a 100 basis point change in the 5-year yield, assuming all other rates do not change.

Practice Question 6

Suppose that an $85 million portfolio consists of the following five issues:

Issue	Maturity	Market value
1	2 years	$20 million
2	5 years	$15 million
3	10 years	$30 million
4	15 years	$5 million
5	28 years	$15 million

A. The portfolio manager computed a duration for the portfolio of 5. Approximately how much will the value of the portfolio decline if interest rates increase by 50 basis points?

B. In your calculation in part A, what is the assumption made in using the duration of 5 to compute the decline in the portfolio's value?

C. Suppose that the portfolio manager computes a 5-year rate duration of 1.5. What does that mean?

Consequently, in theory, there is not one rate duration but a rate duration for each maturity. In practice, a rate duration is not computed for all maturities. Instead, the rate duration is computed for several key maturities on the yield curve and this is referred to as **key rate duration.** Key rate duration is therefore simply the rate duration with respect to a change in a "key" maturity sector. Vendors of analytical systems report key rate durations for the maturities that in their view are the key maturity sectors. Key rate duration will be discussed further at Level II.

CALL AND PREPAYMENT RISK   4

As explained in Reading 62, a bond may include a provision that allows the issuer to retire, or call, all or part of the issue before the maturity date. From the investor's perspective, there are three disadvantages to call provisions:

Disadvantage 1: The cash flow pattern of a callable bond is not known with certainty because it is not known when the bond will be called.

Disadvantage 2: Because the issuer is likely to call the bonds when interest rates have declined below the bond's coupon rate, the investor is exposed to reinvestment risk, i.e., the investor will have to reinvest the proceeds when the bond is called at interest rates lower than the bond's coupon rate.

Disadvantage 3: The price appreciation potential of the bond will be reduced relative to an otherwise comparable option-free bond. (This is called **price compression.**)

We explained the third disadvantage in Section 2 when we discussed how the price of a callable bond may not rise as much as an otherwise comparable option-free bond when interest rates decline.

Because of these three disadvantages faced by the investor, a callable bond is said to expose the investor to **call risk.** The same disadvantages apply to mortgage-backed and asset-backed securities where the borrower can prepay principal prior to scheduled principal payment dates. This risk is referred to as **prepayment risk.**

REINVESTMENT RISK   5

Reinvestment risk is the risk that the proceeds received from the payment of interest and principal (i.e., scheduled payments, called proceeds, and principal prepayments) that are available for reinvestment must be reinvested at a lower interest rate than the security that generated the proceeds. We already saw how reinvestment risk is present when an investor purchases a callable or principal prepayable bond. When the issuer calls a bond, it is typically done to lower the issuer's interest expense because interest rates have declined after the bond is issued. The investor faces the problem of having to reinvest the called bond proceeds received from the issuer in a lower interest rate environment.

Reinvestment risk also occurs when an investor purchases a bond and relies on the yield of that bond as a measure of return. We have not yet explained how to compute the "yield" for a bond. When we do, it will be demonstrated that for the yield computed at the time of purchase to be realized, the investor must be able to reinvest any coupon payments at the computed yield. So, for example, if an investor purchases a 20-year bond with a yield of 6%, to realize the yield of 6%, every time a coupon interest payment is made, it is necessary to reinvest the payment at an interest rate of at 6% until maturity. So, it is assumed that the first coupon payment can be reinvested for the next 19.5 years at 6%; the second coupon payment can be reinvested for the next 19 years at 6%, and so on. The risk that the coupon payments will be reinvested at less than 6% is also reinvestment risk.

When dealing with amortizing securities (i.e., securities that repay principal periodically), reinvestment risk is even greater. Typically, amortizing securities pay interest and principal monthly and permit the borrower to prepay principal prior to schedule payment dates. Now the investor is more concerned with reinvestment risk due to principal prepayments usually resulting from a decline in interest rates, just as in the case of a callable bond. However, since payments are monthly, the investor has to make sure that the interest and principal can be reinvested at no less than the computed yield every month as opposed to semiannually.

This reinvestment risk for an amortizing security is important to understand. Too often it is said by some market participants that securities that pay both interest and principal monthly are advantageous because the investor has the opportunity to reinvest more frequently and to reinvest a larger amount (because principal is received) relative to a bond that pays only semiannual coupon payments. This is not the case in a declining interest rate environment, which will cause borrowers to accelerate their principal prepayments and force the investor to reinvest at lower interest rates.

With an understanding of reinvestment risk, we can now appreciate why zero-coupon bonds may be attractive to certain investors. Because there are no coupon payments to reinvest, there is no reinvestment risk. That is, zero-coupon bonds eliminate reinvestment risk. Elimination of reinvestment risk is important to some investors. That's the plus side of the risk equation. The minus side is that, as explained in Section 2, the lower the coupon rate the greater the interest rate risk for two bonds with the same maturity. Thus, zero-coupon bonds of a given maturity expose investors to the greatest interest rate risk.

Once we cover our basic analytical tools in later readings, we will see how to quantify a bond issue's reinvestment risk.

6   CREDIT RISK

An investor who lends funds by purchasing a bond issue is exposed to **credit risk.** There are three types of credit risk:

1. default risk
2. credit spread risk
3. downgrade risk

We discuss each type below.

6.1 Default Risk

Default risk is defined as the risk that the issuer will fail to satisfy the terms of the obligation with respect to the timely payment of interest and principal.

Studies have examined the probability of issuers defaulting. The percentage of a population of bonds that is expected to default is called the **default rate.** If a default occurs, this does not mean the investor loses the entire amount invested. An investor can expect to recover a certain percentage of the investment. This is called the **recovery rate.** Given the default rate and the recovery rate, the estimated expected loss due to a default can be computed. We will explain the findings of studies on default rates and recovery rates in Reading 64.

6.2 Credit Spread Risk

Even in the absence of default, an investor is concerned that the market value of a bond will decline and/or the price performance of a bond will be worse than that of other bonds. To understand this, recall that the price of a bond changes in the opposite direction to the change in the yield required by the market. Thus, if yields in the economy increase, the price of a bond declines, and vice versa.

As we will see in Reading 64, the yield on a bond is made up of two components: (1) the yield on a similar default-free bond issue and (2) a premium above the yield on a default-free bond issue necessary to compensate for the risks associated with the bond. The risk premium is referred to as a **yield spread.** In the United States, Treasury issues are the benchmark yields because they are believed to be default free, they are highly liquid, and they are not callable (with the exception of some old issues). The part of the risk premium or yield spread attributable to default risk is called the **credit spread.**

The price performance of a non-Treasury bond issue and the return over some time period will depend on how the credit spread changes. If the credit spread increases, investors say that the spread has "widened" and the market price of the bond issue will decline (assuming U.S. Treasury rates have not changed). The risk that an issuer's debt obligation will decline due to an increase in the credit spread is called **credit spread risk.**

This risk exists for an individual issue, for issues in a particular industry or economic sector, and for all non-Treasury issues in the economy. For example, in general during economic recessions, investors are concerned that issuers will face a decline in cash flows that would be used to service their bond obligations. As a result, the credit spread tends to widen for U.S. non-Treasury issuers and the prices of all such issues throughout the economy will decline.

6.3 Downgrade Risk

While portfolio managers seek to allocate funds among different sectors of the bond market to capitalize on anticipated changes in credit spreads, an analyst investigating the credit quality of an individual issue is concerned with the prospects of the credit spread increasing for that particular issue. But how does the analyst assess whether he or she believes the market will change the credit spread associated with an individual issue?

One tool investors use to gauge the default risk of an issue is the credit ratings assigned to issues by rating companies, popularly referred to as **rating agencies.** There are three rating agencies in the United States: Moody's Investors Service, Inc., Standard & Poor's Corporation, and Fitch Ratings.

A **credit rating** is an indicator of the potential default risk associated with a particular bond issue or issuer. It represents in a simplistic way the credit rating agency's assessment of an issuer's ability to meet the payment of principal and interest in accordance with the terms of the indenture. Credit rating symbols or characters are uncomplicated representations of more complex ideas. In effect, they are summary opinions. Exhibit 63-3 identifies the ratings assigned by Moody's, S&P, and Fitch for bonds and the meaning of each rating.

In all systems, the term **high grade** means low credit risk, or conversely, a high probability of receiving future payments is promised by the issuer. The highest-grade bonds are designated by Moody's by the symbol Aaa, and by S&P and Fitch by the symbol AAA. The next highest grade is denoted by the symbol Aa (Moody's) or AA (S&P and Fitch); for the third grade, all three rating companies use A. The next three grades are Baa or BBB, Ba or BB, and B, respectively. There are also C grades. Moody's uses 1, 2, or 3 to provide a narrower credit quality breakdown within each class, and S&P and Fitch use plus and minus signs for the same purpose.

Bonds rated triple A (AAA or Aaa) are said to be **prime grade;** double A (AA or Aa) are of **high quality grade;** single A issues are called **upper medium grade,** and triple B are **lower medium grade.** Lower-rated bonds are said to have **speculative grade** elements or to be **distinctly speculative grade.**

Bond issues that are assigned a rating in the top four categories (that is, AAA, AA, A, and BBB) are referred to as **investment-grade bonds.** Issues that carry a rating below the top four categories are referred to as **non-investment-grade bonds** or **speculative bonds,** or more popularly as **high yield bonds** or **junk bonds.** Thus, the bond market can be divided into two sectors: the investment grade and non-investment grade markets as summarized below:

Investment grade bonds	AAA, AA, A, and BBB
Non-investment grade bonds (speculative/high yield)	Below BBB

Once a credit rating is assigned to a debt obligation, a rating agency monitors the credit quality of the issuer and can reassign a different credit rating. An improvement in the credit quality of an issue or issuer is rewarded with a better credit rating, referred to as an **upgrade;** a deterioration in the credit rating of an issue or issuer is penalized by the assignment of an inferior credit rating, referred to as a **downgrade.** An unanticipated downgrading of an issue or issuer increases the credit spread and results in a decline in the price of the issue or the issuer's bonds. This risk is referred to as **downgrade risk** and is closely related to credit spread risk.

As we have explained, the credit rating is a measure of potential default risk. An analyst must be aware of how rating agencies gauge default risk for purposes of assigning ratings in order to understand the other aspects of credit risk. The agencies' assessment of potential default drives downgrade risk, and in turn, both default potential and credit rating changes drive credit spread risk.

A popular tool used by managers to gauge the prospects of an issue being downgraded or upgraded is a **rating transition matrix.** This is simply a table constructed by the rating agencies that shows the percentage of issues that were downgraded or upgraded in a given time period. So, the table can be used to approximate downgrade risk and default risk.

EXHIBIT 63-3 Bond Rating Symbols and Summary Description

Moody's	S&P	Fitch	Summary Description
Investment Grade—High Credit Worthiness			
Aaa	AAA	AAA	Gilt edge, prime, maximum safety
Aa1	AA+	AA+	
Aa2	AA	AA	High-grade, high-credit quality
Aa3	AA−	AA−	
A1	A+	A+	
A2	A	A	Upper-medium grade
A3	A−	A−	
Baa1	BBB+	BBB+	
Baa2	BBB	BBB	Lower-medium grade
Baa3	BBB−	BBB−	
Speculative—Lower Credit Worthiness			
Ba1	BB+	BB+	
Ba2	BB	BB	Low grade, speculative
Ba3	BB−	BB−	
B1		B+	
B2	B	B	Highly speculative
B3		B−	
Predominantly Speculative, Substantial Risk, or in Default			
	CCC+	CCC+	
Caa	CCC	CCC	Substantial risk, in poor standing
Ca	CC	CC	May be in default, very speculative
C	C	C	Extremely speculative
	CI		Income bonds—no interest being paid
		DDD	
		DD	Default
	D	D	

Exhibit 63-4 shows a hypothetical rating transition matrix for a 1-year period. The first column shows the ratings at the start of the year and the top row shows the rating at the end of the year. Let's interpret one of the numbers. Look at the cell where the rating at the beginning of the year is AA and the rating at the end of the year is AA. This cell represents the percentage of issues rated AA at the beginning of the year that did not change their rating over the year. That is, there were no downgrades or upgrades. As can be seen, 92.75% of the issues rated AA at the start of the year were rated AA at the end of the year. Now look at the cell where the rating at the beginning of the year is AA and at the end of the year is A. This shows the percentage of issues rated AA at the beginning of the year that were downgraded to A by the end of the year. In our hypothetical 1-year rating

EXHIBIT 63-4 Hypothetical 1-Year Rating Transition Matrix

Rating at start of year	Rating at end of year								Total
	AAA	AA	A	BBB	BB	B	CCC	D	
AAA	93.20	6.00	0.60	0.12	0.08	0.00	0.00	0.00	100
AA	1.60	92.75	5.07	0.36	0.11	0.07	0.03	0.01	100
A	0.18	2.65	91.91	4.80	0.37	0.02	0.02	0.05	100
BBB	0.04	0.30	5.20	87.70	5.70	0.70	0.16	0.20	100
BB	0.03	0.11	0.61	6.80	81.65	7.10	2.60	1.10	100
B	0.01	0.09	0.55	0.88	7.90	75.67	8.70	6.20	100
CCC	0.00	0.01	0.31	0.84	2.30	8.10	62.54	25.90	100

transition matrix, this percentage is 5.07%. One can view these percentages as probabilities. There is a probability that an issue rated AA will be downgraded to A by the end of the year and it is 5.07%. One can estimate total downgrade risk as well. Look at the row that shows issues rated AA at the beginning of the year. The cells in the columns A, BBB, BB, B, CCC, and D all represent downgrades from AA. Thus, if we add all of these columns in this row (5.07%, 0.36%, 0.11%, 0.07%, 0.03%, and 0.01%), we get 5.65% which is an estimate of the probability of an issue being downgraded from AA in one year. Thus, 5.65% can be viewed as an estimate of downgrade risk.

A rating transition matrix also shows the potential for upgrades. Again, using Exhibit 63-4 look at the row that shows issues rated AA at the beginning of the year. Looking at the cell shown in the column AAA rating at the end of the year, one finds 1.60%. This is the percentage of issues rated AA at the beginning of the year that were upgraded to AAA by the end of the year.

Finally, look at the D rating category. These are issues that go into default. We can use the information in the column with the D rating at the end of the year to estimate the probability that an issue with a particular rating will go into default at the end of the year. Hence, this would be an estimate of default risk. So, for example, the probability that an issue rated AA at the beginning of the year will go into default by the end of the year is 0.01%. In contrast, the probability of an issue rated CCC at the beginning of the year will go into default by the end of the year is 25.9%.

7 LIQUIDITY RISK

When an investor wants to sell a bond prior to the maturity date, he or she is concerned with whether or not the bid price from broker/dealers is close to the indicated value of the issue. For example, if recent trades in the market for a particular issue have been between $90 and $90.5 and market conditions have not changed, an investor would expect to sell the bond somewhere in the $90 to $90.5 range.

Liquidity risk is the risk that the investor will have to sell a bond below its indicated value, where the indication is revealed by a recent transaction. The primary measure of liquidity is the size of the spread between the bid price (the price at which a dealer is willing to buy a security) and the ask price (the price at which a dealer is willing to sell a security). The wider the bid-ask spread, the greater the liquidity risk.

EXHIBIT 63-5 Broker/Dealer Bid-Ask Spreads for a Specific Security

	Dealer			
	1	**2**	**3**	**4**
Bid price	1	1	2	2
Ask price	4	3	4	5

Bid-ask spread for each dealer (in 32nds):

	Dealer			
	1	**2**	**3**	**4**
Bid-ask spread	3	2	2	3

A liquid market can generally be defined by "small bid-ask spreads which do not materially increase for large transactions."[6] How to define the bid-ask spread in a multiple dealer market is subject to interpretation. For example, consider the bid-ask prices for four dealers. Each quote is for $92 plus the number of 32nds shown in Exhibit 63-5. The bid-ask spread shown in the exhibit is measured relative to a specific dealer. The best bid-ask spread is for $2/32$ Dealers 2 and 3.

From the perspective of the overall market, the bid-ask spread can be computed by looking at the best bid price (high price at which a broker/dealer is willing to buy a security) and the lowest ask price (lowest offer price at which a broker/dealer is willing to sell the same security). This liquidity measure is called the **market bid-ask spread.** For the four dealers, the highest bid price is $92^2/_{32}$ and the lowest ask price is $92^3/_{32}$. Thus, the market bid-ask spread is $1/_{32}$.

7.1 Liquidity Risk and Marking Positions to Market

For investors who plan to hold a bond until maturity and need *not* mark the position to market, liquidity risk is not a major concern. An institutional investor who plans to hold an issue to maturity but is periodically marked to market is concerned with liquidity risk. By marking a position to market, the security is revalued in the portfolio based on its current market price. For example, mutual funds are required to mark to market at the end of each day the investments in their portfolio in order to compute the mutual fund's net asset value (NAV). While other institutional investors may not mark to market as frequently as mutual funds, they are marked to market when reports are periodically sent to clients or the board of directors or trustees.

Where are the prices obtained to mark a position to market? Typically, a portfolio manager will solicit bids from several broker/dealers and then use some process to determine the bid price used to mark (i.e., value) the position. The less liquid the issue, the greater the variation there will be in the bid prices obtained from broker/dealers. With an issue that has little liquidity, the price may have to be determined from a pricing service (i.e., a service company that employs models to determine the fair value of a security) rather than from dealer bid prices.

---

[6] Robert I. Gerber, "A User's Guide to Buy-Side Bond Trading," Chapter 16 in Frank J. Fabozzi (ed.), *Managing Fixed Income Portfolios* (New Hope, PA: Frank J. Fabozzi Associates, 1997), p. 278.

In Reading 62 we discussed the use of repurchase agreements as a form of borrowing funds to purchase bonds. The bonds purchased are used as collateral. The bonds purchased are marked to market periodically in order to determine whether or not the collateral provides adequate protection to the lender for funds borrowed (i.e., the dealer providing the financing). When liquidity in the market declines, a portfolio manager who has borrowed funds must rely solely on the bid prices determined by the dealer lending the funds.

7.2 Changes in Liquidity Risk

Bid-ask spreads, and therefore liquidity risk, change over time. Changing market liquidity is a concern to portfolio managers who are contemplating investing in new complex bond structures. Situations such as an unexpected change in interest rates might cause a widening of the bid-ask spread, as investors and dealers are reluctant to take new positions until they have had a chance to assess the new market level of interest rates.

Here is another example of where market liquidity may change. While there are opportunities for those who invest in a new type of bond structure, there are typically few dealers making a market when the structure is so new. If subsequently the new structure becomes popular, more dealers will enter the market and liquidity improves. In contrast, if the new bond structure turns out to be unappealing, the initial buyers face a market with less liquidity because some dealers exit the market and others offer bids that are unattractive because they do not want to hold the bonds for a potential new purchaser.

Thus, we see that the liquidity risk of an issue changes over time. An actual example of a change in market liquidity occurred during the Spring of 1994. One sector of the mortgage-backed securities market, called the derivative mortgage market, saw the collapse of an important investor (a hedge fund) and the resulting exit from the market of several dealers. As a result, liquidity in the market substantially declined and bid-ask spreads widened dramatically.

8   EXCHANGE RATE OR CURRENCY RISK

A bond whose payments are not in the domestic currency of the portfolio manager has unknown cash flows in his or her domestic currency. The cash flows in the manager's domestic currency are dependent on the exchange rate at the time the payments are received from the issuer. For example, suppose a portfolio manager's domestic currency is the U.S. dollar and that manager purchases a bond whose payments are in Japanese yen. If the yen depreciates relative to the U.S. dollar at the time a payment is made, then fewer U.S. dollars can be exchanged.

As another example, consider a portfolio manager in the United Kingdom. This manager's domestic currency is the pound. If that manager purchases a U.S. dollar denominated bond, then the manager is concerned that the U.S. dollar will depreciate relative to the British pound when the issuer makes a payment. If the U.S. dollar does depreciate, then fewer British pounds will be received on the foreign exchange market.

The risk of receiving less of the domestic currency when investing in a bond issue that makes payments in a currency other than the manager's domestic currency is called **exchange rate risk** or **currency risk.**

INFLATION OR PURCHASING POWER RISK · 9

Inflation risk or **purchasing power risk** arises from the decline in the value of a security's cash flows due to inflation, which is measured in terms of purchasing power. For example, if an investor purchases a bond with a coupon rate of 5%, but the inflation rate is 3%, the purchasing power of the investor has not increased by 5%. Instead, the investor's purchasing power has increased by only about 2%.

For all but inflation protection bonds, an investor is exposed to inflation risk because the interest rate the issuer promises to make is fixed for the life of the issue.

VOLATILITY RISK · 10

In our discussion of the impact of embedded options on the interest rate risk of a bond in Section 2, we said that a change in the factors that affect the value of the embedded options will affect how the bond's price will change. Earlier, we looked at how a change in the level of interest rates will affect the price of a bond with an embedded option. But there are other factors that will affect the price of an embedded option.

While we discuss these other factors at Level II, we can get an appreciation of one important factor from a general understanding of option pricing. A major factor affecting the value of an option is "expected volatility." In the case of an option on common stock, expected volatility refers to "expected price volatility." The relationship is as follows: the greater the expected price volatility, the greater the value of the option. The same relationship holds for options on bonds. However, instead of expected price volatility, for bonds it is the "expected yield volatility." The greater the expected yield volatility, the greater the value (price) of an option. The interpretation of yield volatility and how it is estimated are explained at Level II.

Now let us tie this into the pricing of a callable bond. We repeat the formula for the components of a callable bond below:

> Price of callable bond = Price of option-free bond − Price of embedded call option

If expected yield volatility increases, holding all other factors constant, the price of the embedded call option will increase. As a result, the price of a callable bond will decrease (because the former is subtracted from the price of the option-free bond).

To see how a change in expected yield volatility affects the price of a putable bond, we can write the price of a putable bond as follows:

> Price of putable bond = Price of option-free bond + Price of embedded put option

A decrease in expected yield volatility reduces the price of the embedded put option and therefore will decrease the price of a putable bond. Thus, the volatility risk of a putable bond is that expected yield volatility will decrease.

This risk that the price of a bond with an embedded option will decline when expected yield volatility changes is called **volatility risk.** Below is a summary of the effect of changes in expected yield volatility on the price of callable and putable bonds:

Type of embedded option	Volatility risk due to
Callable bonds	an increase in expected yield volatility
Putable bonds	a decrease in expected yield volatility

11   EVENT RISK

Occasionally the ability of an issuer to make interest and principal payments changes dramatically and unexpectedly because of factors including the following:

1. a natural disaster (such as an earthquake or hurricane) or an industrial accident that impairs an issuer's ability to meet its obligations
2. a takeover or corporate restructuring that impairs an issuer's ability to meet its obligations
3. a regulatory change

These factors are commonly referred to as **event risk.**

11.1 Corporate Takeover/Restructurings

The first type of event risk results in a credit rating downgrade of an issuer by rating agencies and is therefore a form of downgrade risk. However, downgrade risk is typically confined to the particular issuer whereas event risk from a natural disaster usually affects more than one issuer.

The second type of event risk also results in a downgrade and can also impact other issuers. An excellent example occurred in the fall of 1988 with the leveraged buyout (LBO) of RJR Nabisco, Inc. The entire industrial sector of the bond market suffered as bond market participants withdrew from the market, new issues were postponed, and secondary market activity came to a standstill as a result of the initial LBO bid announcement. The yield that investors wanted on Nabisco's bonds increased by about 250 basis points. Moreover, because the RJR LBO demonstrated that size was not an obstacle for an LBO, other large industrial firms that market participants previously thought were unlikely candidates for an LBO were fair game. The spillover effect to other industrial companies of the RJR LBO resulted in required yields' increasing dramatically.

11.2 Regulatory Risk

The third type of risk listed above is **regulatory risk.** This risk comes in a variety of forms. Regulated entities include investment companies, depository institutions, and insurance companies. Pension funds are regulated by ERISA. Regulation of these entities is in terms of the acceptable securities in which they may invest and/or the treatment of the securities for regulatory accounting purposes.

Changes in regulations may require a regulated entity to divest itself from certain types of investments. A flood of the divested securities on the market will adversely impact the price of similar securities.

SOVEREIGN RISK   12

When an investor acquires a bond issued by a foreign entity (e.g., a French investor acquiring a Brazilian government bond), the investor faces **sovereign risk.** This is the risk that, as a result of actions of the foreign government, there may be either a default or an adverse price change even in the absence of a default. This is analogous to the forms of credit risk described in Section 6—credit risk spread and downgrade risk. That is, even if a foreign government does not default, actions by a foreign government can increase the credit risk spread sought by investors or increase the likelihood of a downgrade. Both of these will have an adverse impact on a bond's price.

Sovereign risk consists of two parts. First is the unwillingness of a foreign government to pay. A foreign government may simply repudiate its debt. The second is the inability to pay due to unfavorable economic conditions in the country. Historically, most foreign government defaults have been due to a government's inability to pay rather than unwillingness to pay.

13   SUMMARY

▷ The price of a bond changes inversely with a change in market interest rates.

▷ Interest rate risk refers to the adverse price movement of a bond as a result of a change in market interest rates; for the bond investor typically it is the risk that interest rates will rise.

▷ A bond's interest rate risk depends on the features of the bond—maturity, coupon rate, yield, and embedded options.

▷ All other factors constant, the longer the bond's maturity, the greater is the bond's price sensitivity to changes in interest rates.

▷ All other factors constant, the lower the coupon rate, the greater the bond's price sensitivity to changes in interest rates.

▷ The price of a callable bond is equal to the price of an option-free bond minus the price of any embedded call option.

▷ When interest rates rise, the price of a callable bond will not fall by as much as an otherwise comparable option-free bond because the price of the embedded call option decreases.

▷ The price of a putable bond is equal to the price of an option-free bond plus the price of the embedded put option.

▷ All other factors constant, the higher the level of interest rate at which a bond trades, the lower is the price sensitivity when interest rates change.

▷ The price sensitivity of a bond to changes in interest rates can be measured in terms of (1) the percentage price change from initial price or (2) the dollar price change from initial price.

▷ The most straightforward way to calculate the percentage price change is to average the percentage price change due to the same increase and decrease in interest rates.

▷ Duration is a measure of interest rate risk; it measures the price sensitivity of a bond to interest rate changes.

▷ Duration can be interpreted as the approximate percentage price change of a bond for a 100 basis point change in interest rates.

▷ The computed duration is only as good as the valuation model used to obtain the prices when interest rates are shocked up and down by the same number of basis points.

▷ There can be substantial differences in the duration of complex bonds because valuation models used to obtain prices can vary.

▷ Given the duration of a bond and its market value, the dollar price change can be computed for a given change in interest rates.

▷ Yield curve risk for a portfolio occurs when, if interest rates increase by different amounts at different maturities, the portfolio's value will be different than if interest rates had increased by the same amount.

▷ A portfolio's duration measures the sensitivity of the portfolio's value to changes in interest rates assuming the interest rates for all maturities change by the same amount.

▷ Any measure of interest rate risk that assumes interest rates change by the same amount for all maturities (referred to as a "parallel yield curve shift") is only an approximation.

▷ One measure of yield curve risk is rate duration, which is the approximate percentage price change for a 100 basis point change in the interest rate for one maturity, holding all other maturity interest rates constant.

- Call risk and prepayment risk refer to the risk that a security will be paid prior to the scheduled principal payment dates.

- Reinvestment risk is the risk that interest and principal payments (scheduled payments, called proceeds, or prepayments) available for reinvestment must be reinvested at a lower interest rate than the security that generated the proceeds.

- From an investor's perspective, the disadvantages to call and prepayment provisions are (1) the cash flow pattern is uncertain, (2) reinvestment risk increases because proceeds received will have to be reinvested at a relatively lower interest rate, and (3) the capital appreciation potential of a bond is reduced.

- Reinvestment risk for an amortizing security can be significant because of the right to prepay principal and the fact that interest and principal are repaid monthly.

- A zero-coupon bond has no reinvestment risk but has greater interest rate risk than a coupon bond of the same maturity.

- There are three forms of credit risk: default risk, credit spread risk, and downgrade risk.

- Default risk is the risk that the issuer will fail to satisfy the terms of indebtedness with respect to the timely payment of interest and principal.

- Credit spread risk is the risk that the price of an issuer's bond will decline due to an increase in the credit spread.

- Downgrade risk is the risk that one or more of the rating agencies will reduce the credit rating of an issue or issuer.

- There are three rating agencies in the United States: Standard & Poor's Corporation, Moody's Investors Service, Inc., and Fitch.

- A credit rating is an indicator of the potential default risk associated with a particular bond issue that represents in a simplistic way the credit rater's assessment of an issuer's ability to pay principal and interest in accordance with the terms of the debt contract.

- A rating transition matrix is prepared by rating agencies to show the change in credit ratings over some time period.

- A rating transition matrix can be used to estimate downgrade risk and default risk.

- Liquidity risk is the risk that the investor will have to sell a bond below its indicated value.

- The primary measure of liquidity is the size of the spread between the bid and ask price quoted by dealers.

- A market bid-ask spread is the difference between the highest bid price and the lowest ask price from among dealers.

- The liquidity risk of an issue changes over time.

- Exchange rate risk arises when interest and principal payments of a bond are not denominated in the domestic currency of the investor.

- Exchange rate risk is the risk that the currency in which the interest and principal payments are denominated will decline relative to the domestic currency of the investor.

- Inflation risk or purchasing power risk arises from the decline in value of a security's cash flows due to inflation, which is measured in terms of purchasing power.

- Volatility risk is the risk that the price of a bond with an embedded option will decline when expected yield volatility changes.

▶ For a callable bond, volatility risk is the risk that expected yield volatility will increase; for a putable bond, volatility risk is the risk that expected yield volatility will decrease.

▶ Event risk is the risk that the ability of an issuer to make interest and principal payments changes dramatically and unexpectedly because of certain events such as a natural catastrophe, corporate takeover, or regulatory changes.

▶ Sovereign risk is the risk that a foreign government's actions cause a default or an adverse price decline on its bond issue.

PROBLEMS

1. For each of the following issues, indicate whether the price of the issue should be par value, above par value, or below par value:

	Issue	Coupon rate	Yield required by market
A.	A	5¼%	7.25%
B.	B	6⅝%	7.15%
C.	C	0%	6.20%
D.	D	5⅞%	5.00%
E.	E	4½%	4.50%

2. Explain why a callable bond's price would be expected to decline less than an otherwise comparable option-free bond when interest rates rise.

3. **A.** Short-term investors such as money market mutual funds invest in floating-rate securities having maturities greater than 1 year. Suppose that the coupon rate is reset everyday. Why is the interest rate risk small for such issues?

   B. Why would it be improper to say that a floating-rate security whose coupon rate resets every day has no interest rate risk?

4. John Smith and Jane Brody are assistant portfolio managers. The senior portfolio manager has asked them to consider the acquisition of one of two option-free bond issues with the following characteristics:

   Issue 1 has a lower coupon rate than Issue 2
   Issue 1 has a shorter maturity than Issue 2

   Both issues have the same credit rating.
      Smith and Brody are discussing the interest rate risk of the two issues. Smith argues that Issue 1 has greater interest rate risk than Issue 2 because of its lower coupon rate. Brody counters by arguing that Issue 2 has greater interest rate risk because it has a longer maturity than Issue 1.

   A. Which assistant portfolio manager is correct with respect to their selection to the issue with the greater interest rate risk?

   B. Suppose that you are the senior portfolio manager. How would you suggest that Smith and Brody determine which issue has the greater interest rate risk?

5. A portfolio manager wants to estimate the interest rate risk of a bond using duration. The current price of the bond is 82. A valuation model found that if interest rates decline by 30 basis points, the price will increase to 83.50 and if interest rates increase by 30 basis points, the price will decline to 80.75. What is the duration of this bond?

6. A portfolio manager purchased $8 million in market value of a bond with a duration of 5. For this bond, determine the estimated change in its market value for the change in interest rates shown below:

   A. 100 basis points

   B. 50 basis points

   C. 25 basis points

   D. 10 basis points

7. A portfolio manager of a bond fund is considering the acquisition of an extremely complex bond issue. It is complex because it has multiple embedded options. The manager wants to estimate the interest rate risk of the bond issue so that he can determine the impact of including it in his current portfolio. The portfolio manager contacts the dealer who created the bond issue to obtain an estimate for the issue's duration. The dealer estimates the duration to be 7. The portfolio manager solicited his firm's in-house quantitative analyst and asked her to estimate the issue's duration. She estimated the duration to be 10. Explain why there is such a dramatic difference in the issue's duration as estimated by the dealer's analysts and the firm's in-house analyst.

8. Duration is commonly used as a measure of interest rate risk. However, duration does not consider yield curve risk. Why?

9. What measure can a portfolio manager use to assess the interest rate risk of a portfolio to a change in the 5-year yield?

10. For the investor in a callable bond, what are the two forms of reinvestment risk?

11. Investors are exposed to credit risk when they purchase a bond. However, even if an issuer does not default on its obligation prior to its maturity date, there is still a concern about how credit risk can adversely impact the performance of a bond. Why?

12. Using the hypothetical rating transition matrix shown in Exhibit 4 of the reading, answer the following questions:

    A. What is the probability that a bond rated BBB will be downgraded?

    B. What is the probability that a bond rated BBB will go into default?

    C. What is the probability that a bond rated BBB will be upgraded?

    D. What is the probability that a bond rated B will be upgraded to investment grade?

    E. What is the probability that a bond rated A will be downgraded to non-investment grade?

    F. What is the probability that a AAA rated bond will *not* be downgraded at the end of one year?

13. Suppose that the bid and ask prices of five dealers for Issue XYX is 96 plus the number of 32nds shown:

	Dealer				
	1	2	3	4	5
Bid price	14	14	15	15	13
Ask price	18	17	18	20	19

What is the market bid-ask spread for Issue XYX?

14. A portfolio manager is considering the purchase of a new type of bond. The bond is extremely complex in terms of its embedded options. Currently, there is only one dealer making a market in this type of bond. In addition, the manager plans to finance the purchase of this bond by using the bond as collateral. The bond matures in five years and the manager plans to hold the bond for five years. Because the manager plans to hold the bond to its maturity, he has indicated that he is not concerned with liquidity risk. Explain why you agree or disagree with the manager's view that he is not concerned with liquidity risk.

15. Identify the difference in the major risks associated with the following investment alternatives:

   A. For an investor who plans to hold a security for one year, purchasing a Treasury security that matures in one year versus purchasing a Treasury security that matures in 30 years.

   B. For an investor who plans to hold an investment for 10 years, purchasing a Treasury security that matures in 10 years versus purchasing an AAA corporate security that matures in 10 years.

   C. For an investor who plans to hold an investment for two years, purchasing a zero-coupon Treasury security that matures in one year versus purchasing a zero-coupon Treasury security that matures in two years.

   D. For an investor who plans to hold an investment for five years, purchasing an AA sovereign bond (with dollar denominated cash flow payments) versus purchasing a U.S. corporate bond with a B rating.

   E. For an investor who plans to hold an investment for four years, purchasing a less actively traded 10-year AA rated bond versus purchasing a 10-year AA rated bond that is actively traded.

   F. For a U.S. investor who plans to hold an investment for six years, purchasing a Treasury security that matures in six years versus purchasing an Italian government security that matures in six years and is denominated in lira.

16. Sam Stevens is the trustee for the Hole Punchers Labor Union (HPLU). He has approached the investment management firm of IM Associates (IMA) to manage its $200 million bond portfolio. IMA assigned Carol Peters as the portfolio manager for the HPLU account. In their first meeting, Mr. Stevens told Ms. Peters:

> "We are an extremely conservative pension fund. We believe in investing in only investment grade bonds so that there will be minimal risk that the principal invested will be lost. We want at least 40% of the portfolio to be held in bonds that will mature within the next three years. I would like your thoughts on this proposed structure for the portfolio."

How should Ms. Peters respond?

17. A. A treasurer of a municipality with a municipal pension fund has required that its in-house portfolio manager invest all funds in the highest investment grade securities that mature in one month or less. The treasurer believes that this is a safe policy. Comment on this investment policy.

   B. The same treasurer requires that the in-house portfolio municipality's operating fund (i.e., fund needed for day-to-day operations of the municipality) follow the same investment policy. Comment on the appropriateness of this investment policy for managing the municipality's operating fund.

18. In January 1994, General Electric Capital Corporation (GECC) had outstanding $500 million of Reset Notes due March 15, 2018. The reset notes were floating-rate securities. In January 1994, the bonds had an 8% coupon rate for three years that ended March 15, 1997. On January 26, 1994, GECC notified the noteholders that it would redeem the issue on March 15th at par value. This was within the required 30 to 60 day prior notice period. Investors who sought investments with very short-term instruments (e.g., money market investors) bought the notes after GECC's planned redemption announcement. The notes were viewed as short-term because they would be redeemed in six weeks or so. In early February, the Federal Reserve started to boost interest rates and on February 15th, GECC canceled the proposed redemption. Instead, it decided to reset the new interest rate based on the indenture at 108% of the three-year Treasury rate in effect on the tenth day preceding the date of the new interest period of March 15th. *The Wall Street Journal* reported that the notes dropped from par to 98 ($1,000 to $980 per note) after the cancellation of the proposed redemption.*

Why did the price decline?

19. A British portfolio manager is considering investing in Japanese government bonds denominated in yen. What are the major risks associated with this investment?

20. Explain how certain types of event risk can result in downgrade risk.

21. Comment on the following statement: "Sovereign risk is the risk that a foreign government defaults on its obligation."

---

* To complete this story, investors were infuriated and they protested to GECC. On March 8th the new interest rate of 5.61% was announced in the financial press. On the very next day GECC announced a tender offer for the notes commencing March 17th. It would buy them back at par plus accrued interest on April 15th. This bailed out many investors who had faith in GECC's original redemption announcement.

OVERVIEW OF BOND SECTORS AND INSTRUMENTS

LEARNING OUTCOMES

The candidate should be able to:

a. describe the different types of international bonds (e.g., Eurobonds, global bonds, sovereign debt);

b. describe the types of securities issued by the U.S. Department of the Treasury (e.g. bills, notes, bonds, and inflation protection securities), differentiate between on-the-run and off-the-run Treasury securities, discuss how stripped Treasury securities are created, and distinguish between coupon strips and principal strips;

c. describe a mortgage-backed security, and explain the cash flows for a mortgage-backed security, define prepayments and explain prepayment risk;

d. describe the types and characteristics of securities issued by federal agencies (including mortgage passthroughs and collateralized mortgage obligations);

e. state the motivation for creating a collateralized mortgage obligation, describe the types of securities issued by municipalities in the United States, distinguish between tax-backed debt and revenue bonds;

f. describe insured bonds and prefunded bonds;

g. summarize the bankruptcy process and bondholder rights, explain the factors considered by rating agencies in assigning a credit rating to a corporate debt instrument, and describe secured debt, unsecured debt, and credit enhancements for corporate bonds;

h. distinguish between a corporate bond and a medium-term note;

i. describe a structured note and explain the motivation for their issuance by corporations, describe commercial paper, and distinguish between directly-placed paper and dealer-placed paper, and describe the salient features, uses and limitations of bank obligations (negotiable CDs and bankers acceptances);

j. define an asset-backed security, describe the role of a special purpose vehicle in an asset-backed securities transaction, state the motivation for a corporation to issue an asset-backed security, and describe the types of external credit enhancements for asset-backed securities;

k. describe collateralized debt obligations;

l. contrast the structures of the primary and secondary markets in bonds.

Fixed Income Analysis for the Chartered Financial Analyst® Program, Second Edition, by Frank J. Fabozzi. Reprinted with permission.

1 INTRODUCTION

Thus far we have covered the general features of bonds and the risks associated with investing in bonds. In this reading, we will review the major sectors of a country's bond market and the securities issued. This includes sovereign bonds, semi-government bonds, municipal or province securities, corporate debt securities, mortgage-backed securities, asset-backed securities, and collateralized debt obligations. Our coverage in this reading is to describe the instruments found in these sectors.

2 SECTORS OF THE BOND MARKET

While there is no uniform system for classifying the sectors of the bond markets throughout the world, we will use the classification shown in Exhibit 64-1. From the perspective of a given country, the bond market can be classified into two markets: an **internal bond market** and an **external bond market.**

2.1 Internal Bond Market

The internal bond market of a country is also called the **national bond market.** It is divided into two parts: the **domestic bond market** and the **foreign bond market.** The domestic bond market is where issuers domiciled in the country issue bonds and where those bonds are subsequently traded.

The foreign bond market of a country is where bonds of issuers not domiciled in the country are issued and traded. For example, in the United States, the foreign bond market is the market where bonds are issued by non–U.S. entities and then subsequently traded in the United States. In the U.K., a sterling-denominated bond issued by a Japanese corporation and subsequently traded in the U.K. bond market is part of the U.K. foreign bond market. Bonds in the foreign sector of a bond market have nicknames. For example, foreign bonds in the U.S. market are nicknamed "Yankee bonds" and sterling-denominated bonds in the U.K. foreign bond market are nicknamed "Bulldog bonds." Foreign bonds can be denominated in any currency. For example, a foreign bond issued by an Australian corporation in the United States can be denominated in U.S. dollars, Australian dollars, or euros.

EXHIBIT 64-1 Overview of the Sectors of the Bond Market

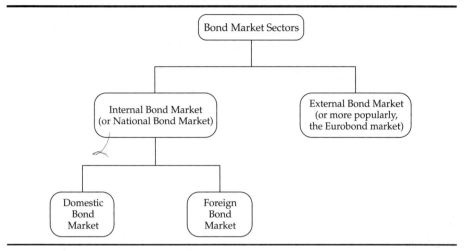

Issuers of foreign bonds include central governments and their subdivisions, corporations, and supranationals. A **supranational** is an entity that is formed by two or more central governments through international treaties. Supranationals promote economic development for the member countries. Two examples of supranationals are the International Bank for Reconstruction and Development, popularly referred to as the World Bank, and the Inter-American Development Bank.

2.2 External Bond Market

The external bond market includes bonds with the following distinguishing features:

- they are underwritten by an international syndicate
- at issuance, they are offered simultaneously to investors in a number of countries
- they are issued outside the jurisdiction of any single country
- they are in unregistered form.

The external bond market is referred to as the **international bond market,** the **offshore bond market,** or, more popularly, the **Eurobond market.**[1] Throughout this book we will use the term Eurobond market to describe this sector of the bond market.

Eurobonds are classified based on the currency in which the issue is denominated. For example, when Eurobonds are denominated in U.S. dollars, they are referred to as Eurodollar bonds. Eurobonds denominated in Japanese yen are referred to as Euroyen bonds.

A **global bond** is a debt obligation that is issued and traded in the foreign bond market of one or more countries and the Eurobond market.

---

[1] It should be noted that the classification used here is by no means universally accepted. Some market observers refer to the external bond market as consisting of the foreign bond market and the Eurobond market.

SOVEREIGN BONDS

In many countries that have a bond market, the largest sector is often bonds issued by a country's central government. These bonds are referred to as **sovereign bonds.** A government can issue securities in its national bond market which are subsequently traded within that market. A government can also issue bonds in the Eurobond market or the foreign sector of another country's bond market. While the currency denomination of a government security is typically the currency of the issuing country, a government can issue bonds denominated in any currency.

3.1 Credit Risk

An investor in any bond is exposed to credit risk. The perception throughout the world is that the credit risk of bonds issued by the U.S. government are virtually free of credit risk. Consequently, the market views these bonds as default-free bonds. Sovereign bonds of non-U.S. central governments are rated by the credit rating agencies. These ratings are referred to as **sovereign ratings.** Standard & Poor's and Moody's rate sovereign debt. We will discuss the factors considered in rating sovereign bonds at Level II.

The rating agencies assign two types of ratings to sovereign debt. One is a **local currency debt rating** and the other a **foreign currency debt rating.** The reason for assigning two ratings is, historically, the default frequency differs by the currency denomination of the debt. Specifically, defaults have been greater on foreign currency denominated debt. The reason for the difference in default rates for local currency debt and foreign currency debt is that if a government is willing to raise taxes and control its domestic financial system, it can generate sufficient local currency to meet its local currency debt obligation. This is not the case with foreign currency denominated debt. A central government must purchase foreign currency to meet a debt obligation in that foreign currency and therefore has less control with respect to its exchange rate. Thus, a significant depreciation of the local currency relative to a foreign currency denominated debt obligation will impair a central government's ability to satisfy that obligation.

3.2 Methods of Distributing New Government Securities

Four methods have been used by central governments to distribute new bonds that they issue: (1) regular auction cycle/multiple-price method, (2) regular auction cycle/single-price method, (3) ad hoc auction method, and (4) tap method.

With the **regular auction cycle/multiple-price method,** there is a regular auction cycle and winning bidders are allocated securities at the yield (price) they bid. For the **regular auction cycle/single-price method,** there is a regular auction cycle and all winning bidders are awarded securities at the highest yield accepted by the government. For example, if the highest yield for a single-price auction is 7.14% and someone bid 7.12%, that bidder would be awarded the securities at 7.14%. In contrast, with a multiple-price auction that bidder would be awarded securities at 7.12%. U.S. government bonds are currently issued using a regular auction cycle/single-price method.

In the **ad hoc auction system,** governments announce auctions when prevailing market conditions appear favorable. It is only at the time of the auction that the amount to be auctioned and the maturity of the security to be offered is announced. This is one of the methods used by the Bank of England in distributing British government bonds. In a **tap system,** additional bonds of a previously outstanding bond issue are auctioned. The government announces periodically that it is adding this new supply. The tap system has been used in the United Kingdom, the United States, and the Netherlands.

3.2.1 United States Treasury Securities

U.S. Treasury securities are issued by the U.S. Department of the Treasury and are backed by the full faith and credit of the U.S. government. As noted above, market participants throughout the world view U.S. Treasury securities as having no credit risk. Because of the importance of the U.S. government securities market, we will take a close look at this market.

Treasury securities are sold in the primary market through sealed-bid auctions on a regular cycle using a single-price method. Each auction is announced several days in advance by means of a Treasury Department press release or press conference. The auction for Treasury securities is conducted on a competitive bid basis.

The secondary market for Treasury securities is an over-the-counter market where a group of U.S. government securities dealers offer continuous bid and ask prices on outstanding Treasuries. There is virtually 24-hour trading of Treasury securities. The most recently auctioned issue for a maturity is referred to as the **on-the-run issue** or the **current issue.** Securities that are replaced by the on-the-run issue are called **off-the-run issues.**

Exhibit 64-2 provides a summary of the securities issued by the U.S. Department of the Treasury. U.S. Treasury securities are categorized as **fixed-principal securities** or **inflation-indexed securities.**

3.2.1.1 Fixed-Principal Treasury Securities

Fixed principal securities include Treasury bills, Treasury notes, and Treasury bonds. **Treasury bills** are issued at a discount to par value, have no coupon rate, mature at par value, and have a maturity date of less than 12 months. As discount securities, Treasury bills do not pay coupon interest; the return to the investor is the difference between the maturity value and the purchase price. We will explain how the price and the yield for a Treasury bill are computed in Reading 67.

EXHIBIT 64-2 Overview of U.S. Treasury Debt Instruments

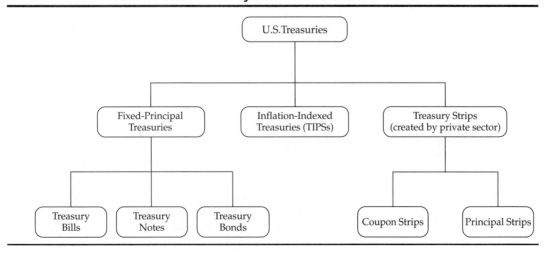

Treasury coupon securities issued with original maturities of more than one year and no more than 10 years are called **Treasury notes.** Coupon securities are issued at approximately par value and mature at par value. Treasury coupon securities with original maturities greater than 10 years are called **Treasury bonds.** While a few issues of the outstanding bonds are callable, the U.S. Treasury has not issued callable Treasury securities since 1984. As of this writing, the U.S. Department of the Treasury has stopped issuing Treasury bonds.

3.2.1.2 Inflation-Indexed Treasury Securities

The U.S. Department of the Treasury issues Treasury notes and bonds that provide protection against inflation. These securities are popularly referred to as **Treasury inflation protection securities** or TIPS. (The Treasury refers to these securities as **Treasury inflation indexed securities,** TIIS.)

TIPS work as follows. The coupon rate on an issue is set at a fixed rate. That rate is determined via the auction process described later in this section. The coupon rate is called the "real rate" because it is the rate that the investor ultimately earns above the inflation rate. The inflation index that the government uses for the inflation adjustment is the non-seasonally adjusted U.S. City Average All Items Consumer Price Index for All Urban Consumers (CPI-U).

The principal that the Treasury Department will base both the dollar amount of the coupon payment and the maturity value on is adjusted semiannually. This is called the **inflation-adjusted principal.** The adjustment for inflation is as follows. Suppose that the coupon rate for a TIPS is 3.5% and the annual inflation rate is 3%. Suppose further that an investor purchases on January 1, $100,000 of par value (principal) of this issue. The semiannual inflation rate is 1.5% (3% divided by 2). The inflation-adjusted principal at the end of the first six-month period is found by multiplying the original par value by (1 + the semiannual inflation rate). In our example, the inflation-adjusted principal at the end of the first six-month period is $101,500. It is this inflation-adjusted principal that is the basis for computing the coupon interest for the first six-month period. The coupon payment is then 1.75% (one half the real rate of 3.5%) multiplied by the inflation-adjusted principal at the coupon payment date ($101,500). The coupon payment is therefore $1,776.25

Let's look at the next six months. The inflation-adjusted principal at the beginning of the period is $101,500. Suppose that the semiannual inflation rate for the second six-month period is 1%. Then the inflation-adjusted principal at the end of the second six-month period is the inflation-adjusted principal at the beginning of the six-month period ($101,500) increased by the semiannual inflation rate (1%). The adjustment to the principal is $1,015 (1% times $101,500). So, the inflation-adjusted principal at the end of the second six-month period (December 31 in our example) is $102,515 ($101,500 + $1,015). The coupon interest that will be paid to the investor at the second coupon payment date is found by multiplying the inflation-adjusted principal on the coupon payment date ($102,515) by one half the real rate (i.e., one half of 3.5%). That is, the coupon payment will be $1,794.01.

Practice Question 1

Suppose an investor purchases $10,000 of par value of a Treasury inflation protection security. The real rate (determined at the auction) is 3.8%.

A. Assume that at the end of the first six months the CPI-U is 2.4% (annual rate). Compute the (i) inflation adjustment to principal at the end of the first six months, (ii) the inflation-adjusted principal at the end of the first six months, and (iii) the coupon payment made to the investor at the end of the first six months.

B. Assume that at the end of the second six months the CPI-U is 2.8% (annual rate). Compute the (i) inflation adjustment to principal at the end of the second six months, (ii) the inflation-adjusted principal at the end of the second six months, and (iii) the coupon payment made to the investor at the end of the second six months.

As can be seen, part of the adjustment for inflation comes in the coupon payment since it is based on the inflation-adjusted principal. However, the U.S. government taxes the adjustment each year. This feature reduces the attractiveness of TIPS as investments for tax-paying entities.

Because of the possibility of disinflation (i.e., price declines), the inflation-adjusted principal at maturity may turn out to be less than the initial par value. However, the Treasury has structured TIPS so that they are redeemed at the greater of the inflation-adjusted principal and the initial par value.

An inflation-adjusted principal must be calculated for a settlement date. The inflation-adjusted principal is defined in terms of an index ratio, which is the ratio of the reference CPI for the settlement date to the reference CPI for the issue date. The reference CPI is calculated with a 3-month lag. For example, the reference CPI for May 1 is the CPI-U reported in February. The U.S. Department of the Treasury publishes and makes available on its website (www.publicdebt.treas.gov) a daily index ratio for an issue.

3.2.1.3 Treasury STRIPs

The Treasury does not issue zero-coupon notes or bonds. However, because of the demand for zero-coupon instruments with no credit risk and a maturity greater than one year, the private sector has created such securities.

To illustrate the process, suppose $100 million of a Treasury note with a 10-year maturity and a coupon rate of 10% is purchased to create zero-coupon Treasury securities (see Exhibit 64-3). The cash flows from this Treasury note are 20 semiannual payments of $5 million each ($100 million times 10% divided by 2) and the repayment of principal ("corpus") of $100 million 10 years from now. As there are 21 different payments to be made by the Treasury, a receipt representing a single payment claim on each payment is issued at a discount, creating 21 zero-coupon instruments. The amount of the maturity value for a receipt on a particular payment, whether coupon or principal, depends on the amount of the payment to be made by the Treasury on the underlying Treasury note. In our example, 20 coupon receipts each have a maturity value of $5 million, and one receipt, the principal, has a maturity value of $100 million. The maturity dates for the receipts coincide with the corresponding payment dates for the Treasury security.

Zero-coupon instruments are issued through the Treasury's Separate Trading of Registered Interest and Principal Securities (STRIPS) program, a program designed to facilitate the stripping of Treasury securities. The zero-coupon Treasury securities created under the STRIPS program are direct obligations of the U.S. government.

Stripped Treasury securities are simply referred to as **Treasury strips.** Strips created from coupon payments are called **coupon strips** and those created from the principal payment are called **principal strips.** The reason why a distinction is made between coupon strips and the principal strips has to do with the tax treatment by non-U.S. entities as discussed below.

A disadvantage of a taxable entity investing in Treasury coupon strips is that accrued interest is taxed each year even though interest is not paid until maturity. Thus, these instruments have negative cash flows until the maturity date because tax payments must be made on interest earned but not received in cash must be made. One reason for distinguishing between strips created from the principal and coupon is that some foreign buyers have a preference for the strips created from the principal (i.e., the principal strips). This preference is due to the tax treatment of the interest in their home country. Some country's tax laws treat the interest as a capital gain if the principal strip is purchased. The capital gain receives a preferential tax treatment (i.e., lower tax rate) compared to ordinary income.

EXHIBIT 64-3 Coupon Stripping: Creating Zero-Coupon Treasury Securities

Security

| Par: $100 million |
| Coupon: 10%, semiannual |
| Maturity: 10 years |

Security

| Coupon: $5 million Receipt in: 6 months | Coupon: $5 million Receipt in: 1 year | Coupon: $5 million Receipt in: 1.5 years | .... | Coupon: $5 million Receipt in: 10 years | Principal: $100 million Receipt in: 10 years |

Zero-coupon securities created

| Maturity value: $5 million Maturity: 6 months | Maturity value: $5 million Maturity: 1 year | Maturity value: $5 million Maturity: 1.5 years | .... | Maturity value: $5 million Maturity: 10 years | Maturity value: $100 million Maturity: 10 years |

3.2.2 Non-U.S. Sovereign Bond Issuers

It is not possible to discuss the bonds/notes of all governments in the world. Instead, we will take a brief look at a few major sovereign issuers.

The German government issues bonds (called *Bunds*) with maturities from 8–30 years and notes (*Bundesobligationen*, Bobls) with a maturity of five years. Ten-year Bunds are the largest sector of the German government securities market in terms of amount outstanding and secondary market turnover. Bunds and Bobls have a fixed-rate coupons and are bullet structures.

The bonds issued by the United Kingdom are called "gilt-edged stocks" or simply *gilts*. There are more types of gilts than there are types of issues in other government bond markets. The largest sector of the gilt market is straight fixed-rate coupon bonds. The second major sector of the gilt market is index-linked issues, referred to as "linkers." There are a few issues of outstanding gilts called "irredeemables." These are issues with no maturity date and are therefore called "undated gilts." Government designated gilt issues may be stripped to create gilt strips, a process that began in December 1997.

The French Treasury issues long-dated bonds, *Obligation Assimilable du Trésor* (OATS), with maturities up to 30 years and notes, *Bons du Trésor á Taux Fixe et á Intérét Annuel* (BTANs), with maturities between 2 and 5 years. OATs are not callable. While most OAT issues have a fixed-rate coupon, there are some special issues with a floating-rate coupon. Long-dated OATs can be stripped to create OAT strips. The French government was one of the first countries after the United States to allow stripping.

The Italian government issues (1) bonds, *Buoni del Tresoro Poliennali* (BTPs), with a fixed-rate coupon that are issued with original maturities of 5, 10, and 30 years, (2) floating-rate notes, *Certificati di Credito del Tresoro* (CCTs), typically with a 7-year maturity and referenced to the Italian Treasury bill rate, (3) 2-year zero-coupon notes, *Certificati di Tresoro a Zero Coupon* (CTZs), and (4) bonds with put options, *Certificati del Tresoro con Opzione* (CTOs). The putable bonds are issued with the same maturities as the BTPs. The investor has the right to put the bond to the Italian government halfway through its stated maturity date. The Italian government has not issued CTOs since 1992.

The Canadian government bond market has been closely related to the U.S. government bond market and has a similar structure, including types of issues. Bonds have a fixed coupon rate except for the inflation protection bonds (called "real return bonds"). All new Canadian bonds are in "bullet" form; that is, they are not callable or putable.

About three quarters of the Australian government securities market consists of fixed-rate bonds and inflation protections bonds called "Treasury indexed bonds." Treasury indexed bonds have either interest payments or capital linked to the Australian Consumer Price Index. The balance of the market consists of floating-rate issues, referred to as "Treasury adjustable bonds," that have a maturity between 3 to 5 years and the reference rate is the Australian Bank Bill Index.

There are two types of Japanese government securities (referred to as JGBs) issued publicly: (1) medium-term bonds and (2) long-dated bonds. There are two types of medium-term bonds: bonds with coupons and zero-coupon bonds. Bonds with coupons have maturities of 2, 3, and 4 years. The other type of medium-term bond is the 5-year zero-coupon bond. Long-dated bonds are interest bearing.

The financial markets of Latin America, Asia with the exception of Japan, and Eastern Europe are viewed as "emerging markets." Investing in the government bonds of emerging market countries entails considerably more credit risk than investing in the government bonds of major industrialized countries. A good amount of secondary trading of government debt of emerging markets is in **Brady bonds** which represent a restructuring of nonperforming bank loans to emerging market governments into marketable securities. There are two types of Brady bonds. The first type covers the interest due on these loans ("past-due interest bonds"). The second type covers the principal amount owed on the bank loans ("principal bonds").

SEMI-GOVERNMENT/AGENCY BONDS   4

A central government can establish an agency or organization that issues bonds. The bonds of such entities are not issued directly by the central government but may have either a direct or implied government guarantee. These bonds are generically referred to as **semi-government bonds** or **government agency bonds.** In some countries, semi-government bonds include bonds issued by regions of the country.

Here are a few examples of semi-government bonds. In Australia, there are the bonds issued by Telstra or a State electric power supplier such as Pacific Power.

These bonds are guaranteed by the full faith and credit of the Commonwealth of Australia. Government agency bonds are issued by Germany's Federal Railway (*Bundesbahn*) and the Post Office (*Bundespost*) with the full faith and credit of the central government.

In the United States, semi-government bonds are referred to as **federal agency securities.** They are further classified by the types of issuer-those issued by **federally related institutions** and those issued by **government-sponsored enterprises.** Our focus in the remainder of this section is on U.S. federal agency securities. Exhibit 64-4 provides an overview of the U.S. federal agency securities market.

Federally related institutions are arms of the federal government. They include the Export-Import Bank of the United States, the Tennessee Valley Authority (TVA), the Commodity Credit Corporation, the Farmers Housing Administration, the General Services Administration, the Government National Mortgage Association (Ginnie Mae), the Maritime Administration, the Private Export Funding Corporation, the Rural Electrification Administration, the Rural Telephone Bank, the Small Business Administration, and the Washington Metropolitan Area Transit Authority. With the exception of securities of the TVA and the Private Export Funding Corporation, the securities are backed by the full faith and credit of the U.S. government. In recent years, the TVA has been the only issuer of securities directly into the marketplace.

Government-sponsored enterprises (GSEs) are privately owned, publicly chartered entities. They were created by Congress to reduce the cost of capital for certain borrowing sectors of the economy deemed to be important enough to warrant assistance. The entities in these sectors include farmers, homeowners, and students. The enabling legislation dealing with a GSE is reviewed periodically. GSEs issue securities directly in the marketplace. The market for these securities, while

EXHIBIT 64-4 Overview of U.S. Federal Agency Securities

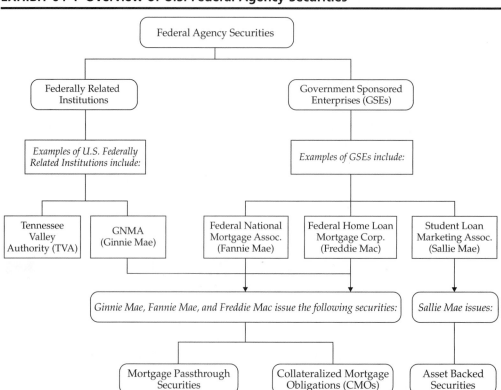

smaller than that of Treasury securities, has in recent years become an active and important sector of the bond market.

Today there are six GSEs that currently issue securities: Federal National Mortgage Association (Fannie Mae), Federal Home Loan Mortgage Corporation (Freddie Mac), Federal Agricultural Mortgage Corporation (Farmer Mac), Federal Farm Credit System, Federal Home Loan Bank System, and Student Loan Marketing Association (Sallie Mae). Fannie Mae, Freddie Mac, and the Federal Home Loan Bank are responsible for providing credit to the residential housing sector. Farmer Mac provides the same function for farm properties. The Federal Farm Credit Bank System is responsible for the credit market in the agricultural sector of the economy. Sallie Mae provides funds to support higher education.

4.1 U.S. Agency Debentures and Discount Notes

Generally, GSEs issue two types of debt: debentures and discount notes. Debentures and discount notes do not have any specific collateral backing the debt obligation. The ability to pay debtholders depends on the ability of the issuing GSE to generate sufficient cash flows to satisfy the obligation.

Debentures can be either notes or bonds. GSE issued notes, with minor exceptions, have 1 to 20 year maturities and bonds have maturities longer than 20 years. **Discount notes** are short-term obligations, with maturities ranging from overnight to 360 days.

Several GSEs are frequent issuers and therefore have developed regular programs for the securities that they issue. For example, let's look at the debentures issued by Federal National Mortgage Association (Fannie Mae) and Freddie Mac (Federal Home Loan Mortgage Corporation). Fannie Mae issues **Benchmark Notes, Benchmark Bonds, Callable Benchmark Notes,** medium-term notes, and global bonds. The debentures issued by Freddie Mac are **Reference Notes, Reference Bonds, Callable Reference Notes,** medium-term notes, and global bonds. (We will discuss medium-term notes and global bonds in Section 6 and Section 8, respectively.) Callable Reference Notes have maturities of 2 to 10 years. Both Benchmark Notes and Bonds and Reference Notes and Bonds are eligible for stripping to create zero-coupon bonds.

4.2 U.S. Agency Mortgage-Backed Securities

The two GSEs charged with providing liquidity to the mortgage market—Fannie Mae and Freddie Mac—also issue securities backed by the mortgage loans that they purchase. That is, they use the mortgage loans they underwrite or purchase as collateral for the securities they issue. These securities are called **agency mortgage-backed securities** and include mortgage passthrough securities, collateralized mortgage obligations (CMOs), and stripped mortgage-backed securities. The latter two mortgage-backed securities are referred to as derivative mortgage-backed securities because they are created from mortgage passthrough securities.

While we confine our discussion to the U.S. mortgage-backed securities market, most developed countries have similar mortgage products.

4.2.1 Mortgage Loans

A mortgage loan is a loan secured by the collateral of some specified real estate property which obliges the borrower to make a predetermined series of payments. The mortgage gives the lender the right, if the borrower defaults, to "foreclose" on the loan and seize the property in order to ensure that the debt is paid off. The interest rate on the mortgage loan is called the **mortgage rate** or **contract rate.**

There are many types of mortgage designs available in the United States. A mortgage design is a specification of the mortgage rate, term of the mortgage, and the manner in which the borrowed funds are repaid. For now, we will use the most common mortgage design to explain the characteristics of a mortgage-backed security: a fixed-rate, level-payment, fully amortizing mortgage.

The basic idea behind this mortgage design is that each monthly mortgage payment is the same dollar amount and includes interest and principal payment. The monthly payments are such that at the end of the loan's term, the loan has been fully amortized (i.e., there is no mortgage principal balance outstanding).

Each monthly mortgage payment for this mortgage design is due on the first of each month and consists of:

1. interest of $1/12$ of the fixed annual interest rate times the amount of the outstanding mortgage balance at the end of the previous month, and

2. a payment of a portion of the outstanding mortgage principal balance.

The difference between the monthly mortgage payment and the portion of the payment that represents interest equals the amount that is applied to reduce the outstanding mortgage principal balance. This amount is referred to as the **amortization.** We shall also refer to it as the **scheduled principal payment.**

To illustrate this mortgage design, consider a 30-year (360-month), $100,000 mortgage with an 8.125% mortgage rate. The monthly mortgage payment would be $742.50.[2] Exhibit 64-5 shows for selected months how each monthly mortgage payment is divided between interest and scheduled principal payment. At the beginning of month 1, the mortgage balance is $100,000, the amount of the original loan. The mortgage payment for month 1 includes interest on the $100,000 borrowed for the month. Since the interest rate is 8.125%, the monthly interest rate is 0.0067708 (0.08125 divided by 12). Interest for month 1 is therefore $677.08 ($100,000 times 0.0067708). The $65.41 difference between the monthly mortgage payment of $742.50[2] and the interest of $677.08 is the portion of the monthly mortgage payment that represents the scheduled principal payment (i.e., amortization). This $65.41 in month 1 reduces the mortgage balance.

The mortgage balance at the end of month 1 (beginning of month 2) is then $99,934.59 ($100,000 minus $65.41). The interest for the second monthly mortgage payment is $676.64, the monthly interest rate (0.0066708) times the mortgage balance at the beginning of month 2 ($99,934.59). The difference between the $742.50 monthly mortgage payment and the $676.64 interest is $65.86, representing the amount of the mortgage balance paid off with that monthly mortgage payment. Notice that the mortgage payment in month 360—the final payment—is sufficient to pay off the remaining mortgage principal balance.

---

[2] The calculation of the monthly mortgage payment is simply an application of the present value of an annuity. The formula as applied to mortgage payments is as follows:

$$MP = B \left[\frac{r(1 + r)^n}{(1 + r)^n - 1} \right]$$

where

    MP = monthly mortgage payment

    B = amount borrowed (i.e., original loan balance)

    r = monthly mortgage rate (annual rate divided by 12)

    n = number of months of the mortgage loan

    In our example,

    B = $100,000 $r = 0.0067708 \ (0.08125/12)$ $n = 360$

Then

$$MP = \$100,000 \left[\frac{0.0067708(1.0067708)^{360}}{(1.0067708)^{360} - 1} \right] = \$742.50$$

EXHIBIT 64-5 Amortization Schedule for a Level-Payment, Fixed-Rate, Fully Amortized Mortgage (Selected Months)

Mortgage loan: $100,000			Monthly payment: $742.50		
Mortgage rate: 8.125%			Term of loan:	30 years (360 months)	

(1)	(2)	(3)	(4)	(5)	(6)
Month	Beginning of Month Mortgage Balance	Mortgage Payment	Interest	Scheduled Principal Repayment	End of Month Mortgage Balance
1	$100,000.00	$742.50	$677.08	$65.41	$99,934.59
2	99,934.59	742.50	676.64	65.86	99,868.73
3	99,868.73	742.50	676.19	66.30	99,802.43
4	99,802.43	742.50	675.75	66.75	99,735.68
. . .	. . .	. . .	. . .	. . .	. . .
25	98,301.53	742.50	665.58	76.91	98,224.62
26	98,224.62	742.50	665.06	77.43	98,147.19
27	98,147.19	742.50	664.54	77.96	98,069.23
. . .	. . .	. . .	. . .	. . .	. . .
184	76,446.29	742.50	517.61	224.89	76,221.40
185	76,221.40	742.50	516.08	226.41	75,994.99
186	75,994.99	742.50	514.55	227.95	75,767.04
. . .	. . .	. . .	. . .	. . .	. . .
289	42,200.92	742.50	285.74	456.76	41,744.15
290	41,744.15	742.50	282.64	459.85	41,284.30
291	41,284.30	742.50	279.53	462.97	40,821.33
. . .	. . .	. . .	. . .	. . .	. . .
358	2,197.66	742.50	14.88	727.62	1,470.05
359	1,470.05	742.50	9.95	732.54	737.50
360	737.50	742.50	4.99	737.50	0.00

As Exhibit 64-5 clearly shows, the portion of the monthly mortgage payment applied to interest declines each month and the portion applied to principal repayment increases. The reason for this is that as the mortgage balance is reduced with each monthly mortgage payment, the interest on the mortgage balance declines. Since the monthly mortgage payment is a fixed dollar amount, an increasingly larger portion of the monthly payment is applied to reduce the mortgage principal balance outstanding in each subsequent month.

To an investor in a mortgage loan (or a pool of mortgage loans), the monthly mortgage payments as described above do not equal an investor's cash flow. There are two reasons for this: (1) servicing fees and (2) prepayments.

Every mortgage loan must be serviced. Servicing of a mortgage loan involves collecting monthly payments and forwarding proceeds to owners of the loan; sending payment notices to mortgagors; reminding mortgagors when payments are overdue; maintaining records of principal balances; administering an escrow balance for real estate taxes and insurance; initiating foreclosure proceedings if necessary; and, furnishing tax information to mortgagors when applicable. The servicing fee is a portion of the mortgage rate. If the mortgage rate is 8.125% and the servicing fee is 50 basis points, then the investor receives interest of 7.625%. The interest rate that the investor receives is said to be the **net interest.**

Our illustration of the cash flow for a level-payment, fixed-rate, fully amortized mortgage assumes that the homeowner does not pay off any portion of the mortgage principal balance prior to the scheduled payment date. But homeowners do pay off all or part of their mortgage balance prior to the scheduled payment date. A payment made in excess of the monthly mortgage payment is called a **prepayment.** The prepayment may be for the entire principal outstanding principal balance or a partial additional payment of the mortgage principal balance. When a prepayment is not for the entire amount, it is called a **curtailment.** Typically, there is no penalty for prepaying a mortgage loan.

Thus, the cash flows for a mortgage loan are monthly and consist of three components: (1) net interest, (2) scheduled principal payment, and (3) prepayments. The effect of prepayments is that the amount and timing of the cash flow from a mortgage is not known with certainty. This is the risk that we referred to as **prepayment risk** in Reading 63.[3]

For example, all that the investor in a $100,000, 8.125% 30-year mortgage knows is that as long as the loan is outstanding and the borrower does not default, interest will be received and the principal will be repaid at the scheduled date each month; then at the end of the 30 years, the investor would have received $100,000 in principal payments. What the investor does not know—the uncertainty—is for how long the loan will be outstanding, and therefore what the timing of the principal payments will be. This is true for all mortgage loans, not just the level-payment, fixed-rate, fully amortized mortgage.

Practice Question 2

Suppose that a mortgage loan for $100,000 is obtained for 30 years. The mortgage is a level-payment, fixed-rate, fully amortized mortgage. The mortgage rate is 7.5% and the monthly mortgage payment is $699.21. Compute an amortization schedule as shown in Exhibit 64-5 for the first six months.

4.2.2 Mortgage Passthrough Securities

A **mortgage passthrough security,** or simply passthrough, is a security created when one or more holders of mortgages form a collection (pool) of mortgages and sell shares or participation certificates in the pool. A pool may consist of several thousand or only a few mortgages. When a mortgage is included in a pool of mortgages that is used as collateral for a passthrough, the mortgage is said to be **securitized.**

The cash flow of a passthrough depends on the cash flow of the underlying pool of mortgages. As we just explained, the cash flow consists of monthly mortgage payments representing net interest, the scheduled principal payment, and any principal prepayments. Payments are made to security holders each month. Because of prepayments, the amount of the cash flow is uncertain in terms of the timing of the principal receipt.

To illustrate the creation of a passthrough look at Exhibits 64-6 and 64-7. Exhibit 64-6 shows 2,000 mortgage loans and the cash flows from these loans. For the sake of simplicity, we assume that the amount of each loan is $100,000 so that the aggregate value of all 2,000 loans is $200 million.

---

[3] Factors affecting prepayments will be discussed at Level II.

EXHIBIT 64-6 Mortgage Loans

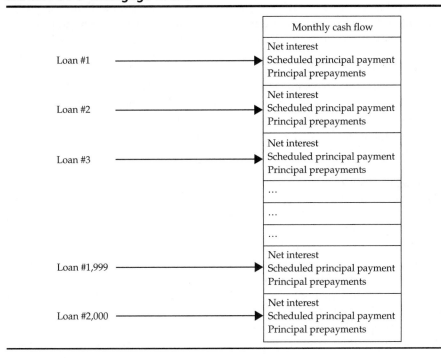

EXHIBIT 64-7 Creation of a Passthrough Security

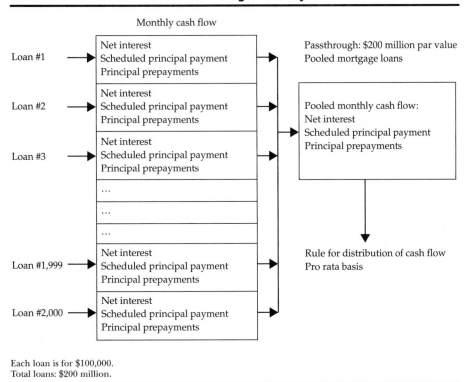

Each loan is for $100,000.
Total loans: $200 million.

An investor who owns any one of the individual mortgage loans shown in Exhibit 64-6 faces prepayment risk. In the case of an individual loan, it is particularly difficult to predict prepayments. If an individual investor were to purchase all 2,000 loans, however, prepayments might become more predictable based on historical prepayment experience. However, that would call for an investment of $200 million to buy all 2,000 loans.

Suppose, instead, that some entity purchases all 2,000 loans in Exhibit 64-6 and pools them. The 2,000 loans can be used as collateral to issue a security whose cash flow is based on the cash flow from the 2,000 loans, as depicted in Exhibit 64-7. Suppose that 200,000 certificates are issued. Thus, each certificate is initially worth $1,000 ($200 million divided by 200,000). Each certificate holder would be entitled to 0.0005% (1/200,000) of the cash flow. The security created is a mortgage passthrough security.

Let's see what has been accomplished by creating the passthrough. The total amount of prepayment risk has not changed. Yet, the investor is now exposed to the prepayment risk spread over 2,000 loans rather than one individual mortgage loan and for an investment of less than $200 million.

Let's compare the cash flow for a mortgage passthrough security (an amortizing security) to that of a noncallable coupon bond (a nonamortizing security). For a standard coupon bond, there are no principal payments prior to maturity while for a mortgage passthrough security the principal is paid over time. Unlike a standard coupon bond that pays interest semiannually, a mortgage passthrough makes monthly interest and principal payments. Mortgage pass-through securities are similar to coupon bonds that are callable in that there is uncertainty about the cash flows due to uncertainty about when the entire principal will be paid.

Passthrough securities are issued by Ginnie Mae, Fannie Mae, and Freddie Mac. They are guaranteed with respect to the timely payment of interest and principal.[4] The loans that are permitted to be included in the pool of mortgage loans issued by Ginnie Mae, Fannie Mae, and Freddie Mac must meet the underwriting standards that have been established by these entities. Loans that satisfy the underwriting requirements are referred to as **conforming loans.** Mortgage-backed securities not issued by agencies are backed by pools of nonconforming loans.

4.2.3 Collateralized Mortgage Obligations

Now we will show how one type of agency mortgage derivative security is created— a **collateralized mortgage obligation** (CMO). The motivation for creation of a CMO is to distribute prepayment risk among different classes of bonds.

The investor in our passthrough in Exhibit 64-7 remains exposed to the total prepayment risk associated with the underlying pool of mortgage loans, regardless of how many loans there are. Securities can be created, however, where investors do not share prepayment risk equally. Suppose that instead of distributing the monthly cash flow on a pro rata basis, as in the case of a passthrough, the distribution of the principal (both scheduled principal and prepayments) is carried out on some prioritized basis. How this is done is illustrated in Exhibit 64-8.

The exhibit shows the cash flow of our original 2,000 mortgage loans and the passthrough. Also shown are three classes of bonds, commonly referred to as **tranches,**[5] the par value of each tranche, and a set of payment rules indicating how the principal from the passthrough is to be distributed to each tranche. Note that the sum of the par value of the three tranches is equal to $200 million.

---

[4] Freddie Mac previously issued passthrough securities that guaranteed the timely payment of interest but guaranteed only the eventual payment of principal (when it is collected or within one year).

[5] "Tranche" is from an old French word meaning "slice." (The pronunciation of tranche rhymes with the English word "launch," as in launch a ship or a rocket.)

Although it is not shown in the exhibit, for each of the three tranches, there will be certificates representing a proportionate interest in a tranche. For example, suppose that for Tranche A, which has a par value of $80 million, there are 80,000 certificates issued. Each certificate would receive a proportionate share (0.00125%) of payments received by Tranche A.

The rule for the distribution of principal shown in Exhibit 64-8 is that Tranche A will receive all principal (both scheduled and prepayments) until that tranche's remaining principal balance is zero. Then, Tranche B receives all principal payments until its remaining principal balance is zero. After Tranche B is completely paid, Tranche C receives principal payments. The rule for the distribution of the cash flows in Exhibit 64-8 indicates that each of the three tranches receives interest on the basis of the amount of the par value outstanding.

EXHIBIT 64-8 Creation of a Collateralized Mortgage Obligation

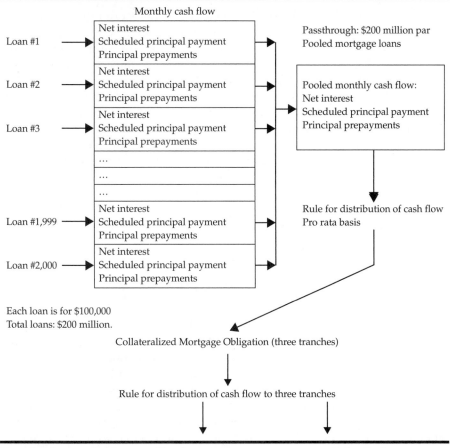

Tranche (par value)	Net interest	Principal
A ($80 million)	Pay each month based on par amount outstanding	Receives all monthly principal until completely paid off
B ($70 million)	Pay each month based on par amount outstanding	After Tranche A paid off, receives all monthly principal
C ($50 million)	Pay each month based on par amount outstanding	After Tranche B paid off, receives all monthly principal

The mortgage-backed security that has been created is called a CMO. The collateral for a CMO issued by the agencies is a pool of passthrough securities which is placed in a trust. The ultimate source for the CMO's cash flow is the pool of mortgage loans.

Let's look now at what has been accomplished. Once again, the total prepayment risk for the CMO is the same as the total prepayment risk for the 2,000 mortgage loans. However, the prepayment risk has been distributed differently across the three tranches of the CMO. Tranche A absorbs prepayments first, then Tranche B, and then Tranche C. The result of this is that Tranche A effectively is a shorter term security than the other two tranches; Tranche C will have the longest maturity. Different institutional investors will be attracted to the different tranches, depending on the nature of their liabilities and the effective maturity of the CMO tranche. Moreover, there is less uncertainty about the maturity of each tranche of the CMO than there is about the maturity of the pool of passthroughs from which the CMO is created. Thus, redirection of the cash flow from the underlying mortgage pool creates tranches that satisfy the asset/liability objectives of certain institutional investors better than a passthrough. Stated differently, the rule for distributing principal repayments redistributes prepayment risk among the tranches.

The CMO we describe in Exhibit 64-8 has a simple set of rules for the distribution of the cash flow. Today, much more complicated CMO structures exist. The basic objective is to provide certain CMO tranches with less uncertainty about prepayment risk. Note, of course, that this can occur only if the reduction in prepayment risk for some tranches is absorbed by other tranches in the CMO structure. A good example is one type of CMO tranche called a **planned amortization class tranche** or PAC tranche. This is a tranche that has a schedule for the repayment of principal (hence the name "planned amortization") if prepayments are realized at a certain prepayment rate.[6] As a result, the prepayment risk is reduced (not eliminated) for this type of CMO tranche. The tranche that realizes greater prepayment risk in order for the PAC tranche to have greater prepayment protection is called the **support tranche.**

We will describe in much more detail PAC tranches and supports tranches, as well as other types of CMO tranches at Level II.

5 STATE AND LOCAL GOVERNMENTS

Non-central government entities also issue bonds. In the United States, this includes state and local governments and entities that they create. These securities are referred to as **municipal securities** or **municipal bonds.** Because the U.S. bond market has the largest and most developed market for non-central government bonds, we will focus on municipal securities in this market.

In the United States, there are both tax-exempt and taxable municipal securities. "Tax-exempt" means that interest on a municipal security is exempt from federal income taxation. The tax-exemption of municipal securities applies to interest income, not capital gains. The exemption may or may not extend to taxation at the state and local levels. Each state has its own rules as to how interest on municipal securities is taxed. Most municipal securities that have been issued are tax-exempt. Municipal securities are commonly referred to as **tax-exempt securities** despite the fact that there are taxable municipal securities that have been issued and are traded in the market. Municipal bonds are traded in the over-the-counter market supported by municipal bond dealers across the country.

---

[6] We will explain what is meant by "prepayment rate" at Level II.

Like other non-Treasury fixed income securities, municipal securities expose investors to credit risk. The nationally recognized rating organizations rate municipal securities according to their credit risk. In Level II, we look at the factors rating agencies consider in assessing credit risk.

There are basically two types of municipal security structures: **tax-backed debt** and **revenue bonds.** We describe each below, as well as some variants.

5.1 Tax-Backed Debt

Tax-backed debt obligations are instruments issued by states, counties, special districts, cities, towns, and school districts that are secured by some form of tax revenue. Exhibit 64-9 provides an overview of the types of tax-backed debt issued in the U.S. municipal securities market. Tax-backed debt includes **general obligation debt, appropriation-backed obligations**, and **debt obligations supported by public credit enhancement programs.** We discuss each below.

5.1.1 General Obligation Debt

The broadest type of tax-backed debt is general obligation debt. There are two types of general obligation pledges: unlimited and limited. An **unlimited tax general obligation debt** is the stronger form of general obligation pledge because it is secured by the issuer's unlimited taxing power. The tax revenue sources include corporate and individual income taxes, sales taxes, and property taxes. Unlimited tax general obligation debt is said to be secured by the full faith and credit of the issuer. A **limited tax general obligation debt** is a limited tax pledge because, for such debt, there is a statutory limit on tax rates that the issuer may levy to service the debt.

EXHIBIT 64-9 Tax-Backed Debt Issues in the U.S. Municipal Securities Market

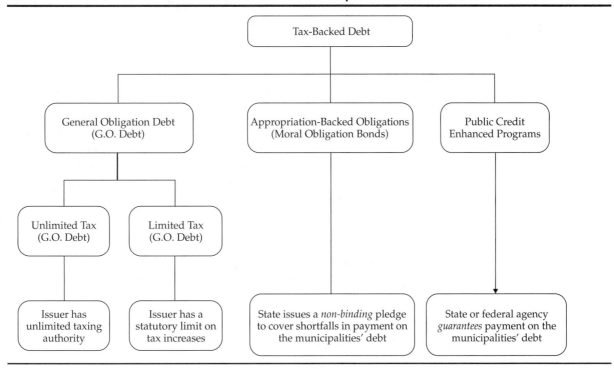

Certain general obligation bonds are secured not only by the issuer's general taxing powers to create revenues accumulated in a general fund, but also by certain identified fees, grants, and special charges, which provide additional revenues from outside the general fund. Such bonds are known as **double-barreled in security** because of the dual nature of the revenue sources. For example, the debt obligations issued by special purpose service systems may be secured by a pledge of property taxes, a pledge of special fees/operating revenue from the service provided, or a pledge of both property taxes and special fees/operating revenues. In the last case, they are double-barreled.

5.1.2 Appropriation-Backed Obligations

Agencies or authorities of several states have issued bonds that carry a potential state liability for making up shortfalls in the issuing entity's obligation. The appropriation of funds from the state's general tax revenue must be approved by the state legislature. However, the state's pledge is not binding. Debt obligations with this nonbinding pledge of tax revenue are called **moral obligation bonds.** Because a moral obligation bond requires legislative approval to appropriate the funds, it is classified as an appropriation-backed obligation. The purpose of the moral obligation pledge is to enhance the credit worthiness of the issuing entity. However, the investor must rely on the best-efforts of the state to approve the appropriation.

5.1.3 Debt Obligations Supported by Public Credit Enhancement Programs

While a moral obligation is a form of credit enhancement provided by a state, it is not a legally enforceable or legally binding obligation of the state. There are entities that have issued debt that carries some form of public credit enhancement that is legally enforceable. This occurs when there is a guarantee by the state or a federal agency or when there is an obligation to automatically withhold and deploy state aid to pay any defaulted debt service by the issuing entity. Typically, the latter form of public credit enhancement is used for debt obligations of a state's school systems.

Some examples of state credit enhancement programs include Virginia's bond guarantee program that authorizes the governor to withhold state aid payments to a municipality and divert those funds to pay principal and interest to a municipality's general obligation holders in the event of a default. South Carolina's constitution requires mandatory withholding of state aid by the state treasurer if a school district is not capable of meeting its general obligation debt. Texas created the Permanent School Fund to guarantee the timely payment of principal and interest of the debt obligations of qualified school districts. The fund's income is obtained from land and mineral rights owned by the state of Texas.

More recently, states and local governments have issued increasing amounts of bonds where the debt service is to be paid from so-called "dedicated" revenues such as sales taxes, tobacco settlement payments, fees, and penalty payments. Many are structured to mimic the asset-backed bonds that are discussed later in this reading (Section 7).

5.2 Revenue Bonds

The second basic type of security structure is found in a revenue bond. Revenue bonds are issued for enterprise financings that are secured by the revenues generated by the completed projects themselves, or for general public-purpose financings in which the issuers pledge to the bondholders the tax and revenue resources that were previously part of the general fund. This latter type of revenue bond is usually created to allow issuers to raise debt outside general obligation debt limits and without voter approval.

Revenue bonds can be classified by the type of financing. These include utility revenue bonds, transportation revenue bonds, housing revenue bonds, higher education revenue bonds, health care revenue bonds, sports complex and convention center revenue bonds, seaport revenue bonds, and industrial revenue bonds.

5.3 Special Bond Structures

Some municipal securities have special security structures. These include **insured bonds** and **prerefunded bonds.**

5.3.1 Insured Bonds

Insured bonds, in addition to being secured by the issuer's revenue, are also backed by insurance policies written by commercial insurance companies. Insurance on a municipal bond is an agreement by an insurance company to pay the bondholder principal and/or coupon interest that is due on a stated maturity date but that has not been paid by the bond issuer. Once issued, this municipal bond insurance usually extends for the term of the bond issue and cannot be canceled by the insurance company.

5.3.2 Prerefunded Bonds

Although originally issued as either revenue or general obligation bonds, municipals are sometimes prerefunded and thus called **prerefunded municipal bonds.** A prerefunding usually occurs when the original bonds are escrowed or collateralized by direct obligations guaranteed by the U.S. government. By this, it is meant that a portfolio of securities guaranteed by the U.S. government is placed in a trust. The portfolio of securities is assembled such that the cash flows from the securities match the obligations that the issuer must pay. For example, suppose that a municipality has a 7% $100 million issue with 12 years remaining to maturity. The municipality's obligation is to make payments of $3.5 million every six months for the next 12 years and $100 million 12 years from now. If the issuer wants to prerefund this issue, a portfolio of U.S. government obligations can be purchased that has a cash flow of $3.5 million every six months for the next 12 years and $100 million 12 years from now.

Once this portfolio of securities whose cash flows match those of the municipality's obligation is in place, the prerefunded bonds are no longer secured as either general obligation or revenue bonds. The bonds are now supported by cash flows from the portfolio of securities held in an escrow fund. Such bonds, if escrowed with securities guaranteed by the U.S. government, have little, if any, credit risk. They are the safest municipal bonds available.

The escrow fund for a prerefunded municipal bond can be structured so that the bonds to be refunded are to be called at the first possible call date or a subsequent call date established in the original bond indenture. While prerefunded bonds are usually retired at their first or subsequent call date, some are structured to match the debt obligation to the maturity date. Such bonds are known as **escrowed-to-maturity bonds.**

6   CORPORATE DEBT SECURITIES

Corporations throughout the world that seek to borrow funds can do so through either bank borrowing or the issuance of debt securities. The securities issued include bonds (called corporate bonds), medium term notes, asset-backed securities, and commercial paper. Exhibit 64-10 provides an overview of the structures found in the corporate debt market. In many countries throughout the world, the principal form of borrowing is via bank borrowing and, as a result, a well-developed market for non-bank borrowing has not developed or is still in its infancy stage. However, even in countries where the market for corporate debt securities is small, large corporations can borrow outside of their country's domestic market.

Because in the United States there is a well developed market for corporations to borrow via the public issuance of debt obligations, we will look at this market. Before we describe the features of corporate bonds in the United States, we will discuss the rights of bondholders in a bankruptcy and the factors considered by rating agencies in assigning a credit rating.

EXHIBIT 64-10 Overview of Corporate Debt Securities

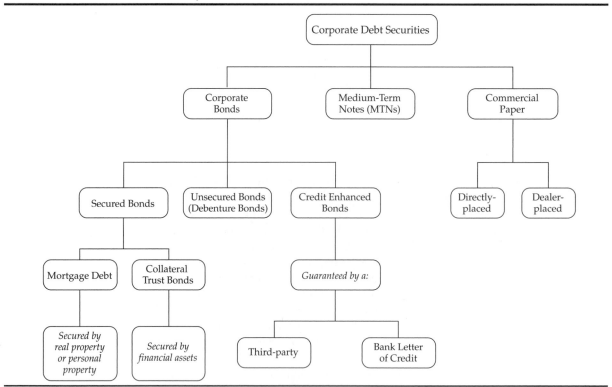

6.1 Bankruptcy and Bondholder Rights in the United States

Every country has securities laws and contract laws that govern the rights of bondholders and a bankruptcy code that covers the treatment of bondholders in the case of a bankruptcy. There are principles that are common in the legal arrangements throughout the world. Below we discuss the features of the U.S. system.

The holder of a U.S. corporate debt instrument has priority over the equity owners in a bankruptcy proceeding. Moreover, there are creditors who have priority over other creditors. The law governing bankruptcy in the United States is the Bankruptcy Reform Act of 1978 as amended from time to time. One purpose of the act is to set forth the rules for a corporation to be either liquidated or reorganized when filing bankruptcy.

The **liquidation** of a corporation means that all the assets will be distributed to the claim holders of the corporation and no corporate entity will survive. In a **reorganization,** a new corporate entity will emerge at the end of the bankruptcy proceedings. Some security holders of the bankrupt corporation will receive cash in exchange for their claims, others may receive new securities in the corporation that results from the reorganization, and others may receive a combination of both cash and new securities in the resulting corporation.

Another purpose of the bankruptcy act is to give a corporation time to decide whether to reorganize or liquidate and then the necessary time to formulate a plan to accomplish either a reorganization or liquidation. This is achieved because when a corporation files for bankruptcy, the act grants the corporation protection from creditors who seek to collect their claims. The petition for bankruptcy can be filed either by the company itself, in which case it is called a **voluntary bankruptcy,** or be filed by its creditors, in which case it is called an **involuntary bankruptcy.** A company that files for protection under the bankruptcy act generally becomes a "debtor-in-possession" and continues to operate its business under the supervision of the court.

The bankruptcy act is comprised of 15 chapters, each chapter covering a particular type of bankruptcy. Chapter 7 deals with the liquidation of a company; Chapter 11 deals with the reorganization of a company.

When a company is liquidated, creditors receive distributions based on the **absolute priority rule** to the extent assets are available. The absolute priority rule is the principle that senior creditors are paid in full before junior creditors are paid anything. For secured and unsecured creditors, the absolute priority rule guarantees their seniority to equity holders. In liquidations, the absolute priority rule generally holds. In contrast, there is a good body of literature that argues that strict absolute priority typically has not been upheld by the courts or the SEC in reorganizations.

6.2 Factors Considered in Assigning a Credit Rating

In the previous reading, we explained that there are companies that assign credit ratings to corporate issues based on the prospects of default. These companies are called rating agencies. In conducting a credit examination, each rating agency, as well as credit analysts employed by investment management companies, consider the four C's of credit—**character, capacity, collateral,** and **covenants.**

It is important to understand that a credit analysis can be for an entire company or a particular debt obligation of that company. Consequently, a rating agency may assign a different rating to the various issues of the same corporation depending on the level of seniority of the bondholders of each issue in the case of bankruptcy. For example, we will explain below that there is senior debt and subordinated debt. Senior debtholders have a better position relative to subordinated debtholders in the case of a bankruptcy for a given issuer. So, a rating agency, for example, may assign a rating of "A" to the senior debt of a corporation and a lower rating, "BBB," to the subordinated debt of the same corporation.

Character analysis involves the analysis of the quality of management. In discussing the factors it considers in assigning a credit rating, Moody's Investors Service notes the following regarding the quality of management:

> Although difficult to quantify, management quality is one of the most important factors supporting an issuer's credit strength. When the

unexpected occurs, it is a management's ability to react appropriately that will sustain the company's performance.[7]

In assessing management quality, the analysts at Moody's, for example, try to understand the business strategies and policies formulated by management. Moody's considers the following factors: (1) strategic direction, (2) financial philosophy, (3) conservatism, (4) track record, (5) succession planning, and (6) control systems.[8]

In assessing the ability of an issuer to pay (i.e., capacity), the analysts conduct financial statement analysis as discussed at Level II. In addition to financial statement analysis, the factors examined by analysts at Moody's are (1) industry trends, (2) the regulatory environment, (3) basic operating and competitive position, (4) financial position and sources of liquidity, (5) company structure (including structural subordination and priority of claim), (6) parent company support agreements, and (7) special event risk.[9]

The third C, collateral, is looked at not only in the traditional sense of assets pledged to secure the debt, but also to the quality and value of those unpledged assets controlled by the issuer. Unpledged collateral is capable of supplying additional sources of funds to support payment of debt. Assets form the basis for generating cash flow which services the debt in good times as well as bad. We discuss later the various types of collateral used for a corporate debt issue and features that analysts should be cognizant of when evaluating an investor's secured position.

Covenants deal with limitations and restrictions on the borrower's activities. **Affirmative covenants** call upon the debtor to make promises to do certain things. **Negative covenants** are those which require the borrower not to take certain actions. Negative covenants are usually negotiated between the borrower and the lender or their agents. Borrowers want the least restrictive loan agreement available, while lenders should want the most restrictive, consistent with sound business practices. But lenders should not try to restrain borrowers from accepted business activities and conduct. A borrower might be willing to include additional restrictions (up to a point) if it can get a lower interest rate on the debt obligation. When borrowers seek to weaken restrictions in their favor, they are often willing to pay more interest or give other consideration. We will see examples of positive and negative covenants later in this reading.

6.3 Corporate Bonds

In Reading 62, we discussed the features of bonds including the wide range of coupon types, the provisions for principal payments, provisions for early retirement, and other embedded options. Also, in Reading 63, we reviewed the various forms of credit risk and the ratings assigned by rating agencies. In our discussion of corporate bonds here, we will discuss secured and unsecured debt and information about default and recovery rates.

6.3.1 Secured Debt, Unsecured Debt, and Credit Enhancements

A corporate debt obligation may be secured or unsecured. **Secured debt** means that there is some form of collateral pledged to ensure payment of the debt. Remove the pledged collateral and we have **unsecured debt.**

---

[7] "Industrial Company Rating Methodology," *Moody's Investors Service: Global Credit Research* (July 1998), p. 6.

[8] "Industrial Company Rating Methodology," p. 7.

[9] "Industrial Company Rating Methodology," p. 3.

It is important to recognize that while a superior legal status will strengthen a bondholder's chance of recovery in case of default, it will not absolutely prevent bondholders from suffering financial loss when the issuer's ability to generate sufficient cash flow to pay its obligations is seriously eroded. Claims against a weak lender are often satisfied for less than par value.

6.3.1.1 Secured Debt

Either **real property** or **personal property** may be pledged as security for secured debt. With **mortgage debt,** the issuer grants the bondholders a lien against pledged assets. A lien is a legal right to sell mortgaged property to satisfy unpaid obligations to bondholders. In practice, foreclosure and sale of mortgaged property is unusual. If a default occurs, there is usually a financial reorganization of the issuer in which provision is made for settlement of the debt to bondholders. The mortgage lien is important, though, because it gives the mortgage bondholders a strong bargaining position relative to other creditors in determining the terms of a reorganization.

Some companies do not own fixed assets or other real property and so have nothing on which they can give a mortgage lien to secure bondholders. Instead, they own securities of other companies; they are holding companies and the other companies are subsidiaries. To satisfy the desire of bondholders for security, the issuer grants investors a lien on stocks, notes, bonds or other kind of financial asset they own. Bonds secured by such assets are called **collateral trust bonds.** The eligible collateral is periodically marked to market by the trustee to ensure that the market value has a liquidation value in excess of the amount needed to repay the entire outstanding bonds and accrued interest. If the collateral is insufficient, the issuer must, within a certain period, bring the value of the collateral up to the required amount. If the issuer is unable to do so, the trustee would then sell collateral and redeem bonds.

Mortgage bonds have many different names. The following names have been used: **first mortgage bonds** (most common name), **first and general mortgage bonds, first refunding mortgage bonds,** and **first mortgage and collateral trusts.** There are instances (excluding prior lien bonds as mentioned above) when a company might have two or more layers of mortgage debt outstanding with different priorities. This situation usually occurs because companies cannot issue additional first mortgage debt (or the equivalent) under the existing indentures. Often this secondary debt level is called **general and refunding mortgage bonds** (G&R). In reality, this is mostly second mortgage debt. Some issuers may have third mortgage bonds.

Although an indenture may not limit the total amount of bonds that may be issued with the same lien, there are certain **issuance tests** that usually have to be satisfied before the company may sell more bonds. Typically there is an **earnings test** that must be satisfied before additional bonds may be issued with the same lien.

6.3.1.2 Unsecured Debt

Unsecured debt is commonly referred to as **debenture bonds.** Although a debenture bond is not secured by a specific pledge of property, that does not mean that bondholders have no claim on property of issuers or on their earnings. Debenture bondholders have the claim of general creditors on all assets of the issuer not pledged specifically to secure other debt. And they even have a claim on pledged assets to the extent that these assets generate proceeds in liquidation that are greater than necessary to satisfy secured creditors. **Subordinated debenture bonds** are issues that rank after secured debt, after debenture bonds, and often after some general creditors in their claim on assets and earnings.

One of the important protective provisions for unsecured debt holders is the **negative pledge clause.** This provision, found in most senior unsecured debt issues and a few subordinated issues, prohibits a company from creating or assuming any lien to secure a debt issue without equally securing the subject debt issue(s) (with certain exceptions).

6.3.1.3 Credit Enhancements

Some debt issuers have other companies guarantee their loans. This is normally done when a subsidiary issues debt and the investors want the added protection of a **third-party guarantee.** The use of guarantees makes it easier and more convenient to finance special projects and affiliates, although guarantees are also extended to operating company debt.

An example of a third-party (but related) guarantee was US West Capital Funding, Inc. 8% Guaranteed Notes that were due October 15, 1996 (guaranteed by US West, Inc.). The principal purpose of Capital Funding was to provide financing to US West and its affiliates through the issuance of debt guaranteed by US West. PepsiCo, Inc. has guaranteed the debt of its financing affiliate, PepsiCo Capital Resources, Inc., and The Standard Oil Company (an Ohio Corporation) has unconditionally guaranteed the debt of Sohio Pipe Line Company.

Another credit enhancing feature is the **letter of credit** (LOC) issued by a bank. A LOC requires the bank make payments to the trustee when requested so that monies will be available for the bond issuer to meet its interest and principal payments when due. Thus the credit of the bank under the LOC is substituted for that of the debt issuer. Specialized insurance companies also lend their credit standing to corporate debt, both new issues and outstanding secondary market issues. In such cases, the credit rating of the bond is usually no better than the credit rating of the guarantor.

While a guarantee or other type of credit enhancement may add some measure of protection to a debtholder, caution should not be thrown to the wind. In effect, one's job may even become more complex as an analysis of both the issuer and the guarantor should be performed. In many cases, only the latter is needed if the issuer is merely a financing conduit without any operations of its own. However, if both concerns are operating companies, it may very well be necessary to analyze both, as the timely payment of principal and interest ultimately will depend on the stronger party. Generally, a downgrade of the credit enhancer's claims-paying ability reduces the value of the credit-enhanced bonds.

6.3.2 Default Rates and Recovery Rates

Now we turn our attention to the various aspects of the historical performance of corporate issuers with respect to fulfilling their obligations to bondholders. Specifically, we will review two aspects of this performance. First, we will review the default rate of corporate borrowers. Second, we will review the default loss rate of corporate borrowers. From an investment perspective, default rates by themselves are not of paramount significance: it is perfectly possible for a portfolio of bonds to suffer defaults and to outperform Treasuries at the same time, provided the yield spread of the portfolio is sufficiently high to offset the losses from default. Furthermore, because holders of defaulted bonds typically recover some percentage of the face amount of their investment, the **default loss rate** is substantially lower than the default rate. Therefore, it is important to look at default loss rates or, equivalently, **recovery rates.**

6.3.2.1 Default Rates

A default rate can be measured in different ways. A simple way to define a default rate is to use the issuer as the unit of study. A default rate is then measured as the number of issuers that default divided by the total number of issuers at the beginning of the year. This measure—referred to as the **issuer default rate**—gives no recognition to the amount defaulted nor the total amount of issuance. Moody's, for example, uses this default rate statistic in its study of default rates. The rationale for ignoring dollar amounts is that the credit decision of an investor does not increase with the size of the issuer. The second measure—called the **dollar default rate**—defines the default rate as the par value of all bonds that defaulted in a given calendar year, divided by the total par value of all bonds outstanding during the year. With either default rate statistic, one can measure the default for a given year or an average annual default rate over a certain number of years.

There have been several excellent studies of corporate bond default rates. All of the studies found that the lower the credit rating, the greater the probability of a corporate issuer defaulting.

There have been extensive studies focusing on default rates for non-investment grade corporate bonds (i.e., speculative-grade issuer or high yield bonds). Studies by Edward Altman suggest that the annual default rate for speculative-grade corporate debt has been between 2.15% and 2.4% per year.[10] Asquith, Mullins, and Wolff, however, found that nearly one out of every three speculative-grade bonds defaults.[11] The large discrepancy arises because researchers use three different definitions of "default rate"; even if applied to the same universe of bonds (which they are not), the results of these studies could be valid simultaneously.[12]

Altman defines the default rate as the dollar default rate. His estimates (2.15% and 2.40%) are simple averages of the annual dollar default rates over a number of years. Asquith, Mullins, and Wolff use a cumulative dollar default rate statistic. While both measures are useful indicators of bond default propensity, they are not directly comparable. Even when restated on an annualized basis, they do not all measure the same quantity. The default statistics reported in both studies, however, are surprisingly similar once cumulative rates have been annualized. A majority of studies place the annual dollar default rates for all original issue high-yield bonds between 3% and 4%.

6.3.1.2 Recovery Rates

There have been several studies that have focused on recovery rates or default loss rates for corporate debt. Measuring the amount recovered is not a simple task. The final distribution to claimants when a default occurs may consist of cash and securities. Often it is difficult to track what was received and then determine the present value of any non-cash payments received.

Here we review recovery information as reported in a study by Moody's which uses the trading price at the time of default as a proxy for the amount recovered.[13] The recovery rate is the trading price at that time divided by the par value. Moody's found that the recovery rate was 38% for all bonds. Moreover, the study found that the higher the level of seniority, the greater the recovery rate.

6.4 Medium-Term Notes

A **medium-term note** (MTN) is a debt instrument, with the unique characteristic that notes are offered continuously to investors by an agent of the issuer. Investors

---

[10] Edward I. Altman and Scott A. Nammacher, *Investing in Junk Bonds* (New York: John Wiley, 1987) and Edward I. Altman, "Research Update: Mortality Rates and Losses, Bond Rating Drift," unpublished study prepared for a workshop sponsored by Merrill Lynch Merchant Banking Group, High Yield Sales and Trading, 1989.

[11] Paul Asquith, David W. Mullins, Jr., and Eric D. Wolff, "Original Issue High Yield Bonds: Aging Analysis of Defaults, Exchanges, and Calls," *Journal of Finance* (September 1989), pp. 923-952.

[12] As a parallel, we know that the mortality rate in the United States is currently less than 1% per year, but we also know that 100% of all humans (eventually) die.

[13] Moody's Investors Service, *Corporate Bond Defaults and Default Rates: 1970-1994*, Moody's Special Report, January 1995, p. 13.

can select from several maturity ranges: 9 months to 1 year, more than 1 year to 18 months, more than 18 months to 2 years, and so on up to 30 years. Medium-term notes are registered with the Securities and Exchange Commission under Rule 415 (the shelf registration rule) which gives a borrower (corporation, agency, sovereign, or supranational) the maximum flexibility for issuing securities on a continuous basis. As with corporate bonds, MTNs are rated by the nationally recognized statistical rating organizations.

The term "medium-term note" used to describe this debt instrument is misleading. Traditionally, the term "note" or "medium-term" was used to refer to debt issues with a maturity greater than one year but less than 15 years. Certainly this is not a characteristic of MTNs since they have been sold with maturities from nine months to 30 years, and even longer. For example, in July 1993, Walt Disney Corporation issued a security with a 100-year maturity off its medium-term note shelf registration. From the perspective of the borrower, the initial purpose of the MTN was to fill the funding gap between commercial paper and long-term bonds. It is for this reason that they are referred to as "medium term."

Borrowers have flexibility in designing MTNs to satisfy their own needs. They can issue fixed- or floating-rate debt. The coupon payments can be denominated in U.S. dollars or in a foreign currency. MTNs have been designed with the same features as corporate bonds.

6.4.1 The Primary Market

Medium-term notes differ from bonds in the manner in which they are distributed to investors when they are initially sold. Although some corporate bond issues are sold on a "best-efforts basis" (i.e., the underwriter does not purchase the securities from the issuer but only agrees to sell them),[14] typically corporate bonds are underwritten by investment bankers. When "underwritten," the investment banker purchases the bonds from the issuer at an agreed upon price and yield and then attempts to sell them to investors. This is discussed further in Section 9. MTNs have been traditionally distributed on a best-efforts basis by either an investment banking firm or other broker/dealers acting as agents. Another difference between bonds and MTNs is that when offered, MTNs are usually sold in relatively small amounts on either a continuous or an intermittent basis, while bonds are sold in large, discrete offerings.

An entity that wants to initiate a MTN program will file a shelf registration[15] with the SEC for the offering of securities. While the SEC registration for MTN offerings are between $100 million and $1 billion, once completely sold, the issuer can file another shelf registration for a new MTN offering. The registration will include a list of the investment banking firms, usually two to four, that the borrower has arranged to act as agents to distribute the MTNs.

The issuer then posts rates over a range of maturities: for example, nine months to one year, one year to 18 months, 18 months to two years, and annually thereafter. In an offering rate schedule, an issuer will post rates as a spread over a Treasury security of comparable maturity. Rates will not be posted for maturity ranges that the issuer does not desire to sell.

---

[14] The primary market for bonds is described in Section 9.1.

[15] SEC Rule 415 permits certain issuers to file a single registration document indicating that it intends to sell a certain amount of a certain class of securities at one or more times within the next two years. Rule 415 is popularly referred to as the "shelf registration rule" because the securities can be viewed as sitting on the issuer's "shelf" and can be taken off that shelf and sold to the public without obtaining additional SEC approval. In essence, the filing of a single registration document allows the issuer to come to market quickly because the sale of the security has been preapproved by the SEC. Prior to establishment of Rule 415, there was a lengthy period required before a security could be sold to the public. As a result, in a fast-moving market, issuers could not come to market quickly with an offering to take advantage of what it perceived to be attractive financing opportunities.

The agents will then make the offering rate schedule available to their investor base interested in MTNs. An investor who is interested in the offering will contact the agent. In turn, the agent contacts the issuer to confirm the terms of the transaction. Since the maturity range in an offering rate schedule does not specify a specific maturity date, the investor can chose the final maturity subject to approval by the issuer.

The rate offering schedule can be changed at any time by the issuer either in response to changing market conditions or because the issuer has raised the desired amount of funds at a given maturity. In the latter case, the issuer can either not post a rate for that maturity range or lower the rate.

6.4.2 Structured MTNs

At one time, the typical MTN was a fixed-rate debenture that was noncallable. It is common today for issuers of MTNs to couple their offerings with transactions in the derivative markets (options, futures/forwards, swaps, caps, and floors) so they may create debt obligations with more complex risk/return features than are available in the corporate bond market. Specifically, an issue can have a floating-rate over all or part of the life of the security and the coupon formula can be based on a benchmark interest rate, equity index, individual stock price, foreign exchange rate, or commodity index. There are MTNs with inverse floating coupon rates and can include various embedded options.

MTNs created when the issuer simultaneously transacts in the derivative markets are called **structured notes.** The most common derivative instrument used in creating structured notes is a swap, an instrument described at Level II. By using the derivative markets in combination with an offering, issuers are able to create investment vehicles that are more customized for institutional investors to satisfy their investment objectives, but who are forbidden from using swaps for hedging or speculating. Moreover, it allows institutional investors who are restricted to investing in investment grade debt issues the opportunity to participate in other asset classes such as the equity market. Hence, structured notes are sometimes referred to as "rule busters." For example, an investor who buys an MTN whose coupon rate is tied to the performance of the S&P 500 (the reference rate) is participating in the equity market without owning common stock. If the coupon rate is tied to a foreign stock index, the investor is participating in the equity market of a foreign country without owning foreign common stock. In exchange for creating a structured note product, issuers can reduce their funding costs.

Common structured notes include: step-up notes, inverse floaters, deleveraged floaters, dual-indexed floaters, range notes, and index amortizing notes.

6.4.2.1 Deleveraged Floaters

A **deleveraged floater** is a floater that has a coupon formula where the coupon rate is computed as a fraction of the reference rate plus a quoted margin. The general formula for a deleveraged floater is:

$$\text{coupon rate} = b \times (\text{reference rate}) + \text{quoted margin}$$

where b is a value between zero and one.

6.4.2.2 Dual-Indexed Floaters

The coupon rate for a **dual-indexed floater** is typically a fixed percentage plus the difference between two reference rates. For example, the Federal Home Loan Bank System issued a floater whose coupon rate (reset quarterly) as follows:

$$(\text{10-year Constant Maturity Treasury rate}) - (\text{3-month LIBOR}) + 160 \text{ basis points}$$

6.4.2.3 Range Notes

A **range note** is a type of floater whose coupon rate is equal to the reference rate as long as the reference rate is within a certain range at the reset date. If the reference rate is outside of the range, the coupon rate is zero for that period. For example, a 3-year range note might specify that the reference rate is the 1-year Treasury rate and that the coupon rate resets every year. The coupon rate for the year is the Treasury rate as long as the Treasury rate at the coupon reset date falls within the range as specified below:

	Year 1	Year 2	Year 3
Lower limit of range	4.5%	5.25%	6.00%
Upper limit of range	6.5%	7.25%	8.00%

If the 1-year Treasury rate is outside of the range, the coupon rate is zero. For example, if in Year 1 the 1-year Treasury rate is 5% at the coupon reset date, the coupon rate for the year is 5%. However, if the 1-year Treasury rate is 7%, the coupon rate for the year is zero since the 1-year Treasury rate is greater than the upper limit for Year 1 of 6.5%.

6.4.2.4 Index Amortizing Notes

An **index amortizing note** (IAN) is a structured note with a fixed coupon rate but whose principal payments are made prior to the stated maturity date based on the prevailing value for some reference interest rate. The principal payments are structured so that the time to maturity of an IAN increases when the reference interest rate increases and the maturity decreases when the reference interest rate decreases.

From our understanding of reinvestment risks, we can see the risks associated with investing in an IAN. Since the coupon rate is fixed, when interest rates rise, an investor would prefer to receive principal back faster in order to reinvest the proceeds received at the prevailing higher rate. However, with an IAN, the rate of principal repayment is decreased. In contrast, when interest rates decline, an investor does not want principal repaid quickly because the investor would then be forced to reinvest the proceeds received at the prevailing lower interest rate. With an IAN, when interest rates decline, the investor will, in fact, receive principal back faster.

6.5 Commercial Paper

Commercial paper is a short-term unsecured promissory note that is issued in the open market and represents the obligation of the issuing corporation. Typically, commercial paper is issued as a zero-coupon instrument. In the United States, the maturity of commercial paper is typically less than 270 days and the most common maturity is 50 days or less.

To pay off holders of maturing paper, issuers generally use the proceeds obtained from selling new commercial paper. This process is often described as "rolling over" short-term paper. The risk that the investor in commercial paper faces is that the issuer will be unable to issue new paper at maturity. As a safeguard against this "roll-over risk," commercial paper is typically backed by unused bank credit lines.

There is very little secondary trading of commercial paper. Typically, an investor in commercial paper is an entity that plans to hold it until maturity.

This is understandable since an investor can purchase commercial paper in a direct transaction with the issuer which will issue paper with the specific maturity the investor desires.

Corporate issuers of commercial paper can be divided into financial companies and nonfinancial companies. There has been significantly greater use of commercial paper by financial companies compared to nonfinancial companies. There are three types of financial companies: captive finance companies, bank-related finance companies, and independent finance companies. Captive finance companies are subsidiaries of manufacturing companies. Their primary purpose is to secure financing for the customers of the parent company. For example, U.S. automobile manufacturers have captive finance companies. Furthermore, a bank holding company may have a subsidiary that is a finance company, providing loans to enable individuals and businesses to acquire a wide range of products. Independent finance companies are those that are not subsidiaries of equipment manufacturing firms or bank holding companies.

EXHIBIT 64-11 Commercial Paper Ratings

Category	Commercial rating company		
	Fitch	Moody's	S&P
Investment grade	F-1+		A-1+
	F-1	P-1	A-1
	F-2	P-2	A-2
	F-3	P-3	A-3
Noninvestment grade	F-S	NP(Not Prime)	B
			C
In default	D		D

Commercial paper is classified as either directly placed paper or dealer-placed paper. **Directly placed paper** is sold by the issuing firm to investors without the help of an agent or an intermediary. A large majority of the issuers of directly placed paper are financial companies. These entities require continuous funds in order to provide loans to customers. As a result, they find it cost effective to establish a sales force to sell their commercial paper directly to investors. General Electric Capital Corporation (GE Capital)—the principal financial services arm of General Electric Company—is the largest and most active direct issuer of commercial paper in the United States. **Dealer-placed commercial paper** requires the services of an agent to sell an issuer's paper.

The three nationally recognized statistical rating organizations that rate corporate bonds and medium-term notes also rate commercial paper. The ratings are shown in Exhibit 64-11. Commercial paper ratings, as with the ratings on other securities, are categorized as either investment grade or noninvestment grade.

6.6 Bank Obligations

Commercial banks are special types of corporations. Larger banks will raise funds using the various debt obligations described earlier. In this section, we describe two other debt obligations of banks—negotiable certificates of deposit and bankers acceptances—that are used by banks to raise funds.

6.6.1 Negotiable CDs

A **certificate of deposit** (CD) is a financial asset issued by a bank (or other deposit-accepting entity) that indicates a specified sum of money has been deposited at the issuing depository institution. A CD bears a maturity date and a specified interest rate; it can be issued in any denomination. In the United States, CDs issued by most banks are insured by the Federal Deposit Insurance Corporation (FDIC), but only for amounts up to $100,000. There is no limit on the maximum maturity. A CD may be nonnegotiable or negotiable. In the former case, the initial depositor must wait until the maturity date of the CD to obtain the funds. If the depositor chooses to withdraw funds prior to the maturity date, an early withdrawal penalty is imposed. In contrast, a **negotiable CD** allows the initial depositor (or any subsequent owner of the CD) to sell the CD in the open market prior to the maturity date. Negotiable CDs are usually issued in denominations of $1 million or more. Hence, an investor in a negotiable CD issued by an FDIC insured bank is exposed to the credit risk for any amount in excess of $100,000.

An important type of negotiable CD is the **Eurodollar CD,** which is a U.S. dollar-denominated CD issued primarily in London by U.S., European, Canadian, and Japanese banks. The interest rates paid on Eurodollar CDs play an important role in the world financial markets because they are viewed globally as the cost of bank borrowing. This is due to the fact that these interest rates represent the rates at which major international banks offer to pay each other to borrow money by issuing a Eurodollar CD with given maturities. The interest rate paid is called the **London interbank offered rate** (LIBOR). The maturities for the Eurodollar CD range from overnight to five years. So, references to "3-month LIBOR" indicate the interest rate that major international banks are offering to pay to other such banks on a Eurodollar CD that matures in three months. During the 1990s, LIBOR has increasingly become the reference rate of choice for borrowing arrangements—loans and floating-rate securities.

6.6.2 Bankers Acceptances

Simply put, a **bankers acceptance** is a vehicle created to facilitate commercial trade transactions. The instrument is called a bankers acceptance because a bank accepts the ultimate responsibility to repay a loan to its holder. The use of bankers acceptances to finance a commercial transaction is referred to as "acceptance financing." In the United States, the transactions in which bankers acceptances are created include (1) the importing of goods; (2) the exporting of goods to foreign entities; (3) the storing and shipping of goods between two foreign countries where neither the importer nor the exporter is a U.S. firm; and (4) the storing and shipping of goods between two U.S. entities in the United States. Bankers acceptances are sold on a discounted basis just as Treasury bills and commercial paper.

The best way to explain the creation of a bankers acceptance is by an illustration. Several entities are involved in our hypothetical transaction:

- Luxury Cars USA (Luxury Cars), a firm in Pennsylvania that sells automobiles
- Italian Fast Autos Inc. (IFA), a manufacturer of automobiles in Italy
- First Doylestown Bank (Doylestown Bank), a commercial bank in Doylestown, Pennsylvania
- *Banco di Francesco*, a bank in Naples, Italy
- The Izzabof Money Market Fund, a U.S. mutual fund

Luxury Cars and IFA are considering a commercial transaction. Luxury Cars wants to import 45 cars manufactured by IFA. IFA is concerned with the ability of Luxury Cars to make payment on the 45 cars when they are received.

Acceptance financing is suggested as a means for facilitating the transaction. Luxury Cars offers $900,000 for the 45 cars. The terms of the sale stipulate payment to be made to IFA 60 days after it ships the 45 cars to Luxury Cars. IFA determines whether it is willing to accept the $900,000. In considering the offering price, IFA must calculate the present value of the $900,000, because it will not be receiving payment until 60 days after shipment. Suppose that IFA agrees to these terms.

Luxury Cars arranges with its bank, Doylestown Bank, to issue a letter of credit. The letter of credit indicates that Doylestown Bank will make good on the payment of $900,000 that Luxury Cars must make to IFA 60 days after shipment. The letter of credit, or time draft, will be sent by Doylestown Bank to IFA's bank, *Banco di Francesco*. Upon receipt of the letter of credit, *Banco di Francesco* will notify IFA, which will then ship the 45 cars. After the cars are shipped, IFA presents the shipping documents to *Banco di Francesco* and receives the present value of $900,000. IFA is now out of the picture.

Banco di Francesco presents the time draft and the shipping documents to Doylestown Bank. The latter will then stamp "accepted" on the time draft. By doing so, Doylestown Bank has created a bankers acceptance. This means that Doylestown Bank agrees to pay the holder of the bankers acceptance $900,000 at the maturity date. Luxury Cars will receive the shipping documents so that it can procure the 45 cars once it signs a note or some other type of financing arrangement with Doylestown Bank.

At this point, the holder of the bankers acceptance is *Banco di Francesco*. It has two choices. It can continue to hold the bankers acceptance as an investment in its loan portfolio, or it can request that Doylestown Bank make a payment of the present value of $900,000. Let's assume that *Banco di Francesco* requests payment of the present value of $900,000. Now the holder of the bankers acceptance is Doylestown Bank. It has two choices: retain the bankers acceptance as an investment as part of its loan portfolio or sell it to an investor. Suppose that Doylestown Bank chooses the latter, and that The Izzabof Money Market Fund is seeking a high-quality investment with the same maturity as that of the bankers acceptance. Doylestown Bank sells the bankers acceptance to the money market fund at the present value of $900,000. Rather than sell the instrument directly to an investor, Doylestown Bank could sell it to a dealer, who would then resell it to an investor such as a money market fund. In either case, at the maturity date, the money market fund presents the bankers acceptance to Doylestown Bank, receiving $900,000, which the bank in turn recovers from Luxury Cars.

Investing in bankers acceptances exposes the investor to credit risk and liquidity risk. Credit risk arises because neither the borrower nor the accepting bank may be able to pay the principal due at the maturity date. When the bankers acceptance market was growing in the early 1980s, there were over 25 dealers. By 1989, the decline in the amount of bankers acceptances issued drove many one-time major dealers out of the business. Today, there are only a few major dealers and therefore bankers acceptances are considered illiquid. Nevertheless, since bankers acceptances are typically purchased by investors who plan to hold them to maturity, liquidity risk is not a concern to such investors.

ASSET-BACKED SECURITIES 7

In Section 4.2 we described how residential mortgage loans have been securitized. While residential mortgage loans is by far the largest type of asset that has been securitized, the major types of assets that have been securitized in many countries have included the following:

- auto loans and leases
- consumer loans
- commercial assets (e.g., including aircraft, equipment leases, trade receivables)
- credit cards
- home equity loans
- manufactured housing loans

Asset-backed securities are securities backed by a pool of loans or receivables. Our objective in this section is to provide a brief introduction to asset-backed securities.

7.1 The Role of the Special Purpose Vehicle

The key question for investors first introduced to the asset-backed securities market is why doesn't a corporation simply issue a corporate bond or medium-term note rather than an asset-backed security? To understand why, consider a triple B rated corporation that manufactures construction equipment. We will refer to this corporation as XYZ Corp. Some of its sales are for cash and others are on an installment sales basis. The installment sales are assets on the balance sheet of XYZ Corp., shown as "installment sales receivables."

Suppose XYZ Corp. wants to raise $75 million. If it issues a corporate bond, for example, XYZ Corp.'s funding cost would be whatever the benchmark Treasury yield is plus a yield spread for BBB issuers. Suppose, instead, that XYZ Corp. has installment sales receivables that are more than $75 million. XYZ Corp. can use the installment sales receivables as collateral for a bond issue. What will its funding cost be? It will probably be the same as if it issued a corporate bond. The reason is if XYZ Corp. defaults on any of its obligations, the creditors will have claim on all of its assets, including the installment sales receivables to satisfy payment of their bonds.

However, suppose that XYZ Corp. can create another corporation or legal entity and sell the installment sales receivables to that entity. We'll refer to this entity as SPV Corp. If the transaction is done properly, SPV Corp. owns the installment sales receivables, not XYZ Corp. It is important to understand that SPV Corp. is *not* a subsidiary of XYZ Corp.; therefore, the assets in SPV Corp. (i.e., the installment sales receivables) are not owned by XYZ Corp. This means that if XYZ Corp. is forced into bankruptcy, its creditors cannot claim the installment sales receivables because they are owned by SPV Corp. What are the implications?

Suppose that SPV Corp. sells securities backed by the installment sales receivables. Now creditors will evaluate the credit risk associated with collecting the receivables independent of the credit rating of XYZ Corp. What credit rating will be received for the securities issued by SPV Corp.? Whatever SPV Corp. wants the rating to be! It may seem strange that the issuer (SPV Corp.) can get any rating it wants, but that is the case. The reason is that SPV Corp. will show the characteristics of the collateral for the security (i.e., the installment sales receivables) to a rating agency. In turn, the rating agency will evaluate the credit quality of the collateral and inform the issuer what must be done to obtain specific ratings.

More specifically, the issuer will be asked to "credit enhance" the securities. There are various forms of credit enhancement. Basically, the rating agencies will look at the potential losses from the pool of installment sales receivables and make a determination of how much credit enhancement is needed for it to issue a specific rating. The higher the credit rating sought by the issuer, the greater the credit enhancement. Thus, XYZ Corp. which is BBB rated can obtain funding using its installment sales receivables as collateral to obtain a better credit rating for the securities issued. In fact, with enough credit enhancement, it can issue a AAA-rated security.

The key to a corporation issuing a security with a higher credit rating than the corporation's own credit rating is using SPV Corp. as the issuer. Actually, this legal entity that a corporation sells the assets to is called a **special purpose vehicle** or **special purpose corporation.** It plays a critical role in the ability to create a security—an asset-backed security—that separates the assets used as collateral from the corporation that is seeking financing.

Why doesn't a corporation always seek the highest credit rating (AAA) for its securities backed by collateral? The answer is that credit enhancement does not come without a cost. Credit enhancement mechanisms increase the costs associated with a securitized borrowing via an asset-backed security. So, the corporation must monitor the trade-off when seeking a higher rating between the additional cost of credit enhancing the security versus the reduction in funding cost by issuing a security with a higher credit rating.

Additionally, if bankruptcy occurs, there is the risk that a bankruptcy judge may decide that the assets of the special purpose vehicle are assets that the creditors of the corporation seeking financing (XYZ Corp. in our example) may claim after all. This is an important but unresolved legal issue in the United States. Legal experts have argued that this is unlikely. In the prospectus of an asset-backed security, there will be a legal opinion addressing this issue. This is the reason why special purpose vehicles in the United States are referred to as "bankruptcy remote" entities.

7.2 Credit Enhancement Mechanisms

In Level II, we will review how rating agencies analyze collateral in order to assign ratings. What is important to understand is that the amount of credit enhancement will be determined relative to a particular rating. There are two general types of credit enhancement structures: external and internal.

External credit enhancements come in the form of third-party guarantees. The most common forms of external credit enhancements are (1) a corporate guarantee, (2) a letter of credit, and (3) bond insurance. A corporate guarantee could be from the issuing entity seeking the funding (XYZ Corp. in our illustration above) or its parent company. Bond insurance provides the same function as in municipal bond structures and is referred to as an insurance "wrap."

A disadvantage of an external credit enhancement is that it is subject to the credit risk of the third-party guarantor. Should the third-party guarantor be downgraded, the issue itself could be subject to downgrade even if the collateral is performing as expected. This is based on the "weak link" test followed by rating agencies. According to this test, when evaluating a proposed structure, the credit quality of the issue is only as good as the weakest link in credit enhancement regardless of the quality of the underlying loans. Basically, an external credit enhancement exposes the investor to event risk since the downgrading of one entity (the third-party guarantor) can result in a downgrade of the asset-backed security.

Internal credit enhancements come in more complicated forms than external credit enhancements. The most common forms of internal credit enhancements are reserve funds, over collateralization, and senior/subordinate structures. We discuss each of these at Level II.

8   COLLATERALIZED DEBT OBLIGATIONS

A fixed income product that is also classified as part of the asset-backed securities market is the **collateralized debt obligation** (CDO). CDOs deserve special attention because of their growth since 2000. Moreover, while a CDO is backed by various assets, it is managed in a way that is not typical in other asset-backed security transactions. CDOs have been issued in both developed and developing countries.

A CDO is a product backed by a diversified pool of one or more of the following types of debt obligations:

- ▷ U.S. domestic investment-grade and high-yield corporate bonds
- ▷ U.S. domestic bank loans
- ▷ emerging market bonds
- ▷ special situation loans and distressed debt
- ▷ foreign bank loans
- ▷ asset-backed securities
- ▷ residential and commercial mortgage-backed securities
- ▷ other CDOs

When the underlying pool of debt obligations consists of bond-type instruments (corporate and emerging market bonds), a CDO is referred to as a **collateralized bond obligation** (CBO). When the underlying pool of debt obligations are bank loans, a CDO is referred to as a **collateralized loan obligation** (CLO).

In a CDO structure, an asset manager is responsible for managing the portfolio of assets (i.e., the debt obligations in which it invests). The funds to purchase the underlying assets (i.e., the bonds and loans) are obtained from the issuance of a CDO. The CDO is structured into notes or *tranches* similar to a CMO issue. The tranches are assigned ratings by a rating agency. There are restrictions as to how the manager manages the CDO portfolio, usually in the form of specific tests that must be satisfied. If any of the restrictions are violated by the asset manager, the notes can be downgraded and it is possible that the trustee begin paying principal to the senior noteholders in the CDO structure.

CDOs are categorized based on the motivation of the sponsor of the transaction. If the motivation of the sponsor is to earn the spread between the yield offered on the fixed income products held in the portfolio of the underlying pool (i.e., the collateral) and the payments made to the noteholders in the structure, then the transaction is referred to as an **arbitrage transaction.** (Moreover, a CDO is a vehicle for a sponsor that is an investment management firm to gather additional assets to manage and thereby generate additional management fees.) If the motivation of the sponsor is to remove debt instruments (primarily loans) from its balance sheet, then the transaction is referred to as a **balance sheet transaction.** Sponsors of balance sheet transactions are typically financial institutions such as banks and insurance companies seeking to reduce their capital requirements by removing loans due to their higher risk-based capital requirements.

9   PRIMARY MARKET AND SECONDARY MARKET FOR BONDS

Financial markets can be categorized as those dealing with financial claims that are newly issued, called the primary market, and those for exchanging financial claims previously issued, called the secondary market.

9.1 Primary Market

The primary market for bonds involves the distribution to investors of newly issued securities by central governments, its agencies, municipal governments, and corporations. Investment bankers work with issuers to distribute newly issued securities. The traditional process for issuing new securities involves investment bankers performing one or more of the following three functions: (1) advising the issuer on the terms and the timing of the offering, (2) buying the securities from the issuer, and (3) distributing the issue to the public. The advisor role may require investment bankers to design a security structure that is more palatable to investors than a particular traditional instrument.

In the sale of new securities, investment bankers need not undertake the second function—buying the securities from the issuer. An investment banker may merely act as an advisor and/or distributor of the new security. The function of buying the securities from the issuer is called underwriting. When an investment banking firm buys the securities from the issuer and accepts the risk of selling the securities to investors at a lower price, it is referred to as an underwriter. When the investment banking firm agrees to buy the securities from the issuer at a set price, the underwriting arrangement is referred to as a firm commitment. In contrast, in a best efforts arrangement, the investment banking firm only agrees to use its expertise to sell the securities—it does not buy the entire issue from the issuer. The fee earned from the initial offering of a security is the difference between the price paid to the issuer and the price at which the investment bank reoffers the security to the public (called the reoffering price).

9.1.1 Bought Deal and Auction Process

Not all bond issues are underwritten using the traditional firm commitment or best effort process we just described. Variations in the United States, the Euromarkets, and foreign markets for bonds include the **bought deal** and the **auction process.** The mechanics of a bought deal are as follows. The underwriting firm or group of underwriting firms offers a potential issuer of debt securities a firm bid to purchase a specified amount of securities with a certain coupon rate and maturity. The issuer is given a day or so (maybe even a few hours) to accept or reject the bid. If the bid is accepted, the underwriting firm has "bought the deal." It can, in turn, sell the securities to other investment banking firms for distribution to their clients and/or distribute the securities to its clients. Typically, the underwriting firm that buys the deal will have presold most of the issue to its institutional clients. Thus, the risk of capital loss for the underwriting firm in a bought deal may not be as great as it first appears. There are some deals that are so straightforward that a large underwriting firm may have enough institutional investor interest to keep the risks of distributing the issue at the reoffering price quite small. Moreover, hedging strategies using interest rate risk control tools can reduce or eliminate the risk of realizing a loss of selling the bonds at a price below the reoffering price.

In the auction process, the issuer announces the terms of the issue and interested parties submit bids for the entire issue. This process is more commonly referred to as a competitive bidding underwriting. For example, suppose that a public utility wishes to issue $400 million of bonds. Various underwriters will form syndicates and bid on the issue. The syndicate that bids the lowest yield (i.e., the lowest cost to the issuer) wins the entire $400 million bond issue and then reoffers it to the public.

9.1.2 Private Placement of Securities

Public and private offerings of securities differ in terms of the regulatory requirements that must be satisfied by the issuer. For example, in the United States, the Securities Act of 1933 and the Securities Exchange Act of 1934 require that all securities offered to the general public must be registered with the SEC, unless there is a specific exemption. The Securities Acts allow certain exemptions from federal registration. Section 4(2) of the 1933 Act exempts from registration "transactions by an issuer not involving any public offering."

The exemption of an offering does not mean that the issuer need not disclose information to potential investors. The issuer must still furnish the same information deemed material by the SEC. This is provided in a private placement memorandum, as opposed to a prospectus for a public offering. The distinction between the private placement memorandum and the prospectus is that the former does not include information deemed by the SEC as "non-material," whereas such information is required in a prospectus. Moreover, unlike a prospectus, the private placement memorandum is not subject to SEC review.

In the United States, one restriction that was imposed on buyers of privately placed securities is that they may not be sold for two years after acquisition. Thus, there was no liquidity in the market for that time period. Buyers of privately placed securities must be compensated for the lack of liquidity which raises the cost to the issuer of the securities. SEC Rule 144A, which became effective in 1990, eliminates the two-year holding period by permitting large institutions to trade securities acquired in a private placement among themselves without having to register these securities with the SEC. Private placements are therefore now classified as Rule 144A offerings or non-Rule 144A offerings. The latter are more commonly referred to as traditional private placements. Rule 144A offerings are underwritten by investment bankers.

9.2 Secondary Market

In the secondary market, an issuer of a bond—whether it is a corporation or a governmental unit—may obtain regular information about the bond's value. The periodic trading of a bond reveals to the issuer the consensus price that the bond commands in an open market. Thus, issuers can discover what value investors attach to their bonds and the implied interest rates investors expect and demand from them. Bond investors receive several benefits from a secondary market. The market obviously offers them liquidity for their bond holdings as well as information about fair or consensus values. Furthermore, secondary markets bring together many interested parties and thereby reduces the costs of searching for likely buyers and sellers of bonds.

A bond can trade on an exchange or in an over-the-counter market. Traditionally, bond trading has taken place predominately in the over-the-counter market where broker-dealer trading desks take principal positions to fill customer buy and sell orders. In recent years, however, there has been an evolution away from this form of traditional bond trading and toward electronic bond trading. This evolution toward electronic bond trading is likely to continue.

There are several related reasons for the transition to the electronic trading of bonds. First, because the bond business has been a principal business (where broker-dealer firms risk their own capital) rather than an agency business (where broker-dealer firms act merely as an agent or broker), the capital of the market makers is critical. The amount of capital available to institutional investors to invest throughout the world has placed significant demands on the capital of broker-dealer firms. As a result, making markets in bonds has become more risky for broker-dealer firms. Second, the increase in bond market volatility has increased the capital required of broker-dealer firms in the bond business. Finally, the profitability of bond market trading has declined since many of the products have become more commodity-like and their bid-offer spreads have decreased.

The combination of the increased risk and the decreased profitability of bond market trading has induced the major broker-dealer firms to deemphasize this business in the allocation of capital. Broker-dealer firms have determined that it is more efficient to employ their capital in other activities such as underwriting and asset management, rather than in principal-type market-making businesses. As a result, the liquidity of the traditionally principal-oriented bond markets has declined, and this decline in liquidity has opened the way for other market-making mechanisms. This retreat by traditional market-making firms opened the door for electronic trading. In fact, the major broker-dealer firms in bonds have supported electronic trading in bonds.

Electronic trading in bonds has helped fill this developing vacuum and provided liquidity to the bond markets. In addition to the overall advantages of electronic trading in providing liquidity to the markets and price discovery (particularly for less liquid markets) is the resulting trading and portfolio management efficiencies that have been realized. For example, portfolio managers can load their buy/sell orders into a web site, trade from these orders, and then clear these orders.

There are a variety of types of electronic trading systems for bonds. The two major types of electronic trading systems are **dealer-to-customer systems** and **exchange systems.** Dealer-to-customer systems can be a single-dealer system or multiple-dealer system. Single-dealer systems are based on a customer dealing with a single, identified dealer over the computer. The single-dealer system simply computerizes the traditional customer-dealer market-making mechanism. Multi-dealer systems provide some advancement over the single-dealer method. A customer can select from any of several identified dealers whose bids and offers are provided on a computer screen. The customer knows the identity of the dealer.

In an exchange system, dealer and customer bids and offers are entered into the system on an anonymous basis, and the clearing of the executed trades is done through a common process. Two different major types of exchange systems are those based on continuous trading and call auctions. Continuous trading permits trading at continuously changing market-determined prices throughout the day and is appropriate for liquid bonds, such as Treasury and agency securities. Call auctions provide for fixed price auctions (that is, all the transactions or exchanges occur at the same "fixed" price) at specific times during the day and are appropriate for less liquid bonds such as corporate bonds and municipal bonds.

10   SUMMARY

- The bond market of a country consists of an internal bond market (also called the national bond market) and an external bond market (also called the international bond market, the offshore bond market, or, more popularly, the Eurobond market).

- A country's national bond market consists of the domestic bond market and the foreign bond market.

- Eurobonds are bonds which generally have the following distinguishing features:(1)they are underwritten by an international syndicate,(2) at issuance they are offered simultaneously to investors in a number of countries,(3)they are issued outside the jurisdiction of any single country, and (4) they are in unregistered form.

- Sovereign debt is the obligation of a country's central government.

- Sovereign credits are rated by Standard & Poor's and Moody's.

- There are two ratings assigned to each central government: a local currency debt rating and a foreign currency debt rating.

- Historically, defaults have been greater on foreign currency denominated debt.

- There are various methods of distribution that have been used by central governments when issuing securities: regular auction cycle/single-price system; regular auction cycle/multiple-price system, ad hoc auction system, and the tap system.

- In the United States, government securities are issued by the Department of the Treasury and include fixed-principal securities and inflation-indexed securities.

- The most recently auctioned Treasury issue for a maturity is referred to as the on-the-run issue or current coupon issue; off-the-run issues are issues auctioned prior to the current coupon issue.

- Treasury discount securities are called bills and have a maturity of one year or less.

- A Treasury note is a coupon-bearing security which when issued has an original maturity between two and 10 years; a Treasury bond is a coupon-bearing security which when issued has an original maturity greater than 10 years.

- The Treasury issues inflation-protection securities (TIPS) whose principal and coupon payments are indexed to the Consumer Price Index.

- Zero-coupon Treasury instruments are created by dealers stripping the coupon payments and principal payment of a Treasury coupon security.

- Strips created from the coupon payments are called coupon strips; those created from the principal payment are called principal strips.

- A disadvantage for a taxable entity investing in Treasury strips is that accrued interest is taxed each year even though interest is not received.

- The bonds of an agency or organization established by a central government are called semi-government bonds or government agency bonds and may have either a direct or implied credit guarantee by the central government.

- In the U.S. bond market, federal agencies are categorized as either federally related institutions or government sponsored enterprises.

- Federally related institutions are arms of the U.S. government and, with the exception of securities of the Tennessee Valley Authority and the

Private Export Funding Corporation, are backed by the full faith and credit of the U.S. government.

▷ Government sponsored enterprises (GSEs) are privately owned, publicly chartered entities that were created by Congress to reduce the cost of capital for certain borrowing sectors of the economy deemed to be important enough to warrant assistance.

▷ A mortgage loan is a loan secured by the collateral of some specified real estate property.

▷ Mortgage loan payments consist of interest, scheduled principal payment, and prepayments.

▷ Prepayments are any payments in excess of the required monthly mortgage payment.

▷ Prepayment risk is the uncertainty about the cash flows due to prepayments.

▷ Loans included in an agency issued mortgage-backed security are conforming loans—loans that meet the underwriting standards established by the issuing entity.

▷ For a mortgage passthrough security the monthly payments are passed through to the certificate holders on a pro rata basis.

▷ In a collateralized mortgage obligation (CMO), there are rules for the payment of interest and principal (scheduled and prepaid) to the bond classes (tranches) in the CMO.

▷ The payment rules in a CMO structure allow for the redistribution of prepayment risk to the tranches comprising the CMO.

▷ In the U.S. bond market, municipal securities are debt obligations issued by state governments, local governments, and entities created by state and local governments.

▷ There are both tax-exempt and taxable municipal securities, where "tax-exempt" means that interest is exempt from federal income taxation; most municipal securities that have been issued are tax-exempt.

▷ There are basically two types of municipal security structures: tax-backed debt and revenue bonds.

▷ Tax-backed debt obligations are instruments secured by some form of tax revenue.

▷ Tax-backed debt includes general obligation debt (the broadest type of tax-backed debt), appropriation-backed obligations, and debt obligations supported by public credit enhancement programs.

▷ Revenue bonds are issued for enterprise financings that are secured by the revenues generated by the completed projects themselves, or for general public-purpose financings in which the issuers pledge to the bondholders the tax and revenue resources that were previously part of the general fund.

▷ Insured bonds, in addition to being secured by the issuer's revenue, are backed by insurance policies written by commercial insurance companies.

▷ Prefunded bonds are supported by a portfolio of Treasury securities held in an escrow fund.

▷ In the United States, the Bankruptcy Reform Act of 1978 as amended governs the bankruptcy process.

▷ Chapter 7 of the bankruptcy act deals with the liquidation of a company; Chapter 11 of the bankruptcy act deals with the reorganization of a company.

▷ In theory, creditors should receive distributions based on the absolute priority rule to the extent assets are available; this rule means that senior creditors are paid in full before junior creditors are paid anything.

▷ Generally, the absolute priority rule holds in the case of liquidations and is typically violated in reorganizations.

▷ In analyzing a corporate bond, a credit analyst must consider the four C's of credit—character, capacity, collateral, and covenants.

▷ Character relates to the ethical reputation as well as the business qualifications and operating record of the board of directors, management, and executives responsible for the use of the borrowed funds and their repayment.

▷ Capacity deals with the ability of an issuer to pay its obligations.

▷ Collateral involves not only the traditional pledging of assets to secure the debt, but also the quality and value of unpledged assets controlled by the issuer.

▷ Covenants impose restrictions on how management operates the company and conducts its financial affairs.

▷ A corporate debt issue is said to be secured debt if there is some form of collateral pledged to ensure payment of the debt.

▷ Mortgage debt is debt secured by real property such as land, buildings, plant, and equipment.

▷ Collateral trust debentures, bonds, and notes are secured by financial assets such as cash, receivables, other notes, debentures or bonds, and not by real property.

▷ Unsecured debt, like secured debt, comes in several different layers or levels of claim against the corporation's assets.

▷ Some debt issues are credit enhanced by having other companies guarantee their payment.

▷ One of the important protective provisions for unsecured debt holders is the negative pledge clause which prohibits a company from creating or assuming any lien to secure a debt issue without equally securing the subject debt issue(s) (with certain exceptions).

▷ Investors in corporate bonds are interested in default rates and, more importantly, default loss rates or recovery rates.

▷ There is ample evidence to suggest that the lower the credit rating, the higher the probability of a corporate issuer defaulting.

▷ Medium-term notes are corporate debt obligations offered on a continuous basis and are offered through agents.

▷ The rates posted for medium-term notes are for various maturity ranges, with maturities as short as nine months to as long as 30 years.

▷ MTNs have been issued simultaneously with transactions in the derivatives market to create structured MTNs allowing issuers greater flexibility in creating MTNs that are attractive to investors who seek to hedge or take a market position that they might otherwise be prohibited from doing.

▷ Common structured notes include: step-up notes, inverse floaters, deleveraged floaters, dual-indexed floaters, range notes, and index amortizing notes.

▷ Commercial paper is a short-term unsecured promissory note issued in the open market that is an obligation of the issuing entity.

▷ Commercial paper is sold on a discount basis and has a maturity less than 270 days.

▷ Bank obligations in addition to the traditional corporate debt instruments include certificates of deposits and bankers acceptances.

- Asset-backed securities are securities backed by a pool of loans or receivables.

- The motivation for issuers to issue an asset-backed security rather than a traditional debt obligation is that there is the opportunity to reduce funding cost by separating the credit rating of the issuer from the credit quality of the pool of loans or receivables.

- The separation of the pool of assets from the issuer is accomplished by means of a special purpose vehicle or special purpose corporation.

- In obtaining a credit rating for an asset-backed security, the rating agencies require that the issue be credit enhanced; the higher the credit rating sought, the greater the credit enhancement needed.

- There are two general types of credit enhancement structures: external and internal.

- A collateralized debt obligation is a product backed by a pool of one or more of the following types of fixed income securities: bonds, asset-backed securities, mortgage-backed securities, bank loans, and other CDOs.

- The asset manager in a collateralized debt obligation is responsible for managing the portfolio of assets (i.e.,the debt obligations backing the transaction) and there are restrictions imposed on the activities of the asset manager.

- The funds to purchase the underlying assets in a collateral debt obligation are obtained from the CDO issuance with ratings assigned by a rating agency.

- Collateralized debt obligations are categorized as either arbitrage transactions or balance sheet transactions, the classification being based on the motivation of the sponsor of the transaction.

- Bonds have traditionally been issued via an underwriting as a firm commitment or on a best efforts basis; bonds are also underwritten via a bought deal or an auction process.

- A bond can be placed privately with an institutional investor rather than issued via a public offering.

- In the United States, private placements are now classified as Rule 144A offerings (underwritten by an investment bank) and non-Rule 144A offerings (a traditional private placement).

- Bonds typically trade in the over-the-counter market.

- The two major types of electronic trading systems for bonds are the dealer-to-customer systems and the exchange systems.higher the probability of a corporate issuer defaulting.

PROBLEMS

1. Explain whether you agree or disagree with each of the following statements:

   A. "The foreign bond market sector of the Japanese bond market consists of bonds of Japanese entities that are issued outside of Japan."

   B. "Because bonds issued by central governments are backed by the full faith and credit of the issuing country, these bonds are not rated."

   C. "A country's semi-government bonds carry the full faith and credit of the central government."

   D. "In the United States, all federal agency bonds carry the full faith and credit of the U.S. government."

2. Why do rating agencies assign two types of ratings to the debt of a sovereign entity?

3. When issuing bonds, a central government can select from several distribution methods.

   A. What is the difference between a single-price auction and a multiple-price auction?

   B. What is a tap system?

4. Suppose a portfolio manager purchases $1 million of par value of a Treasury inflation protection security. The real rate (determined at the auction) is 3.2%.

   A. Assume that at the end of the first six months the CPI-U is 3.6% (annual rate). Compute the (i) inflation adjustment to principal at the end of the first six months, (ii) the inflation-adjusted principal at the end of the first six months, and (iii) the coupon payment made to the investor at the end of the first six months.

   B. Assume that at the end of the second six months the CPI-U is 4.0% (annual rate). Compute the (i) inflation adjustment to principal at the end of the second six months, (ii) the inflation-adjusted principal at the end of the second six months, and (iii) the coupon payment made to the investor at the end of the second six months.

5. A. What is the measure of the rate of inflation selected by the U.S. Treasury to determine the inflation adjustment for Treasury inflation protection securities?

   B. Suppose that there is deflation over the life of a Treasury inflation protection security resulting in an inflation-adjusted principal at the maturity date that is less than the initial par value. How much will the U.S. Treasury pay at the maturity date to redeem the principal?

   C. Why is it necessary for the U.S. Treasury to report a daily index ratio for each TIPS issue?

6. What is a U.S. federal agency debenture?

7. Suppose that a 15-year mortgage loan for $200,000 is obtained. The mortgage is a level-payment, fixed-rate, fully amortized mortgage. The mortgage rate is 7.0% and the monthly mortgage payment is $1,797.66.

   A. Compute an amortization schedule for the first six months.

   B. What will the mortgage balance be at the end of the 15th year?

   C. If an investor purchased this mortgage, what will the timing of the cash flow be assuming that the borrower does not default?

8. **A.** What is a prepayment?

   B. What do the monthly cash flows of a mortgage-backed security consist of?

   C. What is a curtailment?

9. What is prepayment risk?

10. **A.** What is the difference between a mortgage passthrough security and a collateralized mortgage obligation?

    B. Why is a collateralized mortgage obligation created?

11. Name two U.S. government-sponsored enterprises that issue mortgage-backed securities.

12. What is the difference between a limited and unlimited general obligation bond?

13. What is a moral obligation bond?

14. What is an insured municipal bond?

15. **A.** What is a prefunded bond?

    B. Why does a properly structured prefunded municipal bond have no credit risk?

16. **A.** What is the difference between a liquidation and a reorganization?

    B. What is the principle of absolute priority?

    C. Comment on the following statement: "An investor who purchases a mortgage bond issued by a corporation knows that should the corporation become bankrupt, mortgage bondholders will be paid in full before the stockholders receive any proceeds."

17. **A.** What is a subordinated debenture corporate bond?

    B. What is negative pledge clause?

18. **A.** Why is the default rate alone not an adequate measure of the potential performance of corporate bonds?

    B. One study of default rates for speculative grade corporate bonds has found that one-third of all such issues default. Other studies have found that the default rate is between 2.15% and 2.4% for speculative grade corporate bonds. Why is there such a difference in these findings for speculative grade corporate bonds?

    C. Comment on the following statement: "Most studies have found that recovery rates are less than 15% of the trading price at the time of default and the recovery rate does not vary with the level of seniority."

19. **A.** What is the difference between a medium-term note and a corporate bond?

    B. What is a structured note?

    C. What factor determines the principal payment for an index amortizing note and what is the risk of investing in this type of structured note?

20. **A.** What is the risk associated with investing in a negotiable certificate of deposit issued by a U.S. bank?

    B. What is meant by "1-month LIBOR"?

21. What are the risks associated with investing in a bankers acceptance?

22. A financial corporation with a BBB rating has a consumer loan portfolio. An investment banker has suggested that this corporation consider issuing an asset-backed security where the collateral for the security is the consumer loan portfolio. What would be the advantage of issuing an asset-backed security rather than a straight offering of corporate bonds?

23. What is the role played by a special purpose vehicle in an asset-backed security structure?

24. A. What are the various forms of external credit enhancement for an asset-backed security?

   B. What is the disadvantage of using an external credit enhancement in an asset-backed security structure?

25. A. What is a collateralized debt obligation?

   B. Explain whether you agree or disagree with the following statement: "The asset manager in a collateralized debt obligation is free to manage the portfolio as aggressively or passively as he or she deems appropriate."

   C. What distinguishes an arbitrage transaction from a balance sheet transaction?

26. What is a bought deal?

27. How are private placements classified?

28. Explain the two major types of electronic bond trading systems.

UNDERSTANDING YIELD SPREADS

LEARNING OUTCOMES

The candidate should be able to:

a. identify the interest rate policy tools available to a central bank (such as the U.S. Federal Reserve or European Central Bank);

b. describe a yield curve and the different yield curve shapes observed and explain the basic theories of the term structure of interest rates (i.e., pure expectations theory, liquidity preference theory, and market segmentation theory) and describe the implications of each theory for the shape of the yield curve; explain the different types of yield spread measures (e.g., absolute yield spread, relative yield spread, yield ratio), and compute yield spread measures given the yields for two securities;

c. explain why investors may find a relative yield spread to be a better measure of yield spread than the absolute yield spread, distinguish between an intermarket and intramarket sector spread, and describe a credit spread and discuss the suggested relationship between credit spreads and the economic well being of the economy;

d. identify how embedded options affect yield spreads;

e. explain how the liquidity of an issue affects its yield spread relative to Treasury securities and relative to other issues that are comparable in all other ways except for liquidity and describe the relationships that are argued to exist among the size of an issue, liquidity, and yield spread;

f. compute the after-tax yield of a taxable security and the tax-equivalent yield of a tax-exempt security;

g. define LIBOR and why it is an important measure to funded investors who borrow short-term.

INTRODUCTION 1

The interest rate offered on a particular bond issue depends on the interest rate that can be earned on (1) risk-free instruments and (2) the perceived risks associated with the issue. We refer to the interest rates on risk-free instruments as the

Fixed Income Analysis for the Chartered Financial Analyst ®Program, Second Edition, by Frank J. Fabozzi. Reprinted with permission.

"level of interest rates." The actions of a country's central bank influence the level of interest rates as does the state of the country's economy. In the United States, the level of interest rates depends on the state of the economy, the interest rate policies implemented by the Board of Governors of the Federal Reserve Board, and the government's fiscal policies.

A casual examination of the financial press and dealer quote sheets shows a wide range of interest rates reported at any given point in time. Why are there differences in interest rates among debt instruments? We provided information on this topic in Reading 62 and 63. In Reading 62, we explained the various features of a bond while in Reading 63 we explained how those features affect the risk characteristics of a bond relative to bonds without that feature.

In this reading, we look more closely at the differences in yields offered by bonds in different sectors of the bond market and within a sector of the bond market. This information is used by investors in assessing the "relative value" of individual securities within a bond sector, or among sectors of the bond market. Relative value analysis is a process of ranking individual securities or sectors with respect to expected return potential. We will continue to use the terms "interest rate" and "yield" interchangeably.

2   INTEREST RATE DETERMINATION

Our focus in this reading is on (1) the relationship between interest rates offered on different bond issues at a point in time and (2) the relationships among interest rates offered in different sectors of the economy at a given point in time. We will provide a brief discussion of the role of the U.S. Federal Reserve (the Fed), the policy making body whose interest rate policy tools directly influence short-term interest rates and indirectly influence long-term interest rates.

Once the Fed makes a policy decision it immediately announces the policy in a statement issued at the close of its meeting. The Fed also communicates its future intentions via public speeches or its Chairman's testimony before Congress. Managers who pursue an active strategy of positioning a portfolio to take advantage of expected changes in interest rates watch closely the same key economic indicators that the Fed watches in order to anticipate a change in the Fed's monetary policy and to assess the expected impact on short-term interest rates. The indicators that are closely watched by the Fed include non-farm payrolls, industrial production, housing starts, motor vehicle sales, durable good orders, National Association of Purchasing Management supplier deliveries, and commodity prices.

In implementing monetary policy, the Fed uses the following interest rate policy tools:

1. open market operations
2. the discount rate
3. bank reserve requirements
4. verbal persuasion to influence how bankers supply credit to businesses and consumers

Engaging in open market operations and changing the discount rate are the tools most often employed. Together, these tools can raise or lower the cost of funds in the economy. Open market operations do this through the Fed's buying and selling of U.S. Treasury securities. This action either adds funds to the market (when Treasury securities are purchased) or withdraws funds from the market (when Treasury securities are sold). Fed open market operations influence the federal funds rate, the rate at which banks borrow and lend funds from each other. The discount rate is the interest rate at which banks can borrow on a collateralized basis at the Fed's discount window. Increasing the discount rate makes the cost of funds more expensive for banks; the cost of funds is reduced when the discount rate is lowered. Changing bank reserve requirements is a less frequently used policy, as is the use of verbal persuasion to influence the supply of credit.

U.S. TREASURY RATES   ◣ 3 ◢

The securities issued by the U.S. Department of the Treasury are backed by the full faith and credit of the U.S. government. Consequently, market participants throughout the world view these securities as being "default risk-free" securities. However, there are risks associated with owning U.S. Treasury securities.

The Treasury issues the following securities:

Treasury bills: Zero-coupon securities with a maturity at issuance of one year or less. The Treasury currently issues 1-month, 3-month, and 6-month bills.

Treasury notes: Coupon securities with maturity at issuance greater than 1 year but not greater than 10 years. The Treasury currently issues 2-year, 5-year, and 10-year notes.

Treasury bonds: Coupon securities with maturity at issuance greater than 10 years. Although Treasury bonds have traditionally been issued with maturities up to 30 years, the Treasury suspended issuance of the 30-year bond in October 2001.

Inflation-protection securities: Coupon securities whose principal's reference rate is the Consumer Price Index.

The on-the-run issue or current issue is the most recently auctioned issue of Treasury notes and bonds of each maturity. The off-the-run issues are securities that were previously issued and are replaced by the on-the-run issue. Issues that have been replaced by several more recent issues are said to be "well off-the-run issues."

The secondary market for Treasury securities is an over-the-counter market where a group of U.S. government securities dealers provides continuous bids and offers on specific outstanding Treasuries. This secondary market is the most liquid financial market in the world. Off-the-run issues are less liquid than on-the-run issues.

3.1 Risks of Treasury Securities

With this brief review of Treasury securities, let's look at their risks. We listed the general risks in Reading 63 and repeat them here: (1) interest rate risk, (2) call and prepayment risk, (3) yield curve risk, (4) reinvestment risk, (5) credit risk, (6) liquidity risk, (7) exchange-rate risk, (8) volatility risk, (9) inflation or purchasing power risk, and (10) event risk.

All fixed income securities, including Treasury securities, expose investors to interest rate risk.[1] However, the degree of interest rate risk is not the same for all securities. The reason is that maturity and coupon rate affect how much the price changes when interest rates change. One measure of a security's interest rate risk is its *duration*.[2] Since Treasury securities, like other fixed income securities, have different durations, they have different exposures to interest rate risk as measured by duration.

Technically, yield curve risk and volatility risk are risks associated with Treasury securities. However, at this early stage of our understanding of fixed income analysis, we will not attempt to explain these risks. It is not necessary to understand these risks at this point in order to appreciate the material that follows in this section.

Because Treasury securities are noncallable, there is no reinvestment risk due to an issue being called.[3] Treasury coupon securities carry reinvestment risk because in order to realize the yield offered on the security, the investor must reinvest the coupon payments received at an interest rate equal to the computed yield. So, all Treasury coupon securities are exposed to reinvestment risk. Treasury bills are not exposed to reinvestment risk because they are zero-coupon instruments.

As for credit risk, the perception in the global financial community is that Treasury securities have no credit risk. In fact, when market participants and the popular press state that Treasury securities are "risk free," they are referring to credit risk.

Treasury securities are highly liquid. However, on-the-run and off-the-run Treasury securities trade with different degrees of liquidity. Consequently, the yields offered by on-the-run and off-the-run issues reflect different degrees of liquidity.

Since U.S. Treasury securities are dollar denominated, there is no exchange-rate risk for an investor whose domestic currency is the U.S. dollar. However, non-U.S. investors whose domestic currency is not the U.S. dollar are exposed to exchange-rate risk.

Fixed-rate Treasury securities are exposed to inflation risk. Treasury inflation protection securities (TIPS) have a coupon rate that is effectively adjusted for the rate of inflation and therefore have protection against inflation risk.

Finally, the yield on Treasury securities is impacted by a myriad of events that can be classified as political risk, a form of event risk. The actions of monetary and fiscal policy in the United States, as well as the actions of other central banks and governments, can have an adverse or favorable impact on U.S. Treasury yields.

3.2 The Treasury Yield Curve

Given that Treasury securities do not expose investors to credit risk, market participants look at the yield offered on an on-the-run Treasury security as the minimum interest rate required on a non-Treasury security with the same maturity. The relationship between yield and maturity of on-the-run Treasury securities on February 8, 2002 is displayed in Exhibit 1 in tabular form. The relationship shown in Exhibit 65-1 is called the **Treasury yield curve**—even though the "curve" shown in the exhibit is presented in tabular form.

---

[1] Interest rate risk is the risk of an adverse movement in the price of a bond due to changes in interest rates.

[2] Duration is a measure of a bond's price sensitivity to a change in interest rates.

[3] The Treasury no longer issues callable bonds. The Treasury issued callable bonds in the early 1980s and all of these issues will mature no later than November 2014 (assuming that they are not called before then). Moreover, as of 2004, the longest maturity of these issues is 10 years. Consequently, while outstanding callable issues of the Treasury are referred to as "bonds," based on their current maturity these issues would not be compared to long-term bonds in any type of relative value analysis. Therefore, because the Treasury no longer issues callable bonds and the outstanding issues do not have the maturity characteristics of a long-term bond, we will ignore these callable issues and simply treat Treasury bonds as noncallable.

EXHIBIT 65-1 Relationship Between Yield and Maturity for On-the-Run Treasury Issues on February 8, 2002

Issue (maturity)	Yield (%)
1 month	1.68
3 months	1.71
6 months	1.81
1 year[1]	2.09
2 years	2.91
5 years	4.18
10 years	4.88
30 years[2]	5.38

[1] The 1-year issue is based on the 2-year issue closest to maturing in one year.

[2] The 30-year issue shown is based on the last 30-year issue before the Treasury suspended issuance of Treasury bonds in October 2001.

Source: Global Relative Value, Lehman Brothers, Fixed Income Research, February 11, 2002, p. 128.

The information presented in Exhibit 65-1 indicates that the longer the maturity the higher the yield and is referred to as an **upward sloping yield** curve. Since this is the most typical shape for the Treasury yield curve, it is also referred to as a **normal yield curve.** Other relationships have been observed. An inverted yield curve indicates that the longer the maturity, the lower the yield. For a **flat yield curve** the yield is approximately the same regardless of maturity.

Exhibit 65-2 provides a graphic example of the variants of these shapes and also shows how a yield curve can change over time. In the exhibit, the yield curve at the beginning of 2001 was inverted up to the 5-year maturity but was upward sloping beyond the 5-year maturity. By December 2001, all interest rates had declined. As seen in the exhibit, interest rates less than the 10-year maturity dropped substantially more than longer-term rates resulting in an upward sloping yield curve.

The number of on-the-run securities available in constructing the yield curve has decreased over the last two decades. While the 1-year and 30-year yields are shown in the February 8, 2002 yield curve, as of this writing there is no 1-year Treasury bill and the maturity of the 30-year Treasury bond (the last one issued before suspension of the issuance of 30-year Treasury bonds) will decline over time. To get a yield for maturities where no on-the-run Treasury issue exists, it is necessary to interpolate from the yield of two on-the-run issues. Several methodologies are used in practice. (The simplest is just a linear interpolation.) Thus, when market participants talk about a yield on the Treasury yield curve that is not one of the available on-the-run maturities—for example, the 8-year yield—it is only an approximation.

It is critical to understand that any non-Treasury issue must offer a premium above the yield offered for the same maturity on-the-run Treasury issue. For example, if a corporation wanted to offer a 10-year noncallable issue on February 8, 2002, the issuer must offer a yield greater than 4.88% (the yield for the 10-year on-the-run Treasury issue). How much greater depends on the additional risks associated with investing in the 10-year corporate issue compared to investors in the 10-year on-the-run Treasury issue. Even off-the-run Treasury issues must offer a premium to reflect differences in liquidity.

EXHIBIT 65-2 U.S. Treasury Yield Curve: December 2000 and December 2001

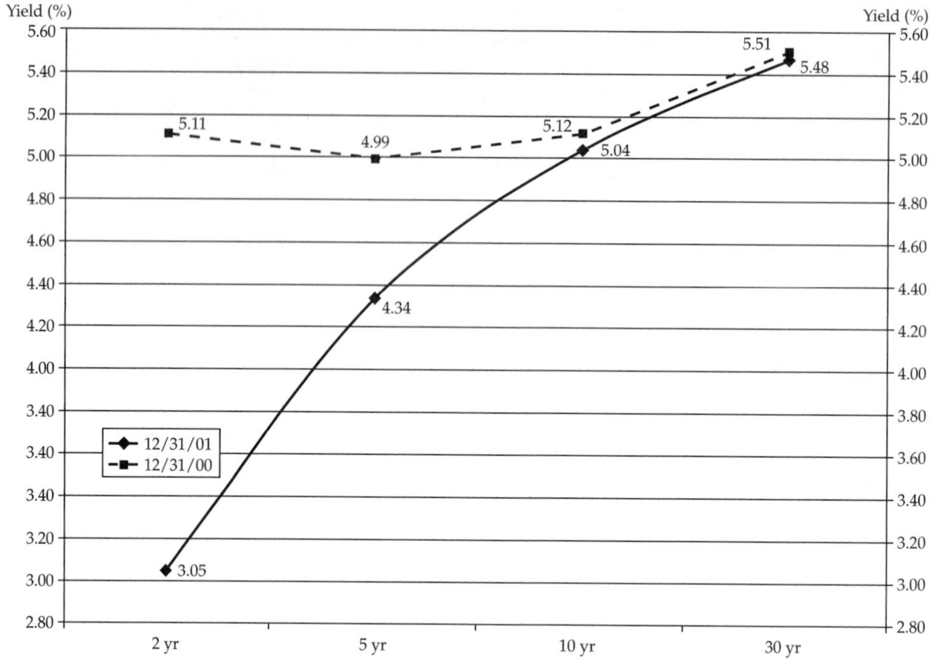

Source: Lehman Brothers Fixed Income Research, *Global Fixed Income Strategy "Playbook,"* January 2002.

Two factors complicate the relationship between maturity and yield as portrayed by the yield curve. The first is that the yield for on-the-run issues may be distorted by the fact that purchase of these securities can be financed at lower rates and as a result these issues offer artificially low yields. To clarify, some investors purchase securities with borrowed funds and use the securities purchased as collateral for the loan. This type of collateralized borrowing is called a repurchase agreement. Since dealers want to obtain use of these securities for their own trading activities, they are willing to lend funds to investors at a lower interest rate than is otherwise available for borrowing in the market. Consequently, incorporated into the price of an on-the-run Treasury security is the cheaper financing available, resulting in a lower yield for an on-the-run issue than would prevail in the absence of this financing advantage.

The second factor complicating the comparison of on-the-run and off-the-run Treasury issues (in addition to liquidity differences) is that they have different interest rate risks and different reinvestment risks. So, for example, if the coupon rate for the 5-year on-the-run Treasury issue in February 2002 is 4.18% and an off-the-run Treasury issue with just less than 5 years to maturity has a 5.25% coupon rate, the two bonds have different degrees of interest rate risk. Specifically, the on-the-run issue has greater interest rate risk (duration) because of the lower coupon rate. However, it has less reinvestment risk because the coupon rate is lower.

Because of this, when market participants talk about interest rates in the Treasury market and use these interest rates to value securities they look at another relationship in the Treasury market: the relationship between yield and maturity for zero-coupon Treasury securities. But wait, we said that the Treasury only issues three zero-coupon securities—1-month, 3-month, and 6-month Treasury bills. Where do we obtain the relationship between yield and maturity for zero-coupon Treasury securities? We discuss this next.

3.2.1 Theories of the Term Structure of Interest Rates

What information do the yield curve reveal? How can we explain and interpret changes in the yield curve? These questions are of great interest to anyone concerned with such tasks as the valuation of multiperiod securities, economic forecasting, and risk management. Theories of the term structure of interest rates[4] address these questions. Here we introduce the three main theories or explanations of the term structure. We shall present these theories intuitively.[5]

The three main term structure theories are:

- the pure expectations theory (unbiased expectations theory)
- the liquidity preference theory (or liquidity premium theory)
- the market segmentation theory

Each theory is explained below.

3.2.1.1 Pure Expectations Theory

The pure expectations theory makes the simplest and most direct link between the yield curve and investors' expectations about future interest rates, and, because long-term interest rates are plausibly linked to investor expectations about future inflation, it also opens the door to some interesting economic interpretations.

The **pure expectations theory** explains the term structure in terms of expected future short-term interest rates. According to the pure expectations theory, the market sets the yield on a two-year bond so that the return on the two-year bond is approximately equal to the return on a one-year bond plus the expected return on a one-year bond purchased one year from today.

Under this theory, a rising term structure indicates that the market expects short-term rates to rise in the future. For example, if the yield on the two-year bond is higher than the yield on the one-year bond, according to this theory, investors expect the one-year rate a year from now to be sufficiently higher than the one-year rate available now so that the two ways of investing for two years have the same expected return. Similarly, a flat term structure reflects an expectation that future short-term rates will be unchanged from today's short-term rates, while a falling term structure reflects an expectation that future short-term rates will decline. This is summarized below:

Shape of term structure	Implication according to pure expectations theory
upward sloping (normal)	rates expected to rise
downward sloping (inverted)	rates expected to decline
flat	rates not expected to change

The implications above are the broadest interpretation of the theory.

---

[4] Term structure means the same as maturity—structure a description of how a bond's yield changes as the bond's maturity changes. In other words, term structure asks the question: Why do long-term bonds have a different yield than short-term bonds?

[5] At level II, we provide a more mathematical treatment of these theories in terms of forward rates that we will discuss in Reading 67.

How does the pure expectations theory explain a humped yield curve? According to the theory, this can result when investors expect the returns on one-year securities to rise for a number of years, then fall for a number of years.

The relationships that the table above illustrates suggest that the shape of the yield curve contains information regarding investors' expectations about future inflation. A pioneer of the theory of interest rates (the economist Irving Fisher) asserted that interest rates reflect the sum of a relatively stable real rate of interest plus a premium for expected inflation. Under this hypothesis, if short-term rates are expected to rise, investors expect inflation to rise as well. An upward (downward) sloping term structure would mean that investors expected rising (declining) future inflation. Much economic discussion in the financial press and elsewhere is based on this interpretation of the yield curve.

The shortcoming of the pure expectations theory is that it assumes investors are indifferent to interest rate risk and any other risk factors associated with investing in bonds with different maturities.

3.2.1.2 Liquidity Preference Theory

The **liquidity preference theory** asserts that market participants want to be compensated for the interest rate risk associated with holding longer-term bonds. The longer the maturity, the greater the price volatility when interest rates change and investors want to be compensated for this risk. According to the liquidity preference theory, the term structure of interest rates is determined by (1) expectations about future interest rates and (2) a yield premium for interest rate risk.[6] Because interest rate risk increases with maturity, the liquidity preference theory asserts that the yield premium increases with maturity.

Consequently, based on this theory, an upward-sloping yield curve may reflect expectations that future interest rates either (1) will rise, or (2) will be unchanged or even fall, but with a yield premium increasing with maturity fast enough to produce an upward sloping yield curve. Thus, for an upward sloping yield curve (the most frequently observed type), the liquidity preference theory by itself has nothing to say about expected future short-term interest rates. For flat or downward sloping yield curves, the liquidity preference theory is consistent with a forecast of declining future short-term interest rates, given the theory's prediction that the yield premium for interest rate risk increases with maturity.

Because the liquidity preference theory argues that the term structure is determined by both expectations regarding future interest rates and a yield premium for interest rate risk, it is referred to as **biased expectations theory.**

3.2.1.3 Market Segmentation Theory

Proponents of the **market segmentation theory** argue that within the different maturity sectors of the yield curve the supply and demand for funds determine the interest rate for that sector. That is, each maturity sector is an independent or segmented market for purposes of determining the interest rate in that maturity sector. Thus, positive sloping, inverted, and humped yield curves are all possible. In fact, the market segmentation theory can be used to explain any shape that one might observe for the yield curve.

Let's understand why proponents of this theory view each maturity sector as independent or segmented. In the bond market, investors can be divided into two groups based on their return needs: investors that manage funds versus a broad-based bond market index and those that manage funds versus their liabilities. The easiest case is for those that manage funds against liabilities. Investors

---

[6] In the liquidity preference theory, "liquidity" is measured in terms of interest rate risk. Specifically, the more interest rate risk, the less the liquidity.

managing funds where liabilities represent the benchmark will restrict their activities to the maturity sector that provides the best match with the maturity of their liabilities.[7] This is the basic principle of asset-liability management. If these investors invest funds outside of the maturity sector that provides the best match against liabilities, they are exposing themselves to the risks associated with an asset-liability mismatch. For example, consider the manager of a defined benefit pension fund. Since the liabilities of a defined benefit pension fund are long-term, the manager will invest in the long-term maturity sector of the bond market. Similarly, commercial banks whose liabilities are typically short-term focus on short-term fixed-income investments. Even if the rate on long-term bonds were considerably more attractive than that on short-term investments, according to the market segmentation theory commercial banks will restrict their activities to investments at the short end of the yield curve. Reinforcing this notion of a segmented market are restrictions imposed on financial institutions that prevent them from mismatching the maturity of assets and liabilities.

A variant of the market segmentation theory is the **preferred habitat theory.** This theory argues that investors prefer to invest in particular maturity sectors as dedicated by the nature of their liabilities. However, proponents of this theory do not assert that investors would be unwilling to shift out of their preferred maturity sector; instead, it is argued that if investors are given an inducement to do so in the form of a yield premium they will shift out of their preferred habitat. The implication of the preferred habitat theory for the shape of the yield curve is that any shape is possible.

3.3 Treasury Strips

Although the U.S. Department of the Treasury does not issue zero-coupon Treasury securities with maturity greater than one year, government dealers can synthetically create zero-coupon securities, which are effectively guaranteed by the full faith and credit of the U.S. government, with longer maturities. They create these securities by separating the coupon payments and the principal payment of a coupon-bearing Treasury security and selling them off separately. The process, referred to as **stripping a Treasury security,** results in securities called **Treasury strips.** The Treasury strips created from coupon payments are called Treasury coupon strips and those created from the principal payment are called Treasury principal strips. We explained the process of creating Treasury strips in Reading 64.

Because zero-coupon instruments have no reinvestment risk, Treasury strips for different maturities provide a superior relationship between yield and maturity than do securities on the on-the-run Treasury yield curve. The lack of reinvestment risk eliminates the bias resulting from the difference in reinvestment risk for the securities being compared. Another advantage is that the duration of a zero-coupon security is approximately equal to its maturity. Consequently, when comparing bond issues against Treasury strips, we can compare them on the basis of duration.

The yield on a zero-coupon security has a special name: the **spot rate.** In the case of a Treasury security, the yield is called a **Treasury spot rate.** The relationship between maturity and Treasury spot rates is called **the term structure of interest rates.** Sometimes discussions of the term structure of interest rates in the Treasury market get confusing. The Treasury yield curve and the Treasury **term structure of interest rates** are often used interchangeably. While there is a technical difference between the two, the context in which these terms are used should be understood.

---

[7] One of the principles of finance is the "matching principle:" short-term assets should be financed with (or matched with) short-term liabilities; long-term assets should be financed with (or matched with) long-term sources of financing.

---

4   YIELDS ON NON-TREASURY SECURITIES

Despite the imperfections of the Treasury yield curve as a benchmark for the minimum interest rate that an investor requires for investing in a non-Treasury security, it is commonplace to refer to the additional yield over the benchmark Treasury issue of the same maturity as the **yield spread.** In fact, because non-Treasury sectors of the fixed income market offer a yield spread to Treasury securities, non-Treasury sectors are commonly referred to as **spread sectors** and non-Treasury securities in these sectors are referred to as **spread products.**

4.1 Measuring Yield Spreads

While it is common to talk about spreads relative to a Treasury security of the same maturity, a yield spread between any two bond issues can be easily computed. In general, the yield spread between any two bond issues, bond X and bond Y, is computed as follows:

$$\text{yield spread} = \text{yield on bond X} - \text{yield on bond Y}$$

where bond Y is considered the reference bond (or benchmark) against which bond X is measured.

When a yield spread is computed in this manner it is referred to as an **absolute yield spread** and it is measured in basis points. For example, on February 8, 2002, the yield on the 10-year on-the-run Treasury issue was 4.88% and the yield on a single A rated 10-year industrial bond was 6.24%. If bond X is the 10-year industrial bond and bond Y is the 10-year on-the-run Treasury issue, the absolute yield spread was:

$$\text{yield spread} = 6.24\% - 4.88\% = 1.36\% \text{ or } 136 \text{ basis points}$$

Unless otherwise specified, yield spreads are typically measured in this way. Yield spreads can also be measured on a relative basis by taking the ratio of the yield spread to the yield of the reference bond. This is called a **relative yield spread** and is computed as shown below, assuming that the reference bond is bond Y:

$$\text{relative yield spread} = \frac{\text{yield on bond X} - \text{yield on bond Y}}{\text{yield on bond Y}}$$

Sometimes bonds are compared in terms of a **yield ratio,** the quotient of two bond yields, as shown below:

$$\text{yield ratio} = \frac{\text{yield on bond X}}{\text{yield on bond Y}}$$

Typically, in the U.S. bond market when these measures are computed, bond Y (the reference bond) is a Treasury issue. In that case, the equations for the yield spread measures are as follows:

$$\text{absolute yield spread} = \text{yield on bond X} - \text{yield of on-the-run Treasury}$$

$$\text{relative yield spread} = \frac{\text{yield on bond X} - \text{yield of on-the-run Treasury}}{\text{yield of on-the-run Treasury}}$$

$$\text{yield ratio} = \frac{\text{yield on bond X}}{\text{yield of on-the-run Treasury}}$$

For the above example comparing the yields on the 10-year single A rated industrial bond and the 10-year on-the-run Treasury, the relative yield spread and yield ratio are computed below:

$$\text{absolute yield spread} = 6.24\% - 4.88\% = 1.36\% = 136 \text{ basis points}$$

$$\text{relative yield spread} = \frac{6.24\% - 4.88\%}{4.88\%} = 0.279 = 27.9\%$$

$$\text{yield ratio} = \frac{6.24\%}{4.88\%} = 1.279$$

The reason for computing yield spreads in terms of a relative yield spread or a yield ratio is that the magnitude of the yield spread is affected by the level of interest rates. For example, in 1957 the yield on Treasuries was about 3%. At that time, the absolute yield spread between triple B rated utility bonds and Treasuries was 40 basis points. This was a relative yield spread of 13% (0.40% divided by 3%). However, when the yield on Treasuries exceeded 10% in 1985, an absolute yield spread of 40 basis points would have meant a relative yield spread of only 4% (0.40% divided by 10%). Consequently, in 1985 an absolute yield spread greater than 40 basis points would have been required in order to produce a similar relative yield spread.

In this reading, we will focus on the yield spread as most commonly measured, the absolute yield spread. So, when we refer to yield spread, we mean absolute yield spread.

Whether we measure the yield spread as an absolute yield spread, a relative yield spread, or a yield ratio, the question to answer is what causes the yield spread between two bond issues. Basically, active bond portfolio strategies involve assessing the factors that cause the yield spread, forecasting how that yield spread may change over an investment horizon, and taking a position to capitalize on that forecast.

Practice Question 1

The following table gives the yield for the 5-year Treasury and for two 5-year corporate bonds as of February 8, 2002.

Issue	Yield
5-year on-run-Treasury issue:	4.18%
5-year yield for GE (Aaa/AAA)	4.93%
5-year yield for Verizon Communications (A1/A+)	5.11%

A. Compute the following yield spread measures between the 5-year GE yield and the 5-year on-the-run Treasury yield: absolute yield spread, relative yield spread, and yield ratio.

B. Compute the following yield spread measures between the 5-year Verizon Communications yield and the 5-year on-the-run Treasury yield: absolute yield spread, relative yield spread, and yield ratio.

4.2 Intermarket Sector Spreads and Intramarket Spreads

The bond market is classified into sectors based on the type of issuer. In the United States, these sectors include the U.S. government sector, the U.S. government agencies sector, the municipal sector, the corporate sector, the mortgage-backed securities sector, the asset-backed securities sector, and the foreign (sovereign, supranational, and corporate) sector. Different sectors are generally perceived as offering different risks and rewards.

The major market sectors are further divided into sub-sectors reflecting common economic characteristics. For example, within the corporate sector, the subsectors are: (1) industrial companies, (2) utility companies, (3) finance companies, and (4) banks. In the market for asset-backed securities, the sub-sectors are based on the type of collateral backing the security. The major types are securities backed by pools of (1) credit card receivables, (2) home equity loans, (3) automobile loans, (4) manufactured housing loans, and (5) student loans. Excluding the Treasury market sector, the other market sectors have a wide range of issuers, each with different abilities to satisfy their contractual obligations. Therefore, a key feature of a debt obligation is the nature of the issuer.

The yield spread between the yields offered in two sectors of the bond market with the same maturity is referred to as an **intermarket sector spread.** The most common intermarket sector spread calculated by market participants is the yield spread between a non-Treasury sector and Treasury securities with the same maturity.

The yield spread between two issues within a market sector is called an **intramarket sector spread.** As with Treasury securities, a yield curve can be estimated for a given issuer. The yield spread typically increases with maturity. The yield spreads for a given issuer can be added to the yield for the corresponding maturity of the on-the-run Treasury issue. The resulting yield curve is then an **issuer's on-the-run yield curve.**

The factors other than maturity that affect the intermarket and intramarket yield spreads are (1) the relative credit risk of the two issues, (2) the presence of embedded options, (3) the liquidity of the two issues, and (4) the taxability of interest received by investors.

4.3 Credit Spreads

The yield spread between non-Treasury securities and Treasury securities that are identical in all respects except for credit rating is referred to as a **credit spread** or **quality spread.** "Identical in all respects except credit rating" means that the maturities are the same and that there are no embedded options.

For example, Exhibit 65-3 shows information on the yield spread within the corporate sector by credit rating and maturity, for the 90-day period ending February 8, 2002. The high, low, and average spreads for the 90-day period are reported. Note that the lower the credit rating, the higher the credit spread. Also note that, for a given sector of the corporate market and a given credit rating, the credit spread increases with maturity.

It is argued that credit spreads between corporates and Treasuries change systematically with changes in the economy. Credit spreads widen (i.e., become larger) in a declining or contracting economy and narrow (i.e., become smaller) during economic expansion. The economic rationale is that, in a declining or contracting economy, corporations experience declines in revenue and cash flow, making it more difficult for corporate issuers to service their contractual debt obligations.

To induce investors to hold spread products as credit quality deteriorates, the credit spread widens. The widening occurs as investors sell off corporates and invest the proceeds in Treasury securities (popularly referred to as a "flight to quality"). The converse is that, during economic expansion and brisk economic activity, revenue and cash flow increase, increasing the likelihood that corporate issuers will have the capacity to service their contractual debt obligations.

Exhibit 65-4 provides evidence of the impact of the business cycle on credit spreads since 1919. The credit spread in the exhibit is the difference between Baa rated and Aaa rated corporate bonds; the shaded areas in the exhibit represent periods of economic recession as defined by the National Bureau of Economic Research (NBER). In general, corporate credit spreads tightened during the early stages of economic expansion, and spreads widened sharply during economic recessions. In fact, spreads typically begin to widen before the official beginning of an economic recession.[8]

EXHIBIT 65-3 Credit Spreads (in Basis Points) in the Corporate Sector on February 8, 2002

Maturity (years)	AA–90-day			A–90-day			BBB–90-day		
	High	Low	Avg	High	Low	Avg	High	Low	Avg
Industrials									
5	87	58	72	135	85	112	162	117	140
10	102	73	90	158	109	134	180	133	156
30	114	93	106	170	132	152	199	154	175
Utilities									
5	140	0	103	153	112	134	200	163	184
10	160	0	121	168	132	153	220	182	204
30	175	0	132	188	151	171	240	200	222
Finance									
5	103	55	86	233	177	198			
10	125	78	103	253	170	209			
30	148	100	130	253	207	228			
Banks									
5	97	60	81	113	83	100			
10	120	78	95	127	92	110			
30	138	105	121	170	127	145			

Source: Abstracted from *Global Relative Value,* Lehman Brothers, Fixed Income Research, February 11, 2002, p. 133.

---

[8] For a further discussion and evidence regarding business cycles and credit spreads, see Chapter 10 in Leland E. Crabbe and Frank J. Fabozzi, *Managing a Corporate Portfolio* (Hoboken, NJ: John Wiley & Sons, 2002).

EXHIBIT 65-4 Credit Spreads Between Baa and Aaa Corporate Bonds Over the Business Cycle Since 1919

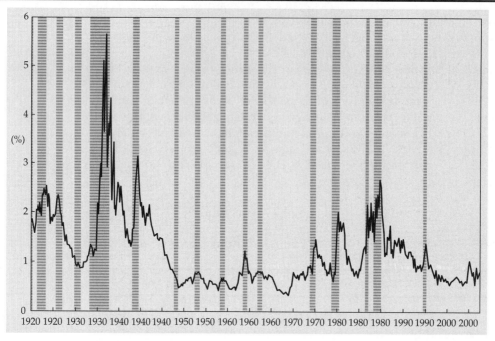

Shaded areas = economic recession as defined by the NBER

Source: Exhibit 1 in Leland E. Crabbe and Frank J. Fabozzi, *Managing a Corporate Portfolio* (Hoboken, NJ: John Wiley & Sons, 2002), p. 154.

Some market observers use the yield spread between issuers in cyclical and non-cyclical industry sectors as a proxy for yield spreads due to expected economic conditions. The rationale is as follows. While companies in both cyclical and non-cyclical industries are adversely affected by expectations of a recession, the impact is greater for cyclical industries. As a result, the yield spread between issuers in cyclical and non-cyclical industry sectors will widen with expectations of a contracting economy.

4.4 Including Embedded Options

It is not uncommon for a bond issue to include a provision that gives either the issuer and/or the bondholder an option to take some action against the other party. The most common type of option in a bond issue is the call provision that grants the issuer the right to retire the debt, fully or partially, before the scheduled maturity date.

The presence of an embedded option has an effect on both the yield spread of an issue relative to a Treasury security and the yield spread relative to otherwise comparable issues that do not have an embedded option. In general, investors require a larger yield spread to a comparable Treasury security for an issue with an embedded option that is favorable to the issuer (e.g. a call option) than for an issue without such an option. In contrast, market participants require a smaller yield spread to a comparable Treasury security for an issue with an embedded option that is favorable to the investor (e.g., put option or conversion option). In fact, for a bond with an option favorable to an investor, the interest rate may be less than that on a comparable Treasury security.

Even for callable bonds, the yield spread depends on the type of call feature. For a callable bond with a deferred call, the longer the deferred call period, the greater the call protection provided to the investor. Thus, all other factors equal, the longer the deferred call period, the lower the yield spread attributable to the call feature.

A major part of the bond market is the mortgage-backed securities sector.[9] These securities expose an investor to prepayment risk and the yield spread between a mortgage-backed security and a comparable Treasury security reflects this prepayment risk. To see this, consider a basic mortgage-backed security called a Ginnie Mae passthrough security. This security is backed by the full faith and credit of the U.S. government. Consequently, the yield spread between a Ginnie Mae passthrough security and a comparable Treasury security is not due to credit risk. Rather, it is primarily due to prepayment risk. For example, Exhibit 65-5 reports the yield on 30-year Ginnie Mae passthrough securities with different coupon rates. The first issue to be addressed is the maturity of the comparable Treasury issue against which the Ginnie Mae should be benchmarked in order to calculate a yield spread. This is an issue because a mortgage passthrough security is an amortizing security that repays principal over time rather than just at the stated maturity date (30 years in our illustration). Consequently, while the stated maturity of a Ginnie Mae passthrough is 30 years, its yield should not be compared to the yield on a 30-year Treasury issue. For now, you can see that the Treasury benchmark in Exhibit 65-5 depends on the coupon rate. The yield spread, shown in the second column, depends on the coupon rate.

In general, when a yield spread is cited for an issue that is callable, part of the spread reflects the risk associated with the embedded option. Reported yield spreads do not adjust for embedded options. The raw yield spreads are sometimes referred to as **nominal spreads**—nominal in the sense that the value of embedded options has not been removed in computing an adjusted yield spread. The yield spread that adjusts for the embedded option is OAS.

The last four columns in Exhibit 65-5 show Lehman Brothers' estimate of the option-adjusted spread for the 30-year Ginnie Mae passthroughs shown in the exhibit—the option-adjusted spread on February 8, 2002 and for the prior 90-day period (high, low, and average). The nominal spread is the yield spread shown in the second column. Notice that the option-adjusted spread is considerably less than the nominal spread. For example, for the 7.5% coupon issue the nominal spread is 155 basis points. After adjusting for the prepayment risk (i.e., the embedded option), the spread as measured by the option-adjusted spread is considerably less, 63 basis points.

Practice Question 2

Below are the yield spreads estimated between 10-year federal agency securities and the 10-year on-the-run Treasury issue on June 30, 1998 as reported in the July 20, 1998 issue of *Spread Talk* published by Prudential Securities (p. 7):

Issue	Yield spread (bps)
noncallable	40
callable, 1 year deferred call	110
callable, 2 year deferred call	95
callable, 3 year deferred call	75

A. Why is the yield spread for the noncallable issue less than for the three callable issues?

B. Why is it that, for the callable issues, the longer the deferred call period, the smaller the yield spread?

---

[9] The mortgage-backed securities sector is often referred to as simply the "mortgage sector."

EXHIBIT 65-5 Yield Spreads and Option-Adjusted Spread (OAS) for Ginnie Mae 30-year Passthrough Securities (February 8, 2002)

Coupon Rate (%)	Yield Spread (bps)	Benchmark Treasury	OAS on 2/8/02 (bps)	90-Day OAS (bps)		
				High	Low	Avg.
6.5	203	5 year	52	75	46	59
7.0	212	5 year	57	83	54	65
7.5	155	3 year	63	94	62	74
8.0	105	3 year	73	108	73	88
9.0	244	2 year	131	160	124	139

Source: Abstracted from *Global Relative Value*, Lehman Brothers, Fixed Income Research, February 11, 2002, p.132.

4.5 Liquidity

Even within the Treasury market, a yield spread exists between off-the-run Treasury issues and on-the-run Treasury issues of similar maturity due to differences in liquidity and the effects of the repo market. Similarly, in the spread sectors, generic on-the-run yield curves can be estimated and the liquidity spread due to an off-the-run issue can be computed.

A Lehman Brother's study found that one factor that affects liquidity (and therefore the yield spread) is the size of an issue—the larger the issue, the greater the liquidity relative to a smaller issue, and the greater the liquidity, the lower the yield spread.[10]

4.6 Taxability of Interest Income

In the United States, unless exempted under the federal income tax code, interest income is taxable at the federal income tax level. In addition to federal income taxes, state and local taxes may apply to interest income.

The federal tax code specifically exempts interest income from qualified municipal bond issues from taxation.[11] Because of the tax-exempt feature of these municipal bonds, the yield on municipal bonds is less than that on Treasuries with the same maturity. Exhibit 65-6 shows this relationship on February 12, 2002, as reported by Bloomberg Financial Markets. The yield ratio shown for municipal bonds is the ratio of AAA general obligation bond yields to yields for the same maturity on-the-run Treasury issue.[12]

The difference in yield between tax-exempt securities and Treasury securities is typically measured not in terms of the absolute yield spread but as a yield ratio. More specifically, it is measured as the quotient of the yield on a tax-exempt security relative to the yield on a comparable Treasury security. This is reported in Exhibit 65-6. The yield ratio has changed over time due to changes in tax rates, as well as other factors. The higher the tax rate, the more attractive the tax-exempt feature and the lower the yield ratio.

The U.S. municipal bond market is divided into two bond sectors: general obligation bonds and revenue bonds. For the tax-exempt bond market, the benchmark

[10] *Global Relative Value*, Lehman Brothers, Fixed Income Research, June 28, 1999, COR-2 AND 3.

[11] As explained in Reading 64, some municipal bonds are taxable.

[12] Some maturities for Treasury securities shown in the exhibit are not on-the-run issues. These are estimates for the market yields.

for calculating yield spreads is not Treasury securities, but rather a generic AAA general obligation yield curve constructed by dealer firms active in the municipal bond market and by data/analytics vendors.

EXHIBIT 65-6 Yield Ratio for AAA General Obligation Municipal Bonds to U.S. Treasuries of the Same Maturity (February 12, 2002)

Maturity	Yield on AAA General Obligation (%)	Yield on U.S. Treasury (%)	Yield Ratio
3 months	1.29	1.72	0.75
6 months	1.41	1.84	0.77
1 year	1.69	2.16	0.78
2 years	2.20	3.02	0.73
3 years	2.68	3.68	0.73
4 years	3.09	4.13	0.75
5 years	3.42	4.42	0.77
7 years	3.86	4.84	0.80
10 years	4.25	4.95	0.86
15 years	4.73	5.78	0.82
20 years	4.90	5.85	0.84
30 years	4.95	5.50	0.90

Source: Bloomberg Financial Markets

4.6.1 After-Tax Yield and Taxable-Equivalent Yield

The yield on a taxable bond issue after federal income taxes are paid is called the **after-tax yield** and is computed as follows:

$$\text{after-tax yield} = \text{pre-tax yield} \times (1 - \text{marginal tax rate})$$

Of course, the marginal tax rate[13] varies among investors. For example, suppose a taxable bond issue offers a yield of 5% and is acquired by an investor facing a marginal tax rate of 31%. The after-tax yield would then be:

$$\text{after-tax yield} = 0.05 \times (1 - 0.31) = 0.0345 = 3.45\%$$

Alternatively, we can determine the yield that must be offered on a taxable bond issue to give the same after-tax yield as a tax-exempt issue. This yield is called the **taxable-equivalent yield** or **tax-equivalent yield** and is computed as follows:

$$\text{taxable-equivalent yield} = \frac{\text{tax-exempt yield}}{(1 - \text{marginal tax rate})}$$

For example, consider an investor facing a 31% marginal tax rate who purchases a tax-exempt issue with a yield of 4%. The taxable-equivalent yield is then:

$$\text{taxable equivalent yield} = \frac{0.04}{(1 - 0.31)} = 0.058 = 5.80\%$$

---

[13] The marginal tax rate is the tax rate at which an additional dollar is taxed.

Notice that the higher the marginal tax rate, the higher the taxable equivalent yield. For instance, in our last example if the marginal tax rate is 40% rather than 31%, the taxable-equivalent yield would be 6.67% rather than 5.80%, as shown below:

$$\text{taxable-equivalent yield} = \frac{0.04}{(1 - 0.40)} = 0.0667 = 6.67\%$$

Practice Question 3

Following is information about two investors, Ms. High and Mr. Low:

	Marginal tax bracket
Ms. High	40%
Mr. Low	15%

A. Suppose that these two investors are considering investing in a taxable bond that offers a yield of 6.8%. What is the after-tax yield for each investor?

B. Suppose that these two investors can purchase a tax-exempt security offering a yield of 4.8%. What is the taxable-equivalent yield for each investor?

Some state and local governments tax interest income from bond issues that are exempt from federal income taxes. Some municipalities exempt interest income from all municipal issues from taxation, while others do not. Some states exempt interest income from bonds issued by municipalities within the state but tax the interest income from bonds issued by municipalities outside of the state. The implication is that two municipal securities with the same credit rating and the same maturity may trade at different yield spreads because of the relative demand for bonds of municipalities in different states. For example, in a high income tax state such as New York, the demand for bonds of New York municipalities drives down their yields relative to bonds issued by municipalities in a zero income tax state such as Texas.

4.7 Technical Factors

At times, deviations from typical yield spreads are caused by temporary imbalances between supply and demand. For example, in the second quarter of 1999, issuers became concerned that the Fed would pursue a policy to increase interest rates. In response, a record issuance of corporate securities resulted in an increase in the yield spread between corporates and Treasuries.

In the municipal market, yield spreads are affected by the temporary oversupply of issues within a market sector. For example, a substantial new issue volume of high-grade state general obligation bonds may tend to decrease the yield spread between high-grade and low-grade revenue bonds. In a weak market environment, it is easier for high-grade municipal bonds to come to market than for weaker credits. So at times high grades flood weak markets even when there is a relative scarcity of medium- and low-grade municipal bond issues.

Since technical factors cause temporary misalignments of the yield spread relationship, some investors look at the forward calendar of planned offerings to project the impact on future yield spreads. Some corporate analysts identify the risk of yield spread changes due to the supply of new issues when evaluating issuers or sectors.

NON-U.S. INTEREST RATES   5

The same factors that affect yield spreads in the United States are responsible for yield spreads in other countries and between countries. Major non-U.S. bond markets have a government benchmark yield curve similar to that of the U.S. Treasury yield curve. Exhibit 65-7 shows the government yield curve as of the beginning and end of 2001 for Germany, Japan, the U.K., and France. These yield curves are presented to illustrate the different shapes and the way in which they can change. Notice that only the Japanese yield curve shifted in an almost parallel fashion (i.e., the rate for all maturities changed by approximately the same number of basis points).

The German bond market is the largest market for publicly issued bonds in Europe. The yields on German government bonds are viewed as benchmark interest rates in Europe. Because of the important role of the German bond market, nominal spreads are typically computed relative to German government bonds (German bunds).

Institutional investors who borrow funds on a short-term basis to invest (referred to as "funded investors") obviously desire to earn an amount in excess of their borrowing cost. The most popular borrowing cost reference rate is the **London interbank offered rate** (LIBOR). LIBOR is the interest rate at which banks pay to borrow funds from other banks in the London interbank market. The borrowing occurs via a cash deposit of one bank (the lender) into a certificate of deposit (CD) in another bank (the borrower). The maturity of the CD can be from overnight to five years. So, 3-month LIBOR represents the interest rate paid on a CD that matures in three months. The CD can be denominated in one of several currencies. The currencies for which LIBOR is reported are the U.S. dollar, the British pound, the Euro, the Canadian dollar, the Australian dollar, the Japanese yen, and Swiss francs. When it is denominated in U.S. dollars, it is referred to as a Eurodollar CD. LIBOR is determined for every London business day by the British Bank Association (BBA) by maturity and for each currency and is reported by various services.

Entities seeking to borrow funds pays a spread over LIBOR and seek to earn a spread over that funding cost when they invest the borrowed funds. So, for example, if the 3-month borrowing cost for a funded investor is 3-month LIBOR plus 25 basis points and the investor can earn 3-month LIBOR plus 125 basis points for three months, then the investor earns a spread of 100 basis points for three months (125 basis points − 25 basis points).

EXHIBIT 65-7 Yield Curves in Germany, Japan, the U.K., and France: 2001

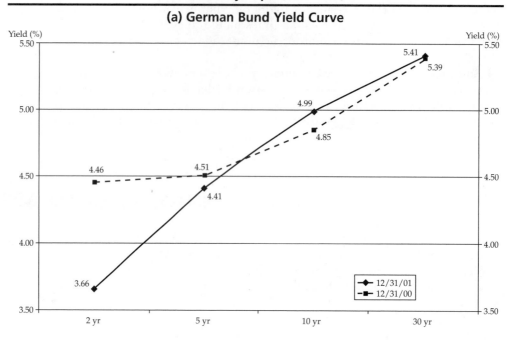

(a) German Bund Yield Curve

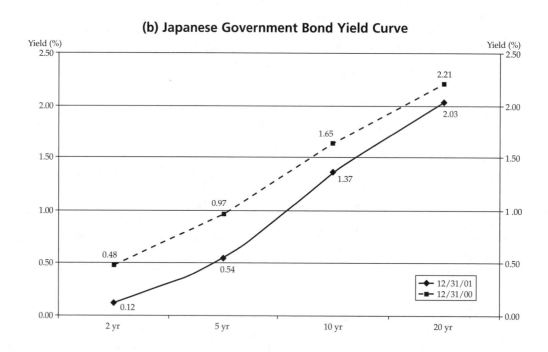

(b) Japanese Government Bond Yield Curve

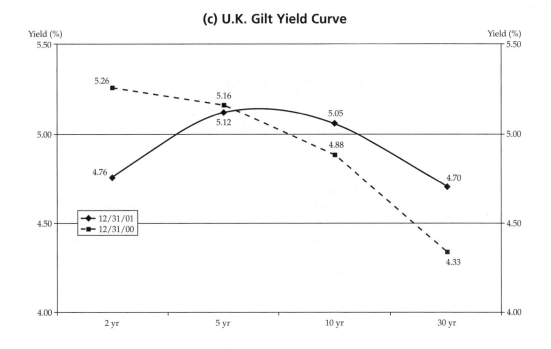

(c) U.K. Gilt Yield Curve

Yield (%)

Yield (%)

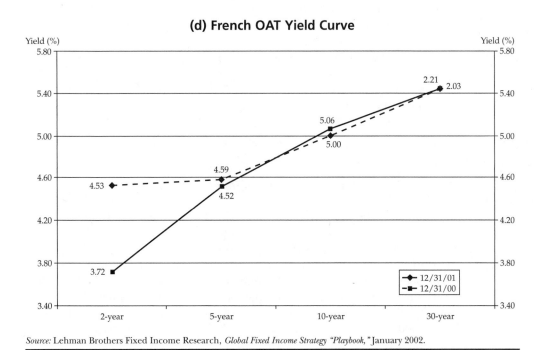

(d) French OAT Yield Curve

Yield (%)

Yield (%)

Source: Lehman Brothers Fixed Income Research, *Global Fixed Income Strategy "Playbook,"* January 2002.

6   SWAP SPREADS

Another important spread measure is the **swap spread**.

6.1 Interest Rate Swap and the Swap Spread

In an interest rate swap, two parties (called **counterparties**) agree to exchange periodic interest payments. The dollar amount of the interest payments exchanged is based on a predetermined dollar principal, which is called the **notional principal** or **notional amount.** The dollar amount each counterparty pays to the other is the agreed-upon periodic interest rate times the notional principal. The only dollars exchanged between the parties are the interest payments, not the notional principal. In the most common type of swap, one party agrees to pay the other party fixed interest payments at designated dates for the life of the swap. This party is referred to as the **fixed-rate payer.** The fixed rate that the fixed-rate payer pays is called the **swap rate.** The other party, who agrees to make interest rate payments that float with some reference rate, is referred to as the **fixed-rate receiver.**

The reference rates used for the floating rate in an interest rate swap is one of various money market instruments: LIBOR (the most common reference rate used in swaps), Treasury bill rate, commercial paper rate, bankers' acceptance rate, federal funds rate, and prime rate.

The convention that has evolved for quoting a swap rate is that a dealer sets the floating rate equal to the reference rate and then quotes the fixed rate that will apply. The fixed rate has a specified "spread" above the yield for a Treasury with the same term to maturity as the swap. This specified spread is called the **swap spread.** The **swap rate** is the sum of the yield for a Treasury with the same maturity as the swap plus the swap spread.

To illustrate an interest rate swap in which one party pays fixed and receives floating, assume the following:

- term of swap: 5 years
- swap spread: 50 basis points
- reference rate: 3-month LIBOR
- notional amount: $50 million
- frequency of payments: every three months

Suppose also that the 5-year Treasury rate is 5.5% at the time the swap is entered into. Then the swap rate will be 6%, found by adding the swap spread of 50 basis points to the 5-year Treasury yield of 5.5%.

This means that the fixed-rate payer agrees to pay a 6% annual rate for the next five years with payments made quarterly and receive from the fixed-rate receiver 3-month LIBOR with the payments made quarterly. Since the notional amount is $50 million, this means that every three months, the fixed-rate payer pays $750,000 (6% times $50 million divided by 4). The fixed-rate receiver pays 3-month LIBOR times $50 million divided by 4. The table below shows the payment made by the fixed-rate receiver to the fixed-rate payer for different values of 3-month LIBOR:[14]

---

[14] The amount of the payment is found by dividing the annual dollar amount by four because payments are made quarterly. In a real world application, both the fixed-rate and floating-rate payments are adjusted for the number of days in a quarter, but it is unnecessary for us to deal with this adjustment here.

If 3-month LIBOR is	Annual dollar amount	Quarterly payment
4%	$2,000,000	$500,000
5	2,500,000	625,000
6	3,000,000	750,000
7	3,500,000	875,000
8	4,000,000	1,000,000

In practice, the payments are netted out. For example, if 3-month LIBOR is 4%, the fixed-rate receiver would receive $750,000 and pay to the fixed-rate payer $500,000. Netting the two payments, the fixed-rate payer pays the fixed-rate receiver $250,000 ($750,000 − $500,000).

6.2 Role of Interest Rate Swaps

Interest rate swaps have many important applications in fixed income portfolio management and risk management. They tie together the fixed-rate and floating-rate sectors of the bond market. As a result, investors can convert a fixed-rate asset into a floating-rate asset with an interest rate swap.

Suppose a financial institution has invested in 5-year bonds with a $50 million par value and a coupon rate of 9% and that this bond is selling at par value. Moreover, this institution borrows $50 million on a quarterly basis (to fund the purchase of the bonds) and its cost of funds is 3-month LIBOR plus 50 basis points. The "income spread" between its assets (i.e., 5-year bonds) and its liabilities (its funding cost) for any 3-month period depends on 3-month LIBOR. The following table shows how the annual spread varies with 3-month LIBOR:

Asset yield	3-month LIBOR	Funding cost	Annual income spread
9.00%	4.00%	4.50%	4.50%
9.00%	5.00%	5.50%	3.50%
9.00%	6.00%	6.50%	2.50%
9.00%	7.00%	7.50%	1.50%
9.00%	8.00%	8.50%	0.50%
9.00%	8.50%	9.00%	0.00%
9.00%	9.00%	9.50%	−0.50%
9.00%	10.00%	10.50%	−1.50%
9.00%	11.00%	11.50%	−2.50%

As 3-month LIBOR increases, the income spread decreases. If 3-month LIBOR exceeds 8.5%, the income spread is negative (i.e., it costs more to borrow than is earned on the bonds in which the borrowed funds are invested).

This financial institution has a mismatch between its assets and its liabilities. An interest rate swap can be used to hedge this mismatch. For example, suppose the manager of this financial institution enters into a 5-year swap with a $50 million notional amount in which it agrees to pay a fixed rate (i.e., to be the fixed-rate payer) in exchange for 3-month LIBOR. Suppose further that the swap rate is 6%. Then the annual income spread taking into account the swap payments is as follows for different values of 3-month LIBOR:

Asset yield	3-month LIBOR	Funding cost	Fixed rate paid in swap	3-month LIBOR rec. in swap	Annual income spread
9.00%	4.00%	4.50%	6.00%	4.00%	2.50%
9.00%	5.00%	5.50%	6.00%	5.00%	2.50%
9.00%	6.00%	6.50%	6.00%	6.00%	2.50%
9.00%	7.00%	7.50%	6.00%	7.00%	2.50%
9.00%	8.00%	8.50%	6.00%	8.00%	2.50%
9.00%	8.50%	9.00%	6.00%	8.50%	2.50%
9.00%	9.00%	9.50%	6.00%	9.00%	2.50%
9.00%	10.00%	10.50%	6.00%	10.00%	2.50%
9.00%	11.00%	11.50%	6.00%	11.00%	2.50%

Assuming the bond does not default and is not called, the financial institution has locked in a spread of 250 basis points.

Effectively, the financial institution using this interest rate swap converted a fixed-rate asset into a floating-rate asset. The reference rate for the synthetic floaing-rate asset is 3-month LIBOR and the liabilities are in terms of 3-month LIBOR. Alternatively, the financial institution could have converted its liabilities to a fixed-rate by entering into a 5-year $50 million notional amount swap by being the fixed-rate payer and the results would have been the same.

This simple illustration shows the critical importance of an interest rate swap. Investors and issuers with a mismatch of assets and liabilities can use an interest rate swap to better match assets and liabilities, thereby reducing their risk.

Practice Question 4

Assume that the asset yield in the illustration is 8.6% instead of 9% and the funding cost is 3-month LIBOR plus 60 basis points. Demonstrate the spread that has been locked in by the interest rate swap (assuming the issuer of the assets does not default) by completing the following table:

Asset yield	3-month LIBOR	Funding cost	Fixed rate paid in swap	3-month LIBOR rec. in swap	Annual income spread
	4.00%				
	5.00%				
	6.00%				
	7.00%				
	8.00%				
	8.50%				
	9.00%				
	10.00%				
	11.00%				

6.3 Determinants of the Swap Spread

Market participants throughout the world view the swap spread as the appropriate spread measure for valuation and relative value analysis. Here we discuss the determinants of the swap spread.

We know that

swap rate = Treasury rate + swap spread

where Treasury rate is equal to the yield on a Treasury with the same maturity as the swap. Since the parties are swapping the future reference rate for the swap rate, then:

reference rate = Treasury rate + swap spread

Solving for the swap spread we have:

swap spread = reference rate − Treasury rate

Since the most common reference rate is LIBOR, we can substitute this into the above formula getting:

swap spread = LIBOR − Treasury rate

Thus, the swap spread is a spread of the global cost of short-term borrowing over the Treasury rate.

The swap spread primarily reflects the credit spreads in the corporate bond market.[15] Studies have found a high correlation between swap spreads and credit spreads in various sectors of the fixed income market. This can be seen in Exhibit 65-8 which shows the 3-year trailing correlation from June 1992 to December 2001 between swap spreads and AA, A, and BBB credit spreads. Note from the exhibit that the highest correlation is with AA credit spreads.

---

[15] We say primarily because there are also technical factors that affect the swap spread. For a discussion of these factors, see Richard Gordon, "The Truth about Swap Spreads," in Frank J. Fabozzi (ed.), *Professional Perspectives on Fixed Income Portfolio Management: Volume 1* (New Hope, PA: Frank J. Fabozzi Associates, 2000), pp. 97–104.

EXHIBIT 65-8 Three-Year Trailing Correlation Between Swap Spreads and Credit Spreads (AA, A, and BB): June 1992 to December 2001

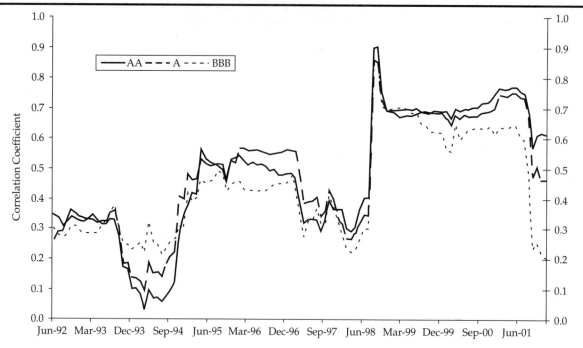

Source: Lehman Brothers Fixed Income Research, *Global Fixed Income Strategy "Playbook,"* January 2002.

EXHIBIT 65-9 January and December 2001 Swap Spread Curves for Germany, Japan, U.K., and U.S.

	Germany				Japan				U.K.				U.S.			
	2-Year	5-Year	10-Year	30-Year	2-Year	5-Year	10-Year	30-Year	2-Year	5-Year	10-Year	30-Year	2-Year	5-Year	10-Year	30-Year
Jan-01	23	40	54	45	8	10	14	29	40	64	83	91	63	82	81	73
Dec-01	22	28	28	14	3	(2)	(1)	8	36	45	52	42	46	76	77	72

Source: Lehman Brothers Fixed Income Research, *Global Fixed Income Strategy "Playbook,"* January 2002.

6.4 Swap Spread Curve

A **swap spread curve** shows the relationship between the swap rate and swap maturity. A swap spread curve is available by country. The swap spread is the amount added to the yield of the respective country's government bond with the same maturity as the maturity of the swap. Exhibit 65-9 shows the swap spread curves for Germany, Japan, the U.K., and the U.S. for January 2001 and December 2001. The swap spreads move together. For example, Exhibit 65-10 shows the daily 5-year swap spreads from December 2000 to December 2001 for the U.S. and Germany.

EXHIBIT 65-10 Daily 5-Year Swap Spreads in Germany and the United States: 2001

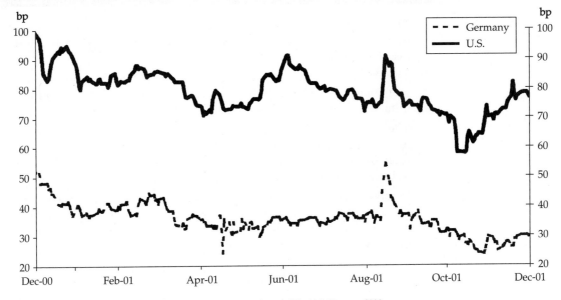

Source: Lehman Brothers Fixed Income Research, *Global Fixed Income Strategy "Playbook,"* January 2002.

7   SUMMARY

▸ The interest rate offered on a particular bond issue depends on the interest rate that can be earned on risk-free instruments and the perceived risks associated with the issue.

▸ The U.S. Federal Reserve Board is the policy making body whose interest rate policy tools directly influence short-term interest rates and indirectly influence long-term interest rates in the United States.

▸ The Fed's most frequently employed interest rate policy tools are open market operations and changing the discount rate; less frequently used tools are changing bank reserve requirements and verbal persuasion to influence how bankers supply credit to businesses and consumers.

▸ Because Treasury securities have no credit risk, market participants look at the interest rate or yield offered on an on-the-run Treasury security as the minimum interest rate required on a non-Treasury security with the same maturity.

▸ The Treasury yield curve shows the relationship between yield and maturity of on-the-run Treasury issues.

▸ The typical shape for the Treasury yield curve is upward sloping—yield increases with maturity—which is referred to as a normal yield curve.

▸ Inverted yield curves (yield decreasing with maturity) and flat yield curves (yield roughly the same regardless of maturity) have been observed for the yield curve.

▸ Two factors complicate the relationship between maturity and yield as indicated by the Treasury yield curve: (1) the yield for on-the-run issues is distorted since these securities can be financed at cheaper rates and, as a result, offer a lower yield than in the absence of this financing advantage and (2) on-the-run Treasury issues and off-the-run issues have different interest rate reinvestment risks.

▸ The yields on Treasury strips of different maturities provide a superior relationship between yield and maturity compared to the on-the-run Treasury yield curve.

▸ The yield on a zero-coupon or stripped Treasury security is called the Treasury spot rate.

▸ The term structure of interest rates is the relationship between maturity and Treasury spot rates.

▸ Three theories have been offered to explain the shape of the yield curve: pure expectations theory, liquidity preference theory, and market segmentation theory.

▸ The pure expectations theory asserts that the market sets yields based solely on expectations for future interest rates.

▸ According to the pure expectations theory: (1) a rising term structure reflects an expectation that future short-term rates will rise, (2) a flat term structure reflects an expectation that future short-term rates will be mostly constant, and (3) a falling term structure reflects an expectation that future short-term rates will decline.

▸ The liquidity preference theory asserts that market participants want to be compensated for the interest rate risk associated with holding longer-term bonds.

▸ The market segmentation theory asserts that there are different maturity sectors of the yield curve and that each maturity sector is independent or segmented from the other maturity sectors. Within each maturity sector, the interest rate is determined by the supply and demand for funds.

▷ According to the market segmentation theory, any shape is possible for the yield curve.

▷ Despite the imperfections of the Treasury yield curve as a benchmark for the minimum interest rate that an investor requires for investing in a non-Treasury security, it is common to refer to a non-Treasury security's additional yield over the nearest maturity on-the-run Treasury issue as the "yield spread."

▷ The yield spread can be computed in three ways: (1) the difference between the yield on two bonds or bond sectors (called the absolute yield spread), (2) the difference in yields as a percentage of the benchmark yield (called the relative yield spread), and (3) the ratio of the yield relative to the benchmark yield (called the yield ratio).

▷ An intermarket yield spread is the yield spread between two securities with the same maturity in two different sectors of the bond market.

▷ The most common intermarket sector spread calculated is the yield spread between the yield on a security in a non-Treasury market sector and a Treasury security with the same maturity.

▷ An intramarket sector spread is the yield spread between two issues within the same market sector.

▷ An issuer specific yield curve can be computed given the yield spread, by maturity, for an issuer and the yield for on-the-run Treasury securities.

▷ The factors other than maturity that affect the intermarket and intramarket yield spreads are (1) the relative credit risk of the two issues; (2) the presence of embedded options; (3) the relative liquidity of the two issues; and, (4) the taxability of the interest.

▷ A credit spread or quality spread is the yield spread between a non-Treasury security and a Treasury security that are "identical in all respects except for credit rating."

▷ Some market participants argue that credit spreads between corporates and Treasuries change systematically because of changes in economic prospects—widening in a declining economy ("flight to quality") and narrowing in an expanding economy.

▷ Generally investors require a larger spread to a comparable Treasury security for issues with an embedded option favorable to the issuer, and a smaller spread for an issue with an embedded option favorable to the investor.

▷ For mortgage-backed securities, one reason for the increased yield spread relative to a comparable Treasury security is exposure to prepayment risk.

▷ The option-adjusted spread of a security seeks to measure the yield spread after adjusting for embedded options.

▷ A yield spread exists due to the difference in the perceived liquidity of two issues.

▷ One factor that affects liquidity (and therefore the yield spread) is the size of an issue—the larger the issue, the greater the liquidity relative to a smaller issue, and the greater the liquidity, the lower the yield spread.

▷ Because of the tax-exempt feature of municipal bonds, the yield on municipal bonds is less than that on Treasuries with the same maturity.

▷ The difference in yield between tax-exempt securities and Treasury securities is typically measured in terms of a yield ratio—the yield on a tax-exempt security as a percentage of the yield on a comparable Treasury security.

▷ The after-tax yield is computed by multiplying the pre-tax yield by one minus the marginal tax rate.

▷ In the tax-exempt bond market, the benchmark for calculating yield spreads is a generic AAA general obligation bond with a specified maturity.

▷ Technical factors having to do with temporary imbalances between the supply of and demand for new issues affect yield spreads.

▷ The same factors that affect yield spreads in the United States affect yield spreads in other countries and between countries.

▷ Major non-U.S. bond markets have government benchmark yield curves similar to the U.S. Treasury yield curve.

▷ Because of the important role of the German bond market, nominal spreads in the European bond market are typically computed relative to German government bonds.

▷ Funded investors who borrow short term typically measure the relative value of a security using borrowing rates rather than the Treasury rate.

▷ The most popular borrowing cost reference rate is the London interbank offered rate (LIBOR), which is the interest rate banks pay to borrow funds from other banks in the London interbank market.

▷ Funded investors typically pay a spread over LIBOR and seek to earn a spread over that funding cost when they invest the borrowed funds.

▷ In an interest rate swap, two parties agree to exchange periodic interest payments with the dollar amount of the interest payments exchanged based on a notional principal (also called a notional amount).

▷ In a typical interest rate swap, one party (the fixed-rate payer) agrees to pay to the counterparty fixed interest payments at designated dates for the life of the contract and the counterparty (the fixed-rate receiver) agrees to make interest rate payments that float with some reference rate.

▷ In an interest rate swap, the fixed rate paid by the fixed-rate payer is called the swap rate.

▷ The most common reference rate used in a swap is LIBOR.

▷ The swap spread is the spread that the fixed-rate payer agrees to pay above the Treasury yield with the same term to maturity as the swap.

▷ The swap rate is the sum of the yield of a Treasury with the same maturity as the swap plus the swap spread.

▷ Institutional investors can use an interest rate swap to convert a fixed-rate asset (or liability) into a floating- rate asset (or liability) and vice versa.

▷ The swap spread is viewed by market participants throughout the world as the appropriate spread measure for valuation and relative value analysis.

▷ The swap spread is the spread of the global cost of short-term borrowing over the Treasury rate.

▷ There is a high correlation between swap spreads and credit spreads in various sectors of the bond market.

▷ A swap spread curve shows the relationship between the swap rate and swap maturity for a given country.

PROBLEMS

1. The following statement appears on page 2 of the August 2, 1999 issue of Prudential Securities' *Spread Talk*.

   > The market appears to be focusing all of its energy on predicting whether or not the Fed will raise rates again at the August and/or October FOMC [Federal Open Market Committee] meetings.

   How do market observers try to predict "whether or not the Fed will raise rates"?

2. Ms. Peters is a financial advisor. One of her clients called and asked about a recent change in the shape of the yield curve from upward sloping to downward sloping. The client told Ms. Peters that she thought that the market was signaling that interest rates were expected to decline in the future. What should Ms. Peters' response be to her client?

3. How does the liquidity preference theory differ from the pure expectations theory?

4. According to the pure expectations theory, what does a humped yield curve suggest about the expectations of future interest rates?

5. Assume the following information pertaining to federal agency spreads was reported:

Agency Spreads versus Benchmark Treasury (basis points)

	Last 12 months			
	Yield spread	High	Low	Average
Noncallable				
3-year	70	70	28	44.1
5-year	80	80	32	55.4
10-year	95	95	45	71.2
Callable				
3-year (NC1)	107	107	50	80.2
5-year (NC1)	145	145	77	112.1
5-year (NC2)	132	132	65	96.9
5-year (NC3)	124	124	—	33.6
10-year (NC3)	178	178	99	132.9
10-year (NC5)	156	156	79	112.5

	Last 12 months		
Yield spread	**High**	**Low**	**Average**
Callable OAS (volatility = 14%)			
3-year (NC1)	75	75	20	50.0
5-year (NC1)	100	100	20	63.8
5-year (NC2)	100	100	23	60.7
5-year (NC3)	100	100	29	59.6
10-year (NC3)	115	115	34	77.0
10-year (NC5)	115	115	36	77.4

Note: NCX = *X*-year deferred call;—= not available

    A. Relative to the previous 12 months, what does the yield spread data above indicate about yield spreads?

    B. Explain what causes the yield spread relationship between callable and noncallable issues for a given maturity?

    C. Explain what causes the yield spread relationship among the different callable issues for a given maturity?

    D. Why are the yield spreads shown in the second panel referred to as nominal spreads?

    E. Explain what causes the yield spread relationship between the callable yield spread and the callable OAS for a given maturity and given deferred call?

6. Comment on the following statement by a representative of an investment management firm who is working with a client in selecting sectors in which the manager for the account will be permitted to invest:

> Mortgage-backed securities give our managers the opportunity to increase yield because these securities offer a higher yield than comparable Treasury securities. In particular, our managers prefer Ginnie Mae mortgage-backed securities because they have no credit risk since they are backed by the full faith and credit of the U.S. government. Therefore, our managers can pick up additional yield with no additional credit risk. While Ginnie Mae mortgage-backed securities may not be as liquid as U.S. Treasury securities, the yield spread is more than adequate to compensate for the lesser liquidity.

7. A. Why is the yield spread between a bond with an embedded option and an otherwise comparable Treasury security referred to as a "nominal spread"?

    B. What is an option-adjusted spread and why is it superior to a nominal spread as a yield spread measure for a bond with an embedded option?

8. Suppose that the yield on a 10-year noncallable corporate bond is 7.25% and the yield for the on-the-run 10-year Treasury is 6.02%. Compute the following:

    A. the absolute yield spread

    B. the relative yield spread

    C. the yield ratio

9. Following is a quote that appeared in the May 19, 1999 *Global Relative Value* by Lehman Brothers (COR-1):

As we have written in the past, percent yield spreads (spread as a percent of Treasury yields) are still cheap on an historical basis. As an illustration, the average single A 10-year industrial percent yield spread was 17% on April 30 compared to a 10 year monthly average of 12%.

A. What is another name for the yield spread measure cited in the quote?
B. Why would the analysts at Lehman Brothers focus on "percent yield spreads" rather than absolute yield spread?

10. If proposals are being considered by Congress to reduce tax rates and the market views that passage of such legislation is likely, what would you expect to happen to municipal bond yields?

11. A. Why isn't the Treasury yield curve used as a benchmark in measuring yield spreads between different sectors of the municipal bond market?
B. What benchmark is used?

12. A. What is the after-tax yield for an investor in the 40% tax bracket if the taxable yield is 5%?
B. What is the taxable-equivalent yield for an investor in the 39% tax bracket if the tax-exempt yield on an investment is 3.1%?

13. Why are funded investors who borrow short term interested in a LIBOR yield curve rather than the Treasury yield curve?

14. If the swap spread for a 5-year interest rate swap is 120 basis points and the yield on the 5-year Treasury is 4.4%, what is the swap rate?

15. Why is the swap spread an important spread measure?

16. Suppose that an institutional investor has entered into an interest rate swap, as the fixed-rate payer, with the following terms:

Term of swap:	2 years
Frequency of payments:	quarterly
Notional amount:	$10 million
Reference rate:	3-month LIBOR
Swap spread:	100 basis points

At the time of the swap, the Treasury yield curve is as follows:

3-month rate:	4.0%	3-year rate:	6.5%
6-month rate:	4.4%	4-year rate:	7.1%
1-year rate:	4.9%	5-year rate:	7.8%
2-year rate:	5.8%		

A. What is the swap rate?
B. What is the dollar amount of the quarterly payment that will be made by the fixed-rate payer?
C. Complete the following table showing the quarterly payment that will be received by the fixed-rate payer, based on 3-month LIBOR:

If 3-month LIBOR is	Annual dollar amount	Amount of payment
5.00%		
5.50%		
6.00%		
6.50%		
7.00%		
7.50%		
8.00%		
8.50%		

D. Complete the following table showing the quarterly net payment that the fixed-rate payer must make, based on 3-month LIBOR:

If 3-month LIBOR is	Floating-rate received	Net payment by fixed-rate payer
5.00%		
5.50%		
6.00%		
6.50%		
7.00%		
7.50%		
8.00%		
8.50%		

17. An investor has purchased a floating-rate security with a 5-year maturity. The coupon formula for the floater is 6-month LIBOR plus 200 basis points and the interest payments are made *semiannually*. The floater is not callable. At the time of purchase, 6-month LIBOR is 7.5%. The investor borrowed the funds to purchase the floater by issuing a 5-year note at par value with a fixed coupon rate of 7%.

A. Ignoring credit risk, what is the risk that this investor faces?

B. Explain why an interest rate swap can be used to offset this risk?

C. Suppose that the investor can enter into a 5-year interest rate swap in which the investor pays LIBOR (i.e., the investor is the fixed-rate receiver). The swap rate is 7.3% and the frequency of the payments is *semiannual*. What annual income spread can the investor lock in?

Reading 66 Introduction to the Valuation of Debt Securities
Reading 67 Yield Measures, Spot Rates, and Forward Rates
Reading 68 Introduction to the Measurement of Interest Rate Risk

Note:
Candidates are responsible
for the questions at the end
of the readings.

LEARNING OUTCOMES

Reading 66: Introduction to the Valuation of Debt Securities

The candidate should be able to:

a. describe the fundamental principles of bond valuation;

b. identify the types of bonds for which estimating the expected cash flows is difficult, and explain the problems encountered when estimating the cash flows for these bonds;

c. determine the appropriate interest rates for valuing a bond's cash flows, compute the value of a bond, given the expected annual or semiannual cash flows and the appropriate single (constant) or multiple (arbitrage-free rate curve) discount rates, explain how the value of a bond changes if the discount rate increases or decreases, and compute the change in value that is attributable to the rate change, and explain how the price of a bond changes as the bond approaches its maturity date, and compute the change in value that is attributable to the passage of time;

d. compute the value of a zero-coupon bond, explain the arbitrage-free valuation approach and the market process that forces the price of a bond toward its arbitrage-free value, determine whether a bond is undervalued or overvalued, given the bond's cash flows, appropriate spot rates or yield to maturity, and current market price, and explain how a dealer could generate an arbitrage profit.

Reading 67: Yield Measures, Spot Rates, and Forward Rates

The candidate should be able to:

a. explain the sources of return from investing in a bond (i.e., coupon interest payments, capital gain/loss, reinvestment income);

b. compute the traditional yield measures for fixed-rate bonds (e.g., current yield, yield to maturity, yield to first call, yield to first par call date, yield to refunding, yield to put, yield to worst, cash flow yield) and explain the assumptions underlying traditional yield measures and the limitations of the traditional yield measures;

c. explain the importance of reinvestment income in generating the yield computed at the time of purchase, and calculate the amount of income required to generate that yield and discuss the factors that affect reinvestment risk;

d. compute the bond equivalent yield of an annual-pay bond, and compute the annual-pay yield of a semiannual-pay bond;

e. compute the theoretical Treasury spot rate curve, using the method of bootstrapping and given the Treasury par yield curve and compute the value of a bond using spot rates;

f. explain the limitations of the nominal spread and differentiate among the nominal spread, the zero-volatility spread, and the option-adjusted spread for a bond with an embedded option, and explain the option cost;

g. explain a forward rate, and compute the value of a bond using forward rates;

h. explain and illustrate the relationship between short-term forward rates and spot rates, and compute spot rates given forward rates, and forward rates given spot rates.

Reading 68: Introduction to the Measurement of Interest Rate Risk

The candidate should be able to:

a. distinguish between the full valuation approach (the scenario analysis approach) and the duration/convexity approach for measuring interest rate risk, and explain the advantage of using the full valuation approach;

b. compute the interest rate risk exposure of a bond position or of a bond portfolio, given a change in interest rates;

c. demonstrate the price volatility characteristics for option-free bonds when interest rates change (including the concept of "positive convexity"), demonstrate the price volatility characteristics of callable bonds and prepayable securities when interest rates change (including the concept of "negative convexity"), and describe the price volatility characteristics of putable bonds;

d. compute the effective duration of a bond, given information about how the bond's price will increase and decrease for given changes in interest rates, and compute the approximate percentage price change for a bond, given the bond's effective duration and a specified change in yield;

e. distinguish among the alternative definitions of duration (modified, effective or option-adjusted, and Macaulay) explain why effective duration is the most appropriate measure of interest rate risk for bonds with embedded options, describe why duration is best interpreted as a measure of a bond's or portfolio's sensitivity to changes in interest rates, compute the duration of a portfolio, given the duration of the bonds comprising the portfolio, and discuss the limitations of portfolio duration;

f. discuss the convexity measure of a bond and estimate a bond's percentage price change, given the bond's duration and convexity and a specified change in interest rates;

g. differentiate between modified convexity and effective convexity;

h. compute the price value of a basis point (PVBP), and explain its relationship to duration.

INTRODUCTION TO THE VALUATION OF DEBT SECURITIES

READING 66

LEARNING OUTCOMES

The candidate should be able to:

a. describe the fundamental principles of bond valuation;

b. identify the types of bonds for which estimating the expected cash flows is difficult, and explain the problems encountered when estimating the cash flows for these bonds;

c. determine the appropriate interest rates for valuing a bond's cash flows, compute the value of a bond, given the expected annual or semiannual cash flows and the appropriate single (constant) or multiple (arbitrage-free rate curve) discount rates, explain how the value of a bond changes if the discount rate increases or decreases, and compute the change in value that is attributable to the rate change, and explain how the price of a bond changes as the bond approaches its maturity date, and compute the change in value that is attributable to the passage of time;

d. compute the value of a zero-coupon bond, explain the arbitrage-free valuation approach and the market process that forces the price of a bond toward its arbitrage-free value, determine whether a bond is undervalued or overvalued, given the bond's cash flows, appropriate spot rates or yield to maturity, and current market price, and explain how a dealer could generate an arbitrage profit.

INTRODUCTION 1

Valuation is the process of determining the fair value of a financial asset. The process is also referred to as "valuing" or "pricing" a financial asset. In this reading, we will explain the general principles of fixed income security valuation. In this reading, we will limit our discussion to the valuation of option-free bonds.

Fixed Income Analysis for the Chartered Financial Analyst® Program, Second Edition, by Frank J. Fabozzi. Reprinted with permission.

2   GENERAL PRINCIPLES OF VALUATION

The fundamental principle of financial asset valuation is that its value is equal to the present value of its expected cash flows. This principle applies regardless of the financial asset. Thus, the valuation of a financial asset involves the following three steps:

Step 1: Estimate the expected cash flows.

Step 2: Determine the appropriate interest rate or interest rates that should be used to discount the cash flows.

Step 3: Calculate the present value of the expected cash flows found in step 1 using the interest rate or interest rates determined in step 2.

2.1 Estimating Cash Flows

Cash flow is simply the cash that is expected to be received in the future from an investment. In the case of a fixed income security, it does not make any difference whether the cash flow is interest income or payment of principal. The **cash flows** of a security are the collection of each period's cash flow. Holding aside the risk of default, the cash flows for few fixed income securities are simple to project. Noncallable U.S. Treasury securities have known cash flows. For Treasury coupon securities, the cash flows are the coupon interest payments every six months up to and including the maturity date and the principal payment at the maturity date.

At times, investors will find it difficult to estimate the cash flows when they purchase a fixed income security. For example, if

1. the issuer or the investor has the option to change the contractual due date for the payment of the principal, or

2. the coupon payment is reset periodically by a formula based on some value or values of reference rates, prices, or exchange rates, or

3. the investor has the choice to convert or exchange the security into common stock.

Callable bonds, putable bonds, mortgage-backed securities, and asset-backed securities are examples of (1). Floating-rate securities are an example of (2). Convertible bonds and exchangeable bonds are examples of (3).

For securities that fall into the first category, future interest rate movements are the key factor to determine if the option will be exercised. Specifically, if interest rates fall far enough, the issuer can sell a new issue of bonds at the lower interest rate and use the proceeds to pay off (call) the older bonds that have the higher coupon rate. (This assumes that the interest savings are larger than the costs involved in refunding.) Similarly, for a loan, if rates fall enough that the interest savings outweigh the refinancing costs, the borrower has an incentive to refinance. For a putable bond, the investor will put the issue if interest rates rise enough to drive the market price below the put price (i.e., the price at which it must be repurchased by the issuer).

What this means is that to properly estimate the cash flows of a fixed income security, it is necessary to incorporate into the analysis how, in the future, changes in interest rates and other factors affecting the embedded option may affect cash flows.

2.2 Determining the Appropriate Rate or Rates

Once the cash flows for a fixed income security are estimated, the next step is to determine the appropriate interest rate to be used to discount the cash flows. As we did in the previous reading, we will use the terms *interest rate* and *yield* interchangeably. The minimum interest rate that an investor should require is the yield available in the marketplace on a default-free cash flow. In the United States, this is the yield on a U.S. Treasury security. This is *one* of the reasons that the Treasury market is closely watched. What is the *minimum* interest rate U.S. investors demand? At this point, we can assume that it is the yield on the on-the-run Treasury security with the same as the security being valued.[1] We will qualify this shortly.

For a security that is not issued by the U.S. government, investors will require a yield premium over the yield available on an on-the-run Treasury issue. This yield premium reflects the additional risks that the investor accepts.

For each cash flow estimated, the same interest rate can be used to calculate the present value. However, since each cash flow is unique, it is more appropriate to value each cash flow using an interest rate specific to that cash flow's maturity. In the traditional approach to valuation a single interest rate is used. In Section IV, we will see that the proper approach to valuation uses multiple interest rates each specific to a particular cash flow. In that section, we will also demonstrate why this must be the case.

2.3 Discounting the Expected Cash Flows

Given expected (estimated) cash flows and the appropriate interest rate or interest rates to be used to discount the cash flows, the final step in the valuation process is to value the cash flows.

What is the value of a single cash flow to be received in the future? It is the amount of money that must be invested today to generate that future value. The resulting value is called the **present value** of a cash flow. (It is also called the **discounted value.**) The present value of a cash flow will depend on (1) when a cash flow will be received (i.e., the **timing** of a cash flow) and (2) the interest rate used to calculate the present value. The interest rate used is called the **discount rate.**

First, we calculate the present value for each expected cash flow. Then, to determine the value of the security, we calculate the sum of the present values (i.e., for all of the security's expected cash flows).

If a discount rate i can be earned on any sum invested today, the present value of the expected cash flow to be received t years from now is:

$$\text{present value}_t = \frac{\text{expected cash flow in period } t}{(1 + i)^t}$$

The value of a financial asset is then the sum of the present value of all the expected cash flows. That is, assuming that there are N expected cash flows:

$$\text{value} = \text{present value}_1 + \text{present value}_2 + \dots + \text{present value}_N$$

To illustrate the present value formula, consider a simple bond that matures in four years, has a coupon rate of 10%, and has a maturity value of $100. For simplicity, let's assume the bond pays interest annually and a discount rate of 8%

---

[1] As explained in Reading 64, the on-the-run Treasury issues are the most recently auctioned Treasury issues.

should be used to calculate the present value of each cash flow. The cash flow for this bond is:

Year	Cash Flow
1	$10
2	10
3	10
4	110

The present value of each cash flow is:

Year 1: present value$_1$ $= \dfrac{\$10}{(1.08)^1} = \$9.2593$

Year 2: present value$_2$ $= \dfrac{\$10}{(1.08)^2} = \$8.5734$

Year 3: present value$_3$ $= \dfrac{\$10}{(1.08)^3} = \$7.9383$

Year 4: present value$_4$ $= \dfrac{\$110}{(1.08)^4} = \$80.8533$

The value of this security is then the sum of the present values of the four cash flows. That is, the present value is $106.6243 ($9.2593 + $8.5734 + $7.9383 + $80.8533).

Practice Question 1

A. What is the present value of a 5-year security with a coupon rate of 7% that pays annually assuming a discount rate of 5% and a par value of $100?

B. A 5-year amortizing security with a par value of $10,000 and a coupon rate of 5% has an expected cash flow of $2,309.75 per year, assuming there are no principal prepayments. The annual cash flow includes interest and principal payment. What is the present value of this amortizing security assuming a discount rate of 6%?

2.3.1 Present Value Properties

An important property about the present value can be seen from the above illustration. For the first three years, the cash flow is the same ($10) and the discount rate is the same (8%). The present value decreases as we go further into the future. *This is an important property of the present value: for a given discount rate, the further into the future a cash flow is received, the lower its present value.* This can be seen in the present value formula. As t increases, present value$_t$ decreases.

Suppose that instead of a discount rate of 8%, a 12% discount rate is used for each cash flow. Then, the present value of each cash flow is:

Year 1: present value$_1$ $= \dfrac{\$10}{(1.12)^1} = \$8.9286$

$$\text{Year 2:} \quad \text{present value}_2 = \frac{\$10}{(1.12)^2} = \$7.9719$$

$$\text{Year 3:} \quad \text{present value}_3 = \frac{\$10}{(1.12)^3} = \$7.1178$$

$$\text{Year 4:} \quad \text{present value}_4 = \frac{\$110}{(1.12)^4} = \$69.9070$$

EXHIBIT 66-1 Price/Discount Rate Relationship for an Option-Free Bond

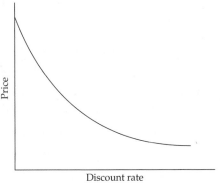

Maximum price = sum of undiscounted cash flows

The value of this security is then $93.9253 ($8.9286 + $7.9719 + $7.1178 + $69.9070). The security's value is lower if a 12% discount rate is used compared to an 8% discount rate ($93.9253 versus $106.6243). This is another general property of present value: *the higher the discount rate, the lower the present value.* Since the value of a security is the present value of the expected cash flows, this property carries over to the value of a security: *the higher the discount rate, the lower a security's value.* The reverse is also true: *the lower the discount rate, the higher a security's value.*

Exhibit 66-1 shows, for an option-free bond, this inverse relationship between a security's value and the discount rate. The shape of the curve in Exhibit 66-1 is referred to as **convex.** By convex, it is meant the curve is bowed in from the origin. As we will see in Reading 68, this convexity or bowed shape has implications for the price volatility of a bond when interest rates change. What is important to understand is that the relationship is not linear.

Practice Question 2

What is the present value of the cash flow of the 5-year 7% coupon security in Practice Question 1 assuming a discount rate of 4% rather than 5%?

2.3.2 Relationship between Coupon Rate, Discount Rate, and Price Relative to Par Value

In Reading 63, we described the relationship between a bond's coupon rate, required market yield, and price relative to its par value (i.e., premium, discount, or equal to par). The required yield is equivalent to the discount rate discussed above. We stated the following relationship:

> coupon rate = yield required by market, *therefore* price = par value
> coupon rate < yield required by market, *therefore* price < par value (discount)
> coupon rate > yield required by market, *therefore* price > par value (premium)

Now that we know how to value a bond, we can demonstrate the relationship. The coupon rate on our hypothetical bond is 10%. When an 8% discount rate is used, the bond's value is $106.6243. That is, the price is greater than par value (premium). This is because the coupon rate (10%) is greater than the required yield (the 8% discount rate). We also showed that when the discount rate is 12% (i.e., greater than the coupon rate of 10%), the price of the bond is $93.9253. That is, the bond's value is less than par value when the coupon rate is less than the required yield (discount). When the discount rate is the same as the coupon rate, 10%, the bond's value is equal to par value as shown below:

Year	Cash flow	Present value at 10%
1	$10	$9.0909
2	10	8.2645
3	10	7.5131
4	110	75.1315
	Total	$100.0000

Practice Question 3

A. What is the value of a 5-year 7% coupon bond per $100 of par value when the discount rate is (i) 6%, (ii) 7%, and (iii) 8%?

B. Show that the results obtained in part A are consistent with the relationship between the coupon rate, discount rate, and price relative to par value given in the text.

2.3.3 Change in a Bond's Value as it Moves Toward Maturity

As a bond moves closer to its maturity date, its value changes. More specifically, assuming that the discount rate does not change, a bond's value:

1. decreases over time if the bond is selling at a premium

2. increases over time if the bond is selling at a discount

3. is unchanged if the bond is selling at par value

At the maturity date, the bond's value is equal to its par value. So, over time as the bond moves toward its maturity date, its price will move to its par value—a characteristic sometimes referred to as a "pull to par value."

To illustrate what happens to a bond selling at a premium, consider once again the 4-year 10% coupon bond. When the discount rate is 8%, the bond's price is 106.6243. Suppose that one year later, the discount rate is still 8%. There are only three cash flows remaining since the bond is now a 3-year security. The cash flow and the present value of the cash flows are given on the following page:

Year	Cash flow	Present value at 8%
1	$10	$9.2593
2	10	8.5734
3	110	87.3215
	Total	$105.1542

The price has declined from $106.6243 to $105.1542.

Now suppose that the bond's price is initially below par value. For example, as stated earlier, if the discount rate is 12%, the 4-year 10% coupon bond's value is $93.9253. Assuming the discount rate remains at 12%, one year later the cash flow and the present value of the cash flow would be as shown below:

Year	Cash flow	Present value at 12%
1	$10	$8.9286
2	10	7.9719
3	110	78.2958
	Total	$95.1963

The bond's price increases from $93.9253 to $95.1963.

To understand how the price of a bond changes as it moves towards maturity, consider the following three 20-year bonds for which the yield required by the market is 8%: a premium bond (10% coupon), a discount bond (6% coupon), and a par bond (8% coupon). To simplify the example, it is assumed that each bond pays interest annually. Exhibit 66-2 shows the price of each bond as it moves toward maturity, assuming that the 8% yield required by the market does not change. The premium bond with an initial price of 119.6363 decreases in price until it reaches par value at the maturity date. The discount bond with an initial price of 80.3637 increases in price until it reaches par value at the maturity date.

In practice, over time the discount rate will change. So, the bond's value will change due to both the change in the discount rate and the change in the cash flow as the bond moves toward maturity. For example, again suppose that the discount rate for the 4-year 10% coupon is 8% so that the bond is selling for $106.6243. One year later, suppose that the discount rate appropriate for a 3-year 10% coupon bond increases from 8% to 9%. Then the cash flow and present value of the cash flows are shown below:

Year	Cash flow	Present value at 9%
1	$10	$9.1743
2	10	8.4168
3	110	84.9402
	Total	$102.5313

The bond's price will decline from $106.6243 to $102.5313. As shown earlier, if the discount rate did not increase, the price would have declined to only $105.1542. The price decline of $4.0930 ($106.6243 − $102.5313) can be decomposed as follows:

Price change attributable to moving to
    maturity (no change in discount rate) $1.4701   (106.6243 − 105.1542)

Price change attribute to an increase in
    the discount rate from 8% to 9% $2.6229   (105.1542 − 102.5313)

Total price change $4.0930

EXHIBIT 66-2 Movement of a Premium, Discount, and Par Bond as a Bond Moves Towards Maturity

Information about the three bonds:
All bonds mature in 20 years and have a yield required by the market of 8%
Coupon payments are annual

Premium bond = 10% coupon selling for 119.6363
Discount bond = 6% coupon selling for 80.3637
Par bond = 8% coupon selling at par value

Assumption: The yield required by the market is unchanged over the life of the bond at 8%.

Time to maturity in years	Premium bond	Discount bond	Par bond
20	119.6363	80.3637	100.0000
19	119.2072	80.7928	100.0000
18	118.7438	81.2562	100.0000
17	118.2433	81.7567	100.0000
16	117.7027	82.2973	100.0000
15	117.1190	82.8810	100.0000
14	116.4885	83.5115	100.0000
13	115.8076	84.1924	100.0000
12	115.0722	84.9278	100.0000
11	114.2779	85.7221	100.0000
10	113.4202	86.5798	100.0000
9	112.4938	87.5062	100.0000
8	111.4933	88.5067	100.0000
7	110.4127	89.5873	100.0000
6	109.2458	90.7542	100.0000
5	107.9854	92.0146	100.0000
4	106.6243	93.3757	100.0000
3	105.1542	94.8458	100.0000
2	103.5665	96.4335	100.0000
1	101.8519	98.1481	100.0000
0	100.0000	100.0000	100.0000

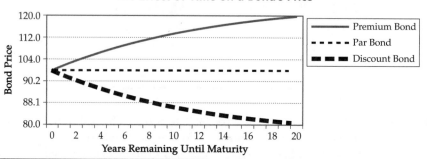

The Effect of Time on a Bond's Price

2.4 Valuation Using Multiple Discount Rates

Thus far, we have used one discount rate to compute the present value of each cash flow. As we will see shortly, the proper way to value the cash flows of a bond is to use a different discount rate that is unique to the time period in which a cash flow will be received. So, let's look at how we would value a security using a different discount rate for each cash flow.

Suppose that the appropriate discount rates are as follows:

year 1   6.8%
year 2   7.2%
year 3   7.6%
year 4   8.0%

Then, for the 4-year 10% coupon bond, the present value of each cash flow is:

Year 1: $\text{present value}_1 = \dfrac{\$10}{(1.068)^1} = \$9.3633$

Year 2: $\text{present value}_2 = \dfrac{\$10}{(1.072)^2} = \$8.7018$

Year 3: $\text{present value}_3 = \dfrac{\$10}{(1.076)^3} = \$8.0272$

Year 4: $\text{present value}_4 = \dfrac{\$110}{(1.080)^4} = \$80.8533$

The present value of this security, assuming the above set of discount rates, is $106.9456.

Practice Question 4

Compute the value per $100 of par value of a 5-year 7% coupon bond, assuming the payments are annual and the discount rate for each year is as follows:

Year	Discount rate (%)
1	3.5
2	3.9
3	4.2
4	4.5
5	5.0

2.5 Valuing Semiannual Cash Flows

In our illustrations, we assumed coupon payments are paid once per year. For most bonds, the coupon payments are semiannual. This does not introduce any complexities into the calculation. The procedure is to simply adjust the coupon payments by dividing the annual coupon payment by 2 and adjust the discount rate by dividing the annual discount rate by 2. The time period t in the present value formula is treated in terms of 6-month periods rather than years.

For example, consider once again the 4-year 10% coupon bond with a maturity value of $100. The cash flow for the first 3.5 years is equal to $5 ($10/2). The last cash flow is equal to the final coupon payment ($5) plus the maturity value ($100). So the last cash flow is $105.

Now the tricky part. If an annual discount rate of 8% is used, how do we obtain the semiannual discount rate? We will simply use one-half the annual rate, 4% (or 8%/2). The reader should have a problem with this: a 4% semiannual rate is not an 8% effective annual rate. That is correct. However, as we will see in the next reading, the *convention* in the bond market is to quote annual interest rates that are just double semiannual rates. This will be explained more fully in the next reading. Don't let this throw you off here. For now, just accept the fact that one-half an annual discount rate is used to obtain a semiannual discount rate in the balance of the reading.

Given the cash flows and the semiannual discount rate of 4%, the present value of each cash flow is shown below:

Period 1: present value$_1 = \dfrac{\$5}{(1.04)^1} = \$4.8077$

Period 2: present value$_2 = \dfrac{\$5}{(1.04)^2} = \$4.6228$

Period 3: present value$_3 = \dfrac{\$5}{(1.04)^3} = \$4.4450$

Period 4: present value$_4 = \dfrac{\$5}{(1.04)^4} = \$4.2740$

Period 5: present value$_5 = \dfrac{\$5}{(1.04)^5} = \$4.1096$

Period 6: present value$_6 = \dfrac{\$5}{(1.04)^6} = \$3.9516$

Period 7: present value$_7 = \dfrac{\$5}{(1.04)^7} = \$3.7996$

Period 8: present value$_8 = \dfrac{\$105}{(1.04)^8} = \$76.7225$

The security's value is equal to the sum of the present value of the eight cash flows, $106.7327. Notice that this price is greater than the price when coupon payments are annual ($106.6243). This is because one-half the annual coupon payment is received six months sooner than when payments are annual. This produces a higher present value for the semiannual coupon payments relative to the annual coupon payments.

The value of a non-amortizing bond can be divided into two components: (1) the present value of the coupon payments and (2) the present value of the maturity value. For a fixed-rate coupon bond, the coupon payments represent an annuity. A short-cut formula can be used to compute the value of a bond when using a single discount rate: compute the present value of the annuity and then add the present value of the maturity value.[2]

---

[2] Note that in our earlier illustration, we computed the present value of the semiannual coupon payments before the maturity date and then added the present value of the last cash flow (last semiannual coupon payment plus the maturity value). In the presentation of how to use the short-cut formula, we are computing the present value of all the semiannual coupon payments and then adding the present value of the maturity value. Both approaches will give the same answer for the value of a bond.

The present value of an annuity is equal to:

$$\text{annuity payment} \times \left[\frac{1 - \dfrac{1}{(1 + i)^{\text{no. of periods}}}}{i} \right]$$

For a bond with annual interest payments, i is the annual discount rate and the "no. of periods" is equal to the number of years.

Applying this formula to a semiannual-pay bond, the annuity payment is one half the annual coupon payment and the number of periods is double the number of years to maturity. So, the present value of the coupon payments can be expressed as:

$$\text{semiannual coupon payment} \times \left[\frac{1 - \dfrac{1}{(1 + i)^{\text{no. of years} \times 2}}}{i} \right]$$

where i is the semiannual discount rate (annual rate/2). Notice that in the formula, we use the number of years multiplied by 2 since a period in our illustration is six months.

The present value of the maturity value is equal to

$$\text{present value of maturity value} = \frac{\$100}{(1 + i)^{\text{no. of years} \times 2}}$$

To illustrate this computation, consider once again the 4-year 10% coupon bond with an annual discount rate of 8% and a semiannual discount rate of one half this rate (4%) for the reason cited earlier. Then:

semiannual coupon payment = $5
semiannual discount rate (i) = 4%
number of years   = 4

then the present value of the coupon payments is

$$\$5 \times \left[\frac{1 - \dfrac{1}{(1.04)^{4 \times 2}}}{0.04} \right] = \$33.6637$$

To determine the price, the present value of the maturity value must be added to the present value of the coupon payments. The present value of the maturity value is

$$\text{present value of maturity value} = \frac{\$100}{(1.04)^{4 \times 2}} = \$73.0690$$

The price is then $106.7327 ($33.6637 + $73.0690). This agrees with our previous calculation for the price of this bond.

Practice Question 5

What is the value of a 5-year 7% coupon bond that pays interest semi-annually assuming that the annual discount rate is 5%?

2.6 Valuing a Zero-Coupon Bond

For a zero-coupon bond, there is only one cash flow—the maturity value. The value of a zero-coupon bond that matures N years from now is

$$\frac{\text{maturity value}}{(1 + i)^{\text{no. of years} \times 2}}$$

where i is the semiannual discount rate.

It may seem surprising that the number of periods is double the number of years to maturity. In computing the value of a zero-coupon bond, the number of 6-month periods (i.e., "no. of years × 2") is used in the denominator of the formula. The rationale is that the pricing of a zero-coupon bond should be consistent with the pricing of a semiannual coupon bond. Therefore, the use of 6-month periods is required in order to have uniformity between the present value calculations.

To illustrate the application of the formula, the value of a 5-year zero-coupon bond with a maturity value of $100 discounted at an 8% interest rate is $67.5564, as shown below:

$$i = 0.04 \ (= 0.08/2)$$
$$N = 5$$
$$\frac{\$100}{(1.04)^{5 \times 2}} = \$67.5564$$

Practice Question 6

A. Complete the following table for a 10-year zero-coupon bond with a maturity value of $1,000 for each of the following *annual* discount rates.

Annual rate	Semiannual rate	Price
1%		
2%		
3%		
4%		
5%		
6%		
7%		
8%		
9%		
10%		
11%		
12%		
13%		
14%		

B. Given the prices for the bond in part A, draw a graph of the price/yield relationship. On the horizontal axis (*x*-axis) should be the annual rate and on the vertical axis (*y*-axis) should be the price.

2.7 Valuing a Bond Between Coupon Payments

For coupon-paying bonds, a complication arises when we try to price a bond between coupon payments. The amount that the buyer pays the seller in such cases is the present value of the cash flow. But one of the cash flows, the very next cash flow, encompasses two components as shown below:

1. interest earned by the seller

2. interest earned by the buyer

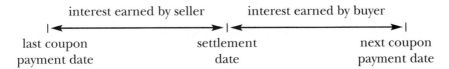

The interest earned by the seller is the interest that has accrued[3] between the last coupon payment date and the settlement date.[4] This interest is called **accrued interest.** At the time of purchase, the buyer must compensate the seller for the accrued interest. The buyer recovers the accrued interest when the next coupon payment is received.

When the price of a bond is computed using the present value calculations described earlier, it is computed with accrued interest embodied in the price. This price is referred to as the **full price.** (Some market participants refer to it as the **dirty price.**) It is the full price that the buyer pays the seller. From the full price, the accrued interest must be deducted to determine the **price** of the bond, sometimes referred to as the **clean price.**

Below, we show how the present value formula is modified to compute the full price when a bond is purchased between coupon periods.

2.7.1 Computing the Full Price

To compute the full price, it is first necessary to determine the fractional periods between the settlement date and the next coupon payment date. This is determined as follows:

$$w \text{ periods} = \frac{\text{days between settlement date and next coupon payment date}}{\text{days in coupon period}}$$

Then the present value of the expected cash flow to be received t periods from now using a discount rate i assuming the first coupon payment is w periods from now is:

$$\text{present value}_t = \frac{\text{expected cash flow}}{(1 + i)^{t-1+w}}$$

This procedure for calculating the present value when a security is purchased between coupon payments is called the "Street method."

To illustrate the calculation, suppose that there are five semiannual coupon payments remaining for a 10% coupon bond. Also assume the following:

1. 78 days between the settlement date and the next coupon payment date

2. 182 days in the coupon period

---

[3] "Accrued" means that the interest is earned but not distributed to the bondholder.

[4] The settlement date is the date a transaction is completed.

Then w is 0.4286 periods (= 78/182). The present value of each cash flow assuming that each is discounted at 8% annual discount rate is

$$\textit{Period 1:} \quad \text{present value}_1 = \frac{\$5}{(1.04)^{0.4286}} = \$4.9167$$

$$\textit{Period 2:} \quad \text{present value}_2 = \frac{\$5}{(1.04)^{1.4286}} = \$4.7276$$

$$\textit{Period 3:} \quad \text{present value}_3 = \frac{\$5}{(1.04)^{2.4286}} = \$4.5457$$

$$\textit{Period 4:} \quad \text{present value}_4 = \frac{\$5}{(1.04)^{3.4286}} = \$4.3709$$

$$\textit{Period 5:} \quad \text{present value}_5 = \frac{\$105}{(1.04)^{4.4286}} = \$88.2583$$

The full price is the sum of the present value of the cash flows, which is $106.8192. Remember that the full price includes the accrued interest that the buyer is paying the seller.

Practice Question 7

Suppose that a bond is purchased between coupon periods. The days between the settlement date and the next coupon period is 58. There are 183 days in the coupon period. Suppose that the bond purchased has a coupon rate of 7% and there are 10 semiannual coupon payments remaining. What is the full price for this bond if a 5% annual discount rate is used?

2.7.2 Computing the Accrued Interest and the Clean Price

To find the price without accrued interest, called the **clean price** or simply **price**, the accrued interest must be computed. To determine the accrued interest, it is first necessary to determine the number of days in the accrued interest period. The number of days in the accrued interest period is determined as follows:

days in accrued interest period =
    days in coupon period − days between settlement and next coupon payment

The percentage of the next semiannual coupon payment that the seller has earned as accrued interest is found as follows:

$$\frac{\text{days in accrued interest period}}{\text{days in coupon period}}$$

So, for example, returning to our illustration where the full price was computed, since there are 182 days in the coupon period and there are 78 days from the settlement date to the next coupon payment, the days in the accrued interest period is 182 minus 78, or 104 days. Therefore, the percentage of the coupon payment that is accrued interest is:

$$\frac{104}{182} = 0.5714 = 57.14\%$$

This is the same percentage found by simply subtracting w from 1. In our illustration, w was 0.4286. Then $1 - 0.4286 = 0.5714$.

Given the value of w, the amount of accrued interest (AI) is equal to:

AI = semiannual coupon payment $\times$ $(1 - w)$

So, for the 10% coupon bond whose full price we computed, since the semiannual coupon payment per $100 of par value is $5 and w is 0.4286, the accrued interest is:

$5 $\times$ $(1 - 0.4286)$ = $2.8570

The clean price is then:

full price $-$ accrued interest

In our illustration, the clean price is[5]

$106.8192 $-$ $2.8570 = $103.9622

Practice Question 8

What is the accrued interest and the clean price for the bond whose full price is computed in Practice Question 7?

2.7.3 Day Count Conventions

The practice for calculating the number of days between two dates depends on *day count conventions* used in the bond market. The convention differs by the type of security. Day count conventions are also used to calculate the number of days in the numerator and denominator of the ratio w.

The accrued interest (AI) assuming semiannual payments is calculated as follows:

$$AI = \frac{\text{annual coupon}}{2} \times \frac{\text{days in AI period}}{\text{days in coupon period}}$$

In calculating the number of days between two dates, the actual number of days is not always the same as the number of days that should be used in the accrued interest formula. The number of days used depends on the day count convention for the particular security. Specifically, day count conventions differ for Treasury securities and government agency securities, municipal bonds, and corporate bonds.

For coupon-bearing Treasury securities, the day count convention used is to determine the actual number of days between two dates. This is referred to

---

[5] Notice that in computing the full price the present value of the next coupon payment is computed. However, the buyer pays the seller the accrued interest now despite the fact that it will be recovered at the next coupon payment date.

as the "actual/actual" day count convention. For example, consider a coupon-bearing Treasury security whose previous coupon payment was March 1. The next coupon payment would be on September 1. Suppose this Treasury security is purchased with a settlement date of July 17th. The actual number of days between July 17 (the settlement date) and September 1 (the date of the next coupon payment) is 46 days, as shown below:

July 17 to July 31	14 days
August	31 days
September 1	1 day
	46 days

Note that the settlement date (July 17) is not counted. The number of days in the coupon period is the actual number of days between March 1 and September 1, which is 184 days. The number of days between the last coupon payment (March 1) through July 17 is therefore 138 days (184 days − 46 days).

For coupon-bearing agency, municipal, and corporate bonds, a different day count convention is used. It is assumed that every month has 30 days, that any 6-month period has 180 days, and that there are 360 days in a year. This day count convention is referred to as "30/360." For example, consider once again the Treasury security purchased with a settlement date of July 17, the previous coupon payment on March 1, and the next coupon payment on September 1. If the security is an agency, municipal, or corporate bond, the number of days until the next coupon payment is 44 days as shown below:

July 17 to July 31	13 days
August	30 days
September 1	1 day
	44 days

Note that the settlement date, July 17, is not counted. Since July is treated as having 30 days, there are 13 days (30 days minus the first 17 days in July). The number of days from March 1 to July 17 is 136, which is the number of days in the accrued interest period.

3 TRADITIONAL APPROACH TO VALUATION

The traditional approach to valuation has been to discount every cash flow of a fixed income security by the same interest rate (or discount rate). For example, consider the three hypothetical 10-year Treasury securities shown in Exhibit 66-3: a 12% coupon bond, an 8% coupon bond, and a zero-coupon bond. The cash flows for each bond are shown in the exhibit. Since the cash flows of all three bonds are viewed as default free, the traditional practice is to use the same discount rate to calculate the present value of all three bonds and use the same discount rate for the cash flow for each period. The discount rate used is the yield for the on-the-run issue obtained from the Treasury yield curve. For example, suppose that the yield for the 10-year on-the-run Treasury issue is 10%. Then, the practice is to discount each cash flow for each bond using a 10% discount rate.

For a non-Treasury security, a yield premium or yield spread is added to the on-the-run Treasury yield. The yield spread is the same regardless of when a cash flow is to be received in the traditional approach. For a 10-year non-Treasury security, suppose that 90 basis points is the appropriate yield spread. Then all cash flows would be discounted at the yield for the on-the-run 10-year Treasury issue of 10% plus 90 basis points.

EXHIBIT 66-3 Cash Flows for Three 10-Year Hypothetical Treasury Securities Per $100 of Par Value

	Each Period Is Six Months		
	Coupon Rate		
Period	12%	8%	0%
1-19	$6	$4	$0
20	106	104	100

THE ARBITRAGE-FREE VALUATION APPROACH   4

The fundamental flaw of the traditional approach is that it views each security as the same package of cash flows. For example, consider a 10-year U.S. Treasury issue with an 8% coupon rate. The cash flows per $100 of par value would be 19 payments of $4 every six months and $104 twenty 6-month periods from now. The traditional practice would discount each cash flow using the same discount rate.

The proper way to view the 10-year 8% coupon Treasury issue is as a package of zero-coupon bonds whose maturity value is equal to the amount of the cash flow and whose maturity date is equal to each cash flow's payment date. Thus, the 10-year 8% coupon Treasury issue should be viewed as 20 zero-coupon bonds. The reason this is the proper way to value a security is that it does not allow arbitrage profit by taking apart or "stripping" a security and selling off the stripped securities at a higher aggregate value than it would cost to purchase the security in the market. We'll illustrate this later. We refer to this approach to valuation as the **arbitrage-free valuation approach.**[6]

By viewing any financial asset as a package of zero-coupon bonds, a consistent valuation framework can be developed. Viewing a financial asset as a package of zero-coupon bonds means that any two bonds would be viewed as different packages of zero-coupon bonds and valued accordingly.

The difference between the traditional valuation approach and the arbitrage-free approach is illustrated in Exhibit 66-4, which shows how the three bonds whose cash flows are depicted in Exhibit 66-3 should be valued. With the traditional approach, the discount rate for all three bonds is the yield on a 10-year U.S. Treasury security. With the arbitrage-free approach, the discount rate for a cash flow is the theoretical rate that the U.S. Treasury would have to pay if it issued a zero-coupon bond with a maturity date equal to the maturity date of the cash flow.

Therefore, to implement the arbitrage-free approach, it is necessary to determine the theoretical rate that the U.S. Treasury would have to pay on a zero-coupon Treasury security for each maturity. As explained in the previous reading, the name given to the zero-coupon Treasury rate is the **Treasury spot rate.** In Reading 67, we will explain how the Treasury spot rate can be calculated. The

---

[6] In its simple form, arbitrage is the simultaneous buying and selling of an asset at two different prices in two different markets. The arbitrageur profits without risk by buying cheap in one market and simultaneously selling at the higher price in the other market. Such opportunities for arbitrage are rare. Less obvious arbitrage opportunities exist in situations where a package of assets can produce a payoff (expected return) identical to an asset that is priced differently. This arbitrage relies on a fundamental principle of finance called the "law of one price" which states that a given asset must have the same price regardless of the means by which one goes about creating that asset. The law of one price implies that if the payoff of an asset can be synthetically created by a package of assets, the price of the package and the price of the asset whose payoff it replicates must be equal.

spot rate for a Treasury security is the interest rate that should be used to discount a default-free cash flow with the same maturity. We call the value of a bond based on spot rates the **arbitrage-free value.**

EXHIBIT 66-4 Comparison of Traditional Approach and Arbitrage-Free Approach in Valuing a Treasury Security

Each Period Is Six Months

| Period | Discount (Base Interest) Rate | | Cash Flows For* | | |
	Traditional Approach	Arbitrage-Free Approach	12%	8%	0%
1	10-year Treasury rate	1-period Treasury spot rate	$6	$4	$0
2	10-year Treasury rate	2-period Treasury spot rate	6	4	0
3	10-year Treasury rate	3-period Treasury spot rate	6	4	0
4	10-year Treasury rate	4-period Treasury spot rate	6	4	0
5	10-year Treasury rate	5-period Treasury spot rate	6	4	0
6	10-year Treasury rate	6-period Treasury spot rate	6	4	0
7	10-year Treasury rate	7-period Treasury spot rate	6	4	0
8	10-year Treasury rate	8-period Treasury spot rate	6	4	0
9	10-year Treasury rate	9-period Treasury spot rate	6	4	0
10	10-year Treasury rate	10-period Treasury spot rate	6	4	0
11	10-year Treasury rate	11-period Treasury spot rate	6	4	0
12	10-year Treasury rate	12-period Treasury spot rate	6	4	0
13	10-year Treasury rate	13-period Treasury spot rate	6	4	0
14	10-year Treasury rate	14-period Treasury spot rate	6	4	0
15	10-year Treasury rate	15-period Treasury spot rate	6	4	0
16	10-year Treasury rate	16-period Treasury spot rate	6	4	0
17	10-year Treasury rate	17-period Treasury spot rate	6	4	0
18	10-year Treasury rate	18-period Treasury spot rate	6	4	0
19	10-year Treasury rate	19-period Treasury spot rate	6	4	0
20	10-year Treasury rate	20-period Treasury spot rate	106	104	100

* Per $100 of par value.

4.1 Valuation Using Treasury Spot Rates

For the purposes of our discussion, we will take the Treasury spot rate for each maturity as given. To illustrate how Treasury spot rates are used to compute the arbitrage-free value of a Treasury security, we will use the hypothetical Treasury spot rates shown in the third column of Exhibit 66-5 to value an 8% 10-year Treasury security. The present value of each period's cash flow is shown in the last column. The sum of the present values is the arbitrage-free value for the Treasury security. For the 8% 10-year Treasury, it is $115.2619.

As a second illustration, suppose that a 4.8% coupon 10-year Treasury bond is being valued based on the Treasury spot rates shown in Exhibit 66-5. The arbitrage-free value of this bond is $90.8428 as shown in Exhibit 66-6.

In the next reading, we discuss yield measures. The yield to maturity is a measure that would be computed for this bond. We won't show how it is computed in this reading, but simply state the result. The yield for the 4.8% coupon 10-year Treasury bond is 6.033%. Notice that the spot rates are used to obtain the price and the price is then used to compute a conventional yield measure. *It is important to understand that there are an infinite number of spot rate curves that can generate the same price of $90.8428 and therefore the same yield.* (We return to this point in the next reading.)

EXHIBIT 66-5 Determination of the Arbitrage-Free Value of an 8% 10-Year Treasury

Period	Years	Cash Flow ($)	Spot Rate (%)*	Present Value ($)**
1	0.5	4	3.0000	3.9409
2	1.0	4	3.3000	3.8712
3	1.5	4	3.5053	3.7968
4	2.0	4	3.9164	3.7014
5	2.5	4	4.4376	3.5843
6	3.0	4	4.7520	3.4743
7	3.5	4	4.9622	3.3694
8	4.0	4	5.0650	3.2747
9	4.5	4	5.1701	3.1791
10	5.0	4	5.2772	3.0829
11	5.5	4	5.3864	2.9861
12	6.0	4	5.4976	2.8889
13	6.5	4	5.6108	2.7916
14	7.0	4	5.6643	2.7055
15	7.5	4	5.7193	2.6205
16	8.0	4	5.7755	2.5365
17	8.5	4	5.8331	2.4536
18	9.0	4	5.9584	2.3581
19	9.5	4	6.0863	2.2631
20	10.0	104	6.2169	56.3830
			Total	$115.2621

* The spot rate is an annual discount rate. The convention to obtain a semiannual discount rate is to take one-half the annual discount rate. So, for period 6 (i.e., 3 years), the spot rate is 4.7520%. The semiannual discount rate is 2.376%.

** The present value for the cash flow is equal to:

$$\frac{\text{Cash flow}}{(1 + \text{Spot rate}/2)^{\text{period}}}$$

Practice Question 9

A. Using the Treasury spot rates shown in Exhibit 66-5, what is the arbitrage-free value of a 7.4% coupon 8-year Treasury security?

B. Using the Treasury spot rates shown in Exhibit 66-5, what is the arbitrage-free value of a 4% coupon 8-year Treasury security?

4.2 Reason for Using Treasury Spot Rates

Thus far, we simply asserted that the value of a Treasury security should be based on discounting each cash flow using the corresponding Treasury spot rate. But what if market participants value a security using the yield for the on-the-run Treasury with a maturity equal to the maturity of the Treasury security being valued? (In other words, what if participants use the yield on coupon-bearing securities rather than the yield on zero-coupon securities?) Let's see why a Treasury security will have to trade close to its arbitrage-free value.

4.2.1 Stripping and the Arbitrage-Free Valuation

The key in the process is the existence of the Treasury strips market. As explained in Reading 64, a dealer has the ability to take apart the cash flows of a Treasury coupon security (i.e., strip the security) and create zero-coupon securities. These zero-coupon securities, which we called Treasury strips, can be sold to investors.

EXHIBIT 66-6 Determination of the Arbitrage-Free Value of a 4.8% 10-Year Treasury

Period	Years	Cash Flow ($)	Spot Rate (%)*	Present Value ($)**
1	0.5	2.4	3.0000	2.3645
2	1.0	2.4	3.3000	2.3227
3	1.5	2.4	3.5053	2.2781
4	2.0	2.4	3.9164	2.2209
5	2.5	2.4	4.4376	2.1506
6	3.0	2.4	4.7520	2.0846
7	3.5	2.4	4.9622	2.0216
8	4.0	2.4	5.0650	1.9648
9	4.5	2.4	5.1701	1.9075
10	5.0	2.4	5.2772	1.8497
11	5.5	2.4	5.3864	1.7916
12	6.0	2.4	5.4976	1.7334
13	6.5	2.4	5.6108	1.6750
14	7.0	2.4	5.6643	1.6233
15	7.5	2.4	5.7193	1.5723
16	8.0	2.4	5.7755	1.5219
17	8.5	2.4	5.8331	1.4722
18	9.0	2.4	5.9584	1.4149
19	9.5	2.4	6.0863	1.3578
20	10.0	102.4	6.2169	55.5156
			Total	90.8430

* The spot rate is an annual discount rate. The convention to obtain a semiannual discount rate is to take one-half the annual discount rate. So, for period 6 (i.e., 3 years), the spot rate is 4.7520%. The semiannual discount rate is 2.376%.

** The present value for the cash flow is equal to:

$$\frac{\text{Cash flow}}{(1 + \text{Spot rate}/2)^{\text{period}}}$$

EXHIBIT 66-7 Price of an 8% 10-Year Treasury Valued at a 6% Discount Rate

Period	Years	Cash Flow ($)	Discount Rate (%)*	Present Value ($)**
1	0.5	4	6.0000	3.8835
2	1.0	4	6.0000	3.7704
3	1.5	4	6.0000	3.6606
4	2.0	4	6.0000	3.5539
5	2.5	4	6.0000	3.4504
6	3.0	4	6.0000	3.3499
7	3.5	4	6.0000	3.2524
8	4.0	4	6.0000	3.1576
9	4.5	4	6.0000	3.0657
10	5.0	4	6.0000	2.9764
11	5.5	4	6.0000	2.8897
12	6.0	4	6.0000	2.8055
13	6.5	4	6.0000	2.7238
14	7.0	4	6.0000	2.6445
15	7.5	4	6.0000	2.5674
16	8.0	4	6.0000	2.4927
17	8.5	4	6.0000	2.4201
18	9.0	4	6.0000	2.3496
19	9.5	4	6.0000	2.2811
20	10.0	104	6.0000	57.5823
			Total	114.8775

* The discount rate is an annual discount rate. The convention to obtain a semiannual discount rate is to take one-half the annual discount rate. So, since the discount rate for each period is 6%, the semiannual discount rate is 3%.

** The present value for the cash flow is equal to:

$$\frac{\text{Cash flow}}{(1.03)^{\text{period}}}$$

At what interest rate or yield can these Treasury strips be sold to investors? They can be sold at the Treasury spot rates. If the market price of a Treasury security is less than its value using the arbitrage-free valuation approach, then a dealer can buy the Treasury security, strip it, and sell off the Treasury strips so as to generate greater proceeds than the cost of purchasing the Treasury security. The resulting profit is an arbitrage profit. Since, as we will see, the value determined by using the Treasury spot rates does not allow for the generation of an arbitrage profit, this is the reason why the approach is referred to as an "arbitrage-free" approach.

To illustrate this, suppose that the yield for the on-the-run 10-year Treasury issue is 6%. (We will see in Reading 67 that the Treasury spot rate curve in Exhibit 66-5 was generated from a yield curve where the on-the-run 10-year Treasury issue was 6%.) Suppose that the 8% coupon 10-year Treasury issue is valued using the traditional approach based on 6%. Exhibit 66-7 shows the value based on discounting all the cash flows at 6% is $114.8775.

Consider what would happen if the market priced the security at $114.8775. The value based on the Treasury spot rates (Exhibit 66-5) is $115.2621. What can the dealer do? The dealer can buy the 8% 10-year issue for $114.8775, strip it,

EXHIBIT 66-8 Arbitrage Profit from Stripping the 8% 10-Year Treasury

Period	Years	Sell for	Buy for	Arbitrage profit
1	0.5	3.9409	3.8835	0.0574
2	1.0	3.8712	3.7704	0.1008
3	1.5	3.7968	3.6606	0.1363
4	2.0	3.7014	3.5539	0.1475
5	2.5	3.5843	3.4504	0.1339
6	3.0	3.4743	3.3499	0.1244
7	3.5	3.3694	3.2524	0.1170
8	4.0	3.2747	3.1576	0.1170
9	4.5	3.1791	3.0657	0.1134
10	5.0	3.0829	2.9764	0.1065
11	5.5	2.9861	2.8897	0.0964
12	6.0	2.8889	2.8055	0.0834
13	6.5	2.7916	2.7238	0.0678
14	7.0	2.7055	2.6445	0.0611
15	7.5	2.6205	2.5674	0.0531
16	8.0	2.5365	2.4927	0.0439
17	8.5	2.4536	2.4201	0.0336
18	9.0	2.3581	2.3496	0.0086
19	9.5	2.2631	2.2811	−0.0181
20	10.0	56.3830	57.5823	−1.1993
		115.2621	114.8775	0.3846

and sell the Treasury strips at the spot rates shown in Exhibit 66-5. By doing so, the proceeds that will be received by the dealer are $115.2621. This results in an arbitrage profit of $0.3846 (= $115.2621 − $114.8775).[7] Dealers recognizing this arbitrage opportunity will bid up the price of the 8% 10-year Treasury issue in order to acquire it and strip it. At what point will the arbitrage profit disappear? When the security is priced at $115.2621, the value that we said is the arbitrage-free value.

To understand in more detail where this arbitrage profit is coming from, look at Exhibit 66-8. The third column shows how much each cash flow can be sold for by the dealer if it is stripped. The values in the third column are simply the present values in Exhibit 66-5 based on discounting the cash flows at the Treasury spot rates. The fourth column shows how much the dealer is effectively purchasing the cash flow if each cash flow is discounted at 6%. This is the last column in Exhibit 66-7. The sum of the arbitrage profit from each cash flow stripped is the total arbitrage profit.

4.2.2 Reconstitution and Arbitrage-Free Valuation

We have just demonstrated how coupon stripping of a Treasury issue will force its market value to be close to the value determined by arbitrage-free valuation

---

[7] This may seem like a small amount, but remember that this is for a single $100 par value bond. Multiply this by thousands of bonds and you can see a dealer's profit potential.

EXHIBIT 66-9 Price of a 4.8% 10-Year Treasury Valued at a 6% Discount Rate

Period	Years	Cash Flow ($)	Discount Rate (%)	Present Value ($)
1	0.5	2.4	6.0000	2.3301
2	1.0	2.4	6.0000	2.2622
3	1.5	2.4	6.0000	2.1963
4	2.0	2.4	6.0000	2.1324
5	2.5	2.4	6.0000	2.0703
6	3.0	2.4	6.0000	2.0100
7	3.5	2.4	6.0000	1.9514
8	4.0	2.4	6.0000	1.8946
9	4.5	2.4	6.0000	1.8394
10	5.0	2.4	6.0000	1.7858
11	5.5	2.4	6.0000	1.7338
12	6.0	2.4	6.0000	1.6833
13	6.5	2.4	6.0000	1.6343
14	7.0	2.4	6.0000	1.5867
15	7.5	2.4	6.0000	1.5405
16	8.0	2.4	6.0000	1.4956
17	8.5	2.4	6.0000	1.4520
18	9.0	2.4	6.0000	1.4097
19	9.5	2.4	6.0000	1.3687
20	10.0	102.4	6.0000	56.6964
			Total	91.0735

when the market price is less than the arbitrage-free value. What happens when a Treasury issue's market price is greater than the arbitrage-free value? Obviously, a dealer will not want to strip the Treasury issue since the proceeds generated from stripping will be less than the cost of purchasing the issue.

When such situations occur, the dealer will follow a procedure called **reconstitution.**[8] Basically, the dealer can purchase a package of Treasury strips so as to create a synthetic (i.e., artificial) Treasury coupon security that is worth more than the same maturity and same coupon Treasury issue.

To illustrate this, consider the 4.8% 10-year Treasury issue whose arbitrage-free value was computed in Exhibit 66-6. The arbitrage-free value is $90.8430. Exhibit 66-9 shows the price assuming the traditional approach where all the cash flows are discounted at a 6% interest rate. The price is $91.0735. What the dealer can do is purchase the Treasury strip for each 6-month period at the prices shown in Exhibit 66-6 and sell short the 4.8% 10-year Treasury coupon issue whose cash flows are being replicated. By doing so, the dealer has the cash flow of a 4.8% coupon 10-year Treasury security at a cost of $90.8430, thereby generating an arbitrage profit

---

[8] The definition of *reconstitute* is to provide with a new structure, often by assembling various parts into a whole. *Reconstitution* then, as used here, means to assemble the parts (the Treasury strips) in such a way that a new whole (a Treasury coupon bond) is created. That is, it is the opposite of *stripping* a coupon bond.

of $0.2305 ($91.0735 − $90.8430). The cash flows from the package of Treasury strips purchased is used to make the payments for the Treasury coupon security shorted. Actually, in practice, this can be done in a more efficient manner using a procedure for reconstitution provided for by the Department of the Treasury.

What forces the market price to the arbitrage-free value of $90.8430? As dealers sell short the Treasury coupon issue (4.8% 10-year issue), the price of the issue decreases. When the price is driven down to $90.8430, the arbitrage profit no longer exists.

This process of stripping and reconstitution assures that the price of a Treasury issue will not depart materially from its arbitrage-free value. In other countries, as governments permit the stripping and reconstitution of their issues, the value of non-U.S. government issues have also moved toward their arbitrage-free value.

4.3 Credit Spreads and the Valuation of Non-Treasury Securities

The Treasury spot rates can be used to value any default-free security. For a non-Treasury security, the theoretical value is not as easy to determine. The value of a non-Treasury security is found by discounting the cash flows by the Treasury spot rates plus a yield spread to reflect the additional risks.

The spot rate used to discount the cash flow of a non-Treasury security can be the Treasury spot rate plus a constant credit spread. For example, suppose the 6-month Treasury spot rate is 3% and the 10-year Treasury spot rate is 6%. Also suppose that a suitable credit spread is 90 basis points. Then a 3.9% spot rate is used to discount a 6-month cash flow of a non-Treasury bond and a 6.9% discount rate to discount a 10-year cash flow. (Remember that when each semiannual cash flow is discounted, the discount rate used is one-half the spot rate—1.95% for the 6-month spot rate and 3.45% for the 10-year spot rate.)

The drawback of this approach is that there is no reason to expect the credit spread to be the same regardless of when the cash flow is received. We actually observed this in the previous reading when we saw how credit spreads increase with maturity. Consequently, it might be expected that credit spreads increase with the maturity of the bond. That is, there is a **term structure of credit spreads.**

Dealer firms typically estimate a term structure for credit spreads for each credit rating and market sector. Generally, the credit spread increases with maturity. This is a typical shape for the term structure of credit spreads. In addition, the shape of the term structure is not the same for all credit ratings. Typically, the lower the credit rating, the steeper the term structure of credit spreads.

When the credit spreads for a given credit rating and market sector are added to the Treasury spot rates, the resulting term structure is used to value bonds with that credit rating in that market sector. This term structure is referred to as the **benchmark spot rate curve** or **benchmark zero-coupon rate curve.**

For example, Exhibit 66-10 reproduces the Treasury spot rate curve in Exhibit 66-5. Also shown in the exhibit is a hypothetical credit spread for a non-Treasury security. The resulting benchmark spot rate curve is in the next-to-the-last column. It is this spot rate curve that is used to value the securities that have the same credit rating and are in the same market sector. This is done in Exhibit 66-10 for a hypothetical 8% 10-year issue. The arbitrage-free value is $108.4616. Notice that the theoretical value is less than that for an otherwise comparable Treasury security. The arbitrage-free value for an 8% 10-year Treasury is $115.2621 (see Exhibit 66-5).

VALUATION MODELS ◥ 4 ◢

A **valuation model** provides the fair value of a security. Thus far, the two valuation approaches we have presented have dealt with valuing simple securities. By simple we mean that it assumes the securities do not have an embedded option. A Treasury security and an option-free non-Treasury security can be valued using the arbitrage-free valuation approach.

More general valuation models handle securities with embedded options. In the fixed income area, two common models used are the **binomial model** and the **Monte Carlo simulation model.** The former model is used to value callable bonds, putable bonds, floating-rate notes, and structured notes in which the coupon formula is based on an interest rate. The Monte Carlo simulation model is used to value mortgage-backed securities and certain types of asset-backed securities.[9]

In very general terms, the following five features are common to the binomial and Monte Carlo simulation valuation models:

EXHIBIT 66-10 Calculation of Arbitrage-Free Value of a Hypothetical 8% 10-Year Non-Treasury Security Using Benchmark Spot Rate Curve

Period	Years	Cash flow ($)	Treasury spot rate (%)	Credit spread (%)	Benchmark spot (%)	Present value ($)
1	0.5	4	3.0000	0.20	3.2000	3.9370
2	1.0	4	3.3000	0.20	3.5000	3.8636
3	1.5	4	3.5053	0.25	3.7553	3.7829
4	2.0	4	3.9164	0.30	4.2164	3.6797
5	2.5	4	4.4376	0.35	4.7876	3.5538
6	3.0	4	4.7520	0.35	5.1020	3.4389
7	3.5	4	4.9622	0.40	5.3622	3.3237
8	4.0	4	5.0650	0.45	5.5150	3.2177
9	4.5	4	5.1701	0.45	5.6201	3.1170
10	5.0	4	5.2772	0.50	5.7772	3.0088
11	5.5	4	5.3864	0.55	5.9364	2.8995
12	6.0	4	5.4976	0.60	6.0976	2.7896
13	6.5	4	5.6108	0.65	6.2608	2.6794
14	7.0	4	5.6643	0.70	6.3643	2.5799
15	7.5	4	5.7193	0.75	6.4693	2.4813
16	8.0	4	5.7755	0.80	6.5755	2.3838
17	8.5	4	5.8331	0.85	6.6831	2.2876
18	9.0	4	5.9584	0.90	6.8584	2.1801
19	9.5	4	6.0863	0.95	7.0363	2.0737
20	10.0	104	6.2169	1.00	7.2169	51.1835
					Total	$108.4616

---

[9] A short summary reason is: mortgage-backed securities and certain asset-backed securities are interest rate path dependent securities and the binomial model cannot value such securities.

1. Each model begins with the yields on the on-the-run Treasury securities and generates Treasury spot rates.

2. Each model makes an assumption about the expected volatility of short-term interest rates. This is a critical assumption in both models since it can significantly affect the security's fair value.

3. Based on the volatility assumption, different "branches" of an interest rate tree (in the case of the binomial model) and interest rate "paths" (in the case of the Monte Carlo model) are generated.

4. The model is calibrated to the Treasury market. This means that if an "on-the-run" Treasury issue is valued using the model, the model will produce the observed market price.

5. Rules are developed to determine when an issuer/borrower will exercise embedded options—a call/put rule for callable/putable bonds and a pre-payment model for mortgage-backed and certain asset-backed securities.

The user of any valuation model is exposed to **modeling risk.** This is the risk that the output of the model is incorrect because the assumptions upon which it is based are incorrect. Consequently, it is imperative the results of a valuation model be stress-tested for modeling risk by altering assumptions.

SUMMARY 6

- Valuation is the process of determining the fair value of a financial asset.

- The fundamental principle of valuation is that the value of any financial asset is the present value of the expected cash flows, where a cash flow is the amount of cash expected to be received at some future periods.

- The valuation process involves three steps: (1) estimating the expected cash flows, (2) determining the appropriate interest rate or interest rates to be used to discount the cash flows, and (3) calculating the present value of the expected cash flows.

- For any fixed income security which neither the issuer nor the investor can alter the payment of the principal before its contractual due date, the cash flows can easily be determined assuming that the issuer does not default.

- The difficulty in determining cash flows arises for securities where either the issuer or the investor can alter the cash flows, or the coupon rate is reset by a formula dependent on some reference rate, price, or exchange rate.

- On-the-run Treasury yields are viewed as the minimum interest rate an investor requires when investing in a bond.

- The risk premium or yield spread over the interest rate on a Treasury security investors require reflects the additional risks in a security that is not issued by the U.S. government.

- For a given discount rate, the present value of a single cash flow received in the future is the amount of money that must be invested today that will generate that future value.

- The present value of a cash flow will depend on when a cash flow will be received (i.e., the timing of a cash flow) and the discount rate (i.e., interest rate) used to calculate the present value

- The sum of the present values for a security's expected cash flows is the value of the security.

- The present value is lower the further into the future the cash flow will be received.

- The higher the discount rate, the lower a cash flow's present value and since the value of a security is the sum of the present value of the cash flows, the higher the discount rate, the lower a security's value.

- The price/yield relationship for an option-free bond is convex.

- The value of a bond is equal to the present value of the coupon payments plus the present value of the maturity value.

- When a bond is purchased between coupon periods, the buyer pays a price that includes accrued interest, called the full price or dirty price.

- The clean price or simply price of a bond is the full price minus accrued interest.

- In computing accrued interest, day count conventions are used to determine the number of days in the coupon payment period and the number of days since the last coupon payment date.

- The traditional valuation methodology is to discount every cash flow of a security by the same interest rate (or discount rate), thereby incorrectly viewing each security as the same package of cash flows.

- The arbitrage-free approach values a bond as a package of cash flows, with each cash flow viewed as a zero-coupon bond and each cash flow discounted at its own unique discount rate.

▷ The Treasury zero-coupon rates are called Treasury spot rates.

▷ The Treasury spot rates are used to discount the cash flows in the arbitrage-free valuation approach.

▷ To value a security with credit risk, it is necessary to determine a term structure of credit rates.

▷ Adding a credit spread for an issuer to the Treasury spot rate curve gives the benchmark spot rate curve used to value that issuer's security.

▷ Valuation models seek to provide the fair value of a bond and accommodate securities with embedded options.

▷ The common valuation models used to value bonds with embedded options are the binomial model and the Monte Carlo simulation model.

▷ The binomial model is used to value callable bonds, putable bonds, floating-rate notes, and structured notes in which the coupon formula is based on an interest rate.

▷ The Monte Carlo simulation model is used to value mortgage-backed and certain asset-backed securities.

▷ The user of a valuation model is exposed to modeling risk and should test the sensitivity of the model to alternative assumptions.

PROBLEMS

1. Compute the value of a 5-year 7.4% coupon bond that pays interest annually assuming that the appropriate discount rate is 5.6%.

2. A 5-year amortizing security with a par value of $100,000 and a coupon rate of 6.4% has an expected cash flow of $23,998.55 per year assuming no prepayments. The annual cash flow includes interest and principal payment. What is the value of this amortizing security assuming no principal prepayments and a discount rate of 7.8%.

3. A. Assuming annual interest payments, what is the value of a 5-year 6.2% coupon bond when the discount rate is (i) 4.5%, (ii) 6.2%, and (iii) 7.3%?

B. Show that the results obtained in part A are consistent with the relationship between the coupon rate, discount rate, and price relative to par value.

4. A client is reviewing a year-end portfolio report. Since the beginning of the year, market yields have increased slightly. In comparing the beginning-of-the-year price for the bonds selling at a discount from par value to the end-of-year prices, the client observes that all the prices are higher. The client is perplexed since he expected that the price of all bonds should be lower since interest rates increased. Explain to the client why the prices of the bonds in the portfolio selling at discount have increased in value.

5. A 4-year 5.8% coupon bond is selling to yield 7%. The bond pays interest annually. One year later interest rates decrease from 7% to 6.2%.

A. What is the price of the 4-year 5.8% coupon bond selling to yield 7%?

B. What is the price of this bond one year later assuming the yield is unchanged at 7%?

C. What is the price of this bond one year later if instead of the yield being unchanged the yield decreases to 6.2%?

D. Complete the following:

Price change attributable to moving to maturity
(no change in discount rate)

Price change attribute to an increase in the
discount rate from 7% to 6.2%

Total price change

6. What is the value of a 5-year 5.8% annual coupon bond if the appropriate discount rate for discounting each cash flow is as follows:

Year	Discount rate
1	5.90%
2	6.40%
3	6.60%
4	6.90%
5	7.30%

7. What is the value of a 5-year 7.4% coupon bond selling to yield 5.6% assuming the coupon payments are made semiannually?

8. What is the value of a zero-coupon bond paying semiannually that matures in 20 years, has a maturity of $1 million, and is selling to yield 7.6%?

9. Suppose that a bond is purchased between coupon periods. The days between the settlement date and the next coupon period is 115. There are 183 days in the coupon period. Suppose that the bond purchased has a coupon rate of 7.4% and there are 10 semiannual coupon payments remaining.

   A. What is the dirty price for this bond if a 5.6% discount rate is used?

   B. What is the accrued interest for this bond?

   C. What is the clean price?

10. Suppose that the prevailing Treasury spot rate curve is the one shown in Exhibit 66-5.

   A. What is the value of a 7.4% 8-year Treasury issue?

   B. Suppose that the 7.4% 8-year Treasury issue is priced in the market based on the on-the-run 8-year Treasury yield. Assume further that yield is 5.65%, so that each cash flow is discounted at 5.65% divided by 2. What is the price of the 7.4% 8-year Treasury issue based on a 5.65% discount rate?

   C. Given the arbitrage-free value found in part A and the price in part B, what action would a dealer take and what would the arbitrage profit be if the market priced the 7.4% 8-year Treasury issue at the price found in part B?

   D. What process assures that the market price will not differ materially from the arbitrage-free value?

11. Suppose that the prevailing Treasury spot rate curve is the one shown in Exhibit 66-5.

   A. What is the value of a 4% 8-year Treasury issue?

   B. Suppose that the 4% 8-year Treasury issue is priced in the market based on the on-the-run 8-year Treasury yield. Assume further that yield is 5.65%, so that each cash flow is discounted at 5.65% divided by 2. What is the price of the 4% 8-year Treasury issue based on a 5.65% discount rate?

   C. Given the arbitrage-free value found in part A and the price in part B, what action would a dealer take and what would the arbitrage profit be if the market priced the 4% 8-year Treasury issue at the price found in part B?

   D. What process assures that the market price will not differ materially from the arbitrage-free value?

YIELD MEASURES, SPOT RATES, AND FORWARD RATES

LEARNING OUTCOMES

The candidate should be able to:

a. explain the sources of return from investing in a bond (i.e., coupon interest payments, capital gain/loss, reinvestment income);

b. compute the traditional yield measures for fixed-rate bonds (e.g., current yield, yield to maturity, yield to first call, yield to first par call date, yield to refunding, yield to put, yield to worst, cash flow yield) and explain the assumptions underlying traditional yield measures and the limitations of the traditional yield measures;

c. explain the importance of reinvestment income in generating the yield computed at the time of purchase, and calculate the amount of income required to generate that yield and discuss the factors that affect reinvestment risk;

d. compute the bond equivalent yield of an annual-pay bond, and compute the annual-pay yield of a semiannual-pay bond;

e. compute the theoretical Treasury spot rate curve, using the method of bootstrapping and given the Treasury par yield curve and compute the value of a bond using spot rates;

f. explain the limitations of the nominal spread and differentiate among the nominal spread, the zero-volatility spread, and the option-adjusted spread for a bond with an embedded option, and explain the option cost;

g. explain a forward rate, and compute the value of a bond using forward rates,

h. explain and illustrate the relationship between short-term forward rates and spot rates and compute spot rates given forward rates, and forward rates given spot rates.

INTRODUCTION 1

Frequently, investors assess the relative value of a security by some yield or yield spread measure quoted in the market. These measures are based on assumptions

Fixed Income Analysis for the Chartered Financial Analyst® Program, Second Edition, by Frank J. Fabozzi. Reprinted with permission.

that limit their use to gauge relative value. This reading explains the various yield and yield spread measures and their limitations.

In this reading, we will see a basic approach to computing the spot rates from the on-the-run Treasury issues. We will see the limitations of the nominal spread measure and explain two measures that overcome these limitations— zero-volatility spread and option-adjusted spread.

2   SOURCES OF RETURN

When an investor purchases a fixed income security, he or she can expect to receive a dollar return from one or more of the following sources:

1. the coupon interest payments made by the issuer
2. any capital gain (or capital loss—a negative dollar return) when the security matures, is called, or is sold
3. income from reinvestment of interim cash flows (interest and/or principal payments prior to stated maturity)

Any yield measure that purports to measure the potential return from a fixed income security should consider all three sources of return described above.

2.1 Coupon Interest Payments

The most obvious source of return on a bond is the periodic coupon interest payments. For zero-coupon instruments, the return from this source is zero. By purchasing a security below its par value and receiving the full par value at maturity, the investor in a zero-coupon instrument is effectively receiving interest in a lump sum.

2.2 Capital Gain or Loss

An investor receives cash when a bond matures, is called, or is sold. If these proceeds are greater than the purchase price, a capital gain results. For a bond held to maturity, there will be a capital gain if the bond is purchased below its par value. For example, a bond purchased for $94.17 with a par value of $100 will generate a capital gain of $5.83 ($100 − $94.17) if held to maturity. For a callable bond, a capital gain results if the price at which the bond is called (i.e., the call price) is greater than the purchase price. For example, if the bond in our previous example is callable and subsequently called at $100.50, a capital gain of $6.33 ($100.50 − $94.17) will be realized. If the same bond is sold prior to its maturity or before it is called, a capital gain will result if the proceeds exceed the purchase price. So, if our hypothetical bond is sold prior to the maturity date for $103, the capital gain would be $8.83 ($103 − $94.17).

Similarly, for all three outcomes, a capital loss is generated when the proceeds received are less than the purchase price. For a bond held to maturity, there will be a capital loss if the bond is purchased for more than its par value (i.e., purchased at a premium). For example, a bond purchased for $102.50 with a par value of $100 will generate a capital loss of $2.50 ($102.50 − $100) if held to maturity. For a callable bond, a capital loss results if the price at which the bond is called is less than the purchase price. For example, if the bond in our example is callable and subsequently called at $100.50, a capital loss of $2 ($102.50 − $100.50) will be realized. If the same bond is sold prior to its maturity or before it is called, a capital loss will result if the sale price is less than the purchase price. So, if our hypothetical bond is sold prior to the maturity date for $98.50, the capital loss would be $4 ($102.50 − $98.50).

2.3 Reinvestment Income

Prior to maturity, with the exception of zero-coupon instruments, fixed income securities make periodic interest payments that can be reinvested. Amortizing securities (such as mortgage-backed securities and asset-backed securities) make periodic principal payments that can be reinvested prior to final maturity. The interest earned from reinvesting the interim cash flows (interest and/or principal payments) prior to final or stated maturity is called **reinvestment income.**

TRADITIONAL YIELD MEASURES ▰ 3

Yield measures cited in the bond market include current yield, yield to maturity, yield to call, yield to put, yield to worst, and cash flow yield. These yield measures are expressed as a percent return rather than a dollar return. Below we explain how each measure is calculated and its limitations.

3.1 Current Yield

The **current yield** relates the annual dollar coupon interest to a bond's market price. The formula for the current yield is:

$$\text{current yield} = \frac{\text{annual dollar coupon interest}}{\text{price}}$$

For example, the current yield for a 7% 8-year bond whose price is $94.17 is 7.43% as shown below:

annual dollar coupon interest = 0.07 × $100 = $7
price = $94.17

$$\text{current yield} = \frac{\$7}{\$94.17} = 0.0743 \text{ or } 7.43\%$$

The current yield will be greater than the coupon rate when the bond sells at a discount; the reverse is true for a bond selling at a premium. For a bond selling at par, the current yield will be equal to the coupon rate.

The drawback of the current yield is that it considers only the coupon interest and no other source for an investor's return. No consideration is given to the capital gain an investor will realize when a bond purchased at a discount is held to maturity; nor is there any recognition of the capital loss an investor will realize if a bond purchased at a premium is held to maturity. No consideration is given to reinvestment income.

3.2 Yield to Maturity

The most popular measure of yield in the bond market is the **yield to maturity.** The yield to maturity is the interest rate that will make the present value of a bond's cash flows equal to its market price plus accrued interest. To find the yield to maturity, we first determine the expected cash flows and then search, by trial and error, for the interest rate that will make the present value of cash flows equal to the market price plus accrued interest. (This is simply a special case of an **internal rate of return** (IRR) calculation where the cash flows are those received if the bond is held to the maturity date.) In the illustrations presented in this reading, we assume that the next coupon payment will be six months from now so that there is no accrued interest.

To illustrate, consider a 7% 8-year bond selling for $94.17. The cash flows for this bond are (1) 16 payments every 6-months of $3.50 and (2) a payment sixteen 6-month periods from now of $100. The present value using various *semi-annual* discount (interest) rates is:

Semiannual interest rate	3.5%	3.6%	3.7%	3.8%	3.9%	4.0%
Present value	100.00	98.80	97.62	96.45	95.30	94.17

When a 4.0% interest rate is used, the present value of the cash flows is equal to $94.17, which is the price of the bond. Hence, 4.0% is the *semiannual* yield to maturity.

The market convention adopted to annualize the semiannual yield to maturity is to double it and call that the yield to maturity. Thus, the yield to maturity for the above bond is 8% (2 times 4.0%). The yield to maturity computed using this convention—doubling the semiannual yield—is called a **bond-equivalent yield.**

The following relationships between the price of a bond, coupon rate, current yield, and yield to maturity hold:

Bond selling at	Relationship
par	coupon rate = current yield = yield to maturity
discount	coupon rate < current yield < yield to maturity
premium	coupon rate > current yield > yield to maturity

Practice Question 1

Determine whether the yield to maturity of a 6% 15-year bond selling for $84.25 is either 7.2%, 7.6%, or 7.8%.

3.2.1 The Bond-Equivalent Yield Convention

The *convention* developed in the bond market to move from a semiannual yield to an annual yield is to simply double the semiannual yield. As just noted, this is called the bond-equivalent yield. In general, when one doubles a semiannual yield (or a semiannual return) to obtain an annual measure, one is said to be computing the measure on a **bond-equivalent basis.**

Students of the bond market are troubled by this convention. The two questions most commonly asked are: First, why is the practice of simply doubling a semiannual yield followed? Second, wouldn't it be more appropriate to compute the effective annual yield by compounding the semiannual yield?[1]

The answer to the first question is that it is simply a convention. There is no danger with a convention unless you use it improperly. The fact is that market participants recognize that a yield (or return) is computed on a semiannual basis by convention and adjust accordingly when using the number. So, if the bond-equivalent yield on a security purchased by an investor is 6%, the investor knows the semiannual yield is 3%. Given that, the investor can use that semiannual yield to compute an effective annual yield or any other annualized measure desired. For a manager comparing the yield on a security as an asset purchased to a yield required on a liability to satisfy, the yield figure will be measured in a manner consistent with that of the yield required on the liability.

The answer to the second question is that it is true that computing an effective annual yield would be better. But so what? Once we discover the limitations of yield measures in general, we will question whether or not an investor should use a bond-equivalent yield measure or an effective annual yield measure in making investment decisions. That is, when we identify the major problems with yield measures, the doubling of a semiannual yield is the least of our problems.

So, don't lose any sleep over this convention. Just make sure that you use a bond-equivalent yield measure properly.

3.2.2 Limitations of Yield-to-Maturity Measure

The yield to maturity considers not only the coupon income but any capital gain or loss that the investor will realize by holding the bond to maturity. The yield to maturity also considers the timing of the cash flows. *It does consider reinvestment income; however, it assumes that the coupon payments can be reinvested at an interest rate equal to the yield to maturity.* So, if the yield to maturity for a bond is 8%, for example, to earn that yield the coupon payments must be reinvested at an interest rate equal to 8%.

The illustrations below clearly demonstrate this. In the illustrations, the analysis will be in terms of dollars. Be sure you keep in mind the difference between the **total future dollars,** which is equal to all the dollars an investor expects to receive (including the recovery of the principal), and the **total dollar return,** which is equal to the dollars an investor expects to realize from the three sources of return (coupon payments, capital gain/loss, and reinvestment income).

Suppose an investor has $94.17 and places the funds in a certificate of deposit (CD) that matures in 8 years. Let's suppose that the bank agrees to pay 4% interest every six months. This means that the bank is agreeing to pay 8% on a bond equivalent basis (i.e., doubling the semiannual yield). We can translate all of this into the total future dollars that will be generated by this investment at the end of 8 years. From the standard formula for the future value of an investment today, we can determine the total future dollars as:

$$\$94.17 \times (1.04)^{16} = \$176.38$$

So, to an investor who invests $94.17 for 8 years at an 8% yield on a bond equivalent basis and interest is paid semiannually, the investment will generate $176.38. Decomposing the total future dollars we see that:

---

[1] By compounding the semiannual yield it is meant that the annual yield is computed as follows:

$$\text{effective annual yield} = (1 + \text{semiannual yield})^2 - 1$$

Total future dollars	=	$176.38
Return of principal	=	$94.17
Total interest from CD	=	$82.21

Thus, any investment that promises a yield of 8% on a bond equivalent basis for 8 years on an investment of $94.17 must generate total future dollars of $176.38 or equivalently a return from all sources of $82.21. That is, if we look at the three sources of a bond return that offered an 8% yield with semiannual coupon payments and sold at a price of $94.17, the following would have to hold:

	Coupon interest
+	Capital gain
+	Reinvestment income
=	Total dollar return = Total interest from CD = $82.21

Now, instead of a certificate of deposit, suppose that an investor purchases a bond with a coupon rate of 7% that matures in 8 years. We know that the three sources of return are coupon income, capital gain/loss, and reinvestment income. Suppose that the price of this bond is $94.17. The yield to maturity for this bond (on a bond equivalent basis) is 8%. Notice that this is the same type of investment as the certificate of deposit—the bank offered an 8% yield on a bond equivalent basis for 8 years and made payments semiannually. So, what should the investor in this bond expect in terms of *total future dollars*? As we just demonstrated, an investment of $94.17 must generate $176.38 in order to say that it provided a yield of 8%. Or equivalently, the total dollar return that must be generated is $82.21. Let's look at what in fact is generated in terms of dollar return.

The coupon is $3.50 every six months. So the dollar return from the coupon interest is $3.50 for 16 six-month periods, or $56. When the bond matures, there is a capital gain of $5.83 ($100 − $94.17). Therefore, based on these two sources of return we have:

Coupon interest	=	$56.00
Capital gain	=	$ 5.83
Dollar return *without reinvestment income*	=	$61.83

Something's wrong here. Only $61.83 is generated from the bond whereas $82.21 is needed in order to say that this bond provided an 8% yield. That is, there is a dollar return shortfall of $20.38 ($82.21 − $61.83). How is this dollar return shortfall generated?

Recall that in the case of the certificate of deposit, the bank does the reinvesting of the principal and interest, and pays 4% every six months or 8% on a bond equivalent basis. In contrast, for the bond, the investor has to reinvest any coupon interest until the bond matures. It is the reinvestment income that must generate the dollar return shortfall of $20.38. But at what yield will the investor have to reinvest the coupon payments in order to generate the $20.38? The answer is: the yield to maturity.[2] That is, the reinvestment income will be $20.38 if each

---

[2] This can be verified by using the future value of an annuity. The future of an annuity is given by the following formula:

$$\text{Annuity payment} = \left[\frac{(1 + i)^n - 1}{i}\right]$$

where i is the interest rate and n is the number of periods.

In our example, i is 4%, n is 16, and the amount of the annuity is the semiannual coupon of $3.50. Therefore, the future value of the coupon payment is

$$\$3.50\left[\frac{(1.04)^{16} - 1}{0.04}\right] = \$76.38$$

Since the coupon payments are $56, the reinvestment income is $20.38 ($76.38 − $56). This is the amount that is necessary to produce the dollar return shortfall in our example.

semiannual coupon payment of $3.50 can be reinvested at a semiannual yield of 4% (one half the yield to maturity). The reinvestment income earned on a given coupon payment of $3.50, if it is invested from the time of receipt in period t to the maturity date (16 periods in our example) at a 4% semiannual rate, is:

$$\$3.50\ (1.04)^{16-t} - \$3.50$$

The first coupon payment ($t = 1$) can be reinvested for 15 periods. Applying the formula above we find the reinvestment income earned on the first coupon payment is:

$$\$3.50\ (1.04)^{16-1} - \$3.50 = \$2.80$$

Similarly, the reinvestment income for all coupon payments is shown below:

Period	Periods reinvested	Coupon payment	Reinvestment income
1	15	$3.5	$2.80
2	14	3.5	2.56
3	13	3.5	2.33
4	12	3.5	2.10
5	11	3.5	1.89
6	10	3.5	1.68
7	9	3.5	1.48
8	8	3.5	1.29
9	7	3.5	1.11
10	6	3.5	0.93
11	5	3.5	0.76
12	4	3.5	0.59
13	3	3.5	0.44
14	2	3.5	0.29
15	1	3.5	0.14
16	0	3.5	0.00
		Total	$20.39

The total reinvestment income is $20.39 (differing from $20.38 due to rounding).
So, with the reinvestment income of $20.38 at 4% semiannually (i.e., one half the yield to maturity on a bond-equivalent basis), the total dollar return is

Coupon interest	=	$56.00
Capital gain	=	$5.83
Reinvestment income	=	$20.38
Total dollar return	=	$82.21

In our illustration, we used an investment in a certificate of deposit to show what the total future dollars will have to be in order to obtain a yield of 8% on an investment of $94.17 for 8 years when interest payments are semiannual. However, this holds for any type of investment, not just a certificate of deposit. For example, if an investor is told that he or she can purchase a debt instrument for $94.17 that offers an 8% yield (on a bond-equivalent basis) for 8 years and makes interest payments semiannually, then the investor should translate this yield into the following:

> I should be receiving total future dollars of $176.38
> I should be receiving a total dollar return of $82.21

It is always important to think in terms of dollars (or pound sterling, yen, or other currency) because "yield measures" are misleading.

We can also see that the reinvestment income can be a significant portion of the total dollar return. In our example, the total dollar return is $82.21 and the total dollar return from reinvestment income to make up the shortfall is $20.38. This means that reinvestment income is about 25% of the total dollar return.

This is such an important point that we should go through this one more time for another bond. Suppose an investor purchases a 15-year 8% coupon bond at par value ($100). The yield for this bond is simple to determine since the bond is trading at par. The yield is equal to the coupon rate, 8%. Let's translate this into dollars. We know that if an investor makes an investment of $100 for 15 years that offers an 8% yield and the interest payments are semiannual, the total future dollars will be:

$$\$100 \times (1.04)^{30} = 324.34$$

Decomposing the total future dollars we see that:

Total future dollars	=	$324.34
Return of principal	=	$100.00
Total dollar return	=	$224.34

Without reinvestment income, the dollar return is:

Coupon interest	=	$120
Capital gain	=	$ 0
Dollar return *without reinvestment income*	=	$120

Note that the capital gain is $0 because the bond is purchased at par value.

The dollar return shortfall is therefore $104.34 ($224.34 − $120). This shortfall is made up if the coupon payments can be reinvested at a yield of 8% (the yield on the bond at the time of purchase). For this bond, the reinvestment income is 46.5% of the total dollar return needed to produce a yield of 8% ($104.34/$224.34).[3]

Clearly, the investor will only realize the yield to maturity stated at the time of purchase if the following two assumptions hold:

> *Assumption 1:* the coupon payments can be reinvested at the yield to maturity
>
> *Assumption 2:* the bond is held to maturity

With respect to the first assumption, the risk that an investor faces is that future interest rates will be less than the yield to maturity at the time the bond is pur-

---

[3] The future value of the coupon payments of $4 for 30 six-month periods is:

$$\$4.00\left[\frac{(1.04)^{30} - 1}{0.04}\right] = \$224.34$$

Since the coupon payments are $120 and the capital gain is $0, the reinvestment income is $104.34. This is the amount that is necessary to produce the dollar return shortfall in our example.

chased, known as **reinvestment risk.** If the bond is not held to maturity, the investor faces the risk that he may have to sell for less than the purchase price, resulting in a return that is less than the yield to maturity, known as **interest rate risk.**

Practice Question 2

A. Suppose that an investor purchases a 6% coupon bond with 20 years to maturity at a price of $89.32 per $100 par value. The yield to maturity for this bond is 7%. Determine the dollar return that must be generated from reinvestment income in order to generate a yield of 7% and the percentage of the reinvestment income relative to the total dollar return needed to generate a 7% yield.

B. Suppose that a zero-coupon bond that matures in 10 years is selling to yield 7%. Determine the dollar return that must be generated from reinvestment income in order to generate a yield of 7% and the percentage of the reinvestment income relative to the total dollar return needed to generate a 7% yield.

3.2.3 Factors Affecting Reinvestment Risk

There are two characteristics of a bond that affect the degree of reinvestment risk:

Characteristic 1. For a given yield to maturity and a given non-zero coupon rate, the longer the maturity, the more the bond's total dollar return depends on reinvestment income to realize the yield to maturity at the time of purchase. That is, the greater the reinvestment risk.

The implication is the yield to maturity measure for long-term maturity coupon bonds tells little about the potential return that an investor may realize if the bond is held to maturity. For long-term bonds, in high interest rate environments, the reinvestment income component may be as high as 70% of the bond's total dollar return.

Characteristic 2. For a coupon paying bond, for a given maturity and a given yield to maturity, the higher the coupon rate, the more dependent the bond's total dollar return will be on the reinvestment of the coupon payments in order to produce the yield to maturity at the time of purchase.

This means that holding maturity and yield to maturity constant, bonds selling at a premium will be more dependent on reinvestment income than bonds selling at par. This is because the reinvestment income has to make up the capital loss due to amortizing the price premium when holding the bond to maturity. In contrast, a bond selling at a discount will be less dependent on reinvestment income than a bond selling at par because a portion of the return is coming from the capital gain due to accrediting the price discount when holding the bond to maturity. For zero-coupon bonds, none of the bond's total dollar return is dependent on reinvestment income. So, a zero-coupon bond has no reinvestment risk if held to maturity.

The dependence of the total dollar return on reinvestment income for bonds with different coupon rates and maturities is shown in Exhibit 67-1.

EXHIBIT 67-1   **Percentage of Total Dollar Return from Reinvestment Income for a Bond to Generate an 8% Yield (BEY)**

	\multicolumn{5}{c}{Years to maturity}				
	2	**3**	**5**	**8**	**15**
Bond with a 7% coupon					
Price	98.19	97.38	95.94	94.17	91.35
% of total	5.2%	8.6%	15.2%	24.8%	44.5%
Bond with an 8% coupon					
Price	100.00	100.00	100.00	100.00	100.00
% of total	5.8%	9.5%	16.7%	26.7%	46.5%
Bond with a 12% coupon					
Price	107.26	110.48	116.22	122.30	134.58
% of total	8.1%	12.9%	21.6%	31.0%	51.8%

3.2.4 Comparing Semiannual-Pay and Annual-Pay Bonds

In our yield calculations, we have been dealing with bonds that pay interest semi-annually. A non-U.S. bond may pay interest annually rather than semiannually. This is the case for many government bonds in Europe and Eurobonds. In such instances, an adjustment is required to make a direct comparison between the yield to maturity on a U.S. fixed-rate bond and that on an annual-pay non-U.S. fixed-rate bond.

Given the yield to maturity on an annual-pay bond, its bond-equivalent yield is computed as follows:

bond-equivalent yield of an annual-pay bond = $2[(1 + \text{yield on annual-pay bond})^{0.5} - 1]$

The term in the square brackets involves determining what semiannual yield, when compounded, produces the yield on an annual-pay bond. Doubling this semiannual yield (i.e., multiplying the term in the square brackets by 2), gives the bond-equivalent yield.

For example, suppose that the yield to maturity on an annual-pay bond is 6%. Then the bond-equivalent yield is:

$2[(1.06)^{0.5} - 1] = 5.91\%$

Notice that the bond-equivalent yield will always be less than the annual-pay bond's yield to maturity.

To convert the bond-equivalent yield of a U.S. bond issue to an annual-pay basis so that it can be compared to the yield on an annual-pay bond, the following formula can be used:

$$\text{yield on an annual-pay basis} = \left[\left(1 + \frac{\text{yield on a bond-equivalent basis}}{2}\right)^2 - 1\right]$$

By dividing the yield on a bond-equivalent basis by 2 in the above expression, the semiannual yield is computed. The semiannual yield is then compounded to get the yield on an annual-pay basis.

For example, suppose that the yield of a U.S. bond issue quoted on a bond-equivalent basis is 6%. The yield to maturity on an annual-pay basis would be:

$$[(1.03)^2 - 1] = 6.09\%$$

The yield on an annual-pay basis is always greater than the yield on a bond-equivalent basis because of compounding.

3.3 Yield to Call

When a bond is callable, the practice has been to calculate a yield to call as well as a yield to maturity. A callable bond may have a call schedule.[4] The yield to call assumes the issuer will call a bond on some assumed call date and that the call price is the price specified in the call schedule. Typically, investors calculate a yield to first call or yield to next call, a yield to first par call, and a yield to refunding. The **yield to first call** is computed for an issue that is not currently callable, while the **yield to next call** is computed for an issue that is currently callable.

Yield to refunding is used when bonds are currently callable but have some restrictions on the source of funds used to buy back the debt when a call is exercised. Namely, if a debt issue contains some refunding protection, bonds cannot be called for a certain period of time with the proceeds of other debt issues sold at a lower cost of money. As a result, the bondholder is afforded some protection if interest rates decline and the issuer can obtain lower-cost funds to pay off the debt. It should be stressed that the bonds can be called with funds derived from other sources (e.g., cash on hand) during the refunded-protected period. The refunding date is the first date the bond can be called using lower-cost debt.

The procedure for calculating any yield to call measure is the same as for any yield to maturity calculation: determine the interest rate that will make the present value of the expected cash flows equal to the price plus accrued interest. In the case of yield to first call, the expected cash flows are the coupon payments to the first call date and the call price. For the **yield to first par call,** the expected cash flows are the coupon payments to the first date at which the issuer can call the bond at par and the par value. For the yield to refunding, the expected cash flows are the coupon payments to the first refunding date and the call price at the first refunding date.

To illustrate the computation, consider a 7% 8-year bond with a maturity value of $100 selling for $106.36. Suppose that the first call date is three years from now and the call price is $103. The cash flows for this bond if it is called in three years are (1) 6 coupon payments of $3.50 every six months and (2) $103 in six 6-month periods from now.

---

[4] A call schedule shows the call price that the issuer must pay based on the date when the issue is called. An example of a call schedule is provided in Reading 62.

EXHIBIT 67-2 Yield to Call for an 8-Year 7% Coupon Bond with a Maturity Value of $100, First Call Date is the End of Year 3, and Call Price of $103

Annual interest rate (%)	Semiannual interest rate (%)	Present value of 6 payments of $3.5	Present value of $103 6 periods from now	Present value of cash flows
5.0	2.5	$19.28	$88.82	$108.10
5.2	2.6	19.21	88.30	107.51
5.4	2.7	19.15	87.78	106.93
5.6	2.8	19.09	87.27	106.36

The present value for several semiannual interest rates is shown in Exhibit 67-2. Since a semiannual interest rate of 2.8% makes the present value of the cash flows equal to the price, 2.8% is the yield to first call. Therefore, the yield to first call on a bond-equivalent basis is 5.6%.

For our 7% 8-year callable bond, suppose that the first par call date is 5 years from now. The cash flows for computing the first par call are then: (1) a total 10 coupon payments of $3.50 each paid every six months and (2) $100 in ten 6-month periods. The yield to par call is 5.53%. Let's verify that this is the case. The semiannual yield is 2.765% (one half of 5.53%). The present value of the 10 coupon payments of $3.50 every six months when discounted at 2.765% is $30.22. The present value of $100 (the call price of par) at the end of five years (10 semiannual periods) is $76.13. The present value of the cash flow is then $106.35 (= $30.22 + $76.13). Since the price of the bond is $106.36 and since using a yield of 5.53% produces a value for this callable bond that differs from $106.36 by only 1 penny, 5.53% is the yield to first par call.

Let's take a closer look at the yield to call as a measure of the potential return of a security. The yield to call considers all three sources of potential return from owning a bond. However, as in the case of the yield to maturity, it assumes that all cash flows can be reinvested at the yield to call until the assumed call date. As we just demonstrated, this assumption may be inappropriate. Moreover, the yield to call assumes that

Assumption 1: the investor will hold the bond to the assumed call date
Assumption 2: the issuer will call the bond on that date

These assumptions underlying the yield to call are unrealistic. Moreover, comparison of different yields to call with the yield to maturity are meaningless because the cash flows stop at the assumed call date. For example, consider two bonds, M and N. Suppose that the yield to maturity for bond M, a 5-year noncallable bond, is 7.5% while for bond N the yield to call, assuming the bond will be called in three years, is 7.8%. Which bond is better for an investor with a 5-year investment horizon? It's not possible to tell from the yields cited. If the investor intends to hold the bond for five years and the issuer calls bond N after three years, the total dollar return that will be available at the end of five years will depend on the interest rate that can be earned from investing funds from the call date to the end of the investment horizon.

Practice Question 4

Suppose that a 9% 10-year bond has the following call structure:

> not callable for the next 5 years
>
> first callable at beginning of year 6 (i.e., at the end of the fifth year) at $104.50
>
> first par call date at beginning of year 9 (i.e., at the end of the eighth year)

The price of the bond is $123.04.

A. Is the yield to first call for this bond 4.4%, 4.6%, or 4.8%?

B. Is the yield to first par call for this bond 5.41%, 5.62%, or 5.75%?

3.4 Yield to Put

When a bond is putable, the yield to the first put date is calculated. The yield to put is the interest rate that will make the present value of the cash flows to the first put date equal to the price plus accrued interest. As with all yield measures (except the current yield), yield to put assumes that any interim coupon payments can be reinvested at the yield calculated. Moreover, the yield to put assumes that the bond will be put on the first put date.

For example, suppose that a 6.2% coupon bond maturing in 8 years is putable at par in 3 years. The price of this bond is $102.19. The cash flows for this bond if it is put in three years are: (1) a total of 6 coupon payments of $3.10 each paid every six months and (2) the $100 put price in six 6-month periods from now. The semiannual interest rate that will make the present value of the cash flows equal to the price of $102.19 is 2.7%. Therefore, 2.7% is the semiannual yield to put and 5.4% is the yield to put on a bond equivalent basis.

3.5 Yield to Worst

A yield can be calculated for every possible call date and put date. In addition, a yield to maturity can be calculated. The lowest of all these possible yields is called the **yield to worst.** For example, suppose that there are only four possible call dates for a callable bond, that the yield to call assuming each possible call date is 6%, 6.2%, 5.8%, and 5.7%, and that the yield to maturity is 7.5%. Then the yield to worst is the minimum of these yields, 5.7% in our example.

The yield to worst measure holds little meaning as a measure of potential return. It supposedly states that this is the worst possible yield that the investor will realize. However, as we have noted about any yield measure, it does not identify the potential return over some investment horizon. Moreover, the yield to worst does not recognize that each yield calculation used in determining the yield to worst has different exposures to reinvestment risk.

3.6 Cash Flow Yield

Mortgage-backed securities and asset-backed securities are backed by a pool of loans or receivables. The cash flows for these securities include principal payment as well as interest. The complication that arises is that the individual borrowers whose loans make up the pool typically can prepay their loan in whole or in part prior to the scheduled principal payment dates. Because of principal prepayments, in order to project cash flows it is necessary to make an assumption about the rate at which principal prepayments will occur. This rate is called the **prepayment rate** or **prepayment speed.**

Given cash flows based on an assumed prepayment rate, a yield can be calculated. The yield is the interest rate that will make the present value of the projected cash flows equal to the price plus accrued interest. The yield calculated is commonly referred to as a **cash flow yield.**[5]

3.6.1 Bond-Equivalent Yield

Typically, the cash flows for mortgage-backed and asset-backed securities are monthly. Therefore the interest rate that will make the present value of projected principal and interest payments equal to the market price plus accrued interest is a monthly rate. The monthly yield is then annualized as follows.

First, the semiannual effective yield is computed from the monthly yield by compounding it for six months as follows:

$$\text{effective semiannual yield} = (1 + \text{monthly yield})^6 - 1$$

Next, the effective semiannual yield is doubled to get the annual cash flow yield on a bond-equivalent basis. That is,

$$\text{cash flow yield} = 2 \times \text{effective semiannual yield}$$

$$= 2\big[(1 + \textit{monthly yield})^6 - 1\big]$$

For example, if the monthly yield is 0.5%, then:

$$\text{cash flow yield on a bond-equivalent basis} = 2\big[(1.005)^6 + 1\big] = 6.08\%$$

The calculation of the cash flow yield may seem strange because it first requires the computing of an effective semiannual yield given the monthly yield and then doubling. This is simply a market convention. Of course, the student of the bond market can always ask the same two questions as with the yield to maturity: Why it is done? Isn't it better to just compound the monthly yield to get an effective annual yield? The answers are the same as given earlier for the yield to maturity. Moreover, as we will see next, this is the least of our problems in using a cash flow yield measure for an asset-backed and mortgage-backed security.

3.6.2 Limitations of Cash Flow Yield

As we have noted, the yield to maturity has two shortcomings as a measure of a bond's potential return: (1) it is assumed that the coupon payments can be reinvested at a rate equal to the yield to maturity and (2) it is assumed that the bond is held to maturity. These shortcomings are equally present in application of the cash flow yield measure: (1) the projected cash flows are assumed to be reinvested at the cash flow yield and (2) the mortgage-backed or asset-backed security is assumed to be held until the final payoff of all the loans, based on some prepayment assumption. The significance of reinvestment risk, the risk that the cash flows will be reinvested at a rate less than the cash flow yield, is particularly important for mortgage-backed and asset-backed securities since payments are typically

---

[5] Some firms such as Prudential Securities refer to this yield as yield to maturity rather than cash flow yield.

monthly and include principal payments (scheduled and prepaid), and interest. Moreover, the cash flow yield is dependent on realizing of the projected cash flows according to some prepayment rate. If actual prepayments differ significantly from the prepayment rate assumed, the cash flow yield will not be realized.

3.7 Spread/Margin Measures for Floating-Rate Securities

The coupon rate for a floating-rate security (or floater) changes periodically according to a reference rate (such as LIBOR or a Treasury rate). Since the future value for the reference rate is unknown, it is not possible to determine the cash flows. This means that a yield to maturity cannot be calculated. Instead, "margin" measures are computed. Margin is simply some spread above the floater's reference rate.

Several spread or margin measures are routinely used to evaluate floaters. Two margin measures commonly used are spread for life and discount margin.[6]

3.7.1 Spread for Life

When a floater is selling at a premium/discount to par, investors consider the premium or discount as an additional source of dollar return. **Spread for life** (also called **simple margin**) is a measure of potential return that accounts for the accretion (amortization) of the discount (premium) as well as the constant quoted margin over the security's remaining life. Spread for life (in basis points) is calculated using the following formula:

$$\text{Spread for life} = \left[\frac{100\left(100 - \text{Price}\right)}{\text{Maturity}} + \text{Quoted margin} \right] \times \left(\frac{100}{\text{Price}} \right)$$

where

Price	=	market price per \$100 of par value
Maturity	=	number of years to maturity
Quoted margin	=	quoted margin in the coupon reset formula measured in basis points

For example, suppose that a floater with a quoted margin of 80 basis points is selling for 99.3098 and matures in 6 years. Then,

Price	=	99.3098
Maturity	=	6
Quoted margin	=	80

$$\text{Spread for life} = \left[\frac{100(100 - 99.3098)}{6} + 80 \right] \times \left(\frac{100}{99.3098} \right)$$

$$= 92.14 \text{ Basis points}$$

The limitations of the spread for life are that it considers only the accretion/amortization of the discount/premium over the floater's remaining term to maturity and does not consider the level of the coupon rate or the time value of money.

---

[6] For a discussion of other traditional measures, see Chapter 3 in Frank J. Fabozzi and Steven V. Mann, *Floating Rate Securities* (New Hope, PA; Frank J. Fabozzi Associates, 2000).

3.7.2 Discount Margin

Discount margin estimates the average margin over the reference rate that the investor can expect to earn over the life of the security. The procedure for calculating the discount margin is as follows:

Step 1. Determine the cash flows assuming that the reference rate does *not* change over the life of the security.

Step 2. Select a margin.

Step 3. Discount the cash flows found in Step 1 by the current value of the reference rate plus the margin selected in Step 2.

Step 4. Compare the present value of the cash flows as calculated in Step 3 to the price plus accrued interest. If the present value is equal to the security's price plus accrued interest, the discount margin is the margin assumed in Step 2. If the present value is not equal to the security's price plus accrued interest, go back to Step 2 and try a different margin.

For a security selling at par, the discount margin is simply the quoted margin in the coupon reset formula.

EXHIBIT 67-3 Calculation of the Discount Margin for a Floating-Rate Security

Floating rate security:		
Maturity	=	6 years
Price	=	99.3098
Coupon formula	=	LIBOR + 80 basis points
		Reset every six months

			Present value ($) at assumed margin of**				
Period	**LIBOR (%)**	**Cash flow ($)***	**80 bp**	**84 bp**	**88 bp**	**96 bp**	**100 bp**
1	10	5.4	5.1233	5.1224	5.1214	5.1195	5.1185
2	10	5.4	4.8609	4.8590	4.8572	4.8535	4.8516
3	10	5.4	4.6118	4.6092	4.6066	4.6013	4.5987
4	10	5.4	4.3755	4.3722	4.3689	4.3623	4.3590
5	10	5.4	4.1514	4.1474	4.1435	4.1356	4.1317
6	10	5.4	3.9387	3.9342	3.9297	3.9208	3.9163
7	10	5.4	3.7369	3.7319	3.7270	3.7171	3.7122
8	10	5.4	3.5454	3.5401	3.5347	3.5240	3.5186
9	10	5.4	3.3638	3.3580	3.3523	3.3409	3.3352
10	10	5.4	3.1914	3.1854	3.1794	3.1673	3.1613
11	10	5.4	3.0279	3.0216	3.0153	3.0028	2.9965
12	10	105.4	56.0729	55.9454	55.8182	55.5647	55.4385
		Present value	100.0000	99.8269	99.6541	99.3098	99.1381

* For periods 1-11: cash flow = $100 (0.5) (LIBOR + assumed margin)
For period 12: cash flow = $100 (0.5) (LIBOR + assumed margin) + $100

** The discount rate is found as follows. To LIBOR of 10%, the assumed margin is added. Thus, for an 80 basis point assumed margin, the discount rate is 10.80%. This is an annual discount rate on a bond-equivalent basis. The semiannual discount rate is then half this amount, 5.4%. It is this discount rate that is used to compute the present value of the cash flows for an assumed margin of 80 basis points.

To illustrate the calculation, suppose that the coupon reset formula for a 6-year floating-rate security selling for $99.3098 is 6-month LIBOR plus 80 basis points. The coupon rate is reset every 6 months. Assume that the current value for the reference rate is 10%.

Exhibit 67-3 shows the calculation of the discount margin for this security. The second column shows the current value for 6-month LIBOR. The third column sets forth the cash flows for the security. The cash flow for the first 11 periods is equal to one-half the current 6-month LIBOR (5%) plus the semiannual quoted margin of 40 basis points multiplied by $100. At the maturity date (i.e., period 12), the cash flow is $5.4 plus the maturity value of $100. The column headings of the last five columns show the assumed margin. The rows below the assumed margin show the present value of each cash flow. The last row gives the total present value of the cash flows.

For the five assumed margins, the present value is equal to the price of the floating-rate security ($99.3098) when the assumed margin is 96 basis points. Therefore, the discount margin is 96 basis points. Notice that the discount margin is 80 basis points, the same as the quoted margin, when this security is selling at par.

There are two drawbacks of the discount margin as a measure of the potential return from investing in a floating-rate security. First, the measure assumes that the reference rate will not change over the life of the security. Second, if the floating-rate security has a cap or floor, this is not taken into consideration.

Practice Question 5

Suppose that the price of the floater in our illustration was 99.8269 rather than 99.3098. Without doing any calculation, determine what the discount margin would be.

3.8 Yield on Treasury Bills

Treasury bills are zero-coupon instruments with a maturity of one year or less. The convention in the Treasury bill market is to calculate a bill's **yield on a discount basis.** This yield is determined by two variables:

1. the settlement price per $1 of maturity value (denoted by p)
2. the number of days to maturity which is calculated as the number of days between the settlement date and the maturity date (denoted by N_{SM})

The yield on a discount basis (denoted by d) is calculated as follows:

$$d = (1 - p)\left(\frac{360}{N_{SM}}\right)$$

We will use two actual Treasury bills to illustrate the calculation of the yield on a discount basis assuming a settlement date in both cases of 8/6/97. The first bill has a maturity date of 1/8/98 and a price of 0.97769722. For this bill, the number of days from the settlement date to the maturity date, N_{SM}, is 155. Therefore, the yield on a discount basis is

$$d = (1 - 0.97769722)\left(\frac{360}{155}\right) = 5.18\%$$

For our second bill, the maturity date is 7/23/98 and the price is 0.9490075. Assuming a settlement date of 8/6/97, the number of days from the settlement date to the maturity date is 351. The yield on a discount basis for this bill is

$$d = (1 - 0.9490075)\left(\frac{360}{351}\right) = 5.23\%$$

Given the yield on a discount basis, the price of a bill (per $1 of maturity value) is computed as follows:

$$p = 1 - d(N_{SM}/360)$$

For the 155-day bill selling for a yield on a discount basis of 5.18%, the price per $1 of maturity value is

$$p = 1 - 0.0518\ (155/360) = 0.97769722$$

For the 351-day bill selling for a yield on a discount basis of 5.23%, the price per $1 of maturity value is

$$p = 1 - 0.0523\ (351/360) = 0.9490075$$

The quoted yield on a discount basis is not a meaningful measure of the return from holding a Treasury bill for two reasons. First, the measure is based on a maturity value investment rather than on the actual dollar amount invested. Second, the yield is annualized according to a 360-day year rather than a 365-day year, making it difficult to compare yields on Treasury bills with Treasury notes and bonds which pay interest based on the actual number of days in a year. The use of 360 days for a year is a convention for money market instruments. Despite its shortcomings as a measure of return, this is the method dealers have adopted to quote Treasury bills.

Market participants recognize this limitation of yield on a discount basis and consequently make adjustments to make the yield quoted on a Treasury bill comparable to that on a Treasury coupon security. For investors who want to compare the yield on Treasury bills to that of other money market instruments (i.e., debt obligations with a maturity that does not exceed one year), there is a formula to convert the yield on a discount basis to that of a money market yield. The key point is that while the convention is to quote the yield on a Treasury bill in terms of a yield on a discount basis, no one uses that yield measure other than to compute the price given the quoted yield.

Practice Question 6

A. A Treasury bill with 115 days from settlement to maturity is selling for $0.9825 per $1 of maturity value. What is the yield on a discount basis?

B. A Treasury bill with 162 days from settlement to maturity is quoted as having a yield on a discount basis of 5.9%. What is the price of this Treasury bill?

THEORETICAL SPOT RATES   4

The theoretical spot rates for Treasury securities represent the appropriate set of interest rates that should be used to value default-free cash flows. A default-free theoretical spot rate curve can be constructed from the observed Treasury yield curve. There are several approaches that are used in practice. The approach that we describe below for creating a theoretical spot rate curve is called **bootstrapping.** (The bootstrapping method described here is also used in constructing a theoretical spot rate curve for LIBOR.)

4.1 Bootstrapping

Bootstrapping begins with the yield for the on-the-run Treasury issues because there is no credit risk and no liquidity risk. In practice, however, there is a problem of obtaining a sufficient number of data points for constructing the U.S. Treasury yield curve. In the United States, the U.S. Department of the Treasury currently issues 3-month and 6-month Treasury bills and 2-year, 5-year, and 10-year Treasury notes. Treasury bills are zero-coupon instruments and Treasury notes are coupon-paying instruments. Hence, there are not many data points from which to construct a Treasury yield curve, particularly after two years. At one time, the U.S. Treasury issued 30-year Treasury bonds. Since the Treasury no longer issues 30-year bonds, market participants currently use the last issued Treasury bond (which has a maturity less than 30 years) to estimate the 30-year yield. The 2-year, 5-year, and 10-year Treasury notes and an estimate of the 30-year Treasury bond are used to construct the Treasury yield curve.

On September 5, 2003, Lehman Brothers reported the following values for these four yields:

2 year	1.71%
5 year	3.25%
10 year	4.35%
30 year	5.21%

To fill in the yield for the 25 missing whole year maturities (3 year, 4 year, 6 year, 7 year, 8 year, 9 year, 11 year, and so on to the 29-year maturity), the yield for the 25 whole year maturities are interpolated from the yield on the surrounding maturities. The simplest interpolation, and the one most commonly used in practice, is simple linear interpolation.

For example, suppose that we want to fill in the gap for each one year of maturity. To determine the amount to add to the on-the-run Treasury yield as we go from the lower maturity to the higher maturity, the following formula is used:

$$\frac{\text{Yield at higher maturity} - \text{Yield at lower maturity}}{\text{Number of years between two observed maturity points}}$$

The estimated on-the-run yield for all intermediate whole-year maturities is found by adding the amount computed from the above formula to the yield at the lower maturity.

For example, using the September 5, 2003 yields, the 5-year yield of 3.25% and the 10-year yield of 4.35% are used to obtain the interpolated 6-year, 7-year, 8-year, and 9-year yields by first calculating:

$$\frac{4.35\% - 3.25\%}{5} = 0.22\%$$

Then,

interpolated 6-year yield	=	3.25% + 0.22%	=	3.47%
interpolated 7-year yield	=	3.47% + 0.22%	=	3.69%
interpolated 8-year yield	=	3.69% + 0.22%	=	3.91%
interpolated 9-year yield	=	3.91% + 0.22%	=	4.13%

Thus, when market participants talk about a yield on the Treasury yield curve that is not one of the on-the-run maturities—for example, the 8-year yield—it is only an approximation. Notice that there is a large gap between maturity points. This may result in misleading yields for the interim maturity points when estimated using the linear interpolation method, a point that we return to later in this reading.

To illustrate bootstrapping, we will use the Treasury yields shown in Exhibit 67-4 for maturities up to 10 years using 6-month periods.[7] Thus, there are 20 Treasury yields shown. The yields shown are assumed to have been interpolated from the on-the-run Treasury issues. Exhibit 67-5 shows the Treasury yield curve based on the yields shown in Exhibit 67-4. Our objective is to show how the values in the last column of Exhibit 67-4 (labeled "Spot Rate") are obtained.

Throughout the analysis and illustrations to come, it is important to remember that the basic principle is the value of the Treasury coupon security should be equal to the value of the package of zero-coupon Treasury securities that duplicates the coupon bond's cash flows. We saw this in Reading 66 when we discussed arbitrage-free valuation.

Consider the 6-month and 1-year Treasury securities in Exhibit 67-4. As we explained in Reading 66, these two securities are called Treasury bills and they are issued as zero-coupon instruments. Therefore, the annualized yield (not the discount yield) of 3.00% for the 6-month Treasury security is equal to the 6-month spot rate.[8] Similarly, for the 1-year Treasury security, the cited yield of 3.30% is the 1-year spot rate. Given these two spot rates, we can compute the spot rate for a theoretical 1.5-year zero-coupon Treasury. The value of a theoretical 1.5-year Treasury should equal the present value of the three cash flows from the 1.5-year coupon Treasury, where the yield used for discounting is the spot rate corresponding to the time of receipt of each six-month cash flow. Since all the coupon bonds are selling at par, as explained in the previous section, the yield to maturity for each bond is the coupon rate. Using $100 par, the cash flows for the 1.5-year coupon Treasury are:

0.5 year	0.035	×	$100	×	0.5		=	$1.75
1.0 year	0.035	×	$100	×	0.5		=	$1.75
1.5 years	0.035	×	$100	×	0.5	+ 100	=	$101.75

The present value of the cash flows is then:

$$\frac{1.75}{(1 + z_1)^1} + \frac{1.75}{(1 + z_2)^2} + \frac{101.75}{(1 + z_3)^3}$$

---

[7] Two points should be noted abut the yields reported in Exhibit 67-4. First, the yields are unrelated to our earlier Treasury yields on September 5, 2003 that we used to show how to calculate the yield on interim maturities using linear interpolation. Second, the Treasury yields in our illustration after the first year are all shown at par value. Hence the Treasury yield curve in Exhibit 67-4 is called a *par yield curve.*

[8] We will assume that the annualized yield for the Treasury bill is computed on a bond-equivalent basis. Earlier in this reading, we saw how the yield on a Treasury bill is quoted. The quoted yield can be converted into a bond-equivalent yield; we assume this has already been done in Exhibit 67-4.

EXHIBIT 67-4 Hypothetical Treasury Yields (Interpolated)

Period	Years	Annual Par Yield to Maturity (BEY) (%)*	Price	Spot Rate (BEY) (%)*
1	0.5	3.00	—	3.0000
2	1.0	3.30	—	3.3000
3	1.5	3.50	100.00	3.5053
4	2.0	3.90	100.00	3.9164
5	2.5	4.40	100.00	4.4376
6	3.0	4.70	100.00	4.7520
7	3.5	4.90	100.00	4.9622
8	4.0	5.00	100.00	5.0650
9	4.5	5.10	100.00	5.1701
10	5.0	5.20	100.00	5.2772
11	5.5	5.30	100.00	5.3864
12	6.0	5.40	100.00	5.4976
13	6.5	5.50	100.00	5.6108
14	7.0	5.55	100.00	5.6643
15	7.5	5.60	100.00	5.7193
16	8.0	5.65	100.00	5.7755
17	8.5	5.70	100.00	5.8331
18	9.0	5.80	100.00	5.9584
19	9.5	5.90	100.00	6.0863
20	10.0	6.00	100.00	6.2169

* The yield to maturity and the spot rate are annual rates. They are reported as bond-equivalent yields. To obtain the semiannual yield or rate, one half the annual yield or annual rate is used

EXHIBIT 67-5 Treasury Par Yield Curve

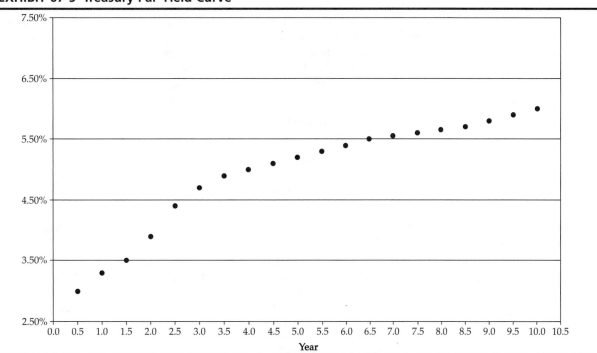

where

z_1 = one-half the annualized 6-month theoretical spot rate
z_2 = one-half the 1-year theoretical spot rate
z_3 = one-half the 1.5-year theoretical spot rate

Since the 6-month spot rate is 3% and the 1-year spot rate is 3.30%, we know that:

$$z_1 = 0.0150 \text{ and } z_2 = 0.0165$$

We can compute the present value of the 1.5-year coupon Treasury security as:

$$\frac{1.75}{(1+z_1)^1} + \frac{1.75}{(1+z_2)^2} + \frac{101.75}{(1+z_3)^3} = \frac{1.75}{(1.015)^1} + \frac{1.75}{(1.0165)^2} + \frac{101.75}{(1+z_3)^3}$$

Since the price of the 1.5-year coupon Treasury security is par value (see Exhibit 67-4), the following relationship must hold:[9]

$$\frac{1.75}{(1.015)^1} + \frac{1.75}{(1.0165)^2} + \frac{101.75}{(1+z_3)^3} = 100$$

We can solve for the theoretical 1.5-year spot rate as follows:

$$1.7241 + 1.6936 + \frac{101.75}{(1+z_3)^3} = 100$$

$$\frac{101.75}{(1+z_3)^3} = 96.5822$$

$$(1+z_3)^3 = \frac{101.75}{96.5822}$$

$$z_3 = 0.0175265 = 1.7527\%$$

Doubling this yield, we obtain the bond-equivalent yield of 3.5053%, which is the theoretical 1.5-year spot rate. That rate is the rate that the market would apply to a 1.5-year zero-coupon Treasury security if, in fact, such a security existed. In other words, all Treasury cash flows to be received 1.5 years from now should be valued (i.e., discounted) at 3.5053%.

Given the theoretical 1.5-year spot rate, we can obtain the theoretical 2-year spot rate. The cash flows for the 2-year coupon Treasury in Exhibit 67-3 are:

0.5 year $0.039 \times \$100 \times 0.5$ = \$1.95
1.0 year $0.039 \times \$100 \times 0.5$ = \$1.95
1.5 years $0.039 \times \$100 \times 0.5$ = \$1.95
2.0 years $0.039 \times \$100 \times 0.5 + 100$ = \$101.95

The present value of the cash flows is then:

$$\frac{1.95}{(1+z_1)^1} + \frac{1.95}{(1+z_2)^2} + \frac{1.95}{(1+z_3)^3} + \frac{101.95}{(1+z_4)^4}$$

where z_4 = one-half the 2-year theoretical spot rate.

---

[9] If we had not been working with a par yield curve, the equation would have been set equal to whatever the market price for the 1.5-year issue is.

Since the 6-month spot rate, 1-year spot rate, and 1.5-year spot rate are 3.00%, 3.30%, and 3.5053%, respectively, then:

$$z_1 = 0.0150 \quad z_2 = 0.0165 \quad z_3 = 0.017527$$

Therefore, the present value of the 2-year coupon Treasury security is:

$$\frac{1.95}{(1.0150)^1} + \frac{1.95}{(1.0165)^2} + \frac{1.95}{(1.017527)^3} + \frac{101.95}{(1 + z_4)^4}$$

Since the price of the 2-year coupon Treasury security is par, the following relationship must hold:

$$\frac{1.95}{(1.0150)^1} + \frac{1.95}{(1.0165)^2} + \frac{1.95}{(1.017527)^3} + \frac{101.95}{(1 + z_4)^4} = 100$$

We can solve for the theoretical 2-year spot rate as follows:

$$\frac{101.95}{(1 + z_4)^4} = 94.3407$$

$$(1 + z_4)^4 = \frac{101.95}{94.3407}$$

$$z_4 = 0.019582 = 1.9582\%$$

Doubling this yield, we obtain the theoretical 2-year spot rate bond-equivalent yield of 3.9164%.

One can follow this approach sequentially to derive the theoretical 2.5-year spot rate from the calculated values of z_1, z_2, z_3, and z_4 (the 6-month-, 1-year-, 1.5-year-, and 2-year rates), and the price and coupon of the 2.5-year bond in Exhibit 67-4. Further, one could derive theoretical spot rates for the remaining 15 half-yearly rates.

EXHIBIT 67-6 Theoretical Spot Rate Curve and Treasury Yield Curve

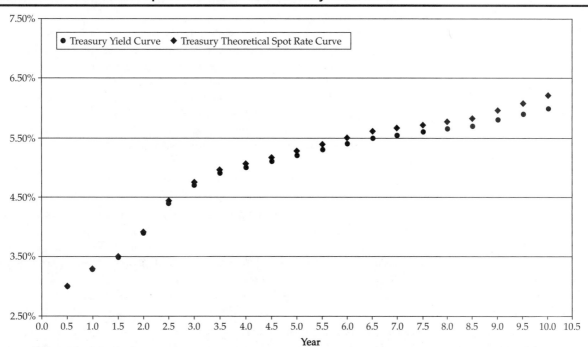

The spot rates thus obtained are shown in the last column of Exhibit 67-4. They represent the term structure of default-free spot rate for maturities up to 10 years at the particular time to which the bond price quotations refer. In fact, it is the default-free spot rates shown in Exhibit 67-4 that were used in our illustrations in the previous reading.

Exhibit 67-6 shows a plot of the spot rates. The graph is called the **theoretical spot rate curve.** Also shown on Exhibit 67-6 is a plot of the par yield curve from Exhibit 67-5. Notice that the theoretical spot rate curve lies above the par yield curve. This will always be the case when the par yield curve is upward sloping. When the par yield curve is downward sloping, the theoretical spot rate curve will lie below the par yield curve.

Practice Question 7

Show how the 2.5-year spot rate reported in Exhibit 67-4 is obtained.

4.2 Yield Spread Measures Relative to a Spot Rate Curve

Traditional analysis of the yield spread for a non-Treasury bond involves calculating the difference between the bond's yield and the yield to maturity of a benchmark Treasury coupon security. The latter is obtained from the Treasury yield curve. For example, consider the following 10-year bonds:

Issue	Coupon	Price	Yield to maturity
Treasury	6%	100.00	6.00%
Non-Treasury	8%	104.19	7.40%

The yield spread for these two bonds as traditionally computed is 140 basis points (7.4% minus 6%). We have referred to this traditional yield spread as the **nominal spread.**

Exhibit 67-7 shows the Treasury yield curve from Exhibit 67-5. The nominal spread of 140 basis points is the difference between the 7.4% yield to maturity for the 10-year non-Treasury security and the yield on the 10-year Treasury, 6%.

What is the nominal spread measuring? It is measuring the compensation for the additional credit risk, option risk (i.e., the risk associated with embedded options),[10] *and liquidity risk an investor is exposed to by investing in a non-Treasury security rather than a Treasury security with the same maturity.*

The drawbacks of the nominal spread measure are

1. for both bonds, the yield fails to take into consideration the term structure of spot rates and

2. in the case of callable and/or putable bonds, expected interest rate volatility may alter the cash flows of the non-Treasury bond.

Let's examine each of the drawbacks and alternative spread measures for handling them.

---

[10] Option risk includes prepayment and call risk.

4.2.1 Zero-Volatility Spread

The **zero-volatility spread** or **Z-spread** is a measure of the spread that the investor would realize over the entire Treasury spot rate curve if the bond is held to maturity. It is not a spread off one point on the Treasury yield curve, as is the nominal spread. The Z-spread, also called the **static spread,** is calculated as the spread that will make the present value of the cash flows from the non-Treasury bond, when discounted at the Treasury spot rate plus the spread, equal to the non-Treasury bond's price. A trial-and-error procedure is required to determine the Z-spread.

To illustrate how this is done, let's use the non-Treasury bond in our previous illustration and the Treasury spot rates in Exhibit 67-4. These spot rates are repeated in Exhibit 67-8. The third column in Exhibit 67-8 shows the cash flows for the 8% 10-year non-Treasury issue. The goal is to determine the spread that, when added to all the Treasury spot rates, will produce a present value for the cash flows of the non-Treasury bond equal to its market price of $104.19.

Suppose we select a spread of 100 basis points. To each Treasury spot rate shown in the fourth column of Exhibit 67-8, 100 basis points is added. So, for example, the 5-year (period 10) spot rate is 6.2772% (5.2772% plus 1%). The spot rate plus 100 basis points is then used to calculate the present values as shown in the fifth column. The total present value of the fifth column is $107.5414. Because the present value is not equal to the non-Treasury issue's price ($104.19), the Z-spread is not 100 basis points. If a spread of 125 basis points is tried, it can be seen from the next-to-the-last column of Exhibit 67-8 that the present value is $105.7165; again, because this is not equal to the non-Treasury issue's price, 125 basis points is not the Z-spread. The last column of Exhibit 67-8 shows the present value when a 146 basis point spread is tried. The present value is equal to the non-Treasury issue's price. Therefore 146 basis points is the Z-spread, compared to the nominal spread of 140 basis points.

A graphical presentation of the Z-spread is shown in Exhibit 67-9. Since the benchmark for computing the Z-spread is the theoretical spot rate curve, that curve is shown in the exhibit. Above each yield at each maturity on the theoretical spot

EXHIBIT 67-7 Illustration of the Nominal Spread

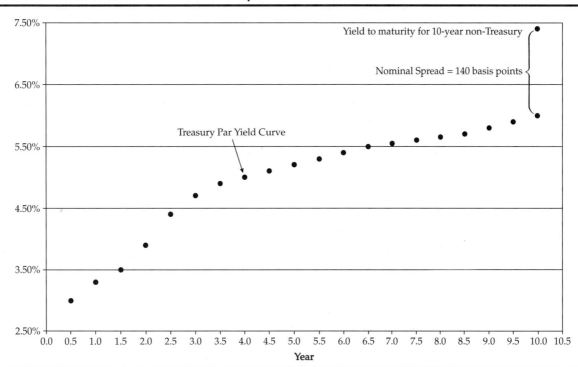

EXHIBIT 67-8 Determining Z-Spread for an 8% Coupon, 10-Year Non-Treasury Issue Selling at $104.19 to Yield 7.4%

Period	Years	Cash flow ($)	Spot rate (%)*	Present value ($) assuming a spread of**		
				100 bp	125 bp	146 bp
1	0.5	4.00	3.0000	3.9216	3.9168	3.9127
2	1.0	4.00	3.3000	3.8334	3.8240	3.8162
3	1.5	4.00	3.5053	3.7414	3.7277	3.7163
4	2.0	4.00	3.9164	3.6297	3.6121	3.5973
5	2.5	4.00	4.4376	3.4979	3.4767	3.4590
6	3.0	4.00	4.7520	3.3742	3.3497	3.3293
7	3.5	4.00	4.9622	3.2565	3.2290	3.2061
8	4.0	4.00	5.0650	3.1497	3.1193	3.0940
9	4.5	4.00	5.1701	3.0430	3.0100	2.9825
10	5.0	4.00	5.2772	2.9366	2.9013	2.8719
11	5.5	4.00	5.3864	2.8307	2.7933	2.7622
12	6.0	4.00	5.4976	2.7255	2.6862	2.6536
13	6.5	4.00	5.6108	2.6210	2.5801	2.5463
14	7.0	4.00	5.6643	2.5279	2.4855	2.4504
15	7.5	4.00	5.7193	2.4367	2.3929	2.3568
16	8.0	4.00	5.7755	2.3472	2.3023	2.2652
17	8.5	4.00	5.8331	2.2596	2.2137	2.1758
18	9.0	4.00	5.9584	2.1612	2.1148	2.0766
19	9.5	4.00	6.0863	2.0642	2.0174	1.9790
20	10.0	104.00	6.2169	51.1835	49.9638	48.9632
			Total	107.5416	105.7165	104.2146

* The spot rate is an annual rate.
** The discount rate used to compute the present value of each cash flow in the third column is found by adding the assumed spread to the spot rate and then dividing by 2. For example, for period 4 the spot rate is 3.9164%. If the assumed spread is 100 basis points, then 100 basis points is added to 3.9164% to give 4.9164%. Dividing this rate by 2 gives the semiannual rate of 2.4582%. The present value is then

$$\frac{\text{cash flow in period } t}{(1.024582)^t}$$

rate curve is a yield that is 146 basis points higher. This is the Z-spread. It is a spread over the entire spot rate curve.

What should be clear is that the difference between the nominal spread and the Z-spread is the benchmark that is being used: the nominal spread is a spread off of one point on the Treasury yield curve (see Exhibit 67-7) while the Z-spread is a spread over the entire theoretical Treasury spot rate curve.

What does the Z-spread represent for this non-Treasury security? Since the Z-spread is measured relative to the Treasury spot rate curve, it represents a spread to compensate for the non-Treasury security's credit risk, liquidity risk, and any option risk (i.e., the risks associated with any embedded options).

EXHIBIT 67-9 Illustration of the Z-Spread

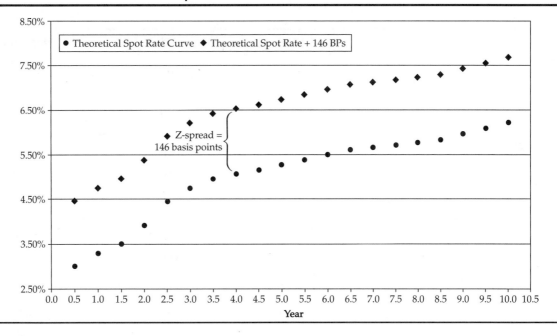

Practice Question 8

Suppose the price of the non-Treasury issue in our example is 105.7165 instead of 104.2145. Without doing computations, what would the Z-spread be?

4.2.1.1 Divergence Between Z-Spread and Nominal Spread

Typically, for standard coupon-paying bonds with a bullet maturity (i.e., a single payment of principal) the Z-spread and the nominal spread will not differ significantly. In our example, it is only 6 basis points. In general terms, the divergence (i.e., amount of difference) is a function of (1) the shape of the term structure of interest rates and (2) the characteristics of the security (i.e., coupon rate, time to maturity, and type of principal payment provision—non-amortizing versus amortizing).

For short-term issues, there is little divergence. The main factor causing any difference is the shape of the Treasury spot rate curve. The steeper the spot rate curve, the greater the difference. To illustrate this, consider the two spot rate curves shown in Exhibit 67-10. The yield for the longest maturity of both spot rate curves is 6%. The first curve is steeper than the one used in Exhibit 67-8; the second curve is flat, with the yield for all maturities equal to 6%. For our 8% 10-year non-Treasury issue, it can be shown that for the first spot rate curve in Exhibit 67-10 the Z-spread is 192 basis points. Thus, with this steeper spot rate curve, the difference between the Z-spread and the nominal spread is 52 basis points. For the flat curve the Z-spread is 140 basis points, the same as the nominal spread. This will always be the case because the nominal spread assumes that the same yield is used to discount each cash flow and, with a flat yield curve, the same yield is being used to discount each flow. Thus, the nominal yield spread and the Z-spread will produce the same value for this security.

The difference between the Z-spread and the nominal spread is greater for issues in which the principal is repaid over time rather than only at maturity. Thus

EXHIBIT 67-10 Two Hypothetical Spot Rate Curves

Period	Years	Steep curve (%)	Flat curve (%)
1	0.5	2.00	6.00
2	1.0	2.40	6.00
3	1.5	2.80	6.00
4	2.0	2.90	6.00
5	2.5	3.00	6.00
6	3.0	3.10	6.00
7	3.5	3.30	6.00
8	4.0	3.80	6.00
9	4.5	3.90	6.00
10	5.0	4.20	6.00
11	5.5	4.40	6.00
12	6.0	4.50	6.00
13	6.5	4.60	6.00
14	7.0	4.70	6.00
15	7.5	4.90	6.00
16	8.0	5.00	6.00
17	8.5	5.30	6.00
18	9.0	5.70	6.00
19	9.5	5.80	6.00
20	10.0	6.00	6.00

the difference between the nominal spread and the Z-spread will be considerably greater for mortgage-backed and asset-backed securities in a steep yield curve
environment. We can see this intuitively if we think in terms of a 10-year zero-
coupon bond and a 10-year amortizing security with equal semiannual cash flows
(that includes interest and principal payment). The Z-spread for the zero-coupon
bond will not be affected by the shape of the term structure but the amortizing
security will be.

4.2.1.2 *Z-Spread Relative to Any Benchmark*

In the same way that a Z-spread relative to a Treasury spot rate curve can be calculated, a Z-spread to any benchmark spot rate curve can be calculated. To illustrate, suppose that a hypothetical non-Treasury security with a coupon rate of
8% and a 10-year maturity is trading at $105.5423. Assume that the *benchmark
spot rate curve for this issuer* is the one given in Exhibit 66-10 of the previous reading. The Z-spread relative to that issuer's benchmark spot rate curve is the spread
that must be added to the spot rates shown in the next-to-last column of that
exhibit that will make the present value of the cash flows equal to the market
price. In our illustration, the Z-spread relative to this benchmark is 40 basis points.

What does the Z-spread mean when the benchmark is not the Treasury spot
rate curve (i.e., default-free spot rate curve)? When the Treasury spot rate curve
is the benchmark, we said that the Z-spread for a non-Treasury issue embodies
credit risk, liquidity risk, and any option risk. When the benchmark is the spot

rate curve for the issuer, the Z-spread is measuring the spread attributable to the liquidity risk of the issue and any option risk.

Thus, when a Z-spread is cited, it must be cited relative to some benchmark spot rate curve. This is necessary because it indicates the credit and sector risks that are being considered when the Z-spread was calculated. While Z-spreads are typically calculated using Treasury securities as the benchmark interest rates, this need not be the case. Vendors of analytical systems commonly allow the user to select a benchmark spot rate curve. Moreover, in non-U.S. markets, Treasury securities are typically not the benchmark. The key point is that an investor should always ask what benchmark was used to compute the Z-spread.

4.2.2 Option-Adjusted Spread

The Z-spread seeks to measure the spread over a spot rate curve thus overcoming the first problem of the nominal spread that we cited earlier. Now let's look at the second shortcoming—failure to take future interest rate volatility into account which could change the cash flows for bonds with embedded options.

4.2.2.1 Valuation Models

What investors seek to do is to buy undervalued securities (securities whose value is greater than their price). Before they can do this though, they need to know what the security is worth (i.e., a fair price to pay). A valuation model is designed to provide precisely this. If a model determines the fair price of a share of common stock is $36 and the market price is currently $24, then the stock is considered to be undervalued. If a bond is selling for less than its fair value, then it too is considered undervalued.

A valuation model need not stop here, however. Market participants find it more convenient to think about yield spread than about price differences. A valuation model can take this difference between the fair price and the market price and convert it into a yield spread measure. Instead of asking, "How much is this security undervalued?", the model can ask, "How much return will I earn in exchange for taking on these risks?"

The **option-adjusted spread** (OAS) was developed as a way of doing just this: taking the dollar difference between the fair price and market price and converting it into a yield spread measure. Thus, the OAS is used to reconcile the fair price (or value) to the market price by finding a return (spread) that will equate the two (using a trial and error procedure). This is somewhat similar to what we did earlier when calculating yield to maturity, yield to call, etc., only in this case, we are calculating a spread (measured in basis points) rather than a percentage rate of return as we did then.

The OAS is model dependent. That is, the OAS computed depends on the valuation model used. In particular, OAS models differ considerably in how they forecast interest rate changes, leading to variations in the level of OAS. What are two of these key modeling differences?

- Interest rate volatility is a critical assumption. Specifically, the higher the interest rate volatility assumed, the lower the OAS. In comparing the OAS of dealer firms, it is important to check on the volatility assumption made.

- The OAS is a spread, but what is it a "spread" over? The OAS is a spread over the Treasury spot rate curve or the issuer's benchmark used in the analysis. In the model, the spot rate curve is actually the result of a series of assumptions that allow for changes in interest rates. Again, different models yield different results.

Why is the spread referred to as "option adjusted"? Because the security's embedded option can change the cash flows; the value of the security should take this change of cash flow into account. Note that the Z-spread doesn't do this—it ignores the fact that interest rate changes can affect the cash flows. In essence, it assumes that interest rate volatility is zero. This is why the Z-spread is also referred to as the **zero-volatility OAS.**

4.2.2.2 Option Cost

The implied cost of the option embedded in any security can be obtained by calculating the difference between the OAS at the assumed interest rate or yield volatility and the Z-spread. That is, since the Z-spread is just the sum of the OAS and option cost, i.e.,

Z-spread = OAS + option cost

it follows that:

option cost = Z-spread − OAS

The reason that the option cost is measured in this way is as follows. In an environment in which interest rates are assumed not to change, the investor would earn the Z-spread. When future interest rates are uncertain, the spread is different because of the embedded option(s); the OAS reflects the spread after adjusting for this option. Therefore, the option cost is the difference between the spread that would be earned in a static interest rate environment (the Z-spread, or equivalently, the zero-volatility OAS) and the spread after adjusting for the option (the OAS).

For callable bonds and most mortgage-backed and asset-backed securities, the option cost is positive. This is because the issuer's ability to alter the cash flows will result in an OAS that is less than the Z-spread. In the case of a putable bond, the OAS is greater than the Z-spread so that the option cost is negative. This occurs because of the investor's ability to alter the cash flows.

In general, when the option cost is positive, this means that the investor has sold an option to the issuer or borrower. This is true for callable bonds and most mortgage-backed and asset-backed securities. A negative value for the option cost means that the investor has purchased an option from the issuer or borrower. A putable bond is an example of this negative option cost. There are certain securities in the mortgage-backed securities market that also have an option cost that is negative.

4.2.2.3 Highlighting the Pitfalls of the Nominal Spread

We can use the concepts presented in this reading to highlight the pitfalls of the nominal spread. First, we can recast the relationship between the option cost, Z-spread, and OAS as follows:

Z-spread = OAS + option cost

Next, recall that the nominal spread and the Z-spread may not diverge significantly. Suppose that the nominal spread is approximately equal to the Z-spread. Then, we can substitute nominal spread for Z-spread in the previous relationship giving:

nominal spread ≈ OAS + option cost

This relationship tells us that a high nominal spread could be hiding a high option cost. The option cost represents the portion of the spread that the investor has given to the issuer or borrower. Thus, while the nominal spread for a security that can be called or prepaid might be, say 200 basis points, the option cost may be 190 and the OAS only 10 basis points. But, an investor is only compensated for the OAS. An investor that relies on the nominal spread may not be adequately compensated for taking on the option risk associated with a security with an embedded option.

4.2.3 Summary of Spread Measures

We have just described three spread measures:

- nominal spread
- zero-volatility spread
- option-adjusted spread

To understand different spread measures we ask two questions:

1. What is the benchmark for computing the spread? That is, what is the spread measured relative to?
2. What is the spread measuring?

The table below provides a summary showing for each of the three spread measures the benchmark and the risks for which the spread is compensating.

Spread measure	Benchmark	Reflects compensation for:
Nominal	Treasury yield curve	Credit risk, option risk, liquidity risk
Zero-volatility	Treasury spot rate curve	Credit risk, option risk, liquidity risk
Option-adjusted	Treasury spot rate curve	Credit risk, liquidity risk

FORWARD RATES 5

We have seen how a default-free theoretical spot rate curve can be extrapolated from the Treasury yield curve. Additional information useful to market participants can be extrapolated from the default-free theoretical spot rate curve: **forward rates.** Under certain assumptions described later, these rates can be viewed as the market's consensus of future interest rates.

Examples of forward rates that can be calculated from the default-free theoretical spot rate curve are the:

- 6-month forward rate six months from now
- 6-month forward rate three years from now
- 1-year forward rate one year from now
- 3-year forward rate two years from now
- 5-year forward rates three years from now

Since the forward rates are implicitly extrapolated from the default-free theoretical spot rate curve, these rates are sometimes referred to as **implied forward**

rates. We begin by showing how to compute the 6-month forward rates. Then we explain how to compute any forward rate.

While we continue to use the Treasury yield curve in our illustrations, as noted earlier, a LIBOR spot rate curve can also be constructed using the bootstrapping methodology and forward rates for LIBOR can be obtained in the same manner as described below.

5.1 Deriving 6-Month Forward Rates

To illustrate the process of extrapolating 6-month forward rates, we will use the yield curve and corresponding spot rate curve from Exhibit 67-4. We will use a very simple arbitrage principle as we did earlier in this reading to derive the spot rates. Specifically, if two investments have the same cash flows and have the same risk, they should have the same value.

Consider an investor who has a 1-year investment horizon and is faced with the following two alternatives:

▷ buy a 1-year Treasury bill, or
▷ buy a 6-month Treasury bill and, when it matures in six months, buy another 6-month Treasury bill.

The investor will be indifferent toward the two alternatives if they produce the same return over the 1-year investment horizon. The investor knows the spot rate on the 6-month Treasury bill and the 1-year Treasury bill. However, he does not know what yield will be on a 6-month Treasury bill purchased six months from now. That is, he does not know the 6-month forward rate six months from now. Given the spot rates for the 6-month Treasury bill and the 1-year Treasury bill, the forward rate on a 6-month Treasury bill is the rate that equalizes the dollar return between the two alternatives.

To see how that rate can be determined, suppose that an investor purchased a 6-month Treasury bill for \$X. At the end of six months, the value of this investment would be:

$$X(1 + z_1)$$

where z_1 is one-half the bond-equivalent yield (BEY) of the theoretical 6-month spot rate.

Let f represent one-half the forward rate (expressed as a BEY) on a 6-month Treasury bill available six months from now. If the investor were to rollover his investment by purchasing that bill at that time, then the future dollars available at the end of one year from the \$X investment would be:

$$X(1 + z_1)(1 + f)$$

EXHIBIT 67-11 Graphical Depiction of the Six-Month Forward Rate Six Months from Now

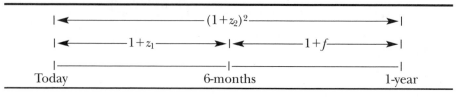

Now consider the alternative of investing in a 1-year Treasury bill. If we let z_2 represent one-half the BEY of the theoretical 1-year spot rate, then the future dollars available at the end of one year from the X investment would be:

$$X(1 + z_2)^2$$

The reason that the squared term appears is that the amount invested is being compounded for two periods. (Recall that each period is six months.)

The two choices are depicted in Exhibit 67-11. Now we are prepared to analyze the investor's choices and what this says about forward rates. The investor will be indifferent toward the two alternatives confronting him if he makes the same dollar investment (X) and receives the same future dollars from both alternatives at the end of one year. That is, the investor will be indifferent if:

$$X(1 + z_1)(1 + f) = X(1 + z_2)^2$$

Solving for f, we get:

$$f = \frac{(1 + z_2)^2}{(1 + z_1)} - 1$$

Doubling f gives the BEY for the 6-month forward rate six months from now.

We can illustrate the use of this formula with the theoretical spot rates shown in Exhibit 67-4. From that exhibit, we know that:

6-month bill spot rate = 0.030, therefore $z_1 = 0.0150$
1-year bill spot rate = 0.033, therefore $z_2 = 0.0165$

Substituting into the formula, we have:

$$f = \frac{(1.0165)^2}{(1.0150)} - 1 = 0.0180 = 1.8\%$$

Therefore, the 6-month forward rate six months from now is 3.6% (1.8% × 2) BEY.

Let's confirm our results. If X is invested in the 6-month Treasury bill at 1.5% and the proceeds then reinvested for six months at the 6-month forward rate of 1.8%, the total proceeds from this alternative would be:

$$X(1.015)(1.018) = 1.03327\ X$$

Investment of X in the 1-year Treasury bill at one-half the 1-year rate, 1.0165%, would produce the following proceeds at the end of one year:

$$X(1.0165)^2 = 1.03327\ X$$

Both alternatives have the same payoff if the 6-month Treasury bill yield six months from now is 1.8% (3.6% on a BEY). This means that, if an investor is guaranteed a 1.8% yield (3.6% BEY) on a 6-month Treasury bill six months from now, he will be indifferent toward the two alternatives.

The same line of reasoning can be used to obtain the 6-month forward rate beginning at any time period in the future. For example, the following can be determined:

▸ the 6-month forward rate three years from now
▸ the 6-month forward rate five years from now

The notation that we use to indicate 6-month forward rates is $_1f_m$ where the subscript 1 indicates a 1-period (6-month) rate and the subscript m indicates the period beginning m periods from now. When m is equal to zero, this means the current rate. Thus, the first 6-month forward rate is simply the current 6-month spot rate. That is, $_1f_0 = z_1$.

The general formula for determining a 6-month forward rate is:

$$_1f_m = \frac{(1 + z_{m+1})^{m+1}}{(1 + z_m)^m} - 1$$

For example, suppose that the 6-month forward rate four years (eight 6-month periods) from now is sought. In terms of our notation, m is 8 and we seek $_1f_8$. The formula is then:

$$_1f_8 = \frac{(1 + z_9)^9}{(1 + z_8)^8} - 1$$

From Exhibit 67-4, since the 4-year spot rate is 5.065% and the 4.5-year spot rate is 5.1701%, z_8 is 2.5325% and z_9 is 2.58505%. Then,

$$_1f_8 = \frac{(1.0258505)^9}{(1.025325)^8} - 1 = 3.0064\%$$

Doubling this rate gives a 6-month forward rate four years from now of 6.01%.

EXHIBIT 67-12 Six-Month Forward Rates (Annualized Rates on a Bond-Equivalent Basis)

Notation	Forward Rate
$_1f_0$	3.00
$_1f_1$	3.60
$_1f_2$	3.92
$_1f_3$	5.15
$_1f_4$	6.54
$_1f_5$	6.33
$_1f_6$	6.23
$_1f_7$	5.79
$_1f_8$	6.01
$_1f_9$	6.24
$_1f_{10}$	6.48
$_1f_{11}$	6.72
$_1f_{12}$	6.97
$_1f_{13}$	6.36
$_1f_{14}$	6.49
$_1f_{15}$	6.62
$_1f_{16}$	6.76
$_1f_{17}$	8.10
$_1f_{18}$	8.40
$_1f_{19}$	8.71

Exhibit 67-12 shows all of the 6-month forward rates for the Treasury yield curve shown in Exhibit 67-4. The forward rates reported in Exhibit 67-12 are the annualized rates on a bond-equivalent basis. In Exhibit 67-13, the short-term forward rates are plotted along with the Treasury par yield curve and theoretical spot rate curve. The graph of the short-term forward rates is called the **short-term forward-rate curve.** Notice that the short-term forward rate curve lies above the other two curves. This will always be the case if the par yield curve is upward sloping. If the par yield curve is downward sloping, the short-term forward rate curve will be the lowest curve. Notice the unusual shape for the short-term forward rate curve. There is a mathematical reason for this shape. In practice, analysts will use statistical techniques to create a smooth short-term forward rate curve.

EXHIBIT 67-13 Graph of Short-Term Forward Rate Curve

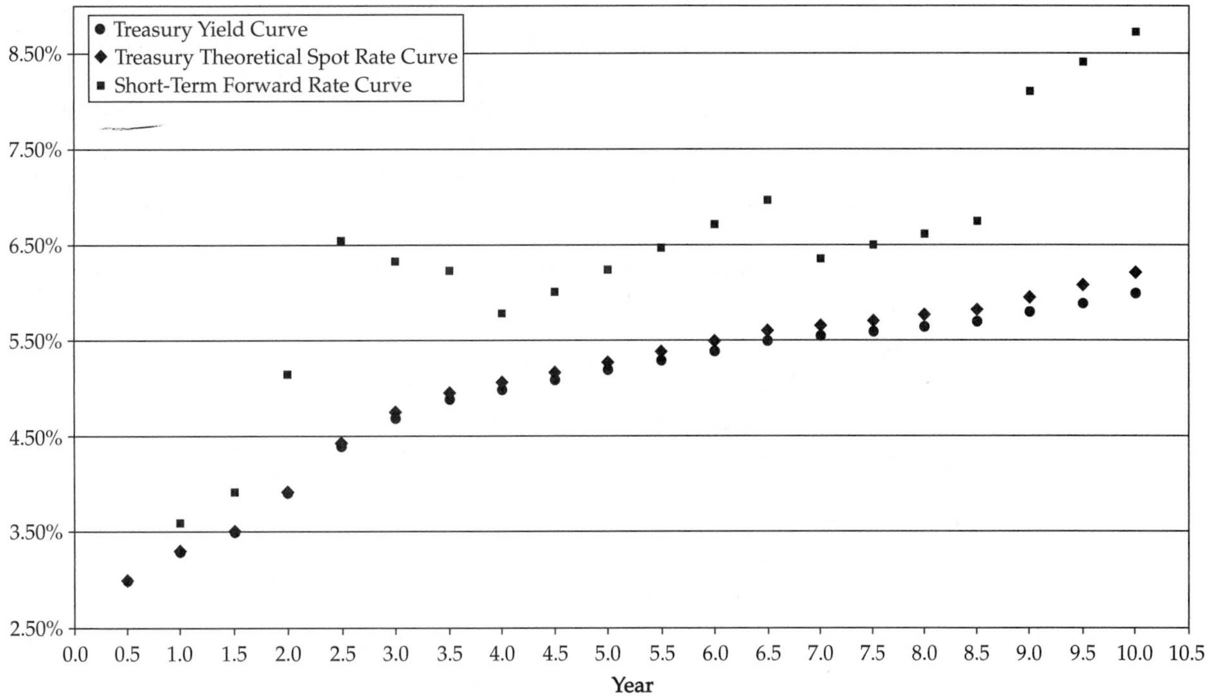

Practice Question 9

Show how the 6-month forward rate 6.5 years (13 periods from now) reported in Exhibit 67-12 is computed.

5.2 Relationship between Spot Rates and Short-Term Forward Rates

Suppose an investor invests X in a 3-year zero-coupon Treasury security. The total proceeds three years (six periods) from now would be:

$$X(1 + z_6)^6$$

The investor could instead buy a 6-month Treasury bill and reinvest the proceeds every six months for three years. The future dollars or dollar return will depend on the 6-month forward rates. Suppose that the investor can actually reinvest the proceeds maturing every six months at the calculated 6-month forward rates shown in Exhibit 67-12. At the end of three years, an investment of X would generate the following proceeds:

$$X (1 + z_1) (1 + {}_1f_1) (1 + {}_1f_2) (1 + {}_1f_3) (1 + {}_1f_4) (1 + {}_1f_5)$$

Since the two investments must generate the same proceeds at the end of three years, the two previous equations can be equated:

$$X (1 + z_6)^6 = X (1 + z_1) (1 + {}_1f_1) (1 + {}_1f_2) (1 + {}_1f_3) (1 + {}_1f_4) (1 + {}_1f_5)$$

Solving for the 3-year (6-period) spot rate, we have:

$$z_6 = [(1 + z_1) (1 + {}_1f_1) (1 + {}_1f_2) (1 + {}_1f_3) (1 + {}_1f_4) (1 + {}_1f_5)]^{1/6} - 1$$

This equation tells us that the 3-year spot rate depends on the current 6-month spot rate and the five 6-month forward rates. In fact, the right-hand side of this equation is a geometric average of the current 6-month spot rate and the five 6-month forward rates.

Let's use the values in Exhibits 67-4 and 67-12 to confirm this result. Since the 6-month spot rate in Exhibit 67-4 is 3%, z_1 is 1.5% and therefore[11]

$$z_6 = [(1.015) (1.018) (1.0196) (1.0257) (1.0327) (1.03165)]^{1/6} - 1$$
$$= 0.023761 = 2.3761\%$$

Doubling this rate gives 4.7522%. This agrees with the spot rate shown in Exhibit 67-4.

In general, the relationship between a T-period spot rate, the current 6-month spot rate, and the 6-month forward rates is as follows:

$$z_T = [(1 + z_1) (1 + {}_1f_1) (1 + {}_1f_2) ... (1 + {}_1f_{T-1})]^{1/T} - 1$$

Therefore, discounting at the forward rates will give the same present value as discounting at spot rates.

5.3 Valuation Using Forward Rates

Since a spot rate is simply a package of short-term forward rates, it will not make any difference whether we discount cash flows using spot rates or forward rates. That is, suppose that the cash flow in period T is $1. Then the present value of the cash flow can be found using the spot rate for period T as follows:

$$\text{PV of \$1 in } T \text{ periods} = \frac{1}{(1 + z_T)^T}$$

Alternatively, since we know that

$$z_T = [(1 + z_1) (1 + {}_1f_1) (1 + {}_1f_2) \cdots (1 + {}_1f_{T-1})]^{1/T} - 1$$

then, adding 1 to both sides of the equation,

---

[11] Actually, the semiannual forward rates are based on annual rates calculated to more decimal places. For example, $f_{1,3}$ is 5.15% in Exhibit 67-12 but based on the more precise value, the semiannual rate is 2.577%.

$$(1 + z_T) = [(1+ z_1)\,(1 + {}_1f_1)\,(1 + {}_1f_2) \cdots (1 + {}_1f_{T-1})]^{1/T}$$

Raising both sides of the equation to the T-th power we get:

$$(1 + z_T)^T = (1+ z_1)\,(1 + {}_1f_1)\,(1 + {}_1f_2) \cdots (1 + {}_1f_{T-1})$$

Substituting the right-hand side of the above equation into the present value formula we get:

$$\text{PV of \$1 in } T \text{ periods} = \frac{1}{(1 + z_1)(1 + {}_1f_1)(1 + {}_1f_2)\cdots(1 + {}_1f_{T-1})}$$

In practice, the present value of \$1 in T periods is called the **forward discount factor for period T.**

For example, consider the forward rates shown in Exhibit 67-12. The forward discount rate for period 4 is found as follows:

$$z_1 = 3\%/2 = 1.5\% \qquad {}_1f_1 = 3.6\%/2 = 1.8\%$$
$${}_1f_2 = 3.92\%/2 = 1.958\% \qquad {}_1f_3 = 5.15\%/2 = 2.577\%$$

$$\text{forward discount factor of \$1 in 4 periods} = \frac{\$1}{(1.015)(1.018)(1.01958)(1.02577)}$$
$$= 0.925369$$

To see that this is the same present value that would be obtained using the spot rates, note from Exhibit 67-4 that the 2-year spot rate is 3.9164%. Using that spot rate, we find:

$$z_4 = 3.9164\%/2 = 1.9582\%$$
$$\text{PV of \$1 in 4 periods} = \frac{\$1}{(1.019582)^4} = 0.925361$$

The answer is the same as the forward discount factor (the slight difference is due to rounding).

Exhibit 67-14 shows the computation of the forward discount factor for each period based on the forward rates in Exhibit 67-12. Let's show how both the forward rates and the spot rates can be used to value a 2-year 6% coupon Treasury bond. The present value for each cash flow is found as follows using spot rates:

$$\frac{\text{cash flow for period } t}{(1 + z_t)^t}$$

The following table uses the spot rates in Exhibit 67-4 to value this bond:

Period	Spot rate BEY (%)	Semiannual spot rate (%)	PV of \$1	Cash flow	PV of cash flow
1	3.0000	1.50000	0.9852217	3	2.955665
2	3.3000	1.65000	0.9677991	3	2.903397
3	3.5053	1.75266	0.9492109	3	2.847633
4	3.9164	1.95818	0.9253619	103	95.312278
				Total	104.018973

Based on the spot rates, the value of this bond is \$104.0190.

EXHIBIT 67-14 Calculation of the Forward Discount Factor for Each Period

Periods	Years	Notation	Forward Rate*	0.5 ×Forward Rate**	1 + Forward Rate	Forward Discount Factor
1	0.5	$_1f_0$	3.00%	1.5000%	1.01500	0.985222
2	1.0	$_1f_1$	3.60%	1.8002%	1.01800	0.967799
3	1.5	$_1f_2$	3.92%	1.9583%	1.01958	0.949211
4	2.0	$_1f_3$	5.15%	2.5773%	1.02577	0.925362
5	2.5	$_1f_4$	6.54%	3.2679%	1.03268	0.896079
6	3.0	$_1f_5$	6.33%	3.1656%	1.03166	0.868582
7	3.5	$_1f_6$	6.23%	3.1139%	1.03114	0.842352
8	4.0	$_1f_7$	5.79%	2.8930%	1.02893	0.818668
9	4.5	$_1f_8$	6.01%	3.0063%	1.03006	0.794775
10	5.0	$_1f_9$	6.24%	3.1221%	1.03122	0.770712
11	5.5	$_1f_{10}$	6.48%	3.2407%	1.03241	0.746520
12	6.0	$_1f_{11}$	6.72%	3.3622%	1.03362	0.722237
13	6.5	$_1f_{12}$	6.97%	3.4870%	1.03487	0.697901
14	7.0	$_1f_{13}$	6.36%	3.1810%	1.03181	0.676385
15	7.5	$_1f_{14}$	6.49%	3.2450%	1.03245	0.655126
16	8.0	$_1f_{15}$	6.62%	3.3106%	1.03310	0.634132
17	8.5	$_1f_{16}$	6.76%	3.3778%	1.03378	0.613412
18	9.0	$_1f_{17}$	8.10%	4.0504%	1.04050	0.589534
19	9.5	$_1f_{18}$	8.40%	4.2009%	1.04201	0.565767
20	10.0	$_1f_{19}$	8.72%	4.3576%	1.04357	0.542142

* The rates in this column are rounded to two decimal places.
** The rates in this column used the forward rates in the previous column carried to four decimal places.

Using forward rates and the forward discount factors, the present value of the cash flow in period t is found as follows:

cash flow in period t × discount factor for period t

The following table uses the forward rates and the forward discount factors in Exhibit 67-14 to value this bond:

Period	Semiannual forward rate	Forward discount factor	Cash flow	PV of cash flow
1	1.5000%	0.985222	3	2.955665
2	1.8002%	0.967799	3	2.903397
3	1.9583%	0.949211	3	2.847633
4	2.5773%	0.925362	103	95.312278
			Total	104.018973

The present value of this bond using forward rates is $104.0190.

So, it does not matter whether one discounts cash flows by spot rates or forward rates, the value is the same.

Practice Question 10

Compute the value of a 10% coupon 3-year bond using the forward rates in Exhibit 67-12.

5.4 Computing Any Forward Rate

Using spot rates, we can compute any forward rate. Using the same arbitrage arguments as used above to derive the 6-month forward rates, any forward rate can be obtained.

There are two elements to the forward rate. The first is when in the future the rate begins. The second is the length of time for the rate. For example, the 2-year forward rate 3 years from now means a rate three years from now for a length of two years. The notation used for a forward rate, f, will have two subscripts—one before f and one after f as shown below:

$$_t f_m$$

The subscript before f is t and is the length of time that the rate applies. The subscript after f is m and is when the forward rate begins. That is,

the length of time of the forward rate f when the forward rate begins

Remember our time periods are still 6-month periods. Given the above notation, here is what the following mean:

Notation	Interpretation for the forward rate
$_1 f_{12}$	6-month (1-period) forward rate beginning 6 years (12 periods) from now
$_2 f_8$	1-year (2-period) forward rate beginning 4 years (8 periods) from now
$_6 f_4$	3-year (6-period) forward rate beginning 2 years (4 periods) from now
$_8 f_{10}$	4-year (8-period) forward rate beginning 5 years (10 periods) from now

To see how the formula for the forward rate is derived, consider the following two alternatives for an investor who wants to invest for $m + t$ periods:

▸ buy a zero-coupon Treasury bond that matures in $m + t$ periods, or

▸ buy a zero-coupon Treasury bond that matures in m periods and invest the proceeds at the maturity date in a zero-coupon Treasury bond that matures in t periods.

The investor will be indifferent between the two alternatives if they produce the same return over the $m + t$ investment horizon.

For $100 invested in the first alternative, the proceeds for this investment at the horizon date assuming that the semiannual rate is z_{m+t} is

$$\$100 \, (1 + z_{m+t})^{m+t}$$

For the second alternative, the proceeds for this investment at the end of m periods assuming that the semiannual rate is z_m is

$$\$100 \, (1 + z_m)^m$$

When the proceeds are received in m periods, they are reinvested at the forward rate, $_tf_m$, producing a value for the investment at the end of $m + t$ periods of

$$\$100 \, (1 + z_m)^m \, (1 + {}_tf_m)^t$$

For the investor to be indifferent to the two alternatives, the following relationship must hold:

$$\$100 \, (1 + z_{m+t})^{m+t} = \$100 \, (1 + z_m)^m \, (1 + {}_tf_m)^t$$

Solving for $_tf_m$ we get:

$$_tf_m = \left[\frac{(1 + z_{m+t})^{m+t}}{(1 + z_m)^m} \right]^{1/t} - 1$$

Notice that if t is equal to 1, the formula reduces to the 1-period (6-month) forward rate.

To illustrate, for the spot rates shown in Exhibit 67-4, suppose that an investor wants to know the 2-year forward rate three years from now. In terms of the notation, t is equal to 4 and m is equal to 6. Substituting for t and m into the equation for the forward rate we have:

$$_4f_6 = \left[\frac{(1 + z_{10})^{10}}{(1 + z_6)^6} \right]^{1/4} - 1$$

This means that the following two spot rates are needed: z_6 (the 3-year spot rate) and z_{10} (the 5-year spot rate). From Exhibit 67-4 we know

z_6 (the 3-year spot rate) = 4.752%/2 = 0.02376
z_{10} (the 5-year spot rate) = 5.2772%/2 = 0.026386

then

$$_4f_6 = \left[\frac{(1.026386)^{10}}{(1.02376)^6} \right]^{1/4} - 1 = 0.030338$$

Therefore, $_4f_6$ is equal to 3.0338% and doubling this rate gives 6.0675% the forward rate on a bond-equivalent basis.

We can verify this result. Investing $100 for 10 periods at the spot rate of 2.6386% will produce the following value:

$$\$100 \, (1.026386)^{10} = \$129.7499$$

By investing $100 for 6 periods at 2.376% and reinvesting the proceeds for 4 periods at the forward rate of 3.030338% gives the same value

$$\$100 \, (1.02376)^6 \, (1.030338)^4 = \$129.75012$$

Practice Question 11

A. Given the spot rates in Exhibit 67-4, compute the 6-year forward rate 4 years from now.

B. Demonstrate that the forward rate computed in part A is correct.

SUMMARY   6

▸ The sources of return from holding a bond to maturity are the coupon interest payments, any capital gain or loss, and reinvestment income.

▸ Reinvestment income is the interest income generated by reinvesting coupon interest payments and any principal payments from the time of receipt to the bond's maturity.

▸ The current yield relates the annual dollar coupon interest to the market price and fails to recognize any capital gain or loss and reinvestment income.

▸ The yield to maturity is the interest rate that will make the present value of the cash flows from a bond equal to the price plus accrued interest.

▸ The market convention to annualize a semiannual yield is to double it and the resulting annual yield is referred to as a bond-equivalent yield.

▸ When market participants refer to a yield or return measure as computed on a bond-equivalent basis it means that a semiannual yield or return is doubled.

▸ The yield to maturity takes into account all three sources of return but assumes that the coupon payments and any principal repayments can be reinvested at an interest rate equal to the yield to maturity.

▸ The yield to maturity will only be realized if the interim cash flows can be reinvested at the yield to maturity and the bond is held to maturity.

▸ Reinvestment risk is the risk an investor faces that future reinvestment rates will be less than the yield to maturity at the time a bond is purchased.

▸ Interest rate risk is the risk that if a bond is not held to maturity, an investor may have to sell it for less than the purchase price.

▸ The longer the maturity and the higher the coupon rate, the more a bond's return is dependent on reinvestment income to realize the yield to maturity at the time of purchase.

▸ The yield to call is the interest rate that will make the present value of the expected cash flows to the assumed call date equal to the price plus accrued interest.

▸ Yield measures for callable bonds include yield to first call, yield to next call, yield to first par call, and yield to refunding.

▸ The yield to call considers all three sources of potential return but assumes that all cash flows can be reinvested at the yield to call until the assumed call date, the investor will hold the bond to the assumed call date, and the issuer will call the bond on the assumed call date.

▸ For a putable bond a yield to put is computed assuming that the issue will be put on the first put date.

▸ The yield to worst is the lowest yield from among all possible yield to calls, yield to puts, and the yield to maturity.

▸ For mortgage-backed and asset-backed securities, the cash flow yield based on some prepayment rate is the interest rate that equates the present value of the projected principal and interest payments to the price plus accrued interest.

▸ The cash flow yield assumes that all cash flows (principal and interest payments) can be reinvested at the calculated yield and that the assumed prepayment rate will be realized over the security's life.

▸ For amortizing securities, reinvestment risk is greater than for standard coupon nonamortizing securities because payments are typically made monthly and include principal as well as interest payments.

▷ For floating-rate securities, instead of a yield measure, margin measures (i.e., spread above the reference rate) are computed.

▷ Two margin measures commonly used are spread for life and discount margin.

▷ The discount margin assumes that the reference rate will not change over the life of the security and that there is no cap or floor restriction on the coupon rate.

▷ The theoretical spot rate is the interest rate that should be used to discount a default-free cash flow.

▷ Because there are a limited number of on-the-run Treasury securities traded in the market, interpolation is required to obtain the yield for interim maturities; hence, the yield for most maturities used to construct the Treasury yield curve are interpolated yields rather than observed yields.

▷ Default-free spot rates can be derived from the Treasury yield curve by a method called bootstrapping.

▷ The basic principle underlying the bootstrapping method is that the value of a Treasury coupon security is equal to the value of the package of zero-coupon Treasury securities that duplicates the coupon bond's cash flows.

▷ The nominal spread is the difference between the yield for a non-Treasury bond and a comparable-maturity Treasury coupon security.

▷ The nominal spread fails to consider the term structure of the spot rates and the fact that, for bonds with embedded options, future interest rate volatility may alter its cash flows.

▷ The zero-volatility spread or Z-spread is a measure of the spread that the investor will realize over the entire Treasury spot rate curve if the bond is held to maturity, thereby recognizing the term structure of interest rates.

▷ Unlike the nominal spread, the Z-spread is not a spread off one point on the Treasury yield curve but is a spread over the entire spot rate curve.

▷ For bullet bonds, unless the yield curve is very steep, the nominal spread will not differ significantly from the Z-spread; for securities where principal is paid over time rather than just at maturity there can be a significant difference, particularly in a steep yield curve environment.

▷ The option-adjusted spread (OAS) converts the cheapness or richness of a bond into a spread over the future possible spot rate curves.

▷ An OAS is said to be option adjusted because it allows for future interest rate volatility to affect the cash flows.

▷ The OAS is a product of a valuation model and, when comparing the OAS of dealer firms, it is critical to check on the volatility assumption (and other assumptions) employed in the valuation model.

▷ The cost of the embedded option is measured as the difference between the Z-spread and the OAS.

▷ Investors should not rely on the nominal spread for bonds with embedded options since it hides how the spread is split between the OAS and the option cost.

▷ OAS is used as a relative value measure to assist in the selection of bonds with embedded options.

▷ Using arbitrage arguments, forward rates can be extrapolated from the Treasury yield curve or the Treasury spot rate curve.

▷ The spot rate for a given period is related to the forward rates; specifically, the spot rate is a geometric average of the current 6-month spot rate and the subsequent 6-month forward rates.

PROBLEMS

1. What are the sources of return any yield measure should incorporate?

2. **A.** Suppose a 10-year 9% coupon bond is selling for $112 with a par value of $100. What is the current yield for the bond?

   B. What is the limitation of the current yield measure?

3. Determine whether the yield to maturity of a 6.5% 20-year bond that pays interest semiannually and is selling for $90.68 is 7.2%, 7.4%, or 7.8%.

4. The following yields and prices were reported in the financial press. Are any of them incorrect assuming that the reported price and coupon rate are correct? If so, explain why. (No calculations are needed to answer this question.)

Bond	Price	Coupon rate	Current Yield	Yield to Maturity
A	100	6.0%	5.0%	6.0%
B	110	7.0%	6.4%	6.1%
C	114	7.5%	7.1%	7.7%
D	95	4.7%	5.2%	5.9%
E	75	5.6%	5.1%	4.1%

5. Comment on the following statement: "The yield to maturity measure is a useless measure because it doubles a semiannual yield (calling the annual yield a bond-equivalent yield) rather than computing an effective annual yield. This is the major shortcoming of the yield-to-maturity measure."

6. **A.** Suppose that an investor invests $108.32 in a 5-year certificate of deposit that pays 7% annually (on a bond-equivalent basis) or 3.5% semiannually and the interest payments are semiannual. What are the total future dollars of this investment at the end of 5 years (i.e., ten 6-month periods)?

   B. How much total interest is generated from the investment in this certificate of deposit?

   C. Suppose an investor can purchase any investment for $108.32 that offers a 7% yield on a bond-equivalent basis and pays interest semiannually. What is the total future dollars and the total dollar return from this investment?

   D. Suppose an investor can purchase a 5-year 9% coupon bond that pays interest semiannually and the price of this bond is $108.32. The yield to maturity for this bond is 7% on a bond-equivalent basis. What is the total future dollars and the total dollar return that will be generated from this bond if it is to yield 7%?

   E. Complete the following for this bond:

   coupon interest   =

   capital gain/loss   =

   reinvestment income =

   ─────────────────────────

   total dollar return   =

   F. What percentage of the total dollar return is dependent on reinvestment income?

   G. How is the reinvestment income in part E realized?

7. A. Which of the following three bonds has the greatest dependence on reinvestment income to generate the computed yield? Assume that each bond is offering the same yield to maturity. (No calculations are needed to answer this question.)

Bond	Maturity	Coupon rate
X	25 years	0%
Y	20 years	7%
Z	20 years	8%

 B. Which of the three bonds in part A has the least dependence on reinvestment income to generate the computed yield? Assume that each bond is offering the same yield to maturity. (No calculations are needed to answer this question.)

8. What is the reinvestment risk and interest rate risk associated with a yield to maturity measure?

9. A. If the yield to maturity on an annual-pay bond is 5.6%, what is the bond-equivalent yield?

 B. If the yield of a U.S. bond issue quoted on a bond-equivalent basis is 5.6%, what is the yield to maturity on an annual-pay basis?

10. Suppose that a 10% 15-year bond has the following call structure:

   not callable for the next 5 years
   first callable in 5 years at $105
   first par call date is in 10 years
   The price of the bond is $127.5880.

 A. Is the yield to maturity for this bond 7.0%, 7.4%, or 7.8%?

 B. Is the yield to first call for this bond 4.55%, 4.65%, or 4.85%?

 C. Is the yield to first par call for this bond 6.25%, 6.55%, or 6.75%?

11. Suppose a 5% coupon 6-year bond is selling for $105.2877 and is putable in four years at par value. The yield to maturity for this bond is 4%. Determine whether the yield to put is 3.38%, 3.44% or 3.57%.

12. Suppose that an amortizing security pays interest monthly. Based on the projected principal payments and interest, suppose that the monthly interest rate that makes the present value of the cash flows equal to the price of the security is 0.41%. What is the cash flow yield on a bond-equivalent basis?

13. Two portfolio managers are discussing the investment characteristics of amortizing securities. Manager A believes that the advantage of these securities relative to nonamortizing securities is that since the periodic cash flows include principal payments as well as coupon payments, the manager can generate greater reinvestment income. In addition, the payments are typically monthly so even greater reinvestment income can be generated. Manager B believes that the need to reinvest monthly and the need to invest larger amounts than just coupon interest payments make amortizing securities less attractive. Who do you agree with and why?

14. An investor is considering the purchase of a 5-year floating-rate note that pays interest semiannually. The coupon formula is equal to 6-month LIBOR plus 30 basis points. The current value for 6-month LIBOR is 5% (annual rate). The price of this note is 99.1360. Is the discount margin 40 basis points, 50 basis points, or 55 basis points?

15. How does the discount margin handle any cap on a floater and the fact that the reference rate may change over time?

16. A. A Treasury bill with 105 days from settlement to maturity is selling for $0.989 per $1 of maturity value. What is the yield on a discount basis?

B. A Treasury bill with 275 days from settlement to maturity is quoted as having a yield on a discount basis of 3.68%. What is the price of this Treasury bill?

C. What are the problems with using the yield on a discount basis as measure of a Treasury bill's yield?

17. Explain how a Treasury yield curve is constructed even though there are only a limited number of on-the-run Treasury issues available in the market.

18. Suppose that the annual yield to maturity for the 6-month and 1-year Treasury bill is 4.6% and 5.0%, respectively. These yields represent the 6-month and 1-year spot rates. Also assume the following Treasury yield curve (i.e., the price for each issue is $100) has been estimated for 6-month periods out to a maturity of 3 years:

Years to maturity	Annual yield to maturity (BEY)
1.5	5.4%
2.0	5.8%
2.5	6.4%
3.0	7.0%

Compute the 1.5-year, 2-year, 2.5-year, and 3-year spot rates.

19. Given the spot rates computed in the previous question and the 6-month and 1-year spot rates, compute the arbitrage-free value of a 3-year Treasury security with a coupon rate of 8%.

20. What are the two limitations of the nominal spread as a measure of relative value of two bonds?

21. Suppose that the Treasury spot rate curve is as follows:

Period	Years to maturity	Spot rate
1	0.5	5.0%
2	1.0	5.4
3	1.5	5.8
4	2.0	6.4
5	2.5	7.0
6	3.0	7.2
7	3.5	7.4
8	4.0	7.8

Suppose that the market price of a 4-year 6% coupon non-Treasury issue is $91.4083. Determine whether the zero-volatility spread (Z-spread) relative to the Treasury spot rate curve for this issue is 80 basis points, 90 basis points, or 100 basis points.

22. The Prestige Investment Management Company sent a report to its pension client. In the report, Prestige indicated that the yield curve is currently flat (i.e., the yield to maturity for each maturity is the same) and then discussed the nominal spread for the corporate bonds held in the client's portfolio. A trustee of the pension fund was concerned that Prestige focused on the nominal spread rather than the zero-volatility spread or option-adjusted spread for these bond issues. Joan Thomas is Prestige's employee who is the contact person for this account. She received a phone call from the trustee regarding his concern. How should she respond regarding the use of nominal spread rather than zero-volatility spread and option-adjusted spread as a spread measure for corporate bonds?

23. John Tinker is a junior portfolio manager assigned to work for Laura Sykes, the manager of the corporate bond portfolio of a public pension fund. Ms. Sykes asked Mr. Tinker to construct a portfolio profile that she could use in her presentation to the trustees. One of the measures Ms. Sykes insisted that Mr. Tinker include was the option-adjusted spread of each issue. In preparing the portfolio profile, Mr. Tinker encountered the following situations that he did not understand. Provide Mr. Tinker with an explanation.

    A. Mr. Tinker checked with several dealer firms to determine the option-adjusted spread for each issue. For several of the issues, there were substantially different option-adjusted spreads reported. For example, for one callable issue one dealer reported an OAS of 100 basis points, one dealer reported 170 basis points, and a third dealer 200 basis points. Mr. Tinker could not understand how the dealers could have substantially different OAS values when in fact the yield to maturity and nominal spread values for each of the issues did not differ from dealer to dealer.

    B. The dealers that Mr. Tinker checked with furnished him with the nominal spread and the Z-spread for each issue in addition to the OAS. For all the bond issues where there were no embedded options, each dealer reported that the Z-spread was equal to the OAS. Mr. Tinker could not understand why.

    C. One dealer firm reported an option cost for each issue. There were positive, negative, and zero values reported. Mr. Tinker observed that for all the bond issues that were putable, the option cost was negative. For all the option-free bond issues, the reported value was zero.

24. Max Dumas is considering the purchase of a callable corporate bond. He has available to him two analytical systems to value the bond. In one system, System A, the vendor uses the on-the-run Treasury issues to construct the theoretical spot rate that is used to construct a model to compute the OAS. The other analytical system, System B, uses the on-the-run issue for the particular issuer in constructing a model to compute the OAS.

    A. Suppose that using System A, Mr. Dumas finds that the OAS for the callable corporate he is considering is 50 basis points. How should he interpret this OAS value?

    B. Suppose that using System B, Mr. Dumas finds that the OAS computed is 15 basis points. How should he interpret this OAS value?

    C. Suppose that a dealer firm shows Mr. Dumas another callable corporate bond of the same credit quality and duration with an OAS of 40 basis points. Should Mr. Dumas view that this bond is more attractive or less attractive than the issue he is considering for acquisition?

25. Assume the following Treasury spot rates:

Period	Years to maturity	Spot rate
1	0.5	5.0%
2	1.0	5.4
3	1.5	5.8
4	2.0	6.4
5	2.5	7.0
6	3.0	7.2
7	3.5	7.4
8	4.0	7.8

Compute the following forward rates:

A. the 6-month forward rate six months from now.

B. the 6-month forward rate one year from now.

C. the 6-month forward rate three years from now.

D. the 2-year forward rate one year from now.

E. the 1-year forward rate two years from now.

26. For the previous question, demonstrate that the 6-month forward rate six months from now is the rate that will produce at the end of one year the same future dollars as investing either (1) at the current 1-year spot rate of 5.4% or (2) at the 6-month spot rate of 5.0% and reinvesting at the 6-month forward rate six months from now.

27. Two sales people of analytical systems are making a presentation to you about the merits of their respective systems. One sales person states that in valuing bonds the system first constructs the theoretical spot rates and then discounts cash flows using these rates. The other sales person interjects that his firm takes a different approach. Rather than using spot rates, forward rates are used to value the cash flows and he believes this is a better approach to valuing bonds compared to using spot rates. How would you respond to the second sales person's comment about his firm's approach?

28. A. Given the following 6-month forward rates, compute the forward discount factor for each period.

Period	Annual forward rate (BEY)
1	4.00%
2	4.40
3	5.00
4	5.60
5	6.00
6	6.40

B. Compute the value of a 3-year 8% coupon bond using the forward rates.

INTRODUCTION TO THE MEASUREMENT OF INTEREST RATE RISK

LEARNING OUTCOMES

The candidate should be able to:

a. distinguish between the full valuation approach (the scenario analysis approach) and the duration/convexity approach for measuring interest rate risk, and explain the advantage of using the full valuation approach;

b. compute the interest rate risk exposure of a bond position or of a bond portfolio, given a change in interest rates;

c. demonstrate the price volatility characteristics for option-free bonds when interest rates change (including the concept of "positive convexity"), demonstrate the price volatility characteristics of callable bonds and prepayable securities when interest rates change (including the concept of "negative convexity"), and describe the price volatility characteristics of putable bonds;

d. compute the effective duration of a bond, given information about how the bond's price will increase and decrease for given changes in interest rates and compute the approximate percentage price change for a bond, given the bond's effective duration and a specified change in yield;

e. distinguish among the alternative definitions of duration (modified, effective or option-adjusted, and Macaulay) explain why effective duration is the most appropriate measure of interest rate risk for bonds with embedded options, describe why duration is best interpreted as a measure of a bond's or portfolio's sensitivity to changes in interest rates, compute the duration of a portfolio, given the duration of the bonds comprising the portfolio, and discuss the limitations of portfolio duration;

f. discuss the convexity measure of a bond, and estimate a bond's percentage price change, given the bond's duration and convexity and a specified change in interest rates;

g. differentiate between modified convexity and effective convexity;

h. compute the price value of a basis point (PVBP), and explain its relationship to duration.

Fixed Income Analysis for the Chartered Financial Analyst® Program, Second Edition, by Frank J. Fabozzi. Reprinted with permission.

1   INTRODUCTION

In Reading 63, we discussed the interest rate risk associated with investing in bonds. We know that the value of a bond moves in the opposite direction to a change in interest rates. If interest rates increase, the price of a bond will decrease. For a short bond position, a loss is generated if interest rates fall. However, a manager wants to know more than simply when a position generates a loss. To control interest rate risk, a manager must be able to quantify that result.

What is the key to measuring the interest rate risk? It is the accuracy in estimating the value of the position after an adverse interest rate change. A valuation model determines the value of a position after an adverse interest rate move. Consequently, if a reliable valuation model is not used, there is no way to properly measure interest rate risk exposure.

There are two approaches to measuring interest rate risk—the full valuation approach and the duration/convexity approach.

2   THE FULL VALUATION APPROACH

The most obvious way to measure the interest rate risk exposure of a bond position or a portfolio is to re-value it when interest rates change. The analysis is performed for different scenarios with respect to interest rate changes. For example, a manager may want to measure the interest rate exposure to a 50 basis point, 100 basis point, and 200 basis point instantaneous change in interest rates. This approach requires the re-valuation of a bond or bond portfolio for a given interest rate change scenario and is referred to as the **full valuation approach.** It is sometimes referred to as **scenario analysis** because it involves assessing the exposure to interest rate change scenarios.

To illustrate this approach, suppose that a manager has a $10 million par value position in a 9% coupon 20-year bond. The bond is option-free. The current price is 134.6722 for a yield (i.e., yield to maturity) of 6%. The market value of the position is $13,467,220 (134.6722% × $10 million). Since the manager owns the bond, she is concerned with a rise in yield since this will decrease the market value of the position. To assess the exposure to a rise in market yields, the manager decides to look at how the value of the bond will change if yields change instantaneously for the following three scenarios: (1) 50 basis point increase, (2) 100 basis point increase, and (3) 200 basis point increase. This means that the manager wants to assess what will happen to the bond position if the yield on the bond increases from 6% to (1) 6.5%, (2) 7%, and (3) 8%. Because this is an option-free bond, valuation is straightforward. In the examples that follow, we will use one yield to discount each of the cash flows. In other words, to simplify the calculations, we will assume a flat yield curve (even though that assumption doesn't fit the examples perfectly). The price of this bond per $100 par value and the market value of the $10 million par position is shown in Exhibit 68-1. Also shown is the new market value and the percentage change in market value.

EXHIBIT 68-1 Illustration of Full Valuation Approach to Assess the Interest Rate Risk of a Bond Position for Three Scenarios

Current bond position: 9% coupon 20-year bond (option-free)
Price: 134.6722
Yield to maturity: 6%
Par value owned: $10 million
Market value of position: $13,467,220.00

Scenario	Yield change (bp)	New yield	New price	New market value ($)	Percentage change in market value (%)
1	50	6.5%	127.7606	12,776,050	−5.13%
2	100	7.0%	121.3551	12,135,510	−9.89%
3	200	8.0%	109.8964	10,989,640	−18.40%

In the case of a portfolio, each bond is valued for a given scenario and then the total value of the portfolio is computed for a given scenario. For example, suppose that a manager has a portfolio with the following two option-free bonds: (1) 6% coupon 5-year bond and (2) 9% coupon 20-year bond. For the shorter term bond, $5 million of par value is owned and the price is 104.3760 for a yield of 5%. For the longer term bond, $10 million of par value is owned and the price is 134.6722 for a yield of 6%. Suppose that the manager wants to assess the interest rate risk of this portfolio for a 50, 100, and 200 basis point increase in interest rates assuming both the 5-year yield and 20-year yield change by the same number of basis points. Exhibit 68-2 shows the interest rate risk exposure. Panel a of the exhibit shows the market value of the 5-year bond for the three scenarios. Panel b does the same for the 20-year bond. Panel c shows the total market value of the two-bond portfolio and the percentage change in the market value for the three scenarios.

In the illustration in Exhibit 68-2, it is assumed that both the 5-year and the 20-year yields changed by the same number of basis points. The full valuation approach can also handle scenarios where the yield curve does not change in a parallel fashion. Exhibit 68-3 illustrates this for our portfolio that includes the 5-year and 20-year bonds. The scenario analyzed is a yield curve shift combined with shifts in the level of yields. In the illustration in Exhibit 68-3, the following yield changes for the 5-year and 20-year yields are assumed:

Scenario	Change in 5-year rate (bp)	Change in 20-year rate (bp)
1	50	10
2	100	50
3	200	100

The last panel in Exhibit 68-3 shows how the market value of the portfolio changes for each scenario.

EXHIBIT 68-2 Illustration of Full Valuation Approach to Assess the Interest Rate Risk of a Two Bond Portfolio (Option-Free) for Three Scenarios Assuming a Parallel Shift in the Yield Curve

Panel a

Bond 1:	6% coupon 5-year bond	Par value:	$5,000,000
Initial price:	104.3760	Initial market value:	$5,218,800
Yield:	5%		

Scenario	Yield change (bp)	New yield	New price	New market value ($)
1	50	5.5%	102.1600	5,108,000
2	100	6.0%	100.0000	5,000,000
3	200	7.0%	95.8417	4,792,085

Panel b

Bond 2:	9% coupon 20-year bond	Par value:	$10,000,000
Initial price:	134.6722	Initial market value:	$13,467,220
Yield:	6%		

Scenario	Yield change (bp)	New yield	New price	New market value ($)
1	50	6.5%	127.7605	12,776,050
2	100	7.0%	121.3551	12,135,510
3	200	8.0%	109.8964	10,989,640

Panel c

Initial Portfolio Market value: $18,686,020.00

Scenario	Yield change (bp)	Market Value of Bond 1 ($)	Market Value of Bond 2 ($)	Market Value of Portfolio ($)	Percentage change in market value (%)
1	50	5,108,000	12,776,050	17,884,020	−4.29%
2	100	5,000,000	12,135,510	17,135,510	−8.30%
3	200	4,792,085	10,989,640	15,781,725	−15.54%

The full valuation approach seems straightforward. If one has a good valuation model, assessing how the value of a portfolio or individual bond will change for different scenarios for parallel and nonparallel yield curve shifts measures the interest rate risk of a portfolio.

A common question that often arises when using the full valuation approach is which scenarios should be evaluated to assess interest rate risk exposure. For some regulated entities, there are specified scenarios established by regulators. For example, it is common for regulators of depository institutions to require entities to determine the impact on the value of their bond portfolio for a 100, 200, and 300 basis point instantaneous change in interest rates (up and down). (Regulators tend to refer to this as "simulating" interest rate scenarios rather than scenario analysis.) Risk managers and highly leveraged investors such as hedge funds tend to look at extreme scenarios to assess exposure to interest rate changes. This practice is referred to as **stress testing.**

EXHIBIT 68-3 Illustration of Full Valuation Approach to Assess the Interest Rate Risk of a Two Bond Portfolio (Option-Free) for Three Scenarios Assuming a Nonparallel Shift in the Yield Curve

Panel a

Bond 1:	6% coupon 5-year bond	Par value:	$5,000,000
Initial price:	104.3760	Initial market value:	$5,218,800
Yield:	5%		

Scenario	Yield change (bp)	New yield	New price	New market value ($)
1	50	5.5%	102.1600	5,108,000
2	100	6.0%	100.0000	5,000,000
3	200	7.0%	95.8417	4,792,085

Panel b

Bond 2:	9% coupon 20-year bond	Par value:	$10,000,000
Initial price:	134.6722	Initial market value:	$13,467,220
Yield:	6%		

Scenario	Yield change (bp)	New yield	New price	New market value ($)
1	10	6.1%	133.2472	13,324,720
2	50	6.5%	127.7605	12,776,050
3	100	7.0%	121.3551	12,135,510

Panel c

Initial Portfolio Market value: $18,686,020.00

Scenario	Market Value of Bond 1 ($)	Bond 2 ($)	Portfolio ($)	Percentage change in market value (%)
1	5,108,000	13,324,720	18,432,720	−1.36%
2	5,000,000	12,776,050	17,776,050	−4.87%
3	4,792,085	12,135,510	16,927,595	−9.41%

Of course, in assessing how changes in the yield curve can affect the exposure of a portfolio, there are an infinite number of scenarios that can be evaluated. The state-of-the-art technology involves using a complex statistical procedure[1] to determine a likely set of yield curve shift scenarios from historical data.

It seems like the reading should end right here. We can use the full valuation approach to assess the exposure of a bond or portfolio to interest rate changes to evaluate any scenario, assuming—and this must be repeated continuously—*that the manager has a good valuation model to estimate what the price of the bonds will be in each interest rate scenario.* However, we are not stopping here. In fact, the balance of this reading is considerably longer than this section. Why? The reason is that the full valuation process can be very time consuming. This is particularly true if the portfolio has a large number of bonds, even if a minority of those bonds are complex (i.e., have embedded options). While the full valuation approach is

---

[1] The procedure used is principal component analysis.

the recommended method, managers want one simple measure that they can use to get an idea of how bond prices will change if rates change in a parallel fashion, rather than having to revalue an entire portfolio. In Reading 63, such a measure was introduced—duration. We will discuss this measure as well as a supplementary measure (convexity) in Sections 4 and 5, respectively. To build a foundation to understand the limitations of these measures, we describe the basic price volatility characteristics of bonds in Section 3. The fact that there are limitations of using one or two measures to describe the interest rate exposure of a position or portfolio should not be surprising. These measures provide a starting point for assessing interest rate risk.

3   PRICE VOLATILITY CHARACTERISTICS OF BONDS

In Reading 63, we described the characteristics of a bond that affect its price volatility: (1) maturity, (2) coupon rate, and (3) presence of embedded options. We also explained how the level of yields affects price volatility. In this section, we will take a closer look at the price volatility of bonds.

3.1 Price Volatility Characteristics of Option-Free Bonds

Let's begin by focusing on option-free bonds (i.e., bonds that do not have embedded options). A fundamental characteristic of an option-free bond is that the price of the bond changes in the opposite direction to a change in the bond's yield. Exhibit 68-4 illustrates this property for four hypothetical bonds assuming a par value of $100.

When the price/yield relationship for any option-free bond is graphed, it exhibits the shape shown in Exhibit 68-5. Notice that as the yield increases, the price of an option-free bond declines. However, this relationship is not linear

EXHIBIT 68-4   Price/Yield Relationship for Four Hypothetical Option-Free Bonds

Yield (%)	Price ($)			
	6%/5 year	6%/20 year	9%/5 year	9%/20 year
4.00	108.9826	127.3555	122.4565	168.3887
5.00	104.3760	112.5514	117.5041	150.2056
5.50	102.1600	106.0195	115.1201	142.1367
5.90	100.4276	101.1651	113.2556	136.1193
5.99	100.0427	100.1157	112.8412	134.8159
6.00	100.0000	100.0000	112.7953	134.6722
6.01	99.9574	99.8845	112.7494	134.5287
6.10	99.5746	98.8535	112.3373	133.2472
6.50	97.8944	94.4479	110.5280	127.7605
7.00	95.8417	89.3225	108.3166	121.3551
8.00	91.8891	80.2072	104.0554	109.8964

EXHIBIT 68-5 Price/Yield Relationship for a Hypothetical Option-Free Bond

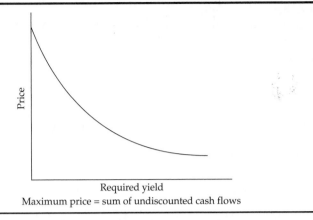

Maximum price = sum of undiscounted cash flows

(i.e., not a straight line relationship). The shape of the price/yield relationship for any option-free bond is referred to as **convex.** This price/yield relationship reflects an instantaneous change in the required yield.

The price sensitivity of a bond to changes in the yield can be measured in terms of the dollar price change or the percentage price change. Exhibit 68-6 uses the four hypothetical bonds in Exhibit 68-4 to show the percentage change in each bond's price for various changes in yield, assuming that the initial yield for all four bonds is 6%. An examination of Exhibit 68-6 reveals the following properties concerning the price volatility of an option-free bond:

Property 1: Although the price moves in the opposite direction from the change in yield, the percentage price change is not the same for all bonds.

Property 2: For small changes in the yield, the percentage price change for a given bond is roughly the same, whether the yield increases or decreases.

Property 3: For large changes in yield, the percentage price change is not the same for an increase in yield as it is for a decrease in yield.

Property 4: For a given large change in yield, the percentage price increase is greater than the percentage price decrease.

EXHIBIT 68-6 Instantaneous Percentage Price Change for Four Hypothetical Bonds (Initial yield for all four bonds is 6%)

| New Yield (%) | Percentage Price Change | | | |
	6%/5 year	6%/20 year	9%/5 year	9%/20 year
4.00	8.98	27.36	8.57	25.04
5.00	4.38	12.55	4.17	11.53
5.50	2.16	6.02	2.06	5.54
5.90	0.43	1.17	0.41	1.07
5.99	0.04	0.12	0.04	0.11
6.01	−0.04	−0.12	−0.04	−0.11
6.10	−0.43	−1.15	−0.41	−1.06
6.50	−2.11	−5.55	−2.01	−5.13
7.00	−4.16	−10.68	−3.97	−9.89
8.00	−8.11	−19.79	−7.75	−18.40

While the properties are expressed in terms of percentage price change, they also hold for dollar price changes.

An explanation for these last two properties of bond price volatility lies in the convex shape of the price/yield relationship. Exhibit 68-7 illustrates this. The following notation is used in the exhibit

$$
\begin{aligned}
Y &= \text{initial yield} \\
Y_1 &= \text{lower yield} \\
Y_2 &= \text{higher yield} \\
P &= \text{initial price} \\
P_1 &= \text{price at lower yield } Y_1 \\
P_2 &= \text{price at higher yield } Y_2
\end{aligned}
$$

What was done in the exhibit was to change the initial yield (Y) up and down by the same number of basis points. That is, in Exhibit 68–7, the yield is decreased from Y to Y_1 and increased from Y to Y_2 such that the change is the same:

$$Y - Y_1 = Y_2 - Y$$

Also, the change in yield is a large number of basis points.

The vertical distance from the horizontal axis (the yield) to the intercept on the graph shows the price. The change in the initial price (P) when the yield declines from Y to Y_1 is equal to the difference between the new price (P_1) and the initial price (P). That is,

$$\text{change in price when yield decreases} = P_1 - P$$

The change in the initial price (P) when the yield increases from Y to Y_2 is equal to the difference between the new price (P_2) and the initial price (P). That is,

$$\text{change in price when yield increases} = P_2 - P$$

EXHIBIT 68-7 Graphical Illustration of Properties 3 and 4 for an Option-Free Bond

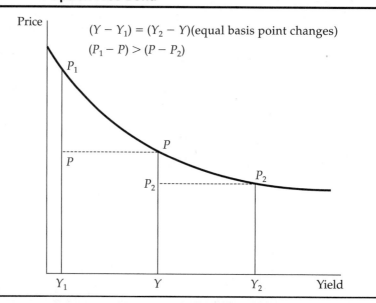

As can be seen in the exhibit, the change in price when yield decreases is not equal to the change in price when yield increases by the same number of basis points. That is,

$$P_1 - P \neq P_2 - P$$

This is what Property 3 states.

A comparison of the price change shows that the change in price when yield decreases is greater than the change in price when yield increases. That is,

$$P_1 - P > P_2 - P$$

This is Property 4.

The implication of Property 4 is that if an investor owns a bond, the capital gain that will be realized if the yield decreases is greater than the capital loss that will be realized if the yield increases by the same number of basis points. For an investor who is short a bond (i.e., sold a bond not owned), the reverse is true: the potential capital loss is greater than the potential capital gain if the yield changes by a given number of basis points.

The convexity of the price/yield relationship impacts Property 4. Exhibit 68-8 shows a less convex price/yield relationship than Exhibit 68-7. That is, the price/yield relationship in Exhibit 68-8 is less bowed than the price/yield relationship in Exhibit 68-7. Because of the difference in the convexities, look at what happens when the yield increases and decreases by the same number of basis points and the yield change is a large number of basis points. We use the same notation in Exhibits 68-8 and 68-9 as in Exhibit 68-7. Notice that while the price gain when the yield decreases is greater than the price decline when the yield increases, the gain is not much greater than the loss. In contrast, Exhibit 68-9 has much greater convexity than the bonds in Exhibits 68-7 and 68-8 and the price gain is significantly greater than the loss for the bonds depicted in Exhibits 68-7 and 68-8.

EXHIBIT 68-8 Impact of Convexity on Property 4: Less Convex Bond

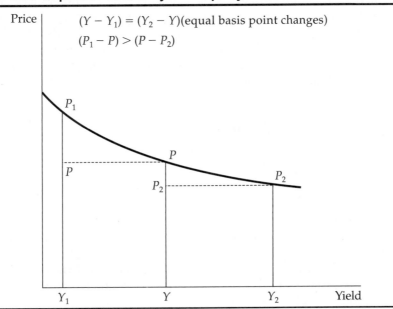

EXHIBIT 68-9 Impact of Convexity on Property 4: Highly Convex Bond

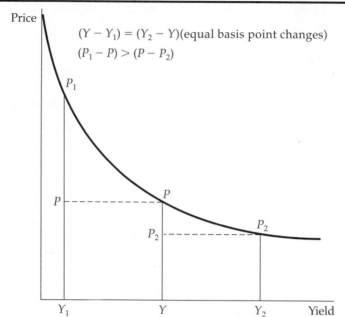

3.2 Price Volatility of Bonds with Embedded Options

Now let's turn to the price volatility of bonds with embedded options. As explained in previous chapters, the price of a bond with an embedded option is comprised of two components. The first is the value of the same bond if it had no embedded option (that is, the price if the bond is option free). The second component is the value of the embedded option. In other words, the value of a bond with embedded options is equal to the value of an option-free bond plus or minus the value of embedded options.

The two most common types of embedded options are call (or prepay) options and put options. As interest rates in the market decline, the issuer may call or prepay the debt obligation prior to the scheduled principal payment date. The other type of option is a put option. This option gives the investor the right to require the issuer to purchase the bond at a specified price. Below we will examine the price/yield relationship for bonds with both types of embedded options (calls and puts) and implications for price volatility.

3.2.1 Bonds with Call and Prepay Options

In the discussion below, we will refer to a bond that may be called or is prepayable as a callable bond. Exhibit 68-10 shows the price/yield relationship for an option-free bond and a callable bond. The convex curve given by *a-a′* is the price/yield relationship for an option-free bond. The unusual shaped curve denoted by *a–b* in the exhibit is the price/yield relationship for the callable bond.

The reason for the price/yield relationship for a callable bond is as follows. When the prevailing market yield for comparable bonds is higher than the coupon rate on the callable bond, it is unlikely that the issuer will call the issue. For example, if the coupon rate on a bond is 7% and the prevailing market yield on comparable bonds is 12%, it is highly unlikely that the issuer will call a 7% coupon bond so that it can issue a 12% coupon bond. Since the bond is unlikely to be called, the callable bond will have a similar price/yield relationship to an otherwise comparable option-free bond. Consequently, the callable bond will be val-

EXHIBIT 68-10 Price/Yield Relationship for a Callable Bond and an Option-Free Bond

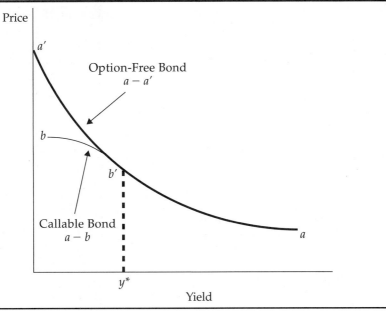

ued as if it is an option-free bond. However, since there is still some value to the call option,[2] the bond won't trade exactly like an option-free bond.

As yields in the market decline, the concern is that the issuer will call the bond. The issuer won't necessarily exercise the call option as soon as the market yield drops below the coupon rate. Yet, the value of the embedded call option increases as yields approach the coupon rate from higher yield levels. For example, if the coupon rate on a bond is 7% and the market yield declines to 7.5%, the issuer will most likely not call the issue. However, market yields are now at a level at which the investor is concerned that the issue may eventually be called if market yields decline further. Cast in terms of the value of the embedded call option, that option becomes more valuable to the issuer and therefore it reduces the price relative to an otherwise comparable option-free bond[3]. In Exhibit 68-10, the value of the embedded call option at a given yield can be measured by the difference between the price of an option-free bond (the price shown on the curve a-a') and the price on the curve a-b. Notice that at low yield levels (below y^* on the horizontal axis), the value of the embedded call option is high.

Using the information in Exhibit 68-10, let's compare the price volatility of a callable bond to that of an option-free bond. Exhibit 68-11 focuses on the portion of the price/yield relationship for the callable bond where the two curves in Exhibit 68-10 depart (segment b'-b in Exhibit 68-10). We know from our earlier discussion that for a large change in yield, the price of an option-free bond increases by more than it decreases (Property 4 above). Is that what happens for a callable bond in the region of the price/yield relationship shown in Exhibit 68-11? No, it is not. In fact, as can be seen in the exhibit, the opposite is true! That is, for a given large change in yield, the price appreciation is less than the price decline.

This very important characteristic of a callable bond—that its price appreciation is less than its price decline when rates change by a large number of basis

---

[2] This is because there is still some chance that interest rates will decline in the future and the issue will be called.

[3] For readers who are already familiar with option theory, this characteristic can be restated as follows: When the coupon rate for the issue is below the market yield, the embedded call option is said to be "out-of-the-money." When the coupon rate for the issue is above the market yield, the embedded call option is said to be "in-the-money."

EXHIBIT 68-11 Negative Convexity Region of the Price/Yield Relationship for a Callable Bond

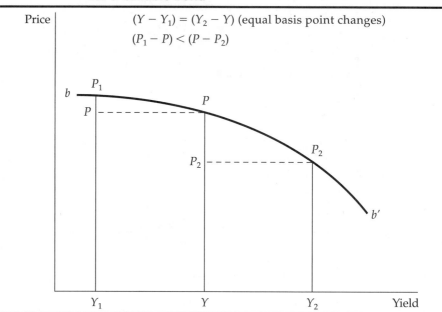

$(Y - Y_1) = (Y_2 - Y)$ (equal basis point changes)
$(P_1 - P) < (P - P_2)$

points—is referred to as **negative convexity.**[4] But notice from Exhibit 68-10 that callable bonds don't exhibit this characteristic at every yield level. When yields are high (relative to the issue's coupon rate), the bond exhibits the same price/yield relationship as an option-free bond; therefore at high yield levels it also has the characteristic that the gain is greater than the loss. Because market participants have referred to the shape of the price/yield relationship shown in Exhibit 68-11 as negative convexity, market participants refer to the relationship for an option-free bond as **positive convexity.** Consequently, a callable bond exhibits negative convexity at low yield levels and positive convexity at high yield levels. This is depicted in Exhibit 68-12.

As can be seen from the exhibits, when a bond exhibits negative convexity, the bond compresses in price as rates decline. That is, at a certain yield level there is very little price appreciation when rates decline. When a bond enters this region, the bond is said to exhibit "price compression."

3.2.2 Bonds with Embedded Put Options

Putable bonds may be redeemed by the bondholder on the dates and at the put price specified in the indenture. Typically, the put price is par value. The advantage to the investor is that if yields rise such that the bond's value falls below the put price, the investor will exercise the put option. If the put price is par value, this means that if market yields rise above the coupon rate, the bond's value will fall below par and the investor will then exercise the put option.

The value of a putable bond is equal to the value of an option-free bond plus the value of the put option. Thus, the difference between the value of a putable bond and the value of an otherwise comparable option-free bond is the value of the embedded put option. This can be seen in Exhibit 68-13 which shows the price/yield relationship for a putable bond is the curve a-c and for an option-free bond is the curve a-a'.

---

[4] Mathematicians refer to this shape as being "concave."

EXHIBIT 68-12 Negative and Positive Convexity Exhibited by a Callable Bond

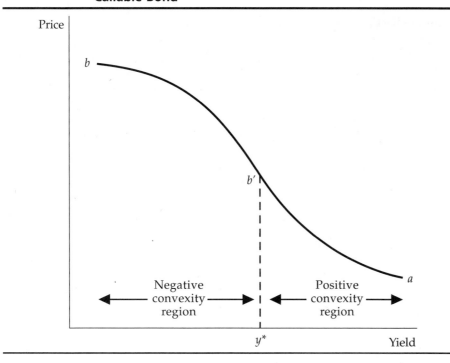

EXHIBIT 68-13 Price/Yield Relationship for a Putable Bond and an Option-Free Bond

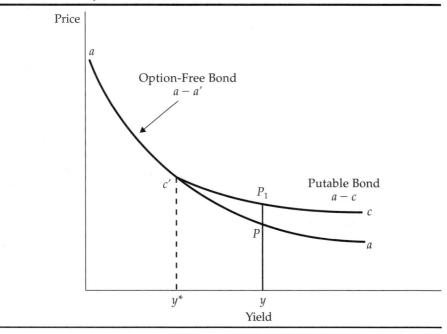

At low yield levels (low relative to the issue's coupon rate), the price of the putable bond is basically the same as the price of the option-free bond because the value of the put option is small. As rates rise, the price of the putable bond declines, but the price decline is less than that for an option-free bond. The divergence in the price of the putable bond and an otherwise comparable option-free bond at a given yield level (y) is the value of the put option (P_1–P). When yields rise to a level where the bond's price would fall below the put price, the price at these levels is the put price.

4   DURATION

With the background about the price volatility characteristics of a bond, we can now turn to an alternate approach to full valuation: the duration/convexity approach. As explained in Reading 63, *duration is a measure of the approximate price sensitivity of a bond to interest rate changes.* More specifically, *it is the approximate percentage change in price for a 100 basis point change in rates.* We will see in this section that duration is the first (linear) approximation of the percentage price change. To improve the approximation provided by duration, an adjustment for "convexity" can be made. Hence, using duration combined with convexity to estimate the percentage price change of a bond caused by changes in interest rates is called the **duration/convexity approach.**

4.1   Calculating Duration

In Reading 63, we explained that the duration of a bond is estimated as follows:

$$\frac{\text{price if yields decline} - \text{price if yields rise}}{2(\text{initial price})(\text{change in yield in decimal})}$$

If we let

$$
\begin{aligned}
\Delta y &= \text{change in yield in decimal} \\
V_0 &= \text{initial price} \\
V_- &= \text{price if yields decline by } \Delta y \\
V_+ &= \text{price if yields increase by } \Delta y
\end{aligned}
$$

then duration can be expressed as

$$\text{duration} = \frac{V_- - V_+}{2\,(V_0)\,(\Delta y)} \qquad \textbf{(68-1)}$$

For example, consider a 9% coupon 20-year option-free bond selling at 134.6722 to yield 6% (see Exhibit 68-4). Let's change (i.e., shock) the yield down and up by 20 basis points and determine what the new prices will be for the numerator. If the yield is decreased by 20 basis points from 6.0% to 5.8%, the price would increase to 137.5888. If the yield increases by 20 basis points, the price would decrease to 131.8439. Thus,

$$
\begin{aligned}
\Delta y &= 0.002 \\
V_0 &= 134.6722 \\
V_- &= 137.5888 \\
V_+ &= 131.8439
\end{aligned}
$$

Then,

$$\text{duration} = \frac{137.5888 - 131.8439}{2 \times (134.6722) \times (0.002)} = 10.66$$

As explained in Reading 63, duration is interpreted as the approximate percentage change in price for a 100 basis point change in rates. Consequently, a duration of 10.66 means that the approximate change in price for this bond is 10.66% for a 100 basis point change in rates.

A common question asked about this interpretation of duration is the consistency between the yield change that is used to compute duration using equation (68-1) and the interpretation of duration. For example, recall that in computing the duration of the 9% coupon 20-year bond, we used a 20 basis point yield change to obtain the two prices to use in the numerator of equation (68-1). Yet, we interpret the duration computed as the approximate percentage price change for a 100 basis point change in yield. The reason is that regardless of the yield change used to estimate duration in equation (68-1), the interpretation is the same. If we used a 25 basis point change in yield to compute the prices used in the numerator of equation (68-1), the resulting duration is interpreted as the approximate percentage price change for a 100 basis point change in yield. Later we will use different changes in yield to illustrate the sensitivity of the computed duration.

Practice Question 1

A. Compute the duration of the 9% coupon 20-year option-free bond by changing the yield down and up by 10 basis points. (The relevant values can be found in Exhibit 68-4.)

B. Suppose a 6% coupon 20-year option-free bond is selling at par value and therefore offering a yield of 6%. Compute the duration by changing the yield down and up by 10 basis points. (The relevant values can be found in Exhibit 68-4.)

4.2 Approximating the Percentage Price Change Using Duration

In Reading 63, we explained how to approximate the percentage price change for a given change in yield and a given duration. Here we will express the process using the following formula:

$$\text{approximate percentage price change} = -\text{duration} \times \Delta y_* \times 100 \quad \textbf{(68-2)}$$

where Δy_* is the yield change (in decimal) for which the estimated percentage price change is sought.[5] The reason for the negative sign on the right-hand side of equation (68-2) is due to the inverse relationship between price change and yield change (e.g., as yields increase, bond prices decrease). The following two examples illustrate how to use duration to estimate a bond's price change.

Example #1: small change in basis point yield. For example, consider the 9% 20-year bond trading at 134.6722 whose duration we just showed is 10.66. The approximate percentage price change for a 10 basis point increase in yield (i.e., $\Delta y_* = +0.001$) is:

$$\text{approximate percentage price change} = -10.66 \times (+0.001) \times 100 = -1.066\%$$

---

[5] The difference between Δy in the duration formula given by equation (68-1) and Δy_* in equation (68-2) to get the approximate percentage price change is as follows. In the duration formula, the Δy is used to estimate duration and, as explained later, for reasonably small changes in yield the resulting value for duration will be the same. We refer to this change as the "rate shock." Given the duration, the next step is to estimate the percentage price change for any change in yield. The Δy_* in equation (68-2) is the specific change in yield for which the approximate percentage price change is sought.

How good is this approximation? The actual percentage price change is −1.06% (as shown in Exhibit 68-6 when yield increases to 6.10%). Duration, in this case, did an excellent job in estimating the percentage price change.

We would come to the same conclusion if we used duration to estimate the percentage price change if the yield declined by 10 basis points (i.e., $\Delta y = -0.001$). In this case, the approximate percentage price change would be +1.066% (i.e., the direction of the estimated price change is the reverse but the magnitude of the change is the same). Exhibit 68-6 shows that the actual percentage price change is +1.07%.

In terms of estimating the new price, let's see how duration performed. The initial price is 134.6722. For a 10 basis point increase in yield, duration estimates that the price will decline by 1.066%. Thus, the price will decline to 133.2366 (found by multiplying 134.6722 by one minus 0.01066). The actual price from Exhibit 68-4 if the yield increases by 10 basis points is 133.2472. Thus, the price estimated using duration is close to the actual price.

For a 10 basis point decrease in yield, the actual price from Exhibit 68-4 is 136.1193 and the estimated price using duration is 136.1078 (a price increase of 1.066%). Consequently, the new price estimated by duration is close to the actual price for a 10 basis point change in yield.

Example #2: large change in basis point yield. Let's look at how well duration does in estimating the percentage price change if the yield increases by 200 basis points instead of 10 basis points. In this case, Δy is equal to +0.02. Substituting into equation (68-2), we have

$$\text{approximate percentage price change} = -10.66 \times (+0.02) \times 100 = -21.32\%$$

How good is this estimate? From Exhibit 68-6, we see that the actual percentage price change when the yield increases by 200 basis points to 8% is −18.40%. Thus, the estimate is not as accurate as when we used duration to approximate the percentage price change for a change in yield of only 10 basis points. If we use duration to approximate the percentage price change when the yield decreases by 200 basis points, the approximate percentage price change in this scenario is +21.32%. The actual percentage price change as shown in Exhibit 68-6 is +25.04%.

Let's look at the use of duration in terms of estimating the new price. Since the initial price is 134.6722 and a 200 basis point increase in yield will decrease the price by 21.32%, the estimated new price using duration is 105.9601 (found by multiplying 134.6722 by one minus 0.2132). From Exhibit 68-4, the actual price if the yield is 8% is 109.8964. Consequently, the estimate is not as accurate as the estimate for a 10 basis point change in yield. The estimated new price using duration for a 200 basis point decrease in yield is 163.3843 compared to the actual price (from Exhibit 68-4) of 168.3887. Once again, the estimation of the price using duration is not as accurate as for a 10 basis point change. *Notice that whether the yield is increased or decreased by 200 basis points, duration underestimates what the new price will be. We will see why shortly.*

Summary. Let's summarize what we found in our application of duration to approximate the percentage price change:

Yield change (bp)	Initial price	New price Based on duration	New price Actual	Percent price change Based on duration	Percent price change Actual	Comment
+10	134.6722	133.2366	133.2472	−1.066	−1.06	estimated price close to new price
−10	134.6722	136.1078	136.1193	+1.066	+1.07	estimated price close to new price
+200	134.6722	105.9601	109.8964	−21.320	−18.40	underestimates new price
−200	134.6722	163.3843	168.3887	+21.320	+25.04	underestimates new price

Should any of this be a surprise to you? No, not after reading Section 3 of this reading and evaluating equation (68-2) in terms of the properties for the price/yield relationship discussed in that section. Look again at equation (68-2). Notice that whether the change in yield is an increase or a decrease, the approximate percentage price change will be the same except that the sign is reversed. This violates Property 3 and Property 4 with respect to the price volatility of option-free bonds when yields change. Recall that Property 3 states that the percentage price change will not be the same for a large increase and decrease in yield by the same number of basis points. Property 4 states the percentage price increase is greater than the percentage price decrease. These are two reasons why the estimate is inaccurate for a 200 basis point yield change.

Why did the duration estimate of the price change do a good job for a small change in yield of 10 basis points? Recall from Property 2 that the percentage price change will be approximately the same whether there is an increase or decrease in yield by a small number of basis points. We can also explain these results in terms of the graph of the price/yield relationship.

Practice Question 2

Using the duration for the 6% coupon 20-year bond found in part B of Practice Question 1, answer the following questions.

1. What is the approximate percentage price change if interest rates increase by 10 basis points?

2. Comment on the approximation compared to the actual price change as given in Exhibit 68-6.

3. What is the approximate percentage price change if interest rates decrease by 10 basis points?

4. Comment on the approximation compared to the actual price change as given in Exhibit 68-6.

5. What is the approximate percentage price change if interest rates increase by 200 basis points?

6. Comment on the approximation compared to the actual price change as given in Exhibit 68-6.

7. What is the approximate percentage price change if interest rates decrease by 200 basis points?

8. Comment on the approximation compared to the actual price change as given in Exhibit 68-6.

4.3 Graphical Depiction of Using Duration to Estimate Price Changes

In Section 3, we used the graph of the price/yield relationship to demonstrate the price volatility properties of bonds. We can also use graphs to illustrate what we observed in our examples about how duration estimates the percentage price change, as well as some other noteworthy points.

The shape of the price/yield relationship for an option-free bond is convex. Exhibit 68-14 shows this relationship. In the exhibit, a tangent line is drawn to the price/yield relationship at yield y^*. (For those unfamiliar with the concept of a tangent line, it is a straight line that just touches a curve at one point within a relevant (local) range. In Exhibit 68-14, the tangent line touches the curve at the point where the yield is equal to y^* and the price is equal to p^*.) The

EXHIBIT 68-14 Price/Yield Relationship for an Option-Free Bond with a Tangent Line

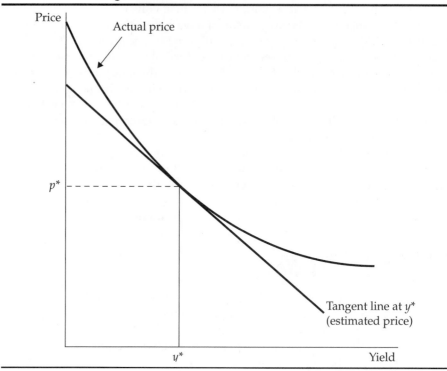

tangent line is used to *estimate* the new price if the yield changes. If we draw a vertical line from any yield (on the horizontal axis), as in Exhibit 68-14, the distance between the horizontal axis and the tangent line represents the price approximated by using duration starting with the initial yield y^*.

Now how is the tangent line related to duration? Given an initial price and a specific yield change, the tangent line tells us the approximate new price of a bond. The approximate percentage price change can then be computed for this change in yield. But this is precisely what duration [using equation (68-2)] gives us: the approximate percentage price change for a given change in yield. Thus, using the tangent line, one obtains the same approximate percentage price change as using equation (68-2).

This helps us understand why duration did an effective job of estimating the percentage price change, or equivalently the new price, when the yield changes by a small number of basis points. Look at Exhibit 68-15. Notice that for a small change in yield, the tangent line does not depart much from the price/yield relationship. Hence, when the yield changes up or down by 10 basis points, the tangent line does a good job of estimating the new price, as we found in our earlier numerical illustration.

Exhibit 68-15 shows what happens to the estimate using the tangent line when the yield changes by a large number of basis points. Notice that the error in the estimate gets larger the further one moves from the initial yield. The estimate is less accurate the more convex the bond as illustrated in Exhibit 68-16.

Also note that, regardless of the magnitude of the yield change, the tangent line always underestimates what the new price will be for an option-free bond because the tangent line is below the price/yield relationship. This explains why we found in our illustration that when using duration, we underestimated what the actual price will be.

EXHIBIT 68-15 Estimating The New Price Using A Tangent Line

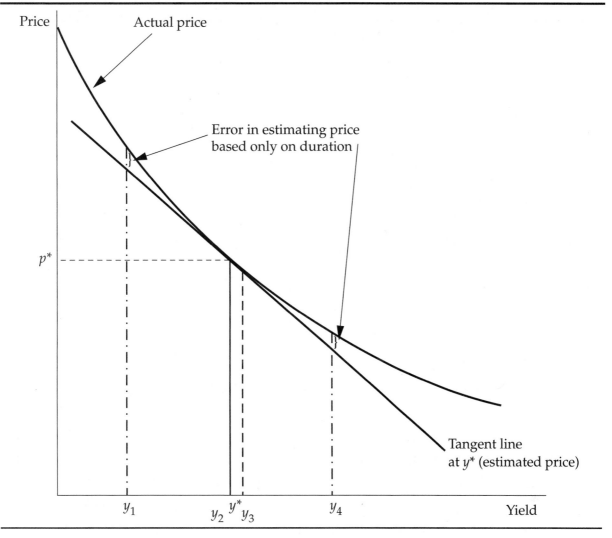

The results reported in Exhibit 68-17 are for option-free bonds. When we deal with more complicated securities, small rate shocks that do not reflect the types of rate changes that may occur in the market do not permit the determination of how prices can change. This is because expected cash flows may change when dealing with bonds with embedded options. In comparison, if large rate shocks are used, we encounter the asymmetry caused by convexity. Moreover, large rate shocks may cause dramatic changes in the expected cash flows for bonds with embedded options that may be far different from how the expected cash flows will change for smaller rate shocks.

There is another potential problem with using small rate shocks for complicated securities. The prices that are inserted into the duration formula as given by equation (68-1) are derived from a valuation model. The duration measure depends crucially on the valuation model. If the rate shock is small and the valuation model used to obtain the prices for equation (68-1) is poor, dividing poor price estimates by a small shock in rates (in the denominator) will have a significant effect on the duration estimate.

EXHIBIT 68-16 Estimating the New Price for a Large Yield Change for Bonds with Different Convexities

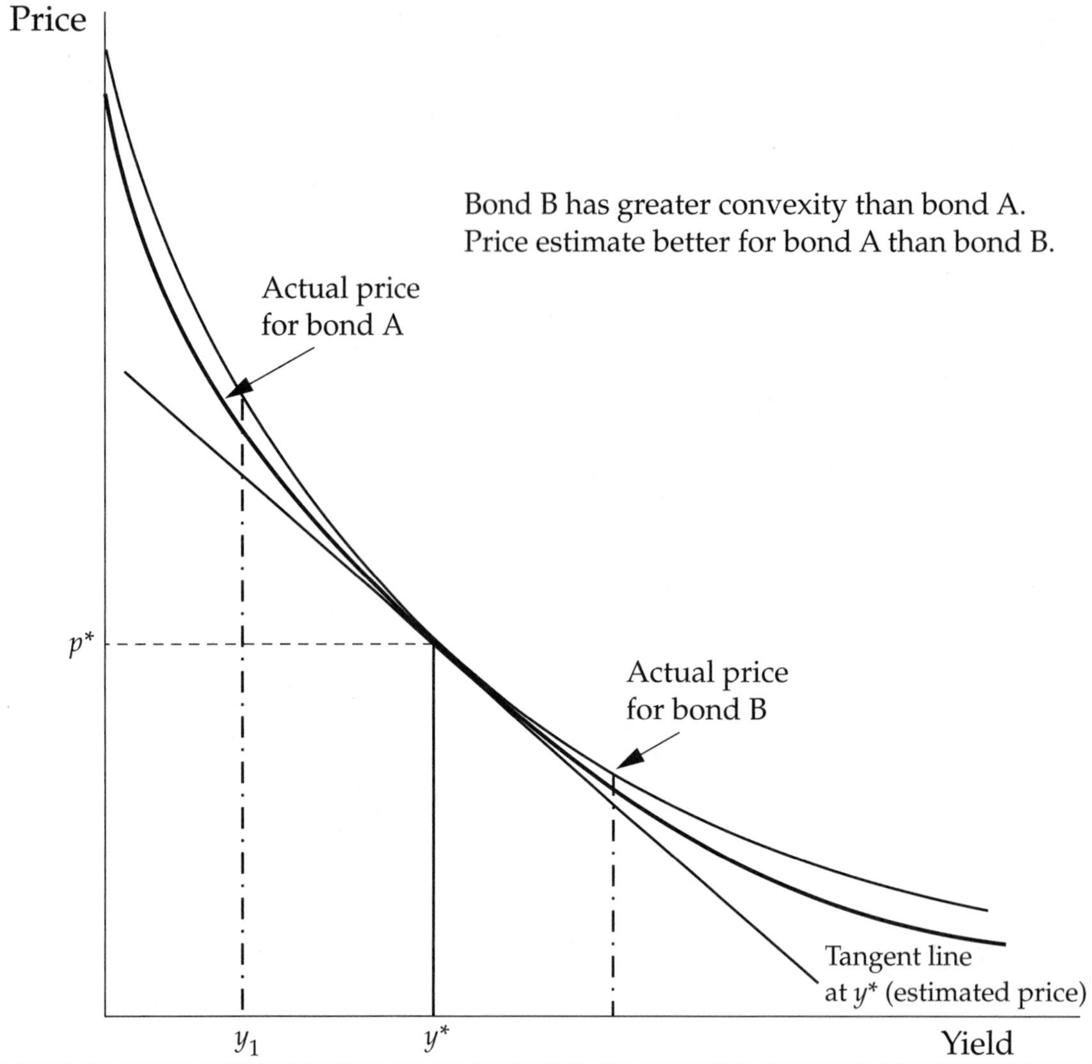

Price

Bond B has greater convexity than bond A.
Price estimate better for bond A than bond B.

Actual price
for bond A

Actual price
for bond B

Tangent line
at y^* (estimated price)

p^*

y_1 y^*

Yield

4.4 Rate Shocks and Duration Estimate

In calculating duration using equation (68-1), it is necessary to shock interest rates (yields) up and down by the same number of basis points to obtain the values for V_- and V_+. In our illustration, 20 basis points was arbitrarily selected. But how large should the shock be? That is, how many basis points should be used to shock the rate?

In Exhibit 68-17, the duration estimates for our four hypothetical bonds using equation (68-1) for rate shocks of 1 basis point to 200 basis points are reported. The duration estimates for the two 5-year bonds are not affected by the size of the shock. The two 5-year bonds are less convex than the two 20-year bonds. But even for the two 20-year bonds, for the size of the shocks reported in Exhibit 68-17, the duration estimates are not materially affected by the greater convexity.

What is done in practice by dealers and vendors of analytical systems? Each system developer uses rate shocks that they have found to be realistic based on historical rate changes.

EXHIBIT 68-17 Duration Estimates for Different Rate Shocks

Assumption: Initial yield is 6%

Bond	1 bp	10 bps	20 bps	50 bps	100 bps	150 bps	200 bps
6% 5 year	4.27	4.27	4.27	4.27	4.27	4.27	4.27
6% 20 year	11.56	11.56	11.56	11.57	11.61	11.69	11.79
9% 5 year	4.07	4.07	4.07	4.07	4.07	4.08	4.08
9% 20 year	10.66	10.66	10.66	10.67	10.71	10.77	10.86

EXHIBIT 68-18 Modified Duration versus Effective Duration

Duration
Interpretation: Generic description of the sensitivity of a bond's price (as a percentage of initial price) to a change in yield

Modified Duration
Duration measure in which it is assumed that yield changes do not change the expected cash flows

Effective Duration
Duration measure in which recognition is given to the fact that yield changes may change the expected cash flows

4.5 Modified Duration versus Effective Duration

One form of duration that is cited by practitioners is **modified duration.** Modified duration is the approximate percentage change in a bond's price for a 100 basis point change in yield *assuming that the bond's expected cash flows do not change when the yield changes.* What this means is that in calculating the values of V_- and V_+ in equation (68-1), the same cash flows used to calculate V_0 are used. Therefore, the change in the bond's price when the yield is changed is due solely to discounting cash flows at the new yield level.

The assumption that the cash flows will not change when the yield is changed makes sense for option-free bonds such as noncallable Treasury securities. This is because the payments made by the U.S. Department of the Treasury to holders of its obligations do not change when interest rates change. However, the same cannot be said for bonds with embedded options (i.e., callable and putable bonds and mortgage-backed securities). For these securities, a change in yield may significantly alter the expected cash flows.

In Section 3, we showed the price/yield relationship for callable and pre-payable bonds. Failure to recognize how changes in yield can alter the expected cash flows will produce two values used in the numerator of equation (68-1) that are not good estimates of how the price will actually change. The duration is then not a good number to use to estimate how the price will change.

Some valuation models for bonds with embedded options take into account how changes in yield will affect the expected cash flows. Thus, when V_- and V_+ are the values produced from these valuation models, the resulting duration takes into account both the discounting at different interest rates and how the expected cash flows may change. When duration is calculated in this manner, it is referred to as **effective duration** or **option-adjusted duration.** (Lehman Brothers refers to this measure in some of its publications as **adjusted duration.**) Exhibit 68-18 summarizes the distinction between modified duration and effective duration.

The difference between modified duration and effective duration for bonds with embedded options can be quite dramatic. For example, a callable bond could have a modified duration of 5 but an effective duration of only 3. For certain collateralized mortgage obligations, the modified duration could be 7 and the effective duration 20! Thus, using modified duration as a measure of the price sensitivity for a security with embedded options to changes in yield would be misleading. Effective duration is the more appropriate measure for any bond with an embedded option.

4.6 Macaulay Duration and Modified Duration

It is worth comparing the relationship between modified duration to the another duration measure, **Macaulay duration.** Modified duration can be written as:[6]

$$\frac{1}{(1 + \text{yield}/k)} \left[\frac{1 \times \text{PVCF}_1 + 2 \times \text{PVCF}_2 + ... + n \times \text{PVCF}_n}{k \times \text{Price}} \right] \qquad \textbf{(68-3)}$$

where

k	= number of periods, or payments, per year (e.g., $k = 2$ for semiannual-pay bonds and $k = 12$ for monthly-pay bonds)
n	= number of periods until maturity (i.e., number of years to maturity times k)
yield	= yield to maturity of the bond
PVCF_t	= present value of the cash flow in period t discounted at the yield to maturity where $t = 1, 2, ..., n$

We know that duration tells us the approximate percentage price change for a bond if the yield changes.

The expression in the brackets of the modified duration formula given by equation (68-3) is a measure formulated in 1938 by Frederick Macaulay.[7] This measure is popularly referred to as Macaulay duration. Thus, modified duration is commonly expressed as:

$$\text{Modified duration} = \frac{\text{Macaulay duration}}{(1 + \text{yield}/k)}$$

The general formulation for duration as given by equation (68-1) provides a short-cut procedure for determining a bond's modified duration. Because it is easier to calculate the modified duration using the short-cut procedure, most vendors of analytical software will use equation (68-1) rather than equation (68-3) to reduce computation time.

However, *modified duration is a flawed measure of a bond's price sensitivity to interest rate changes for a bond with embedded options and therefore so is Macaulay duration.* The duration formula given by equation (68-3) misleads the user because it masks the fact that changes in the expected cash flows must be recognized for bonds with embedded options. Although equation (68-3) will give the same estimate of percent price change for an option-free bond as equation (68-1), equation (68-1) is still better because it acknowledges cash flows and thus value can change due to yield changes.

---

[6] More specifically, this is the formula for the modified duration of a bond on a coupon anniversary date.

[7] Frederick Macaulay, *Some Theoretical Problems Suggested by the Movement of Interest Rates, Bond Yields, and Stock Prices in the U.S. Since 1856* (New York: National Bureau of Economic Research, 1938).

4.7 Interpretations of Duration

Throughout this book, the definition provided for duration is: the approximate percentage price change for a 100 basis point change in rates. That definition is the most relevant for how a manager or investor uses duration. In fact, if you understand this definition, you can easily calculate the change in a bond's value.

For example, suppose we want to know the approximate percentage change in price for a 50 basis point change in yield for our hypothetical 9% coupon 20-year bond selling for 134.6722. Since the duration is 10.66, a 100 basis point change in yield would change the price by about 10.66%. For a 50 basis point change in yield, the price will change by approximately 5.33% (= 10.66%/2). So, if the yield increases by 50 basis points, the price will decrease by about 5.33% from 134.6722 to 127.4942.

Now let's look at some other duration definitions or interpretations that appear in publications and are cited by managers in discussions with their clients.

4.7.1 Duration Is the "First Derivative"

Sometimes a market participant will refer to duration as the "first derivative of the price/yield function" or simply the "first derivative." Wow! Sounds impressive. First, "derivative" here has nothing to do with "derivative instruments" (i.e., futures, swaps, options, etc.). A derivative as used in this context is obtained by differentiating a mathematical function using calculus. There are first derivatives, second derivatives, and so on. When market participants say that duration is the first derivative, here is what they mean. The first derivative calculates the slope of a line—in this case, the slope of the tangent line in Exhibit 68-14. If it were possible to write a mathematical equation for a bond in closed form, the first derivative would be the result of differentiating that equation the first time. Even if you don't know how to do the process of differentiation to get the first derivative, it sounds like you are really smart since it suggests you understand calculus! While it is a correct interpretation of duration, it is an interpretation that in no way helps us understand what the interest rate risk is of a bond. That is, it is an operationally meaningless interpretation.

Why is it an operationally meaningless interpretation? Go back to the $10 million bond position with a duration of 6. Suppose a client is concerned with the exposure of the bond to changes in interest rates. Now, tell that client the duration is 6 and that it is the first derivative of the price function for that bond. What have you told the client? Not much. In contrast, tell that client that the duration is 6 and that duration is the approximate price sensitivity of a bond to a 100 basis point change in rates and you have told the client more relevant information with respect to the bond's interest rate risk.

4.7.2 Duration Is Some Measure of Time

When the concept of duration was originally introduced by Macaulay in 1938, he used it as a gauge of the time that the bond was outstanding. More specifically, Macaulay defined duration as the weighted average of the time to each coupon and principal payment of a bond. Subsequently, duration has too often been thought of in temporal terms, i.e., years. This is most unfortunate for two reasons.

First, in terms of dimensions, there is nothing wrong with expressing duration in terms of years because that is the proper dimension of this value. But the proper interpretation is that duration is the price volatility of a zero-coupon bond with that number of years to maturity. So, when a manager says a bond has a duration of 4 years, it is not useful to think of this measure in terms of time, but that the bond has the price sensitivity to rate changes of a 4-year zero-coupon bond.

Second, thinking of duration in terms of years makes it difficult for managers and their clients to understand the duration of some complex securities. Here are a few examples. For a mortgage-backed security that is an interest-only security (i.e., receives coupons but not principal repayment) discussed at Level II, the duration is negative. What does a negative number, say, -4 mean? In terms of our interpretation as a percentage price change, it means that when rates change by 100 basis points, the price of the bond changes by about 4% but the change is in the same direction as the change in rates.

As a second example, consider an inverse floater created in the collateralized mortgage obligation (CMO) market. The underlying collateral for such a security might be loans with 25 years to final maturity. However, an inverse floater can have a duration that easily exceeds 25. This does not make sense to a manager or client who uses a measure of time as a definition for duration.

As a final example, consider derivative instruments, such as an option that expires in one year. Suppose that it is reported that its duration is 60. What does that mean? To someone who interprets duration in terms of time, does that mean 60 years, 60 days, 60 seconds? It doesn't mean any of these. It simply means that the option tends to have the price sensitivity to rate changes of a 60-year zero-coupon bond.

4.7.3 Forget First Derivatives and Temporal Definitions

The bottom line is that one should not care if it is technically correct to think of duration in terms of years (volatility of a zero-coupon bond) or in terms of first derivatives. There are even some who interpret duration in terms of the "half life" of a security.[8] Subject to the limitations that we will describe as we proceed in this book, duration is the measure of a security's price sensitivity to changes in yield. We will fine tune this definition as we move along.

Users of this interest rate risk measure are interested in what it tells them about the price sensitivity of a bond (or a portfolio) to changes in interest rates. Duration provides the investor with a feel for the dollar price exposure or the percentage price exposure to potential interest rate changes. Try the following definitions on a client who has a portfolio with a duration of 4 and see which one the client finds most useful for understanding the interest rate risk of the portfolio when rates change:

> *Definition 1:* The duration of 4 for your portfolio indicates that the portfolio's value will change by approximately 4% if rates change by 100 basis points.
> *Definition 2:* The duration of 4 for your portfolio is the first derivative of the price function for the bonds in the portfolio.
> *Definition 3:* The duration of 4 for your portfolio is the weighted average number of years to receive the present value of the portfolio's cash flows.

Definition 1 is clearly preferable. It would be ridiculous to expect clients to understand the last two definitions better than the first.

Moreover, interpreting duration in terms of a measure of price sensitivity to interest rate changes allows a manager to make comparisons between bonds regarding their interest rate risk under certain assumptions.

4.8 Portfolio Duration

A portfolio's duration can be obtained by calculating the weighted average of the duration of the bonds in the portfolio. The weight is the proportion of the

---

[8] "Half-life" is the time required for an element to be reduced to half its initial value.

portfolio that a security comprises. Mathematically, a portfolio's duration can be calculated as follows:

$$w_1D_1 + w_2D_2 + w_3D_3 + \dots w_KD_K$$

where

w_i = market value of bond i/market value of the portfolio
D_i = duration of bond i
K = number of bonds in the portfolio

To illustrate this calculation, consider the following 3-bond portfolio in which all three bonds are option free:

Bond	Price ($)	Yield (%)	Par amount owned	Market value	Duration
10% 5-year	100.0000	10	$4 million	$4,000,000	3.861
8% 15-year	84.6275	10	5 million	4,231,375	8.047
14% 30-year	137.8586	10	1 million	1,378,586	9.168

In this illustration, it is assumed that the next coupon payment for each bond is exactly six months from now (i.e., there is no accrued interest). The market value for the portfolio is $9,609,961. Since each bond is option free, modified duration can be used. The market price per $100 par value of each bond, its yield, and its duration are given below:

In this illustration, K is equal to 3 and:

w_1 = $4,000,000/$9,609,961 = 0.416 D_1 = 3.861
w_2 = $4,231,375/$9,609,961 = 0.440 D_2 = 8.047
w_3 = $1,378,586/$9,609,961 = 0.144 D_3 = 9.168

The portfolio's duration is:

0.416 (3.861) + 0.440 (8.047) + 0.144 (9.168) = 6.47

A portfolio duration of 6.47 means that for a 100 basis point change in the yield for each of the three bonds, the market value of the portfolio will change by approximately 6.47%. But keep in mind, the yield for each of the three bonds must change by 100 basis points for the duration measure to be useful. (In other words, there must be a parallel shift in the yield curve.) This is a *critical assumption* and its importance cannot be overemphasized.

An alternative procedure for calculating the duration of a portfolio is to calculate the dollar price change for a given number of basis points for each security in the portfolio and then add up all the price changes. Dividing the total of the price changes by the initial market value of the portfolio produces a percentage price change that can be adjusted to obtain the portfolio's duration.

For example, consider the 3-bond portfolio shown above. Suppose that we calculate the dollar price change for each bond in the portfolio based on its respective duration for a 50 basis point change in yield. We would then have:

Bond	Market value	Duration	Change in value for 50 bp yield change
10% 5-year	$4,000,000	3.861	$77,220
8% 15-year	4,231,375	8.047	170,249
14% 30-year	1,378,586	9.168	63,194
		Total	$310,663

Thus, a 50 basis point change in all rates changes the market value of the 3-bond portfolio by $310,663. Since the market value of the portfolio is $9,609,961, a 50 basis point change produced a change in value of 3.23% ($310,663 divided by $9,609,961). Since duration is the approximate percentage change for a 100 basis point change in rates, this means that the portfolio duration is 6.46 (found by doubling 3.23). This is essentially the same value for the portfolio's duration as found earlier.

5　CONVEXITY ADJUSTMENT

The duration measure indicates that regardless of whether interest rates increase or decrease, the approximate percentage price change is the same. However, as we noted earlier, this is not consistent with Property 3 of a bond's price volatility. Specifically, while for small changes in yield the percentage price change will be the same for an increase or decrease in yield, for large changes in yield this is not true. This suggests that duration is only a good approximation of the percentage price change for small changes in yield.

We demonstrated this property earlier using a 9% 20-year bond selling to yield 6% with a duration of 10.66. For a 10 basis point change in yield, the estimate was accurate for both an increase or decrease in yield. However, for a 200 basis point change in yield, the approximate percentage price change was off *considerably*.

The reason for this result is that duration is in fact a first (linear) approximation for a small change in yield.[9] The approximation can be improved by using a second approximation. This approximation is referred to as the "convexity adjustment." It is used to approximate the change in price that is not explained by duration.

The formula for the convexity adjustment to the percentage price change is

Convexity adjustment to the percentage price change =
$$C \times (\Delta y*)^2 \times 100 \qquad \text{(68-4)}$$

where $\Delta y* =$ the change in yield for which the percentage price change is sought and

$$C = \frac{V_+ + V_- - 2V_0}{2V_0(\Delta y)^2} \qquad \text{(68-5)}$$

The notation is the same as used in equation (68-1) for duration.[10]

---

[9] The reason it is a linear approximation can be seen in Exhibit 68-15 where the tangent line is used to estimate the new price. That is, a straight line is being used to approximate a non-linear (i.e., convex) relationship.

[10] See **footnote 5** for the difference between Δy in the formula for C and $\Delta y*$ in equation (68-4).

For example, for our hypothetical 9% 20-year bond selling to yield 6%, we know from Section 4.1 that for a 20 basis point change in yield ($\Delta y = 0.002$):

$$V_0 = 134.6722, \quad V_- = 137.5888, \text{ and } V_+ = 131.8439$$

Substituting these values into the formula for C:

$$C = \frac{131.8439 + 137.5888 - 2(134.6722)}{2(134.6722)(0.002)^2} = 81.95$$

Suppose that a convexity adjustment is sought for the approximate percentage price change for our hypothetical 9% 20-year bond for a change in yield of 200 basis points. That is, in equation (68-4), Δy_* is 0.02. Then the convexity adjustment is

$$81.95 \times (0.02)^2 \times 100 = 3.28\%$$

If the yield decreases from 6% to 4%, the convexity adjustment to the percentage price change based on duration would also be 3.28%.

The approximate percentage price change based on duration and the convexity adjustment is found by adding the two estimates. So, for example, if yields change from 6% to 8%, the estimated percentage price change would be:

Estimated change using duration	=	−21.32%
Convexity adjustment	=	+3.28%
Total estimated percentage price change	=	−18.04%

The actual percentage price change is −18.40%.

For a decrease of 200 basis points, from 6% to 4%, the approximate percentage price change would be as follows:

Estimated change using duration	=	−21.32%
Convexity adjustment	=	+3.28%
Total estimated percentage price change	=	+24.60%

The actual percentage price change is +125.04%. Thus, duration *combined* with the convexity adjustment does a better job of estimating the sensitivity of a bond's price change to large changes in yield (i.e., better than using duration alone).

5.1 Positive and Negative Convexity Adjustment

Notice that when the convexity adjustment is positive, we have the situation described earlier that the gain is greater than the loss for a given large change in rates. That is, the bond exhibits positive convexity. We can see this in the example above. However, if the convexity adjustment is negative, we have the situation where the loss will be greater than the gain. For example, suppose that a callable bond has an effective duration of 4 and a convexity adjustment for a 200 basis point change of −1.2%.

The bond then exhibits the negative convexity property illustrated in Exhibit 68-11. The approximate percentage price change after adjusting for convexity is:

Estimated change using duration	=	−8.0%
Convexity adjustment	=	−1.2%
Total estimated percentage price change	=	−9.2%

For a decrease of 200 basis points, the approximate percentage price change would be as follows:

Estimated change using duration	=	+8.0%
Convexity adjustment	=	−1.2%
Total estimated percentage price change	=	+6.8%

Notice that the loss is greater than the gain—a property called negative convexity that we discussed in Section 3 and illustrated in Exhibit 68-11.

Practice Question 3

A. What is the value for C in equation (68-4) for a 6% 20-year option-free bond selling at par to yield 6% using an interest rate shock of 10 basis points (i.e., $\Delta y_* = 0.001$)? (The relevant values can be found in Exhibit 68-4.)

B. Using the convexity adjustment for the 6% coupon 20-year option-free bond selling at 100 to yield 6% found in part A, complete the following:

i. For a 10 basis point increase in interest rates (i.e., $\Delta y_* = 0.001$):

Estimated change using duration   = _____ %
Convexity adjustment   = _____ %
Total estimated percentage price change = _____ %

Actual percentage price change*   = _____ %

ii. For a 10 basis point decrease in interest rates (i.e., $\Delta y_* = -0.001$):

Estimated change using duration   = _____ %
Convexity adjustment   = _____ %
Total estimated percentage price change = _____ %

Actual percentage price change*   = _____ %

iii. For a 200 basis point decrease in interest rates (i.e., $\Delta y_* = 0.02$):

Estimated change using duration   = _____ %
Convexity adjustment   = _____ %
Total estimated percentage price change = _____ %

Actual percentage price change*   = _____ %

iv. For a 200 basis point decrease in interest rates (i.e., $\Delta y_* = -0.02$)

Estimated change using duration   = _____ %
Convexity adjustment   = _____ %
Total estimated percentage price change = _____ %

Actual percentage price change*   = _____ %

* See Exhibit 68-6.

5.2 Modified and Effective Convexity Adjustment

The prices used in computing C in equation (68-4) to calculate the convexity adjustment can be obtained by assuming that, when the yield changes, the expected cash flows either do not change or they do change. In the former case, the resulting convexity is referred to as **modified convexity adjustment.** (Actually, in the industry, convexity adjustment is not qualified by the adjective "modified.") In contrast, **effective convexity adjustment** assumes that the cash flows change when yields change. This is the same distinction made for duration.

As with duration, there is little difference between a modified convexity adjustment and an effective convexity adjustment for option-free bonds. However, for bonds with embedded options, there can be quite a difference between the calculated modified convexity adjustment and an effective convexity adjustment. In fact, for all option-free bonds, either convexity adjustment will have a positive value. For bonds with embedded options, the calculated effective convexity adjustment can be negative when the calculated modified convexity adjustment is positive.

PRICE VALUE OF A BASIS POINT 6

Some managers use another measure of the price volatility of a bond to quantify interest rate risk—the **price value of a basis point** (PVBP). This measure, also called the **dollar value of an 01** (DV01), is the absolute value of the change in the price of a bond for a 1 basis point change in yield. That is,

PVBP = | initial price − price if yield is changed by 1 basis point |

Does it make a difference if the yield is increased or decreased by 1 basis point? It does not because of Property 2—the change will be about the same for a small change in basis points.

To illustrate the computation, let's use the values in Exhibit 68-4. If the initial yield is 6%, we can compute the PVBP by using the prices for either the yield at 5.99% or 6.01%. The PVBP for both for each bond is shown below:

Coupon	6.0%	6.0%	9.0%	9.0%
Maturity	5	20	5	20
Initial price	$100.0000	$100.0000	$112.7953	$134.6722
Price at 5.99%	100.0427	100.1157	112.8412	134.8159
PVBP at 5.99%	$0.0427	$0.1157	$0.0459	$0.1437
Price at 6.01%	99.9574	99.8845	112.7494	134.5287
PVBP at 6.01%	$0.0426	$0.1155	$0.0459	$0.1435

The PVBP is related to duration. In fact, PVBP is simply a special case of dollar duration described in Reading 63. We know that the duration of a bond is the approximate percentage price change for a 100 basis point change in interest rates. We also know how to compute the approximate percentage price change for any number of basis points given a bond's duration using equation (68-2). Given the initial price and the approximate percentage price change for 1 basis point, we can compute the change in price for a 1 basis point change in rates.

For example, consider the 9% 20-year bond. The duration for this bond is 10.66. Using equation (68-2), the approximate percentage price change for a 1 basis point increase in interest rates (i.e., $\Delta y = 0.0001$), ignoring the negative sign in equation (68-2), is:

$$10.66 \times (0.0001) \times 100 = 0.1066\%$$

Given the initial price of 134.6722, the dollar price change estimated using duration is

$$0.1066\% \times 134.6722 = \$0.1435$$

This is the same price change as shown above for a PVBP for this bond. Below is (1) the PVBP based on a 1 basis point increase for each bond and (2) the estimated price change using duration for a 1 basis point increase for each bond:

Coupon	6.0%	6.0%	9.0%	9.0%
Maturity	5	20	5	20
PVBP for 1 bp increase	$0.0426	$0.1155	$0.0459	$0.1435
Duration of bond	4.2700	11.5600	4.0700	10.6600
Duration estimate	$0.0427	$0.1156	$0.0459	$0.1436

7   THE IMPORTANCE OF YIELD VOLATILITY

What we have not considered thus far is the volatility of interest rates. For example, as we explained in Reading 63, all other factors equal, the higher the coupon rate, the lower the price volatility of a bond to changes in interest rates. In addition, the higher the level of yields, the lower the price volatility of a bond to changes in interest rates. This is illustrated in Exhibit 68-19 which shows the price/yield relationship for an option-free bond. When the yield level is high (Y_H, for example, in the exhibit), a change in interest rates does not produce a large change in the initial price. For example, as yields change from Y_H to Y_H'', the price changes a *small* amount from P_H to P_H''. However, when the yield level is low and changes (Y_L to Y_L', for example, in the exhibit), a change in interest rates of the same number of basis points as Y_H to Y_H'' produces a *large* change in the initial price (P_L to P_L').

This can also be cast in terms of duration properties: the higher the coupon, the lower the duration; the higher the yield level, the lower the duration. Given these two properties, a 10-year non-investment grade bond has a lower duration than a current coupon 10-year Treasury note since the former has a higher coupon rate and trades at a higher yield level. Does this mean that a 10-year non-investment grade bond has less interest rate risk than a current coupon 10-year Treasury note? Consider also that a 10-year Swiss government bond has a lower coupon rate than a current coupon 10-year U.S. Treasury note and trades at a lower yield level. Therefore, a 10-year Swiss government bond will have a higher duration than a current coupon 10-year Treasury note. Does this mean that a 10-year Swiss government bond has greater interest rate risk than a current coupon 10-year U.S. Treasury note? The missing link is the relative volatility of rates, which we shall refer to as **yield volatility** or **interest rate volatility**.

EXHIBIT 68-19 The Effect of Yield Level on Price Volatility— Option-Free Bond

$$(Y_H' - Y_H) = (Y_H - Y_H'') = (Y_L' - Y_L) = (Y_L - Y_L'')$$
$$(P_H - P_H') < (P_L - P_L') \text{ and}$$
$$(P_H - P_H'') < (P_L - P_L'')$$

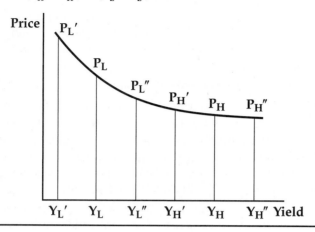

The greater the expected yield volatility, the greater the interest rate risk for a given duration and current value of a position. In the case of non-investment grade bonds, while their durations are less than current coupon Treasuries of the same maturity, the yield volatility of non-investment grade bonds is greater than that of current coupon Treasuries. For the 10-year Swiss government bond, while the duration is greater than for a current coupon 10-year U.S. Treasury note, the yield volatility of 10-year Swiss bonds is considerably less than that of 10-year U.S. Treasury notes.

Consequently, to measure the exposure of a portfolio or position to interest rate changes, it is necessary to measure yield volatility. This requires an understanding of the fundamental principles of probability distributions. The measure of yield volatility is the standard deviation of yield changes. As we will see, depending on the underlying assumptions, there could be a wide range for the yield volatility estimates.

A framework that ties together the price sensitivity of a bond position to interest rate changes and yield volatility is the **value-at-risk (VaR) framework.** Risk in this framework is defined as the maximum estimated loss in market value of a given position that is expected to occur with a specified probability.

8   SUMMARY

▷ To control interest rate risk, a manager must be able to quantify what will occur from an adverse change in interest rates.

▷ A valuation model is used to determine the value of a position after an interest rate movement and therefore, if a reliable valuation model is not used, there is no way to measure interest rate risk exposure.

▷ There are two approaches to measure interest rate risk: full valuation approach and duration/convexity approach.

▷ The full valuation approach involves revaluing a bond position (every position in the case of a portfolio) for a scenario of interest rate changes.

▷ The advantage of the full valuation approach is its accuracy with respect to interest rate exposure for a given interest rate change scenario—accurate relative to the valuation model used—but its disadvantage for a large portfolio is having to revalue each bond for each scenario.

▷ The characteristics of a bond that affect its price volatility are (1) maturity, (2) coupon rate, and (3) presence of any embedded options.

▷ The shape of the price/yield relationship for an option-free bond is convex.

▷ The price sensitivity of a bond to changes in the required yield can be measured in terms of the dollar price change or percentage price change.

▷ One property of an option-free bond is that although its price moves in the opposite direction of a change in yield, the percentage price change is not the same for all bonds.

▷ A second property of an option-free bond is that for small changes in the required yield, the percentage price change for a given bond is roughly the same whether the yield increases or decreases.

▷ A third property of an option-free bond is that for a large change in yield, the percentage price change for an increase in yield is not the same for a decrease in yield.

▷ A fourth property of an option-free bond is that for a large change in yield, the price of an option-free bond increases more than it decreases.

▷ "Negative convexity" means that for a large change in interest rates, the amount of the price appreciation is less than the amount of the price depreciation.

▷ Option-free bonds exhibit positive convexity.

▷ "Positive convexity" means that for a large change in interest rates, the amount of the price appreciation is greater than the amount of the price depreciation.

▷ A callable bond exhibits positive convexity at high yield levels and negative convexity at low yield levels where "high" and "low" yield levels are relative to the issue's coupon rate.

▷ At low yield levels (low relative to the issue's coupon rate), the price of a putable bond is basically the same as the price of an option-free bond because the value of the put option is small; as rates rise, the price of a putable bond declines, but the price decline is less than that for an option-free bond.

▷ Duration is a first approximation of a bond's price or a portfolio's value to interest rate changes.

▷ To improve the estimate provided by duration, a convexity adjustment can be used.

- Using duration combined with a convexity adjustment to estimate the percentage price change of a bond to changes in interest rates is called the duration/convexity approach to interest rate risk measurement.

- Duration does a good job of estimating the percentage price change for a small change in interest rates but the estimation becomes poorer the larger the change in interest rates.

- In calculating duration, it is necessary to shock interest rates (yields) up and down by the same number of basis points to obtain the values when rates change.

- In calculating duration for option-free bonds, the size of the interest rate shock is unimportant for reasonable changes in yield.

- For bonds with embedded options, the problem with using a small shock to estimate duration is that divergences between actual and estimated price changes are magnified by dividing by a small change in rate in the denominator of the duration formula; in addition, small rate shocks that do not reflect the types of rate changes that may occur in the market do not permit the determination of how prices can change because expected cash flows may change.

- For bonds with embedded options, if large rate shocks are used the asymmetry caused by convexity is encountered; in addition, large rate shocks may cause dramatic changes in the expected cash flows for bonds with embedded options that may be far different from how the expected cash flows will change for smaller rate shocks.

- Modified duration is the approximate percentage change in a bond's price for a 100 basis point change in yield assuming that the bond's expected cash flows do not change when the yield changes.

- In calculating the values to be used in the numerator of the duration formula, for modified duration the cash flows are not assumed to change and therefore, the change in the bond's price when the yield is changed is due solely to discounting at the new yield levels.

- Effective duration is the approximate percentage change in a bond's price for a 100 basis point change in yield assuming that the bond's expected cash flows do change when the yield changes.

- Modified duration is appropriate for option-free bonds; effective duration should be used for bonds with embedded options.

- The difference between modified duration and effective duration for bonds with an embedded option can be quite dramatic.

- Macaulay duration is mathematically related to modified duration and is therefore a flawed measure of the duration of a bond with an embedded option.

- Interpretations of duration in temporal terms (i.e., some measure of time) or calculus terms (i.e., first derivative of the price/yield relationship) are operationally meaningless and should be avoided.

- The duration for a portfolio is equal to the market-value weighted duration of each bond in the portfolio.

- In applying portfolio duration to estimate the sensitivity of a portfolio to changes in interest rates, it is assumed that the yield for all bonds in the portfolio change by the same amount.

- The duration measure indicates that regardless of whether interest rates increase or decrease, the approximate percentage price change is the same; however, this is not a property of a bond's price volatility for large changes in yield.

- ▶ A convexity adjustment can be used to improve the estimate of the percentage price change obtained using duration, particularly for a large change in yield.

- ▶ The convexity adjustment is the amount that should be added to the duration estimate for the percentage price change in order to obtain a better estimate for the percentage price change.

- ▶ The same distinction made between modified duration and effective duration applies to modified convexity adjustment and effective convexity adjustment.

- ▶ For a bond with an embedded option that exhibits negative convexity at some yield level, the convexity adjustment will be negative.

- ▶ The price value of a basis point (or dollar value of an 01) is the change in the price of a bond for a 1 basis point change in yield.

- ▶ The price value of a basis point is the same as the estimated dollar price change using duration for a 1 basis point change in yield.

- ▶ Yield volatility must be recognized in estimating the interest rate risk of a bond and a portfolio.

- ▶ Value-at-risk is a measure that ties together the duration of a bond and yield volatility.

PROBLEMS

1. Explain why you agree or disagree with the following statement:

> The disadvantage of the full valuation approach to measuring interest rate risk is that it requires a revaluation of each bond in the portfolio for each interest rate scenario. Consequently, you need a valuation model. In contrast, for the duration/convexity approach there is no need for a valuation model because the duration and convexity adjustment can be obtained without a valuation model.

2. Explain why you agree or disagree with the following statement:

> The problem with both the full valuation approach and the duration/convexity approach is that they fail to take into account how the change in the yield curve can affect a portfolio's value.

3. Explain why you agree or disagree with the following statement:

> If two bonds have the same duration, then the percentage change in price of the two bonds will be the same for a given change in interest rates.

4. James Smith and Donald Robertson are assistant portfolio managers for Micro Management Partners. In a review of the interest rate risk of a portfolio, Smith and Robertson discussed the riskiness of two Treasury securities. Following is the information about these two Treasuries:

Bond	Price	Modified duration
A	90	4
B	50	6

Smith noted that Treasury bond B has more price volatility because of its higher modified duration. Robertson disagreed noting that Treasury bond A has more price volatility despite its lower modified duration. Which manager is correct?

5. At its quarterly meeting, the trustees of the National Baggage Handlers Pension Fund reviewed the status of its bond portfolio. The portfolio is managed by William Renfro of Wiser and Wiser Management Company. The portfolio consists of 20% Treasury bonds, 10% corporate bonds that are noncallable for the life of the bonds, 30% callable corporate bonds, and 40% mortgage-backed securities. The report provided by Wiser and Wiser includes the following information for each bond in the portfolio: (1) modified duration and (2) effective duration. The portfolio's modified duration and effective duration were reported to be 5 and 3, respectively. Renfro attended the board meeting to answer any questions that the trustees might have. Nancy Weston, one of the trustees for the fund, prepared the following list of questions:

A. What does the duration of a bond mean and how should the board interpret the portfolio duration?

B. Why is the modified duration and effective duration for each Treasury bond and noncallable corporate bond the same?

C. What is the appropriate duration measure, effective duration or modified duration?

D. How were the effective duration measures obtained?

E. What are the limitations in using duration?

The minutes of the board meeting indicated the following response by Mr. Renfro to each of these questions:

A. Duration is a measure of the approximate weighted average life of a bond or a bond portfolio. For example, a portfolio duration of 5 means that the fund will realize the return of the amount invested (in present value terms) in about 5 years.

B. Because the Treasury bonds in the portfolio are noncallable, modified duration is the same as effective duration. The same is true for the corporate bonds that are noncallable for life.

C. The appropriate measure is the effective duration since it takes into account the option embedded in the bonds held in the portfolio.

D. We obtained the effective duration from various sources—dealers firms and commercial vendors. There is a standard formula that all of these sources use to obtain the effective duration. Sometimes, a source may provide an effective duration that is not logical and we override the value by using the modified duration. For example, for some of the collateralized mortgage obligations, one vendor reported an effective duration of 40. This value was obviously wrong since the underlying collateral is 30-year loans; therefore, the duration cannot exceed 30. Moreover, for some of the CMOs, the duration is negative and this is obviously wrong. Again, in such instances we use the modified duration.

E. Duration is only a good measure for small changes in yield and assumes that the yield curve will shift in a parallel fashion. However, if these assumptions are satisfied, two portfolios with the same duration will perform in exactly the same way.

You are employed by Pension Consultants, a consultant to the labor union. You have been given the minutes of the meeting of the board of trustees with the responses of Mr. Renfro to the questions of Ms. Weston. Prepare a report indicating whether you agree or disagree with Mr. Renfro's responses.

6. Lewis Marlo, an assistant portfolio manager, was reviewing a potential buy list of corporate bonds. The list provided information on the effective duration and effective convexity adjustment assuming a 200 basis point change in interest rates for each corporate bond on the list. The senior portfolio manager, Jane Zorick, noticed that Mr. Marlo crossed out each bond with a negative convexity adjustment. When Ms. Zorick asked Mr. Marlo why, he responded that a negative value meant that the particular corporate bond was unattractive. How do you think Ms. Zorick should respond?

7. A client is reviewing information about the portfolio. For one of the issues in the portfolio the client sees the following:

Issue	Maturity	Duration
X	10 years	13

The client has questioned you as to whether or not the reported duration of 13 is correct. The client's concern is that he has heard that duration is some measure of time for a bond and as such cannot exceed the maturity of the security. Yet, the duration of Issue X exceeds its maturity. What explanation do you give to the client?

8. Suppose that you are given the following information about two callable bonds of the same issuer that can be called immediately:

	Estimated percentage change in price if interest rates change by:	
	−50 basis points	+50 basis points
Bond ABC	+2%	−5%
Bond XYZ	+11%	−8%

You are told that both bonds have about the same maturity and the coupon rate of one bond is 7% and the other 13%. Suppose that the yield curve for this issuer is flat at 8%. Based on this information, which bond is the lower coupon bond and which is the higher coupon bond? Explain why.

9. **A.** Why is modified duration an inappropriate measure for a high-coupon callable bond?

   B. What would be a better measure than modified duration?

10. Suppose that a 7% coupon corporate bond is immediately callable. Also suppose that if this issuer issued new bonds the coupon rate would be 12%. Why would the modified duration be a good approximation of the effective duration for this bond?

Questions 11–15 are based on the following price information for four bonds and assuming that all four bonds are trading to yield 5%:

	Coupon	5.0%	5.0%	8.0%	8.0%
Yield	Maturity	4	25	4	25
3.00%		107.4859	134.9997	118.7148	187.4992
4.00%		103.6627	115.7118	114.6510	162.8472
4.50%		101.8118	107.4586	112.6826	152.2102
4.75%		100.9011	103.6355	111.7138	147.2621
4.90%		100.3593	101.4324	111.1374	144.4042
5.00%		100.0000	100.0000	110.7552	142.5435
5.10%		99.6423	98.5959	110.3746	140.7175
5.25%		99.1085	96.5416	109.8066	138.0421
5.50%		98.2264	93.2507	108.8679	133.7465
6.00%		96.4902	87.1351	107.0197	125.7298
7.00%		93.1260	76.5444	103.4370	111.7278

Percentage price change based on an initial yield of 5%

Yield	Coupon Maturity	5.0% 4	5.0% 25	8.0% 4	8.0% 25
3.00%		7.49%	35.00%	7.19%	31.54%
4.00%		3.66%	15.71%	3.52%	14.24%
4.50%		1.81%	7.46%	1.74%	6.78%
4.75%		0.90%	3.64%	0.87%	3.31%
4.90%		0.36%	1.43%	0.35%	1.31%
5.00%		0.00%	0.00%	0.00%	0.00%
5.10%		−0.36%	−1.40%	−0.34%	−1.28%
5.25%		−0.89%	−3.46%	−0.86%	−3.16%
5.50%		−1.77%	−6.75%	−1.70%	−6.17%
6.00%		−3.51%	−12.86%	−3.37%	−11.80%
7.00%		−6.87%	−23.46%	−6.61%	−21.62%

11. Assuming all four bonds are selling to yield 5%, compute the following for each bond:

   A. duration based on a 25 basis point rate shock ($\Delta y = 0.0025$)

   B. duration based on a 50 basis point rate shock ($\Delta y = 0.0050$)

12. Assuming all four bonds are selling to yield 5%, compute the value for C in the convexity equation for each bond using a 25 basis point rate shock ($\Delta y = 0.0025$).

13. A. Using the duration computed in question 11A, compute the approximate percentage price change using duration for the two 8% coupon bonds assuming that the yield changes by 10 basis points ($\Delta y_* = 0.0010$).

   B. How does the estimated percentage price change compare to the actual percentage price change?

14. A. Using the duration computed in question 11A, compute the approximate percentage price change using duration for the two 8% coupon bonds assuming that the yield changes by 200 basis points ($\Delta y_* = 0.02$).

   B. How does the estimated percentage price change compare to the actual percentage price change?

15. A. Using the value for C computed in question 12, compute the convexity adjustment for the two 25-year bonds assuming that the yield changes by 200 basis points ($\Delta y_* = 0.02$).

   B. Compute the estimated percentage price change using duration (as computed in question 11A) and convexity adjustment if yield changes by 200 basis points.

   C. How does the estimated percentage price change using duration and convexity adjustment compare to the actual percentage price change for a 200 basis point change in yield?

16. A. Given the information below for a 6.2% 18-year bond compute the price value of a basis point:

   price = 114.1338   yield = 5%   price if yield is 5.01% = 114.0051

   B. If the duration of the 6.2% 18-year bond is 11.28, what is the estimated price change for a 1 basis point change in yield.

17. Why is information about a bond's duration and convexity adjustment insufficient to quantify interest rate risk exposure?

ANALYSIS OF DERIVATIVE INVESTMENTS

The candidate should be able to demonstrate a working knowledge of the analysis of derivative investments, including forwards, futures, options, and swaps.

STUDY SESSION 16
DERIVATIVE INVESTMENTS

LEARNING OUTCOMES

Note:
Candidates are responsible for the problems at the end of the readings.

Reading 69: Derivative Markets and Instruments

The candidate should be able to define a derivative and

a. define a derivative and differentiate between exchange-traded and over-the-counter derivatives;

b. define a forward commitment, identify the types of forward commitments, and describe the basic characteristics of forward contracts, futures contracts, and swaps;

c. define a contingent claim and identify the types of contingent claims;

d. describe the basic characteristics of options, and distinguish between an option to buy (call) and an option to sell (put);

e. discuss the purposes and criticisms of derivative markets;

f. explain the concept of arbitrage and the role it plays in determining prices and in promoting market efficiency.

Reading 70: Forward Markets and Contracts

The candidate should be able to:

a. discuss the differences between the positions held by the long and short parties to a forward contract in terms of delivery/settlement and default risk;

b. describe the procedures for settling a forward contract at expiration and discuss how a party to a forward contract can terminate a position prior to expiration as well as how credit risk is affected by the way in which a position is terminated;

c. differentiate between a dealer and an end user of a forward contract;

261

d. describe the characteristics of equity forward contracts;

e. describe the characteristics of forward contracts on zero-coupon and coupon bonds;

f. explain the characteristics of the Eurodollar time deposit market, define LIBOR and Euribor, and describe the characteristics of forward rate agreements (FRAs);

g. calculate and interpret the payment at expiration of an FRA, explain each of the component terms, and describe the characteristics of currency forward contracts.

Reading 71: Futures Markets and Contracts

The candidate should be able to:

a. identify the institutional features that distinguish futures contracts from forward contracts and describe the characteristics of futures contracts;

b. differentiate between margin in the securities markets and margin in the futures markets;

c. describe how a futures trade takes place;

d. describe how a futures position may be closed out (i.e., offset) prior to expiration;

e. define initial margin, maintenance margin, variation margin, and settlement price;

f. describe the process of marking to market and compute the margin balance, given the previous day's balance and the new futures price;

g. explain price limits, limit move, limit up, limit down, and locked limit;

h. describe how a futures contract can be terminated by a close-out (i.e., offset) at expiration, delivery, an equivalent cash settlement, or an exchange-for-physicals;

i. explain delivery options in futures contracts;

j. distinguish among scalpers, day traders, and position traders;

k. describe the characteristics of the following types of futures contracts: Treasury bill, Eurodollar, Treasury bond, stock index, and currency.

Reading 72: Option Markets and Contracts

The candidate should be able to:

a. identify the basic elements and describe the characteristics of option contracts;

b. define European option, American option, moneyness, payoff, intrinsic value, and time value and differentiate between exchange-traded options and over-the-counter options;

c. identify the different types of options in terms of the underlying instruments;

d. compare and contrast interest rate options to forward rate agreements (FRAs);

e. explain how option payoffs are determined, and show how interest rate option payoffs differ from the payoffs of other types of options;

f. define interest rate caps and floors;

g. identify the minimum and maximum values of European options and American options;

h. explain how the lower bounds of European calls and puts are determined by constructing portfolio combinations that prevent arbitrage, and calculate an option's lower bound;

i. determine the lowest prices of European and American calls and puts based on the rules for minimum values and lower bounds;

j. describe how a portfolio (combination) of options establishes the relationship between options that differ only by exercise price;

k. explain how option prices are affected by the time to expiration of the option;

l. explain put-call parity for European options, given the payoffs on a fiduciary call and a protective put;

m. explain the relationship between American options and European options in terms of the lower bounds on option prices and the possibility of early exercise;

n. explain how cash flows on the underlying asset affect put-call parity and the lower bounds of option prices;

o. identify the directional effect of an interest rate change on an option's price and describe the impact of a change in volatility on an option's price.

Reading 73: Swap Markets and Contracts

The candidate should be able to:

a. describe the characteristics of swap contracts and explain how swaps are terminated;

b. define and give examples of currency swaps and calculate and interpret the payments on a currency swap;

c. define and give an example of a plain vanilla interest rate swap and calculate and interpret the payments on an interest rate swap;

d. define and give examples of equity swaps and calculate and interpret the payments on an equity swap.

Reading 74: Risk Management Applications of Option Strategies

The candidate should be able to:

a. determine the value at expiration, profit, maximum profit, maximum loss, breakeven underlying price at expiration, and general shape of the graph of the strategies of buying and selling calls and buying and selling puts, and explain each strategy's characteristics;

b. determine the value at expiration, profit, maximum profit, maximum loss, breakeven underlying price at expiration, and general shape of the graph of the covered call strategy and the protective put strategy, and explain each strategy's characteristics.

DERIVATIVE MARKETS AND INSTRUMENTS

LEARNING OUTCOMES

The candidate should be able to:

a. define a derivative and differentiate between exchange-traded and over-the-counter derivatives;

b. define a forward commitment, identify the types of forward commitments, and describe the basic characteristics of forward contracts, futures contracts, and swaps;

c. define a contingent claim and identify the types of contingent claims;

d. describe the basic characteristics of options, and distinguish between an option to buy (call) and an option to sell (put);

e. discuss the purposes and criticisms of derivative markets;

f. explain the concept of arbitrage and the role it plays in determining prices and in promoting market efficiency.

INTRODUCTION   1

The concept of risk is at the heart of investment management. Financial analysts and portfolio managers continually identify, measure, and manage risk. In a simple world where only stocks and bonds exist, the only risks are the fluctuations associated with market values and the potential for a creditor to default. Measuring risk often takes the form of standard deviations, betas, and probabilities of default. In the above simple setting, managing risk is limited to engaging in stock and bond transactions that reduce or increase risk. For example, a portfolio manager may hold a combination of a risky stock portfolio and a risk-free bond, with the relative allocations determined by the investor's tolerance for risk. If for some reason the manager desires a lower level of risk, the only transactions available to adjust the risk downward are to reduce the allocation to the risky stock portfolio and increase the allocation to the risk-free bond.

Analysis of Derivatives for the CFA® Program, by Don M. Chance, Copyright © 2003 by Association for Investment Management and Research. Reprinted with permission.

But we do not live in a simple world of only stocks and bonds, and in fact investors can adjust the level of risk in a variety of ways. For example, one way to reduce risk is to use insurance, which can be described as the act of paying someone to assume a risk for you. The financial markets have created their own way of offering insurance against financial loss in the form of contracts called **derivatives.** *A derivative is a financial instrument that offers a return based on the return of some other underlying asset.* In this sense, its return is *derived* from another instrument—hence, the name.

As the definition states, a derivative's performance is based on the performance of an underlying asset. This underlying asset is often referred to simply as the **underlying.**[1] It trades in a market in which buyers and sellers meet and decide on a price; the seller then delivers the asset to the buyer and receives payment. The price for immediate purchase of the underlying asset is called the **cash price** or **spot price** (in this book, we will use the latter term). A derivative also has a defined and limited life: A derivative contract initiates on a certain date and terminates on a later date. Often the derivative's payoff is determined and/or made on the expiration date, although that is not always the case. In accordance with the usual rules of law, a derivative contract is an agreement between two parties in which each does something for the other. In some cases, as in the simple insurance analogy, a derivative contract involves one party paying the other some money and receiving coverage against potential losses. In other cases, the parties simply agree that each will do something for the other at a later date. In other words, no money need change hands up front.

We have alluded to several general characteristics of derivative contracts. Let us now turn to the specific types of derivatives that we will cover in this book.

2   TYPES OF DERIVATIVES

In this section, we take a brief look at the different types of derivative contracts. This brief treatment serves only as a short introduction to familiarize you with the general ideas behind the contracts. We shall examine these derivatives in considerable detail in later readings.

Let us start by noting that derivative contracts are created on and traded in two distinct but related types of markets: exchange traded and over the counter. Exchange-traded contracts have standard terms and features and are traded on an organized derivatives trading facility, usually referred to as a futures exchange or an options exchange. Over-the-counter contracts are any transactions created by two parties anywhere else. We shall examine the other distinctive features of these two types of contracts as we proceed.

Derivative contracts can be classified into two general categories: forward commitments and contingent claims. In the following section, we examine forward commitments, which are contracts in which the two parties enter into an agreement to engage in a transaction at a later date at a price established at the

---

[1] On behalf of the financial world, we apologize to all English teachers. "Underlying" is not a noun, but in the world of derivatives it is commonly used as such. To be consistent with that terminology, we use it in that manner here.

start. Within the category of forward commitments, two major classifications exist: exchanged-traded contracts, specifically futures, and over-the-counter contracts, which consist of forward contracts and swaps.

2.1 Forward Commitments

The **forward contract** is an agreement between two parties in which one party, the buyer, agrees to buy from the other party, the seller, an underlying asset at a future date at a price established at the start. The parties to the transaction specify the forward contract's terms and conditions, such as when and where delivery will take place and the precise identity of the underlying. In this sense, the contract is said to be *customized*. Each party is subject to the possibility that the other party will default.

Many simple, everyday transactions are forms of forward commitments. For example, when you order a pizza for delivery to your home, you are entering into an agreement for a transaction to take place later ("30 minutes or less," as some advertise) at a price agreed on at the outset. Although default is not likely, it could occur—for instance, if the party ordering the pizza decided to go out to eat, leaving the delivery person wondering where the customer went. Or perhaps the delivery person had a wreck on the way to delivery and the pizza was destroyed. But such events are extremely rare.

Forward contracts in the financial world take place in a large and private market consisting of banks, investment banking firms, governments, and corporations. These contracts call for the purchase and sale of an underlying asset at a later date. The underlying asset could be a security (i.e., a stock or bond), a foreign currency, a commodity, or combinations thereof, or sometimes an interest rate. In the case of an interest rate, the contract is not on a bond from which the interest rate is derived but rather on the interest rate itself. Such a contract calls for the exchange of a single interest payment for another at a later date, where at least one of the payments is determined at the later date.[2]

As an example of someone who might use a forward contract in the financial world, consider a pension fund manager. The manager, anticipating a future inflow of cash, could engage in a forward contract to purchase a portfolio equivalent to the S&P 500 at a future date—timed to coincide with the future cash inflow date—at a price agreed on at the start. When that date arrives, the cash is received and used to settle the obligation on the forward contract.[3] In this manner, the pension fund manager commits to the position in the S&P 500 without having to worry about the risk that the market will rise during that period. Other common forward contracts include commitments to buy and sell a foreign currency or a commodity at a future date, locking in the exchange rate or commodity price at the start.

The forward market is a private and largely unregulated market. Any transaction involving a commitment between two parties for the future purchase/sale of an asset is a forward contract. Although pizza deliveries are generally not considered forward contracts, similar transactions occur commonly in the financial world. Yet we cannot simply pick up *The Wall Street Journal* or *The Financial Times* and read about them or determine how many contracts were created the previous day.[4] They are private transactions for a reason: The parties want to keep them private and want little government interference. This need for privacy and the

---

[2] These instruments are called forward rate agreements and will be studied in detail in Reading 70.

[3] The settling of the forward contract can occur through delivery, in which case the buyer pays the agreed-upon price and receives the asset from the seller, or through an equivalent cash settlement. In the latter case, the seller pays the buyer the difference between the market price and the agreed-upon price if the market price is higher. The buyer pays the seller the difference between the agreed-upon price and the market price if the agreed-upon price is higher.

[4] In Section 4 of this reading, we will look at some ways to measure the amount of this type of trading.

absence of regulation does not imply anything illegal or corrupt but simply reflects a desire to maintain a prudent level of business secrecy.

Recall that we described a forward contract as an agreement between two parties in which one party, the buyer, agrees to buy from the other party, the seller, an underlying asset at a future date at a price agreed upon at the start. A **futures contract** is a variation of a forward contract that has essentially the same basic definition but some additional features that clearly distinguish it from a forward contract. For one, a futures contract is not a private and customized transaction. Instead, it is a public, standardized transaction that takes place on a futures exchange. A futures exchange, like a stock exchange, is an organization that provides a facility for engaging in futures transactions and establishes a mechanism through which parties can buy and sell these contracts. The contracts are standardized, which means that the exchange determines the expiration dates, the underlying, how many units of the underlying are included in one contract, and various other terms and conditions.

Probably the most important distinction between a futures contract and a forward contract, however, lies in the default risk associated with the contracts. As noted above, in a forward contract, the risk of default is a concern. Specifically, the party with a loss on the contract could default. Although the legal consequences of default are severe, parties nonetheless sometimes fall into financial trouble and are forced to default. For that reason, only solid, creditworthy parties can generally engage in forward contracts. In a futures contract, however, the futures exchange guarantees to each party that if the other fails to pay, the exchange will pay. In fact, the exchange actually writes itself into the middle of the contract so that each party effectively has a contract with the exchange and not with the other party. The exchange collects payment from one party and disburses payment to the other.

The futures exchange implements this performance guarantee through an organization called the clearinghouse. For some futures exchanges, the clearinghouse is a separate corporate entity. For others, it is a division or subsidiary of the exchange. In either case, however, the clearinghouse protects itself by requiring that the parties settle their gains and losses to the exchange on a daily basis. This process, referred to as the daily settlement or marking to market, is a critical distinction between futures and forward contracts. With futures contracts, profits and losses are charged and credited to participants' accounts each day. This practice prevents losses from accumulating without being collected. For forward contracts, losses accumulate until the end of the contract.[5]

One should not get the impression that forward contracts are rife with credit losses and futures contracts never involve default. Credit losses on forward contracts are extremely rare, owing to the excellent risk management practices of participants. In the case of futures contracts, parties do default on occasion. In fact, it is likely that there are more defaults on futures contracts than on forward contracts.[6] Nonetheless, the exchange guarantee has never failed for the party on the other side of the transaction. Although the possibility of the clearinghouse defaulting does exist, the probability of such a default happening is extremely

---

[5] Although this process of losses accumulating on forward contracts until the expiration day is the standard format for a contract, modern risk management procedures include the possibility of forcing a party in debt to periodically pay losses accrued prior to expiration. In addition, a variety of risk-reducing techniques, such as the use of collateral, are used to mitigate the risk of loss. We discuss these points in more detail in Reading 70 and Chapter 9.

[6] Defaults are more likely for futures contracts than for forward contracts because participants in the forward markets must meet higher creditworthiness standards than those in the futures markets. Indeed, many individuals participate in the futures markets; forward market participants are usually large, creditworthy companies. But the forward markets have no guarantor of performance, while the futures markets do. Therefore, participants in the forward markets have incurred credit losses in the past, while participants in the futures markets have not.

small. Thus, we can generally assume that futures contracts are default-free. In contrast, the possibility of default, although relatively small, exists for forward contracts.

Another important distinction between forward contracts and futures contracts lies in the ability to engage in offsetting transactions. Forward contracts are generally designed to be held until expiration. It is possible, however, for a party to engage in the opposite transaction prior to expiration. For example, a party might commit to purchase one million euros at a future date at an exchange rate of $0.85/€. Suppose that later the euro has a forward price of $0.90/€. The party might then choose to engage in a new forward contract to sell the euro at the new price of $0.90/€. The party then has a commitment to buy the euro at $0.85 and sell it at $0.90. The risk associated with changes in exchange rates is eliminated, but both transactions remain in place and are subject to default.[7]

In futures markets, the contracts have standardized terms and trade in a market that provides sufficient liquidity to permit the parties to enter the market and offset transactions previously created. The use of contracts with standardized terms results in relatively widespread acceptance of these terms as homogeneous agreed-upon standards for trading these contracts. For example, a U.S. Treasury bond futures contract covering $100,000 face value of Treasury bonds, with an expiration date in March, June, September, or December, is a standard contract. In contrast, if a party wanted a contract covering $120,000 of Treasury bonds, he would not find any such instrument in the futures markets and would have to create a nonstandard instrument in the forward market. The acceptance of standardized terms makes parties more willing to trade futures contracts. Consequently, futures markets offer the parties liquidity, which gives them a means of buying and selling the contracts. Because of this liquidity, a party can enter into a contract and later, before the contract expires, enter into the opposite transaction and offset the position, much the same way one might buy or sell a stock or bond and then reverse the transaction later. This reversal of a futures position completely eliminates any further financial consequences of the original transaction.[8]

A **swap** is a variation of a forward contract that is essentially equivalent to a series of forward contracts. Specifically, a swap is an agreement between two parties to exchange a series of future cash flows. Typically at least one of the two series of cash flows is determined by a later outcome. In other words, one party agrees to pay the other a series of cash flows whose value will be determined by the unknown future course of some underlying factor, such as an interest rate, exchange rate, stock price, or commodity price. The other party promises to make a series of payments that could also be determined by a second unknown factor or, alternatively, could be preset. We commonly refer to swap payments as being "fixed" or "floating" (sometimes "variable").

We noted that a forward contract is an agreement to buy or sell an underlying asset at a future date at a price agreed on today. A swap in which one party makes a single fixed payment and the other makes a single floating payment amounts to a forward contract. One party agrees to make known payments to the other and receive something unknown in return. This type of contract is like an agreement to buy at a future date, paying a fixed amount and receiving something of unknown future value. That the swap is a *series* of such payments distinguishes it from a forward contract, which is only a single payment.[9]

---

[7] It is possible for the party engaging in the first transaction to engage in the second transaction with the same party. The two parties agree to cancel their transactions, settling the difference in value in cash and thereby eliminating the risk associated with exchange rates as well as the possibility of default.

[8] A common misconception is that, as a result of their standardized terms, futures contracts are liquid but nonstandardized forward contracts are illiquid. This is not always the case; many futures contracts have low liquidity and many forward contracts have high liquidity.

[9] A few other distinctions exist between swaps and forward contracts, such as the fact that swaps can involve both parties paying a variable amount.

Swaps, like forward contracts, are private transactions and thus not subject to direct regulation.[10] Swaps are arguably the most successful of all derivative transactions. Probably the most common use of a swap is a situation in which a corporation, currently borrowing at a floating rate, enters into a swap that commits it to making a series of interest payments to the swap counterparty at a fixed rate, while receiving payments from the swap counterparty at a rate related to the floating rate at which it is making its loan payments. The floating components cancel, resulting in the effective conversion of the original floating-rate loan to a fixed-rate loan.

Forward commitments (whether forwards, futures, or swaps) are firm and binding agreements to engage in a transaction at a future date. They obligate each party to complete the transaction, or alternatively, to offset the transaction by engaging in another transaction that settles each party's financial obligation to the other. Contingent claims, on the other hand, allow one party the flexibility to not engage in the future transaction, depending on market conditions.

2.2 Contingent Claims

Contingent claims are derivatives in which the payoffs occur if a specific event happens. We generally refer to these types of derivatives as options. Specifically, an **option** is a financial instrument that gives one party the right, but not the obligation, to buy or sell an underlying asset from or to another party at a fixed price over a specific period of time. An option that gives the right to buy is referred to as a call; an option that gives the right to sell is referred to as a put. The fixed price at which the underlying can be bought or sold is called the exercise price, strike price, striking price, or strike, and is determined at the outset of the transaction. In this book, we refer to it as the exercise price, and the action of buying or selling the underlying at the exercise price is called exercising the option. The holder of the option has the right to exercise it and will do so if conditions are advantageous; otherwise, the option will expire unexercised. Thus, the payoff of the option is contingent on an event taking place, so options are sometimes referred to as contingent claims.

In contrast to participating in a forward or futures contract, which represents a *commitment* to buy or sell, owning an option represents the *right* to buy or sell. To acquire this right, the buyer of the option must pay a price at the start to the option seller. This price is called the option premium or sometimes just the option price. In this book, we usually refer to it as the option price.

Because the option buyer has the right to buy or sell an asset, the seller of the option has the potential commitment to sell or buy this asset. If the option buyer has the right to buy, the option seller may be obligated to sell. If the option buyer has the right to sell, the option seller may be obligated to buy. As noted above, the option seller receives the amount of the option price from the option buyer for his willingness to bear this risk.

An important distinction we made between forward and futures contracts was that the former are customized private transactions between two parties without a guarantee against losses from default. The latter are standardized contracts that take place on futures exchanges and are guaranteed by the exchange against losses from default. For options, both types of contracts—over-the-counter customized and exchange-listed standardized—exist. In other words, the buyer and seller of an option can arrange their own terms and create an option contract. Alternatively, the buyer and seller can meet directly, or through their brokers, on an options exchange and trade standardized options. In the case of customized options, the buyer is subject to the possibility of the seller defaulting when and if the buyer

---

[10] Like all over-the-counter derivatives transactions, swaps are subject to indirect regulatory oversight in that the companies using them could be regulated by securities or banking authorities. In addition, swaps, like all contracts, are subject to normal contract and civil law.

decides to exercise the option. Because the option buyer is not obligated to do anything beyond paying the original price, the seller of any type of option is not subject to the buyer defaulting. In the case of a standardized option, the buyer does not face the risk of the seller defaulting. The exchange, through its clearinghouse, guarantees the seller's performance to the buyer.

A variety of other instruments contain options and thus are forms of contingent claims. For instance, many corporations issue convertible bonds offering the holder an optionlike feature that enables the holder to participate in gains on the market price of the corporation's stock without having to participate in losses on the stock. Callable bonds are another example of a common financial instrument that contains an option, in this case the option of the issuer to pay off the bond before its maturity. Options themselves are often characterized in terms of standard or fairly basic options and more advanced options, often referred to as exotic options. There are also options that are not even based on assets but rather on futures contracts or other derivatives. A very widely used group of options is based on interest rates.

Another common type of option is contained in asset-backed securities. An asset-backed security is a claim on a pool of securities. The pool, which might be mortgages, loans, or bonds, is a portfolio assembled by a financial institution that then sells claims on the portfolio. Often, the borrowers who issued the mortgages, loans, or bonds have the right to pay off their debts early, and many choose to do so when interest rates fall significantly. They then refinance their loans by taking out a new loan at a lower interest rate. This right, called a prepayment feature, is a valuable option owned by the borrower. Holders of asset-backed securities bear the risk associated with prepayment options and hence are sellers of those options. The holders, or option sellers, receive a higher promised yield on their bond investment than they would have received on an otherwise equivalent bond without the option.

With an understanding of derivatives, there are no limits to the types of financial instruments that can be constructed, analyzed, and applied to achieve investment objectives. What you learn from this book and the CFA Program will help you recognize and understand the variety of derivatives that appear in many forms in the financial world.

EXHIBIT 69-1 A Classification of Derivatives

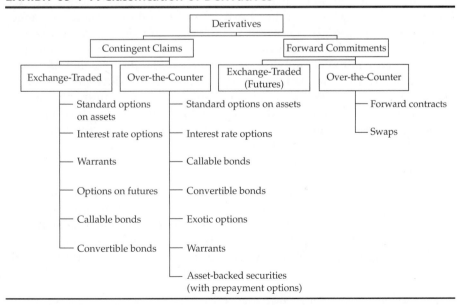

Exhibit 69-1 presents a classification of the types of derivative contracts as we have described them. Note that we have partitioned derivatives into those that are exchange-traded and those that trade in the over-the-counter market. The exhibit also notes some other categories not specifically mentioned above. These instruments are included for completeness, but they are relatively advanced and not covered in this first reading.

We have now looked at the basic characteristics of derivative contracts. In order to better understand and appreciate derivatives, we should take a quick look at where they came from and where they are now. Accordingly, we take a brief look at the history and current state of derivative markets.

3   DERIVATIVE MARKETS: PAST AND PRESENT

Derivative markets have an exciting and colorful history. Examining that history gives insights that help us understand the structure of these markets as they exist today.

The basic characteristics of derivative contracts can be found throughout the history of humankind. Agreements to engage in a commercial transaction as well as agreements that provide the right to engage in a commercial transaction date back hundreds of years. In medieval times, contracts for the future delivery of an asset with the price fixed at the time of the contract initiation were frequent. Early indications of futures markets were seen in Japan many hundreds of years ago. The futures markets generally trace their roots, however, to the 1848 creation of the Chicago Board of Trade, the first organized futures market. Its origins resulted from the burgeoning grain markets in Chicago, which created a need for a farmer to secure a price at one point in time, store the grain, and deliver it at a later point in time. At around the same time, customized option transactions were being offered, including some by the well known financier Russell Sage, who found a clever way to offer combinations of customized options that replicated a loan at a rate that exceeded the maximum allowable rate under the then-existing usury laws.[11]

In the century that followed, the futures industry grew rapidly. Institutions such as the Chicago Board of Trade, the Chicago Mercantile Exchange, and later, the New York Mercantile Exchange and the Chicago Board Options Exchange became the primary forces in the global derivatives industry. These exchanges created and successfully marketed many innovative derivative contracts.[12] Although the first 100 years of futures exchanges were dominated by trading in futures on agricultural commodities, the 1970s saw the introduction of futures on financial instruments such as currencies, bonds, and stock indices. These "financial futures," as well as newly introduced options on individual stocks, currencies, bonds, and stock indices, ushered in a new era in which financial derivatives dominated agricultural derivatives—a situation that continues today. Although the commodity derivatives market includes very active contracts in oil and precious metals, financial derivatives have remained the primary force in the worldwide derivatives market.

Exchange-listed standardized derivatives, however, have hardly been the only instruments in the derivatives world. As noted, customized options have been around since at least the 19th century. The customized-options market flourished until the early 1970s, largely as a retail product. With the introduction of standardized options in 1973, however, the customized options market effectively

---

[11] Sage was perhaps the first options arbitrageur. Of course, usury laws are rare these days and most investors understand put–call parity, so do not expect to make any money copying Sage's scheme.

[12] It is probably also important to note that the futures and options exchanges have introduced many unsuccessful contracts as well.

EXHIBIT 69-2 Global Derivatives Exchanges

North America

American Stock Exchange
Bourse de Montreal
BrokerTec Futures Exchange
Chicago Board Options Exchange
Chicago Board of Trade
Chicago Mercantile Exchange
International Securities Exchange
  (New York)
Kansas City Board of Trade
Minneapolis Grain Exchange
New York Board of Trade
New York Mercantile Exchange
Pacific Exchange (San Francisco)
Philadelphia Stock Exchange
Winnipeg Commodity Exchange

Asia

Central Japan Commodity Exchange
Dalian Commodity Exchange
Hong Kong Exchanges & Clearing
Kansai Commodities Exchange (Osaka)
Korea Futures Exchange
Korea Stock Exchange
Malaysia Derivatives Exchange
New Zealand Futures & Options
  Exchange
Osaka Mercantile Exchange
Shanghai Futures Exchange
Singapore Commodity Exchange
Singapore Exchange
Tokyo Commodity Exchange
Tokyo Grain Exchange
Tokyo International Financial Futures
  Exchange
Tokyo Stock Exchange
Zhengzhou Commodity Exchange

Europe

Bolsa de Valores de Lisboa e Porto
Borsa Italiana
Budapest Commodity Exchange
Eurex Frankfurt
Eurex Zurich
Euronext Amsterdam
Euronext Brussels
Euronext Paris
FUTOP Market (Copenhagen)
Helsinki Exchanges Group
International Petroleum Exchange of
  London
London International Financial Futures
  and Options Exchange
London Metal Exchange
MEFF Renta Fija (Barcelona)
MEFF Renta Variable (Madrid)
OM London Exchange
OM Stockholm Exchange
Romanian Commodity Exchange
Sibiu Monetary–Financial and
  Commodities Exchange (Romania)
Tel Aviv Stock Exchange
Wiener Borse AG (Vienna)

South America

Bolsa de Mercadorias & Futuros
  (Sao Paulo)
Mercado a Termino de Buenos Aires
Santiago Stock Exchange

Africa

South African Futures Exchange

Australia

Australian Stock Exchange
Sydney Futures Exchange

Source: Futures [magazine] *2002 Sourcebook.*

died. But something else was going on at the time that would later revive this market. In the early 1970s, foreign exchange rates were deregulated and allowed to float freely. This deregulation led not only to the development of a futures, and later options, market for currencies but also to a market for customized forward contracts in foreign currencies. This market became known as the interbank market because it was largely operated within the global banking community, and it grew rapidly. Most importantly, it set the stage for the banking industry to engage in other customized derivative transactions.

Spurred by deregulation of their permitted activities during the 1980s, banks discovered that they could create derivatives of all forms and sell them to corporations and institutions that had risks that could best be managed with products specifically tailored for a given situation. These banks make markets in derivative products by assuming the risks that the corporations want to eliminate. But banks are not in the business of assuming unwanted risks. They use their vast resources and global networks to transfer or lay off the risk elsewhere, often in the futures markets. If they successfully lay off these risks, they can profit by buying and selling the derivatives at a suitable bid–ask spread. In addition to banks, investment banking firms also engage in derivatives transactions of this sort. The commercial and investment banks that make markets in derivatives are called **derivatives dealers.** Buying and selling derivatives is a natural extension of the activity these banks normally undertake in financial markets. This market for customized derivatives is what we refer to as the over-the-counter derivatives market.

By the end of the 20th century, the derivatives market reached a mature stage, growing at only a slow pace but providing a steady offering of existing products and a continuing slate of new products. Derivatives exchanges underwent numerous changes, often spurred by growing competition from the over-the-counter market. Some merged; others that were formerly nonprofit corporations have since become profit making. Some derivatives exchanges have even experimented with offering somewhat customized transactions. Nearly all have lobbied heavily for a reduction in the level or structure of the regulations imposed on them. Some derivatives exchanges have altered the manner in which trading takes place, from the old system of face-to-face on a trading floor (in sections called pits) to off-floor electronic trading in which participants communicate through computer screens. This type of transacting, called electronic trading, has even been extended to the Internet and, not surprisingly, is called e-trading. Pit trading is still the primary format for derivatives exchanges in the United States, but electronic trading is clearly the wave of the future. As the dominant form of trading outside the United States, it will likely replace pit trading in the United States in coming years.

Exhibit 69-2 lists all global derivatives exchanges as of January 2002. Note that almost every country with a reasonably advanced financial market system has a derivatives exchange.

We cannot technically identify where over-the-counter derivatives markets exist. These types of transactions can conceivably occur anywhere two parties can agree to engage in a transaction. It is generally conceded, however, that London and New York are the primary markets for over-the-counter derivatives; considerable activity also takes place in Tokyo, Paris, Frankfurt, Chicago, Amsterdam, and many other major world cities.

Now we know where the derivative markets are, but are they big enough for us to care about? We examine this question in Section 4.

4   HOW BIG IS THE DERIVATIVES MARKET?

Good question. And the answer is: We really do not know. Because trading in exchange-listed contracts, such as futures and some options, is recorded, volume figures for those types of contracts are available. Exhibit 69-3 presents summary statistics for contract volume of global futures and options for 2000 and 2001. Note that in 2001, the largest category is equity indices. In 2000, the largest category was individual equities, followed by interest rates. In prior years, the largest category had been interest rates.

Currently, the United States accounts for approximately 35 percent of global futures and options volume. The largest exchange in the world, however, is the Korea Stock Exchange, which trades an exceptionally large volume of options on a Korean stock index. The second-largest exchange (and the largest exchange in terms of futures volume only) is the combined German–Swiss exchange called Eurex. The other largest exchanges (in order of 2001 volume) are the Chicago Mercantile Exchange, the Chicago Board of Trade, the London International Financial Futures and Options Exchange, the Paris Bourse, the New York Mercantile Exchange, the

EXHIBIT 69-3 Global Exchange-Traded Futures and Options Contract Volume (in millions of contracts)

Contract Type	2000	2001
Equity indices	674.8	1,470.3
Interest rates	844.3	1,216.1
Individual equities	969.7	1,112.7
Energy	154.8	166.9
Agricultural	185.7	156.5
Nonprecious metals	75.7	70.2
Currencies	47.0	49.2
Precious metals	36.2	39.1
Other	1.3	0.8
Overall Total	2,989.5	4,281.8

Source: Futures Industry (January/February 2002).

Bolsa de Mercadorias & Futuros of Brazil, and the Chicago Board Options Exchange. All of these exchanges traded at least 70 million contracts in 2001.[13]

One important factor that must be considered, however, in looking at trading volume as a measure of activity is that the futures and options exchanges influence their own volume by designating a contract's size. For example, a standard option in the United States covers 100 shares of the underlying stock. If an investor takes a position in options on 1,000 shares of stock, the investor would trade 10 options. If the options exchange had designated that the contract size be 200 options, then the investor would trade only five contracts. Although there are often good reasons for setting a contract size at a certain level, volume comparisons must be taken with a degree of skepticism.[14]

The over-the-counter derivatives market is much more difficult to measure. Because the transactions are private, unregulated, and can take place virtually anywhere two parties can enter into an agreement, no official tabulation exists that allows us to identify the size of the market. Information is available, however, from semiannual surveys conducted by the Bank for International Settlements (BIS) of Basel, Switzerland, an international organization of central banks. The BIS publishes this data in its semiannual report "Regular OTC Derivatives Market Statistics," available on its website at www.bis.org/publ/regpubl.htm.

Exhibit 69-4 presents two charts constructed from the 30 June 2001 BIS survey and shows figures for foreign exchange, interest rate, equity, and commodity derivatives transactions. The "other" category, however, does include transactions of these types and reflects the BIS's estimates of positions taken by parties that do not report in this survey. It is used primarily to obtain an estimate for the overall size of the market and is not broken down by category.

---

[13] *Futures Industry* (January/February 2002).

[14] For example, in 1999 the volume of Treasury bond futures on the Chicago Board of Trade was about 90 million contracts while the volume of Eurodollar futures on the Chicago Mercantile Exchange was about 93 million contracts. Consequently, at that time these two contracts appeared to have about the same amount of activity. But the Treasury bond contract covers Treasury bonds with a face value of $100,000 while the Eurodollar contract covers Eurodollars with a face value of $1,000,000. Thus, the Eurodollar futures market was arguably 10 times the size of the Treasury bond futures market. In 2002, about three Eurodollar futures contracts were traded for every Treasury bond futures contract traded.

EXHIBIT 69-4A Outstanding Notional Principal of Global Over-the-Counter Derivatives, 30 June 2001 (billions)

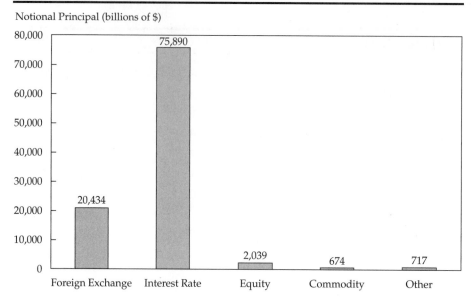

Source: Bank for International Settlements, www.bis.org/publ/regpubl.htm

For over-the-counter derivatives, notional principal is the most widely used measure of market size. Notional principal measures the amount of the underlying asset covered by a derivative contract. For example, a swap involving interest payments on ¥500 million has a notional principal of ¥500 million. The actual payments made in the swap, however, are merely interest payments on ¥500 million and do not come close to ¥500 million.[15] Thus, although notional principal is a commonly used measure of the size of the market, it can give a misleading impression by suggesting that it reflects the amount of money involved.[16]

Nonetheless, we would be remiss if we failed to note the market size as measured by notional principal. Based on Exhibit 69-4A, the total notional principal summing over these five categories is almost $100 trillion. Also note that interest rate derivatives are the most widely used category by far.

Exhibit 69-4B gives another picture of the size of the market by indicating the market value of over-the-counter derivatives. Market value indicates the economic worth of a derivative contract and represents the amount of money that would change hands if these transactions were terminated at the time of the report. The total market value for all categories is about $3 trillion. Market value is a better indication of the size of the market because it more accurately represents the actual money involved. Nonetheless, market value is subject to greater errors in estimation and thus is a less reliable measure than notional principal.

---

[15] In fact, the payments on a swap are even smaller than the interest payments on the notional principal. Swap interest payments usually equal only the difference between the interest payments owed by the two parties.

[16] The over-the-counter derivatives industry originally began the practice of measuring its size by notional principal. This was a deliberate tactic designed to make the industry look larger so it would be more noticed and viewed as a significant and legitimate force. As it turns out, this tactic backfired, resulting in fears that more money was involved and at risk of loss than really was. Calls for increased scrutiny of the industry by government authorities resulted in the industry backpedaling on its use of notional principal and focusing more on market value as a measure of its size. Nonetheless, notional principal continues to be used as one, if not the primary, measure of the industry's size.

EXHIBIT 69-4B Outstanding Market Value of Global Over-the-Counter Derivatives, 30 June 2001 (billions)

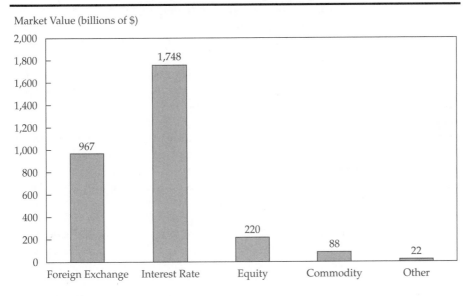

Market Value (billions of $)

Source: Bank for International Settlements, www.bis.org/publ/regpubl.htm

Although it is impossible to determine where these contracts originate, dollar-denominated derivatives represented about 34 percent of the global interest rate derivatives market in 2001, with euro-denominated derivatives accounting for about 27 percent and yen-denominated derivatives representing 17 percent.

Whether notional principal or market value is used, it is clear that the derivatives industry is large by any standard. Derivatives are widely available in global asset markets, and consequently, understanding derivatives is essential to operating in these markets, whether one chooses to use them or not.

Because derivative markets have been created around the world, there must be a reason for their continued existence. Let us now look at why derivative markets exist.

THE PURPOSES OF DERIVATIVE MARKETS   5

Derivative markets serve a variety of purposes in global social and economic systems. One of the primary functions of futures markets is **price discovery.** Futures markets provide valuable information about the prices of the underlying assets on which futures contracts are based. They provide this information in two ways. First, many of these assets are traded in geographically dispersed markets. Recall that the current price of the underlying asset is called the spot price. With geographically dispersed markets, many different spot prices could exist. In the futures markets, the price of the contract with the shortest time to expiration often serves as a proxy for the price of the underlying asset. Second, the prices of all futures contracts serve as prices that can be accepted by those who trade contracts in lieu of facing the risk of uncertain future prices. For example, a company that mines gold can hedge by selling a futures contract on gold expiring in two months, which locks in the price of gold two months later. In this manner, the two-month futures price substitutes for the uncertainty of the price of gold over the next two months.[17]

Futures contracts are not, however, the only derivatives that serve this purpose. In fact, forward contracts and swaps allow users to substitute a single locked-in price for the uncertainty of future spot prices and thereby permit the same form of price discovery as do futures.

Options work in a slightly different manner. They are used in a different form of hedging, one that permits the holder to protect against loss while allowing participation in gains if prices move favorably. Options do not so much reveal *prices* as they reveal *volatility*. As we shall see in Reading 72, the volatility of the underlying asset is a critical factor in the pricing of options. It is possible, therefore, to infer what investors feel about volatility from the prices of options.

Perhaps the most important purpose of derivative markets is **risk management.** We define risk management as the process of identifying the desired level of risk, identifying the actual level of risk, and altering the latter to equal the former. Often this process is described as hedging, which generally refers to the reduction, and in some cases the elimination, of risk. On the other side is the process called speculation. Traditional discussions of derivatives refer to hedging and speculation as complementary activities. In general, hedgers seek to eliminate risk and need speculators to assume risk, but such is not always the case. Hedgers often trade with other hedgers, and speculators often trade with other speculators. All one needs to hedge or speculate is a party with opposite beliefs or opposite risk exposure. For example, a corporation that mines gold could hedge the future sale of gold by entering into a derivative transaction with a company that manufactures jewelry. Both of these companies are hedgers, seeking to avoid the uncertainty of future gold prices by locking in a price for a future transaction. The mining corporation has concerns about a price decrease, and the jewelry manufacturer is worried about a price increase.

An unfortunate consequence of the use of the terms "hedging" and "speculating" is that hedgers are somehow seen as on the high moral ground and speculators are sometimes seen as evil—a distortion of the role of speculators. In fact, there need be very little difference between hedgers and speculators. To restate an example we used when discussing swaps, consider a corporation that currently borrows at a floating rate. A common response to a fear of rising interest rates is for the corporation to use an interest rate swap in which it will make payments at a fixed rate and receive payments at a floating rate. The floating-rate payments it receives from the swap offset the floating-rate payments on the loan, thereby effectively converting the loan to a fixed-rate loan. The company is now borrowing at a fixed rate and, in the eyes of many, hedging.

But is the company really hedging? Or is it simply making a bet that interest rates will increase? If interest rates decrease, the company will be losing money in the sense of the lost opportunity to borrow at a lower rate. From a budgeting and cash flow standpoint, however, its fixed interest payments are set in stone. Moreover, the market value of a fixed-rate loan is considerably more volatile than that of a floating-rate loan. Thus, our "hedging" corporation can be viewed as taking more risk than it originally had.

The more modern view of the reason for using derivatives does not refer to hedging or speculation. Although we shall sometimes use those terms, we shall use them carefully and make our intentions clear. In the grander scheme of things, derivatives are tools that enable companies to more easily practice risk management. In the context of our corporation borrowing at the floating rate, it made

---

[17] Some people view futures prices as revealing expectations of future spot prices of the underlying asset, and in that sense, leading to price discovery. This view, however, is incorrect. Futures prices are not necessarily expectations of future spot prices. As we discussed above, they allow a substitution of the futures price for the uncertainty of future spot prices of the asset. In that sense they permit the acceptance of a sure price and the avoidance of risk.

a conscious decision to borrow at a fixed rate. Engaging in the swap is simply an activity designed to align its risk with the risk it wants, given its outlook for interest rates. Whether one calls this activity hedging or speculation is not even very important. The company is simply managing risk.

Derivative markets serve several other useful purposes. As we show later when exploring the pricing of derivative contracts, they improve market efficiency for the underlying assets. Efficient markets are fair and competitive and do not allow one party to easily take money from another. As a simple example, we shall learn in Reading 3 that buying a stock index fund can be replicated by buying a futures on the fund and investing in risk-free bonds with the money that otherwise would have been spent on the fund. In other words, the fund and the combination of the futures and risk-free bond will have the same performance. But if the fund costs more than the combination of the futures and risk-free bond, investors have the opportunity to avoid the overpriced fund and take the combination.[18] This decreased demand for the fund will lower its price. The benefits to investors who do not even use derivatives should be clear: They can now invest in the fund at a more attractive price, because the derivatives market forced the price back to its appropriate level.

Derivative markets are also characterized by relatively low transaction costs. For example, the cost of investing in a stock index portfolio is as much as 20 times the cost of buying a futures contract on the index and a risk-free bond as described above. One might reasonably ask why derivatives are so much less expensive in terms of transaction costs. The answer is that derivatives are designed to provide a means of managing risk. As we have previously described, they serve as a form of insurance. Insurance cannot be a viable product if its cost is too high relative to the value of the insured asset. In other words, derivatives must have low transaction costs; otherwise, they would not exist.

It would be remiss to overlook the fact that derivative markets have been subject to many criticisms. We next present some of these complaints and the reasons behind them.

CRITICISMS OF DERIVATIVE MARKETS   6

Derivatives have been highly controversial for a number of reasons. For one, they are very complex. Much of the criticism has stemmed from a failure to understand derivatives. When derivatives fail to do their job, it is often the derivatives themselves, rather than the users of derivatives, that take the blame. Yet, in many cases, the critics of derivatives simply do not understand them well enough. As described in Section 2, when homeowners take out mortgages, they usually receive a valuable option: the right to prepay their mortgages. When interest rates fall, homeowners often pay off their mortgages, refinancing them at lower rates. The holders of these mortgages usually sell them to other parties, which can include small organizations and individuals. Thus, we often find unsophisticated investors holding securities based on the payments from mortgages. When homeowners refinance, they capture huge interest savings. Where does this money come from? It comes from the pockets of the holders of mortgage securities. When these unsophisticated investors lose a lot of money, derivatives usually get the blame. Yet these losses went into the pockets of homeowners in the form of interest savings. Who is to blame? Probably the brokers, who sold the securities to investors who

---

[18] Some investors, called arbitrageurs, will even find ways to sell the fund short to eliminate the risk of holding the futures and the bond, earning a profit from any discrepancy in their prices. We shall cover this type of transaction later in this reading.

did not know what they were buying—which leads us to the next common criticism of derivatives.

The complexity of derivatives means that sometimes the parties that use them do not understand them well. As a result, they are often used improperly, leading to potentially large losses. Such an argument can, however, be used to describe fire, electricity, and chemicals. Used improperly, perhaps in the hands of a child or someone who does not know how to use them, all of these can be extremely dangerous. Yet, we know that sufficient knowledge of fire, electricity, and chemicals to use them properly is not very difficult to obtain. The same is true for derivatives; treat them with respect and healthy doses of knowledge.

Derivatives are also mistakenly characterized as a form of legalized gambling. Although gambling is certainly legal in many parts of the world, derivatives are often viewed as a government's sanction of gambling via the financial markets. But there is an important distinction between gambling and derivatives: The benefits of derivatives extend much further across society. By providing a means of managing risk along with the other benefits discussed above, derivatives make financial markets work better. The organized gambling industry affects the participants, the owners of casinos, and perhaps some citizens who benefit from state lotteries. Organized gambling does not, however, make society function better, and it arguably incurs social costs.

We have taken a look at what derivatives are, where they come from, where they are now, why we have them, and what people think of them. Understanding derivatives, however, requires a basic understanding of the market forces that govern derivative prices. Although we shall cover derivative pricing in more detail in later readings, here we take a brief look at the process of pricing derivatives by examining some important fundamental principles.

7 ELEMENTARY PRINCIPLES OF DERIVATIVE PRICING

In this section, we take a preliminary glance at how derivative contracts are priced. First, we introduce the concept of **arbitrage.** Arbitrage occurs when equivalent assets or combinations of assets sell for two different prices. This situation creates an opportunity to profit at no risk with no commitment of money. Let us start with the simplest (and least likely) opportunity for arbitrage: the case of a stock selling for more than one price at a given time. Assume that a stock is trading in two markets simultaneously. Suppose the stock is trading at $100 in one market and $98 in the other market. We simply buy a share for $98 in one market and immediately sell it for $100 in the other. We have no net position in the stock, so it does not matter what price the stock moves to. We make an easy $2 at no risk and we did not have to put up any funds of our own. The sale of the stock at $100 was more than adequate to finance the purchase of the stock at $98. Naturally, many market participants would do this, which would create downward pressure on the price of the stock in the market where it trades for $100 and upward pressure on the price of the stock in the market where it trades for $98. Eventually the two prices must come together so that there is but a single price for the stock. Accordingly, the principle that no arbitrage opportunities should be available is often referred to as the **law of one price.**

Recall that we mentioned in Section 5 that an asset can potentially trade in different geographic markets and, therefore, have several spot prices. This potential would appear to violate the law of one price, but in reality, the law is still upheld. A given asset selling in two different locations is not necessarily the same asset. If a buyer in one location discovered that it is possible to buy the asset more cheaply in another location, the buyer would still have to incur the cost of moving the asset to the buyer's location. Transportation costs could offset any such price differences.[19]

Now suppose we face the situation illustrated in Exhibit 69-5. In Exhibit 69-5A, observe that we have one stock, AXE Electronics, which today is worth $50 and which, one period later, will be worth either $75 or $40. We shall denote these prices as $AXE = 50$, $AXE^+ = 75$, and $AXE^- = 40$. Another stock, BYF Technology, is today worth $38 and one period later will be worth $60 or $32. Thus, $BYF = 38$, $BYF^+ = 60$, and $BYF^- = 32$. Let us assume the risk-free borrowing and lending rate is 4 percent. We assume no dividends on either stock during the period covered by this example.

The opportunity exists to make a profit at no risk without committing any of our funds, as demonstrated in Exhibit 69-5B. Suppose we borrow 100 shares of stock AXE, which is selling for $50, and sell short, thereby receiving $5,000. We take $4,750 and purchase 125 shares of stock BYF. We invest the remaining $250 in risk-free bonds at 4 percent. This transaction will not require us to put up any funds of our own: The short sale will be sufficient to fund the investment in BYF and leave money to invest in risk-free bonds.

If the top outcome in Exhibit 69-5 occurs, we sell the 125 shares of BYF for $125 \times \$60 = \$7,500$. This amount is sufficient to buy back the 100 shares of AXE, which is selling for $75. But we will also have the bonds, which are worth $\$250 \times 1.04 = \$260$. If the bottom outcome occurs, we sell the 125 shares of BYF for $125 \times \$32 = \$4,000$—enough money to buy back the 100 shares of AXE, which is selling for $40. Again, we will have the risk-free bonds, worth $260. Regardless of the outcome, we end up with $260.

Recall that we put up no money of our own and ended up with a sure $260. It should be apparent that this is an extremely attractive transaction, so everyone would do it. The combined actions of multiple investors would drive down the price of AXE and/or drive up the price of BYF until an equilibrium was reached at which this transaction would not be profitable. Assuming stock BYF's price remained constant, stock AXE would fall to $47.50. Or assuming stock AXE's price remained constant, stock BYF would rise to $40.

Of course, this example is extremely simplified. Clearly a stock price can change to more than two other prices. Also, if a given stock is at one price, another stock may be at any other price. We have created a simple case here to illustrate a point. But as you will learn in Reading 72, when derivatives are involved, the simplification here is relatively safe. In fact, it is quite appropriate.

Now we look at another type of arbitrage opportunity, which involves a forward contract and will establish an appropriate price for the forward contract. Let stock AXE sell for $50. We borrow $50 at 4 percent interest by issuing a risk-free bond, use the money to buy one share of stock AXE, and simultaneously enter into a forward contract to sell this share at a price of $54 one period later. The stock will then move to either $75 or $40 in the next period; the forward contract will require that we deliver the stock and accept $54 for it; and we shall owe $50 \times 1.04 = \$52$ on the loan.

Let us look at the two outcomes. Suppose stock AXE goes to $75. We deliver the stock to settle the obligation on the forward contract and receive $54 for it. We use $52 of the $54 to pay back the loan, leaving a gain of $2. Now suppose AXE goes to $40. We deliver the stock, fulfilling the obligation of the forward

---

[19] One might reasonably wonder if finding a consumer article selling in Wal-Mart at a lower price than in Target is not a violation of the law of one price. It certainly is, but we make no claim that the market for consumer products is efficient. Our focus is on the financial markets where, for example, Goldman Sachs can hardly offer shares of IBM at one price while Merrill Lynch offers them at another.

EXHIBIT 69-5A Arbitrage Opportunity with Stock AXE, Stock BYF, and a Risk-Free Bond

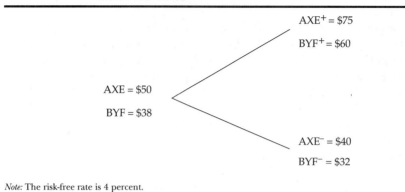

AXE = $50
BYF = $38

AXE$^+$ = $75
BYF$^+$ = $60

AXE$^-$ = $40
BYF$^-$ = $32

Note: The risk-free rate is 4 percent.

EXHIBIT 69-5B Execution of Arbitrage Transaction with Stock AXE, Stock BYF, and a Risk-Free Bond

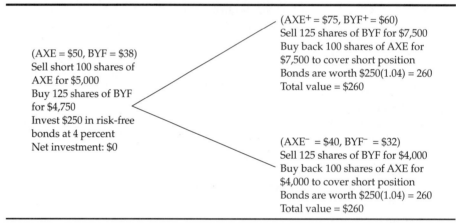

(AXE = $50, BYF = $38)
Sell short 100 shares of
AXE for $5,000
Buy 125 shares of BYF
for $4,750
Invest $250 in risk-free
bonds at 4 percent
Net investment: $0

(AXE$^+$ = $75, BYF$^+$ = $60)
Sell 125 shares of BYF for $7,500
Buy back 100 shares of AXE for
$7,500 to cover short position
Bonds are worth $250(1.04) = 260
Total value = $260

(AXE$^-$ = $40, BYF$^-$ = $32)
Sell 125 shares of BYF for $4,000
Buy back 100 shares of AXE for
$4,000 to cover short position
Bonds are worth $250(1.04) = 260
Total value = $260

contract, and receive $54. Again, we use $52 of the $54 to pay back the loan, leaving a gain of $2.

In either case we made $2, free and clear. In fact, we can even accommodate the possibility of more than two future prices for AXE. The key point is that we faced no risk and did not have to put up any of our own money, but we ended up with $2—clearly a good deal. In fact, this is what we would call an arbitrage profit. But from where did it originate?

It turns out that the forward price we received, $54, was an inappropriate price given current market conditions. In fact, it was just an arbitrary price, made up to illustrate the point. To eliminate the opportunity to earn the $2 profit, the forward price should be $52—equal, not coincidentally, to the amount owed on the loan. It is also no coincidence that $52 is the price of the asset increased by the rate of interest. We will discuss this point further in Reading 70.

In this example, many market participants would do this transaction as long it generates an arbitrage profit. These forces of arbitrage would either force the forward price down or force the price of the stock up until an equilibrium is reached that eliminates the opportunity to profit at no risk with no commitment of one's own funds.

We have just had a taste of not only the powerful forces of arbitrage but also a pricing model for one derivative, the forward contract. In this simple example, according to the pricing model, the forward price should be the spot price increased by the interest rate. Although there is a lot more to derivative pricing than shown here, the basic principle remains the same regardless of the type of instrument or the complexity of the setting: *Prices are set to eliminate the opportunity to profit at no risk with no commitment of one's own funds.* There are no opportunities for arbitrage profits.

Lest we be too naive, however, we must acknowledge that there is a large industry of arbitrageurs. So how can such an industry exist if there are no opportunities for riskless profit? One explanation is that most of the arbitrage transactions are more complex than this simple example and involve estimating information, which can result in differing opinions. Arbitrage involving options, for example, usually requires estimates of a stock's volatility. Different participants have different opinions about this volatility. It is quite possible that two counterparties trading with each other can believe that each is arbitraging against the other.

But more importantly, the absence of arbitrage opportunities is upheld, ironically, only if participants believe that arbitrage opportunities *do* exist. If market traders believe that no opportunities exist to earn arbitrage profits, then they will not follow market prices and compare these prices with what they ought to be, as in the forward contract example given above. Without participants watching closely, prices would surely get out of line and offer arbitrage opportunities. Thus, eliminating arbitrage opportunities requires that participants be vigilant to arbitrage opportunities. In other words, strange as it may sound, disbelief and skepticism concerning the absence of arbitrage opportunities are required in order that it hold as a legitimate principle.

Markets in which arbitrage opportunities are either nonexistent or are quickly eliminated are relatively efficient markets. Recall from your study of portfolio theory and investment analysis that efficient markets are those in which it is not possible, except by chance, to earn returns in excess of those that would be fair compensation for the risk assumed. Although abnormal returns can be earned in a variety of ways, arbitrage profits are definitely examples of abnormal returns, relatively obvious to identify and easy to capture. Thus, they are the most egregious violations of the principle of market efficiency. A market in which arbitrage profits do not exist is one in which the most obvious violations of market efficiency have been eliminated.

Throughout this book, we shall study derivatives by using the principle of arbitrage as a guide. We will assume that arbitrage opportunities cannot exist for any significant length of time. Thus, prices must conform to models that assume no arbitrage. On the other hand, we do not want to take the absence of arbitrage opportunities so seriously that we give up and believe that arbitrage opportunities never exist. Otherwise, they will arise, and someone else will take them from us.

We have now completed this introductory reading, which has touched only lightly on the world of derivatives. The remainder of the book is organized as follows: Reading 70 on forwards, Reading 71 on futures, Reading 72 on options, and Reading 73 on swaps provide details describing the types of instruments and how they are priced. Chapter 6 on forwards and futures, Reading 74 on options, and Chapter 8 on swaps discuss strategies using these instruments. Chapter 9 covers the integrative topic of risk management, introducing concepts and issues related to the management of risk and some tools and techniques for managing risk. We now proceed to Reading 70, which looks at forward markets and contracts.

8   SUMMARY

▷ A derivative contract is a financial instrument with a return that is obtained from or "derived" from the return of another underlying financial instrument.

▷ Exchange-traded derivatives are created, authorized, and traded on a derivatives exchange, an organized facility for trading derivatives. Exchange-traded derivatives are standardized instruments with respect to certain terms and conditions of the contract. They trade in accordance with rules and specifications prescribed by the derivatives exchange and are usually subject to governmental regulation. Exchange-traded derivatives are guaranteed by the exchange against loss resulting from the default of one of the parties. Over-the-counter derivatives are transactions created by any two parties off of a derivatives exchange. The parties set all of their own terms and conditions, and each assumes the credit risk of the other party.

▷ A forward commitment is an agreement between two parties in which one party agrees to buy and the other agrees to sell an asset at a future date at a price agreed on today. The three types of forward commitments are forward contracts, futures contracts, and swaps.

▷ A forward contract is a forward commitment created in the over-the-counter market. A futures contract is a forward commitment created and traded on a futures exchange. A swap is an over-the-counter transaction consisting of a series of forward commitments.

▷ A contingent claim is a derivative contract with a payoff dependent on the occurrence of a future event. The primary types of contingent claims are options, but other types involve variations of options, often combined with other financial instruments or derivatives.

▷ An option is a derivative contract giving one party the right to buy or sell an underlying asset at a fixed price over a period of time or at a specific point in time. The party obtaining the right pays a premium (the option price) at the start and receives the right to buy or sell, as prescribed by the contract. The two types of options are a call (the right to buy) and a put (the right to sell).

▷ The size of the global derivatives market can be measured by notional principal, which is the amount of the underlying on which a derivative is based, and by market value, which is the economic worth of the derivative.

▷ Derivative markets serve many useful purposes such as providing price discovery, facilitating risk management, making markets more efficient, and lowering transaction costs. Derivatives are often criticized as being excessively dangerous for unknowledgeable investors and have been inappropriately likened to gambling.

▷ Arbitrage is a process through which an investor can buy an asset or combination of assets at one price and concurrently sell at a higher price, thereby earning a profit without investing any money or being exposed to any risk. The combined actions of many investors engaging in arbitrage results in rapid price adjustments that eliminate these opportunities, thereby bringing prices back in line and making markets more efficient.

PROBLEMS

1. For all parties involved, which of the following financial instruments is NOT an example of a forward commitment?

    A. Swap

    B. Call option

    C. Futures contract

    D. Forward contract

2. The main risk faced by an individual who enters into a forward contract to buy the S&P 500 Index is that

    A. the market may rise.

    B. the market may fall.

    C. market volatility may rise.

    D. market volatility may fall.

3. Which of the following statements is *most* accurate?

    A. Futures contracts are private transactions.

    B. Forward contracts are marked to market daily.

    C. Futures contracts have more default risk than forward contracts.

    D. Forward contracts require that both parties to the transaction have a high degree of creditworthiness.

4. Which of the following statements is *least* accurate?

    A. Futures contracts are easier to offset than forward contracts.

    B. Forward contracts are generally more liquid than futures contracts.

    C. Forward contracts are easier to tailor to specific needs than futures contracts.

    D. Futures contracts are characterized by having a clearinghouse as an intermediary.

5. A swap is *best* characterized as a

    A. series of forward contracts.

    B. derivative contract that has not gained widespread popularity.

    C. single fixed payment in exchange for a single floating payment.

    D. contract that is binding on only one of the parties to the transaction.

6. Which of the following is *most* representative of forward contracts and contingent claims?

	Forward Contracts	Contingent Claims
A.	Premium paid at inception	Premium paid at inception
B.	Premium paid at inception	No premium paid at inception
C.	No premium paid at inception	Premium paid at inception
D.	No premium paid at inception	No premium paid at inception

7. For the long position, the *most likely* advantage of contingent claims over forward commitments is that contingent claims

    A. are easier to offset than forward commitments.

    B. have lower default risk than forward commitments.

    C. permit gains while protecting against losses.

    D. are typically cheaper to initiate than forward commitments.

8. For derivative contracts, the notional principal is *best* described as
   A. the amount of the underlying asset covered by the contract.
   B. a measure of the actual payments made and received in the contract.
   C. tending to underestimate the actual payments made and received in the contract.
   D. being, conceptually and in aggregate, the best available measure of the size of the market.

9. By volume, the most widely used group of derivatives is the one with contracts written on which of the following types of underlying assets?
   A. Financial
   B. Commodities
   C. Energy-related
   D. Precious metals

10. Which of the following is *least* likely to be a purpose served by derivative markets?
    A. Arbitrage
    B. Price discovery
    C. Risk management
    D. Hedging and speculation

11. The *most likely* reason derivative markets have flourished is that
    A. derivatives are easy to understand and use.
    B. derivatives have relatively low transaction costs.
    C. the pricing of derivatives is relatively straightforward.
    D. strong regulation ensures that transacting parties are protected from fraud.

12. If the risk-free rate of interest is 5 percent and an investor enters into a transaction that has no risk, the rate of return the investor should earn in the absence of arbitrage opportunities is
    A. 0%.
    B. between 0% and 5%.
    C. 5%.
    D. more than 5%.

13. If the spot price of gold is $250 per ounce and the risk-free rate of interest is 10 percent per annum, the six-month forward price per ounce of gold, in equilibrium, should be *closest* to
    A. $250.00.
    B. $256.25.
    C. $262.50.
    D. $275.00.

14. Concerning efficient financial (including derivative) markets, the *most appropriate* description is that
    A. it is often possible to earn abnormal returns.
    B. the law of one price holds only in the academic literature.
    C. arbitrage opportunities rarely exist and are quickly eliminated.
    D. arbitrage opportunities often exist and can be exploited for profit.

15. Stock A costs $10.00 today and its price will be either $7.50 or $12.50 next period. Stock B's price will be either $18.00 or $30.00 next period. If risk-free borrowing and lending are possible at 8 percent per period, neither stock pays dividends, and it is possible to buy and sell fractional shares, Stock B's equilibrium price today should be *closest* to

   A. $19.00.

   B. $21.00.

   C. $24.00.

   D. $26.00.

FORWARD MARKETS AND CONTRACTS

LEARNING OUTCOMES

The candidate should be able to:

a. discuss the differences between the positions held by the long and short parties to a forward contract in terms of delivery/settlement and default risk;

b. describe the procedures for settling a forward contract at expiration and discuss how a party to a forward contract can terminate a position prior to expiration as well as how credit risk is affected by the way in which a position is terminated;

c. differentiate between a dealer and an end user of a forward contract;

d. describe the characteristics of equity forward contracts;

e. describe the characteristics of forward contracts on zero-coupon and coupon bonds;

f. explain the characteristics of the Eurodollar time deposit market, define LIBOR and Euribor, and describe the characteristics of forward rate agreements (FRAs);

g. calculate and interpret the payment at expiration of an FRA, explain each of the component terms and describe the characteristics of currency forward contracts.

INTRODUCTION 1

In Reading 69, we gave a general overview of global derivative markets. We identified those markets as forward markets, futures markets, options markets, and swap markets. The following series of readings focuses individually on those markets. We begin with forward markets.

First recall our definition of a forward contract: *A forward contract is an agreement between two parties in which one party, the buyer, agrees to buy from the other party, the seller, an underlying asset or other derivative, at a future date at a price established at the start of the contract.* Therefore, it is a commitment by two parties to engage in a transaction at a later date with the price set in advance. The buyer is often called the **long** and the seller is often

Analysis of Derivatives for the CFA® Program, by Don M. Chance, Copyright © 2003 by Association for Investment Management and Research. Reprinted with permission.

called the **short.**[1] Although any two parties can agree on such a contract, in this book we are interested only in forward contracts that involve large corporations, financial institutions, nonprofit organizations, or governments.

Recalling an example from Reading 69, a pension fund manager, anticipating the receipt of cash at a future date, might enter into a commitment to purchase a stock portfolio at a later date at a price agreed on today. By doing so, the manager's position is unaffected by any changes in the value of the stock portfolio between today and the date of the actual investment in the stock portfolio. In this sense, the manager is hedged against an increase in stock prices until the cash is received and invested. The disadvantage of such a transaction is that the manager is also hedged against any decreases in stock prices. If stock prices fall between the time the commitment is established and the time the cash is received, the manager will regret having entered into the forward contract because the stock could have been acquired at a lower price. But that is the nature of a forward contract hedge: It locks in a price.

An important feature of a forward contract is that neither party pays any money at the start. In Chapter 9, we shall look at how the parties might require some collateral to minimize the risk of default, but for most of this book, we shall ignore this point. So keep in mind this very important aspect of forward contracts: *No money changes hands at the start.*

1.1 Delivery and Settlement of a Forward Contract

When a forward contract expires, there are two possible arrangements that can be used to settle the obligations of the parties. A deliverable forward contract stipulates that the long will pay the agreed-upon price to the short, who in turn will deliver the underlying asset to the long, a process called **delivery.** An alternative procedure, called **cash settlement,** permits the long and short to pay the net cash value of the position on the delivery date. For example, suppose two parties agree to a forward contract to deliver a zero-coupon bond at a price of $98 per $100 par. At the contract's expiration, suppose the underlying zero-coupon bond is selling at a price of $98.25. The long is due to receive from the short an asset worth $98.25, for which a payment to the short of $98.00 is required. In a cash-settled forward contract, the short simply pays the long $0.25. If the zero-coupon bond were selling for $97.50, the long would pay the short $0.50. Delivery of a zero-coupon bond is not a difficult thing to do, however, and cash-settled contracts are more commonly used in situations where delivery is impractical.[2] For example, if the underlying is the Russell 3000 Index, the short would have to deliver to the long a portfolio containing each of the Russell 3000 stocks proportionate to its weighting in the index. Consequently, cash settlement is much more practical. Cash-settled forward contracts are sometimes called **NDFs,** for **nondeliverable forwards,** although this term is used predominately with respect to foreign exchange forwards.

---

[1] As pointed out in Reading 69 with respect to the word *underlying,* the derivatives industry often uses nouns, verbs, adjectives, and adverbs as parts of speech other than what they are. Hence, words like *long* and *short* are used not as adjectives but as nouns.

[2] Be aware, however, that the choice of delivery or cash settlement is not an option available at expiration. It is negotiated between the parties at the start.

1.2 Default Risk and Forward Contracts

An important characteristic of forward contracts is that they are subject to default. Regardless of whether the contract is for delivery or cash settlement, the potential exists for a party to default. In the zero-coupon bond example above, the long might be unable to pay the $98 or the short might be unable to buy the zero-coupon bond and make delivery of the bond to the long. Generally speaking, however, forward contracts are structured so that only the party owing the greater amount can default. In other words, if the short is obligated to deliver a zero-coupon bond selling for more than $98, then the long would not be obligated to make payment unless the short makes delivery. Likewise, in a cash settled contract, only one party—the one owing the greater amount—can default. We discuss the nature of this credit risk in the following section and in Section 5 after we have determined how to value forward contracts. We also address the topic of credit risk in derivative contracts in Chapter 9.

1.3 Termination of a Forward Contract

Let us note that a forward contract is nearly always constructed with the idea that the participants will hold on to their positions until the contract expires and either engage in delivery of the asset or settle the cash equivalent, as required in the specific contract. The possibility exists, however, that at least one of the participants might wish to terminate the position prior to expiration. For example, suppose a party goes long, meaning that she agrees to buy the asset at the expiration date at the price agreed on at the start, but she subsequently decides to terminate the contract before expiration. We shall assume that the contract calls for delivery rather than cash settlement at expiration.

To see the details of the contract termination, suppose it is part of the way through the life of the contract, and the long decides that she no longer wishes to buy the asset at expiration. She can then re-enter the market and create a new forward contract expiring at the same time as the original forward contract, taking the position of the seller instead. Because of price changes in the market during the period since the original contract was created, this new contract would likely have a different price at which she would have to commit to sell. She would then be long a contract to buy the asset at expiration at one price and short a contract to sell the asset at expiration at a different price. It should be apparent that she has no further exposure to the price of the asset.

For example, suppose she is long to buy at $40 and short to deliver at $42. Depending on the characteristics of the contract, one of several possibilities could occur at expiration. Everything could go as planned—the party holding the short position of the contract on which she is long at $40 delivers the asset to her, and she pays him $40. She then delivers the asset to the party who is long the contract on which she is short at $42. That party pays her $42. She nets $2. The transaction is over.

There is always a possibility that her counterparty on the long contract could default. She is still obligated to deliver the asset on the short contract, for which she will receive $42. But if her counterparty on the long contract defaults, she has to buy the asset in the market and could suffer a significant loss. There is also a possibility that the counterparty on her short contract could fail to pay her the $42. Of course, she would then not deliver the asset but would be exposed to the risk of changes in the asset's price. This type of problem illustrates the credit risk in a forward contract. We shall cover credit risk in more detail in Section 5 of this reading and in Chapter 9.

To avoid the credit risk, when she re-enters the market to go short the forward contract, she could contact the same counterparty with whom she engaged in the long forward contract. They could agree to cancel both contracts. Because she would be owed $2 at expiration, cancellation of the contract would result in the counterparty paying her the present value of $2. This termination or offset of the original forward position is clearly desirable for both counterparties because it eliminates the credit risk.[3] It is always possible, however, that she might receive a better price from another counterparty. If that price is sufficiently attractive and she does not perceive the credit risk to be too high, she may choose to deal with the other counterparty and leave the credit risk in the picture.

2   THE STRUCTURE OF GLOBAL FORWARD MARKETS

The global market for forward contracts is part of a vast network of financial institutions that make markets in these instruments as well as in other related derivatives, such as swaps and options. Some dealers specialize in certain markets and contracts, such as forward contracts on the euro or forward contracts on Japanese equity products. These dealers are mainly large global banking institutions, but many large non-banking institutions, such as Goldman Sachs and Merrill Lynch, are also big players in this market.

Dealers engage in transactions with two types of parties: end users and other dealers. An end user is typically a corporation, nonprofit organization, or government.[4] An end user is generally a party with a risk management problem that is searching for a dealer to provide it with a financial transaction to solve that problem. Although the problem could simply be that the party wants to take a position in anticipation of a market move, more commonly the end user has a risk it wants to reduce or eliminate.

As an example, Hoffman-LaRoche, the large Swiss pharmaceutical company, sells its products globally. Anticipating the receipt of a large amount of cash in U.S. dollars and worried about a decrease in the value of the dollar relative to the Swiss franc, it could buy a forward contract to sell the dollar and buy Swiss francs. It might seek out a dealer such as UBS Warburg, the investment firm affiliated with the large Swiss bank UBS, or it might approach any of the other large multinational banks with which it does business. Or it might end up dealing with a non-bank entity, like Merrill Lynch. Assume that Hoffman-LaRoche enters into this contract with UBS Warburg. Hoffman-LaRoche is the end user; UBS Warburg is the dealer.

Transactions in forward contracts typically are conducted over the phone. Each dealer has a quote desk, whose phone number is well known to the major participants in the market. If a party wishes to conduct a transaction, it simply phones the dealer for a quote. The dealer stands ready to take either side of the transaction, quoting a bid and an ask price or rate. The bid is the price at which the dealer is willing to pay for the future purchase of the asset, and the ask is the price at which the dealer is willing to sell. When a dealer engages in a forward transaction, it has then taken on risk from the other party. For example, in the aforementioned transaction of Hoffman-LaRoche and UBS Warburg, by entering into the contract, UBS Warburg takes on a risk that Hoffman-LaRoche has eliminated. Specifically, UBS Warburg has now committed to buying dollars and

---

[3] This statement is made under the assumption that the parties do not want the credit risk. Credit risk, like other risks, however, can be a risk that some parties want because of the potential for earning attractive returns by using their expertise in measuring the actual credit risk relative to the credit risk as perceived by the market. In addition, credit risk offers diversification benefits. We will discuss these points more fully in Chapter 9.

[4] The U.S. government does not transact in forward contracts or other derivatives, but some foreign governments and central banks do. Within the United States, however, some state and local governments do engage in forward contracts and other derivatives.

selling Swiss francs at a future date. Thus, UBS Warburg is effectively long the dollar and stands to gain from a strengthening dollar/weakening Swiss franc. Typically dealers do not want to hold this exposure. Rather, they find another party to offset the exposure with another derivative or spot transaction. Thus, UBS Warburg is a wholesaler of risk—buying it, selling it, and trying to earn a profit off the spread between its buying price and selling price.

One might reasonably wonder why Hoffman-LaRoche could not avoid the cost of dealing with UBS Warburg. In some cases, it might be able to. It might be aware of another party with the exact opposite needs, but such a situation is rare. The market for financial products such as forward contracts is made up of wholesalers of risk management products who use their technical expertise, their vast network of contacts, and their access to critical financial market information to provide a more efficient means for end users to engage in such risk management transactions.

Dealers such as UBS Warburg lay off the risk they do not wish to assume by transacting with other dealers and potentially other end users. If they do this carefully, quickly, and at accurate prices, they can earn a profit from this market-making activity. One should not get the impression, however, that market making is a highly profitable activity. The competition is fierce, which keeps bid–ask spreads very low and makes it difficult to earn much money on a given transaction. Indeed, many market makers do not make much money on individual transactions—they typically make a small amount of money on each transaction and do a large number of transactions. They may even lose money on some standard transactions, hoping to make up losses on more-complicated, nonstandard transactions, which occur less frequently but have higher bid–ask spreads.

Risk magazine conducts annual surveys to identify the top dealers in various derivative products. Exhibit 70-1 presents the results of those surveys for two of the forward products we cover here, currency and interest rate forwards. Interest rate forwards are called forward rate agreements (FRAs). In the next section, we shall study the different types of forward contracts and note that there are some others not covered in the *Risk* surveys.

One of these surveys was sent to banks and investment banks that are active dealers in over-the-counter derivatives. The other survey was sent to end users. The tabulations are based on respondents' simple rankings of who they think are the best dealers. Although the identities of the specific dealer firms are not critical, it is interesting and helpful to be aware of the major players in these types of contracts. Most of the world's leading global financial institutions are listed, but many other big names are not. It is also interesting to observe that the perceptions of the users of these dealer firms' services differ somewhat from the dealers' self-perceptions. Be aware, however, that the rankings change, sometimes drastically, each year.

EXHIBIT 70-1 *Risk* **Magazine Surveys of Banks, Investment Banks, and Corporate End Users to Determine the Top Three Dealers in Currency and Interest Rate Forwards**

	Respondents	
Currencies	**Banks and Investment Banks**	**Corporate End Users**
Currency Forwards		
$/€	UBS Warburg	Citigroup
	Deutsche Bank	Royal Bank of Scotland
	JP Morgan Chase	JP Morgan Chase/Bank of America

	Respondents	
Currencies	Banks and Investment Banks	Corporate End Users

Currency Forwards (continued)

$/¥	UBS Warburg	Citigroup
	Citigroup	Bank of America
	JP Morgan Chase	JP Morgan Chase/UBS Warburg
$/£	UBS Warburg	Royal Bank of Scotland
	Royal Bank of Scotland	Citigroup
	Hong Kong Shanghai Banking Corporation	UBS Warburg
$/SF	UBS Warburg	UBS Warburg
	Credit Suisse First Boston	Citigroup
	BNP Paribas	Credit Suisse First Boston

Interest Rate Forwards (FRAs)

$	JP Morgan Chase	JP Morgan Chase
	Bank of America	Royal Bank of Scotland
	Deutsche Bank	Bank of America
€	Deutsche Bank	Royal Bank of Scotland
	Intesa BCI	JP Morgan Chase
	Royal Bank of Scotland	Deutsche Bank
¥	Mizuho Securities	Citigroup
	JP Morgan Chase	Merrill Lynch
	BNP Paribas	Hong Kong Shanghai Banking Corporation
£	Royal Bank of Scotland	Royal Bank of Scotland
	Commerzbank	Bank of America/ING Barings
	Deutsche Bank	
SF	Credit Suisse First Boston	UBS Warburg
	UBS Warburg	Credit Suisse First Boston
	Deutsche Bank	Citigroup/ING Barings

Note: $ = US dollar, € = euro, ¥ = Japanese yen, £ = U.K. pound sterling, SF = Swiss franc.

Source: Risk, September 2002, pp. 30–67 for banks and investment banking dealer respondents, and June 2002, pp. 24–34 for end user respondents. The end user survey provides responses from corporations and asset managers. The above results are for corporate respondents only.

3   TYPES OF FORWARD CONTRACTS

In this section, we examine the types of forward contracts that fall within the scope of this book. By the word "types," we mean the underlying asset groups on which these forward contracts are created. Because the CFA Program focuses on the asset management industry, our primary interest is in equity, interest rate and fixed-income, and currency forwards.

3.1 Equity Forwards

An **equity forward** is a contract calling for the purchase of an individual stock, a stock portfolio, or a stock index at a later date. For the most part, the differences in types of equity forward contracts are only slight, depending on whether the contract is on an individual stock, a portfolio of stocks, or a stock index.

3.1.1 Forward Contracts on Individual Stocks

Consider an asset manager responsible for the portfolio of a high-net-worth individual. As is sometimes the case, such portfolios may be concentrated in a small number of stocks, sometimes stocks that have been in the family for years. In many cases, the individual may be part of the founding family of a particular company. Let us say that the stock is called Gregorian Industries, Inc., or GII, and the client is so heavily invested in this stock that her portfolio is not diversified. The client notifies the portfolio manager of her need for $2 million in cash in six months. This cash can be raised by selling 16,000 shares at the current price of $125 per share. Thus, the risk exposure concerns the market value of $2 million of stock. For whatever reason, it is considered best not to sell the stock any earlier than necessary. The portfolio manager realizes that a forward contract to sell GII in six months will accomplish the client's desired objective. The manager contacts a forward contract dealer and obtains a quote of $128.13 as the price at which a forward contract to sell the stock in six months could be constructed.[5] In other words, the portfolio manager could enter into a contract to sell the stock to the dealer in six months at $128.13. We assume that this contract is deliverable, meaning that when the sale is actually made, the shares will be delivered to the dealer. Assuming that the client has some flexibility in the amount of money needed, let us say that the contract is signed for the sale of 15,600 shares at $128.13, which will raise $1,998,828. Of course when the contract expires, the stock could be selling for any price. The client can gain or lose on the transaction. If the stock rises to a price above $128.13 during the six-month period, the client will still have to deliver the stock for $128.13. But if the price falls, the client will still get $128.13 per share for the stock.

3.1.2 Forward Contracts on Stock Portfolios

Because modern portfolio theory and good common sense dictate that investors should hold diversified portfolios, it is reasonable to assume that forward contracts on specific stock portfolios would be useful. Suppose a pension fund manager knows that in three months he will need to sell about $20 million of stock to make payments to retirees. The manager has analyzed the portfolio and determined the precise identities of the stocks he wants to sell and the number of shares of each that he would like to sell. Thus the manager has designated a specific sub-portfolio to be sold. The problem is that the prices of these stocks in three months are uncertain. The manager can, however, lock in the sale prices by entering into a forward contract to sell the portfolio. This can be done one of two ways.

The manager can enter into a forward contract on each stock that he wants to sell. Alternatively, he can enter into a forward contract on the overall portfolio. The first way would be more costly, as each contract would incur administrative costs, whereas the second way would incur only one set of costs.[6] Assume

---

[5] In Section 4, we shall learn how to calculate forward prices such as this one.

[6] Ignoring those costs, there would be no difference in doing forward contracts on individual stocks or a single forward contract on a portfolio. Because of the non-linearity of their payoffs, this is not true for options. A portfolio of options is not the same as an option on a portfolio, but a portfolio of forward contracts is the same as a forward contract on a portfolio, ignoring the aforementioned costs.

that the manager chooses the second method. He provides a list of the stocks and number of shares of each he wishes to sell to the dealer and obtains a quote. The dealer gives him a quote of $20,200,000. So, in three months, the manager will sell the stock to the dealer and receive $20,200,000. The transaction can be structured to call for either actual delivery or cash settlement, but in either case, the client will effectively receive $20,200,000 for the stock.[7]

3.1.3 Forward Contracts on Stock Indices

Many equity forward contracts are based on a stock index. For example, consider a U.K. asset manager who wants to protect the value of her portfolio that is a Financial Times Stock Exchange 100 index fund, or who wants to eliminate a risk for which the FTSE 100 Index is a sufficiently accurate representation of the risk she wishes to eliminate. For example, the manager may be anticipating the sale of a number of U.K. blue chip shares at a future date. The manager could, as in our stock portfolio example, take a specific portfolio of stocks to a forward contract dealer and obtain a forward contract on that portfolio. She realizes, however, that a forward contract on a widely accepted benchmark would result in a better price quote, because the dealer can more easily hedge the risk with other transactions. Moreover, the manager is not even sure which stocks she will still be holding at the later date. She simply knows that she will sell a certain amount of stock at a later date and believes that the FTSE 100 is representative of the stock that she will sell. The manager is concerned with the systematic risk associated with the U.K. stock market, and accordingly, she decides that selling a forward contract on the FTSE 100 would be a good way to manage the risk.

Assume that the portfolio manager decides to protect £15,000,000 of stock. The dealer quotes a price of £6,000 on a forward contract covering £15,000,000. We assume that the contract will be cash settled because such index contracts are nearly always done that way. When the contract expiration date arrives, let us say that the index is at £5,925—a decrease of 1.25 percent from the forward price. Because the manager is short the contract and its price went down, the transaction makes money. But how much did it make on a notional principal of £15,000,000?

The index declined by 1.25 percent. Thus, the transaction should make $0.0125 \times £15,000,000 = £187,500$. In other words, the dealer would have to pay £187,500 in cash. If the portfolio were a FTSE 100 index fund, then it would be viewed as a portfolio initially worth £15,000,000 that declined by 1.25 percent, a loss of £187,500. The forward contract offsets this loss. Of course, in reality, the portfolio is not an index fund and such a hedge is not perfect, but as noted above, there are sometimes reasons for preferring that the forward contract be based on an index.

3.1.4 The Effect of Dividends

It is important to note the effect of dividends in equity forward contracts. Any equity portfolio nearly always has at least a few stocks that pay dividends, and it is inconceivable that any well-known equity index would not have some component stocks that pay dividends. Equity forward contracts typically have payoffs based only on the price of the equity, value of the portfolio, or level of the index.

---

[7] If, for example, the stock is worth $20,500,000 and the transaction calls for delivery, the manager will transfer the stocks to the dealer and receive $20,200,000. The client effectively takes an opportunity loss of $300,000. If the transaction is structured as a cash settlement, the client will pay the dealer $300,000. The client would then sell the stock in the market, receiving $20,500,000 and netting $20,200,000 after settling the forward contract with the dealer. Similarly, if the stock is selling for less than the amount guaranteed by the forward contract, the client will deliver the stock and receive $20,200,000 or, if the transaction is cash settled, the client will sell the stock in the market and receive a cash payment from the dealer, making the effective sale price still $20,200,000.

They do not ordinarily pay off any dividends paid by the component stocks. An exception, however, is that some equity forwards on stock indices are based on total return indices. For example, there are two versions of the well-known S&P 500 Index. One represents only the market value of the stocks. The other, called the S&P 500 Total Return Index, is structured so that daily dividends paid by the stocks are reinvested in additional units of the index, as though it were a portfolio. In this manner, the rate of return on the index, and the payoff of any forward contract based on it, reflects the payment and reinvestment of dividends into the underlying index. Although this feature might appear attractive, it is not necessarily of much importance in risk management problems. The variability of prices is so much greater than the variability of dividends that managing price risk is considered much more important than worrying about the uncertainty of dividends.

In summary, equity forwards can be based on individual stocks, specific stock portfolios, or stock indices. Moreover, these underlying equities often pay dividends, which can affect forward contracts on equities. Let us now look at bond and interest rate forward contracts.

3.2 Bond and Interest Rate Forward Contracts

Forward contracts on bonds are similar to forward contracts on interest rates, but the two are different instruments. Forward contracts on bonds, in fact, are no more difficult to understand than those on equities. Drawing on our experience of Section 3.1, we simply extend the notion of a forward contract on an individual stock, a specific stock portfolio, or a stock index to that of a forward contract on an individual bond, a specific bond portfolio, or a bond index.[8]

3.2.1 Forward Contracts on Individual Bonds and Bond Portfolios

Although a forward contract on a bond and one on a stock are similar, some basic differences nonetheless exist between the two. For example, the bond may pay a coupon, which corresponds somewhat to the dividend that a stock might pay. But unlike a stock, a bond matures, and a forward contract on a bond must expire prior to the bond's maturity date. In addition, bonds often have many special features such as calls and convertibility. Finally, we should note that unlike a stock, a bond carries the risk of default. A forward contract written on a bond must contain a provision to recognize how default is defined, what it means for the bond to default, and how default would affect the parties to the contract.

In addition to forward contracts on individual bonds, there are also forward contracts on portfolios of bonds as well as on bond indices. The technical distinctions between forward contracts on individual bonds and collections of bonds, however, are relatively minor.

The primary bonds for which we shall consider forward contracts are default-free zero-coupon bonds, typically called Treasury bills or T-bills in the United States, which serve as a proxy for the risk-free rate.[9] In a forward contract on a T-bill, one party agrees to buy the T-bill at a later date, prior to the bill's maturity, at a price agreed on today. T-bills are typically sold at a discount from par value and the price is quoted in terms of the discount rate. Thus, if a 180-day T-bill is selling at a discount of 4 percent, its price per $1 par will be $1 - 0.04(180/360) = \$0.98$.

---

[8] It may be useful to review Chapters 1 and 3 of *Fixed Income Analysis for the Chartered Financial Analyst Program* by Frank J. Fabozzi, New Hope, PA: Frank J. Fabozzi Associates (2000).

[9] A government-issued zero-coupon bond is typically used as a proxy for a risk-free asset because it is assumed to be free of default risk. It can be purchased and held to maturity, thereby eliminating any market value risk, and it has no reinvestment risk because it has no coupons. If the bond is liquidated before maturity, however, some market value risk exists in addition to the risk associated with reinvesting the market price.

The use of 360 days is the convention in calculating the discount. So the bill will sell for $0.98. If purchased and held to maturity, it will pay off $1. This procedure means that the interest is deducted from the face value in advance, which is called **discount interest.**

The T-bill is usually traded by quoting the discount rate, not the price. It is understood that the discount rate can be easily converted to the price by the above procedure. A forward contract might be constructed that would call for delivery of a 90-day T-bill in 60 days. Such a contract might sell for $0.9895, which would imply a discount rate of 4.2 percent because $1 - 0.042(90/360) = 0.9895. Later in this reading, we shall see how forward prices of T-bills are derived.

In addition to forward contracts on zero-coupon bonds/T-bills, we shall consider forward contracts on default-free coupon-bearing bonds, also called Treasury bonds in the United States. These instruments pay interest, typically in semiannual installments, and can sell for more (less) than par value if the yield is lower (higher) than the coupon rate. Prices are typically quoted without the interest that has accrued since the last coupon date, but with a few exceptions, we shall always work with the full price—that is, the price including accrued interest. Prices are often quoted by stating the yield. Forward contracts call for delivery of such a bond at a date prior to the bond's maturity, for which the long pays the short the agreed-upon price.

3.2.2 Forward Contracts on Interest Rates: Forward Rate Agreements

So far in Section 3.2 we have discussed forward contracts on actual fixed-income securities. Fixed-income security prices are driven by interest rates. A more common type of forward contract is the interest rate forward contract, more commonly called a **forward rate agreement** or **FRA.** Before we can begin to understand FRAs, however, we must examine the instruments on which they are based.

There is a large global market for time deposits in various currencies issued by large creditworthy banks. This market is primarily centered in London but also exists elsewhere, though not in the United States. The primary time deposit instrument is called the **Eurodollar,** which is a dollar deposited outside the Unites States. Banks borrow dollars from other banks by issuing Eurodollar time deposits, which are essentially short-term unsecured loans. In London, the rate on such dollar loans is called the London Interbank Rate. Although there are rates for both borrowing and lending, in the financial markets the lending rate, called the **London Interbank Offer Rate** or **LIBOR,** is more commonly used in derivative contracts. LIBOR is the rate at which London banks lend dollars to other London banks. Even though it represents a loan outside of the United States, LIBOR is considered to be the best representative rate on a dollar borrowed by a private, i.e., nongovernmental, high-quality borrower. It should be noted, however, that the London market includes many branches of banks from outside the United Kingdom, and these banks are also active participants in the Eurodollar market.

A Eurodollar time deposit is structured as follows. Let us say a London bank such as NatWest needs to borrow $10 million for 30 days. It obtains a quote from the Royal Bank of Scotland for a rate of 5.25 percent. Thus, 30-day LIBOR is 5.25 percent. If NatWest takes the deal, it will owe $10,000,000 \times [1 + 0.0525(30/360)] = $10,043,750$ in 30 days. Note that, like the Treasury bill market, the convention in the Eurodollar market is to prorate the quoted interest rate over 360 days. In contrast to the Treasury bill market, the interest is not deducted from the principal. Rather, it is added on to the face value, a procedure appropriately called **add-on interest.** The market for Eurodollar time deposits is quite large, and the rates on these instruments are assembled by a central organization and quoted in financial newspapers. The British Bankers Association publishes a semi-official Eurodollar rate, compiled from an average of the quotes of London banks.

The U.S. dollar is not the only instrument for which such time deposits exist. Eurosterling, for example, trades in Tokyo, and Euroyen trades in London. You may be wondering about Euroeuro. Actually, there is no such entity as Euroeuro, at least not by that name. The Eurodollar instrument described here has nothing to do with the European currency known as the euro. Eurodollars, Euroyen, Eurosterling, etc. have been around longer than the euro currency and, despite the confusion, have retained their nomenclature. An analogous instrument does exist, however—a euro-denominated loan in which one bank borrows euros from another. Trading in euros and euro deposits occurs in most major world cities, and two similar rates on such euro deposits are commonly quoted. One, called EuroLIBOR, is compiled in London by the British Bankers Association, and the other, called Euribor, is compiled in Frankfurt and published by the European Central Bank. Euribor is more widely used and is the rate we shall refer to in this book.

Now let us return to the world of FRAs. FRAs are contracts in which the underlying is neither a bond nor a Eurodollar or Euribor deposit but simply an interest payment made in dollars, Euribor, or any other currency at a rate appropriate for that currency. Our primary focus will be on dollar LIBOR and Euribor, so we shall henceforth adopt the terminology LIBOR to represent dollar LIBOR and Euribor to represent the euro deposit rate.

Because the mechanics of FRAs are the same for all currencies, for illustrative purposes we shall use LIBOR. Consider an FRA expiring in 90 days for which the underlying is 180-day LIBOR. Suppose the dealer quotes this instrument at a rate of 5.5 percent. Suppose the end user goes long and the dealer goes short. The end user is essentially long the rate and will benefit if rates increase. The dealer is essentially short the rate and will benefit if rates decrease. The contract covers a given notional principal, which we shall assume is $10 million.

The contract stipulates that at expiration, the parties identify the rate on new 180-day LIBOR time deposits. This rate is called 180-day LIBOR. It is, thus, the underlying rate on which the contract is based. Suppose that at expiration in 90 days, the rate on 180-day LIBOR is 6 percent. That 6 percent interest will be paid 180 days later. Therefore, the present value of a Eurodollar time deposit at that point in time would be

$$\frac{\$10,000,000}{1 + 0.06\left(\dfrac{180}{360}\right)}$$

At expiration, then, the end user, the party going long the FRA in our example, receives the following payment from the dealer, which is the party going short:

$$\$10,000,000\left[\frac{(0.06 - 0.055)\left(\dfrac{180}{360}\right)}{1 + 0.06\left(\dfrac{180}{360}\right)}\right] = \$24,272$$

If the underlying rate is less than 5.5 percent, the payment is calculated based on the difference between the 5.5 percent rate and the underlying rate and is paid by the long to the short. It is important to note that even though the contract expires in 90 days, the rate is on a 180-day LIBOR instrument; therefore, the rate calculation adjusts by the factor 180/360. The fact that 90 days have elapsed at expiration is not relevant to the calculation of the payoff.

Before presenting the general formula, let us review the calculations in the numerator and denominator. In the numerator, we see that the contract is obviously paying the difference between the actual rate that exists in the market on the contract expiration date and the agreed-upon rate, adjusted for the fact that the rate applies to a 180-day instrument, multiplied by the notional principal. The divisor appears because when Eurodollar rates are quoted in the market, they are based on the assumption that the rate applies to an instrument that accrues interest at that rate with the interest paid a certain number of days (here 180) later. When participants determine this rate in the London Eurodollar market, it is understood to apply to a Eurodollar time deposit that begins now and matures 180 days later. So the interest on an actual Eurodollar deposit would not be paid until 180 days later. Thus, it is necessary to adjust the FRA payoff to reflect the fact that the rate implies a payment that would occur 180 days later on a standard Eurodollar deposit. This adjustment is easily done by simply discounting the payment at the current LIBOR, which here is 6 percent, prorated over 180 days. These conventions are also followed in the market for FRAs with other underlying rates.

In general, the FRA payoff formula (from the perspective of the party going long) is

$$\text{Notional principal} \left[\frac{(\text{Underlying rate at expiration} - \text{Forward contract rate})\left(\dfrac{\text{Days in underlying rate}}{360}\right)}{1 + \text{Underlying rate at expiration}\left(\dfrac{\text{Days in underlying rate}}{360}\right)} \right]$$

where *forward contract rate* represents the rate the two parties agree will be paid and *days in underlying rate* refers to the number of days to maturity of the instrument on which the underlying rate is based.

One somewhat confusing feature of FRAs is the fact that they mature in a certain number of days and are based on a rate that applies to an instrument maturing in a certain number of days measured from the maturity of the FRA. Thus, there are two day figures associated with each contract. Our example was a 90-day contract on 180-day LIBOR. To avoid confusion, the FRA markets use a special type of terminology that converts the number of days to months. Specifically, our example FRA is referred to as a 3×9, reflecting the fact that the contract expires in three months and that six months later, or nine months from the contract initiation date, the interest is paid on the underlying Eurodollar time deposit on whose rate the contract is based.[10]

FRAs are available in the market for a variety of maturities that are considered somewhat standard. Exhibit 70-2 presents the most common maturities. Most dealers follow the convention that contracts should expire in a given number of exact months and should be on the most commonly traded Eurodollar rates such as 30-day LIBOR, 60-day LIBOR, 90-day LIBOR, 180-day LIBOR, and so on. If a

EXHIBIT 70-2 FRA Descriptive Notation and Interpretation

Notation	Contract Expires in	Underlying Rate
1×3	1 month	60-day LIBOR
1×4	1 month	90-day LIBOR
1×7	1 month	180-day LIBOR
3×6	3 months	90-day LIBOR
3×9	3 months	180-day LIBOR
6×12	6 months	180-day LIBOR
12×18	12 months	180-day LIBOR

Note: This list is not exhaustive and represents only the most commonly traded FRAs.

---

[10] The notation "3×9" is pronounced "three by nine."

party wants a contract expiring in 37 days on 122-day LIBOR, it would be considered an exception to the standard, but most dealers would be willing to make a market in such an instrument. Such nonstandard instruments are called *off the run*. Of course, FRAs are available in all of the leading currencies.

The FRA market is large, but not as large as the swaps market. It is important, however, to understand FRAs before trying to understand swaps. As we will show in Reading 73, a swap is a special combination of FRAs. But let us now turn to another large forward market, the market for currency forwards.

3.3 Currency Forward Contracts

Spurred by the relaxation of government controls over the exchange rates of most major currencies in the early 1970s, a currency forward market developed and grew extremely large. Currency forwards are widely used by banks and corporations to manage foreign exchange risk. For example, suppose Microsoft has a European subsidiary that expects to send it €12 million in three months. When Microsoft receives the euros, it will then convert them to dollars. Thus, Microsoft is essentially long euros because it will have to sell euros, or equivalently, it is short dollars because it will have to buy dollars. A currency forward contract is especially useful in this situation, because it enables Microsoft to lock in the rate at which it will sell euros and buy dollars in three months. It can do this by going short the forward contract, meaning that it goes short the euro and long the dollar. This arrangement serves to offset its otherwise long-euro, short-dollar position. In other words, it needs a forward contract to sell euros and buy dollars.

For example, say Microsoft goes to JP Morgan Chase and asks for a quote on a currency forward for €12 million in three months. JP Morgan Chase quotes a rate of $0.925, which would enable Microsoft to sell euros and buy dollars at a rate of $0.925 in three months. Under this contract, Microsoft would know it could convert its €12 million to 12,000,000 × $0.925 = $11,100,000. The contract would also stipulate whether it will settle in cash or will call for Microsoft to actually deliver the euros to the dealer and be paid $11,100,000. This simplified example is a currency forward hedge, a transaction we explore more thoroughly in Chapter 6.

Now let us say that three months later, the spot rate for euros is $0.920. Microsoft is quite pleased that it locked in a rate of $0.925. It simply delivers the euros and receives $11,100,000 at an exchange rate of $0.925.[11] Had rates risen, however, Microsoft would still have had to deliver the euros and accept a rate of $0.925.

A few variations of currency forward contracts exist, but most of them are somewhat specialized and beyond the objectives of this book. Let us now take a very brief look at a few other types of forward contracts.

3.4 Other Types of Forward Contracts

Although this book focuses primarily on the financial derivatives used by asset managers, we should mention here some of the other types. Commodity forwards—in which the underlying asset is oil, a precious metal, or some other commodity—are widely used. In addition, the derivatives industry has created forward contracts and other derivatives on various sources of energy (electricity, gas, etc.) and even weather, in which the underlying is a measure of the temperature or the amount of disaster damage from hurricanes, earthquakes, or tornados.

---

[11] Had the contract been structured to settle in cash, the dealer would have paid Microsoft 12,000,000 × ($0.925 − $0.920) = $60,000. Microsoft would have converted the euros to dollars at the current spot exchange rate of $0.920, receiving 12,000,000 × $0.920 = $11,040,000. Adding the $60,000 payment from the dealer, Microsoft would have received $11,100,000, an effective rate of $0.925.

Many of these instruments are particularly difficult to understand, price, and trade. Nonetheless, through the use of derivatives and indirect investments, such as hedge funds, they can be useful for managing risk and investing in general. They are not, however, the focus of this book.

In the examples and illustrations used, we have made reference to certain prices. Determining appropriate prices and fair values of financial instruments is a central objective of much of the process of asset management. Accordingly, pricing and valuation occupies a major portion of the CFA Program. As such, we turn our attention to the pricing and valuation of forward contracts.

4   PRICING AND VALUATION OF FORWARD CONTRACTS

Before getting into the actual mechanics of pricing and valuation, the astute reader might wonder whether we are being a bit redundant. Are pricing and valuation not the same thing?

An equity analyst often finds that a stock is priced at more or less than its fair market value and uses this conclusion as the basis for a buy or sell recomendation.[12] In an efficient market, the price of a stock would always equal its value or the price would quickly converge to the value. Thus, for all practical purposes, pricing and valuation would be the same thing. In general, when we speak of the value and price of an *asset*, we are referring to what that asset is worth and what it sells for. With respect to certain *derivatives*, however, value and price take on slightly different meanings.

So let us begin by defining value: *Value is what you can sell something for or what you must pay to acquire something.* This applies to stocks, bonds, derivatives, and used cars.[13] Accordingly, *valuation is the process of determining the value of an asset or service.* Pricing is a related but different concept; let us explore what we mean by pricing a forward contract.

A forward contract price is the fixed price or rate at which the transaction scheduled to occur at expiration will take place. This price is agreed to on the contract initiation date and is commonly called the **forward price** or **forward rate.** Pricing means to determine the forward price or forward rate. Valuation, however, means to determine the amount of money that one would need to pay or would expect to receive to engage in the transaction. Alternatively, if one already held a position, valuation would mean to determine the amount of money one would either have to pay or expect to receive in order to get out of the position. Let us look at a generic example.

4.1 Generic Pricing and Valuation of a Forward Contract

Because derivative contracts have finite lives, it is important to carefully specify the time frame in which we are operating. We denote time in the following manner: Today is identified as time 0. The expiration date is time T. Time t is an arbitrary time between today and the expiration. Usually when we refer to "today," we are referring to the date on which the contract is created. Later we shall move forward to time t and time T, which will then be "today."

---

[12] From your study of equity analysis, you should recall that we often use the discounted cash flow model, sometimes combined with the capital asset pricing model, to determine the fair market value of a stock.

[13] Be careful. You may think the "value" of a certain used car is $5,000, but if no one will give you that price, it can hardly be called the value.

0　　　　　　　　　　　　　　　t　　　　　　　　　　　　　　T
(today)　　　　　　　　　　　　　　　　　　　　　　　(expiration)

The price of the underlying asset in the spot market is denoted as S_0 at time 0, S_t at time t, and S_T at time T. The forward contract price, established when the contract is initiated at time 0, is $F(0,T)$. This notation indicates that $F(0,T)$ is the price of a forward contract initiated at time 0 and expiring at time T. The value of the forward contract is $V_0(0,T)$. This notation indicates that $V_0(0,T)$ is the value at time 0 of a forward contract initiated at time 0 and expiring at time T. In this book, subscripts always indicate that we are at a specific point in time.

We have several objectives in this analysis. First, we want to determine the forward price $F(0,T)$. We also want to determine the forward contract value today, denoted $V_0(0,T)$, the value at a point during the life of the contract such as time t, denoted $V_t(0,T)$, and the value at expiration, denoted $V_T(0,T)$. Valuation is somewhat easier to grasp from the perspective of the party holding the long position, so we shall take that point of view in this example. Once that value is determined, the value to the short is obtained by simply changing the sign.

If we are at expiration, we would observe the spot price as S_T. The long holds a position to buy the asset at the already agreed-upon price of $F(0,T)$. Thus, the value of the forward contract at expiration should be obvious: $S_T - F(0,T)$. If the value at expiration does not equal this amount, then an arbitrage profit can be easily made. For example, suppose the forward price established at the initiation of the contract, $F(0,T)$, is $20. Now at expiration, the spot price, S_T, is $23. The contract value must be $3. If it were more than $3, then the long would be able to sell the contract to someone for more than $3—someone would be paying the long more than $3 to obtain the obligation of buying a $23 asset for $20. Obviously, no one would do that. If the value were less than $3, the long would have to be willing to sell for less than $3 the obligation of buying a $23 asset for $20. Obviously, the long would not do that. Thus, we state that the value at expiration of a forward contract established at time 0 is

$$V_T(0,T) = S_T - F(0,T) \tag{70-1}$$

Note that the value of a forward contract can also be interpreted as its profit, the difference between what the long pays for the underlying asset, $F(0,T)$, and what the long receives, the asset price S_T. Of course, we have still not explained how $F(0,T)$ is determined, but the above equation gives the value of the contract at expiration, at which time $F(0,T)$ would certainly be known because it was agreed on at the initiation date of the contract.

Now let us back up to the time when the contract was originated. Consider a contract that expires in one year. Suppose that the underlying asset is worth $100 and that the forward price is $108. We do not know if $108 is the correct forward price; we will simply try it and see.

Suppose we buy the asset for $100 and sell the forward contract for $108. We hold the position until expiration. We assume that there are no direct costs associated with buying or holding the asset, but we must recognize that we lose interest on the $100 tied up in the asset. Assume that the interest rate is 5 percent.

Recall that no money changes hands at the start with a forward contract. Consequently, the $100 invested in the asset is the full outlay. At the end of the year, the forward contract expires and we deliver the asset, receiving $108 for it—not bad at all. At a 5 percent interest rate, we lose only $5 in interest on the $100 tied up in the asset. We receive $108 for the asset regardless of its price at expiration. We can view $108 − $105 = $3 as a risk-free profit, which more than covered the cost. In fact, if we had also borrowed the $100 at 5 percent, we could have done this transaction without putting up any money of our own. We would have more than covered the interest on the borrowed funds and netted a $3 risk-free profit. This profit is essentially free money—there is no cost and no risk. Thus, it is an arbitrage profit, a concept we introduced in Reading 69 and a dominant theme throughout this book. We would certainly want to execute any transaction that would generate an arbitrage profit.

In the market, the forces of arbitrage would then prevail. Other market participants would execute this transaction as well. Although it is possible that the spot price would bear some of the adjustment, in this book we shall always let the derivative price make the full adjustment. Consequently, the derivative price would have to come down to $105.

If the forward price were below $105, we could also earn an arbitrage profit, although it would be a little more difficult because the asset would have to be sold short. Suppose the forward price is $103. If the asset were a financial asset, we could borrow it and sell it short. We would receive $100 for it and invest that $100 at the 5 percent rate. We would simultaneously buy a forward contract. At expiration, we would take delivery of the asset paying $103 and then deliver it to the party from whom we borrowed it. The short position is now covered, and we still have the $100 invested plus 5 percent interest on it. This transaction offers a clear arbitrage profit of $2. Again, the forces of arbitrage would cause other market participants to undertake the transaction, which would push the forward price up to $105.

If short selling is not permitted, too difficult, or too costly, a market participant who already owns the asset could sell it, invest the $100 at 5 percent, and buy a forward contract. At expiration, he would pay $103 and take delivery on the forward contract, which would return him to his original position of owning the asset. He would now, however, receive not only the stock but also 5 percent interest on $100. Again, the forces of arbitrage would make this transaction attractive to other parties who held the asset, provided they could afford to part with it for the necessary period of time.[14]

Going back to the situation in which the forward contract price was $103, an arbitrage profit could, however, be eliminated if the party going long the forward contract were required to pay some money up front. For example, suppose the party going long the forward contract paid the party going short $1.9048. Then the party going long would lose $1.9048 plus interest on this amount. Notice that $1.9048 compounded at 5 percent interest equals precisely $2, which not surprisingly is the amount of the arbitrage profit.

Thus, if the forward price were $103, the value of the contract would be $1.9048. With T = 1, this value equals

$$V_0(0,T) = V_0(0,1) = \$100 - \$103/1.05 = \$1.9048$$

Therefore, to enter into this contract at this forward price, one party must pay another. Because the value is positive, it must be paid by the party going long the forward contract to the party going short. Parties going long must pay positive values; parties going short pay negative values.[15]

If the forward price were $108, the value would be

$$V_0(0,T) = \$100 - \$108/1.05 = -\$2.8571$$

---

[14] In other words, a party holding the asset must be willing to part with it for the length of time it would take for the forces of arbitrage to bring the price back in line, thereby allowing the party to capture the risk-free profit and return the party to its original state of holding the asset. The period of time required for the price to adjust should be very short if the market is relatively efficient.

[15] For example, when a stock is purchased, its value, which is always positive, is paid from the long to the short. This is true for any asset.

In this case, the value is negative and would have to be paid from the short to the long. Doing so would eliminate the arbitrage profit that the short would have otherwise been able to make, given the forward price of $108.

Arbitrage profits can be eliminated with an up-front payment from long to short or vice versa that is consistent with the forward price the parties select. The parties could simply negotiate a forward price, and any resulting market value could be paid from one party to the other. *It is customary, however, in the forward market for the initial value to be set to zero.* This convention eliminates the necessity of either party making a payment to the other and results in a direct and simple determination of the forward price. Specifically, setting $V_0(0,T) = 0$ and letting r represent the interest rate,

$$V_0(0,T) = S_0 - F(0,T)/(1 + r) = 0$$

which means that $F(0,T) = S_0(1 + r)$. In our example, $F(0,T) = \$100(1.05) = \$105$, which is the forward price that eliminates the arbitrage profit.

Our forward price formula can be interpreted as saying that the forward price is the spot price compounded at the risk-free interest rate. In our example, we had an annual interest rate of r and one year to expiration. With today being time 0 and expiration being time T, the time $T - 0 = T$ is the number of years to expiration of the forward contract. Then we more generally write the forward price as

$$F(0,T) = S_0(1 + r)^T \qquad \textbf{(70-2)}$$

Again, this result is consistent with the custom that no money changes hands at the start of a forward contract, meaning that the value of a forward contract at its start is zero.

Exhibit 70-3 summarizes the process of pricing a forward contract. At time 0, we buy the asset and sell a forward contract for a total outlay of the spot price of the asset.[16] Over the life of the contract, we hold the asset and forgo interest on the money. At expiration, we deliver the asset and receive the forward price for a payoff of $F(0,T)$. The overall transaction is risk free and equivalent to

EXHIBIT 70-3 Pricing a Forward Contract

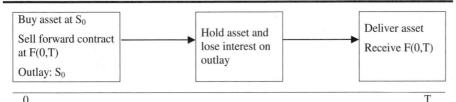

The transaction is risk free and should be equivalent to investing S_0 dollars in a risk-free asset that pays $F(0,T)$ at time T. Thus, the amount received at T must be the future value of the initial outlay invested at the risk-free rate. For this equality to hold, the forward price must be given as

$$F(0,T) = S_0(1 + r)^T$$

Example: The spot price is $72.50, the risk-free rate is 8.25 percent, and the contract is for five years. The forward price would be

$$F(0,T) = F(0,5) = 72.50(1.0825)^5 = 107.76$$

[16] Remember that in a forward contract, neither party pays anything for the forward contract at the start.

investing the spot price of the asset in a risk-free bond that pays $F(0,T)$ at time T. Therefore, the payoff at T must be the future value of the spot price invested at the risk-free rate. This equality can be true only if the forward price is the spot price compounded at the risk-free rate over the life of the asset.

A contract in which the initial value is intentionally set at a nonzero value is called an **off-market FRA.** In such a contract, the forward price is set arbitrarily in the process of negotiation between the two parties. Given the chosen forward price, the contract will have a nonzero value. As noted above, if the value is positive, the long pays that amount up front to the short. If it is negative, the short pays that amount up front to the long. Although off-market FRAs are not common, we shall use them in Reading 73 when studying swaps.

Now suppose we are at a time t, which is a point during the life of the contract. We may want to know the value of the forward contract for several reasons. For one, it makes good business sense to know the monetary value of an obligation to do something at a later date. Also, accounting rules require that a company mark its derivatives to their current market values and report the effects of those values in income statements and balance sheets. In addition, the market value can be used as a gauge of the credit exposure. Finally, the market value can be used to determine how much money one party can pay the other to terminate the contract.

Let us start by assuming that we established a long forward contract at time 0 at the price $F(0,T)$. Of course, its value at time 0 was zero. But now it is time t, and we want to know its new value, $V_t(0,T)$. Let us consider what it means to hold the position of being long at time t a forward contract established at time 0 at the price $F(0,T)$ and expiring at time T:

We will have to pay F(0,T) dollars at T.

We will receive the underlying asset, which will be worth S_T, at T.

At least part of the value will clearly be the present value of a payment of $F(0,T)$, or in other words, $-F(0,T)/(1 + r)^{T-t}$. The other part of the contract value comes from the fact that we have a claim on the asset's value at T. We do not know what S_T (the asset value at T) will be, but we do know that the market tells us its present value is S_t, the current asset price. *By definition, an asset's value today is the present value of its future value.*[17] Thus we can easily value our forward contract at time t during the life of the contract:

$$V_t(0,T) = S_t - F(0,T)/(1 + r)^{(T-t)} \qquad \textbf{(70-3)}$$

Consider our earlier example in which we entered into a one-year forward contract to buy the asset at $105. Now assume it is three months later and the price of the asset is $102. With $t = 0.25$ and $T = 1$, the value of the contract would be

$$V_t(0,T) = V_{0.25}(0,1) = \$102 - \$105/(1.05)^{0.75} = \$0.7728$$

Again, why is this the value? The contract provides the long with a claim on the asset at expiration. That claim is currently worth the current asset value of $102. That claim also obligates the long to pay $105 at expiration, which has a present value of $105/(1.05)^{0.75} = 101.2272. Thus, the long position has a value of $102 - $101.2272 = 0.7728.

As noted above, this market value may well affect the income statement and balance sheet. In addition, it gives an idea of the contract's credit exposure, a topic we have touched on and will cover in more detail in Section 5.

---

[17] This statement is true for any type of asset or financial instrument. It always holds by definition.

Finally, we noted earlier that a party could re-enter the market and offset the contract by paying the counterparty or having the counterparty pay him a cash amount. This cash amount is the market value as calculated here.[18]

Exhibit 70-4 summarizes how we value a forward contract. If we went long a forward contract at time 0 and we are now at time t prior to expiration, we hold a claim on the asset at expiration and are obligated to pay the forward price at expiration. The claim on the asset is worth its current price; the obligation to pay the forward price at expiration is worth the negative of its present value. Thus, the value of the forward contract is the current spot price minus the forward price discounted from expiration back to the present.

EXHIBIT 70-4 Valuing a Forward Contract

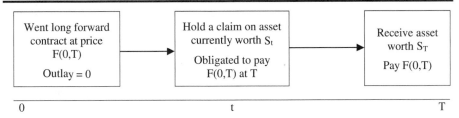

The value of the forward contract at t must be the value of what it will produce at T:

$$V_t(0,T) = S_t - F(0,T)/(1 + r)^{(T-t)}$$

Example: A two-year forward contract was established with a price of \$62.25. Now, a year and a half later (t = 1.5), the spot price is \$71.19 and the risk-free rate is 7 percent. The value of the forward contract is

$$V_t(0,T) = V_{1.5}(0,2) = 71.19 - 62.25/(1.07)^{0.5} = 11.01$$

Therefore, we have seen that the forward contract value is zero today: the asset price minus the present value of the forward price at a time prior to expiration, and the asset price minus the forward price at expiration. It may be helpful to note that in general, we can always say that *the forward contract value is the asset price minus the present value of the exercise price,* because given $V_t(0,T) = S_t - F(0,T)/(1 + r)^{(T-t)}$:

If t = 0, $V_t(0,T) = V_0(0,T) = S_0 - F(0,T)/(1 + r)^T = 0$
    because $F(0,T) = S_0(1 + r)^T$

If t = T, $V_t(0,T) = V_T(0,T) = S_T - F(0,T)/(1 + r)^0 = S_T - F(0,T)$

The formulas for pricing and valuation of a forward contract are summarized in Exhibit 70-5.

In our examples, there were no costs or cash flows associated with holding the underlying assets. In the specific examples below for equity derivatives, fixed-income and interest rate derivatives, and currency derivatives, we present cases in which cash flows on the underlying asset will slightly alter our results. We shall ignore any costs of holding assets. Such costs are primarily associated with commodities, an asset class we do not address in this book.

---

[18] If the market value is positive, the value of the asset exceeds the present value of what the long promises to pay. Thus, it makes sense that the short must pay the long. If the market value is negative, then the present value of what the long promises to pay exceeds the value of the asset. Then, it makes sense that the long must pay the short.

EXHIBIT 70-5 Pricing and Valuation Formulas for a Forward Contract

Today = time 0
Arbitrary point during the contract's life = time t
Expiration = time T

Value of a forward contract at any time t:

$$V_t(0,T) = S_t - F(0,T)/(1 + r)^{(T-t)}$$

Value of a forward contract at expiration (t = T):

$$V_T(0,T) = S_T - F(0,T)$$

Value of a forward contract at initiation (t = 0):

$$V_0(0,T) = S_0 - F(0,T)/(1 + r)^T$$

Customarily, no money changes hands at initiation so $V_0(0,T)$ is set equal to zero. Thus,

$$F(0,T) = S_0(1 + r)^T$$

Practice Problem 1

An investor holds title to an asset worth €125.72. To raise money for an unrelated purpose, the investor plans to sell the asset in nine months. The investor is concerned about uncertainty in the price of the asset at that time. The investor learns about the advantages of using forward contracts to manage this risk and enters into such a contract to sell the asset in nine months. The risk-free interest rate is 5.625 percent.

A. Determine the appropriate price the investor could receive in nine months by means of the forward contract.

B. Suppose the counterparty to the forward contract is willing to engage in such a contract at a forward price of €140. Explain what type of transaction the investor could execute to take advantage of the situation. Calculate the rate of return (annualized), and explain why the transaction is attractive.

C. Suppose the forward contract is entered into at the price you computed in Part A. Two months later, the price of the asset is €118.875. The investor would like to evaluate her position with respect to any gain or loss accrued on the forward contract. Determine the market value of the forward contract at this point in time from the perspective of the investor in Part A.

D. Determine the value of the forward contract at expiration assuming the contract is entered into at the price you computed in Part A and the price of the underlying asset is €123.50 at expiration. Explain how the investor did on the overall position of both the asset and the forward contract in terms of the rate of return.

SOLUTIONS

A. $T = 9/12 = 0.75$
$S_0 = 125.72$
$r = 0.05625$

$F(0,T) = 125.72(1.05625)^{0.75} = 130.99$

B. As found in Part A, the forward contract should be selling at
€130.99, but it is selling for €140. Consequently, it is overpriced—
and an overpriced contract should be sold. Because the investor
holds the asset, she will be hedged by selling the forward contract.
Consequently, her asset, worth €125.72 when the forward contract
is sold, will be delivered in nine months and she will receive €140
for it. The rate of return will be

$$\left(\frac{140}{125.72}\right) - 1 = 0.1136$$

This risk-free return of 11.36 percent for nine months is clearly in
excess of the 5.625 percent annual rate. In fact, a rate of 11.36 percent for nine months annualizes to

$$(1.1136)^{12/9} - 1 = 0.1543$$

An annual risk-free rate of 15.43 percent is clearly preferred over
the actual risk-free rate of 5.625 percent. The position is not only
hedged but also earns an arbitrage profit.

C. $t = 2/12$
$T - t = 9/12 - 2/12 = 7/12$
$S_t = 118.875$
$F(0,T) = 130.99$

$$V_t(0,T) = V_{2/12}(0,9/12) = 118.875 - 130.99/(1.05625)^{7/12} = -8.0$$

The contract has a negative value. Note, however, that in this form,
the answer applies to the holder of the long position. This investor is
short. Thus, the value to the investor in this problem is positive 8.0.

D. $S_T = 123.50$

$$V_T(0,T) = V_{9/12}(0,9/12) = 123.50 - 130.99 = -7.49$$

This amount is the value to the long. This investor is short, so the value
is a positive 7.49. The investor incurred a loss on the asset of 125.72 −
123.50 = 2.22. Combined with the gain on the forward contract, the
net gain is 7.49 − 2.22 = 5.27. A gain of 5.27 on an asset worth 125.72
when the transaction was initiated represents a return of 5.27/125.72 =
4.19 percent. When annualized, the rate of return equals

$$(1.0419)^{12/9} - 1 = 0.05625$$

It should come as no surprise that this number is the annual risk-
free rate. The transaction was executed at the no-arbitrage forward

> price of €130.99. Thus, it would be impossible to earn a return higher or lower than the risk-free rate.

4.2 Pricing and Valuation of Equity Forward Contracts

Equity forward contracts are priced and valued much like the generic contract described above, with one important additional feature. Many stocks pay dividends, and the effects of these dividends must be incorporated into the pricing and valuation process. Our concern is with the dividends that occur over the life of the forward contract, but not with those that may come after the contract ends. Following standard procedure, we assume that these dividends are known or are a constant percentage of the stock price.

We begin with the idea of a forward contract on either a single stock, a portfolio of stocks, or an index in which dividends are to be paid during the life of the contract. Using the time notation that today is time 0, expiration is time T, and there is an arbitrary time t during its life when we need to value the contract, assume that dividends can be paid at various times during the life of the contract between t and T.[19]

In the examples that follow, we shall calculate present and future values of this stream of dividends over the life of the forward contract. Given a series of these dividends of $D_1, D_2, \ldots D_n$, whose values are known, that occur at times $t_1, t_2, \ldots t_n$, the present value will be defined as PV(D,0,T) and computed as

$$PV(D,0,T) = \sum_{i=1}^{n} \frac{D_i}{(1 + r)^{t_i}}$$

The future value will be defined as FV(D,0,T) and computed as

$$FV(D,0,T) = \sum_{i=1}^{n} D_i(1 + r)^{T - t_i}$$

Recall that the forward price is established by eliminating any opportunity to arbitrage from establishing a forward contract without making any cash outlay today, as is customary with forward contracts. We found that the forward price is the spot price compounded at the risk-free interest rate. To include dividends, we adjust our formula slightly to

$$F(0,T) = [S_0 - PV(D,0,T)](1 + r)^T \tag{70-4}$$

In other words, we simply subtract the present value of the dividends from the stock price. Note that the dividends reduce the forward price, a reflection of the fact that holders of long positions in forward contracts do not benefit from dividends in comparison to holders of long positions in the underlying stock.

For example, consider a stock priced at $40, which pays a dividend of $3 in 50 days. The risk-free rate is 6 percent. A forward contract expiring in six months (T = 0.5) would have a price of

$$F(0,T) = F(0,0.5) = [\$40 - \$3/(1.06)^{50/365}](1.06)^{0.5} = \$38.12$$

---

[19] Given the way dividends are typically paid, the right to the dividend leaves the stock on the ex-dividend date, which is prior to the payment date. To precisely incorporate this feature, either the dividend payment date should be the ex-dividend date or the dividend should be the present value at the ex-dividend date of the dividend to be paid at a later date. We shall ignore this point here and assume that it would be taken care of in practice.

If the stock had more than one dividend, we would simply subtract the present value of all dividends over the life of the contract from the stock price, as in the following example.

The risk-free rate is 4 percent. The forward contract expires in 300 days and is on a stock currently priced at \$35, which pays quarterly dividends according to the following schedule:

Days to Ex-Dividend Date	Dividend
10	\$0.45
102	\$0.45
193	\$0.45
283	\$0.45

The present value of the dividends is found as follows:

$$\text{PV(D,0,T)} = \$0.45/(1.04)^{10/365} + \$0.45/(1.04)^{102/365}$$
$$+ \$0.45/(1.04)^{193/365} + \$0.45/(1.04)^{283/365} = \$1.77$$

The time to expiration is $T = 300/365$. Therefore, the forward price equals

$$F(0,T) = F(0,300/365) = (\$35 - \$1.77)(1.04)^{300/365} = \$34.32$$

Another approach to incorporating the dividends is to use the future value of the dividends. With this forward contract expiring in 300 days, the first dividend is reinvested for 290 days, the second for 198 days, the third for 107 days, and the fourth for 17 days. Thus,

$$\text{FV(D,0,T)} = \$0.45(1.04)^{290/365} + \$0.45(1.04)^{198/365}$$
$$+ \$0.45(1.04)^{107/365} + \$0.45(1.04)^{17/365} = \$1.83$$

To obtain the forward price, we compound the stock value to expiration and subtract the future value of the dividends. Thus, the forward price would be

$$F(0,T) = S_0(1 + r)^T - \text{FV(D,0,T)} \qquad \textbf{(70-5)}$$

This formula will give the same answer as the one using the present value of the dividends, as shown below:

$$F(0,300/365) = \$35(1.04)^{300/365} - \$1.83 = \$34.32$$

An alternative way to incorporate dividends is to express them as a fixed percentage of the stock price. The more common version of this formulation is to assume that the stock, portfolio, or index pays dividends continuously at a rate of δ^c. By specifying the dividends in this manner, we are allowing the dividends to be uncertain and completely determined by the stock price at the time the dividends are being paid. In this case, the stock is constantly paying a dividend at the rate δ^c. In Reading 71, we will again discuss how to incorporate dividends.

Because we pay dividends continuously, for consistency we must also compound the interest continuously. The continuously compounded equivalent of the discrete risk-free rate r will be denoted r^c and is found as $r^c = \ln(1 + r)$.[20] The future value of \$1 at time T is $\exp(r^cT)$. Then the forward price is given as

$$F(0,T) = (S_0 e^{-\delta^c T}) e^{r^c T} \qquad\qquad \text{(70-6)}$$

The term in parentheses, the stock price discounted at the dividend yield rate, is equivalent to the stock price minus the present value of the dividends. This value is then compounded at the risk-free rate over the life of the contract, just as we have done in the other versions.

Some people attach significance to whether the forward price is higher than the spot price. It is important to note that the forward price should not be interpreted as a forecast of the future price of the underlying. This misperception is common. If the forward price is higher than the spot price, it merely indicates that the effect of the risk-free rate is greater than the effect of the dividends. In fact, such is usually the case with equity forwards. Interest rates are usually greater than dividend yields.

As an example, consider a forward contract on France's CAC 40 Index. The index is at 5475, the continuously compounded dividend yield is 1.5 percent, and the continuously compounded risk-free interest rate is 4.625 percent. The contract life is two years. With T = 2, the contract price is, therefore,

$$F(0,T) = F(0,2) = (5475 \times e^{-0.015(2)}) e^{0.04625(2)} = 5828.11$$

This specification involving a continuous dividend yield is commonly used when the underlying is a portfolio or stock index. If a single stock in the portfolio pays a dividend, then the portfolio or index can be viewed as paying a dividend. Given the diversity of dividend policies and ex-dividend dates, such an assumption is usually considered a reasonable approximation for stock portfolios or stock indices, but the assumption is not as appropriate for individual stocks. No general agreement exists on the most appropriate approach, and you must become comfortable with all of them. To obtain the appropriate forward price, the most important point to remember is that one way or another, the analysis must incorporate the dividend component of the stock price, portfolio value, or index level. If the contract is not trading at the correct price, then it is mispriced and arbitrage, as described in the generic forward contract pricing section, will force an alignment between the market forward price and the theoretical forward price.

Recall that the value of a forward contract is the asset price minus the forward price discounted back from the expiration date. Regardless of how the dividend is specified or even whether the underlying stock, portfolio, or index pays dividends, the valuation formulas for a forward contract on a stock differ only in that the stock price is adjusted by removing the present value of the remaining dividends:

$$V_t(0,T) = S_t - PV(D,t,T) - F(0,T)/(1 + r)^{(T-t)} \qquad\qquad \text{(70-7)}$$

where we now note that the dividends are only those paid after time t. If we are using continuous compounding,

$$V_t(0,T) = S_t e^{-\delta^c(T-t)} - F(0,T) e^{-r^c(T-t)} \qquad\qquad \text{(70-8)}$$

---

[20] The notation "ln" stands for natural logarithm. A logarithm is the power to which its base must be raised to equal a given number. The base of the natural logarithm system is e, approximately 2.71828. With an interest rate of r = 0.06, we would have $r^c = \ln(1.06) = 0.058$. Then $e^{0.058} = 1.06$ is called the exponential function and often written as $\exp(0.058) = 1.06$. The future value factor is thus $\exp(r^c)$. The present value factor is $1/\exp(r^c)$ or $\exp(-r^c)$. If the period is more or less than one year, we also multiply the rate by the number of years or fraction of a year—that is, $\exp(-r^c T)$ or $\exp(r^c T)$.

At the contract initiation date, t = 0 and $V_0(0,T)$ is set to zero because no cash changes hands. At expiration, t = T and no dividends remain, so the valuation formula reduces to $S_T - F(0,T)$.

The formulas for pricing and valuation of equity forward contracts are summarized in Exhibit 70-6.

EXHIBIT 70-6 Pricing and Valuation Formulas for Equity Forward Contracts

Forward price = (Stock price − Present value of dividends over life of contract) × $(1 + r)^T$

or (Stock price) × $(1 + r)^T$ minus Future value of dividends over life of contract

Discrete dividends over the life of the contract:

$$F(0,T) = [S_0 - PV(D,0,T)](1 + r)^T \text{ or } S_0(1 + r)^T - FV(D,0,T)$$

Continuous dividends at the rate δ^c:

$$F(0,T) = (S_0 e^{-\delta^c T}) e^{r^c T}$$

Value of forward contract:

$$V_t(0,T) = S_t - PV(D,t,T) - F(0,T)/(1 + r)^{(T-t)}$$

or

$$V_t(0,T) = S_t e^{-\delta^c(T-t)} - F(0,T) e^{-r^c(T-t)}$$

Practice Problem 2

An asset manager anticipates the receipt of funds in 200 days, which he will use to purchase a particular stock. The stock he has in mind is currently selling for $62.50 and will pay a $0.75 dividend in 50 days and another $0.75 dividend in 140 days. The risk-free rate is 4.2 percent. The manager decides to commit to a future purchase of the stock by going long a forward contract on the stock.

A. At what price would the manager commit to purchase the stock in 200 days through a forward contract?

B. Suppose the manager enters into the contract at the price you found in Part A. Now, 75 days later, the stock price is $55.75. Determine the value of the forward contract at this point.

C. It is now the expiration day, and the stock price is $58.50. Determine the value of the forward contract at this time.

SOLUTIONS

$$S_0 = \$62.50$$
$$T = 200/365$$
$$D_1 = \$0.75, t_1 = 50/365$$
$$D_2 = \$0.75, t_2 = 140/365$$
$$r = 0.042$$

A. First find the present value of the dividends:

$$\$0.75/(1.042)^{50/365} + \$0.75/(1.042)^{140/365} = \$1.48$$

Then find the forward price:

$$F(0,T) = F(0,200/365) = (\$62.50 - \$1.48)(1.042)^{200/365} = \$62.41$$

B. We must now find the present value of the dividends 75 days after the contract begins. The first dividend has already been paid, so it is not relevant. Because only one remains, the second dividend is now the "first" dividend. It will be paid in 65 days. Thus, $t_1 - t = 65/365$. The present value of this dividend is $\$0.75/(1.042)^{65/365} = \$0.74$. The other information is

$$t = 75/365$$
$$T - t = (200 - 75)/365 = 125/365$$
$$S_t = \$55.75$$

The value of the contract is, therefore,

$$V_t(0,T) = V_{75/365}(0,200/365) = (\$55.75 - \$0.74) - \$62.41$$
$$/(1.042)^{125/365} = -\$6.53$$

Thus, the contract has a negative value.

C. $S_T = \$58.50$

The value of the contract is

$$V_{200/365}(0,200/365) = V_T(0,T) = \$58.50 - \$62.41 = -\$3.91$$

Thus, the contract expires with a value of negative $3.91.

4.3 Pricing and Valuation of Fixed-Income and Interest Rate Forward Contracts

Forward contracts on fixed-income securities are priced and valued in a virtually identical manner to their equity counterparts. We can use the above formulas if S_t represents the bond price at time t and D_i represents a coupon paid at time t_i. We denote B^c as a coupon bond and then use notation to draw attention to those coupons that must be included in the forward contract pricing calculations. We will let $B_t^c(T + Y)$ represent the bond price at time t, T is the expiration date of the forward contract, Y is the remaining maturity of the bond on the forward contract expiration, and $(T + Y)$ is the time to maturity of the bond at the time the forward contract is initiated. Consider a bond with n coupons to occur before its maturity date. Converting our formula for a forward contract on a stock into that for a forward contract on a bond and letting CI be the coupon interest over a specified period of time, we have a forward price of

$$F(0,T) = [B_0^c(T + Y) - PV(CI,0,T)](1 + r)^T \qquad \textbf{(70-9)}$$

where PV(CI,0,T) is the present value of the coupon interest over the life of the forward contract. Alternatively, the forward price can be obtained as

$$F(0,T) = [B_0^c(T + Y)](1 + r)^T - FV(CI,0,T) \qquad \textbf{(70-10)}$$

where FV(CI,0,T) is the future value of the coupon interest over the life of the forward contract.

The value of the forward contract at time t would be

$$V_t(0,T) = B_t^c(T + Y) - PV(CI,t,T) - F(0,T)/(1 + r)^{(T-t)} \qquad \textbf{(70-11)}$$

at time t; note that the relevant coupons are only those remaining as of time t until expiration of the forward contract. As in the case for stock, this formula will reduce to the appropriate values at time 0 and at expiration. For example, at expiration, no coupons would remain, $t = T$, and $V_T(0,T) = B_T^c(T + Y) - F(0,T)$. At time $t = 0$, the contract is being initiated and has a zero value, which leads to the formula for F(0,T) above.

Consider a bond with semiannual coupons. The bond has a current maturity of 583 days and pays four coupons, each six months apart. The next coupon occurs in 37 days, followed by coupons in 219 days, 401 days, and 583 days, at which time the principal is repaid. Suppose that the bond price, which includes accrued interest, is \$984.45 for a \$1,000 par, 4 percent coupon bond. The coupon rate implies that each coupon is \$20. The risk-free interest rate is 5.75 percent. Assume that the forward contract expires in 310 days. Thus, $T = 310$, $T + Y = 583$, and $Y = 273$, meaning that the bond has 273 days remaining after the forward contract expires. Note that only the first two coupons occur during the life of the forward contract.

The present value of the coupons is

$$\$20/(1.0575)^{37/365} + \$20/(1.0575)^{219/365} = \$39.23$$

The forward price if the contract is initiated now is

$$F(0,T) = (\$984.45 - \$39.23)(1.0575)^{310/365} = \$991.18$$

Thus, we assume that we shall be able to enter into this contract to buy the bond in 310 days at the price of \$991.18.

Now assume it is 15 days later and the new bond price is \$973.14. Let the risk-free interest rate now be 6.75 percent. The present value of the remaining coupons is

$$\$20/(1.0675)^{22/365} + \$20/(1.0675)^{204/365} = \$39.20$$

The value of the forward contract is thus

$$\$973.14 - \$39.20 - \$991.19/(1.0675)^{295/365} = -\$6.28$$

The contract has gone from a zero value at the start to a negative value, primarily as a result of the decrease in the price of the underlying bond.

If the bond is a zero-coupon bond/T-bill, we can perform the same analysis as above, but we simply let the coupons equal zero.

Exhibit 70-7 summarizes the formulas for the pricing and valuation of forward contracts on fixed-income securities.

EXHIBIT 70-7 Pricing and Valuation Formulas for Fixed Income Forward Contracts

Forward price = (Bond price − Present value of coupons over life of contract)$(1 + r)^T$
or (Bond price)$(1 + r)^T$ − Future value of coupons over life of contract

Price of forward contract on bond with coupons CI:

$$F(0,T) = [B_0^c(T + Y) − PV(CI,0,T)](1 + r)^T$$
$$\text{or } [B_0^c(T + Y)](1 + r)^T − FV(CI,0,T)$$

Value of forward contract on bond with coupons CI:

$$V_t(0,T) = B_t^c(T + Y) − PV(CI,t,T) − F(0,T)/(1 + r)^{(T−t)}$$

Practice Problem 3

An investor purchased a bond when it was originally issued with a maturity of five years. The bond pays semiannual coupons of $50. It is now 150 days into the life of the bond. The investor wants to sell the bond the day after its fourth coupon. The first coupon occurs 181 days after issue, the second 365 days, the third 547 days, and the fourth 730 days. At this point (150 days into the life of the bond), the price is $1,010.25. The bond prices quoted here include accrued interest.

A. At what price could the owner enter into a forward contract to sell the bond on the day after its fourth coupon? Note that the owner would receive that fourth coupon. The risk-free rate is currently 8 percent.

B. Now move forward 365 days. The new risk-free interest rate is 7 percent and the new price of the bond is $1,025.375. The counterparty to the forward contract believes that it has received a gain on the position. Determine the value of the forward contract and the gain or loss to the counterparty at this time. Note that we have now introduced a new risk-free rate, because interest rates can obviously change over the life of the bond and any calculations of the forward contract value must reflect this fact. The new risk-free rate is used instead of the old rate in the valuation formula.

SOLUTIONS

A. First we must find the present value of the four coupons over the life of the forward contract. At the 150th day of the life of the bond, the coupons occur 31 days from now, 215 days from now, 397 days from now, and 580 days from now. Keep in mind that we need consider only the first four coupons because the owner will sell the bond on the day after the fourth coupon. The present value of the coupons is

$$\$50/(1.08)^{31/365} + \$50/(1.08)^{215/365} + \$50/(1.08)^{397/365} + \$50/(1.08)^{580/365} = \$187.69$$

Because we want the forward contract to expire one day after the fourth coupon, it expires in $731 − 150 = 581$ days. Thus, $T = 581/365$.

$$F(0,T) = F(0,581/365) = (\$1,010.25 − \$187.69)(1.08)^{581/365} = \$929.76$$

B. It is now 365 days later—the 515th day of the bond's life. There are two coupons to go, one occurring in $547 - 515 = 32$ days and the other in $730 - 515 = 215$ days. The present value of the coupons is now

$$\$50/(1.07)^{32/365} + \$50/(1.07)^{215/365} = \$97.75$$

To address the value of the forward contract and the gain or loss to the counterparty, note that $731 - 515 = 216$ days now remain until the contract's expiration. Because the bondholder would sell the forward contract to hedge the future sale price of the bond, the bondholder's counterparty to the forward contract would hold a long position. The value of the forward contract is the current spot price minus the present value of the coupons minus the present value of the forward price:

$$\$1,025.375 - \$97.75 - \$929.76/(1.07)^{216/365} = \$34.36$$

Because the contract was initiated with a zero value at the start and the counterparty is long the contract, the value of $34.36 represents a gain to the counterparty.

Now let us look at the pricing and valuation of FRAs. Previously we used the notations t and T to represent the time to a given date. The expressions t or T were, respectively, the number of days to time point t or T, each divided by 365. In the FRA market, contracts are created with specific day counts. We will use the letter h to refer to the day on which the FRA expires and the letter g to refer to an arbitrary day prior to expiration. Consider the time line shown below. We shall initiate an FRA on day 0. The FRA expires on day h. The rate underlying the FRA is the rate on an m-day Eurodollar deposit. Thus, there are h days from today until the FRA expiration and $h + m$ days until the maturity date of the Eurodollar instrument on which the FRA rate is based. The date indicated by g will simply be a date during the life of the FRA at which we want to determine a value for the FRA.

0	g	h	h + m
(today)		(expiration)	

Now let us specify some notation. We let $L_i(j)$ represent the rate on a j-day LIBOR deposit on an arbitrary day i, which falls somewhere in the above period from 0 to h, inclusive. Remember that this instrument is a j-day loan from one bank to another. For example, the bank borrowing $1 on day i for j days will pay back the amount

$$\$1\left[1 + L_i(j)\left(\frac{j}{360}\right)\right]$$

in j days.

The rate for m-day LIBOR on day h, $L_h(m)$, will determine the payoff of the FRA. We denote the fixed rate on the FRA as FRA(0,h,m), which stands for the rate on an FRA established on day 0, expiring on day h, and based on m-day

LIBOR. We shall use a $1 notional principal for the FRA, which means that at expiration its payoff is

$$\frac{[L_h(m) - \mathrm{FRA}(0,h,m)]\left(\dfrac{m}{360}\right)}{1 + L_h(m)\left(\dfrac{m}{360}\right)} \tag{70-12}$$

The numerator is the difference between the underlying LIBOR on the expiration day and the rate agreed on when the contract was initiated, multiplied by the adjustment factor m/360. Both of these rates are annual rates applied to a Eurodollar deposit of m days; hence, multiplying by m/360 is necessary. The denominator discounts the payoff by the m-day LIBOR in effect at the time of the payoff. As noted earlier, this adjustment is necessary because the rates in the numerator apply to Eurodollar deposits created on day h and paying off m days later. If the notional principal is anything other than $1, we also must multiply the above payoff by the notional principal to determine the actual payoff.

To derive the formula for pricing an FRA, a specific arbitrage transaction involving Eurodollars and FRAs is required. We omit the details of this somewhat complex transaction, but the end result is that the FRA rate is given by the following formula:

$$\mathrm{FRA}(0,h,m) = \left[\frac{1 + L_0(h + m)\left(\dfrac{h + m}{360}\right)}{1 + L_0(h)\left(\dfrac{h}{360}\right)} - 1\right]\left(\frac{360}{m}\right) \tag{70-13}$$

This somewhat awkward-looking formula is actually just the formula for a LIBOR forward rate, given the interest payment conventions in the FRA market. The numerator is the future value of a Eurodollar deposit of h + m days. The denominator is the future value of a shorter-term Eurodollar deposit of h days. This ratio is 1 plus a rate; subtracting 1 and multiplying by 360/m annualizes the rate.[21]

Consider a 3 × 9 FRA. This instrument expires in 90 days and is based on 180-day LIBOR. Thus, the Eurodollar deposit on which the underlying rate is based begins in 90 days and matures in 270 days. Because we are on day 0, h = 90, m = 180, and h + m = 270. Let the current rates be

$L_0(h) = L_0(90) = 0.056$

$L_0(h + m) = L_0(270) = 0.06$

In other words, the 90-day rate is 5.6 percent, and the 270-day rate is 6 percent. With h = 90 and m = 180, using our formula for the FRA rate, we obtain

$$\mathrm{FRA}(0,h,m) = \mathrm{FRA}(0,90,180) = \left[\frac{1 + 0.06\left(\dfrac{270}{360}\right)}{1 + 0.056\left(\dfrac{90}{360}\right)} - 1\right]\left(\frac{360}{180}\right) = 0.0611$$

So to enter into an FRA on day 0, the rate would be 6.11 percent.[22]

---

[21] To compare with the traditional method of calculating a forward rate, consider a two-year rate of 10 percent and a one-year rate of 9 percent. The forward rate is $[(1.10)^2/(1.09)] - 1 = 0.1101$. The numerator is the future value of the longer-term bond, and the denominator is the future value of the shorter-term bond. The ratio is 1 plus the rate. We do not need to annualize in this example, because the forward rate is on a one-year bond.

[22] It is worthwhile to point out again that this rate is the forward rate in the LIBOR term structure.

As noted, the initial outlay for entering the forward contract is zero. Thus, the initial value is zero. Later during the life of the contract, its value will rise above or fall below zero. Now let us determine the value of an FRA during its life. Specifically, we use the notation $V_g(0,h,m)$ to represent the value of an FRA on day g, prior to expiration, which was established on day 0, expires on day h, and is based on m-day LIBOR. Omitting the derivation, the value of the FRA will be

$$V_g(0,h,m) = \frac{1}{1 + L_g(h-g)\left(\dfrac{h-g}{360}\right)} - \frac{1 + FRA(0,h,m)\left(\dfrac{m}{360}\right)}{1 + L_g(h+m-g)\left(\dfrac{h+m-g}{360}\right)} \qquad \textbf{(70-14)}$$

This formula looks complicated, but the ideas behind it are actually quite simple. Recall that we are at day g. The first term on the right-hand side is the present value of \$1 received at day h. The second term is the present value of 1 plus the FRA rate to be received on day h + m, the maturity date of the underlying Eurodollar time deposit.

Assume that we go long the FRA, and it is 25 days later. We need to assign a value to the FRA. First note that g = 25, h − g = 90 − 25 = 65, and h + m − g = 90 + 180 − 25 = 245. In other words, we are 25 days into the contract, 65 days remain until expiration, and 245 days remain until the maturity of the Eurodollar deposit on which the underlying LIBOR is based. First we need information about the new term structure. Let

$$L_g(h-g) = L_{25}(65) = 0.059$$

$$L_g(h+m-g) = L_{25}(245) = 0.065$$

We now use the formula for the value of the FRA to obtain

$$V_g(0,h,m) = V_{25}(0,90,180) = \frac{1}{1 + 0.059\left(\dfrac{65}{360}\right)} - \frac{1 + 0.0611\left(\dfrac{180}{360}\right)}{1 + 0.065\left(\dfrac{245}{360}\right)} = 0.0026$$

Thus, we went long this FRA on day 0. Then 25 days later, the term structure changes to the rates used here and the FRA has a value of \$0.0026 per \$1 notional principal. If the notional principal is any amount other than \$1, we multiply the notional principal by \$0.0026 to obtain the full market value of the FRA.

We summarize the FRA formulas in Exhibit 70-8. We have now looked at the pricing and valuation of equity, fixed-income, and interest rate forward contracts. One of the most widely used types of forward contracts is the currency forward. The pricing and valuation of currency forwards is remarkably similar to that of equity forwards.

EXHIBIT 70-8 Pricing and Valuation Formulas for Interest Rate Forward Contracts (FRAs)

Forward price (rate):

$$FRA(0,h,m) = \left[\frac{1 + L_0(h+m)\left(\dfrac{h+m}{360}\right)}{1 + L_0(h)\left(\dfrac{h}{360}\right)} - 1 \right]\left(\frac{360}{m}\right)$$

Value of FRA on day g:

$$V_g(0,h,m) = \frac{1}{1 + L_g(h-g)\left(\dfrac{h-g}{360}\right)} - \frac{1 + FRA(0,h,m)\left(\dfrac{m}{360}\right)}{1 + L_g(h+m-g)\left(\dfrac{h+m-g}{360}\right)}$$

Practice Problem 4

A corporate treasurer needs to hedge the risk of the interest rate on a future transaction. The risk is associated with the rate on 180-day Euribor in 30 days. The relevant term structure of Euribor is given as follows:

30-day Euribor	5.75%
210-day Euribor	6.15%

A. State the terminology used to identify the FRA in which the manager is interested.

B. Determine the rate that the company would get on an FRA expiring in 30 days on 180-day Euribor.

C. Suppose the manager went long this FRA. Now, 20 days later, interest rates have moved significantly downward to the following:

10-day Euribor	5.45%
190-day Euribor	5.95%

The manager would like to know where the company stands on this FRA transaction. Determine the market value of the FRA for a €20 million notional principal.

D. On the expiration day, 180-day Euribor is 5.72 percent. Determine the payment made to or by the company to settle the FRA contract.

SOLUTIONS

A. This transaction would be identified as a 1×7 FRA.

B. Here the notation would be $h = 30$, $m = 180$, $h + m = 210$. Then

$$FRA(0,h,m) = FRA(0,30,180) = \left[\frac{1 + 0.0615\left(\dfrac{210}{360}\right)}{1 + 0.0575\left(\dfrac{30}{360}\right)} - 1 \right]\left(\frac{360}{180}\right) = 0.0619$$

C. Here g = 20, h − g = 30 − 20 = 10, h + m − g = 30 + 180 − 20 = 190. The value of the FRA for a €1 notional principal would be

$$V_g(0,h,m) = V_{20}(0,30,180) = \frac{1}{1 + 0.0545\left(\frac{10}{360}\right)} - \frac{1 + 0.0619\left(\frac{180}{360}\right)}{1 + 0.0595\left(\frac{190}{360}\right)} = -0.0011$$

Thus, for a notional principal of €20 million, the value would be €20,000,000(−0.0011) = −€22,000.

D. At expiration, the payoff is

$$\frac{[L_h(m) - FRA(0,h,m)]\left(\frac{m}{360}\right)}{1 + L_h(m)\left(\frac{m}{360}\right)} = \frac{(0.0572 - 0.0619)\left(\frac{180}{360}\right)}{1 + 0.0572\left(\frac{180}{360}\right)} = -0.0023$$

For a notional principal of €20 million, the payoff would then be €20,000,000(−0.0023) = −€46,000. Thus, €46,000 would be paid by the company, because it is long and the final rate was lower than the FRA rate.

4.4 Pricing and Valuation of Currency Forward Contracts

Foreign currency derivative transactions as well as spot transactions must be handled with care. The exchange rate can be quoted in terms of units of the domestic currency per unit of foreign currency, or units of the foreign currency per unit of the domestic currency. In this book, we shall always quote exchange rates in terms of units of the domestic currency per unit of the foreign currency, which is also called a direct quote. This approach is in keeping with the way in which other underlying assets are quoted. For example, from the perspective of a U.S. investor, a stock that sells for $50 is quoted in units of the domestic currency per unit (share) of stock. Likewise, if the euro exchange rate is quoted as $0.90, then the euro sells for $0.90 per unit, which is one euro. Alternatively, we could quote that $1 sells for 1/$0.90 = €1.1111—that is, €1.1111 per $1; in this case, units of foreign currency per one unit of domestic currency from the perspective of a U.S. investor. In fact, this type of quote is commonly used and is called an indirect quote. Taking that approach, however, we would quote the stock price as 1/$50 = 0.02 shares per $1, a very unusual and awkward way to quote a stock price.

By taking the approach of quoting prices in terms of units of the domestic currency per unit of foreign currency, we facilitate a comparison of currencies and their derivatives with equities and their derivatives—a topic we have already covered. For example, we have previously discussed the case of a stock selling for S_0, which represents units of the domestic currency per share of stock. Likewise, we shall treat the currency as having an exchange rate of S_0, meaning that it is selling for S_0. We also need the foreign interest rate, denoted as r^f, and the domestic interest rate, denoted as r.[23]

---

[23] We do not use a superscript "d" for the domestic rate, because in all previous examples we have used r to denote the interest rate in the home country of the investor.

Consider the following transactions executed today (time 0), assuming a contract expiration date of T:

Take $S_0/(1 + r^f)^T$ units of the domestic currency and convert it to $1/(1 + r^f)^T$ units of the foreign currency.[24]

Sell a forward contract to deliver one unit of the foreign currency at the rate F(0,T) expiring at time T.

Hold the position until time T. The $(1 + r^f)^T$ units of foreign currency will accrue interest at the rate r^f and grow to one unit of the currency at T as follows:

$$\left(\frac{1}{1 + r^f}\right)^T (1 + r^f) = 1$$

Thus, at expiration we shall have one unit of the foreign currency, which is then delivered to the holder of the long forward contract, who pays the amount F(0,T). This amount was known at the start of the transaction. Because the risk has been hedged away, the exchange rate at expiration is irrelevant. Hence, this transaction is risk-free. Accordingly, the present value of F(0,T), found by discounting at the domestic risk-free interest rate, must equal the initial outlay of $S_0/(1 + r^f)^T$. Setting these amounts equal and solving for F(0,T) gives

$$F(0,T) = \left[\frac{S_0}{(1 + r^f)^T}\right](1 + r)^T \tag{70-15}$$

The term in brackets is the spot exchange rate discounted by the foreign interest rate. This term is then compounded at the domestic interest rate to the expiration day.[25]

Recall that in pricing equity forwards, we always reduced the stock price by the present value of the dividends and then compounded the resulting value to the expiration date. We can view currencies in the same way. The stock makes cash payments that happen to be called dividends; the currency makes cash payments that happen to be called interest. Although the time pattern of how a stock pays dividends is quite different from the time pattern of how interest accrues, the general idea is the same. After reducing the spot price or rate by any cash flows over the life of the contract, the resulting value is then compounded at the risk-free rate to the expiration day.

The formula we have obtained here is simply a variation of the formula used for other types of forward contracts. In international financial markets, however, this formula has acquired its own name: **interest rate parity** (sometimes called covered interest rate parity). It expresses the equivalence, or parity, of spot and forward exchange rates, after adjusting for differences in the interest rates in the two countries. One implication of interest rate parity is that the forward rate will exceed (be less than) the spot rate if the domestic interest rate exceeds (is less than) the foreign interest rate. With a direct quote, if the forward rate exceeds (is less than) the spot rate, the foreign currency is said to be selling at a premium (discount). One should not, on the basis of this information, conclude that

---

[24] In other words, if one unit of the foreign currency costs S_0, then $S_0/(1 + r^f)^T$ units of the domestic currency would, therefore, buy $1/(1 + r^f)^T$ units of the foreign currency.

[25] It is also common to see the above Equation 70-15 written inversely, with the spot rate divided by the domestic interest factor and compounded by the foreign interest factor. This variation would be appropriate if the spot and forward rates were quoted in terms of units of the foreign currency per unit of domestic currency (indirect quotes). As we mentioned earlier, however, it is easier to think of a currency as just another asset, which naturally should have its price quoted in units of the domestic currency per unit of the asset or foreign currency.

a currency selling at a premium is expected to increase or one selling at a discount is expected to decrease. A forward premium or discount is merely an implication of the relationship between interest rates in the two countries. More information would be required to make any assumptions about the outlook for the exchange rate.

If the forward rate in the market does not equal the forward rate given by interest rate parity, then an arbitrage transaction can be executed. Indeed, a similar relationship is true for any of the forward rates we have studied. In the foreign exchange markets, however, this arbitrage transaction has its own name: **covered interest arbitrage.** If the forward rate in the market is higher than the rate given by interest rate parity, then the forward rate is too high. When the price of an asset or derivative is too high, it should be sold. Thus, a trader would 1) sell the forward contract at the market rate, 2) buy $1/(1 + r^f)^T$ units of the foreign currency, 3) hold the position, earning interest on the currency, and 4) at maturity of the forward contract deliver the currency and be paid the forward rate. This arbitrage transaction would earn a return in excess of the domestic risk-free rate without any risk. If the forward rate is less than the rate given by the formula, the trader does the opposite, selling the foreign currency and buying a forward contract, in a similar manner. The combined actions of many traders undertaking this transaction will bring the forward price in the market in line with the forward price given by the model.

In Equation 70-15, both interest rates were annual rates with discrete compounding. In dealing with equities, we sometimes assume that the dividend payments are made continuously. Similarly, we could also assume that interest is compounded continuously. If that is the case, let r^{fc} be the continuously compounded foreign interest rate, defined as $r^{fc} = \ln(1 + r^f)$, and as before, let r^c be the continuously compounded domestic interest rate. Then the forward price is given by the same formula, with appropriately adjusted symbols, as we obtained when working with equity derivatives:

$$F(0,T) = (S_0 e^{-r^{fc}T})e^{r^cT} \qquad \textbf{(70-16)}$$

Now consider how we might value a foreign currency forward contract at some point in time during its life. In fact, we already know how: We simply apply to foreign currency forward contracts what we know about the valuation of equity forwards during the contract's life. Recall that the value of an equity forward is the stock price minus the present value of the dividends over the remaining life of the contract minus the present value of the forward price over the remaining life of the contract. An analogous formula for a currency forward gives us

$$V_t(0,T) = \frac{S_t}{(1 + r^f)^{(T-t)}} - \frac{F(0,T)}{(1 + r)^{(T-t)}} \qquad \textbf{(70-17)}$$

In other words, we take the current exchange rate at time t, S_t, discount it by the foreign interest rate over the remaining life of the contract, and subtract the forward price discounted by the domestic interest rate over the remaining life of the contract. Under the assumption that we are using continuous compounding and discounting, the formula would be

$$V_t(0,T) = (S_t e^{-r^{fc}(T-t)}) - F(0,T)e^{-r^c(T-t)} \qquad \textbf{(70-18)}$$

For example, suppose the domestic currency is the U.S. dollar and the foreign currency is the Swiss franc. Let the spot exchange rate be $0.5987, the U.S. interest rate be 5.5 percent, and the Swiss interest rate be 4.75 percent. We assume these interest rates are fixed and will not change over the life of the forward contract. We also assume that these rates are based on annual compounding and are not quoted as LIBOR-type rates. Thus, we compound using formulas like $(1 + r)^T$, where T is the number of years and r is the annual rate.[26]

Assuming the forward contract has a maturity of 180 days, we have T = 180/365. Using the above formula for the forward rate, we find that the forward price should be

$$F(0,T) = F(0,180/365) = \left[\frac{\$0.5987}{(1.0475)^{180/365}}\right](1.055)^{180/365} = \$0.6008$$

Thus, if we entered into a forward contract, it would call for us to purchase (if long) or sell (if short) one Swiss franc in 180 days at a price of $0.6008.

Suppose we go long this forward contract. It is now 40 days later, or 140 days until expiration. The spot rate is now $0.65. As assumed above, the interest rates are fixed. With t = 40/365 and T − t = 140/365, the value of our long position is

$$V_t(0,T) = V_{40/365}(0,180/365) = \frac{\$0.6500}{(1.0475)^{140/365}} - \frac{\$0.6008}{(1.055)^{140/365}} = \$0.0499$$

So the contract value is $0.0499 per Swiss franc. If the notional principal were more than one Swiss franc, we would simply multiply the notional principal by $0.0499.

If we were working with continuously compounded rates, we would have $r^c = \ln(1.055) = 0.0535$ and $r^{fc} = \ln(1.0475) = 0.0464$. Then the forward price would be $F(0,T) = F(0,180/365) = (0.5987e^{-0.0464(180/365)})e^{0.0535(180/365)} = 0.6008$, and the value 40 days later would be $V_{40/365}(0,180/365) = 0.65e^{-0.0464(140/365)} - 0.6008e^{-0.0535(140/365)} = 0.0499$. These are the same results we obtained working with discrete rates.

Exhibit 70-9 summarizes the formulas for pricing and valuation of currency forward contracts.

EXHIBIT 70-9   Pricing and Valuation Formulas for Currency Forward Contracts

Forward price (rate) = (Spot price discounted by foreign interest rate) compounded at domestic interest rate:

Discrete interest: $F(0,T) = \left[\dfrac{S_0}{(1 + r^f)^T}\right](1 + r)^T$

Continuous interest: $F(0,T) = (S_0 e^{-r^{fc}T})e^{r^c T}$

Value of forward contract:

Discrete interest: $V_t(0,T) = \left[\dfrac{S_t}{(1 + r^f)^{(T-t)}}\right] - \dfrac{F(0,T)}{(1 + r)^{(T-t)}}$

Continuous interest: $V_t(0,T) = [S_t e^{-r^{fc}(T-t)}] - F(0,T)e^{-r^c(T-t)}$

Note: The exchange rate is quoted in units of domestic currency per unit of foreign currency.

---

[26] If these were LIBOR-style rates, the interest would be calculated using the factor 1 + [Rate(Days/360)].

The spot rate for British pounds is $1.76. The U.S. risk-free rate is 5.1 percent, and the U.K. risk-free rate is 6.2 percent; both are compounded annually. One-year forward contracts are currently quoted at a rate of $1.75.

A. Identify a strategy with which a trader can earn a profit at no risk by engaging in a forward contract, regardless of her view of the pound's likely movements. Carefully describe the transactions the trader would make. Show the rate of return that would be earned from this transaction. Assume the trader's domestic currency is U.S. dollars.

B. Suppose the trader simply shorts the forward contract. It is now one month later. Assume interest rates are the same, but the spot rate is now $1.72. What is the gain or loss to the counterparty on the trade?

C. At expiration, the pound is at $1.69. What is the value of the forward contract to the short at expiration?

SOLUTIONS

A. The following information is given:

$S_0 = \$1.76$
$r = 0.051$
$r^f = 0.062$
$T = 1.0$

The forward price should be

$$F(0,T) = \left(\frac{\$1.76}{1.062}\right)(1.051) = \$1.7418$$

With the forward contract selling at $1.75, it is slightly overpriced. Thus, the trader should be able to buy the currency and sell a forward contract to earn a return in excess of the risk-free rate at no risk. The specific transactions are as follows:

Take $1.76/(1.062) = \$1.6573$. Use it to buy $1/1.062 = £0.9416$.

Sell a forward contract to deliver £1.00 in one year at the price of $1.75.

Hold the position for one year, collecting interest at the U.K. risk-free rate of 6.2 percent. The £0.9416 will grow to $(0.9416)(1.062) = £1.00$.

At expiration, deliver the pound and receive $1.75. This is a return of

$$\frac{1.75}{1.6573} - 1 = 0.0559$$

A risk-free return of 5.59 percent is better than the U.S. risk-free rate of 5.1 percent, a result of the fact that the forward contract is overpriced.

B. We now need the value of the forward contract to the counterparty, who went long at $1.75. The inputs are

$$t = 1/12$$
$$S_t = \$1.72$$
$$T - t = 11/12$$
$$F(0,T) = \$1.75$$

The value of the forward contract to the long is

$$V_t(0,T) = \frac{1.72}{(1.062)^{(11/12)}} - \frac{1.75}{(1.051)^{11/12}} = -0.0443$$

which is a loss of $0.0443 to the long and a gain of $0.0443 to the short.

C. The pound is worth $1.69 at expiration. Thus, the value to the long is

$$V_T(0,T) = 1.69 - 1.75 = -0.06$$

and the value to the short is +$0.06. Note the minus sign in the equation $V_T(0,T) = -0.06$. The value to the long is always the spot value at expiration minus the original forward price. The short will be required to deliver the foreign currency and receive $1.75, which is $0.06 more than market value of the pound. The contract's value to the short is thus $0.06, which is the negative of its value to the long.

We have now seen how to determine the price and value of equity, fixed-income and interest rate, and currency forward contracts. We observed that the price is determined such that no arbitrage opportunities exist for either the long or the short. We have found that the value of a forward contract is the amount we would pay or receive to enter or exit the contract. Because no money changes hands up front, the value of a forward contract when initiated is zero. The value at expiration is determined by the difference between the spot price or rate at expiration and the forward contract price or rate. The value prior to expiration can also be determined and is the present value of the claim at expiration.

Determining the value of a forward contract is important for several reasons. One, however, is particularly important: Forward contracts contain the very real possibility that one of the parties might default. By knowing the market value, one can determine the amount of money at risk if a counterparty defaults. Let us now look at how credit risk enters into a forward contract.

5   CREDIT RISK AND FORWARD CONTRACTS

To illustrate how credit risk affects a forward contract, consider the currency forward contract example we just finished in the previous section. It concerns a contract that expires in 180 days in which the long will pay a forward rate of $0.6008 for each Swiss franc to be received at expiration. Assume that the contract covers 10 million Swiss francs. Let us look at the problem from the point of view of the holder of the long position and the credit risk faced by this party.

Assume it is the contract expiration day and the spot rate for Swiss francs is $0.62. The long is due to receive 10 million Swiss francs and pay $0.6008 per Swiss franc, or $6,008,000 in total. Now suppose that perhaps because of bankruptcy or insolvency, the short cannot come up with the $6,200,000 that it would take to purchase the Swiss francs on the open market at the prevailing spot rate.[27] In order to obtain the Swiss francs, the long would have to buy them in the open market. Doing so would incur an additional cost of $6,200,000 − $6,008,000 = $192,000, which can be viewed as the credit risk at the point of expiration when the spot rate is $0.62. Not surprisingly, this amount is also the market value of the contract at this point.

This risk is an immediate risk faced at expiration. Prior to expiration, the long faces a potential risk that the short will default. If the long wanted to gauge the potential exposure, he would calculate the current market value. In the example we used in which the long is now 40 days into the life of the contract, the market value to the long is $0.0499 per Swiss franc. Hence, the long's exposure would be 10,000,000($0.0499) = $499,000. Although no payments are due at this point, $499,000 is the market value of the claim on the payment at expiration. Using an estimate of the probability that the short would default, the long can gauge the expected credit loss from the transaction by multiplying that probability by $499,000.

The market value of a forward contract reflects the current value of the claim at expiration, given existing market conditions. If the Swiss franc rises significantly, the market value will increase along with it, thereby exposing the long to the potential for even greater losses. Many participants in derivatives markets estimate this potential loss by running simulations that attempt to reflect the potential market value of the contract along with the probability of the counterparty defaulting.

We have viewed credit risk from the viewpoint of the long, but what about the short's perspective? In the case in which we went to expiration and the short owed the long the greater amount, the short faces no credit risk. In the case prior to expiration in which the contract's market value was positive, the value of the future claim was greater to the long than to the short. Hence, the short still did not face any credit risk.

The short would face credit risk, however, if circumstances were such that the value of the transaction were negative to the long, which would make the value to the short positive. In that case, the scenario discussed previously in this section would apply from the short's perspective.

In Chapter 9, we shall discuss methods of managing the credit risk of various types of derivatives transactions. At this point, however, it will be helpful to specifically examine one particular method. Let us go back to the long currency forward contract that had a market value of $499,000. As it stands at this time, the holder of the long position has a claim on the holder of the short position that is worth $499,000. Suppose the two parties had agreed when they entered into the transaction that in 40 days, the party owing the greater amount to the other would pay the amount owed and the contract would be repriced at the new forward rate. Now on the 40th day, the short would pay the long $499,000. Recalling that the U.S. interest rate was 5.5 percent and the Swiss interest rate was 4.75 percent, the contract, which now has 140 days to go (T = 140/365), would then be repriced to the rate

$$F(0,T) = F(0,140/365) = \left[\frac{\$0.65}{(1.0475)^{140/365}} \right] (1.055)^{140/365} = \$0.6518$$

In other words, from this point, the contract has a new rate of $0.6518. The long now agrees to pay $0.6518 for the currency from the short in 140 days.

[27] Even if the short already holds the Swiss franc, she might be declaring bankruptcy or otherwise unable to pay debts such that the forward contract claim is combined with the claims of all of the short's other creditors.

What the two parties have done is called **marking to market.** They have settled up the amount owed and marked the contract to its current market rate. If the parties agree in advance, a forward contract can be marked to market at whatever dates the parties feel are appropriate. Marking to market keeps one party from becoming too deeply indebted to the other without paying up. At the dates when the contract is marked to market, the parties restructure the contract so that it remains in force but with an updated price.

Forward contracts and swaps are sometimes marked to market to mitigate credit risk. In Reading 71, we shall examine futures contracts. A distinguishing characteristic of futures contracts is that they are marked to market every day. In essence, they are forward contracts that are marked to market and repriced daily to reduce the credit risk.

6   THE ROLE OF FORWARD MARKETS

In this reading we have discussed many aspects of forward contracts and forward markets. We will conclude the reading (and each of the following readings, which cover futures, options, and swaps) with a brief discussion of the role that these markets play in our financial system. Although forward, futures, options, and swap markets serve similar purposes in our society, each market is unique. Otherwise, these markets would consolidate.

Forward markets may well be the least understood of the various derivative markets. In contrast to their cousins, futures contracts, forward contracts are a far less visible segment of the financial markets. Both forwards and futures serve a similar purpose: They provide a means in which a party can commit to the future purchase or sale of an asset at an agreed-upon price, without the necessity of paying any cash until the asset is actually purchased or sold. In contrast to futures contracts, forward contracts are private transactions, permitting the ultimate in customization. As long as a counterparty can be found, a party can structure the contract completely to its liking. Futures contracts are standardized and may not have the exact terms required by the party. In addition, futures contracts, with their daily marking to market, produce interim cash flows that can lead to imperfections in a hedge transaction designed not to hedge interim events but to hedge a specific event at a target horizon date. Forward markets also provide secrecy and have only a light degree of regulation. In general, forward markets serve a specialized clientele, specifically large corporations and institutions with specific target dates, underlying assets, and risks that they wish to take or reduce by committing to a transaction without paying cash at the start.

As Reading 73 will make clear, however, forward contracts are just miniature versions of swaps. A swap can be viewed as a series of forward contracts. Swaps are much more widely used than forward contracts, suggesting that parties that have specific risk management needs typically require the equivalent of a series of forward contracts. A swap contract consolidates a series of forward contracts into a single instrument at lower cost.

Forward contracts are the building blocks for constructing and understanding both swaps and futures. Swaps and futures are more widely used and better known, but forward contracts play a valuable role in helping us understand swaps and futures. Moreover, as noted, for some parties, forward contracts serve specific needs not met by other derivatives.

In Reading 71 we shall look at futures contracts. We shall demonstrate how similar they are to forward contracts, but the differences are important, and some of their benefits to society are slightly different and less obvious than those of forwards.

SUMMARY 7

- The holder of a long forward contract (the "long") is obligated to take delivery of the underlying asset and pay the forward price at expiration. The holder of a short forward contract (the "short") is obligated to deliver the underlying asset and accept payment of the forward price at expiration.

- At expiration, a forward contract can be terminated by having the short make delivery of the underlying asset to the long or having the long and short exchange the equivalent cash value. If the asset is worth more (less) than the forward price, the short (long) pays the long (short) the cash difference between the market price or rate and the price or rate agreed on in the contract.

- A party can terminate a forward contract prior to expiration by entering into an opposite transaction with the same or a different counterparty. It is possible to leave both the original and new transactions in place, thereby leaving both transactions subject to credit risk, or to have the two transactions cancel each other. In the latter case, the party owing the greater amount pays the market value to the other party, resulting in the elimination of the remaining credit risk. This elimination can be achieved, however, only if the counterparty to the second transaction is the same counterparty as in the first.

- A dealer is a financial institution that makes a market in forward contracts and other derivatives. A dealer stands ready to take either side of a transaction. An end user is a party that comes to a dealer needing a transaction, usually for the purpose of managing a particular risk.

- Equity forward contracts can be written on individual stocks, specific stock portfolios, or stock indices. Equity forward contract prices and values must take into account the fact that the underlying stock, portfolio, or index could pay dividends.

- Forward contracts on bonds can be based on zero-coupon bonds or on coupon bonds, as well as portfolios or indices based on zero-coupon bonds or coupon bonds. Zero-coupon bonds pay their return by discounting the face value, often using a 360-day year assumption. Forward contracts on bonds must expire before the bond's maturity. In addition, a forward contract on a bond can be affected by special features of bonds, such as callability and convertibility.

- Eurodollar time deposits are dollar loans made by one bank to another. Although the term "Eurodollars" refers to dollar-denominated loans, similar loans exist in other currencies. Eurodollar deposits accrue interest by adding it on to the principal, using a 360-day year assumption. The primary Eurodollar rate is called LIBOR.

- LIBOR stands for London Interbank Offer Rate, the rate at which London banks are willing to lend to other London banks. Euribor is the rate on a euro time deposit, a loan made by banks to other banks in Frankfurt in which the currency is the euro.

- An FRA is a forward contract in which one party, the long, agrees to pay a fixed interest payment at a future date and receive an interest payment at a rate to be determined at expiration. FRAs are described by a special notation. For example, a 3×6 FRA expires in three months; the underlying is a Eurodollar deposit that begins in three months and ends three months later, or six months from now.

- The payment of an FRA at expiration is based on the net difference between the underlying rate and the agreed-upon rate, adjusted by the notional principal and the number of days in the instrument on which the underlying rate is based. The payoff is also discounted, however, to reflect the fact that the underlying rate on which the instrument is based assumes that payment will occur at a later date.

▸ A currency forward contract is a commitment for one party, the long, to buy a currency at a fixed price from the other party, the short, at a specific date. The contract can be settled by actual delivery, or the two parties can choose to settle in cash on the expiration day.

▸ A forward contract is priced by assuming that the underlying asset is purchased, a forward contract is sold, and the position is held to expiration. Because the sale price of the asset is locked in as the forward price, the transaction is risk free and should earn the risk-free rate. The forward price is then obtained as the price that guarantees a return of the risk-free rate. If the forward price is too high or too low, an arbitrage profit in the form of a return in excess of the risk-free rate can be earned. The combined effects of all investors executing arbitrage transactions will force the forward price to converge to its arbitrage-free level.

▸ The value of a forward contract is determined by the fact that a long forward contract is a claim on the underlying asset and a commitment to pay the forward price at expiration. The value of a forward contract is, therefore, the current price of the asset less the present value of the forward price at expiration. Because no money changes hands at the start, the value of the forward contract today is zero. The value of a forward contract at expiration is the price of the underlying asset minus the forward price.

▸ Valuation of a forward contract is important because 1) it makes good business sense to know the values of future commitments, 2) accounting rules require that forward contracts be accounted for in income statements and balance sheets, 3) the value gives a good measure of the credit exposure, and 4) the value can be used to determine the amount of money one party would have to pay another party to terminate a position.

▸ An off-market forward contract is established with a nonzero value at the start. The contract will, therefore, have a positive or negative value and require a cash payment at the start. A positive value is paid by the long to the short; a negative value is paid by the short to the long. In an off-market forward contract, the forward price will not equal the price of the underlying asset compounded at the risk-free rate but rather will be set in the process of negotiation between the two parties.

▸ An equity forward contract is priced by taking the stock price, subtracting the present value of the dividends over the life of the contract, and then compounding this amount at the risk-free rate to the expiration date of the contract. The present value of the dividends can be found by assuming the dividends are risk-free and calculating their present value using the risk-free rate of interest. Or one can assume that dividends are paid at a constant continuously compounded rate and then discount the stock price by the exponential function using the continuously compounded dividend rate. Alternatively, an equity forward can be priced by compounding the stock price to the expiration date and then subtracting the future value of the dividends at the expiration date. The value of an equity forward contract is the stock price minus the present value of the dividends minus the present value of the forward price that will be paid at expiration.

▸ To price a fixed-income forward contract, take the bond price, subtract the present value of the coupons over the life of the contract, and compound this amount at the risk-free rate to the expiration date of the contract. The value of a fixed-income forward contract is the bond price minus the present value of the coupons minus the present value of the forward price that will be paid at expiration.

▸ The price of an FRA, which is actually a rate, is simply the forward rate embedded in the term structure of the FRA's underlying rate. The value of an FRA based on a Eurodollar deposit is the present value of $1 to be received at expiration minus the present value of $1 plus the FRA rate to be received at the maturity date of the Eurodollar deposit on which the FRA is based, with appropriate (days/360) adjustments.

▸ The price, which is actually an exchange rate, of a forward contract on a currency is the spot rate discounted at the foreign interest rate over the life of the contract and then compounded at the domestic interest rate to the expiration date of the contract. The value of a currency forward contract is the spot rate discounted at the foreign interest rate over the life of the contract minus the present value of the forward rate at expiration.

▸ Credit risk in a forward contract arises when the counterparty that owes the greater amount is unable to pay at expiration or declares bankruptcy prior to expiration. The market value of a forward contract is a measure of the net amount one party owes the other. Only one party, the one owing the lesser amount, faces credit risk at any given time. Because the market value can change from positive to negative, however, the other party has the potential for facing credit risk at a later date. Counterparties occasionally mark forward contracts to market, with one party paying the other the current market value; they then reprice the contract to the current market price or rate.

▸ Forward markets play an important role in society, providing a means by which a select clientele of parties can engage in customized, private, unregulated transactions that commit them to buying or selling an asset at a later date at an agreed-upon price without paying any cash at the start. Forward contracts also are a simplified version of both futures and swaps and, therefore, form a basis for understanding these other derivatives.

PROBLEMS

1. **A.** Calculate the price for a T-bill with a face value of $10,000, 153 days to maturity, and a discount yield of 1.74 percent.

   B. Calculate the asked discount yield for a T-bill that has 69 days to maturity, a face value of $10,000, and a price of $9,950.

2. Assume that 60-day LIBOR is 4.35 percent. You are based in London and need to borrow $20,000,000 for 60 days. What is the total amount you will owe in 60 days?

3. The treasurer of Company A expects to receive a cash inflow of $15,000,000 in 90 days. The treasurer expects short-term interest rates to fall during the next 90 days. In order to hedge against this risk, the treasurer decides to use an FRA that expires in 90 days and is based on 90-day LIBOR. The FRA is quoted at 5 percent. At expiration, LIBOR is 4.5 percent. Assume that the notional principal on the contract is $15,000,000.

   A. Indicate whether the treasurer should take a long or short position to hedge interest rate risk.

   B. Using the appropriate terminology, identify the type of FRA used here.

   C. Calculate the gain or loss to Company A as a consequence of entering the FRA.

4. Suppose that a party wanted to enter into an FRA that expires in 42 days and is based on 137-day LIBOR. The dealer quotes a rate of 4.75 percent on this FRA. Assume that at expiration, the 137-day LIBOR is 4 percent and the notional principal is $20,000,000.

   A. What is the term used to describe such nonstandard instruments?

   B. Calculate the FRA payoff on a long position.

5. Assume Sun Microsystems expects to receive €20,000,000 in 90 days. A dealer provides a quote of $0.875 for a currency forward contract to expire in 90 days. Suppose that at the end of 90 days, the rate is $0.90. Assume that settlement is in cash. Calculate the cash flow at expiration if Sun Microsystems enters into a forward contract expiring in 90 days to buy dollars at $0.875.

FUTURES MARKETS AND CONTRACTS

LEARNING OUTCOMES

The candidate should be able to:

a. identify the institutional features that distinguish futures contracts from forward contracts and describe the characteristics of futures contracts;

b. differentiate between margin in the securities markets and margin in the futures markets;

c. describe how a futures trade takes place;

d. describe how a futures position may be closed out (i.e., offset) prior to expiration;

e. define initial margin, maintenance margin, variation margin, and settlement price;

f. describe the process of marking to market and compute the margin balance, given the previous day's balance and the new futures price;

g. explain price limits, limit move, limit up, limit down, and locked limit;

h. describe how a futures contract can be terminated by a close-out (i.e., offset) at expiration, delivery, an equivalent cash settlement, or an exchange-for-physicals;

i. explain delivery options in futures contracts;

j. distinguish among scalpers, day traders, and position traders;

k. describe the characteristics of the following types of futures contracts: Treasury bill, Eurodollar, Treasury bond, stock index, and currency.

INTRODUCTION 1

In Reading 69, we undertook a general overview of derivative markets. In Reading 70, we focused on forward markets. Now we explore futures markets in a similar fashion. Although we shall see a clear similarity between forward and futures contracts, critical distinctions nonetheless exist between the two.

In Reading 69 we learned that, like a forward contract, *a futures contract is an agreement between two parties in which one party, the buyer, agrees to buy*

Analysis of Derivatives for the CFA® Program, by Don M. Chance, Copyright © 2003 by Association for Investment Management and Research. Reprinted with permission.

from the other party, the seller, an underlying asset or other derivative, at a future date at a price agreed on today. Unlike a forward contract, however, a futures contract is not a private and customized transaction but rather a public transaction that takes place on an organized futures exchange. In addition, a futures contract is standardized—the exchange, rather than the individual parties, sets the terms and conditions, with the exception of price. As a result, futures contracts have a secondary market, meaning that previously created contracts can be traded. Also, parties to futures contracts are guaranteed against credit losses resulting from the counterparty's inability to pay. A clearinghouse provides this guarantee via a procedure in which it converts gains and losses that accrue on a daily basis into actual cash gains and losses. Futures contracts are regulated at the federal government level; as we noted in Reading 70, forward contracts are essentially unregulated. Futures contracts are created on organized trading facilities referred to as futures exchanges, whereas forward contracts are not created in any specific location but rather initiated between any two parties who wish to enter into such a contract. Finally, each futures exchange has a division or subsidiary called a clearinghouse that performs the specific responsibilities of paying and collecting daily gains and losses as well as guaranteeing to each party the performance of the other.

In a futures transaction, one party, the long, is the buyer and the other party, the short, is the seller. The buyer agrees to buy the underlying at a later date, the expiration, at a price agreed on at the start of the contract. The seller agrees to sell the underlying to the buyer at the expiration, at the price agreed on at the start of the contract. Every day, the futures contract trades in the market and its price changes in response to new information. Buyers benefit from price increases, and sellers benefit from price decreases. On the expiration day, the contract terminates and no further trading takes place. Then, either the buyer takes delivery of the underlying from the seller, or the two parties make an equivalent cash settlement. We shall explore each of these characteristics of futures contracts in more detail. First, however, it is important to take a brief look at how futures markets came into being.

1.1 A Brief History of Futures Markets

Although vestiges of futures markets appear in the Japanese rice markets of the 18th century and perhaps even earlier, the mid-1800s marked the first clear origins of modern futures markets. For example, in the United States in the 1840s, Chicago was becoming a major transportation and distribution center for agricultural commodities. Its central location and access to the Great Lakes gave Chicago a competitive advantage over other U.S. cities. Farmers from the Midwest would harvest their grain and take it to Chicago for sale. Grain production, however, is seasonal. As a result, grain prices would rise sharply just prior to the harvest but then plunge when the grain was brought to the market. Too much grain at one time and too little at another resulted in severe problems. Grain storage facilities in Chicago were inadequate to accommodate the oversupply. Some farmers even dumped their grain in the Chicago River because prices were so low that they could not afford to take their grain to another city to sell.

To address this problem, in 1848 a group of businessmen formed an organization later named the Chicago Board of Trade (CBOT) and created an arrangement called a "to-arrive" contract. These contracts permitted farmers to sell their grain before delivering it. In other words, farmers could harvest the grain and enter into a contract to deliver it at a much later date at a price already agreed on. This transaction allowed the farmer to hold the grain in storage at some other location besides Chicago. On the other side of these contracts were the businessmen who had formed the Chicago Board of Trade.

It soon became apparent that trading in these to-arrive contracts was more important and useful than trading in the grain itself. Soon the contracts began trading in a type of secondary market, which allowed buyers and sellers to discharge their obligations by passing them on, for a price, to other parties. With the addition of the clearinghouse in the 1920s, which provided a guarantee against default, modern futures markets firmly established their place in the financial world. It was left to other exchanges, such as today's Chicago Mercantile Exchange, the New York Mercantile Exchange, Eurex, and the London International Financial Futures Exchange, to develop and become, along with the Chicago Board of Trade, the global leaders in futures markets.

We shall now explore the important features of futures contracts in more detail.

1.2 Public Standardized Transactions

A private transaction is not generally reported in the news or to any price-reporting service. Forward contracts are private contracts. Just as in most legal contracts, the parties do not publicly report that they have engaged in a contract. In contrast, a futures transaction is reported to the futures exchange, the clearinghouse, and at least one regulatory agency. The price is recorded and available from price reporting services and even on the Internet.[1]

We noted that a futures transaction is not customized. Recall from Reading 70 that in a forward contract, the two parties establish all of the terms of the contract, including the identity of the underlying, the expiration date, and the manner in which the contract is settled (cash or actual delivery) as well as the price. The terms are customized to meet the needs of both parties. In a futures contract, the price is the only term established by the two parties; the exchange establishes all other terms. Moreover, the terms that are established by the exchange are standardized, meaning that the exchange selects a number of choices for underlyings, expiration dates, and a variety of other contract-specific items. These standardized terms are well known to all parties. If a party wishes to trade a futures contract, it must accept these terms. The only alternative would be to create a similar but customized contract on the forward market.

With respect to the underlying, for example, a given asset has a variety of specifications and grades. Consider a futures contract on U.S. Treasury bonds. There are many different Treasury bonds with a variety of characteristics. The futures exchange must decide which Treasury bond or group of bonds the contract covers. One of the most actively traded commodity futures contracts is oil, but there are many different types of oil.[2] To which type of oil does the contract apply? The exchange decides at the time it designs the contract.

---

[1] The information reported to the general public does not disclose the identity of the parties to transactions but only that a transaction took place at a particular price.

[2] Some of the main types are Saudi Arabian light crude, Brent crude, and West Texas intermediate crude.

The parties to a forward contract set its expiration at whatever date they want. For a futures contract, the exchange establishes a set of expiration dates. The first specification of the expiration is the month. An exchange might establish that a given futures contract expires only in the months of March, June, September, and December. The second specification determines how far the expirations go out into the future. For example, in January of a given year, there may be expirations of March, June, September, and December. Expirations might also be available for March, June, September, and December of the following year, and perhaps some months of the year after that. The exchange decides which expiration months are appropriate for trading, based on which expirations they believe would be actively traded. Treasury bond futures have expirations going out only about a year. Eurodollar futures, however, have expirations that go out about 10 years.[3] The third specification of the expiration is the specific day of expiration. Many, but not all, contracts expire some time during the third week of the expiration month.

The exchange determines a number of other contract characteristics, including the contract size. For example, one Eurodollar futures contract covers $1 million of a Eurodollar time deposit. One U.S. Treasury bond futures contract covers $100,000 face value of Treasury bonds. One futures contract on crude oil covers 1,000 barrels. The exchange also decides on the price quotation unit. For example, Treasury bond futures are quoted in points and 32nds of par of 100. Hence, you will see a price like 104 21/32, which means 104.65625. With a contract size of $100,000, the actual price is $104,656.25.

The exchange also determines what hours of the day trading takes place and at what physical location on the exchange the contract will be traded. Many futures exchanges have a trading floor, which contains octagonal-shaped pits. A contract is assigned to a certain pit. Traders enter the pits and express their willingness to buy and sell by calling out and/or indicating by hand signals their bids and offers. Some exchanges have electronic trading, which means that trading takes place on computer terminals, generally located in companies' offices. Some exchanges have both floor trading and electronic trading; some have only one or the other.

1.3 Homogenization and Liquidity

By creating contracts with generally accepted terms, the exchange standardizes the instrument. In contrast, forward contracts are quite heterogeneous because they are customized. Standardizing the instrument makes it more acceptable to a broader group of participants, with the advantage being that the instrument can then more easily trade in a type of secondary market. Indeed, the ability to sell a previously purchased contract or purchase a previously sold contract is one of the important features of futures contracts. A futures contract is therefore said to have liquidity in contrast to a forward contract, which does not generally trade after it has been created.[4] This ability to trade a previously opened contract allows participants in this market to offset the position before expiration, thereby obtaining exposure to price movements in the underlying without the actual requirement of holding the position to expiration. We shall discuss this characteristic further when we describe futures trading in Section 2.

---

[3] You may be wondering why some Eurodollar futures contracts have such long expirations. Dealers in swaps and forward rate agreements use Eurodollar futures to hedge their positions. Many of those over-the-counter contracts have very long expirations.

[4] The notion of liquidity here is only that a market exists for futures contracts, but this does not imply a high degree of liquidity. There may be little trading in a given contract, and the bid–ask spread can be high. In contrast, some forward markets can be very liquid, allowing forward contracts to be offset, as described in Reading 70.

1.4 The Clearinghouse, Daily Settlement, and Performance Guarantee

Another important distinction between futures and forwards is that the futures exchange guarantees to each party the performance of the other party, through a mechanism known as the clearinghouse. This guarantee means that if one party makes money on the transaction, it does not have to worry about whether it will collect the money from the other party because the clearinghouse ensures it will be paid. In contrast, each party to a forward contract assumes the risk that the other party will default.

An important and distinguishing feature of futures contracts is that the gains and losses on each party's position are credited and charged on a daily basis. This procedure, called **daily settlement** or **marking to market,** essentially results in paper gains and losses being converted to cash gains and losses each day. It is also equivalent to terminating a contract at the end of each day and reopening it the next day at that settlement price. In some sense, a futures contract is like a strategy of opening up a forward contract, closing it one day later, opening up a new contract, closing it one day later, and continuing in that manner until expiration. The exact manner in which the daily settlement works will be covered in more detail later in Section 3.

1.5 Regulation

In most countries, futures contracts are regulated at the federal government level. State and regional laws may also apply. In the United States, the Commodity Futures Trading Commission regulates the futures market. In the United Kingdom, the Securities and Futures Authority regulates both the securities and futures markets.

Federal regulation of futures markets generally arises out of a concern to protect the general public and other futures market participants, as well as through a recognition that futures markets affect all financial markets and the economy. Regulations cover such matters as ensuring that prices are reported accurately and in a timely manner, that markets are not manipulated, that professionals who offer their services to the public are qualified and honest, and that disputes are resolved. In the United States, the government has delegated some of these responsibilities to an organization called the National Futures Association (NFA). An industry self-regulatory body, the NFA was created with the objective of having the industry regulate itself and reduce the federal government's burden.

FUTURES TRADING   2

In this section, we look more closely at how futures contracts are traded. As noted above, futures contracts trade on a futures exchange either in a pit or on a screen or electronic terminal.

We briefly mentioned pit trading, also known as floor-based trading, in Section 1.2. Pit trading is a very physical activity. Traders stand in the pit and shout out their orders in the form of prices they are willing to pay or accept. They also use hand signals to indicate their bids and offers.[5] They engage in transactions with other traders in the pits by simply agreeing on a price and number of contracts to trade. The activity is fast, furious, exciting, and stressful. The average pit trader is quite young, owing to the physical demands of

---

[5] Hand signals facilitate trading with someone who is too far away in the pit for verbal communication.

the job and the toll it takes on body and mind. In recent years, more trading has come off of the exchange floor to electronic screens or terminals. In electronic or screen-based trading, exchange members enter their bids and offers into a computer system, which then displays this information and allows a trader to consummate a trade electronically. In the United States, pit trading is dominant, owing to its long history and tradition. Exchange members who trade on the floor enjoy pit trading and have resisted heavily the advent of electronic trading. Nonetheless, the exchanges have had to respond to market demands to offer electronic trading. In the United States, both pit trading and electronic trading are used, but in other countries, electronic trading is beginning to drive pit trading out of business.[6]

A person who enters into a futures contract establishes either a long position or a short position. Similar to forward contracts, long positions are agreements to buy the underlying at the expiration at a price agreed on at the start. Short positions are agreements to sell the underlying at a future date at a price agreed on at the start. When the position is established, each party deposits a small amount of money, typically called the margin, with the clearinghouse. Then, as briefly described in Section 1.4, the contract is marked to market, whereby the gains are distributed to and the losses collected from each party. We cover this marking-to-market process in more detail in the next section. For now, however, we focus only on the opening and closing of the position.

A party that has opened a long position collects profits or incurs losses on a daily basis. At some point in the life of the contract prior to expiration, that party may wish to re-enter the market and close out the position. This process, called **offsetting,** is the same as selling a previously purchased stock or buying back a stock to close a short position. The holder of a long futures position simply goes back into the market and offers the identical contract for sale. The holder of a short position goes back into the market and offers to buy the identical contract. It should be noted that when a party offsets a position, it does not necessary do so with the same counterparty to the original contract. In fact, rarely would a contract be offset with the same counterparty. Because of the ability to offset, futures contracts are said to be fungible, which means that any futures contract with any counterparty can be offset by an equivalent futures contract with another counterparty. Fungibility is assured by the fact that the clearinghouse inserts itself in the middle of each contract and, therefore, becomes the counterparty to each party.

For example, suppose in early January a futures trader purchases an S&P 500 stock index futures contract expiring in March. Through 15 February, the trader has incurred some gains and losses from the daily settlement and decides that she wants to close the position out. She then goes back into the market and offers for sale the March S&P 500 futures. Once she finds a buyer to take the position, she has a long and short position in the same contract. The clearinghouse considers that she no longer has a position in that contract and has no remaining exposure, nor any obligation to make or take delivery at expiration. Had she initially gone short the March futures, she might re-enter the market in February offering to buy it. Once she finds a seller to take the opposite position, she becomes long and short the same contract and is considered to have offset the contract and therefore have no net position.

---

[6] For example, in France electronic trading was introduced while pit trading continued. Within two weeks, all of the volume had migrated to electronic trading and pit trading was terminated.

THE CLEARINGHOUSE, MARGINS, AND PRICE LIMITS

As briefly noted in the previous section, when a trader takes a long or short position in a futures, he must first deposit sufficient funds in a margin account. This amount of money is traditionally called the margin, a term derived from the stock market practice in which an investor borrows a portion of the money required to purchase a certain amount of stock.

Margin in the stock market is quite different from margin in the futures market. In the stock market, "margin" means that a loan is made. The loan enables the investor to reduce the amount of his own money required to purchase the securities, thereby generating leverage or gearing, as it is sometimes known. If the stock goes up, the percentage gain to the investor is amplified. If the stock goes down, however, the percentage loss is also amplified. The borrowed money must eventually be repaid with interest. The margin percentage equals the market value of the stock minus the market value of the debt divided by the market value of the stock—in other words, the investor's own equity as a percentage of the value of the stock. For example, in the United States, regulations permit an investor to borrow up to 50 percent of the initial value of the stock. This percentage is called the initial margin requirement. On any day thereafter, the equity or percentage ownership in the account, measured as the market value of the securities minus the amount borrowed, can be less than 50 percent but must be at least a percentage known as the maintenance margin requirement. A typical maintenance margin requirement is 25 to 30 percent.

In the futures market, by contrast, the word **margin** is commonly used to describe the amount of money that must be put into an account by a party opening up a futures position, but the term is misleading. When a transaction is initiated, a futures trader puts up a certain amount of money to meet the **initial margin requirement;** however, the remaining money is not borrowed. The amount of money deposited is more like a down payment for the commitment to purchase the underlying at a later date. Alternatively, one can view this deposit as a form of good faith money, collateral, or a performance bond: The money helps ensure that the party fulfills his or her obligation.[7] Moreover, both the buyer and the seller of a futures contract must deposit margin.

In securities markets, margin requirements are normally set by federal regulators. In the United States, maintenance margin requirements are set by the securities exchanges and the NASD. In futures markets, margin requirements are set by the clearinghouses. In further contrast to margin practices in securities markets, futures margins are traditionally expressed in dollar terms and not as a percentage of the futures price. For ease of comparison, however, we often speak of the futures margin in terms of its relationship to the futures price. In futures markets, the initial margin requirement is typically much lower than the initial margin requirement in the stock market. In fact, futures margins are usually less than 10 percent of the futures price.[8] Futures clearinghouses set their margin requirements by studying historical price movements. They then establish minimum margin levels by taking into account normal price movements and the fact that accounts are marked to market daily. The clearinghouses thus collect and disburse margin money every day. Moreover, they are permitted to do so more often

---

[7] In fact, the Chicago Mercantile Exchange uses the term "performance bond" instead of "margin." Most other exchanges use the term "margin."

[8] For example, the margin requirement of the Eurodollar futures contract at the Chicago Mercantile Exchange has been less than one-tenth of one percent of the futures price. An exception to this requirement, however, is individual stock futures, which in the United States have margin requirements comparable to those of the stock market.

than daily, and on some occasions they have used that privilege. By carefully setting margin requirements and collecting margin money every day, clearinghouses are able to control the risk of default.

In spite of the differences in margin practices for futures and securities markets, the effect of leverage is similar for both. By putting up a small amount of money, the trader's gains and losses are magnified. Given the tremendously low margin requirements of futures markets, however, the magnitude of the leverage effect is much greater in futures markets. We shall see how this works as we examine the process of the daily settlement.

As previously noted, each day the clearinghouse conducts an activity known as the daily settlement, also called marking to market. This practice results in the conversion of gains and losses on paper into actual gains and losses. As margin account balances change, holders of futures positions must maintain balances above a level called the **maintenance margin requirement.** The maintenance margin requirement is lower than the initial margin requirement. On any day in which the amount of money in the margin account at the end of the day falls below the maintenance margin requirement, the trader must deposit sufficient funds to bring the balance back up to the initial margin requirement. Alternatively, the trader can simply close out the position but is responsible for any further losses incurred if the price changes before a closing transaction can be made.

To provide a fair mark-to-market process, the clearinghouse must designate the official price for determining daily gains and losses. This price is called the **settlement price** and represents an average of the final few trades of the day. It would appear that the closing price of the day would serve as the settlement price, but the closing price is a single value that can potentially be biased high or low or perhaps even manipulated by an unscrupulous trader. Hence, the clearinghouse takes an average of all trades during the closing period (as defined by each exchange).

Exhibit 71-1 provides an example of the marking-to-market process that occurs over a period of six trading days. We start with the assumption that the futures price is $100 when the transaction opens, the initial margin requirement is $5, and the maintenance margin requirement is $3. In Panel A, the trader takes a long position of 10 contracts on Day 0, depositing $50 ($5 times 10 contracts) as indicated in Column 3. At the end of the day, his ending balance is $50.[9] Although

EXHIBIT 71-1 Mark-to-Market Example

Initial futures price = $100, Initial margin requirement = $5, Maintenance margin requirement = $3

A. *Holder of Long Position of 10 Contracts*

Day (1)	Beginning Balance (2)	Funds Deposited (3)	Settlement Price (4)	Futures Price Change (5)	Gain/ Loss (6)	Ending Balance (7)
0	0	50	100.00			50
1	50	0	99.20	−0.80	−8	42
2	42	0	96.00	−3.20	−32	10
3	10	40	101.00	5.00	50	100
4	100	0	103.50	2.50	25	125
5	125	0	103.00	−0.50	−5	120
6	120	0	104.00	1.00	10	130

[9] Technically, we are assuming that the position was opened at the settlement price on Day 0. If the position is opened earlier during the day, it would be marked to the settlement price at the end of the day.

B. *Holder of Short Position of 10 Contracts*

Day (1)	Beginning Balance (2)	Funds Deposited (3)	Settlement Price (4)	Futures Price Change (5)	Gain/ Loss (6)	Ending Balance (7)
0	0	50	100.00			50
1	50	0	99.20	−0.80	8	58
2	58	0	96.00	−3.20	32	90
3	90	0	101.00	5.00	−50	40
4	40	0	103.50	2.50	−25	15
5	15	35	103.00	−0.50	5	55
6	55	0	104.00	1.00	−10	45

the trader can withdraw any funds in excess of the initial margin requirement, we shall assume that he does not do so.[10]

The ending balance on Day 0 is then carried forward to the beginning balance on Day 1. On Day 1, the futures price moves down to 99.20, as indicated in Column 4 of Panel A. The futures price change, Column 5, is −0.80 (99.20 − 100). This amount is then multiplied by the number of contracts to obtain the number in Column 6 of −0.80 × 10 = −$8. The ending balance, Column 7, is the beginning balance plus the gain or loss. The ending balance on Day 1 of $42 is above the maintenance margin requirement of $30, so no funds need to be deposited on Day 2.

On Day 2 the settlement price goes down to $96. Based on a price decrease of $3.20 per contract and 10 contracts, the loss is $32, lowering the ending balance to $10. This amount is $20 below the maintenance margin requirement. Thus, the trader will get a margin call the following morning and must deposit $40 to bring the balance up to the initial margin level of $50. This deposit is shown in Column 3 on Day 3.

Here, we must emphasize two important points. First, additional margin that must be deposited is the amount sufficient to bring the ending balance up to the initial margin requirement, not the maintenance margin requirement.[11] This additional margin is called the **variation margin.** In addition, the amount that must be deposited the following day is determined regardless of the price change the following day, which might bring the ending balance well above the initial margin requirement, as it does here, or even well below the maintenance margin requirement. Thus, another margin call could occur. Also note that when the trader closes the position, the account is marked to market to the final price at which the transaction occurs, not the settlement price that day.

Over the six-day period, the trader in this example deposited $90. The account balance at the end of the sixth day is $130—nearly a 50 percent return over six days; not bad. But look at Panel B, which shows the position of a holder of 10 short contracts over that same period. Note that the short gains when prices decrease and loses when prices increase. Here the ending balance falls below the maintenance margin requirement on Day 4, and the short must deposit $35 on Day 5. At the end of Day 6, the short has deposited $85 and the balance is $45, a loss of $40 or nearly 50 percent, which is the same $40 the long made. Both cases illustrate the leverage effect that magnifies gains and losses.

[10] Virtually all professional traders are able to deposit interest-earning assets, although many other account holders are required to deposit cash. If the deposit earns interest, there is no opportunity cost and no obvious necessity to withdraw the money to invest elsewhere.

[11] In the stock market, one must deposit only the amount necessary to bring the balance up to the maintenance margin requirement.

When establishing a futures position, it is important to know the price level that would trigger a margin call. In this case, it does not matter how many contracts one has. The price change would need to fall for a long position (or rise for a short position) by the difference between the initial and maintenance margin requirements. In this example, the difference between the initial and maintenance margin requirements is $5 − $3 = $2. Thus, the price would need to fall from $100 to $98 for a long position (or rise from $100 to $102 for a short position) to trigger a margin call.

As described here, when a trader receives a margin call, he is required to deposit funds sufficient to bring the account balance back up to the initial margin level. Alternatively, the trader can choose to simply close out the position as soon as possible. For example, consider the position of the long at the end of the second day when the margin balance is $10. This amount is $20 below the maintenance level, and he is required to deposit $40 to bring the balance up to the initial margin level. If he would prefer not to deposit the additional funds, he can close out the position as soon as possible the following day. Suppose, however, that the price is moving quickly at the opening on Day 3. If the price falls from $96 to $95, he has lost $10 more, wiping out the margin account balance. In fact, if it fell any further, he would have a negative margin account balance. He is still responsible for these losses. Thus, the trader could lose more than the amount of money he has placed in the margin account. The total amount of money he could lose is limited to the price per contract at which he bought, $100, times the number of contracts, 10, or $1,000. Such a loss would occur if the price fell to zero, although this is not likely. This potential loss may not seem like a lot, but it is certainly large relative to the initial margin requirement of $50. For the holder of the short position, there is no upper limit on the price and the potential loss is theoretically infinite.

Practice Problem 1

Consider a futures contract in which the current futures price is $82. The initial margin requirement is $5, and the maintenance margin requirement is $2. You go long 20 contracts and meet all margin calls but do not withdraw any excess margin. Assume that on the first day, the contract is established at the settlement price, so there is no mark-to-market gain or loss on that day.

A. Complete the table below and provide an explanation of any funds deposited.

Day	Beginning Balance	Funds Deposited	Futures Price	Price Change	Gain/Loss	Ending Balance
0			82			
1			84			
2			78			
3			73			
4			79			
5			82			
6			84			

B. Determine the price level that would trigger a margin call.

SOLUTIONS

A.

Day	Beginning Balance	Funds Deposited	Futures Price	Price Change	Gain/Loss	Ending Balance
0	0	100	82			100
1	100	0	84	2	40	140
2	140	0	78	−6	−120	20
3	20	80	73	−5	−100	0
4	0	100	79	6	120	220
5	220	0	82	3	60	280
6	280	0	84	2	40	320

On Day 0, you deposit $100 because the initial margin requirement is $5 per contract and you go long 20 contracts. At the end of Day 2, the balance is down to $20, which is $20 below the $40 maintenance margin requirement ($2 per contract times 20 contracts). You must deposit enough money to bring the balance up to the initial margin requirement of $100 ($5 per contract times 20 contracts). So on Day 3, you deposit $80. The price change on Day 3 causes a gain/loss of −$100, leaving you with a balance of $0 at the end of Day 3. On Day 4, you must deposit $100 to return the balance to the initial margin level.

B. A price decrease to $79 would trigger a margin call. This calculation is based on the fact that the difference between the initial margin requirement and the maintenance margin requirement is $3. If the futures price starts at $82, it can fall by $3 to $79 before it triggers a margin call.

Some futures contracts impose limits on the price change that can occur from one day to the next. Appropriately, these are called **price limits.** These limits are usually set as an absolute change over the previous day. Using the example above, suppose the price limit was $4. This would mean that each day, no transaction could take place higher than the previous settlement price plus $4 or lower than the previous settlement price minus $4. So the next day's settlement price cannot go beyond the price limit and thus no transaction can take place beyond the limits.

If the price at which a transaction would be made exceeds the limits, then price essentially freezes at one of the limits, which is called a **limit move.** If the price is stuck at the upper limit, it is called **limit up;** if stuck at the lower limit, it is called **limit down.** If a transaction cannot take place because the price would be beyond the limits, this situation is called **locked limit.** By the end of the day, unless the price has moved back within the limits, the settlement price will then be at one of the limits. The following day, the new range of acceptable prices is based on the settlement price plus or minus limits. The exchanges have different rules that provide for expansion or contraction of price limits under some circumstances. In addition, not all contracts have price limits.

Finally, we note that the exchanges have the power to mark contracts to market whenever they deem it necessary. Thus, they can do so during the trading day rather than wait until the end of the day. They sometimes do so when abnormally large market moves occur.

The daily settlement procedure is designed to collect losses and distribute gains in such a manner that losses are paid before becoming large enough to impose a serious risk of default. Recall that the clearinghouse guarantees to each party that it need not worry about collecting from the counterparty. The clearinghouse essentially positions itself in the middle of each contract, becoming the short counterparty to the long and the long counterparty to the short. The clearinghouse collects funds from the parties incurring losses in this daily settlement procedure and distributes them to the parties incurring gains. By doing so each day, the clearinghouse ensures that losses cannot build up. Of course, this process offers no guarantee that counterparties will not default. Some defaults do occur, but the counterparty is defaulting to the clearinghouse, which has never failed to pay off the opposite party. In the unlikely event that the clearinghouse were unable to pay, it would turn to a reserve fund or to the exchange, or it would levy a tax on exchange members to cover losses.

4   DELIVERY AND CASH SETTLEMENT

As previously described, a futures trader can close out a position before expiration. If the trader holds a long position, she can simply enter into a position to go short the same futures contract. From the clearinghouse's perspective, the trader holds both a long and short position in the same contract. These positions are considered to offset and, therefore, there is no open position in place. Most futures contracts are offset before expiration. Those that remain in place are subject to either delivery or a final cash settlement. Here we explore this process, which determines how a futures contract terminates at expiration.

When the exchange designs a futures contract, it specifies whether the contract will terminate with delivery or cash settlement. If the contract terminates in delivery, the clearinghouse selects a counterparty, usually the holder of the oldest long contract, to accept delivery. The holder of the short position then delivers the underlying to the holder of the long position, who pays the short the necessary cash for the underlying. Suppose, for example, that two days before expiration, a party goes long one futures contract at a price of $50. The following day (the day before expiration), the settlement price is $52. The trader's margin account is then marked to market by crediting it with a gain of $2. Then suppose that the next day the contract expires with the settlement price at $53. As the end of the trading day draws near, the trader has two choices. She can attempt to close out the position by selling the futures contract. The margin account would then be marked to market at the price at which she sells. If she sells close enough to the expiration, the price she sold at would be very close to the final settlement price of $53. Doing so would add $1 to her margin account balance.

The other choice is to leave the position open at the end of the trading day. Then she would have to take delivery. If that occurred, she would be required to take possession of the asset and pay the short the settlement price of the previous day. Doing so would be equivalent to paying $52 and receiving the asset. She could then sell the asset for its price of $53, netting a $1 gain, which is equivalent to the final $1 credited to her margin account if she had terminated the position at the settlement price of $53, as described above.[12]

---

[12] The reason she pays the settlement price of the previous day is because on the previous day when her account was marked to market, she essentially created a new futures position at a price of $52. Thus, she committed to purchase the asset at expiration, just one day later, at a price of $52. The next day when the contract expires, it is then appropriate that she buy the underlying for $52.

An alternative settlement procedure, which we described in Reading 70 on forward contracts, is cash settlement. The exchange designates certain futures contracts as cash-settled contracts. If the contract used in this example were cash settled, then the trader would not need to close out the position close to the end of the expiration day. She could simply leave the position open. When the contract expires, her margin account would be marked to market for a gain on the final day of $1. Cash settlement contracts have some advantages over delivery contracts, particularly with respect to significant savings in transaction costs.[13]

Exhibit 71-2 illustrates the equivalence of these three forms of delivery. Note, however, that because of the transaction costs of delivery, parties clearly prefer a closeout or cash settlement over physical delivery, particularly when the underlying asset is a physical commodity.

EXHIBIT 71-2 Closeout versus Physical Delivery versus Cash Settlement

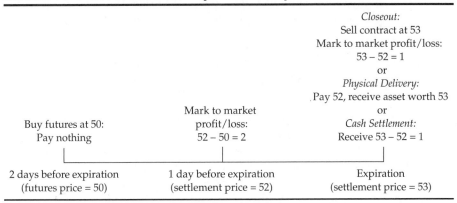

Contracts designated for delivery have a variety of features that can complicate delivery. In most cases, delivery does not occur immediately after expiration but takes place over several days. In addition, many contracts permit the short to choose when delivery takes place. For many contracts, delivery can be made any business day of the month. The delivery period usually includes the days following the last trading day of the month, which is usually in the third week of the month.

In addition, the short often has other choices regarding delivery, a major one being exactly which underlying asset is delivered. For example, a futures contract on U.S. Treasury bonds trading at the Chicago Board of Trade permits the short to deliver any of a number of U.S. Treasury bonds.[14] The wheat futures contract at the Chicago Board of Trade permits delivery of any of several types of wheat. Futures contracts calling for physical delivery of commodities often permit delivery at different locations. A given commodity delivered to one location is not the same as that commodity delivered to another because of the costs involved in transporting the commodity. The short holds the sole right to make decisions about what, when, and where to deliver, and the right to make these decisions can be extremely valuable. The right to make a decision concerning these aspects of delivery is called a **delivery option.**

---

[13] Nonetheless, cash settlement has been somewhat controversial in the United States. If a contract is designated as cash settlement, it implies that the buyer of the contract never intended to actually take possession of the underlying asset. Some legislators and regulators feel that this design is against the spirit of the law, which views a futures contract as a commitment to buy the asset at a later date. Even though parties often offset futures contracts prior to expiration, the possibility of actual delivery is still present in contracts other than those settled by cash. This controversy, however, is relatively minor and has caused no serious problems or debates in recent years.

[14] We shall cover this feature in more detail in Sections 6.2 and 7.2.3.

Some futures contracts that call for delivery require delivery of the actual asset, and some use only a book entry. For example, in this day and age, no one physically handles U.S. Treasury bonds in the form of pieces of paper. Bonds are transferred electronically over the Federal Reserve's wire system. Other contracts, such as oil or wheat, do actually involve the physical transfer of the asset. Physical delivery is more common when the underlying is a physical commodity, whereas book entry is more common when the underlying is a financial asset.

Futures market participants use one additional delivery procedure, which is called **exchange for physicals (EFP).** In an EFP transaction, the long and short arrange an alternative delivery procedure. For example, the Chicago Board of Trade's wheat futures contracts require delivery on certain dates at certain locations either in Chicago or in a few other specified locations in the Midwest. If the long and short agree, they could effect delivery by having the short deliver the wheat to the long in, for example, Omaha. The two parties would then report to the Chicago Board of Trade that they had settled their contract outside of the exchange's normal delivery procedures, which would be satisfactory to the exchange.

5   FUTURES EXCHANGES

A futures exchange is a legal corporate entity whose shareholders are its members. The members own memberships, more commonly called **seats.** Exchange members have the privilege of executing transactions on the exchange. Each member acts as either a **floor trader** or a **broker.** Floor traders are typically called **locals;** brokers are typically called **futures commission merchants (FCMs).** Locals are market makers, standing ready to buy and sell by quoting a bid and an ask price. They are the primary providers of liquidity to the market. FCMs execute transactions for other parties off the exchange.

The locals on the exchange floor typically trade according to one of several distinct styles. The most common is called scalping. A **scalper** offers to buy or sell futures contracts, holding the position for only a brief period of time, perhaps just seconds. Scalpers attempt to profit by buying at the bid price and selling at the higher ask price. A **day trader** holds a position open somewhat longer but closes all positions at the end of the day.[15] A **position trader** holds positions open overnight. Day traders and position traders are quite distinct from scalpers in that they attempt to profit from the anticipated direction of the market; scalpers are trying simply to buy at the bid and sell at the ask.

Recall that futures exchanges have trading either on the floor or off the floor on electronic terminals, or in some cases, both. As previously described, floor trading in the United States takes place in pits, which are octagonal, multi-tiered areas where floor traders stand and conduct transactions. Traders wear jackets of specific colors and badges to indicate such information as what type of trader (FCM or local) they are and whom they represent.[16] As noted, to indicate a willingness to trade, a trader shouts and uses a set of standard hand signals. A trade is consummated by two traders agreeing on a price and a number of contracts. These traders might not actually say anything to each other; they may simply use a combination of hand signals and/or eye contact to agree on a transaction. When a transaction is agreed on, the traders fill out small paper forms and turn them over to clerks, who then see that the transactions are entered into the system and reported.

---

[15] The term "day trader" has been around the futures market for a long time but has recently acquired a new meaning in the broader financial markets. The term is now used to describe individual investors who trade stocks, often over the Internet, during the day for a living or as a hobby. In fact, the term has even been used in a somewhat pejorative manner, in that day traders are often thought of as naïve investors speculating wildly with money they can ill afford to lose.

[16] For example, an FCM or local could be trading for himself or could represent a company.

Each trader is required to have an account at a clearing firm. The clearing firms are the actual members of the clearinghouse. The clearinghouse deals only with the clearing firms, which then deal with their individual and institutional customers.

In electronic trading, the principles remain essentially the same but the traders do not stand in the pits. In fact, they do not see each other at all. They sit at computer terminals, which enable them to see the bids and offers of other traders. Transactions are executed by the click of a computer mouse or an entry from a keyboard.

Exhibit 71-3 lists the world's 20 leading futures exchanges in 2001, ranked by trading volume. Recall from Reading 69 that trading volume can be a misleading measure of the size of futures markets; nonetheless, it is the measure primarily used. The structure of global futures exchanges has changed considerably in recent years. Exchanges in the United States, primarily the Chicago Board of Trade and the Chicago Mercantile Exchange, were clearly the world leaders in the past. Note that the volume leader now, however, is Eurex, the combined German–Swiss exchange. Eurex has been so successful partly because of its decision to be an all-electronic futures exchange, whereas the Chicago exchanges are still primarily pit-trading exchanges. Note the popularity of futures trading in Japan; four of the 20 leading exchanges are Japanese.

EXHIBIT 71-3 The World's 20 Leading Futures Exchanges

Exchange and Location	Volume in 2001 (Number of Contracts)
Eurex (Germany and Switzerland)	435,141,707
Chicago Mercantile Exchange (United States)	315,971,885
Chicago Board of Trade (United States)	209,988,002
London International Financial Futures and Options Exchange (United Kingdom)	161,522,775
Bolsa de Mercadorias & Futuros (Brazil)	94,174,452
New York Mercantile Exchange (United States)	85,039,984
Tokyo Commodity Exchange (Japan)	56,538,245
London Metal Exchange (United Kingdom)	56,224,495
Paris Bourse SA (France)	42,042,673
Sydney Futures Exchange (Australia)	34,075,508
Korea Stock Exchange (Korea)	31,502,184
Singapore Exchange (Singapore)	30,606,546
Central Japan Commodity Exchange (Japan)	27,846,712
International Petroleum Exchange (United Kingdom)	26,098,207
OM Stockholm Exchange (Sweden)	23,408,198
Tokyo Grain Exchange (Japan)	22,707,808
New York Board of Trade (United States)	14,034,168
MEFF Renta Variable (Spain)	13,108,293
Tokyo Stock Exchange (Japan)	12,465,433
South African Futures Exchange (South Africa)	11,868,242

Source: Futures Industry, January/February 2002

6   TYPES OF FUTURES CONTRACTS

The different types of futures contracts are generally divided into two main groups: commodity futures and financial futures. Commodity futures cover traditional agricultural, metal, and petroleum products. Financial futures include stocks, bonds, and currencies. Exhibit 71-4 gives a broad overview of the most active types of futures contracts traded on global futures exchanges. These contracts are those covered by the *Wall Street Journal* on the date indicated.

Our primary focus in this book is on financial and currency futures contracts. Within the financials group, our main interest is on interest rate and bond futures, stock index futures, and currency futures. We may occasionally make reference to a commodity futures contract, but that will primarily be for illustrative purposes. In the following subsections, we introduce the primary contracts we shall focus on. These are U.S. contracts, but they resemble most types of futures contracts found on exchanges throughout the world. Full contract specifications for these and other contracts are available on the Web sites of the futures exchanges, which are easy to locate with most Internet search engines.

6.1 Short-Term Interest Rate Futures Contracts

The primary short-term interest rate futures contracts are those on U.S. Treasury bills and Eurodollars on the Chicago Mercantile Exchange.

6.1.1 Treasury Bill Futures

The Treasury bill contract, launched in 1976, was the first interest rate futures contract. It is based on a 90-day U.S. Treasury bill, one of the most important U.S. government debt instruments (described in Reading 70, Section 3.2.1). The Treasury bill, or T-bill, is a discount instrument, meaning that its price equals the face value minus a discount representing interest. The discount equals the face value multiplied by the quoted rate times the days to maturity divided by 360. Thus, using the example from Reading 70, if a 180-day T-bill is selling at a discount of 4 percent, its price per \$1 par is $1 - 0.04(180/360) = 0.98$. An investor who buys the bill and holds it to maturity would receive \$1 at maturity, netting a gain of \$0.02.

The futures contract is based on a 90-day \$1,000,000 U.S. Treasury bill. Thus, on any given day, the contract trades with the understanding that a 90-day T-bill will be delivered at expiration. While the contract is trading, its price is quoted as 100 minus the rate quoted as a percent priced into the contract by the futures market. This value, 100 − Rate, is known as the IMM Index; IMM stands for International Monetary Market, a division of the Chicago Mercantile Exchange. The IMM Index is a reported and publicly available price; however, it is not the actual futures price, which is

$$100 - (\text{Rate}/100)(90/360)$$

For example, suppose on a given day the rate priced into the contract is 6.25 percent. Then the quoted price will be $100 - 6.25 = 93.75$. The actual futures price would be

$$\$1,000,000[1 - 0.0625(90/360)] = \$984,375$$

Recall, however, that except for the small margin deposit, a futures transaction does not require any cash to be paid up front. As trading takes place, the rate fluctuates with market interest rates and the associated IMM Index price changes

EXHIBIT 71-4 Most-Active Global Futures Contracts as Covered by the *Wall Street Journal*, 18 June 2002

Commodity Futures		Financial Futures
Corn (CBOT)	Treasury Bonds (CBOT)	Euro (CME)
Oats (CBOT)	Treasury Notes (CBOT)	Euro–Sterling (NYBOT)
Soybeans (CBOT)	10-Year Agency Notes (CBOT)	Euro–U.S. Dollar (NYBOT)
Soybean Meal (CBOT)	10-Year Interest Rate Swaps (CBOT)	Euro–Yen (NYBOT)
Soybean Oil (CBOT)	2-Year Agency Notes (CBOT)	Dow Jones Industrial Average (CBOT)
Wheat (CBOT, KCBT, MGE)	5-Year Treasury Notes (CBOT)	Mini Dow Jones Industrial Average (CBOT)
Canola (WPG)	2-Year Treasury Notes (CBOT)	S&P 500 Index (CME)
Barley (WPG)	Federal Funds (CBOT)	Mini S&P 500 Index (CME)
Feeder Cattle (CME)	Municipal Bond Index (CBOT)	S&P Midcap 400 Index (CME)
Live Cattle (CME)	Treasury Bills (CME)	Nikkei 225 (CME)
Lean Hogs (CME)	1-Month LIBOR (CME)	Nasdaq 100 Index (CME)
Pork Bellies (CME)	Eurodollar (CME)	Mini Nasdaq Index (CME)
Milk (CME)	Euroyen (CME, SGX)	Goldman Sachs Commodity Index (CME)
Lumber (CME)	Short Sterling (LIFFE)	Russell 1000 Index (CME)
Cocoa (NYBOT)	Long Gilt (LIFFE)	Russell 2000 Index (CME)
Coffee (NYBOT)	3-Month Euribor (LIFFE)	NYSE Composite Index (NYBOT)
World Sugar (NYBOT)	3-Month Euroswiss (LIFFE)	U.S. Dollar Index (NYBOT)
Domestic Sugar (NYBOT)	Canadian Bankers Acceptance (ME)	Share Price Index (SFE)
Cotton (NYBOT)	10-Year Canadian Government Bond (ME)	CAC 40 Stock Index (MATIF)
Orange Juice (NYBOT)	10-Year Euro Notional Bond (MATIF)	Xetra Dax (EUREX)
Copper (NYMEX)	3-Month Euribor (MATIF)	FTSE 200 Index (LIFFE)
Gold (NYMEX)	3-Year Commonwealth T-Bonds (SFE)	Dow Jones Euro Stoxx 50 Index (EUREX)
Platinum (NYMEX)	5-Year German Euro Government Bond (EUREX)	Dow Jones Stoxx 50 Index (EUREX)
Palladium (NYMEX)	10-Year German Euro Government Bond (EUREX)	
Silver (NYMEX)	2-Year German Euro Government Bond (EUREX)	
Crude Oil (NYMEX)	Japanese Yen (CME)	
No. 2 Heating Oil (NYMEX)	Canadian Dollar (CME)	
Unleaded Gasoline (NYMEX)	British Pound (CME)	
Natural Gas (NYMEX)	Swiss Franc (CME)	
Brent Crude Oil (IPEX)	Australian Dollar (CME)	
Gas Oil (IPEX)	Mexican Peso (CME)	

Exchange codes: CBOT (Chicago Board of Trade), CME (Chicago Mercantile Exchange), LIFFE (London International Financial Futures Exchange), WPG (Winnipeg Grain Exchange), EUREX (Eurex), NYBOT (New York Board of Trade), IPEX (International Petroleum Exchange), MATIF (Marché a Terme International de France), ME (Montreal Exchange), MGE (Minneapolis Grain Exchange), SFE (Sydney Futures Exchange), SGX (Singapore Exchange), KCBT (Kansas City Board of Trade), NYMEX (New York Mercantile Exchange)

Note: These are not the only global futures contracts but are those covered in the *Wall Street Journal* on the date given and represent the most active contracts at that time.

accordingly. The actual futures price, as calculated above, also fluctuates according to the above formula, but interestingly, that price is not very important. The same information can be captured more easily by referencing the IMM Index than by calculating the actual price.

Suppose, for example, that a trader had his account marked to market to the above price, 6.25 in terms of the rate, 93.75 in terms of the IMM Index, and $984,375 in terms of the actual futures price. Now suppose the rate goes to 6.50, an increase of 0.25 or 25 basis points. The IMM Index declines to 93.50, and the actual futures price drops to

$$\$1,000,000[1 - 0.065(90/360)] = \$983,750$$

Thus, the actual futures price decreased by $984,375 - $983,750 = $625. A trader who is long would have a loss of $625; a trader who is short would have a gain of $625.

This $625 gain or loss can be arrived at more directly, however, by simply noting that each basis point move is equivalent to $25.[17] This special design of the contract makes it easy for floor traders to do the necessary arithmetic in their heads. For example, if floor traders observe the IMM Index move from 93.75 to 93.50, they immediately know that it has moved down 25 basis points and that 25 basis points times $25 per basis point is a loss of $625. The minimum tick size is one-half basis point or $12.50.

T-bill futures contracts have expirations of the current month, the next month, and the next four months of March, June, September, and December. Because of the small trading volume, however, only the closest expiration has much trading volume, and even that one is only lightly traded. T-bill futures expire specifically on the Monday of the week of the third Wednesday each month and settle in cash rather than physical delivery of the T-bill, as described in Section 4.

As important as Treasury bills are in U.S. financial markets, however, today this futures contract is barely active. The Eurodollar contract is considered much more important because it reflects the interest rate on a dollar borrowed by a high-quality private borrower. The rates on T-bills are considered too heavily influenced by U.S. government policies, budget deficits, government funding plans, politics, and Federal Reserve monetary policy. Although unquestionably Eurodollar rates are affected by those factors, market participants consider them much less directly influenced. But in spite of this relative inactivity, T-bill futures are useful instruments for illustrating certain principles of futures market pricing and trading. Accordingly, we shall use them on some occasions. For now, however, we turn to the Eurodollar futures contract.

6.1.2 Eurodollar Futures

Recall that in Reading 70, we devoted a good bit of effort to understanding Eurodollar forward contracts, known as FRAs. These contracts pay off based on LIBOR on a given day. The Eurodollar futures contract of the Chicago Mercantile Exchange is based on $1 million notional principal of 90-day Eurodollars. Specifically, the underlying is the rate on a 90-day dollar-denominated time deposit issued by a bank in London. As we described in Reading 70, this deposit is called a Eurodollar time deposit, and the rate is referred to as LIBOR (London Interbank Offer Rate). On a given day, the futures contract trades based on the understanding that at expiration, the official Eurodollar rate, as compiled by the British Bankers

---

[17] Expressed mathematically, $\$1,000,000[0.0001(90/360)] = \$25$. In other words, any move in the last digit of the rate (a basis point) affects the actual futures price by $25.

Association (BBA), will be the rate at which the final settlement of the contract is made. While the contract is trading, its price is quoted as 100 minus the rate priced into the contract by futures traders. Like its counterpart in the T-bill futures market, this value, 100 − Rate, is also known as the IMM Index.

As in the T-bill futures market, on a given day, if the rate priced into the contract is 5.25 percent, the quoted price will be $100 − 5.25 = 94.75$. With each contract based on $1 million notional principal of Eurodollars, the actual futures price is

$$\$1,000,000[1 - 0.0525(90/360)] = \$986,875$$

Like the T-bill contract, the actual futures price moves $25 for every basis point move in the rate or IMM Index price.

As with all futures contracts, the price fluctuates on a daily basis and margin accounts are marked to market according to the exchange's official settlement price. At expiration, the final settlement price is the official rate quoted on a 90-day Eurodollar time deposit by the BBA. That rate determines the final settlement. Eurodollar futures contracts do not permit actual delivery of a Eurodollar time deposit; rather, they settle in cash, as described in Section 4.

The Eurodollar futures contract is one of the most active in the world. Because its rate is based on LIBOR, it is widely used by dealers in swaps, FRAs, and interest rate options to hedge their positions taken in dollar-denominated over-the-counter interest rate derivatives. Such derivatives usually use LIBOR as the underlying rate.

It is important to note, however, that there is a critical distinction between the manner in which the interest calculation is built into the Eurodollar futures contract and the manner in which interest is imputed on actual Eurodollar time deposits. Recall from Reading 70 that when a bank borrows $1 million at a rate of 5 percent for 90 days, the amount it will owe in 90 days is

$$\$1,000,000[1 + 0.05(90/360)] = \$1,012,500$$

Interest on Eurodollar time deposits is computed on an add-on basis to the principal. As described in this section, however, it appears that in computing the futures price, interest is deducted from the principal so that a bank borrowing $1,000,000 at a rate of 5 percent would receive

$$\$1,000,000[1 - 0.05(90/360)] = \$987,500$$

and would pay back $1,000,000. This procedure is referred to as discount interest and is used in the T-bill market.

The discount interest computation associated with Eurodollar futures is merely a convenience contrived by the futures exchange to facilitate quoting prices in a manner already familiar to its traders, who were previously trading T-bill futures. This inconsistency between the ways in which Eurodollar futures and Eurodollar spot transactions are constructed causes some pricing problems, as we shall see in Section 7.2.2.

The minimum tick size for Eurodollar futures is 1 basis point or $25. The available expirations are the next two months plus March, June, September, and December. The expirations go out about 10 years, a reflection of their use by over-the-counter derivatives dealers to hedge their positions in long-term interest rate derivatives. Eurodollar futures expire on the second business day on which London banks are open before the third Wednesday of the month and terminate with a cash settlement.

6.2 Intermediate- and Long-Term Interest Rate Futures Contracts

In U.S. markets, the primary interest-rate-related instruments of intermediate and long maturities are U.S. Treasury notes and bonds. The U.S. government issues both instruments: Treasury notes have an original maturity of 2 to 10 years, and Treasury bonds have an original maturity of more than 10 years. Futures contracts on these instruments are very actively traded on the Chicago Board of Trade. For the most part, there are no real differences in the contract characteristics for Treasury note and Treasury bond futures; the underlying bonds differ slightly, but the futures contracts are qualitatively the same. We shall focus here on one of the most active instruments, the U.S. Treasury bond futures contract.

The contract is based on the delivery of a U.S. Treasury bond with any coupon but with a maturity of at least 15 years. If the deliverable bond is callable, it cannot be callable for at least 15 years from the delivery date.[18] These specifications mean that there are potentially a large number of deliverable bonds, which is exactly the way the Chicago Board of Trade, the Federal Reserve, and the U.S. Treasury want it. They do not want a potential run on a single issue that might distort prices. By having multiple deliverable issues, however, the contract must be structured with some fairly complicated procedures to adjust for the fact that the short can deliver whatever bond he chooses from among the eligible bonds. This choice gives the short a potentially valuable option and puts the long at a disadvantage. Moreover, it complicates pricing the contract, because the identity of the underlying bond is not clear. Although when referring to a futures contract on a 90-day Eurodollar time deposit we are relatively clear about the underlying instrument, a futures contract on a long-term Treasury bond does not allow us the same clarity.

To reduce the confusion, the exchange declares a standard or hypothetical version of the deliverable bond. This hypothetical deliverable bond has a 6 percent coupon. When a trader holding a short position at expiration delivers a bond with a coupon greater (less) than 6 percent, she receives an upward (a downward) adjustment to the price paid for the bond by the long. The adjustment is done by means of a device called the **conversion factor.** In brief, the conversion factor is the price of a $1.00 par bond with a coupon and maturity equal to those of the deliverable bond and a yield of 6 percent. Thus, if the short delivers a bond with a coupon greater (less) than 6 percent, the conversion factor exceeds (is less than) 1.0.[19] The amount the long pays the short is the futures price at expiration multiplied by the conversion factor. Thus, delivery of a bond with coupon greater (less) than the standard amount, 6 percent, results in the short receiving an upward (a downward) adjustment to the amount received. A number of other technical considerations are also involved in determining the delivery price.[20]

The conversion factor system is designed to put all bonds on equal footing. Ideally, application of the conversion factor would result in the short finding no preference for delivery of any one bond over any other. That is not the case, however, because the complex relationships between bond prices cannot be reduced to a simple linear adjustment, such as the conversion factor method. As a result, some bonds are cheaper to deliver than others. When making the delivery decision, the short compares the cost of buying a given bond on the open

---

[18] The U.S. government no longer issues callable bonds but has done so in the past.

[19] This statement is true regardless of the maturity of the deliverable bond. Any bond with a coupon in excess of its yield is worth more than its par value.

[20] For example, the actual procedure for delivery of U.S. Treasury bonds is a three-day process starting with the short notifying the exchange of intention to make delivery. Delivery actually occurs several days later. In addition, as is the custom in U.S. bond markets, the quoted price does not include the accrued interest. Accordingly, an adjustment must be made.

market with the amount she would receive upon delivery of that bond. The former will always exceed the latter; otherwise, a clear arbitrage opportunity would be available. The most attractive bond for delivery would be the one in which the amount received for delivering the bond is largest relative to the amount paid on the open market for the bond. The bond that minimizes this loss is referred to as the **cheapest-to-deliver** bond.

At any time during the life of a Treasury bond futures contract, traders can identify the cheapest-to-deliver bond. Determining the amount received at delivery is straightforward; it equals the current futures price times the conversion factor for a given bond. To determine the amount the bond would cost at expiration, one calculates the forward price of the bond, positioned at the delivery date. Of course, this is just a forward computation; circumstances could change by the expiration date. But this forward calculation gives a picture of circumstances as they currently stand and identifies which bond is currently the cheapest to deliver. That bond is then considered the bond most likely to be delivered. Recall that one problem with this futures contract is that the identity of the underlying bond is unclear. Traders traditionally treat the cheapest to deliver as the bond that underlies the contract. As time passes and interest rates change, however, the cheapest-to-deliver bond can change. Thus, the bond underlying the futures contract can change, adding an element of uncertainty to the pricing and trading of this contract.

With this complexity associated with the U.S. Treasury bond futures contract, one might suspect that it is less actively traded. In fact, the opposite is true: Complexity creates extraordinary opportunities for gain for those who understand what is going on and can identify the cheapest bond to deliver.

The Chicago Board of Trade's U.S. Treasury bond futures contract covers $100,000 par value of U.S. Treasury bonds. The expiration months are March, June, September, and December. They expire on the seventh business day preceding the last business day of the month and call for actual delivery, through the Federal Reserve's wire system, of the Treasury bond. Prices are quoted in points and 32nds, meaning that you will see prices like 98 18/32, which equals 98.5625. For a contract covering $100,000 par value, for example, the price is $98,562.50. The minimum tick size is 1/32, which is $31.25.

In addition to the futures contract on the long-term government bond, there are also very similar futures contracts on intermediate-term government bonds. The Chicago Board of Trade's contracts on 2-, 5-, and 10-year Treasury notes are very actively traded and are almost identical to its long-term bond contract, except for the exact specification of the underlying instrument. Intermediate and long-term government bonds are important instruments in every country's financial markets. They give the best indication of the long-term default-free interest rate and are often viewed as a benchmark bond for various comparisons in financial markets.[21] Accordingly, futures contracts on such bonds play an important role in a country's financial markets and are almost always among the most actively traded contracts in futures markets around the world.

If the underlying instrument is not widely available and not actively traded, the viability of a futures contract on it becomes questionable. The reduction seen in U.S. government debt in the late 1990s has led to a reduction in the supply of intermediate and long-term government bonds, and some concern has arisen over this fact. In the United States, some efforts have been made to promote the

---

[21] For example, the default risk of a corporate bond is often measured as the difference between the corporate bond yield and the yield on a Treasury bond or note of comparable maturity. Fixed rates on interest rate swaps are usually quoted as a spread over the rate on a Treasury bond or note of comparable maturity.

long-term debt of Fannie Mae and Freddie Mac as substitute benchmark bonds.[22] It remains to be seen whether such efforts will be necessary and, if so, whether they will succeed.

6.3 Stock Index Futures Contracts

One of the most successful types of futures contracts of all time is the class of futures on stock indices. Probably the most successful has been the Chicago Mercantile Exchange's contract on the Standard and Poor's 500 Stock Index. Called the S&P 500 Stock Index futures, this contract premiered in 1982 and has benefited from the widespread acceptance of the S&P 500 Index as a stock market benchmark. The contract is quoted in terms of a price on the same order of magnitude as the S&P 500 itself. For example, if the S&P 500 Index is at 1183, a two-month futures contract might be quoted at a price of, say, 1187. We shall explain how to determine a stock index futures price in Section 7.3.

The contract implicitly contains a multiplier, which is (appropriately) multiplied by the quoted futures price to produce the actual futures price. The multiplier for the S&P 500 futures is $250. Thus, when you hear of a futures price of 1187, the actual price is 1187($250) = $296,750.

S&P 500 futures expirations are March, June, September, and December and go out about two years, although trading is active only in the nearest two to three expirations. With occasional exceptions, the contracts expire on the Thursday preceding the third Friday of the month. Given the impracticality of delivering a portfolio of the 500 stocks in the index combined according to their relative weights in the index, the contract is structured to provide for cash settlement at expiration.

The S&P 500 is not the only active stock index futures contract. In fact, the Chicago Mercantile Exchange has a smaller version of the S&P 500 contract, called the Mini S&P 500, which has a multiplier of $50 and trades only electronically. Other widely traded contracts in the United States are on the Dow Jones Industrials, the S&P Midcap 400, and the Nasdaq 100. Virtually every developed country has a stock index futures contract based on the leading equities of that country. Well-known stock index futures contracts around the world include the United Kingdom's FTSE 100 (pronounced "Footsie 100"), Japan's Nikkei 225, France's CAC 40, and Germany's DAX 30.

6.4 Currency Futures Contracts

In Reading 70 we described forward contracts on foreign currencies. There are also futures contracts on foreign currencies. Although the forward market for foreign currencies is much more widely used, the futures market is still quite active. In fact, currency futures were the first futures contracts not based on physical commodities. Thus, they are sometimes referred to as the first financial futures contracts, and their initial success paved the way for the later introduction of interest rate and stock index futures.

---

[22] Fannie Mae is the Federal National Mortgage Association, and Freddie Mac is the Federal Home Loan Mortgage Corporation. These institutions were formerly U.S. government agencies that issued debt to raise funds to buy and sell mortgages and mortgage-backed securities. These institutions are now publicly traded corporations but are considered to have extremely low default risk because of their critical importance in U.S. mortgage markets. It is believed that an implicit Federal government guarantee is associated with their debt. Nonetheless, it seems unlikely that the debt of these institutions could take over that of the U.S. government as a benchmark. The Chicago Board of Trade has offered futures contracts on the bonds of these organizations, but the contracts have not traded actively.

Compared with forward contracts on currencies, currency futures contracts are much smaller in size. In the United States, these contracts trade at the Chicago Mercantile Exchange with a small amount of trading at the New York Board of Trade. In addition there is some trading on exchanges outside the United States. The characteristics we describe below refer to the Chicago Mercantile Exchange's contract.

In the United States, the primary currencies on which trading occurs are the euro, Canadian dollar, Swiss franc, Japanese yen, British pound, Mexican peso, and Australian dollar. Each contract has a designated size and a quotation unit. For example, the euro contract covers €125,000 and is quoted in dollars per euro. A futures price such as $0.8555 is stated in dollars and converts to a contract price of

$$125,000(\$0.8555) = \$106,937.50$$

The Japanese yen futures price is structured somewhat differently. Because of the large number of yen per dollar, the contract covers ¥12,500,000 and is quoted without two zeroes that ordinarily precede the price. For example, a price might be stated as 0.8205, but this actually represents a price of 0.008205, which converts to a contract price of

$$12,500,000(0.008205) = \$102,562.50$$

Alternatively, a quoted price of 0.8205 can be viewed as $1/0.008205 = ¥121.88$ per dollar.

Currency futures contracts expire in the months of March, June, September, and December. The specific expiration is the second business day before the third Wednesday of the month. Currency futures contracts call for actual delivery, through book entry, of the underlying currency.

We have briefly examined the different types of futures contracts of interest to us. Of course there are a variety of similar instruments trading on futures exchanges around the world. The purpose of this book, however, is not to provide institutional details, which can be obtained at the Web sites of the world's futures exchanges, but rather to enhance your understanding of the important principles necessary to function in the world of derivatives.

Until now we have made reference to prices of futures contracts. Accordingly, let us move forward and examine the pricing of futures contracts.

PRICING AND VALUATION OF FUTURES CONTRACTS   7

In Reading 70, we devoted considerable effort to understanding the pricing and valuation of forward contracts. We first discussed the notion of what it means to *price* a forward contract in contrast to what it means to *value* a forward contract. Recall that pricing means to assign a fixed price or rate at which the underlying will be bought by the long and sold by the short at expiration. In assigning a forward price, we set the price such that the value of the contract is zero at the start. A zero-value contract means that the present value of the payments promised by each party to the other is the same, a result in keeping with the fact that neither party pays the other any money at the start. The value of the contract to the long is the present value of the payments promised by the short to the long minus the present value of the payments promised by the long to the short. Although the value is zero at the start, during the life of the contract, the value will fluctuate as market conditions change; the original forward contract price, however, stays the same.

In Reading 70, we presented numerous examples of how to apply the concept of pricing and valuation when dealing with forward contracts on stocks, bonds, currencies, and interest rates. To illustrate the concepts of pricing and valuation, we started with a generic forward contract. Accordingly, we do so here in the futures reading. We assume no transaction costs.

7.1 Generic Pricing and Valuation of a Futures Contract

As we did with forward contracts, we start by illustrating the time frame within which we are working:

0	t − 1	t	T
(today)			(expiration)

Today is time 0. The expiration date of the futures contract is time T. Times $t - 1$ and t are arbitrary times between today and the expiration and are the points at which the contract will be marked to market. Thus, we can think of the three periods depicted above, 0 to $t - 1$, $t - 1$ to t, and t to T, as three distinct trading days with times $t - 1$, t, and T being the end of each of the three days.

The price of the underlying asset in the spot market is denoted as S_0 at time 0, S_{t-1} at time $t - 1$, S_t at time t, and S_T at time T. We denote the futures contract price at time 0 as $f_0(T)$. This notation indicates that $f_0(T)$ is the price of a futures contract at time 0 that expires at time T. Unlike forward contract prices, however, futures prices fluctuate in an open and competitive market. The marking-to-market process results in each futures contract being terminated every day and reinitiated. Thus, we not only have a futures price set at time 0 but we also have a new one at time $t - 1$, at time t, and at time T. In other words,

$$
\begin{aligned}
f_0(T) &= \text{price of a futures contract at time 0 that expires at time T} \\
f_{t-1}(T) &= \text{price of a futures contract at time } t - 1 \text{ that expires at time T} \\
f_t(T) &= \text{price of a futures contract at time t that expires at time T} \\
f_T(T) &= \text{price of a futures contract at time T that expires at time T}
\end{aligned}
$$

Note, however, that $f_{t-1}(T)$ and $f_t(T)$ are also the prices of contracts newly established at times $t - 1$ and t for delivery at time T. Futures contracts are homogeneous and fungible. Any contract for delivery of the underlying at T is equivalent to any other contract, regardless of when the contracts were created.[23]

The value of the futures contract is denoted as $v_0(T)$. This notation indicates that $v_0(T)$ is the value at time 0 of a futures contract expiring at time T. We are also

---

[23] As an analogy from the bond markets, consider a 9 percent coupon bond, originally issued with 10 years remaining. Three years later, that bond is a 9 percent seven-year bond. Consider a newly issued 9 percent coupon bond with seven years maturity and the same issuer. As long as the coupon dates are the same and all other terms are the same, these two bonds are fungible and are perfect substitutes for each other.

interested in the values of the contract prior to expiration, such as at time t, denoted as $v_t(T)$, as well as the value of the contract at expiration, denoted as $v_T(T)$.[24]

7.1.1 The Futures Price at Expiration

Now suppose we are at time T. The spot price is S_T and the futures price is $f_T(T)$. To avoid an arbitrage opportunity, *the futures price must converge to the spot price at expiration*:

$$f_T(T) = S_T \qquad \textbf{(71-1)}$$

Consider what would happen if this were not the case. If $f_T(T) < S_T$, a trader could buy the futures contract, let it immediately expire, pay $f_T(T)$ to take delivery of the underlying, and receive an asset worth S_T. The trader would have paid $f_T(T)$ and received an asset worth S_T, which is greater, at no risk. If $f_T(T) > S_T$, the trader would go short the futures, buy the asset for S_T, make delivery, and receive $f_T(T)$ for the asset, for which he paid a lesser amount. Only if $f_T(T) = S_T$ does this arbitrage opportunity go away. Thus, the futures price must equal the spot price at expiration.

Another way to understand this point is to recall that by definition, a futures contract calls for the delivery of an asset at expiration at a price determined when the transaction is initiated. If expiration is right now, a futures transaction is equivalent to a spot transaction, so the futures price must equal the spot price.

7.1.2 Valuation of a Futures

Let us consider how to determine the value of a futures contract. We already agreed that because no money changes hands, the value of a forward contract at the initiation date is zero. For the same reason, *the value of a futures contract at the initiation date is zero*. Thus,

$$v_0(T) = 0 \qquad \textbf{(71-2)}$$

Now let us determine the value of the contract during its life. Suppose we are at the end of the second day, at time t. In our diagram above, this point would be essentially at time t, but perhaps just an instant before it. So let us call it time t−. An instant later, we call the time point t+. In both cases, the futures price is $f_t(T)$. The contract was previously marked to market at the end of day t − 1 to a price of $f_{t-1}(T)$. An instant later when the futures account is marked to market, the trader will receive a gain of $f_t(T) - f_{t-1}(T)$. We can reasonably ignore the present value difference of receiving this money an instant later. Let us now state more formally that the value of a futures contract is

$$v_{t+}(T) = f_t(T) - f_{t-1}(T) \; \textit{an instant before the account is marked to market} \qquad \textbf{(71-3)}$$

$v_{t-}(T) = 0$ *as soon as the account is marked to market*

---

[24] It is important at this point to make some comments about notation. First, note that in Reading 70 we use an uppercase F and V for forward contracts; here we use lowercase f and v for futures contracts. Also, we follow the pattern of using subscripts to indicate a price or value at a particular point in time. The arguments in parentheses refer to characteristics of a contract. Thus, in Reading 70 we described the price of a forward contract as F(0,T) meaning the price of a forward contract initiated at time 0 and expiring at time T. This price does not fluctuate during the life of the contract. A futures contract, however, reprices on a daily basis. Its original time of initiation does not matter—it is reinitiated every day. Hence, futures prices are indicated by notation such as $f_0(T)$ and $f_t(T)$. We follow a similar pattern for value, using $V_0(0,T)$, $V_t(0,T)$, and $V_T(0,T)$ for forwards and $v_0(T)$, $v_t(T)$, and $v_T(T)$ for futures.

Suppose, however, that the trader is at a time j during the second trading day, between t − 1 and t. The accumulated gain or loss since the account was last marked to market is $f_j(T) − f_{t-1}(T)$. If the trader closes the position out, he would receive or be charged this amount at the end of the day. So the value at time j would be $f_j(T) − f_{t-1}(T)$ discounted back from the end of the day at time t until time j—that is, a fraction of a day. It is fairly routine to ignore this intraday interest. Thus, in general we say that *the value of a futures contract before it has been marked to market is the gain or loss accumulated since the account was last marked to market.*

So to recap, the value of a futures contract is the accumulated gain or loss since the last mark to market. The holder of a futures contract has a claim or liability on this amount. Once that claim is captured or the liability paid through the mark-to-market process, the contract is repriced to its current market price and the claim or liability goes back to a value of zero. Using these results, determining the value of a futures contract at expiration is easy. An instant before expiration, it is simply the accumulated profit since the last mark to market. At expiration, the value goes back to zero. With respect to the value of the futures, expiration is no different from any other day. Exhibit 71-5 summarizes the principles of valuation.

EXHIBIT 71-5 The Value of a Futures Contract Before and After Marking to Market

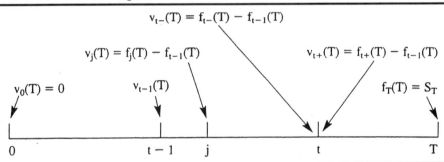

In Reading 70, we devoted considerable effort toward understanding how forward contracts are valued. When holding positions in forward contracts, we are forced to assign values to instruments that do not trade in an open market with widely disseminated prices. Thus, it is important that we understand how forward contracts are valued. When dealing with futures contracts, the process is considerably simplified. Because futures contracts are generally quite actively traded, there is a market with reliable prices that provides all of the information we need. For futures contracts, we see that the value is simply the observable price change since the last mark to market.

7.1.3 Forward and Futures Prices

For all financial instruments, it is important to be able to determine whether the price available in the market is an appropriate one. Hence, we engage in the process of "pricing" the financial instrument. A major objective of this reading is to determine the appropriate price of a futures contract. Given the similarity between futures and forward prices, however, we can benefit from studying forward contract pricing, which was covered in Reading 70. But first, we must look at the similarities and differences between forward and futures contracts.

Recall that futures contracts settle daily and are essentially free of default risk. Forward contracts settle only at expiration and are subject to default risk. Yet both types of contracts allow the party to purchase or sell the underlying asset at a price agreed on in advance. It seems intuitive that futures prices and forward prices would be relatively close to each other.

The issues involved in demonstrating the relationship between futures and forward prices are relatively technical and beyond the scope of this book. We can, however, take a brief and fairly nontechnical look at the question. First let us ignore the credit risk issue. We shall assume that the forward contract participants are prime credit risks. We focus only on the technical distinction caused by the daily marking to market.

The day before expiration, both the futures contract and the forward contract have one day to go. At expiration, they will both settle. These contracts are therefore the same. At any other time prior to expiration, futures and forward prices can be the same or different. If interest rates are constant or at least known, any effect of the addition or subtraction of funds from the marking-to-market process can be shown to be neutral. If interest rates are positively correlated with futures prices, traders with long positions will prefer futures over forwards, because they will generate gains when interest rates are going up, and traders can invest those gains for higher returns. Also, traders will incur losses when interest rates are going down and can borrow to cover those losses at lower rates. Because traders holding long positions prefer the marking to market of futures over forwards when futures prices are positively correlated with interest rates, futures will carry higher prices than forwards. Conversely, when futures prices are negatively correlated with interest rates, traders will prefer not to mark to market, so forward contracts will carry higher prices.

Because interest rates and fixed-income security prices move in opposite directions, interest rate futures are good examples of cases in which forward and futures prices should be inversely related. Alternatively, when inflation is high, interest rates are high and investors oftentimes put their money in such assets as gold. Thus, gold futures prices and interest rates would tend to be positively correlated. It would be difficult to identify a situation in which futures prices are not correlated with interest rates. Zero correlation is rare in the financial world, but we can say that when the correlation is low or close to zero, the difference between forward and futures prices would be very small.

At this introductory level of treatment, we shall make the simplifying assumption that futures prices and forward prices are the same. We do so by ignoring the effects of marking a futures contract to market. In practice, some significant issues arise related to the marking-to-market process, but they detract from our ability to understand the important concepts in pricing and trading futures and forwards.

Therefore, based on the equivalence we are assuming between futures and forwards, we can assume that the value of a futures contract at expiration, before marking to market, is

$$v_T(T) = f_T(T) - f_0(T) = S_T - f_0(T)$$

with the spot price substituted for the futures price at T, given what we know about their convergence.

7.1.4 Pricing Futures Contracts

Now let us proceed to the pricing of futures contracts. As we did with forward contracts, we consider the case of a generic underlying asset priced at $100. A futures contract calls for delivery of the underlying asset in one year at a price of $108. Let us see if $108 is the appropriate price for this futures contract.

Suppose we buy the asset for $100 and sell the futures contract. We hold the position until expiration. For right now, we assume no costs are involved in holding the asset. We do, however, lose interest on the $100 tied up in the asset for one year. We assume that this opportunity cost is at the risk-free interest rate of 5 percent.

Recall that no money changes hands at the start of a futures contract. Moreover, we can reasonably ignore the rather small margin deposit that would be required. In addition, margin deposits can generally be met by putting up interest-earning securities, so there is really no opportunity cost. As discussed in the previous section, we also will assume away the daily settlement procedure; in other words, the value of the futures contract paid out at expiration is the final futures price minus the original futures price. Because the final futures price converges to the spot price, the final payout is the spot price minus the original futures price.

So at the contract expiration, we are short the futures and must deliver the asset, which we own. We do so and receive the original futures price for it. So we receive $108 for an asset purchased a year ago at $100. At a 5 percent interest rate, we lose only $5 in interest, so our return in excess of the opportunity cost is 3 percent risk free. This risk-free return in excess of the risk-free rate is clearly attractive and would induce traders to buy the asset and sell the futures. This arbitrage activity would drive the futures price down until it reaches $105.

If the futures price falls below $105, say to $102, the opposite arbitrage would occur. The arbitrageur would buy the futures, but either we would need to be able to borrow the asset and sell it short, or investors who own the asset would have to be willing to sell it and buy the futures. They would receive the asset price of $100 and invest it at 5 percent interest. Then at expiration, those investors would get the asset back upon taking delivery, paying $102. This transaction would net a clear and risk-free profit of $3, consisting of interest of $5 minus a $2 loss from selling the asset at $100 and buying it back at $102. Again, through the buying of the futures and shorting of the asset, the forces of arbitrage would cause prices to realign to $105.

Some difficulties occur with selling short certain assets. Although the financial markets make short selling relatively easy, some commodities are not easy to sell short. In such a case, it is still possible for arbitrage to occur. If investors who already own the asset sell it and buy the futures, they can reap similar gains at no risk. Because our interest is in financial instruments, we shall ignore these commodity market issues and assume that short selling can be easily executed.[25]

If the market price is not equal to the price given by the model, it is important to note that regardless of the asset price at expiration, the above arbitrage guarantees a risk-free profit. That profit is known at the time the parties enter the transaction. Exhibit 71-6 summarizes and illustrates this point.

EXHIBIT 71-6 The Risk-Free Nature of Long and Short Futures Arbitrage

Asset is priced at $100, futures is priced at $f_0(T)$ and expires in one year. Interest rate over the life of the futures is 5 percent.

Time	Long Asset, Short Futures Arbitrage	Short Asset, Long Futures Arbitrage
Today (time 0)	Buy asset at $100 Sell futures at $f_0(T)$	Sell short asset for $100 Buy futures for $f_0(T)$
Expiration (time T)	Asset price is S_T Futures price converges to asset price	Asset price is S_T Futures price converges to asset price
	Deliver asset	Take delivery of asset
	Profit on asset after accounting for the 5 percent ($5) interest lost from $100 tied up in the investment in the asset: $S_T - 100 - 5$	Profit on asset after accounting for the 5 percent ($5) interest earned on the $100 received from the short sale of the asset: $100 + 5 - S_T$
	Profit on futures: $f_0(T) - S_T$	Profit on futures: $S_T - f_0(T)$
	Total profit: $f_0(T) - 100 - 5$	Total profit: $100 + 5 - f_0(T)$

Conclusion: The asset price at expiration has no effect on the profit captured at expiration for either transaction. The profit is known today. To eliminate arbitrage, the futures price today, $f_0(T)$, must equal $100 + 5 = \$105$.

---

[25] Keep in mind that there are some restrictions on the short selling of financial instruments, such as uptick rules and margin requirements, but we will not concern ourselves with these impediments here.

The transactions we have described are identical to those using forward contracts. We did note with forward contracts, however, that one can enter into an off-market forward contract, having one party pay cash to another to settle any difference resulting from the contract not trading at its arbitrage-free value up front. In the futures market, this type of arrangement is not permitted; all contracts are entered into without any cash payments up front.

So in general, through the forces of arbitrage, we say that *the futures price is the spot price compounded at the risk-free rate:*

$$f_0(T) = S_0(1 + r)$$

It is important, however, to write this result in a form we are more likely to use. In the above form, we specify r as the interest rate over the life of the futures contract. In financial markets, however, interest rates are nearly always specified as annual rates. Therefore, to compound the asset price over the life of the futures, we let r equal an annual rate and specify the life of the futures as T years. Then the futures price is found as

$$f_0(T) = S_0(1 + r)^T \qquad \textbf{(71-4)}$$

The futures price is the spot price compounded over the life of the contract, T years, at the annual risk-free rate, r. From this point on, we shall use this more general specification.

As an example, consider a futures contract that has a life of 182 days; the annual interest rate is 5 percent. Then $T = 182/365$ and $r = 0.05$. If the spot price is \$100, the futures price would then be

$$f_0(T) = S_0(1 + r)^T$$
$$f_0(182/365) = 100(1.05)^{182/365}$$
$$= 102.46$$

If the futures is selling for more than \$102.46, an arbitrageur can buy the asset for \$100 and sell the futures for whatever its price is, hold the asset (losing interest on \$100 at an annual rate of 5 percent) and deliver it to receive the futures price. The overall strategy will net a return in excess of 5 percent a year at no risk. If the futures is selling for less than \$102.46, the arbitrageur can borrow the asset, sell it short, and buy the futures. She will earn interest on the funds obtained from the short sale and take delivery of the asset at the futures expiration, paying the original futures price. The overall transaction results in receiving \$100 up front and paying back an amount less than the 5 percent risk-free rate, making the transaction like a loan that is paid back at less than the risk-free rate. If one could create such a loan, one could use it to raise funds and invest the funds at the risk-free rate to earn unlimited gains.

7.1.5 Pricing Futures Contracts When There Are Storage Costs

Except for opportunity costs, we have until now ignored any costs associated with holding the asset. In many asset markets, there are significant costs, other than the opportunity cost, to holding an asset. These costs are referred to as **storage costs** or **carrying costs** and are generally a function of the physical characteristics of the underlying asset. Some assets are easy to store; some are difficult. For example, assume the underlying is oil, which has significant storage costs but a very long storage life.[26] One would not expect to incur costs associated

---

[26] After all, oil has been stored by nature for millions of years.

with a decrease in quality of the oil. Significant risks do exist, however, such as spillage, fire, or explosion. Some assets on which futures are based are at risk for damage. For example, cattle and pigs can become ill and die during storage. Grains are subject to pest damage and fire. All of these factors have the potential to produce significant storage costs, and protection such as insurance leads to higher storage costs for these assets. On the other hand, financial assets have virtually no storage costs. Of course, all assets have one significant storage cost, which is the opportunity cost of money tied up in the asset, but this effect is covered in the present value calculation.

It is reasonable to assume that the storage costs on an asset are a function of the quantity of the asset to be stored and the length of time in storage. Let us specify this cost with the variable $FV(SC,0,T)$, which denotes the value at time T (expiration) of the storage costs (excluding opportunity costs) associated with holding the asset over the period 0 to T. By specifying these costs as of time T, we are accumulating the costs and compounding the interest thereon until the end of the storage period. We can reasonably assume that when storage is initiated, these costs are known.[27]

Revisiting the example we used previously, we would buy the asset at S_0, sell a futures contract at $f_0(T)$, store the asset and accumulate costs of $FV(SC,0,T)$, and deliver the asset at expiration to receive the futures price. The total payoff is $f_0(T) - FV(SC,0,T)$. This amount is risk free. To avoid an arbitrage opportunity, its present value should equal the initial outlay, S_0, required to establish the position. Thus,

$$[f_0(T) - FV(SC,0,T)]/(1 + r)^T = S_0$$

Solving for the futures price gives

$$f_0(T) = S_0(1 + r)^T + FV(SC,0,T) \qquad \textbf{(71-5)}$$

This result says that *the futures price equals the spot price compounded over the life of the futures contract at the risk-free rate, plus the future value of the storage costs over the life of the contract.* In the previous example with no storage costs, we saw that the futures price was the spot price compounded at the risk-free rate. With storage costs, we must add the future value of the storage costs. The logic behind this adjustment should make sense. The futures price should be higher by enough to cover the storage costs when a trader buys the asset and sells a futures to create a risk-free position.[28]

Consider the following example. The spot price of the asset is \$50, the interest rate is 6.25 percent, the future value of the storage costs is \$1.35, and the futures expires in 15 months. Then $T = 15/12 = 1.25$. The futures price would, therefore, be

$$f_0(T) = S_0(1 + r)^T + FV(SC,0,T)$$

$$f_0(1.25) = 50(1.0625)^{1.25} + 1.35$$

$$= 55.29$$

If the futures is selling for more than \$55.29, the arbitrageur would buy the asset and sell the futures, holding the position until expiration, at which time he would deliver the asset and collect the futures price, earning a return that covers the

---

[27] There may be reason to suggest that storage costs have an element of uncertainty in them, complicating the analysis.

[28] We did not cover assets that are storable at significant cost when we studied forward contracts because such contracts are less widely used for these assets. Nonetheless, the formula given here would apply for forward contracts as well, given our assumption of no credit risk on forward contracts.

6.25 percent cost of the money and the storage costs of $1.35. If the futures is selling for less than $55.29, the arbitrageur would sell short the asset and buy the futures, reinvesting the proceeds from the short sale at 6.25 percent and saving the storage costs. The net effect would be to generate a cash inflow today plus the storage cost savings and a cash outflow at expiration that would replicate a loan with a rate less than the risk-free rate. Only if the futures sells for exactly $55.29 do these arbitrage opportunities go away.

7.1.6 *Pricing Futures Contracts When There Are Cash Flows on the Underlying Asset*

In each case we have considered so far, the underlying asset did not generate any positive cash flows to the holder. For some assets, there will indeed be positive cash flows to the holder. Recall that in Reading 70, we examined the pricing and valuation of forward contracts on stocks and bonds and were forced to recognize that stocks pay dividends, bonds pay interest, and these cash flows affect the forward price. A similar concept applies here and does so in a symmetric manner to what we described in the previous section in which the asset incurs a cash cost. As we saw in that section, a cash cost incurred from holding the asset increases the futures price. Thus, we might expect that cash generated from holding the asset would result in a lower futures price and, as we shall see in this section, that is indeed the case. But in the next section, we shall also see that it is even possible for an asset to generate nonmonetary benefits that must also be taken into account when pricing a futures contract on it.

Let us start by assuming that over the life of the futures contract, the asset generates positive cash flows of $FV(CF,0,T)$. It is no coincidence that this notation is similar to the one we used in the previous section for the storage costs of the underlying asset over the life of the futures. Cash inflows and storage costs are just different sides of the same coin. We must remember, however, that $FV(CF,0,T)$ represents a positive flow in this case. Now let us revisit our example.

We would buy the asset at S_0, sell a futures contract at $f_0(T)$, store the asset and generate positive cash flows of $FV(CF,0,T)$, and deliver the asset at expiration, receiving the futures price. The total payoff is $f_0(T) + FV(CF,0,T)$. This amount is risk free and known at the start. To avoid an arbitrage opportunity, its present value should equal the initial outlay, S_0, required to establish the position. Thus,

$$[f_0(T) + FV(CF,0,T)]/(1 + r)^T = S_0$$

Solving for the futures price gives

$$f_0(T) = S_0(1 + r)^T - FV(CF,0,T) \hspace{2cm} \textbf{(71-6)}$$

In the previous example that included storage costs, we saw that the futures price was the spot price compounded at the risk-free rate plus the future value of the storage costs. With positive cash flows, we must subtract the future value of these cash flows. The logic behind this adjustment should make sense. The futures price should be reduced by enough to account for the positive cash flows when a trader buys the asset and sells a futures to create a risk-free position. Otherwise, the trader would receive risk-free cash flows from the asset *and* the equivalent amount from the sale of the asset at the futures price. Reduction of the futures price by this amount avoids overcompensating the trader.

As noted, these cash flows can be in the form of dividends from a stock or coupon interest from a bond. When we specifically examine the pricing of bond and stock futures, we shall make this specification a little more precise and work an example.

7.1.7 Pricing Futures Contracts When There Is a Convenience Yield

Now consider the possibility that the asset might generate nonmonetary benefits that must also be taken into account. The notion of nonmonetary benefits that could affect futures prices might sound strange, but upon reflection, it makes perfect sense. For example, a house is a common and normally desirable investment made by individuals and families. The house generates no monetary benefits and incurs significant costs. As well as being a possible monetary investment if prices rise, the house generates some nonmonetary benefits in the form of serving as a place to live. These benefits are quite substantial; many people consider owning a residence preferable to renting, and people often sell their homes for monetary gains far less than any reasonable return on a risky asset. Clearly the notion of a nonmonetary benefit to owning an asset is one most people are familiar with.

In a futures contract on an asset with a nonmonetary gain, that gain must be taken into account. Suppose, for the purpose of understanding the effect of nonmonetary benefits on a futures contract, we create a hypothetical futures contract on a house. An individual purchases a house and sells a futures contract on it. We shall keep the arguments as simple as possible by ignoring the operating or carrying costs. What should be the futures price? If the futures is priced at the spot price plus the risk-free rate, as in the original case, the homeowner receives a guaranteed sale price, giving a return of the risk-free rate *and* the use of the home. This is clearly a good deal. Homeowners would be eager to sell futures contracts, leading to a decrease in the price of the futures. Thus, any nonmonetary benefits ought to be factored into the futures price and logically would lead to a lower futures price.

Of course, in the real world of standardized futures contracts, there are no futures contracts on houses. Nonetheless, there are futures contracts on assets that have nonmonetary benefits. Assets that are often in short supply, particularly those with seasonal and highly risky production processes, are commonly viewed as having such benefits. The nonmonetary benefits of these assets are referred to as the **convenience yield.** Formally, a convenience yield is the nonmonetary return offered by an asset when in short supply. When an asset is in short supply, its price tends to be high. Holders of the asset earn an implicit incremental return from having the asset on hand. This return enables them, as commercial enterprises, to avoid the cost and inconvenience of not having their primary product or resource input on hand. Because shortages are generally temporary, the spot price can be higher than the futures price, even when the asset incurs storage costs. If a trader buys the asset, sells a futures contract, and stores the asset, the return is risk free and will be sufficient to cover the storage costs and the opportunity cost of money, but it will be reduced by an amount reflecting the benefits of holding the asset during a period of shortage or any other nonmonetary benefits.

Now, let the notation FV(CB,0,T) represent the future value of the costs of storage minus the benefits:

FV(CB,0,T) = Costs of storage − Nonmonetary benefits (Convenience yield)

where all terms are expressed in terms of their future value at time T and are considered to be known at time 0. If the costs exceed the benefits, FV(CB,0,T) is a positive number.[29] We refer to FV(CB,0,T) as the **cost of carry.**[30] The general futures pricing formula is

$$f_0(T) = S_0(1 + r)^T + FV(CB,0,T) \qquad \text{(71-7)}$$

The futures price is the spot price compounded at the risk-free rate plus the cost of carry. This model is often called the **cost-of-carry model.**

---

[29] In other words, FV(CB,0,T) has to be positive to refer to it as a "cost."

[30] In some cases, such as in inventory storage, it is customary to include the opportunity cost in the definition of cost of carry; but we keep it separate in this text.

Consider an asset priced at $75; the risk-free interest rate is 5.15 percent, the net of the storage costs, interest, and convenience yield is $3.20, and the futures expires in nine months. Thus, $T = 9/12 = 0.75$. Then the futures price should be

$$f_0(T) = S_0(1 + r)^T + FV(CB,0,T)$$
$$f_0(0.75) = 75(1.0515)^{0.75} + 3.20$$
$$= 81.08$$

As we have always done, we assume that this price will prevail in the marketplace. If it does not, the forces of arbitrage will drive the market price to the model price. If the futures price exceeds $81.08, the arbitrageur can buy the asset and sell the futures to earn a risk-free return in excess of the risk-free rate. If the futures price is less than $81.08, the arbitrageur can either sell the asset short or sell it if he already owns it, and then also buy the futures, creating a risk-free position equivalent to a loan that will cost less than the risk-free rate. The gains from both of these transactions will have accounted for any nonmonetary benefits. This arbitrage activity will force the market price to converge to the model price.

The above equation is the most general form of the futures pricing formula we shall encounter. Exhibit 71-7 reviews and illustrates how we obtained this formula and provides another example.

EXHIBIT 71-7 Pricing a Futures Contract

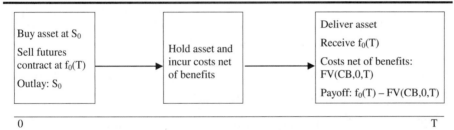

The transaction is risk-free and should be equivalent to investing S_0 dollars in a risk-free asset that pays $f_0(T) - FV(CB,0,T)$ at time T. Therefore, the payoff at T must be the future value of the initial outlay invested at the risk-free rate. For this relationship to hold, the futures price must be given as

$$f_0(T) = S_0(1 + r)^T + FV(CB,0,T)$$

Example: An asset is selling for $225. A futures contract expires in 150 days (T = 150/365 = 0.411). The risk-free rate is 7.5 percent, and the net cost of carry is $5.75. The futures price will be

$$f_0(T) = f_0(0.411) = \$225(1.075)^{0.411} + \$5.75 = \$237.54$$

Some variations of this general formula are occasionally seen. Sometimes the opportunity cost of interest is converted to dollars and imbedded in the cost of carry. Then we say that $f_0(T) = S_0 + FV(CB,0,T)$; the futures price is the spot price plus the cost of carry. This is a perfectly appropriate way to express the formula if the interest is imbedded in the cost of carry, but we shall not do so in this book.

Another variation of this formula is to specify the cost of carry in terms of a rate, such as y. Then we have $f_0(T) = S_0(1 + r)^T(1 + y)^T$. Again, this variation is certainly appropriate but is not the version we shall use.[31]

Note that when we get into the specifics of pricing certain types of futures contracts, we must fine-tune the formulas a little more. First, however, we explore some general characterizations of the relationship between futures and spot prices.

---

[31] Yet another variation of this formula is to use $(1 + r + y)^T$ as an approximation for $(1 + r)^T(1 + y)^T$. We do not, however, consider this expression an acceptable way to compute the futures price as it is an approximation of a formula that is simple enough to use without approximating.

Practice Problem 2

Consider an asset priced at $50. The risk-free interest rate is 8 percent, and a futures contract on the asset expires in 45 days. Answer the following, with questions A, B, C, and D independent of the others.

A. Find the appropriate futures price if the underlying asset has no storage costs, cash flows, or convenience yield.

B. Find the appropriate futures price if the future value of storage costs on the underlying asset at the futures expiration equals $2.25.

C. Find the appropriate futures price if the future value of positive cash flows on the underlying asset equals $0.75.

D. Find the appropriate futures price if the future value of the net overall cost of carry on the underlying asset equals $3.55.

E. Using Part D above, illustrate how an arbitrage transaction could be executed if the futures contract is trading at $60.

F. Using Part A above, determine the value of a long futures contract an instant before marking to market if the previous settlement price was $49.

SOLUTIONS

A. First determine that $T = 45/365 = 0.1233$. Then the futures price is

$$f_0(0.1233) = \$50(1.08)^{0.1233} = \$50.48$$

B. Storage costs must be covered in the futures price, so we add them:

$$f_0(0.1233) = \$50(1.08)^{0.1233} + \$2.25 = \$52.73$$

C. A positive cash flow, such as interest or dividends on the underlying, reduces the futures price:

$$f_0(0.1233) = \$50(1.08)^{0.1233} - \$0.75 = \$49.73$$

D. The net overall cost of carry must be covered in the futures price, so we add it:

$$f_0(0.1233) = \$50(1.08)^{0.1233} + \$3.55 = \$54.03$$

E. Follow these steps:

Sell the futures at $60.

Buy the asset at $50.

Because the asset price compounded at the interest rate is $50.48, the interest forgone is $0.48. So the asset price is effectively $50.48 by the time of the futures expiration.

Incur costs of $3.55.

At expiration, deliver the asset and receive $60. The net investment in the asset is $50.48 + $3.55 = $54.03. If the asset is sold for $60, the net gain is $5.97.

F. If the last settlement price was $49.00 and the price is now $50.48 (our answer in Part A), the value of a long futures contract equals the difference between these prices: $50.48 − $49.00 = $1.48.

7.1.8 Backwardation and Contango

Because the cost of carry, FV(CB,0,T), can be either positive or negative, the futures price can be greater or less than the spot price. Because the costs plus the interest tend to exceed the benefits, it is more common for the futures price to exceed the spot price, a situation called **contango.** In contrast, when the benefits exceed the costs plus the interest, the futures price will be less than the spot price, called **backwardation.** These terms are not particularly important in understanding the necessary concepts, but they are so commonly used that they are worthwhile to remember.

7.1.9 Futures Prices and Expected Spot Prices

An important concept when examining futures prices is the relationship between futures prices and expected spot prices. In order to fully understand the issue, let us first consider the relationship between spot prices and expected spot prices. Consider an asset with no risk, but which incurs carrying costs. At time 0, the holder of the asset purchases it with the certainty that she will cover her opportunity cost and carrying cost. Otherwise, she would not purchase the asset. Thus, the spot price at time 0 is the present value of the total of the spot price at time T less costs minus benefits:

$$S_0 = \frac{S_T - FV(CB,0,T)}{(1 + r)^T}$$

$$= \frac{S_T}{(1 + r)^T} - \frac{FV(CB,0,T)}{(1 - r)^T}$$

Because FV(CB,0,T) is the future value of the carrying cost, $FV(CB,0,T)/(1 + r)^T$ is the present value of the carrying cost. So on the one hand, we can say that the spot price is the future spot price minus the future value of the carrying cost, all discounted to the present. On the other hand, we can also say that the spot price is the discounted value of the future spot price minus the present value of the carrying cost.

If, however, the future price of the asset is uncertain, as it nearly always is, we must make some adjustments. For one, we do not know at time 0 what S_T will be. We must form an expectation, which we will denote as $E_0(S_T)$. But if we simply replace S_T above with $E_0(S_T)$ we would not be acting rationally. We would be paying a price today and expecting compensation only at the risk-free rate along with coverage of our carrying cost. Indeed, one of the most important and intuitive elements of all we know about finance is that risky assets require a risk premium. Let us denote this risk premium with the symbol, $\phi_0(S_T)$. It represents a discount off of the expected value that is imbedded in the current price, S_0. Specifically, the current price is now given as

$$S_0 = \frac{E_0(S_T) - FV(CB,0,T) - \phi_0(S_T)}{(1 + r)^T}$$

where we see that the risk premium lowers the current spot price. Intuitively, investors pay less for risky assets, all other things equal.

Until now, we have worked only with the spot price, but nothing we have said so far violates the rule of no arbitrage. Hence, our futures pricing formula, $f_0(T) = S_0(1 + r)^T + FV(CB,0,T)$, still applies. If we rearrange the futures pricing formula for FV(CB,0,T), substitute this result into the formula for S_0, and solve for the futures price, $f_0(T)$, we obtain $f_0(T) = E_0(S_T) - \phi_0(S_T)$. This equation says that the futures price equals the expected future spot price minus the risk premium.

An important conclusion to draw from this formula is that the futures price does not equal the expectation of the future spot price. The futures price would be biased on the low side. If one felt that the futures price were an unbiased predictor of the future spot price, $f_0(T) = E_0(S_T)$, one could expect on average to be able to predict the future spot price of oil by looking at the futures price of oil. But that is not likely to be the case.

The intuition behind this result is easy to see. We start with the assumption that all units of the asset must be held by someone. Holders of the asset incur the risk of its future selling price. If a holder of the asset wishes to transfer that risk by selling a futures contract, she must offer a futures contract for sale. But if the futures contract is offered at a price equal to the expected spot price, the buyer of the futures contract takes on the risk but expects to earn only a price equal to the price paid for the futures. Thus, the futures trader incurs the risk without an expected gain in the form of a risk premium. On the opposite side of the coin, the holder of the asset would have a risk-free position with an expected gain in excess of the risk-free rate. Clearly, the holder of the asset would not be able to do such a transaction. Thus, she must lower the price to a level sufficient to compensate the futures trader for the risk he is taking on. This process will lead to a futures price that equals the expected spot price minus the risk premium, as shown in the above equation. In effect, the risk premium transfers from the holder of the asset to the buyer of the futures contract.

In all fairness, however, we must acknowledge that this view is not without its opponents. Some consider the futures price an unbiased predictor of the future spot price. In such a case, the futures price would tend to overshoot and undershoot the future spot price but on average would be equal to it. For such a situation to exist would require the unreasonable assumption that there is no risk or that investors are risk neutral, meaning that they are indifferent to risk. There is, however, one other situation in which the risk premium could disappear or even turn negative. Suppose holders of the asset who want to hedge their holdings could find other parties who need to purchase the asset and who would like to hedge by going long. In that case, it should be possible for the two parties to consummate a futures transaction with the futures price equal to the expected spot price. In fact, if the parties going long exerted greater pressure than the parties going short, it might even be possible for the futures price to exceed the expected spot price.

When futures prices are lower than expected spot prices, the situation is called **normal backwardation.** When futures prices are higher than expected spot prices, it is called **normal contango.** Note the contrast with the terms backwardation and contango, which we encountered in Section 7.1.8. Backwardation means that the futures price is lower than the spot price; contango means that the futures price exceeds the spot price. Normal backwardation means that the futures price is lower than the expected spot price; normal contango means that the futures price exceeds the expected spot price.

Generally speaking, we should favor the notion that futures prices are biased predictors of future spot prices because of the transferal of the risk premium from holders of the asset to buyers of futures. Intuitively, this is the more likely case, but the other interpretations are possible. Fortunately, for our purposes, it is not critical to resolve the issue, but we do need to be aware of it.

7.2 Pricing Interest Rate Futures

We shall examine the pricing of three classes of interest rate futures contracts: Treasury bill futures, Eurodollar futures, and Treasury bond futures. In Section 6.1, we described the characteristics of these instruments and contracts. Now we look at their pricing, keeping in mind that we established the general foundations for pricing—the cost-of-carry model—in the previous section. Recall that in the cost-of-carry model, we buy the underlying asset, sell a futures contract, store the asset (which incurs costs and could generate benefits), and deliver the asset at expiration. To prevent arbitrage, the futures price is found in general as

$$\text{Futures price} = \text{Spot price of underlying asset} \times \text{Compounding factor} \\ + \text{Costs net of monetary and nonmonetary benefits}$$

When the underlying is a financial instrument, there will be no nonmonetary benefits and no costs other than the opportunity cost.

7.2.1 Pricing T-Bill Futures

Consider the following time line of our problem:

0	h	h + m
(today)	(expiration)	(maturity of underlying T-bill)

Time 0 is today, and time h is the expiration day of the futures contract. The T-bill underlying the contract is an m-day T-bill. Thus, when the futures expires, the T-bill is required to have m days to go before maturity. So from our perspective today, the underlying T-bill is an (h + m)-day T-bill.[32] As in Reading 70 for FRAs, h and m represent a particular number of days. In accordance with common practice, m is traditionally 90. We now introduce some necessary notation. First, where necessary, we use a simple expression, r, for the risk-free interest rate. But when pricing Treasury bill futures, we need a more flexible notation. Here we need the rates for T-bills maturing on day h and on day h + m. In addition, because interest rates can change from day 0 to day h, we need notation that distinguishes rates for different maturities and rates at different points in time.[33]

To find the spot price of the underlying asset, we need the discount rate on an (h + m)-day T-bill. Suppose we have

$$r_0^d(h), r_0^d(h + m) = \text{Discount rates in effect on day 0 of h-day and} \\ (h + m)\text{-day T-bills}$$

As described in Section 6, these are discount rates and convert to prices by the following formula: $B_0(j) = 1 - r_0^d(j)(j/360)$, where in this case j will either be h or h + m. Thus, the prices of h- and (h + m)-day spot T-bills on day 0 (assuming \$1 face amounts) are

$$B_0(h) = 1 - r_0^d(h)\left(\frac{h}{360}\right)$$

$$B_0(h + m) = 1 - r_0^d(h + m)\left(\frac{h + m}{360}\right)$$

In other words, the h- or (h + m)-day discount rate is multiplied by the number of days in the life of the T-bill over 360 and subtracted from the face value of \$1.

---

[32] It is common practice in the T-bill futures market to refer to the underlying as an m-day T-bill, but at time 0, the underlying must be an (h + m)-day T-bill in order for it to be an m-day T-bill at time h.

[33] When we assume that the interest rates are the same for all maturities and cannot change over time, which is considered acceptable when working with stock index and currency futures, we can use the simpler notation of r for the rate.

Now let us turn to the futures market. We define

$r_0^{df}(h)$ = implied discount rate on day 0 of futures contract expiring on day h, where the deliverable instrument is an m-day T-bill

$f_0(h)$ = price on day 0 of futures contract expiring on day h

The relationship between $r_0^{df}(h)$ and $f_0(h)$ is

$$f_0(h) = 1 - r_0^{df}(h)\left(\frac{m}{360}\right)$$

It is important to note that the futures price, not the implied discount rate, is the more important variable. Like any price, the futures price is determined in a market of buyers and sellers. Any rate is simply a way of transforming a price into a number that can be compared with rates on various other fixed-income instruments.[34] Do not think that a futures contract pays an interest rate. It is more appropriate to think of such a rate imbedded in a futures price as an *implied rate*, hence our use of the term *implied discount rate*. Although knowing this rate does not tell us any more than knowing the futures price, traders often refer to the futures contract in terms of the rate rather than the price.

Finally, let us note that at expiration, the futures price is the price of the underlying T-bill

$$f_h(h) = B_h(h + m)$$
$$= 1 - r_h^d(h + m)\left(\frac{m}{360}\right)$$

where $B_h(h + m)$ is the price on day h of the T-bill maturing on day $h + m$, and $r_h^d(h + m)$ is the discount rate on day h on the T-bill maturing on day $h + m$.

We now derive the futures price by constructing a risk-free portfolio that permits no arbitrage profits to be earned. This transaction is referred to as a cash-and-carry strategy, because the trader buys the asset in the cash (spot) market and carries (holds) it.

On day 0, we buy the $(h + m)$-day T-bill, investing $B_0(h + m)$. We simultaneously sell a futures contract at the price $f_0(h)$. On day h, we are required to deliver an m-day T-bill. The bill we purchased, which originally had $h + m$ days to maturity, now has m days to maturity. We therefore deliver that bill and receive the original futures price. We can view this transaction as having paid $B_0(h + m)$ on day 0 and receiving $f_0(h)$. Because $f_0(h)$ is known on day 0, this transaction is risk free. It should thus earn the same return per dollar invested as would a T-bill purchased on day 0 that matures on day h. The return per dollar invested from the arbitrage transaction would be $f_0(h)/B_0(h + m)$, and the return per dollar invested in an h-day T-bill would be $1/B_0(h)$.[35] Consequently, we set these values equal:

$$\frac{f_0(h)}{B_0(h + m)} = \frac{1}{B_0(h)}$$

---

[34] To further reinforce the notion that an interest rate is just a transformation of a price, consider a zero-coupon bond selling at $95 and using 360 days as a year. The price can be transformed into a rate in the manner of $1/0.95 - 1 = 0.0526$ or 5.26 percent. But using the convention of the Treasury bill market, the rate is expressed as a discount rate. Then $0.95 = 1 - \text{Rate} \times (360/360)$, and the rate would be 0.05 or 5 percent. A price can be converted into a rate in a number of other ways, such as by assuming different compound periods. The price of any asset is determined in a market-clearing process. The rate is just a means of transforming the price so that interest rate instruments and their derivatives can be discussed in a more comparable manner.

[35] For example, if a one-year $1 face value T-bill is selling for $0.90, the return per dollar invested is $1/\$0.90 = 1.1111$.

Solving for the futures price, we obtain

$$f_0(h) = \frac{B_0(h + m)}{B_0(h)}$$

In words, the futures price is the ratio of the longer-term bill price to the shorter-term bill price. This price is, in fact, the same as the forward price from the term structure. In fact, as we noted above, futures prices and forward prices will be equal under the assumptions we have made so far and will follow throughout this book.

Recall that we previously demonstrated that the futures price should equal the spot price plus the cost of carry. Yet the above formula looks nothing like this result. In fact, however, it is consistent with the cost-of-carry formula. First, the above formula can be written as

$$f_0(h) = B_0(h + m)\left[\frac{1}{B_0(h)}\right]$$

As noted above, the expression $1/B_0(h)$ can be identified as the return per dollar invested over h days, which simplifies to $[1 + r_0(h)]^{h/365}$, which is essentially a compound interest factor for h days at the rate $r_0(h)$. Note that h is the number of days, assuming 365 in a year. For the period ending at day h, the above formula becomes

$$f_0(h) = B_0(h + m)[1 + r_0(h)]^{h/365} \qquad \textbf{(71-8)}$$

and the futures price is seen to equal the spot price of the underlying compounded at the interest rate, which simply reflects the opportunity cost of the money tied up for h days.

Note that what we have been doing is deriving the appropriate price for a futures contract. In a market with no arbitrage opportunities, the actual futures price would be this theoretical price. Let us suppose for a moment, however, that the actual futures price is something else, say $f_0(h)^*$. The spot price is, of course, $B_0(h + m)$. Using these two numbers, we can infer the implied rate of return from a transaction involving the purchase of the T-bill and sale of the futures. We have

$$f_0(h)^* = B_0(h + m)[1 + r_0(h)^*]^{h/365}$$

where $r_0(h)^*$ is the implied rate of return. Solving for $r_0(h)^*$ we obtain

$$r_0(h)^* = \left[\frac{f_0(h)^*}{B_0(h + m)}\right]^{365/h} - 1 \qquad \textbf{(71-9)}$$

This rate of return, $r_0(h)^*$, has a special name, the **implied repo rate.** It is the rate of return from a cash-and-carry transaction that is implied by the futures price relative to the spot price. Traders who engage in such transactions often obtain the funds to do so in the repurchase agreement (repo) market. The implied repo rate tells the trader what rate of return to expect from the strategy. If the financing rate available in the repo market is less than the implied repo rate, the strategy is worthwhile and would generate an arbitrage profit. If the trader could lend in the repo market at greater than the implied repo rate, the appropriate strategy would be to reverse the transaction—selling the T-bill short and buying the futures—turning the strategy into a source of financing that would cost less than the rate at which the funds could be lent in the repo market.[36]

---

[36] The concepts of a cash-and-carry strategy and the implied repo rate are applicable to any type of futures contract, but we cover them only with respect to T-bill futures.

The implied repo rate is the rate of return implied by the strategy of buying the asset and selling the futures. As noted above, the futures price is often expressed in terms of an implied discount rate. Remember that the buyer of a futures contract is committing to buy a T-bill at the price $f_0(h)$. In the convention of pricing a T-bill by subtracting a discount rate from par value, the implied discount rate would be

$$r_0^{df}(h) = [1 - f_0(h)]\left(\frac{360}{m}\right)$$

(71-10)

We can also determine this implied discount rate from the discount rates on the h- and (h + m)-day T-bills as follows:[37]

$$r_0^{df}(h) = \left\{1 - \left[\frac{1 - r_0^d(h + m)\left(\dfrac{h + m}{360}\right)}{1 - r_0^d(h)\left(\dfrac{h}{360}\right)}\right]\right\}\left(\frac{360}{m}\right)$$

Now let us look at an example. We are interested in pricing a futures contract expiring in 30 days. A 30-day T-bill has a discount rate of 6 percent, and a 120-day T-bill has a discount rate of 6.6 percent. With h = 30 and h + m = 120, we have

$$r_0^d(h) = r_0^d(30) = 0.06$$
$$r_0^d(h + m) = r_0^d(120) = 0.066$$

The prices of these T-bills will, therefore, be

$$B_0(h) = 1 - r_0^d(h)\left(\frac{h}{360}\right)$$
$$B_0(30) = 1 - 0.06\left(\frac{30}{360}\right) = 0.9950$$
$$B_0(h + m) = 1 - r_0^d(h + m)\left(\frac{h + m}{360}\right)$$
$$B_0(120) = 1 - 0.066\left(\frac{120}{360}\right) = 0.9780$$

Using the formula we derived, we have the price of a futures expiring in 30 days as

$$f_0(h) = \frac{B_0(h + m)}{B_0(h)}$$
$$f_0(30) = \frac{B_0(120)}{B_0(30)} = \frac{0.9780}{0.9950} = 0.9829$$

The discount rate implied by the futures price would be

$$r_0^{df}(h) = [1 - f_0(h)]\left(\frac{360}{m}\right)$$
$$r_0^{df}(30) = (1 - 0.9829)\left(\frac{360}{90}\right) = 0.0684$$

---

[37] This formula is found by substituting $1 - r_0^d(h + m)[(h + m)/360]$ for $B_0(h + m)$ and $1 - r_0^d(h)(h/360)$ for $B_0(h)$ in the above equation for $r_0^{df}(h)$. This procedure expresses the spot prices in terms of their respective discount rates.

In other words, in the T-bill futures market, the rate would be stated as 6.84 percent, which would imply a futures price of 0.9829.[38] Alternatively, the implied futures discount rate could be obtained from the spot discount rates as

$$
r_0^{df}(h) = \left\{ 1 - \left[\frac{1 - r_0^d(h+m)\left(\frac{h+m}{360}\right)}{1 - r_0^d(h)\left(\frac{h}{360}\right)} \right] \right\} \left(\frac{360}{m}\right)
$$

$$
r_0^{df}(30) = \left\{ 1 - \left[\frac{1 - 0.066\left(\frac{120}{360}\right)}{1 - 0.06\left(\frac{30}{360}\right)} \right] \right\} \left(\frac{360}{90}\right) = 0.0683
$$

with a slight difference due to rounding.

To verify this result, one would buy the 120-day T-bill for 0.9780 and sell the futures at a price of 0.9829. Then, 30 days later, the T-bill would be a 90-day T-bill and would be delivered to settle the futures contract. The trader would receive the original futures price of 0.9829. The return per dollar invested would be

$$
\frac{0.9829}{0.9780} = 1.0050
$$

If, instead, the trader had purchased a 30-day T-bill at the price of 0.9950 and held it for 30 days, the return per dollar invested would be

$$
\frac{1}{0.9950} = 1.0050
$$

Thus, the purchase of the 120-day T-bill with its price in 30 days hedged by the sale of the futures contract is equivalent to purchasing a 30-day T-bill and holding it to maturity. Each transaction has the same return per dollar invested and is free of risk.

Suppose in the market, the futures price is 0.9850. The implied repo rate would be

$$
r_0(h)^* = \left[\frac{f_0(h)^*}{B_0(h+m)} \right]^{365/h} - 1
$$

$$
= \left(\frac{0.9850}{0.9780} \right)^{365/30} - 1 = 0.0906
$$

Buying the 120-day T-bill for 0.9780 and selling a futures for 0.9850 generates a rate of return of $0.9850/0.9780 - 1 = 0.007157$. Annualizing this rate, $(1.007157)^{365/30} - 1 = 0.0906$. If financing could be obtained in the repo market for less than this annualized rate, the strategy would be attractive. If the trader could lend in the repo market at higher than this rate, he should buy the futures and sell short the T-bill to implicitly borrow at 9.06 percent and lend in the repo market at a higher rate.

---

[38] We should also probably note that the IMM Index would be $100 - 6.84 = 93.16$. Thus, the futures price would be quoted in the market as 93.16.

Let us now recap the pricing of Treasury bill futures. We buy an (h + m)-day bond and sell a futures expiring on day h, which calls for delivery of an m-day T-bill. The futures price should be the price of the (h + m)-day T-bill compounded at the h-day risk-free rate. That rate is the rate of return on an h-day bill. The futures price can also be obtained as the ratio of the price of the (h + m)-day T-bill to the price of the h-day T-bill. Alternatively, we can express the futures price in terms of an implied discount rate, and we can derive the price in terms of the discount rates on the (h + m)-day T-bill and the h-day T-bill. Finally, remember that the actual futures price in the market relative to the price of the (h + m)-day T-bill implies a rate of return called the implied repo rate. The implied repo rate can be compared with the rate in the actual repo market to determine the attractiveness of an arbitrage transaction.

Exhibit 71-8 summarizes the important formulas involved in the pricing of T-bill futures. We then turn to the pricing of another short-term interest rate futures contract, the Eurodollar futures.

EXHIBIT 71-8 Pricing Formulas for T-Bill Futures Contract

Futures price = Underlying T-bill price compounded at risk-free rate

Futures price in terms of spot T-bills:

$$f_0(h) = \frac{B_0(h + m)}{B_0(h)}$$

Futures price as spot price compounded at risk-free rate:

$$f_0(h) = B_0(h + m)[1 + r_0(h)]^{h/365}$$

Discount rate implied by futures price:

$$r_0^{df}(h) = [1 - f_0(h)]\left(\frac{360}{m}\right) = \left\{1 - \left[\frac{1 - r_0^d(h + m)\left(\dfrac{h + m}{360}\right)}{1 - r_0^d(h)\left(\dfrac{h}{360}\right)}\right]\right\}\left(\frac{360}{m}\right)$$

Implied repo rate:

$$r_0(h)* = \left[\frac{f_0(h)*}{B_0(h + m)}\right]^{365/h} - 1$$

Practice Problem 3

A futures contract on a Treasury bill expires in 50 days. The T-bill matures in 140 days. The discount rates on T-bills are as follows:

    50-day bill: 5.0 percent
    140-day bill: 4.6 percent

A. Find the appropriate futures price by using the prices of the 50- and 140-day T-bills.

B. Find the futures price in terms of the underlying spot price compounded at the appropriate risk-free rate.

C. Convert the futures price to the implied discount rate on the futures.

D. Now assume that the futures contract is trading in the market at an implied discount rate 10 basis points lower than is appropriate, given the pricing model and the rule of no arbitrage. Demonstrate how an arbitrage transaction could be executed and show the outcome. Calculate the implied repo rate and discuss how it would be used to determine the profitability of the arbitrage.

SOLUTIONS

A. First, find the prices of the 50- and 140-day bonds:

$$B_0(50) = 1 - 0.05(50/360) = 0.9931$$
$$B_0(140) = 1 - 0.046(140/360) = 0.9821$$

The futures price is, therefore,

$$f_0(50) = \frac{0.9821}{0.9931} = 0.9889$$

B. First, find the rate at which to compound the spot price of the 140-day T-bill. This rate is obtained from the 50-day T-bill:

$$[1 + r_0(h)]^{h/365} = \frac{1}{0.9931} = 1.0069$$

We actually do not need to solve for $r_0(h)$. The above says that based on the rate $r_0(h)$, every dollar invested should grow to a value of 1.0069. Thus, the futures price should be the spot price (the price of the 140-day T-bill) compounded by the factor 1.0069:

$$f_0(50) = 0.9821(1.0069) = 0.9889$$

Annualized, this rate would equal $(1.0069)^{365/50} - 1 = 0.0515$.

C. Given the futures price of 0.9889, the implied discount rate is

$$r_0^{df}(50) = (1 - 0.9889)\left(\frac{360}{90}\right)$$
$$= 0.0444$$

D. If the futures is trading for 10 basis points lower, it trades at a rate of 4.34 percent, so the futures price would be

$$f_0(50) = 1 - 0.0434\left(\frac{90}{360}\right)$$
$$= 0.9892$$

Do the following:

Buy the 140-day bond at 0.9821
Sell the futures at 0.9892

This strategy provides a return per dollar invested of

$$\frac{0.9892}{0.9821} = 1.0072$$

which compares favorably with a return per dollar invested of 1.0069 if the futures is correctly priced.

The implied repo rate is simply the annualization of this rate: $(1.0072)^{365/50} - 1 = 0.0538$. The cash-and-carry transaction would, therefore, earn 5.38 percent. Because the futures appears to be mispriced, we could likely obtain financing in the repo market at less than this rate.

7.2.2 *Pricing Eurodollar Futures*

Based on the T-bill case, it is tempting to argue that the interest rate implied by the Eurodollar futures price would be the forward rate in the term structure of LIBOR. Unfortunately, that is not quite the case. In fact, the unusual construction of the Eurodollar futures contract relative to the Eurodollar spot market means that no risk-free combination of a Eurodollar time deposit and a Eurodollar futures contract can be constructed. Recall that the Eurodollar time deposit is an add-on instrument. Using $L_0(j)$ as the rate (LIBOR) on a j-day Eurodollar time deposit on day 0, if one deposits \$1, the deposit will grow to a value of $1 + L_0(j)(j/360)$ j days later. So, the present value of \$1 in j days is $1/[1 + L_0(j)(j/360)]$. The Eurodollar futures contract, however, is structured like the T-bill contract—as though the underlying were a discount instrument. So its price is stated in the form of $1 - L_0(j)(j/360)$. If we try the same arbitrage with Eurodollars that we did with T-bills, we cannot get the LIBOR that determines the spot price of a Eurodollar at expiration to offset the LIBOR that determines the futures price at expiration.

In other words, suppose that on day 0 we buy an (h + m)-day Eurodollar deposit that pays \$1 on day (h + m) and sell a futures at a price of $f_0(h)$. On day h, the futures expiration, the Eurodollar deposit has m days to go and is worth $1/[1 + L_h(m)(m/360)]$. The futures price at expiration is $f_h(h) = 1 - L_h(m)(m/360)$. The profit from the futures is $f_0(h) - [1 - L_h(m)(m/360)]$. Adding this amount to the value of the m-day Eurodollar deposit we are holding gives a total position value of

$$\frac{1}{1 + L_h(m)\left(\dfrac{m}{360}\right)} + f_0(h) - [1 - L_h(m)]\left(\frac{m}{360}\right)$$

Although $f_0(h)$ is known when the transaction is initiated, $L_h(m)$ is not determined until the futures expiration. There is no way for the $L_h(m)$ terms to offset. This problem does not occur in the T-bill market because the spot price is a discount instrument and the futures contract is designed as a discount instrument.[39] It is, nonetheless, common for participants in the futures market to treat the Eurodollar rate as equivalent to the implied forward rate. Such an assumption would require the ability to conduct the risk-free arbitrage, which, as we have shown, is impossible. The differences are fairly small, but we shall not assume that the Eurodollar futures rate should equal the implied forward rate. In that case, it would take a more advanced model to solve the pricing problem. The essential points in pricing interest rate futures on short-term instruments can be understood by studying the T-bill futures market.

---

[39] It is not clear why the Chicago Mercantile Exchange designed the Eurodollar contract as a discount instrument when the underlying Eurodollar deposit is an add-on instrument. The most likely reason is that the T-bill futures contract was already trading, was successful, and its design was well understood and accepted by traders. The CME most likely felt that this particular design was successful and should be continued with the Eurodollar contract. Ironically, the Eurodollar contract became exceptionally successful and the T-bill contract now has virtually no trading volume.

This mismatch in the design of spot and futures instruments in the Eurodollar market would appear to make the contract difficult to use as a hedging instrument. Although we cover hedging futures and forwards in Chapter 6, we should note that in the above equation for the payoff of the portfolio combining a spot Eurodollar time deposit and a short Eurodollar futures contract, an increase (decrease) in LIBOR lowers (raises) the value of the spot Eurodollar deposit and raises (lowers) the payoff from the short Eurodollar futures. Thus, the Eurodollar futures contract can still serve as a hedging tool. The hedge will not be perfect but can still be quite effective. Indeed, the Eurodollar futures contract is a major hedging tool of dealers in over-the-counter derivatives.

We have now completed the treatment of futures contracts on short-term interest rate instruments. Now let us look at the pricing of Treasury bond futures.

7.2.3 Pricing Treasury Note and Bond Futures

Recall that in Section 6.2, we described the bond futures contract as one in which there are a number of deliverable bonds. When a given bond is delivered, the long pays the short the futures price times an adjustment term called the conversion factor. The conversion factor is the price of a $1 bond with coupon equal to that of the deliverable bond and yield equal to 6 percent, with calculations based on semiannual compounding. Bonds with a coupon greater (less) than 6 percent will have a conversion factor greater (less) than 1. Before we delve into the complexities added by this feature, however, let us start off by assuming a fairly generic type of contract: one in which the underlying is a single, specific bond.

When examining bond forward contracts in Reading 70, we specified a time line and notation. We return to that specific time line and notation, which differs from those we used for examining short-term interest rate futures.

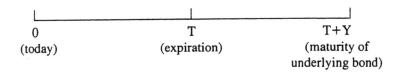

Recall our notation from Reading 70:

$B_0^c(T + Y)$ = price at time 0 of coupon bond that matures at time $T + Y$. The bond has a maturity of Y at the futures expiration.

CI_i = coupon at time t_i, where the coupons occur at times $t_1, t_2, \ldots, t_n$. Note that we care only about coupons prior to the futures expiration at T.

$f_0(T)$ = price at time 0 of futures expiring at time T.

$B_0(T)$ = price at time 0 of zero-coupon bond maturing at T.

We also need to know at time T the accumulated value of all coupons received over the period from 0 to T. We need the compound value from 0 to T of any coupons paid during the time the futures contract is alive. This value is denoted as $FV(CI,0,T)$. We introduced this variable in Reading 70 and showed how to compute it, so you may wish to review that material. It is traditionally assumed that the interest rate at which these coupons are reinvested is known. We also assume that this interest rate applies to the period from 0 to T for money borrowed or lent. We denote this rate as

$r_0(T)$ = Interest rate at time 0 for period until time T

As described in the section on T-bill futures pricing, this is the rate that determines the price of a zero-coupon bond maturing at T.[40] Hence,

$$B_0(T) = \frac{1}{[1 + r_0(T)]^T}$$

The futures price at expiration is the price of the deliverable bond at expiration:

$$f_T(T) = B_T(T + Y)$$

Now we are ready to price this bond futures contract. On day 0, we buy the bond at the price $B_0^c(T + Y)$ and sell the futures at the price $f_0(T)$. Because the futures does not require any cash up front, its initial value is zero. The current value of the overall transaction is, therefore, just the value of the bond, $B_0^c(T + Y)$. This value represents the amount of money we must invest to engage in this transaction.

We hold this position until the futures expiration. During this time, we collect and reinvest the coupons. On day T, the futures expires. We deliver the bond and receive the futures price, $f_0(T)$. We also have the reinvested coupons, which have a value at T of FV(CI,0,T). These two amounts, $f_0(T)$ and FV(CI,0,T), are known when the transaction was initiated at time 0, so the transaction is risk-free. Therefore, the current value of the transaction, $B_0^c(T + Y)$, should be the discounted value of its value at T of $f_0(T)$ + FV(CI,0,T):

$$B_0^c(T + Y) = \frac{f_0(T) + FV(CI, 0, T)}{[1 + r_0(T)]^T}$$

Note that we are simply discounting the known future value at T of the transaction at the risk-free rate of $r_0(T)$.[41]

We are, of course, more interested in the futures price, which is the only unknown in the above equation. Solving, we obtain

$$f_0(T) = B_0^c(T + Y)[1 + r_0(T)]^T - FV(CI,0,T) \qquad \textbf{(71-11)}$$

This equation is a variation of our basic cost-of-carry formula. The spot price, $B_0^c(T + Y)$, is compounded at the risk-free interest rate. We then subtract the compound future value of the reinvested coupons over the life of the contract. The coupon interest is like a negative cost of carry; it is a positive cash flow associated with holding the underlying bond.

Now let us work an example. Consider a $1 face value Treasury bond that pays interest at 7 percent semiannually. Thus, each coupon is $0.035. The bond has exactly five years remaining, so during that time it will pay 10 coupons, each six months apart. The yield on the bond is 8 percent. The price of the bond is found by calculating the present value of both the 10 coupons and the face value: The price is $0.9594.

Now consider a futures contract that expires in one year and three months: T = 1.25. The risk-free rate, $r_0(T)$, is 6.5 percent. The accumulated value of the coupons and the interest on them is

$$\$0.035(1.065)^{0.75} + \$0.035(1.065)^{0.25} = \$0.0722$$

---

[40] Keep in mind, however, that this rate is not the discount rate that determines the price of the zero-coupon bond maturing at T. It is the rate of return, expressed as an annual rate. When working with T-bills, the symbol "T" represented Days/365, which is consistent with its use here with T-bonds.

[41] We shall not take up the topic of the implied repo rate again, but note that if the futures is selling for $f_0(T)$, then $r_0(T)$ would be the implied repo rate.

The first coupon is paid in one-half a year and reinvests for three-quarters of a year. The second coupon is paid in one year and reinvests for one-quarter of a year.

Now the futures price is obtained as

$$f_0(T) = B_0^c(T + Y)[1 + r_0(T)]^T - FV(CI,0,T)$$

$$f_0(1.25) = \$0.9594(1.065)^{1.25} - \$0.0722 = \$0.9658$$

This is the price at which the futures should trade, given current market conditions. To verify this result, buy the five-year bond for $0.9594 and sell the futures for $0.9658. Hold the position for 15 months until the futures expiration. Collect and reinvest the coupons. When the futures expires, deliver the bond and receive the futures price of $0.9658. Then add the reinvested coupons of $0.0722 for a total of $0.9658 + $0.0722 = $1.0380. If we invest $0.9594 and end up with $1.0380 15 months later, the return is $1.0380/$0.9594 = 1.0819. For comparison purposes, we should determine the annual equivalent of this rate, which is found as $(1.0819)^{1/1.25} - 1 = 0.065$. This is the same 6.5 percent risk-free rate. If the futures contract trades at a higher price, the above transaction would result in a return greater than 6.5 percent. The amount available at expiration would be higher, clearly leading to a rate of return higher than 6.5 percent. If the futures trades at a lower price, the arbitrageur would sell short the bond and buy the futures, which would generate a cash inflow today. The amount paid back would be at less than the risk-free rate of 6.5 percent.[42]

Unfortunately, we now must complicate the matter a little by moving to the more realistic case with a delivery option. Bond futures contracts traditionally permit the short to choose which bond to deliver. This feature reduces the possibility of unusual price behavior of the deliverable bond caused by holders of short positions scrambling to buy a single deliverable bond at expiration. By allowing more than one bond to be deliverable, such problems are avoided. The contract is structured as though there is a standard hypothetical deliverable bond, which has a given coupon rate. The Chicago Board of Trade's contract uses a 6 percent rate. If the short delivers a bond with a higher (lower) coupon rate, the price received at delivery is adjusted upward (downward). The conversion factor is defined and calculated as the price of a $1 face value bond with a coupon and maturity equal to that of the deliverable bond and a yield of 6 percent. Each deliverable bond has its own conversion factor. The short designates which bond he will deliver, and that bond's conversion factor is multiplied by the final futures price to determine the amount the long will pay the short for the bond.

The availability of numerous deliverable bonds creates some confusion in pricing the futures contract, arising from the fact that the underlying cannot be uniquely identified, at least not on the surface. This confusion has given rise to the concept that one bond is always the best one to deliver. If a trader buys a given bond and sells the futures, he creates a risk-free hedge. If there are no arbitrage opportunities, the return from that hedge cannot exceed the risk-free rate. That return can, however, be *less* than the risk-free rate. How can this be? In all previous cases, if a return from a risk-free transaction is less than the risk-free rate, it should be a simple matter to reverse the transaction and capture an arbitrage profit. In this case, however, a reverse transaction would not work. If the arbitrageur sells short the bond and buys the futures, she must be assured that the short will deliver the bond from which the potential arbitrage profit was computed. But the short makes the delivery decision and in all likelihood would not deliver that particular bond.

---

[42] Again, as in the section on T-bill futures, this analysis could be conducted in terms of the implied repo rate.

Thus, the short can be long a bond and short futures and earn a return less than the risk-free rate. One bond, however, results in a return closest to the risk-free rate. Clearly that bond is the best bond to deliver. The terminology in the business is that this bond is the cheapest to deliver.

The cheapest-to-deliver bond is determined by selecting a given bond and computing the rate of return from buying that bond and selling the futures to hedge its delivery at expiration. This calculation is performed for all bonds. The one with the highest rate of return is the cheapest to deliver.[43] The cheapest-to-deliver bond can change, however, which can benefit the short and not the long. We ignore the details of determining the cheapest-to-deliver bond and assume that it has been identified. From here, we proceed to price the futures.

Let $CF(T)$ be the conversion factor for the bond we have identified as the cheapest to deliver. Now we go back to the arbitrage transaction described for the case where there is only one deliverable bond. Recall that we buy the bond, sell a futures, and reinvest the coupons on the bond. At expiration, we deliver the bond, receive the futures price $f_0(T)$, and have the reinvested coupons, which are worth $FV(CI,0,T)$. Now, in the case where the futures contract has many deliverable bonds, we must recognize that when the bond is delivered, the long pays $f_0(T)$ times $CF(T)$. This adjustment does not add any risk to this risk-free transaction. Thus, the present value of the amount received at delivery, $f_0(T)CF(T) + FV(CI,0,T)$, should still equal the original price of the bond, which was the amount we invested to initiate the transaction:

$$B_0^c(T + Y) = \frac{f_0(T)CF(T) + FV(CI,0,T)}{[1 + r_0(T)]^T}$$

Solving for the futures price, we obtain

$$f_0(T) = \frac{B_0^c(T + Y)[1 + r_0(T)]^T - FV(CI,0,T)}{CF(T)} \tag{71-12}$$

Note that when we had only one deliverable bond, the formula did not have the $CF(T)$ term, but a better way to look at it is that for only one deliverable bond, the conversion factor is effectively 1, so Equation 71-12 would still apply.

Consider the same example we previously worked, but now we need a conversion factor. As noted above, the conversion factor is the price of a $1 bond with coupon and maturity equal to that of the deliverable bond on the expiration day and yield of 6 percent, with all calculations made assuming semiannual interest payments. As noted, we shall skip the specifics of this calculation here; it is simply a present value calculation. For this example, the 7 percent bond with maturity of three and three-quarter years on the delivery day would have a conversion factor of 1.0505. Thus, the futures price would be

$$f_0(T) = \frac{B_0^c(T + Y)[1 + r_0(T)]^T - FV(CI,0,T)}{CF(T)}$$

$$f_0(1.25) = \frac{0.9594(1.065)^{1.25} - 0.0722}{1.0505} = 0.9193$$

If the futures is priced higher than 0.9193, one can buy the bond and sell the futures to earn more than the risk-free rate. If the futures price is less than 0.9193,

---

[43] As noted, this rate of return will not exceed the risk-free rate but will be the highest rate below the risk-free rate.

one can sell short the bond and buy the futures to end up borrowing at less than the risk-free rate. As noted previously, however, this transaction has a complication: If one goes short the bond and long the futures, this bond must remain the cheapest to deliver. Otherwise, the short will not deliver this particular bond and the arbitrage will not be successful.

Exhibit 71-9 reviews the important formulas for pricing Treasury bond futures contracts.

EXHIBIT 71-9 Pricing Formulas for Treasury Bond Futures Contract

Futures price = Underlying T-bond price compounded at risk-free rate less Compound future value of reinvested coupons.

Futures price if underlying bond is the only deliverable bond:

$$f_0(T) = B_0^c(T + Y)[1 + r_0(T)]^T - FV(CI,0,T)$$

Futures price when there are multiple deliverable bonds:

$$f_0(T) = \frac{B_0^c(T + Y)[1 + r_0(T)]^T - FV(CI,0,T)}{CF(T)}$$

Practice Problem 4

Consider a three-year $1 par Treasury bond with a 7.5 percent annual yield and 8 percent semiannual coupon. Its price is $1.0132. A futures contract calling for delivery of this bond only expires in one year. The one-year risk-free rate is 7 percent.

A. Find the future value in one year of the coupons on this bond. Assume a reinvestment rate of 3.75 percent per six-month period.

B. Find the appropriate futures price.

C. Now suppose the bond is one of many deliverable bonds. The contract specification calls for the use of a conversion factor to determine the price paid for a given deliverable bond. Suppose the bond described here has a conversion factor of 1.0372. Now determine the appropriate futures price.

SOLUTIONS

A. One coupon of 0.04 will be invested for half a year at 3.75 percent (half of the rate of 7.5 percent). The other coupon is not reinvested but is still counted. Thus, $FV(CI,0,1) = 0.04(1.0375) + 0.04 = 0.0815$.

B. $f_0(1) = 1.0132(1.07) - 0.0815 = 1.0026$

C. $f_0(1) = \dfrac{1.0132(1.07) - 0.0815}{1.0372} = 0.9667$

7.3 Pricing Stock Index Futures

Now let the underlying be either a portfolio of stocks or an individual stock.[44] The former are normally referred to as stock index futures, in which the portfolio is identical in composition to an underlying index of stocks. In this material, we focus on the pricing of stock index futures, but the principles are the same if the underlying is an individual stock.

In pricing stock index futures, we must account for the fact that the underlying stocks pay dividends.[45] Recall that in our previous discussions about the generic pricing of futures, we demonstrated that the futures price is lower as a result of the compound future value of any cash flows paid on the asset. Such cash flows consist of coupon interest payments if the underlying is a bond, or storage costs if the underlying incurs costs to store.[46] Dividends work exactly like coupon interest.

Consider the same time line we used before. Today is time 0, and the futures expires at time T. During the life of the futures, there are n dividends of D_j, $j = 1, 2, \ldots, n$. We assume these dividends are all known when the futures contract is initiated. Let

$$FV(D,0,T) = \text{the compound value over the period of 0 to T of all dividends collected and reinvested}$$

We introduced this variable in Reading 70 and showed how to compute it, so you may wish to review that material. The other notation is the same we have previously used:

$$S_0 = \text{current value of the stock index}$$
$$f_0(T) = \text{futures price today of a contract that expires at T}$$
$$r = \text{risk-free interest rate over the period 0 to T}$$

Now that we are no longer working with interest rate futures, we do not need the more flexible notation for interest rates on bonds of different maturities or interest rates at different time points. So we can use the simple notation of r as the risk-free interest rate, but we must keep in mind that it is the risk-free rate for the time period from 0 to T.

We undertake the following transaction: On day 0, we buy the stock portfolio that replicates the index. This transaction will require that we invest the amount S_0. We simultaneously sell the futures at the price $f_0(T)$.

On day T, the futures expires. We deliver the stock and receive the original futures price $f_0(T)$.[47] We also have the accumulated value of the reinvested dividends, $FV(D,0,T)$ for a total of $f_0(T) + FV(D,0,T)$. Because this amount is known at time 0, the transaction is risk free. Therefore, we should discount its value at the risk-free rate and set this equal to the initial value of the portfolio, S_0, as follows:

---

[44] Futures on individual stocks have taken a long time to develop, primarily because of regulatory hurdles. They were introduced in the United States in late 2002 and, as of the publication date of this book, have achieved only modest trading volume. They currently trade in a few other countries such as the United Kingdom and Australia.

[45] Even if not all of the stocks pay dividends, at least some of the stocks almost surely pay dividends.

[46] We also allowed for the possibility of noncash costs, which we called the convenience yield, but there are no implicit costs or benefits associated with stock index futures.

[47] Virtually all stock index futures contracts call for cash settlement at expiration. See the explanation of the equivalence of delivery and cash settlement in Section 4 and Exhibit 71-2.

$$S_0 = \frac{f_0(T) + FV(D,0,T)}{(1 + r)^T}$$

Solving for the futures price gives

$$f_0(T) = S_0(1 + r)^T - FV(D,0,T)$$ **(71-13)**

which is the cost-of-carry formula for stock index futures. Notice that it is virtually identical to that for bond futures. Ignoring the conversion factor necessitated by the delivery option, the only difference is that we use the compound future value of the dividends instead of the compound future value of the coupon interest.

Consider the following example. A stock index is at 1,452.45, and a futures contract on the index expires in three months. Thus, $T = 3/12 = 0.25$. The risk-free interest rate is 5.5 percent. The value of the dividends reinvested over the life of the futures is 7.26. The futures price should, therefore, be

$$f_0(T) = S_0(1 + r)^T - FV(D,0,T)$$
$$f_0(0.25) = 1,452.45(1.055)^{0.25} - 7.26$$
$$= 1,464.76$$

Thus, if the futures contract is selling for more than this price, an arbitrageur can buy the stocks and sell the futures. The arbitrageur would collect and reinvest the dividends and at expiration would receive a gain that would exceed the risk-free rate of 5.5 percent, a result of receiving more than 1,464.76 for the stocks. If the futures contract is selling for less than this price, the arbitrageur can sell short the stocks and buy the futures. After paying the dividends while holding the stocks,[48] the arbitrageur will end up buying back the stocks at a price that implies that he has borrowed money and paid it back at a rate less than the risk-free rate. The combined activities of all arbitrageurs will force the futures price to 1,464.76.

The stock index futures pricing formula has a number of variations. Suppose we define $FV(D,0,T)/(1 + r)^T$ as the present value of the dividends, $PV(D,0,T)$:

$$FV(D,0,T) = PV(D,0,T)(1 + r)^T$$

Substituting in the futures pricing formula above for $FV(D,0,T)$, we obtain

$$f_0(T) = [S_0 - PV(D,0,T)](1 + r)^T$$ **(71-14)**

Notice here that the stock price is reduced by the present value of the dividends. This adjusted stock price is then compounded at the risk-free rate over the life of the futures.

In the problem we worked above, the present value of the dividends is found as

$$PV(D,0,T) = \frac{FV(D,0,T)}{(1 + r)^T}$$

$$PV(D,0,0.25) = \frac{7.26}{(1.055)^{0.25}} = 7.16$$

---

[48] Remember that a short seller must make restitution for any dividends paid while the position is short.

Then the futures price would be

$$f_0(T) = [S_0 - PV(D,0,T)](1 + r)^T$$
$$f_0(0.25) = (1,452.45 - 7.16)(1.055)^{0.25}$$
$$= 1,464.76$$

Another variation of the formula defines the yield as δ in the following manner:

$$\frac{1}{(1 + \delta)^T} = 1 - \frac{FV(D,0,T)}{S_0(1 + r)^T}$$

The exact solution for δ is somewhat complex, so we shall just leave it in the form above. Using this specification, we find that the futures pricing formula would be

$$f_0(T) = \left(\frac{S_0}{(1 + \delta)^T}\right)(1 + r)^T \qquad \textbf{(71-15)}$$

The stock price is, thus, discounted at the dividend yield, and this adjusted stock price is then compounded at the risk-free rate over the life of the futures.[49]

In the example above, the yield calculation is

$$\frac{1}{(1 + \delta)^T} = 1 - \frac{FV(D,0,T)}{S_0(1 + r)^T}$$

$$\frac{1}{(1 + \delta)^T} = 1 - \frac{7.26}{1,452.45(1.055)^{0.25}} = 0.9951$$

Then $(1 + \delta)^T$ is $1/0.9951 = 1.0049$ and the futures price is

$$f_0(T) = \left(\frac{S_0}{(1 + \delta)^T}\right)(1 + r)^T$$

$$f_0(0.25) = \left(\frac{1,452.45}{1.0049}\right)(1.055)^{0.25}$$

$$= 1,464.84$$

The difference between this and the answer we previously obtained is strictly caused by a rounding error.

Another variation of this formula is to express the yield as

$$\delta^* = \frac{PV(D,0,T)}{S_0} = \frac{FV(D,0,T)/(1 + r)^T}{S_0}$$

This means that $FV(D,0,T) = S_0(1 + r)^T\delta^*$. Substituting into our futures pricing formula for $FV(D,0,T)$, we obtain

$$f_0(T) = S_0(1 - \delta^*)(1 + r)^T \qquad \textbf{(71-16)}$$

Here again, the stock price is reduced by the yield, and this "adjusted" stock price is compounded at the risk-free rate.

---

[49] Sometimes the futures price is written as $f_0(T) = S_0(1 + r - \delta)^T$ where the dividend yield is simply subtracted from the risk-free rate to give a net cost of carry. This formula is a rough approximation that we do not consider acceptable.

In the problem we worked above, the yield would be found as

$$\delta^* = \frac{PV(D,0,T)}{S_0}$$

$$\delta^* = \frac{7.16}{1,452.45} = 0.0049$$

Then the futures price would be

$$f_0(T) = S_0(1 - \delta^*)(1 + r)^T$$
$$f_0(0.25) = 1,452.45(1 - 0.0049)(1.055)^{0.25}$$
$$= 1,464.81$$

Again, the difference between the two prices comes from rounding.

A common variation uses the assumption of continuous compounding. The continuously compounded risk-free rate is defined as $r^c = \ln(1 + r)$. The continuously compounded dividend yield is $\delta^c = \ln(1 + \delta)$. When working with discrete dividends, we obtained the relationship

$$\frac{1}{(1 + \delta)^T} = 1 - \frac{FV(D,0,T)}{S_0(1 + r)^T}$$

We calculated $(1 + \delta)^T$. To obtain δ^c, we take the natural log of this value and divide by T: $\delta^c = (1/T)\ln[(1 + \delta)^T]$. The formula for the futures price is

$$f_0(T) = S_0 e^{(r^c - \delta^c)T}$$

In the above formula, the opportunity cost, expressed as the interest rate, is reduced by the dividend yield. Thus, the formula compounds the spot price by the interest cost less the dividend benefits. An equivalent variation of the above formula is

$$f_0(T) = (S_0 e^{-\delta^c T}) e^{r^c T} \qquad \text{(71-17)}$$

The expression in parentheses is the stock price discounted at the dividend yield rate. The result is an adjusted stock price with the present value of the dividends removed. This adjusted stock price is then compounded at the risk-free rate. So, as we have previously seen, the stock price less the present value of the dividends is compounded at the risk-free rate to obtain the futures price.

In the previous problem, $(1 + \delta)^T = 1.0049$. Then $\delta^c = (1/0.25)\ln(1.0049) = 0.0196$. The continuously compounded risk-free rate is $\ln(1.055) = 0.0535$. The futures price is, therefore, $f_0(0.25) = (1452.45 e^{-0.0196(0.25)}) e^{0.0535(0.25)} = 1464.81$; again the difference comes from rounding.

Exhibit 71-10 summarizes the formulas for pricing stock index futures contracts. Each of these formulas is consistent with the general formula for pricing futures. They are each based on the notion that a futures price is the spot price compounded at the risk-free rate, plus the compound future value of any other costs minus any cash flows and benefits. Alternatively, one can convert the compound future value of the costs net of benefits or cash flows of holding the asset to their current value and subtract this amount from the spot price before compounding the spot price at the interest rate. In this manner, the spot price adjusted for any costs or benefits is then compounded at the risk-free interest rate to give the futures price. These costs, benefits, and cash flows thus represent the linkage between spot and futures prices.

EXHIBIT 71-10 Pricing Formulas for Stock Index Futures Contract

Futures price = Stock index compounded at risk-free rate − Future value of dividends, or (Stock index − Present value of dividends) compounded at risk-free rate.

Futures price as stock index compounded at risk-free rate − Future value of dividends:

$$f_0(T) = S_0(1 + r)^T - FV(D,0,T)$$

Futures price as stock index − Present value of dividends compounded at risk-free rate:

$$f_0(T) = [S_0 - PV(D,0,T)](1 + r)^T$$

Futures price as stock index discounted at dividend yield, compounded at risk-free rate:

$$f_0(T) = \left(\frac{S_0}{(1 + \delta)^T}\right)(1 + r)^T \quad \text{or}$$
$$f_0(T) = S_0(1 - \delta^*)(1 + r)^T$$

Futures price in terms of continuously compounded rate and yield:

$$f_0(T) = S_0 e^{(r^c - \delta^c)T} \qquad \text{or}$$
$$f_0(T) = (S_0 e^{-\delta^c T})e^{r^c T}$$

Practice Problem 5

A stock index is at 755.42. A futures contract on the index expires in 57 days. The risk-free interest rate is 6.25 percent. At expiration, the value of the dividends on the index is 3.94.

A. Find the appropriate futures price, using both the future value of the dividends and the present value of the dividends.

B. Find the appropriate futures price in terms of the two specifications of the dividend yield.

C. Using your answer in Part B, find the futures price under the assumption of continuous compounding of interest and dividends.

SOLUTIONS

A. $T = 57/365 = 0.1562$

$$f_0(0.1562) = 755.42(1.0625)^{0.1562} - 3.94 = 758.67$$

Alternatively, we can find the present value of the dividends:

$$PV(D,0,0.1562) = \frac{3.94}{(1.0625)^{0.1562}} = 3.90$$

Then we can find the futures price as $f_0(0.1562) = (755.42 - 3.90)$ $(1.0625)^{0.1562} = 758.67$.

B. Under one specification of the yield, we have

$$\frac{1}{(1 + \delta)^T} = 1 - \frac{3.94}{755.42(1.0625)^{0.1562}} = 0.9948$$

We need the inverse of this amount, which is $1/0.9948 = 1.0052$. Then the futures price is

$$f_0(0.1562) = \left(\frac{755.42}{1.0052}\right)(1.0625)^{0.1562} = 758.66$$

Under the other specification of the dividend yield, we have

$$\delta^* = \frac{3.90}{755.42} = 0.0052$$

The futures price is $f_0(0.1562) = 755.42(1 - 0.0052)(1.0625)^{0.1562} = 758.64$, with the difference caused by rounding.

C. The continuously compounded risk-free rate is $r^c = \ln(1.0625) = 0.0606$. The continuously compounded dividend yield is

$$\frac{1}{0.1562} \ln(1.0052) = 0.0332$$

The futures price would then be

$$f_0(0.1562) = 755.42 e^{(0.0606 - 0.0332)(0.1562)}$$
$$= 758.66$$

7.4 Pricing Currency Futures

Given our assumptions about no marking to market, it will be a simple matter to learn how to price currency futures: We price them the same as currency forwards. Recall that in Reading 70 we described a currency as an asset paying a yield of r^f, which can be viewed as the foreign risk-free rate. Thus, in this sense, a currency futures can also be viewed like a stock index futures, whereby the dividend yield is analogous to the foreign interest rate.

Therefore, an arbitrageur can buy the currency for the spot exchange rate of S_0 and sell a futures expiring at T for $f_0(T)$, holding the position until expiration, collecting the foreign interest, and delivering the currency to receive the original futures price. An important twist, however, is that the arbitrageur must be careful to have the correct number of units of the currency on hand to deliver.

Consider a futures contract on one unit of the currency. If the arbitrageur purchases one unit of the currency up front, the accumulation of interest on the currency will result in having more than one unit at the futures expiration. To adjust for this problem, the arbitrageur should take $S_0/(1 + r^f)^T$ units of his own currency and buy $1/(1 + r^f)^T$ units of the foreign currency.[50] The arbitrageur holds this position and collects interest at the foreign rate. The accumulation of interest is accounted for by multiplying by the interest factor $(1 + r^f)^T$. At expiration, the number of units of the currency will have grown to $[1/(1 + r^f)^T]$ $[1 + r^f]^T = 1$. So, the arbitrageur would then have 1 unit of the currency. He delivers that unit and receives the futures price of $f_0(T)$.

---

[50] In other words, if S_0 buys 1 unit, then $S_0/(1 + r^f)^T$ buys $1/(1 + r^f)^T$ units.

To avoid an arbitrage opportunity, the present value of the payoff of $f_0(T)$ must equal the amount initially invested. To find the present value of the payoff, we must discount at the domestic risk-free rate, because that rate reflects the opportunity cost of the arbitrageur's investment of his own money. So, first we equate the present value of the future payoff, discounting at the domestic risk-free rate, to the amount initially invested:

$$\frac{f_0(T)}{(1 + r)^T} = \frac{S_0}{(1 + r^f)^T}$$

Then we solve for the futures price to obtain

$$f_0(T) = \left(\frac{S_0}{(1 + r^f)^T}\right)(1 + r)^T \qquad \text{(71-18)}$$

This formula is the same one we used for currency forwards.

An alternative variation of this formula would apply when we use continuously compounded interest rates. The adjustment is very slight. In the formula above, dividing S_0 by $(1 + r^f)^T$ finds a present value by discounting at the foreign interest rate. Multiplying by $(1 + r)^T$ is finding a future value by compounding at the domestic interest rate. The continuously compounded analogs to those rates are $r^{fc} = \ln(1 + r^f)$ and $r^c = \ln(1 + r)$. Then the formula becomes

$$f_0(T) = (S_0 e^{-r^{fc}T}) e^{r^c T} \qquad \text{(71-19)}$$

We also saw this formula in Reading 70.

Consider a futures contract expiring in 55 days on the euro. Therefore, $T = 55/365 = 0.1507$. The spot exchange rate is \$0.8590. The foreign interest rate is 5.25 percent, and the domestic risk-free rate is 6.35 percent. The futures price should, therefore, be

$$f_0(T) = \left(\frac{S_0}{(1 + r^f)^T}\right)(1 + r)^T$$

$$f_0(0.1507) = \left(\frac{0.8590}{(1.0525)^{0.1507}}\right)(1.0635)^{0.1507} = 0.8603$$

If the futures is selling for more than this amount, the arbitrageur can buy the currency and sell the futures. He collects the foreign interest and converts the currency back at a higher rate than 0.8603, resulting in a risk-free return that exceeds the domestic risk-free rate. If the futures is selling for less than this amount, the arbitrageur can borrow the currency and buy the futures. The end result will be to receive money at the start and pay back money at a rate less than the domestic risk-free rate.

If the above problem were structured in terms of continuously compounded rates, the domestic rate would be $\ln(1.0635) = 0.0616$ and the foreign rate would be $\ln(1.0525) = 0.0512$. The futures price would then be

$$f_0(T) = (S_0 e^{-r^{fc}T}) e^{r^c T}$$

$$f_0(0.1507) = (0.85890 e^{-0.0512(0.1507)}) e^{0.0616(0.1507)} = 0.8603$$

which, of course, is the same price we calculated above.

Exhibit 71-11 summarizes the formulas for pricing currency futures.

EXHIBIT 71-11 Pricing Formulas for Currency Futures Contract

Futures price = (Spot exchange rate discounted by Foreign interest rate) compounded at Domestic interest rate:

Discrete interest: $f_0(T) = \left(\dfrac{S_0}{(1 + r^f)^T}\right)(1 + r)^T$

Continuous interest: $f_0(T) = (S_0 e^{-r^{fc}T}) e^{r^c T}$

Practice Problem 6

The spot exchange rate for the Swiss franc is \$0.60. The U.S. interest rate is 6 percent, and the Swiss interest rate is 5 percent. A futures contract expires in 78 days.

A. Find the appropriate futures price.

B. Find the appropriate futures price under the assumption of continuous compounding.

C. Using Part A, execute an arbitrage resulting from a futures price of \$0.62.

SOLUTIONS

$T = 78/365 = 0.2137$

A. $f_0(0.2137) = \dfrac{\$0.60}{(1.05)^{0.2137}} (1.06)^{0.2137} = \$0.6012$

B. The continuously compounded equivalent rates are

$$r^{fc} = \ln(1.05) = 0.0488$$
$$r^c = \ln(1.06) = 0.0583$$

The futures price is

$$f_0(0.2137) = (\$0.60 e^{-0.0488(0.2137)}) e^{0.0583(0.2137)}$$
$$= \$0.6012$$

C. At \$0.62, the futures price is too high, so we will need to sell the futures. First, however, we must determine how many units of the currency to buy. It should be

$$\frac{1}{(1.05)^{0.2137}} = 0.9896$$

So we buy this many units, which costs $0.9896(\$0.60) = \$0.5938$. We sell the futures at \$0.62. We hold the position until expiration. During that time the accumulation of interest will make the 0.9896 units of the currency grow to 1.0000 unit. We convert the Swiss franc to dollars at the futures rate of \$0.62. The return per dollar invested is

$$\frac{0.62}{0.5938} = 1.0441$$

This is a return of 1.0441 per dollar invested over 78 days. At the risk-free rate of 6 percent, the return over 78 days should be $(1.06)^{0.2137} =$ 1.0125. Obviously, the arbitrage transaction is much better.

7.5 Futures Pricing: A Recap

We have now examined the pricing of short-term interest rate futures, intermediate- and long-term interest rate futures, stock index futures, and currency futures. Let us recall the intuition behind pricing a futures contract and see the commonality in each of those special cases. First recall that under the assumption of no marking to market, at expiration the short makes delivery and we assume that the long pays the full futures price at that point. An arbitrageur buys the asset and sells a futures contract, holds the asset for the life of the futures, and delivers it at expiration of the futures, at which time he is paid the futures price. In addition, while holding the asset, the arbitrageur accumulates costs and accrues cash flows, such as interest, dividends, and benefits such as a convenience yield. The value of the position at expiration will be the futures price net of these costs minus benefits and cash flows. The overall value of this transaction at expiration is known when the transaction is initiated; thus, the value at expiration is risk-free. The return from a risk-free transaction should equal the risk-free rate, which is the rate on a zero-coupon bond whose maturity is the futures expiration day. If the return is indeed this risk-free rate, then the futures price must equal the spot price compounded at the risk-free rate plus the compound value of these costs net of benefits and cash flows.

It should also be noted that although we have taken the more natural approach of buying the asset and selling the futures, we could just as easily have sold short the asset and bought the futures. Because short selling is usually a little harder to do as well as to understand, the approach we take is preferable from a pedagogical point of view. It is important, nonetheless, to remember that the ability to sell short the asset or the willingness of parties who own the asset to sell it to offset the buying of the futures is critical to establishing the results we have shown here. Otherwise, the futures pricing formulas would be inequalities—limited on one side but not restricted on the other.

We should remind ourselves that this general form of the futures pricing model also applied in Reading 70 in our discussion of forward contracts. Futures contracts differ from forward contracts in that the latter are subject to credit risk. Futures contracts are marked to market on a daily basis and guaranteed against losses from default by the futures clearinghouse, which has never defaulted. Although there are certain institutional features that distinguish futures from forwards, we consider those features separately from the material on pricing. Because the general economic and financial concepts are the same, for pricing purposes, we treat futures and forwards as the same.

8   THE ROLE OF FUTURES MARKETS AND EXCHANGES

We conclude this reading with a brief look at the role that futures markets and exchanges play in global financial systems and in society. Virtually all participants in the financial markets have heard of futures markets, but many do not understand the role that futures markets play. Some participants do not understand how futures markets function in global financial systems and often look at futures with suspicion, if not disdain.

In Reading 69, we discussed the purposes of derivative markets. We found that derivative markets provide price discovery and risk management, make the markets for the underlying assets more efficient, and permit trading at low transaction costs. These characteristics are also associated with futures markets. In fact, price discovery is often cited by others as the primary advantage of futures markets. Yet, all derivative markets provide these benefits. What characteristics do futures markets have that are not provided by comparable markets as forward markets?

First recall that a major distinction between futures and forwards is that futures are standardized instruments. By having an agreed-upon set of homogeneous contracts, futures markets can provide an orderly, liquid market in which traders can open and close positions without having to worry about holding these positions to expiration. Although not all futures contracts have a high degree of liquidity, an open position can nonetheless be closed on the exchange where the contract was initiated.[51] More importantly, however, futures contracts are guaranteed against credit losses. If a counterparty defaults, the clearinghouse pays and, as we have emphasized, no clearinghouse has ever defaulted. In this manner, a party can engage in a transaction to lock in a future price or rate without having to worry about the credit quality of the counterparty. Forward contracts are subject to default risk, but of course they offer the advantage of customization, the tailoring of a contract's terms to meet the needs of the parties involved.

With an open, standardized, and regulated market for futures contracts, their prices can be disseminated to other investors and the general public. Futures prices are closely watched by a vast number of market participants, many trying to discern an indication of the direction of future spot prices and some simply trying to determine what price they could lock in for future purchase or sale of the underlying asset. Although forward prices provide similar information, forward contracts are private transactions and their prices are not publicly reported. Futures markets thus provide transparency to the financial markets. They reveal the prices at which parties contract for future transactions.

Therefore, futures prices contribute an important element to the body of information on which investors make decisions. In addition, they provide opportunities to transact for future purchase or sale of an underlying asset without having to worry about the credit quality of the counterparty.

In Readings 70 and 71, we studied forward and futures contracts and showed that they have a lot in common. Both are commitments to buy or sell an asset at a future date at a price agreed on today. No money changes hands at the start of either transaction. We learned how to determine appropriate prices and values for these contracts. In Chapter 6, we shall look at a variety of strategies and applications using forward and futures contracts. For now, however, we take a totally different approach and look at contracts that provide not the obligation but rather the right to buy or sell an asset at a later date at a price agreed on today. To obtain such a right, in contrast to agreeing to an obligation, one must pay money at the start. These instruments, called options, are the subject of Reading 72.

---

[51] Recall that there is no liquid market for previously opened forward contracts to be closed, but the holder of a forward contract can re-enter the market and establish a position opposite to the one previously established. If one holds a long forward contract to buy an asset in six months, one can then do a short forward contract to sell the asset in six months, and this transaction offsets the risk of changing market prices. The credit risk on both contracts remains. In some cases, the offsetting contract can be done with the same counterparty as in the original contract, permitting the two parties to arrange a single cash settlement to offset both contracts.

9   SUMMARY

▷ Futures contracts are standardized instruments that trade on a futures exchange, have a secondary market, and are guaranteed against default by means of a daily settling of gains and losses. Forward contracts are customized instruments that are not guaranteed against default and are created anywhere off of an exchange.

▷ Modern futures markets primarily originated in Chicago out of a need for grain farmers and buyers to be able to transact for delivery at future dates for grain that would, in the interim, be placed in storage.

▷ Futures transactions are standardized and conducted in a public market, are homogeneous, have a secondary market giving them an element of liquidity, and have a clearinghouse, which collects margins and settles gains and losses daily to provide a guarantee against default. Futures markets are also regulated at the federal government level.

▷ Margin in the securities markets is the deposit of money, the margin, and a loan for the remainder of the funds required to purchase a stock or bond. Margin in the futures markets is much smaller and does not involve a loan. Futures margin is more like a performance bond or down payment.

▷ Futures trading occurs on a futures exchange, which involves trading either in a physical location called a pit or via a computer terminal off of the floor of the futures exchange as part of an electronic trading system. In either case, a party to a futures contract goes long, committing to buy the underlying asset at an agreed-upon price, or short, committing to sell the underlying asset at an agreed-upon price.

▷ A futures trader who has established a position can re-enter the market and close out the position by doing the opposite transaction (sell if the original position was long or buy if the original position was short). The party has offset the position, no longer has a contract outstanding, and has no further obligation.

▷ Initial margin is the amount of money in a margin account on the day of a transaction or when a margin call is made. Maintenance margin is the amount of money in a margin account on any day other than when the initial margin applies. Minimum requirements exist for the initial and maintenance margins, with the initial margin requirement normally being less than 10 percent of the futures price and the maintenance margin requirement being smaller than the initial margin requirement. Variation margin is the amount of money that must be deposited into the account to bring the balance up to the required level. The settlement price is an average of the last few trades of the day and is used to determine the gains and losses marked to the parties' accounts.

▷ The futures clearinghouse engages in a practice called marking to market, also known as the daily settlement, in which gains and losses on a futures position are credited and charged to the trader's margin account on a daily basis. Thus, profits are available for withdrawal and losses must be paid quickly before they build up and pose a risk that the party will be unable to cover large losses.

▷ The margin balance at the end of the day is determined by taking the previous balance and accounting for any gains or losses from the day's activity, based on the settlement price, as well as any money added or withdrawn.

▷ Price limits are restrictions on the price of a futures trade and are based on a range relative to the previous day's settlement price. No trade can take place outside of the price limits. A limit move is when the price at which two parties would like to trade is at or beyond the price limit. Limit up is when the market price would be at or above the upper limit. Limit down is when the market price would be at or below the lower limit. Locked limit occurs when a trade cannot take place because the price would be above the limit up or below the limit down prices.

▸ A futures contract can be terminated by entering into an offsetting position very shortly before the end of the expiration day. If the position is still open when the contract expires, the trader must take delivery (if long) or make delivery (if short), unless the contract requires that an equivalent cash settlement be used in lieu of delivery. In addition, two participants can agree to alternative delivery terms, an arrangement called exchange for physicals.

▸ Delivery options are features associated with a futures contract that permit the short some flexibility in what to deliver, where to deliver it, and when in the expiration month to make delivery.

▸ Scalpers are futures traders who take positions for very short periods of time and attempt to profit by buying at the bid price and selling at the ask price. Day traders close out all positions by the end of the day. Position traders leave their positions open overnight and potentially longer.

▸ Treasury bill futures are contracts in which the underlying is $1,000,000 of a U.S. Treasury bill. Eurodollar futures are contracts in which the underlying is $1,000,000 of a Eurodollar time deposit. Treasury bond futures are contracts in which the underlying is $100,000 of a U.S. Treasury bond with a minimum 15-year maturity. Stock index futures are contracts in which the underlying is a well-known stock index, such as the S&P 500 or FTSE 100. Currency futures are contracts in which the underlying is a foreign currency.

▸ An expiring futures contract is equivalent to a spot transaction. Consequently, at expiration the futures price must converge to the spot price to avoid an arbitrage opportunity in which one can buy the asset and sell a futures or sell the asset and buy a futures to capture an immediate profit at no risk.

▸ The value of a futures contract just prior to marking to market is the accumulated price change since the last mark to market. The value of a futures contract just after marking to market is zero. These values reflect the claim a participant has as a result of her position in the contract.

▸ The price of a futures contract will equal the price of an otherwise equivalent forward contract one day prior to expiration, or if interest rates are known or constant, or if interest rates are uncorrelated with futures prices.

▸ A futures price is derived by constructing a combination of a long position in the asset and a short position in the futures. This strategy guarantees that the price received from the sale of the asset is known when the transaction is initiated. The futures price is then derived as the unknown value that eliminates the opportunity to earn an arbitrage profit off of the transaction.

▸ Futures prices are affected by the opportunity cost of funds tied up in the investment in the underlying asset, the costs of storing the underlying asset, any cash flows paid on the underlying asset, such as interest or dividends, and nonmonetary benefits of holding the underlying asset, referred to as the convenience yield.

▸ Backwardation describes a condition in which the futures price is lower than the spot price. Contango describes a condition in which the futures price is higher than the spot price.

▸ The futures price will not equal the expected spot price if the risk premium in the spot price is transferred from hedgers to futures traders. If the risk premium is transferred, then the futures price will be biased high or low relative to the expected future spot price. When the futures price is biased low (high), it is called normal backwardation (normal contango).

▷ T-bill futures prices are determined by going short a futures contract and going long a T-bill that will have the desired maturity at the futures expiration. At expiration, the T-bill is delivered or cash settled to a price locked in when the transaction was initiated through the sale of the futures. The correct futures price is the one that prohibits this combination from earning an arbitrage profit. Under the assumptions we make, the T-bill futures price is the same as the T-bill forward price.

▷ The implied repo rate is the rate of return implied by a transaction of buying a spot asset and selling a futures contract. If financing can be obtained in the repo market at less than the implied repo rate, the transaction should be undertaken. If financing can be supplied to the repo market at greater than the implied repo rate, the transaction should be reversed.

▷ Eurodollar futures cannot be priced as easily as T-bill futures, because the expiration price of a Eurodollar futures is based on a value computed as 1 minus a rate, whereas the value of the underlying Eurodollar time deposit is based on 1 divided by a rate. The difference is small but not zero. Hence, Eurodollar futures do not lend themselves to an exact pricing formula based on the notion of a cost of carry of the underlying.

▷ Treasury bond futures prices are determined by first identifying the cheapest bond to deliver, which is the bond that the short would deliver under current market conditions. Then one must construct a combination of a short futures contract and a long position in that bond. The bond is held, and the coupons are collected and reinvested. At expiration, the underlying bond is delivered and the futures price times the conversion factor for that bond is received. The correct futures price is the one that prevents this transaction from earning an arbitrage profit.

▷ Stock index futures prices are determined by constructing a combination of a long portfolio of stocks identical to the underlying index and a short futures contract. The stocks are held and the dividends are collected and reinvested. At expiration, the cash settlement results in the effective sale of the stock at the futures price. The correct futures price is the one that prevents this transaction from earning an arbitrage profit.

▷ Currency futures prices are determined by buying the underlying currency and selling a futures on the currency. The position is held, and the underlying currency pays interest at the foreign risk-free rate. At expiration, the currency is delivered and the futures price is received. The correct futures price is the one that prevents this transaction from earning an arbitrage profit.

▷ Futures markets serve our financial systems by making the markets for the underlying assets more efficient, by providing price discovery, by offering opportunities to trade at lower transaction costs, and by providing a means of managing risk. Futures markets also provide a homogeneous, standardized, and tradable instrument through which participants who might not have access to forward markets can make commitments to buy and sell assets at a future date at a locked-in price with no fear of credit risk. Because futures markets are so visible and widely reported on, they are also an excellent source of information, contributing greatly to the transparency of financial markets.

PROBLEMS

1. **A.** In February, Dave Parsons purchased a June futures contract on the Nasdaq 100 Index. He decides to close out his position in April. Describe how he would do so.

   B. Peggy Smith is a futures trader. In early August, she took a short position in an S&P 500 Index futures contract expiring in September. After a week, she decides to close out her position. Describe how she would do so.

2. A gold futures contract requires the long trader to buy 100 troy ounces of gold. The initial margin requirement is $2,000, and the maintenance margin requirement is $1,500.

   A. Matthew Evans goes long one June gold futures contract at the futures price of $320 per troy ounce. When could Evans receive a maintenance margin call?

   B. Chris Tosca sells one August gold futures contract at a futures price of $323 per ounce. When could Tosca receive a maintenance margin call?

3. A copper futures contract requires the long trader to buy 25,000 lbs of copper. A trader buys one November copper futures contract at a price of $0.75/lb. Theoretically, what is the maximum loss this trader could have? Another trader sells one November copper futures contract. Theoretically, what is the maximum loss this trader with a short position could have?

4. Consider a hypothetical futures contract in which the current price is $212. The initial margin requirement is $10, and the maintenance margin requirement is $8. You go long 20 contracts and meet all margin calls but do not withdraw any excess margin.

   A. When could there be a margin call?

   B. Complete the table below and explain any funds deposited. Assume that the contract is purchased at the settlement price of that day so there is no mark-to-market profit or loss on the day of purchase.

Day	Beginning Balance	Funds Deposited	Futures Price	Price Change	Gain/Loss	Ending Balance
0			212			
1			211			
2			214			
3			209			
4			210			
5			204			
6			202			

   C. How much are your total gains or losses by the end of day 6?

5. Sarah Moore has taken a short position in one Chicago Board of Trade Treasury bond futures contract with a face value of $100,000 at the price of 96 6/32. The initial margin requirement is $2,700, and the maintenance margin requirement is $2,000. Moore would meet all margin calls but would not withdraw any excess margin.

A. Complete the table below and provide an explanation of any funds deposited. Assume that the contract is purchased at the settlement price of that day, so there is no mark-to-market profit or loss on the day of purchase.

Day	Beginning Balance	Funds Deposited	Futures Price	Price Change	Gain/Loss	Ending Balance
0			96-06			
1			96-31			
2			97-22			
3			97-18			
4			97-24			
5			98-04			
6			97-31			

B. How much are Moore's total gains or losses by the end of day 6?

6. A. The IMM index price in yesterday's newspaper for a September Eurodollar futures contract is 95.23. What is the actual price of this contract?

B. The IMM index price in today's newspaper for the contract mentioned above is 95.25. How much is the change in the actual futures price of the contract since the previous day?

OPTION MARKETS AND CONTRACTS

72

The candidate should be able to:

a. identify the basic elements and describe the characteristics of option contracts;

b. define European option, American option, moneyness, payoff, intrinsic value, and time value and differentiate between exchange-traded options and over-the-counter options;

c. identify the different types of options in terms of the underlying instruments;

d. compare and contrast interest rate options to forward rate agreements (FRAs);

e. explain how option payoffs are determined, and show how interest rate option payoffs differ from the payoffs of other types of options;

f. define interest rate caps and floors;

g. identify the minimum and maximum values of European options and American options;

h. explain how the lower bounds of European calls and puts are determined by constructing portfolio combinations that prevent arbitrage, and calculate an option's lower bound;

i. determine the lowest prices of European and American calls and puts based on the rules for minimum values and lower bounds;

j. describe how a portfolio (combination) of options establishes the relationship between options that differ only by exercise price;

k. explain how option prices are affected by the time to expiration of the option;

l. explain put-call parity for European options, given the payoffs on a fiduciary call and a protective put;

m. explain the relationship between American options and European options in terms of the lower bounds on option prices and the possibility of early exercise;

n. explain how cash flows on the underlying asset affect put-call parity and the lower bounds of option prices;

o. identify the directional effect of an interest rate change on an option's price and describe the impact of a change in volatility on an option's price.

Analysis of Derivatives for the CFA® Program, by Don M. Chance, Copyright © 2003 by Association for Investment Management and Research. Reprinted with permission.

1   INTRODUCTION

In Reading 69, we provided a general introduction to derivative markets. In Reading 70 we examined forward contracts, and in Reading 71 we looked at futures contracts. We noted how similar forward and futures contracts are: Both are commitments to buy an underlying asset at a fixed price at a later date. Forward contracts, however, are privately created, over-the-counter customized instruments that carry credit risk. Futures contracts are publicly traded, exchange-listed standardized instruments that effectively have no credit risk. Now we turn to options. Like forwards and futures, they are derivative instruments that provide the opportunity to buy or sell an underlying asset with a specific expiration date. But in contrast, buying an option gives the *right*, not the obligation, to buy or sell an underlying asset. And whereas forward and futures contracts involve no exchange of cash up front, options require a cash payment from the option buyer to the option seller.

Yet options contain several features common to forward and futures contracts. For one, options can be created by any two parties with any set of terms they desire. In this sense, options can be privately created, over-the-counter, customized instruments that are subject to credit risk. In addition, however, there is a large market for publicly traded, exchange-listed, standardized options, for which credit risk is essentially eliminated by the clearinghouse.

Just as we examined the pricing of forwards and futures in the last two readings, we shall examine option pricing in this reading. We shall also see that options can be created out of forward contracts, and that forward contracts can be created out of options. With some simplifying assumptions, options can be created out of futures contracts and futures contracts can be created out of options.

Finally, we note that options also exist that have a futures or forward contract as the underlying. These instruments blend some of the features of both options and forwards/futures.

As background, we discuss the definitions and characteristics of options.

2   BASIC DEFINITIONS AND ILLUSTRATIONS OF OPTIONS CONTRACTS

In Reading 69, we defined an option as a financial derivative contract that provides a party the right to buy or sell an underlying at a fixed price by a certain time in the future. The party holding the right is the option buyer; the party granting the right is the option seller. There are two types of options, a **call** and a **put.** A call is an option granting the right to buy the underlying; a put is an option granting the right to sell the underlying. With the exception of some advanced types of options, a given option contract is either a call, granting the right to buy, or a put, granting the right to sell, but not both.[1] We emphasize that this right to buy or sell is held by the option buyer, also called the long or option holder, and granted by the option seller, also called the short or option writer.

To obtain this right, the option buyer pays the seller a sum of money, commonly referred to as the **option price.** On occasion, this option price is called the **option premium** or just the **premium.** This money is paid when the option contract is initiated.

2.1 Basic Characteristics of Options

The fixed price at which the option holder can buy or sell the underlying is called the **exercise price, strike price, striking price,** or **strike.** The use of this right to buy or sell the underlying is referred to as **exercise** or **exercising the option.** Like all derivative contracts, an option has an **expiration date,** giving rise to the notion of an option's **time to expiration.** When the expiration date arrives, an option that is not exercised simply expires.

What happens at exercise depends on whether the option is a call or a put. If the buyer is exercising a call, she pays the exercise price and receives either the underlying or an equivalent cash settlement. On the opposite side of the transaction is the seller, who receives the exercise price from the buyer and delivers the underlying, or alternatively, pays an equivalent cash settlement. If the buyer is exercising a put, she delivers the stock and receives the exercise price or an equivalent cash settlement. The seller, therefore, receives the underlying and must pay the exercise price or the equivalent cash settlement.

As noted in the above paragraph, cash settlement is possible. In that case, the option holder exercising a call receives the difference between the market value of the underlying and the exercise price from the seller in cash. If the option holder exercises a put, she receives the difference between the exercise price and the market value of the underlying in cash.

There are two primary exercise styles associated with options. One type of option has **European-style exercise,** which means that the option can be exercised only on its expiration day. In some cases, expiration could occur during that day; in others, exercise can occur only when the option has expired. In either case, such an option is called a **European option.** The other style of exercise is **American-style exercise.** Such an option can be exercised on any day through the expiration day and is generally called an **American option.**[2]

Option contracts specify a designated number of units of the underlying. For exchange-listed, standardized options, the exchange establishes each term, with the exception of the price. The price is negotiated by the two parties. For an over-the-counter option, the two parties decide each of the terms through negotiation.

In an over-the-counter option—one created off of an exchange by any two parties who agree to trade—the buyer is subject to the possibility of the writer defaulting. When the buyer exercises, the writer must either deliver the stock or cash if a call, or pay for the stock or pay cash if a put. If the writer cannot do so for financial reasons, the option holder faces a credit loss. Because the option holder paid the price up front and is not required to do anything else, the seller does not face any credit risk. Thus, although credit risk is bilateral in forward contracts—the long assumes the risk of the short defaulting, and the short assumes

---

[1] Of course, a party could buy both a call and a put, thereby holding the right to buy *and* sell the underlying.

[2] It is worthwhile to be aware that these terms have nothing to do with Europe or America. Both types of options are found in Europe and America. The names are part of the folklore of options markets, and there is no definitive history to explain how they came into use.

the risk of the long defaulting—the credit risk in an option is unilateral. Only the buyer faces credit risk because only the seller can default. As we discuss later, in exchange-listed options, the clearinghouse guarantees payment to the buyer.

2.2 Some Examples of Options

Consider some call and put options on Sun Microsystems (SUNW). The date is 13 June and Sun is selling for $16.25. Exhibit 72-1 gives information on the closing prices of four options, ones expiring in July and October and ones with exercise prices of 15.00 and 17.50. The July options expire on 20 July and the October options expire on 18 October. In the parlance of the profession, these are referred to as the July 15 calls, July 17.50 calls, October 15 calls, and October 17.50 calls, with similar terminology for the puts. These particular options are American style.

EXHIBIT 72-1 Closing Prices of Selected Options on SUNW, 13 June

Exercise Price	July Calls	October Calls	July Puts	October Puts
15.00	2.35	3.30	0.90	1.85
17.50	1.00	2.15	2.15	3.20

Note: Stock price is $16.25; July options expire on 20 July; October options expire on 18 October.

Consider the July 15 call. This option permits the holder to buy SUNW at a price of $15 a share any time through 20 July. To obtain this option, one would pay a price of $2.35. Therefore, a writer received $2.35 on 13 June and must be ready to sell SUNW to the buyer for $15 during the period through 20 July. Currently, SUNW trades above $15 a share, but as we shall see in more detail later, the option holder has no reason to exercise the option right now.[3] To justify purchase of the call, the buyer must be anticipating that SUNW will increase in price before the option expires. The seller of the call must be anticipating that SUNW will not rise sufficiently in price before the option expires.

Note that the option buyer could purchase a call expiring in July but permitting the purchase of SUNW at a price of $17.50. This price is more than the $15.00 exercise price, but as a result, the option, which sells for $1.00, is considerably cheaper. The cheaper price comes from the fact that the July 17.50 call is less likely to be exercised, because the stock has a higher hurdle to clear. A buyer is not willing to pay as much and a seller is more willing to take less for an option that is less likely to be exercised.

Alternatively, the option buyer could choose to purchase an October call instead of a July call. For any exercise price, however, the October calls would be more expensive than the July calls because they allow a longer period for the stock to make the move that the buyer wants. October options are more likely to be

---

[3] The buyer paid $2.35 for the option. If he exercised it right now, he would pay $15.00 for the stock, which is worth only $16.25. Thus, he would have effectively paid $17.35 (the cost of the option of $2.35 plus the exercise price of $15) for a stock worth $16.25. Even if he had purchased the option previously at a much lower price, the current option price of $2.35 is the opportunity cost of exercising the option—that is, he can always sell the option for $2.35. Therefore, if he exercised the option, he would be throwing away the $2.35 he could receive if he sold it.

exercised than July options; therefore, a buyer would be willing to pay more and the seller would demand more for the October calls.

Suppose the buyer expects the stock price to go down. In that case, he might buy a put. Consider the October 17.50 put, which would cost the buyer $3.20. This option would allow the holder to sell SUNW at a price of $17.50 any time up through 18 October.[4] He has no reason to exercise the option right now, because it would mean he would be buying the option for $3.20 and selling a stock worth $16.25 for $17.50. In effect, the option holder would part with $19.45 (the cost of the option of $3.20 plus the value of the stock of $16.25) and obtain only $17.50.[5] The buyer of a put obviously must be anticipating that the stock will fall before the expiration day.

If he wanted a cheaper option than the October 17.50 put, he could buy the October 15 put, which would cost only $1.85 but would allow him to sell the stock for only $15.00 a share. The October 15 put is less likely to be exercised than the October 17.50, because the stock price must fall below a lower hurdle. Thus, the buyer is not willing to pay as much and the seller is willing to take less.

For either exercise price, purchase of a July put instead of an October put would be much cheaper but would allow less time for the stock to make the downward move necessary for the transaction to be worthwhile. The July put is cheaper than the October put; the buyer is not willing to pay as much and the seller is willing to take less because the option is less likely to be exercised.

In observing these option prices, we have obtained our first taste of some principles involved in pricing options.

Call options have a lower premium the higher the exercise price.
Put options have a lower premium the lower the exercise price.
Both call and put options are cheaper the shorter the time to expiration.[6]

These results should be intuitive, but later in this reading we show unequivocally why they must be true.

2.3 The Concept of Moneyness of an Option

An important concept in the study of options is the notion of an option's **moneyness,** which refers to the relationship between the price of the underlying and the exercise price.

We use the terms **in-the-money, out-of-the-money,** and **at-the-money.** We explain the concept in Exhibit 72-2 with examples from the SUNW options. Note that in-the-money options are those in which exercising the option would produce a cash inflow that exceeds the cash outflow. Thus, calls are in-the-money when the value of the underlying exceeds the exercise price. Puts are in-the-money when the exercise price exceeds the value of the underlying. In our example, there are no at-the-money SUNW options, which would require that the stock value equal the exercise price; however, an at-the-money option can effectively be viewed as an out-of-the-money option, because its exercise would not bring in more money than is paid out.

---

[4] Even if the option holder did not own the stock, he could use the option to sell the stock short.

[5] Again, even if the option were purchased in the past at a much lower price, the $3.20 current value of the option is an opportunity cost. Exercise of the option is equivalent to throwing away the opportunity cost.

[6] There is an exception to the rule that put options are cheaper the shorter the time to expiration. This statement is always true for American options but not always for European options. We explore this point later.

EXHIBIT 72-2 Moneyness of an Option

In-the-Money		Out-of-the-Money	
Option	Justification	Option	Justification
July 15 call	$16.25 > 15.00$	July 17.50 call	$16.25 < 17.50$
October 15 call	$16.25 > 15.00$	October 17.50 call	$16.25 < 17.50$
July 17.50 put	$17.50 > 16.25$	July 15 put	$15.00 < 16.25$
October 17.50 put	$17.50 > 16.25$	October 15 put	$15.00 < 16.25$

Notes: Sun Microsystems options on 13 June; stock price is 16.25. See Exhibit 72-1 for more details. There are no options with an exercise price of 16.25, so no options are at-the-money.

As explained above, *one would not necessarily exercise an in-the-money option, but one would never exercise an out-of-the-money option.*

We now move on to explore how options markets are organized.

3 THE STRUCTURE OF GLOBAL OPTIONS MARKETS

Although no one knows exactly how options first got started, contracts similar to options have been around for thousands of years. In fact, insurance is a form of an option. The insurance buyer pays the insurance writer a premium and receives a type of guarantee that covers losses. This transaction is similar to a put option, which provides coverage of a portion of losses on the underlying and is often used by holders of the underlying. The first true options markets were over-the-counter options markets in the United States in the 19th century.

3.1 Over-the-Counter Options Markets

In the United States, customized over-the-counter options markets were in existence in the early part of the 20th century and lasted well into the 1970s. An organization called the Put and Call Brokers and Dealers Association consisted of a group of firms that served as brokers and dealers. As brokers, they attempted to match buyers of options with sellers, thereby earning a commission. As dealers, they offered to take either side of the option transaction, usually laying off (hedging) the risk in another transaction. Most of these transactions were retail, meaning that the general public were their customers.

As we discuss in Section 3.2 below, the creation of the Chicago Board Options Exchange was a revolutionary event, but it effectively killed the Put and Call Brokers and Dealers Association. Subsequently, the increasing use of swaps facilitated a rebirth of the customized over-the-counter options market. Currency options, a natural extension to currency swaps, were in much demand. Later, interest rate options emerged as a natural outgrowth of interest rate swaps. Soon bond, equity, and index options were trading in a vibrant over-the-counter market. In contrast to the previous over-the-counter options market, however, the current one emerged as a largely wholesale market. Transactions are usually made with institutions and corporations and are rarely conducted directly with individuals. This market is much like the forward market described in Reading 70, with dealers offering to take either the long or short position in options and hedging that risk with transactions in other options or derivatives. There are no guarantees that the seller will perform; hence, the buyer faces credit risk. As such, option buyers must scrutinize sellers' credit risk and may require some risk reduction measures, such as collateral.

As previously noted, customized options have *all* of their terms—such as price, exercise price, time to expiration, identification of the underlying, settlement or delivery terms, size of the contract, and so on—determined by the two parties.

Like forward markets, over-the-counter options markets are essentially unregulated. In most countries, participating firms, such as banks and securities firms, are regulated by the appropriate authorities but there is usually no particular regulatory body for the over-the-counter options markets. In some countries, however, there are regulatory bodies for these markets.

Exhibit 72-3 provides information on the leading dealers in over-the-counter currency and interest rate options as determined by *Risk* magazine in its annual surveys of banks and investment banks and also end users.

EXHIBIT 72-3 *Risk* **Magazine Surveys of Banks, Investment Banks, and Corporate End Users to Determine the Top Three Dealers in Over-the-Counter Currency and Interest Rate Options**

	Respondents	
Currencies	**Banks and Investment Banks**	**Corporate End Users**
Currency Options		
$/€	UBS Warburg	Citigroup
	Citigroup/Deutsche Bank	Royal Bank of Scotland
		Deutsche Bank
$/¥	UBS Warburg	Citigroup
	Credit Suisse First Boston	JP Morgan Chase
	JP Morgan Chase/Royal Bank of Scotland	UBS Warburg
$/£	Royal Bank of Scotland	Royal Bank of Scotland
	UBS Warburg	Citigroup
	Citigroup	Hong Kong Shanghai Banking Corp.
$/SF	UBS Warburg	UBS Warburg
	Credit Suisse First Boston	Credit Suisse First Boston
	Citigroup	Citigroup
Interest Rate Options		
$	JP Morgan Chase	JP Morgan Chase
	Deutsche Bank	Citigroup
	Bank of America	Deutsche Bank/ Lehman Brothers
€	JP Morgan Chase	JP Morgan Chase
	Credit Suisse First Boston/ Morgan Stanley	Citigroup
		UBS Warburg

	Respondents	
Currencies	**Banks and Investment Banks**	**Corporate End Users**
¥	JP Morgan Chase/ Deutsche Bank	UBS Warburg
	Bank of America	Barclays Capital
		Citigroup
£	Barclays Capital	Royal Bank of Scotland
	Societe Generale Groupe	Citigroup
	Bank of America/Royal Bank of Scotland	Hong Kong Shanghai Banking Corp.
SF	UBS Warburg	UBS Warburg
	JP Morgan Chase	JP Morgan
	Credit Suisse First Boston	Goldman Sachs

Notes: $ = U.S. dollar, € = euro, ¥ = Japanese yen, £ = U.K. pound sterling, SF = Swiss franc

Source: Risk, September 2002, pp. 30–67 for Banks and Investment Banking dealer respondents, and June 2002, pp. 24–34 for Corporate End User respondents.

Results for Corporate End Users for Interest Rate Options are from *Risk,* July 2001, pp. 38–46. *Risk* omitted this category from its 2002 survey.

3.2 Exchange Listed Options Markets

As briefly noted above, the Chicago Board Options Exchange was formed in 1973. Created as an extension of the Chicago Board of Trade, it became the first organization to offer a market for standardized options. In the United States, standardized options also trade on the Amex–Nasdaq, the Philadelphia Stock Exchange, and the Pacific Stock Exchange.[7] On a worldwide basis, standardized options are widely traded on such exchanges as LIFFE (the London International Financial Futures and Options Exchange) in London, Eurex in Frankfurt, and most other foreign exchanges. Exhibit 72-4 shows the 20 largest options exchanges in the world. Note, perhaps surprisingly, that the leading options exchange is in Korea.

EXHIBIT 72-4 World's 20 Largest Options Exchanges

Exchange and Location	Volume in 2001
Korea Stock Exchange (Korea)	854,791,792
Chicago Board Options Exchange (United States)	306,667,851
MONEP (France)	285,667,686
Eurex (Germany and Switzerland)	239,016,516

---

[7] You may wonder why the New York Stock Exchange is not mentioned. Standardized options did trade on the NYSE at one time but were not successful, and the right to trade these options was sold to another exchange.

Exchange and Location	Volume in 2001
American Stock Exchange (United States)	205,103,884
Pacific Stock Exchange (United States)	102,701,752
Philadelphia Stock Exchange (United States)	101,373,433
Chicago Mercantile Exchange (United States)	95,740,352
Amsterdam Exchange (Netherlands)	66,400,654
LIFFE (United Kingdom)	54,225,652
Chicago Board of Trade (United States)	50,345,068
OM Stockholm (Sweden)	39,327,619
South African Futures Exchange (South Africa)	24,307,477
MEFF Renta Variable (Spain)	23,628,446
New York Mercantile Exchange (United States)	17,985,109
Korea Futures Exchange (Korea)	11,468,991
Italian Derivatives Exchange (Italy)	11,045,804
Osaka Securities Exchange (Japan)	6,991,908
Bourse de Montreal (Canada)	5,372,930
Hong Kong Futures Exchange (China)	4,718,880

Note: Volume given is in number of contracts.
Source: Data supplied by *Futures Industry* magazine.

As described in Reading 71 on futures, the exchange fixes all terms of standardized instruments except the price. Thus, the exchange establishes the expiration dates and exercise prices as well as the minimum price quotation unit. The exchange also determines whether the option is European or American, whether the exercise is cash settlement or delivery of the underlying, and the contract size. In the United States, an option contract on an individual stock covers 100 shares of stock. Terminology such as "one option" is often used to refer to one option contract, which is really a set of options on 100 shares of stock. Index option sizes are stated in terms of a multiplier, indicating that the contract covers a hypothetical number of shares, as though the index were an individual stock. Similar specifications apply for options on other types of underlyings.

The exchange generally allows trading in exercise prices that surround the current stock price. As the stock price moves, options with exercise prices around the new stock price are usually added. The majority of trading occurs in options that are close to being at-the-money. Options that are far in-the-money or far out-of-the-money, called **deep-in-the-money** and **deep-out-of-the-money** options, are usually not very actively traded and are often not even listed for trading.

Most exchange-listed options have fairly short-term expirations, usually the current month, the next month, and perhaps one or two other months. Most of the trading takes place for the two shortest expirations. Some exchanges list options with expirations of several years, which have come to be called LEAPS, for **long-term equity anticipatory securities.** These options are fairly actively purchased, but most investors tend to buy and hold them and do not trade them as often as they do the shorter-term options.

The exchanges also determine on which companies they will list options for trading. Although specific requirements do exist, generally the exchange will list the options of any company for which it feels the options would be actively traded. The company has no voice in the matter. Options of a company can be listed on more than one exchange in a given country.

In Reading 71, we described the manner in which futures are traded. The procedure is very similar for exchange-listed options. Some exchanges have pit trading, whereby parties meet in the pit and arrange a transaction. Some exchanges use electronic trading, in which transactions are conducted through computers. In either case, the transactions are guaranteed by the clearinghouse. In the United States, the clearinghouse is an independent company called the Options Clearing Corporation or OCC. The OCC guarantees to the buyer that the clearinghouse will step in and fulfill the obligation if the seller reneges at exercise.

When the buyer purchases the option, the premium, which one might think would go to the seller, instead goes to the clearinghouse, which maintains it in a margin account. In addition, the seller must post some margin money, which is based on a formula that reflects whether the seller has a position that hedges the risk and whether the option is in- or out-of-the-money. If the price moves against the seller, the clearinghouse will force the seller to put up additional margin money. Although defaults are rare, the clearinghouse has always been successful in paying when the seller defaults. Thus, exchange-listed options are effectively free of credit risk.

Because of the standardization of option terms and participants' general acceptance of these terms, exchange-listed options can be bought and sold at any time prior to expiration. Thus, a party who buys or sells an option can re-enter the market before the option expires and offset the position with a sale or a purchase of the identical option. From the clearinghouse's perspective, the positions cancel.

As in futures markets, traders on the options exchange are generally either market makers or brokers. Some slight technical distinctions exist between different types of market makers in different options markets, but the differences are minor and do not concern us here. Like futures traders, option market makers attempt to profit by scalping (holding positions very short term) to earn the bid–ask spread and sometimes holding positions longer, perhaps closing them overnight or leaving them open for days or more.

When an option expires, the holder decides whether or not to exercise it. When the option is expiring, there are no further gains to waiting, so in-the-money options are always exercised, assuming they are in-the-money by more than the transaction cost of buying or selling the underlying or arranging a cash settlement when exercising. Using our example of the SUNW options, if at expiration the stock is at 16, the calls with an exercise price of 15 would be exercised. Most exchange-listed stock options call for actual delivery of the stock. Thus, the seller delivers the stock and the buyer pays the seller, through the clearinghouse, $15 per share. If the exchange specifies that the contract is cash settled, the seller simply pays the buyer $1. For puts requiring delivery, the buyer tenders the stock and receives the exercise price from the seller. If the option is out-of-the-money, it simply expires unexercised and is removed from the books. If the put is cash settled, the writer pays the buyer the equivalent cash amount.

Some nonstandardized exchange-traded options exist in the United States. In an attempt to compete with the over-the-counter options market, some exchanges permit some options to be individually customized and traded on the exchange, thereby benefiting from the advantages of the clearinghouse's credit guarantee. These options are primarily available only in large sizes and tend to be traded only by large institutional investors.

Like futures markets, exchange-listed options markets are typically regulated at the federal level. In the United States, federal regulation of options markets is the responsibility of the Securities and Exchange Commission; similar regulatory structures exist in other countries.

TYPES OF OPTIONS　　4

Almost anything with a random outcome can have an option on it. Note that by using the word *anything*, we are implying that the underlying does not even need to be an asset. In this section, we shall discover the different types of options, identified by the nature of the underlying. Our focus in this book is on financial options, but it is important, nonetheless, to gain some awareness of other types of options.

4.1 Financial Options

Financial options are options in which the underlying is a financial asset, interest rate, or a currency.

4.1.1 Stock Options

Options on individual stocks, also called **equity options,** are among the most popular. Exchange-listed options are available on most widely traded stocks and an option on any stock can potentially be created on the over-the-counter market. We have already given examples of stock options in an earlier section; we now move on to index options.

4.1.2 Index Options

Stock market indices are well known, not only in the investment community but also among many individuals who are not even directly investing in the market. Because a stock index is just an artificial portfolio of stocks, it is reasonable to expect that one could create an option on a stock index. Indeed, we have already covered forward and futures contracts on stock indices; options are no more difficult in structure.

For example, consider options on the S&P 500 Index, which trade on the Chicago Board Options Exchange and have a designated index contract multiplier of 100. On 13 June of a given year, the S&P 500 closed at 1241.60. A call option with an exercise price of $1,250 expiring on 20 July was selling for $28. The option is European style and settles in cash. The underlying, the S&P 500, is treated as though it were a share of stock worth $1,241.60, which can be bought, using the call option, for $1,250 on 20 July. At expiration, if the option is in-the-money, the buyer exercises it and the writer pays the buyer the $250 contract multiplier times the difference between the index value at expiration and $1,250.

In the United States, there are also options on the Dow Jones Industrial Average, the Nasdaq, and various other indices. There are nearly always options on the best-known stock indices in most countries.

Just as there are options on stocks, there are also options on bonds.

4.1.3 Bond Options

Options on bonds, usually called **bond options,** are primarily traded in the over-the-counter markets. Options exchanges have attempted to generate interest in options on bonds, but have not been very successful. Corporate bonds are not very actively traded; most are purchased and held to expiration. Government bonds, however, are very actively traded; nevertheless, options on them have not gained widespread acceptance on options exchanges. Options exchanges generate much of their trading volume from individual investors, who have far more interest in and understanding of stocks than bonds.

Thus, bond options are found almost exclusively in the over-the-counter market and are almost always options on government bonds. Consider, for example, a U.S. Treasury bond maturing in 27 years. The bond has a coupon of 5.50 percent, a yield of 5.75 percent, and is selling for \$0.9659 per \$1 par. An over-the-counter options dealer might sell a put or call option on the bond with an exercise price of \$0.98 per \$1.00 par. The option could be European or American. Its expiration day must be significantly before the maturity date of the bond. Otherwise, as the bond approaches maturity, its price will move toward par, thereby removing much of the uncertainty in its price. The option could be specified to settle with actual delivery of the bond or with a cash settlement. The parties would also specify that the contract covered a given notional principal, expressed in terms of a face value of the underlying bond.

Continuing our example, let us assume that the contract covers \$5 million face value of bonds and is cash settled. Suppose the buyer exercises a call option when the bond price is at \$0.995. Then the option is in-the-money by \$0.995 − \$0.98 = \$0.015 per \$1 par. The seller pays the buyer 0.015(\$5,000,000) = \$75,000. If instead the contract called for delivery, the seller would deliver \$5 million face value of bonds, which would be worth \$5,000,000(\$0.995) = \$4,975,000. The buyer would pay \$5,000,000(\$0.98) = \$4,900,000. Because the option is created in the over-the-counter market, the option buyer would assume the risk of the seller defaulting.

Even though bond options are not very widely traded, another type of related option is widely used, especially by corporations. This family of options is called **interest rate options.** These are quite different from the options we have previously discussed, because the underlying is not a particular financial instrument.

4.1.4 Interest Rate Options

In Reading 70, we devoted considerable effort to understanding the Eurodollar spot market and forward contracts on the Eurodollar rate or LIBOR, called FRAs. In this reading, we cover options on LIBOR. Although these are not the only interest rate options, their characteristics are sufficiently general to capture most of what we need to know about options on other interest rates. First recall that a Eurodollar is a dollar deposited outside of the United States. The primary Eurodollar rate is LIBOR, and it is considered the best measure of an interest rate paid in dollars on a nongovernmental borrower. These Eurodollars represent dollar-denominated time deposits issued by banks in London borrowing from other banks in London.

Before looking at the characteristics of interest rate options, let us set the perspective by recalling that FRAs are forward contracts that pay off based on the difference between the underlying rate and the fixed rate embedded in the contract when it is constructed. For example, consider a 3 × 9 FRA. This contract expires in three months. The underlying rate is six-month LIBOR. Hence, when the contract is constructed, the underlying Eurodollar instrument matures in nine months. *When the contract expires, the payoff is made immediately,* but the rate on which it is based, 180-day LIBOR, is set in the spot market, where it is assumed that interest will be paid 180 days later. Hence, the payoff on an FRA is discounted by the spot rate on 180-day LIBOR to give a present value for the payoff as of the expiration date.

Just as an FRA is a forward contract in which the underlying is an interest rate, an **interest rate option** is an option in which the underlying is an interest rate. Instead of an exercise price, it has an **exercise rate** (or **strike rate**), which is expressed on an order of magnitude of an interest rate. At expiration, the option payoff is based on the difference between the underlying rate in the market and the exercise rate. Whereas an FRA is a *commitment* to make one interest payment and receive another at a future date, an interest rate option is the *right* to make one interest payment and receive another. And just as there are call and put options, there is also an **interest rate call** and an **interest rate put.**

An interest rate call is an option in which the holder has the right to make a known interest payment and receive an unknown interest payment. The underlying is the unknown interest rate. If the unknown underlying rate turns out to be higher than the exercise rate at expiration, the option is in-the-money and is exercised; otherwise, the option simply expires. *An interest rate put is an option in which the holder has the right to make an unknown interest payment and receive a known interest payment.* If the unknown underlying rate turns out to be lower than the exercise rate at expiration, the option is in-the-money and is exercised; otherwise, the option simply expires. All interest rate option contracts have a specified size, which, as in FRAs, is called the notional principal. An interest rate option can be European or American style, but most tend to be European style. Interest rate options are settled in cash.

As with FRAs, these options are offered for purchase and sale by dealers, which are financial institutions, usually the same ones who offer FRAs. These dealers quote rates for options of various exercise prices and expirations. When a dealer takes an option position, it usually then offsets the risk with other transactions, often Eurodollar futures.

To use the same example we used in introducing FRAs, consider options expiring in 90 days on 180-day LIBOR. The option buyer specifies whatever exercise rate he desires. Let us say he chooses an exercise rate of 5.5 percent and a notional principal of $10 million.

Now let us move to the expiration day. Suppose that 180-day LIBOR is 6 percent. Then the call option is in-the-money. The payoff to the holder of the option is

$$(\$10,000,000)(0.06 - 0.055)\left(\frac{180}{360}\right) = \$25,000$$

This money is not paid at expiration, however; it is paid 180 days later. There is no reason why the payoff could not be made at expiration, as is done with an FRA. The delay of payment associated with interest rate options actually makes more sense, because these instruments are commonly used to hedge floating-rate loans in which the rate is set on a given day but the interest is paid later. We shall see examples of the convenience of this type of structure in Reading 74.

Note that the difference between the underlying rate and the exercise rate is multiplied by 180/360 to reflect the fact that the rate quoted is a 180-day rate but is stated as an annual rate. Also, the interest calculation is multiplied by the notional principal.

In general, the payoff of an interest rate call is

$$(\text{Notional Principal})\,\text{Max}\left(0,\text{Underlying rate at expiration} - \text{Exercise rate}\right)\left(\frac{\text{Days in underlying rate}}{360}\right) \qquad \textbf{(72-1)}$$

The expression Max(0,Underlying rate at expiration − Exercise rate) is similar to a form that we shall commonly see throughout this reading for all options. The payoff of a call option at expiration is based on the maximum of zero or the underlying minus the exercise rate. If the option expires out-of-the-money, then "Underlying rate at expiration − Exercise rate" is negative; consequently, zero is greater. Thus, the option expires with no value. If the option expires in-the-money, "Underlying rate at expiration − Exercise rate" is positive. Thus, the option expires worth this difference (multiplied by the notional principal and the Days/360 adjustment). The expression "Days in underlying rate," which we used in Reading 70, refers to the fact that the rate is specified as the rate on an instrument of a specific number of days to maturity, such as a 90-day or 180-day rate, thereby requiring that we multiply by 90/360 or 180/360 or some similar adjustment.

For an interest rate put option, the general formula is

$$\text{(Notional Principal)}\,\text{Max}(0,\text{Exercise rate} - \text{Underlying rate at expiration})\left(\frac{\text{Days in underlying rate}}{360}\right) \tag{72-2}$$

For an exercise rate of 5.5 percent and an underlying rate at expiration of 6 percent, an interest rate put expires out-of-the-money. Only if the underlying rate is less than the exercise rate does the put option expire in-the-money.

As noted above, borrowers often use interest rate call options to hedge the risk of rising rates on floating-rate loans. Lenders often use interest rate put options to hedge the risk of falling rates on floating-rate loans. The form we have seen here, in which the option expires with a single payoff, is not the more commonly used variety of interest rate option. Floating-rate loans usually involve multiple interest payments. Each of those payments is set on a given date. To hedge the risk of interest rates increasing, the borrower would need options expiring on each rate reset date. Thus, the borrower would require a combination of interest rate call options. Likewise, a lender needing to hedge the risk of falling rates on a multiple-payment floating-rate loan would need a combination of interest rate put options.

A combination of interest rate calls is referred to as an **interest rate cap** or sometimes just a **cap.** A combination of interest rate puts is called an **interest rate floor** or sometimes just a **floor.**[8] Specifically, *an interest rate cap is a series of call options on an interest rate, with each option expiring at the date on which the floating loan rate will be reset, and with each option having the same exercise rate.*[9] Each option is independent of the others; thus, exercise of one option does not affect the right to exercise any of the others. Each component call option is called a **caplet.** *An interest rate floor is a series of put options on an interest rate, with each option expiring at the date on which the floating loan rate will be reset, and with each option having the same exercise rate.* Each component put option is called a **floorlet.** The price of an interest rate cap or floor is the sum of the prices of the options that make up the cap or floor.

A special combination of caps and floors is called an **interest rate collar.** *An interest rate collar is a combination of a long cap and a short floor or a short cap and a long floor.* Consider a borrower in a floating rate loan who wants to hedge the risk of rising interest rates but is concerned about the requirement that this hedge must have a cash outlay up front: the option premium. A collar, which adds a short floor to a long cap, is a way of reducing and even eliminating the up-front cost of the cap. The sale of the floor brings in cash that reduces the cost of the cap. It is possible to set the exercise rates such that the price received for the sale of the floor precisely offsets the price paid for the cap, thereby completely eliminating the up-front cost. This transaction is sometimes called a **zero-cost collar.** The term is a bit misleading, however, and brings to mind the importance of noting the true cost of a collar. Although the cap allows the borrower to be paid from the call options when rates are high, the sale of the floor requires the borrower to pay the counterparty when rates are low. Thus, the cost of protection against rising rates is the loss of the advantage of falling rates. Caps, floors, and

---

[8] It is possible to construct caps and floors with options on any other type of underlying, but they are very often used when the underlying is an interest rate.

[9] Technically, each option need not have the same exercise rate, but they generally do.

collars are popular instruments in the interest rate markets. We shall explore strategies using them in Reading 74.

Although interest rate options are primarily written on such rates as LIBOR, Euribor, and Euroyen, the underlying can be any interest rate.

4.1.5 Currency Options

As we noted in Reading 70, the currency forward market is quite large. The same is true for the currency options market. A **currency option** allows the holder to buy (if a call) or sell (if a put) an underlying currency at a fixed exercise rate, expressed as an exchange rate. Many companies, knowing that they will need to convert a currency X at a future date into a currency Y, will buy a call option on currency Y specified in terms of currency X. For example, say that a U.S. company will be needing €50 million for an expansion project in three months. Thus, it will be buying euros and is exposed to the risk of the euro rising against the dollar. Even though it has that concern, it would also like to benefit if the euro weakens against the dollar. Thus, it might buy a call option on the euro. Let us say it specifies an exercise rate of $0.90. So it pays cash up front for the right to buy €50 million at a rate of $0.90 per euro. If the option expires with the euro above $0.90, it can buy euros at $0.90 and avoid any additional cost over $0.90. If the option expires with the euro below $0.90, it does not exercise the option and buys euros at the market rate.

Note closely these two cases:

Euro expires above $0.90
   Company buys €50 million at $0.90

Euro expires at or below $0.90
   Company buys €50 million at the market rate

These outcomes can also be viewed in the following manner:

Dollar expires below €1.1111, that is, €1 > $0.90
   Company sells $45 million (€50 million × $0.90) at €1.1111, equivalent to buying €50 million

Dollar expires above €1.1111, that is, €1 < $0.90
   Company sells sufficient dollars to buy €50 million at the market rate

This transaction looks more like a put in which the underlying is the dollar and the exercise rate is expressed as €1.1111. Thus, the call on the euro can be viewed as a put on the dollar. Specifically, a call to buy €50 million at an exercise price of $0.90 is also a put to sell €50 million × $0.90 = $45 million at an exercise price of 1/$0.90, or €1.1111.

Most foreign currency options activity occurs on the customized over-the-counter markets. Some exchange-listed currency options trade on a few exchanges, but activity is fairly low.

4.2 Options on Futures

In Reading 70 we covered futures markets. One of the important innovations of futures markets is options on futures. These contracts originated in the United States as a result of a regulatory structure that separated exchange-listed options and futures markets. The former are regulated by the Securities and Exchange Commission, and the latter are regulated by the Commodity Futures Trading

Commission (CFTC). SEC regulations forbid the trading of options side by side with their underlying instruments. Options on stocks trade on one exchange, and the underlying trades on another or on Nasdaq.

The futures exchanges got the idea that they could offer options in which the underlying is a futures contract; no such prohibitions for side-by-side trading existed under CFTC rules. As a result, the futures exchanges were able to add an attractive instrument to their product lines. The side-by-side trading of the option and its underlying futures made for excellent arbitrage linkages between these instruments. Moreover, some of the options on futures are designed to expire on the same day the underlying futures expires. Thus, the options on the futures are effectively options on the spot asset that underlies the futures.

A call option on a futures gives the holder the right to enter into a long futures contract at a fixed futures price. A put option on a futures gives the holder the right to enter into a short futures contract at a fixed futures price. The fixed futures price is, of course, the exercise price. Consider an option on the Eurodollar futures contract trading at the Chicago Mercantile Exchange. On 13 June of a particular year, an option expiring on 13 July was based on the July Eurodollar futures contract. That futures contract expires on 16 July, a few days after the option expires.[10] The call option with exercise price of 95.75 had a price of $4.60. The underlying futures price was 96.21. Recall that this price is the IMM index value, which means that the price is based on a discount rate of $100 - 96.21 = 3.79$. The contract size is $1 million.

The buyer of this call option on a futures would pay $0.046(\$1,000,000) = \$46,000$ and would obtain the right to buy the July futures contract at a price of 95.75. Thus, at that time, the option was in the money by $96.21 - 95.75 = 0.46$ per $100 face value. Suppose that when the option expires, the futures price is 96.00. Then the holder of the call would exercise it and obtain a long futures position at a price of 95.75. The price of the underlying futures is 96.00, so the margin account is immediately marked to market with a credit of 0.25 or $625.[11] The party on the short side of the contract is immediately set up with a short futures contract at the price of 95.75. That party will be charged the $625 gain that the long made. If the option is a put, exercise of it establishes a short position. The exchange assigns the put writer a long futures position.

4.3 Commodity Options

Options in which the asset underlying the futures is a commodity, such as oil, gold, wheat, or soybeans, are also widely traded. There are exchange-traded as well as over-the-counter versions. Over-the-counter options on oil are widely used.

Our focus in this book is on financial instruments so we will not spend any time on commodity options, but readers should be aware of the existence and use of these instruments by companies whose business involves the buying and selling of these commodities.

---

[10] Some options on futures expire a month or so before the futures expires. Others expire very close to, if not at, the futures expiration.

[11] If the contract is in-the-money by $96 - 95.75 = 0.25$ per $100 par, it is in-the-money by $0.25/100 = 0.0025$, or 0.25 percent of the face value. Because the face value is $1 million, the contract is in the money by $(0.0025)(90/360)(\$1,000,000) = \$625$. (Note the adjustment by 90/360.) Another way to look at this calculation is that the futures price at 95.75 is $1 - (0.0425)(90/360) = \$0.989375$ per $1 par, or $989,375. At 96, the futures price is $1 - 0.04(90/360) = \$0.99$ per $1 par or $990,000. The difference is $625. So, exercising this option is like entering into a futures contract at a price of $989,375 and having the price immediately go to $990,000, a gain of $625. The call holder must deposit money to meet the Eurodollar futures margin, but the exercise of the option gives him $625. In other words, assuming he meets the minimum initial margin requirement, he is immediately credited with $625 more.

4.4 Other Types of Options

As derivative markets develop, options (and even some other types of derivatives) have begun to emerge on such underlyings as electricity, various sources of energy, and even weather. These instruments are almost exclusively customized over-the-counter instruments. Perhaps the most notable feature of these instruments is how the underlyings are often instruments that cannot actually be held. For example, electricity is not considered a storable asset because it is produced and almost immediately consumed, but it is nonetheless an asset and certainly has a volatile price. Consequently, it is ideally suited for options and other derivatives trading.

Consider weather. It is hardly an asset at all but simply a random factor that exerts an enormous influence on economic activity. The need to hedge against and speculate on the weather has created a market in which measures of weather activity, such as economic losses from storms or average temperature or rainfall, are structured into a derivative instrument. Option versions of these derivatives are growing in importance and use. For example, consider a company that generates considerable revenue from outdoor summer activities, provided that it does not rain. Obviously a certain amount of rain will occur, but the more rain, the greater the losses for the company. It could buy a call option on the amount of rainfall with the exercise price stated as a quantity of rainfall. If actual rainfall exceeds the exercise price, the company exercises the option and receives an amount of money related to the excess of the rainfall amount over the exercise price.

Another type of option, which is not at all new but is increasingly recognized in practice, is the real option. A real option is an option associated with the flexibility inherent in capital investment projects. For example, companies may invest in new projects that have the option to defer the full investment, expand or contract the project at a later date, or even terminate the project. In fact, most capital investment projects have numerous elements of flexibility that can be viewed as options. Of course, these options do not trade in markets the same way as financial and commodity options, and they must be evaluated much more carefully. They are, nonetheless, options and thus have the potential for generating enormous value.

Again, our emphasis is on financial options, but readers should be aware of the growing role of these other types of options in our economy. Investors who buy shares in companies that have real options are, in effect, buying real options. In addition, commodity and other types of options are sometimes found in investment portfolios in the form of "alternative investments" and can provide significant diversification benefits.

To this point, we have examined characteristics of options markets and contracts. Now we move forward to the all-important topic of how options are priced.

PRINCIPLES OF OPTION PRICING   5

In Readings 70 and 71, we discussed the pricing and valuation of forward and futures contracts. Recall that the value of a contract is what someone must pay to buy into it or what someone would receive to sell out of it. A forward or futures contract has zero value at the start of the contract, but the value turns positive or negative as prices or rates change. A contract that has positive value to one party and negative value to the counterparty can turn around and have negative value to the former and positive value to the latter as prices or rates change. The forward or futures price is the price that the parties agree will be paid on the future date to buy and sell the underlying.

With options, these concepts are different. An option has a positive value at the start. The buyer must pay money and the seller receives money to initiate the contract. Prior to expiration, the option always has positive value to the buyer and negative value to the seller. In a forward or futures contract, the two parties agree on the fixed price the buyer will pay the seller. This fixed price is set such that the buyer and seller do not exchange any money. The corresponding fixed price at which a call holder can buy the underlying or a put holder can sell the underlying is the exercise price. It, too, is negotiated between buyer and seller but still results in the buyer paying the seller money up front in the form of an option premium or price.[12]

Thus, what we called the forward or futures price corresponds more to the exercise price of an option. The option price *is* the option value: With a few exceptions that will be clearly noted, in this reading we do not distinguish between the option price and value.

In this section of the reading, we examine the principles of option pricing. These principles are characteristics of option prices that are governed by the rationality of investors. These principles alone do not allow us to calculate the option price. We do that in Section 6.

Before we begin, it is important to remind the reader that we assume all participants in the market behave in a rational manner such that they do not throw away money and that they take advantage of arbitrage opportunities. As such, we assume that markets are sufficiently competitive that no arbitrage opportunities exist.

Let us start by developing the notation, which is very similar to what we have used previously. Note that time 0 is today and time T is the expiration.

S_0, S_T = price of the underlying asset at time 0 (today) and time T (expiration)

X = exercise price

r = risk-free rate

T = time to expiration, equal to number of days to expiration divided by 365

c_0, c_T = price of European call today and at expiration

C_0, C_T = price of American call today and at expiration

p_0, p_T = price of European put today and at expiration

P_0, P_T = price of American put today and at expiration

On occasion, we will introduce some variations of the above as well as some new notation. For example, we start off with no cash flows on the underlying, but we shall discuss the effects of cash flows on the underlying in Section 5.7.

5.1 Payoff Values

The easiest time to determine an option's value is at expiration. At that point, there is no future. Only the present matters. An option's value at expiration is called its **payoff**. We introduced this material briefly in our basic descriptions of types of options; now we cover it in more depth.

At expiration, a call option is worth either zero or the difference between the underlying price and the exercise price, whichever is greater:

$$c_T = \text{Max}(0, S_T - X)$$
$$C_T = \text{Max}(0, S_T - X)$$

(72-3)

Note that at expiration, a European option and an American option have the same payoff because they are equivalent instruments at that point.

---

[12] For a call, there is no finite exercise price that drives the option price to zero. For a put, the unrealistic example of a zero exercise price would make the put price be zero.

The expression $\text{Max}(0, S_T - X)$ means to take the greater of zero or $S_T - X$. Suppose the underlying price exceeds the exercise price, $S_T > X$. In this case, the option is expiring in-the-money and the option is worth $S_T - X$. Suppose that at the instant of expiration, it is possible to buy the option for less than $S_T - X$. Then one could buy the option, immediately exercise it, and immediately sell the underlying. Doing so would cost c_T (or C_T) for the option and X to buy the underlying but would bring in S_T for the sale of the underlying. If c_T (or C_T) $< S_T - X$, this transaction would net an immediate risk-free profit. The collective actions of all investors doing this would force the option price up to $S_T - X$. The price could not go higher than $S_T - X$, because all that the option holder would end up with an instant later when the option expires is $S_T - X$. If $S_T < X$, meaning that the call is expiring out-of-the-money, the formula says the option should be worth zero. It cannot sell for less than zero because that would mean that the option seller would have to pay the option buyer. A buyer would not pay more than zero, because the option will expire an instant later with no value.

At expiration, a put option is worth either zero or the difference between the exercise price and the underlying price, whichever is greater:

$$p_T = \text{Max}(0, X - S_T)$$
$$P_T = \text{Max}(0, X - S_T)$$

(72-4)

Suppose $S_T < X$, meaning that the put is expiring in-the-money. At the instant of expiration, suppose the put is selling for less than $X - S_T$. Then an investor buys the put for p_T (or P_T) and the underlying for S_T and exercises the put, receiving X. If p_T (or P_T) $< X - S_T$, this transaction will net an immediate risk-free profit. The combined actions of participants doing this will force the put price up to $X - S_T$. It cannot go any higher, because the put buyer will end up an instant later with only $X - S_T$ and would not pay more than this. If $S_T > X$, meaning that the put is expiring out-of the-money, it is worth zero. It cannot be worth less than zero because the option seller would have to pay the option buyer. It cannot be worth more than zero because the buyer would not pay for a position that, an instant later, will be worth nothing.

These important results are summarized along with an example in Exhibit 72-5. The payoff diagrams for the short positions are also shown and are obtained as the negative of the long positions. For the special case of $S_T = X$, meaning that both call and put are expiring at-the-money, we can effectively treat the option as out-of-the-money because it is worth zero at expiration.

The value $\text{Max}(0, S_T - X)$ for calls or $\text{Max}(0, X - S_T)$ for puts is also called the option's intrinsic value or exercise value. We shall use the former terminology. Intrinsic value is what the option is worth to exercise it based on current conditions. In this section, we have talked only about the option at expiration. Prior to expiration, an option will normally sell for more than its intrinsic value.[13] The difference between the market price of the option and its intrinsic value is called its time value or speculative value. We shall use the former terminology. The time value reflects the potential for the option's intrinsic value at expiration to be greater than its current intrinsic value. At expiration, of course, the time value is zero.

There is no question that everyone agrees on the option's intrinsic value; after all, it is based on the current stock price and exercise price. It is the time value that we have more difficulty estimating. So remembering that Option price = Intrinsic value + Time value, let us move forward and attempt to determine the value of an option today, prior to expiration.

---

[13] We shall later see an exception to this statement for European puts, but for now take it as the truth.

EXHIBIT 72-5 Option Values at Expiration (Payoffs)

Option	Value	Example (X = 50)	
		$S_T = 52$	$S_T = 48$
European call	$c_T = \text{Max}(0, S_T - X)$	$c_T = \text{Max}(0, 52 - 50) = 2$	$c_T = \text{Max}(0, 48 - 50) = 0$
American call	$C_T = \text{Max}(0, S_T - X)$	$C_T = \text{Max}(0, 52 - 50) = 2$	$C_T = \text{Max}(0, 48 - 50) = 0$
European put	$p_T = \text{Max}(0, X - S_T)$	$p_T = \text{Max}(0, 50 - 52) = 0$	$p_T = \text{Max}(0, 50 - 48) = 2$
American put	$P_T = \text{Max}(0, X - S_T)$	$P_T = \text{Max}(0, 50 - 52) = 0$	$P_T = \text{Max}(0, 50 - 48) = 2$

Notes: Results for the European and American calls correspond to Graph A. Results for Graph B are the negative of Graph A. Results for the European and American puts correspond to Graph C, and results for Graph D are the negative of Graph C.

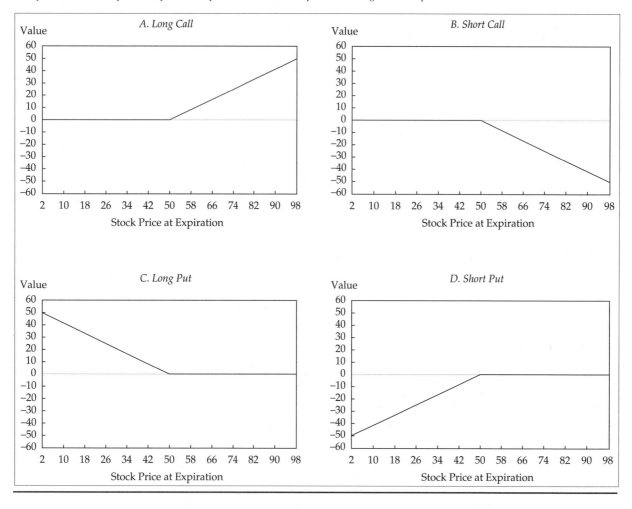

Practice Problem 1

For Parts A through E, determine the payoffs of calls and puts under the conditions given.

A. The underlying is a stock index and is at 5,601.19 when the options expire. The multiplier is 500. The exercise price is
  i. 5,500
  ii. 6,000

B. The underlying is a bond and is at $1.035 per $1 par when the options expire. The contract is on $100,000 face value of bonds. The exercise price is
  i. $1.00
  ii. $1.05

C. The underlying is a 90-day interest rate and is at 9 percent when the options expire. The notional principal is $50 million. The exercise rate is
  i. 8 percent
  ii. 10.5 percent

D. The underlying is the Swiss franc and is at $0.775 when the options expire. The options are on SF500,000. The exercise price is
  i. $0.75
  ii. $0.81

E. The underlying is a futures contract and is at 110.5 when the options expire. The options are on a futures contract covering $1 million of the underlying. These prices are percentages of par. The exercise price is
  i. 110
  ii. 115

For Parts F and G, determine the payoffs of the strategies indicated and describe the payoff graph.

F. The underlying is a stock priced at $40. A call option with an exercise price of $40 is selling for $7. You buy the stock and sell the call. At expiration, the stock price is
  i. $52
  ii. $38

G. The underlying is a stock priced at $60. A put option with an exercise price of $60 is priced at $5. You buy the stock and buy the put. At expiration, the stock price is
  i. $68
  ii. $50

SOLUTIONS

A. **i.** Calls: $\text{Max}(0,5601.19 - 5500) \times 500 = 50{,}595$
      Puts: $\text{Max}(0,5500 - 5601.19) \times 500 = 0$
  ii. Calls: $\text{Max}(0,5601.19 - 6000) \times 500 = 0$
      Puts: $\text{Max}(0,6000 - 5601.19) \times 500 = 199{,}405$

B. **i.** Calls: $\text{Max}(0,1.035 - 1.00) \times \$100{,}000 = \$3{,}500$
      Puts: $\text{Max}(0,1.00 - 1.035) \times \$100{,}000 = \$0$
  ii. Calls: $\text{Max}(0,1.035 - 1.05) \times \$100{,}000 = \$0$
      Puts: $\text{Max}(0,1.05 - 1.035) \times \$100{,}000 = \$1{,}500$

C. **i.** Calls: $\text{Max}(0, 0.09 - 0.08) \times (90/360) \times \$50{,}000{,}000 = \$125{,}000$
　　　Puts: $\text{Max}(0, 0.08 - 0.09) \times (90/360) \times \$50{,}000{,}000 = \$0$
　　ii. Calls: $\text{Max}(0, 0.09 - 0.105) \times (90/360) \times \$50{,}000{,}000 = \$0$
　　　Puts: $\text{Max}(0, 0.105 - 0.09) \times (90/360) \times \$50{,}000{,}000 = \$187{,}500$

D. **i.** Calls: $\text{Max}(0, 0.775 - 0.75) \times \text{SF}500{,}000 = \$12{,}500$
　　　Puts: $\text{Max}(0, 0.75 - 0.775) \times \text{SF}500{,}000 = \$0$
　　ii. Calls: $\text{Max}(0, 0.775 - 0.81) \times \text{SF}500{,}000 = \$0$
　　　Puts: $\text{Max}(0, 0.81 - 0.775) \times \text{SF}500{,}000 = \$17{,}500$

E. **i.** Calls: $\text{Max}(0, 110.5 - 110) \times (1/100) \times \$1{,}000{,}000 = \$5{,}000$
　　　Puts: $\text{Max}(0, 110 - 110.5) \times (1/100) \times \$1{,}000{,}000 = \$0$
　　ii. Calls: $\text{Max}(0, 110.5 - 115) \times (1/100) \times \$1{,}000{,}000 = \$0$
　　　Puts: $\text{Max}(0, 115 - 110.5) \times (1/100) \times \$1{,}000{,}000 = \$45{,}000$

F. **i.** $52 - \text{Max}(0, 52 - 40) = 40$
　　ii. $38 - \text{Max}(0, 38 - 40) = 38$

For any value of the stock price at expiration of 40 or above, the payoff is constant at 40. For stock price values below 40 at expiration, the payoff declines with the stock price. The graph would look similar to the short put in Panel D of Exhibit 72-5. This strategy is known as a covered call and is discussed in Reading 74.

G. **i.** $68 + \text{Max}(0, 60 - 68) = 68$
　　ii. $50 + \text{Max}(0, 60 - 50) = 60$

For any value of the stock price at expiration of 60 or below, the payoff is constant at 60. For stock price values above 60 at expiration, the payoff increases with the stock price at expiration. The graph will look similar to the long call in Panel A of Exhibit 72-5. This strategy is known as a protective put and is covered later in this reading and in Reading 74.

5.2 Boundary Conditions

We start by examining some simple results that establish minimum and maximum values for options prior to expiration.

5.2.1 Minimum and Maximum Values

The first and perhaps most obvious result is one we have already alluded to: *The minimum value of any option is zero.* We state this formally as

$$c_0 \geq 0, C_0 \geq 0$$
$$p_0 \geq 0, P_0 \geq 0$$

(72-5)

No option can sell for less than zero, for in that case the writer would have to pay the buyer.

　　Now consider the maximum value of an option. It differs somewhat depending on whether the option is a call or a put and whether it is European or American. *The maximum value of a call is the current value of the underlying:*

$$c_0 \leq S_0, C_0 \leq S_0$$

(72-6)

A call is a means of buying the underlying. It would not make sense to pay more for the right to buy the underlying than the value of the underlying itself.

For a put, it makes a difference whether the put is European or American. One way to see the maximum value for puts is to consider the best possible outcome for the put holder. The best outcome is that the underlying goes to a value of zero. Then the put holder could sell a worthless asset for X. For an American put, the holder could sell it immediately and capture a value of X. For a European put, the holder would have to wait until expiration; consequently, we must discount X from the expiration day to the present. Thus, *the maximum value of a European put is the present value of the exercise price. The maximum value of an American put is the exercise price,*

$$p_0 \le X/(1 + r)^T, P_0 \le X \tag{72-7}$$

where r is the risk-free interest rate and T is the time to expiration. These results for the maximums and minimums for calls and puts are summarized in Exhibit 72-6, which also includes a numerical example.

EXHIBIT 72-6 Minimum and Maximum Values of Options

Option	Minimum Value	Maximum Value	Example ($S_0 = 52$, $X = 50$, $r = 5\%$, $T = 1/2$ year)
European call	$c_0 \ge 0$	$c_0 \le S_0$	$0 \le c_0 \le 52$
American call	$C_0 \ge 0$	$C_0 \le S_0$	$0 \le C_0 \le 52$
European put	$p_0 \ge 0$	$p_0 \le X/(1 + r)^T$	$0 \le p_0 \le 48.80 \ [48.80 = 50/(1.05)^{0.5}]$
American put	$P_0 \ge 0$	$P_0 \le X$	$0 \le P_0 \le 50$

5.2.2 Lower Bounds

The results we established in Section 5.2.1 do not put much in the way of restrictions on the option price. They tell us that the price is somewhere between zero and the maximum, which is either the underlying price, the exercise price, or the present value of the exercise price—a fairly wide range of possibilities. Fortunately, we can tighten the range up a little on the low side: We can establish a **lower bound** on the option price.

For American options, which are exercisable immediately, we can state that the lower bound of an American option price is its current intrinsic value:[14]

$$C_0 \ge Max(0, S_0 - X)$$
$$P_0 \ge Max(0, X - S_0) \tag{72-8}$$

The reason these results hold today is the same reason we have already shown for why they must hold at expiration. If the option is in-the-money and is selling for less than its intrinsic value, it can be bought and exercised to net an immediate

---

[14] Normally we have italicized sentences containing important results. This one, however, is a little different: We are stating it temporarily. We shall soon show that we can override one of these results with a lower bound that is higher and, therefore, is a better lower bound.

risk-free profit.[15] The collective actions of market participants doing this will force the American option price up to at least the intrinsic value.

Unfortunately, we cannot make such a statement about European options— but we can show that the lower bound is either zero or the current underlying price minus the present value of the exercise price, whichever is greater. They cannot be exercised early; thus, there is no way for market participants to exercise an option selling for too little with respect to its intrinsic value. Fortunately, however, there is a way to establish a lower bound for European options. We can combine options with risk-free bonds and the underlying in such a way that a lower bound for the option price emerges.

First, we need the ability to buy and sell a risk-free bond with a face value equal to the exercise price and current value equal to the present value of the exercise price. This procedure is simple but perhaps not obvious. If the exercise price is X (say, 100), we buy a bond with a face value of X (100) maturing on the option expiration day. The current value of that bond is the present value of X, which is $X/(1 + r)^T$. So we buy the bond today for $X/(1 + r)^T$ and hold it until it matures on the option expiration day, at which time it will pay off X. We assume that we can buy or sell (issue) this type of bond. Note that this transaction involves borrowing or lending an amount of money equal to the present value of the exercise price with repayment of the full exercise price.

Exhibit 72-7 illustrates the construction of a special combination of instruments. We buy the European call and the risk-free bond and sell short the underlying asset. Recall that short selling involves borrowing the asset and selling it. At expiration, we shall buy back the asset. In order to illustrate the logic behind the lower bound for a European call in the simplest way, we assume that we can sell short without any restrictions.

EXHIBIT 72-7 A Lower Bound Combination for European Calls

Transaction	Current Value	Value at Expiration	
		$S_T \leq X$	$S_T > X$
Buy call	c_0	0	$S_T - X$
Sell short underlying	$-S_0$	$-S_T$	$-S_T$
Buy bond	$X/(1 + r)^T$	X	X
Total	$c_0 - S_0 + X/(1 + r)^T$	$X - S_T \geq 0$	0

In Exhibit 72-7 the two right-hand columns contain the value of each instrument when the option expires. The rightmost column is the case of the call expiring in-the-money, in which case it is worth $S_T - X$. In the other column, the out-of-the-money case, the call is worth zero. The underlying is worth $-S_T$ (the negative of its current value) in either case, reflecting the fact that we buy it back to cover the short position. The bond is worth X in both cases. The sum of all the positions is positive when the option expires out-of-the-money and zero when the option

---

[15] Consider, for example, an in-the-money call selling for less than $S_0 - X$. One can buy the call for C_0, exercise it, paying X, and sell the underlying netting a gain of $S_0 - X - C_0$. This value is positive and represents an immediate risk-free gain. If the option is an in-the-money put selling for less than $X - S_0$, one can buy the put for P_0, buy the underlying for S_0, and exercise the put to receive X, thereby netting an immediate risk-free gain of $X - S_0 - P_0$.

expires in-the-money. Therefore, in no case does this combination of instruments have a negative value. That means that we never have to pay out any money at expiration. We are guaranteed at least no loss at expiration and possibly something positive.

If there is a possibility of a positive outcome from the combination and if we know we shall never have to pay anything out from holding a combination of instruments, the cost of that combination must be positive—it must cost us something to enter into the position. We cannot take in money to enter into the position. In that case, we would be receiving money up front and never having to pay anything out. The cost of entering the position is shown in the second column, labeled the "Current Value." Because that value must be positive, we therefore require that $c_0 - S_0 + X/(1 + r)^T \geq 0$. Rearranging this equation, we obtain $c_0 \geq S_0 - X/(1 + r)^T$. Now we have a statement about the minimum value of the option, which can serve as a lower bound. This result is solid, because if the call is selling for less than $S_0 - X/(1 + r)^T$, an investor can buy the call, sell short the underlying, and buy the bond. Doing so would bring in money up front and, as we see in Exhibit 72-7, an investor would not have to pay out any money at expiration and might even get a little more money. Because other investors would do the same, the call price would be forced up until it is at least $S_0 - X/(1 + r)^T$.

But we can improve on this result. Suppose $S_0 - X/(1 + r)^T$ is negative. Then we are stating that the call price is greater than a negative number. But we already know that the call price cannot be negative. So we can now say that

$$c_0 \geq \text{Max}[0, S_0 - X/(1 + r)^T]$$

In other words, *the lower bound on a European call price is either zero or the underlying price minus the present value of the exercise price, whichever is greater.* Notice how this lower bound differs from the minimum value for the American call, $\text{Max}(0, S_0 - X)$. For the European call, we must wait to pay the exercise price and obtain the underlying. Therefore, the expression contains the current underlying value—the present value of its future value—as well as the present value of the exercise price. For the American call, we do not have to wait until expiration; therefore, the expression reflects the potential to immediately receive the underlying price minus the exercise price. We shall have more to say, however, about the relationship between these two values.

To illustrate the lower bound, let $X = 50$, $r = 0.05$, and $T = 0.5$. If the current underlying price is 45, then the lower bound for the European call is

$$\text{Max}[0, 45 - 50/(1.05)^{0.5}] = \text{Max}(0, 45 - 48.80) = \text{Max}(0, -3.80) = 0$$

All this calculation tells us is that the call must be worth no less than zero, which we already knew. If the current underlying price is 54, however, the lower bound for the European call is

$$\text{Max}(0, 54 - 48.80) = \text{Max}(0, 5.20) = 5.20$$

which tells us that the call must be worth no less than 5.20. With European puts, we can also see that the lower bound differs from the lower bound on American puts in this same use of the present value of the exercise price.

EXHIBIT 72-8 A Lower Bound Combination for European Puts

		Value at Expiration	
Transaction	Current Value	$S_T < X$	$S_T \geq X$
Buy put	p_0	$X - S_T$	0
Buy underlying	S_0	S_T	S_T
Issue bond	$-X/(1 + r)^T$	$-X$	$-X$
Total	$p_0 + S_0 - X/(1 + r)^T$	0	$S_T - X \geq 0$

Exhibit 72-8 constructs a similar type of portfolio for European puts. Here, however, we buy the put and the underlying and borrow by issuing the zero-coupon bond. The payoff of each instrument is indicated in the two rightmost columns. Note that the total payoff is never less than zero. Consequently, the initial value of the combination must not be less than zero. Therefore, $p_0 + S_0 - X/(1 + r)^T \geq 0$. Isolating the put price gives us $p_0 \geq X/(1 + r)^T - S_0$. But suppose that $X/(1 + r)^T - S_0$ is negative. Then, the put price must be greater than a negative number. We know that the put price must be no less than zero. So we can now formally say that

$$p_0 \geq \text{Max}[0, X/(1 + r)^T - S_0]$$

In other words, *the lower bound of a European put is the greater of either zero or the present value of the exercise price minus the underlying price.* For the American put, recall that the expression was $\text{Max}(0, X - S_0)$. So for the European put, we adjust this value to the present value of the exercise price. The present value of the asset price is already adjusted to S_0.

Using the same example we did for calls, let $X = 50$, $r = 0.05$, and $T = 0.5$. If the current underlying price is 45, then the lower bound for the European put is

$$\text{Max}(0, 50/(1.05)^{0.5} - 45) = \text{Max}(0, 48.80 - 45) = \text{Max}(0, 3.80) = 3.80$$

If the current underlying price is 54, however, the lower bound is

$$\text{Max}(0, 48.80 - 54) = \text{Max}(0, -5.20) = 0$$

At this point let us reconsider what we have found. The lower bound for a European call is $\text{Max}[0, S_0 - X/(1 + r)^T]$. We also observed that an American call must be worth at least $\text{Max}(0, S_0 - X)$. But except at expiration, the European lower bound is greater than the minimum value of the American call.[16] We could not, however, expect an American call to be worth less than a European call. Thus the lower bound of the European call holds for American calls as well. Hence, we can conclude that

$$c_0 \geq \text{Max}[0, S_0 - X/(1 + r)^T]$$
$$C_0 \geq \text{Max}[0, S_0 - X/(1 + r)^T]$$

(72-9)

---

[16] We discuss this point more formally and in the context of whether it is ever worthwhile to exercise an American call early in Section 5.6.

For European puts, the lower bound is $\text{Max}[0,X/(1 + r)^T - S_0]$. For American puts, the minimum price is $\text{Max}(0,X - S_0)$. The European lower bound is lower than the minimum price of the American put, so the American put lower bound is not changed to the European lower bound, the way we did for calls. Hence,

$$p_0 \geq \text{Max}[0,X/(1 + r)^T - S_0]$$
$$P_0 \geq \text{Max}(0,X - S_0)$$

(72-10)

These results tell us the lowest possible price for European and American options.

Recall that we previously referred to an option price as having an intrinsic value and a time value. For American options, the intrinsic value is the value if exercised, $\text{Max}(0,S_0 - X)$ for calls and $\text{Max}(0,X - S_0)$ for puts. The remainder of the option price is the time value. For European options, the notion of a time value is somewhat murky, because it first requires recognition of an intrinsic value. Because a European option cannot be exercised until expiration, in a sense, all of the value of a European option is time value. The notion of an intrinsic value and its complement, a time value, is therefore inappropriate for European options, though the concepts are commonly applied to European options. Fortunately, understanding European options does not require that we separate intrinsic value from time value. We shall include them together as they make up the option price.

Practice Problem 2

Consider call and put options expiring in 42 days, in which the underlying is at 72 and the risk-free rate is 4.5 percent. The underlying makes no cash payments during the life of the options.

A. Find the lower bounds for European calls and puts with exercise prices of 70 and 75.

B. Find the lower bounds for American calls and puts with exercise prices of 70 and 75.

SOLUTIONS

A. 70 call: $\text{Max}[0,72 - 70/(1.045)^{0.1151}] = \text{Max}(0,2.35) = 2.35$
75 call: $\text{Max}[0,72 - 75/(1.045)^{0.1151}] = \text{Max}(0,-2.62) = 0$
70 put: $\text{Max}[0,70/(1.045)^{0.1151} - 72] = \text{Max}(0,-2.35) = 0$
75 put: $\text{Max}[0,75/(1.045)^{0.1151} - 72] = \text{Max}(0,2.62) = 2.62$

B. 70 call: $\text{Max}[0,72 - 70/(1.045)^{0.1151}] = \text{Max}(0,2.35) = 2.35$
75 call: $\text{Max}[0,72 - 75/(1.045)^{0.1151}] = \text{Max}(0,-2.62) = 0$
70 put: $\text{Max}(0,70 - 72) = 0$
75 put: $\text{Max}(0,75 - 72) = 3$

5.3 The Effect of a Difference in Exercise Price

Now consider two options on the same underlying with the same expiration day but different exercise prices. Generally, the higher the exercise price, the lower the value of a call and the higher the price of a put. To see this, let the two exercise prices be X_1 and X_2, with X_1 being the smaller. Let $c_0(X_1)$ be the price of a European call with exercise price X_1 and $c_0(X_2)$ be the price of a European call with exercise price X_2. We refer to these as the X_1 call and the X_2 call. In Exhibit 72-9, we construct a combination in which we buy the X_1 call and sell the X_2 call.[17]

EXHIBIT 72-9 Portfolio Combination for European Calls Illustrating the Effect of Differences in Exercise Prices

Transaction	Current Value	Value at Expiration		
		$S_T \leq X_1$	$X_1 < S_T < X_2$	$S_T \geq X_2$
Buy call ($X = X_1$)	$c_0(X_1)$	0	$S_T - X_1$	$S_T - X_1$
Sell call ($X = X_2$)	$-c_0(X_2)$	0	0	$-(S_T - X_2)$
Total	$c_0(X_1) - c_0(X_2)$	0	$S_T - X_1 > 0$	$X_2 - X_1 > 0$

Note first that the three outcomes are all non-negative. This fact establishes that the current value of the combination, $c_0(X_1) - c_0(X_2)$ has to be non-negative. We have to pay out at least as much for the X_1 call as we take in for the X_2 call; otherwise, we would get money up front, have the possibility of a positive value at expiration, and never have to pay any money out. Thus, because $c_0(X_1) - c_0(X_2) \geq 0$, we restate this result as

$$c_0(X_1) \geq c_0(X_2)$$

This expression is equivalent to the statement that *a call option with a higher exercise price cannot have a higher value than one with a lower exercise price.* The option with the higher exercise price has a higher hurdle to get over; therefore, the buyer is not willing to pay as much for it. Even though we demonstrated this result with European calls, it is also true for American calls. Thus,[18]

$$C_0(X_1) \geq C_0(X_2)$$

In Exhibit 72-10 we construct a similar portfolio for puts, except that we buy the X_2 put (the one with the higher exercise price) and sell the X_1 put (the one with the lower exercise price).

EXHIBIT 72-10 Portfolio Combination for European Puts Illustrating the Effect of Differences in Exercise Prices

Transaction	Current Value	Value at Expiration		
		$S_T \leq X_1$	$X_1 < S_T < X_2$	$S_T \geq X_2$
Buy put ($X = X_2$)	$p_0(X_2)$	$X_2 - S_T$	$X_2 - S_T$	0
Sell put ($X = X_1$)	$-p_0(X_1)$	$-(X_1 - S_T)$	0	0
Total	$p_0(X_2) - p_0(X_1)$	$X_2 - X_1 > 0$	$X_2 - S_T > 0$	0

---

[17] In Reading 74, when we cover option strategies, this transaction will be known as a bull spread.

[18] It is possible to use the results from this table to establish a limit on the difference between the prices of these two options, but we shall not do so here.

Observe that the value of this combination is never negative at expiration; therefore, it must be non-negative today. Hence, $p_0(X_2) - p_0(X_1) \geq 0$. We restate this result as

$$p_0(X_2) \geq p_0(X_1)$$

Thus, *the value of a European put with a higher exercise price must be at least as great as the value of a European put with a lower exercise price*. These results also hold for American puts. Therefore,

$$P_0(X_2) \geq P_0(X_1)$$

Even though it is technically possible for calls and puts with different exercise prices to have the same price, *generally we can say that the higher the exercise price, the lower the price of a call and the higher the price of a put*. For example, refer back to Exhibit 72-1 and observe how the most expensive calls and least expensive puts have the lower exercise prices.

5.4 The Effect of a Difference in Time to Expiration

Option prices are also affected by the time to expiration of the option. Intuitively, one might expect that the longer the time to expiration, the more valuable the option. A longer-term option has more time for the underlying to make a favorable move. In addition, if the option is in-the-money by the end of a given period of time, it has a better chance of moving even further in-the-money over a longer period of time. If the additional time gives it a better chance of moving out-of-the-money or further out-of-the-money, the limitation of losses to the amount of the option premium means that the disadvantage of the longer time is no greater. In most cases, a longer time to expiration is beneficial for an option. We will see that longer-term American and European calls and longer-term American puts are worth no less than their shorter-term counterparts.

First let us consider each of the four types of options: European calls, American calls, European puts, and American puts. We shall introduce options otherwise identical except that one has a longer time to expiration than the other. The one expiring earlier has an expiration of T_1 and the one expiring later has an expiration of T_2. The prices of the options are $c_0(T_1)$ and $c_0(T_2)$ for the European calls, $C_0(T_1)$ and $C_0(T_2)$ for the American calls, $p_0(T_1)$ and $p_0(T_2)$ for the European puts, and $P_0(T_1)$ and $P_0(T_2)$ for the American puts.

When the shorter-term call expires, the European call is worth $Max(0, S_{T_1} - X)$, but we have already shown that the longer-term European call is worth *at least* $Max(0, S_{T_1} - X/(1 + r)^{(T_2 - T_1)})$, which is at least as great as this amount.[19] Thus, the longer-term European call is worth at least the value of the shorter-term European call. These results are not altered if the call is American. When the shorter-term American call expires, it is worth $Max(0, S_{T_1} - X)$. The longer-term American call must be worth at least the value of the European call, so it is worth *at least* $Max[0, S - X/(1 + r)^{T_2 - T_1}]$. Thus, the longer-term call, European or American, is worth no less than the shorter-term call when the shorter-term call expires. Because this statement is always true, the longer-term call, European or American, is worth no less than the shorter-term call at any time prior to expiration. Thus,

$$c_0(T_2) \geq c_0(T_1)$$
$$C_0(T_2) \geq C_0(T_1)$$
    (72-11)

---

[19] Technically, we showed this calculation using a time to expiration of T, but here the time to expiration is $T_2 - T_1$.

Notice that these statements do not mean that the longer-term call is always worth more; it means that the longer-term call can be worth no less. With the exception of the rare case in which both calls are so far out-of-the-money or in-the-money that the additional time is of no value, the longer-term call will be worth more.

For European puts, we have a slight problem. For calls, the longer term gives additional time for a favorable move in the underlying to occur. For puts, this is also true, but there is one disadvantage to waiting the additional time. When a put is exercised, the holder receives money. The lost interest on the money is a disadvantage of the additional time. For calls, there is no lost interest. In fact, a call holder earns additional interest on the money by paying out the exercise price later. Therefore, it is not always true that additional time is beneficial to the holder of a European put. It is true, however, that the additional time is beneficial to the holder of an American put. An American put can always be exercised; there is no penalty for waiting. Thus, we have

$$p_0(T_2) \text{ can be either greater or less than } p_0(T_1)$$
$$P_0(T_2) \geq P_0(T_1)$$

(72-12)

So for European puts, either the longer-term or the shorter-term option can be worth more. The longer-term European put will tend to be worth more when volatility is greater and interest rates are lower.

Referring back to Exhibit 72-1, observe that the longer-term put and call options are more expensive than the shorter-term ones. As noted, we might observe an exception to this rule for European puts, but these are all American options.

5.5 Put–Call Parity

So far we have been working with puts and calls separately. To see how their prices must be consistent with each other and to explore common option strategies, let us combine puts and calls with each other or with a risk-free bond. We shall put together some combinations that produce equivalent results.

5.5.1 Fiduciary Calls and Protective Puts

First we consider an option strategy referred to as a **fiduciary call.** It consists of a European call and a risk-free bond, just like the ones we have been using, that matures on the option expiration day and has a face value equal to the exercise price of the call. The upper part of the table in Exhibit 72-11 shows the payoffs at expiration of the fiduciary call. We see that if the price of the underlying is below X at expiration, the call expires worthless and the bond is worth X. If the price of the underlying is above X at expiration, the call expires and is worth S_T (the underlying price) $- X$. So at expiration, the fiduciary call will end up worth X or S_T, whichever is greater.

EXHIBIT 72-11 Portfolio Combinations for Equivalent Packages of Puts and Calls

Transaction	Current Value	Value at Expiration	
		$S_T \leq X$	$S_T > X$
Fiduciary Call			
Buy call	c_0	0	$S_T - X$

Transaction	Current Value	Value at Expiration	
		$S_T \leq X$	$S_T > X$
Buy bond	$X/(1 + r)^T$	X	X
Total	$c_0 + X/(1 + r)^T$	X	S_T
Protective Put			
Buy put	p_0	$X - S_T$	0
Buy underlying asset	S_0	S_T	S_T
Total	$p_0 + S_0$	X	S_T

Value of Fiduciary Call and
Protective Put at Expiration

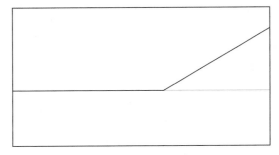

Stock Price at Expiration

This type of combination is called a fiduciary call because it allows protection against downside losses and is thus faithful to the notion of preserving capital.

Now we construct a strategy known as a **protective put,** which consists of a European put and the underlying asset. If the price of the underlying is below X at expiration, the put expires and is worth $X - S_T$ and the underlying is worth S_T. If the price of the underlying is above X at expiration, the put expires with no value and the underlying is worth S_T. So at expiration, the protective put is worth X or S_T, whichever is greater. The lower part of the table in Exhibit 72-11 shows the payoffs at expiration of the protective put.

Thus, the fiduciary call and protective put end up with the same value. They are, therefore, identical combinations. To avoid arbitrage, their values today must be the same. The value of the fiduciary call is the cost of the call, c_0, and the cost of the bond, $X/(1 + r)^T$. The value of the protective put is the cost of the put, p_0, and the cost of the underlying, S_0. Thus,

$$c_0 + X/(1 + r)^T = p_0 + S_0 \qquad \text{(72-13)}$$

This equation is called **put–call parity** and is one of the most important results in options. It does not say that puts and calls are equivalent, but it does show an equivalence (parity) of a call/bond portfolio and a put/underlying portfolio.

Put–call parity can be written in a number of other ways. By rearranging the four terms to isolate one term, we can obtain some interesting and important results. For example,

$$c_0 = p_0 + S_0 - X/(1 + r)^T$$

means that a call is equivalent to a long position in the put, a long position in the asset, and a short position in the risk-free bond. The short bond position simply means to borrow by issuing the bond, rather than lend by buying the bond as we did in the fiduciary call portfolio. We can tell from the sign whether we should go long or short. Positive signs mean to go long; negative signs mean to go short.

5.5.2 Synthetics

Because the right-hand side of the above equation is equivalent to a call, we often refer to it as a **synthetic call.** To see that the synthetic call is equivalent to the actual call, look at Exhibit 72-12:

EXHIBIT 72-12 Call and Synthetic Call

Transaction	Current Value	Value at Expiration $S_T \leq X$	Value at Expiration $S_T > X$
Call			
Buy call	c_0	0	$S_T - X$
Synthetic Call			
Buy put	p_0	$X - S_T$	0
Buy underlying asset	S_0	S_T	S_T
Issue bond	$-X/(1 + r)^T$	$-X$	$-X$
Total	$p_0 + S_0 - X/(1 + r)^T$	0	$S_T - X$

The call produces the value of the underlying minus the exercise price or zero, whichever is greater. The synthetic call does the same thing, but in a different way. When the call expires in-the-money, the synthetic call produces the underlying value minus the payoff on the bond, which is X. When the call expires out-of-the-money, the put covers the loss on the underlying and the exercise price on the put matches the amount of money needed to pay off the bond.

Similarly, we can isolate the put as follows:

$$p_0 = c_0 - S_0 + X/(1 + r)^T$$

which says that a put is equivalent to a long call, a short position in the underlying, and a long position in the bond. Because the left-hand side is a put, it follows that the right-hand side is a **synthetic put.** The equivalence of the put and synthetic put is shown in Exhibit 72-13.

EXHIBIT 72-13 Put and Synthetic Put

Transaction	Current Value	Value at Expiration $S_T \leq X$	Value at Expiration $S_T > X$
Put			
Buy put	p_0	$X - S_T$	0

Transaction	Current Value	Value at Expiration	
		$S_T \leq X$	$S_T > X$
Synthetic Put			
Buy call	c_0	0	$S_T - X$
Short underlying asset	$-S_0$	$-S_T$	$-S_T$
Buy bond	$X/(1+r)^T$	X	X
Total	$c_0 - S_0 + X/(1+r)^T$	$X - S_T$	0

EXHIBIT 72-14 Alternative Equivalent Combinations of Calls, Puts, the Underlying, and Risk-Free Bonds

Strategy	Consisting of	Worth	Equates to	Strategy	Consisting of	Worth
Fiduciary call	Long call + Long bond	$c_0 + X/(1+r)^T$	=	Protective put	Long put + Long underlying	$p_0 + S_0$
Long call	Long call	c_0	=	Synthetic call	Long put + Long underlying + Short bond	$p_0 + S_0 - X/(1+r)^T$
Long put	Long put	p_0	=	Synthetic put	Long call + Short underlying + Long bond	$c_0 - S_0 + X/(1+r)^T$
Long underlying	Long underlying	S_0	=	Synthetic underlying	Long call + Long bond + Short put	$c_0 + X/(1+r)^T - p_0$
Long bond	Long bond	$X/(1+r)^T$	=	Synthetic bond	Long put + Long underlying + Short call	$p_0 + S_0 - c_0$

As you can well imagine, there are numerous other combinations that can be constructed. Exhibit 72-14 shows a number of the more important combinations. There are two primary reasons that it is important to understand synthetic positions in option pricing. Synthetic positions enable us to price options, because they produce the same results as options and have known prices. Synthetic positions also tell how to exploit mispricing of options relative to their underlying assets. Note that we can not only synthesize a call or a put, but we can also synthesize the underlying or the bond. As complex as it might seem to do this, it is really quite easy. First, we learn that *a fiduciary call is a call plus a risk-free bond maturing on the option expiration day with a face value equal to the exercise price of the option.* Then we learn that *a protective put is the underlying plus a put.* Then we learn the basic put–call parity equation: *A fiduciary call is equivalent to a protective put:*

$$c_0 + X/(1+r)^T = p_0 + S_0$$

Learn the put–call parity equation this way, because it is the easiest form to remember and has no minus signs.

Next, we decide which instrument we want to synthesize. We use simple algebra to isolate that instrument, with a plus sign, on one side of the equation, moving all other instruments to the other side. We then see what instruments are on the other side, taking plus signs as long positions and minus signs as short positions. Finally, to check our results, we should construct a table like Exhibits 72-11 or 72-12, with the expiration payoffs of the instrument we wish to synthesize compared with the expiration payoffs of the equivalent combination of instruments. We then check to determine that the expiration payoffs are the same.

5.5.3 An Arbitrage Opportunity

In this section we examine the arbitrage strategies that will push prices to put–call parity. Suppose that in the market, prices do not conform to put–call parity. This is a situation in which price does not equal value. Recalling our basic equation, $c_0 + X/(1 + r)^T = p_0 + S_0$, we should insert values into the equation and see if the equality holds. If it does not, then obviously one side is greater than the other. We can view one side as overpriced and the other as underpriced, which suggests an arbitrage opportunity. To exploit this mispricing, we buy the underpriced combination and sell the overpriced combination.

Consider the following example involving call options with an exercise price of $100 expiring in half a year (T = 0.5). The risk-free rate is 10 percent. The call is priced at $7.50, and the put is priced at $4.25. The underlying price is $99.

The left-hand side of the basic put–call parity equation is $c_0 + X/(1 + r)^T = 7.50 + 100/(1.10)^{0.5} = 7.50 + 95.35 = 102.85$. The right-hand side is $p_0 + S_0 = 4.25 + 99 = 103.25$. So the right-hand side is greater than the left-hand side. This means that the protective put is overpriced. Equivalently, we could view this as the fiduciary call being underpriced. Either way will lead us to the correct strategy to exploit the mispricing.

We sell the overpriced combination, the protective put. This means that we sell the put and sell short the underlying. Doing so will generate a cash inflow of $103.25. We buy the fiduciary call, paying out $102.85. This series of transactions nets a cash inflow of $103.25 − $102.85 = $0.40. Now, let us see what happens at expiration.

The options expire with the underlying above 100:
    The bond matures, paying $100.
    Use the $100 to exercise the call, receiving the underlying.
    Deliver the underlying to cover the short sale.
    The put expires with no value.
    Net effect: No money in or out.
The options expire with the underlying below 100:
    The bond matures, paying $100.
    The put expires in-the-money; use the $100 to buy the underlying.
    Use the underlying to cover the short sale.
    The call expires with no value.
    Net effect: No money in our out.

So we receive $0.40 up front and do not have to pay anything out. The position is perfectly hedged and represents an arbitrage profit. The combined effects of other investors performing this transaction will result in the value of the protective put going down and/or the value of the covered call going up until the two strategies are equivalent in value. Of course, it is possible that transaction costs might consume any profit, so small discrepancies will not be exploited.

It is important to note that regardless of which put–call parity equation we use, we will arrive at the same strategy. For example, in the above problem, the synthetic put (a long call, a short position in the underlying, and a long bond) is worth $7.50 − $99 + $95.35 = $3.85. The actual put is worth $4.25. Thus, we would conclude that we should sell the actual put and buy the synthetic put. To buy the synthetic put, we would buy the call, short the underlying, and buy the bond—precisely the strategy we used to exploit this price discrepancy.

In all of these examples based on put–call parity, we used only European options. Put–call parity using American options is considerably more complicated. The resulting parity equation is a complex combination of inequalities. Thus, we cannot say that a given combination exactly equals another; we can say only that one combination is more valuable than another. Exploitation of any such mispricing is somewhat more complicated, and we shall not explore it here.

Practice Problem 3

European put and call options with an exercise price of 45 expire in 115 days. The underlying is priced at 48 and makes no cash payments during the life of the options. The risk-free rate is 4.5 percent. The put is selling for 3.75, and the call is selling for 8.00.

A. Identify the mispricing by comparing the price of the actual call with the price of the synthetic call.

B. Based on your answer in Part A, demonstrate how an arbitrage transaction is executed.

SOLUTIONS

A. Using put–call parity, the following formula applies:

$$c_0 = p_0 + S_0 - X/(1 + r)^T$$

The time to expiration is $T = 115/365 = 0.3151$. Substituting values into the right-hand side:

$$c_0 = 3.75 + 48 - 45/(1.045)^{0.3151} = 7.37$$

Hence, the synthetic call is worth 7.37, but the actual call is selling for 8.00 and is, therefore, overpriced.

B. Sell the call for 8.00 and buy the synthetic call for 7.37. To buy the synthetic call, buy the put for 3.75, buy the underlying for 48.00, and issue a zero-coupon bond paying 45.00 at expiration. The bond will bring in $45.00/(1.045)^{0.3151} = 44.38$ today. This transaction will bring in $8.00 - 7.37 = 0.63$.

At expiration, the following payoffs will occur:

	$S_T < 45$	$S_T \geq 45$
Short call	0	$-(S_T - 45)$
Long put	$45 - S_T$	0
Underlying	S_T	S_T
Bond	-45	-45
Total	0	0

Thus there will be no cash in or out at expiration. The transaction will net a risk-free gain of $8.00 - 7.37 = 0.63$ up front.

5.6 American Options, Lower Bounds, and Early Exercise

As we have noted, American options can be exercised early and in this section we specify cases in which early exercise can have value. Because early exercise is never mandatory, the right to exercise early may be worth something but could never hurt the option holder. Consequently, the prices of American options must be no less than the prices of European options:

$$C_0 \geq c_0$$
$$P_0 \geq p_0$$

(72-14)

Recall that we already used this result in establishing the minimum price from the lower bounds and intrinsic value results in Section 5.2.2. Now, however, our concern is understanding the conditions under which early exercise of an American option might occur.

Suppose today, time 0, we are considering exercising early an in-the-money American call. If we exercise, we pay X and receive an asset worth S_0. But we already determined that a European call is worth at least $S_0 - X/(1 + r)^T$—that is, the underlying price minus the present value of the exercise price, which is more than $S_0 - X$. Because we just argued that the American call must be worth no less than the European call, it therefore must also be worth at least $S_0 - X/(1 + r)^T$. This means that the value we could obtain by selling it to someone else is more than the value we could obtain by exercising it. Thus, there is no reason to exercise the call early.

Some people fail to see the logic behind not exercising early. Exercising a call early simply gives the money to the call writer and throws away the right to decide at expiration if you want the underlying. It is like renewing a magazine subscription before the current subscription expires. Not only do you lose the interest on the money, you also lose the right to decide later if you want to renew. Without offering an early exercise incentive, the American call would have a price equal to the European call price. Thus, we must look at another case to see the value of the early exercise option.

If the underlying makes a cash payment, there may be reason to exercise early. If the underlying is a stock and pays a dividend, there may be sufficient reason to exercise just before the stock goes ex-dividend. By exercising, the option holder throws away the time value but captures the dividend. We shall skip the technical details of how this decision is made and conclude by stating that

▷ *When the underlying makes no cash payments, $C_0 = c_0$.*

▷ *When the underlying makes cash payments during the life of the option, early exercise can be worthwhile and C0 can thus be higher than c_0.*

We emphasize the word *can*. It is possible that the dividend is not high enough to justify early exercise.

For puts, there is nearly always a possibility of early exercise. Consider the most obvious case, an investor holding an American put on a bankrupt company. The stock is worth zero. It cannot go any lower. Thus, the put holder would exercise immediately. As long as there is a possibility of bankruptcy, the American put will be worth more than the European put. But in fact, bankruptcy is not required for early exercise. The stock price must be very low, although we cannot say exactly how low without resorting to an analysis using option pricing models. Suffice it to say that *the American put is nearly always worth more than the European put: $P_0 > p_0$.*

5.7 The Effect of Cash Flows on the Underlying Asset

Both the lower bounds on puts and calls and the put–call parity relationship must be modified to account for cash flows on the underlying asset. In Readings 70 and 71, we discussed situations in which the underlying has cash flows. Stocks pay dividends, bonds pay interest, foreign currencies pay interest, and commodities have carrying costs. As we have done in the previous readings, we shall assume that these cash flows are either known or can be expressed as a percentage of the asset price. Moreover, as we did previously, we can remove the present value of those cash flows from the price of the underlying and use this adjusted underlying price in the results we have obtained above.

In the previous readings, we specified these cash flows in the form of the accumulated value at T of all cash flows incurred on the underlying over the life of the derivative contract. When the underlying is a stock, we specified these cash flows more precisely in the form of dividends, using the notation $FV(D,0,T)$ as the future value, or alternatively $PV(D,0,T)$ as the present value, of these dividends. When the underlying was a bond, we used the notation $FV(CI,0,T)$ or $PV(CI,0,T)$, where CI stands for "coupon interest." When the cash flows can be specified in terms of a yield or rate, we used the notation δ where $S_0/(1 + \delta)^T$ is the underlying price reduced by the present value of the cash flows.[20] Using continuous compounding, the rate can be specified as dc so that $S_0 e^{-\delta^c T}$ is the underlying price reduced by the present value of the dividends. For our purposes in this reading on options, let us just write this specification as $PV(CF,0,T)$, which represents the present value of the cash flows on the underlying over the life of the options. Therefore, we can restate the lower bounds for European options as

$$c_0 \geq Max\{0,[S_0 - PV(CF,0,T)] - X/(1 + r)^T\}$$
$$p_0 \geq Max\{0,X/(1 + r)^T - [S_0 - PV(CF,0,T)]\}$$

and put–call parity as

$$c_0 + X/(1 + r)^T = p_0 + [S_0 - PV(CF,0,T)]$$

which reflects the fact that, as we said, we simply reduce the underlying price by the present value of its cash flows over the life of the option.

5.8 The Effect of Interest Rates and Volatility

It is important to know that interest rates and volatility exert an influence on option prices. *When interest rates are higher, call option prices are higher and put option prices are lower.* This effect is not obvious and strains the intuition somewhat. When investors buy call options instead of the underlying, they are effectively buying an indirect leveraged position in the underlying. When interest rates are higher, buying the call instead of a direct leveraged position in the underlying is more attractive. Moreover, by using call options, investors save more money by not paying for the underlying until a later date. For put options, however, higher interest rates are disadvantageous. When interest rates are higher, investors lose more interest while waiting to sell the underlying when using puts. Thus, the opportunity cost of waiting is higher when interest rates are higher. Although these points may not seem completely clear, fortunately they are not critical. Except when the underlying is a bond or interest rate, interest rates do not have a very strong effect on option prices.

---

[20] We actually used several specifications of the dividend yield in Reading 71, but we shall use just one here.

Volatility, however, has an extremely strong effect on option prices. *Higher volatility increases call and put option prices because it increases possible upside values and increases possible downside values of the underlying.* The upside effect helps calls and does not hurt puts. The downside effect does not hurt calls and helps puts. The reason calls are not hurt on the downside and puts are not hurt on the upside is that when options are out-of-the-money, it does not matter if they end up more out-of-the-money. But when options are in-the-money, it does matter if they end up more in-the-money.

Volatility is a critical variable in pricing options. It is the only variable that affects option prices that is not directly observable either in the option contract or in the market. It must be estimated. We shall have more to say about volatility later in this reading.

5.9 Option Price Sensitivities

Later in this reading, we will study option price sensitivities in more detail. These sensitivity measures have Greek names:

- *Delta* is the sensitivity of the option price to a change in the price of the underlying.
- *Gamma* is a measure of how well the delta sensitivity measure will approximate the option price's response to a change in the price of the underlying.
- *Rho* is the sensitivity of the option price to the risk-free rate.
- *Theta* is the rate at which the time value decays as the option approaches expiration.
- *Vega* is the sensitivity of the option price to volatility.

6   DISCRETE-TIME OPTION PRICING: THE BINOMIAL MODEL

Until now, we have looked only at some basic principles of option pricing. Other than put–call parity, all we examined were rules and conditions, often suggesting limitations, on option prices. With put–call parity, we found that we could price a put or a call based on the prices of the combinations of instruments that make up the synthetic version of the instrument. If we wanted to determine a call price, we had to have a put; if we wanted to determine a put price, we had to have a call. What we need to be able to do is price a put or a call without the other instrument. In this section, we introduce a simple means of pricing an option. It may appear that we oversimplify the situation, but we shall remove the simplifying assumptions gradually, and eventually reach a more realistic scenario.

The approach we take here is called the **binomial model.** The word "binomial" refers to the fact that there are only two outcomes. In other words, we let the underlying price move to only one of two possible new prices. As noted, this framework oversimplifies things, but the model can eventually be extended to encompass all possible prices. In addition, we refer to the structure of this model as **discrete time,** which means that time moves in distinct increments. This is much like looking at a calendar and observing only the months, weeks, or days. Even at its smallest interval, we know that time moves forward at a rate faster than one day at a time.

It moves in hours, minutes, seconds, and even fractions of seconds, and fractions of fractions of seconds. When we talk about time moving in the tiniest increments, we are talking about **continuous time.** We will see that the discrete time model can be extended to become a continuous time model. Although we present the continuous time model (Black–Scholes–Merton) in Section 7, we must point out that the binomial model has the advantage of allowing us to price American options. In addition, the binomial model is a simple model requiring a minimum of mathematics. Thus it is worthy of study in its own right.

6.1 The One-Period Binomial Model

We start off by having only one binomial period. This means that the underlying price starts off at a given level, then moves forward to a new price, at which time the option expires. Here we need to change our notation slightly from what we have been using previously. We let S be the current underlying price. One period later, it can move up to S^+ or down to S^-. Note that we are removing the time subscript, because it will not be necessary here. We let X be the exercise price of the option and r be the one period risk-free rate. The option is European style.

6.1.1 The Model

We start with a call option. If the underlying goes up to S^+, the call option will be worth c^+. If the underlying goes down to S^-, the option will be worth c^-. We know that if the option is expiring, its value will be the intrinsic value. Thus,

$$c^+ = \text{Max}(0, S^+ - X)$$
$$c^- = \text{Max}(0, S^- - X)$$

Exhibit 72-15 illustrates this scenario with a diagram commonly known as a **binomial tree.** Note how we indicate that the current option price, c, is unknown.

EXHIBIT 72-15 One-Period Binomial Model

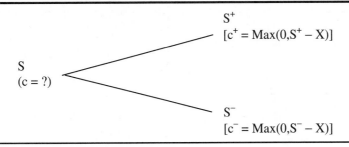

Now let us specify how the underlying moves. We identify a factor, u, as the up move on the underlying and d as the down move:

$$u = \frac{S^+}{S}$$

$$d = \frac{S^-}{S}$$

so that u and d represent 1 plus the rate of return if the underlying goes up and down, respectively. Thus, $S^+ = Su$ and $S^- = Sd$. To avoid an obvious arbitrage opportunity, we require that[21]

$$d < 1 + r < u$$

We are now ready to determine how to price the option. We assume that we have all information except for the current option price. In addition, we do not know in what direction the price of the underlying will move. We start by constructing an arbitrage portfolio consisting of one short call option. Let us now purchase an unspecified number of units of the underlying. Let that number be n. Although at the moment we do not know the value of n, we can figure it out quickly. We call this portfolio a hedge portfolio. In fact, n is sometimes called the **hedge ratio.** Its current value is H, where

$$H = nS - c$$

This specification reflects the fact that we own n units of the underlying worth S and we are short one call.[22] One period later, this portfolio value will go to either H^+ or H^-:

$$H^+ = nS^+ - c^+$$
$$H^- = nS^- - c^-$$

Because we can choose the value of n, let us do so by setting H^+ equal to H^-. This specification means that regardless of which way the underlying moves, the portfolio value will be the same. Thus, the portfolio will be hedged. We do this by setting

$$H^+ = H^-, \text{ which means that}$$
$$nS^+ - c^+ = nS^- - c^-$$

We then solve for n to obtain

$$n = \frac{c^+ - c^-}{S^+ - S^-} \tag{72-15}$$

Because the values on the right-hand side are known, we can easily set n according to this formula. If we do so, the portfolio will be hedged. A hedged portfolio should grow in value at the risk-free rate.

$$H^+ = H(1 + r), \text{ or}$$
$$H^- = H(1 + r)$$

We know that $H^+ = nS^+ - c^+$, $H^- = nS^- - c^-$, and $H = nS - c$. We know the values of n, S^+, S^-, c^+, and c^-, as well as r. We can substitute and solve either of the above for c to obtain

$$c = \frac{\pi c^+ + (1 - \pi)c^-}{1 + r} \tag{72-16}$$

---

[21] This statement says that if the price of the underlying goes up, it must do so at a rate better than the risk-free rate. If it goes down, it must do so at a rate lower than the risk-free rate. If the underlying always does better than the risk-free rate, it would be possible to buy the underlying, financing it by borrowing at the risk-free rate, and be assured of earning a greater return from the underlying than the cost of borrowing. This would make it possible to generate an unlimited amount of money. If the underlying always does worse than the risk-free rate, one can buy the risk-free asset and finance it by shorting the underlying. This would also make it possible to earn an unlimited amount of money. Thus, the risky underlying asset cannot dominate or be dominated by the risk-free asset.

[22] Think of this specification as a plus sign indicating assets and a minus sign indicating liabilities.

where

$$\pi = \frac{1 + r - d}{u - d}$$

(72-17)

We see that the call price today, c, is a weighted average of the next two possible call prices, c^+ and c^-. The weights are π and $1 - \pi$. This weighted average is then discounted one period at the risk-free rate.

It might appear that π and $1 - \pi$ are probabilities of the up and down movements, but they are not. In fact, the probabilities of the up and down movements are not required. It is important to note, however, that π and $1 - \pi$ are the probabilities that would exist if investors were risk neutral. Risk-neutral investors value assets by computing the expected future value and discounting that value at the risk-free rate. Because we are discounting at the risk-free rate, it should be apparent that π and $1 - \pi$ would indeed be the probabilities if the investor were risk neutral. In fact, we shall refer to them as **risk-neutral probabilities** and the process of valuing an option is often called **risk-neutral valuation.**[23]

6.1.2 One-Period Binomial Example

Suppose the underlying is a non-dividend-paying stock currently valued at $50. It can either go up by 25 percent or go down by 20 percent. Thus, u = 1.25 and d = 0.80.

$$S^+ = Su = 50(1.25) = 62.50$$
$$S^- = Sd = 50(0.80) = 40$$

Assume that the call option has an exercise price of 50 and the risk-free rate is 7 percent. Thus, the option values one period later will be

$$c^+ = \text{Max}(0, S^+ - X) = \text{Max}(0, 62.50 - 50) = 12.50$$
$$c^- = \text{Max}(0, S^- - X) = \text{Max}(0, 40 - 50) = 0$$

Exhibit 72-16 depicts the situation.

Exhibit 72-16 One-Period Binomial Example

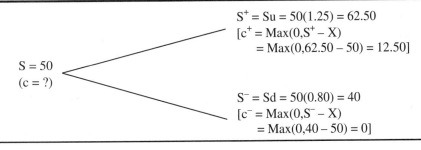

---

[23] It may be helpful to contrast risk neutrality with risk aversion, which characterizes nearly all individuals. People who are risk neutral value an asset, such as an option or stock, by discounting the expected value at the risk-free rate. People who are risk averse discount the expected value at a higher rate, one that consists of the risk-free rate plus a risk premium. In the valuation of options, we are not making the assumption that people are risk neutral, but the fact that options can be valued by finding the expected value, using these special probabilities, and discounting at the risk-free rate creates the *appearance* that investors are assumed to be risk neutral. We emphasize the word "appearance," because no such assumption is being made. The terms "risk neutral probabilities" and "risk neutral valuation" are widely used in options valuation, although they give a misleading impression of the assumptions underlying the process.

First we calculate π:

$$\pi = \frac{1 + r - d}{u - d} = \frac{1.07 - 0.80}{1.25 - 0.80} = 0.6$$

and, hence, $1 - \pi = 0.4$. Now, we can directly calculate the option price:

$$c = \frac{0.6(12.50) + 0.4(0)}{1.07} = 7.01$$

Thus, the option should sell for $7.01.

6.1.3 One-Period Binomial Arbitrage Opportunity

Suppose the option is selling for $8. If the option should be selling for $7.01 and it is selling for $8, it is overpriced—a clear case of price not equaling value. Investors would exploit this opportunity by selling the option and buying the underlying. The number of units of the underlying purchased for each option sold would be the value n:

$$n = \frac{c^+ - c^-}{S^+ - S^-} = \frac{12.50 - 0}{62.50 - 40} = 0.556$$

Thus, for every option sold, we would buy 0.556 units of the underlying. Suppose we sell 1,000 calls and buy 556 units of the underlying. Doing so would require an initial outlay of H = 556($50) − 1,000($8) = $19,800. One period later, the portfolio value will be either

$$H^+ = nS^+ - c^+ = 556(\$62.50) - 1,000(\$12.50) = \$22,250, \text{ or}$$
$$H^- = nS^- - c^- = 556(\$40) - 1,000(\$0) = \$22,240$$

These two values are not exactly the same, but the difference is due only to rounding the hedge ratio, n. We shall use the $22,250 value. If we invest $19,800 and end up with $22,250, the return is

$$\frac{\$22,250}{\$19,800} - 1 = 0.1237$$

that is, a risk-free return of more than 12 percent in contrast to the actual risk-free rate of 7 percent. Thus we could borrow $19,800 at 7 percent to finance the initial net cash outflow, capturing a risk-free profit of $(0.1237 - 0.07) \times \$19,800 = \$1,063$ (to the nearest dollar) without any net investment of money. Other investors will recognize this opportunity and begin selling the option, which will drive down its price. When the option sells for $7.01, the initial outlay would be H = 556($50) − 1,000($7.01) = $20,790. The payoffs at expiration would still be $22,250. This transaction would generate a return of

$$\frac{\$22,250}{\$20,790} - 1 \approx 0.07$$

Thus, when the option is trading at the price given by the model, a hedge portfolio would earn the risk-free rate, which is appropriate because the portfolio would be risk free.

If the option sells for less than $7.01, investors would buy the option and sell short the underlying, which would generate cash up front. At expiration, the investor would have to pay back an amount less than 7 percent. All investors would perform this transaction, generating a demand for the option that would push its price back up to $7.01.

Practice Problem 4

Consider a one-period binomial model in which the underlying is at 65 and can go up 30 percent or down 22 percent. The risk-free rate is 8 percent.

A. Determine the price of a European call option with exercise prices of 70.

B. Assume that the call is selling for 9 in the market. Demonstrate how to execute an arbitrage transaction and calculate the rate of return. Use 10,000 call options.

SOLUTIONS

A. First find the underlying prices in the binomial tree. We have u = 1.30 and d = 1 − 0.22 = 0.78.

$$S^+ = Su = 65(1.30) = 84.50$$
$$S^- = Sd = 65(0.78) = 50.70$$

Then find the option values at expiration:

$$c^+ = Max(0, 84.50 − 70) = 14.50$$
$$c^- = Max(0, 50.70 − 70) = 0$$

The risk-neutral probability is

$$\pi = \frac{1.08 − 0.78}{1.30 − 0.78} = 0.5769$$

and $1 − \pi = 0.4231$. The call's price today is

$$n = \frac{0.5769(14.50) + 0.4231(0)}{1.08} = 7.75$$

B. We need the value of n for calls:

$$n = \frac{c^+ − c^-}{S^+ − S^-} = \frac{14.50 − 0}{84.50 − 50.70} = 0.4290$$

The call is overpriced, so we should sell 10,000 call options and buy 4,290 units of the underlying.

Sell 10,000 calls at 9	+90,000
Buy 4,290 units of the underlying at 65	−278,850
Net cash flow	−188,850

So we invest 188,850. The value of this combination at expiration will be

If $S_T = 84.50$,
$$4{,}290(84.50) - 10{,}000(14.50) = 217{,}505$$

If $S_T = 50.70$,
$$4{,}290(50.70) - 10{,}000(0) = 217{,}503$$

These values differ by only a rounding error.
The rate of return is

$$\frac{217{,}505}{188{,}850} - 1 = 0.1517$$

Thus, we receive a risk-free return almost twice the risk-free rate. We could borrow the initial outlay of \$188,850 at the risk-free rate and capture a risk-free profit without any net investment of money.

6.2 The Two-Period Binomial Model

In the example above, the movements in the underlying were depicted over one period, and there were only two outcomes. We can extend the model and obtain more-realistic results with more than two outcomes. Exhibit 72-17 shows how to do so with a two-period binomial tree.

EXHIBIT 72-17 Two-Period Binomial Model

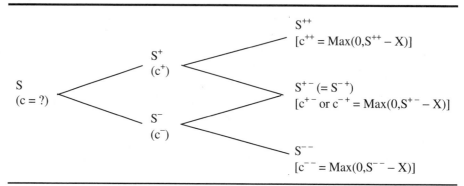

In the first period, we let the underlying price move from S to S^+ or S^- in the manner we did in the one-period model. That is, if u is the up factor and d is the down factor,

$$S^+ = Su$$
$$S^- = Sd$$

Then, with the underlying at S^+ after one period, it can either move up to S^{++} or down to S^{+-}. Thus,

$$S^{++} = S^+u$$
$$S^{+-} = S^+d$$

If the underlying is at S^- after one period, it can either move up to S^{-+} or down to S^{--}.

$$S^{-+} = S^-u$$
$$S^{--} = S^-d$$

We now have three unique final outcomes instead of two. Actually, we have four final outcomes, but S^{+-} is the same as S^{-+}. We can relate the three final outcomes to the starting price in the following manner:

$$S^{++} = S^+u = Suu = Su^2$$
$$S^{+-} \ (\text{or } S^{-+}) = S^+d \ (\text{or } S^-u) = Sud \ (\text{or } Sdu)$$
$$S^{--} = S^-d = Sdd = Sd^2$$

Now we move forward to the end of the first period. Suppose we are at the point where the underlying price is S^+. Note that now we are back into the one-period model we previously derived. There is one period to go and two outcomes. The call price is c^+ and can go up to c^{++} or down to c^{+-}. Using what we know from the one-period model, the call price must be

$$c^+ = \frac{\pi c^{++} + (1 - \pi)c^{+-}}{1 + r} \qquad \textbf{(72-18)}$$

where again we see that the call price is a weighted average of the next two possible call prices, then discounted back one period. If the underlying price is at S^-, the call price would be

$$c^- = \frac{\pi c^{-+} + (1 - \pi)c^{--}}{1 + r} \qquad \textbf{(72-19)}$$

where in both cases the formula for π is still Equation 72-17:

$$\pi = \frac{1 + r - d}{u + d}$$

Now we step back to the starting point and find that the option price is still given as Equation 72-16:

$$c = \frac{\pi c^+ + (1 - \pi)c^-}{1 + r}$$

again, using the general form that the call price is a weighted average of the next two possible call prices, discounted back to the present. Other than requiring knowledge of the formula for π, the call price formula is simple and intuitive. It is an average, weighted by the risk-neutral probabilities, of the next two outcomes, then discounted to the present.[24]

Recall that the hedge ratio, n, was given as the difference in the next two call prices divided by the difference in the next two underlying prices. This will be true in all cases throughout the binomial tree. Hence, we have different hedge ratios at each time point:

---

[24] It is also possible to express the price today as a weighted average of the three final option prices discounted two periods, thereby skipping the intermediate step of finding c^+ and c^-; but little is gained by doing so and this approach is somewhat more technical.

$$n = \frac{c^+ - c^-}{S^+ - S^-}$$

$$n^+ = \frac{c^{++} - c^{+-}}{S^{++} - S^{--}}$$

$$n^- = \frac{c^{-+} - c^{--}}{S^{-+} - S^{--}}$$

(72-20)

6.2.1 Two-Period Binomial Example

We can continue with the example presented in Section 6.1.2 in which the underlying goes up 25 percent or down 20 percent. Let us, however, alter the example a little. Suppose the underlying goes up 11.8 percent and down 10.56 percent, and we extend the number of periods to two. So, the up factor is 1.118 and the down factor is $1 - 0.1056 = 0.8944$. If the underlying goes up for two consecutive periods, it rises by a factor of $1.118(1.118) = 1.25$ (25 percent). If it goes down in both periods, it falls by a factor of $(0.8944)(0.8944) = 0.80$ (20 percent). This specification makes the highest and lowest prices unchanged. Let the risk-free rate be 3.44 percent per period. The π becomes $(1.0344 - 0.8944)/(1.118 - 0.8944) = 0.6261$. The underlying prices at expiration will be

$$S^{++} = Su^2 = 50(1.118)(1.118) = 62.50$$
$$S^{+-} = Sud = 50(1.118)(0.8944) = 50$$
$$S^{--} = Sd^2 = 50(0.8944)(0.8944) = 40$$

When the options expire, they will be worth

$$c^{++} = Max(0, S^{++} - 50) = Max(0, 62.50 - 50) = 12.50$$
$$c^{+-} = Max(0, S^{+-} - 50) = Max(0, 50 - 50) = 0$$
$$c^{--} = Max(0, S^{--} - 50) = Max(0, 40 - 50) = 0$$

The option values after one period are, therefore,

$$c^+ = \frac{\pi c^{++} + (1 - \pi)c^{+-}}{1 + r} = \frac{0.6261(12.50) + 0.3739(0)}{1.0344} = 7.57$$

$$c^- = \frac{\pi c^{-+} + (1 - \pi)c^{--}}{1 + r} = \frac{0.6261(0) + 0.3739(0)}{1.0344} = 0.0$$

So the option price today is

$$c = \frac{\pi c^+ + (1 - \pi)c^-}{1 + r} = \frac{0.6261(7.57) + 0.3739(0)}{1.0344} = 4.58$$

These results are summarized in Exhibit 72-18.

EXHIBIT 72-18 Two-Period Binomial Example

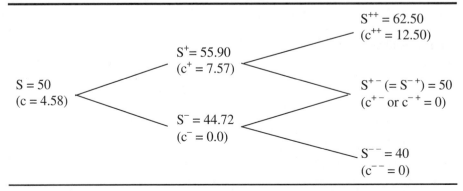

We shall not illustrate an arbitrage opportunity, because doing so requires a very long and detailed example that goes beyond our needs. Suffice it to say that if the option is mispriced, one can construct a hedged portfolio that will capture a return in excess of the risk-free rate.

Practice Problem 5

Consider a two-period binomial model in which the underlying is at 30 and can go up 14 percent or down 11 percent each period. The risk-free rate is 3 percent per period.

A. Find the value of a European call option expiring in two periods with an exercise price of 30.

B. Find the number of units of the underlying that would be required at each point in the binomial tree to construct a risk-free hedge using 10,000 calls.

SOLUTIONS

A. First find the underlying prices in the binomial tree: We have $u = 1.14$ and $d = 1 - 0.11 = 0.89$.

$$S^+ = Su = 30(1.14) = 34.20$$
$$S^- = Sd = 30(0.89) = 26.70$$
$$S^{++} = Su^2 = 30(1.14)^2 = 38.99$$
$$S^{+-} = Sud = 30(1.14)(0.89) = 30.44$$
$$S^{--} = Sd^2 = 30(0.89)^2 = 23.76$$

Then find the option prices at expiration:

$$c^{++} = Max(0, 38.99 - 30) = 8.99$$
$$c^{+-} = Max(0, 30.44 - 30) = 0.44$$
$$c^{--} = Max(0, 23.76 - 30) = 0$$

We will need the value of π:

$$\pi = \frac{1.03 - 0.89}{1.14 - 0.89} = 0.56$$

and $1 - \pi = 0.44$. Then step back and find the option prices at time 1:

$$c^+ = \frac{0.56(8.99) + 0.44(0.44)}{1.03} = 5.08$$

$$c^- = \frac{0.56(0.44) + 0.44(0)}{1.03} = 0.24$$

The price today is

$$c = \frac{0.56(5.08) + 0.44(0.24)}{1.03} = 2.86$$

B. The number of units of the underlying at each point in the tree is found by first computing the values of n.

$$n = \frac{5.08 - 0.24}{34.20 - 26.70} = 0.6453$$

$$n^+ = \frac{8.99 - 0.44}{38.99 - 30.44} = 1.00$$

$$n^- = \frac{0.44 - 0}{30.44 - 23.76} = 0.0659$$

The number of units of the underlying required for 10,000 calls would thus be 6,453 today, 10,000 at time 1 if the underlying is at 34.20, and 659 at time 1 if the underlying is at 26.70.

6.3 Binomial Put Option Pricing

In Section 6.2, the option was a call. It is a simple matter to make the option a put. We could step back through the entire example, changing all c's to p's and using the formulas for the payoff values of a put instead of a call. We should note, however, that if the same formula used for a call is used to calculate the hedge ratio, the minus sign should be ignored as it would suggest being long the stock (put) and short the put (stock) when the hedge portfolio should actually be long both instruments or short both instruments. The put moves opposite to the stock in the first place; hence, long or short positions in both instruments are appropriate.

Practice Problem 6

Repeating the data from Practice Problem 4, consider a one-period binomial model in which the underlying is at 65 and can go up 30 percent or down 22 percent. The risk-free rate is 8 percent. Determine the price of a European put option with exercise price of 70.

SOLUTION

First find the underlying prices in the binomial tree. We have $u = 1.30$ and $d = 1 - 0.22 = 0.78$.

$S^+ = Su = 65(1.30) = 84.50$
$S^- = Sd = 65(0.78) = 50.70$

Then find the option values at expiration:

$p^+ = \text{Max}(0, 70 - 84.50) = 0$
$p^- = \text{Max}(0, 70 - 50.70) = 19.30$

The risk-neutral probability is

$$\pi = \frac{1.08 - 0.78}{1.30 - 0.78} = 0.5769$$

and $1 - \pi = 0.4231$. The put price today is

$$p = \frac{0.5769(0) + 0.423(19.30)}{1.08} = 7.56$$

6.4 Binomial Interest Rate Option Pricing

In the examples above, the applications were appropriate for options on a stock, currency, or commodity.[25] Now we take a brief look at options on bonds and interest rates. A model for pricing these options must start with a model for the one-period interest rate and the prices of zero-coupon bonds.

We look at such a model in Exhibit 72-19. Note that this binomial tree is the first one we have seen with more than two time periods. At each point in the tree, we see a group of numbers. The first number is the one-period interest rate. The second set of numbers, which are in parentheses, represents the prices of $1 face value zero-coupon bonds of various maturities. At time 0, 0.9048 is the price of a one-period zero-coupon bond, 0.8106 is the price of a two-period zero-coupon bond, 0.7254 is the price of a three-period zero-coupon bond, and 0.6479 is the price of a four-period zero-coupon bond. The one-period bond price can be determined from the one-period rate—that is, $0.9048 = 1/1.1051$, subject to some rounding off. The other prices cannot be determined solely from the one-period rate; we would have to see a tree of the two-, three-, and four-period rates. As we move forward in time, we lose one bond as the one-period bond matures.[26] Thus, at time 1, when the one-period rate is 13.04 percent, the two-period bond from the previous period, whose price was 0.8106, is now a one-period bond whose price is $1/1.1304 = 0.8846$. Although we present these prices and rates here without derivation, they were determined using a model that prevents arbitrage opportunities in buying and selling bonds. We do not cover the actual derivation of the model here.

EXHIBIT 72-19 Binomial Interest Rate Tree

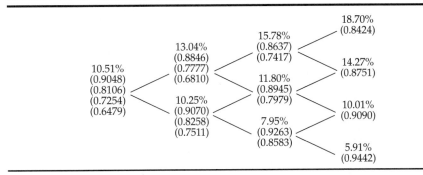

---

[25] We have also been assuming that there are no cash flows on the underlying.

[26] Technically we could show the bond we are losing as a bond with a price of $1.00, its face value, at its point of maturity.

Now let us price a European option on a zero-coupon bond. First note that we need the option to expire before the bond matures, and it should have a reasonable exercise price. We shall work with the four-period zero-coupon bond. Exhibit 72-20 contains its price and the price of a two-period call option with an exercise price of $0.80 per $1 of par, as well as the one-period interest rate. The binomial interest rate tree in Exhibit 72-20 is based on the data in Exhibit 72-19. In parentheses in Exhibit 72-20 are the prices of the call option expiring at time 2.

EXHIBIT 72-20 Four-Period Zero-Coupon Bond and Two-Period Call Option with Exercise Price of 0.80

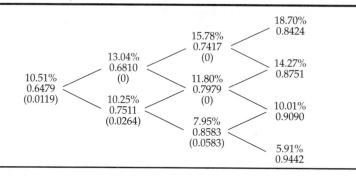

First note that in binomial term structure models, the models are usually fit such that the risk-neutral probability, π, is 0.5. Thus we do not have to calculate π, as in the examples above. We must, however, do one thing quite differently. Whereas we have used a constant interest rate, we must now discount at a different interest rate, the one-period rate, given in Exhibit 72-19, depending on where we are in the tree.

The payoff values at time 2 of the call with exercise price of 0.80 are

$$c^{++} = \text{Max}(0, 0.7417 - 0.80) = 0$$
$$c^{+-} = \text{Max}(0, 0.7979 - 0.80) = 0$$
$$c^{--} = \text{Max}(0, 0.8583 - 0.80) = 0.0583$$

These numbers appear in Exhibit 72-20 at time 2 along with the underlying bond prices and the one-period interest rates. Stepping back to time 1, we find the option prices as follows:

$$c^{+} = \frac{0.5(0) + 0.5(0)}{1.1304} = 0$$
$$c^{-} = \frac{0.5(0) + 0.5(0.0583)}{1.1025} = 0.0264$$

Note how we discount by the appropriate one-period rate, which is 10.25 percent for the bottom outcome at time 1 and 13.04 percent for the top outcome at time 1. Stepping back to time 0, the option price is, therefore,

$$c = \frac{0.5(0) + 0.5(0.0264)}{1.1051} = 0.0119$$

using the one-period rate of 10.51 percent. The call option is thus worth $0.0119 when the underlying zero-coupon bond paying $1 at time 4 is currently worth $0.6479.

Now let us price an option on a coupon bond. First, however, we must construct the tree of coupon bond prices. Exhibit 72-21 illustrates the price of a $1 face value, 11 percent coupon bond maturing at time 4 along with a call option expiring at time 2 with an exercise price of $0.95 per $1 of par.

EXHIBIT 72-21 Four-Period 11 Percent Coupon Bond and Two-Period Call Option with Exercise Price of 0.95

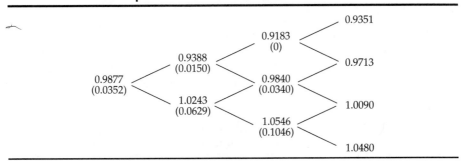

We obtain the prices of the coupon bond from the prices of zero-coupon bonds. For example, at time 0, a four-period 11 percent coupon bond is equivalent to a combination of zero-coupon bonds with face value of 0.11 maturing at times 1, 2, and 3, and a zero-coupon bond with face value of 1.11 maturing at time 4. Thus, its price can be found by multiplying these face values by the prices of one-, two-, three-, and four-period zero-coupon bonds respectively, the prices of which are taken from Exhibit 72-19.

$$0.11(0.9048) + 0.11(0.8106) + 0.11(0.7254) + 1.11(0.6479) = 0.9877$$

At any other point in the tree, we use the same procedure, but of course fewer coupons remain.[27] Of course, pricing a coupon bond by decomposing it into a combination of zero-coupon bonds is basic fixed income material, which you have learned elsewhere in the CFA curriculum.

Now let us find the option prices. At time 2, the prices are

$$c^{++} = Max(0, 0.9183 - 0.95) = 0$$
$$c^{+-} = Max(0, 0.9840 - 0.95) = 0.0340$$
$$c^{--} = Max(0, 1.0546 - 0.95) = 0.1046$$

Stepping back to time 1, the prices are

$$c^{+} = \frac{0.5(0) + 0.5(0.0340)}{1.1304} = 0.0150$$

$$c^{-} = \frac{0.5(0.0340) + 0.5(0.1046)}{1.1025} = 0.0629$$

Stepping back to time 0, the option price is

$$c = \frac{0.5(0.0150) + 0.5(0.0629)}{1.1051} = 0.0352$$

---

[27] For example, consider the middle node at time 2. The coupon bond is now a two-period bond. The one- and two-period zero-coupon bond prices are 0.8945 and 0.7979, respectively (from Exhibit 72-19). Thus, the coupon bond price is 0.11(0.8945) + 1.11(0.7979) = 0.9840 as shown in Exhibit 72-21.

Now let us look at options on interest rates. Recall that in Section 4.1.4, we illustrated how these options work. Their payoffs are based on the difference between the interest rate and an exercise rate. When the option expires, the payoff does not occur for one additional period. Thus, we have to discount the intrinsic value at expiration by the one-period interest rate. Recall that an interest rate cap is a set of interest rate call options expiring at various points in the life of a loan. The cap is generally set up to hedge the interest rate risk on a floating rate loan.

Exhibit 72-22 illustrates the pricing of a two-period cap with an exercise rate of 10.5 percent. This contract consists of two caplets: a one-period call option on the one-period interest rate with an exercise rate of 10.5 percent, and a two-period call option on the one-period interest rate with an exercise rate of 10.5 percent. We price the cap by pricing these two component options.

EXHIBIT 72-22 Two-Period Cap on One-Period Interest Rate with Exercise Rate of 10.5 Percent

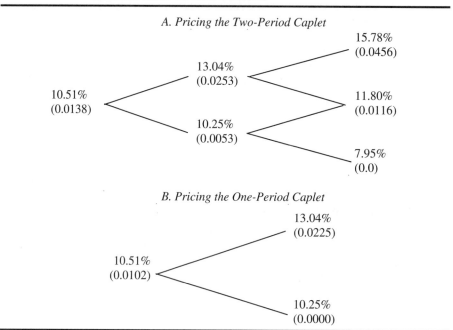

A. Pricing the Two-Period Caplet

B. Pricing the One-Period Caplet

In Panel A, we price the two-period caplet. The values at time 2 are

$$c^{++} = \frac{\text{Max}(0, 0.1578 - 0.105)}{1.1578} = 0.0456$$

$$c^{+-} = \frac{\text{Max}(0, 0.1180 - 0.105)}{1.1180} = 0.0116$$

$$c^{--} = \frac{\text{Max}(0, 0.0795 - 0.105)}{1.0795} = 0.0$$

Note especially that we discount the payoff one period at the appropriate one-period rate, because the payoff does not occur until one period later. Stepping back to time 1:

$$c^{+} = \frac{0.5(0.0456) + 0.5(0.0116)}{1.1304} = 0.0253$$

$$c^- = \frac{0.5(0.0116) + 0.5(0.0)}{1.1025} = 0.0053$$

At time 0, the option price is

$$c = \frac{0.5(0.0253) + 0.5(0.0053)}{1.1051} = 0.0138$$

Panel B illustrates the same procedure for the one-period caplet. We shall omit the details because they follow precisely the pattern above. The one-period caplet price is 0.0102; thus the cap costs $0.0138 + 0.0102 = 0.0240$.

If the option is a floor, the procedure is precisely the same but the payoffs are based on the payoffs of a put instead of a call. Pricing a zero-cost collar, however, is considerably more complex. Remember that a zero-cost collar is a long cap and a short floor with the exercise rates set such that the premium on the cap equals the premium on the floor. We can arbitrarily choose the exercise rate on the cap or the floor, but the exercise rate on the other would have to be found by trial and error so that the premium offsets the premium on the other instrument.

Practice Problem 7

The diagram below is a two-period binomial tree containing the one-period interest rate and the prices of zero-coupon bonds. The first price is a one-period zero-coupon bond, the second is a two-period zero-coupon bond, and the third is a three-period zero-coupon bond. As we move forward, one bond matures and its price is removed. The maturity of each bond is then shorter by one period.

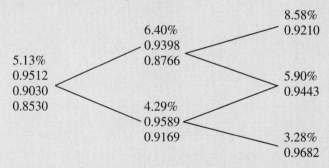

A. Find the price of a European put expiring in two periods with an exercise price of 1.01 on a three-period 6 percent coupon bond with $1.00 face value.

B. Find the price of a European put option expiring at time 2 with an exercise rate of 6 percent where the underlying is the one-period rate.

SOLUTIONS

A. First we have to find the price of the three-period $1.00 par, 6 percent coupon bond at expiration of the option (t = 2). We break the coupon bond up into zero-coupon bonds of one, two, and three periods to maturity. The face values of these zero-coupon bonds are 0.06, 0.06, and 1.06, respectively. The bond price at t =2 is $1.06 discounted one period at the appropriate discount rate:

Bond prices at time 2:

$+ +$ outcome: $1.06(0.9210) = 0.9763$
$+ -$ outcome: $1.06(0.9443) = 1.0010$
$- -$ outcome: $1.06(0.9682) = 1.0263$

Now compute the put option values at expiration:

$+ +$ outcome: $\text{Max}(0, 1.01 - 0.9763) = 0.0337$
$+ -$ outcome: $\text{Max}(0, 1.01 - 1.0010) = 0.0090$
$- -$ outcome: $\text{Max}(0, 1.01 - 1.0263) = 0.0000$

Now step back and compute the option values at time 1:

$$+ \text{ outcome:} \quad \frac{0.5(0.0337) + 0.5(0.0090)}{1.064} = 0.0201$$

$$- \text{ outcome:} \quad \frac{0.5(0.0090) + 0.5(0.0000)}{1.0429} = 0.0043$$

Now step back and compute the option values at time 0:

$$\frac{0.5(0.201) + 0.5(0.0043)}{1.0513} = 0.0116$$

B. First compute the put option values at expiration:

$$p^{++} = \frac{\text{Max}(0, 0.06 - 0.0858)}{1.0858} = 0.0000$$

$$p^{+-} = \frac{\text{Max}(0, 0.06 - 0.0590)}{1.059} = 0.0009$$

$$p^{--} = \frac{\text{Max}(0, 0.06 - 0.0328)}{1.0328} = 0.0263$$

Step back to time 2 and compute the option values:

$$p^{+} = \frac{0.5(0.0000) + 0.5(0.0009)}{1.064} = 0.0004$$

$$p^{-} = \frac{0.5(0.0009) + 0.5(0.0263)}{1.0429} = 0.0130$$

Now step back to time 0 and compute the option price as

$$p = \frac{0.5(0.0004) + 0.5(0.0130)}{1.0513} = 0.0064$$

6.5 American Options

The binomial model is also well suited for handling American-style options. At any point in the binomial tree, we can see whether the calculated value of the option is exceeded by its value if exercised early. If that is the case, we replace the calculated value with the exercise value.[28]

6.6 Extending the Binomial Model

In the examples in this reading, we divided an option's life into a given number of periods. Suppose we are pricing a one-year option. If we use only one binomial period, it will give us only two prices for the underlying, and we are unlikely to get a very good result. If we use two binomial periods, we will have three prices for the underlying at expiration. This result would probably be better but still not very good. But as we increase the number of periods, the result should become more accurate. In fact, in the limiting case, we are likely to get a very good result. By increasing the number of periods, we are moving from discrete time to continuous time.

Consider the following example of a one-period binomial model for a nine-month option. The asset is priced at 52.75. It can go up by 35.41 percent or down by 26.15 percent, so u = 1.3541 and d = 1 − 0.2615 = 0.7385. The risk-free rate is 4.88 percent. A call option has an exercise price of 50 and expires in nine months. Using a one-period binomial model would obtain an option price of 10.0259. Exhibit 72-23 shows the results we obtain if we divide the nine-month option life into an increasing number of periods of smaller and smaller length. The manner in which we fit the binomial tree is not arbitrary, however, because we have to alter the values of u, d, and the risk-free rate so that the underlying price move is reasonable for the life of the option. How we alter u and d is related to the volatility, a topic we cover in the next section. In fact, we need not concern ourselves with exactly how to alter any of these values. We need only to observe that our binomial option price appears to be converging to a value of around 8.62.

In the same way a sequence of rapidly taken still photographs converges to what appears to be a continuous sequence of a subject's movements, the binomial model converges to a continuous-time model, the subject of which is in our next section.

EXHIBIT 72-23 Binomial Option Prices for Different Numbers of Time Periods

Number of Time Periods	Option Price
1	10.0259
2	8.4782
5	8.8305
10	8.6983
25	8.5862
50	8.6438
100	8.6160
500	8.6162
1000	8.6190

Notes: Call option with underlying price of 52.75, up factor of 1.3541, down factor of 0.7385, risk-free rate of 4.88 percent, and exercise price of 50. The variables u, d, and r are altered accordingly as the number of time periods increases.

---

[28] See Chapter 4 of *An Introduction to Derivatives and Risk Management*, 6th edition, Don M. Chance (South-Western College Publishing, 2004) for a treatment of this topic.

7 CONTINUOUS-TIME OPTION PRICING: THE BLACK–SCHOLES–MERTON MODEL

When we move to a continuous-time world, we price options using the famous Black–Scholes–Merton model. Named after its founders Fischer Black, Myron Scholes, and Robert Merton, this model resulted in the award of a Nobel Prize to Scholes and Merton in 1997.[29] (Fischer Black had died in 1995 and thus was not eligible for the prize.) The model can be derived either as the continuous limit of the binomial model, or through taking expectations, or through a variety of highly complex mathematical procedures. We are not concerned with the derivation here and instead simply present the model and its applications. First, however, let us briefly review its underlying assumptions.

7.1 Assumptions of the Model

7.1.1 The Underlying Price Follows a Geometric Lognormal Diffusion Process

This assumption is probably the most difficult to understand, but in simple terms, *the underlying price follows a lognormal probability distribution as it evolves through time.* A lognormal probability distribution is one in which the log return is normally distributed. For example, if a stock moves from 100 to 110, the return is 10 percent but the log return is $\ln(1.10) = 0.0953$ or 9.53 percent. Log returns are often called *continuously compounded returns.* If the log or continuously compounded return follows the familiar normal or bell-shaped distribution, the return is said to be lognormally distributed. The distribution of the return itself is skewed, reaching further out to the right and truncated on the left side, reflecting the limitation that an asset cannot be worth less than zero.

The lognormal distribution is a convenient and widely used assumption. It is almost surely not an exact measure in reality, but it suffices for our purposes.

7.1.2 The Risk-Free Rate Is Known and Constant

The Black–Scholes–Merton model does not allow interest rates to be random. Generally, we assume that *the risk-free rate is constant.* This assumption becomes a problem for pricing options on bonds and interest rates, and we will have to make some adjustments then.

7.1.3 The Volatility of the Underlying Asset Is Known and Constant

The volatility of the underlying asset, specified in the form of the standard deviation of the log return, is assumed to be known at all times and does not change over the life of the option. This assumption is the most critical, and we take it up again in a later section. In reality, the volatility is definitely not known and must be estimated or obtained from some other source. In addition, volatility is generally not constant. Obviously, the stock market is more volatile at some times than at others. Nonetheless, the

---

[29] The model is more commonly called the Black–Scholes model, but we choose to give Merton the credit he is due that led to his co-receipt of the Nobel Prize.

assumption is critical for this model. Considerable research has been conducted with the assumption relaxed, but this topic is an advanced one and does not concern us here.

7.1.4 There Are No Taxes or Transaction Costs

We have made this assumption all along in pricing all types of derivatives. Taxes and transaction costs greatly complicate our models and keep us from seeing the essential financial principles involved in the models. It is possible to relax this assumption, but we shall not do so here.

7.1.5 There Are No Cash Flows on the Underlying

We have discussed this assumption at great length in pricing futures and forwards and earlier in this reading in studying the fundamentals of option pricing. The basic form of the Black–Scholes–Merton model makes this assumption, but it can easily be relaxed. We will show how to do this in Section 7.4.

7.1.6 The Options Are European

With only a few very advanced variations, the Black–Scholes–Merton model does not price American options. Users of the model must keep this in mind, or they may badly misprice these options. For pricing American options, the best approach is the binomial model with a large number of time periods.

7.2 The Black–Scholes–Merton Formula

Although the mathematics underlying the Black–Scholes–Merton formula are quite complex, the formula itself is not difficult, although it may appear so at first glance. The input variables are some of those we have already used: S_0 is the price of the underlying, X is the exercise price, r^c is the continuously compounded risk-free rate, and T is the time to expiration. The one other variable we need is the standard deviation of the log return on the asset. We denote this as σ and refer to it as the volatility. Then, the Black–Scholes–Merton formulas for the prices of call and put options are

$$c = S_0 N(d_1) - X e^{-r^c T} N(d_2)$$
$$p = X e^{-r^c T} [1 - N(d_2)] - S_0 [1 - N(d_1)]$$

(72-21)

where

$$d_1 = \frac{\ln(S_0/X) + [r^c + (\sigma^2/2)]T}{\sigma\sqrt{T}}$$

(72-22)

$$d_2 = d_1 - \sigma\sqrt{T}$$

σ = the annualized standard deviation of the continuously compounded return on the stock

r^c = the continuously compounded risk-free rate of return

Of course, we have already seen the terms "ln" and "e" in previous readings. We do, however, introduce two new and somewhat unusual looking terms, $N(d_1)$ and $N(d_2)$. These terms represent normal probabilities based on the values of d_1 and d_2. We compute the normal probabilities associated with values of d_1 and d_2 using the second equation above and insert these values into the formula as $N(d_1)$

and $N(d_2)$. Exhibit 72-24 presents a brief review of the normal probability distribution and explains how to obtain a probability value. Once we know how to look up a number in a normal probability table, we can then easily calculate d_1 and d_2, look them up in the table to obtain $N(d_1)$ and $N(d_2)$, and then insert the values of $N(d_1)$ and $N(d_2)$ into the above formula.

EXHIBIT 72-24 The Normal Probability Distribution

The normal probability distribution, or bell-shaped curve, gives the probability that a standard normal random variable will be less than or equal to a given value. The graph below shows the normal probability distribution; note that the curve is centered around zero. The values on the horizontal axis run from $-\infty$ to $+\infty$. If we were interested in a value of x of positive infinity, we would have $N(+\infty) = 1$. This expression means that the probability is 1.0 that we would obtain a value less than $+\infty$. If we were interested in a value of x of negative infinity, then $N(-\infty) = 0.0$. This expression means that there is zero probability of a value of x of less than negative infinity. Below, we are interested in the probability of a value less than x, where x is not infinite. We want $N(x)$, which is the area under the curve to the left of x.

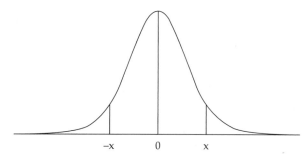

We obtain the values of $N(x)$ by looking them up in a table. Below is an excerpt from a table of values of x (the full table is given as Appendix 72A). Suppose $x = 1.12$. Then we find the row containing the value 1.1 and move over to the column containing 0.02. The sum of the row value and the column value is the value of x.

x	0	0.01	0.02	0.03	0.04	0.05	0.06	0.07	0.08	0.09
0.60	0.7257	0.7291	0.7324	0.7357	0.7389	0.7422	0.7454	0.7486	0.7517	0.7549
0.70	0.7580	0.7611	0.7642	0.7673	0.7704	**0.7734**	0.7764	0.7794	0.7823	0.7852
0.80	0.7881	0.7910	0.7939	0.7967	0.7995	0.8023	0.8051	0.8078	0.8106	0.8133
0.90	0.8159	0.8186	0.8212	0.8238	0.8264	0.8289	0.8315	0.8340	0.8365	0.8389
1.00	0.8413	0.8438	0.8461	0.8485	0.8508	0.8531	0.8554	0.8577	0.8599	0.8621
1.10	0.8643	0.8665	**0.8686**	0.8708	0.8729	0.8749	0.8770	0.8790	0.8810	0.8830
1.20	0.8849	0.8869	0.8888	0.8907	0.8925	0.8944	0.8962	0.8980	0.8997	0.9015

The corresponding probability is seen as the value 0.8686. Thus, $N(1.12) = 0.8686$. This means that the probability of obtaining a value of less than 1.12 in a normal distribution is 0.8686.

Now, suppose the value of x is negative. Observe in the figure above that the area to the left of $-x$ is the same as the area to the right of $+x$. Therefore, if x is a negative number, $N(x)$ is found as $1 - N(-x)$. For example, let $x = -0.75$. We simply look up $N(-x) = N[-(-0.75)] = N(0.75) = 0.7734$. Then $N(-0.75) = 1 - 0.7734 = 0.2266$.

Consider the following example. The underlying price is 52.75 and has a volatility of 0.35. The continuously compounded risk-free rate is 4.88 percent. The option expires in nine months; therefore, $T = 9/12 = 0.75$. The exercise price is 50. First we calculate the values of d1 and d2:

$$d_1 = \frac{\ln(52.75/50) + (0.0488 + (0.35)^2/2)0.75}{0.35\sqrt{0.75}} = 0.4489$$

$$d_2 = 0.4489 - 0.35\sqrt{0.75} = 0.1458$$

To use the normal probability table in Appendix 72A, we must round off d_1 and d_2 to two digits to the right of the decimal. Thus we have $d_1 = 0.45$ and $d_2 = 0.15$. From the table, we obtain

$$N(0.45) = 0.6736$$
$$N(0.15) = 0.5596$$

Then we plug everything into the equation for c:

$$c = 52.75(0.6736) - 50e^{-0.0488(0.75)}(0.5596) = 8.5580$$

The value of a put with the same terms would be

$$p = 50e^{-0.0488(0.75)}(1 - 0.5596) - 52.75(1 - 0.6736) = 4.0110$$

At this point, we should note that the Black–Scholes–Merton model is extremely sensitive to rounding errors. In particular, the process of looking up values in the normal probability table is a major source of error. A number of other ways exist to obtain $N(d_1)$ and $N(d_2)$, such as using Microsoft Excel's function "=normsdist()". Using a more precise method, such as Excel, the value of the call would be 8.619. Note that this is the value to which the binomial option price converged in the example we showed with 1,000 time periods in Exhibit 72-23. Indeed, the Black–Scholes–Merton model is said to be the continuous limit of the binomial model.

Practice Problem 8

Use the Black–Scholes–Merton model to calculate the prices of European call and put options on an asset priced at 68.5. The exercise price is 65, the continuously compounded risk-free rate is 4 percent, the options expire in 110 days, and the volatility is 0.38. There are no cash flows on the underlying.

SOLUTION

The time to expiration will be $T = 110/365 = 0.3014$. Then d_1 and d_2 are

$$d_1 = \frac{\ln(68.5/65) + (0.04 + (0.38)^2/2)(0.3014)}{0.38\sqrt{0.3014}} = 0.4135$$

$$d_2 = 0.4135 - 0.38\sqrt{0.3014} = 0.2049$$

Looking up in the normal probability table, we have

$$N(0.41) = 0.6591$$
$$N(0.20) = 0.5793$$

Plugging into the option price formula,

$$c = 68.5(0.6591) - 65e^{-0.04(0.3014)}(0.5793) = 7.95$$
$$p = 65e^{-0.04(0.3014)}(1 - 0.5793) - 68.5(1 - 0.6591) = 3.67$$

Let us now take a look at the various inputs required in the Black–Scholes–Merton model. We need to know where to obtain the inputs and how the option price varies with these inputs.

7.3 Inputs to the Black–Scholes–Merton Model

The Black–Scholes–Merton model has five inputs: the underlying price, the exercise price, the risk-free rate, the time to expiration, and the volatility.[30] As we have previously seen, call option prices should be higher the higher the underlying price, the longer the time to expiration, the higher the volatility, and the higher the risk-free rate. They should be lower the higher the exercise price. Put option prices should be higher the higher the exercise price and the higher the volatility. They should be lower the higher the underlying price and the higher the risk-free rate. As we saw, European put option prices can be either higher or lower the longer the time to expiration. American put option prices are always higher the longer the time to expiration, but the Black–Scholes–Merton model does not apply to American options.

These relationships are general to any European and American options and do not require the Black–Scholes–Merton model to understand them. Nonetheless, the Black–Scholes–Merton model provides an excellent opportunity to examine these relationships more closely. We can calculate and plot relationships such as those mentioned, which are usually called the option Greeks, because they are often referred to with Greek names. Let us now look at each of the inputs and the various option Greeks.

7.3.1 The Underlying Price: Delta and Gamma

The price of the underlying is generally one of the easiest sources of input information. Suffice it to say that if an investor cannot obtain the price of the underlying, then she should not even be considering the option. The price should generally be obtained as a quote or trade price from a liquid, open market.

The relationship between the option price and the underlying price has a special name: It is called the option **delta.** In fact, the delta can be obtained approximately from the Black–Scholes–Merton formula as the value of $N(d_1)$ for calls and $N(d_1) - 1$ for puts. More formally, the delta is defined as

$$\text{Delta} = \frac{\text{Change in option price}}{\text{Change in underlying price}} \qquad \text{(72-23)}$$

The above definition for delta is exact; the use of $N(d_1)$ for calls and $N(d_1) - 1$ for puts is approximate. Later in this section, we shall see why $N(d_1)$ and $N(d_2)$ are approximations and when they are good or bad approximations.

Let us consider the example we previously worked, where S = 52.75, X = 50, r^c = 0.0488, T = 0.75, and σ = 0.35. Using a computer to obtain a more precise Black–Scholes–Merton answer, we get a call option price of 8.6186 and a put option price of 4.0717. $N(d_1)$, the call delta, is 0.6733, so the put delta is $0.6733 - 1 = -0.3267$. Given that Delta = (Change in option price/Change in underlying price), we should expect that

Change in option price = Delta × Change in underlying price.

Therefore, for a $1 change in the price of the underlying, we should expect

---

[30] Later we shall add one more input, cash flows on the underlying.

Change in call option price $= 0.6733(1) = 0.6733$
Change in put option price $= -0.3267(1) = -0.3267$

This calculation would mean that

Approximate new call option price $= 8.6186 + 0.6733 = 9.2919$
Approximate new put option price $= 4.0717 - 0.3267 = 3.7450$

To test the accuracy of this approximation, we let the underlying price move up $1 to $53.75 and re-insert these values into the Black–Scholes–Merton model. We would then obtain

Actual new call option price $= 9.3030$
Actual new put option price $= 3.7560$

The delta approximation is fairly good, but not perfect.

Delta is important as a risk measure. *The delta defines the sensitivity of the option price to a change in the price of the underlying.* Traders, especially dealers in options, use delta to construct hedges to offset the risk they have assumed by buying and selling options. For example, recall from Reading 70 that FRA dealers offer to take either side of an FRA transaction. They then usually hedge the risk they have assumed by entering into other transactions. These same types of dealers offer to buy and sell options, hedging that risk with other transactions. For example, suppose we are a dealer offering to sell the call option we have been working with above. A customer buys 1,000 options for 8.619. We now are short 1,000 call options, which exposes us to considerable risk if the underlying goes up. So we must buy a certain number of units of the underlying to hedge this risk. We previously showed that the delta is 0.6733, so we would buy 673 units of the underlying at 52.75.[31] Assume for the moment that the delta tells us precisely the movement in the option for a movement in the underlying. Then suppose the underlying moves up $1:

Change in value of 1,000 long units of the underlying: $673(+\$1) = \$673$
Change in value of 1,000 short options: $1,000(+\$1)(0.6733) \approx \$673$

Because we are long the underlying and short the options, these values offset. At this point, however, the delta has changed. If we recalculate it, we would find it to be 0.6953. This would require that we have 695 units of the underlying, so we would need to buy an additional 22 units. We would borrow the money to do this. In some cases, we would need to sell off units of the underlying, in which case we would invest the money in the risk-free asset.

We shall return to the topic of delta hedging in Reading 74. For now, however, let us consider how changes in the underlying price will change the delta. In fact, even if the underlying price does not change, the delta would still change as the option moves toward expiration. For a call, the delta will increase toward 1.0 as the underlying price moves up and will decrease toward 0.0 as the underlying price moves down. For a put, the delta will decrease toward -1.0 as the underlying price moves down and increase towards 0.0 as the underlying price moves up.[32] If the underlying price does not move, a call delta will move toward 1.0 if the call is in-the-money or 0.0 if the call is out-of-the-money as the call moves

---

[31] This transaction would require $673(\$52.75) = \$35,500$, less the $1,000(\$8.619) = \$8,619$ received from the sale of the option, for a total investment required of $26,881. We would probably borrow this money.

[32] Remember that the put delta is negative; hence, its movement is down toward -1.0 or up toward 0.0.

toward the expiration day. A put delta will move toward -1.0 if the put is in-the-money or 0.0 if the put is out-of-the-money as it moves toward expiration.

So the delta is constantly changing, which means that delta hedging is a dynamic process. In fact, delta hedging is often referred to as **dynamic hedging.** In theory, the delta is changing continuously and the hedge should be adjusted continuously, but continuous adjustment is not possible in reality. When the hedge is not adjusted continuously, we are admitting the possibility of much larger moves in the price of the underlying. Let us see what happens in that case.

Using our previous example, we allow an increase in the underlying price of $10 to $62.75. Then the call price should change by $0.6733(10) = 6.733$, and the put option price should change by $-0.3267(10) = -3.267$. Thus, the approximate prices would be

Approximate new call option price = $8.619 + 6.733 = 15.3520$
Approximate new put option price = $4.0717 - 3.267 = 0.8047$

The actual prices are obtained by recalculating the option values using the Black–Scholes–Merton model with an underlying price of 62.75. Using a computer for greater precision, we find that these prices are

Actual new call option price = 16.3026
Actual new put option price = 1.7557

The approximations based on delta are not very accurate. In general, the larger the move in the underlying, the worse the approximation. This will make delta hedging less effective.

Exhibit 72-25 shows the relationship between the option price and the underlying price. Panel A depicts the relationship for calls and Panel B shows the corresponding relationship for puts. Notice the curvature in the relationship between the option price and the underlying price. Call option values definitely increase the greater the underlying value, and put option values definitely decrease. But the amount of change is not the same in each direction. $N(d_1)$ measures the slope of this line at a given point. As such, it measures only the slope for a very small change in the underlying. When the underlying changes by more than a very small amount, the curvature of the line comes into play and distorts the relationship between the option price and underlying price that is explained by the delta. The problem here is much like the relationship between a bond price and its yield. This first-order relationship between a bond price and its yield is called the duration; therefore, duration is similar to delta.

The curvature or second-order effect is known in the fixed income world as the convexity. In the options world, this effect is called **gamma.** Gamma is a numerical measure of how sensitive the delta is to a change in the underlying—in other words, how much the delta changes. When gamma is large, the delta changes rapidly and cannot provide a good approximation of how much the option moves for each unit of movement in the underlying. We shall not concern ourselves with measuring and using gamma, but we should know a few things about the gamma and, therefore, about the behavior of the delta.

Gamma is larger when there is more uncertainty about whether the option will expire in- or out-of-the-money. This means that *gamma will tend to be large when the option is at-the-money and close to expiration.* In turn, this statement means that delta will be a poor approximation for the option's price sensitivity when it is at-the-money and close to the expiration day. Thus, a delta hedge will work poorly. When the gamma is large, we may need to use a gamma-based hedge, which would require that we add a position in another option to the delta-hedge position of the underlying and the option. We shall not take up this advanced topic here.

EXHIBIT 72-25 The Relationship between Option Price and Underlying Price X = 50, r^c = 0.0488, T = 0.75, σ = 0.35

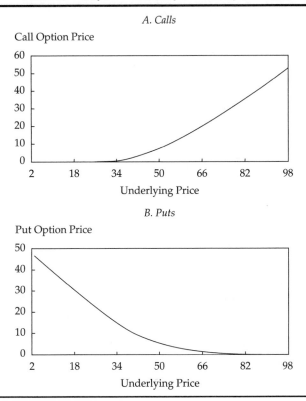

A. Calls

B. Puts

7.3.2 The Exercise Price

The exercise price is easy to obtain. It is specified in the option contract and does not change. Therefore, it is not worthwhile to speak about what happens when the exercise price changes, but we can talk about how the option price would differ if we choose an option with a different exercise price. As we have previously seen, the call option price will be lower the higher the exercise price and the put option price will be higher. This relationship is confirmed for our sample option in Exhibit 72-26.

EXHIBIT 72-26 The Relationship between Option Price and Exercise Price S = 52.75, r^c = 0.0488, T = 0.75, σ = 0.35

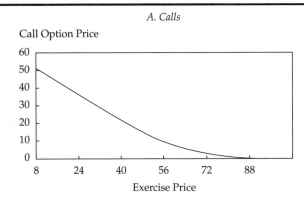

A. Calls

EXHIBIT 72-26 The Relationship between Option Price and Exercise Price
S = 52.75, r^c = 0.0488, T = 0.75, σ = 0.35 (continued)

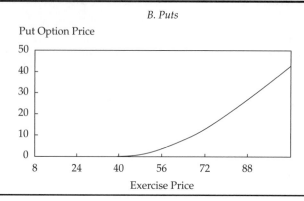

7.3.3 The Risk-Free Rate: Rho

The risk-free rate is the continuously compounded rate on the risk-free security whose maturity corresponds to the option's life. We have used the risk-free rate in previous readings; sometimes we have used the discrete version and sometimes the continuous version. As we have noted, the continuously compounded risk-free rate is the natural log of 1 plus the discrete risk-free rate.

For example, suppose the discrete risk-free rate quoted in annual terms is 5 percent. Then the continuous rate is

$$r^c = \ln(1 + r) = \ln(1.05) = 0.0488$$

Let us recall the difference in these two specifications. Suppose we want to find the present value of $1 in six months using both the discrete and continuous risk-free rates.

$$\text{Present value using discrete rate} = \frac{1}{(1 + r)^T} = \frac{1}{(1.05)^{0.5}} = 0.9759$$

$$\text{Present value using continuous rate} = e^{-r^cT} = e^{-0.0488(0.5)} = 0.9759$$

Obviously either specification will work. Because of how it uses the risk-free rate in the calculation of d_1, however, the Black–Scholes–Merton model requires the continuous risk-free rate.

The sensitivity of the option price to the risk-free rate is called the **rho.** We shall not concern ourselves with the calculation of rho. Technically, the Black–Scholes–Merton model assumes a constant risk-free rate, so it is meaningless to talk about the risk-free rate changing over the life of the option. We can, however, explore how the option price would differ if the current rate were different. Exhibit 72-27 depicts this effect. Note how little change occurs in the option price over a very broad range of the risk-free rate. Indeed, *the price of a European option on an asset is not very sensitive to the risk-free rate.*[33]

---

[33] When the underlying is an interest rate, however, there is a strong relationship between the option price and interest rates.

EXHIBIT 72-27 The Relationship between Option Price and Risk-Free Rate
S = 52.75, X = 50, T = 0.75, σ = 0.35

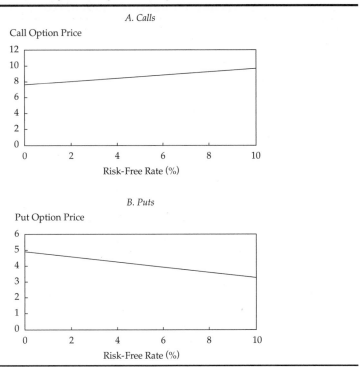

7.3.4 Time to Expiration: Theta

Time to expiration is an easy input to determine. An option has a definite expiration date specified in the contract. We simply count the number of days until expiration and divide by 365, as we have done previously with forward and futures contracts.

Obviously, the time remaining in an option's life moves constantly towards zero. Even if the underlying price is constant, the option price will still change. We noted that American options have both an intrinsic value and a time value. For European options, all of the price can be viewed as time value. In either case, time value is a function of the option's moneyness, its time to expiration, and its volatility. The more uncertainty there is, the greater the time value. As expiration approaches, the option price moves toward the payoff value of the option at expiration, a process known as **time value decay.** The rate at which the time value decays is called the option's **theta.** We shall not concern ourselves with calculating the specific value of theta, but be aware that if the option price decreases as time moves forward, the theta will be negative. Exhibit 72-28 shows the time value decay for our sample option.

Note that both call and put values decrease as the time to expiration decreases. We previously noted that European put options do not necessarily do this. For some cases, European put options can increase in value as the time to expiration decreases, the case of a positive theta, but that is not so for our put.[34] *Most of the time, option prices are higher the longer the time to expiration. For European puts, however, some exceptions exist.*

---

[34] Positive put thetas tend to occur when the put is deep in-the-money, the volatility is low, the interest rate is high, and the time to expiration is low.

EXHIBIT 72-28 The Relationship between Option Price and Time to Expiration S = 52.75, X = 50, r^c = 0.0488, σ = 0.35. T Starts at 0.75 and Goes toward 0.0

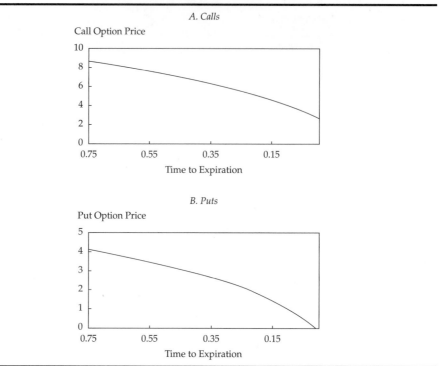

7.3.5 Volatility: Vega

As we have previously noted, volatility is the standard deviation of the continuously compounded return on the stock. We have also noted that the volatility is an extremely important variable in the valuation of an option. It is the only variable that cannot be obtained easily and directly from another source. In addition, as we illustrate here, option prices are extremely sensitive to the volatility. We take up the subject of estimating volatility in Section 7.5.

The relationship between option price and volatility is called the **vega,** which—albeit considered an option Greek—is not actually a Greek word.[35] We shall not concern ourselves with the actual calculation of the vega, but know that the vega is positive for both calls and puts, meaning that if the volatility increases, both call and put prices increase. Also, the vega is larger the closer the option is to being at-the-money.

In the problem we previously worked (S_0 = $52.75, X = $50, r^c = 0.0488, T = 0.75), at a volatility of 0.35, the option price was 8.619. Suppose we erroneously use a volatility of 0.40. Then the call price would be 9.446. An error in the volatility of this magnitude would not be difficult to make, especially for a variable that is not directly observable. Yet the result is a very large error in the option price.

Exhibit 72-29 displays the relationship between the option price and the volatility. Note that this relationship is nearly linear and that the option price varies over a very wide range, although this near-linearity is not the case for all options.

---

[35] So that all of these effects ("the Greeks") be named after Greek words, the term *kappa* is sometimes used to represent the relationship between an option price and its volatility. As it turns out, however, vega is used far more often than kappa and is probably easier to remember, given the "v" in vega and the "v" in volatility. Vega, however, is a star, not a letter, and its origin is Latin.

EXHIBIT 72-29 The Relationship between Option Price and Volatility
$$S = 52.75, X = 50, r^c = 0.0488, T = 0.75$$

A. Calls

Call Option Price

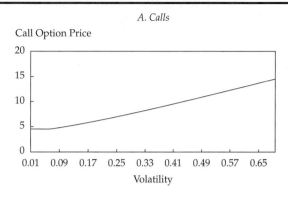

Volatility

B. Puts

Put Option Price

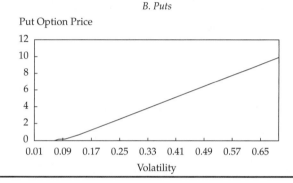

Volatility

7.4 The Effect of Cash Flows on the Underlying

As we saw in Readings 70 and 71, cash flows on the underlying affect the prices of forward and futures contracts. It should follow that they would affect the prices of options. In studying the option boundary conditions and put–call parity earlier in this reading, we noted that we subtract the present value of the dividends from the underlying price and use this adjusted price to obtain the boundary conditions or to price the options using put–call parity. We do the same using the Black–Scholes–Merton model. Specifically, we introduced the expression PV(CF,0,T) for the present value of the cash flows on the underlying over the life of the option. So, we simply use $S_0 - PV(CF,0,T)$ in the Black–Scholes–Merton model instead of S_0.

Recall that in previous readings, we also used continuous compounding to express the cash flows. For stocks, we used a continuously compounded dividend yield; for currencies, we used a continuously compounded interest rate. In the case of stocks, we let δ^c represent the continuously compounded dividend rate. Then we substituted for $S_0 e^{-\delta^c T}$ for S_0 in the Black–Scholes–Merton formula. For a foreign currency, we let S_0 represent the exchange rate, which we discount using r^{fc}, the continuously compounded foreign risk-free rate. Let us work an example involving a foreign currency option.

Let the exchange rate of U.S. dollars for euros be $0.8475. The continuously compounded U.S. risk-free rate, which in this example is r^c, is 5.10 percent. The continuously compounded euro risk-free rate, r^{fc}, is 4.25 percent. A call option expires in 125 days (T = 125/365 = 0.3425) and has an exercise price of $0.90. The volatility of the continuously compounded exchange rate is 0.055.

The first thing we do is obtain the adjusted price of the underlying: $0.8475e^{-0.0425(0.3425)} = 0.8353$. We then use this value as S_0 in the formula for d_1 and d_2:

$$d_1 = \frac{\ln(0.8353/0.90) + [0.051 + (0.055)^2/2](0.3425)}{0.055\sqrt{0.3425}} = -1.7590$$

$$d_2 = -1.7590 - 0.055\sqrt{0.3425} = -1.7912$$

Using the normal probability table, we find that

$$N(d_1) = N(-1.76) = 1 - 0.9608 = 0.0392$$
$$N(d_2) = N(-1.79) = 1 - 0.9633 = 0.0367$$

In discounting the exercise rate to evaluate the second term in the Black–Scholes–Merton expression, we use the domestic (here, U.S.) continuously compounded risk-free rate. The call option price would thus be

$$c = 0.8353(0.0392) - 0.90e^{-0.051(0.3425)}(0.0367) = 0.0003$$

Therefore, this call option on an asset worth \$0.8575 would cost \$0.0003.

Practice Problem 9

Use the Black–Scholes–Merton model adjusted for cash flows on the underlying to calculate the price of a call option in which the underlying is priced at 225, the exercise price is 200, the continuously compounded risk-free rate is 5.25 percent, the time to expiration is three years, and the volatility is 0.15. The effect of cash flows on the underlying is indicated below for two alternative approaches:

A. The present value of the cash flows over the life of the option is 19.72.

B. The continuously compounded dividend yield is 2.7 percent.

SOLUTIONS

A. Adjust the price of the underlying to $S_0 = 225 - 19.72 = 205.28$. Then insert into the Black–Scholes–Merton formula as follows:

$$d_1 = \frac{\ln(205.28/200) + [0.0525 + (0.15)^2/2](3.0)}{0.15\sqrt{3.0}} = 0.8364$$

$$d_2 = 0.8364 - 0.15\sqrt{3.0} = 0.5766$$
$$N(0.84) = 0.7995$$
$$N(0.58) = 0.7190$$
$$c = 205.28(0.7995) - 200e^{-0.0525(3.0)}(0.7190) = 41.28$$

B. Adjust the price of the underlying to $S_0 = 225e^{-0.027(3.0)} = 207.49$

$$d_1 = \frac{\ln(207.49/200) + [0.0525 + (0.15)^2/2](3.0)}{0.15\sqrt{3.0}} = 0.8776$$

$$d_2 = 0.8776 - 0.15\sqrt{3.0} = 0.6178$$
$$N(0.88) = 0.8106$$
$$N(0.62) = 0.7324$$
$$c = 207.49(0.8106) - 200e^{-0.0525(3.0)}(0.7324) = 43.06$$

7.5 The Critical Role of Volatility

As we have previously stressed, volatility is an extremely important variable in the pricing of options. In fact, with the possible exception of the cash flows on the underlying, it is the only variable that cannot be directly observed and easily obtained. It is, after all, the volatility over the life of the option; therefore, it is not past or current volatility but rather the future volatility. Differences in opinion on option prices nearly always result from differences of opinion about volatility. But how does one obtain a number for the future volatility?

7.5.1 Historical Volatility

The most logical starting place to look for an estimate of future volatility is past volatility. When the underlying is a publicly traded asset, we usually can collect some data over a recent past period and estimate the standard deviation of the continuously compounded return.

Exhibit 72-30 illustrates this process for a sample of 12 monthly prices of a particular stock. We convert these prices to returns, convert the returns to continuously compounded returns, find the variance of the series of continuously compounded returns, and then convert the variance to the standard deviation. In this example, the data are monthly returns, so we must annualize the variance by multiplying it by 12. Then we take the square root to obtain the historical estimate of the annual standard deviation or volatility.

EXHIBIT 72-30 Estimating Historical Volatility

Month	Price	Return	Log Return	(Log Return-Average)^2
0	100			
1	102	0.020000	0.019803	0.000123
2	99	−0.029412	−0.029853	0.001486
3	97	−0.020202	−0.020409	0.000847
4	89	−0.082474	−0.086075	0.008982
5	103	0.157303	0.146093	0.018878
6	104	0.009709	0.009662	0.000001
7	102	−0.019231	−0.019418	0.000790
8	99	−0.029412	−0.029853	0.001486
9	104	0.050505	0.049271	0.001646
10	102	−0.019231	−0.019418	0.000790
11	105	0.029412	0.028988	0.000412
12	111	0.057143	0.055570	0.002197
		Sum	0.104360	0.037639
		Average	0.008697	

EXHIBIT 72-30 Estimating Historical Volatility (continued)

The variance is estimated as follows:

$$\sigma^2 = \frac{\sum_{i=1}^{N} (R_i^c - \overline{R}^c)^2}{N-1}$$

where R_i^c is the continuously compounded return for observation i (shown above in the fourth column and calculated as $\ln(1 + R_i)$, where i goes from 1 to 12) and R_i is the ith return, $\overline{R}^c$ is the average return over the entire sample, and N is the number of observations in the sample (here, N = 12). Then

$$\sigma^2 = \frac{0.037639}{11} = 0.003422$$

Because this sample consists of monthly returns, to obtain the annual variance, we must multiply this number by 12 (or 52 for weekly, or 250—the approximate number of trading days in a year—for daily). Thus

$$\sigma^2 = 12(0.003422) = 0.041064$$

The annual standard deviation or volatility is, therefore,

$$\sigma = \sqrt{0.041064} = 0.2026$$

So the historical volatility estimate is 20.26 percent.

The historical estimate of the volatility is based only on what happened in the past. To get the best estimate, we must use a lot of prices, but that means going back farther in time. The farther back we go, the less current the data become, and the less reliable our estimate of the volatility. We now look at a way of obtaining a more current estimate of the volatility, but one that raises questions as well as answers them.

7.5.2 Implied Volatility

In a market in which options are traded actively, we can reasonably assume that the market price of the option is an accurate reflection of its true value. Thus, by setting the Black–Scholes–Merton price equal to the market price, we can work backwards to infer the volatility. This procedure enables us to determine the volatility that option traders are using to price the option. This volatility is called the **implied volatility.**

Unfortunately, determining implied volatility is not a simple task. We cannot simply solve the Black–Scholes–Merton equation for the volatility. It is a complicated function with the volatility appearing several times, in some cases as σ^2. There are some mathematical techniques that speed up the estimation of the implied volatility. Here, however, we shall look at only the most basic method: trial and error.

Recall the option we have been working with. The underlying price is 52.75, the exercise price is 50, the risk-free rate is 4.88 percent, and the time to expiration is 0.75. In our previous examples, the volatility was 0.35. Using these values in the Black–Scholes–Merton model, we obtained a call option price of 8.619. Suppose we observe the option selling in the market for 9.25. What volatility would produce this price?

We have already calculated a price of 8.619 at a volatility of 0.35. Because the call price varies directly with the volatility, we know that it would take a volatility greater than 0.35 to produce a price higher than 8.619. We do not know how much higher, so we should just take a guess. Let us try a volatility of 0.40. Using the Black–Scholes–Merton formula with a volatility of 0.40, we obtain a price of 9.446. This is too high, so we try a lower volatility. We keep doing this in the following manner:

Volatility	Black–Scholes–Merton Price
0.35	8.619
0.40	9.446
0.39	9.280
0.38	9.114

So now we know that the correct volatility lies between 0.38 and 0.39, closer to 0.39. In solving for the implied volatility, we must decide either how close to the option price we want to be or how many significant digits we want in the implied volatility. If we choose four significant digits in the implied volatility, a value of 0.3882 would produce the option price of 9.2500. Alternatively, if we decide that we want to be within 0.01 of the option price, we would find that the implied volatility is in the range of 38.76 to 38.88 percent.

Thus, if the option is selling for about 9.25, we say that the market is pricing it at a volatility of 0.3882. This number represents the market's best estimate of the true volatility of the underlying asset; it can be viewed as a more current source of volatility information than the past volatility. Unfortunately, a circularity exists in the argument. If one uses the Black–Scholes–Merton model to determine if an option is over- or underpriced, the procedure for extracting the implied volatility assumes that the market correctly prices the option. The only way to use the implied volatility in identifying mispriced options is to interpret the implied volatility as either too high or too low, which would require an estimate of true volatility. Nonetheless, the implied volatility is a source of valuable information on the uncertainty in the underlying, and option traders use it routinely.

All of this material on continuous-time option pricing has been focused on options in which the underlying is an asset. As we described earlier in this reading, there are also options on futures. Let us take a look at the pricing of options on futures, which will pave the way for a continuous-time pricing model for options on interest rates, another case in which the underlying is not an asset.

8

PRICING OPTIONS ON FORWARD AND FUTURES CONTRACTS AND AN APPLICATION TO INTEREST RATE OPTION PRICING

Earlier in this reading, we discussed how options on futures contracts are active, exchange-traded options in which the underlying is a futures contract. In addition, there are over-the-counter options in which the underlying is a forward contract. In our treatment of these instruments, we assume constant interest rates. As we learned in Readings 70 and 71, this assumption means that futures and forward contracts will have the same prices. European options on futures and forward contracts will, therefore, have the same prices. American options on forwards will differ in price from American options on futures, and we discuss this later.

First we take a quick look at the basic rules that we previously developed for options on underlying assets. If the underlying asset is a futures contract, the payoff values of the options at expiration are

$$c_T = Max[0, f_T(T) - X]$$
$$p_T = Max[0, X - f_T(T)]$$

(72-24)

where $f_T(T)$ is the price of a futures contract at T in which the contract expires at T. Thus, $f_T(T)$ is the futures price at expiration. These formulas are, of course, the same as for options when the underlying is an asset, with the futures price substituted for the asset price. When the option and the futures expire simultaneously, the futures price at expiration, $f_T(T)$, converges to the asset price, S_T, making the above payoffs precisely the same as those of the option on the underlying asset.

The minimum and maximum values for options on forwards or futures are the same as those we obtained for options on assets, substituting the futures price for the asset price. Specifically,

$$0 \leq c_0 \leq f_0(T)$$
$$0 \leq C_0 \leq f_0(T)$$
$$0 \leq p_0 \leq X/(1 + r)^T$$
$$0 \leq P_0 \leq X$$

(72-25)

We also established lower bounds for European options and intrinsic values for American options and used these results to establish the minimum prices of these options. For options on futures, the lower bounds are

$$c_0 \geq Max\{0, [f_0(T) - X]/(1 + r)^T\}$$
$$p_0 \geq Max\{0, [X - f_0(T)]/(1 + r)^T\}$$

(72-26)

where $f_0(T)$ is the price at time 0 of a futures contract expiring at T. Therefore, the price of a European call or put on the futures is either zero or the difference between the futures price and exercise price, as formulated above, discounted to the present. For American options on futures, early exercise is possible. Thus, we express their lowest prices as the intrinsic values:

$$C_0 \geq Max[0, f_0(T) - X]$$
$$P_0 \geq Max[0, X - f_0(T)]$$

(72-27)

Because these values are greater than the lower bounds, we maintain these values as the minimum prices of American calls.[36]

---

[36] In other words, we cannot use the European lower bound as the lowest price of an American call or put, as we could with calls when the underlying was an asset instead of a futures.

As we have previously pointed out, with the assumption of constant interest rates, futures prices and forward prices are the same. We can treat European options on futures the same way as options on forwards. American options on futures will differ from American options on forwards. Now we explore how put–call parity works for options on forwards.

8.1 Put–Call Parity for Options on Forwards

In an earlier section, we examined put–call parity. Now we take a look at the parity between puts and calls on forward contracts and their underlying forward contracts. First recall the notation: $F(0,T)$ is the price established at time 0 for a forward contract expiring at time T. Let c_0 and p_0 be the prices today of calls and puts on the forward contract. We shall assume that the puts and calls expire when the forward contract expires. The exercise price of the options is X. The payoff of the call is $\text{Max}(0, S_T - X)$, and the payoff of the put is $\text{Max}(0, X - S_T)$.[37] We construct a combination consisting of a long call and a long position in a zero-coupon bond with face value of $X - F(0,T)$. We construct another combination consisting of a long position in a put and a long position in a forward contract. Exhibit 72-31 shows the results.

EXHIBIT 72-31 Portfolio Combinations for Equivalent Packages of Puts, Calls, and Forward Contracts (Put–Call Parity for Forward Contracts

Transaction	Current Value	Value at Expiration $S_T \leq X$	Value at Expiration $S_T > X$
Call and Bond			
Buy call	c_0	0	$S_T - X$
Buy bond	$[X - F(0,T)]/(1 + r)^T$	$X - F(0,T)$	$X - F(0,T)$
Total	$c_0 + [X - F(0,T)]/(1 + r)^T$	$X - F(0,T)$	$S_T - F(0,T)$
Put and Forward			
Buy put	p_0	$X - S_T$	0
Buy forward contract	0	$S_T - F(0,T)$	$S_T - F(0,T)$
Total	p_0	$X - F(0,T)$	$S_T - F(0,T)$

As the exhibit demonstrates, both combinations produce a payoff of either $X - F(0,T)$ or $S_T - F(0,T)$, whichever is greater. The call and bond combination is thus equivalent to the put and forward contract combination. Hence, to prevent an arbitrage opportunity, the initial values of these combinations must be the same. The initial value of the call and bond combination is $c_0 + [X - F(0,T)]/(1 + r)^T$. The forward contract has zero initial value, so the initial value of the put and forward contract combination is only the initial value of the put, p_0. Therefore,

$$c_0 + [X - F(0,T)]/(1 + r)^T = p_0 \qquad \text{(72-28)}$$

This equation is **put–call parity for options on forward contracts.**

---

[37] Recall that the option payoffs are given by the underlying price at expiration, because the forward contract expires when the option expires. Therefore, the forward price at expiration is the underlying price at expiration.

Note that we seem to have implied that the bond is a long position, but that might not be the case. The bond should have a face value of $X - F(0,T)$. We learned in Reading 70 that $F(0,T)$ is determined in the market as the underlying price compounded at the risk-free rate.[38] Because there are a variety of options with different exercise prices, any one of which could be chosen, it is clearly possible for X to exceed or be less than $F(0,T)$. If $X > F(0,T)$, we are long the bond, because the payoff of $X - F(0,T)$ is greater than zero, meaning that we get back money from the bond. If $X < F(0,T)$, we issue the bond, because the payoff of $X - F(0,T)$ is less than zero, meaning that we must pay back money. Note the special case when $X = F(0,T)$. The bond is effectively out of the picture. Then $c_0 = p_0$.

Now recall from Reading 70 that with discrete interest compounding and no storage costs, the forward price is the spot price compounded at the risk-free rate. So,

$$F(0,T) = S_0(1 + r)^T$$

If we substitute this result for $F(0,T)$ in the put–call parity equation for options on forwards, we obtain

$$p_0 + S_0 = c_0 + X/(1 + r)^T$$

which is the put–call parity equation for options on the underlying that we learned earlier in this reading. Indeed, put–call parity for options on forwards and put–call parity for options on the underlying asset are the same. The only difference is that in the former, the forward contract and the bond replace the underlying. Given the equivalence of options on the forward contract and options on the underlying, we can refer to put–call parity for options on forwards as **put–call–forward parity.** The equation

$$c_0 + [X - F(0,T)]/(1 + r)^T = p_0$$

expresses the relationship between the forward price and the prices of the options on the underlying asset, or alternatively between the forward price and the prices of options on the forward contract. We can also rearrange the equation to isolate the forward price and obtain

$$F(0,T) = (c_0 - p_0)(1 + r)^T + X$$

which shows how the forward price is related to the put and call prices and to the exercise price.

Now observe in Exhibit 72-32 how a synthetic forward contract can be created out of options. In the top half of the exhibit is a forward contract. Its payoff at expiration is $S_T - F(0,T)$. In the bottom half of the exhibit is a **synthetic forward contract,** which consists of a long call, a short put, and a long risk-free bond with a face value equal to the exercise price minus the forward price. Note that this bond can actually be short if the exercise price of these options is lower than the forward price. The forward contract and synthetic forward contract have the same payoffs, so their initial values must be equal. The initial value of the forward contract is zero, so the initial value of the synthetic forward contract must be zero. Thus,

$$c_0 - p_0 + [X - F(0,T)]/(1 + r)^T = 0$$

---

[38] We are, of course, assuming no cash flows or costs on the underlying asset.

EXHIBIT 72-32 Forward Contract and Synthetic Forward Contract

Transaction	Current Value	Value at Expiration $S_T \le X$	Value at Expiration $S_T > X$
Forward Contract			
Long forward contract	0	$S_T - F(0,T)$	$S_T - F(0,T)$
Synthetic Forward Contract			
Buy call	c_0	0	$S_T - X$
Sell put	$-p_0$	$-(X - S_T)$	0
Buy (or sell) bond	$[X - F(0,T)]/(1 + r)^T$	$X - F(0,T)$	$X - F(0,T)$
Total	$c_0 - p_0 + [X - F(0,T)]/(1 + r)^T$	$S_T - F(0,T)$	$S_T - F(0,T)$

Solving for $F(0,T)$, we obtain the equation for the forward price in terms of the call, put, and bond that was given previously. So a synthetic forward contract is a combination consisting of a long call, a short put, and a zero-coupon bond with face value of $X - F(0,T)$.

Consider the following example: The options and a forward contract expire in 50 days, so $T = 50/365 = 0.1370$. The risk-free rate is 6 percent, and the exercise price is 95. The call price is 5.50, the put price is 10.50, and the forward price is 90.72. Substituting in the above equation, we obtain

$$5.50 - 10.50 + \frac{95 - 90.72}{(1.06)^{0.1370}} = -0.7540$$

which is supposed to be zero. The left-hand side replicates a forward contract. Thus, the synthetic forward is underpriced. We buy it and sell the actual forward contract. So if we buy the call, sell the put, and buy the bond with face value $95 - 90.72 = 4.28$, we bring in 0.7540. At expiration, the payoffs are as follows.

The options and forward expire with the underlying above 95:
>   The bond matures and pays off $95 - 90.72 = 4.28$.
>   Exercise the call, paying 95 and obtaining the underlying.
>   Deliver the underlying and receive 90.72 from the forward contract.
>   The put expires with no value.
>   Net effect: No money in or out.

The options and forward expire with the underlying at or below 95:
>   The bond matures and pays off $95 - 90.72 = 4.28$.
>   Buy the underlying for 95 with the short put.
>   Deliver the underlying and receive 90.72 from the forward contract.
>   The call expires with no value.
>   Net effect: No money in or out.

So we take in 0.7540 up front and never have to pay anything out. The pressure of other investors doing this will cause the call price to increase and the put price to decrease until the above equation equals zero or is at least equal to the transaction costs that would be incurred to exploit any discrepancy from zero.

Practice Problem 10

Determine if a forward contract is correctly priced by using put–call–forward parity. The option exercise price is 90, the risk-free rate is 5 percent, the options and the forward contract expire in two years, the call price is 15.25, the put price is 3.00, and the forward price is 101.43.

SOLUTION

First note that the time to expiration is $T = 2.0$. There are many ways to express put–call–forward parity. We use the following specification:

$$p_0 = c_0 + [X - F(0,T)]/(1 + r)^T$$

The right-hand side is the synthetic put and consists of a long call, a short forward contract, and a bond with face value of $X - F(0,T)$. Substituting the values into the right-hand side, we obtain

$$p_0 = 15.25 + (90 - 101.43)/(1.05)^{2.0} = 4.88$$

Because the actual put is selling for 3.00, it is underpriced. So we should buy the put and sell the synthetic put. To sell the synthetic put we should sell the call, buy the forward contract, and hold a bond with face value $F(0,T) - X$. Doing so will generate the following cash flow up front:

Buy put:	−3.00
Sell call:	+15.25
Buy bond:	$-(101.43 - 90)/(1.05)^{2.0} = -10.37$
Total:	+1.88

Thus the transaction brings in 1.88 up front. The payoffs at expiration are

	$S_T < 90$	$S_T \geq 90$
Long put	$90 - S_T$	0
Short call	0	$-(S_T - 90)$
Long bond	$101.43 - 90$	$101.43 - 90$
Long forward	$S_T - 101.43$	$S_T - 101.43$
Total	0	0

Therefore, no money flows in or out at expiration.

Similarly, an option can be created from a forward contract. If a long forward contract is equivalent to a long call, short put, and zero-coupon bond with face value of $X - F(0,T)$, then a long call is a long forward, long put, and a zero-coupon bond with face value of $F(0,T) - X$. A long put is a long call, short forward, and a bond with face value of $X - F(0,T)$. These results are obtained just by rearranging what we learned here about forwards and options.

These results hold strictly for European options; some additional considerations exist for American options, but we do not cover them here.

8.2 Early Exercise of American Options on Forward and Futures Contracts

As we noted earlier, the holder of an American put option may want to exercise it early. For American call options on underlying assets that make no cash payments, however, there is no justification for exercising the option early. If the underlying asset makes a cash payment, such as a dividend on a stock or interest on a bond, it may be justifiable to exercise the call option early.

For American options on futures, it may be worthwhile to exercise both calls and puts early. Even though early exercise is never justified for American calls on underlying assets that make no cash payments, early exercise can be justified for American call options on futures. Deep-in-the money American call options on futures behave almost identically to the underlying, but the investor has money tied up in the call. If the holder exercises the call and establishes a futures position, he earns interest on the futures margin account. A similar argument holds for deep-in-the-money American put options on futures. The determination of the timing of early exercise is a specialist topic so we do not explore it here.

If the option is on a forward contract instead of a futures contract, however, these arguments are overshadowed by the fact that a forward contract does not pay off until expiration, in contrast to the mark-to-market procedure of futures contracts. Thus, if one exercised either a call or a put on a forward contract early, doing so would only establish a long or short position in a forward contract. This position would not pay any cash until expiration. No justification exists for exercising early if one cannot generate any cash from the exercise. Therefore, an American call on a forward contract is the same as a European call on a forward contract, but American calls on futures are different from European calls on futures and carry higher prices.

8.3 The Black Model

The usual model for pricing European options on futures is called the Black model, named after Fischer Black of Black–Scholes–Merton fame. The formula is

$$c = e^{-r^c T}[f_0(T)N(d_1) - XN(d_2)]$$

$$p = e^{-r^c T}(X[1 - N(d_2)] - f_0(T)[1 - N(d_1)])$$

where

$$d_1 = \frac{\ln(f_0(T)/X) + (\sigma^2/2)T}{\sigma\sqrt{T}}$$

$$d_2 = d_1 - \sigma\sqrt{T}$$

$$f_0(T) = \text{the futures price}$$

and the other terms are those we have previously used. The volatility, σ, is the volatility of the continuously compounded change in the futures price.[39]

Although the Black model may appear to give a somewhat different formula, it can be obtained directly from the Black–Scholes–Merton formula. Recall that

---

[39] If we were using the model to price options on forward contracts, we would insert $F(0,T)$, the forward price, instead of the futures price. Doing so would produce some confusion because we have never subscripted the forward price, arguing that it does not change. Therefore, although we could use the formula to price options on forwards at time 0, how could we use the formula to price options on forwards at a later time, say time t, prior to expiration? In that case, we would have to use the price of a newly constructed forward contract that expires at T, $F(t,T)$. Of course, with constant interest rates, these forward prices, $F(0,T)$ and $F(t,T)$, would be identical to the analogous futures price, $f_0(T)$ and $f_t(T)$. So, for ease of exposition we use the futures price.

the futures price in terms of the underlying spot price would be $f_0(T) = S_0 e^{r^cT}$. If we substitute the right-hand-side for $f_0(T)$ in the Black formula for d_1, we obtain the Black–Scholes–Merton formula for d_1.[40] Then if we substitute the right-hand side of the above for $f_0(T)$ in the Black formula for c_0 and p_0, we obtain the Black–Scholes–Merton formula for c_0 and p_0. These substitutions should make sense: The prices of options on futures equal the prices of options on the asset when the options and futures expire simultaneously.

The procedure should be straightforward if you have mastered substituting the asset price and other inputs into the Black–Scholes–Merton formula. Also, note that as with the Black–Scholes–Merton formula, the formula applies only to European options. As we noted in the previous section, early exercise of American options on futures is often justified, so we cannot get away with using this formula for American options on futures. We can, however, use the formula for American options on forwards, because they are never exercised early.

Practice Problem 11

The price of a forward contract is 139.19. A European option on the forward contract expires in 215 days. The exercise price is 125. The continuously compounded risk-free rate is 4.25 percent. The volatility is 0.15.

A. Use the Black model to determine the price of the call option.

B. Determine the price of the underlying from the above information and use the Black–Scholes–Merton model to show that the price of an option on the underlying is the same as the price of the option on the forward.

SOLUTIONS

The time to expiration is T = 215/365 = 0.5890.

A. First find d_1 and d_2, then $N(d_1)$ and $N(d_2)$, and then the call price:

$$d_1 = \frac{\ln(139.19/125) + [(0.15)^2/2]0.5890}{0.15\sqrt{0.5890}} = 0.9916$$

$d_2 = 0.9916 - 0.15\sqrt{0.5890} = 0.8765$

$N(0.99) = 0.8389$

$N(0.88) = 0.8106$

$c = e^{-0.0425(0.5890)}[139.19(0.8389) - 125(0.8106)] = 15.06$

B. We learned in Reading 70 that if there are no cash flows on the underlying and the interest is compounded continuously, the forward price is given by the formula $F(0, T) = S_0 e^{r^cT}$. We can thus find the spot price as

$$S_0 = F(0,T)e^{-r^cT} = 139.19e^{-0.0425(0.5890)} = 135.75$$

---

[40] This action requires us to recognize that $\ln(S_0 e^{r^cT}/X) = \ln(S_0/X) + r^cT$.

Then we simply use the Black–Scholes–Merton formula:

$$d_1 = \frac{\ln(135.75/125) + (0.0425 + (0.15)^2/2)(0.5890)}{0.15\sqrt{0.5890}} = 0.9916$$

$$d_2 = 0.9916 - 0.15\sqrt{0.5890} = 0.8765$$

These are the same values as in Part A, so $N(d_1)$ and $N(d_2)$ will be the same. Plugging into the formula for the call price gives

$$c = 135.75(0.8389) - 125e^{-0.0425(0.5890)}(0.8106) = 15.06$$

This price is the same as in Part A.

8.4 Application of the Black Model to Interest Rate Options

Earlier in this reading, we described options on interest rates. These derivative instruments parallel the FRAs that we covered in Reading 70, in that they are derivatives in which the underlying is not a bond but rather an interest rate. Pricing options on interest rates is a challenging task. We showed how this is done using binomial trees. It would be nice if the Black–Scholes–Merton model could be easily used to price interest rate options, but the process is not so straightforward. Pricing options on interest rates requires a sophisticated model that prohibits arbitrage among interest-rate related instruments and their derivatives. The Black–Scholes–Merton model is not sufficiently general to use in this manner. Nonetheless, practitioners often employ the Black model to price interest rate options. Somewhat remarkably, perhaps, it is known to give satisfactory results. Therefore, we provide a quick overview of this practice here.

Suppose we wish to price a one-year interest rate cap, consisting of three caplets. One caplet expires in 90 days, one 180 days, and one in 270 days.[41] The exercise rate is 9 percent. To use the Black model, we use the forward rate as though it were $f_0(T)$.

Therefore, we also require its volatility and the risk-free rate for the period to the option's expiration.[42] Recalling that there are three caplets and we have to price each one individually, let us first focus on the caplet expiring in 90 days. We first specify that $T = 90/365 = 0.2466$. Then we need the forward rate today for the period day 90 to day 180. Let this rate be 9.25 percent. We shall assume its volatility is 0.03. We then need the continuously compounded risk-free rate for

---

[41] A one-year cap will have three individual caplets. The first expires in 90 days and pays off in 180 days, the second expires in 180 days and pays off in 270 days, and the third expires in 270 days and pays off in 360 days. The tendency to think that a one-year cap using quarterly periods should have four caplets is incorrect because there is no caplet expiring right now and paying off in 90 days. It would make no sense to create an option that expires immediately. Also, in a one-year loan, the rate is set at the start and reset only three times; hence, only three caplets are required.

[42] It is important to note here that the Black model requires that all inputs be in continuous compounding format. Therefore, the forward rate and risk-free rate would need to be the continuously compounded analogs to the discrete rates. Because the underlying is usually LIBOR, which is a discrete rate quoted on the basis of a 360-day year, some adjustments must be made to convert to a continuous rate quoted on the basis of a 365-day year. We will not address these adjustments here.

90 days, which we assume to be 9.60 percent. So now we have the following input variables:

$T = 0.2466$
$f_0(T) = 0.0925$
$\sigma = 0.03$
$X = 0.09$
$r^c = 0.096$

Inserting these inputs into the Black model produces

$$d_1 = \frac{\ln(0.0925/0.09) + [(0.03)^2/2](0.2466)}{0.03\sqrt{0.2466}} = 1.8466$$

$$d_2 = 1.8466 - 0.03\sqrt{0.2466} = 1.8317$$

$$N(1.85) = 0.9678$$

$$N(1.83) = 0.9664$$

$$c_0 = e^{-0.096(0.2466)}[0.0925(0.9678) - 0.09(0.9664)] = 0.00248594$$

(Because of the order of magnitude of the inputs, we carry the answer out to eight decimal places.) But this answer is not quite what we need. The formula gives the answer under the assumption that the option payoff occurs at the option expiration. As we know, interest rate options pay off later than their expirations. This option expires in 90 days and pays off 90 days after that. Therefore, we need to discount this result back from day 180 to day 90 using the forward rate of 9.25 percent.[43] We thus have

$$0.00248594 e^{-0.0925(0.2466)} = 0.00242988$$

Another adjustment is necessary. Because the underlying price and exercise price are entered as rates, the resulting answer is a rate. Moreover, the underlying rate and exercise rate are expressed as annual rates, so the answer is an annual rate. Interest rate option prices are always quoted as periodic rates (which are prices for $1 notional principal). We would adjust this rate by multiplying by 90/360.[44] The price would thus be

$$0.00242988(90/360) = 0.00060747$$

Finally, we should note that this price is valid for a $1 notional principal option. If the notional principal were $1 million, the option price would be

$$\$1,000,000(0.00060747) = \$607.47$$

We have just priced the first caplet of this cap. To price the second caplet, we need the forward rate for the period 180 days to 270 days, we would use $180/365 = 0.4932$ as the time to expiration, and we need the risk-free rate for 180 days. To

---

[43] Be very careful in this discounting procedure. The exponent in the exponential should have a time factor of the number of days between the option expiration and its payoff. Because there are 90 days between days 90 and 180, we use $90/365 = 0.2466$. This value is not quite the same as the time until the option expiration, which today is 90 but which will count down to zero.

[44] It is customary in the interest rate options market to use 360 in the denominator to make this adjustment, even though we have used 365 in other places.

price the third caplet, we need the forward rate for the period 270 days to 360 days, we would use $270/365 = 0.7397$ as the time to expiration, and we need the risk-free rate for 270 days. The price of the cap would be the sum of the prices of the three component caplets. If we were pricing a floor, we would price the component floorlets using the Black model for puts.

Although the Black model is frequently used to price interest rate options, binomial models, as we illustrated earlier, are somewhat more widely used in this area. These models are more attuned to deriving prices that prohibit arbitrage opportunities using any of the diverse instruments whose prices are given by the term structure. When you use the Black model to price interest rate options, there is some risk, perhaps minor, of having a counterparty be able to do arbitrage against you. Yet somehow the Black model is used often, and professionals seem to agree that it works remarkably well.

Practice Problem 12

Use the Black model to price an interest rate put that expires in 280 days. The forward rate is currently 6.8 percent, the 280-day continuously compounded risk-free rate is 6.25 percent, the exercise rate is 7 percent, and the volatility is 0.02. The option is based on a 180-day underlying rate, and the notional principal is $10 million.

SOLUTION

The time to expiration is $T = 280/365 = 0.7671$. Calculate the value of d_1, d_2, and $N(d_1)$, $N(d_2)$, and p_0 using the Black model:

$$d_1 = \frac{\ln(0.068/0.07) + [0.02)^2/2]0.7671}{0.02\sqrt{0.7671}} = -1.6461$$

$d_2 = -1.6461 - 0.02\sqrt{0.7671} = -1.6636$

$N(-1.65) = 1 - N(1.65) = 1 - 0.9505 = 0.0495$

$N(-1.66) = 1 - N(1.66) = 1 - 0.9515 = 0.0485$

$p_0 = e^{-0.0625(0.7671)}[0.07(1 - 0.0485) - 0.068(1 - 0.0495)] = 0.00187873$

This formula assumes the option payoff is made at expiration. For an interest rate option, that assumption is false. This is a 180-day rate, so the payoff is made 180 days later. Therefore, we discount the payoff over 180 days using the forward rate:

$e^{-0.068(180/365)}(0.00187873) = 0.00181677$

Interest rate option prices must reflect the fact that the rate used in the formula is quoted as an annual rate. So, we must multiply by $180/360$ because the transaction is based on a 180-day rate:

$0.00181677(180/360) = 0.00090839$

Then we multiply by the notional principal:

$\$10,000,000(0.00090839) = \$9,084$

9   THE ROLE OF OPTIONS MARKETS

As we did with futures markets, we conclude the reading by looking at the important role options markets play in the financial system. Recall from Reading 69 that we looked at the purposes of derivative markets. We noted that derivative markets provide price discovery and risk management, make the markets for the underlying assets more efficient, and permit trading at low transaction costs. These features are also associated with options markets. Yet, options offer further advantages that some other derivatives do not offer.

For example, forward and futures contracts have bidirectional payoffs. They have the potential for a substantial gain in one direction and a substantial loss in the other direction. The advantage of taking such a position lies in the fact that one need pay no cash up front. In contrast, options offer the feature that, if one is willing to pay cash up front, one can limit the loss in a given direction. In other words, options have unidirectional payoffs. This feature can be attractive to the holder of an option. To the writer, options offer the opportunity to be paid cash up front for a willingness to assume the risk of the unidirectional payoff. An option writer can assume the risk of potentially a large loss unmatched by the potential for a large gain. In fact, the potential gain is small. But for this risk, the option writer receives money up front.

Options also offer excellent devices for managing the risk of various exposures. An obvious one is the protective put, which we saw earlier and which can protect a position against loss by paying off when the value of the underlying is down. We shall see this and other such applications in Reading 74.

Recall that futures contracts offer price discovery, the revelation of the prices at which investors will contract today for transactions to take place later. Options, on the other hand, provide volatility discovery. Through the implied volatility, investors can determine the market's assessment of how volatile it believes the underlying asset is. This valuable information can be difficult to obtain from any other source.

Futures offer advantages over forwards, in that futures are standardized, tend to be actively traded in a secondary market, and are protected by the exchange's clearinghouse against credit risk. Although some options, such as interest rate options, are available only in over-the-counter forms, many options exist in both over-the-counter and exchange-listed forms. Hence, one can often customize an option if necessary or trade it on an exchange.

In Reading 70, we covered forward contracts; in Reading 71, we covered futures contracts; and in this reading we covered option contracts. We have one more major class of derivative instruments, swaps, which we now turn to in Reading 73. We shall return to options in Reading 74, where we explore option trading strategies.

▷ Options are rights to buy or sell an underlying at a fixed price, the exercise price, for a period of time. The right to buy is a call; the right to sell is a put. Options have a definite expiration date. Using the option to buy or sell is the action of exercising it. The buyer or holder of an option pays a price to the seller or writer for the right to buy (a call) or sell (a put) the underlying instrument. The writer of an option has the corresponding potential obligation to sell or buy the underlying.

▷ European options can be exercised only at expiration; American options can be exercised at any time prior to expiration. Moneyness refers to the characteristic that an option has positive intrinsic value. The payoff is the value of the option at expiration. An option's intrinsic value is the value that can be captured if the option is exercised. Time value is the component of an option's price that reflects the uncertainty of what will happen in the future to the price of the underlying.

▷ Options can be traded as standardized instruments on an options exchange, where they are protected from default on the part of the writer, or as customized instruments on the over-the-counter market, where they are subject to the possibility of the writer defaulting. Because the buyer pays a price at the start and does not have to do anything else, the buyer cannot default.

▷ The underlying instruments for options are individual stocks, stock indices, bonds, interest rates, currencies, futures, commodities, and even such random factors as the weather. In addition, a class of options called real options is associated with the flexibility in capital investment projects.

▷ Like FRAs, which are forward contracts in which the underlying is an interest rate, interest rate options are options in which the underlying is an interest rate. However, FRAs are commitments to make one interest payment and receive another, whereas interest rate options are rights to make one interest payment and receive another.

▷ Option payoffs, which are the values of options when they expire, are determined by the greater of zero or the difference between underlying price and exercise price, if a call, or the greater of zero or the difference between exercise price and underlying price, if a put. For interest rate options, the exercise price is a specified rate and the underlying price is a variable interest rate.

▷ Interest rate options exist in the form of caps, which are call options on interest rates, and floors, which are put options on interest rates. Caps consist of a series of call options, called caplets, on an underlying rate, with each option expiring at a different time. Floors consist of a series of put options, called floorlets, on an underlying rate, with each option expiring at a different time.

▷ The minimum value of European and American calls and puts is zero. The maximum value of European and American calls is the underlying price. The maximum value of a European put is the present value of the exercise price. The maximum value of an American put is the exercise price.

▷ The lower bound of a European call is established by constructing a portfolio consisting of a long call and risk-free bond and a short position in the underlying asset. This combination produces a non-negative value at expiration, so its current value must be non-negative. For this situation to occur, the call price has to be worth at least the underlying price minus the present value of the exercise price. The lower bound of a European put is established by constructing a portfolio consisting of a long put, a long position in the underlying, and the issuance of a zero-coupon bond. This combination produces a non-negative value at expiration so its current value must be non-negative. For this to occur, the put price has to be at least as much as the present value of the exercise price minus the underlying price. For both calls and puts, if this lower bound is negative, we invoke the rule that an option price can be no lower than zero.

▸ The lowest price of a European call is referred to as the lower bound. The lowest price of an American call is also the lower bound of a European call. The lowest price of a European put is also referred to as the lower bound. The lowest price of an American put, however, is its intrinsic value.

▸ Buying a call with a given exercise price and selling an otherwise identical call with a higher exercise price creates a combination that always pays off with a non-negative value. Therefore, its current value must be non-negative. For this to occur, the call with the lower exercise price must be worth at least as much as the other call. A similar argument holds for puts, except that one would buy the put with the higher exercise price. This line of reasoning shows that the put with the higher exercise price must be worth at least as much as the one with the lower exercise price.

▸ A longer-term European or American call must be worth at least as much as a corresponding shorter-term European or American call. A longer-term American put must be worth at least as much as a shorter-term American put. A longer-term European put, however, can be worth more or less than a shorter-term European put.

▸ A fiduciary call, consisting of a European call and a zero-coupon bond, produces the same payoff as a protective put, consisting of the underlying and a European put. Therefore, their current values must be the same. For this equivalence to occur, the call price plus bond price must equal the underlying price plus put price. This relationship is called put–call parity and can be used to identify combinations of instruments that synthesize another instrument by rearranging the equation to isolate the instrument you are trying to create. Long positions are indicated by positive signs, and short positions are indicated by negative signs. One can create a synthetic call, a synthetic put, a synthetic underlying, and a synthetic bond, as well as synthetic short positions in these instruments for the purpose of exploiting mispricing in these instruments.

▸ Put–call parity violations exist when one side of the equation does not equal the other. An arbitrageur buys the lower-priced side and sells the higher-priced side, thereby earning the difference in price, and the positions offset at expiration. The combined actions of many arbitrageurs performing this set of transactions would increase the demand and price for the underpriced instruments and decrease the demand and price for the overpriced instruments, until the put–call parity relationship is upheld.

▸ American option prices must always be no less than those of otherwise equivalent European options. American call options, however, are never exercised early unless there is a cash flow on the underlying, so they can sell for the same as their European counterparts in the absence of such a cash flow. American put options nearly always have a possibility of early exercise, so they ordinarily sell for more than their European counterparts.

▸ Cash flows on the underlying affect an option's boundary conditions and put–call parity by lowering the underlying price by the present value of the cash flows over the life of the option.

▸ A higher interest rate increases a call option's price and decreases a put option's price.

▷ In a one-period binomial model, the underlying asset can move up to one of two prices. A portfolio consisting of a long position in the underlying and a short position in a call option can be made risk-free and, therefore, must return the risk-free rate. Under this condition, the option price can be obtained by inferring it from a formula that uses the other input values. The option price is a weighted average of the two option prices at expiration, discounted back one period at the risk-free rate.

▷ If an option is trading for a price higher than that given in the binomial model, one can sell the option and buy a specific number of units of the underlying, as given by the model. This combination is risk free but will earn a return higher than the risk-free rate. If the option is trading for a price lower than the price given in the binomial model, a short position in a specific number of units of the underlying and a long position in the option will create a risk-free loan that costs less than the risk-free rate.

▷ In a two-period binomial model, the underlying can move to one of two prices in each of two periods; thus three underlying prices are possible at the option expiration. To price an option, start at the expiration and work backward, following the procedure in the one-period model in which an option price at any given point in time is a weighted average of the next two possible prices discounted at the risk-free rate.

▷ To calculate the price of an option on a zero-coupon bond or a coupon bond, one must first construct a binomial tree of the price of the bond over the life of the option. To calculate the price of an option on an interest rate, one should use a binomial tree of interest rates. Then the option price is found by starting at the option expiration, determining the payoff and successively working backwards by computing the option price as the weighted average of the next two option prices discounted back one period. For the case of options on bonds or interest rates, a different discount rate is used at different parts of the tree.

▷ For an option of a given expiration, a greater pricing accuracy is obtained by dividing the option's life into a greater number of time periods in a binomial tree. As more time periods are added, the discrete-time binomial price converges to a stable value as though the option is being modeled in a continuous-time world.

▷ The assumptions under which the Black–Scholes–Merton model is derived state that the underlying asset follows a geometric lognormal diffusion process, the risk-free rate is known and constant, the volatility of the underlying asset is known and constant, there are no taxes or transaction costs, there are no cash flows on the underlying, and the options are European.

▷ To calculate the value of an option using the Black–Scholes–Merton model, enter the underlying price, exercise price, risk-free rate, volatility, and time to expiration into a formula. The formula will require you to look up two normal probabilities, obtained from either a table or preferably a computer routine.

▷ The change in the option price for a change in the price of the underlying is called the delta. The change in the option price for a change in the risk-free rate is called the rho. The change in the option price for a change in the time to expiration is called the theta. The change in the option price for a change in the volatility is called the vega.

▷ The delta is defined as the change in the option price divided by the change in the underlying price. The option price change can be approximated by the delta times the change in the underlying price. To construct a delta-hedged position, a short (long) position in each call is matched with a long (short) position in delta units of the underlying. Changes in the underlying price will generate offsetting changes in the value of the option position, provided the changes in the underlying price are small and occur over a short time period. A delta-hedged position should be adjusted as the delta changes and time passes.

▶ If changes in the price of the underlying are large or the delta hedge is not adjusted over a longer time period, the hedge may not be effective. This effect is due to the instability of the delta and is called the gamma effect. If the gamma effect is large, option price changes will not be very close to the changes as approximated by the delta times the underlying price change.

▶ Cash flows on the underlying are accommodated in option pricing models by reducing the price of the underlying by the present value of the cash flows over the life of the option.

▶ Volatility can be estimated by calculating the standard deviation of the continuously compounded returns from a sample of recent data for the underlying. This is called the historical volatility. An alternative measure, called the implied volatility, can be obtained by setting the Black–Scholes–Merton model price equal to the market price and inferring the volatility. The implied volatility is a measure of the volatility the market is using to price the option.

▶ The payoffs of a call on a forward contract and an appropriately chosen zero-coupon bond are equivalent to the payoffs of a put on the forward contract and the forward contract. Thus, their current values must be the same. For this equality to occur, the call price plus the bond price must equal the put price. The appropriate zero-coupon bond is one with a face value equal to the exercise price minus the forward price. This relationship is called put–call–forward (or futures) parity.

▶ There is no justification for exercising American options on forward contracts early, so they are equivalent to European options on forwards. American options on futures, both calls and puts, can sometimes be exercised early, so they are different from European options on futures and carry a higher price.

▶ The Black model can be used to price European options on forwards or futures by entering the forward price, exercise price, risk-free rate, time to expiration, and volatility into a formula that will also require the determination of two normal probabilities.

▶ The Black model can be used to price European options on interest rates by entering the forward interest rate into the model for the forward or futures price and the exercise rate for the exercise price.

▶ Options are useful in financial markets because they provide a way to limit losses to the premium paid while permitting potentially large gains. They can be used for hedging purposes, especially in the case of puts, which can be used to limit the loss on a long position in an asset. Options also provide information on the volatility of the underlying asset. Options can be standardized and exchange-traded or customized in the over-the-counter market.

APPENDIX

72A Cumulative Probabilities for a Standard Normal Distribution
$P(X \leq x) = N(x)$ for $x \geq 0$ or $1 - N(-x)$ for $x < 0$

x	0	0.01	0.02	0.03	0.04	0.05	0.06	0.07	0.08	0.09
0.00	0.5000	0.5040	0.5080	0.5120	0.5160	0.5199	0.5239	0.5279	0.5319	0.5359
0.10	0.5398	0.5438	0.5478	0.5517	0.5557	0.5596	0.5636	0.5675	0.5714	0.5753
0.20	0.5793	0.5832	0.5871	0.5910	0.5948	0.5987	0.6026	0.6064	0.6103	0.6141
0.30	0.6179	0.6217	0.6255	0.6293	0.6331	0.6368	0.6406	0.6443	0.6480	0.6517
0.40	0.6554	0.6591	0.6628	0.6664	0.6700	0.6736	0.6772	0.6808	0.6844	0.6879
0.50	0.6915	0.6950	0.6985	0.7019	0.7054	0.7088	0.7123	0.7157	0.7190	0.7224
0.60	0.7257	0.7291	0.7324	0.7357	0.7389	0.7422	0.7454	0.7486	0.7517	0.7549
0.70	0.7580	0.7611	0.7642	0.7673	0.7704	0.7734	0.7764	0.7794	0.7823	0.7852
0.80	0.7881	0.7910	0.7939	0.7967	0.7995	0.8023	0.8051	0.8078	0.8106	0.8133
0.90	0.8159	0.8186	0.8212	0.8238	0.8264	0.8289	0.8315	0.8340	0.8365	0.8389
1.00	0.8413	0.8438	0.8461	0.8485	0.8508	0.8531	0.8554	0.8577	0.8599	0.8621
1.10	0.8643	0.8665	0.8686	0.8708	0.8729	0.8749	0.8770	0.8790	0.8810	0.8830
1.20	0.8849	0.8869	0.8888	0.8907	0.8925	0.8944	0.8962	0.8980	0.8997	0.9015
1.30	0.9032	0.9049	0.9066	0.9082	0.9099	0.9115	0.9131	0.9147	0.9162	0.9177
1.40	0.9192	0.9207	0.9222	0.9236	0.9251	0.9265	0.9279	0.9292	0.9306	0.9319
1.50	0.9332	0.9345	0.9357	0.9370	0.9382	0.9394	0.9406	0.9418	0.9429	0.9441
1.60	0.9452	0.9463	0.9474	0.9484	0.9495	0.9505	0.9515	0.9525	0.9535	0.9545
1.70	0.9554	0.9564	0.9573	0.9582	0.9591	0.9599	0.9608	0.9616	0.9625	0.9633
1.80	0.9641	0.9649	0.9656	0.9664	0.9671	0.9678	0.9686	0.9693	0.9699	0.9706
1.90	0.9713	0.9719	0.9726	0.9732	0.9738	0.9744	0.9750	0.9756	0.9761	0.9767
2.00	0.9772	0.9778	0.9783	0.9788	0.9793	0.9798	0.9803	0.9808	0.9812	0.9817
2.10	0.9821	0.9826	0.9830	0.9834	0.9838	0.9842	0.9846	0.9850	0.9854	0.9857
2.20	0.9861	0.9864	0.9868	0.9871	0.9875	0.9878	0.9881	0.9884	0.9887	0.9890
2.30	0.9893	0.9896	0.9898	0.9901	0.9904	0.9906	0.9909	0.9911	0.9913	0.9916
2.40	0.9918	0.9920	0.9922	0.9925	0.9927	0.9929	0.9931	0.9932	0.9934	0.9936
2.50	0.9938	0.9940	0.9941	0.9943	0.9945	0.9946	0.9948	0.9949	0.9951	0.9952
2.60	0.9953	0.9955	0.9956	0.9957	0.9959	0.9960	0.9961	0.9962	0.9963	0.9964
2.70	0.9965	0.9966	0.9967	0.9968	0.9969	0.9970	0.9971	0.9972	0.9973	0.9974
2.80	0.9974	0.9975	0.9976	0.9977	0.9977	0.9978	0.9979	0.9979	0.9980	0.9981
2.90	0.9981	0.9982	0.9982	0.9983	0.9984	0.9984	0.9985	0.9985	0.9986	0.9986
3.00	0.9987	0.9987	0.9987	0.9988	0.9988	0.9989	0.9989	0.9989	0.9990	0.9990

PROBLEMS

1. A. Calculate the payoff at expiration for a call option on the S&P 100 stock index in which the underlying price is 579.32 at expiration, the multiplier is 100, and the exercise price is

    i. 450

    ii. 650

   B. Calculate the payoff at expiration for a put option on the S&P 100 in which the underlying is at 579.32 at expiration, the multiplier is 100, and the exercise price is

    i. 450

    ii. 650

2. A. Calculate the payoff at expiration for a call option on a bond in which the underlying is at $0.95 per $1 par at expiration, the contract is on $100,000 face value bonds, and the exercise price is

    i. $0.85

    ii. $1.15

   B. Calculate the payoff at expiration for a put option on a bond in which the underlying is at $0.95 per $1 par at expiration, the contract is on $100,000 face value bonds, and the exercise price is

    i. $0.85

    ii. $1.15

3. A. Calculate the payoff at expiration for a call option on an interest rate in which the underlying is a 180-day interest rate at 6.53 percent at expiration, the notional principal is $10 million, and the exercise price is

    i. 5 percent

    ii. 8 percent

   B. Calculate the payoff at expiration for a put option on an interest rate in which the underlying is a 180-day interest rate at 6.53 percent at expiration, the notional principal is $10 million, and the exercise price is

    i. 5 percent

    ii. 8 percent

4. A. Calculate the payoff at expiration for a call option on the British pound in which the underlying is at $1.438 at expiration, the options are on 125,000 British pounds, and the exercise price is

    i. $1.35

    ii. $1.55

   B. Calculate the payoff at expiration for a put option on the British pound where the underlying is at $1.438 at expiration, the options are on 125,000 British pounds, and the exercise price is

    i. $1.35

    ii. $1.55

5. A. Calculate the payoff at expiration for a call option on a futures contract in which the underlying is at 1136.76 at expiration, the options are on a futures contract for $1,000, and the exercise price is

    i. 1130

    ii. 1140

   B. Calculate the payoff at expiration for a put option on a futures contract in which the underlying is at 1136.76 at expiration, the options are on a futures contract for $1000, and the exercise price is

     i. 1130

     ii. 1140

6. Consider a stock index option that expires in 75 days. The stock index is currently at 1240.89 and makes no cash payments during the life of the option. Assume that the stock index has a multiplier of 1. The risk-free rate is 3 percent.

   A. Calculate the lowest and highest possible prices for European-style call options on the above stock index with exercise prices of

     i. 1225

     ii. 1255

   B. Calculate the lowest and highest possible prices for European-style put options on the above stock index with exercise prices of

     i. 1225

     ii. 1255

7. A. Consider American-style call and put options on a bond. The options expire in 60 days. The bond is currently at $1.05 per $1 par and makes no cash payments during the life of the option. The risk-free rate is 5.5 percent. Assume that the contract is on $1 face value bonds. Calculate the lowest and highest possible prices for the calls and puts with exercise prices of

     i. $0.95

     ii. $1.10

   B. Consider European style call and put options on a bond. The options expire in 60 days. The bond is currently at $1.05 per $1 par and makes no cash payments during the life of the option. The risk-free rate is 5.5 percent. Assume that the contract is on $1 face value bonds. Calculate the lowest and highest possible prices for the calls and puts with exercise prices of

     i. $0.95

     ii. $1.10

8. You are provided with the following information on put and call options on a stock:

Call price, $c_0 = \$6.64$

Put price, $p_0 = \$2.75$

Exercise price, $X = \$30$

Days to option expiration = 219

Current stock price, $S_0 = \$33.19$

Put–call parity shows the equivalence of a call/bond portfolio (fiduciary call) and a put/underlying portfolio (protective put). Illustrate put–call parity assuming stock prices at expiration (S_T) of $20 and of $40. Assume that the risk-free rate, r, is 4 percent.

SWAP MARKETS AND CONTRACTS

LEARNING OUTCOMES

The candidate should be able to:

a. describe the characteristics of swap contracts and explain how swaps are terminated;

b. define and give examples of currency swaps and calculate and interpret the payments on a currency swap;

c. define and give an example of a plain vanilla interest rate swap and calculate and interpret the payments on an interest rate swap;

d. define and give examples of equity swaps and calculate and interpret the payments on an equity swap.

INTRODUCTION   1

This reading completes the survey of the main types of derivative instruments. The three preceding readings covered forward contracts, futures contracts, and options. This reading covers swaps. Although swaps were the last of the main types of derivatives to be invented, they are clearly not the least important. In fact, judging by the size of the swap market, they are probably the most important. In Reading 69, we noted that the Bank for International Settlements had estimated the notional principal of the global over-the-counter derivatives market as of 30 June 2001 at $100 trillion. Of that amount, interest rate and currency swaps account for about $61 trillion, with interest rate swaps representing about $57 trillion of that total.[1] Indeed, interest rate swaps have had overwhelming success as a derivative product. They are widely used by corporations, financial institutions, and governments.

---

[1] Equity and commodity swaps account for less than the notional principal of currency swaps.

Analysis of Derivatives for the CFA® Program, by Don M. Chance, Copyright © 2003 by Association for Investment Management and Research. Reprinted with permission.

In Reading 69, we briefly described the characteristics of swaps, but now we explore this subject in more detail. Recall first that *a swap is an agreement between two parties to exchange a series of future cash flows*. For most types of swaps, one party makes payments that are determined by a random outcome, such as an interest rate, a currency rate, an equity return, or a commodity price. These payments are commonly referred to as variable or *floating*. The other party either makes variable or floating payments determined by some other random factor or makes fixed payments. At least one type of swap involves both parties making fixed payments, but the values of those payments vary due to random factors.

In forwards, futures, and options, the terminology of *long* and *short* has been used to describe buyers and sellers. These terms are not used as often in swaps. The preferred terminology usually designates a party as being the floating- (or variable-) rate payer or the fixed-rate payer. Nonetheless, in swaps in which one party receives a floating rate and the other receives a fixed rate, the former is usually said to be long and the latter is said to be short. This usage is in keeping with the fact that parties who go long in other instruments pay a known amount and receive a claim on an unknown amount. In some swaps, however, both sides are floating or variable, and this terminology breaks down.

1.1 Characteristics of Swap Contracts

Although technically a swap can have a single payment, most swaps involve multiple payments. Thus, we refer to a swap as a *series* of payments. In fact, we have already covered a swap with one payment, which is just a forward contract. Hence, a swap is basically a series of forward contracts. We will elaborate further in Section 4.1.2, but with this idea in mind, we can see that a swap is like an agreement to buy something over a period of time. We might be paying a variable price or a price that has already been fixed; we might be paying an uncertain price, or we might already know the price we shall pay.

When a swap is initiated, neither party pays any amount to the other. Therefore, a swap has zero value at the start of the contract. Although it is not absolutely necessary for this condition to be true, swaps are typically done in this fashion. Neither party pays anything up front. There is, however, a technical exception to this point in regard to currency swaps. Each party pays the notional principal to the other, but the amounts exchanged are equivalent, though denominated in two different currencies.

Each date on which the parties make payments is called a **settlement date,** sometimes called a payment date, and the time between settlement dates is called the **settlement period.** On a given settlement date when payments are due, one party makes a payment to the other, which in turn makes a payment to the first party. With the exception of currency swaps and a few variations associated with other types of swaps, both sets of payments are made in the same currency. Consequently, the parties typically agree to exchange only the net amount owed from one party to the other, a practice called **netting.** In currency swaps and a few other special cases, the payments are not made in the same currency; hence, the parties usually make separate payments without netting. Note the implication that swaps are generally settled in cash. It is quite rare for swaps to call for actual physical delivery of an underlying asset.

A swap always has a **termination date,** the date of the final payment. We can think of this date as its expiration date, as we do with other derivatives. The original time to maturity is sometimes called the *tenor* of a swap.

The swap market is almost exclusively an over-the-counter market, so swaps contracts are customized to the parties' specific needs. Several of the leading futures exchanges have created futures contracts on swaps. These contracts allow participants to hedge and speculate on the rates that will prevail in the swap market at future dates. Of course, these contracts are not swaps themselves but, as derivatives of swaps, they can in some ways serve as substitutes for swaps. These futures contracts have been moderately successful, but their volume is insignificant compared with the over-the-counter market for swaps.

As we have discussed in previous readings, over-the-counter instruments are subject to default risk. Default is possible whenever a payment is due. When a series of payments is made, there is default risk potential throughout the life of the contract, depending on the financial condition of the two parties. But default can be somewhat complicated in swaps. Suppose, for example, that on a settlement date, Party A owes Party B a payment of $50,000 and Party B owes Party A a payment of $12,000. Agreeing to net, Party A owes Party B $38,000 for that particular payment. Party A may be illiquid, or perhaps even bankrupt, and unable to make the payment. But it may be the case that the market value of the swap, which reflects the present value of the remaining payments, could be positive from the perspective of Party A and negative from the perspective of Party B. In that case, Party B owes Party A more for the remaining payments. We will learn how to determine the market value of a swap in Section 4.2 of this reading.

The handling of default in swaps can be complicated, depending on the contract specifications and the applicable laws under which the contract was written. In most cases, the above situation would be resolved by having A be in default but possessing an asset, the swap, that can be used to help settle its other liabilities. We shall discuss the default risk of swaps in more detail in Section 7.

1.2 Termination of a Swap

As we noted earlier, a swap has a termination or expiration date. Sometimes, however, a party could want to terminate a swap before its formal expiration. This scenario is much like a party selling a bond before it matures or selling an exchange-traded option or futures contract before its expiration. With swaps, early termination can take place in several ways.

As we mentioned briefly and will cover in more detail later, a swap has a market value that can be calculated during its life. If a party holds a swap with a market value of $125,000, for example, it can settle the swap with the counterparty by having the counterparty pay it $125,000 in cash. This payment terminates the transaction for both parties. From the opposite perspective, a party holding a swap with a negative market value can terminate the swap by paying the market value to the counterparty. Terminating a swap in this manner is possible only if the counterparties specify in advance that such a transaction can be made, or if they reach an agreement to do so without having specified in advance. In other words, this feature is not automatically available and must be agreed to by both parties.

Many swaps are terminated early by entering into a separate and offsetting swap. For example, suppose a corporation is engaged in a swap to make fixed payments of 5 percent and receive floating payments based on LIBOR, with the payments made each 15 January and 15 July. Three years remain on the swap. That corporation can offset the swap by entering into an entirely new swap in which it makes payments based on LIBOR and receives a fixed rate with the payments made each 15 January and 15 July for three years. The swap fixed rate is determined by market conditions at the time the swap is initiated. Thus, the fixed rate on the new swap is not likely to match the fixed rate on the old swap, but the effect of this transaction is simply to have the floating payments offset; the fixed payments will net out to a known amount. Hence, the risk associated with the floating rate is eliminated. The default risk, however, is not eliminated because both swaps remain in effect.

Another way to terminate a swap early is sell the swap to another counterparty. Suppose a corporation holds a swap worth $75,000. If it can obtain the counterparty's permission, it can find another party to take over its payments. In effect, it sells the swap for $75,000 to that party. This procedure, however, is not commonly used.

A final way to terminate a swap early is by using a swaption. This instrument is an option to enter into a swap at terms that are established in advance. Thus, a party could use a swaption to enter into an offsetting swap, as described above. We shall cover swaptions in more detail in Section 6.

2   THE STRUCTURE OF GLOBAL SWAP MARKETS

The global swaps market is much like the global forward and over-the-counter options markets, which we covered in some detail in Readings 69, 70, and 72. It is made up of dealers, which are banks and investment banking firms. These dealers make markets in swaps, quoting bid and ask prices and rates, thereby offering to take either side of a swap transaction. Upon taking a position in a swap, the dealer generally offsets the risk by making transactions in other markets. The counterparties to swaps are either end users or other dealers. The end users are often corporations with risk management problems that can be solved by engaging in a swap—a corporation or other end user is usually exposed to or needs an exposure to some type of risk that arises from interest rates, exchange rates, stock prices, or commodity prices. The end user contacts a dealer that makes a market in swaps. The two engage in a transaction, at which point the dealer assumes some risk from the end user. The dealer then usually lays off the risk by engaging in a transaction with another party. That transaction could be something as simple as a futures contract, or it could be an over-the-counter transaction with another dealer.

Risk magazine conducts annual surveys of participants in various derivative products. Exhibit 73-1 presents the results of those surveys for currency and interest rate swaps. One survey provides opinions of banks and investment banks that are swaps dealers. In the other survey, the respondents are end users. The results give a good idea of the major players in this market. It is interesting to note the disagreement between how dealers view themselves and how end users view them. Also, note that the rankings change, sometimes drastically, from year to year.

EXHIBIT 73-1 *Risk* **Magazine Surveys of Banks, Investment Banks, and Corporate End Users to Determine the Top Three Dealers in Currency and Interest Rate Swaps**

	Respondents	
Currencies	Banks and Investment Banks	Corporate End Users
Currency Swaps		
$/€	UBS Warburg	Citigroup
	JP Morgan Chase	Royal Bank of Scotland
	Deutsche Bank	Bank of America
$/¥	JP Morgan Chase	Citigroup
	UBS Warburg	Bank of America
	Credit Suisse First Boston/Deutsche Bank	JP Morgan Chase
$/£	Royal Bank of Scotland	Royal Bank of Scotland

	JP Morgan Chase	Citigroup
	Goldman Sachs	Deutsche Bank
$/SF	UBS Warburg	UBS Warburg
	Goldman Sachs	Citigroup
	Credit Suisse First Boston	Credit Suisse First Boston

Interest Rate Swaps (2–10 years)

$	JP Morgan Chase	JP Morgan Chase
	Bank of America	Bank of America
	Morgan Stanley	Royal Bank of Scotland
€	JP Morgan Chase	Royal Bank of Scotland
	Deutsche Bank	Deutsche Bank
	Morgan Stanley	Citigroup
¥	JP Morgan Chase	Royal Bank of Scotland
	Deutsche Bank	Barclays Capital
	Bank of America	Citigroup/JP Morgan Chase
£	Royal Bank of Scotland	Royal Bank of Scotland
	Barclays Capital	Barclays Capital
	UBS Warburg	Deutsche Bank
SF	UBS Warburg	UBS Warburg
	Credit Suisse First Boston	Credit Suisse First Boston
	Zürcher Kantonalbank	Zürcher Kantonalbank

Note: $ = U.S. dollar, € = euro, ¥ = Japanese yen, £ = U.K. pound sterling, SF = Swiss franc

Source: Risk, September 2002, pp. 30–67 for banks and investment banking dealer respondents, and June 2002, pp. 24–34 for corporate end user respondents. Ratings for swaps with maturities less than 2 years and greater than 10 years are also provided in the September 2002 issue of *Risk.*

TYPES OF SWAPS   3

We alluded to the fact that the underlying asset in a swap can be a currency, interest rate, stock, or commodity. We now take a look at these types of swaps in more detail.

3.1 Currency Swaps

In a currency swap, each party makes interest payments to the other in different currencies.[2] Consider this example. The U.S. retailer Target Corporation (NYSE: TGT) does not have an established presence in Europe. Let us say that it has decided to begin opening a few stores in Germany and needs €9 million to fund construction and initial operations. TGT would like to issue a fixed-rate euro-denominated bond with face value of €9 million, but the company is not very well known in Europe. European investment bankers have given it a quote for such a

---

[2] It is important at this point to clear up some terminology confusion. Foreign currency is often called *foreign exchange* or sometimes *FX*. There is another transaction called an *FX swap*, which sounds as if it might be referring to a currency swap. In fact, an FX swap is just a long position in a forward contract on a foreign currency and a short position in a forward contract on the same currency with a different expiration. Why this transaction is called a swap is not clear, but this transaction existed before currency swaps were created. In futures markets, the analogous transaction is called a *spread*, reflecting as it does the risk associated with the spread between the prices of futures contracts with different expirations.

bond. Deutsche Bank, AG (NYSE: DB), however, tells TGT that it should issue the bond in dollars and use a swap to convert it into euros.

Suppose TGT issues a five-year US$10 million bond at a rate of 6 percent. It then enters into a swap with DB in which DB will make payments to TGT in U.S. dollars at a fixed rate of 5.5 percent and TGT will make payments to DB in euros at a fixed rate of 4.9 percent each 15 March and 15 September for five years. The payments are based on a notional principal of 10 million in dollars and 9 million in euros. We assume the swap starts on 15 September of the current year. The swap specifies that the two parties exchange the notional principal at the start of the swap and at the end. Because the payments are made in different currencies, netting is not practical, so each party makes its respective payments.[3]

Thus, the swap is composed of the following transactions:
15 September:

  ▸ DB pays TGT €9 million
  ▸ TGT pays DB $10 million

Each 15 March and 15 September for five years:

  ▸ DB pays TGT 0.055(180/360)$10 million = $275,000
  ▸ TGT pays DB 0.049(180/360) €9 million = €220,500

15 September five years after initiation:

  ▸ DB pays TGT $10 million
  ▸ TGT pays DB €9 million

Note that we have simplified the interest calculations a little. In this example, we calculated semiannual interest using the fraction 180/360. Some parties might choose to use the exact day count in the six-month period divided by 365 days. LIBOR and Euribor transactions, the predominant rates used in interest rate swaps, nearly always use 360 days, as mentioned in previous readings. Exhibit 73-2 shows the stream of cash flows from TGT's perspective.

EXHIBIT 73-2 Cash Flows to TGT on Swap with DB

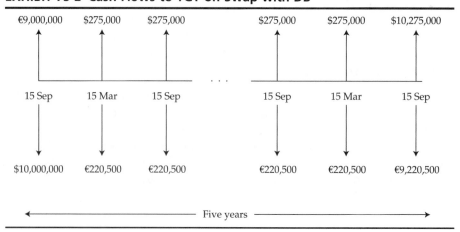

---

[3] In this example, we shall assume 180 days between payment dates. In practice, exact day counts are usually used, leading to different fixed payment amounts in one six-month period from those of another. In the example here, we are only illustrating the idea behind swap cash flows, so it is convenient to keep the fixed payments the same. Later in the reading, we shall illustrate situations in which the exact day count is used, leading to fixed payments that vary slightly.

Note that the Target–Deutsche Bank transaction looks just like TGT is issuing a bond with face value of €9 million and that bond is purchased by DB. TGT converts the €9 million to $10 million and buys a dollar-denominated bond issued by DB. Note that TGT, having issued a bond denominated in euros, accordingly makes interest payments to DB in euros. DB, appropriately, makes interest payments in dollars to TGT. At the end, they each pay off the face values of the bonds they have issued. We emphasize that the Target–Deutsche Bank transaction *looks like* what we have just described. In fact, neither TGT nor DB actually issues or purchases a bond. They exchange only a series of cash flows that replicated the issuance and purchase of these bonds.

Exhibit 73-3 illustrates how such a combined transaction would work. TGT issues a bond in dollars (Exhibit 73-3, Panel A). It takes the dollars and passes

EXHIBIT 73-3 Issuing a Dollar-Denominated Bond and Using a Currency Swap to Convert a Euro-Denominated Bond

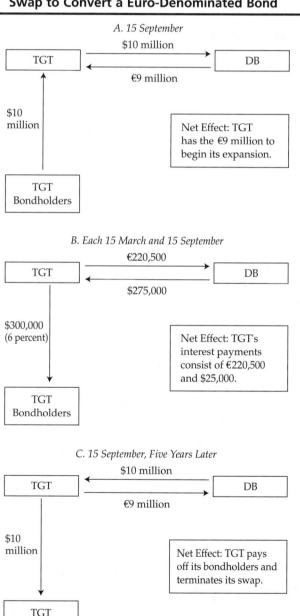

them through to DB, which gives TGT the €9 million it needs. On the interest payment dates, the swap generates $275,000 of the $300,000 in interest TGT needs to pay its bondholders (Panel B). In turn, TGT makes interest payments in euros. Still, small dollar interest payments are necessary because TGT cannot issue a dollar bond at the swap rate. At the end of the transaction, TGT receives $10 million back from DB and passes it through to its bondholders (Panel C). TGT pays DB €9 million, thus effectively paying off a euro-denominated bond.

TGT has effectively issued a dollar-denominated bond and converted it to a euro-denominated bond. In all likelihood, it can save on interest expense by funding its need for euros in this way, because TGT is better known in the United States than in Europe. Its swap dealer, DB, knows TGT well and also obviously has a strong presence in Europe. Thus, DB can pass on its advantage in euro bond markets to TGT. In addition, had TGT issued a euro-denominated bond, it would have assumed no credit risk. By entering into the swap, TGT assumes a remote possibility of DB defaulting. Thus, TGT saves a little money by assuming some credit risk.

Practice Problem 1

Consider a currency swap in which the domestic party pays a fixed rate in the foreign currency, the British pound, and the counterparty pays a fixed rate in U.S. dollars. The notional principals are $50 million and £30 million. The fixed rates are 5.6 percent in dollars and 6.25 percent in pounds. Both sets of payments are made on the basis of 30 days per month and 365 days per year, and the payments are made semiannually.

A. Determine the initial exchange of cash that occurs at the start of the swap.

B. Determine the semiannual payments.

C. Determine the final exchange of cash that occurs at the end of the swap.

D. Give an example of a situation in which this swap might be appropriate.

SOLUTIONS

A. At the start of the swap:
Domestic party pays counterparty $50 million
Counterparty pays domestic party £30 million

B. Semiannually:
Domestic party pays counterparty £30,000,000(0.0625)(180/365) = £924,658
Counterparty pays domestic party $50,000,000(0.056)(180/365) = $1,380,822

C. At the end of the swap:
Domestic party pays counterparty £30,000,000
Counterparty pays domestic party $50,000,000

D. This swap would be appropriate for a U.S. company that issues a dollar-denominated bond but would prefer to borrow in British pounds.

Returning to the Target swap, recall that Target effectively converted a fixed-rate loan in dollars to a fixed-rate loan in euros. Suppose instead that TGT preferred to borrow in euros at a floating rate. It then would have specified that the swap required it to make payments to DB at a floating rate. Had TGT preferred to issue the dollar-denominated bond at a floating rate, it would have specified that DB pay it dollars at a floating rate.

Although TGT and DB exchanged notional principal, some scenarios exist in which the notional principals are not exchanged. For example, suppose many years later, TGT is generating €10 million in cash semi-annually and converting it back to dollars on 15 January and 15 July. It might then wish to lock in the conversion rate by entering into a currency swap that would require it to pay a dealer €10 million and receive a fixed amount of dollars. If the euro fixed rate were 5 percent, a notional principal of €400 million would generate a payment of $0.05(180/360)€400$ million $= €10$ million. If the exchange rate is, for example, $0.85, the equivalent dollar notional principal would be $340 million. If the dollar fixed rate is 6 percent, TGT would receive $0.06(180/360)$340$ million $= $10.2 million.[4] These payments would occur twice a year for the life of the swap. TGT might then lock in the conversion rate by entering into a currency swap with notional principal amounts that would allow it to receive a fixed amount of dollars on 15 January and 15 July. There would be no reason to specify an exchange of notional principal. As we previously described, there are four types of currency swaps. Using the original Target–Deutsche Bank swap as an example, the semi-annual payments would be

A. TGT pays euros at a fixed rate; DB pays dollars at a fixed rate.

B. TGT pays euros at a fixed rate; DB pays dollars at a floating rate.

C. TGT pays euros at a floating rate; DB pays dollars at a floating rate.

D. TGT pays euros at a floating rate; DB pays dollars at a fixed rate.

Or, reversing the flow, TGT could be the payer of dollars and DB could be the payer of euros:

E. TGT pays dollars at a fixed rate; DB pays euros at a fixed rate.

F. TGT pays dollars at a fixed rate; DB pays euros at a floating rate.

G. TGT pays dollars at a floating rate; DB pays euros at a floating rate.

H. TGT pays dollars at a floating rate; DB pays euros at a fixed rate.

Suppose we combine Swap A with Swap H. With TGT paying euros at a fixed rate and DB paying euros at a fixed rate, the euro payments wash out and the net effect is

I. TGT pays dollars at a floating rate; DB pays dollars at a fixed rate.

Suppose we combine Swap B with Swap E. Similarly, the euro payments again wash out, and the net effect is

J. TGT pays dollars at a fixed rate; DB pays dollars at a floating rate.

Suppose we combine Swap C with Swap F. Likewise, the euro floating payments wash out, and the net effect is

---

[4] It might appear that TGT has somehow converted cash flows worth €10 million($0.085) = $8.5 million into cash flows worth $10.2 million. Recall, however, that the €10 million cash flows are generated yearly and $0.85 is the *current* exchange rate. We cannot apply the current exchange rate to a series of cash flows over various future dates. We would apply the respective forward exchange rates, not the spot rate, to the series of future euro cash flows.

   K. TGT pays dollars at a fixed rate; DB pays dollars at a floating rate.

Lastly, suppose we combine Swap D with Swap G. Again, the euro floating payments wash out, and the net effect is

   L. TGT pays dollars at a floating rate; DB pays dollars at a fixed rate.

Of course, the net results of I and L are equivalent, and the net results of J and K are equivalent. What we have shown here, however, is that combinations of currency swaps eliminate the currency flows and leave us with transactions in only one currency. A swap in which both sets of interest payments are made in the same currency is an interest rate swap.

3.2 Interest Rate Swaps

As we discovered in the above paragraph, an interest rate swap can be created as a combination of currency swaps. Of course, no one would create an interest rate swap that way; doing so would require two transactions when only one would suffice. Interest rate swaps evolved into their own market. In fact, the interest rate swap market is much bigger than the currency swap market, as we have seen in the notional principal statistics.

As previously noted, one way to look at an interest rate swap is that it is a currency swap in which both currencies are the same. Consider a swap to pay Currency A fixed and Currency B floating. Currency A could be dollars, and B could be euros. But what if A and B are both dollars, or A and B are both euros? The first case is a dollar-denominated plain vanilla swap; the second is a euro-denominated plain vanilla swap. A **plain vanilla swap** *is simply an interest rate swap in which one party pays a fixed rate and the other pays a floating rate, with both sets of payments in the same currency.* In fact, the plain vanilla swap is probably the most common derivative transaction in the global financial system.

Note that because we are paying in the same currency, there is no need to exchange notional principals at the beginning and at the end of an interest rate swap. In addition, the interest payments can be, and nearly always are, netted. If one party owes $X and the other owes $Y, the party owing the greater amount pays the net difference, which greatly reduces the credit risk (as we discuss in more detail in Section 7). Finally, we note that there is no reason to have both sides pay a fixed rate. The two streams of payments would be identical in that case. So in an interest rate swap, either one side always pays fixed and the other side pays floating, or both sides paying floating, but never do both sides pay fixed.[5]

Thus, in a plain vanilla interest rate swap, one party makes interest payments at a fixed rate and the other makes interest payments at a floating rate. Both sets of payments are on the same notional principal and occur on regularly scheduled dates. For each payment, the interest rate is multiplied by a fraction representing the number of days in the settlement period over the number of days in a year. In some cases, the settlement period is computed assuming 30 days in each month; in others, an exact day count is used. Some cases assume a 360-day year; others use 365 days.

Let us now illustrate an interest rate swap. Suppose that on 15 December, General Electric Company (NYSE: GE) borrows money for one year from a bank such as Bank of America (NYSE: BAC). The loan is for $25 million and specifies that GE will make interest payments on a quarterly basis on the 15th of March, June, September, and December for one year at the rate of LIBOR plus 25 basis

---

[5] The case of both sides paying floating is called a basis swap, which we shall cover in Section 5.

points. At the end of the year, it will pay back the principal. On the 15th of December, March, June, and September, LIBOR is observed and sets the rate for that quarter. The interest is then paid at the end of the quarter.[6]

GE believes that it is getting a good rate, but fearing a rise in interest rates, it would prefer a fixed-rate loan. It can easily convert the floating-rate loan to a fixed-rate loan by engaging in a swap. Suppose it approaches JP Morgan Chase (NYSE: JPM), a large dealer bank, and requests a quote on a swap to pay a fixed rate and receive LIBOR, with payments on the dates of its loan payments. The bank prices the swap (a procedure we cover in Section 4) and quotes a fixed rate of 6.2 percent.[7] The fixed payments will be made based on a day count of 90/365, and the floating payments will be made based on 90/360. Current LIBOR is 5.9 percent. Therefore, the first fixed payment, which GE makes to JPM, is $25,000,000(0.062)(90/365) = $382,192. This is also the amount of each remaining fixed payment.

The first floating payment, which JPM makes to GE, is $25,000,000(0.059)(90/360) = $368,750. Of course, the remaining floating payments will not be known until later. Exhibit 73-4 shows the pattern of cash flows on the swap from GE's perspective.

EXHIBIT 73-4 Cash Flows to GE on Swap with JPM

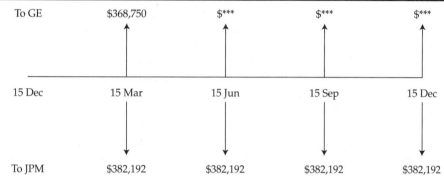

***Computed as $25,000,000(L)90/360, where L is LIBOR on the previous settlement date.

Practice Problem 2

Determine the upcoming payments in a plain vanilla interest rate swap in which the notional principal is €70 million. The end user makes semi-annual fixed payments at the rate of 7 percent, and the dealer makes semi-annual floating payments at Euribor, which was 6.25 percent on the last settlement period. The floating payments are made on the basis of 180

---

[6] Again, we assume 90 days in each interest payment period for this example. The exact payment dates are not particularly important for illustrative purposes.

[7] Typically the rate is quoted as a spread over the rate on a U.S. Treasury security with a comparable maturity. Suppose the yield on a two-year Treasury note is 6 percent. Then the swap would be quoted as 20 basis points over the two-year Treasury rate. By quoting the rate in the this manner, GE knows what it is paying over the Treasury rate, a differential called the swap spread, which is a type of credit risk premium we discuss in Section 7. In addition, a quote in this form protects the bank from the rate changing drastically either during the phone conversation or shortly thereafter. Thus, the quote can stay in effect for a reasonable period of time while GE checks out quotes from other dealers.

days in the settlement period and 360 days in a year. The fixed payments are made on the basis of 180 days in the settlement period and 365 days in a year. Payments are netted, so determine which party pays which and what amount.

SOLUTION

The fixed payments are €70,000,000(0.07)(180/365) = €2,416,438.

The upcoming floating payment is €70,000,000(0.0625)(180/360) = €2,187,500.

The net payment is that the party paying fixed will pay the party paying floating €2,416,438 − €2,187,500 = €228,938.

Note in Exhibit 73-4 that we did not show the notional principal, because it was not exchanged. We could implicitly show that GE received $25 million from JPM and paid $25 million to JPM at the start of the swap. We could also show that the same thing happens at the end. If we look at it that way, it appears as if GE has issued a $25 million fixed-rate bond, which was purchased by JPM, which in turn issued a $25 million floating-rate bond, which was in turn purchased by GE. We say that *it appears* as if this is what happened: In fact, neither party actually issued a bond, but they have generated the cash flows that would occur if GE had issued such a fixed-rate bond, JPM had issued such a floating-rate bond, and each purchased the bond of the other. In other words, we could include the principals on both sides to make each set of cash flows look like a bond, yet the overall cash flows would be the same as on the swap.

So let us say that GE enters into this swap. Exhibit 73-5 shows the net effect of the swap and the loan. GE pays LIBOR plus 25 basis points to Bank of America on its loan, pays 6.2 percent to JPM, and receives LIBOR from JPM. The net effect is that GE pays 6.2 + 0.25 = 6.45 percent fixed.

EXHIBIT 73-5 GE's Conversion of a Floating-Rate Loan to a Fixed-Rate Loan Using an Interest Rate Swap with JPM

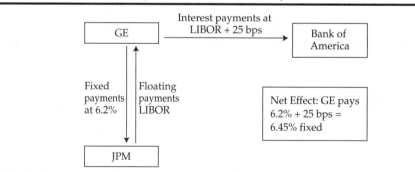

Now, JPM is engaged in a swap to pay LIBOR and receive 6.2 percent. It is exposed to the risk of LIBOR increasing. It would, therefore, probably engage in some other type of transaction to offset this risk. One transaction commonly used in this situation is to sell Eurodollar futures. As discussed in Reading 71, Eurodollar futures prices move $25 in value for each basis point move in LIBOR. JPM will determine how sensitive its position is to a move in LIBOR and sell an appropriate number of futures to offset the risk. Note that Bank of America is exposed to LIBOR as well, but in the banking industry, floating-rate loans are often made because the funding that the bank obtained to make the loan was probably already at LIBOR or a comparable floating rate.

It is possible but unlikely that GE could get a fixed-rate loan at a better rate. The swap involves some credit risk: the possibility, however small, that JPM will default. In return for assuming that risk, GE in all likelihood would get a better rate than it would if it borrowed at a fixed rate. JPM is effectively a wholesaler of risk, using its powerful position as one of the world's leading banks to facilitate the buying and selling of risk for companies such as GE. Dealers profit from the spread between the rates they quote to pay and the rates they quote to receive. The swaps market is, however, extremely competitive and the spreads have been squeezed very tight, which makes it very challenging for dealers to make a profit. Of course, this competition is good for end users, because it gives them more attractive rates.

3.3 Equity Swaps

By now, it should be apparent that a swap requires at least one variable rate or price underlying it. So far, that rate has been an interest rate.[8] In an equity swap, the rate is the return on a stock or stock index. This characteristic gives the equity swap two features that distinguish it from interest rate and currency swaps.

First, the party making the fixed-rate payment could also have to make a variable payment based on the equity return. Suppose the end user pays the equity payment and receives the fixed payment, i.e., it pays the dealer the return on the S&P 500 Index, and the dealer pays the end user a fixed rate. If the S&P 500 increases, the return is positive and the end user pays that return to the dealer. If the S&P 500 goes down, however, its return is obviously negative. In that case, the end user would pay the dealer the *negative return on the S&P 500*, which means that it would receive that return from the dealer. For example, if the S&P 500 falls by 1 percent, the dealer would pay the end user 1 percent, in addition to the fixed payment the dealer makes in any case. So the dealer, or in general the party receiving the equity return, could end up making *both* a fixed-rate payment and an equity payment.

The second distinguishing feature of an equity swap is that the payment is not known until the end of the settlement period, at which time the return on the stock is known. In an interest rate or currency swap, the floating interest rate is set at the beginning of the period.[9] Therefore, one always knows the amount of the upcoming floating interest payment.[10]

Another important feature of some equity swaps is that the rate of return is often structured to include both dividends and capital gains. In interest rate and currency swaps, capital gains are not paid.[11] Finally, we note that in some equity swaps, the notional principal is indexed to change with the level of the stock, although we will not explore such swaps in this book.[12]

Equity swaps are commonly used by asset managers. Let us consider a situation in which an asset manager might use such a swap. Suppose that the Vanguard Asset Allocation Fund (Nasdaq: VAAPX) is authorized to use swaps. On the last day of December, it would like to sell $100 million in U.S. large-cap equities and

---

[8] Currency swaps also have the element that the exchange rate is variable.

[9] Technically, there are interest rate swaps in which the floating rate is set at the end of the period, at which time the payment is made. We shall briefly mention these swaps in Section 5.

[10] In a currency swap, however, one does not know the exchange rate until the settlement date.

[11] In some kinds of interest rate swaps, the total return on a bond, which includes dividends and capital gains, is paid. This instrument is called a **total return swap** and is a common variety of a credit derivative, which we cover in Chapter 9.

[12] Some interest rate swaps also have a notional principal that changes, which we shall briefly discuss in Section 5.

invest the proceeds at a fixed rate. It believes that a swap allowing it to pay the total return on the S&P 500, while receiving a fixed rate, would achieve this objective. It would like to hold this position for one year, with payments to be made on the last day of March, June, September, and December. It enters into such a swap with Morgan Stanley (NYSE: MWD).

Specifically, the swap covers a notional principal of $100 million and calls for VAAPX to pay MWD the return on the S&P 500 Total Return Index and for MWD to pay VAAPX a fixed rate on the last day of March, June, September, and December for one year. MWD prices the swap at a fixed rate of 6.5 percent. The fixed payments will be made using an actual day count/365 days convention. There are 90 days between 31 December and 31 March, 91 days between 31 March and 30 June, 92 days between 30 June and 30 September, and 92 days between 30 September and 31 December. Thus, the fixed payments will be

31 March:	$100,000,000(0.065)(90/365) = \$1,602,740$
30 June:	$100,000,000(0.065)(91/365) = \$1,620,548$
30 September:	$100,000,000(0.065)(92/365) = \$1,638,356$
31 December:	$100,000,000(0.065)(92/365) = \$1,638,356$

Exhibit 73-6 shows the cash flow stream to VAAPX.

Suppose that on the day the swap is initiated, 31 December, the S&P 500 Total Return Index is at 3,517.76. Now suppose that on 31 March, the index is at 3,579.12. The return on the index is

$$\frac{3,579.12}{3,517.76} - 1 = 0.0174$$

EXHIBIT 73-6 Cash Flows to VAAPX on Equity Swap with MWD

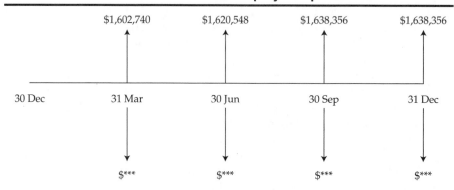

***Computed as $100,000,000R, where R is the return on the S&P 500 Total Return Index from the previous settlement date.

Thus, the return is 1.74 percent. The equity payment that VAAPX would make to MWD would be $100,000,000(0.0174) = \$1,740,000$.

Of course, this amount would not be known until 31 March, and only the difference between this amount and the fixed payment would be paid. Then on 31 March, the index value of 3,579.12 would be the base for the following period. Suppose that on 30 June, the index declines to 3,452.78. Then the return for the second quarter would be

$$\frac{3{,}452.78}{3{,}579.12} - 1 = -0.0353$$

Therefore, the loss is 3.53 percent, requiring a payment of $100,000,000(0.0353) = $3,530,000.

Because this amount represents a loss on the S&P 500, MWD would make a payment to VAAPX. In addition, MWD would also owe VAAPX the fixed payment of $1,620,548. It is as though VAAPX sold out of its position in stock, thereby avoiding the loss of about $3.5 million, and moved into a fixed-income position, thereby picking up a gain of about $1.6 million.

Practice Problem 3

A mutual fund has arranged an equity swap with a dealer. The swap's notional principal is $100 million, and payments will be made semiannually. The mutual fund agrees to pay the dealer the return on a small-cap stock index, and the dealer agrees to pay the mutual fund based on one of the two specifications given below. The small-cap index starts off at 1,805.20; six months later, it is at 1,796.15.

A. The dealer pays a fixed rate of 6.75 percent to the mutual fund, with payments made on the basis of 182 days in the period and 365 days in a year. Determine the first payment for both parties and, under the assumption of netting, determine the net payment and which party makes it.

B. The dealer pays the return on a large-cap index. The index starts off at 1155.14 and six months later is at 1148.91. Determine the first payment for both parties and, under the assumption of netting, determine the net payment and which party makes it.

SOLUTIONS

A. The fixed payment is $100,000,000(0.0675)182/365 = $3,365,753
The equity payment is

$$\left(\frac{1796.15}{1805.20} - 1\right)\$100{,}000{,}000 = -\$501{,}329$$

Because the fund pays the equity return and the equity return is negative, the dealer must pay the equity return. The dealer also pays the fixed return, so the dealer makes both payments, which add up to $3,365,753 + $501,329 = $3,867,082. The net payment is $3,867,082, paid by the dealer to the mutual fund.

B. The large-cap equity payment is

$$\left(\frac{1148.91}{1155.14} - 1\right)\$100{,}000{,}000 = -\$539{,}329$$

The fund owes −$501,329, so the dealer owes the fund $501,329. The dealer owes −$539,329, so the fund owes the dealer $539,329. Therefore, the fund pays the dealer the net amount of $539,329 − $501,329 = $38,000.

Exhibit 73-7 illustrates what VAAPX has accomplished. It is important to note that the conversion of its equity assets into fixed income is not perfect. VAAPX does not hold a portfolio precisely equal to the S&P 500 Total Return Index. To the extent that VAAPX's portfolio generates a return that deviates from the index, some mismatching can occur, which can be a problem. As an alternative, VAAPX can request that MWD give it a swap based on the precise portfolio that VAAPX wishes to sell off. In that case, however, MWD would assess a charge by lowering the fixed rate it pays or raising the rate VAAPX pays to it.[13]

EXHIBIT 73-7 VAAPX's Conversion of an Equity Position into a Fixed-Income Position

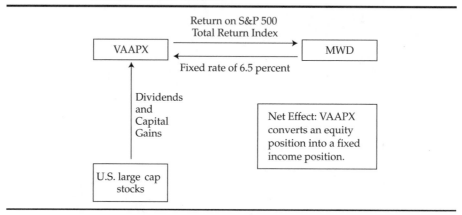

In our previous VAAPX example, the fund wanted to move some money out of a large-cap equity position and invest the proceeds at a fixed rate. Suppose instead that they do not want to move the proceeds into a fixed-rate investment. VAAPX could structure a swap to pay it a floating rate or the return on some other equity index. For example, an asset allocation from U.S. large-cap stocks to U.S. small-cap stocks could be accomplished by having MWD pay the return on the S&P 500 Small Cap 600 Index.

Suppose VAAPX wanted to move out of a position in U.S. stocks and into a position in U.K. large-cap stocks. It could structure the swap to have MWD pay it the return on the FTSE (Financial Times Stock Exchange) 100 Index. Note, however, that this index is based on the prices of U.K. stocks as quoted in pounds sterling. If VAAPX wanted the exposure in pounds—that is, it wanted the currency risk as well as the risk of the U.K. stock market—the payments from MWD to VAAPX would be made in pounds. VAAPX could, however, ask for the payments in dollars. In that case, MWD would hedge the currency risk and make payments in dollars.

Although our focus in this book is on currency, interest rate, and equity products, we shall take a very brief look at some other types of swaps.

3.4 Commodity and Other Types of Swaps

Just as currencies, interest rates, and equities can be used to structure swaps, so too can commodities and just about anything that has a random outcome and to which a corporation, financial institution, or even an individual is exposed.

---

[13] Note, however, that VAAPX is converting not its entire portfolio but simply a $100 million portion of it.

Commodity swaps are very commonly used. For example, airlines enter into swaps to hedge their future purchases of jet fuel. They agree to make fixed payments to a swap dealer on regularly scheduled dates and receive payments determined by the price of jet fuel. Gold mining companies use swaps to hedge future deliveries of gold. Other parties dealing in such commodities as natural gas and precious metals often use swaps to lock in prices for future purchases and sales. In addition, swaps can be based on non-storable commodities, like electricity and the weather. In the case of the weather, payments are made based on a measure of a particular weather factor, such as amounts of rain, snowfall, or weather-related damage.

We have now introduced and described the basic structure of swaps. We have made many references to the pricing and valuation of swaps, and we now move on to explore how this is done.

PRICING AND VALUATION OF SWAPS   4

In Reading 70, we took our first look at the concepts of pricing and valuation when we examined forward contracts on assets and FRAs, which are essentially forward contracts on interest rates. Recall that a forward contract requires no cash payment at the start and commits one party to buy and another to sell an asset at a later date. An FRA commits one party to make a single fixed-rate interest payment and the other to make a single floating-rate interest payment. A swap extends that concept by committing one party to making a series of floating payments. The other party commits to making a series of fixed or floating payments. For swaps containing any fixed terms, such as a fixed rate, pricing the swap means to determine those terms at the start of the swap. Some swaps do not contain any fixed terms; we explore examples of both types of swaps.

All swaps have a market value. Valuation of a swap means to determine the market value of the swap based on current market conditions. The fixed terms, such as the fixed rate, are established at the start to give the swap an initial market value of zero. As we have already discussed, a zero market value means that neither party pays anything to the other at the start. Later during the life of the swap, as market conditions change, the market value will change, moving from zero from both parties' perspective to a positive value for one party and a negative value for the other. When a swap has zero value, it is neither an asset nor a liability to either party. When the swap has positive value to one party, it is an asset to that party; from the perspective of the other party, it thus has negative value and is a liability.

We begin the process of pricing and valuing swaps by learning how swaps are comparable to other instruments. If we know that one financial instrument is equivalent to another, we can price one instrument if we know or can determine the price of the other instrument.

4.1 Equivalence of Swaps and Other Instruments

In this section, we look at how swaps are similar to other instruments. Because our focus is on currency, interest rate, and equity swaps, we do not discuss commodity swaps here.

4.1.1 Swaps and Assets

We have already alluded to the similarity between swaps and assets. For example, a currency swap is identical to issuing a fixed- or floating-rate bond in one currency, converting the proceeds to the other currency, and using the proceeds to purchase a fixed- or floating-rate bond denominated in the other currency. An interest rate swap is identical to issuing a fixed- or floating-rate bond and using the proceeds to purchase a floating- or fixed-rate bond. The notional principal is equivalent to the face value on these hypothetical bonds.

Equity swaps appear to be equivalent to issuing one type of security and using the proceeds to purchase another, where at least one of the types of securities is a stock or stock index. For example, a pay-fixed, receive-equity swap looks like issuing a fixed-rate bond and using the proceeds to buy a stock or index portfolio. As it turns out, however, these two transactions are not exactly the same, although they are close. The stock position in the transaction is not the same as a buy-and-hold position; some adjustments are required on the settlement dates to replicate the cash flows of a swap. We shall take a look at this process of replicating an equity swap in Section 4.2.3. For now, simply recognize that an equity swap is like issuing bonds and buying stock, but not buying and holding stock.

The equivalence of a swap to transactions we are already familiar with, such as owning assets, is important because it allows us to price and value the swap using simple instruments, such as the underlying currency, interest rate, or stock. We do not require other derivatives to replicate the cash flows of a swap. Nonetheless, other derivatives can be used to replicate the cash flows of a swap, and it is worth seeing why this is true.

4.1.2 Swaps and Forward Contracts

Recall that a forward contract, whether on an interest rate, a currency, or an equity, is an agreement for one party to make a fixed payment to the other, while the latter party makes a variable payment to the former. A swap extends this notion by combining a series of forward contracts into a single transaction. There are, however, some subtle differences between swaps and forward contracts. For example, swaps are a series of equal fixed payments, whereas the component contracts of a series of forward contracts would almost always be priced at different fixed rates.[14] In this context we often refer to a swap as a series of off-market forward contracts, reflecting the fact that the implicit forward contracts that make up the swap are all priced at the swap fixed rate and not at the rate at which they would normally be priced in the market. In addition, in interest rate swaps, the next payment that each party makes is known. That would obviously not be the case for a single forward contract. Other subtleties distinguish currency swaps from a series of currency forwards and equity swaps from a series of equity forwards, but in general, it is acceptable to view a swap as a series of forward contracts.

4.1.3 Swaps and Futures Contracts

It is a fairly common practice to equate swaps to futures contracts. This practice is partially correct, but only to the extent that futures contracts can be equated to forward contracts. We saw in Reading 71 that futures contracts are equivalent to forward contracts only when future interest rates are known. Obviously this condition can never truly be met, and because swaps are often used to manage

---

[14] For example, a series of FRAs would have different fixed rates unless the term structure is flat.

uncertain interest rates, the equivalence of futures with swaps is not always appropriate. Moreover, swaps are highly customized contracts, whereas futures are standardized with respect to expiration and the underlying instrument. Although it is common to equate a swap with a series of futures contracts, this equality holds true only in very limited cases.[15]

4.1.4 Swaps and Options

Finally, we note that swaps can be equated to combinations of options. Buying a call and selling a put would force the transacting party to make a net payment if the underlying is below the exercise rate at expiration, and would result in receipt of a payment if the underlying is above the exercise rate at expiration. This payment will be equivalent to a swap payment if the exercise rate is set at the fixed rate on the swap. Therefore, a swap is equivalent to a combination of options with expirations at the swap payment dates. The connection between swaps and options is relatively straightforward for interest rate instruments, but less so for currency and equity instruments. Nonetheless, we can generally consider swaps as equivalent to combinations of options.

In this section, we have learned that swaps can be shown to be equivalent to combinations of assets, combinations of forward contracts, combinations of futures contracts, and combinations of options. Thus, to price and value swaps we can choose any of these approaches. We choose the simplest: swaps and assets.

4.2 Pricing and Valuation

As in previous readings, our goal is to determine the market value of the derivative transaction of interest, in this case, swaps. At the start of a swap, the market value is set to zero. The process of pricing the swap involves finding the terms that force that market value to zero. To determine the market value of a swap, we replicate the swap using other instruments that produce the same cash flows. Knowing the values of these other instruments, we are able to value the swap. This value can be thought of as what the swap is worth if we were to sell it to someone else. In addition, we can think of the value as what we might assign to it on our balance sheet. The swap can have a positive value, making it an asset, or a negative value, making it a liability.

As we noted in Section 4.1, swaps are equivalent to a variety of instruments, but we prefer to use the simplest instruments to replicate the swap. The simplest instruments are the underlying assets: bonds, stocks, and currencies. Therefore, we shall use these underlying instruments to replicate the swap.

To understand the pricing of currency, interest rate, and equity swaps, we shall have to first take a brief digression to examine an instrument that plays an important role in their pricing. We shall see that the floating-rate security will have a value of 1.0, its par, at the start and on any coupon reset date. Recall that we have made numerous references to floating rates and floating payments. Accordingly, we must first obtain a solid understanding of floating-rate notes.

---

[15] It is possible only in extremely rare circumstances for futures expirations to line up with swap settlement dates and thereby provide perfect equivalence. That does not mean, however, that futures cannot be used to hedge in a delta-hedging sense, as described in Reading 72. A futures price has a given sensitivity to the underlying, and futures are often highly liquid. A dealer, having entered into a swap, can determine the swap's sensitivity to the underlying and execute the appropriate number of futures transactions to balance the volatility of the swap to that of the futures. Indeed, this method is standard for hedging plain vanilla swaps using the Eurodollar futures contract.

As we did in Reading 70, let us first set up a time line that indicates where we are and where the interest payments on the floating-rate note will occur:

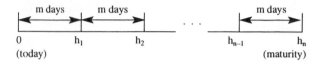

We start at time 0. The interest payments will occur on days $h_1, h_2, \ldots, h_{n-1}$, and h_n, so there are n interest payments in all. Day h_n is the maturity date of the floating-rate note. The time interval between payments is m days. The underlying rate is an m-day interest rate.

For simplicity, we will use LIBOR as the underlying rate and denote it with the symbol we have previously used, $L_i(m)$, which stands for the m-day LIBOR on day i. If i = 1, we are referring to day h_1, which might, for example, be 180 days after day 0. Thus, $h_1 = 180$. $L_0(180)$ is the 180-day LIBOR on day 0. Then h_2 would likely be 360 and $L_0(2m) = L_0(360)$, the 360-day LIBOR on day 0. We denote $B_0(h_j)$ as the present value factor on a zero-coupon instrument paying \$1 at its maturity date. As an example, to discount payments 180 and 360 days later, we multiply the payment amount by the following respective factors:

$$B_0(180) = \frac{1}{1 + L_0(180) \times (180/360)}$$

$$B_0(360) = \frac{1}{1 + L_0(360) \times (360/360)}$$

We can think of these discount factors as the values of spot LIBOR deposits that pay \$1 at maturity, 180 and 360 days later.

On day 0, the floating rate is set for the first period and the interest to be paid at that rate is paid on day h_1. Then on day h_1, the rate is set for the second period and the interest is paid on day h_2. This process continues so that on day h_{n-1} the rate is set for the last period, and the final interest payment and the principal are paid on day h_n. Let the principal be 1.0.

Suppose today is day h_{n-1} and LIBOR on that day is $L_{n-1}(m)$. Remember that this rate is the m-day LIBOR in the market at that time. Therefore, looking ahead to day h_n, we anticipate receiving 1.0, the final principal payment, plus $L_{n-1}(m) \times (m/360)$. What is the value of this amount on day h_{n-1}? We would discount it by the appropriate m-day LIBOR in the following manner:

$$\text{Value at } h_{n-1} = (\text{Payment at } h_n)(\text{One-period discount factor})$$

$$= [1.0 + L_{n-1}(m) \times (m/360)]\left[\frac{1}{1.0 + L_{n-1}(m) \times (m/360)}\right]$$

$$= 1.0$$

The value is 1.0, its par value. Now step back to day h_{n-2}, at which time the rate is $L_{n-2}(m)$. Looking ahead to day h_{n-1} we shall receive an interest payment of $L_{n-2}(m) \times (m/360)$. We do not receive the principal on day h_{n-1}, but it is appropriate to discount the market value on day h_{n-1}, which we just determined is 1.0.[16]

---

[16] All we are doing here is discounting the upcoming cash flow and the market value of the security on the next payment date. This procedure is not unique to floating-rate securities; it is standard valuation procedure for any type of security. What is special and different for floating-rate securities is that the market value goes back to par on each payment date.

Thus, the value of the floating-rate security will be

Value at h_{n-2} = (Payment at $h_n - 1$)(One-period discount factor)

$$= [1.0 + L_{n-2}(m) \times (m/360)] \left[\frac{1}{1.0 + L_{n-2}(m) \times (m/360)} \right]$$

$$= 1.0$$

We continue this procedure, stepping back until we reach time 0. The floating-rate security will have a value of 1.0, its par, at the start and on any coupon reset date.[17] We shall use this result to help us price and value swaps.

In previous material in this reading, we have covered currency swaps first. We did so because we showed that an interest rate swap is just a currency swap in which both currencies are the same. A currency swap is thus the more general instrument of the two. For the purposes of this section, however, it will be easier to price and value a currency swap if we first price and value an interest rate swap.

4.2.1 *Interest Rate Swaps*

Pricing an interest rate swap means finding the fixed rate that equates the present value of the fixed payments to the present value of the floating payments, a process that sets the market value of the swap to zero at the start. Using the time line illustrated earlier, the swap cash flows will occur on days $h_1, h_2, \ldots, h_{n-1}$, and h_n, so there are n cash flows in the swap. Day h_n is the expiration date of the swap. The time interval between payments is m days. We can thus think of the swap as being on an m-day interest rate, which will be LIBOR in our examples.

As previously mentioned, the payments in an interest rate swap are a series of fixed and floating interest payments. They do not include an initial and final exchange of notional principals. As we already observed, such payments would be only an exchange of the same money. But if we introduce the notional principal payments as though they were actually made, we have not done any harm. The cash flows on the swap are still the same. The advantage of introducing the notional principal payments is that we can now treat the fixed and floating sides of the swap as though they were fixed- and floating-rate bonds.

So we introduce a hypothetical final notional principal payment of $1 on a swap starting at day 0 and ending on day h_n, in which the underlying is an m-day rate. The fixed swap interest payment *rate*, FS(0,n,m), gives the fixed payment *amount* corresponding to the $1 notional principal. Thus, the present value of a series of fixed interest payments at the swap rate FS(0,n,m) plus a final principal payment of 1.0 is

$$\sum_{j=1}^{n} FS(0,n,m)B_0(h_j) + \$1 \times B_0(h_n), \text{ or}$$

$$FS(0,n,m) \sum_{j=1}^{n} B_0(h_j) + B_0(h_n)$$

Here the summation simply represents the sum of the present value factors for each payment. The expression $B_0(h_n)$ is the present value factor for the final hypothetical notional principal payment of 1.0.

Now we must find the present value of the floating payments, and here we use what we learned about floating-rate notes. Remember that a floating-rate note

---

[17] Floating-rate securities are designed to allow the coupon to catch up with market interest rates on a regularly scheduled basis. The price can deviate from par during the period between reset dates. In addition, if there is any credit risk and that risk changes during the life of the security, its price can deviate from par at any time, including at the coupon reset date. We are assuming no credit risk here.

with $1 face will have a value of $1 at the start and at any coupon reset date. If the swap's floating payments include a final principal payment, we can treat them like a floating-rate note. Hence, we know their value is $1.

Now all we have to do is equate the present value of the fixed payments to the present value of the floating payments

$$FS(0,n,m)\sum_{j=1}^{n} B_0(h_j) + B_0(h_n) = 1.0$$

and solve for the fixed rate FS(0,n,m) that will result in equality of these two streams of payments. The solution is as follows:

$$FS(0,n,m) = \frac{1.0 - B_0(h_n)}{\sum_{j=1}^{n} B_0(h_j)} \tag{73-1}$$

The swap fixed payment is 1.0 minus the last present value factor divided by the sum of the present value factors for each payment. Thus, we have priced the swap.

One can use several other ways to find the fixed payment on a swap, but this method is unquestionably the simplest. In fact, this formulation shows that the fixed rate on a swap is simply the coupon rate on a par bond whose payments coincide with those on the swap.[18]

Let us now work a problem. Consider a one-year swap with quarterly payments on days 90, 180, 270, and 360. The underlying is 90-day LIBOR. The annualized LIBOR spot rates today are

$$L_0(90) \quad = 0.0345$$
$$L_0(180) = 0.0358$$
$$L_0(270) = 0.0370$$
$$L_0(360) = 0.0375$$

The present value factors are obtained as follows:

$$B_0(90) = \frac{1}{1 + 0.0345(90/360)} = 0.9914$$

$$B_0(180) = \frac{1}{1 + 0.0358(180/360)} = 0.9824$$

$$B_0(270) = \frac{1}{1 + 0.0370(270/360)} = 0.9730$$

$$B_0(360) = \frac{1}{1 + 0.0375(360/360)} = 0.9639$$

The fixed payment is found as

$$FS(0,n,m) = FS(0,4,90) = \frac{1 - 0.9639}{0.9914 + 0.9824 + 0.9730 + 0.9639} = 0.0092$$

Therefore, the quarterly fixed payment will be 0.0092 for each $1 notional principal. Of course, this rate is quarterly; it is customary to quote it as an annual rate.

---

[18] Technically, bond interest payments are usually found by dividing the annual rate by 2 if the payments are semiannual, whereas swap payments do, on occasion, use day counts such as 181/365 to determine semiannual payments. When we refer to a par bond, we are assuming the payments are structured exactly like those on the swap.

We would thus see the rate quoted as $0.0092 \times (360/90) = 0.0368$, or 3.68 percent. We would also have to adjust our payment by multiplying by the actual notional principal. For example, if the actual notional principal were $30 million, the payment would be $(0.0092)\$30$ million $= \$276,000$.

In determining the fixed rate on the swap, we have essentially found the fixed payment that sets the present value of the floating payments plus a hypothetical notional principal of 1.0 equal to the present value of the fixed payments plus a hypothetical notional principal of 1.0. We have thus made the market value of the swap equal to zero at the start of the transaction. This equality makes sense, because neither party pays any money to the other.

Now suppose we have entered into the swap. Let us move forward into the life of the swap, at which time interest rates have changed, and determine its market value. Rather than present mathematical equations for determining its value, we shall work through this example informally. We shall see that the procedure is simple and intuitive. Suppose we have now moved 60 days into the life of the swap. At day 60, we face a new term structure of LIBORs. Because the upcoming payments occur in 30, 120, 210, and 300 days, we want the term structure for 30, 120, 210, and 300 days, which is given as follows:

$$L_{60}(30) = 0.0425$$
$$L_{60}(120) = 0.0432$$
$$L_{60}(210) = 0.0437$$
$$L_{60}(300) = 0.0444$$

The new set of discount factors is

$$B_{60}(30) = \frac{1}{1 + 0.0425(30/360)} = 0.9965$$

$$B_{60}(120) = \frac{1}{1 + 0.0432(120/360)} = 0.9858$$

$$B_{60}(210) = \frac{1}{1 + 0.0437(210/360)} = 0.9751$$

$$B_{60}(300) = \frac{1}{1 + 0.0444(300/360)} = 0.9643$$

We must value the swap from the perspective of one of the parties. Let us look at it as though we were the party paying fixed and receiving floating. Finding the present value of the remaining fixed payments of 0.0092 is straightforward. This present value, including the hypothetical notional principal, is $0.0092(0.9965 + 0.9858 + 0.9751 + 0.9643) + 1.0(0.9643) = 1.0004$.

Now we must find the present value of the floating payments. Recall that on day 0, the 90-day LIBOR was 3.45 percent. Thus, the first floating payment will be $0.0345(90/360) = 0.0086$. We know that we should discount this payment back 30 days, but what about the remaining floating payments? Remember that we know that the market value of the remaining payments on day 90, including the hypothetical final notional principal, is 1.0. So, we can discount $1.00 + 0.0086 = 1.0086$ back 30 days to obtain $1.0086(0.9965) = 1.0051$.

The present value of the remaining floating payments, plus the hypothetical notional principal, is 1.0051, and the present value of the remaining fixed payments, plus the hypothetical notional principal, is 1.0004. Therefore, the value of the swap is $1.0051 - 1.0004 = 0.0047$ per $1 notional principal. If, for example, the actual swap were for a notional principal of $30 million, the market value would be $30 million$(0.0047) = \$141,000$.

Consider a one-year interest rate swap with semiannual payments.

A. Determine the fixed rate on the swap and express it in annualized terms. The term structure of LIBOR spot rates is given as follows:

Days	Rate
180	7.2%
360	8.0%

B. Ninety days later, the term structure is as follows:

Days	Rate
90	7.1%
270	7.4%

Determine the market value of the swap from the perspective of the party paying the floating rate and receiving the fixed rate. Assume a notional principal of $15 million.

SOLUTIONS

A. First calculate the present value factors for 180 and 360 days:

$$B_0(180) = \frac{1}{1 + 0.072(180/360)} = 0.9653$$

$$B_0(360) = \frac{1}{1 + 0.08(360/360)} = 0.9259$$

The fixed rate is $\dfrac{1 - 0.9259}{0.9653 + 0.9259} = 0.0392$. The fixed payment would,

therefore, be 0.0392 per $1 notional principal. The annualized rate would be 0.0392(360/180) = 0.0784.

B. Calculate the new present value factors for 90 and 270 days:

$$B_{90}(90) = \frac{1}{1 + 0.071(90/360)} = 0.9826$$

$$B_{90}(270) = \frac{1}{1 + 0.0074(270/360)} = 0.9474$$

The present value of the remaining fixed payments plus the hypothetical $1 notional principal is 0.0392(0.9826 + 0.9474) + 1.0(0.9474) = 1.0231.

The 180-day rate at the start was 7.2 percent, so the first floating payment would be 0.072(180/360) = 0.036. The present value of the floating payments plus the hypothetical $1 notional principal will be 1.036(0.9826) = 1.0180. The market value of a pay-floating, receive-fixed swap is, therefore, 1.0231 − 1.0180 = 0.0051. For a notional principal of $15 million, the market value is $15,000,000(0.0051) = $76,500.

Note that we valued the swap from the perspective of the party paying the fixed rate. From the counterparty's perspective, the value of the swap would be the negative of the value to the fixed-rate payer.

Although an interest rate swap is like a series of FRAs, or a long position in an interest rate cap and a short position in an interest rate floor with the exercise rate set at the fixed rate on a swap, pricing and valuing an interest rate swap as either of these instruments is more difficult than what we have done here. To price the swap as a series of FRAs, we would need to calculate the forward rates, which is not difficult but would add another step. If we priced a swap as a combination of caps and floors, we would need to price these options. As we saw in Reading 72, interest rate option pricing can be somewhat complex. In addition, we would have to find the exercise rate on the cap and floor that equated their values, which would require trial and error. What we have seen here is the trick that if we add the notional principal to both sides of an interest rate swap, we do not change the swap payments, but we make the cash flows on each side of the swap equivalent to those of a bond. Then we can price the swap as though it were a pair of bonds, one long and the other short. One side is like a floating-rate bond, which we know is priced at par value at the time of issuance as well as on any reset date. The other side is like a fixed-rate bond. Because the value of the fixed-rate bond must equal that of the floating-rate bond at the start, we know that the coupon on a par value bond is the fixed rate on the swap.

Having discussed the pricing and valuation of interest rate swaps, we can now move on to currency swaps, taking advantage of what we know about pricing interest rate swaps. As we have already noted, an interest rate swap is just like a currency swap in which both currencies are the same.

4.2.2 Currency Swaps

Recall the four types of currency swaps: (1) pay one currency fixed, receive the other fixed, (2) pay one currency fixed, receive the other floating, (3) pay one currency floating, receive the other fixed, and (4) pay one currency floating, receive the other floating. In determining the fixed rate on a swap, we must keep in mind one major point: The fixed rate is the rate that makes the present value of the payments made equal the present value of the payments received. In the fourth type of currency swap mentioned here, both sides pay floating so there is no need to find a fixed rate. But all currency swaps have two notional principals, one in each currency. We can arbitrarily set the notional principal in the domestic currency at one unit. We then must determine the equivalent notional principal in the other currency. This task is straightforward: We simply convert the one unit of domestic currency to the equivalent amount of foreign currency, dividing 1.0 by the exchange rate.

Consider the first type of currency swap, in which we pay the foreign currency at a fixed rate and receive the domestic currency at a fixed rate. What are the two fixed rates? We will see that they are the fixed rates on plain vanilla interest rate swaps in the respective countries.

Because we know that the value of a floating-rate security with $1 face value is $1, we know that the fixed rate on a plain vanilla interest rate swap is the rate on a $1 par bond in the domestic currency. That rate results in the present value of the interest payments and the hypothetical notional principal being equal to 1.0 unit of the domestic currency. Moreover, for a currency swap, the notional principal is typically paid, so we do not even have to call it hypothetical. We know that the fixed rate on the domestic leg of an interest rate swap is the appropriate domestic fixed rate for a currency swap in which the domestic notional principal is 1.0 unit of the domestic currency.

What about the fixed rate for the foreign payments on the currency swap? To answer that question, let us assume the point of view of a resident of the foreign country. Given the term structure in the foreign country, we might be interested in first pricing plain vanilla interest rate swaps in that country. So, we know that the fixed rate on interest rate swaps in that country would make the present value of the interest and principal payments equal 1.0 unit of that currency.

Now let us return to our domestic setting. We know that the fixed rate on interest rate swaps in the foreign currency makes the present value of the foreign interest and principal payments equal to 1.0 unit of the foreign currency. We multiply by the spot rate, S_0, to obtain the value of those payments in our domestic currency: 1.0 times S_0 equals S_0, which is now in terms of the domestic currency. This amount does not equal the present value of the domestic payments, but if we set the notional principal on the foreign side of the swap equal to $1/S_0$, then the present value of the foreign payments will be $S_0(1/S_0) = 1.0$ unit of our domestic currency, which is what we want.

Let us now summarize this argument:

▸ The fixed rate on plain vanilla swaps in our country makes the present value of the domestic interest and principal payments equal 1.0 unit of the domestic currency.

▸ The fixed rate on plain vanilla swaps in the foreign country makes the present value of the foreign interest and principal payments equal 1.0 unit of the foreign currency.

▸ A notional principal of $1/S_0$ units of foreign currency makes the present value of the foreign interest and principal payments equal $1/S_0$ units of the foreign currency.

▸ Conversion of $1/S_0$ units of foreign currency at the current exchange rate of S_0 gives 1.0 unit of domestic currency.

▸ Therefore, the present value of the domestic payments equals the present value of the foreign payments.

▸ The fixed rates on a currency swap are, therefore, the fixed rates on plain vanilla interest rate swaps in the respective countries.

Of course, if the domestic notional principal is any amount other than 1.0, we multiply the domestic notional principal by $1/S_0$ to obtain the foreign notional principal. Then the actual swap payments are calculated by multiplying by the overall respective notional principals.

The second and third types of currency swaps each involve one side paying fixed and the other paying floating. The rate on the fixed side of each of these swaps is, again, just the fixed rate on an interest rate swap in the given country. The payments on the floating side automatically have the same present value as the payments on the fixed side. We again use 1.0 unit of domestic currency and $1/S_0$ units of foreign currency as the notional principal.

For the last type of currency swap, in which both sides pay floating, we do not need to price the swap because both sides pay a floating rate. Again, the notional principals are 1.0 unit of domestic currency and $1/S_0$ units of foreign currency.

In the example we used in pricing interest rate swaps, we were given a term structure for a one-year swap with quarterly payments. We found that the fixed payment was 0.0092, implying an annual rate of 3.68 percent. Let us now work through a currency swap in which the domestic currency is the dollar and the foreign currency is the Swiss franc. The current exchange rate is $0.80. We shall use the same term structure used previously for the domestic term structure: $L_0(90) = 0.0345$, $L_0(180) = 0.0358$, $L_0(270) = 0.0370$, and $L_0(360) = 0.0375$.

The Swiss term structure, denoted with a superscript SF, is

$$L_0^{SF}(90) = 0.0520$$
$$L_0^{SF}(180) = 0.0540$$
$$L_0^{SF}(270) = 0.0555$$
$$L_0^{SF}(360) = 0.0570$$

The present value factors are

$$B_0^{SF}(90) = \frac{1}{1 + 0.0520(90/360)} = 0.9872$$

$$B_0^{SF}(180) = \frac{1}{1 + 0.0540(180/360)} = 0.9737$$

$$B_0^{SF}(270) = \frac{1}{1 + 0.0555(270/360)} = 0.9600$$

$$B_0^{SF}(360) = \frac{1}{1 + 0.0570(360/360)} = 0.9461$$

The fixed payment is easily found as

$$FS^{SF}(0, n, m) = FS^{SF}(0,4,90) = \frac{1 - 0.9461}{0.9872 + 0.9737 + 0.9600 + 0.9461} = 0.0139$$

The quarterly fixed payment is thus SF0.0139 for each SF1.00 of notional principal. This translates into an annual rate of 0.0139(360/90) = 0.0556 or 5.56 percent, so in Switzerland we would quote the fixed rate on a plain vanilla interest rate swap in Swiss francs as 5.56 percent.

Our currency swap involving dollars for Swiss francs would have a fixed rate of 3.68 percent in dollars and 5.56 percent in Swiss francs. The notional principal would be $1.0 and 1/$0.80 = SF1.25. Summarizing, we have the following terms for the four swaps:

Swap 1: Pay dollars fixed at 3.68 percent, receive SF fixed at 5.56 percent.

Swap 2: Pay dollars fixed at 3.68 percent, receive SF floating.

Swap 3: Pay dollars floating, receive SF fixed at 5.56 percent.

Swap 4: Pay dollars floating, receive SF floating.

In each case, the notional principal is $1 and SF1.25, or more generally, SF1.25 for every dollar of notional principal.

As we did with interest rate swaps, we move 60 days forward in time. We have a new U.S. term structure, given in the interest rate swap problem, and a new Swiss franc term structure, which is given below:

$$L_{60}^{SF}(30) = 0.0600$$
$$L_{60}^{SF}(120) = 0.0615$$
$$L_{60}^{SF}(210) = 0.0635$$
$$L_{60}^{SF}(300) = 0.0653$$

The new set of discount factors is

$$B_{60}^{SF}(30) = \frac{1}{1 + 0.0600(30/360)} = 0.9950$$

$$B_{60}^{SF}(120) = \frac{1}{1 + 0.0615(120/360)} = 0.9799$$

$$B_{60}^{SF}(210) = \frac{1}{1 + 0.0635(210/360)} = 0.9643$$

$$B_{60}^{SF}(300) = \frac{1}{1 + 0.0653(300/360)} = 0.9484$$

The new exchange rate is $0.82. Now let us value each swap in turn, taking advantage of what we already know about the values of the U.S. dollar interest rate swaps calculated in the previous section. Recall we found that

Present value of dollar fixed payments = 1.0004

Present value of dollar floating payments = 1.0051

Let us find the comparable numbers for the Swiss franc payments. In other words, we position ourselves as a Swiss resident or institution and obtain the values of the fixed and floating streams of Swiss franc payments per SF1 notional principal. The present value of the remaining Swiss fixed payments is

$$0.0139(0.9950 + 0.9799 + 0.9643 + 0.9484) + 1.0(0.9484) = 1.0024$$

Recall that in finding the present value of the floating payments, we simply recognize that on the next payment date, we shall receive a floating payment of $0.052(90/360) = 0.013$, and the market value of the remaining payments will be $1.0.$[19] Thus, we can discount 1.0130 back 30 days to obtain $1.0130(0.9950) = 1.0079$.

These two figures are based on SF1 notional principal. We convert them to the actual notional principal in Swiss francs by multiplying by SF1.25. Thus,

Present value of SF fixed payments = 1.0024(1.25) = SF1.2530

Present value of SF floating payments = 1.0079(1.25) = SF1.2599

Now we need to convert these figures to dollars by multiplying by the current exchange rate of $0.82. Thus,

Present value of SF fixed payments in dollars = 1.2530($0.82) = $1.0275

Present value of SF floating payments in dollars = 1.2599($0.82) = $1.0331

Now we can value the four currency swaps:

Value of swap to pay SF fixed, receive $ fixed = −$1.0275 + $1.0004 = −$0.0271

Value of swap to pay SF floating, receive $ fixed = −$1.0331 + $1.0004 = −$0.0327

Value of swap to pay SF fixed, receive $ floating = −$1.0275 + $1.0051 = −$0.0224

Value of swap to pay SF floating, receive $ floating = −$1.0331 + $1.0051 = −$0.0280

Note that all of these numbers are negative. Therefore, our swaps are showing losses as a result of the combination of interest rate changes in the two countries

---

[19] The first floating payment was set when the swap was initiated at the 90-day rate of 5.2 percent times 90/360.

as well as the exchange rate change. To the counterparty, the swaps are worth these same numerical amounts, but the signs are positive.

Practice Problem 5

Consider a one-year currency swap with semiannual payments. The two currencies are the U.S. dollar and the euro. The current exchange rate is $0.75.

A. The term structure of interest rates for LIBOR and Euribor are

Days	LIBOR	Euribor
180	7.2%	6.0%
360	8.0%	6.6%

Determine the fixed rate in euros and express it in annualized terms. Note that the LIBOR rates are the same as in Practice Problem 4, in which we found that the fixed payment in dollars was 0.0392.

B. Ninety days later, the term structure is as follows:

Days	LIBOR	Euribor
90	7.1%	5.5%
270	7.4%	6.0%

The new exchange rate is $0.70. Determine the market values of swaps to pay dollars and receive euros. Consider all four swaps that are covered in the reading. Assume a notional principal of $20 million and the appropriate amount for euros. Note that the LIBOR rates are the same as in Practice Problem 4, in which we found that the present value of the fixed payments (floating payments) plus the hypothetical $1 notional principal was $1.0231 ($1.0180).

SOLUTIONS

A. The fixed payment in dollars is the same as in Practice Problem 4: 0.0392. To determine the fixed rate in euros, we first compute the discount factors:

$$B_0^{€}(180) = \frac{1}{1 + 0.06(180/360)} = 0.9709$$

$$B_0^{€}(360) = \frac{1}{1 + 0.066(360/360)} = 0.9381$$

The fixed rate in euros is, therefore, $\frac{1 - 0.9381}{0.9709 + 0.9381} = 0.0324$.

On an annual basis, this rate would be $0.0324(360/180) = 0.0648$.

B. Recalculate the euro discount factors:

$$B_{90}^{\text{€}}(90) = \frac{1}{1 + 0.055(90/360)} = 0.9864$$

$$B_{90}^{\text{€}}(270) = \frac{1}{1 + 0.060(270/360)} = 0.9569$$

The present value of the fixed payments plus hypothetical €1 notional principal is €0.0324(0.9864 + 0.9569) + €1.0(0.9569) = €1.0199.

The 180-day rate at the start of the swap was 6 percent, so the first floating payment would be 0.06(180/360) = 0.03. The present value of the floating payments plus hypothetical notional principal of €1 is €1.03(0.9864) = €1.0160.

The euro notional principal, established at the start of the swap, is 1/$0.75 = €1.3333. Converting the euro payments to dollars at the new exchange rate and multiplying by the euro notional principal, we obtain the following values for the four swaps (where we use the present values of U.S. dollar fixed and floating payments as found in Practice Problem 4, repeated in the statement of Part B above).

Pay $ fixed, receive € fixed = −$1.0231 + €1.3333($0.70)1.0199 = −$0.0712

Pay $ fixed, receive € floating = −$1.0231 + €1.3333($0.70)1.0160 = −$0.0749

Pay $ floating, receive € fixed = −$1.0180 + €1.3333($0.70)1.0199 = −$0.0661

Pay $ floating, receive € floating = −$1.0180 + €1.3333($0.70)1.0160 = −$0.0698

Now we turn to equity swaps. It is tempting to believe that we will not use any more information regarding the term structure in pricing and valuing equity swaps. In fact, for equity swaps in which one side pays either a fixed or floating rate, the results we have obtained for interest rate swaps will be very useful.

4.2.3 Equity Swaps

In this section, we explore how to price and value three types of equity swaps: (1) a swap to pay a fixed rate and receive the return on the equity, (2) a swap to pay a floating rate and receive the return on the equity, and (3) a swap to pay the return on one equity and receive the return on another.

To price or value an equity swap, we must determine a combination of stock and bonds that replicates the cash flows on the swap. As we saw with interest rate and currency swaps, such a replication is not difficult to create. We issue a bond and buy a bond, with one being a fixed-rate bond and the other being a floating-rate bond. If we are dealing with a currency swap, we require that one of the bonds be denominated in one currency and the other be denominated in the other currency. With an equity swap, it would appear that a replicating strategy would involve issuing a bond and buying the stock or vice versa, but this is not exactly how to replicate an equity swap. Remember that in an equity swap, we receive cash payments representing the return on the stock, and that is somewhat different from payments based on the price.

Pricing a Swap to Pay a Fixed Rate and Receive the Return on the Equity: By example, we will demonstrate how to price an n-payment m-day rate swap to pay a fixed rate and receive the return on equity. Suppose the notional principal is $1, the swap involves annual settlements and lasts for two years (n = 2), and the returns on the stock for each of the two years are 10 percent for the first year and 15 percent for the second year. The equity payment on the swap would be $0.10 the first year and $0.15 the second. If, however, we purchased the stock instead of doing the equity swap, we would have to sell the stock at the end of the first year or we would not generate any cash. Suppose at the end of the first year, the stock is at $1.10. We sell the stock, withdraw $0.10, and reinvest $1.00 in the stock. At the end of the second year the stock would be at $1.15. We then sell the stock, taking cash of $0.15. But we have $1.00 left over. To get rid of, or off-set, this cash flow, suppose that when we purchased the stock we borrowed the present value of $1.00 for two years. Then two years later, we would pay back $1.00 on that loan. This procedure would offset the $1.00 in cash we have from the stock. The fixed payments on the swap can be easily replicated. If the fixed payment is denoted as $FS(0,n,m)$, we simply borrow the present value of $FS(0,n,m)$ for one year and also borrow the present value of $FS(0,n,m)$ for two years. When we pay those loans back, we will have replicated the fixed payments on the swap.

For the more general case of n payments, we do the following to replicate the swap whose fixed payments are $FS(0,n,m)$:

1. Invest $1.00 in the stock.
2. Borrow the present value of $1.00 to be paid back at the swap expiration, day h_n. This is the amount $B_0(h_n)$.
3. Take out a series of loans requiring that we pay back $FS(0,n,m)$ at time h_1, and also at time h_2, and at all remaining times through time h_n.

Note that this transaction is like issuing debt and buying stock. The amount of money required to do this is

$$\$1 - B_0(h_n) - FS(0,n,m) \sum_{j=1}^{n} B_0(h_j)$$

Because no money changes hands at the start, the initial value of the swap is zero. We set the expression above to zero and solve for the fixed payment $FS(0,n,m)$ to obtain

$$FS(0,n,m) = \frac{1.0 - B_0(h_j)}{\sum_{j=1}^{n} B_0(h_j)}$$

This is precisely the formula (Equation 73-1) for the fixed rate on an interest rate swap or a currency swap.

Pricing a Swap to Pay a Floating Rate and Receive the Return on the Equity: If, instead, the swap involves the payment of a floating rate for the equity return, no further effort is needed because there is no fixed rate for which we must solve. We know from our understanding of interest rate swaps that the present value of the floating payments equals the present value of the fixed payments, which equals the notional principal of 1.0. The market value of the swap is zero at the start, as it should be.

Pricing a Swap to Pay the Return on One Equity and Receive the Return on Another Equity: Let $S_0(1)$ and $S_1(1)$ be the level of Stock Index 1 at times 0 and 1, and let $S_0(2)$ and $S_1(2)$ be the level of Stock Index 2 at times 0 and 1. Assume we pay the return on Index 2 and receive the return on Index 1. We need to replicate the cash flows on this swap by investing in these two stocks using some type of strategy. Suppose we sell short $1.00 of Index 2, taking the proceeds and investing in $1.00 of Index 1. Then at time 1, we liquidate the position in Index 1, as described above, withdrawing the cash and reinvesting the $1.00 back into Index 1. We cover the short position in Index 2, taking the proceeds and re-shorting Index 2. We continue in this manner throughout the life of the swap. This strategy replicates the cash flows on the swap. Thus, going long one stock and short the other replicates this swap. Of course, there is no fixed rate and thus no need to price the swap. The market value at the start is zero as it should be.

Now let us look at how to determine the market values of each of these swaps during their lives. In other words, after the swap has been initiated, we move forward in time. We must take into account where we are in the life of the swap and how interest rates and the equity price have changed.

Valuing a Swap to Pay the Fixed Rate and Receive the Return on the Equity: Let us use the same U.S. term structure we have already been using for interest rate and currency swaps. Our equity swap is for one year and will involve fixed quarterly payments. Recall that the fixed payment on the interest rate swap is 0.0092, corresponding to an annual rate of 3.68 percent. This will be the rate on the swap to pay fixed and receive the equity payment.

Now let us move 60 days into the life of the swap, at which time we have a new term structure as given in the interest rate swap example. We started off with a stock price of S_0, and now the stock price is S_{60}. The stock payment we will receive at the first settlement in 30 days is $S_{90}/S_0 - 1$. Let us write this amount as

$$\left(\frac{1}{S_0}\right)S_{90} - 1$$

Sixty days into the life of the swap, we could replicate this payment by purchasing $1/S_0$ shares of stock, currently at S_{60}. Doing so will cost $(1/S_0)S_{60}$. Then at the first settlement, we shall have stock worth $(1/S_0)S_{90}$. We sell that stock, withdrawing cash of $(1/S_0)S_{90} - 1$. We then take the $1 left over and roll it into the stock again, which will replicate the return the following period, as described above. This procedure will leave $1 left over at the end. Thus, sixty days into the swap, to replicate the remaining cash flows, we do the following:

1. Invest $(1/S_0)S_{60}$ in the stock.
2. Borrow the present value of $1.00 to be paid back at the swap expiration, time h_n. This is the amount $B_{60}(h_n)$.
3. Take out a series of loans requiring that we pay back $FS(0,n,m)$ at time h_1, and also at time h_2, and at all remaining times through time h_n.

For the general case of day t, the market value of the swap is

$$\left(\frac{S_t}{S_0}\right) - B_t(h_n) - FS(0,n,m)\sum_{j=1}^{n}B_t(h_j) \qquad \textbf{(73-2)}$$

The first term reflects the investment in the stock necessary to replicate the equity return. The second term is the loan for the present value of $1.00 due at the expiration date of the swap. The third term is the series of loans of the amount $FS(0,n,m)$ due at the various swap settlement dates. Note that all discounting is done using the new term structure. Of course, the overall market value figure would then be multiplied by the notional principal.

Let us calculate these results for our pay-fixed, receive-equity swap 60 days into its life. Suppose the stock index was at 1405.72 when the swap was initiated. Now it is at 1436.59. We use the same term structure at 60 days that we used for the interest rate swap example. The market value of the swap is

$$\left(\frac{1436.59}{1405.72}\right) - 0.9643 - (0.0092)(0.9965 + 0.9858 + 0.9751 + 0.9643) = 0.0216$$

Thus, 60 days into its life, the market value of this fixed-for-equity swap is positive at $0.0216 per $1 notional principal.

Valuing a Swap to Pay a Floating Rate and Receive the Return on the Equity: We can value this swap in two ways. The first will require that we discount the next floating rate and the par value, as we did with interest rate swaps. We can do this because we recognize that a floating-rate security is worth its par value on the payment date. As long as we add the notional principal, we can assume the floating payments are those of a floating-rate bond. The notional principal offsets the $1 left over at the end from holding the stock and withdrawing all of the profits on each settlement date. The calculation of the market value of this swap is simple. We just determine the value of $1 invested in the stock since the last settlement period, minus the present value of the floating leg. With the upcoming floating payment being 0.0086, the market value of the swap is, therefore,

$$\left(\frac{1436.59}{1405.72}\right) - (1.0086)(0.9965) = 0.0169$$

Another, and probably easier, way to arrive at this answer is to recognize that

- ▷ a swap to pay fixed and receive the equity return is worth 0.0216, and
- ▷ a swap to pay floating and receive fixed is worth -0.0047.[20]

If we did both of these swaps, the fixed payments would offset and would leave the equivalent of the equity swap. The value would then be $0.0216 - 0.0047 = 0.0169$.

Valuing a Swap to Pay One Equity Return and Receive Another: Now we need to value the swap to pay the return on Index 2 and receive the return on Index 1, 60 days into the swap's life. Let the following be the values of the indices on days 0 and 60.

	Day 0	Day 60
Index 1	1405.72	1436.59
Index 2	5255.18	5285.73

As we previously described, this swap can be replicated by going long Index 1 and short Index 2. The market value calculation is simple: We find the value of $1 invested in Index 1 since the last settlement day minus the value of $1 invested in Index 2 since the last settlement day. Thus, the market value of the position is

---

[20] In Section 4.2.1, we found the value of a swap to pay fixed and receive floating to be 0.0047. Therefore, a swap to pay floating and receive fixed is worth -0.0047.

$$\left(\frac{1436.59}{1405.72}\right) - \left(\frac{5285.73}{5255.18}\right) = 0.0161$$

Of course, all of these results are per $1 notional principal, so we would have to multiply by the actual notional principal to get the overall market value of this equity-for-equity swap.

Practice Problem 6

Consider an equity swap that calls for semiannual payments for one year. The party will receive the return on the Dow Jones Industrial Average (DJIA), which starts off at 10033.27. The current LIBOR term structure is

Days	Rate
180	7.2%
360	8.0%

A. In Practice Problem 4, we determined that the fixed rate for a one-year interest rate swap given the above term structure was 0.0392. Given this term structure data, what is the fixed rate in an equity swap calling for the party to pay a fixed rate and receive the return on the DJIA?

B. Find the market value of the swap 90 days later if the new term structure is

Days	Rate
90	7.1%
270	7.4%

The notional principal of the swap is $60 million. The DJIA is at 9955.14. Again, these are the same rates as in Practice Problem 4, for which we computed $B_{90}(180) = 0.9826$ and $B_{90}(360) = 0.9474$.

C. Recompute the market value under the assumption that the counterparty pays a floating rate instead of a fixed rate.

D. Recompute the market value under the assumption that the counterparty pays the return on the Dow Jones Transportation Index, which started off at 2835.17 and 90 days later is 2842.44.

SOLUTIONS

A. Because this term structure is the same as in Practice Problem 4, the fixed rate is the same at 0.0392. The fact that the party here receives an equity return rather than a floating interest rate does not affect the magnitude of the fixed payment.

B. Using the 180- and 360-day discount factors at 90 days from Practice Problem 4, the market value of the swap to pay a fixed rate and receive the equity return is

$$\left(\frac{9955.14}{10033.27}\right) - 0.9474 - 0.0392(0.9826 + 0.9474) = -0.0309$$

Multiplying by the notional principal of $60 million, we obtain a market value of $60,000,000(-0.0309) = -\$1,854,000$.

C. Because the first floating payment would be at the rate of 7.2 percent and is, therefore, 0.036, the market value of the swap to pay a floating rate and receive the equity return is

$$\left(\frac{9955.14}{10033.27}\right) - 1.036(0.9826) = -0.0258$$

Adjusting for the notional principal, the market value is $60,000,000(-0.0258) = -\$1,548,000$.

D. The market value of the swap to pay the return on the Dow Jones Transportation Average and receive the return on the DJIA is

$$\left(\frac{9955.14}{10033.27}\right) - \left(\frac{2842.44}{2835.17}\right) = -0.0104$$

Adjusting for the notional principal, the market value is $60,000,000(-0.0104) = -\$624,000$.

4.3 Some Concluding Comments on Swap Valuation

Let us review some important results on swap valuation and pricing. Because the market value of the swap when initiated is zero, pricing the swap means to find the terms of the swap that will make its market value be zero. If the swap pays a fixed rate, we must find the fixed rate that makes the present value of the fixed payments equal the present value of the floating payments. If both sides of the swap involve floating payments, there are no terms to determine. For currency swaps, we also have to determine the notional principal in one currency that is equivalent to a given notional principal in another currency.

The market value of a swap starts off at zero but changes to either a positive or negative value as the swap evolves through its life and market conditions change. To determine the market value of a swap, we must determine the present value of the remaining stream of payments, netting one against the other.

The market value of a swap gives a number that represents what the swap is worth to each party. If the market value is positive, the swap is like an asset. The amount due to one party is worth more than the amount that party owes. If it is negative, the swap is like a liability. The amount that party owes is worth more than the amount owed to it. The market value of a swap is also sometimes known as the **replacement value.** This notion views the swap as an instrument whose value can potentially be lost through default. If a party is holding a positive value swap and the other party defaults, that value is lost and would require that amount of money to replace it. We discuss this point further in Section 7.

5   VARIATIONS OF SWAPS

So far we have covered the most common types of swaps: fixed-for-floating interest rate swaps, various combinations of fixed and floating currency swaps, and equity swaps involving fixed payments, floating payments, or the returns on another equity. We must also mention some other types of swaps.

We briefly referred to the **basis swap,** in which both sides pay a floating rate. A typical basis swap involves one party paying LIBOR and the other paying the T-bill rate. As we learned in Reading 71, the term *basis* refers to the spread between two prices, usually the spot and futures prices. Here it is simply the spread between two rates, LIBOR and the T-bill rate. Because LIBOR is always more than the T-bill rate, the two parties negotiate a fixed spread such that the party paying LIBOR actually pays LIBOR minus the spread.[21] LIBOR is the borrowing rate of high-quality London banks, and the T-bill rate is the default-free borrowing rate of the U.S. government. The difference between LIBOR and the T-bill rate is thus a reflection of investors' perception of the general level of credit risk in the market. Basis swaps are usually employed for speculative purposes by end users who believe the spread between LIBOR and the T-bill rate will change.[22] A basis swap of this type is, therefore, usually a position taken in anticipation of a change in the relative level of credit risk in the market. As noted, both sides are floating, and typically both sides use 360-day years in their calculations.[23]

Another type of swap we sometimes encounter is not all that different from a plain vanilla or basis swap. In a **constant maturity swap,** one party pays a fixed rate, or a short-term floating rate such as LIBOR, and the other party pays a floating rate that is the rate on a security known as a **constant maturity treasury (CMT)** security. The transaction is also sometimes known as a CMT swap. This underlying instrument is a hypothetical U.S. Treasury note, meaning that its maturity is in the 2- to 10-year range, with a constant maturity. Obviously the reference to a particular CMT cannot be referring to a single note, because the maturity of any security decreases continuously. As mentioned, the note is hypothetical. For example, for a two-year CMT security, when there is an actual two-year note, that note is the CMT security. Otherwise, the yield on a CMT security is interpolated from the yields of securities with surrounding maturities. The distinguishing characteristic of a constant maturity swap is that the maturity of the underlying security exceeds the length of the settlement period. For example, a CMT swap might call for payments every six months, with the rate based on the one-year CMT security. In contrast, a standard swap settling every six months would nearly always be based on a six-month security. Otherwise, however, a constant maturity swap possesses the general characteristics of a plain vanilla swap.

One interesting variant of an interest rate swap is an **overnight index swap (OIS).** This instrument commits one party to paying a fixed rate as usual. The floating rate, however, is the cumulative value of a single unit of currency invested at an overnight rate during the settlement period. The overnight rate changes daily. This instrument is used widely in Europe but not in the United States.

Amortizing and **accreting swaps** are those in which the notional principal changes according to a formula related to the underlying. The more common of the two is the amortizing swap, sometimes called an **index amortizing swap.**

---

[21] Alternatively, the counterparty could pay the T-bill rate plus the spread. .

[22] The spread between LIBOR and the T-bill rate is called the TED spread. It is considered an indicator of the relative state of credit risk in the markets. LIBOR represents the rate on a private borrower (London banks); the T-bill rate is the U.S. government borrowing rate. When the global economy weakens, the TED spread tends to widen because rates based on the credit risk of private borrowers will increase while the U.S. government remains a risk-free borrower.

[23] Of course, a basis swap need not be based on LIBOR and the T-bill rate, so other conventions can be used.

In this type of interest rate swap, the notional principal is indexed to the level of interest rates. The notional principal declines with the level of interest rates according to a predefined schedule. This feature makes the swap similar to certain asset-backed securities, such as mortgage-backed securities, which prepay some of their principal as rates fall. An index amortizing swap is often used to hedge this type of security.

Diff swaps combine elements of interest rate, currency, and equity swaps. In a typical diff swap, one party pays the floating interest rate of one country and the other pays the floating interest rate of another country. Both sets of payments, however, are made in a single currency. So one set of payments is based on the interest rate of one country, but the payment is made in the currency of another country. This swap is a pure play on the interest rate differential between two countries and is basically a currency swap with the currency risk hedged. Alternatively, in equity diff swaps, the return on a foreign stock index is paid in the domestic currency.

An **arrears swap** is a special type of interest rate swap in which the floating payment is set at the end of the period and the interest is paid at that same time. This procedure stands in contrast to the typical interest rate swap, in which the payment is set on one settlement date and the interest is paid on the next settlement date.

In a **capped swap,** the floating payments have a limit as to how high they can be. Similarly, a **floored swap** has a limit on how low the floating payments can be.

There is no limit to the number of variations that can be found in swaps, and it is not worthwhile to examine them beyond the basic, most frequently used types. We must, however, cover an important variation of a swap that combines elements of both swaps and options.

SWAPTIONS   6

A **swaption** *is an option to enter into a swap.* Although swaptions can be designed in a variety of ways, we shall focus exclusively on the most widely used swaption, the plain vanilla interest rate swaption. This is a swaption to pay the fixed rate and receive the floating rate or the other way around. It allows the holder to establish a fixed rate on the underlying swap in advance and have the option of entering into the swap with that fixed rate or allowing the swaption to expire and entering into the swap at the fixed rate that prevails in the market.

6.1 Basic Characteristics of Swaptions

The two types of swaptions are a **payer swaption** and a **receiver swaption.** A payer swaption allows the holder to enter into a swap as the fixed-rate payer and floating-rate receiver. A receiver swaption allows the holder to enter into a swap as the fixed-rate receiver and floating-rate payer. Therefore, these terms refer to the fixed rate and are comparable to the terms *call* and *put* used for other types of options. Although it is not apparent at this point, a payer swaption is a put and a receiver swaption is a call.

Swaptions have specific expiration dates. Like ordinary options, swaptions can be European style (exercisable only at expiration) or American style (exercisable at any time prior to expiration). A swaption is based on a specific underlying swap. For example, consider a European payer swaption that expires in two years and allows the holder to enter into a three-year swap with semiannual payments every 15 January and 15 July. The payments will be made at the rate of 6.25 percent and will be computed using the 30/360 adjustment. The underlying swap is based on LIBOR, and the notional principal is $10 million. Of course, a swaption has a price or premium, which is an amount paid by the buyer to the seller up front.

Note that this swaption expires in two years and the underlying swap expires three years after that. This arrangement is called a 2×5 swaption, a terminology we used in explaining FRAs. The underlying can be viewed as a five-year swap at the time the swaption is initiated and will be a three-year swap when the swaption expires.

Finally, there are a number of ways to settle a swaption at expiration. Recall that ordinary options can allow for either physical delivery or cash settlement. We will explore the comparable concepts for swaptions in Section 6.3.

6.2 Uses of Swaptions

Swaptions have a variety of purposes, which we shall cover in more detail in Chapter 8 when we discuss swap applications and strategies. For right now, however, we take a brief glance at why swaptions exist.

Swaptions are used by parties who anticipate the need for a swap at a later date but would like to establish the fixed rate today, while providing the flexibility to not engage in the swap later or engage in the swap at a more favorable rate in the market. These parties are often corporations that expect to need a swap later and would like to hedge against unfavorable interest rate moves while preserving the flexibility to gain from favorable moves.

Swaptions are used by parties entering into a swap to give them the flexibility to terminate the swap. In Section 1.2, we discussed why a party engaged in a swap might wish to terminate it before expiration. Suppose the party in a swap is paying fixed and receiving floating. If it owned a receiver swaption, it could exercise the swaption, thereby entering into a swap to receive a fixed rate and pay a floating rate. It would then have offset the floating parts of the swap, effectively removing any randomness from the position.[24] But the only way the party could do so would require having previously purchased a swaption. Similarly, parties engaged in a receive-fixed, pay-floating swap can effectively offset it by exercising a payer swaption.

Swaptions are used by parties to speculate on interest rates. As with any interest rate sensitive instrument, swaptions can be used to speculate. Their prices move with interest rates and, like all options, they contain significant leverage. Thus, they are appropriate instruments for interest rate speculators.

6.3 Swaption Payoffs

When a swaption is exercised, it effectively creates a stream of equivalent payments, commonly referred to in the financial world as an annuity. This stream is a series of interest payments equal to the difference between the exercise rate and the market rate on the underlying swap when the swaption is exercised.

Consider a European payer swaption that expires in two years and is exercisable into a one-year swap with quarterly payments, using 90/360 as the day-count adjustment. The exercise rate is 3.60 percent. The notional principal is

---

[24] Note, however, that both swaps are still in effect even though the floating sides offset. Because both swaps remain in effect, there is credit risk on the two transactions.

$20 million. Now, suppose we are at the swaption expiration and the term structure is the one we obtained when pricing the interest rate swap earlier in this reading. We repeat that information here:

Maturity	Rate	Discount Factor
90 days	3.45%	0.9914
180 days	3.58%	0.9824
270 days	3.70%	0.9730
360 days	3.75%	0.9639

Under these conditions, we found that the swap fixed payment is 0.0092, equating to an annual fixed rate of 3.68 percent.

The holder of the swaption has the right to enter into a swap to pay 3.60 percent, whereas in the market such a swap would require payment at a rate of 3.68 percent. Therefore, here at expiration this swaption does appear to offer an advantage over the market rate. Let us consider the three possible ways to exercise this swaption.

The holder can exercise the swaption, thereby entering into a swap to pay 3.60 percent. The quarterly payment at the rate of 3.60 percent would be $20,000,000 × (0.0360)(90/360) = $180,000. The swaption holder would then be engaged in a swap to pay $180,000 quarterly and receive LIBOR. The first floating payment would be at 3.45 percent[25] and would be $20,000,000(0.0345)(90/360) = $172,500. The remaining floating payments would, of course, be determined later. The payment stream is illustrated in Exhibit 73-8, Panel A.

Alternatively, the holder can exercise the swaption, thereby entering into a swap to pay 3.60 percent, and then enter into a swap in the market to receive fixed and pay floating. The fixed rate the holder would receive is 3.68 percent, the market-determined fixed rate at the time the swaption expires. The quarterly fixed payment at 3.68 percent would be $20,000,000(0.0368)(90/360) = $184,000. Technically, the LIBOR payments are still made, but the same amount is paid and received. Hence, they effectively offset. Panel B illustrates this payment stream. This arrangement would be common if the counterparty to the second swap is not the same as the counterparty to the swaption.

The holder can arrange to receive a net payment stream of $184,000 − $180,000 = $4,000. Panel C illustrates this payment stream. In this case, the counterparty to the second swap is probably the same as the counterparty to the swap created by exercising the swaption, who would be the counterparty to the swaption. Because the floating payments are eliminated, the amount of cash passing between the parties is reduced, which mitigates the credit risk.

The holder can receive an up-front cash payment. We can easily determine the amount. It is simply the present value of the payment stream shown in Panel C, which we can obtain using the discount factors shown above:

$4,000(0.9914 + 0.9824 + 0.9730 + 0.9639) = $15,643

This pure cash settlement is illustrated in Panel D.

---

[25] The first floating payment is at 3.45 percent because this is the 90-day rate in effect at the time the swap is initiated.

EXHIBIT 73-8 Cash Flows from Swaptions

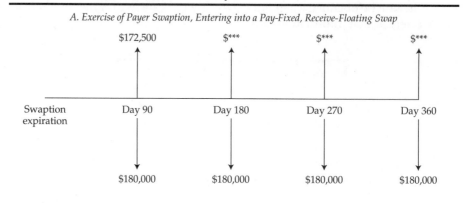

A. Exercise of Payer Swaption, Entering into a Pay-Fixed, Receive-Floating Swap

	$172,500	$***	$***	$***
Swaption expiration	Day 90	Day 180	Day 270	Day 360
	$180,000	$180,000	$180,000	$180,000

***Computed as $20,000,000(L)90/360, where L is LIBOR on the previous settlement date.

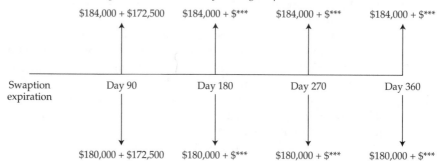

B. Exercise of Payer Swaption, Entering into a Pay-Fixed, Receive-Floating Swap and Entering into a Receive-Fixed, Pay-Floating Swap at the Market Rate

	$184,000 + $172,500	$184,000 + $***	$184,000 + $***	$184,000 + $***
Swaption expiration	Day 90	Day 180	Day 270	Day 360
	$180,000 + $172,500	$180,000 + $***	$180,000 + $***	$180,000 + $***

***Computed as $20,000,000(L)90/360, where L is LIBOR on the previous settlement date.

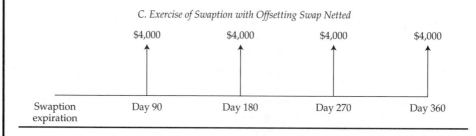

C. Exercise of Swaption with Offsetting Swap Netted

	$4,000	$4,000	$4,000	$4,000
Swaption expiration	Day 90	Day 180	Day 270	Day 360

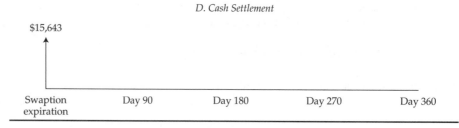

D. Cash Settlement

$15,643				
Swaption expiration	Day 90	Day 180	Day 270	Day 360

Other than transaction costs and the credit risk associated with the newly created swaps, each of these means of exercising a swaption has the same value. Of course, the two parties would have to agree up front which of these means to use at expiration. Cash settlement is the most common.

Therefore, the payoff of a payer swaption in which the exercise rate is x and the market rate on the underlying swap is FS(0,n,m) is

$$\text{Max}[0, FS(0,n,m) - x] \sum_{j=1}^{n} B_0(h_j) \qquad \textbf{(73-3)}$$

Similarly, the payoff of a receiver swaption would be

$$\text{Max}[0, x - FS(0,n,m)] \sum_{j=1}^{n} B_0(h_j) \qquad \textbf{(73-4)}$$

Of course, these figures would be multiplied by the actual notional principal. So we see that a swaption effectively creates an annuity. The present value factors are not relevant in determining whether the swaption will be exercised. Exercise is determined solely on the relationship between the swap rate at expiration and the exercise rate. The present value factors are used to convert the stream of net payments obtained upon exercise of the swap into a current value. Now, let us take a brief look at how a swaption is priced.

6.4 Pricing and Valuation of Swaptions

We shall show here, perhaps somewhat surprisingly, that an interest rate swaption is like an option on a coupon bond. Restating our result given above, the payoff of a payer swaption is

$$\text{Max}[0, FS(0,n,m) - x] \sum_{j=1}^{n} B_0(h_j)$$

This expression finds the present value of the difference between the fixed rate on the swap and the exercise rate on the swaption if that difference is positive. Otherwise, the payoff is zero. Recall from Section 4.2.1 (Equation 73-1) that the fixed rate on an interest rate swap is

$$FS(0,n,m) = \frac{1.0 - B_0(h_n)}{\sum_{j=1}^{n} B_0(h_j)}$$

Substituting the fixed rate into the payoff equation, we obtain

$$\text{Max}\left[0, \frac{1.0 - B_0(h_n)}{\sum_{j=1}^{n} B_0(h_j)} - x\right] \sum_{j=1}^{n} B_0(h_j)$$

which can be rewritten as

$$\text{Max}\left\{0, 1.0 - \left[x \sum_{j=1}^{n} B_0(h_j) + B_0(h_N)\right]\right\}$$

Note the term in brackets,

$$x \sum_{j=1}^{n} B_0(h_j) + B_0(h_N)$$

which is the same as the market value at the swaption expiration of a coupon bond of $1.00 par value, in which the coupon is x. Thus, the swaption payoff is effectively $Max(0, 1.0 - \text{Market value of coupon bond})$. This amount is the payoff of a put option on a coupon bond with coupon of x, a face value of 1.0, and a maturity of the swap expiration date. The exercise price is the par value of 1.0, and the exercise rate of the swaption is the coupon rate on the bond. Hence, we can value the swaption as though it were simply a put on a bond. In a similar manner, the payoff of a receiver swaption can be shown to be that of a call option on this coupon bond.

Now you can see why, as we stated earlier, a payer swaption is a put option and a receiver swaption is a call option. More specifically, a payer swaption is a put option on a bond and a receiver swaption is a call option on a bond.

Practice Problem 7

Calculate the market value of a receiver swaption at the expiration if the exercise rate is 4 percent and the term structure is given below:

Days	Rate
180	7.2%
360	8.0%

These are the same rates as in Practice Problem 4. The swaption is on a swap that will make payments in 180 and 360 days, and the notional principal is $25 million. Also, show that this payoff is equivalent to that of a call option on a bond.

SOLUTION

Based on a fixed rate of 0.0392 from Practice Problem 4, the market value is $Max(0, 0.04 - 0.0392)(0.9653 + 0.9259) = 0.0015$.

Based on a notional principal of $25 million, this is a market value of $25,000,000(0.0015) = \$37,500$.

This payoff is equivalent to that of a call option on a bond with an exercise price of 1.0, its par value. At this point in time, the expiration of the option, the bond on which this call is based would have a market value of $0.04(0.9653 + 0.9259) + 1.0(0.9259) = 1.0015$.

Therefore, the payoff of a call on this bond is $Max(0, 1.0015 - 1.0) = 0.0015$—the same as that of the swaption.

With that result in mind, we could value the swaption using any of a number of approaches to valuing bond options. We shall not take up the pricing of swaptions here, as it is a somewhat advanced topic and the issues are somewhat complicated. It is not a straightforward matter to apply the Black–Scholes–Merton or Black models to pricing bond options. We discussed the valuation of options on bonds in Reading 72, noting that the binomial model is probably the best way to do so.

6.5 Forward Swaps

We have seen in this book that options represent rights and forward contracts represent commitments. Just as there are options to enter swaps, there are also forward contracts to enter into swaps, called forward swaps. They are not as widely used as swaptions but do offer the advantage, as is always the case with forwards, that one does not have to pay any cash up front as with an option premium. Forward swaps are priced by pricing the swap off of the forward term structure instead of the spot term structure.

CREDIT RISK AND SWAPS   7

In this reading, we have mentioned on a few occasions that swaps are subject to credit risk. Indeed, as we have emphasized throughout the book, *all* over-the-counter derivatives are subject to credit risk. In this section, we examine some of the issues involved in the credit risk of swaps.

Recall that a swap has zero market value at the start. It starts off as neither an asset nor a liability. Once the swap is engaged and market conditions change, the market value becomes positive for one party and negative for the other. The party holding the positive value swap effectively owns an asset, which represents a claim against the counterparty. This claim is a netting of the amount owed by the counterparty and the amount that the party owes, with the former exceeding the latter. The party holding the positive-value swap thus assumes credit risk. The counterparty could declare bankruptcy, leaving the party holding the positive-value swap with a claim that is subject to the legal process of bankruptcy. In most swap arrangements, netting is legally recognized, so the claim has a value based on the net amount. Of course, as we described in the reading, currency swaps are generally not netted so the credit risk is greater on currency swaps.

The party to which the swap has a negative value is not subject to credit risk. It owes more than is owed to it, so the other party faces the risk.

During the life of the swap, however, the market value to a given party can change from positive to negative or vice versa. Hence, the party not facing credit risk at a given moment is not entirely free of risk, because the swap value could turn positive for it later.

The timing of credit risk is in the form of immediate or **current credit risk** and deferred or **potential credit risk.** The former arises when a payment is immediately due and cannot be made by one party. The latter reflects the ever-present possibility that, although a counterparty may currently be able to make payments, it may be unable to make future payments.

Let us work through an example illustrating these points. Consider two parties A and B who are engaged in a swap. At a given payment date, the payment of Party A to Party B is $100,000 and the payment of Party B to Party A is $35,000. As is customarily the case, Party A must pay $65,000 to Party B. Once the payment is made, we shall assume that the market value of the swap is $1,250,000, which is an asset to A and a liability to B.

Suppose Party A is unable to pay and declares bankruptcy. Then Party B does not make any payment to Party A. Party A is bankrupt, but the swap is an asset to A. Given the $65,000 owed by A to B, the claim of A against B is $1,250,000 − $65,000 = $1,185,000. We emphasize in this example that A is the bankrupt party, but the swap is an asset to A, representing its claim against B. If B were holding the positive market value of the swap, it would have a claim of $1,250,000 + $65,000 = $1,315,000 on A as A enters into the bankruptcy process.

Let us change the example a little by having A not be bankrupt on the payment date. It makes its payment of $65,000 to B and moves forward. But a few months later, before the next payment, A declares bankruptcy. Its payment is not immediately due, but it has essentially stated that it will not make its next payment or any payments thereafter. To determine the financial implications of the event, the two parties must compute the market value of the swap. Suppose the value is now $1,100,000 and is positive to A. Then A, the bankrupt party, holds a claim against B of $1,100,000. The fact that A is bankrupt does not mean that it cannot have a claim against someone else, just as a bankrupt corporation can be owed money for inventory it has sold but on which it has not yet collected payment.

Of course, A could be bankrupt and B's claim against A could be the greater. In fact, with A bankrupt, there is a very good possibility that this scenario would be the case. Then, of course, B would simply be another of A's many creditors.

Exactly what happens to resolve these claims in each of these situations is a complex legal issue and is beyond the scope of our level of treatment. In addition, the bankruptcy laws vary somewhat around the world, so the potential exists for different treatments of the same situation. Most countries do recognize the legality of netting, however, so it would be rare that a party would be able to claim the full amount owed it without netting out the amount it owes.

The credit risk in a swap varies during its life. An interest rate or equity swap has no final principal payments. The credit risk in either of these swap types is greater during the middle of its life. This occurs because near the end of the life of the swap, not many payments remain, so there is not much money at risk. And at the beginning of the life of the swap, the credit risk is usually low because the parties would probably not engage in the swap if a great deal of credit risk already were present at the start. Therefore, the greatest potential for credit losses is during the middle of the life of the swap. For currency swaps, in which the notional principals are typically exchanged at the end of the life of the swap, the credit risk is concentrated between the middle and the end of its life.

The parties that engage in swaps are generally of good credit quality, but the fear of default is still a significant concern. Yet, perhaps surprisingly, the rates that all parties pay on swaps are the same, regardless of either party's credit quality. As we have illustrated here, a plain vanilla swap, in which one party pays a floating rate and the other pays a fixed rate, has the fixed rate determined by the term structure for that underlying rate. Therefore, if a party wanted to engage in a swap to pay LIBOR and receive a fixed rate, it would get the fixed rate based on the LIBOR term structure, regardless of its credit quality or that of the counterparty, provided that the two parties agreed to do the transaction. Implicit in the fixed rate, however, is the spread between LIBOR and the default-free rate. As we described earlier in the reading, swap rates are quoted with respect to a spread over the equivalent default-free rate. Thus, a one-year swap rate of 3.68 percent as in our example might be quoted as 50 basis points over the rate on a one-year U.S. Treasury note, implying that the one-year U.S. Treasury note rate was 3.18 percent. This differential is called the **swap spread.**

It is important to note that the swap spread is not a measure of the credit risk on a given swap but rather a reflection of the general level of credit risk in the global economy. The LIBOR term structure reflects the borrowing rate for

London banks, which are generally highly rated but not default free. Whenever a recession approaches or credit concerns arise, this spread widens and fixed-rate payers on swaps end up paying more. Of course, floating-rate payers end up paying more as well, but the additional cost to them is less obvious up front because the floating rates change over the life of the swap.

So all parties pay the same rate, but clearly some parties are better credit risks than others. In addition, virtually no parties are default free, and many are of lower credit quality than the typical London bank on which LIBOR is based. How do parties manage the credit risk in swaps? There are a number of methods, which we shall discuss in more detail in Chapter 9. For right now, however, we cover one such method that we have seen before with respect to forward contracts and that is routinely used in the futures market: marking to market.

Reconsider the interest rate swap we covered earlier in the reading in which the payments are made quarterly in the amount of 0.0092 per \$1 notional principal. The swap lasts for one year, so there are four payments. Suppose the parties agree to mark the contract to market halfway through its life—that is, in six months, immediately after the payment is made. Suppose we are at that point and the term structure is as follows:

$$L_{180}(90) = 0.0390$$
$$L_{180}(180) = 0.0402$$

Note that we are at day 180, and the upcoming payments occur in 90 and 180 days. We thus need to calculate $B_{180}(270)$ and $B_{180}(360)$. These present value factors are

$$B_{180}(270) = \frac{1}{1 + 0.039(90/360)} = 0.9903$$
$$B_{180}(360) = \frac{1}{1 = 0.0402(180/360)} = 0.9803$$

Now we can compute the market value of the swap. The present value of the remaining fixed payments, plus the hypothetical notional principal, is $0.0092(0.9903 + 0.9803) + 1.0(0.9803) = 0.9984$.

Because the 90-day floating rate is 3.90 percent, the next floating payment will be $0.0390(90/360) = 0.00975$. Of course, we do not know the last floating payment, but it does not matter because the present value of the remaining floating payments, plus the hypothetical notional principal, is automatically 1.0 because we are on the coupon reset date. Therefore, the market value of the swap to the party receiving floating and paying fixed is the present value of the floating payments, 1.0, minus the present value of the fixed payments, 0.9984, or $1.0 - 0.9984 = 0.0016$.

If the two parties marked this swap to market, the party paying floating and receiving fixed would pay the other party a lump sum cash payment of \$0.0016 per \$1 notional principal. The two parties would then reprice the swap. The new payment would be

$$FS(0,n,m) = FS(0,2,90) = \frac{1 - 0.9803}{0.9903 + 0.9803} = 0.01$$

Thus, the fixed payment would be 0.01 for the rest of the swap.

Practice Problem 8

Consider a two-year swap to pay a fixed rate and receive a floating rate with semiannual payments. The fixed rate is 0.0462. Now, 360 days later, the term structure is

Days	Rate
180	10.1%
360	10.4%

The next floating payment will be 0.045. The swap calls for marking to market after 180 days, and, therefore, will now be marked to market. Determine the market value, identify which party pays which, and calculate the new fixed rate.

SOLUTION

First find the discount factors:

$$B_{360}(540) = \frac{1}{1 + 0.0101(180/360)} = 0.9519$$

$$B_{360}(720) = \frac{1}{1 + 0.104(360/360)} = 0.9058$$

The market value of the fixed payments plus $1 hypothetical notional principal is $0.0462(0.9519 + 0.9058) + 1.0(0.9058) = 0.9916$.

The market value of the floating payments plus $1 hypothetical notional principal is $1.045(0.9519) = 0.9947$.

Therefore, the market value to the party paying fixed and receiving floating is $0.9947 - 0.9916 = 0.0031$.

This amount would be paid by the party paying floating and receiving fixed. The new fixed rate would then be

$$\frac{1 - 0.9058}{0.9519 + 0.9058} = 0.0507$$

This rate would be quoted as an annual rate of $5.07\%(360/180) = 10.14\%$.

As in the futures market, marking a swap contract to market results in the two parties terminating the contract and automatically engaging in a new swap. In essence, the arrangement commits the two parties to terminating the swap and re-establishing it on a predetermined schedule. This process reduces the credit risk by requiring one party to pay the other any amount due at a time prior to the expiration date of the swap. The effect is to reduce the extent to which the swap can go deeply underwater to one of the parties, who may be facing financial problems.

A number of other techniques can be used to control credit risk in swaps. We shall return to the general subject of credit risk and derivatives in Chapter 9.

THE ROLE OF SWAP MARKETS 8

In each of the preceding three readings, we have discussed the role played by the markets represented by the various derivative instruments. The swap market is extremely large, consisting of dealers and end users engaging in customized transactions that involve a series of payments. As we showed in this reading, swaps can be equivalent to various other derivative instruments. Moreover, we used transactions in assets to replicate swaps. Hence, an obvious question is why swaps exist when the same results can be obtained using other instruments.

First let us ignore the obvious counter-question of why other instruments exist when swaps serve the same purpose. In the race to see which derivative instrument is more popular, swaps have clearly won. We can only surmise the reason why.

The tremendous popularity of swaps results largely from the popularity of interest rate swaps. For several reasons, these instruments have been embraced by corporations as tools for managing interest rate risk. One is that interest rate swaps, certainly the plain vanilla type, are simple instruments, rarely requiring technology, computational skills, or financial know-how beyond what exists in most corporate treasury offices. In short, they are easy to understand. In addition, interest rate swaps can easily be viewed as a pair of loans. Borrowing and lending money is second nature to corporations. Corporations view engaging in swaps as nothing more than an extension of their regular practice of borrowing and lending money. Many corporations are restricted in their use of options and futures, but they can usually justify swaps as nothing more than variations of loans. Also, swaps are so easily tailored to alter the interest rate patterns on most corporate loans that they seem to go hand in hand with the typical fixed- and floating-rate loans that corporations take out. Many corporations borrow money and combine the loan with a swap right from the start. Finally, we should note that some dealer firms have exploited the attractions of swaps by aggressive selling. In some cases, corporations entered into ill-advised and occasionally complex, exotic swaps. We do not suggest that most dealers have engaged in unethical actions (although some certainly have) but rather that, as in all sales-oriented activities, customers do not always get impartial advice from sales personnel. In some cases, corporations have used swaps to step over the line from good risk management into speculation on risks they know nothing about. In short, at least part of the success of swaps has probably not been for the right reasons.

But using swaps for the wrong reason does not sufficiently explain the success of these instruments. If it were the primary motivation for their use, swaps would die out as a risk management tool. Instead, swaps have grown in popularity. Swaps provide a mechanism for managing the risks associated with a series of payments. Although forward contracts and other instruments can manage that risk, a swap is more of a portfolio approach to managing risk—a package of risk management tools all rolled up into one. Given that risk often exists in a series, swaps are ideal instruments for managing it. Other instruments may be able to do the job, but they must be carefully constructed with a certain amount of financial ingenuity.

We have now completed Readings 70, 71, 72, and 73, each of which deals with specific types of derivatives. We have obtained a good description of each derivative and examined how to price and value them. We have briefly alluded to how they are used. In the following three readings we shall examine strategies and applications using these instruments.

9   SUMMARY

▷ Swaps are over-the-counter contracts in which two parties agree to pay a series of cash flows to each other. At least one series is floating or variable and related to an interest rate, exchange rate, equity price, or commodity price; the other can be fixed or floating. Swaps have zero value at the start and have payments made on scheduled payment or settlement dates and a final termination or expiration date. When swap payments are made in the same currency, the payments are usually netted. Swaps are subject to default on the part of either party.

▷ Swaps can be terminated by having one party pay the market value of the swap to the other party, by entering into a swap in which the variable payments offset, by selling the swap to another party, or by exercising a swaption to enter into an offsetting swap.

▷ In a currency swap, each party makes payments to the other in different currencies. A currency swap can have one party pay a fixed rate in one currency and the other pay a fixed rate in the other currency; have both pay a floating rate in their respective currencies; have the first party pay a fixed rate in one currency and the second party pay a floating rate in the other currency; or have the first party pay a floating rate in one currency and the second pay a fixed rate in the other currency. In currency swaps, the notional principal is usually exchanged at the beginning and at the end of the life of the swap, although this exchange is not mandatory.

▷ The payments on a currency swap are calculated by multiplying the notional principal by the fixed or floating interest rate times a day-count adjustment. This procedure is done in each currency, and the respective parties make their separate payments to each other. The payments are not netted.

▷ In a plain vanilla interest rate swap, one party makes payments at a fixed rate and the other makes payments at a floating rate, with no exchange of notional principal. A typical plain vanilla swap involves one party paying a fixed rate and the other paying a floating rate such as LIBOR. Swaps are often done by a party borrowing floating at a rate tied to LIBOR; that party then uses a pay-fixed, receive-floating swap to offset the risk of its exposure to LIBOR and effectively convert its loan to a fixed-rate loan.

▷ The payments on an interest rate swap are calculated by multiplying the notional principal by the fixed or floating interest rate times a day-count adjustment. The respective amounts are netted so that the party owing the greater amount makes a net payment to the other.

▷ The three types of equity swaps involve one party paying a fixed rate, a floating rate, or the return on another equity, while the other party pays an equity return. Therefore, an equity swap is a swap in which at least one party pays the return on a stock or stock index.

▷ The equity payment (or payments, if both sides of the swap are related to an equity return) on an equity swap is calculated by multiplying the return on the stock over the settlement period by the notional principal. If there is a fixed or floating payment, it is calculated in the same manner as in an interest rate swap. With payments in a single currency, the two sets of payments are netted.

▷ Swap pricing means to determine the fixed rate and any relevant terms, such as the foreign notional principal on a currency swap, at the start of the swap. Valuation means to determine the market value of the swap, which is the present value of one stream of payments less the present value of the other stream of payments. The market value of a swap is zero at the start but will change to positive for one party and negative for the other during the life of the swap, as market conditions change and time passes.

▶ Swaps can be viewed as combinations of assets. Currency swaps are like issuing a bond denominated in one currency and using the proceeds to buy a bond denominated in another currency. Interest rate swaps are like issuing a fixed-rate bond and using the proceeds to buy a floating-rate bond or vice versa. Equity swaps are like issuing a bond and using the proceeds to buy stock or vice versa. Equity swaps with both sides paying an equity return are like selling short one stock and using the proceeds to buy another stock. The stock position is not, however, a buy-and-hold position and requires some rebalancing.

▶ An interest rate swap is like a series of off-market FRAs, meaning that the rate on each FRA is set at the swap rate, not at the rate it would be set at if priced as an FRA with zero market value at the start. In addition, the first payment on a swap is just an exchange of known amounts of cash. Currency swaps and equity swaps are similar to forward contracts, but the connection is not as straightforward as in interest rate swaps.

▶ Interest rate swaps are like being long (short) interest rate calls and short (long) interest rate puts. Currency swaps and equity swaps are also similar to combinations of options, but the connection is not as straightforward.

▶ The fixed rate on an interest rate swap equates the present value of the fixed payments plus a hypothetical notional principal to the present value of the floating payments plus a hypothetical notional principal. The notional principals offset but permit these swaps to be treated like bonds. The fixed rate is then equivalent to the fixed rate on a par bond with the same payments as on the swap. The market value of the swap during its life is found by determining the difference in the market values of the floating- and fixed-rate bonds later during their lives under the new term structure.

▶ The fixed rates on a currency swap are the same as the fixed rates on plain vanilla interest rate swaps in the given countries. The foreign notional principal for a domestic notional principal of one unit is the inverse of the exchange rate. In other words, it is the foreign currency equivalent of the domestic notional principal. Because a currency swap is like issuing a bond in one currency and using the proceeds to buy a bond in another currency, the market value of a currency swap during its life is found by determining the difference in the market values of the two bonds during their lives using the new term structures in the two countries. The foreign bond value must be converted to its domestic equivalent by using the new exchange rate.

▶ The fixed rate on an equity swap is the same as the fixed rate on a plain vanilla interest rate swap. The market value of an equity swap involving fixed or floating payments during its life is found as the present value of the equity payments less the present value of the fixed or floating payments necessary to replicate the equity swap payment. The market value of an equity swap in which both sides make equity payments is the market value of a long position in one equity and a short position in the other, assuming the positions are liquidated at each settlement date and gains and losses are paid out.

▶ A swaption is an option to enter into a swap. The two types of interest rate swaptions are payer swaptions, which allow the holder to enter into a swap to pay the fixed rate and receive the floating rate, and receiver swaptions, which allow the holder to enter into a swap to receive the fixed rate and pay the floating rate. Swaptions are based on a specific underlying swap and have an exercise rate and an expiration date. At expiration, they can be exercised to enter into the underlying swap. Swaptions require an up-front premium.

▸ Swaptions exist to allow users the flexibility to enter into swaps at later dates but establish the terms in advance. If market conditions are not favorable to exercising a swaption, the holder can allow the swaption to expire and obtain more favorable terms by entering into a swap at the market rate. Swaptions are used by parties who anticipate a need to enter into a swap at a later date, who anticipate the need to terminate an already-existing swap, or who wish to speculate on interest rates.

▸ The payoffs of an interest rate swaption are like those of an option on a coupon-bearing bond. The option has an exercise price of par value, and the coupon rate is the exercise rate on the swaption. A payer swaption is like a put on the bond, and a receiver swaption is like a call on the bond.

▸ At expiration, an interest rate payer swaption is worth the maximum of zero or the present value of the difference between the market swap rate and the exercise rate, valued as an annuity extending over the remaining life of the underlying swap. To value a receiver swaption at expiration, we take the difference between the exercise rate and the market swap rate, adjusted for its present value over the life of the underlying swap. These figures must be multiplied by the notional principal.

▸ The market value of a swaption at expiration can be received in one of four ways: by exercising the swaption to enter into the underlying swap, by exercising the swaption and entering into an offsetting swap that keeps both swaps in force, by exercising the swaption and entering into an offsetting swap that eliminates both swaps and pays a series of payments equal to the net difference in the fixed rates on the two swaps, or by exercising the swaption and receiving a lump sum cash payment.

▸ A forward swap is a forward contract to enter into a swap. It commits both parties to entering into a swap at a later date at a fixed rate agreed on today. In contrast to a swaption, which is the right to enter into a swap, a forward swap is a binding commitment to enter into a swap.

▸ Credit risk arises in a swap due to the possibility that a party will not be able to make its payments. Current credit risk is the risk of a party being unable to make the upcoming payment. Potential credit risk is the risk of a party being unable to make future payments. Credit risk is faced only by the party that is owed the greater amount.

▸ The credit risk in an interest rate or equity swap is greatest during the middle of the swap's life. The risk is small at the beginning of the swap because the parties would not engage in the swap if the credit risk were significant at the start. The risk is low at the end of the life of the swap because of the small number of remaining payments. For currency swaps, the payment of notional principal shifts the credit risk more toward the end of the life of the swap. In addition, because the payments are typically not netted, the credit risk on currency swaps is greater than on interest rate swaps.

▸ The swap spread is the difference between the fixed rate on a swap and the yield on a default-free security of the same maturity as the swap. The spread indicates the average credit risk in the global economy but not the credit risk in a given swap.

▸ Netting reduces the credit risk in a swap by reducing the amount of money passing from any one party to another. The amount owed by a party is deducted from the amount due to a party, and only the net is paid. Marking a swap to market is a process in which the parties agree to periodically calculate the market value of the swap and have the party owing the greater amount pay the market value to the other party. The fixed rate is then reset on the swap until it is marked to market again or terminates.

This procedure forces the party to which the swap is losing money to pay the other party before getting too deeply in debt.

▶ Swaps play an important role in the financial system by providing a simple means of managing a series of risks. Their popularity has arisen largely from corporate use in managing interest rate exposure.

PROBLEMS

1. A U.S. company enters into a currency swap in which it pays a fixed rate of 5.5 percent in euros and the counterparty pays a fixed rate of 6.75 percent in dollars. The notional principals are $100 million and €116.5 million. Payments are made semiannually and on the basis of 30 days per month and 360 days per year.

   A. Calculate the initial exchange of payments that takes place at the beginning of the swap.

   B. Calculate the semiannual payments.

   C. Calculate the final exchange of payments that takes place at the end of the swap.

2. A British company enters into a currency swap in which it pays a fixed rate of 6 percent in dollars and the counterparty pays a fixed rate of 5 percent in pounds. The notional principals are £75 million and $105 million. Payments are made semiannually and on the basis of 30 days per month and 360 days per year.

   A. Calculate the initial exchange of payments that takes place at the beginning of the swap.

   B. Calculate the semiannual payments.

   C. Calculate the final exchange of payments that takes place at the end of the swap.

3. A U.S. company has entered into an interest rate swap with a dealer in which the notional principal is $50 million. The company will pay a floating rate of LIBOR and receive a fixed rate of 5.75 percent. Interest is paid semiannually, and the current LIBOR is 5.15 percent. Calculate the first payment and indicate which party pays which. Assume that floating-rate payments will be made on the basis of 180/360 and fixed-rate payments will be made on the basis of 180/365.

4. A German company that has issued floating-rate notes now believes that interest rates will rise. It decides to protect itself against this possibility by entering into an interest rate swap with a dealer. In this swap, the notional principal is €25 million and the company will pay a fixed rate of 5.5 percent and receive Euribor. The current Euribor is 5 percent. Calculate the first payment and indicate which party pays which. Assume that floating-rate payments will be made on the basis of 90/360 and fixed-rate payments will be made on the basis of 90/365.

5. An asset manager wishes to reduce his exposure to large-cap stocks and increase his exposure to small-cap stocks. He seeks to do so using an equity swap. He agrees to pay a dealer the return on a large-cap index, and the dealer agrees to pay the manager the return on a small-cap index. For each of the scenarios listed below, calculate the first overall payment and indicate which party makes the payment. Assume that payments are made semiannually. The notional principal is $100 million.

   A. The value of the small-cap index starts off at 689.40, and the large-cap index starts at 1130.20. In six months, the small-cap index is at 625.60 and the large-cap index is at 1251.83.

   B. The value of the small-cap index starts off at 689.40 and the large-cap index starts at 1130.20. In six months, the small-cap index is at 703.23 and the large-cap index is at 1143.56.

6. An asset manager wishes to reduce her exposure to small-cap stocks and increase her exposure to fixed-income securities. She seeks to do so using

an equity swap. She agrees to pay a dealer the return on a small-cap index and the dealer agrees to pay the manager a fixed rate of 5.5 percent. For each of the scenarios listed below, calculate the overall payment six months later and indicate which party makes the payment. Assume that payments are made semiannually (180 days per period) and there are 365 days in each year. The notional principal is $50 million.

A. The value of the small-cap index starts off at 234.10 and six months later is at 238.41.

B. The value of the small-cap index starts off at 234.10 and six months later is at 241.27.

7. An asset manager wishes to reduce his exposure to fixed-income securities and increase his exposure to large-cap stocks. He seeks to do so using an equity swap. He agrees to pay a dealer a fixed rate of 4.5 percent, and the dealer agrees to pay the manager the return on a large-cap index. For each of the scenarios listed below, calculate the overall payment six months later and indicate which party makes it. Assume that payments are made semiannually (180 days per period) and there are 365 days in a year. The notional principal is $25 million.

A. The value of the large-cap index starts off at 578.50 and six months later is at 622.54.

B. The value of the large-cap index starts off at 578.50 and six months later is at 581.35.

RISK MANAGEMENT APPLICATIONS OF OPTION STRATEGIES

LEARNING OUTCOMES

The candidate should be able to:

a. determine the value at expiration, profit, maximum profit, maximum loss, breakeven underlying price at expiration, and general shape of the graph of the strategies of buying and selling calls and buying and selling puts, and explain each strategy's characteristics;

b. determine the value at expiration, profit, maximum profit, maximum loss, breakeven underlying price at expiration, and general shape of the graph of the covered call strategy and the protective put strategy, and explain each strategy's characteristics.

INTRODUCTION 1

In the previous reading, we examined strategies that employ forward and futures contracts. Recall that forward and futures contracts have linear payoffs and do not require an initial outlay. Options, on the other hand, have nonlinear payoffs and require the payment of cash up front. By having nonlinear payoffs, options permit their users to benefit from movements in the underlying in one direction and to not be harmed by movements in the other direction. In many respects, they offer the best of all worlds, a chance to profit if expectations are realized with minimal harm if expectations turn out to be wrong. The price for this opportunity is the cash outlay required to establish the position. From the standpoint of the holder of the short position, options can lead to extremely large losses. Hence, sellers of options must be well compensated in the form of an adequate up-front premium and must skillfully manage the risk they assume.

In this reading we examine the most widely used option strategies. The reading is divided into three parts. In the first part, we look at option strategies that are typically used in equity investing, which include standard strategies involving single options and strategies that combine options with the underlying. In the second part, we look at the specific strategies that are commonly used in managing interest rate risk. In the third part, we examine option strategies that are used primarily by dealers and sophisticated traders to manage the risk of option positions.

Let us begin by reviewing the necessary notation. These symbols are the same ones we have previously used. First recall that time 0 is the time at which the strategy is initiated and time T is the time the option expires, stated as a fraction of a year. Accordingly, the amount of time until expiration is simply $T - 0 = T$, which is (Days to expiration)/365. The other symbols are

c_0, c_T = price of the call option at time 0 and time T
p_0, p_T = price of the put option at time 0 and time T[1]
X = exercise price
S_0, S_T = price of the underlying at time 0 and time T
V_0, V_T = value of the position at time 0 and time T
Π = profit from the transaction: $V_T - V_0$
r = risk-free rate

Some additional notation will be introduced when necessary.

Note that we are going to measure the profit from an option transaction, which is simply the final value of the transaction minus the initial value of the transaction. Profit does not take into account the time value of money or the risk. Although a focus on profit is not completely satisfactory from a theoretical point of view, it is nonetheless instructive, simple, and a common approach to examining options. Our primary objective here is to obtain a general picture of the manner in which option strategies perform. With that in mind, discussing profit offers probably the best trade-off in terms of gaining the necessary knowledge with a minimum of complexity.

In this reading, we assume that the option user has a view regarding potential movements of the underlying. In most cases that view is a prediction of the direction of the underlying, but in some cases it is a prediction of the volatility of the underlying. In all cases, we assume this view is specified over a horizon that corresponds to the option's life or that the option expiration can be tailored to the horizon date. Hence, for the most part, these options should be considered customized, over-the-counter options.[2] Every interest rate option is a customized option.

---

[1] As in Reading 72, lower case indicates European options, and upper case indicates American options. In this reading, all options are European.

[2] If the options discussed were exchange-listed options, it would not significantly alter the material in this reading.

Because the option expiration corresponds to the horizon date for which a particular view is held, there is no reason to use American options. Accordingly, all options in this reading are European options. Moreover, we shall not consider terminating the strategy early. Putting an option in place and closing the position prior to expiration is certainly a legitimate strategy. It could reflect the arrival of new information over the holding period, but it requires an understanding of more complex issues, such as valuation of the option and the rate at which the option loses its time value. Thus, we shall examine the outcome of a particular strategy over a range of possible values of the underlying only on the expiration day.

Section 2 of this reading focuses on option strategies that relate to equity investments. Section 3 concentrates on strategies using interest rate options. In Section 4, we focus on managing an option portfolio.

OPTION STRATEGIES FOR EQUITY PORTFOLIOS   2

Many typical illustrations of option strategies use individual stocks, but we shall use options on a stock index, the Nasdaq 100, referred to simply as the Nasdaq. We shall assume that in addition to buying and selling options on the Nasdaq, we can also buy the index, either through construction of the portfolio itself, through an index mutual fund, or an exchange-traded fund.[3] We shall simply refer to this instrument as a stock. We are given the following numerical data:

$S_0 = 2000$, value of the Nasdaq 100 when the strategy is initiated
$T = 0.0833$, the time to expiration (one month = $1/12$)

The options available will be the following:[4]

Exercise Price	Call Price	Put Price
1950	108.43	56.01
2000	81.75	79.25
2050	59.98	107.39

Let us start by examining an initial strategy that is the simplest of all: to buy or sell short the underlying. Panel A of Exhibit 74-1 illustrates the profit from the transaction of buying a share of stock. We see the obvious result that if you buy the stock and it goes up, you make a profit; if it goes down, you incur a loss. Panel B shows the case of selling short the stock. Recall that this strategy involves borrowing the shares from a broker, selling them at the current price, and then

---

[3] Exchange-traded shares on the Nasdaq 100 are called Nasdaq 100 Trust Shares and QQQs, for their ticker symbol. They are commonly referred to as Qubes, trade on the Amex, and are the most active exchange-traded fund and often the most actively traded of all securities. Options on the Nasdaq 100 are among the most actively traded as well.

[4] These values were obtained using the Black–Scholes–Merton model. By using this model, we know we are working with reasonable values that do not permit arbitrage opportunities.

EXHIBIT 74-1 Simple Stock Strategies

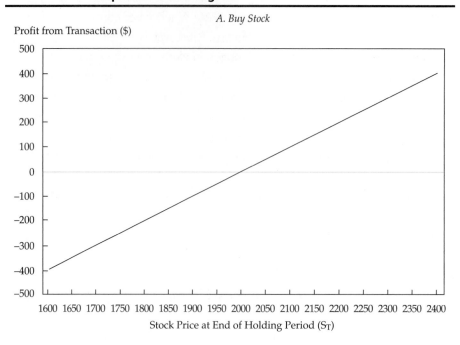

A. Buy Stock

Profit from Transaction ($)

Stock Price at End of Holding Period (S_T)

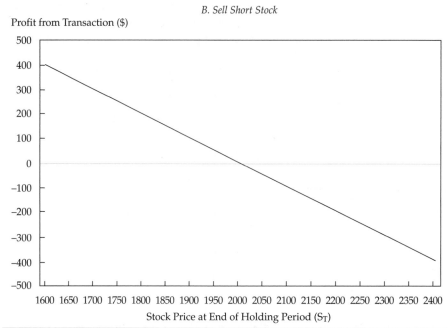

B. Sell Short Stock

Profit from Transaction ($)

Stock Price at End of Holding Period (S_T)

buying them back at a later date. In this case, if you sell short the stock and it goes down, you make a profit. Conversely, if it goes up, you incur a loss. Now we shall move on to strategies involving options, but we shall use the stock strategies again when we combine options with stock.

In this section we examine option strategies in the context of their use in equity portfolios. Although these strategies are perfectly applicable for fixed-income portfolios, corporate borrowing scenarios, or even commodity risk management situations, they are generally more easily explained and understood in the context of investing in equities or equity indices.

To analyze an equity option strategy, we first assume that we establish the position at the current price. We then determine the value of the option at expiration for a specific value of the index at expiration. We calculate the profit as the value at expiration minus the current price. We then generate a graph to illustrate the value at expiration and profit for a range of index values at expiration. Although the underlying is a stock index, we shall just refer to it as the underlying to keep things as general as possible. We begin by examining the most fundamental option transactions, long and short positions in calls and puts.

2.1 Standard Long and Short Positions

2.1.1 Calls

Consider the purchase of a call option at the price c_0. The value at expiration, c_T, is $c_T = \max(0, S_T - X)$. Broken down into parts,

$$c_T = 0 \qquad \text{if } S_T \le X$$
$$c_T = S_T - X \qquad \text{if } S_T > X$$

The profit is obtained by subtracting the option premium, which is paid to purchase the option, from the option value at expiration, $\Pi = c_T - c_0$. Broken down into parts,

$$\Pi = -c_0 \qquad \text{if } S_T \le X$$
$$\Pi = S_T - X - c_0 \qquad \text{if } S_T > X$$

Now consider this example. We buy the call with the exercise price of 2000 for 81.75. Consider values of the index at expiration of 1900 and 2100. For $S_T = 1900$,

$$c_T = \max(0, 1900 - 2000) = 0$$
$$\Pi = 0 - 81.75 = -81.75$$

For $S_T = 2100$,

$$c_T = \max(0, 2100 - 2000) = 100$$
$$\Pi = 100 - 81.75 = 18.25$$

Exhibit 74-2 illustrates the value at expiration and profit when S_T, the underlying price at expiration, ranges from 1600 to 2400. We see that buying a call results in a limited loss of the premium, 81.75. For an index value at expiration greater than the exercise price of 2000, the value and profit move up one-for-one with the index value, and there is no upper limit.

It is important to identify the breakeven index value at expiration. Recall that the formula for the profit is $\Pi = \max(0, S_T - X) - c_0$. We would like to know the value of S_T for which $\Pi = 0$. We shall call that value S_T^*. It would be nice to be able to solve $\Pi = \max(0, S_T^* - X) - c_0 = 0$ for S_T^*, but that is not directly possible. Instead, we observe that there are two ranges of outcomes, one in which $\Pi = S_T^* - X - c_0$ for $S_T^* > X$, the case of the option expiring in-the-money, and the other in which $\Pi = -c_0$ for $S_T \le X$, the case of the option expiring out-of-the-money. It is obvious from the equation and by observing Exhibit 74-2 that in the latter case, there is no possibility of breaking even. In the former case, we see that we can solve for S_T^*. Setting $\Pi = S_T^* - X - c_0 = 0$, we obtain $S_T^* = X + c_0$.

Thus, the breakeven is the exercise price plus the option premium. This result should be intuitive: The value of the underlying at expiration must exceed the exercise price by the amount of the premium to recover the cost of the premium. In this problem, the breakeven is $S_T^* = 2000 + 81.75 = 2081.75$. Observe in Exhibit 74-2 that the profit line crosses the axis at this value.

In summarizing the strategy, we have the following results for the option buyer:

$c_T = \max(0, S_T - X)$
Value at expiration $= c_T$
Profit: $\Pi = c_T - c_0$
Maximum profit $= \infty$
Maximum loss $= c_0$
Breakeven: $S_T^* = X + c_0$

EXHIBIT 74-2 Buy Call

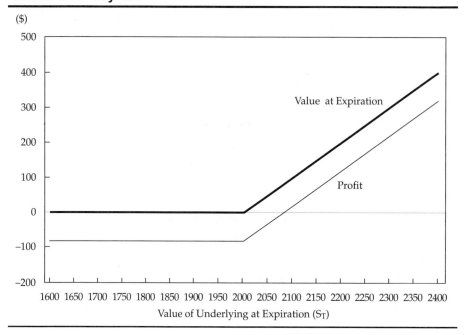

Call options entice naive speculators, but it is important to consider the *likely* gains and losses more than the *potential* gains and losses. For example, in this case, the underlying must go up by about 4.1 percent in one month to cover the cost of the call. This increase equates to an annual rate of almost 50 percent and is an unreasonable expectation by almost any standard. If the underlying does not move at all, the loss is 100 percent of the premium.

For the seller of the call, the results are just the opposite. The sum of the positions of the seller and buyer is zero. Hence, we can take the value and profit results for the buyer and change the signs. The results for the maximum profit and maximum loss are changed accordingly, and the breakeven is the same. Hence, for the option seller,

$c_T = \max(0, S_T - X)$
Value at expiration $= -c_T$
Profit: $\Pi = -c_T + c_0$
Maximum profit $= c_0$
Maximum loss $= \infty$
Breakeven: $S_T^* = X + c_0$

Exhibit 74-3 shows the results for the seller of the call. Note that the value and profit have a fixed maximum. The worst case is an infinite loss. Just as there is no upper limit to the buyer's potential gain, there is no upper limit to how much the seller can lose.

Call options are purchased by investors who are bullish. We now turn to put options, which are purchased by investors who are bearish.

EXHIBIT 74-3 Sell Call

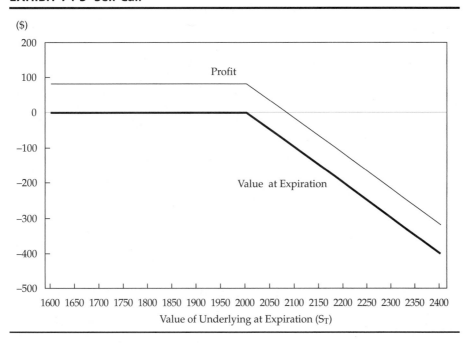

Practice Problem 1

Consider a call option selling for $7 in which the exercise price is $100 and the price of the underlying is $98.

A. Determine the value at expiration and the profit for a buyer under the following outcomes:
  i. The price of the underlying at expiration is $102.
  ii. The price of the underlying at expiration is $94.

B. Determine the value at expiration and the profit for a seller under the following outcomes:
  i. The price of the underlying at expiration is $91.
  ii. The price of the underlying at expiration is $101.

C. Determine the following:
  i. The maximum profit to the buyer (maximum loss to the seller)
  ii. The maximum loss to the buyer (maximum profit to the seller)

D. Determine the breakeven price of the underlying at expiration.

SOLUTIONS

A. Call buyer

    i. Value at expiration $= c_T = \max(0, S_T - X) = \max(0, 102 - 100) = 2$
$$\Pi = c_T - c_0 = 2 - 7 = -5$$

    ii. Value at expiration $= c_T = \max(0, S_T - X) = \max(0, 94 - 100) = 0$
$$\Pi = c_T - c_0 = 0 - 7 = -7$$

B. Call seller

    i. Value at expiration $= -c_T = -\max(0, S_T - X) = -\max(0, 91 - 100) = 0$
$$\Pi = -c_T + c_0 = -0 + 7 = 7$$

    ii. Value at expiration $= -c_T = -\max(0, S_T - X) = -\max(0, 101 - 100) = -1$
$$\Pi = -c_T + c_0 = -1 + 7 = 6$$

C. Maximum and minimum

    i. Maximum profit to buyer (loss to seller) $= \infty$

    ii. Maximum loss to buyer (profit to seller) $= c_0 = 7$

D. $S_T^* = X + c_0 = 100 + 7 = 107$

2.1.2 Puts

The value of a put at expiration is $p_T = \max(0, X - S_T)$. Broken down into parts,

$$
\begin{aligned}
p_T &= X - S_T &&\text{if } S_T < X \\
p_T &= 0 &&\text{if } S_T \ge X
\end{aligned}
$$

The profit is obtained by subtracting the premium on the put from the value at expiration:

$$\Pi = p_T - p_0$$

Broken down into parts,

$$
\begin{aligned}
\Pi &= X - S_T - p_0 &&\text{if } S_T < X \\
\Pi &= -p_0 &&\text{if } S_T \ge X
\end{aligned}
$$

For our example and outcomes of $S_T = 1900$ and 2100, the results are as follows:

$S_T = 1900$:

$$
\begin{aligned}
p_T &= \max(0, 2000 - 1900) = 100 \\
\Pi &= 100 - 79.25 = 20.75
\end{aligned}
$$

$S_T = 2100$:

$$
\begin{aligned}
p_T &= \max(0, 2000 - 2100) = 0 \\
\Pi &= 0 - 79.25 = -79.25
\end{aligned}
$$

These results are shown in Exhibit 74-4. We see that the put has a maximum value and profit and a limited loss, the latter of which is the premium. The maximum

EXHIBIT 74-4 Buy Put

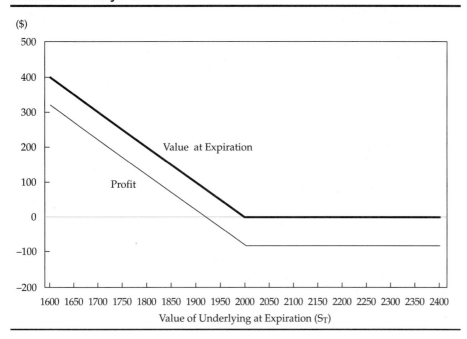

value is obtained when the underlying goes to zero.[5] In that case, $p_T = X$. So the maximum profit is $X - p_0$. Here that will be $2000 - 79.25 = 1920.75$.

The breakeven is found by breaking up the profit equation into its parts, $\Pi = X - S_T - p_0$ for $S_T < X$ and $\Pi = -p_0$ for $S_T \geq X$. In the latter case, there is no possibility of breaking even. It refers to the range over which the entire premium is lost. In the former case, we denote the breakeven index value as S_T^*, set the equation to zero, and solve for S_T^* to obtain $S_T^* = X - p_0$. In our example, the breakeven is $S_T^* = 2000 - 79.25 = 1920.75$.

In summary, for the strategy of buying a put we have

$p_T = \max(0, X - S_T)$
Value at expiration $= p_T$
Profit: $\Pi = p_T - p_0$
Maximum profit $= X - p_0$
Maximum loss $= p_0$
Breakeven: $S_T^* = X - p_0$

Now consider the *likely* outcomes for the holder of the put. In this case, the underlying must move down by almost 4 percent in one month to cover the premium. One would hardly ever expect the underlying to move down at an annual rate of almost 50 percent. Moreover, if the underlying does not move downward at all (a likely outcome given the positive expected return on most assets), the loss is 100 percent of the premium.

For the sale of a put, we simply change the sign on the value at expiration and profit. The maximum profit for the buyer becomes the maximum loss for the seller and the maximum loss for the buyer becomes the maximum profit for the seller. The breakeven for the seller is the same as for the buyer. So, for the seller,

---

[5] The maximum value and profit are not visible on the graph because we do not show S_T all the way down to zero.

$$p_T = \max(0, X - S_T)$$
Value at expiration $= -p_T$
Profit: $\Pi = -p_T + p_0$
Maximum profit $= p_0$
Maximum loss $= X - p_0$
Breakeven: $S_T^* = X - p_0$

Exhibit 74-5 graphs the value at expiration and the profit for this transaction.

EXHIBIT 74-5 Sell Put

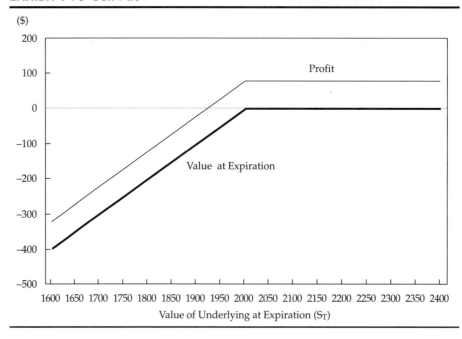

Practice Problem 2

Consider a put option selling for $4 in which the exercise price is $60 and the price of the underlying is $62.

A. Determine the value at expiration and the profit for a buyer under the following outcomes:

  i. The price of the underlying at expiration is $62.

  ii. The price of the underlying at expiration is $55.

B. Determine the value at expiration and the profit for a seller under the following outcomes:

  i. The price of the underlying at expiration is $51.

  ii. The price of the underlying at expiration is $68.

C. Determine the following:

  i. The maximum profit to the buyer (maximum loss to the seller)

  ii. The maximum loss to the buyer (maximum profit to the seller)

D. Determine the breakeven price of the underlying at expiration.

SOLUTIONS

A. Put buyer

   i. Value at expiration = p_T = max$(0, X - S_T)$ = max$(0, 60 - 62)$ = 0

     $\Pi = p_T - p_0 = 0 - 4 = -4$

   ii. Value at expiration = p_T = max$(0, X - S_T)$ = max$(0, 60 - 55)$ = 5

     $\Pi = p_T - p_0 = 5 - 4 = 1$

B. Put seller

   i. Value at expiration = $-p_T$ = $-$max$(0, X - S_T)$ = $-$max$(0, 60 - 51)$ = -9

     $\Pi = -p_T + p_0 = -9 + 4 = -5$

   ii. Value at expiration = $-p_T$ = $-$max$(0, X - S_T)$ = $-$max$(0, 60 - 68)$ = 0

     $\Pi = -p_T + p_0 = 0 + 4 = 4$

C. Maximum and minimum

   i. Maximum profit to buyer (loss to seller) = $X - p_0 = 60 - 4 = 56$

   ii. Maximum loss to buyer (profit to seller) = $p_0 = 4$

D. $S_T^* = X - p_0 = 60 - 4 = 56$

It may be surprising to find that we have now covered all of the information we need to examine all of the other option strategies. We need to learn only a few basic facts. We must know the formula for the value at expiration of a call and a put. Then we need to know how to calculate the profit for the purchase of a call and a put, but that calculation is simple: the value at expiration minus the initial value. If we know these results, we can calculate the value at expiration of the option and the profit for any value of the underlying at expiration. If we can do that, we can graph the results for a range of possible values of the underlying at expiration. Because graphing can take a long time, however, it is probably helpful to learn the basic shapes of the value and profit graphs for calls and puts. Knowing the profit equation and the shapes of the graphs, it is easy to determine the maximum profit and maximum loss. The breakeven can be determined by setting the profit equation to zero for the case in which the profit equation contains S_T. Once we have these results for the long call and put, it is an easy matter to turn them around and obtain the results for the short call and put. Therefore, little if any memorization is required. From there, we can go on to strategies that combine an option with another option and combine options with the underlying.

2.2 Risk Management Strategies with Options and the Underlying

In this section, we examine two of the most widely used option strategies, particularly for holders of the underlying. One way to reduce exposure without selling the underlying is to sell a call on the underlying; the other way is to buy a put.

2.2.1 Covered Calls

A **covered call** is a relatively conservative strategy, but it is also one of the most misunderstood strategies. A covered call is a position in which you own the underlying and sell a call. The value of the position at expiration is easily found as the value of the underlying plus the value of the short call:

$$V_T = S_T - \max(0, S_T - X)$$

Therefore,

$$V_T = S_T \qquad\qquad\qquad \text{if } S_T \le X$$
$$V_T = S_T - (S_T - X) = X \quad \text{if } S_T > X$$

We obtain the profit for the covered call by computing the change in the value of the position, $V_T - V_0$. First recognize that V_0, the value of the position at the start of the contract, is the initial value of the underlying minus the call premium. We are long the underlying and short the call, so we must subtract the call premium that was received from the sale of the call. The initial investment in the position is what we pay for the underlying less what we receive for the call. Hence, $V_0 = S_0 - c_0$. The profit is thus

$$\Pi = S_T - \max(0, S_T - X) - (S_0 - c_0)$$
$$= S_T - S_0 - \max(0, S_T - X) + c_0$$

With the equation written in this manner, we see that the profit for the covered call is simply the profit from buying the underlying, $S_T - S_0$, plus the profit from selling the call, $-\max(0, S_T - X) + c_0$. Breaking it down into ranges,

$$\Pi = S_T - S_0 + c_0 \qquad\qquad\qquad \text{if } S_T \le X$$
$$\Pi = S_T - S_0 - (S_T - X) + c_0 = X - S_0 + c_0 \quad \text{if } S_T > X$$

In our example, $S_0 = 2000$. In this section we shall use a call option with the exercise price of 2050. Thus $X = 2050$, and the premium, c_0, is 59.98. Let us now examine two outcomes: $S_T = 2100$ and $S_T = 1900$. The value at expiration when $S_T = 2100$ is $V_T = 2100 - (2100 - 2050) = 2050$, and when $S_T = 1900$, the value of the position is $V_T = 1900$.

In the first case, we hold the underlying worth 2100 but are short a call worth 50. Thus, the net value is 2050. In the second case, we hold the underlying worth 1900 and the option expires out-of-the-money.

In the first case, $S_T = 2100$, the profit is $\Pi = 2050 - 2000 + 59.98 = 109.98$. In the second case, $S_T = 1900$, the profit is $\Pi = 1900 - 2000 + 59.98 = -40.02$. These results are graphed for a range of values of S_T in Exhibit 74-6. Note that for all values of S_T greater than 2050, the value and profit are maximized. Thus, 2050 is the maximum value and 109.98 is the maximum profit.[6]

As evident in Exhibit 74-6 and the profit equations, the maximum loss would occur when S_T is zero. Hence, the profit would be $S_T - S_0 + c_0$. The profit is $-S_0 + c_0$ when $S_T = 0$. This means that the maximum loss is $S_0 - c_0$. In this example, $-S_0 + c_0$ is $-2000 + 59.98 = -1940.02$. Intuitively, this would mean that you purchased the underlying for 2000 and sold the call for 59.98. The underlying value went to zero, resulting in a loss of 2000, but the call expired with no value, so the gain from the option is the option premium. The total loss is 1940.02.

---

[6] Note in Exhibit 74-6 that there is a large gap between the value at expiration and profit, especially compared with the graphs of buying and selling calls and puts. This difference occurs because a covered call is mostly a position in the underlying asset. The initial value of the asset, S_0, accounts for most of the difference in the two lines. Note also that because of the put–call parity relationship we covered in Reading 72, a covered call looks very similar to a short put.

EXHIBIT 74-6 Covered Call (Buy Underlying, Sell Call)

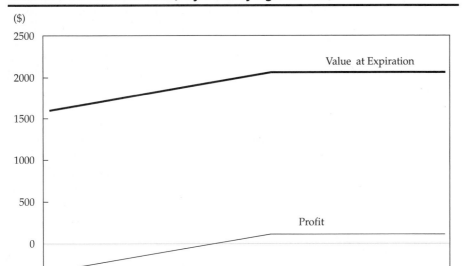

The breakeven underlying price is found by examining the profit equations and focusing on the equation that contains S_T. In equation form, $\Pi = S_T - S_0 + c_0$ when $S_T \leq X$. We let S_T^* denote the breakeven value of S_T, set the equation to zero, and solve for S_T^* to obtain $S_T^* = S_0 - c_0$. The breakeven and the maximum loss are identical. In this example, the breakeven is $S_T^* = 2000 - 59.98 = 1940.02$, which is seen in Exhibit 74-6.

To summarize the covered call, we have the following:

Value at expiration: $V_T = S_T - \max(0, S_T - X)$
Profit: $\Pi = V_T - S_0 + c_0$
Maximum profit $= X - S_0 + c_0$
Maximum loss $= S_0 - c_0$
Breakeven: $S_T^* = S_0 - c_0$

Because of the importance and widespread use of covered calls, it is worthwhile to discuss this strategy briefly to dispel some misunderstandings. First of all, some investors who do not believe in using options fail to see that selling a call on a position in the underlying reduces the risk of that position. Options do not automatically increase risk. The option part of this strategy alone, viewed in isolation, seems an extremely risky strategy. We noted in Section 2.1.1 that selling a call without owning the stock exposes the investor to unlimited loss potential. But selling a covered call—adding a short call to a long position in a stock—reduces the overall risk. Thus, any investor who holds a stock cannot say he is too conservative to use options.

Following on that theme, however, one should also view selling a covered call as a strategy that reduces not only the risk but also the expected return compared with simply holding the underlying. Hence, one should not expect to make a lot of money writing calls on the underlying. It should be apparent that in fact the covered call writer could miss out on significant gains in a strong bull market. The compensation for this willingness to give up potential upside gains, however, is that in a bear market the losses on the underlying will be cushioned by the option premium.

It may be disconcerting to some investors to look at the profit profile of a covered call. The immediate response is to think that no one in their right mind would invest in a strategy that has significant downside risk but a limited upside. Just owning the underlying has significant downside risk, but at least there is an upside. But it is important to note that the visual depiction of the strategy, as in Exhibit 74-6, does not tell the whole story. It says nothing about the likelihood of certain outcomes occurring.

For example, consider the covered call example we looked at here. The underlying starts off at 2000. The maximum profit occurs when the option expires with the underlying at 2050 or above, an increase of 2.5 percent over the life of the option. We noted that this option has a one-month life. Thus, the underlying would have to increase at an approximate annual rate of at least $2.5\%(12) = 30\%$ for the covered call writer to forgo all of the upside gain. There are not many stocks, indices, or other assets in which an investor would expect the equivalent of an annual move of at least 30 percent. Such movements obviously do occur from time to time, but they are not common. Thus, covered call writers do not often give up large gains.

But suppose the underlying did move to 2050 or higher. As we previously showed, the value of the position would be 2050. Because the initial value of the position is $2000 - 59.98 = 1940.02$, the rate of return would be 5.7 percent for one month. Hence, the maximum return is still outstanding by almost anyone's standards.[7]

Many investors believe that the initial value of a covered call should not include the value of the underlying if the underlying had been previously purchased. Suppose, for example, that this asset, currently worth 2000, had been bought several months ago at 1900. It is tempting to ignore the current value of the underlying; there is no current outlay. This view, however, misses the notion of opportunity cost. If an investor currently holding an asset chooses to write a call on it, she has made a conscious decision not to sell the asset. Hence, the current value of the asset should be viewed as an opportunity cost that is just as real as the cost to an investor buying the underlying at this time.

Sellers of covered calls must make a decision about the chosen exercise price. For example, one could sell the call with an exercise price of 1950 for 108.43, or sell the call with an exercise price of 2000 for 81.75, or sell the call with an exercise price of 2050 for 59.98. The higher the exercise price, the less one receives for the call but the more room for gain on the upside. There is no clear-cut solution to deciding which call is best; the choice depends on the risk preferences of the investor.

Finally, we should note that anecdotal evidence suggests that writers of call options make small amounts of money, but make it often. The reason for this phenomenon is generally thought to be that buyers of calls tend to be overly optimistic, but that argument is fallacious. The real reason is that the expected profits come from rare but large payoffs. For example, consider the call with exercise price of 2000 and a premium of 81.75. As we learned in Section 2.1, the breakeven underlying price is 2081.75—a gain of about 4.1 percent in a one-month period, which would be an exceptional return for almost any asset. These prices were obtained using the Black–Scholes–Merton model, so they are fair prices. Yet the required underlying price movement to profit on the call is exceptional. Obviously someone buys calls, and naturally, someone must be on the other side of the transaction. Sellers of calls tend to be holders of the underlying or other calls, which reduces the enormous risk they would assume if they sold calls without any other

---

[7] Of course, we are not saying that the performance reflects a positive alpha. We are saying only that the upside performance given up reflects improbably high returns, and therefore the limits on the upside potential are not too restrictive.

position.[8] Hence, it is reasonable to expect that sellers of calls would make money often, because large underlying price movements occur only rarely. Following this line of reasoning, however, it would appear that sellers of calls can consistently take advantage of buyers of calls. That cannot possibly be the case. What happens is that buyers of calls make money less often than sellers, but when they do make money, the leverage inherent in call options amplifies their returns. Therefore, when call writers lose money, they tend to lose big, but most call writers own the underlying or are long other calls to offset the risk.

Practice Problem 3

Consider a bond selling for $98 per $100 face value. A call option selling for $8 has an exercise price of $105. Answer the following questions about a covered call.

A. Determine the value of the position at expiration and the profit under the following outcomes:

   i. The price of the bond at expiration is $110.

   ii. The price of the bond at expiration is $88.

B. Determine the following:

   i. The maximum profit

   ii. The maximum loss

C. Determine the breakeven bond price at expiration.

SOLUTIONS

A. i. $V_T = S_T - \max(0,S_T - X) = 110 - \max(0,110 - 105)$
$$= 110 - 110 + 105 = 105$$
$$\Pi = V_T - V_0 = 105 - (S_0 - c_0) = 105 - (98 - 8) = 15$$

   ii. $V_T = S_T - \max(0,S_T - X) = 88 - \max(0,88 - 105) = 88 - 0 = 88$
$$\Pi = V_T - V_0 = 88 - (S_0 - c_0) = 88 - (98 - 8) = -2$$

B. i. Maximum profit $= X - S_0 + c_0 = 105 - 98 + 8 = 15$

   ii. Maximum loss $= S_0 - c_0 = 98 - 8 = 90$

C. $S_T^* = S_0 - c_0 = 98 - 8 = 90$

Covered calls represent one widely used way to protect a position in the underlying. Another popular means of providing protection is to buy a put.

2.2.2 Protective Puts

Because selling a call provides some protection to the holder of the underlying against a fall in the price of the underlying, buying a put should also provide protection. A put, after all, is designed to pay off when the price of the underlying moves down. In some ways, buying a put to add to a long stock position is much better than selling a call. As we shall see here, it provides downside protection while retaining the upside potential, but it does so at the expense of

---

[8] Sellers of calls who hold other calls are engaged in transactions called spreads. We discuss several types of spreads in Section 2.3.

requiring the payment of cash up front. In contrast, a covered call generates cash up front but removes some of the upside potential.

Holding an asset and a put on the asset is a strategy known as a **protective put.** The value at expiration and the profit of this strategy are found by combining the value and profit of the two strategies of buying the asset and buying the put. The value is $V_T = S_T + max(0, X - S_T)$. Thus, the results can be expressed as

$$V_T = S_T + (X - S_T) = X \quad \text{if } S_T \leq X$$
$$V_T = S_T \quad \text{if } S_T > X$$

When the underlying price at expiration exceeds the exercise price, the put expires with no value. The position is then worth only the value of the underlying. When the underlying price at expiration is less than the exercise price, the put expires in-the-money and is worth $X - S_T$, while the underlying is worth S_T. The combined value of the two instruments is X. When the underlying is worth less than the exercise price at expiration, the put can be used to sell the underlying for the exercise price.

The initial value of the position is the initial price of the underlying, S_0, plus the premium on the put, p_0. Hence, the profit is $\Pi = S_T + max(0, X - S_T) - (S_0 + p_0)$. The profit can be broken down as follows:

$$\Pi = X - (S_0 + p_0) \quad \text{if } S_T \leq X$$
$$\Pi = S_T - (S_0 + p_0) \quad \text{if } S_T > X$$

In this example, we are going to use the put with an exercise price of 1950. Its premium is 56.01. Recalling that the initial price of the underlying is 2000, the value at expiration and profit for the case of $S_T = 2100$ are

$$V_T = 2100$$
$$\Pi = 2100 - (2000 + 56.01) = 43.99$$

For the case of $S_T = 1900$, the value at expiration and profit are

$$V_T = 1950$$
$$\Pi = 1950 - (2000 + 56.01) = -106.01$$

The results for a range of outcomes are shown in Exhibit 74-7. Note how the protective put provides a limit on the downside with no limit on the upside.[9] Therefore, we can say that the upper limit is infinite. The lower limit is a loss of 106.01. In the worst possible case, we can sell the underlying for the exercise price, but the up-front cost of the underlying and put are 2056.01, for a maximum loss of 106.01.

Now let us find the breakeven price of the underlying at expiration. Note that the two profit equations are $\Pi = S_T - (S_0 + p_0)$ if $S_T > X$ and $\Pi = X - (S_0 + p_0)$ if $S_T \leq X$. In the latter case, there is no value of the underlying that will allow us to break even. In the former case, $S_T > X$, we change the notation on S_T to $S_T{*}$ to denote the breakeven value, set this expression equal to zero, and solve for $S_T{*}$:

$$S_T{*} = S_0 + p_0$$

---

[9] Note that the graph for a protective put looks like the graph for a call. This result is due to put–call parity, as covered in Reading 72.

EXHIBIT 74-7 Protective Put (Buy Underlying, Buy Put)

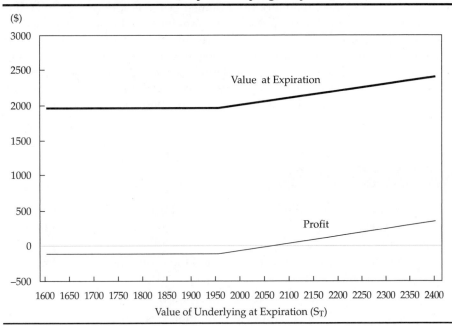

To break even, the underlying must be at least as high as the amount expended up front to establish the position. In this problem, this amount is $2000 + 56.01 = 2056.01$.

To summarize the protective put, we have the following:

Value at expiration: $V_T = S_T + \max(0, X - S_T)$
Profit: $\Pi = V_T - S_0 - p_0$
Maximum profit $= \infty$
Maximum loss $= S_0 + p_0 - X$
Breakeven: $S_T^* = S_0 + p_0$

A protective put can appear to be a great transaction with no drawbacks. It provides downside protection with upside potential, but let us take a closer look. First recall that this is a one-month transaction and keep in mind that the option has been priced by the Black–Scholes–Merton model and is, therefore, a fair price. The maximum loss of 106.01 is a loss of $106.01/2056.01 = 5.2\%$. The breakeven of 2056.01 requires an upward move of 2.8 percent, which is an annual rate of about 34 percent. From this angle, the protective put strategy does not look quite as good, but in fact, these figures simply confirm that protection against downside loss is expensive. When the protective put is fairly priced, the protection buyer must give up considerable upside potential that may not be particularly evident from just looking at a graph.

The purchase of a protective put also presents the buyer with some choices. In this example, the buyer bought the put with exercise price of 1950 for 56.01. Had he bought the put with exercise price of 2000, he would have paid 79.25. The put with exercise price of 2050 would have cost 107.39. The higher the price for which the investor wants to be able to sell the underlying, the more expensive the put will be.

The protective put is often viewed as a classic example of insurance. The investor holds a risky asset and wants protection against a loss in value. He then buys insurance in the form of the put, paying a premium to the seller of the insurance, the put writer. The exercise price of the put is like the insurance deductible because the magnitude of the exercise price reflects the risk assumed by the party holding the underlying. The higher the exercise price, the less risk assumed by the holder of the underlying and the more risk assumed by the put seller. The lower the exercise price, the more risk assumed by the holder of the underlying and the less risk assumed by the put seller. In insurance, the higher the deductible, the more risk assumed by the insured party and the less risk assumed by the insurer. Thus, a higher exercise price is analogous to a lower insurance deductible.

Like traditional insurance, this form of insurance provides coverage for a period of time. At the end of the period of time, the insurance expires and either pays off or not. The buyer of the insurance may or may not choose to renew the insurance by buying another put.

Practice Problem 4

Consider a currency selling for $0.875. A put option selling for $0.075 has an exercise price of $0.90. Answer the following questions about a protective put.

A. Determine the value at expiration and the profit under the following outcomes:

  i. The price of the currency at expiration is $0.96.

  ii. The price of the currency at expiration is $0.75.

B. Determine the following:

  i. The maximum profit

  ii. The maximum loss

C. Determine the breakeven price of the currency at expiration.

SOLUTIONS

A. **i.** $V_T = S_T + \max(0, X - S_T) = 0.96 + \max(0, 0.90 - 0.96) = 0.96$
       $\Pi = V_T - V_0 = 0.96 - (S_0 + p_0) = 0.96 - (0.875 + 0.075) = 0.01$

   ii. $V_T = S_T + \max(0, X - S_T) = 0.75 + \max(0, 0.90 - 0.75) = 0.90$
       $\Pi = V_T - V_0 = 0.90 - (S_0 + p_0) = 0.90 - (0.875 + 0.075) = -0.05$

B. **i.** Maximum profit $= \infty$

   ii. Maximum loss $= S_0 + p_0 - X = 0.875 + 0.075 - 0.90 = 0.05$

C. $S_T^* = S_0 + p_0 = 0.875 + 0.075 = 0.95$

Finally, we note that a protective put can be modified in a number of ways. One in particular is to sell a call to generate premium income to pay for the purchase of the put. This strategy is known as a collar. We shall cover collars in detail in Section 2.4.1 when we look at combining puts and calls. For now, however, let us proceed with strategies that combine calls with calls and puts with puts. These strategies are called spreads.

2.3 Money Spreads

A spread is a strategy in which you buy one option and sell another option that is identical to the first in all respects except either exercise price or time to expiration. If the options differ by time to expiration, the spread is called a time spread. Time spreads are strategies designed to exploit differences in perceptions of volatility of the underlying. They are among the more specialized strategies, and we do not cover them here. Our focus is on money spreads, which are spreads in which the two options differ only by exercise price. The investor buys an option with a given expiration and exercise price and sells an option with the same expiration but a different exercise price. Of course, the options are on the same underlying asset. The term *spread* is used here because the payoff is based on the difference, or spread, between option exercise prices.

2.3.1 Bull Spreads

A **bull spread** is designed to make money when the market goes up. In this strategy we combine a long position in a call with one exercise price and a short position in a call with a higher exercise price. Let us use X_1 as the lower of the two exercise prices and X_2 as the higher. Following the notation we introduced in Reading 72, the European call prices would be denoted as $c(X_1)$ and $c(X_2)$, but we shall simplify this notation somewhat in this reading by using the symbols c_1 and c_2, respectively. We found that the value of a call at expiration is $c_T = \max(0, S_T - X)$. So, the value of the spread at expiration is

$$V_T = \max(0, S_T - X_1) - \max(0, S_T - X_2)$$

Therefore,

$$
\begin{aligned}
V_T &= 0 - 0 = 0 & &\text{if } S_T \leq X_1 \\
V_T &= S_T - X_1 - 0 = S_T - X_1 & &\text{if } X_1 < S_T < X_2 \\
V_T &= S_T - X_1 - (S_T - X_2) = X_2 - X_1 & &\text{if } S_T \geq X_2
\end{aligned}
$$

The profit is obtained by subtracting the initial outlay for the spread from the above value of the spread at expiration. To determine the initial outlay, recall that a call option with a lower exercise price will be more expensive than a call option with a higher exercise price. Because we are buying the call with the lower exercise price and selling the call with the higher exercise price, the call we buy will cost more than the call we sell. Hence, the spread will require a net outlay of funds. This net outlay is the initial value of the position of $V_0 = c_1 - c_2$, which we call the net premium. The profit is $V_T - V_0$. Therefore,

$$\Pi = \max(0, S_T - X_1) - \max(0, S_T - X_2) - (c_1 - c_2)$$

In this manner, we see that the profit is the profit from the long call, $\max(0, S_T - X_1) - c_1$, plus the profit from the short call, $-\max(0, S_T - X_2) + c_2$. Broken down into ranges, the profit is

$$
\begin{aligned}
\Pi &= -c_1 + c_2 & &\text{if } S_T \leq X_1 \\
\Pi &= S_T - X_1 - c_1 + c_2 & &\text{if } X_1 < S_T < X_2 \\
\Pi &= X_2 - X_1 - c_1 + c_2 & &\text{if } S_T \geq X_2
\end{aligned}
$$

If S_T is below X_1, the strategy will lose a limited amount of money. The profit on the upside, if S_T is at least X_2, is also limited. When both options expire out-of-the-money, the investor loses the net premium, $c_1 - c_2$.

In this example, we use exercise prices of 1950 and 2050. Thus $X_1 = 1950$, $c_1 = 108.43$, $X_2 = 2050$, and $c_2 = 59.98$. Let us examine the outcomes in which the asset price at expiration is 2100, 2000, and 1900. In one outcome, the underlying is above the upper exercise price at expiration, and in one, the underlying is below the lower exercise price at expiration. Let us also examine one case between the exercise prices with S_T equal to 2000.

When $S_T = 2100$, the value at expiration is $V_T = 2050 - 1950 = 100$.
When $S_T = 2000$, the value at expiration is $V_T = 2000 - 1950 = 50$.
When $S_T = 1900$, the value at expiration is $V_T = 0$.

EXHIBIT 74-8 Bull Spread (Buy Call with Exercise Price X₁, Sell Call with Exercise Price X₂)

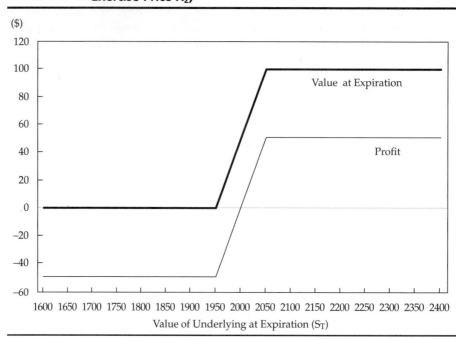

To calculate the profit, we simply subtract the initial value for the call with exercise price X_1 and add the initial value for the call with exercise price X_2.

When $S_T = 2100$, the profit is $\Pi = 100 - 108.43 + 59.98 = 51.55$.
When $S_T = 2000$, the profit is $\Pi = 50 - 108.43 + 59.98 = 1.55$.
When $S_T = 1900$, the profit is $\Pi = -108.43 + 59.98 = -48.45$.

When S_T is greater than 2100, we would obtain the same outcome as when S_T equals 2100. When S_T is less than 1900, we would obtain the same outcome as when S_T equals 1900.

Exhibit 74-8 depicts these results graphically. Note how the bull spread provides a limited gain as well as a limited loss. Of course, just purchasing a call provides a limited loss. But when selling the call in addition to buying the call, the investor gives up the upside in order to reduce the downside. In the bull spread, the investor sells gains from the call beyond the higher exercise price. Thus, a bull spread has some similarities to the covered call. With a covered call, the long position in the underlying "covers" the short position in the call. In a bull spread, the long position in the call with the lower exercise price "covers" the short position in the call with the higher exercise price. For both strategies, the short call can be viewed as giving up the gains beyond its exercise price. The upside gain can also be viewed as paying a premium of $c_1 - c_2$ to buy the underlying for X_1 and sell it for X_2. Accordingly, the maximum gain is $X_2 - X_1 - c_1 + c_2 = 2050 - 1950 - 108.43 + 59.98 = 51.55$, as computed above. This amount represents a maximum return of about 106 percent.[10] The maximum loss is the net premium, 48.45, which is a 100 percent loss.

As can be seen from the graph and the profit equations, there is a breakeven asset price at expiration that falls between the two exercise prices. We let S_T^* be the breakeven asset price at expiration and set the profit for the case of $X_1 < S_T < X_2$ to zero:

---

[10] This calculation is based on the fact that the initial value of the position is $108.43 - 59.98 = 48.45$ and the maximum value is 100, which is a gain of 106.4 percent.

$$S_T^* = X_1 + c_1 - c_2$$

To achieve a profit of zero or more, the asset price at expiration must exceed the lower exercise price by at least the net premium paid for the options. The long option must expire in-the-money by enough to cover the net premium. In our example,

$$S_T^* = 1950 + 108.43 - 59.98 = 1{,}998.45$$

What this result means is that the underlying must not move down by more than 0.08 percent.

To summarize the bull spread, we have

Value at expiration: $V_T = \max(0, S_T - X_1) - \max(0, S_T - X_2)$
Profit: $\Pi = V_T - c_1 + c_2$
Maximum profit $= X_2 - X_1 - c_1 + c_2$
Maximum loss $= c_1 - c_2$
Breakeven: $S_T^* = X_1 + c_1 - c_2$

Practice Problem 5

Consider two call options on a stock selling for $72. One call has an exercise price of $65 and is selling for $9. The other call has an exercise price of $75 and is selling for $4. Both calls expire at the same time. Answer the following questions about a bull spread:

A. Determine the value at expiration and the profit under the following outcomes:

  i. The price of the stock at expiration is $78.

  ii. The price of the stock at expiration is $69.

  iii. The price of the stock at expiration is $62.

B. Determine the following:

  i. The maximum profit

  ii. The maximum loss

C. Determine the breakeven stock price at expiration.

SOLUTIONS

A. **i.** $V_T = \max(0, S_T - X_1) - \max(0, S_T - X_2) = \max(0, 78 - 65) - \max(0, 78 - 75) = 13 - 3 = 10$
     $\Pi = V_T - V_0 = V_T - (c_1 - c_2) = 10 - (9 - 4) = 5$

  ii. $V_T = \max(0, S_T - X_1) - \max(0, S_T - X_2) = \max(0, 69 - 65) - \max(0, 69 - 75) = 4 - 0 = 4$
     $\Pi = V_T - V_0 = V_T - (c_1 - c_2) = 4 - (9 - 4) = -1$

  iii. $V_T = \max(0, S_T - X_1) - \max(0, S_T - X_2) = \max(0, 62 - 65) - \max(0, 62 - 75) = 0 - 0 = 0$
     $\Pi = V_T - V_0 = 0 - (c_1 - c_2) = 0 - (9 - 4) = -5$

B. **i.** Maximum profit $= X_2 - X_1 - (c_1 - c_2) = 75 - 65 - (9 - 4) = 5$

  ii. Maximum loss $= c_1 - c_2 = 9 - 4 = 5$

C. $S_T^* = X_1 + c_1 - c_2 = 65 + 9 - 4 = 70$

Bull spreads are used by investors who think the underlying price is going up. There are also bear spreads, which are used by investors who think the underlying price is going down.

2.3.2 Bear Spreads

If one uses the opposite strategy, selling a call with the lower exercise price and buying a call with the higher exercise price, the opposite results occur. The graph is completely reversed: The gain is on the downside and the loss is on the upside. This strategy is called a **bear spread.** The more intuitive way of executing a bear spread, however, is to use puts. Specifically, we would buy the put with the higher exercise price and sell the put with the lower exercise price.

The value of this position at expiration would be $V_T = \max(0, X_2 - S_T) - \max(0, X_1 - S_T)$. Broken down into ranges, we have the following relations:

$$
\begin{array}{ll}
V_T = X_2 - S_T - (X_1 - S_T) = X_2 - X_1 & \text{if } S_T \leq X_1 \\
V_T = X_2 - S_T - 0 = X_2 - S_T & \text{if } X_1 < S_T < X_2 \\
V_T = 0 - 0 = 0 & \text{if } S_T \geq X_2
\end{array}
$$

To obtain the profit, we subtract the initial outlay. Because we are buying the put with the higher exercise price and selling the put with the lower exercise price, the put we are buying is more expensive than the put we are selling. The initial value of the bear spread is $V_0 = p_2 - p_1$. The profit is, therefore, $V_T - V_0$, which is

$$
\Pi = \max(0, X_2 - S_T) - \max(0, X_1 - S_T) - p_2 + p_1
$$

We see that the profit is the profit from the long put, $\max(0, X_2 - S_T) - p_2$, plus the profit from the short put, $-\max(0, X_1 - S_T) + p_1$. Broken down into ranges, the profit is

$$
\begin{array}{ll}
\Pi = X_2 - X_1 - p_2 + p_1 & \text{if } S_T \leq X_1 \\
\Pi = X_2 - S_T - p_2 + p_1 & \text{if } X_1 < S_T < X_2 \\
\Pi = -p_2 + p_1 & \text{if } S_T \geq X_2
\end{array}
$$

In contrast to the profit in a bull spread, the bear spread profit occurs on the downside; the maximum profit occurs when $S_T \leq X_1$. This profit reflects the purchase of the underlying at X_1, which occurs when the short put is exercised, and the sale of the underlying at X_2, which occurs when the long put is exercised. The worst outcome occurs when $S_T > X_2$, in which case both puts expire out-of-the-money and the net premium is lost.

In the example, we again use options with exercise prices of 1950 and 2050. Their premiums are $p_1 = 56.01$ and $p_2 = 107.39$. We examine the three outcomes we did with the bull spread: S_T is 1900, 2000, or 2100.

> With $S_T = 1900$, the value at expiration is $V_T = 2050 - 1950 = 100$.
> With $S_T = 2000$, the value at expiration is $V_T = 2050 - 2000 = 50$.
> With $S_T = 2100$, the value at expiration is $V_T = 0$.

The profit is obtained by taking the value at expiration, subtracting the premium of the put with the higher exercise price, and adding the premium of the put with the lower exercise price:

> When $S_T = 1900$, the profit is $\Pi = 100 - 107.39 + 56.01 = 48.62$.
> When $S_T = 2000$, the profit is $\Pi = 50 - 107.39 + 56.01 = -1.38$.
> When $S_T = 2100$, the profit is $\Pi = -107.39 + 56.01 = -51.38$.

EXHIBIT 74-9 Bear Spread (Buy Put with Exercise Price X₂, Sell Put with Exercise Price X₁)

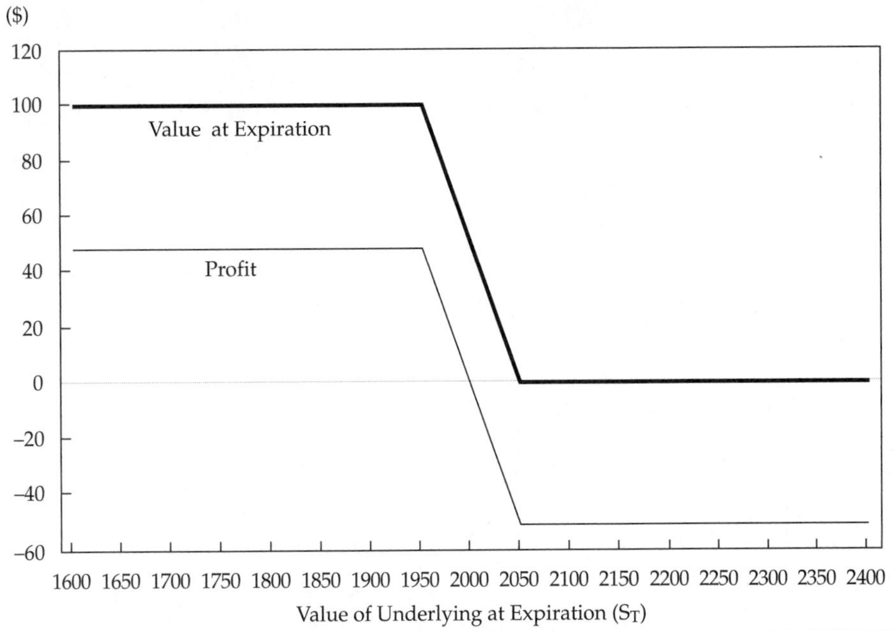

Value of Underlying at Expiration (S_T)

When S_T is less than 1900, the outcome is the same as when S_T equals 1900. When S_T is greater than 2100, the outcome is the same as when S_T equals 2100.

The results are graphed in Exhibit 74-9. Note how this strategy is similar to a bull spread but with opposite outcomes. The gains are on the downside underlying moves and the losses are on the upside underlying. The maximum profit occurs when both puts expire in-the-money. You end up using the short put to buy the asset and the long put to sell the asset. The maximum profit is $X_2 - X_1 - p_2 + p_1$, which in this example is $100 - 107.39 + 56.01 = 48.62$, a return of 94 percent.[11] The maximum loss of $p_2 - p_1$ occurs when both puts expire out-of-the-money, and in this case is $107.39 - 56.01 = 51.38$, a loss of 100 percent.

The breakeven asset price occurs between the two exercise prices. Let S_T^* be the breakeven asset price at expiration, set the profit equation for the middle case to zero, and solve for S_T^* to obtain $S_T^* = X_2 - p_2 + p_1$. In this case, the breakeven is $S_T^* = 2050 - 107.39 + 56.01 = 1{,}998.62$. The underlying need move down only as little as 0.07 percent to make a profit.

To summarize the bear spread, we have

Value at expiration: $V_T = \max(0, X_2 - S_T) - \max(0, X_1 - S_T)$
Profit: $\Pi = V_T - p_2 + p_1$
Maximum profit $= X_2 - X_1 - p_2 + p_1$
Maximum loss $= p_2 - p_1$
Breakeven: $S_T^* = X_2 - p_2 + p_1$

---

[11] The net premium is $107.39 - 56.01 = 51.38$, so the maximum value of 100 is a return of about 94 percent.

Practice Problem 6

Consider two put options on a bond selling for $92 per $100 par. One put has an exercise price of $85 and is selling for $3. The other put has an exercise price of $95 and is selling for $11. Both puts expire at the same time. Answer the following questions about a bear spread:

A. Determine the value at expiration and the profit under the following outcomes:

    i. The price of the bond at expiration is $98.

    ii. The price of the bond at expiration is $91.

    iii. The price of the bond at expiration is $82.

B. Determine the following:

    i. The maximum profit

    ii. The maximum loss

C. Determine the breakeven bond price at expiration.

SOLUTIONS

A. **i.** $V_T = \max(0, X_2 - S_T) - \max(0, X_1 - S_T) = \max(0, 95 - 98) - \max(0, 85 - 98) = 0 - 0 = 0$

      $\Pi = V_T - V_0 = V_T - (p_2 - p_1) = 0 - (11 - 3) = -8$

  ii. $V_T = \max(0, X_2 - S_T) - \max(0, X_1 - S_T) = \max(0, 95 - 91) - \max(0, 85 - 91) = 4 - 0 = 4$

      $\Pi = V_T - V_0 = V_T - (p_2 - p_1) = 4 - (11 - 3) = -4$

  iii. $V_T = \max(0, X_2 - S_T) - \max(0, X_1 - S_T) = \max(0, 95 - 82) - \max(0, 85 - 82) = 13 - 3 = 10$

      $\Pi = V_T - V_0 = 10 - (p_2 - p_1) = 10 - (11 - 3) = 2$

B. **i.** Maximum profit $= X_2 - X_1 - (p_2 - p_1) = 95 - 85 - (11 - 3) = 2$

  ii. Maximum loss $= p_2 - p_1 = 11 - 3 = 8$

C. $S_T^* = X_2 - p_2 + p_1 = 95 - 11 + 3 = 87$

The bear spread with calls involves selling the call with the lower exercise price and buying the one with the higher exercise price. Because the call with the lower exercise price will be more expensive, there will be a cash inflow at initiation of the position and hence a profit if the calls expire worthless.

Bull and bear spreads are but two types of spread strategies. We now take a look at another strategy, which combines bull and bear spreads.

2.3.3 Butterfly Spreads

In both the bull and bear spread, we used options with two different exercise prices. There is no limit to how many different options one can use in a strategy. As an example, the **butterfly spread** combines a bull and bear spread. Consider three different exercise prices, X_1, X_2, and X_3. Suppose we first construct a bull spread, buying the call with exercise price of X_1 and selling the call with exercise price of X_2. Recall that we could construct a bear spread using calls instead of puts. In that case, we would buy the call with the higher exercise price and sell the call with the lower exercise price. This bear spread is identical to the sale of a bull spread.

Suppose we sell a bull spread by buying the call with exercise price X_3 and selling the call with exercise price X_2. We have now combined a long bull spread and a short bull spread (or a bear spread). We own the calls with exercise price X_1 and X_3 and have sold two calls with exercise price X_2. Combining these results, we obtain a value at expiration of

$$V_T = max(0, S_T - X_1) - 2max(0, S_T - X_2) + max(0, S_T - X_3)$$

This can be broken down into ranges of

$$
\begin{aligned}
V_T &= 0 - 2(0) + 0 = 0 & \text{if } S_T \le X_1 \\
V_T &= S_T - X_1 - 2(0) + 0 = S_T - X_1 & \text{if } X_1 < S_T < X_2 \\
V_T &= S_T - X_1 - 2(S_T - X_2) + 0 = -S_T + 2X_2 - X_1 & \text{if } X_2 \le S_T < X_3 \\
V_T &= S_T - X_1 - 2(S_T - X_2) + S_T - X_3 = 2X_2 - X_1 - X_3 & \text{if } S_T \ge X_3
\end{aligned}
$$

If the exercise prices are equally spaced, $2X_2 - X_1 - X_3$ would equal zero.[12] In virtually all cases in practice, the exercise prices are indeed equally spaced, and we shall make that assumption. Therefore,

$$V_T = 2X_2 - X_1 - X_3 = 0 \quad \text{if } S_T \ge X_3$$

To obtain the profit, we must subtract the initial value of the position, which is $V_0 = c_1 - 2c_2 + c_3$. Is this value positive or negative? It turns out that it will always be positive. The bull spread we buy is more expensive than the bull spread we sell, because the lower exercise price on the bull spread we buy (X_1) is lower than the lower exercise price on the bull spread we sell (X_2). Because the underlying is more likely to move higher than X_1 than to move higher than X_2, the bull spread we buy is more expensive than the bull spread we sell.

The profit is thus $V_T - V_0$, which is

$$\Pi = max(0, S_T - X_1) - 2max(0, S_T - X_2) + max(0, S_T - X_3) - c_1 + 2c_2 - c_3$$

Broken down into ranges,

$$
\begin{aligned}
\Pi &= -c_1 + 2c_2 - c_3 & \text{if } S_T \le X_1 \\
\Pi &= S_T - X_1 - c_1 + 2c_2 - c_3 & \text{if } X_1 < S_T < X_2 \\
\Pi &= -S_T + 2X_2 - X_1 - c_1 + 2c_2 - c_3 & \text{if } X_2 \le S_T < X_3 \\
\Pi &= -c_1 + 2c_2 - c_3 & \text{if } S_T \ge X_3
\end{aligned}
$$

Note that in the lowest and highest ranges, the profit is negative; a loss. It is not immediately obvious what happens in the middle two ranges. Let us look at our example. In this example, we buy the calls with exercise prices of 1950 and 2050 and sell two calls with exercise price of 2000. So, $X_1 = 1950$, $X_2 = 2000$, and $X_3 = 2050$. Their premiums are $c_1 = 108.43$, $c_2 = 81.75$, and $c_3 = 59.98$. Let us examine the outcomes in which $S_T = 1900$, 1975, 2025, and 2100. These outcomes fit into each of the four relevant ranges.

When $S_T = 1900$, the value at expiration is $V_T = 0 - 2(0) + 0 = 0$.
When $S_T = 1975$, the value at expiration is $V_T = 1975 - 1950 = 25$.
When $S_T = 2025$, the value at expiration is $V_T = -2025 + 2(2000) - 1950 = 25$.
When $S_T = 2100$, the value at expiration is $V_T = 0$.

---

[12] For example, suppose the exercise prices are equally spaced with $X_1 = 30$, $X_2 = 40$, and $X_3 = 50$. Then $2X_2 - X_3 - X_1 = 2(40) - 50 - 30 = 0$.

Now, turning to the profit,

> When $S_T = 1900$, the profit will be $\Pi = 0 - 108.43 + 2(81.75) - 59.98 = -4.91$.
> When $S_T = 1975$, the profit will be $\Pi = 25 - 108.43 + 2(81.75) - 59.98 = 20.09$.
> When $S_T = 2025$, the profit will be $\Pi = 25 - 108.43 + 2(81.75) - 59.98 = 20.09$.
> When $S_T = 2100$, the profit will be $\Pi = 0 - 108.43 + 2(81.75) - 59.98 = -4.91$.

Exhibit 74-10 depicts these results graphically. Note that the strategy is based on the expectation that the volatility of the underlying will be relatively low. The expectation must be that the underlying will trade near the middle exercise price. The maximum loss of 4.91 occurs if the underlying ends up below the lower strike, 1950, or above the upper strike, 2050. The maximum profit occurs if the underlying ends up precisely at the middle exercise price. This maximum profit is found by examining either of the middle two ranges with S_T set equal to X_2:

$$\begin{aligned}
\Pi \text{ (maximum)} &= S_T - X_1 - c_1 + 2c_2 - c_3 \\
&= X_2 - X_1 - c_1 + 2c_2 - c_3 \qquad \text{if } S_T = X_2 \\
\Pi \text{ (maximum)} &= -S_T + 2X_2 - X_1 - c_1 + 2c_2 - c_3 \\
&= X_2 - X_1 - c_1 + 2c_2 - c_3 \qquad \text{if } S_T = X_2
\end{aligned}$$

In this case, the maximum profit is Π (maximum) $= 2000 - 1950 - 108.43 + 2(81.75) - 59.98 = 45.09$, which is a return of 918 percent.[13]

EXHIBIT 74-10 Butterfly Spread (Buy Calls with Exercise Price X₁ and X₃, Sell Two Calls with Exercise Price X₂)

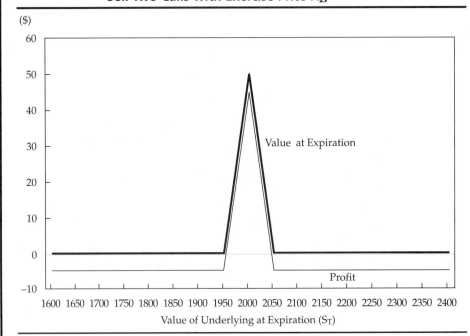

---

[13] This return is based on a maximum value of $2000 - 1950 = 50$ versus the initial value of 4.91, a return of 918 percent.

There are two breakeven prices, and they lie within the two middle profit ranges. We find them as follows:

For $X_1 < S_T < X_2$:
$$\Pi = S_T{}^* - X_1 - c_1 + 2c_2 - c_3 = 0$$
$$S_T{}^* = X_1 + c_1 - 2c_2 + c_3$$
For $X_2 \leq S_T < X_3$:
$$\Pi = -S_T{}^* + 2X_2 - X_1 - c_1 + 2c_2 - c_3 = 0$$
$$S_T{}^* = 2X_2 - X_1 - c_1 + 2c_2 - c_3$$

In this example, therefore, the breakeven prices are

$$S_T{}^* = X_1 + c_1 - 2c_2 + c_3$$
$$= 1950 + 108.43 - 2(81.75) + 59.98 = 1954.91$$
$$S_T{}^* = 2X_2 - X_1 - c_1 + 2c_2 - c_3$$
$$= 2(2000) - 1950 - 108.43 + 2(81.75) - 59.98 = 2045.09$$

These movements represent a range of roughly ± 2.3 percent from the starting value of 2000. Therefore, if the underlying stays within this range, the strategy will be profitable.

In summary, for the butterfly spread

Value at expiration: $V_T = \max(0, S_T - X_1) - 2\max(0, S_T - X_2) + \max(0, S_T - X_3)$
Profit: $\Pi = V_T - c_1 + 2c_2 - c_3$
Maximum profit $= X_2 - X_1 - c_1 + 2c_2 - c_3$
Maximum loss $= c_1 - 2c_2 + c_3$
Breakeven: $S_T{}^* = X_1 + c_1 - 2c_2 + c_3$ and $S_T{}^* = 2X_2 - X_1 - c_1 + 2c_2 - c_3$

As we noted, a butterfly spread is a strategy based on the expectation of low volatility in the underlying. Of course, for a butterfly spread to be an appropriate strategy, the user must believe that the underlying will be less volatile than the market expects. If the investor buys into the strategy and the market is more volatile than expected, the strategy is likely to result in a loss. If the investor expects the market to be more volatile than he believes the market expects, the appropriate strategy could be to sell the butterfly spread. Doing so would involve selling the calls with exercise prices of X_1 and X_3 and buying two calls with exercise prices of X_2.[14]

Alternatively, a butterfly spread can be executed using puts. Note that the initial value of the spread using calls is $V_0 = c_1 - 2c_2 + c_3$. Recall that from put–call parity, $c = p + S - X/(1 + r)^T$. If we use the appropriate subscripts and substitute $p_i + S - X_i/(1 + r)^T$ for c_i where $i = 1, 2$, and 3, we obtain $V_0 = p_1 - 2p_2 + p_3$. The positive signs on p_1 and p_3 and the negative sign on $2p_2$ mean that we could buy the puts with exercise prices X_1 and X_3 and sell two puts with exercise price of X_2 to obtain the same result. We would, in effect, be buying a bear spread with puts consisting of buying the put with exercise price of X_3 and selling the put with exercise price of X_2, and also selling a bear spread by selling the put with exercise price of X_2 and buying the put with exercise price of X_1. If the options are priced correctly, it does not really matter whether we use puts or calls.[15]

---

[14] A short butterfly spread is sometimes called a **sandwich spread.**

[15] If puts were underpriced, it would be better to buy the butterfly spread using puts. If calls were underpriced, it would be better to buy the butterfly spread using calls. Of course, other strategies could also be used to take advantage of any mispricing.

Practice Problem 7

Consider three put options on a currency that is currently selling for $1.45. The exercise prices are $1.30, $1.40, and $1.50. The put prices are $0.08, $0.125, and $0.18, respectively. The puts all expire at the same time. Answer the following questions about a butterfly spread.

A. Determine the value at expiration and the profit under the following outcomes:

  i. The price of the currency at expiration is $1.26.

  ii. The price of the currency at expiration is $1.35.

  iii. The price of the currency at expiration is $1.47.

  iv. The price of the currency at expiration is $1.59.

B. Determine the following:

  i. The maximum profit

  ii. The maximum loss

C. Determine the breakeven currency price at expiration.

SOLUTIONS

A. **i.** $V_T = \max(0, X_1 - S_T) - 2\max(0, X_2 - S_T) + \max(0, X_3 - S_T) = \max(0, 1.30 - 1.26) - 2\max(0, 1.40 - 1.26) + \max(0, 1.50 - 1.26) = 0.04 - 2(0.14) + 0.24 = 0.0$

$\Pi = V_T - V_0 = V_T - (p_1 - 2p_2 + p_3) = 0.0 - [0.08 - 2(0.125) + 0.18] = -0.01$

  ii. $V_T = \max(0, X_1 - S_T) - 2\max(0, X_2 - S_T) + \max(0, X_3 - S_T) = \max(0, 1.30 - 1.35) - 2\max(0, 1.40 - 1.35) + \max(0, 1.50 - 1.35) = 0.0 - 2(0.05) + 0.15 = 0.05$

$\Pi = V_T - V_0 = V_T - (p_1 - 2p_2 + p_3) = 0.05 - [0.08 - 2(0.125) + 0.18] = 0.04$

  iii. $V_T = \max(0, X_1 - S_T) - 2\max(0, X_2 - S_T) + \max(0, X_3 - S_T) = \max(0, 1.30 - 1.47) - 2\max(0, 1.40 - 1.47) + \max(0, 1.50 - 1.47) = 0.0 - 2(0) + 0.03 = 0.03$

$\Pi = V_T - V_0 = V_T - (p_1 - 2p_2 + p_3) = 0.03 - [0.08 - 2(0.125) + 0.18] = 0.02$

  iv. $V_T = \max(0, X_1 - S_T) - 2\max(0, X_2 - S_T) + \max(0, X_3 - S_T) = \max(0, 1.30 - 1.59) - 2\max(0, 1.40 - 1.59) + \max(0, 1.50 - 1.59) = 0.0 - 2(0) + 0.0 = 0.0$

$\Pi = V_T - V_0 = V_T - (p_1 - 2p_2 + p_3) = 0.0 - [0.08 - 2(0.125) + 0.18] = -0.01$

B. **i.** Maximum profit $= X_2 - X_1 - (p_1 - 2p_2 + p_3) = 1.40 - 1.30 - [0.08 - 2(0.125) + 0.18] = 0.09$

  ii. Maximum loss $= p_1 - 2p_2 + p_3 = 0.08 - 2(0.125) + 0.18 = 0.01$

C. $S_T^* = X_1 + p_1 - 2p_2 + p_3 = 1.30 + 0.08 - 2(0.125) + 0.18 = 1.31$

$S_T^* = 2X_2 - X_1 - p_1 + 2p_2 - p_3 = 2(1.40) - 1.30 - 0.08 + 2(0.125) - 0.18 = 1.49$

So far, we have restricted ourselves to the use of either calls or puts, but not both. We now look at strategies that involve positions in calls *and* puts.

2.4 Combinations of Calls and Puts

2.4.1 Collars

Recall that in Section 2.2 we examined the protective put. In that strategy, the holder of the underlying asset buys a put to provide protection against downside loss. Purchasing the put requires the payment of the put premium. One way to get around paying the put premium is to sell another option with a premium equal to the put premium, which can be done by selling a call with an exercise price above the current price of the underlying.

Although it is not necessary that the call premium offset the put premium, and the call premium can even be more than the put premium, the typical collar has the call and put premiums offset. When this offsetting occurs, no net premium is required up front. In effect, the holder of the asset gains protection below a certain level, the exercise price of the put, and pays for it by giving up gains above a certain level, the exercise price of the call. This strategy is called a **collar.** When the premiums offset, it is sometimes called a **zero-cost collar.** This term is a little misleading, however, as it suggests that there is no "cost" to this transaction. The cost takes the form of forgoing upside gains. The term "zero-cost" refers only to the fact that no cash is paid up front.

A collar is a modified version of a protective put and a covered call and requires different exercise prices for each. Let the put exercise price be X_1 and the call exercise price be X_2. With X_1 given, it is important to see that X_2 is not arbitrary. If we want the call premium to offset the put premium, the exercise price on the call must be set such that the price of the call equals the price of the put. We thus can select any exercise price of the put. Then the call exercise price is selected by determining which exercise price will produce a call premium equal to the put premium. Although the put can have any exercise price, typically the put exercise price is lower than the current value of the underlying. The call exercise price then must be above the current value of the underlying.[16]

So let X_1 be set. The put with this exercise price has a premium of p_1. We now need to set X_2 such that the premium on the call, c_2, equals the premium on the put, p_1. To do so, we need to use an option valuation model, such as Black–Scholes–Merton, to find the exercise price of the call that will make $c_2 = p_1$. Recall that the Black–Scholes–Merton formula is

$$c = S_0 N(d_1) - X e^{-r^c T} N(d_2)$$

where

$$d_1 = \frac{\ln(S_0/X) + (r^c + \sigma^2/2)T}{\sigma\sqrt{T}}$$
$$d_2 = d_1 - \sigma\sqrt{T}$$

and where r^c is the continuously compounded risk-free rate and $N(d_1)$ and $N(d_2)$ are normal probabilities associated with the values d_1 and d_2. Ideally we would turn the equation around and solve for X in terms of c, but the equation is too complex to be able to isolate X on one side. So, we must solve for X by trial and error.

---

[16] It can be proven in general that the call exercise price would have to be above the current value of the underlying. Intuitively, it can be shown through put–call parity that if the call and put exercise prices were equal to the current value of the underlying, the call would be worth more than the put. If we lower the put exercise price below the price of the underlying, the put price would decrease. Then the gap between the call and put prices would widen further. We would then need to raise the call exercise price above the current price of the underlying to make its premium come down.

We substitute in values of X until the option price equals c, where c is the call premium that we want to equal the put premium.

Consider the Nasdaq example. Suppose we use the put with exercise price of 1950. Its premium is 56.01. So now we need a call with a premium of 56.01. The call with exercise price of 2000 is worth 81.75. So to get a lower call premium, we need a call with an exercise price higher than 2000. By trial and error, we insert higher and higher exercise prices until the call premium falls to 56.01, which occurs at an exercise price of about 2060.[17] So now we have it. We buy the put with an exercise price of 1950 for 56.01 and sell the call with exercise price of 2060 for 56.01. This transaction requires no cash up front.

The value of the position at expiration is the sum of the value of the underlying asset, the value of the put, and the value of the short call:

$$V_T = S_T + \max(0, X_1 - S_T) - \max(0, S_T - X_2)$$

Broken down into ranges, we have

$$\begin{aligned}
V_T &= S_T + X_1 - S_T - 0 = X_1 &&\text{if } S_T \le X_1 \\
V_T &= S_T + 0 - 0 = S_T &&\text{if } X_1 < S_T < X_2 \\
V_T &= S_T + 0 - (S_T - X_2) = X_2 &&\text{if } S_T \ge X_2
\end{aligned}$$

The initial value of the position is simply the value of the underlying asset, S_0. The profit is $V_T - V_0$:

$$\Pi = S_T + \max(0, X_1 - S_T) - \max(0, S_T - X_2) - S_0$$

Broken down into ranges, we have

$$\begin{aligned}
\Pi &= X_1 - S_0 &&\text{if } S_T \le X_1 \\
\Pi &= S_T - S_0 &&\text{if } X_1 < S_T < X_2 \\
\Pi &= X_2 - S_0 &&\text{if } S_T \ge X_2
\end{aligned}$$

Using our example where $X_1 = 1950$, $p_1 = 56.01$, $X_2 = 2060$, $c_2 = 56.01$, and $S_0 = 2000$, we obtain the following values at expiration:

If $S_T = 1900$, $V_T = 1950$
If $S_T = 2000$, $V_T = 2000$
If $S_T = 2100$, $V_T = 2060$

The profit for $S_T = 1900$ is $\Pi = 1950 - 2000 = -50$.

If $S_T = 2000$, $\Pi = 2000 - 2000 = 0$
If $S_T = 2100$, $\Pi = 2060 - 2000 = 60$

A graph of this strategy is shown in Exhibit 74-11. Note that the lines are flat over the range of S_T up to the put exercise price of 1950 and in the range beyond the call exercise price of 2060. Below 1950, the put provides protection against loss. Above 2060, the short call forces a relinquishment of the gains, which are earned by the buyer of the call. In between these ranges, neither the put nor the

---

[17] The other necessary information to obtain the exercise price of the call are that the volatility is 0.35, the risk-free rate is 0.02, and the dividend yield is 0.005. The actual call price at a stock price of 2060 is 56.18. At 2061, the call price is 55.82. Thus, the correct exercise price lies between 2060 and 2061; we simply round to 2060.

EXHIBIT 74-11 Zero-Cost Collar (Buy Put with Exercise Price X₁, Sell Call with Exercise Price X₂, Put and Call Premiums Offset)

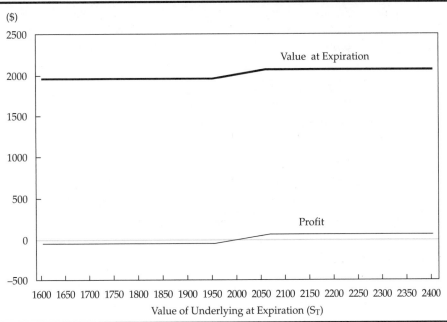

call has value. The profit is strictly determined by the underlying and moves directly with the value of the underlying. The maximum profit is $X_2 - S_0$, which here is $2060 - 2000 = 60$, a return of 3 percent. The maximum loss is $S_0 - X_1$, which here is $2000 - 1950 = 50$, a loss of 2.5 percent. Keep in mind that these options have lives of one month, so those numbers represent one-month returns. The breakeven is simply the original underlying price of 2000.

In summary, for the collar

Value at expiration: $V_T = S_T + \max(0, X_1 - S_T) - \max(0, S_T - X_2)$
Profit: $\Pi = V_T - S_0$
Maximum profit $= X_2 - S_0$
Maximum loss $= S_0 - X_1$
Breakeven: $S_T^* = S_0$

Collars are also known as range forwards and risk reversals.[18] Asset managers often use them to guard against losses without having to pay cash up front for the protection. Clearly, however, they are virtually the same as bull spreads. The latter has a cap on the gain and a floor on the loss but does not involve actually holding the underlying. In Section 3.0, we shall encounter this strategy again in the form of an interest rate collar, which protects floating-rate borrowers against high interest rates.

---

[18] It is not clear why a collar is sometimes called a risk reversal. It is clear, however, why a collar is sometimes called a range forward. Like a forward contract, it requires no initial outlay other than for the underlying. Unlike a forward contract, which has a strictly linear payoff profile, the collar payoff breaks at the two exercise prices, thus creating a range.

Practice Problem 8

The holder of a stock worth $42 is considering placing a collar on it. A put with an exercise price of $40 costs $5.32. A call with the same premium would require an exercise price of $50.59.

A. Determine the value at expiration and the profit under the following outcomes:

   i. The price of the stock at expiration is $55.

   ii. The price of the stock at expiration is $48.

   iii. The price of the stock at expiration is $35.

B. Determine the following:

   i. The maximum profit

   ii. The maximum loss

C. Determine the breakeven stock price at expiration.

SOLUTIONS

A. **i.** $V_T = S_T + max(0, X_1 - S_T) - max(0, S_T - X_2) = 55 + max(0, 40 - 55) - max(0, 55 - 50.59) = 55 + 0 - (55 - 50.59) = 50.59$

    $\Pi = V_T - S_0 = 50.59 - 42 = 8.59$

  ii. $V_T = S_T + max(0, X_1 - S_T) - max(0, S_T - X_2) = 48 + max(0, 40 - 48) - max(0, 48 - 50.59) = 48 + 0 - 0 = 48$

    $\Pi = V_T - S_0 = 48 - 42 = 6$

  iii. $V_T = S_T + max(0, X_1 - S_T) - max(0, S_T - X_2) = 35 + max(0, 40 - 35) - max(0, 35 - 50.59) = 35 + 5 - 0 = 40$

    $\Pi = V_T - S_0 = 40 - 42 = -2$

B. **i.** Maximum profit $= X_2 - S_0 = 50.59 - 42 = 8.59$

  ii. Maximum loss $= S_0 - X_1 = 42 - 40 = 2$

C. $S_T^* = S_0 = 42$

Collars are one of the many directional strategies, meaning that they perform based on the direction of the movement in the underlying. Of course, butterfly spreads perform based on the volatility of the underlying. Another strategy in which performance is based on the volatility of the underlying is the straddle.

2.4.2 Straddle

To justify the purchase of a call, an investor must be bullish. To justify the purchase of a put, an investor must be bearish. What should an investor do if he believes the market will be volatile but does not feel particularly strongly about the direction? We discussed earlier that a short butterfly spread is one strategy. It benefits from extreme movements, but its gains are limited. There are other, more-complex strategies, such as time spreads, that can benefit from high volatility; however, one simple strategy, the **straddle,** also benefits from high volatility.

Suppose the investor buys both a call and a put with the same exercise price on the same underlying with the same expiration. This strategy enables the investor to profit from upside or downside moves. Its cost, however, can be quite heavy. In fact, a straddle is a wager on a large movement in the underlying.

The value of a straddle at expiration is the value of the call and the value of the put: $V_T = \max(0, S_T - X) + \max(0, X - S_T)$. Broken down into ranges,

$$V_T = X - S_T \quad \text{if } S_T < X$$
$$V_T = S_T - X \quad \text{if } S_T \geq X$$

The initial value of the straddle is simply $V_0 = c_0 + p_0$. The profit is $V_T - V_0$ or $\Pi = \max(0, S_T - X) + \max(0, X - S_T) - c_0 - p_0$. Broken down into ranges,

$$\Pi = X - S_T - c_0 - p_0 \quad \text{if } S_T < X$$
$$\Pi = S_T - X - c_0 - p_0 \quad \text{if } S_T \geq X$$

In our example, let $X = 2000$. Then $c_0 = 81.75$ and $p_0 = 79.25$.

    If $S_T = 2100$, the value of the position at expiration is $V_T = 2100 - 2000 = 100$.
    If $S_T = 1900$, the value of the position at expiration is $V_T = 2000 - 1900 = 100$.
    If $S_T = 2100$, the profit is $\Pi = 100 - 81.75 - 79.25 = -61$.
    If $S_T = 1900$, the profit is $\Pi = 100 - 81.75 - 79.25 = -61$.

Note the symmetry, whereby a move of 100 in either direction results in a change in value of 61. The put and call payoffs are obviously symmetric. It is also apparent that these outcomes are below breakeven.

Observe the results in Exhibit 74-12. Note that the value and profit are V-shaped, thereby benefiting from large moves in the underlying in either direction. Like the call option the straddle contains, the gain on the upside is unlimited. Like the put, the downside gain is not unlimited, but it is quite large. The underlying can go down no further than zero. Hence, on the downside the maximum profit is $X - c_0 - p_0$, which in this case is $2000 - 81.75 - 79.25 = 1839$. The maximum loss occurs if the underlying ends up precisely at the exercise price. In that case, neither the call nor the put expires with value and the premiums are lost on both. Therefore, the maximum loss is $c_0 + p_0$, which is $81.75 + 79.25 = 161$.

EXHIBIT 74-12 Straddle (Buy Call and Put with Exercise Price X)

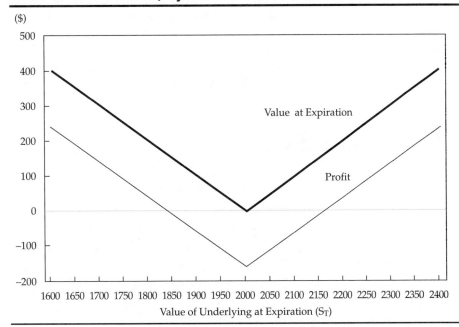

There are two breakevens. Using S_T^* to denote the breakevens, we set each profit equation to zero and solve for S_T^*:

If $S_T \geq X$,
$$\Pi = S_T^* - X - c_0 - p_0 = 0$$
$$S_T^* = X + c_0 + p_0$$

If $S_T < X$,
$$\Pi = X - S_T^* - c_0 - p_0 = 0$$
$$S_T^* = X - c_0 - p_0$$

The breakevens thus equal the exercise price plus or minus the premiums. So in this case, the breakevens are $2000 \pm 161 = 2161$ and 1839. A move of 161 is a percentage move of 8.1 percent over a one-month period. Hence, in this example, the purchase of a straddle is a bet that the underlying will move at nearly a 100 percent annual rate over a one-month period, quite a risky bet. An investor would make such a bet only when he felt that the underlying would be exceptionally volatile. An obvious time to use a straddle would be around major events such as earnings announcements. But because earnings announcements are known and anticipated events, the greater uncertainty surrounding them should already be reflected in the options' prices. Recall that the greater the volatility, the higher the prices of both puts and calls. Therefore, using a straddle in anticipation of an event that everyone knows is coming is not necessarily a good idea. Only when the investor believes the market will be more volatile than everyone else believes would a straddle be advised.

In summary, for a straddle

Value at expiration: $V_T = \max(0, S_T - X) + \max(0, X - S_T)$
Profit: $\Pi = V_T - (c_0 + p_0)$
Maximum profit = ∞
Maximum loss = $c_0 + p_0$
Breakeven: $S_T^* = X \pm (c_0 + p_0)$

As we have noted, a straddle would tend to be used by an investor who is expecting the market to be volatile but does not have strong feelings one way or the other on the direction. An investor who leans one way or the other might consider adding a call or a put to the straddle. Adding a call to a straddle is a strategy called a **strap,** and adding a put to a straddle is called a **strip.** It is even more difficult to make a gain from these strategies than it is for a straddle, but if the hoped-for move does occur, the gains are leveraged. Another variation of the straddle is a **strangle,** in which the put and call have different exercise prices. This strategy creates a graph similar to a straddle but with a flat section instead of a point on the bottom.

Practice Problem 9

Consider a stock worth $49. A call with an exercise price of $50 costs $6.25 and a put with an exercise price of $50 costs $5.875. An investor buys a straddle.

A. Determine the value at expiration and the profit under the following outcomes:

   i. The price of the stock at expiration is $61.

   ii. The price of the stock at expiration is $37.

B. Determine the following:

   i. The maximum profit

> **ii.** The maximum loss
>
> **C.** Determine the breakeven stock price at expiration.
>
> **SOLUTIONS**
>
> **A.** **i.** $V_T = \max(0,S_T - X) + \max(0,X - S_T) = \max(0,61 - 50) + \max(0,50 - 61) = 11 - 0 = 11$
> $\Pi = V_T - (c_0 + p_0) = 11 - (6.25 + 5.875) = -1.125$
>
> **ii.** $V_T = \max(0,S_T - X) + \max(0,X - S_T) = \max(0,37 - 50) + \max(0,50 - 37) = 0 + 13 = 13$
> $\Pi = V_T - S_0 = 13 - (6.25 + 5.875) = 0.875$
>
> **B.** **i.** Maximum profit $= \infty$
>
> **ii.** Maximum loss $= c_0 + p_0 = 6.25 + 5.875 = 12.125$
>
> **C.** $S_T^* = X \pm (c_0 + p_0) = 50 \pm (6.25 + 5.875) = 62.125, 37.875$

Now we turn to a strategy that combines more than one call and more than one put. It should not be surprising that we shall recognize this strategy as just a combination of something we have already learned.

2.4.3 Box Spreads

In Reading 72 we exploited an arbitrage opportunity with a neutral position three alternative ways: using put–call parity, using the binomial model, or using the Black–Scholes–Merton model. Exploiting put–call parity requires a position in the underlying. Using the binomial or Black–Scholes–Merton model requires that the model holds in the market. In addition, both models require a position in the underlying and an estimate of the volatility.

A **box spread** can also be used to exploit an arbitrage opportunity but it requires that neither the binomial nor Black–Scholes–Merton model holds, it needs no estimate of the volatility, and all of the transactions can be executed within the options market, making implementation of the strategy simpler, faster, and with lower transaction costs.

In basic terms, a box spread is a combination of a bull spread and a bear spread. Suppose we buy the call with exercise price X_1 and sell the call with exercise price X_2. This set of transactions is a bull spread. Then we buy the put with exercise price X_2 and sell the put with exercise price X_1. This is a bear spread. Intuitively, it should sound like a combination of a bull spread and a bear spread would leave the investor with a fairly neutral position, and indeed, that is the case.

The value of the box spread at expiration is

$$V_T = \max(0,S_T - X_1) - \max(0,S_T - X_2) + \max(0,X_2 - S_T) - \max(0,X_1 - S_T)$$

Broken down into ranges, we have

$$V_T = 0 - 0 + X_2 - S_T - (X_1 - S_T) = X_2 - X_1 \quad \text{if } S_T \leq X_1$$
$$V_T = S_T - X_1 - 0 + X_2 - S_T - 0 = X_2 - X_1 \quad \text{if } X_1 < S_T < X_2$$
$$V_T = S_T - X_1 - (S_T - X_2) + 0 - 0 = X_2 - X_1 \quad \text{if } S_T \geq X_2$$

These outcomes are all the same. In each case, two of the four options expire in-the-money, and the other two expire out-of-the-money. In each case, the holder of the box spread ends up buying the underlying with one option, using either the long call at X_1 or the short put at X_1, and selling the underlying with another option, using either the long put at X_2 or the short call at X_2. The box spread thus results in buying the underlying at X_1 and selling it at X_2. This outcome is known at the start.

The initial value of the transaction is the value of the long call, short call, long put, and short put, $V_0 = c_1 - c_2 + p_2 - p_1$. The profit is, therefore, $\Pi = X_2 - X_1 - c_1 + c_2 - p_2 + p_1$.

In contrast to all of the other strategies, the outcome is simple. In all cases, we end up with the same result. Using the options with exercise prices of 1950 and 2050, which have premiums of $c_1 = 108.43$, $c_2 = 59.98$, $p_1 = 56.01$, and $p_2 = 107.39$, the value at expiration is always $2050 - 1950 = 100$ and the profit is always $\Pi = 100 - 108.43 + 59.98 - 107.39 + 56.01 = 0.17$. This value may seem remarkably low. We shall see why momentarily.

The initial value of the box spread is $c_1 - c_2 + p_2 - p_1$. The payoff at expiration is $X_2 - X_1$. Because the transaction is risk free, the present value of the payoff, discounted using the risk-free rate, should equal the initial outlay. Hence, we should have

$$(X_2 - X_1)/(1 + r)^T = c_1 - c_2 + p_2 - p_1$$

If the present value of the payoff exceeds the initial value, the box spread is underpriced and should be purchased.

In this example, the initial outlay is $V_0 = 108.43 - 59.98 + 107.39 - 56.01 = 99.83$. To obtain the present value of the payoff, we need an interest rate and time to expiration. The prices of these options were obtained using a time to expiration of one month and a risk-free rate of 2.02 percent. The present value of the payoff is

$$(X_2 - X_1)/(1 + r)^r = (2050 - 1950)/(1.0202)^{1/12} = 99.83$$

In other words, this box spread is correctly priced. This result should not be surprising, because we noted that we used the Black–Scholes–Merton model to price these options. The model should not allow arbitrage opportunities of any form.

Recall that the profit from this transaction is 0.17, a very low value. This profit reflects the fact that the box spread is purchased at 99.83 and matures to a value of 100, a profit of 0.17, which is a return of the risk-free rate for one month.[19] The reason the profit seems so low is that it is just the risk-free rate.

Let us assume that one of the long options, say the put with exercise price of 2050, is underpriced. Let its premium be 105 instead of 107.39. Then the net premium would be $108.43 - 59.98 + 105 - 56.01 = 97.44$. Again, the present value of the payoff is 99.83. Hence, the box spread would generate a gain in value clearly in excess of the risk-free rate. If some combination of the options was such that the net premium is more than the present value of the payoff, then the box spread would be overpriced. Then we should sell the X_1 call and X_2 put and buy the X_2 call and X_1 put. Doing so would generate an outlay at expiration with a present value less than the initial value.

So to summarize the box spread, we say that

Value at expiration: $V_T = X_2 - X_1$
Profit: $\Pi = X_2 - X_1 - (c_1 - c_2 + p_2 - p_1)$
Maximum profit = (same as profit)
Maximum loss = (no loss is possible, given fair option prices)

---

[19] That is, $99.83(1.0202)^{1/12} \approx 100$. Hence, the profit of 0.17 is about 2.02 percent, for one month.

Breakeven: no breakeven; the transaction always earns the risk-free rate, given fair option prices.

Practice Problem 10

Consider a box spread consisting of options with exercise prices of 75 and 85. The call prices are 16.02 and 12.28 for exercise prices of 75 and 85, respectively. The put prices are 9.72 and 15.18 for exercise prices of 75 and 85, respectively. The options expire in six months and the discrete risk-free rate is 5.13 percent.

A. Determine the value of the box spread and the profit for any value of the underlying at expiration.

B. Show that this box spread is priced such that an attractive opportunity is available.

SOLUTIONS

A. The box spread always has a value at expiration of $X_2 - X_1 =$
85 − 75 = 10
$\Pi = V_T - (c_1 - c_2 + p_2 - p_1) = 10 - (16.02 - 12.28 + 15.18 - 9.72) = 0.80$

B. The box spread should be worth $(X_2 - X_1)/(1 + r)^T$, or

$$(85 - 75)/(1.0513)^{0.5} = 9.75$$

The cost of the box spread is 16.02 − 12.28 + 15.18 − 9.72 = 9.20. The box spread is thus underpriced. At least one of the long options is priced too low or at least one of the short options is priced too high; we cannot tell which. Nonetheless, we can execute this box spread, buying the call with exercise price $X_1 = 75$ and put with exercise price $X_2 = 85$ and selling the call with exercise price $X_2 = 85$ and put with exercise price $X_1 = 75$. This would cost 9.20. The present value of the payoff is 9.75. Therefore, the box spread would generate an immediate increase in value of 0.55.

We have now completed our discussion of equity option strategies. Although the strategies are applicable, with minor changes, to fixed-income securities, we shall not explore that area here. We shall, however, look at interest rate option strategies, which require some significant differences in presentation and understanding compared with equity option strategies.

INTEREST RATE OPTION STRATEGIES   3

In Reading 72 we examined options, which included a group of options in which the underlying is an interest rate and the exercise price is expressed in terms of a rate. Recall that this group of options consists of calls, which pay off if the option expires with the underlying interest rate above the exercise rate, and puts, which pay off if the option expires with the underlying interest rate below the exercise rate. Interest rate call and put options are usually purchased to protect against changes in interest rates. For dollar-based interest rate derivatives, the underlying is usually LIBOR but is always a specific rate, such as the rate on a 90- or 180-day underlying instrument. An interest rate option is based on a specific notional principal, which determines the payoff when the option is exercised. Traditionally, the payoff does not occur immediately upon exercise but is delayed by a period corresponding to the life of the underlying instrument from which the interest rate is taken, an issue we review below.

Recall from Reading 72 that the payoff of an interest rate call option (Equation 72-1) is

$$(\text{Notional principal}) \max(0, \text{Underlying rate at expiration} - \text{Exercise rate}) \left(\frac{\text{Days in underlying rate}}{360} \right)$$

where "days in underlying" refers to the maturity of the instrument from which the underlying rate is taken. In some cases, "days in underlying" may be the exact day count during a period. For example, if an interest rate option is used to hedge the interest paid over an m-day period, then "days in underlying" would be m. Even though LIBOR of 30, 60, 90, 180 days, etc., whichever is closest to m, might be used as the underlying rate, the actual day count would be m, the exact number of days. In such cases, the payment date is usually set at 30, 60, 90, 180, etc. days after the option expiration date. So, for example, 180-day LIBOR might be used as the underlying rate, and "days in underlying" could be 180 or perhaps 182, 183, etc. The most important point, however, is that the rate is determined on one day, the option expiration, and payment is made m days later. This practice is standard in floating-rate loans and thus is used with interest rate options, which are designed to manage the risk of floating-rate loans.

Likewise, the payoff of an interest rate put (Equation 72-2) is

$$(\text{Notional principal}) \max(0, \text{Exercise rate} - \text{Underlying rate at expiration}) \left(\frac{\text{Days in underlying rate}}{360} \right)$$

Now let us take a look at some applications of interest rate options.

3.1 Using Interest Rate Calls with Borrowing

Let us examine an application of an interest rate call to establish a maximum interest rate for a loan to be taken out in the future. In brief, a company can buy an interest rate call that pays off from increases in the underlying interest rate beyond a chosen level. The call pay-off then compensates for the higher interest rate the company has to pay on the loan.

Consider the case of a company called Global Computer Technology (GCT), which occasionally takes out short-term loans in U.S. dollars with the rate tied to LIBOR. Anticipating that it will take out a loan at a later date, GCT recognizes the potential for an interest rate increase by that time. In this example, today is 14 April, and GCT expects to borrow $40 million on 20 August at LIBOR plus 200 basis points. The loan will involve the receipt of the money on 20 August with full repayment of principal and interest 180 days later on 16 February. GCT would like protection against higher interest rates, so it purchases an interest rate call on 180-day LIBOR to expire on 20 August. GCT chooses an exercise rate of 5 percent. This option gives it the right to receive an interest payment of the difference between the 20 August LIBOR and 5 percent. If GCT exercises the option on 20 August, the payment will occur 180 days later on 16 February when the loan is paid off. The cost of the call is $100,000, which is paid on 14 April. LIBOR on 14 April is 5.5 percent.

The transaction is designed such that if LIBOR is above 5 percent on 20 August, GCT will benefit and be protected against increases in interest rates. To determine how the transaction works, we need to know the effective rate on the loan. Note that the sequence of events is as follows:

14 April ———————→ 20 August ———————→ 16 February
GCT buys call   Call expires; loan starts   Loan repaid and call payoff made

So cash is paid for the call on 14 April. Cash proceeds from the loan are received on 20 August. On 16 February, the loan is repaid and the call payoff (if any) is made.

To evaluate the effectiveness of the overall transaction, we need to determine how the call affects the loan. Therefore, we need to incorporate the payment of the call premium on 14 April into the cash flow on the loan. So, it would be appropriate to compound the call premium from 14 April to 20 August. In effect, we need to know what the call, purchased on 14 April, effectively costs on 20 August. We compound its premium for the 128 days from 14 April to 20 August at the rate at which GCT would have to borrow on 14 April. This rate would be LIBOR on 14 April plus 200 basis points, or 7.5 percent. The call premium thus effectively costs

$$\$100,000\left[1 + 0.075\left(\frac{128}{360}\right)\right] = \$102,667$$

on 20 August.[20] On that date, GCT takes out the loan, thereby receiving $40 million. We should, however, reduce this amount by $102,667, because GCT effectively receives less money because it must buy the call. So, the loan proceeds are effectively $40,000,000 − $102,667 = $39,897,333.

Next we must calculate the amount of interest paid on the loan and the amount of any call payoff. Let us assume that LIBOR on 20 August is 8 percent. In that case, the loan rate will be 10 percent. The interest on the loan will be

$$\$40,000,000(0.10)\left(\frac{128}{360}\right) = \$2,000,000$$

This amount, plus $40 million principal, is repaid on 16 February. With LIBOR assumed to be 8 percent on 20 August, the option payoff is

$$\$40,000,000 \max(0, 0.08 - 0.05)\left(\frac{128}{360}\right) = \$40,000,000(0.03)\left(\frac{128}{360}\right) = \$600,000$$

This amount is paid on 16 February. The effective interest paid on 16 February is thus $2,000,000 − $600,000 = $1,400,000. So, GCT effectively receives $39,897,333 on 20 August and pays back $40,000,000 plus $1,400,000 or $41,400,000 on 16 February. The effective annual rate is

$$\left(\frac{\$41,400,000}{\$39,897,333}\right)^{365/180} - 1 = 0.0779$$

---

[20] The interpretation of this calculation is that GCT's cost of funds is 7.5 percent, making the option premium effectively $102,667 by the time the loan is taken out.

Exhibit 74-13 presents a complete description of the transaction and the results for a range of possible LIBORs on 20 August. Exhibit 74-14 illustrates the effective loan rate compared with LIBOR on 20 August. We see that the strategy places an effective ceiling on the rate on the loan of about 7.79 percent while enabling GCT to benefit from decreases in LIBOR. Of course, a part of this maximum rate is the 200 basis point spread over LIBOR that GCT must pay.[21] In effect, the company's maximum rate without the spread is 5.79 percent. This reflects the exercise rate of 5.5 percent plus the effect of the option premium.

EXHIBIT 74-13 Outcomes for an Anticipated Loan Protected with an Interest Rate Call

Scenario (14 April)

Global Computer Technology (GCT) is a U.S. corporation that occasionally undertakes short-term borrowings in U.S. dollars with the rate tied to LIBOR. To facilitate its cash flow planning, it buys an interest rate call to put a ceiling on the rate it pays while enabling it to benefit if rates fall. A call gives GCT the right to receive the difference between LIBOR on the expiration date and the exercise rate it chooses when it purchases the option. The payoff of the call is determined on the expiration date, but the payment is not received until a certain number of days later, corresponding to the maturity of the underlying LIBOR. This feature matches the timing of the interest payment on the loan.

Action

GCT determines that it will borrow $40 million at LIBOR plus 200 basis points on 20 August. The loan will be repaid with a single payment of principal and interest 180 days later on 16 February.

To protect against increases in LIBOR between 14 April and 20 August, GCT buys a call option on LIBOR with an exercise rate of 5 percent to expire on 20 August with the underlying being 180-day LIBOR. The call premium is $100,000. We summarize the information as follows:

Loan amount:	$40,000,000
Underlying:	180-day LIBOR
Spread:	200 basis points over LIBOR
Current LIBOR:	5.5 percent
Expiration:	20 August (128 days later)
Exercise rate:	5 percent
Call premium:	$100,000

Scenario (20 August)

LIBOR on 20 August is 8 percent.

Outcome and Analysis

For any LIBOR, the call payoff at expiration is given below and will be received 180 days later:

$$\$40,000,000 \max(0, \text{LIBOR} - 0.05)\left(\frac{180}{360}\right)$$

For LIBOR of 8 percent, the payoff is

$$\$40,000,000 \max(0, 0.08 - 0.05)\left(\frac{180}{360}\right) = \$600,000$$

---

[21] It should be noted that the effective annual rate is actually more than 200 basis points. For example, if someone borrows $100 at 2 percent for 180 days, the amount repaid would be $100[1 + 0.02(180/360)] = $101. The effective annual rate would be $(\$101/\$100)^{365/180} - 1 = 0.0204$.

The premium compounded from 14 April to 20 August at the original LIBOR of 5.5 percent plus 200 basis points is

$$\$100{,}000\left[1 + (0.055 + 0.02)\left(\frac{128}{360}\right)\right] - \$102{,}667$$

So the call costs $100,000 on 14 April, which is equivalent to $102,667 on 20 August. The effective loan proceeds are $40,000,000 − $102,667 = $39,897,333. The loan interest is

$$\$40{,}000{,}000(\text{LIBOR on 20 August} + 200 \text{ basis points})\left(\frac{180}{360}\right)$$

For LIBOR of 8 percent, the loan interest is

$$\$40{,}000{,}000(0.08 + 0.02)\left(\frac{180}{360}\right) = \$2{,}000{,}000$$

The call payoff was given above. The loan interest minus the call payoff is the effective interest. The effective rate on the loan is

$$\left(\frac{\$40{,}000.000 \text{ plus effective interest}}{\$39{,}897{,}333}\right)^{365/180} - 1$$

$$= \left(\frac{\$40{,}000{,}000 + \$2{,}000{,}000 - \$600{,}000}{\$39{,}897{,}333}\right)^{365/180} - 1 = 0.0779$$

or 7.79 percent.

The results are shown below for a range of LIBORs on 20 August.

LIBOR on 20 August	Loan Rate	Loan Interest Paid on 16 February	Call Payoff	Effective Interest	Effective Loan Rate
0.010	0.030	$600,000	$0	$600,000	0.0360
0.015	0.035	700,000	0	700,000	0.0412
0.020	0.040	800,000	0	800,000	0.0464
0.025	0.045	900,000	0	900,000	0.0516
0.030	0.050	1,000,000	0	1,000,000	0.0568
0.035	0.055	1,100,000	0	1,100,000	0.0621
0.040	0.060	1,200,000	0	1,200,000	0.0673
0.045	0.065	1,300,000	0	1,300,000	0.0726
0.050	0.070	1,400,000	0	1,400,000	0.0779
0.055	0.075	1,500,000	100,000	1,400,000	0.0779
0.060	0.080	1,600,000	200,000	1,400,000	0.0779
0.065	0.085	1,700,000	300,000	1,400,000	0.0779
0.070	0.090	1,800,000	400,000	1,400,000	0.0779
0.075	0.095	1,900,000	500,000	1,400,000	0.0779
0.080	0.100	2,000,000	600,000	1,400,000	0.0779
0.085	0.105	2,100,000	700,000	1,400,000	0.0779
0.090	0.110	2,200,000	800,000	1,400,000	0.0779

EXHIBIT 74-14 The Effective Rate on an Anticipated Future Loan Protected with an Interest Rate Call Option

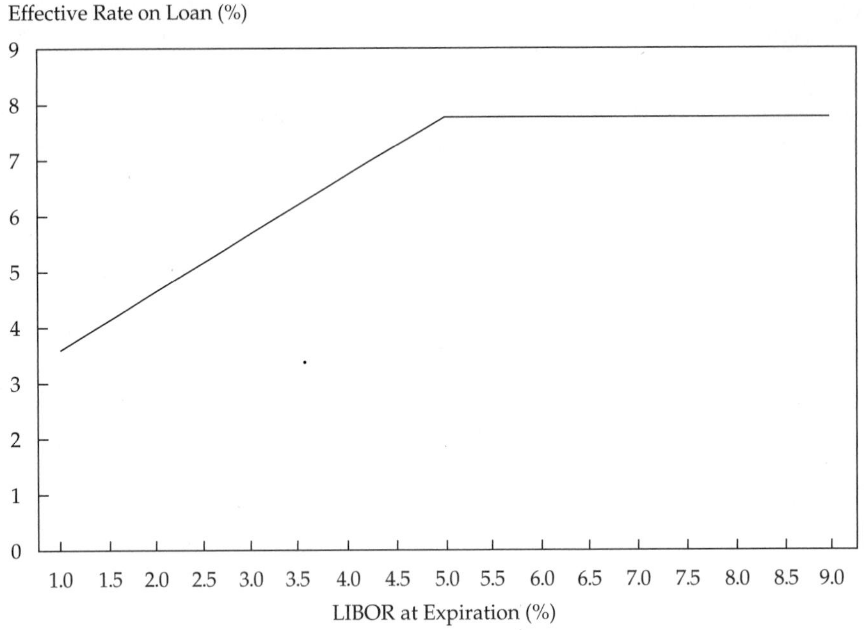

Practice Problem 11

On 10 January, ResTex Ltd. determines that it will need to borrow $5 million on 15 February at 90-day LIBOR plus 300 basis points. The loan will be an add-on interest loan in which ResTex will receive $5 million and pay it back plus interest on 16 May. To manage the risk associated with the interest rate on 15 February, ResTex buys an interest rate call that expires on 15 February and pays off on 16 May. The exercise rate is 5 percent, and the option premium is $10,000. The current 90-day LIBOR is 5.25 percent. Assume that this rate, plus 300 basis points, is the rate it would borrow at for any period of up to 90 days if the loan were taken out today. Interest is computed on the exact number of days divided by 360.

Determine the effective annual rate on the loan for each of the following outcomes:

i. 90-day LIBOR on 15 February is 6 percent.

ii. 90-day LIBOR on 15 February is 4 percent.

SOLUTION

First we need to compound the premium from 10 January to 15 February, which is 36 days. This calculation tells us the effective cost of the call as of the time the loan is taken out:

$$\$10,000\left[1 + (0.0525 + 0.03)\left(\frac{36}{360}\right)\right] = \$10,083$$

The loan proceeds will therefore be $5,000,000 − $10,083 = $4,989,917.

    i. LIBOR is 6 percent. The loan rate will be 9 percent.

    The interest on the loan will be $\$5,000,000(0.06 + 0.03)(90/360) = \$112,500$.

    The option payoff will be $\$5,000,000 \max(0, 0.06 - 0.05)(90/360) = \$12,500$.

    Therefore, the effective interest will be $\$112,500 - \$12,500 = \$100,000$.

    The effective rate on the loan will be $\left(\dfrac{\$5,000,000 + \$1,000,000}{\$4,989,917}\right)^{365/90} - 1 = 0.0925$.

    Of course, a little more than 300 basis points of this amount is the spread.

    ii. LIBOR is 4 percent. The loan rate will be 7 percent.

    The interest on the loan will be $\$5,000,000(0.04 + 0.03)(90/360) = \$87,500$.

    The option payoff will be $\$5,000,000 \max(0, 0.04 - 0.05)(90/360) = \$0.00$.

    The effective interest will, therefore, be $\$87,500$.

    The effective rate on the loan will be $\left(\dfrac{\$5,000,000 + \$87,500}{\$4,989,917}\right)^{365/90} - 1 = 0.0817$.

    Of course, a little more than 300 basis points of this amount is the spread.

Whereas interest rate call options are appropriate for borrowers, lenders also face the risk of interest rates changing. As you may have guessed, they make use of interest rate puts.

3.2 Using Interest Rate Puts with Lending

Now consider an application of an interest rate put to establish a minimum interest rate for a commitment to give a loan in the future. A lender can buy a put that pays off if the interest rate falls below a chosen level. The put payoff then compensates the bank for the lower interest rate on the loan.

    For example, consider Arbitrage Bank Inc. (ABInc) which makes loan commitments to corporations. It stands ready to make a loan at LIBOR at a future date. To protect itself against decreases in interest rates between the time of the commitment and the time the loan is taken out, it buys interest rate puts. These options pay off if LIBOR is below the exercise rate at expiration. If LIBOR is above the exercise rate at expiration, the option expires unexercised and the lender benefits from the higher rate on the loan.

    In this example, ABInc makes a commitment on 15 March to lend $50 million at 90-day LIBOR plus 2.5 percent on 1 May, which is 47 days later. Current LIBOR is 7.25 percent. It buys a put with an exercise rate of 7 percent for $62,500. Assume that the opportunity cost of lending in the LIBOR market is LIBOR plus a spread of 2.5 percent. Therefore, the effective cost of the premium compounded to the option's expiration is[22]

$$\$62,500\left[1 + (0.0725 + 0.025)\left(\frac{47}{360}\right)\right] = \$63,296$$

---

[22] The interpretation of this calculation is that the bank could have otherwise made a loan of $62,500, which would have paid back $63,296 on 1 May.

When it lends $50 million on 1 May, it effectively has an outlay of $50,000,000 + $63,296 = $50,063,296. The loan rate is set on 1 May and the interest, paid 90 days later on 30 July, is

$$\$50,000,000\left[\text{LIBOR on 1 May plus 250 basis points}\left(\frac{90}{360}\right)\right]$$

The put payoff is

$$\$50,000,000\max(0,0.07-\text{LIBOR on 1 May})\left(\frac{90}{360}\right)$$

The loan interest plus the put payoff make up the effective interest. The effective rate on the loan is

$$\left(\frac{\text{Principal plus effective interest}}{\$50,063,296}\right)^{365/90}-1$$

Suppose LIBOR on 1 May is 6 percent. In that case, the loan rate will be 8.5 percent, and the interest on the loan will be

$$\$50,000,000\left[(0.06+0.025)\left(\frac{90}{360}\right)\right]=\$1,062,500$$

The put payoff is

$$\$50,000,000\max(0,0.07-0.06)\left(\frac{90}{360}\right)=\$125,000$$

This amount is paid on 30 July. The put cost of $62,500 on 15 March is equivalent to paying $63,296 on 1 May. Thus, on 1 May the bank effectively commits $50,000,000 + $63,296 = $50,063,296. The effective interest it receives is the loan interest of $1,062,500 plus the put payoff of $125,000, or $1,187,500. The effective annual rate is

$$\left(\frac{\$50,000,000+\$1,187,500}{\$1,187,500}\right)^{365/90}-1=0.0942$$

Exhibit 74-15 presents the results for a range of possible LIBORs at expiration, and Exhibit 74-16 graphs the effective loan rate against LIBOR on 1 May. Note how there is a minimum effective loan rate of 9.42 percent. Of this rate, 250 basis points is automatically built in as the loan spread.[23] The remaining amount reflects the exercise rate on the put of 7 percent minus the cost of the put premium.

EXHIBIT 74-15 Outcomes for an Anticipated Loan Protected with an Interest Rate Put

Scenario (15 March)

Arbitrage Bank Inc. (ABInc) is a U.S. bank that makes loan commitments to corporations. When ABInc makes these commitments, it recognizes the risk that LIBOR will fall by the date the loan is taken out. ABInc protects itself against interest rate decreases by purchasing interest rate puts, which give it the right to receive the difference between the exercise rate it chooses and LIBOR at expiration. LIBOR is currently 7.25 percent.

---

[23] As in the case of the borrower, the spread is effectively more than 250 basis points when the effective annual rate is determined. For this 90-day loan, this effectively amounts to 256 basis points

Action

ABInc commits to lending $50 million to a company at 90-day LIBOR plus 250 basis points. The loan will be a single-payment loan, meaning that it will be made on 1 May and the principal and interest will be repaid 90 days later on 30 July.

To protect against decreases in LIBOR between 15 March and 1 May, ABInc buys a put option with an exercise rate of 7 percent to expire on 1 May with the underlying being 90-day LIBOR. The put premium is $62,500. We summarize the information as follows:

Loan amount:	$50,000,000
Underlying:	90-day LIBOR
Spread:	250 basis points over LIBOR
Current LIBOR:	7.25 percent
Expiration:	1 May
Exercise rate:	7 percent
Put premium:	$62,500

Scenario (1 May)

LIBOR is now 6 percent.

Outcome and Analysis

For any LIBOR, the payoff at expiration is given below and will be received 90 days later:

$$\$50,000,000 \max(0,0.07 - \text{LIBOR})\left(\frac{90}{360}\right)$$

For LIBOR of 6 percent, the payoff is

$$\$50,000,000 \max(0,0.07 - 0.060)\left(\frac{90}{360}\right) = \$125,000$$

The premium compounded from 15 March to 1 May at current LIBOR plus 250 basis points is

$$\$62,500\left[1 + (0.0725 + 0.025)\left(\frac{47}{360}\right)\right] = \$63,296$$

So the put costs $62,500 on 15 March, which is equivalent to $63,296 on 1 May. The effective amount loaned is $50,000,000 + $63,296 = $50,063,296. For any LIBOR, the loan interest is

$$\$50,000,000\left[\text{LIBOR on 1 May plus 250 basis points}\left(\frac{90}{360}\right)\right]$$

With LIBOR at 6 percent, the interest is

$$\$50,000,000\left[(0.06 + 0.025)\left(\frac{90}{360}\right)\right] = \$1,062,500$$

The loan interest plus the put payoff is the effective interest on the loan. The effective rate on the loan is

$$\left(\frac{\text{Principal plus effective interest}}{\$50,063,296}\right)^{365/90} - 1$$

$$= \left(\frac{\$50,000,000 + \$1,062,500 + \$125,000}{\$50,063,296}\right)^{365/90} - 1 = 0.0942$$

or 9.42 percent. The results are shown below for a range of LIBORs on 1 May.

EXHIBIT 74-15 Outcomes for an Anticipated Loan Protected with an Interest Rate Put (continued)

LIBOR on 1 May	Loan Rate	Loan Interest Paid on 30 July	Put Payoff	Effective Interest	Effective Loan Rate
0.030	0.055	$687,500	$500,000	$1,187,500	0.0942
0.035	0.060	750,000	437,500	1,187,500	0.0942
0.040	0.065	812,500	375,000	1,187,500	0.0942
0.045	0.070	875,000	312,500	1,187,500	0.0942
0.050	0.075	937,500	250,000	1,187,500	0.0942
0.055	0.080	1,000,000	187,500	1,187,500	0.0942
0.060	0.085	1,062,500	125,000	1,187,500	0.0942
0.065	0.090	1,125,000	62,500	1,187,500	0.0942
0.070	0.095	1,187,500	0	1,187,500	0.0942
0.075	0.100	1,250,000	0	1,250,000	0.0997
0.080	0.105	1,312,500	0	1,312,500	0.1051
0.085	0.110	1,375,000	0	1,375,000	0.1106
0.090	0.115	1,437,500	0	1,437,500	0.1161
0.095	0.120	1,500,000	0	1,500,000	0.1216
0.100	0.125	1,562,500	0	1,562,500	0.1271
0.105	0.130	1,625,000	0	1,625,000	0.1327
0.110	0.135	1,687,500	0	1,687,500	0.1382

EXHIBIT 74-16 The Effective Rate on an Anticipated Loan with an Interest Rate Put Option

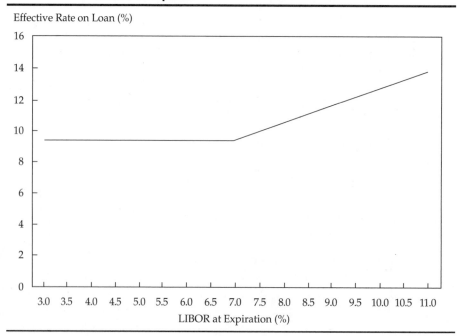

Practice Problem 12

State Bank and Trust (SBT) is a lender in the floating-rate instrument market, but it has been hurt by recent interest rate decreases. SBT often makes loan commitments for its customers and then accepts the rate in effect on the day the loan is taken out. SBT has avoided floating-rate financing in the past. It takes out a certain amount of fixed-rate financing in advance to cover its loan commitments. One particularly large upcoming loan has it worried. This is a $100 million loan to be made in 65 days at 180-day LIBOR plus 100 basis points. The loan will be paid back 182 days after being taken out, and interest will be based on an exact day count and 360 days in a year. Current LIBOR is 7.125 percent, which is the rate it could borrow at now for any period less than 180 days. SBT considers the purchase of an interest rate put to protect it against an interest rate decrease over the next 65 days. The put will have an exercise price of 7 percent and a premium of $475,000.

Determine the effective annual rate on the loan for the following outcomes:

i. 180-day LIBOR at the option expiration is 9 percent.
ii. 180-day LIBOR at the option expiration is 5 percent.

SOLUTION

First we need to compound the premium for 65 days. This calculation tells us the effective cost of the put as of the time the loan is made:

$$\$475,000\left[1 + (0.07125 + 0.01)\left(\frac{65}{360}\right)\right] = \$481,968$$

The outlay will effectively be $100,000,000 + $481,968 = $100,481,968.

i. LIBOR is 9 percent. The loan rate will be 10 percent.
The interest on the loan will be $100,000,000(0.09 + 0.01) (182/360) = $5,055,556.
The option payoff will be $100,000,000 max(0,0.07 − 0.09) (182/360) = $0.0.
Because there is no option payoff, the effective interest will be $5,055,556.
The effective rate on the loan will be
$$\left(\frac{\$100,000,000 + \$5,055,556}{\$100,481,968}\right)^{365/182} - 1 = 0.0934.$$
Of course, a little more than 100 basis points of this amount is the spread.

ii. LIBOR is 5 percent. The loan will be 6 percent.
The interest on the loan will be $100,000,000(0.05 + 0.01) (182/360) = $3,033,333.
The option payoff will be $100,000,000 max(0,0.07 − 0.05) (182/360) = $1,011,111.
The effective interest will, therefore, be $3,033,333 + $1,011,111 = $4,044,444.
The effective rate on the loan will be
$$\left(\frac{\$100,000,000 + \$4,044,444}{\$100,481,968}\right)^{365/182} - 1 = 0.0724.$$
Of course, a little more than 100 basis points of this amount is the spread.

Interest rate calls and puts can be combined into packages of multiple options, which are widely used to manage the risk of floating-rate loans.

3.3 Using an Interest Rate Cap with a Floating-Rate Loan

As we have described previously in this book, many corporate loans are floating-rate loans. They require periodic interest payments in which the rate is reset on a regularly scheduled basis. Because there is more than one interest payment, there is effectively more than one distinct risk. If a borrower wanted to use an interest rate call to place a ceiling on the effective borrowing rate, it would require more than one call. In effect, it would require a distinct call option expiring on each interest rate reset date. As described in Reading 72, a combination of interest rate call options designed to align with the rates on a loan is called a **cap.** The component options are called **caplets.** Each caplet is distinct in having its own expiration date, but typically the exercise rate on each caplet is the same.

To illustrate the use of a cap, consider a company called Measure Technology (MesTech), which borrows in the floating-rate loan market. It usually takes out a loan for several years at a spread over LIBOR, paying the interest semiannually and the full principal at the end. On 15 April, MesTech takes out a $10 million three-year loan at 100 basis points over 180-day LIBOR from a bank called SenBank. Current 180-day LIBOR is 9 percent, which sets the rate for the first six-month period at 10 percent. Interest payments will be on the 15th of October and April for three years. This means that the day counts for the six payments will be 183, 182, 183, 182, 183, and 182.

To protect against increases in interest rates, MesTech purchases an interest rate cap with an exercise rate of 8 percent. The component caplets expire on 15 October, the following 15 April, and so forth until the last caplet expires on a subsequent 15 October. The loan has six interest payments, but because the first rate is already set, there are only five risky payments so the cap will contain five caplets. The payoff of each caplet will be determined on its expiration date, but the caplet payoff, if any, will actually be made on the next payment date. This enables the caplet payoff to line up with the date on which the loan interest is paid. The cap premium, paid up front on 15 April, is $75,000.

In the example of a single interest rate call, we looked at a range of outcomes several hundred basis points around the exercise rate. In a cap, however, many more outcomes are possible. Ideally we would examine a range of outcomes for each caplet. In the example of a single cap, we looked at the exercise rate and 8 rates above and below for a total of 17 rates. For five distinct rate resets, this same procedure would require 5^{17} or more than 762 billion different possibilities. So, we shall just look at one possible combination of rates.

We shall examine a set of outcomes in which LIBOR is

8.50 percent on 15 October
7.25 percent on 15 April the following year
7.00 percent on the following 15 October
6.90 percent on the following 15 April
8.75 percent on the following 15 October

The loan interest is computed as

$$\$10,000,000(\text{LIBOR on previous reset date} + 100 \text{ basis points})\left(\frac{\text{Days in settlement period}}{360}\right)$$

Thus, the first interest payment is

$$\$10,000,000(0.10)\left(\frac{183}{360}\right) = \$508,333$$

which is based on 183 days between 15 April and 15 October. This amount is certain, because the first interest rate has already been set. The remaining interest payments are based on the assumption we made above about the course of LIBOR over the life of the loan.

The results for these assumed rates are shown in the table at the end of Exhibit 7-17. Note several things about the effective interest, displayed in the last column. First, the initial interest payment is much higher than the other interest payments because the initial rate is somewhat higher than the remaining rates that prevailed over the life of the loan. Also, recall that the initial rate is already set, and it would make no sense to add a caplet to cover the initial rate, because the caplet would have to expire immediately in order to pay off on the first 15 October. If the caplet expired immediately, the amount MesTech would have to pay for it would be the amount of the caplet payoff, discounted for the deferral of the payoff. In other words, it would make no sense to have an option, or any derivative for that matter, that is purchased and expires immediately. Note also the variation in the effective interest payments, which occurs for two reasons. One is that, in contrast to previous examples, interest is computed over the exact number of days in the period. Thus, even if the rate were the same, the interest could vary by the effect of one or two days of interest. The other reason is that in some cases the caplets do expire with value, thereby reducing the effective interest paid.

EXHIBIT 74-17 Interest Rate Cap

Scenario (15 April)

Measure Technology (MesTech) is a corporation that borrows in the floating-rate instrument market. It typically takes out a loan for several years at a spread over LIBOR. MesTech pays the interest semiannually and the full principal at the end.

To protect against rising interest rates over the life of the loan, MesTech usually buys an interest rate cap in which the component caplets expire on the dates on which the loan rate is reset. The cap seller is a derivatives dealer.

Action

MesTech takes out a $10 million three-year loan at 100 basis points over LIBOR. The payments will be made semiannually. The lender is SenBank. Current LIBOR is 9 percent, which means that the first rate will be at 10 percent. Interest will be based on 1/360 of the exact number of days in the six-month period. MesTech selects an exercise rate of 8 percent. The caplets will expire on 15 October, 15 April of the following year, and so on for three years, but the caplet payoffs will occur on the next payment date to correspond with the interest payment based on LIBOR that determines the cap payoff. The cap premium is $75,000. We thus have the following information:

Loan amount:	$10,000,000
Underlying:	180-day LIBOR
Spread:	100 basis points over LIBOR
Current LIBOR:	9 percent
Interest based on:	actual days/360
Component caplets:	five caplets expiring 15 October, 15 April, etc.
Exercise rate:	8 percent
Cap premium:	$75,000

EXHIBIT 74-17 Interest Rate Cap (continued)

Scenario (various dates throughout the loan)

Shown below is one particular set of outcomes for LIBOR:

8.50 percent on 15 October
7.25 percent on 15 April the following year
7.00 percent on the following 15 October
6.90 percent on the following 15 April
8.75 percent on the following 15 October

Outcome and Analysis

The loan interest due is computed as

$$\$10,000,000(\text{LIBOR on previous reset date} + 100 \text{ basis points})\left(\frac{\text{Days in settlement period}}{360}\right)$$

The caplet payoff is

$$\$10,000,000 \max(0,\text{LIBOR on previous reset date} - 0.08)\left(\frac{\text{Days in settlement period}}{360}\right)$$

The previous reset date is the expiration date of the caplet. The effective interest is the interest due minus the caplet payoff.

The first caplet expires on the first 15 October and pays off the following April, because LIBOR on 15 October was 8.5 percent. The payoff is computed as

$$\$10,000,000 \max(0,0.085 - 0.08)\left(\frac{182}{360}\right) = \$10,000,000(0.005)\left(\frac{182}{360}\right) = \$25,278$$

which is based on 182 days between 15 October and 15 April. The following table shows the payments on the loan and cap:

Date	LIBOR	Loan Rate	Days in Period	Interest Due	Caplet Payoffs	Effective Interest
15 April	0.0900	0.1000				
15 October	0.0850	0.0950	183	$508,333		$508,333
15 April	0.0725	0.0825	182	480,278	$25,278	455,000
15 October	0.0700	0.0800	183	419,375	0	419,375
15 April	0.0690	0.0790	182	404,444	0	404,444
15 October	0.0875	0.0975	183	401,583	0	401,583
15 April			182	492,917	37,917	455,000

Note that on the following three dates, the caplets are out-of-the-money, because the LIBORs are all lower than 8 percent. On the final 15 October, however, LIBOR is 8.75 percent, which leads to a final caplet payoff of $37,917 on the following 15 April, at which time the loan principal is repaid.

We do not show the effective rate on the loan. Because the loan has multiple payments, the effective rate would be analogous to the internal rate of return on a capital investment project or the yield-to-maturity on a bond. This rate would have to be found with a financial calculator or spreadsheet, and we would have to account for the principal received up front and paid back at maturity, as well as the cap premium. It is sufficient for us to see that the cap protects the borrower any time the rate rises above the exercise rate and allows the borrower to benefit from rates lower than the exercise rate.

Finally, there is one circumstance under which this cap might contain a sixth caplet, one expiring on the date on which the loan is taken out. If the borrower purchased the cap in advance of taking out the loan, the first loan rate would not be set until the day the loan is actually taken out. The borrower would thus have an incentive to include a caplet that would protect the first rate setting.

Practice Problem 13

Healthy Biosystems (HBIO) is a typical floating-rate borrower, taking out loans at LIBOR plus a spread. On 15 January 2002, it takes out a loan of $25 million for one year with quarterly payments on 12 April, 14 July, 16 October, and the following 14 January. The underlying rate is 90-day LIBOR, and HBIO will pay a spread of 250 basis points. Interest is based on the exact number of days in the period. Current 90-day LIBOR is 6.5 percent. HBIO purchases an interest rate cap for $20,000 that has an exercise rate of 7 percent and has caplets expiring on the rate reset dates.

Determine the effective interest payments if LIBOR on the following dates is as given:

    12 April: 7.250 percent
    14 July: 6.875 percent
    16 October: 7.125 percent

SOLUTION

The interest due for each period is computed as $25,000,000(LIBOR on previous reset date + 0.0250)(Days in period/360). For example, the first interest payment is calculated as $25,000,000(0.065 + 0.025)(87/360) = $543,750, based on the fact that there are 87 days between 15 January and 12 April. Each caplet payoff is computed as $25,000,000 max(0,LIBOR on previous reset date − 0.07)(Days in period/360), where the "previous reset date" is the caplet expiration. Payment is deferred until the date on which the interest is paid at the given LIBOR. For example, the caplet expiring on 12 April is worth $25,000,000 max(0,0.0725 − 0.07)(93/360) = $16,145, which is paid on 14 July and is based on the fact that there are 93 days between 12 April and 14 July.

The effective interest is the actual interest minus the caplet payoff. The payments are shown in the table below:

Date	LIBOR	Loan Rate	Days in Period	Interest Due	Caplet Payoff	Effective Interest
15 January	0.065	0.09				
12 April	0.0725	0.0975	87	$543,750		$543,750
14 July	0.06875	0.09375	93	629,688	$16,146	613,542
16 October	0.07125	0.09625	94	611,979	0	611,979
14 January			90	601,563	7,813	593,750

Lenders who use floating-rate loans face the same risk as borrowers. As such they can make use of combinations of interest rate puts.

3.4 Using an Interest Rate Floor with a Floating-Rate Loan

Let us now consider the same problem from the point of view of the lender, which is Sen-Bank in this example. It would be concerned about falling interest rates. It could, there-fore, buy a combination of interest rate put options that expire on the various interest rate reset dates. This combination of puts is called a **floor,** and the component options are called **floorlets.** Specifically, let SenBank buy a floor with floorlets expiring on the interest rate reset dates and with an exercise rate of 8 percent. The premium is $72,500.[24] Exhibit 7-18 illustrates the results using the same outcomes we looked at when examining the interest rate cap. Note that the floorlet expires in-the-money on three dates when LIBOR is less than 8 percent, and out-of-the-money on two dates when LIBOR is greater than 8 percent. In those cases in which the floorlet expires in-the-money, the actual payoff does not occur until the next settlement period. This structure aligns the floorlet payoffs with the interest payments they are designed to protect. We see that the floor protects the lender against falling interest rates. Any time the rate is below 8 percent, the floor compensates the bank for any difference between the rate and 8 percent. When the rate is above 8 percent, the floorlets simply expire unused.

EXHIBIT 74-18 Interest Rate Floor

Scenario (15 April)

SenBank lends in the floating-rate instrument market. Often it uses floating-rate financing, thereby protecting itself against decreases in the floating rates on its loans. Sometimes, however, it finds it can get a better rate with fixed-rate financing, but it then leaves itself exposed to interest rate decreases on its floating-rate loans. Its loans are typically for several years at a spread over LIBOR with interest paid semiannually and the full principal paid at the end.

To protect against falling interest rates over the life of the loan, SenBank buys an interest rate floor in which the component floorlets expire on the dates on which the loan rate is reset. The floor seller is a derivatives dealer.

Action

SenBank makes a $10 million three-year loan at 100 basis points over LIBOR to MesTech (see cap example). The payments will be made semiannually. Current LIBOR is 9 percent, which means that the first interest payment will be at 10 percent. Interest will be based on the exact number of days in the six-month period divided by 360. SenBank selects an exercise rate of 8 percent. The floorlets will expire on 15 October, 15 April of the following year, and so on for three years, but the floorlet payoffs will occur on the next payment date so as to correspond with the interest payment based on LIBOR that determines the floorlet payoff. The floor premium is $72,500. We thus have the following information:

Loan amount:	$10,000,000
Underlying:	180-day LIBOR
Spread:	100 basis points over LIBOR
Current LIBOR:	9 percent
Interest based on:	actual days/360

---

[24] Note that the premiums for the cap and floor are not the same. This difference occurs because the premiums for a call and a put with the same exercise price are not the same, as can be seen by examining put–call parity.

Component floorlets: five floorlets expiring 15 October, 15 April, etc.

Exercise rate: 8 percent

Floor premium: $72,500

Outcomes (various dates throughout the loan)

Shown below is one particular set of outcomes for LIBOR:

8.50 percent on 15 October

7.25 percent on 15 April the following year

7.00 percent on the following 15 October

6.90 percent on the following 15 April

8.75 percent on the following 15 October

Outcome and Analysis

The loan interest is computed as

$$\$10,000,000(\text{LIBOR on previous reset date} + 100 \text{ basis points})\left(\frac{\text{Day in settlement period}}{360}\right)$$

The floorlet payoff is

$$\$10,000,000\max(0,0.08 - \text{LIBOR on previous reset date})\left(\frac{\text{Days in settlement period}}{360}\right)$$

The effective interest is the interest due plus the floorlet payoff. The following table shows the payments on the loan and floor:

Date	LIBOR	Loan Rate	Days in Period	Interest Due	Floorlet Payoffs	Effective Interest
15 April	0.0900	0.1000				
15 October	0.0850	0.0950	183	$508,333		$508,333
15 April	0.0725	0.0825	182	480,278	$0	480,278
15 October	0.0700	0.0800	183	419,375	38,125	457,500
15 April	0.0690	0.0790	182	404,444	50,556	455,000
15 October	0.0875	0.0975	183	401,583	55,917	457,500
15 April			182	492,917	0	492,917

Practice Problem 14

Capitalized Bank (CAPBANK) is a lender in the floating-rate loan market. It uses fixed-rate financing on its floating-rate loans and buys floors to hedge the rate. On 1 May 2002, it makes a loan of $40 million at 180-day LIBOR plus 150 basis points. Interest will be paid on 1 November, the following 5 May, the following 1 November, and the following 2 May, at which time the principal will be repaid. The exercise rate is 4.5 percent, the floorlets expire on the rate reset dates, and the premium will be $120,000. Interest will be calculated based on the actual number of days in the period over 360. The current 180-day LIBOR is 5 percent.

Determine the effective interest payments CAPBANK will receive if LIBOR on the following dates is as given:

1 November: 4.875 percent
5 May: 4.25 percent
1 November: 5.125 percent

SOLUTION

The interest due for each period is computed as $40,000,000(LIBOR on previous reset date + 0.0150)(Days in period/360). For example, the first interest payment is $40,000,000(0.05 + 0.0150)(184/360) = $1,328,889, based on the fact that there are 184 days between 1 May and 1 November. Each floorlet payoff is computed as $40,000,000 max(0,0.045 − LIBOR on previous reset date)(Days in period/360), where the "previous reset date" is the floorlet expiration. Payment is deferred until the date on which the interest is paid at the given LIBOR. For example, the floorlet expiring on 5 May is worth $40,000,000 max(0,0.045 − 0.0425)(180/360) = $50,000, which is paid on 1 November and is based on the fact that there are 180 days between 5 May and 1 November.

The effective interest is the actual interest plus the floorlet payoff. The payments are shown in the table below:

Date	LIBOR	Loan Rate	Days in Period	Interest Due	Caplet Payoff	Effective Interest
1 May	0.05	0.065				
1 November	0.04875	0.06375	184	$1,328,889		$1,328,889
5 May	0.0425	0.0575	185	1,310,417	$0	1,310,417
1 November	0.05125	0.06625	180	1,150,000	50,000	1,200,000
2 May			182	1,339,722	0	1,339,722

When studying equity option strategies, we combined puts and calls into a single transaction called a collar. In a similar manner, we now combine caps and floors into a single transaction, also called a collar.

3.5 Using an Interest Rate Collar with a Floating-Rate Loan

As we showed above, borrowers are attracted to caps because they protect against rising interest rates. They do so, however, at the cost of having to pay a premium in cash up front. A collar combines a long position in a cap with a short position in a floor. The sale of the floor generates a premium that can be used to offset the premium on the cap. Although it is not necessary that the floor premium completely offset the cap premium, this arrangement is common.[25] The exercise

---

[25] It is even possible for the floor premium to be greater than the cap premium, thereby *generating cash* up front.

rate on the floor is selected such that the floor premium is precisely the cap premium. As with equity options, this type of strategy is called a zero-cost collar. Recall, however, that this term is a bit misleading because it suggests that this transaction has no true "cost." The cost is simply not up front in cash. The sale of the floor results in the borrower giving up any gains from interest rates below the exercise rate on the floor. Therefore, the borrower pays for the cap by giving away some of the gains from the possibility of falling rates.

Recall that for equity investors, the collar typically entails ownership of the underlying asset and the purchase of a put, which is financed with the sale of a call. In contrast, an interest rate collar is more commonly seen from the borrower's point of view: a position as a borrower and the purchase of a cap, which is financed by the sale of a floor. It is quite possible, however, that a lender would want a collar. The lender is holding an asset, the loan, and wants protection against falling interest rates, which can be obtained by buying a floor, which itself can be financed by selling a cap. Most interest rate collars, however, are initiated by borrowers.

In the example we used previously, MesTech borrows $10 million at LIBOR plus 100 basis points. The cap exercise rate is 8 percent, and the premium is $75,000. We now change the numbers a little and let MesTech set the exercise rate at 8.625 percent. To sell a floor that will generate the same premium as the cap, the exercise rate is set at 7.5 percent. It is not necessary for us to know the amounts of the cap and floor premiums; it is sufficient to know that they offset.

Exhibit 74-19 shows the collar results for the same set of interest rate outcomes we have been previously using. Note that on the first 15 October, LIBOR is between the cap and floor exercise rates, so neither the caplet nor the floorlet expires in-the-money. On the following 15 April, 15 October, and the next 15 April, the rate is below the floor exercise rate, so MesTech has to pay up on the expiring floorlets. On the final 15 October, LIBOR is above the cap exercise rate, so MesTech gets paid on its cap.

EXHIBIT 74-19 Interest Rate Collar

Scenario (15 April)

Consider the Measure Technology (MesTech) scenario described in the cap and floor example in Exhibits 74-17 and 74-18. MesTech is a corporation that borrows in the floating-rate instrument market. It typically takes out a loan for several years at a spread over LIBOR. MesTech pays the interest semiannually and the full principal at the end.

To protect against rising interest rates over the life of the loan, MesTech usually buys an interest rate cap in which the component caplets expire on the dates on which the loan rate is reset. To pay for the cost of the interest rate cap, MesTech can sell a floor at an exercise rate lower than the cap exercise rate.

Action

Consider the $10 million three-year loan at 100 basis points over LIBOR. The payments are made semiannually. Current LIBOR is 9 percent, which means that the first rate will be at 10 percent. Interest is based on the exact number of days in the six-month period divided by 360. MesTech selects an exercise rate of 8.625 percent for the cap. Generating a floor premium sufficient to offset the cap premium requires a floor exercise rate of 7.5 percent. The caplets and floorlets will expire on 15 October, 15 April of the following year, and so on for three years, but the payoffs will occur on the following payment date to correspond with the interest payment based on LIBOR that determines the caplet and floorlet payoffs. Thus, we have the following information:

Loan amount: $10,000,000
Underlying: 180-day LIBOR
Spread: 100 basis points over LIBOR
Current LIBOR: 9 percent

EXHIBIT 74-19 Interest Rate Collar (continued)

Interest based on: actual days/360
Component options: five caplets and floorlets expiring 15 October, 15 April, etc.
Exercise rate: 8.625 percent on cap, 7.5 percent on floor
Premium: no net premium

Scenario (various dates throughout the loan)
Shown below is one particular set of outcomes for LIBOR:

8.50 percent on 15 October
7.25 percent on 15 April the following year
7.00 percent on the following 15 October
6.90 percent on the following 15 April
8.75 percent on the following 15 October

Outcome and Analysis
The loan interest is computed as

$$\$10,000,000(\text{LIBOR on previous reset date} + 100 \text{ basis points})\left(\frac{\text{Days in settlement period}}{360}\right)$$

The caplet payoff is

$$\$10,000,000 \max(0,\text{LIBOR on previous reset date} - 0.08625)\left(\frac{\text{Days in settlement period}}{360}\right)$$

The floorlet payoff is

$$\$10,000,000 \max(0,0.075 - \text{LIBOR on previous reset date})\left(\frac{\text{Days in settlement period}}{360}\right)$$

The effective interest is the interest due minus the caplet payoff minus the floorlet payoff. Note that because the floorlet was sold, the floorlet payoff is either negative (so we would subtract a negative number, thereby adding an amount to obtain the total interest due) or zero.

The following table shows the payments on the loan and collar:

Date	LIBOR	Loan Rate	Days in Period	Interest Due	Caplet Payoffs	Floorlet Payoffs	Effective Interest
15 April	0.0900	0.1000					
15 October	0.0850	0.0950	183	$508,333			$508,333
15 April	0.0725	0.0825	182	480,278	$0	$0	480,278
15 October	0.0700	0.0800	183	419,375	0	−12,708	432,083
15 April	0.0690	0.0790	182	404,444	0	−25,278	429,722
15 October	0.0875	0.0975	183	401,583	0	−30,500	432,083
15 April			182	492,917	6,319	0	486,598

A collar establishes a range, the cap exercise rate minus the floor exercise rate, within which there is interest rate risk. The borrower will benefit from falling rates and be hurt by rising rates within that range. Any rate increases above the cap exercise rate will have no net effect, and any rate decreases below the floor exercise rate will have no net effect. The net cost of this position is zero, provided that the floor exercise rate is set such that the floor premium offsets the cap premium.[26] It is probably easy to see that collars are popular among borrowers.

Practice Problem 15

Exegesis Systems (EXSYS) is a floating-rate borrower that manages its interest rate risk with collars, purchasing a cap and selling a floor in which the cost of the cap and floor are equivalent. EXSYS takes out a $35 million one-year loan at 90-day LIBOR plus 200 basis points. It establishes a collar with a cap exercise rate of 7 percent and a floor exercise rate of 6 percent. Current 90-day LIBOR is 6.5 percent. The interest payments will be based on the exact day count over 360. The caplets and floorlets expire on the rate reset dates. The rates will be set on the current date (5 March), 4 June, 5 September, and 3 December, and the loan will be paid off on the following 3 March.

Determine the effective interest payments if LIBOR on the following dates is as given:

    4 June: 7.25 percent
    5 September: 6.5 percent
    3 December: 5.875 percent

SOLUTION

The interest due for each period is computed as $35,000,000(LIBOR on previous reset date + 0.02)(Days in period/360). For example, the first interest payment is $35,000,000(0.065 + 0.02)(91/360) = $752,014, based on the fact that there are 91 days between 5 March and 4 June. Each caplet payoff is computed as $35,000,000 max(0,LIBOR on previous reset date − 0.07)(Days in period/360), where the "previous reset date" is the caplet expiration. Payment is deferred until the date on which the interest is paid at the given LIBOR. For example, the caplet expiring on 4 June is worth $35,000,000 max(0,0.0725 − 0.07) (93/360) = $22,604, which is paid on 5 September and is based on the fact that there are 93 days between 4 June and 5 September. Each floorlet payoff is computed as $35,000,000 max(0,0.06 − LIBOR on previous reset date)(Days in period/360). For example, the floorlet expiring on 3 December is worth $35,000,000 max(0,0.06 − 0.05875)(90/360) = $10,938, based on the fact that there are 90 days between 3 December and 3 March. The effective interest is the actual interest minus the caplet payoff plus the floorlet payoff. The payments are shown in the table on the following page:

---

[26] It is certainly possible that the floor exercise rate would be set first, and the cap exercise rate would then be set to have the cap premium offset the floor premium. This would likely be the case if a lender were doing the collar. We assume, however, the case of a borrower who wants protection above a certain level and then decides to give up gains below a particular level necessary to offset the cost of the protection.

Date	LIBOR	Loan Rate	Days in Period	Interest Due	Caplet Payoff	Floorlet Payoff	Effective Interest
5 March	0.065	0.085					
4 June	0.0725	0.0925	91	$752,014			$752,014
5 September	0.065	0.085	93	836,354	$22,604	$0	813,750
3 December	0.05875	0.07875	89	735,486	0	0	735,486
3 March			90	689,063	0	−10,938	700,001

Of course, caps, floors, and collars are not the only forms of protection against interest rate risk. We have previously covered FRAs and interest rate futures. The most widely used protection, however, is the interest rate swap. We cover swap strategies in the next reading.

In the final section of this reading, we examine the strategies used to manage the risk of an option portfolio.

4   OPTION PORTFOLIO RISK MANAGEMENT STRATEGIES

So far we have looked at examples of how companies and investors use options. As we have described previously, many options are traded by dealers who make markets in these options, providing liquidity by first taking on risk and then hedging their positions in order to earn the bid–ask spread without taking the risk. In this section, we shall take a look at the strategies dealers use to hedge their positions.[27]

Let us assume that a customer contacts a dealer with an interest in purchasing a call option. The dealer, ready to take either side of the transaction, quotes an acceptable ask price and the customer buys the option. Recall from earlier in this reading that a short position in a call option is a very dangerous strategy, because the potential loss on an upside underlying move is open ended. The dealer would not want to hold a short call position for long. The ideal way to lay off the risk is to find someone else who would take the exact opposite position, but in most cases, the dealer will not be so lucky.[28] Another ideal possibility is for the dealer to lay off the risk using put–call parity. Recall that put–call parity says that $c = p + S - X/(1 + r)^T$. The dealer that has sold a call needs to buy a call to hedge the position. The put–call parity equation means that a long call is equivalent to a long put, a long position in the asset, and issuing a zero-coupon bond with a face value equal to the option exercise price and maturing on the option expiration date. Therefore, if the dealer could buy a put with the same exercise price and expiration, buy the asset, and sell a bond or take out a loan with face value equal to the exercise price and maturity equal to that of the option's expiration, it would have the position hedged. Other than buying an identical call, as described above, this hedge would be the best because it is static: No change to the position is required as time passes.

---

[27] For over-the-counter options, these dealers are usually the financial institutions that make markets in these options. For exchange-traded options, these dealers are the traders at the options exchanges, who may trade for their own accounts or could represent firms.

[28] Even luckier would be the dealer's original customer who might stumble across a party who wanted to sell the call option. The two parties could then bypass the dealer and negotiate a transaction directly between each other, which would save each party half of the bid–ask spread.

Unfortunately, neither of these transactions can be commonly employed. The necessary options may not be available or may not be favorably priced. As the next best alternative, dealers **delta hedge** their positions using an available and attractively priced instrument. The dealer is short the call and will need an offsetting position in another instrument. An obvious offsetting instrument would be a long position of a certain number of units of the underlying. The size of that long position will be related to the option's delta. In Reading 72, we discussed the concept of an option's delta. Let us briefly review delta here. By definition,

$$\text{Delta} = \frac{\text{Change in option price}}{\text{Change in underlying price}}$$

Delta expresses how the option price changes relative to the price of the underlying. Technically, we should use an approximation sign ($\approx$) in the above equation, but for now we shall assume the approximation is exact. Let ΔS be the change in the underlying price and Δc be the change in the option price. Then Delta = $\Delta c / \Delta S$. Recall from Reading 72 that the delta usually lies between 0.0 and 1.0.[29] Delta will be 1.0 only at expiration and only if the option expires in-the-money. Delta will be 0.0 only at expiration and only if the option expires out-of-the-money. So most of the time, the delta will be between 0.0 and 1.0. Hence, 0.5 is often given as an "average" delta, but one must be careful because even before expiration the delta will tend to be higher than 0.5 if the option is in-the-money.

Now, let us assume that we construct a portfolio consisting of N_S units of the underlying and N_c call options. The value of the portfolio is, therefore,

$$V = N_S S + N_c c$$

The change in the value of the portfolio is

$$\Delta V = N_S \Delta S + N_c \Delta c$$

If we want to hedge the portfolio, then we want the change in V, given a change in S, to be zero. Dividing by ΔS, we obtain

$$\frac{\Delta V}{\Delta S} = N_S \frac{\Delta S}{\Delta S} + N_c \frac{\Delta c}{\Delta S}$$

$$= N_S + N_c \frac{\Delta c}{\Delta S}$$

Setting this result equal to zero and solving for N_c / N_S, we obtain

$$\frac{N_c}{N_S} = -\frac{1}{\Delta c / \Delta S}$$

The ratio of calls to shares has to be the negative of 1 over the delta. Thus, if the dealer sells a given number of calls, say 100, it will need to own 100(Delta) shares.

How does delta hedging work? Let us say that we sell call options on 200 shares (this quantity is 2 standardized call contracts on an options exchange) and the delta is 0.5. We would, therefore, need to hold 200(0.5) = 100 shares. Say the underlying falls by \$1. Then we lose \$100 on our position in the underlying. If

---

[29] In the following text, we always make reference to the delta lying between 0.0 and 1.0, which is true for calls. For puts, the delta is between −1.0 and 0.0. It is common, however, to refer to a put delta of −1.0 as just 1.0, in effect using its absolute value and ignoring the negative. In all discussions in this reading, we shall refer to delta as ranging between 1.0 and 0.0, recalling that a put delta would range from −1.0 to 0.0.

the delta is accurate, the option should decline by $0.50. By having 200 options, the loss in value of the options collectively is $100. Because we are short the options, the loss in value of the options is actually a gain. Hence, the loss on the underlying is offset by the gain on the options. If the dealer were long the option, it would need to sell short the shares.

This illustration may make delta hedging sound simple: Buy (sell) delta shares for each option short (long). But there are three complicating issues. One is that delta is only an approximation of the change in the call price for a change in the underlying. A second issue is that the delta changes if anything else changes. Two factors that change are the price of the underlying and time. When the price of the underlying changes, delta changes, which affects the number of options required to hedge the underlying. Delta also changes as time changes; because time changes continuously, delta also changes continuously. Although a dealer can establish a delta-hedged position, as soon as anything happens—the underlying price changes or time elapses—the position is no longer delta hedged. In some cases, the position may not be terribly out of line with a delta hedge, but the more the underlying changes, the further the position moves away from being delta hedged. The third issue is that the number of units of the underlying per option must be rounded off, which leads to a small amount of imprecision in the balancing of the two opposing positions.

In Reading 72, we took a basic look at the concept of delta hedging. In the following section, we examine how a dealer delta hedges an option position, carrying the analysis through several days with the additional feature that excess cash will be invested in bonds and any additional cash needed will be borrowed.

4.1 Delta Hedging an Option Over Time

In the previous section, we showed how to set up a delta hedge. As we noted, a delta-hedged position will not remain delta hedged over time. The delta will change as the underlying changes and as time elapses. The dealer must account for these effects.

Let us first examine how actual option prices are sensitive to the underlying and what the delta tells us about that sensitivity. Consider a call option in which the underlying is worth 1210, the exercise price is 1200, the continuously compounded risk-free rate is 2.75 percent, the volatility of the underlying is 20 percent, and the expiration is 120 days. There are no dividends or cash flows on the underlying. Substituting these inputs into the Black–Scholes–Merton model, the option is worth 65.88. Recall from our study of the Black–Scholes–Merton model that delta is the term "$N(d_1)$" in the formula and represents a normal probability associated with the value d_1, which is provided as part of the Black–Scholes–Merton formula. In this example, the delta is 0.5826.[30]

Suppose that the underlying price instantaneously changes to 1200, a decline of 10. Using the delta, we would estimate that the option price would be

$$65.88 + (1200 - 1210)(0.5826) = 60.05$$

If, however, we plugged into the Black–Scholes–Merton model the same parameters but with a price of the underlying of 1200, we would obtain a new option price of 60.19—not much different from the previous result. But observe in Exhibit 74-20 what we obtain for various other values of the underlying. Two patterns become apparent: (1) The further away we move from the current price,

---

[30] All calculations were done on a computer for best precision.

the worse the delta-based approximation, and (2) the effects are asymmetric. A given move in one direction does not have the same effect on the option as the same move in the other direction. Specifically, for calls, the delta underestimates the effects of increases in the underlying and overestimates the effects of decreases in the underlying.[31] Because of this characteristic, the delta hedge will not be perfect. The larger the move in the underlying, the worse the hedge. Moreover, whenever the underlying price changes, the delta changes, which requires a rehedging or adjustment to the position. Observe in the last column of the table in Exhibit 74-20 we have recomputed the delta using the new price of the underlying. A dealer must adjust the position according to this new delta.

EXHIBIT 74-20 Delta and Option Price Sensitivity

S = 1210
X = 1200
r^c = 0.0275 (continuously compounded)
σ = 0.20
T = 0.328767 (based on 120 days/365)
No dividends
c = 65.88 (from the Black–Scholes–Merton model)

New Price of Underlying	Delta-Estimated Call Price[a]	Actual Call Price[b]	Difference (Actual − Estimated)	New Delta
1180	48.40	49.69	1.29	0.4959
1190	54.22	54.79	0.57	0.5252
1200	60.05	60.19	0.14	0.5542
1210	65.88	65.88	0.00	0.5826
1220	71.70	71.84	0.14	0.6104
1230	77.53	78.08	0.55	0.6374
1240	83.35	84.59	1.24	0.6635

[a] Delta-estimated call price = Original call price + (New price of underlying − Original price of underlying)Delta.
[b] Actual call price obtained from Black–Scholes–Merton model using new price of underlying; all other inputs are the same.

Now let us consider the effect of time on the delta. Exhibit 74-21 shows the delta and the number of units of underlying required to hedge 1,000 short options when the option has 120 days, 119, etc. on down to 108. A critical assumption is that we are holding the underlying price constant. Of course, this constancy would not occur in practice, but to focus on understanding the effect of time on the delta, we must hold the underlying price constant. Observe that the delta changes slowly and the number of units of the underlying required changes gradually over this 12-day period. Another not-so-obvious effect is also present: When we round up, we have more units of the underlying than needed, which has a negative effect that hurts when the underlying goes down. When we round down, we have fewer units of the underlying than needed, which hurts when the underlying goes up.

---

[31] For puts, delta underestimates the effects of price decreases and overestimates the effects of price increases.

EXHIBIT 74-21 The Effect of Time on the Delta

$S = 1210$

$X = 1200$

$r^c = 0.0275$ (continuously compounded)

$\sigma = 0.20$

$T = 0.328767$ (based on 120 days/365)

No dividends

$c = 65.88$ (from the Black–Scholes–Merton model)

Delta $= 0.5826$

Delta hedge 1,000 short options by holding $1,000(0.5826) = 582.6$ units of the underlying.

Time to Expiration (days)	Delta	Number of Units of Underlying Required
120	0.5826	582.6
119	0.5825	582.5
118	0.5824	582.4
117	0.5823	582.3
116	0.5822	582.2
115	0.5821	582.1
114	0.5820	582.0
113	0.5819	581.9
112	0.5818	581.8
111	0.5817	581.7
110	0.5816	581.6
109	0.5815	581.5
108	0.5814	581.4

The combined effects of the underlying price changing and the time to expiration changing interact to present great challenges for delta hedgers. Let us set up a delta hedge and work through a few days of it. Recall that for the option we have been working with, the underlying price is $1,200, the option price is $65.88, and the delta is 0.5826. Suppose a customer comes to us and asks to buy calls on 1,000 shares. We need to buy a sufficient number of shares to offset the sale of the 1,000 calls. Because we are short 1,000 calls, and this number is fixed, we need 0.5826 shares per call or about 583 shares. So we buy 583 shares to balance the 1,000 short calls. The value of this portfolio is

$$583(\$1,210) - 1,000(\$65.88) = \$639,550$$

So, to initiate this delta hedge, we would need to invest $639,550. To determine if this hedge is effective, we should see this value grow at the risk-free rate. Because the Black–Scholes–Merton model uses continuously compounded interest, the formula for compounding a value at the risk-free rate for one day is $\exp(r^c/365)$, where r^c is the continuously compounded risk-free rate. One day later, this value should be $\$639,550 \exp(0.0275/365) = \$639,598$. This value becomes our benchmark.

Now, let us move forward one day and have the underlying go to $1,215. We need a new value of the call option, which now has one less day until expiration and is based on an underlying with a price of $1,215. The market would tell us the option price, but we do not have the luxury here of asking the market for the price. Instead, we have to appeal to a model that would tell us an appropriate price. Naturally, we turn to the Black–Scholes–Merton model. We recalculate the value of the call option using Black–Scholes–Merton, with the price of the underlying at $1,215 and the time to expiration at $119/365 = 0.3260$. The option value is $68.55, and the new delta is 0.5966. The portfolio is now worth

$$583(\$1,215) - 1,000(\$68.55) = \$639,795$$

This value differs from the benchmark by a small amount: $\$639,795 - \$639,598 = \$197$. Although the hedge is not perfect, it is off by only about 0.03 percent.

Now, to move forward and still be delta hedged, we need to revise the position. The new delta is 0.5966. So now we need $1,000(0.5966) = 597$ units of the underlying and must buy 14 units of the underlying. This purchase will cost $14(\$1,215) = \$17,010$. We obtain this money by borrowing it at the risk-free rate. So we issue bonds in the amount of $17,010. Now our position is 597 units of the underlying, 1,000 short calls, and a loan of $17,010. The value of this position is still

$$597(\$1,215) - 1,000(\$68.55) - \$17,010 = \$639,795$$

Of course, this is the same value we had before adjusting the position. We could not expect to generate or lose money just by rearranging our position. As we move forward to the next day, we should see this value grow by one day's interest to $\$639,795 \exp(0.0275/365) = \$639,843$. This amount is the benchmark for the next day.

Suppose the next day the underlying goes to $1,198, the option goes to 58.54, and its delta goes to 0.5479. Our loan of $17,010 will grow to $17,010 $\exp(0.0275/365) = \$17,011$. The new value of the portfolio is

$$597(\$1,198) - 1,000(\$58.54) - \$17,011 = \$639,655$$

This amount differs from the benchmark by $\$639,655 - \$639,843 = -\$188$, an error of about 0.03 percent.

With the new delta at 0.5479, we now need 548 shares. Because we have 597 shares, we now must sell $597 - 548 = 49$ shares. Doing so would generate $49(\$1,198) = \$58,702$. Because the value of our debt was $17,011 and we now have $58,702 in cash, we can pay back the loan, leaving $\$58,702 - \$17,011 = \$41,691$ to be invested at the risk-free rate. So now we have 548 units of the underlying, 1,000 short calls, and bonds of $41,691. The value of this position is

$$548(\$1,198) - 1,000(\$58.54) + \$41,691 = \$639,655$$

Of course, this is the same value we had before buying the underlying. Indeed, we cannot create or destroy any wealth by just rearranging the position.

Exhibit 74-22 illustrates the delta hedge, carrying it through one more day. After the third day, the value of the position should be $639,655 $\exp(0.0275/365) = \$639,703$. The actual value is $639,870, a difference of $\$639,870 - \$639,703 = \$167$.

EXHIBIT 74-22 Delta Hedge of a Short Options Position

S = \$1,210
X = \$1,200
r^c = 0.0275 (continuously compounded)
σ = 0.20
T = 0.328767 (based on 120 days/365)
No dividends
c = \$65.88 (from the Black–Scholes–Merton model)
Delta = 0.5826

Units of option constant at 1,000
Units of underlying required = 1000 × Delta
Units of underlying purchased = (Units of underlying required one day) − (Units of underlying required previous day)
Bonds purchased = −S(Units of underlying purchased)
Bond balance = (Previous balance) exp(r^c/365) + Bonds purchased
Value of portfolio = (Units of underlying)S + (Units of options)c + Bond balance

Day	S	c	Delta	Options Sold	Units of Underlying Required	Units of Underlying Purchased	Value of Bonds Purchased	Bond Balance	Value of Portfolio
0	\$1,210	\$65.88	0.5826	1,000	583	583	\$0	\$0	\$639,550
1	1,215	68.55	0.5965	1,000	597	14	−17,010	−17,010	639,795
2	1,198	58.54	0.5479	1,000	548	−49	58,702	41,691	639,655
3	1,192	55.04	0.5300	1,000	530	−18	21,456	63,150	639,870

As we can see, the delta hedge is not perfect, but it is pretty good. After three days, we are off by \$167, only about 0.03 percent of the benchmark.

In our example and the discussions here, we have noted that the dealer would typically hold a position in the underlying to delta-hedge a position in the option. Trading in the underlying would not, however, always be the preferred hedge vehicle. In fact, we have stated quite strongly that trading in derivatives is often easier and more cost effective than trading in the underlying. As noted previously, ideally a short position in a particular option would be hedged by holding a long position in that same option, but such a hedge requires that the dealer find another customer or dealer who wants to sell that same option. It is possible, however, that the dealer might be able to more easily buy a different option on the same underlying and use that option as the hedging instrument.

For example, suppose one option has a delta of Δ_1 and the other has a delta of Δ_2. These two options are on the same underlying but are not identical. They differ by exercise price, expiration, or both. Using c_1 and c_2 to represent their prices and N_1 and N_2 to represent the quantity of each option in a portfolio that hedges the value of one of the options, the value of the position is

$$V = N_1c_1 + N_2c_2$$

Dividing by ΔS, we obtain

$$\frac{\Delta V}{\Delta S} = N_1 \frac{\Delta c_1}{\Delta S} + N_2 \frac{\Delta c_2}{\Delta S}$$

To delta hedge, we set this amount to zero and solve for N_1/N_2 to obtain

$$\frac{N_1}{N_2} = -\frac{\Delta c_2}{\Delta c_1}$$

The negative sign simply means that a long position in one option will require a short position in the other. The desired quantity of Option 1 relative to the quantity of Option 2 is the ratio of the delta of Option 2 to the delta of Option 1. As in the standard delta-hedge example, however, these deltas will change and will require monitoring and modification of the position.[32]

Practice Problem 16

DynaTrade is an options trading company that makes markets in a variety of derivative instruments. DynaTrade has just sold 500 call options on a stock currently priced at $125.75. Suppose the trade date is 18 November. The call has an exercise price of $125, 60 days until expiration, a price of $10.89, and a delta of 0.5649. DynaTrade will delta-hedge this transaction by purchasing an appropriate number of shares. Any additional transactions required to adjust the delta hedge will be executed by borrowing or lending at the continuously compounded risk-free rate of 4 percent.

DynaTrade has begun delta hedging the option. Two days later, 20 November, the following information applies:

Stock price:	$122.75
Option price:	$9.09
Delta:	0.5176
Number of options:	500
Number of shares:	328
Bond balance:	−$6,072
Market value:	$29,645

A. At the end of 19 November, the delta was 0.6564. Based on this number, show how 328 shares of stock is used to delta hedge 500 call options.

B. Show the allocation of the $29,645 market value of DynaTrade's total position among stock, options, and bonds on 20 November.

C. Show what transactions must be done to adjust the portfolio to be delta hedged for the following day (21 November).

D. On 21 November, the stock is worth $120.50 and the call is worth $7.88. Calculate the market value of the delta-hedged portfolio and compare it with a benchmark, based on the market value on 20 November.

SOLUTIONS

A. If the stock moves up (down) $1, the 328 shares should change by $328. The 500 calls should change by 500(0.6564) = $328.20, rounded off to $328. The calls are short, so any change in the value of the stock position is an opposite change in the value of the options.

---

[32] Because the position is long one option and short another, whenever the options differ by exercise price, expiration, or both, the position has the characteristics of a spread. In fact, it is commonly called a **ratio spread.**

B. Stock worth 328($122.75) = $40,262

Options worth −500($9.09) = −$4,545

Bonds worth −$6,072

   Total of $29,645

C. The new required number of shares is 500(0.5176) = 258.80. Round this number to 259. So we need to have 259 shares instead of 328 shares and must sell 69 shares, generating 69($122.75) = $8,470. We invest this amount in risk-free bonds. We had a bond balance of −$6,072, so the proceeds from the sale will pay off all of this debt, leaving a balance of $8,470 −$6,072 = $2,398 going into the next day. The composition of the portfolio would then be as follows:

Shares worth 259($122.75) = $31,792

Options worth −500($9.09) = −$4,545

Bonds worth $2,398

   Total of $29,645

D. The benchmark is $29,645 exp(0.04/365) = $29,648. Also, the value of the bond one day later will be $2,398 exp(0.04/365) = $2,398. (This is less than a half-dollar's interest, so it essentially leaves the balance unchanged.) Now we have

Shares worth 259($120.50) = $31,210

Options worth −500($7.88) = −$3,940

Bonds worth $2,398

   Total of $29,668

This is about $20 more than the benchmark.

EXHIBIT 74-23 Actual Option Price (−) and Delta-Estimated Option Price (−)

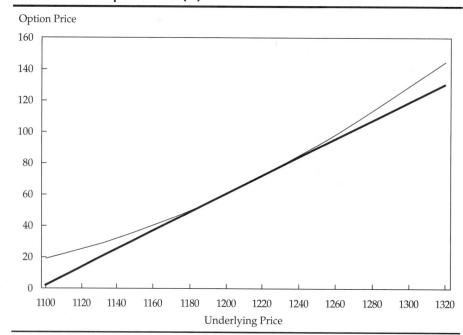

As previously noted, the delta is a fairly good approximation of the change in the option price for a very small and rapid change in the price of the underlying. But the underlying does not always change in such a convenient manner, and this possibility introduces a risk into the process of delta hedging.

Note Exhibit 74-23, a graph of the actual option price and the delta-estimated option price from the perspective of day 0 in Exhibit 74-20. At the underlying price of $1,210, the option price is $65.88. The curved line shows the exact option price, calculated with the Black–Scholes–Merton model, for a range of underlying prices. The heavy line shows the option price estimated using the delta as we did in Exhibit 74-20. In that exhibit, we did not stray too far from the current underlying price. In Exhibit 74-23, we let the underlying move a little further. Note that the further we move from the current price of the underlying of $1,210, the further the heavy line deviates from the solid line. As noted earlier, the actual call price moves up more than the delta approximation and moves down less than the delta approximation. This effect occurs because the option price is convex with respect to the underlying price, a point we discussed in Section 7.3.1 of Reading 72. This convexity, which is quite similar to the convexity of a bond price with respect to its yield, means that a first-order price sensitivity measure like delta, or its duration analog for bonds, is accurate only if the underlying moves by a small amount. With duration, a second-order measure called convexity reflects the extent of the deviation of the actual pricing curve from the approximation curve. With options, the second-order measure is called **gamma.**

4.2 Gamma and the Risk of Delta

As noted, in Reading 72 we introduced the concept of the gamma, which is a measure of several effects. We already mentioned that it reflects the deviation of the exact option price change from the price change as approximated by the delta. It also measures the sensitivity of delta to a change in the underlying. In effect, it is the delta of the delta. Specifically,

$$\text{Gamma} = \frac{\text{Change in delta}}{\text{Change in underlying price}}$$

Like delta, gamma is actually an approximation, but we shall treat it as exact. Although a formula exists for gamma, we need to understand only the concept.

If a delta-hedged position were risk free, its gamma would be zero. The larger the gamma, the more the delta-hedged position deviates from being risk free. Because gamma reflects movements in the delta, let us first think about how delta moves. Focusing on call options, recall that the delta is between 0.0 and 1.0. At expiration, the delta is 1.0 if the option expires in-the-money and 0.0 if it expires out-of-the-money. During its life, the delta will tend to be above 0.5 if the option is in-the-money and below 0.5 if the option is out-of-the-money. As expiration approaches, the deltas of in-the-money options will move toward 1.0 and the deltas of out-of-the-money options will move toward 0.0.[33] They will, however, move slowly in their respective directions. The largest moves occur near expiration, when the deltas of at-the-money options move quickly toward 1.0 or 0.0. These rapid movements are the ones that cause the most problems for delta hedgers. Options that are deep in-the-money or deep out-of-the-money tend to have their deltas move closer to 1.0 or 0.0 well before expiration. Their movements are slow and pose fewer problems for delta hedgers. Thus, it is the rapid movements in delta that

---

[33] The deltas of options that are very slightly in-the-money will temporarily move down as expiration approaches. Exhibit 74-21 illustrates this effect. But they will eventually move up toward 1.0.

concern delta hedgers. These rapid movements are more likely to occur on options that are at-the-money and/or near expiration. Under these conditions, the gammas tend to be largest and delta hedges are hardest to maintain.

When gammas are large, some delta hedgers choose to also gamma hedge. This somewhat advanced strategy requires adding a position in another option, combining the underlying and the two options in such a manner that the delta is zero and the gamma is zero. Because it is a somewhat advanced and specialized topic, we do not cover the details of how this is done.

The delta is not the only important factor that changes in the course of managing an option position. The volatility of the underlying can also change.

4.3   Vega and Volatility Risk

As we covered in Reading 72, the sensitivity of the option price to the volatility is called the vega and is defined as

$$\text{Vega} = \frac{\text{Change in option price}}{\text{Change in volatility}}$$

As with delta and gamma, the relationship above is an approximation, but we shall treat it as exact. As we noted in Reading 72, an option price is very sensitive to the volatility of the underlying. Moreover, the volatility is the only unobservable variable required to value an option. Hence, volatility is the most critical variable. When we examined option-pricing models, we studied the Black–Scholes–Merton and binomial models. In neither of these models is the volatility allowed to change. Yet no one believes that volatility is constant; on some days the stock market is clearly more volatile than on other days. This risk of changing volatility can greatly affect a dealer's position in options. A delta-hedged position with a zero or insignificant gamma can greatly change in value if the volatility changes. If, for example, the dealer holds the underlying and sells options to delta hedge, an increase in volatility will raise the value of the options, generating a potentially large loss for the dealer.

Measuring the sensitivity of the option price to the volatility is difficult. The vega from the Black–Scholes–Merton or binomial models is a somewhat artificial construction. It represents how much the model price changes if one changes the volatility by a small amount. But in fact, the model itself is based on the assumption that volatility does not change. Forcing the volatility to change in a model that does not acknowledge that volatility can change has unclear implications.[34] It is clear, however, that an option price is more sensitive to the volatility when it is at-the-money.

Dealers try to measure the vega, monitor it, and in some cases hedge it by taking on a position in another option, using that option's vega to offset the vega on the original option. Managing vega risk, however, cannot be done independently of managing delta and gamma risk. Thus, the dealer is required to jointly monitor and manage the risk associated with the delta, gamma, and vega. We should be aware of the concepts behind managing these risks.

---

[34] If this point seems confusing, consider this analogy. In the famous Einstein equation $E = mc^2$, E is energy, m is mass, and c is the constant representing the speed of light. For a given mass, we could change c, which would change E. The equation allows this change, but in fact the speed of light is constant at 186,000 miles per second. So far as scientists know, it is a universal constant and can never change. In the case of option valuation, the model assumes that volatility of a given stock is like a universal constant. We can change it, however, and the equation would give us a new option price. But are we allowed to do so? Unlike the speed of light, volatility does indeed change, even though our model says that it does not. What happens when we change volatility in our model? We do not know.

FINAL COMMENTS   5

In Chapter 6, we examined forward and futures strategies. These types of contracts provide gains from movements of the underlying in one direction but result in losses from movements of the underlying in the other direction. The advantage of a willingness to incur losses is that no cash is paid at the start. Options offer the advantage of having one-directional effects: The buyer of an option gains from a movement in one direction and loses only the premium from movements in the other direction. The cost of this advantage is that options require the payment of cash at the start. Some market participants choose forwards and futures because they do not have to pay cash at the start. They can justify taking positions without having to come up with the cash to do so. Others, however, prefer the flexibility to benefit when their predictions are right and suffer only a limited loss when wrong. The trade-off between the willingness to pay cash at the start versus incurring losses, given one's risk preferences, is the deciding factor in whether to use options or forwards/futures.

All option strategies are essentially rooted in the transactions of buying a call or a put. Understanding a short position in either type of option means understanding the corresponding long position in the option. All remaining strategies are just combinations of options, the underlying, and risk-free bonds. We looked at a number of option strategies associated with equities, which can apply about equally to index options or options on individual stocks. The applicability of these strategies to bonds is also fairly straightforward. The options must expire before the bonds mature, but the general concepts associated with equity option strategies apply similarly to bond option strategies.

Likewise, strategies that apply to equity options apply in nearly the same manner to interest rate options. Nonetheless, significant differences exist between interest rate options and equity or bond options. If nothing else, the notion of bullishness is quite opposite. Bullish (bearish) equity investors buy calls (puts). In interest rate markets, bullish (bearish) investors buy puts (calls) on interest rates, because being bullish (bearish) on interest rates means that one thinks rates are going down (up). Interest rate options pay off as though they were interest payments. Equity or bond options pay off as though the holder were selling or buying stocks or bonds. Finally, interest rate options are very often combined into portfolios in the form of caps and floors for the purpose of hedging floating-rate loans. Standard option strategies such as straddles and spreads are just as applicable to interest rate options.

Recall that in Reading 72, we examined one other slightly different type of option, one in which the underlying is a futures contract. Despite some subtle differences between the option strategies examined in this reading and comparable strategies using options on futures, the differences are relatively minor and do not warrant separate coverage here. If you have a good grasp of the basics of the option strategies presented in this reading, you can easily adapt those strategies to ones in which the underlying is a futures contract.

In Chapter 8, we take up strategies using swaps. As we have so often mentioned, interest rate swaps are the most widely used financial derivative. They are less widely used with currencies and equities than are forwards, futures, and options. Nonetheless, there are many applications of swaps to currencies and equities, and we shall certainly look at them. To examine swaps, however, we must return to the types of instruments with two-directional payoffs and no cash payments at the start. Indeed, as we showed in Reading 73, swaps are a lot like forward contracts, which themselves are a lot like futures.

6

▷ The profit from buying a call is the value at expiration, $\max(0, S_T - X)$, minus c_0, the option premium. The maximum profit is infinite, and the maximum loss is the option premium. The breakeven underlying price at expiration is the exercise price plus the option premium. When one sells a call, these results are reversed.

▷ The profit from buying a put is the value at expiration, $\max(0, X - S_T)$, minus p_0, the option premium. The maximum profit is the exercise price minus the option premium, and the maximum loss is the option premium. The breakeven underlying price at expiration is the exercise price minus the option premium. When one sells a put, these results are reversed.

▷ The profit from a covered call—the purchase of the underlying and sale of a call—is the value at expiration, $S_T - \max(0, S_T - X)$, minus $S_0 - c_0$, the cost of the underlying minus the option premium. The maximum profit is the exercise price minus the original underlying price plus the option premium, and the maximum loss is the cost of the underlying less the option premium. The breakeven underlying price at expiration is the original price of the underlying minus the option premium.

▷ The profit from a protective put—the purchase of the underlying and a put—is the value at expiration, $S_T + \max(0, X - S_T)$, minus the cost of the underlying plus the option premium, $S_0 + p_0$. The maximum profit is infinite, and the maximum loss is the cost of the underlying plus the option premium minus the exercise price. The breakeven underlying price at expiration is the original price of the underlying plus the option premium.

▷ The profit from a bull spread—the purchase of a call at one exercise price and the sale of a call with the same expiration but a higher exercise price—is the value at expiration, $\max(0, S_T - X_1) - \max(0, S_T - X_2)$, minus the net premium, $c_1 - c_2$, which is the premium of the long option minus the premium of the short option. The maximum profit is $X_2 - X_1$ minus the net premium, and the maximum loss is the net premium. The breakeven underlying price at expiration is the lower exercise price plus the net premium.

▷ The profit from a bear spread—the purchase of a put at one exercise price and the sale of a put with the same expiration but a lower exercise price—is the value at expiration, $\max(0, X_2 - S_T) - \max(0, X_1 - S_T)$, minus the net premium, $p_2 - p_1$, which is the premium of the long option minus the premium of the short option. The maximum profit is $X_2 - X_1$ minus the net premium, and the maximum loss is the net premium. The breakeven underlying price at expiration is the higher exercise price minus the net premium.

▷ The profit from a butterfly spread—the purchase of a call at one exercise price, X_1, sale of two calls at a higher exercise price, X_2, and the purchase of a call at a higher exercise price, X_3—is the value at expiration, $\max(0, S_T - X_1) - 2\max(0, S_T - X_2), + \max(0, S_T - X_3)$, minus the net premium, $c_1 - 2c_2 + c_3$. The maximum profit is $X_2 - X_1$ minus the net premium, and the maximum loss is the net premium. The breakeven underlying prices at expiration are $2X_2 - X_1$ minus the net premium and X_1 plus the net premium. A butterfly spread can also be constructed by trading the corresponding put options.

▷ The profit from a collar—the holding of the underlying, the purchase of a put at one exercise price, X_1, and the sale of a call with the same expiration and a higher exercise price, X_2, and in which the premium on the put equals the premium on the call—is the value at expiration, $S_T + \max(0,X_1 - S_T) - \max(0,S_T - X_2)$, minus S_0, the original price of the underlying. The maximum profit is $X_2 - S_0$, and the maximum loss is $S_0 - X_1$. The breakeven underlying price at expiration is the initial price of the underlying.

▷ The profit from a straddle—a long position in a call and a put with the same exercise price and expiration—is the value at expiration, $\max(0,S_T - X) + \max(0,X - S_T)$, minus the premiums on the call and put, $c_0 + p_0$. The maximum profit is infinite, and the maximum loss is the sum of the premiums on the call and put, $c_0 + p_0$. The breakeven prices at expiration are the exercise price plus and minus the premiums on the call and put.

▷ A box spread is a combination of a bull spread using calls and a bear spread using puts, with one call and put at an exercise price of X_1 and another call and put at an exercise price of X_2. The profit is the value at expiration, $X_2 - X_1$, minus the net premiums, $c_1 - c_2 + p_2 - p_1$. The transaction is risk free, and the net premium paid should be the present value of this risk-free payoff.

▷ A long position in an interest rate call can be used to place a ceiling on the rate on an anticipated loan from the perspective of the borrower. The call provides a payoff if the interest rate at expiration exceeds the exercise rate, thereby compensating the borrower when the rate is higher than the exercise rate. The effective interest paid on the loan is the actual interest paid minus the call payoff. The call premium must be taken into account by compounding it to the date on which the loan is taken out and deducting it from the initial proceeds received from the loan.

▷ A long position in an interest rate put can be used to lock in the rate on an anticipated loan from the perspective of the lender. The put provides a payoff if the interest rate at expiration is less than the exercise rate, thereby compensating the lender when the rate is lower than the exercise rate. The effective interest paid on the loan is the actual interest received plus the put payoff. The put premium must be taken into account by compounding it to the date on which the loan is taken out and adding it to initial proceeds paid out on the loan.

▷ An interest rate cap can be used to place an upper limit on the interest paid on a floating rate loan from the perspective of the borrower. A cap is a series of interest rate calls, each of which is referred to as a caplet. Each caplet provides a payoff if the interest rate on the loan reset date exceeds the exercise rate, thereby compensating the borrower when the rate is higher than the exercise rate. The effective interest paid is the actual interest paid minus the caplet payoff. The premium is paid at the start and is the sum of the premiums on the component caplets.

▷ An interest rate floor can be used to place a lower limit on the interest received on a floating-rate loan from the perspective of the lender. A floor is a series of interest rate puts, each of which is called a floorlet. Each floorlet provides a payoff if the interest rate at the loan reset date is less than the exercise rate, thereby compensating the lender when the rate is lower than the exercise rate. The effective interest received is the actual interest plus the floorlet payoff. The premium is paid at the start and is the sum of the premiums on the component floorlets.

▷ An interest rate collar, which consists of a long interest rate cap at one exercise rate and a short interest rate floor at a lower exercise rate, can be used to place an upper limit on the interest paid on a floating-rate loan. The floor, however, places a lower limit on the interest paid on the floating-rate loan. Typically the floor exercise rate is set such that the premium on the floor equals the premium on the cap, so that no cash outlay is required to initiate the transaction. The effective interest is the actual interest paid minus any payoff from the long caplet plus any payoff from the short floorlet.

▶ Dealers offer to take positions in options and typically hedge their positions by establishing delta-neutral combinations of options and the underlying or other options. These positions require that the sensitivity of the option position with respect to the underlying be offset by a quantity of the underlying or another option. The delta will change, moving toward 1.0 for in-the-money calls (-1.0 for puts) and 0.0 for out-of-the-money options as expiration approaches. Any change in the underlying price will also change the delta. These changes in the delta necessitate buying and selling options or the underlying to maintain the delta-hedged position. Any additional funds required to buy the underlying or other options are obtained by issuing risk-free bonds. Any additional funds released from selling the underlying or other options are invested in risk-free bonds.

▶ The delta of an option changes as the underlying changes and as time elapses. The delta will change more rapidly with large movements in the underlying and when the option is approximately at-the-money and near expiration. These large changes in the delta will prevent a delta-hedged position from being truly risk free. Dealers usually monitor their gammas and in some cases hedge their gammas by adding other options to their positions such that the gammas offset.

▶ The sensitivity of an option to volatility is called the vega. An option's volatility can change, resulting in a potentially large change in the value of the option. Dealers monitor and sometimes hedge their vegas so that this risk does not impact a delta-hedged portfolio.

1. Consider a call option selling for $4 in which the exercise price is $50.

   A. Determine the value at expiration and the profit for a buyer under the following outcomes:

   i. The price of the underlying at expiration is $55.
   ii. The price of the underlying at expiration is $51.
   iii. The price of the underlying at expiration is $48.

   B. Determine the value at expiration and the profit for a seller under the following outcomes:
   i. The price of the underlying at expiration is $49.
   ii. The price of the underlying at expiration is $52.
   iii. The price of the underlying at expiration is $55.

   C. Determine the following:
   i. The maximum profit to the buyer (maximum loss to the seller)
   ii. The maximum loss to the buyer (maximum profit to the seller)

   D. Determine the breakeven price of the underlying at expiration.

2. Suppose you believe that the price of a particular underlying, currently selling at $99, is going to increase substantially in the next six months. You decide to purchase a call option expiring in six months on this underlying. The call option has an exercise price of $105 and sells for $7.

   A. Determine the profit under the following outcomes for the price of the underlying six months from now.
   i. $99
   ii. $104
   iii. $105
   iv. $109
   v. $112
   vi. $115

   B. Determine the breakeven price of the underlying at expiration. Check that your answer is consistent with the solution to Part A of this problem.

3. Consider a put option on the Nasdaq 100 selling for $106.25 in which the exercise price is 2100.

   A. Determine the value at expiration and the profit for a buyer under the following outcomes:
   i. The price of the underlying at expiration is 2125.
   ii. The price of the underlying at expiration is 2050.
   iii. The price of the underlying at expiration is 1950.

   B. Determine the value at expiration and the profit for a seller under the following outcomes:
   i. The price of the underlying at expiration is 1975.
   ii. The price of the underlying at expiration is 2150.

   C. Determine the following:
   i. The maximum profit to the buyer (maximum loss to the seller)
   ii. The maximum loss to the buyer (maximum profit to the seller)

   D. Determine the breakeven price of the underlying at expiration.

4. Suppose you believe that the price of a particular underlying, currently selling at $99, will decrease considerably in the next six months. You decide to purchase a put option expiring in six months on this underlying. The put option has an exercise price of $95 and sells for $5.

A. Determine the profit for you under the following outcomes for the price of the underlying six months from now:
  i. $100
  ii. $95
  iii. $93
  iv. $90
  v. $85

B. Determine the breakeven price of the underlying at expiration. Check that your answer is consistent with the solution to Part A of this problem.

C. i. What is the maximum profit that you can have?
   ii. At what expiration price of the underlying would this profit be realized?

5. You simultaneously purchase an underlying priced at $77 and write a call option on it with an exercise price of $80 and selling at $6.

A. What is the term commonly used for the position that you have taken?

B. Determine the value at expiration and the profit for your strategy under the following outcomes:
  i. The price of the underlying at expiration is $70.
  ii. The price of the underlying at expiration is $75.
  iii. The price of the underlying at expiration is $80.
  iv. The price of the underlying at expiration is $85.

C. Determine the following:
  i. The maximum profit
  ii. The maximum loss
  iii. The expiration price of the underlying at which you would realize the maximum profit
  iv. The expiration price of the underlying at which you would incur the maximum loss

D. Determine the breakeven price at expiration.

6. Suppose you simultaneously purchase an underlying priced at $77 and a put option on it, with an exercise price of $75 and selling at $3.

A. What is the term commonly used for the position that you have taken?

B. Determine the value at expiration and the profit for your strategy under the following outcomes:
  i. The price of the underlying at expiration is $70.
  ii. The price of the underlying at expiration is $75.
  iii. The price of the underlying at expiration is $80.
  iv. The price of the underlying at expiration is $85.
  v. The price of the underlying at expiration is $90.

C. Determine the following:
  i. The maximum profit
  ii. The maximum loss
  iii. The expiration price of the underlying at which you would incur the maximum loss

D. Determine the breakeven price at expiration.

ANALYSIS OF ALTERNATIVE INVESTMENTS

The candidate should be able to demonstrate a working knowledge of the analysis of alternative investments, including mutual funds, exchange traded funds, real estate, venture capital, hedge funds, closely held companies, distressed securities, and commodities and commodity derivatives.

Reading 75 Alternative Investments

Reading 75: Alternative Investments

The candidate should be able to:

a. distinguish between an open-end and a closed-end fund;

b. explain how the net asset value of a fund is calculated;

c. explain the nature of various fees charged by investment companies;

d. distinguish among style, sector, index, global, and stable value strategies in equity investment;

e. distinguish among exchange traded funds (ETFs), traditional mutual funds, and closed-end funds;

f. explain the advantages and risks of ETFs;

g. describe the forms of real estate investment;

h. explain the characteristics of real estate as an investable asset class;

i. describe the various approaches to the valuation of real estate;

j. calculate the net operating income (NOI) from a real estate investment;

k. calculate the value of a property using the sales comparison and income approaches;

l. calculate the after-tax cash flows, net present value, and yield of a real estate investment;

m. explain the various stages in venture capital investing;

n. discuss venture capital investment characteristics and the challenges to venture capital valuation and performance measurement;

o. calculate the net present value (NPV) of a venture capital project, given the project's possible payoff and conditional failure probabilities;

p. discuss the descriptive accuracy of the term "hedge fund," define hedge fund in terms of objectives, legal structure, and fee structure, and describe the various classifications of hedge funds;

Note:
Candidates are responsible for the problems at the end of the reading.

617

q. discuss the benefits and drawbacks to fund of funds investing;

r. discuss the leverage and unique risks of hedge funds;

s. discuss the performance of hedge funds, the biases present in hedge fund performance measurement and explain the effect of survivorship bias on the reported return and risk measures for a hedge fund data base;

t. explain how the legal environment affects the valuation of closely held companies;

u. describe alternative valuation methods for closely held companies and distinguish among the bases for the discounts and premiums for these companies;

v. discuss distressed securities investing and the similarities between venture capital investing and distressed securities investing;

w. discuss the role of commodities as a vehicle for investing in production and consumption;

x. discuss the motivation for investing in commodities, commodities derivatives, and commodity-linked securities;

y. discuss the sources of return on a collateralized commodity futures position.

ALTERNATIVE INVESTMENTS

LEARNING OUTCOMES

The candidate should be able to:

a. distinguish between an open-end and a closed-end fund;

b. explain how the net asset value of a fund is calculated;

c. explain the nature of various fees charged by investment companies;

d. distinguish among style, sector, index, global, and stable value strategies in equity investment;

e. distinguish among exchange traded funds (ETFs), traditional mutual funds, and closed-end funds;

f. explain the advantages and risks of ETFs;

g. describe the forms of real estate investment;

h. explain the characteristics of real estate as an investable asset class;

i. describe the various approaches to the valuation of real estate;

j. calculate the net operating income (NOI) from a real estate investment;

k. calculate the value of a property using the sales comparison and income approaches;

l. calculate the after-tax cash flows, net present value, and yield of a real estate investment;

m. explain the various stages in venture capital investing;

n. discuss venture capital investment characteristics and the challenges to venture capital valuation and performance measurement;

o. calculate the net present value (NPV) of a venture capital project, given the project's possible payoff and conditional failure probabilities;

p. discuss the descriptive accuracy of the term "hedge fund," define hedge fund in terms of objectives, legal structure, and fee structure, and describe the various classifications of hedge funds;

q. discuss the benefits and drawbacks to fund of funds investing;

r. discuss the leverage and unique risks of hedge funds;

s. discuss the performance of hedge funds, the biases present in hedge fund performance measurement and the effect of survivorship bias on the reported return and risk measures for a hedge fund data base;

International Investments, Fifth Edition, by Bruno Solnik and Dennis McLeavey, Copyright © 2004. Reprinted with permission of Pearson Education, publishing as Pearson Addison Wesley.

619

t. explain how the legal environment affects the valuation of closely held companies;

u. describe alternative valuation methods for closely held companies and distinguish among the bases for the discounts and premiums for these companies;

v. discuss distressed securities investing and the similarities between venture capital investing and distressed securities investing;

w. discuss the role of commodities as a vehicle for investing in production and consumption;

x. discuss the motivation for investing in commodities, commodities derivatives, and commodity-linked securities;

y. discuss the sources of return on a collateralized commodity futures position.

1 INTRODUCTION

Alternative investments complement stocks, bonds, and other traditional financial instruments traded on international financial markets. There is a large variety of alternative investments, and the list evolves over time. Both alternative assets (such as real estate) and alternative strategies (hedge funds) are classified as alternative investments. Alternative investments generally have lower liquidity, sell in less efficient markets, and require a longer time horizon than publicly traded stocks and bonds. Sharpe, Alexander, and Bailey (1999) provide a nice summary of the common features of alternative investments:

▶ Illiquidity
▶ Difficulty in determining current market values
▶ Limited historical risk and return data
▶ Extensive investment analysis required

When present, liquidity can make alternative investments, such as real estate, attractive; but are there cases in which the general illiquidity of alternative investments can be attractive? Alternative investments beckon investors to areas of the market where alpha[1] is more likely to be found than in more liquid and efficient markets. Illiquidity, limited information, and less efficiency do not suit all investors, but can be attractive features to those looking for likely places to add value through investment expertise.

Terhaar, Staub, and Singer (2003) discuss two additional features of alternative investments:

▶ A liquidity premium compensates the investor for the investor's inability to continuously rebalance the alternative investments in the portfolio.

▶ A segmentation premium compensates investors for the risk of alternative assets that, by nature, are generally not priced in a fully integrated global market.

---

[1] *Alpha* is risk-adjusted return in excess of the required rate of return, but, more colloquially, stands for positive excess risk-adjusted return, the goal of active managers.

It is difficult to give a broad characterization of alternative investments, but they are often equity investments in some nonpublicly traded asset. In some cases, however, they may look more like an investment strategy than an asset class. Whatever the nature of alternative investments, specialized intermediaries often link the investor to the investments. Whether the investor invests directly or through an intermediary, he must know the investment's characteristics. In the case of investing through an intermediary, he must make sure that the incentive structure for any intermediary suits his investor needs.

Finally, alternative investments can be characterized as raising unique legal and tax considerations. A financial advisor would coordinate with an attorney and a tax accountant before recommending any specific real estate investment. Also, many forms of alternative investments involve special legal structures that avoid some taxes (exchange traded funds) or avoid some regulations (hedge funds).

INVESTMENT COMPANIES   2

Investment companies are financial intermediaries that earn fees to pool and invest investors' funds, giving the investors rights to a proportional share of the pooled fund performance. Both managed and unmanaged companies pool investor funds in this manner. Unmanaged investment companies (unit investment trusts in the United States) hold a fixed portfolio of investments (often tax exempt) for the life of the company and usually stand ready to redeem the investor's shares at market value. Managed investment companies are classified according to whether or not they stand ready to redeem investor shares. Open-end investment companies (mutual funds) offer this redemption feature, but closed-end funds do not. Closed-end investment companies issue shares that are then traded in the secondary markets.

2.1 Valuing Investment Company Shares

The basis for valuing investment company shares is net asset value (NAV). NAV is the per-share value of the investment company's assets minus its liabilities. Liabilities may come from fees owed to investment managers, for example. Share value equals NAV for unmanaged and open-end investment companies because they stand ready to redeem their shares at NAV. The price of a closed-end investment company's shares is determined in the secondary markets in which they trade, and, consequently, can be at a premium or discount to NAV.

2.2 Fund Management Fees

Investment companies charge fees, some as one-time charges and some as annual charges. By setting an initial selling price above the NAV, the unmanaged company charges a fee for the effort of setting up the fund. For managed funds, loads are simply sales commissions charged at purchase (front-end) as a percentage of the investment. A redemption fee (back-end load) is a charge to exit the fund. Redemption fees discourage quick trading turnover and are often set up so that the fees decline the longer the shares are held (in this case, the fees are sometimes called contingent deferred sales charges). Loads and redemption fees provide sales incentives but not portfolio management performance incentives.

Annual charges are composed of operating expenses including management fees, administrative expenses, and continuing distribution fees (12b-1 fees in the U.S.). The ratio of operating expenses to average assets is often referred to as the fund's "expense ratio." Distribution fees are fees paid back to the party that arranged the initial sale of the shares and are thus another type of sales incentive fee. Only management fees can be considered a portfolio management incentive fee. Example 75-1 is an illustration of the effects of investment company fees on fund performance.

2.3 Investment Strategies

Investment companies primarily invest in equity. Investment strategies can be characterized as style, sector, index, global, or stable value strategies. Style strategies focus on the underlying characteristics common to certain investments. Growth is a different style than value, and large capitalization investing is a different style than small stock investing. A growth strategy may focus on high price-to-earnings stocks, and a value strategy on low price-to-earnings stocks. Clearly, there are many styles.[2] A sector investment fund focuses on a particular industry. An index fund tracks an index. In the simplest implementation, the fund owns the securities in the index in exactly the same proportion as the market value weights of those securities in the index. A global fund includes securities from around the world and might keep portfolio weights similar to world market capitalization weights. An international fund is one that does not include the home country's securities, whereas a global fund includes the securities from the home country. A stable value fund invests in securities such as short-term fixed income instruments and guaranteed investment contracts which are guaranteed by the issuing insurance company and pay principal and a set rate of interest.

Example 75-1

Investment Company Fees: Effects on Performance

An investor is considering the purchase of TriGroup International Equity Fund (TRIEF) for her portfolio. Like many U.S.-based mutual funds today, TRIEF has more than one class of shares. Although all classes hold the same portfolio of securities, each class has a different expense structure. This particular mutual fund has three classes of shares, A, B, and C. The expenses of these classes are summarized in the following table:

Expense Comparison for Three Classes of TRIEF

	Class A	Class B*	Class C
Sales charge (load) on purchases	3%	None	None
Deferred sales charge (load) on redemptions	None	5% in the first year, declining by 1 percentage point each year thereafter	1% for the initial two years

---

[2] See, for example, Richard Bernstein, *Style Investing*, Wiley, 1995, and Richard Michaud, *Investment Styles, Market Anomalies, and Global Stock Selection*, The Research Foundation of AIMR, 1999.

	Class A	Class B*	Class C
Annual expenses:			
Distribution fee	0.25%	0.50%	0.50%
Management fee	0.75%	0.75%	0.75%
Other expenses	0.25%	0.25%	0.25%
	1.25%	1.50%	1.50%

*Class B shares automatically convert to Class A shares 72 months (6 years) after purchase, reducing future annual expenses.

The time horizon associated with the investor's objective in purchasing TRIEF is six years. She expects equity investments with risk characteristics similar to TRIEF to earn 8 percent per year, and she decides to make her selection of fund share class based on an assumed 8 percent return each year, gross of any of the expenses given in the preceding table.

A. Based on only the information provided here, determine the class of shares that is most appropriate for this investor. Assume that expense percentages given will be constant at the given values. Assume that the deferred sales charges are computed on the basis of NAV.

B. Suppose that, as a result of an unforeseen liquidity need, the investor needs to liquidate her investment at the end of the first year. Assume an 8 percent rate of return has been earned. Determine the relative performance of the three fund classes, and interpret the results.

C. Based on your answers to A and B, discuss the appropriateness of these share classes as it relates to an investor's time horizon; for example, a one-, six- and ten-year horizon.

SOLUTIONS

A. To address this question, we compute the terminal value of $1 invested at the end of year 6. The share class with the highest terminal value, net of all expenses, would be the most appropriate for this investor, as all classes are based on the same portfolio and thus have the same portfolio risk characteristics.

Class A. $1 \times (1 - 0.03) = \$0.97$ is the amount available for investment at $t = 0$, after paying the front-end sales charge. Because this amount grows at 8 percent for six years, reduced by annual expenses of 0.0125, the terminal value per $1 invested after six years is $\$0.97 \times 1.08^6 \times (1 - 0.0125)^6 = \$1.4274$.

Class B. After six years, $1 invested grows to $\$1 \times 1.08^6 \times (1 - 0.015)^6 = \$1.4493$. According to the table, the deferred sales charge disappears after year 5; therefore, the terminal value is $1.4493.

Class C. After six years, $1 invested grows to $\$1 \times 1.08^6 \times (1 - 0.015)^6 = \$1.4493$. There is no deferred sales charge in the sixth year, so $1.4493 is the terminal value.

In summary, the ranking by terminal value after six years is Class B and Class C ($1.4493), followed by Class A ($1.4274). Class B or Class C appears to be the most appropriate for this investor with a six-year horizon.

B. For Class A shares, the terminal value per $1 invested is $0.97 \times 1.08 \times (1 - 0.0125) = \$1.0345$. For Class B shares, it is $\$1 \times 1.08 \times (1 - 0.015) \times (1 - 0.05) = \$1.0106$, reflecting a 5 percent redemption charge; for Class C shares, it is $\$1 \times 1.08 \times (1 - 0.015) \times (1 - 0.01) = \$1.0532$, reflecting a 1 percent redemption charge. Thus, the ranking is Class C ($1.0532), Class A ($1.0345), and Class B ($1.0106).

C. Although Class B is appropriate given a six-year investment horizon, it is a costly choice if the fund shares need to be liquidated soon after investment. That eventuality would need to be assessed by the investor we are discussing. Class B, like Class A, is more attractive the longer the holding period, in general. Because Class C has higher annual expenses than Class A and Class B (after six years), it becomes less attractive the longer the holding period, in general.

After 10 years Class B shares would return $\$1 \times 1.08^{10} \times (1 - 0.015)^6 \times (1 - 0.0125)^4 = \$1.8750$, reflecting conversion to Class A after six years. Class C would return $\$1 \times 1.08^{10} \times (1 - 0.0150)^{10} = \$1.8561$. Class A shares would return the smallest amount, $\$0.97 \times 1.08^{10} \times (1 - 0.0125)^{10} = \$1.8466$. Though Class A underperforms Class C for a ten-year investment horizon, one could verify that Class A outperforms Class C for an investment horizon of 13 years or more. Also, in practice, the sales charge for Class A shares may be lower for purchases over certain sizes, making them more attractive in such comparisons.

2.4 Exchange Traded Funds

Exchange traded funds (ETFs) are index-based investment products that allow investors to buy or sell exposure to an index through a single financial instrument. ETFs are funds that trade on a stock market like shares of any individual companies. Gastineau (2001) gives a good introduction to ETFs. They can be traded at any time during market hours, can be sold short or margined. But they are shares of a portfolio, not of an individual company. They represent shares of ownership in either open-end funds or unit investment trusts that hold portfolios of stocks or bonds in custody, which are designed to track the price and yield performance of their underlying indexes—broad market, sector/industry, single country/region (multiple countries), or fixed income. Although many investors regard ETFs simply as a form of diversified equity investment, their novelty and legal specificity suggested their inclusion in this reading.

2.4.1 Recent Developments of ETFs

ETFs first appeared as TIP 35 (Toronto Index Participation Fund) in Canada in 1989, and appeared in the United States in 1993 with the introduction of Standard & Poor's 500 (S&P 500) Depositary Receipts. The first Asian ETF, the Hong Kong Tracker Fund, was launched in 1999. The first ETF launched in Europe, Euro STOXX 50, did not appear until 2000. Japan did not trade ETFs until 2001, when eight were listed. Their popularity has grown so quickly that they have become one of the most successful financial products of the decade.

According to Merrill Lynch (2002), there were 102 ETFs listed in the United States as of June 2002, 14 in Canada, 106 in Europe, and approximately 24 in Asia, including Japan—a total of 246.[3] Total global assets under management approached $130 billion, 75 percent of which are invested in U.S.-listed products. Although ETFs had a slow trading start in the United States, the trading volume of ETFs has grown rapidly in the last few years. According to Goldman Sachs (2002), the total shares outstanding for U.S. ETFs amounts to 1.9 million shares, with total assets of $92 billion, while average daily trading volume reached $7.0 billion, or 146.6 million shares per day, in mid-2002. ETFs based on international indexes have shown a strong growth and now represent almost 10 percent of total U.S.-listed ETF assets. The latest additions to the universe of ETFs are fixed-income ETFs, which started trading in July 2002 on the American Stock Exchange.

In Europe, the first ETF was launched by Merrill Lynch in April 2000 to track the Euro STOXX 50, which is the most actively replicated index in Europe. Listings of multiple ETFs on the same underlying index are common in Europe. In general, ETFs traded in Europe fall into four categories: single-country ETFs, regional ETFs based mostly on some pan-European or Eurozone indexes, European-sector ETFs, and global ETFs. The most popular ETFs are based on Euro STOXX 50, CAC 40, and the DAX. Although assets under management ($8 billion in mid-2002) and average daily volumes are still small compared with U.S. figures, the growth in terms of volume and number of outstanding products has been impressive. The daily trading volume grew from $6 million in the third quarter of 2000 to over $250 million in the first quarter of 2002 (Mussavian and Hirsch, 2002).

In Asia, the growth in ETFs comes primarily from Japan. Merrill Lynch (2002) estimates that the total assets under management in Asian ETFs were in excess of $13.9 billion in mid-2002.

2.4.2 ETF Structure

The usual ETF structure adopted worldwide is that of open-end funds with special characteristics, such as the "in-kind" process for creation and redemption of shares described subsequently (see Gastineau, 2001). Details of the legal structure vary depending on the country where the ETF is incorporated. In the United States, ETFs have adopted three different legal structures:

▶ *Managed investment companies:* Managed investment companies are open-ended investment companies registered under the Investment Company Act of 1940. They offer the most flexible ETF structure. The index can be tracked using various techniques, such as holding only a sample of the underlying securities in the index, lending of securities, and trading in derivatives. Dividends paid on the securities can be immediately reinvested in the fund. Sector SPDRs, iShares, and WEBS use this legal structure.

▶ *Unit investment trusts:* Unit investment trusts (UITs) are also registered investment companies, but they operate under more constraints, because they do not have a manager per se (but trustees). UITs are required to be fully invested in all underlying securities forming the index and must hold dividends received on securities in cash until the ETF pays a dividend to shareholders. This could result in a slight cash drag on performance. UITs

---

[3] Complete listings of ETFs can be found at www.indexfunds.com.

are not permitted to lend securities and do not generally use derivatives. S&P 500 SPDR, Midcap 400 SPDR and NASDAQ-100 QQQ use this legal structure.

▶ *Grantor trusts:* Grantor trusts are not registered investment companies. Accordingly, owning a grantor trust is substantially similar to holding a basket of securities. A grantor trust often takes the form of an American Depositary Receipt (ADR) and trades as such. Because a grantor trust is fully invested in the basket of securities, no investment discretion is exercised by the trust. This is basically an unmanaged (and unregistered) investment company with a limited life. The trust passes all dividends on the underlying securities to shareholders as soon as practicable. Securities lending and use of derivatives are generally not practiced. HOLDRs use this legal structure. Grantor trusts are a structure that allows investors to indirectly own an unmanaged basket of stocks rather than tracking an index, and some do not classify them as ETFs.

We will now introduce the unique "in-kind" creation and redemption process used by open-end and UIT ETFs. This in-kind process is a major distinguishing feature of ETFs. Creation/redemption units are created in large multiples of individual ETF shares, for example, 50,000 shares. These units are available to exchange specialists (*authorized participants* or *creation agents*) that are authorized by the fund and who will generally act as market makers on the individual ETF shares. The fund publishes the index tracking portfolio that it is willing to accept for in-kind transactions. When there is excess demand for ETF shares, an authorized participant will create a *creation unit* (a large block of ETF shares) by depositing with the trustee of the fund the specified portfolio of stocks used to track the index. In return, the authorized participant will receive ETF shares that can be sold to investors on the stock market. The redemption process is the same but in reverse. If there is an excess number of ETF shares sold by investors, an authorized participant will decide to redeem ETF shares; it will do so by exchanging with the fund a *redemption unit* (a large block of ETF shares) for a portfolio of stocks held by the fund and used to track the index. Exhibit 75-1 depicts the ETF structure and the creation/redemption process.

As opposed to traditional open-end funds, the in-kind redemption means that no capital gain will be realized in the fund's portfolio on redemption. If the redemption were in cash, the fund would have to sell stocks held in the fund's portfolio. If their price had appreciated, the fund would realize a capital gain, and the tax burden would have to be passed to all existing fund shareholders. This is not the case with ETFs. This in-kind transfer for redemptions does not create a tax burden for the remaining ETF shareholders under current U.S. tax law, unlike the capital gains distributions on traditional mutual fund shareholders that could result from the sale of securities to meet redemption demand.[4] As in any open-end fund, individual ETF shareholders[5] can require in-cash redemption based on the NAV. Redemption in cash by individual ETF shareholders is discouraged in two ways:

▶ Redemption is based on the NAV computed a couple of days after the shareholder commits to redemption. So, the redemption value is unknown when the investor decides to redeem. This is a common feature of mutual funds.

▶ A large fee is assessed on in-cash redemptions.

---

[4] As pointed out by Chamberlain and Jordan (2002), there are situations in which capital gains distributions are generated for the ETF, such as capital gains resulting from selling securities directly to the capital markets due to an index reconstitution. Thus, zero capital gains distributions are not guaranteed.

[5] But authorized participants commit to redeem only in kind.

It is more advantageous for individual shareholders to sell their shares on the market than to redeem them in cash. Arbitrage[6] by authorized participants ensures that the listed price is close to the fund's NAV, and the sale can take place immediately based on observed share prices and at a low transaction cost. Authorized participants maintain a market in the ETF share by posting bid-and-ask prices with a narrow spread, or by entering in an electronic order book buy-and-sell limit orders, which play the same role. The transaction cost of ETFs can be estimated as the sum of the commission charged by the broker plus half this bid–ask spread.

EXHIBIT 75-1 Creation/Redemption Process of Exchange Traded Funds

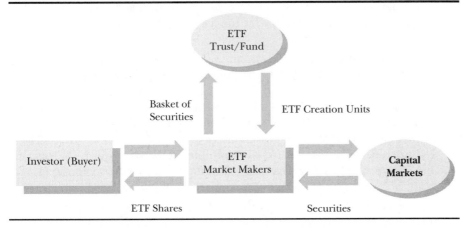

In comparing the ETF structure presented in Exhibit 75-1 with that of the traditional mutual fund structure, it is clear that market makers in the ETF structure play an instrumental role in the creation and redemption process. In the traditional mutual fund structure, an increase in demand for the shares of the mutual fund is met by the mutual fund, which simply issues new shares to the investor, and the fund manager will take the cash to the capital markets and buy securities appropriate to the fund's objective. When the customer wants to sell the mutual fund shares, the fund manager may need to raise cash by selling securities back to the capital markets. In contrast, when a customer wants to buy ETF shares, the order is not directed to the fund but to the market makers on the exchange. The market maker will exchange ETF shares for cash with the customer (via broker/dealer) and, when necessary, replenish the supply of ETFs through the creation process outlined earlier.

2.4.3 Advantages/Disadvantages of ETFs

ETFs are used by a wide spectrum of investors, both individual and institutional, in a wide variety of investment strategies. This is because ETFs have the following advantages:

▷ Diversification can be obtained easily with a single ETF transaction. With equity-oriented ETFs, investors can gain instant exposure to different market capitalizations, style (value or growth), sector or industries, countries or geographic regions. With fixed income ETFs, they can gain exposure to different maturity segments and bond market sectors. Thus, ETFs provide a convenient way to diversify.

---

[6] ETFs usually publish an indicative intraday NAV every 15 seconds that is available from major data providers.

▷ Although ETFs represent interests in a portfolio of securities, they trade similarly to a stock on an organized exchange. For example, ETFs can be sold short and also bought on margin.

▷ ETFs trade throughout the whole trading day at market prices that are updated continuously, rather than only trading once a day at closing market prices, as do the traditional open-end mutual funds.

▷ For many ETFs, there exist futures and options contracts on the same index, which is convenient for risk management.

▷ Portfolio holdings of ETFs are transparent. The ETF sponsor publishes the constituents of the fund on a daily basis. This should closely resemble the constituents of the underlying index. This is in contrast to other funds, for which the manager publishes only the list of assets in the fund from time to time.

▷ ETFs are cost effective. There are no load fees. Moreover, because the ETFs are passively managed, the expense ratio (which includes management fee for open-end funds, trustee fee for UITs, and custody fee for HOLDRs) can be kept low relative to actively managed funds. The expense ratio is comparable to that of an index mutual fund. For example, management fee can be as low as 8 basis points for the most successful U.S. ETFs, and up to 90 basis points for sector and international products (Mussavian and Hirsch, 2002). ETFs have a cost advantage over traditional mutual funds because there is no shareholder accounting at the fund level.

▷ ETFs have an advantage over closed-end index funds because their structure can prevent a significant premium/discount. Although supply and demand determine the market price of an ETF just like any other security, arbitrage helps keep the traded price of an ETF much more in line with its underlying value. By simultaneously buying (or selling) the ETF basket of securities and selling (or buying) the ETF shares in the secondary market, and creating (or redeeming) ETF shares to be delivered against the sale, market makers can capture the price discrepancy and make an arbitrage profit. Thus, UIT and open-end ETFs have the capability to avoid trading at large premiums and discounts to the NAVs. This is in contrast to closed-end index funds, which offer a fixed supply of shares, and as demand changes, they frequently trade at appreciable discounts from—and sometimes premiums to—their NAVs.

▷ The exposure to capital gains distribution taxes is lower than for traditional funds, so the consequences of other shareholders' redemptions are limited. As mentioned, capital gains resulting from in-kind transfer for redemptions do not create a tax burden for the remaining ETF shareholders. For this reason, capital gains tax liability is expected to be lower for ETF shareholders than for mutual fund shareholders.

▷ Dividends are reinvested immediately for open-end ETFs (but not for UIT ETFs), whereas for index mutual funds, timing of dividend reinvestment varies.

However, ETFs are not necessarily the most efficient alternative for investing in a market segment.

▷ In many countries, actively traded ETFs track a narrow-based market index, including only stocks with large market capitalization. So, no ETF is available for mid or low market-cap stocks. This is not the case in the United States, where a variety of ETF products trade actively.

▷ Many investors do not require the intraday trading opportunity provided by ETFs, because they have a long investment horizon.

- Some ETFs do not have large trading volumes and the bid–ask spread can be quite large. For example, some U.S. ETFs based on some sector indexes or on some foreign indexes (e.g., emerging markets) do not trade actively, and directly investing in a managed fund can be a less costly alternative, especially for large investors. Sector and international ETFs have an expense ratio that can be substantial (close to 1 percent) compared with that of a managed portfolio.

- For large institutional investors, the alternative to international ETFs is to invest directly in an indexed, or actively managed, international portfolio; the costs could be less, and the tax situation equivalent or better.

2.4.4 Types of ETFs

ETFs can be grouped by investment category, based on their investment target (broad domestic market index, style, sector/industry, country or region). For a given investment target, ETFs can be created based on different indexes of the same market, as well as by different sponsors. The number of ETFs keeps growing, and the diversity of investment targets increases, although all ETFs launched are not successful. We only cite some notable examples under each of the following categories:

- *Broad domestic market index:* In many countries, the most active ETFs are those launched on the major local stock index. Hong Kong Tracker Fund was the first ETF listed in Asia and the largest ever IPO in Asia excluding Japan. In Japan, Nikkei 225 and TOPIX ETFs have amassed significant assets under management, and there are several competing sponsors offering ETFs on the same indexes. In Europe, ETFs based on the French CAC 40 index and the German DAX 30 index are, by far, the most actively traded. In the United States, there are many market indexes followed by investors, so there are many competing ETFs; the most notable examples in this category include S&P 500 Depositary Receipts (SPDRs or "spiders"), Nasdaq-100 Index Tracking Stock (QQQs or "cubes"), and Diamonds Trust Series (DIAs or "diamonds"). There are also ETFs based on very broad U.S. market indexes, such as the Russell 1000, Russell 3000, or Wilshire 5000 indexes. It is fair to say that ETFs based on local market indexes now exist in most countries, including in many emerging countries.

- *Style:* Some ETFs track a specific investment style. This type of ETF is mostly found in the United States, because investors from other countries are less accustomed to style investing. ETFs exist on growth and value indexes developed by S&P/BARRA and Russell. Investors can also find ETFs specialized by market capitalization (large, mid, and small cap).

- *Sector or industry:* Some ETFs track a sector index or invest in baskets of stocks from specific industry sectors, including consumer, cyclicals, energy, financial, heath care, industrials, insurance, materials, media, staples, technology, telecommunications, transportation, and utilities. Sector and industry ETFs can be found in the United States, Europe, and Japan. Many European funds track pan-European or global-sector indexes. In the United States, industry HOLDRs offer a series of investment portfolios that are based not on an index, but on a basket of 20 to 50 companies in the same industry.

- *Country or region (multiple countries):* A fast-growing segment of the ETF market is funds tracking foreign-country indexes and regional indexes. In the United States, iShares are indexed to several developed and emerging equity markets, as well as to international indexes such as MSCI Europe and EAFE. Fresco introduced on the NYSE an ETF indexed on the Euro STOXX 50 index of the major 50 stocks of the Eurozone. Country and regional ETFs have also been launched in Europe and Japan. Again, several sponsors are competing for products on the same international indexes.

▶ *Fixed income:* This category is the latest addition to the universe of ETFs, and mostly in the United States. They have had limited success so far.

As stressed in Chapter 5, international ETFs have distinguishing features. An ETF indexed on some less-liquid emerging market is bound to have high bid–ask spreads. Managing an ETF on a broad international index means holding stocks from numerous countries with different custodial arrangement and time zones. Again, the bid–ask spreads are bound to be larger than for plain-vanilla ETFs. But the size (assets under management) of the ETF is an important factor influencing costs. The effect of non-overlapping time zones should be taken into account when comparing the ETF price and its NAV. Take the example of an ETF on a Japanese stock index, traded in New York. During Wall Street opening hours, the Tokyo stock market is closed. The NAV available in the morning in America is based on the closing prices in Tokyo several hours before New York opened. Except for currency fluctuations, the NAV will remain unchanged because Tokyo is closed throughout the New York trading session. However, the ETF price will be affected by expectations about future stock prices in Tokyo, so it could differ significantly from the official NAV. This is not an inefficiency and there are no arbitrage opportunities, because the NAV is stale and does not correspond to current market pricing.

2.4.5 Risks in ETFs

Listed next are the major risks faced by ETFs. They, however, do not affect all ETFs to the same extent. For example, market risk, trading risk, and tracking error risk affect all ETFs, while sector risk, currency risk, and country risk may affect sector and country ETFs. Likewise, derivatives risk affects only those funds that employ derivatives in their investment strategies. In addition, different ETFs may face risks that are unique to the fund (not discussed in this reading).

▶ *Market risk:* ETF shareholders are subject to risks similar to those of holders of other diversified portfolios. The NAV of the ETF will change with changes in the market index tracked by the fund.

▶ *Asset class/sector risk:* Some ETFs invest in some market segment. The returns from the type of securities in which an ETF invests may underperform returns from the general securities markets or different asset classes. For example, the performance of a sector ETF may be susceptible to any single economic, market, political, or regulatory occurrence. Thus, a sector ETF also may be adversely affected by the performance of that specific sector or group of industries on which it is based. This risk is directly implied by the investment strategy offered by the fund.

▶ *Trading risk:* Although an ETF is designed to make it likely that it will trade close to its NAV, impediments to the securities markets may result in trading prices that differ, sometimes significantly, from NAV. Moreover, there is no assurance that an active trading market will always exist for the ETF on the exchange, so the bid–ask spread can be large for some ETFs. The overall depth and liquidity of the secondary market also may fluctuate.

▶ *Tracking error risk:* Although ETFs are designed to provide investment results that generally correspond to the price and yield performance of their respective underlying indexes, the funds/trusts may not be able to exactly replicate the performance of the indexes because of fund/trust expenses and other factors. Tracking risk comes from trading risk (the ETF market price deviates from its NAV), but also from the fact that the ETF NAV differs from the index value.

▷ *Derivatives risk:* ETFs that invest in index futures contracts and other derivatives to track an index are subject to additional risks that accrue to derivatives, for example, counterparty credit risk and higher leverage.

▷ *Currency risk and country risk:* ETFs that are based on international indexes may involve risk of capital loss from unfavorable fluctuations in currency values or from economic and political instability in other nations. ETFs invested in emerging markets bear greater risk of market shutdown and of the imposition of capital controls than those typically found in a developed market. Country risk also includes the risk of expropriation. It could be that foreign investors are discriminated against, so that the return of an ETF will significantly underperform the local market index return achieved by a local investor.

2.4.6 Applications of ETFs

ETFs can be used in a wide variety of investment strategies. Following are some suggested popular applications:

▷ *Implementing asset allocation:* ETFs can be used to effect asset allocation among baskets of stocks and bonds at either the strategic or the tactical level.

▷ *Diversifying sector/industry exposure:* ETFs on broad market indexes can be used to diversify away the sector- or industry-specific event risks borne in an otherwise undiversified portfolio. Such ETF exposure is a natural complement to an investment strategy of holding only a few attractive stocks.

▷ *Gaining exposure to international markets:* Money managers can quickly and easily purchase ETFs for instant and extensive international exposure to a single country or multiple countries within a geographic region, compared with the expense and difficulty of assembling a portfolio of foreign securities.

▷ *Equitizing cash:* By investing in ETFs, money managers can put idle cash to work temporarily while determining where to invest for the longer term. For example, a fund manager using the Nikkei 225 as its benchmark could invest cash inflows into one of the ETFs tied to this benchmark before he decides which stocks to buy. This can minimize cash drag or benchmark risk. It is a convenient alternative to buying futures contract on the market index.

▷ *Managing cash flows:* Investment managers can take advantage of ETFs' liquidity during periods of cash inflows and outflows. A portfolio manager can establish a position in an ETF that corresponds to the portfolio's benchmark or investment strategy, investing inflows into the ETF and liquidating the position as needed to meet redemptions or invest in specific stocks or bonds.

▷ *Completing overall investment strategy:* Fund or money managers can use ETFs to quickly establish or increase exposure to an industry or sector to "fill holes" in an overall investment strategy.

▷ *Bridging transitions in fund management:* Pension plan assets can often lie dormant during times of investment manager appointments, replacements, or shifts. Institutions can use ETFs as a cost-effective method to keep assets invested in the interim.

▷ *Managing portfolio risk:* Because ETFs can be sold short in a declining equity market (or rising interest rate market for fixed-income ETFs), portfolio managers can use ETFs to hedge overall portfolio risk or sector/industry exposure.

▷ *Applying relative value, long/short strategies:* Institutions can take advantage of ETF features to apply long/short strategies aimed at increasing returns. For example, an institution can establish a long position in a broad market, country, sector, or bond index expected to outperform while shorting an index expected to underperform. Doubling the size of the long position versus the short position can leverage the total position. Market makers can use ETFs to exploit price discrepancies between ETFs, the underlying index, the futures, and/or options.

3   REAL ESTATE

Real estate is usually considered to be buildings and buildable land, including offices, industrial warehouses, multifamily buildings, and retail space. Real estate is a form of tangible asset, one that can be touched and seen, as opposed to financial claims that are recorded as pieces of paper. Other forms of tangible assets are available for investment purposes. These include natural resources, timber, containers, artwork, and many others. We will focus on real estate, which is, by far, the most common form of investment in tangible assets.

Real estate as an investment has several unique characteristics as well as several characteristics common to other types of investments. Even the definition of real estate isolates it as a unique investment. Real estate is an immovable asset—land (earth surface) and the permanently attached improvements to it. Graaskamp defines real estate as artificially delineated space with a fourth dimension of time referenced to a fixed point on the face of the earth.[7] This astrophysical definition stresses the idea that ownership rights to earth areas can be divided up not only in the three dimensions of space, but also in a time dimension, as well as divided up among investors. One plot of land with its building can be divided into above ground (e.g., buildings) and below ground (e.g., minerals), into areas within the building (e.g., rooms), and into periods of time (timesharing). Different investors can own the different divisions. Many classifications can be adopted for real estate. Real estate can be classified by usage (office space, multifamily housing, retail space) and location. It can also be classified into four quadrants by form of ownership, public or private, and by form of financing, debt or equity.[8] Clearly, it is not possible to adopt a simple classification of real estate, because this asset class covers so many different investment products.

Real estate is an important investment category. In many countries, domestic real estate is a common investment vehicle for pension funds and life insurance companies. It is not uncommon to have private European investors owning and renting directly a few real estate units, such as houses, condominium apartments, or parking spaces. But there are some obstacles for institutions and individuals wishing to invest in foreign real estate. First, it is difficult to monitor properties located abroad. Second, taxes, paperwork, and unforeseen risks may make foreign real estate investment impractical on a large scale, although investments can be made through specialized managers in the countries of interest. To be sure, private deals can be arranged for special projects, but these are well beyond the scope of this book. There is, however, a definite trend toward the development of negotiable forms for real

---

[7] Jarchow (1991), p. 42.

[8] See, for example, Hudson-Wilson (2001).

property interest. In many countries, pooled funds have been created with the specific purpose of real estate investment. Mortgage-backed Eurobonds are rapidly growing in popularity. Many institutional investors, especially in Europe, have started to invest in international real estate. The time may not be too far off when real estate will be a normal component of international investment strategies.

3.1 Forms of Real Estate Investment

There are several forms of real estate investment: free and clear equity, leveraged equity, mortgages, and aggregation vehicles.

3.1.1 Free and Clear Equity

"Free and clear equity," sometimes called "fee simple," refers to full ownership rights for an indefinite period of time, giving the owner the right, for example, to lease the property to tenants and resell the property at will. This is straightforward purchase of some real estate property.

3.1.2 Leveraged Equity

Leveraged equity refers to the same ownership rights but subject to debt (a promissory note) and a pledge (mortgage) to hand over real estate ownership rights if the loan terms are not met. A mortgage is a pledge of real estate ownership rights to another party as security for debt owed to that party. Thus, leveraged equity involves equity ownership plus a debt and a requirement to transfer ownership of the equity in case of default on the debt. The debt and the mortgage are usually packaged together into a mortgage loan.

3.1.3 Mortgages

Mortgages (or more precisely, mortgage loans) themselves are another real estate investment vehicle, representing a type of debt investment. Investing in a mortgage provides the investor with a stream of bondlike payments. These payments include net interest, net of mortgage servicing fees, and a scheduled repayment of principal. This is a form of real estate investment because the creditor may end up owning the property being mortgaged. Mortgage loans often include a clause of early repayment (at a cost) at the option of the debtor. So, the debtholder may also receive excess principal repayments, called mortgage prepayments. These prepayments produce uncertainty in the amount and timing of mortgage cash flows.

To diversify risks, a typical investor does not invest in one mortgage, but in securities issued against a pool of mortgages. An intermediary buys a pool of mortgages and then issues securities backed by the mortgages, but with the securities passing through the net mortgage payments to the investors.

3.1.4 Aggregation Vehicles

Aggregation vehicles aggregate investors and serve the purpose of giving investors collective access to real estate investments. *Real estate limited partnerships (RELPs)* allow investors (the limited partners) to participate in real estate projects while preserving limited liability (the initial investment) and leaving management to the general partners who are real estate experts. *Commingled funds* are pools of capital created largely by like-minded institutional investors organized together by an intermediary to invest chiefly in real estate investment projects. The investors share in the investment rewards according to the amount of capital they invest. Commingled funds can be either open or closed end. Closed-end funds have a set termination date, typically allow no new investors after initiation of the fund, and typically buy and hold a real estate portfolio for the life of the fund, with no reinvestment as sales occur. By contrast, open-end funds have indefinite lives, accept new investors, and revise their real estate portfolios over time. Finally, *real estate investment trusts (REITs)* are a type of closed-end investment company. They issue shares that are traded on a stock market, and they invest in various types of real estate. Thus, they aggregate individual investors and provide them easy access to real estate and diversification within real estate. Of course, the risk and return characteristics of REITs depend on the type of investment they make. Mortgage REITs, which invest primarily in mortgages, are more akin to a bond investment, while equity REITs, which invest primarily in commercial or residential properties using leverage, are more akin to an investment in leveraged equity real estate. The shares of REITs trade freely on the stock market, so they are liquid investments, but their share price can trade at a discount (or premium) to the NAV of the properties in their portfolio.

3.2 Valuation Approaches

Real estate assets are quite different from securities traded on a financial market: "Because the real estate market is not an auction market offering divisible shares in every property, and information flows in the market are complex, these features place a premium on investment judgment. Managers who want to own some of IBM simply buy some shares. Managers who want to participate in the returns on, say, a $300 million office building, must take a significant position in the property."[9] Following are some characteristics of real estate as an investable asset class:

▷ Properties are immovable, basically indivisible, and unique assets, as contrasted to fungible (perfectly interchangeable) and divisible assets such as currencies. Though unique, even art is movable and thus not as unique as real estate.

▷ Properties are only approximately comparable to other properties.

▷ Properties are generally illiquid, due to their immobility and indivisibility.

▷ There is no national, or international, auction market for properties. Hence, the "market" value of a given property is difficult to assess.

▷ Transaction costs and management fees for real estate investments are high.

▷ Real estate markets suffer inefficiencies because of the nature of real estate itself and because information is not freely available.

Valuation of real estate focuses on intrinsic value just as does the valuation of any asset. In real estate, the term *appraisal* is used for the process of estimating the market and the investment value of the property. The market value estimate is independent of the particular investor, but the investment value depends on the particular use that the investor plans for the property.

To estimate a property's value, a real estate appraiser generally uses one of three approaches or a combination of the approaches. The approaches are the cost approach, the sales comparison approach, and the income approach.

---

[9] Firstenberg, Ross, and Zisler (1988).

An investor can further take into account her specific tax situation to value the property using a discounted after-tax cash flow approach. These four approaches are used worldwide.

3.2.1 The Cost Approach

The cost approach is analogous to the use of replacement cost of total assets in the calculation of Tobin's Q for equity valuation. What would it cost to replace the building in its present form? Of course, an estimate of the land value must be added to the building replacement cost estimate. The replacement cost approach is relatively easy to implement because it is based on current construction costs, but it suffers from severe limitations. First, an appraisal of the land value is required and that is not always an easy task. Second, the market value of an existing property could differ markedly from its construction cost. An office building could be very valuable because it has some prestigious and stable tenants that pay high rents, not because of the value of the construction. Conversely, an office building in poor condition, with a large vacancy rate and in a bad neighborhood, could be worth much less than its replacement cost.

3.2.2 The Sales Comparison Approach

The sales comparison approach is similar to the "price multiple comparables" approach in equity valuation. Market value is estimated relative to a benchmark value. The benchmark value may be the market price of a similar property, or the average or median value of the market prices of similar properties, in transactions made near the time of the appraisal. The benchmark-based estimate needs to be adjusted for changing market conditions, the possibility that the benchmark itself is mispriced, and the unique features of the property relative to the benchmark. Properties with comparable characteristics might not have traded recently.

One formal variation of the sales comparison approach is the method of *hedonic price estimation*. In this method, the major characteristics of a property that can affect its value are identified. The characteristics of a residential property that are relevant to its value can be the age of the building, its size, its location, its vacancy rate, its amenities, and so on. Individual properties are given a quantitative rating for each of the characteristics. For example, location could be ranked from 1 (very bad) to 10 (very good). The sales price for all recent transactions of the properties in the benchmark are then regressed on their characteristics ratings. This is a regression in which there is one observation for each transaction. The dependent (left-hand side) variable is the transaction price, and the independent (right-hand side) variables are the ratings for each of the characteristics. The estimated slope coefficients are the valuation of each characteristic in the transaction price. The result is a benchmark monetary value associated with each characteristic's rating. It is then possible to estimate the selling price of a specific property by taking into account its rating on each feature. Although this has become a standard technique in residential property appraisal, it has also been applied to income producing property.[10]

---

[10] See Söderberg (2002), pp. 157–180.

Example 75-2

Sales Comparison Approach: Hedonic Price Model

A real estate company has prepared a simple hedonic model to value houses in a specific area. A summary list of the house's characteristics that can affect pricing are:

- the number of main rooms,
- the surface area of the garden,
- the presence of a swimming pool, and
- the distance to a shopping center.

A statistical analysis of a large number of recent transactions in the area allowed the company to estimate the following slope coefficients:

Characteristics	Units	Slope Coefficient in Pounds per Unit
Number of rooms	Number	20,000
Surface area of the garden	Square feet	5
Swimming pool	0 or 1	20,000
Distance to shopping center	In miles	−10,000

A typical house in the area has five main rooms, a garden of 10,000 square feet, a swimming pool, and a distance of one mile to the nearest shopping center. The transaction price for a typical house was £160,000.

You wish to value a house that has seven rooms, a garden of 10,000 square feet, a swimming pool, and a distance of two miles to the nearest shopping center. What is the appraisal value based on this sales comparison approach of hedonic price estimation?

SOLUTION

The appraised value is given by the equation

$$
\begin{aligned}
\text{Value} &= 20{,}000 \times (\text{\# Rooms}) + 5 \times (\text{Garden surface}) + 20{,}000 \times \\
&\quad (\text{Pool}) - 10{,}000 \times (\text{Distance to shopping center}) \\
&= 20{,}000 \times 7 + 5 \times 10{,}000 + 20{,}000 \times 1 - 10{,}000 \times 2 \\
&= £190{,}000
\end{aligned}
$$

This specific house has an appraised value of £190,000. Compared to the typical house in the area, it has two more rooms but is one mile farther from the nearest shopping center.

3.2.3 The Income Approach

The income approach to real estate valuation values property using a perpetuity discount type of model. The perpetuity is the annual net operating income (NOI).

This perpetual stream is discounted at a market required rate of return (the market capitalization or cap rate). NOI is gross potential income minus expenses, which include estimated vacancy and collection losses, insurance, taxes, utilities, and repairs and maintenance. Technically, the market cap rate is the rate used by the market in recent transactions to capitalize future income into a present market value. For a constant and perpetual stream of annual NOI, we have

$$\text{Appraisal price} = \frac{\text{NOI}}{\text{Market cap rate}}$$

And the market cap rate is calculated on the benchmark transactions as

$$\text{Market cap rate} = \frac{\text{Benchmark NOI}}{\text{Benchmark transaction price}}$$

Benchmark may refer to a single comparable property or the median or mean of several comparable properties, with any appropriate adjustments.

It must be stressed that the income approach makes the simplifying assumption of a constant and perpetual amount of annual income. The income approach can also be adjusted for the special cases of a constant growth rate in rentals or a constant growth rate in rentals coupled with long-term leases. Valuation with a constant growth rate in rentals parallels the constant growth dividend discount model. Inflation could make NOI grow at the inflation rate over time. As long as inflation can be passed through, it will not affect valuation, because the market cap rate also incorporates the inflation rate. In the long-term lease case, the growth in rentals is not fully reflected in the NOI growth rate. The rent remains fixed over the term of the lease, while costs grow at the inflation rate. This is analogous to the inflation pass-through question raised in equity valuation (see Chapter 6). If expected inflation will cause operating expenses to rise, how much of the inflation can the owner pass through to the tenants? Longer lease terms delay the pass-through. Another limitation of this approach is that all calculations are performed before tax.

Example 75-3

The Income Approach

An investor wants to evaluate an apartment complex using the income approach. Recent sales in the area consist of an office building and an apartment complex. He gathers the following data on the apartment complex, as well as on recent sales in the area. All income items are on an annual basis. According to the income approach, what is the value of the apartment complex?

	Apartment Investment under Consideration	Office Building Recently Sold	Apartment Complex Recently Sold
Gross potential rental income	$120,000		
Estimated vacancy and collection losses	6%		
Insurance and taxes	$10,000		

	Apartment Investment under Consideration	Office Building Recently Sold	Apartment Complex Recently Sold
Utilities	$7,000		
Repairs and maintenance	$12,000		
Depreciation	$14,000		
Interest on proposed financing	$11,000		
Net operating income		$300,000	$60,000
Sales price		$2,000,000	$500,000

SOLUTION

The NOI for the apartment complex is gross potential rental income minus estimated vacancy and collection costs minus insurance and taxes minus utilities minus repairs and maintenance.

$$NOI = 120,000 - 0.06 \times 120,000 - 10,000 - 7,000 - 12,000 = 83,800$$

The other apartment complex is the comparable property, and that has a capitalization rate of

$$NOI/(\text{Transaction price}) = 60,000/500,000 = 0.12$$

Applying this cap rate to the apartment complex under consideration gives an appraisal price of

$$NOI/(\text{Cap rate}) = 83,800/0.12 = \$698,333$$

Note that we do not use the financing costs to determine the NOI, because we wish to appraise the value of the property independently of its financing. Neither do we subtract depreciation. The implicit assumption is that repairs and maintenance will allow the investor to keep the building in good condition forever.

3.2.4 The Discounted After-Tax Cash Flow Approach

Supplementing the cost, sales comparison, and income approach used for market value appraisals, the discounted after-tax cash flow approach is a check on investment valuation. If the investor can deduct depreciation and any interest payments from NOI, then the investor's after-tax cash flows depend on the investor's marginal tax rate. Hence, the value of a property for a specific investor depends on the investor's marginal tax rate. Once these cash flows and after-tax proceeds from future property disposition are estimated, the net present value of the property to an equity investor is obtained as the present value of the cash flows, discounted at the investor's required rate of return on equity, minus the amount of equity required to make the investment.

For an equity investment to be worthwhile, its expected net present value must be positive. Alternatively, the investment's yield (internal rate of return) should exceed the investor's required rate of return.

Example 75-4

The Discounted Cash Flow Approach

An analyst is assigned the task of evaluating a real estate investment project. The purchase price is $700,000, which is financed 20 percent by equity and 80 percent by a mortgage loan at a 10 percent pretax interest rate. According to the applicable country's tax rules, the interest on real estate financing for this project is tax deductible. The mortgage loan has a long maturity and level annual payments of $59,404. This includes interest payments on the remaining principal at a 10 percent interest rate and a variable principal repayment that steps up with time. The analyst calculated NOI in the first year to be $83,800. NOI is expected to grow at a rate of 5 percent every year.

The analyst faces the following valuation tasks: determining the first year's after-tax cash flow, determining interim after-tax cash flows, determining the final year's after-tax cash flow, and calculating two measures of the project's profitability, the investment's net present value (NPV) and the investment's yield (internal rate of return).

i. Determine the first year's after-tax cash flow, using the following data:

Net operating income (NOI) for first year	$83,800
Straight-line depreciation	18,700
Mortgage payment	59,404
Purchase price	700,000
80% financing at a 10% interest rate	
NOI growth rate	5%
Marginal income tax rate	31%

ii. Determine the second year's after-tax cash flow, using the preceding table and with a growth rate of 5% in NOI.

iii. The property is sold at the end of the fifth year. Determine the after-tax cash flow for that property sale year, using the following data (the after-tax cash flow without property sale has been calculated as previously).

After-tax cash flow without property sale	$33,546
Straight-line depreciation	18,700
Mortgage payment	59,404
Cumulative mortgage principal repayments by end of fifth year	20,783
Purchase price	700,000
80% financing at 10% interest rate	
NOI growth factor	5%
Marginal income tax rate	31%

Capital gains tax rate	20%
Forecasted sales price	$875,000
Property sales expense as a percentage of sales price	6%

Use the information below to answer Parts iv and v.

The following data summarize the after-tax cash flows for all five years of the project's life (the table includes the results we have calculated previously for years 1, 2, and 5, as well as results for years 3 and 4):

Year	1	2	3	4	5
Cash flow	21.575	24,361	27.280	30,339	273,629

The analyst now turns to evaluating whether the project should be undertaken. She estimates the required rate of return for an equity investment in projects of similar risk as 16 percent. The purchase price for the property is $700,000. The financing plan calls for 80 percent debt financing, so the equity investment is only $140,000. The investor's cost of equity for projects with this level of risk is 16 percent, but a sensitivity analysis on cost of equity helps provide some perspective for the analyst. She decides to conduct a sensitivity analysis, calculating the present value of the year 1 to year 5 after-tax cash flows using a range of discount rates other than 16 percent; the results appear in the following table:

Discount Rate	Present Value
0.10	$250,867
0.14	$216,161
0.18	$187,637
0.22	$164,012
0.26	$144,303
0.30	$127,747
0.34	$113,750

iv. Determine the real estate project's NPV, using the analyst's required rate of return, and make a purchase recommendation based only on this analysis.

v. Determine an approximate yield for the real estate project, and make a purchase recommendation based only on this analysis.

SOLUTION TO i

Because interest is tax deductible here, calculate the first year's interest, and then calculate after-tax net income. The amount borrowed is

$560,000 = 700,000 \times 0.8$. The first year's interest at 10 percent is then $56,000 = 0.1 \times \$560,000$. After-tax net income is then ($83,800 − $18,700 − $56,000) × (1 − 0.31) = $6,279.

To get after-tax cash flow from after-tax net income, depreciation must be added and the principal repayment component of the $59,404 mortgage payment must be subtracted. The principal repayment is the mortgage payment minus the interest payment, or $3,404 = $59,404 − $56,000. Thus, the after-tax cash flow is $21,575 = $6,279 + $18,700 − $3,404.

SOLUTION TO ii

First we calculate the new NOI, equal to $87,990 = $83,800 × (1.05).

Second, we calculate after-tax net income. We need to calculate the second year's interest payment on the mortgage balance after the first year's payment. This mortgage balance is the original principal balance minus the first year's principal repayment, or $556,596. The interest on this balance is then $55,660. After-tax net income is then ($87,990 − $18,700 − $55,660) × (1 − 0.31) = $9,405.

Third, the second year's principal repayment is the mortgage payment minus the interest payment, or $3,744 = $59,404 − $55,660.

Finally, then calculate the second year's after-tax cash flow, which equals the second year's after-tax net income plus depreciation minus the principal repayment, or $24,361 = $9,405 + $18,700 − $3,744.

SOLUTION TO iii

The after-tax cash flow for the property sale year is equal to the sum of the after-tax cash flow without the property sale plus the after-tax cash flow from the property sale. When a property is sold, the outstanding mortgage principal balance (the outstanding mortgage, for short) must be paid to the lender. In the following calculations, we incorporate that effect into the after-tax cash flow from the property sale.

To begin, we calculate the capital gains on the sale of the property. To do that, first determine the ending book value as the original purchase price minus five years' worth of depreciation, or $606,500 = $700,000 − 5 × $18,700. The net sale price is equal to the forecasted sale price, $875,000, minus sales expenses of 6 percent, or $52,500. Capital gains taxes are paid on the difference between the net sales price and the book value, or a difference of $216,000 = ($875,000 − $52,500) − $606,500. The capital gains taxes are then $43,200 = 0.2 × $216,000. The after-tax cash flow from the property sale is then the net sales price minus the outstanding mortgage minus the capital gains taxes. The outstanding mortgage is the original mortgage minus five years' worth of principal repayments, or $539,217 = $560,000 − $20,783. Thus the after-tax cash flow from the property sale is $240,083 = ($875,000 − $52,500) − $539,217 − $43,200. The after-tax cash flow for the property sale year is then $273,629 = $33,546 + $240,083.

SOLUTION TO iv

At a cost of equity of 16 percent, the present value of the cash flow is $201,215 = $21,575/1.16 + $24,361/1.16^2 + $27,280/1.16^3 + $30,339/1.16^4 + $273,629/1.16^5. The investment requires equity of

$140,000 = 0.2 \times \$700,000$. Thus, the NPV is $\$61,215 = \$201,215 - \$140,000$. The analyst recommends this investment because it has a positive NPV.

SOLUTION TO v

We can address the question using the results of the analyst's sensitivity analysis. The yield or internal rate of return is the discount rate that makes the project's NPV equal to zero. The yield must be between 26 percent and 30 percent because discounting at 26 percent gives a present value ($144,303) that is larger than the initial investment (of $140,000), or a positive NPV, while discounting at 30 percent gives a present value ($127,747) that is smaller than the initial investment, or a negative NPV. Consequently, the project's yield must lie between 26 percent and 30 percent. Actually, the internal rate of return of this project is slightly below 27 percent. The analyst recommends the investment because the investment's yield exceeds the investor's required rate of return (16 percent).

3.3 Real Estate in a Portfolio Context

Some real estate indexes have been developed to attempt to measure the average return on real estate investment. Good-quality indexes with a long-term historical record exist in the United States and United Kingdom, but they are more recent or even nonexistent in other countries.

Real estate returns consist of income and capital gain or loss. The income on a property can usually be measured in a straightforward fashion. The value appreciation is more difficult to assess. The most common method is to use changes in appraised value. Appraisal of each property is conducted by specialists fairly infrequently (typically once a year). Appraisals are generally based on the approaches discussed previously. In practice, appraisal prices exhibit remarkable inertia. The value of a real estate portfolio is further smoothed because properties are appraised infrequently, so their prices remain constant between appraisals.

Following are the major U.S. real estate indexes, based on appraisal values:

▷ The *Frank Russell Company (FRC)* and the *National Council of Real Estate Investment Fiduciaries (NCREIF)* indexes. These are quarterly indexes, starting in 1978 and broken down by regions and property types.

▷ The *Commingled Real Estate Equity Fund (CREF)* index, published by Evaluation Associates. This is a quarterly index of major tax-exempt funds, starting in 1969.

Another method of measuring price appreciation is to use a reference to REITs. The total return on a REIT is made up of the income paid to shareholders, as well as of the stock market appreciation of the REIT share price. Various REIT indexes are used to proxy the average total return on real estate investments. They are easier to construct, because they are simply some weighted average of market-traded shares. The major REIT indexes are as follows:

▷ The *National Association of Real Estate Investment Trusts (NAREIT)*, a monthly equal-weighted index of some one hundred REITs, starting in 1972.

▶ REIT indexes published by various institutions, for example, Wilshire or Goldman Sachs.

The two types of indexes provide very different performance and risk characteristics, which have been studied by Firstenberg, Ross, and Zisler (1988), Goetzmann and Ibbotson (1990), and Gyourko and Keim (1993). Appraisal-based indexes are much less volatile than REIT indexes. For example, Goetzman and Ibbotson found that a REIT index had an annual standard deviation of 15.4 percent, comparable to that of the S&P 500 index, but six times larger than that of the CREF index, of 2.6 percent. Furthermore, appraisal-based indexes and REIT indexes have very little correlation. Appraisal-based indexes exhibit persistent returns (returns are correlated over time), showing the inertia in appraisals. REIT indexes are strongly correlated with the rest of the stock market.

In summary, real estate returns can be calculated using either appraisal indexes or REIT indexes. Appraisals do not provide continuous price data and they do not provide market prices but only market price estimates. REIT indexes provide continuous market prices of REITs but not of the underlying real estate. Thus, they reflect the amount of leverage used in the REITs. Therefore neither approach to calculating returns is entirely satisfactory. In any case, the issue in investment is one of forecasting returns, standard deviations, and correlations. For example, in analyzing a particular real estate project, an investor would supplement cash flow forecasts and discounted cash flow analysis with considerations of how the project's cash flows will covary with his existing portfolio. An individual investor will not receive diversification benefits from a real estate project whose returns are highly correlated with his own business employment income.

A few studies have looked at real estate from a global viewpoint. These studies examine the proposed portfolio benefits of real estate, risk reduction (through diversification) and inflation protection. Eichholtz (1996) looked at the diversification benefits of real estate shares quoted in many countries. He found that international diversification strongly reduces the risk of a real estate portfolio. However, Mull and Soenen (1997) showed that REITs are strongly correlated with other U.S. stocks, so that foreign investors who buy U.S. REITs do not gain much diversification benefit, beyond the U.S. stock market exposure. Liu, Hartzell, and Hoesli (1997) looked at real estate securities traded on seven national stock markets and concluded that their correlation with inflation is low, so they do not provide a good hedge against inflation. Quan and Titman (1997) studied commercial real estate values in 17 countries, where property values and rents are calculated using an appraisal-based approach. Commercial real estate prices and stock prices are both affected by the general level of economic activity, so they should be strongly correlated. Pooling their international data, Quan and Titman did find that the relation between stock returns and changes in real estate values is very strong.

Although research studies have not provided overwhelming evidence to support the risk reduction and inflation protection benefits of real estate, such studies are always limited by the use of either appraisal indexes or REIT indexes. Judgment is needed in assessing the impact of real estate on a portfolio. First, what are the projected cash flows and what are the predicted covariances of the cash flows with the current portfolio? Second, what are the inflation pass-through characteristics of the real estate investment?

PRIVATE EQUITY: VENTURE CAPITAL 　　4

Venture capital is one of the main categories of private equity investing. Private equity investments are equity investments that are not traded on exchanges.

Venture capital investments are private equity investments in business ventures from idea stage through expansion of a company already producing and selling a product and through preparation for exit from the investment via buyout or initial public offering. Venture capital investing may be done at stages along the way, but eventual exit is a primary consideration. By its very nature, such investing requires a horizon of several years and the willingness to accept several failures for every success in the venture capital portfolio: The possibly enormous return on the winning venture must compensate for many likely failed ventures.

Institutional and individual investors usually invest in private equity through limited partnerships. Limited partnerships allow investors (the limited partners) to participate in a portfolio of venture capital projects while preserving limited liability (the initial investment) and leaving management to the general partners who are private equity experts. Typically, the general partners are associated with a firm that specializes in private equity or with the private equity department of a financial institution. Funds of funds are also offered that pool investments in several ventures.

CONCEPTS IN ACTION Global Investing: Mounting Overseas Interest Keeps U.S. Real Estate Prices Above Water

As stock markets continue to offer weak returns, foreign investors have poured money into US real estate at a fast pace this year, attracted by superior yields and the transparency and liquidity of the market.

Jacques Gordon, international director of investment strategy and research for LaSalle Investment Management, said US real estate has always been attractive to foreign money, but the magnitude of the sums incoming has been particularly noteworthy this year.

Much of the attraction is based on the higher yields from US properties, which average between 7 and 8 per cent compared with 4 to 5 per cent in Europe.

Real Capital Analytics, a real estate monitoring group, estimates foreign investors will have acquired nearly $9bn of US commercial property by the end of 2002, double the $4.5bn seen in 2001.

Overseas money is largely being spent on office space in metropolitan areas such as New York and Washington. Foreigners bought $6.7bn of office properties, representing 16 per cent of total office investments in the US in 2002. German-based Jamestown Immobilien is just about to close a $745m deal to buy the Axa Financial Center on Sixth Avenue in New York.

Of greatest interest to foreigners have been "trophy" buildings in the central business districts of big cities. That heightened interest has boosted property prices to new records, despite rising vacancies and falling rents.

This discrepancy in the fundamentals is raising concerns for the future profitability of current investments, especially in light of continuing weakness in the US economy. "There is a disconnect between the price of commercial real estate and if there is a renewed recession that disconnect cannot persist," said Hugh Kelly, professor of real estate at New York University.

But Mr Gordon said that although record prices are being paid for office properties, he sees limited risk to the downside, given that the amounts being paid are only about 10 per cent higher than previous records.

"Although record amounts are being paid, it is not anything like the tech frenzy we saw in the stock market. [The record prices] do not trouble me in the sense that there's a bubble about to burst," Mr Gordon said.

Interest in the US market has been heaviest from Germany, accounting for 51 per cent of total foreign capital in US real estate this year. Germans invested $4.9bn in US property in 2002 compared with just $2.7bn a year earlier.

The main reason for the increased interest is that money is flowing at an unprecedented rate into German open-ended and closed-end funds, and analysts say investing large sums in high-profile buildings in the US is an easy way to invest the funds quickly and efficiently.

Markus Derkum of Jamestown, a real estate investment company that raises money in Germany for investments in the US, says weak stock-market performance already saw German investors turning to US real estate in 2001. He said the terrorist attacks in the World Trade Center and the Pentagon in September only caused a minor blip on the flow.

"We thought nobody would touch US real estate any more, especially the international capital. We were wrong," he said.

In 2001, foreign acquisitions in apartment, industrial and retail properties totaled $1bn and that is set to jump to $2.2bn this year.

Non-German European investors account for about 22 per cent of the foreign interest in the US, and Middle Eastern investors, Israeli and Arab, account for about 14 per cent. Canadians invested 8 per cent of total foreign investment and Australians, with 5 per cent, have this year emerged as a significant new source of capital, particularly in the retail sector.

Source: Global Investing, Zarina Rijnen, *Financial Times*, 10 December 2002.

4.1 Stages of Venture Capital Investing

Schilit (1996) provides a good review of the various stages of venture capital investing. Several rounds of financing take place, and these can be characterized by where they occur in the development of the venture itself. Here, Schilit's classification review is adapted and blended with other common industry terminology.[11] Each stage of financing is matched by investments, so that aggregate investment activity is often reported by the amount in different stage funds.

1. *Seed-stage* financing is capital provided for a business idea. The capital generally supports product development and market research.

2. *Early-stage* financing is capital provided for companies moving into operation and before commercial manufacturing and sales have occurred.

   ▷ *Start-up* is capital provided for companies just moving into operation but without any commercial product or service sales. The capital generally supports product development and initial marketing.

   ▷ *First-stage* financing is capital provided to initiate commercial manufacturing and sales.

3. *Formative-stage* financing includes seed stage and early stage.

4. *Later-stage* financing is capital provided after commercial manufacturing and sales have begun but before any initial public offering.

   ▷ *Second-stage* financing refers to capital used for initial expansion of a company already producing and selling a product but perhaps not yet profitably.

   ▷ *Third-stage* financing is capital provided for major expansion, such as physical plant expansion, product improvement, or a major marketing campaign.

---

[11] See, for example, Thomson Venture Economics, the National Venture Capital Association (in the United States), the European Venture Capital Association, and the British Venture Capital Association.

> *Mezzanine* (bridge) financing is capital provided to prepare for the step of going public and represents the bridge between the expanding company and the initial public offering (IPO).

Expansion-stage financing includes second and third stage. *Balanced-stage* financing is a term used to refer to all the stages, seed through mezzanine.

CONCEPTS IN ACTION   **Venture Capital Investments Continue to Decline in Q3 2002: Economic Realities Return Investing to pre-1998 levels**

Stage of Development

Expansion stage companies continue to receive the most venture capital, receiving 56% of all capital invested and 55% of the number of deals in the third quarter. At the same time, investors continued to fund earlier stage companies. In Q3, companies in the "formative" stages of development (early stage and startup/seed) received similar levels as last quarter, 23% of dollars invested and 30% of the number of deals. This stability in earlier stage investing indicates venture capital firms continue to take longer-term views.

Later stage investing became more dominant in the third quarter, representing 20% of the dollars invested and 15% of the number of deals compared to 13% of the dollars invested and 9% of the number of deals in Q2. This increase in later stage deals demonstrates that venture capitalists have remained committed to their existing portfolio companies and continue to finance their development during this difficult economic period.

According to Jesse Reyes, vice president at Thomson Venture Economics, "Venture funds that focus on later stage deals are finding fewer traditional later stage opportunities—that is, deals a couple of years from exit—because the time to exit has lengthened. As a result, VCs are finding that the only new investments that fit their focus are expansion stage deals that require even more time to mature before exit is a possibility."

Source: PricewaterhouseCoopers, Venture Economics, National Venture Capital Association MoneyTree™ Survey.

4.2 Investment Characteristics

Venture capital investing has several characteristics, some of which are common to alternative investing in general, but many of which are unique:

> *Illiquidity:* Venture capital investments do not provide an easy or short-term path for cashing out. Liquidation or divestment of each venture within a portfolio is dependent on the success of the fund manager in creating a buyout or initial public offering (IPO) opportunity. One particular risk is that inexperienced venture fund managers will "grandstand" and bring ventures to the market too early, especially when the IPO market is good. Conversely, a poor IPO market may mean that otherwise successful ventures may afford no immediate path to liquidity.

> *Long-term commitment required:* Venture capital requires a long-term commitment because of the time lag to liquidity. If the average investor is averse to illiquidity, this will create a liquidity risk premium on venture capital. Thus, an investor with a longer than average time horizon can expect to profit from this liquidity risk premium. It is not surprising that university endowments (with their long horizons) have sought venture capital vehicles.

▸ *Difficulty in determining current market values:* Because there is no continuous trading of the investments within a venture fund portfolio, there is no objective way of determining the current market value of the portfolio. This poses a problem for reporting the market value exposure of the current venture capital portion of an investor's portfolio.

▸ *Limited historical risk and return data:* Because there is no continuous market in venture capital, historical risk and return data have limitations.

▸ *Limited information:* Because entrepreneurs operate in previously uncharted territory, there is little information on which to base estimates of cash flows or the probability of success of their ventures

▸ *Entrepreneurial/management mismatches:* Although surely profit motivated, some entrepreneurs may be more wedded to the success of their favorite idea than to the financial success of the venture. During the early life of a firm, there are also two major problems that may arise. First, the entrepreneur may not be a good manager, so the existence or creation of a good management team is critical. Second, rapid growth produces a change in the type of managerial expertise required, so that entrepreneurs/managers who can succeed with small ventures need the ability to adapt to the different demands of larger companies, or the investors must be in a position to replace them.

▸ *Fund manager incentive mismatches:* Fund managers may be rewarded by size of their fund rather than by performance of their fund. Investors interested in performance must look for fund managers whose incentives are aligned with theirs.

▸ *Lack of knowledge of how many competitors exist:* Because entrepreneurs operate in uncharted territory, there is often little way for them or for analysts to know how many other entrepreneurs are developing substitute ideas or products at the same time. Thus, competitive analysis for venture capital investments is even more difficult than for investments in established companies in established industries.

▸ *Vintage cycles:* Some years are better than others. Both entry and exit are factors here. If too many entrepreneurial firms enter at the prompt of increased venture capital availability, the economics of perfect competition will prevail and returns will be weak. On the exit side, poor financial market conditions can cause venture capital to dry up, and perhaps some firms that could be successful will not find the financing needed for their success. Thus, some years provide better firm planting and growing conditions than others.

▸ *Extensive operations analysis and advice may be required:* More than financial engineering skill is required of fund managers. Venture capital investments require extensive investment analysis, but they also require extensive operating management experience. Thus, a venture capital manager who can add value will be the one who has both financial and operating experience, and knowledge of the emerging industry in which the entrepreneur is operating. The venture capital manager must be able to act as both a financial and an operations management consultant to the venture. Reflecting David Swensen's philosophy[12] at the Yale Endowment, the investor is well advised to choose a fund manager who knows the business and can add value.

---

[12] See pages 17 and 18 in Lerner (2000).

4.3 Types of Liquidation/Divestment[13]

Exit strategies are critical for venture capital investing. The main types of liquidation/divestment are trade sales, initial public offerings (IPOs) followed by the sale of quoted equity, and write-offs. Trade sales are sales or mergers of the private company for cash or stock of the acquirer. An IPO is the initial issuance of shares registered for public trading. Shares are distributed to the private equity investors who can sell them in the marketplace only after the expiration of a lock-up period. (In rare cases, a sale or merger of the private company follows the IPO.) Write-offs are voluntary liquidations that may or may not produce any proceeds. In addition to the main types of liquidation, there are also cases of bankruptcy as well as the situation in which the founder/entrepreneur buys out the outside venture capital investors and takes the company back to a privately held company without institutional shareholders.

Participating in a venture capital fund, investors get distributions of public stock or cash from realized venture capital investments. The fund may require additional investments (drawdowns) from limited partners and may make cash or share distributions at random times during the life of the fund. Investors might also be able to sell their interests if they can find a buyer. Also, at the end of the fund's life, there are often illiquid, barely alive companies (living dead) that are transferred to a liquidating vehicle with minimal fees. A very few funds have an evergreen type of structure, which rolls old fund investments into a new fund that has new cash commitments.

In the following Concepts in Action, note that divestment by flotation and sale of quoted equity together constitute the second main exit mechanism (exit via a public market).

CONCEPTS IN ACTION European Divestment Reported Through the Third Quarter of 2002

Excluding write-offs, the highest amount divested at cost this year was in quarter three. A total of €1.5bn was divested at cost in Q3, up from €1.3bn in Q2 and just over €1bn in Q1. A total of 502 companies were divested in Q3, down from the 774 divested in Q2. Trade sales remained the most significant route to exit and accounted for 28.8% of total divestment at cost (€434m), a 5% decrease in amount on the previous quarter. At €342m, write-offs remained significant in Q3, but fell by 18% on the previous quarter. IPOs as an exit were still a rare option, but the slow trickle of activity (2 companies divested through IPO in Q3) showed that some practitioners still managed to use the IPO, even in the prevailing difficult climate. Between Q1 and Q3 of 2002, a total of €3.9bn was divested at cost.

	Q3 2002				
	Amount at Cost (€m)	%	No of Divestments	%	No of Co.s
Divestment by Trade Sale	433.6	28.8	118	17.5	81
Divestment by Flotation (IPO)	5.1	0.3	6	0.9	2
Sale of Quoted Equity	62.0	4.1	99	14.7	58
Divestment by Write-Off	342.0	22.7	194	28.8	177

---

[13] This section has benefited from correspondence with Dean Takahashi.

	Amount at Cost (€m)	%	No of Divestments	%	No of Co.s
Other	664.7	44.1	257	38.1	184
Total	**1,507.5**	**100.0**	**674**	**100.0**	**502**

Source: Reprinted with permission from European Venture Capital & Private Equity Association, Thomson Economics and PricewaterhouseCoopers.

(Quarterly Activity Indicator, Q3 2002).

4.4 Valuation and Performance Measurement

In the venture capital area, valuation and performance measurement is a difficult exercise. This is true at the level of a single venture project, but also at the level of an investment in a venture capital fund.

4.4.1 Valuation and Project Risk

Valuing a prospective venture capital project is a challenging task. Although some valuation methods can be applied, quantifying future cash flows is difficult. Investing in a particular venture capital project is motivated by an anticipated large payoff at time of exit. But many projects will fail along the way. In addition to the normal risk of equity investments, the particular risk of venture capital stems from the increased uncertainty created by possibly inexperienced entrepreneurs with innovative products or product ideas and uncertain time to success, even if successful. Some of the unique risks of venture capital projects come from their investment characteristics, as described. Of course, the risk of a portfolio of venture capital investments is less than the risk of any individual venture project, because of risk diversification.

So, there are three main parameters that enter into valuing a venture capital project:

▷ An assessment of the expected payoff at time of exit, if the venture is successful;

▷ An assessment of the time it will take to exit the venture successfully; and

▷ An assessment of the probability of failure.

This is illustrated in Example 75-5.

Example 75-5

Venture Capital Valuation And Risk

An investor estimates that investing $1 million in a particular venture capital project will pay $16 million at the end of seven years if it succeeds; however, she realizes that the project may fail at any time between now and the end of seven years. The investor is considering an equity investment in the project and her cost of equity for a project with this level of risk is 18 percent. In the following table are the investor's estimates of some probabilities of failure for the project. First, 0.25 is the probability of failure in year 1. For year 2, 0.25 is the probability that the project fails in the second year, given that it has survived through year 1. For year 3, 0.20 is the probability that the project fails, given that it has survived through year 2, and so forth.

Year	1	2	3	4	5	6	7
Failure probability	0.25	0.22	0.20	0.20	0.20	0.20	0.20

   i. Determine the probability that the project survives to the end of the seventh year.

   ii. Determine the expected NPV of the project.

   iii. Make a recommendation.

SOLUTION

   i. The probability that the project survives to the end of the first year is $(1 - 0.25) = 1$ minus the probability of failure in the first year; the probability that it survives the end of second year is the product of the probability it survives the first year times the probability it survives the second year, or $(1 - 0.25)(1 - 0.22)$. Using this pattern, the probability that the firm survives to end of the seventh year is $(1 - 0.25)(1 - 0.22)(1 - 0.20)^5 = (0.75)(0.78)(0.80)^5 = 0.192$ or 19.2%.

   ii. The NPV of the project, given that it survives to the end of the seventh year and thus earns $16 million, equals $4.02 million = $-$1 million + $16 million$/1.18^7$. The NPV of project given that it fails is $-$1 million. Thus, the project's expected NPV is a probability-weighted average of these two amounts, or $(0.192)($4.02 million) + (0.808)(-$1 million) = -$36,160$.

   iii. Based on its negative NPV, the recommendation is to decline the investment.

The payoff structure of actual projects is generally more complex than that of Example 75-5. Practitioners may use a multiple-scenario approach to valuation. In this approach, payoffs are simulated under each scenario (from optimistic to pessimistic) and weighted by the probability of occurrence of the scenario.

4.4.2 Performance Measurement

Investors in a venture capital fund need to evaluate the performance of their investment, not only at time of liquidation, but also during the life of their investment. This is usually done by calculating an internal rate of return based on cash flows since inception and the end-of-period valuation of the unliquidated remaining holdings (residual value or net asset value). The European Venture Capital Association (www.evca.com), the British Venture Capital Association (www.bvca.co.uk), and AIMR have valuation guidelines bearing on this.

There are several challenges to performance measurement in the venture capital area. Lerner (2000) points these out in a discussion of future directions for an endowment fund:

▸ The difficulty in determining precise valuations. Venture capital funds do not have market prices to value their holdings, so they use some arbitrary technique to value their portfolios of ongoing projects. For example, some managers apply an average internal rate of return to the historical investment costs of their ongoing projects. Of course, the actual exit value is used at the time of exit of a project, or a zero value is used if a project failed.

▸ The lack of meaningful benchmarks against which fund manager and investment success can be measured.

▸ The long-term nature of any reliable performance feedback in the venture capital asset class.

HEDGE FUNDS AND ABSOLUTE RETURN STRATEGIES

5

The early 1990s saw the explosive development of *hedge funds*. Even though the attraction of these funds was tempered by many huge losses suffered in 1994 and 1998, the hedge fund industry continued to prosper. The number of global hedge funds, estimated to be 1,373 in 1988 grew to an estimated 7,000 at the end of 2001. The assets under management of hedge funds grew from $42 billion in 1988 to $311 billion in 1998, and to about $600 billion by the end of 2001.[14] The asset base of U.S. and non-U.S. hedge funds are of the same order of magnitude.

CONCEPTS IN ACTION Losses in Private Equity Business Reach $10bn

Financial services companies' private equity operations have lost more than $10bn in total since the bear market in technology began in 2000, according to their financial reports.

Many institutions—including Deutsche Bank, which has lost $1.7bn, and GE Capital Services, which has taken a $592m hit to earnings—are planning to leave the business, while those that remain are radically changing their practices.

The banks with the largest private equity operations, JP Morgan Chase and Credit Suisse First Boston—both of which have assets of more than $20bn in their groups—remain committed to their business.

But JP Morgan, which has lost at least $1.8bn during the downturn, will have a much reduced presence in the market.

In a memo last week, Bill Harrison, chief executive, reiterated his support for the private equity group, but also set a multi-year target of halving private equity exposure to 10 percent of common equity from 20 percent.

He also noted that the private equity group would have to seek more outside money to support their efforts. The bank recently launched a private equity fund with $1.7bn of outside money, but that fell well short of the initial $5bn target.

JP Morgan also intends to sell its interests in other people's private equity partnerships. Both JP Morgan and CSFB, among others, bought into the idea of investing in buyout funds to cement their growing relationships with buyout firms, which are important Wall Street clients.

---

[14] The source for this is Van Hedge Fund Advisors International at www.vanhedge.com, accessed on 12 December 2002.

But the fall in some funds injected unwanted volatility into banks' income statements and bankers now acknowledge those positions were less useful in attracting buyout business.

Banks have reacted to those losses by turning to the secondary and securitization markets in an effort to find an exit. JP Morgan sold more than $1bn of partnerships 18 months ago and CSFB is in the process of concluding a $100m sale.

Deutsche Bank plans to securitize its investments in other private equity partnerships, as well as allowing its own group to launch a management buyout.

Many firms have found it difficult to divest their private equity exposures, however.

Secondary private equity funds have raised billions of dollars to buy unwanted private equity partnerships.

But after a year when the average buyout fund declined 11 percent in value and the average venture capital fund has fallen 27 percent, according to Thomson Venture Economics, secondary funds are cautious about what they will pay for other people's portfolios.

Source: Robert Clow, *Financial Times: Companies & Markets,* 13 December 2002, p. 19.

Although individual investors have been the traditional client bases of hedge funds, institutional investors, especially endowments and foundations, have started to invest en masse. We start this section by a description of the different types of hedge funds available, including funds of funds. A discussion of the leverage and unique risk characteristics of hedge funds will complete this description. Hedge funds follow strategies that promise a large absolute return, and deserve a close investigation of the actual performance and risk of those strategies. We therefore present the case for investing in hedge funds in some detail, but also provide the caveats.

CONCEPTS IN ACTION   Endowments, Foundations Move More to Hedge Funds

WILTON, Conn.—Endowments and foundations increased their allocations to hedge funds in the year ended June 30, a Commonfund report shows.

Among those that altered their asset allocations during the year, hedge fund exposure rose to 35% of the average alternatives portfolio from 22%.

Increased use of hedge funds helped boost alternative investments to 15% of total assets as of June 30, from 11% a year earlier among the funds that changed their asset allocations.

Of the 97 endowments and foundations surveyed, 29% reported changes in the asset allocation in the previous year.

The $197 million University of Connecticut foundation in Storrs is among those hiking hedge fund exposure. The foundation doubled its hedge fund allocation to 10% of total assets following an asset allocation study by Wilshire Associates, Santa Monica, Calif.

"We've been adding diversification," said Kevin Edwards, director of treasury services.

Of those institutions that made changes, the average allocation to domestic equities dropped three percentage points to 47%; the average allocation to international equities dropped one point to 10%.

John Griswold, executive director of Commonfund Institute, said while he's pleased endowments and foundations largely "are sticking to their guns" on asset allocation, he expects more shifts soon.

"This fall, there will be meetings of committees with a lot of concern," he said.

This is the second consecutive year that endowments and foundations showed negative returns. The average return was −5.4% for the year ended

June 30 and −3% for the previous one-year period. For the year ended June 30, 2000, the average return was 13.2%.

The smaller the fund, the worse the return, the survey shows. Respondents with assets between $51 million and $100 million reported an average return of −7.4%, while those assets between $101 million and $500 million reported an average −6.1% return.

By contrast, funds with more than $1 billion in assets returned an average −3.4% for the year ended June 30.

The findings are from the interim edition of Commonfund's benchmark study, an annual survey of higher-education endowments and foundations. The interim study covers 97 endowments and foundations that were surveyed through an Internet questionnaire. The final results of the study will be released in 2003.

Source: Mike Kennedy, *Pensions & Investments,* 30 September 2002, p. 33. Reprinted with permission, *Pensions & Investments,* September 30, 2002. Copyright Crain Communications Inc.

5.1 Definition

5.1.1 Objective

It is difficult to provide a general definition of hedge funds. The original concept of a hedge fund was to offer plays *against* the markets, using shortselling, futures, and other derivative products. Today, funds using the "hedge fund" appellation follow all kinds of strategies and cannot be considered a homogeneous asset class. Some funds are highly leveraged; others are not. Some engage in hedging activities, and others do not. Some focus on making macroeconomic bets on commodities, currencies, interest rates, and so on. Some are mostly "technical" funds trying to take advantage of the mispricing of some securities within their market. Futures funds belong to the world of hedge funds. In fact, the common denominator of hedge funds is not their investment strategy but the *search for absolute returns.*

Money management has progressively moved toward a focus on performance *relative to preassigned benchmarks.* An institutional money manager's performance is generally evaluated relative to some market index that is assigned as a mandate. In turn, these benchmarks guide (some would say "unduly constrain") the money manager's investment policy. The risk of deviating from the performance of the benchmark has become huge, given all of the publicity surrounding relative performance in a very competitive money management industry. The development of hedge funds can be seen as a reaction against this trend, with the search for absolute return in all directions. In practice, this means that hedge funds might have more appropriately been termed *isolation* funds. They generally try to isolate specific bets for the purpose of generating alpha. One can infer the particular bet from each hedge fund position. Hedge fund managers seek freedom to achieve high absolute returns and wish to be rewarded for their performance. These objectives are apparent in the legal organization and the fee structure of hedge funds. These two aspects are probably the only uniform characteristics of hedge funds.

5.1.2 Legal Structure

Hedge funds are typically set up as a *limited partnership,* as a limited liability corporation (in the United States), or as an *offshore corporation.* These legal structures allow the fund manager to take short and long positions in any asset, to use all kinds of derivatives, and to leverage the fund without restrictions. Hedge funds based in the United States most often take the form of a limited partnership organized under section 3(c)(1) of the Investment Company Act, thereby gaining exemption from most U.S. Securities and Exchange Commission (SEC) regulations. The fund is limited to no more than 100 partners, who must be "accredited investors,"[15] and is prohibited from advertising. Some U.S. hedge funds are organized under section 3(c)(7) of the Investment Company Act, and are also exempt from most SEC regulations. In that case, the fund is limited to no more than 500 investors, who must be "qualified purchasers,"[16] and is prohibited from advertising. Given the small number of partners, a minimum investment is typically more than $200,000. Institutional investors can become partners. U.S. hedge funds are typically incorporated in a "fund-friendly" state, such as Delaware. *Offshore funds* have also proved to be an attractive legal structure. These are incorporated in locations such as the British Virgin Islands, Cayman Islands, Bermuda, or other locations attractive from a fiscal and legal point of view. A hedge fund might consider using "feeders" (vehicles that have an ownership interest in the hedge fund) that enable the hedge fund to solicit funds from investors in every imaginable tax and legal domain—one feeder for ordinary U.S. investors; another for tax-free pensions; another for Japanese who want their profits hedged in yen; still another for European institutions, which invest only in shares that are listed on an exchange (i.e., a dummy listing on the Irish Stock Exchange). These feeders don't keep the money; they are used as paper conduits that channel the money to a central fund, typically a Cayman Islands partnership.

5.1.3 Fee Structure

The manager is compensated through a *base* management fee based on the value of assets under management (at one time as much as 2 to 3 percent, now more typically 1 percent of the asset base) plus an *incentive fee* proportional to the realized profits (ranging from 15 percent to 30 percent, typically 20 percent of total profits).[17] The base fee is paid whatever the performance of the fund. The incentive fee cannot be negative, so a negative return on the funds implies a zero incentive fee. The incentive fee is sometimes applied to profits measured above a risk-free rate applied to the assets. In other words, the hedge fund return has to be greater than the risk-free rate before the incentive fee is activated. The fee structure sometimes includes a "high water mark" stating that following a year in which the fund declined in value, the hedge fund would first have to recover those losses before any incentive fee would be paid. Example 75-6 shows the effect of a hedge fund's fee structure on its net return.

Example 75-6

Hedge Fund Fee

A hedge fund has an annual fee of 1 percent base management fee plus a 20 percent incentive fee applied to profits above the risk-free rate, taken to be the Treasury Bill rate. Hence the incentive fee is applied to annual profits after deduction of the Treasury bill rate applied to the amount of assets under management at the start of the year. The gross return during the year is 40 percent. What is the net return (the return after fees) for an investor, if the risk-free rate is 5 percent?

---

[15] An accredited investor under the Securities and Exchange Act is an individual with a net worth in excess of $1 million or an annual income in excess of $200,000; or an entity with total assets of $5 million or more.

[16] A qualified purchaser (or qualified investor) is an individual with at least $5 million in investments or an entity with at least $25 million in investments.

[17] Besides the management and incentive fees that almost all hedge funds charge their clients, hedge funds may charge other fees, such as surrender fees, ticket charges, and financing fees.

SOLUTION

Fee = 1% + 20% × (40% − 5%) = 8%
Net return = 40% − 8% = 32%

5.2 Classification

Hedge funds have become quite global, as evidenced by the wide array of global investments used by these hedge funds and the international diversity of their client base. Some classifications of hedge funds by investment strategy is provided in the media and by hedge funds databases. These classifications are somewhat arbitrary, exhibit a large degree of overlap, and differ extensively across sources. Following is one possible classification system:

▷ *Long/short funds* are the traditional types of hedge funds, taking short and long bets in common stocks. They vary their short and long exposures according to forecasts, use leverage, and now operate on numerous markets throughout the world. These funds often maintain net positive or negative market exposures; so they are not necessarily market-neutral. In fact, a subgroup within this category is funds that have a systematic short bias, known as dedicated short funds, or short-seller funds. Long/short funds represent a large amount of hedge fund assets.

▷ *Market-neutral funds* are a form of long/short funds that attempt to be hedged against a general market movement. They take bets on valuation differences of individual securities within some market segment. This could involve simultaneous long and short positions in closely related securities with a zero net exposure to the market itself. A market-neutral long-short portfolio is constructed so that the total value of the positions held long equals the total value of the positions sold short (dollar neutrality) and so that the total sensitivity of the long positions equals and offsets the total sensitivity of the short positions (beta neutrality). The long position would be in stocks considered undervalued, and the short position would be in stocks considered overvalued. Leverage is generally used, so that the investment in the long position (or the short position) is a multiple of the hedge fund equity. Another alternative is to use derivatives to hedge market risk. For example, a manager could buy some bond deemed to be underpriced with a simultaneous short position in bond futures or other fixed-income derivatives. This type of fund is sometimes called a fixed-income arbitrage fund. Other types of arbitrage make use of complex securities with option-like clauses, such as convertibles, warrants, or collateralized mortgage obligations (CMOs). Among the various techniques used by market-neutral funds are

  ▷ equity long/short,
  ▷ fixed-income hedging,
  ▷ pairs trading,
  ▷ warrant arbitrage,
  ▷ mortgage arbitrage,
  ▷ convertible bond arbitrage,
  ▷ closed-end fund arbitrage, and
  ▷ statistical arbitrage.

It must be stressed that despite their labels ("arbitrage," "neutral"), these funds are not riskless because hedges can never be perfect. Loss can be incurred if the model used is imperfect, and can be high because hedge funds tend to be highly leveraged.

Example 75-7

Long/Short Market-Neutral Strategy

A hedge fund has a capital of $10 million and invests in a market-neutral long/short strategy on the British equity market. Shares can be borrowed from a primary broker with a cash margin deposit equal to 18 percent of the value of the shares. No additional costs are charged to borrow the shares. The hedge fund has drawn up a list of shares regarded as undervalued (list A) and a list of shares regarded as overvalued (list B). The hedge fund expects that shares in list A will outperform the British index by 5 percent over the year, while shares in list B will underperform the British index by 5 percent over the year. The hedge fund wishes to retain a cash cushion of $1 million for unforeseen events. What specific investment actions would you suggest?

SOLUTION

The hedge fund would sell short shares from list B and use the proceeds to buy shares from list A for an equal amount such that the overall beta of the portfolio with respect to the market equals zero. Some capital needs to be invested in the margin deposit. The hedge funds could take long/short positions for $50 million:

- Keep $1 million in cash.
- Deposit $9 million in margin.
- Borrow $50 million of Shares B from a broker, and sell those shares short.
- Use the sale proceeds to buy $50 million worth of shares A.

The positions in shares A and B are established so that the portfolio's beta is zero. Also, note that the invested assets of $50 million equals $9 million divided by 0.18. The ratio of invested assets to equity capital is roughly 5:1.

If expectations materialize, the return for investors in the hedge fund will be high. The long/short portfolio of shares should have a gain over the year of 10 percent on $50 million, whatever the movement in the general market index. This $5 million gain will translate into an annual return before fees of 50 percent on the invested capital of $10 million. This calculation does not take into account the return on invested cash ($1 million) and assumes that the dividends on long positions will offset dividends on short positions.

▶ *Global macro funds* take bets on the direction of a market, a currency, an interest rate, a commodity, or any macroeconomic variable. These funds tend to be highly leveraged and make extensive use of derivatives. There are many subgroups in this category, including the following:

▷ *Futures funds* (or *managed futures funds*) are commodity pools that include commodity trading advisor funds (CTAs). They take bets on directional moves in the positions they hold (long and short) in a single asset class, such as currency, fixed income, or commodities and tend to use many actively traded futures contracts.

▷ *Emerging-market funds* primarily take bets on all types of securities in emerging markets. The securities markets in these economies are typically less efficient and less liquid than those in developed markets. There typically is not an organized lending market for securities, so it is difficult to sell short most issues. Emerging market investments tend to be fairly volatile and greatly influenced by economic and political factors.

▷ *Event-driven funds* take bets on some event specific to a company or a security. Typically the events are special situations or opportunities to capitalize on price fluctuations. These include the following, among others:

▷ *Distressed securities funds:* The manager invests in the debt and/or equity of companies having financial difficulty. Such companies are generally in bankruptcy reorganization or are emerging from reorganization or appear likely to declare bankruptcy in the near future. Because of their distressed situations, the manager can buy such companies' securities at deeply discounted prices. The manager stands to make money should the company successfully reorganize and return to profitability. The manager may take short positions in companies whose situations he believes will worsen, rather than improve, in the short term.

▷ *Risk arbitrage in mergers and acquisitions:* Before the effective date of a merger, the stock of the acquired company will typically sell at a discount to its acquisition value as officially announced. A hedge fund manager simultaneously buys stock in a company being acquired and sells stock in its acquirers. Even though a merger has been accepted by the board of directors of the two companies, there is always a chance that the merger will not go through, possibly because of objections by regulatory authorities. This is a reason for the existence of the discount. If the takeover falls through, fund managers can be left with large losses.

Example 75-8

Merger Risk Arbitrage and Long/Short Market-Neutral Strategy

A merger has been announced between a French company A and a German company B. A will acquire B by offering one share of A for two shares of B. Shares of B were trading in a €15 to €20 range prior to the merger announcement. Shares of B currently trade at €24, while shares of A trade at €50. The merger has been approved by both boards of directors but is awaiting ratification by all shareholders (which is extremely likely) and approval by the EU commission (there is a slight risk of non-approval because the combined company has a large European market share in some products). How could a hedge fund take advantage of the situation? What are the risks?

SOLUTION

The hedge fund should construct a hedged position whereby it buys two shares of B for every share of A that it sells short. Because the proceeds of the short sale of one share of A (€50) can be used to buy two shares of B (€48), the position can be highly leveraged. Of course, the cost of securities lending and margin deposit should also be taken into account. When the merger is completed, the hedge fund will make a profit of approximately two euros for each share of A.

The risk is that the merger will fall through. If it does, the stock price of B will drop sharply, because it was to be acquired at a price well above its premerger market value. If the stock price of A also falls, it should be by less than for B, resulting in an overall loss. The stock price of A might also rise, adding to the loss related to the position in B. That would mean a sizable loss for the hedge fund.

5.3 Funds of Funds

Funds of funds (FOF) have been created to allow easier access to small investors, but also to institutional investors. An FOF is open to investors and, in turn, invests in a selection of hedge funds. If an FOF has a large client base, it can invest large sums of money in each hedge fund. With their attractive benefits, FOF have grown rapidly and now compose more than a quarter of all hedge fund assets (McCrary [2002]). An FOF provides investors with several benefits:

▸ *Retailing:* Typically, a single hedge fund requires an investment of one to several hundred thousand dollars or euros. For the same amount, an investor can get exposure to a large number of hedge funds.

▸ *Access:* FOF managers may be able to offer investments in successful hedge funds that are closed to individual investors because the maximum number of investors has been reached. As long-time investors, they may have "old" money invested with funds that have been closed to new investment. They are also privileged clients that will have priority in buying shares of individual investors who cash out from the hedge fund for personal reasons.

▸ *Diversification:* An FOF allows investors to diversify the risk of a single hedge fund. The good performance of a single hedge fund could be due to specific market conditions prevailing in the past. An FOF can diversify across several types of hedge funds that may have good performance in different market conditions.

▸ *Expertise:* The manager of the FOF is supposed to have expertise in finding reliable and good-quality hedge funds in a world where information on the investment strategies of hedge funds is difficult to obtain. Selecting the right hedge fund and strategy requires a large database and intimate knowledge of strategies, and their advantages and potential pitfalls.

▸ *Due diligence process:* The due diligence (both at the outset and ongoing) that has to be performed by an institutional investor when selecting a hedge fund is highly specialized and time consuming, given the secretive nature of hedge funds and their complex investment strategies. An FOF may be better equipped to perform this due diligence than is a typical institutional investor.

However, there are drawbacks with an FOF:

▸ *Fee:* The fee charged by its manager is in addition to that charged by each hedge fund. The total fee can be quite hefty.

▸ *Performance:* Individual hedge funds are mostly selected by the FOF on the basis of past performance, which in practice often gives little indication of future performance. Biases of the existing databases on hedge funds used by FOFs in their selection process are described subsequently. There is little evidence of persistence in the performance delivered by FOFs.

▷ *Diversification is a two-edged sword:* Blending a high expected return hedge fund with many others for risk reduction purposes means that the overall FOF expected return will be lowered by this diversification. But the fees paid are still very high.

5.4 Leverage and Unique Risks of Hedge Funds

Prior to discussing the performance of hedge funds, we review the use of leverage by hedge funds and the unique risks for hedge funds. Some people regard the use of leverage as one of the main sources of risk for hedge funds, while others maintain that proper use of leverage with appropriate risk management benefits hedge fund investors. In addition, risks that are unique to hedge funds may make hedge funds look unduly risky. Thus, we can usefully discuss hedge funds' risks prior to presenting their historical track record.

5.4.1 Use of Leverage

One of the common characteristics of hedge funds is their use of leverage as part of their trading strategy, although some hedge funds do not use leverage at all.[18] For certain strategies (such as arbitrage strategies), leverage is essential because the arbitrage return is so small that leverage is needed for amplifying the profit. However, leverage is a double-edged sword that also magnifies losses on the downside. In this traditional sense, leveraged investments are more aggressive than those without leverage, and to some people, this may mean high risk.

Leverage in hedge funds often runs from 2:1 to 10:1 (depending on the type of assets held and strategies used) and can run higher than 100:1 (e.g., at one point in time, a well known hedge fund, Long Term Capital Managment or LTCM, had leverage that stood over 500:1 [Lhabitant, 2002]). Thus, some hedge funds may specifically limit the leverage they will employ in the limited partnership agreement so that hedge fund managers are legally bound by that limit. Within the limit, however, hedge fund managers have considerable flexibility.

In general, hedge fund managers can create leverage in trading by:

▷ borrowing external funds to invest more or sell short more than the equity capital they put in,

▷ borrowing through a brokerage margin account, and

▷ using financial instruments and derivatives that require posting margins (typically a fraction of the full value of the position) in lieu of trading in the cash securities that require full payment.

5.4.2 Unique Risks for Hedge Funds

In addition to market and trading risks in different markets, hedge funds face the following unique risks:

---

[18] According to survey results, more than 70 percent of hedge funds use leverage to some degree (McCrary, 2002; Van Hedge Fund Advisors International, 2002).

▷ *Liquidity risk:* The liquidity risk is common to all investors who trade in illiquid or thin markets. However, the lack of liquidity under extreme market conditions can cause irreversible damage to hedge funds whose strategies rely on the presence of liquidity in specific markets. For example, the demise of LTCM was attributed to the unexpected absence of normal liquidity.

▷ *Pricing risk:* Hedge funds often invest in complex securities traded over-the-counter. Pricing securities that trade infrequently is a difficult task, especially in periods of high volatility. Broker-dealers tend to adopt an extremely conservative pricing policy to protect themselves in periods of high volatility. The marking-to-market (margin calls) of positions based on these prices can create severe cash needs for hedge funds, even if the funds do not try to liquidate their positions. For example, it is widely believed that the cash drain of marking-to-market positions based on brokers' conservative pricing of derivatives compounded the problems of LTCM. A similar problem arose for Askin Capital's market-neutral funds (see Concepts in Action on page 418). Pricing risk compounds liquidity risk.

▷ *Counterparty credit risk:* Because hedge funds deal with broker-dealers in most transactions—from buying securities on margin to mortgage trading—counterparty credit risk can arise from many sources. Thus, hedge funds face significant counterparty risk.

▷ *Settlement risk:* Settlement risk refers to the failure to deliver the specified security or money by one of the parties to the transaction on the settlement day.

▷ *Short squeeze risk:* A short squeeze arises when short sellers must buy in their positions at rising prices, for example because owners of the borrowed stock demand their shares back. Because some hedge fund strategies require short selling (e.g., long/short strategies), this risk can affect fund performance significantly.

▷ *Financing squeeze:* If a hedge fund has reached or is near its borrowing capacity, its ability to borrow cash is constrained. Margin calls and marking position to market might result in a cash need for the fund. This risk puts the hedge fund in a vulnerable position when it is forced to reduce the levered positions, say, in an illiquid market at substantial losses, in order to stop the leverage from rising. If the hedge fund were able to borrow more cash, these substantial losses could be avoided.

5.5 The Case for Hedge Funds

The case for investing in hedge funds is based on their historical track record and managerial talent. Hedge funds use their track record to support the claim of superior returns, with low risk and low correlation with conventional investments.

5.5.1 Track Record

Because of their heterogeneity, it is impossible to talk about the performance of hedge funds as an asset class. Some indexes of hedge fund performance are available from consultants or fund managers. They are constructed from a database on hedge funds.[19] Among the many indexes, one can list CISDM (by the Center for International Securities and Derivatives Markets at the University of Massachusetts),

---

[19] For a description of hedge fund indexes, see McCarthy and Spurgin (1998), Amenc and Martellini (2002), and Lhabitant (2002).

a successor of indexes by Zurich Capital Management and MAR (Managed Account Reports); CSFB/Tremont (by Credit Suisse First Boston and Tremont, a company producing the TASS database); VAN (by Van Hedge Funds Advisor International); Henessee (by Henessee Group); EACM 100 (Evaluation Associates Capital Market); HFR (by Hedge Fund Research); and Carr/Barclays for CTAs. These indexes are also broken down in subindexes for various classifications of hedge funds. Some indexes are equal-weighted, while others are weighted by the assets under management for each fund. Some are audited, but others are not. The criteria for inclusion vary; in many cases, all that is required is that the hedge fund volunteers to be included in the database used for the index construction. Any index only includes a (small) number of the existing hedge funds. For any month, the performance reported by the various indexes varies widely. For example, Amenc and Martellini (2002) indicate that Zurich Capital Management reported a 20.48 percent return on long/short strategies in February 2000, while EACM reported a −1.56 percent return in the same month.

CONCEPTS IN ACTION The Collapse of Askin's Granite Market-Neutral Funds and Pricing Problems

The Askin Capital debacle carries with it some sobering lessons for any pension sponsor who invests in specialized corners of the OTC markets.

It does not seem plausible that the collective brainpower brought to bear on David Askin's adventure in high-yield investing could have produced such costly errors. But in piecing together the story from dozens of interviews with investors, money managers, consultants, broker-dealers, and Wall Street risk control specialists, a cautionary tale emerges for plan sponsors in an era of increasingly arcane, specialized investment strategies.

Foremost is a simple lesson about the perils of markets that grow up around esoteric financial instruments like the ones Askin held. Combining illiquid securities—the ones Askin held were priced by very few dealers—with leverage is extremely risky.

The limited liquidity available for esoteric CMO tranches permitted the development of a pricing pattern peculiar to a few OTC markets. Traders call it "free finesse," a term credited to former junk bond king Michael Milken. It means that when a few dealers—some 13 sell esoteric CMOs—are pricing securities for a small group of buyers and extending full financing, price levels achieve an artificial buoyancy.

In such a setting, disasters can happen easily. Askin was trying to make as much money as possible for himself and his investors. Dealers who were eager to deal and extend credit a short time before, in March suddenly demanded repayment from Askin's highly leveraged funds—leaving the end investor in the lurch. An intimate circle of over-the-counter buyers and sellers, which seemed small and comfortable weeks before, suddenly turned into pitiless adversaries.

Another lesson is the importance of knowing how specific money managers value portfolios. Askin's holdings were so highly structured that some bonds had taken as long as a week to create. With this degree of complexity, first, investors were unable to create shadow portfolios; then, changes to a few elements of the formula resulted in large shifts in prices.

Askin could and did argue with dealers about pricing—until he finally took matters into his own hands. By late December, Askin reportedly was using his own "internal manager marks" to price his portfolio.

Such situations are a danger not only to highly sophisticated institutional investors like the ones who bet on Askin Capital's three hedge funds, but to any fund sponsors who invest in specialized corners of the OTC markets. Despite the complexities of Askin's "market neutral" strategy, the crisis that enveloped his funds—an interest rate shift, sparking a turnaround in expectations for mortgages—is all too familiar in the burgeoning CMO market.

Source: Jinny St Goar, *Pension Sponsor,* June 1994.

However, the study of performance and risk of all of these hedge fund indexes yields a strong case for investing in hedge funds:

▷ Hedge funds tend to have a net return (after fees) that is higher than equity markets and bond markets. For example, Exhibit 75-2 reports the average U.S. hedge fund net returns for various indexes over the period January 1996 to September 2002, as calculated by CISDM. The mean annual return for U.S. hedge funds is 10.92 percent based on the HFR Fund Weighted Composite index, compared with 5.86 percent for the S&P 500, and 7.24 percent for the Lehman Brothers government/corporate bond index.

▷ Hedge funds tend to have lower risk (measured by the volatility of return or standard deviation) than equity investments. Their investment strategies appear to provide more stable return than traditional equity investments. This is shown on Exhibit 75-2.

EXHIBIT 75-2 Net Return and Risk of Hedge Funds and Conventional Investments
        January 1996 to September 2002, Annualized

	HFR Fund Weighted Composite	HFR Fund of Funds	EACM 100	CSFB/ Tremont	S&P 500	Lehman Government/ Corporate Bond Index
Annualized Return	10.92%	8.29%	9.96%	11.55%	5.86%	7.24%
Standard Deviation	8.59%	7.00%	4.93%	9.34%	17.49%	3.99%
Sharpe Ratio	0.74	0.54	1.10	0.75	0.08	0.68
Correlation with HFR Fund Weighted Composite	1.00	0.91	0.88	0.77	0.73	−0.11
Correlation with HFR Fund of Funds	0.91	1.00	0.94	0.91	0.56	−0.04
Correlation with EACM 100	0.88	0.94	1.00	0.88	0.52	0.01
Correlation with CSFB/ Tremont	0.77	0.91	0.88	1.00	0.51	0.13
Correlation with S&P 500	0.73	0.56	0.52	0.51	1.00	−0.04
Correlation with Lehman Government/Corporate Bond Index	−0.11	−0.04	0.01	0.13	−0.04	1.00

Source: CISDM, University of Massachusetts at Amherst, Winter 2002.

▷ The Sharpe ratio is the reward-to-risk ratio measured as the mean return in excess of the risk-free rate and divided by the standard deviation. Services that follow hedge funds frequently report this metric which may not be appropriate, however, when returns have option-like characteristics as discussed later. Over the period 1996–2002, the Sharpe ratio of hedge funds (represented by all indexes) was higher than that of equity investments and that of bonds (except for the HFR fund of funds index).

▷ The correlation of hedge funds with conventional investments is generally low, though still positive. In periods of bear equity markets, hedge funds tend to produce returns that are positive (or less negative than equity). Note, however, in Exhibit 75-2, that the correlation of major fund indexes with the S&P 500 is still positive and fairly large over the period 1996–2002. Exhibit 75-3 reports the correlations of hedge fund subindexes (including a CTA subindex) with the S&P 500 index and the Lehman Brothers government/corporate bond index over the same 1996–2002 period. Although some correlations with the S&P 500 are low, especially for market-neutral funds (only 0.15), the correlation for equity hedge funds is a fairly large 0.70. The correlations of hedge fund subindexes with the bond markets are low and mostly negative, with the CTA dollar-weighted index being the highest at 0.45.

EXHIBIT 75-3 Correlation of Hedge Fund Subindexes with S&P 500 Index and Lehman Government/Corporate Bond Index *January 1996 to September 2002*

Hedge Fund Subindex	Correlation with S&P 500	Correlation with Lehman Government/ Corporate Bond Index
HFR Convertible Arbitrage	0.35	−0.08
HFR Equity Hedged	0.70	−0.08
HFR Fixed Income Arbitrage	−0.13	−0.12
HFR Emerging Markets	0.61	−0.20
HFR Event Driven	0.66	−0.14
HFR Merger Arbitrage	0.52	−0.15
HFR Equity Market Neutral	0.15	0.18
HFR Macro	0.40	0.21
CISDM CTA Dollar Weighted	−0.11	0.45

Source: CISDM, University of Massachusetts at Amherst, Winter 2002.

5.5.2 Talent

The fee structure and flexibility of hedge funds attract talented fund managers. Someone having an outstanding investment idea can apply it in a hedge fund with few constraints. The investment idea can be leveraged to generate high returns for investors and for the manager. So, the search for an attractive hedge fund is based on its track record and also on the perceived talent of the manager to generate superior performance.

5.6 Caveats

Investors should exercise caution when using the historical track record of hedge funds in reaching asset allocation decisions. The hedge fund industry does not adhere to rigorous performance presentation standards. Biases in historical performance data can make it difficult to interpret hedge fund performance; past winners may also not repeat.

5.6.1 Biases

The performance data from hedge fund databases and indexes suffer from serious biases that are listed here. Both performance and risk measures are affected.

▶ *Self-selection bias:* Hedge fund managers decide themselves whether they want to be included in a database. Managers that have funds with an unimpressive track record will not wish to have that information exposed.

▶ *Instant history bias:* When a hedge fund enters a database, it brings with it its track record. Because only hedge funds with good track records enter the database, this creates a positive bias in past performance in the database, as stressed by Fung and Hsieh (2002).

▶ *Survivorship bias: Return:* In the investment industry, unsuccessful funds and managers tend to disappear over time. Only successful ones search for new clients and present their track records. This creates a survivor bias. This problem is acute with hedge funds because they often do not have to comply with performance presentation standards. It is not uncommon to see hedge fund managers present the track records of only their successful funds, omitting those that have been closed. If a fund begins to perform poorly, perhaps even starting to go out of business, it may stop reporting its performance entirely, thus inflating the reported average performance of hedge funds. Hedge fund indexes and databases may only include funds that have survived. Funds with bad performance disappear and are removed from the database that is used by investors to select among existing funds. Some data bases are now available that may be free from survivorship bias as defunct hedge funds are left in the data base; however, funds that simply stop reporting still pose a problem.

▶ *Survivorship bias: Risk:* Biases also affect risk measures. A similar survivorship bias applies to risk measures. Investors shy away from high risk, as well as from negative returns. Hedge funds that exhibited highly volatile returns in the past tend to disappear. Only strategies that have experienced low volatility in the past survive. So, reported volatility of existing funds will tend to be low. There is no guarantee that the same strategy will also be low risk in the future. Examples abound of hedge funds that were regarded as low risk but lost all of their capital.

▶ *Smoothed pricing: Infrequently traded assets:* Some assets trade infrequently. This is the case for many alternative assets that are not exchange-traded, such as real estate or private equity. This is also the case for illiquid exchange-traded securities or OTC instruments often used by hedge funds. Because prices used are often not up-to-date market prices, but estimates of fair value, their volatility is reduced (smoothing effect). The infrequent nature of price updates for alternative investments, induces a significant downward bias to the measured risk of the assets. In addition, correlations of alternative investment returns with

Example 75-9

Biases in Reported Performance

A manager without any expertise has decided to launch five long/short hedge funds with some seed money. The investment strategies of the five funds are quite different. Actually, the investment strategy of fund A is just the opposite of that of fund E. After a couple of years, some have performed well and some badly, as could be expected by pure chance. The annualized gross returns on the five funds are listed in the following table. All have an annualized standard deviation of 10 percent and the annual risk-free rate is 3 percent. The manager decides to close funds A, B, and C and to enter funds D and E in a well-known hedge fund database. The marketing pitch of the manager is that the funds have superior performance (Sharpe ratio of 1.7 and 2.7). What do you think?

Fund Name	Mean Annual Return	Standard Deviation	Sharpe Ratio
Fund A	−30%	10%	−3.3
Fund B	−20%	10%	−2.3
Fund C	0%	10%	−0.3
Fund D	+20%	10%	1.7
Fund E	+30%	10%	2.7

SOLUTION

The performance on the funds is purely random. But only the good-performing funds are included in the hedge fund database. The performance reported for a selection of funds is misleading. There is obvious survivorship and self-selection bias. Similarly, the performance of the hedge fund index is biased upward and misleading.

conventional equity and fixed income returns, and correlations among the alternative investments, are often artificially low simply because of the smoothing effect and the absence of market-observable returns. The bias can be very large,[20] so the true risk is much larger than the reported estimates.

▹ *Option-like investment strategies:* Traditional risk measures used in performance appraisal assume that portfolio returns are drawn from normal or, at least symmetric, distributions. Many investment strategies followed by hedge funds have some option-like features that violate these distributional assumptions. For example, hedge funds following so-called arbitrage strategies will generally make a small profit when asset prices converge to their estimated fair value, but they run the risk of a huge loss if their arbitrage model fails. Standard deviation or traditional value at risk (VaR) measures understate the true risk of losses, and the Sharpe ratio can be an inappropriate performance measure.

▹ *Fee structure and gaming:* It is also important to remember the high fees charged by hedge funds: Typically a fixed fee of 1 percent plus an incentive fee of 20 percent of the total return, if positive. This compensation structure is option-like. Clearly, fund managers are paid to take risks. One can argue that they have strong incentives to take a huge amount of risk if their recent performance has been bad. However, one can also argue that because of the high water mark provision, hedge fund managers may not want to ruin their chance to stage a comeback by taking more risk as their performance diminishes. In either case, past risk measures may be misleading for forecasting future performance and risk for a fund that has performed badly in the recent past.

5.6.2 Persistence of Performance

Because of various biases, judging the average performance of the hedge fund industry by using the indexes discussed can be difficult. To appraise individual

---

[20] See, for example, Asness, Krail, and Liew (2001).

hedge funds, investors should look at their persistence of performance. Before a specific hedge fund is purchased, investors should judge whether their good track record will persist in the future. A similar attitude must be adopted when considering an FOF.[21]

Talented hedge fund managers can exploit market inefficiencies that cannot be exploited by conventional asset managers and/or design innovative investment strategies that may yield excellent returns. But, again, two caveats are in order. First, the size of the hedge fund industry is huge (some $600 billion by the end of 2001), and the leverage used means that the industry is a very large player in capital markets. But the existence of pricing inefficiencies, for which many managers search, is necessarily limited. Thus there is a very large pool of capital chasing after what is likely to be a limited supply of pricing inefficiencies. Second, any successful strategy will quickly be imitated by many other investors, thereby reducing its future profitability.

To summarize, investors need to exercise great caution in interpreting the reported performance of hedge funds; the risks in hedge fund investments are easily underestimated.

6   CLOSELY HELD COMPANIES AND INACTIVELY TRADED SECURITIES

Investments in closely held companies and inactively traded securities require analysis of legal, financial, and ownership considerations with account taken of the effects of illiquidity. Closely held companies are those that are not publicly traded. Inactively traded securities are securities of companies that are infrequently traded; they generally do not trade on major exchanges. Illiquidity, limited information availability, and minority ownership issues are common to such companies.

6.1 Legal Environment

Closely held companies may be organized in various legal forms, such as special tax-advantaged corporations (subchapter S corporations in the United States), regular corporations, general partnerships, limited partnerships, and sole proprietorships. These forms have tax implications, as well as ownership differences, for the investor. Ownership is a bundle of rights, and these rights differ, depending on the business form. Because valuations can be required to provide evidence in litigation—for example, minority shareholder claims—much case law defines terms such as *intrinsic value, fundamental value,* and *fair value.* These definitions may vary in different jurisdictions. Even what is judged as evidence for a valuation can vary. There has long been a tension between the theory of value as based on projected cash flows and the acceptance of the *hard* evidence of recent cash flows. In a real sense, then, valuation of closely held and inactively traded securities requires extensive knowledge of the law and the purposes of the valuation.[22]

---

[21] In a study that may come as a surprise to proponents of hedge funds, Brown, Goetzmann, and Ibbotson (1999) found "no evidence of performance persistence in raw returns or risk-adjusted returns, even when we break funds down according to their returns-based style classification." They conclude that "the hedge fund arena provides no evidence that past performance forecasts future performance." It's important to note, however, that this study covers a relatively short time period and that determining accurate and comparable performance figures in the hedge fund arena is extremely complex.

[22] See Pratt, Reilly, and Schweihs (1996) for an extensive treatment of the analysis and appraisal of closely held companies.

6.2 Valuation Alternatives

The basic types of valuation are the cost approach, the comparables approach, and the income approach.

6.2.1 The Cost Approach

This approach attempts to determine what it would cost to replace the company's assets in their present form.

6.2.2 The Comparables Approach

In the company comparison approach, market value is estimated relative to a benchmark value. The benchmark value may be the market price of a similar but actively traded company, or the average or median value of the market prices of similar companies, in transactions made near the time of the appraisal. The benchmark-based estimate needs to be adjusted for changing market conditions, the possibility that the benchmark itself is mispriced, and the unique features of the company relative to the benchmark. Companies with comparable characteristics might not have traded recently.

6.2.3 The Income Approach

For business valuation, Pratt, Reilly, and Schweihs (1996) essentially define the income approach as one of appropriately discounting any anticipated future economic income stream.

6.3 Bases for Discounts/Premiums

Because closely held companies and inactively traded securities are illiquid, some discount must be made for that illiquidity. For infrequently traded stocks, share prices should reflect a liquidity discount compensating investors for illiquidity in the market for the shares. Shares of closely held companies lack a public market (lack marketability) and so their valuation should reflect a marketability discount to account for the extra return investors should require on those shares. In addition to a discount for lack of marketability for a closely held company, the analyst may also need to apply a discount for minority interest, or a premium for control. The minority interest discount is applied if the interest will not be able to influence corporate strategy and other business decisions. To estimate a marketability discount, minority discount, or control premium, the analyst must carefully define the amount or base to which the discount or premium should be applied.

To estimate a marketability discount for a closely held company, the analyst identifies a publicly traded comparable company with a liquid market. The comparable's market value of equity is the base to which the marketability discount is applied.

To estimate a minority interest discount for a company, the base is an estimate of that company's value of equity inclusive of the value arising from ownership of all rights of control. To estimate a control premium, the base is an estimate of that company's value of equity not reflecting control (the value of equity from a minority shareholder perspective).

7 DISTRESSED SECURITIES/BANKRUPTCIES

Distressed securities are securities of companies that have filed or are close to filing for bankruptcy court protection, or that are seeking out-of-court debt restructuring to avoid bankruptcy.[23] The legal framework of bankruptcy proceedings differs across countries. In the United States, two types of bankruptcy protection are available: protection for liquidation (called Chapter 7) and protection for reorganization (called Chapter 11). Valuation of such securities requires legal, operational, and financial analysis.

To understand distressed securities, one must appreciate the inherent divergence of interests between the stockholders and bondholders of a company. Stockholders own the successful company, but bondholders have a prior claim to the assets of the bankrupt company. In reorganizations, bondholders' prior claim can allow them to negotiate for ownership in the postbankruptcy company, thus diluting the original shareholders' claims. Investing in distressed securities, then, usually means investing in distressed company bonds with a view toward equity ownership in the eventually reconstituted company. In this regard, such investments have characteristics somewhat similar to those of venture capital investing. For example, they are illiquid and require a long horizon, as well as intense investor participation in guiding the venture to a successful outcome. Another similarity, though, is the possibility of mispricing. Hooke (1998) reports on the disappointment of some traditional distressed-securities investors that these investments are attracting attention and efficient prices; but he suggests that business volatility and high leverage will guarantee many problem companies with inevitable value discrepancies (mispricing).

Distressed-security investing may be viewed as the ultimate in value investing. A distressed company with low enterprise value (EV) to earnings before interest, taxes, depreciation, and amortization (EBITDA) will attract the attention of an investor looking for positive, postrestructuring cash flows. The primary question for any distressed security is the question of the distress source. Is the company operationally sound but financially hampered by too much gearing (leverage), or is the company weak operationally? If the company is weak operationally, is it a candidate to be turned around by cost cutting and improvement in the business cycle or else by new management and/or a new competitive strategy? Distressed-security investing requires intense industry analysis, as well as analysis of business strategies and of the management team that will conduct the restructuring.

8 COMMODITY MARKETS AND COMMODITY DERIVATIVES

Commodities present an unusual investment alternative. Investing in commodities complements the investment opportunities offered by shares of corporations that extensively use those commodities in their production process. Investing directly in agricultural products and other commodities gives the investor a share in the commodity components of the country's production and consumption. Money managers and average investors, however, usually prefer commodity derivatives (financial instruments that derive their value from the value of the underlying commodity) rather than commodities themselves. The average investor does not want to store grains, cattle, crude oil, or metals. A common investment objective is to

---

[23] See Tremont Advisers, 2002.

purchase indirectly those real assets that should provide a good hedge against inflation risk. There are several indirect ways to invest in commodities:

▶ Futures contracts: A commodity futures contract is a standardized, exchange-traded agreement between two parties in which the buyer agrees to buy a commodity from the seller at a future date at a price agreed upon today.

▶ Bonds indexed on some commodity price.

▶ Stocks of companies producing the commodity.

CONCEPTS IN ACTION UAL Strategy Chief Outlines Plans

Competitive costs, services for range of customers will form basis of revival

The business plan that UAL Corp.'s United Airlines hopes will be the foundation for its emergence from bankruptcy-court protection features competitive costs and a suite of discrete air-service products designed to make the airline "relevant" to as many customers as possible.

In a message to employees, Doug Hacker, UAL's new executive vice president of strategy, said the company intends to develop a "mainline" jet service that has the lowest costs among its peers. United will court international travelers through increased reliance on its airline partners in the Star Alliance, he said.

To serve small domestic cities, United intends to continue to build up small-jet flights offered by its regional affiliates. And to cater to leisure fliers, it expects to operate a separate airline that offers "a low-cost, no-frills" product in markets dominated by leisure customers and low-cost competition, Mr. Hacker said.

Lenders set conditions

UAL, the world's second-largest carrier, filed for protection from its creditors Monday in U.S. Bankruptcy Court in Chicago. As part of its filing, the company said it arranged $1.5 billion in interim financing to help it operate while under court protection. The lenders, who next week will extend an initial $800 million of that funding, insist that the airline meet strict financial benchmarks if it is to receive the balance.

Mr. Hacker, who served for several years as UAL's chief financial officer before leaving to head a United subsidiary, on Wednesday was named to the new post as strategy chief. Yesterday, he presented an overview of United's business plan to leaders of the carrier's union. In a telephone message to employees, he noted that the terms of the interim bankruptcy financing require lower labor costs "under very tight time frames."

In discussions with union leaders yesterday, it wasn't clear whether the company spelled out specific savings targets. A United spokesman last night declined to discuss details on the business plan or the savings targets.

Possible low-fare product

"We want to make the United brand relevant to as many customers as we can," Mr. Hacker told employees. "We'll do that through a family of products that meets customers' different needs."

Glenn Tilton, UAL's chairman and chief executive, has hinted in recent days that United would revive a product similar to its low-fare shuttle service that operated in the Western U.S. in the late 1990s to help the carrier fight off competition from Southwest Airlines. Mr. Tilton also hinted in employee meetings the past few days in the airline's hubs that UAL may seek government aid to facilitate its exit from Chapter 11.

The Air Transportation Stabilization Board, whose refusal to grant government-loan backing forced the airline into bankruptcy, has indicated it would consider a revised application from United for loan guarantees to back up financing to help the airline emerge from reorganization.

Source: Susan Carey, *The Wall Street Journal*, 13 December 2002, p. A2.

Investing in commodity futures is the most common strategy. Commodity trading advisers (CTAs) offer *managed futures funds* that take positions in exchange-traded derivatives on commodities and financials.[24]

8.1 Commodity Futures

Futures contracts are the easiest and cheapest way to invest in commodities. Commodities can be grouped into three major categories:

▷ *Agricultural products,* including fibers (wool, cotton), grains (wheat, corn, soybeans), food (coffee, cocoa, orange juice), and livestock (cattle, hogs, pork bellies). These are often called soft commodities by professionals.

▷ *Energy,* including crude oil, heating oil, and natural gas

▷ *Metals,* such as copper, aluminum, gold, silver, and platinum

Numerous commodity indexes have been developed. Some traditional indexes are broadly based, with a global economic perspective; they aim to track the evolution of input prices. Other indexes have been developed as *investable* indexes. They are based on the most liquid commodity futures contracts, so they can easily be replicated by taking positions in individual commodities. For example, the Goldman Sachs Commodity Index (GSCI) is a world-production weighted index of 26 commodities with liquid futures contracts. Futures contracts on the GSCI trade in Chicago. The composition and weights of the various commodity indexes differ widely, and so do their performances.

8.2 Motivation and Investment Vehicles

Commodities are sometimes treated as an asset class because they represent a direct participation in the real economy. The motivation for investing in commodities ranges from the diversification benefits achievable by a passive investor to the speculative profits sought by an *active* investor. The design of the investment vehicle used reflects these different motivations.

8.2.1 Passive Investment

A passive investor would buy commodities for their risk-diversification benefits. When inflation accelerates, commodity prices go up, whereas bond and stock prices tend to go down. A passive investor would typically invest through a collateralized position in a futures contract. Many banks and money managers offer collateralized futures funds based on one of the investable commodity indexes. A collateralized position in futures is a portfolio in which an investor takes a long position in futures for a given amount of underlying value and simultaneously invests the same amount in government securities, such as Treasury bills. The various investable indexes and collateralized futures indexes are published both in excess-return and in total-return form. The indexes reported assume that the *total return* on the index is continuously reinvested. The *excess return* is the return above the risk-free rate. The total return is the risk-free rate plus the excess return.

---

[24] See Jaeger (2002) p. 18.

Example 75-10

Collateralized Futures

Assume that the futures price is currently $100. If $100 million is added to the fund, the manager will take a long position in the futures contract for $100 million of underlying value and simultaneously buy $100 million worth of Treasury bills (part of this will be deposited as margin). If the futures price drops to $95 the next day, the futures position will be marked to market, and the manager will have to sell $5 million of the Treasury bills to cover the loss. Conversely, if the futures price rises to $105, the manager will receive a marked-to-market profit of $5 million, which will be invested in additional Treasury bills. Discuss the sources of total return from such an investment.

SOLUTION

The total return on the collateralized futures position comes from the change in futures price and the interest income on the Treasury bills.

Generally, the volatility of commodity futures is higher than that of domestic or international equity, but commodities have a negative correlation with stock and bond returns and a desirable positive correlation with inflation. Nevertheless, the excellent long-term performance of some commodity indexes requires a word of caution. The commodities and weights selected to enter indexes reflect a selection bias when they include data from time periods prior to the initiation of the index, which biases any back-calculated performance.

8.3 Active Investment

Besides making inflation bets, another motivation for investing in commodities is that they provide good performance in periods of economic growth. In periods of rapid economic growth, commodities are in strong demand to satisfy production needs, and their prices go up. Because of productivity gains, the prices of finished goods are unlikely to rise as fast as those of raw materials. This suggests an active management strategy in which specific commodities are bought and sold at various times. Managed futures are proposed by a large number of institutions.

As with any investments, the return–risk characteristics of managed futures must be analyzed carefully. Schneeweis (2002) discusses the proposed attraction of managed futures: the possibility of positive returns in months when the market does well and in the months when it does poorly. Jaeger (2002) proposes several principles for the risk management of managed futures portfolios:

- Diversification
- Liquidity monitoring, because diversification into a larger universe of contracts can include illiquid contracts
- Volatility dependent allocation where the weight of the different contracts in the portfolio is determined by their historical or implied volatility
- Quantitative risk management techniques such as value at risk (VaR) and stress tests

▷ Risk budgeting on various aggregation levels to detect undesired risk concentrations

▷ Limits on leverage

▷ Use of derivatives to hedge any unwanted currency risk

▷ Care in model selection with respect to data mining, in and out of sample performance, and adequate performance adjustments for risk

8.4 The Example of Gold

Gold has always played a special role in investments. It is a commodity traded worldwide, but more important, it has been regarded by many Europeans and Asians as the ultimate store of value. It is considered an international monetary asset that offers protection in case of a major disruption. Furthermore, central banks and most non-U.S. investors regard gold as a monetary asset because it has been the core of domestic and international monetary systems for many centuries. This section focuses on gold investment because of the historical importance of gold in investment strategies, and as an example of a real asset investment. Of course, precious stones, stamps, or paintings could also be profitable long-term investments, but they usually require high transaction costs; moreover, each stone or painting is in a sense unique, which reduces its marketability. Gold is offered in a wide variety of investment vehicles that can be used in passive or active strategies. Gold-linked investments include gold bullion, coins, bonds, mining equity, futures, and options on gold and on mining equity or bonds.

8.4.1 The Motivation for Investing in Gold

The traditional role of gold as the ultimate hedge and store of value is well known. For centuries, Europeans and Asians alike have regarded gold as the best possible protection against inflation and social, political, or economic crises because it can easily be traded worldwide at any time, and its real value increases during crises. Europeans and others who have suffered revolutions, invasions, and periods of hyperinflation need no correlation coefficients to be convinced of this attractive portfolio hedge characteristic. For example, gold kept its real value during the U.S. stock market crash from 1929 to 1932 and the London Stock Exchange collapse in equity and bonds from 1973 to 1975. Furthermore, the central role gold has played in domestic and international monetary systems for thousands of years makes it, in part, a monetary asset with exceptional liquidity. Other real assets, such as diamonds or stamps, do not have this characteristic.

In general, gold often allows investors to diversify against the kinds of risks that affect all stock markets simultaneously. For example, in 1973 and 1974, the price of bullion tripled when stock markets worldwide dropped dramatically during the oil crisis; the NYSE dropped approximately 50 percent.

A theoretical comment is in order here. In modern portfolio theory, a small or negative beta implies that the expected return on gold should be small. For example, a negative beta caused by a negative correlation between gold and the market portfolio implies that in the capital asset pricing model (CAPM) framework, the expected return on gold should be less than the risk-free interest rate. Indeed, it can be claimed that we should expect a modest long-term performance in gold and a greater return on the other assets in the portfolio; however, gold assets will reduce the risk of the portfolio in the event of adverse economic conditions. The question for a prudent portfolio manager, then, is whether these hedge benefits are worth the implicit cost she must pay in the form of a smaller expected long-term return for a small part of the portfolio.

8.4.2 Gold Price Determinants

The following material is intended to indicate the kind of information and methods that analysts and investment managers use to analyze real asset investments. Commodities other than gold could also serve as examples.

Gold is a tangible international asset in limited supply. Gold can be extracted at a cost but cannot be produced artificially. Although gold is immune to the effects of weather, water, and oxygen, it suffers from human habits. The tradition of hiding gold treasures in the ground is consistent with the observation that gold is the ultimate physical store of value during major disruptions such as civil unrest, coup d'état, and war. During World War II, most Europeans dug a hole in their gardens or cellars to hide their gold holdings. Part of this hidden gold is never recovered if the owner dies. Most of the gold used in dentistry also disappears with the owner. Despite these losses, the stock of gold keeps slowly increasing with the amount extracted.

In a sense, the price of gold should be easy to forecast: The product is well defined. The supply sources are well identified, and reserves can be reasonably estimated. The major demands are clearly identified: carat jewelry, industrial needs, coins, and investment.

Supply and demand clearly determine the price of gold. It is therefore necessary to study the various components of supply and demand to forecast the price of gold. A different model may be required for each component. For example, Western mine production is affected by technological considerations, South African extraction policy, and political situations in sensitive countries. Russia's gold sales depend on their need for hard currencies. Official sales may also be induced by monetary and balance of payments problems. Industrial demand depends on technological innovation and the discovery of cheaper substitutes. Jewelry demand is sensitive to short-term gold price movements, as well as fashion; the investment motivation is often present in jewelry purchases. Investment demand for bullion and coins is a component of the total demand affecting gold price but is also determined by expectations of future price movements.

So, although gold is a single, well-identified, extensively researched product, its analysis and valuation is not a simple exercise. This difficulty may add another dimension to gold's mystical attraction.

8.5 Commodity-Linked Securities

Holding commodities provides no income, so the sole return to the owner is through price increase. Investors can also select securities that are linked to some commodity prices and also provide some income. This can be an attractive alternative for investors who wish to, or must, hold financial investments rather than real assets. The two major types of commodity-linked securities are bonds and equity. The indexation clause is explicit for commodity-linked bonds but implicit for equity. Again, we focus on the example of gold.

8.5.1 Commodity-Linked Bonds

There are many examples of commodity-linked bonds in the world capital markets.[25] In periods of high inflation, governments have often been forced to offer loans with coupons or principal indexed to either the price of a specific good or a global inflation index. Inflation-indexed gilts became popular in the United Kingdom during the 1980s. The capital and coupons of these bonds are indexed to British retail prices.

In 1997, the U.S. Treasury started to offer Inflation-Indexed Securities, also known as Treasury Inflation Protected Securities (TIPS).[26] The first such security was a 10-year bond, issued with a real yield of 3.45 percent. The principal value is adjusted for changes in the consumer price index (CPI) on each semiannual coupon payment date. So, the nominal coupon, equal to the real yield times the CPI-adjusted principal, increases with inflation. At maturity, the CPI-adjusted principal is reimbursed. In the United States, some government agencies, municipalities, and corporations have also issued inflation-indexed bonds. Often, the inflation adjustment to the principal is paid out immediately rather than at final maturity. This structure has been adopted because seeing their nominal credit exposure on non-government issues accumulate automatically over time worried investors.

Several countries have issued inflation-indexed bonds, and corporations and governments have issued bonds indexed to a variety of specific prices, such as oil prices. Gold bonds, and bonds with warrants on gold, have been an attractive alternative to holding gold ingots.

8.5.2 Commodity-Linked Equity

The value of some companies is directly affected by commodity prices. This is clearly the case with the so-called *energy companies*. For example, companies in the oil and gas industries are affected by the evolution of oil prices. The link between commodity prices and stock prices is more evident for small, undiversified companies that specialize in one type of activity, for example, oil and gas exploration and production. However, large oil companies tend to be quite diversified across activities and the link between commodity prices and stock prices is weaker. An integrated exploration, production, and refining company will be less affected by oil price increases than a company operating in only one of the industry segments.

Gold mining companies are another example of commodity-linked equity. Gold mining shares differ from commodity-linked bonds in that the indexation clause is not fixed by contract but depends on mining economics. In fact, the mining industry is probably the simplest activity to describe in a valuation model. The economics of mining can be described by a simple discounted cash flow model. The principal relationship in the model is the cost structure of the mine as measured by the ratio of costs to revenues. The cost to remove an ounce or a gram of gold from so-called storage and refine it depends on several factors: technology, wage rates, power rates, and the grade and depth of the mine. Revenues depend on the world price of gold. Any movement in the market price of gold will directly affect the cash flows of a mine and therefore its market value; the higher the ratio of costs to revenues, the more sensitive will be the cash flows to gold price movements. However, note that the correlation between gold mine share prices and the price of gold is far from perfect. Gold mine values are influenced by factors other than gold prices; for example, social and political factors have strongly affected South African share prices over time.

---

[25] Jacquillat and Roll (1979) provide an empirical analysis of the benefits of commodity-linked bonds. Schwartz (1982) provides a theoretical model for an index-linked bond with an option to repay the bond at face value or at an index-linked price. Such a model was tested on a silver-linked bond issued by Sunshine Mining in Brauer and Ravichandran (1986). An interesting analysis of oil-linked securities is provided by Gibson and Schwartz (1990).

[26] McFall Lamm (1998) and Anderson and Moore (1998) provide an analysis of TIPS.

SUMMARY

9

▶ Alternative investments usually involve illiquidity, difficulty in the determination of current market values, limited historical risk and return data, the requirement for extensive investment analysis, a liquidity risk premium, and a segmentation risk premium. Alternative assets are assets not traded on exchanges. Alternative strategies are strategies that mostly use traded assets for the purpose of isolating bets and generating alpha.

▶ An open-end fund stands ready to redeem investor shares at market value, but a closed-end fund does not. A load fund has sales commission charges, and a no-load fund does not. Sales fees may also appear in annual distribution fees.

▶ The net asset value of a fund is calculated as the per-share value of the investment company's assets minus liabilities.

▶ Mutual funds may charge several different fees: Loads and redemption fees provide sales incentives; distribution and operating fees are annual fees; the part of the operating fee that is allocated to the fund manager can be considered an investment performance incentive.

▶ An exchange traded fund (ETF) is a special type of fund that tracks some market index but that is traded on a stock market as any common share.

▶ A mutual fund's purchases and sales of stocks held in the fund lead to taxable gains at the level of the fund, but this is not the case for an ETF because of its in-kind creation and redemption process.

▶ The advantages of ETFs are diversification; trading similarly to a stock; management of their risk augmented by futures and options contracts on them; transparency; cost effectiveness; avoidance of significant premiums or discounts to NAV; tax savings from payment of in-kind redemption; and immediate dividend reinvestment for open-end ETFs. The disadvantages are only a narrow-based market index tracked in some countries; intraday trading opportunity is not important for long-horizon investors; large bid–ask spreads on some ETFs; and possibly better cost structures and tax advantages to direct index investing for large institutions.

▶ Some characteristics of real estate as an investable asset class are that each property is immovable, basically indivisible, and unique; not directly comparable to other properties; illiquid; and bought and sold intermittently in a generally local marketplace, with high transaction costs and market inefficiencies.

▶ The main approaches to real estate valuation are the cost approach, the sales comparison approach, the income approach, and the discounted after-tax cash flow approach.

▶ The net operating income from a real estate investment is gross potential income minus expenses, which include estimated vacancy and collection costs, insurance, taxes, utilities, and repairs and maintenance.

▶ The value of a property can be calculated as the cost to replace the building in its present form in the cost approach; an adjusted value from a benchmark of comparable sales in the sales comparison approach; or a hedonic price estimate from a regression model in the sales comparison approach; and capitalized net operating income in the income approach.

▶ The net present value of a property to an equity investor is obtained as the present value of the after tax cash flows, discounted at the investor's required rate of return on equity, minus the amount of equity required to make the investment.

- ▷ Venture capital investing is done in many stages from seed through mezzanine.

- ▷ Venture capital investment characteristics include illiquidity; long-term commitment required; difficulty in determining current market values; limited historical risk and return data; limited information; entrepreneurial/management mismatches; fund manager incentive mismatches; lack of knowledge of how many competitors exist; vintage cycles; and the requirement for extensive operations analysis and advice. The challenges to venture capital performance measurement are the difficulty in determining precise valuations, the lack of meaningful benchmarks, and the long-term nature of any performance feedback.

- ▷ The expected net present value of a venture capital project with a single, terminal payoff and a single, initial investment can be calculated, given its possible payoff and its conditional failure probabilities, as the present value of the expected payoff minus the required initial investment.

- ▷ The term *hedge fund* is not fully descriptive, because the hedged position is generally designed to isolate a bet rather than to reduce risk. Hedge funds can be defined as funds that seek absolute returns; have a legal structure avoiding some government regulations; and have option-like fees, including a base management fee and an incentive fee proportional to realized profits.

- ▷ The net performance of a hedge fund can be calculated by subtracting its fees from its gross performance.

- ▷ Hedge funds can be classified in a variety of ways. One classification of hedge funds comprises the categories: long/short, market neutral, global macro, and event driven.

- ▷ The advantages of fund of funds investing are availability to the small investor, access to funds closed to new investors, diversification, managerial expertise, and a due diligence process. The disadvantages to fund of funds investing are high fees, little evidence of persistent performance, and the absolute return loss through diversification.

- ▷ High leverage is often present in hedge funds as part of the trading strategy and is an essential part of some strategies in which the arbitrage return is so small that leverage is needed to amplify the profit. The unique risks of hedge funds are liquidity risk, pricing risk, counterparty credit risk, settlement risk, short squeeze risk, and financing squeeze risk.

- ▷ In terms of performance, hedge funds are generally viewed as having a net return higher than available for equity or bond investments, lower standard deviation of return than equity investments, a Sharpe ratio that is comparable to bonds and higher than that of equity investments, and a low correlation with conventional investments. The biases present in hedge fund performance reporting include self-selection bias, instant history bias, survivorship bias on return, survivorship bias on risk, smoothed pricing on infrequently traded assets, option-like investment strategies, and fee structure–induced gaming.

- ▷ For closely held companies and inactively traded securities, a discount is used for lack of liquidity, lack of marketability, and for a minority interest, but a control premium is added for controlling ownership. The base for the marketability discount is the market value of equity for a comparable publicly traded company.

- ▷ Distressed-securities investing usually means investing in distressed company bonds with a view to equity ownership in the eventually reconstituted company. Such investments are similar to venture capital investments because they are illiquid; they require a long investment horizon; they require intense investor participation/consulting; and they offer the possibility of alpha because of mispricing.

▷ As a vehicle for investing in production and consumption, commodities complement the investment opportunities offered by shares of corporations that extensively use these as raw materials in their production processes. Investing directly in agricultural products and other commodities gives the investor exposure to the commodity components of the country's production and consumption.

▷ Commodity trading advisors (CTAs) offer managed futures funds that take positions in exchange traded derivatives on commodities and financials.

▷ The return on a collateralized futures position comes from the change in the futures price plus the interest income on risk-free government securities.

▷ The motivation for investing in commodities, commodity derivatives, and commodity-linked securities is that they may have negative correlation with stock and bond returns and a desirable positive correlation with inflation. In the case of commodity-linked securities, the investor can receive some income rather than depending solely on commodity price changes.

▷ The risk of managed futures can be managed through diversification, liquidity monitoring, volatility dependent allocation, quantitative techniques such as VaR, risk budgeting on various aggregation levels, limits on leverage, use of derivatives, and care in model selection.

PROBLEMS

Use the following information for Problems 1 and 2: Global Leveraged Equity Fund (GLEF) has three classes of shares, each holding the same portfolio of securities but having a different expense structure. The following table summarizes the expenses of these classes of shares.

Expense Comparison for Four Classes of GLEF

	Class A	Class B*	Class C
Sales charge (load) on purchases	5%	None	None
Deferred sales charge (load) on redemptions	None	4% in the first year, declining by 1% each year thereafter	1% for the initial 2 years only
Annual expenses:			
Distribution fee	0.25%	0.50%	0.50%
Management fee	0.50%	0.50%	0.50%
Other expenses	0.50%	0.50%	0.50%
	1.25%	1.50%	1.50%

*Class B shares automatically convert to Class A shares 72 months (6 years) after purchase.

Assume that expense percentages given will be constant at the given values. Assume that the deferred sales charges are computed on the basis of NAV.

An investor is considering the purchase of GLEF shares. The investor expects equity investments with risk characteristics similar to GLEF to earn 9 percent per year. He decides to make his selection of fund share class based on an assumed 9 percent return each year, gross of any of the expenses given in the preceding table.

1. Decide which class of shares of GLEF is best for the investor if he plans to liquidate his investment toward the end of
   A. Year 1
   B. Year 3
   C. Year 5
   D. Year 15

2. You have analyzed the relative performance of different classes of GLEF shares for liquidation in several years. Specifically, you have looked at liquidation in years 1, 3, 5, and 15. Your results are as follows. (The > symbol implies that the class preceding the sign performs better than the class following and the = symbol implies equal performance of the two classes.)

   ▷ Liquidation in year 1: Class C > Class B > Class A
   ▷ Liquidation in year 3: Class C > Class B > Class A
   ▷ Liquidation in year 5: Class B = Class C > Class A
   ▷ Liquidation in year 15: Class B > Class C > Class A

Provide an intuitive explanation for the pattern of relative performance that you observe.

3. Using the price data for several houses recently sold in a particular area, a real estate firm has identified the main characteristics that affect the prices of houses in that area. The characteristics identified include the living area, the number of bathrooms, whether the house has a fireplace, and how old the house is. The estimated slope coefficient for each of these characteristics and the constant term are as follows:

Characteristic	Units	Coefficient in Euros per Unit
Intercept	—	140,000
Living area	Square meters	210
Number of bathrooms	Number	10,000
Fireplace	0 or 1	15,000
Age of the house	Years	−6,000

Use these above estimates to value a five-year-old house with a living area of 500 square meters, three bathrooms, and a fireplace.

4. A real estate firm is evaluating an office building, using the income approach. The real estate firm has compiled the following information for the office building. All information is on an annual basis.

Gross potential rental income	$350,000
Estimated vacancy and collection losses*	4%
Insurance and taxes	$26,000
Utilities	$18,000
Repairs and maintenance	$23,000
Depreciation	$40,000
Interest on proposed financing	$18,000

*As a percentage of gross potential rental income

There have been two recent sales of office buildings in the area. The first building had a net operating income of $500,000 and was sold at $4 million. The second building had a net operating income of $225,000 and was sold at $1.6 million.

A. Compute the net operating income for the office building to be valued.

B. Use the income approach to compute the appraisal price of the office building.

5. An analyst is evaluating a real estate investment project using the discounted cash flow approach. The purchase price is $3 million, which is financed 15 percent by equity and 85 percent by a mortgage loan. It is expected that the property will be sold in five years. The analyst has estimated the following after-tax cash flows during the first four years of the five-year life of the real estate investment project.

Year	1	2	3	4
Cash flow	$60,000	$75,000	$91,000	$108,000

For the fifth year, that is, the year when the property would be sold by the investor, the after-tax cash flow without the property sale is estimated to be $126,000 and the after-tax cash flow from the property sale is estimated to be $710,000.

Compute the NPV of this project. State whether the investor should undertake the project. The investor's cost of equity for projects with level of risk comparable to this real estate investment project is 18 percent.

6. An investment firm is evaluating a real estate investment project, using the discounted cash flow approach. The purchase price is $1.5 million, which is financed 20 percent by equity and 80 percent by a mortgage loan at a 9 percent pre-tax interest rate. The mortgage loan has a long maturity and constant annual payments of $120,000. This includes interest payments on the remaining principal at a 9 percent interest rate and a variable principal repayment that steps up with time. The net operating income (NOI) in the first year is estimated to be $170,000. NOI is expected to grow at a rate of 4 percent every year. The interest on real estate financing for the project is tax deductible. The marginal income tax rate for the investment firm is 30 percent. Using straight-line depreciation, the annual depreciation of the property is $37,500.

A. Compute the after-tax cash flows in years 1, 2, and 3 of the project.

B. It is expected that the property will be sold at the end of three years. The projected sale price is $1.72 million. The property's sales expenses are 6.5 percent of the sale price. The capital gains tax rate is 20 percent. Compute the after-tax cash flow from the property sale in year 3.

C. The investor's cost of equity for projects with level of risk comparable to this real estate investment project is 19 percent. Recommend whether to invest in the project or not, based on the NPV of the project.

7. Would you suggest using real estate appraisal-based indexes in a global portfolio optimization?

8. Suppose the estimated correlation matrix of the Wilshire 5000 U.S. stock index and two real estate indexes, the Federal Russell Company index (FRC) and the National Association of Real Estate Investment Trusts (NAREIT) is as follows:

	Wilshire 5000	NAREIT	FRC
Wilshire 5000	1.00	0.79	0.18
NAREIT	0.79	1.00	0.02
FRC	0.18	0.02	1.00

Based on this above matrix, compare the expected price behavior of the two real estate indexes.

9. An investor is evaluating a venture capital project that will require an investment of $1.4 million. The investor estimates that she will be able to exit the venture successfully in eight years. She also estimates that there is an 80 percent chance that the venture will not survive until the end of the eighth year. If the venture does survive until then, she expects to exit the project then, and it is equally likely that the payoff at the time of exit will be either $25 million or $35 million. The investor is considering an equity investment in the project, and her cost of equity for a project with similar risk is 20 percent.

A. Compute the net present value of the venture capital project.

B. Recommend whether to accept or reject the project.

10. VenCap, Inc. is a venture capital financier. It estimates that investing €4.5 million in a particular venture capital project can return €60 million at the end of six years if it succeeds; however, it realizes that the project may fail at any time between now and the end of six years. The following table has VenCap's estimates of probabilities of failure for the project. First, 0.28 is the probability of failure in year 1. The probability that the project fails in the second year, given that it has survived through year 1, is 0.25. The probability that the project fails in the third year, given that it has survived through year 2, is 0.22; and so forth. VenCap is considering an equity investment in the project, and its cost of equity for a project with this level of risk is 22 percent.

Year	1	2	3	4	5	6
Failure probability	0.28	0.25	0.22	0.18	0.18	0.10

Compute the expected net present value of the venture capital project and recommend whether VenCap should accept or reject the project.

11. Consider a hedge fund that has an annual fee structure of 1.5 percent base management fee plus a 15 percent incentive fee applied to profits above the risk-free rate. If the risk-free rate is 5.5 percent, compute the net percentage return for an investor if the gross return during the year is

A. 35%

B. 5%

C. −6%

12. A hedge fund currently has assets of $2 billion. The annual fee structure of this fund consists of a fixed fee of 1 percent of portfolio assets plus a 20 percent incentive fee. The fund applies the incentive fee to the gross return each year in excess of the portfolio's previous high watermark, which is the maximum portfolio value since the inception of the fund. The maximum value the fund has achieved so far since its inception was a little more than a year ago when its value was $2.1 billion. Compute the fee that the manager would earn in dollars if the return on the fund this year turns out to be

A. 29%

B. 4.5%

C. −1.8%

13. Consider a hedge fund whose annual fee structure has a fixed fee and an incentive fee with a high watermark provision. The fund manager earns an incentive fee only if the fund is above the high watermark of the maximum portfolio value since the inception of the fund. Discuss the positive and negative implications of the high watermark provision for the investors of the hedge fund.

14. The shares of an Italian firm have been trading earlier around €6. Recently, a Spanish firm entered into talks with the Italian firm to acquire it. The Spanish firm offered two of its shares for every three shares of the Italian firm. The boards of directors of both firms have approved the merger, and ratification by shareholders is expected soon. The shares of

the Spanish firm are currently trading at €12.50, and the shares of the Italian firm are trading at €8.

A. Should the shares of the Italian firm trade at a discount? Explain.

B. What position do you think a hedge fund that specializes in risk arbitrage in mergers and acquisitions will take in the two firms? Assume that the hedge fund's position will involve 250,000 shares of the Italian firm.

C. It turns out that the European Union commission does not approve the merger because it fears that the merged firm will have a monopolistic position in its industry. After this announcement, the shares of the Italian firm fell to €6.10 each. The shares of the Spanish firm are still trading at €12.50 each. Discuss the consequences for the hedge fund. Ignore the cost of securities lending and margins deposit.

15. Global group manages hedge funds, and has three hedge funds invested in the stock market of a particular emerging country. These three hedge funds have very different investment strategies. As expected, the 2000 returns on the three funds were quite different. Over the year 2000, an index based on the overall stock market of the emerging country went up by 20 percent. Here are the performances of the three funds before management fees set at 15 percent of gross profits:

Fund	Gross Return
A	50%
B	20%
C	−10%

At year end, most clients had left fund C, and Global group closed this fund. At the start of 2001, Global group launched an aggressive publicity campaign among portfolio managers, stressing the remarkable return on fund A. If potential clients asked whether the firm had other hedge funds invested in the particular emerging market, it mentioned the only other fund, fund B, and claimed that the group's average gross performance during 2000 was 35 percent.

A. Compare the average gross return and the average net return on the three hedge funds with the percentage increase in the stock market index.

B. Comment on the publicity campaign launched by Global group.

16. An analyst is examining the performance of hedge funds. He looks at the 90 hedge funds that are in existence today, and notes that the average annual return on these funds during the last 10 years is 25.17 percent. The standard deviation of these returns is 17.43 percent and the Sharpe ratio is 1.15. The analyst also observes that the average of the annual returns on a stock market index during the last 10 years is 14.83 percent. The standard deviation of these returns is 11.87 percent and the Sharpe ratio is 0.81. The analyst concludes that the hedge funds have substantially outperformed the stock market index. Discuss why the comparison by the analyst could be misleading.

17. Consider the four major commodities traded on a commodity futures exchange today (year 10). The following table lists the average annualized price movements from year 1 to year 10, as well as the production volumes, expressed in the local currency unit, today (year 10) and ten years ago (year 1).

Commodity	Average Return	Annual Production	
		Year 1	Year 10
A	20%	10	50
B	20%	5	20
C	−10%	50	10
D	0%	35	20

The futures exchange has now decided to create a commodity index based on the four commodities, with weights equal to their current relative importance in economic production. These indexes are back-calculated till year 1 using today's weights.

A. Would such an index give unbiased indications over the past 10 years?

B. What suggestions do you have regarding weights that can be used to back-calculate the indexes?

18. The beta of gold relative to the market portfolio is −0.3. The risk-free rate is 7 percent, and the market risk premium is 4 percent.

A. What is the expected return on gold based on the capital asset pricing model (CAPM)?

B. Give an intuitive explanation for the magnitude of the expected return on gold.

PORTFOLIO MANAGEMENT

The candidate should be able to demonstrate a working knowledge of the key elements of the portfolio management process, including the investment setting, investment policy, and asset allocation.

STUDY SESSION 18
PORFOLIO MANAGEMENT

LEARNING OUTCOMES

Reading 76: The Investment Setting

The candidate should be able to:

a. explain the concept of required rate of return and discuss the components of an investor's required rate of return;

b. differentiate between the real risk-free rate of return and the nominal risk-free rate of return and compute both return measures;

c. explain the risk premium, the associated fundamental sources of risk, and why these sources are complementary to systematic risk;

d. define the security market line, and discuss the factors that cause movements along, changes in the slope of, and shifts of the security market line.

Reading 77: The Asset Allocation Decision

The candidate should be able to:

a. describe the steps in the portfolio management process and explain the reasons for a policy statement;

b. explain why investment objectives should be expressed in terms of both risk and return and list the factors that may affect an investor's risk tolerance;

c. describe the return objectives of capital preservation, capital appreciation, current income, and total return and describe the investment constraints of liquidity, time horizon, tax concerns, legal and regulatory factors, and unique needs and preferences;

Note:
Candidates are responsible for the problems at the end of Readings 78 and 79.

Note:
Although this reading addresses the taxation of individual investors from the viewpoint of a U.S. investor, candidates are not expected to know the U.S. tax code. This reading is intended to illustrate the importance of taxation to investors, particularly individual investors.

d. describe the importance of asset allocation, in terms of the percentage of a portfolio's return that can be explained by the target asset allocation and list reasons for the differences in the average asset allocation among citizens of different countries.

Reading 78: An Introduction to Portfolio Management

The candidate should be able to:

a. define risk aversion and cite evidence that suggests that individuals are generally risk averse;

b. list the assumptions about individuals' investment behavior of the Markowitz Portfolio Theory;

c. compute expected return for an individual investment and for a portfolio;

d. compute the variance and standard deviation for an individual investment;

e. compute the covariance of rates of return, and show how it is related to the correlation coefficient;

f. list the components of the portfolio standard deviation formula, and explain which component is most important to consider when adding an investment to a portfolio;

g. describe the efficient frontier and explain the implications for incremental returns as an investor assumes more risk;

h. define optimal portfolio and show how each investor may have a different optimal portfolio.

Reading 79: An Introduction to Asset Pricing Models

The candidate should be able to:

a. list the assumptions of the capital market theory;

b. explain what happens to the expected return, the standard deviation of returns, and possible risk-return combinations when a risk-free asset is combined with a portfolio of risky assets;

c. identify the market portfolio, and describe the role of the market portfolio in the formation of the capital market line (CML);

d. define systematic and unsystematic risk and explain why an investor should not expect to receive additional return for assuming unsystematic risk;

e. describe the capital asset pricing model, diagram the security market line (SML), and define beta;

f. calculate and interpret, using the SML, the expected return on a security, and evaluate whether the security is undervalued, overvalued, or properly valued;

g. explain how the systematic risk of an asset is estimated using the characteristic line.

THE INVESTMENT SETTING

LEARNING OUTCOMES

The candidate should be able to:

a. explain the concept of required rate of return and discuss the components of an investor's required rate of return;

b. differentiate between the real risk-free rate of return and the nominal risk-free rate of return and, compute both return measures;

c. explain the risk premium, the associated fundamental sources of risk, and why these sources are complementary to systematic risk;

d. define the security market line, and discuss the factors that cause movements along, changes in the slope of, and shifts of the security market line.

INTRODUCTION   1

This initial reading discusses several topics basic to the subsequent readings. We begin by defining the term *investment* and discussing the returns and risks related to investments. This leads to a presentation of how to measure the expected and historical rates of returns for an individual asset or a portfolio of assets. In addition, we consider how to measure risk not only for an individual investment but also for an investment that is part of a portfolio.

The third section of the reading discusses the factors that determine the required rate of return for an individual investment. The factors discussed are those that contribute to an asset's *total* risk. Because most investors have a portfolio of investments, it is necessary to consider how to measure the risk of an asset when it is a part of a large portfolio of assets. The risk that prevails when an asset is part of a diversified portfolio is referred to as its *systematic risk*.

The final section deals with what causes *changes* in an asset's required rate of return over time. Changes occur because of both macroeconomic events that affect all investment assets and microeconomic events that affect the specific asset.

2　WHAT IS AN INVESTMENT?

For most of your life, you will be earning and spending money. Rarely, though, will your current money income exactly balance with your consumption desires. Sometimes, you may have more money than you want to spend; at other times, you may want to purchase more than you can afford. These imbalances will lead you either to borrow or to save to maximize the long-run benefits from your income.

When current income exceeds current consumption desires, people tend to save the excess. They can do any of several things with these savings. One possibility is to put the money under a mattress or bury it in the backyard until some future time when consumption desires exceed current income. When they retrieve their savings from the mattress or backyard, they have the same amount they saved.

Another possibility is that they can give up the immediate possession of these savings for a future larger amount of money that will be available for future consumption. This tradeoff of *present* consumption for a higher level of *future* consumption is the reason for saving. What you do with the savings to make them increase over time is *investment*.[1]

Those who give up immediate possession of savings (that is, defer consumption) expect to receive in the future a greater amount than they gave up. Conversely, those who consume more than their current income (that is, borrow) must be willing to pay back in the future more than they borrowed.

The rate of exchange between *future consumption* (future dollars) and *current consumption* (current dollars) is the *pure rate of interest*. Both people's willingness to pay this difference for borrowed funds and their desire to receive a surplus on their savings give rise to an interest rate referred to as the *pure time value of money*. This interest rate is established in the capital market by a comparison of the supply of excess income available (savings) to be invested and the demand for excess consumption (borrowing) at a given time. If you can exchange $100 of certain income today for $104 of certain income one year from today, then the pure rate of exchange on a risk-free investment (that is, the time value of money) is said to be 4 percent (104/100 – 1).

The investor who gives up $100 today expects to consume $104 of goods and services in the future. This assumes that the general price level in the economy stays the same. This price stability has rarely been the case during the past several decades when inflation rates have varied from 1.1 percent in 1986 to 13.3 percent in 1979, with an average of about 5.4 percent a year from 1970 to 2001. If investors expect a change in prices, they will require a higher rate of return to compensate for it. For example, if an investor expects a rise in prices (that is, he or she expects inflation) at the rate of 2 percent during the period of investment, he or she will increase the required interest rate by 2 percent. In our example, the investor would require $106 in the future to defer the $100 of consumption during an inflationary period (a 6 percent nominal, risk-free interest rate will be required instead of 4 percent).

Further, if the future payment from the investment is not certain, the investor will demand an interest rate that exceeds the pure time value of money plus the inflation rate. The uncertainty of the payments from an investment is the *investment risk*. The additional return added to the nominal, risk-free interest rate is called a *risk premium*. In our previous example, the investor would require more than $106 one year from today to compensate for the uncertainty. As an example, if the required amount were $110, $4, or 4 percent, would be considered a risk premium.

---

[1] In contrast, when current income is less than current consumption desires, people borrow to make up the difference. Although we will discuss borrowing on several occasions, the major emphasis of this text is how to invest savings.

2.1 Investment Defined

From our discussion, we can specify a formal definition of investment. Specifically, an **investment** is the current commitment of dollars for a period of time in order to derive future payments that will compensate the investor for (1) the time the funds are committed, (2) the expected rate of inflation, and (3) the uncertainty of the future payments. The "investor" can be an individual, a government, a pension fund, or a corporation. Similarly, this definition includes all types of investments, including investments by corporations in plant and equipment and investments by individuals in stocks, bonds, commodities, or real estate. This text emphasizes investments by individual investors. In all cases, the investor is trading a *known* dollar amount today for some *expected* future stream of payments that will be greater than the current outlay.

At this point, we have answered the questions about why people invest and what they want from their investments. They invest to earn a return from savings due to their deferred consumption. They want a rate of return that compensates them for the time, the expected rate of inflation, and the uncertainty of the return. This return, the investor's **required rate of return,** is discussed throughout this book. A central question of this book is how investors select investments that will give them their required rates of return.

The next section of this reading describes how to measure the expected or historical rate of return on an investment and also how to quantify the uncertainty of expected returns. You need to understand these techniques for measuring the rate of return and the uncertainty of these returns to evaluate the suitability of a particular investment. Although our emphasis will be on financial assets, such as bonds and stocks, we will refer to other assets, such as art and antiques. Chapter 3 discusses the range of financial assets and also considers some nonfinancial assets.

MEASURES OF RETURN AND RISK   3

The purpose of this book is to help you understand how to choose among alternative investment assets. This selection process requires that you estimate and evaluate the expected risk-return trade-offs for the alternative investments available. Therefore, you must understand how to measure the rate of return and the risk involved in an investment accurately. To meet this need, in this section we examine ways to quantify return and risk. The presentation will consider how to measure both *historical* and *expected* rates of return and risk.

We consider historical measures of return and risk because this book and other publications provide numerous examples of historical average rates of return and risk measures for various assets, and understanding these presentations is important. In addition, these historical results are often used by investors when attempting to estimate the *expected* rates of return and risk for an asset class.

The first measure is the historical rate of return on an individual investment over the time period the investment is held (that is, its holding period). Next, we consider how to measure the *average* historical rate of return for an individual investment over a number of time periods. The third subsection considers the average rate of return for a *portfolio* of investments.

Given the measures of historical rates of return, we will present the traditional measures of risk for a historical time series of returns (that is, the variance and standard deviation).

Following the presentation of measures of historical rates of return and risk, we turn to estimating the *expected* rate of return for an investment. Obviously, such an estimate contains a great deal of uncertainty, and we present measures of this uncertainty or risk.

3.1 Measures of Historical Rates of Return

When you are evaluating alternative investments for inclusion in your portfolio, you will often be comparing investments with widely different prices or lives. As an example, you might want to compare a $10 stock that pays no dividends to a stock selling for $150 that pays dividends of $5 a year. To properly evaluate these two investments, you must accurately compare their historical rates of returns. A proper measurement of the rates of return is the purpose of this section.

When we invest, we defer current consumption in order to add to our wealth so that we can consume more in the future. Therefore, when we talk about a return on an investment, we are concerned with the *change in wealth* resulting from this investment. This change in wealth can be either due to cash inflows, such as interest or dividends, or caused by a change in the price of the asset (positive or negative).

If you commit $200 to an investment at the beginning of the year and you get back $220 at the end of the year, what is your return for the period? The period during which you own an investment is called its *holding period,* and the return for that period is the **holding period return (HPR).** In this example, the HPR is 1.10, calculated as follows:

$$\text{HPR} = \frac{\text{Ending Value of Investment}}{\text{Beginning Value of Investment}} = \frac{\$220}{\$200} = 1.10 \qquad \textbf{(76-1)}$$

This value will always be zero or greater—that is, it can never be a negative value. A value greater than 1.0 reflects an increase in your wealth, which means that you received a positive rate of return during the period. A value less than 1.0 means that you suffered a decline in wealth, which indicates that you had a negative return during the period. An HPR of zero indicates that you lost all your money.

Although HPR helps us express the change in value of an investment, investors generally evaluate returns in *percentage terms on an annual basis.* This conversion to annual percentage rates makes it easier to directly compare alternative investments that have markedly different characteristics. The first step in converting an HPR to an annual percentage rate is to derive a percentage return, referred to as the **holding period yield (HPY).** The HPY is equal to the HPR minus 1.

$$\text{HPY} = \text{HPR} - 1 \qquad \textbf{(76-2)}$$

In our example:

$$\begin{aligned}\text{HPY} &= 1.10 - 1 = 0.10 \\ &= 10\%\end{aligned}$$

To derive an *annual* HPY, you compute an *annual* HPR and subtract 1. Annual HPR is found by:

$$\text{Annual HPR} = \text{HPR}^{1/n} \qquad \textbf{(76-3)}$$

where:

n = **number of years the investment is held**

Consider an investment that cost $250 and is worth $350 after being held for two years:

$$\text{HPR} = \frac{\text{Ending Value of Investment}}{\text{Beginning Value of Investment}} = \frac{\$350}{\$250}$$
$$= 1.40$$
$$\text{Annual HPR} = 1.40^{1/n}$$
$$= 1.40^{1/2}$$
$$= 1.1832$$
$$\text{Annual HPY} = 1.1832 - 1 = 0.1832$$
$$= 18.32\%$$

If you experience a decline in your wealth value, the computation is as follows:

$$\text{HPR} = \frac{\text{Ending Value}}{\text{Beginning Value}} = \frac{\$400}{\$500} = 0.80$$
$$\text{HPY} = 0.80 - 1.00 = -0.20 = -20\%$$

A multiple year loss over two years would be computed as follows:

$$\text{HPR} = \frac{\text{Ending Value}}{\text{Beginning Value}} = \frac{\$750}{\$1,000} = 0.75$$
$$\text{Annual HPR} = (0.75)^{1/n} = 0.75^{1/2}$$
$$= 0.866$$
$$\text{Annual HPY} = 0.866 - 1.00 = -0.134 = -13.4\%$$

In contrast, consider an investment of $100 held for only six months that earned a return of $12:

$$\text{HPR} = \frac{\$112}{\$100} = 1.12 (n = 0.5)$$
$$\text{Annual HPR} = 1.12^{1/.5}$$
$$= 1.12^2$$
$$= 1.2544$$
$$\text{Annual HPY} = 1.2544 - 1 = 0.2544$$
$$= 25.44\%$$

Note that we made some implicit assumptions when converting the HPY to an annual basis. This annualized holding period yield computation assumes a constant annual yield for each year. In the two-year investment, we assumed an 18.32 percent rate of return each year, compounded. In the partial year HPR that was annualized, we assumed that the return is compounded for the whole year. That is, we assumed that the rate of return earned during the first part of the year is likewise earned on the value at the end of the first six months. The 12 percent rate of return for the initial six months compounds to 25.44 percent for the full year.[2] Because of the uncertainty of being able to earn the same return in the future six months, institutions will typically not compound partial year results.

Remember one final point: The ending value of the investment can be the result of a positive or negative change in price for the investment alone (for example, a stock going from $20 a share to $22 a share), income from the investment

---

[2] To check that you understand the calculations, determine the annual HPY for a three-year HPR of 1.50. (Answer: 14.47 percent.) Compute the annual HPY for a three-month HPR of 1.06. (Answer: 26.25 percent.)

alone, or a combination of price change and income. Ending value includes the value of everything related to the investment.

3.2 Computing Mean Historical Returns

Now that we have calculated the HPY for a single investment for a single year, we want to consider **mean rates of return** for a single investment and for a portfolio of investments. Over a number of years, a single investment will likely give high rates of return during some years and low rates of return, or possibly negative rates of return, during others. Your analysis should consider each of these returns, but you also want a summary figure that indicates this investment's typical experience, or the rate of return you should expect to receive if you owned this investment over an extended period of time. You can derive such a summary figure by computing the mean annual rate of return for this investment over some period of time.

Alternatively, you might want to evaluate a portfolio of investments that might include similar investments (for example, all stocks or all bonds) or a combination of investments (for example, stocks, bonds, and real estate). In this instance, you would calculate the mean rate of return for this portfolio of investments for an individual year or for a number of years.

3.2.1 Single Investment

Given a set of annual rates of return (HPYs) for an individual investment, there are two summary measures of return performance. The first is the arithmetic mean return, the second the geometric mean return. To find the **arithmetic mean (AM),** the sum (Σ) of annual HPYs is divided by the number of years (n) as follows:

$$AM = \Sigma HPY/n \qquad \text{(76-4)}$$

where:

ΣHPY = the sum of annual holding period yields

An alternative computation, the **geometric mean (GM),** is the nth root of the product of the HPRs for n years.

$$GM = [\pi\, HPR]^{1/n} - 1 \qquad \text{(76-5)}$$

where:

π = the product of the annual holding period returns as follows:

$$(HPR_1) \times (HPR_2) \cdots (HPR_n)$$

To illustrate these alternatives, consider an investment with the following data:

Year	Beginning Value	Ending Value	HPR	HPY
1	100.0	115.0	1.15	0.15
2	115.0	138.0	1.20	0.20
3	138.0	110.4	0.80	−0.20

$$AM = [(0.15) + (0.20) + (-0.20)]/3$$
$$= 0.15/3$$
$$= 0.05 = 5\%$$

$$GM = [(1.15) \times (1.20) \times (0.80)]^{1/3} - 1$$
$$= (1.104)^{1/3} - 1$$
$$= 1.03353 - 1$$
$$= 0.03353 = 3.353\%$$

Investors are typically concerned with long-term performance when comparing alternative investments. GM is considered a superior measure of the long-term mean rate of return because it indicates the compound annual rate of return based on the ending value of the investment versus its beginning value.[3] Specifically, using the prior example, if we compounded 3.353 percent for three years, $(1.03353)^3$, we would get an ending wealth value of 1.104.

Although the arithmetic average provides a good indication of the expected rate of return for an investment during a future individual year, it is biased upward if you are attempting to measure an asset's long-term performance. This is obvious for a volatile security. Consider, for example, a security that increases in price from \$50 to \$100 during year 1 and drops back to \$50 during year 2. The annual HPYs would be:

Year	Beginning Value	Ending Value	HPR	HPY
1	50	100	2.00	1.00
2	100	50	0.50	−0.50

This would give an AM rate of return of:

$$[(1.00) + (-0.50)]/2 = .50/2$$
$$= 0.25 = 25\%$$

This investment brought no change in wealth and therefore no return, yet the AM rate of return is computed to be 25 percent.

The GM rate of return would be:

$$(2.00 \times 0.50)^{1/2} - 1 = (1.00)^{1/2} - 1$$
$$= 1.00 - 1 = 0\%$$

This answer of a 0 percent rate of return accurately measures the fact that there was no change in wealth from this investment over the two-year period.

When rates of return are the same for all years, the GM will be equal to the AM. If the rates of return vary over the years, the GM will always be lower than the AM. The difference between the two mean values will depend on the year-to-year changes in the rates of return. Larger annual changes in the rates of return—that is, more volatility—will result in a greater difference between the alternative mean values.

---

[3] Note that the GM is the same whether you compute the geometric mean of the individual annual holding period yields or the annual HPY for a three-year period, comparing the ending value to the beginning value, as discussed earlier under annual HPY for a multiperiod case.

An awareness of both methods of computing mean rates of return is important because published accounts of investment performance or descriptions of financial research will use both the AM and the GM as measures of average historical returns. We will also use both throughout this book. Currently most studies dealing with long-run historical rates of return include both AM and GM rates of return.

3.2.2 A Portfolio of Investments

The mean historical rate of return (HPY) for a portfolio of investments is measured as the weighted average of the HPYs for the individual investments in the portfolio, or the overall change in value of the original portfolio. The weights used in computing the averages are the relative *beginning* market values for each investment; this is referred to as *dollar-weighted* or *value-weighted* mean rate of return. This technique is demonstrated by the examples in Exhibit 76-1. As shown, the HPY is the same (9.5 percent) whether you compute the weighted average return using the beginning market value weights or if you compute the overall change in the total value of the portfolio.

Although the analysis of historical performance is useful, selecting investments for your portfolio requires you to predict the rates of return you *expect* to prevail. The next section discusses how you would derive such estimates of expected rates of return. We recognize the great uncertainty regarding these future expectations, and we will discuss how one measures this uncertainty, which is referred to as the risk of an investment.

3.3 Calculating Expected Rates of Return

Risk is the uncertainty that an investment will earn its expected rate of return. In the examples in the prior section, we examined *realized* historical rates of return. In contrast, an investor who is evaluating a future investment alternative expects or anticipates a certain rate of return. The investor might say that he or she *expects* the investment will provide a rate of return of 10 percent, but this is actually the

---

EXHIBIT 76-1 Computation of Holding Period Yield for a Portfolio

Investment	Number of Shares	Beginning Price	Beginning Market Value	Ending Price	Ending Market Value	HPR	HPY	Market Weight[a]	Weighted HPY
A	100,000	$10	$ 1,000,000	$12	$ 1,200,000	1.20	20%	0.05	0.01
B	200,000	20	4,000,000	21	4,200,000	1.05	5	0.20	0.01
C	500,000	30	15,000,000	33	16,500,000	1.10	10	0.75	0.075
Total			$20,000,000		$21,900,000				0.095

$$\text{HPR} = \frac{21,900,000}{20,000,000} = 1.095$$

$$\text{HPY} = 1.095 - 1 = 0.095$$
$$= 9.5\%$$

---

[a] Weights are based on beginning values.

investor's most likely estimate, also referred to as a *point estimate*. Pressed further, the investor would probably acknowledge the uncertainty of this point estimate return and admit the possibility that, under certain conditions, the annual rate of return on this investment might go as low as –10 percent or as high as 25 percent. The point is, the specification of a larger range of possible returns from an investment reflects the investor's uncertainty regarding what the actual return will be. Therefore, a larger range of expected returns makes the investment riskier.

An investor determines how certain the expected rate of return on an investment is by analyzing estimates of expected returns. To do this, the investor assigns probability values to all *possible* returns. These probability values range from zero, which means no chance of the return, to one, which indicates complete certainty that the investment will provide the specified rate of return. These probabilities are typically subjective estimates based on the historical performance of the investment or similar investments modified by the investor's expectations for the future. As an example, an investor may know that about 30 percent of the time the rate of return on this particular investment was 10 percent. Using this information along with future expectations regarding the economy, one can derive an estimate of what might happen in the future.

The *expected* return from an investment is defined as:

$$\text{Expected Return} = \sum_{i=1}^{n} (\text{Probability of Return}) \times (\text{Possible Return})$$

$$E(R_i) = [(P_1)(R_1) + (P_2)(R_2) + (P_3)(R_3) + \cdots + (P_n R_n)] \qquad \textbf{(76-6)}$$

$$E(R_i) = \sum_{i=1}^{n} (P_i)(R_i)$$

Let us begin our analysis of the effect of risk with an example of perfect certainty wherein the investor is absolutely certain of a return of 5 percent. Exhibit 76-2 illustrates this situation.

Perfect certainty allows only one possible return, and the probability of receiving that return is 1.0. Few investments provide certain returns. In the case of perfect certainty, there is only one value for $P_i R_i$:

$$E(R_i) = (1.0)(0.05) = 0.05$$

In an alternative scenario, suppose an investor believed an investment could provide several different rates of return depending on different possible economic conditions. As an example, in a strong economic environment with high corporate profits and little or no inflation, the investor might expect the rate of return on common stocks during the next year to reach as high as 20 percent. In contrast, if there is an economic decline with a higher-than-average rate of inflation, the investor might expect the rate of return on common stocks during the next year to be –20 percent. Finally, with no major change in the economic environment, the rate of return during the next year would probably approach the long-run average of 10 percent.

EXHIBIT 76-2 Probability Distribution for Risk-Free Investment

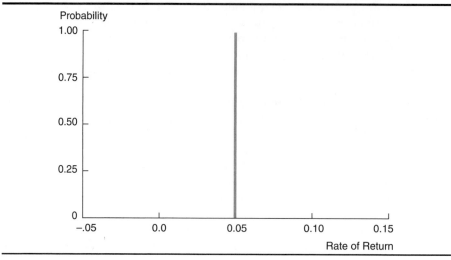

The investor might estimate probabilities for each of these economic scenarios based on past experience and the current outlook as follows:

Economic Conditions	Probability	Rate of Return
Strong economy, no inflation	0.15	0.20
Weak economy, above-average inflation	0.15	−0.20
No major change in economy	0.70	0.10

This set of potential outcomes can be visualized as shown in exhibit 76-3.

The computation of the expected rate of return $[E(R_i)]$ is as follows:

$$E(R_i) = [(0.15)(0.20)] + [(0.15)(-0.20)] + [(0.70)(0.10)]$$
$$= 0.07$$

Obviously, the investor is less certain about the expected return from this investment than about the return from the prior investment with its single possible return.

A third example is an investment with 10 possible outcomes ranging from −40 percent to 50 percent with the same probability for each rate of return. A graph of this set of expectations would appear as shown in exhibit 76-4.

In this case, there are numerous outcomes from a wide range of possibilities. The expected rate of return $[E(R_i)]$ for this investment would be:

$$E(R_i) = (0.10)(-0.40) + (0.10)(-0.30) + (0.10)(-0.20) + (0.10)(-0.10) +$$
$$(0.10)(0.0) + (0.10)(0.10) + (0.10)(0.20) + (0.10)(0.30) +$$
$$(0.10)(0.40) + (0.10)(0.50)$$
$$= (-0.04) + (-0.03) + (-0.02) + (-0.01) + (0.00) + (0.01) +$$
$$(0.02) + (0.03) - (0.04) + (0.05)$$
$$= 0.05$$

The *expected* rate of return for this investment is the same as the certain return discussed in the first example; but, in this case, the investor is highly uncertain about the *actual* rate of return. This would be considered a risky investment because of that uncertainty. We would anticipate that an investor faced with the

EXHIBIT 76-3 Probability Distribution for Risky Investment with Three Possible Rates of Return

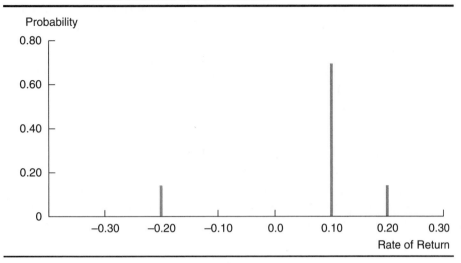

EXHIBIT 76-4 Probability Distribution for Risky Investment with 10 Possible Rates of Return

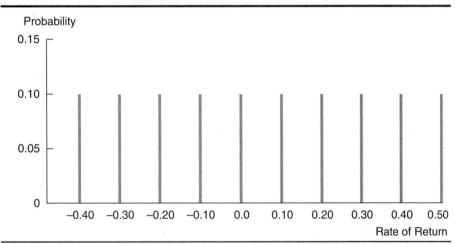

choice between this risky investment and the certain (risk-free) case would select the certain alternative. This expectation is based on the belief that most investors are **risk averse,** which means that if everything else is the same, they will select the investment that offers greater certainty.

3.4 Measuring the Risk of Expected Rates of Return

We have shown that we can calculate the expected rate of return and evaluate the uncertainty, or risk, of an investment by identifying the range of possible returns from that investment and assigning each possible return a weight based on the probability that it will occur. Although the graphs help us visualize the dispersion of possible returns, most investors want to quantify this dispersion using statistical techniques. These statistical measures allow you to compare the return and risk measures for alternative investments directly. Two possible measures of risk (uncertainty) have received support in theoretical work on portfolio theory: the *variance* and the *standard deviation* of the estimated distribution of expected returns.

In this section, we demonstrate how variance and standard deviation measure the dispersion of possible rates of return around the expected rate of return. We will work with the examples discussed earlier. The formula for variance is as follows:

$$\text{Variance } (\sigma^2) = \sum_{i=1}^{n} (\text{Probability}) \times \left(\begin{array}{c} \text{Possible} \\ \text{Return} \end{array} - \begin{array}{c} \text{Expected} \\ \text{Return} \end{array} \right)^2 \qquad \textbf{(76-7)}$$

$$= \sum_{i=1}^{n} (P_i)[R_i - E(R_i)]^2$$

3.4.1 Variance

The larger the **variance** for an expected rate of return, the greater the dispersion of expected returns and the greater the uncertainty, or risk, of the investment. The variance for the perfect-certainty example would be:

$$(\sigma^2) = \sum_{i=1}^{n} (P_i)[R_i - E(R_i)]^2$$

$$= 1.0(0.05 - 0.05)^2 = 1.0(0.0) = 0$$

Note that, in perfect certainty, there is *no variance of return* because there is no deviation from expectations and, therefore, *no risk* or *uncertainty*. The variance for the second example would be:

$$(\sigma^2) = \sum_{i=1}^{n} (P_i)[R_i - E(R_i)]^2$$

$$= [(0.15)(0.20 - 0.07)^2 + (0.15)(-0.20 - 0.07)^2 + (0.70)(0.10 - 0.07)^2]$$

$$= [0.010935 + 0.002535 + 0.00063]$$

$$= 0.0141$$

3.4.2 Standard Deviation

The **standard deviation** is the square root of the variance:

$$\text{Standard Deviation} = \sqrt{\sum_{i=1}^{n} P_i[R_i - E(R_i)]} \qquad \textbf{(76-8)}$$

For the second example, the standard deviation would be:

$$\sigma = \sqrt{0.0141}$$

$$= 0.11874 = 11.874\%$$

Therefore, when describing this example, you would contend that you expect a return of 7 percent, but the standard deviation of your expectations is 11.87 percent.

3.4.3 A Relative Measure of Risk

In some cases, an unadjusted variance or standard deviation can be misleading. If conditions for two or more investment alternatives are not similar—that is, if there are major differences in the expected rates of return—it is necessary to use a measure of *relative variability* to indicate risk per unit of expected return. A widely used relative measure of risk is the **coefficient of variation (CV)**, calculated as follows:

$$\begin{aligned} \text{Coefficient of} \atop \text{Variation (CV)} &= \frac{\text{Standard Deviation of Returns}}{\text{Expected Rate of Return}} \\ &= \frac{\sigma_i}{E(R)} \end{aligned} \qquad \text{(76-9)}$$

The *CV* for the preceding example would be:

$$\begin{aligned} CV &= \frac{0.11874}{0.07000} \\ &= 1.696 \end{aligned}$$

This measure of relative variability and risk is used by financial analysts to compare alternative investments with widely different rates of return and standard deviations of returns. As an illustration, consider the following two investments:

	Investment A	Investment B
Expected return	0.07	0.12
Standard deviation	0.05	0.07

Comparing absolute measures of risk, investment B appears to be riskier because it has a standard deviation of 7 percent versus 5 percent for investment A. In contrast, the CV figures show that investment B has less relative variability or lower risk per unit of expected return because it has a substantially higher expected rate of return:

$$CV_A = \frac{0.05}{0.07} = 0.714$$

$$CV_B = \frac{0.07}{0.12} = 0.583$$

3.5 Risk Measures for Historical Returns

To measure the risk for a series of historical rates of returns, we use the same measures as for expected returns (variance and standard deviation) except that we consider the historical holding period yields (HPYs) as follows:

$$\sigma^2 = \sum_{i=1}^{n} [\text{HPY}_i - E(\text{HPY})]^{2/n} \qquad \text{(76-10)}$$

where:

$$\sigma^2 = \text{the variance of the series}$$
$$\text{HPY}_i = \text{the holding period yield during period } i$$
$$E(\text{HPY}) = \text{the expected value of the holding period yield that is equal to the arithmetic mean of the series}$$
$$n = \text{the number of observations}$$

The standard deviation is the square root of the variance. Both measures indicate how much the individual HPYs over time deviated from the expected value of the series. An example computation is contained in the appendix to this reading. As is shown in subsequent readings where we present historical rates of return for alternative asset classes, presenting the standard deviation as a measure of risk for the series or asset class is fairly common.

4   DETERMINANTS OF REQUIRED RATES OF RETURN

In this section, we continue our consideration of factors that you must consider when selecting securities for an investment portfolio. You will recall that this selection process involves finding securities that provide a rate of return that compensates you for: (1) the time value of money during the period of investment, (2) the expected rate of inflation during the period, and (3) the risk involved.

The summation of these three components is called the *required rate of return*. This is the minimum rate of return that you should accept from an investment to compensate you for deferring consumption. Because of the importance of the required rate of return to the total investment selection process, this section contains a discussion of the three components and what influences each of them.

The analysis and estimation of the required rate of return are complicated by the behavior of market rates over time. First, a wide range of rates is available for alternative investments at any time. Second, the rates of return on specific assets change dramatically over time. Third, the difference between the rates available (that is, the spread) on different assets changes over time.

EXHIBIT 76-5 Promised Yields on Alternative Bonds

Type of Bond	1995	1996	1997	1998	1999	2000	2001
U.S. government 3-month Treasury bills	5.49%	5.01%	5.06%	4.78%	4.64%	5.82%	3.80%
U.S. government long-term bonds	6.93	6.80	6.67	5.69	6.14	6.41	6.18
Aaa corporate bonds	7.59	7.37	7.27	6.53	7.05	7.62	7.32
Baa corporate bonds	7.83	8.05	7.87	7.22	7.88	8.36	8.19

Source: Federal Reserve Bulletin, various issues.

The yield data in Exhibit 76-5 for alternative bonds demonstrate these three characteristics. First, even though all these securities have promised returns based upon bond contracts, the promised annual yields during any year differ substantially. As an example, during 1999 the average yields on alternative assets ranged from 4.64 percent on T-bills to 7.88 percent for Baa corporate bonds. Second, the changes in yields for a specific asset are shown by the three-month Treasury bill rate that went from 4.64 percent in 1999 to 5.82 percent in 2000. Third, an example of a change in the difference between yields over time (referred to as a spread) is shown by the Baa–Aaa spread.[4] The yield spread in 1995 was only 24 basis points (7.83 – 7.59), but the spread in 1999 was 83 basis points (7.88 – 7.05). (A basis point is 0.01 percent.)

Because differences in yields result from the riskiness of each investment, you must understand the risk factors that affect the required rates of return and include them in your assessment of investment opportunities. Because the required returns on all investments change over time, and because large differences separate individual investments, you need to be aware of the several components that determine the required rate of return, starting with the risk-free rate. The discussion in this reading considers the three components of the required rate of return and briefly discusses what affects these components. The presentation in Chapter 11 on valuation theory will discuss the factors that affect these components in greater detail.

4.1 The Real Risk-Free Rate

The **real risk-free rate (RRFR)** is the basic interest rate, assuming no inflation and no uncertainty about future flows. An investor in an inflation-free economy who knew with certainty what cash flows he or she would receive at what time would demand the RRFR on an investment. Earlier, we called this the *pure time value of money*, because the only sacrifice the investor made was deferring the use of the money for a period of time. This RRFR of interest is the price charged for the exchange between current goods and future goods.

Two factors, one subjective and one objective, influence this exchange price. The subjective factor is the time preference of individuals for the consumption of income. When individuals give up $100 of consumption this year, how much consumption do they want a year from now to compensate for that sacrifice? The strength of the human desire for current consumption influences the rate of compensation required. Time preferences vary among individuals, and the market creates a composite rate that includes the preferences of all investors. This composite rate changes gradually over time because it is influenced by all the investors in the economy, whose changes in preferences may offset one another.

The objective factor that influences the RRFR is the set of investment opportunities available in the economy. The investment opportunities are determined in turn by the *long-run real growth rate of the economy*. A rapidly growing economy produces more and better opportunities to invest funds and experience positive rates of return. A change in the economy's long-run real growth rate causes a change in all investment opportunities and a change in the required rates of return on all investments. Just as investors supplying capital should demand a higher rate of return when growth is higher, those looking for funds to invest should be willing and able to pay a higher rate of return to use the funds for investment because of the higher growth rate. Thus, a *positive* relationship exists between the real growth rate in the economy and the RRFR.

---

[4] Bonds are rated by rating agencies based upon the credit risk of the securities, that is, the probability of default. Aaa is the top rating Moody's (a prominent rating service) gives to bonds with almost no probability of default. (Only U.S. Treasury bonds are considered to be of higher quality.) Baa is a lower rating Moody's gives to bonds of generally high quality that have some possibility of default under adverse economic conditions.

4.2 Factors Influencing the Nominal Risk-Free Rate (NRFR)

Earlier, we observed that an investor would be willing to forgo current consumption in order to increase future consumption at a rate of exchange called the *risk-free rate of interest*. This rate of exchange was measured in real terms because the investor wanted to increase the consumption of actual goods and services rather than consuming the same amount that had come to cost more money. Therefore, when we discuss rates of interest, we need to differentiate between *real* rates of interest that adjust for changes in the general price level, as opposed to *nominal* rates of interest that are stated in money terms. That is, nominal rates of interest that prevail in the market are determined by real rates of interest, plus factors that will affect the nominal rate of interest, such as the expected rate of inflation and the monetary environment. It is important to understand these factors.

As noted earlier, the variables that determine the RRFR change only gradually over the long term. Therefore, you might expect the required rate on a risk-free investment to be quite stable over time. As discussed in connection with Exhibit 76-5, rates on three-month T-bills were *not* stable over the period from 1995 to 2001. This is demonstrated with additional observations in Exhibit 76-6, which contains yields on T-bills for the period 1980 to 2001.

Investors view T-bills as a prime example of a default-free investment because the government has unlimited ability to derive income from taxes or to create money from which to pay interest. Therefore, rates on T-bills should change only gradually. In fact, the data show a highly erratic pattern. Specifically, there was an increase from about 11.4 percent in 1980 to more than 14 percent in 1981 before declining to less than 6 percent in 1987 and 3.33 percent in 1993. In sum, T-bill rates increased almost 23 percent in one year and then declined by almost 60 percent in six years. Clearly, the nominal rate of interest on a default-free investment is *not* stable in the long run or the short run, even though the underlying determinants of the RRFR are quite stable. The point is, two other factors influence the *nominal risk-free rate (NRFR)*: (1) the relative ease or tightness in the capital markets, and (2) the expected rate of inflation.

EXHIBIT 76-6 Three-Month Treasury Bill Yields and Rates of Inflation

Year	3-Month T-Bills	Rate of Inflation	Year	3-Month T-Bills	Rate of Inflation
1980	11.43%	7.70%	1991	5.38%	3.06%
1981	14.03	10.40	1992	3.43	2.90
1982	10.61	6.10	1993	3.33	2.75
1983	8.61	3.20	1994	4.25	2.67
1984	9.52	4.00	1995	5.49	2.54
1985	7.48	3.80	1996	5.01	3.32
1986	5.98	1.10	1997	5.06	1.70
1987	5.78	4.40	1998	4.78	1.61
1988	6.67	4.40	1999	4.64	2.70
1989	8.11	4.65	2000	5.82	3.40
1990	7.50	6.11	2001	3.80	1.55

Source: Federal Reserve Bulletin, various issues; Economic Report of the President, various issues.

4.2.1 Conditions in the Capital Market

You will recall from prior courses in economics and finance that the purpose of capital markets is to bring together investors who want to invest savings with companies or governments who need capital to expand or to finance budget deficits. The cost of funds at any time (the interest rate) is the price that equates the current supply and demand for capital. A change in the relative ease or tightness in the capital market is a short-run phenomenon caused by a temporary disequilibrium in the supply and demand of capital.

As an example, disequilibrium could be caused by an unexpected change in monetary policy (for example, a change in the growth rate of the money supply) or fiscal policy (for example, a change in the federal deficit). Such a change in monetary policy or fiscal policy will produce a change in the NRFR of interest, but the change should be short-lived because, in the longer run, the higher or lower interest rates will affect capital supply and demand. As an example, a decrease in the growth rate of the money supply (a tightening in monetary policy) will reduce the supply of capital and increase interest rates. In turn, this increase in interest rates (for example, the price of money) will cause an increase in savings and a decrease in the demand for capital by corporations or individuals. These changes in market conditions will bring rates back to the long-run equilibrium, which is based on the long-run growth rate of the economy.

4.2.2 Expected Rate of Inflation

Previously, it was noted that if investors expected the price level to increase during the investment period, they would require the rate of return to include compensation for the expected rate of inflation. Assume that you require a 4 percent real rate of return on a risk-free investment but you expect prices to increase by 3 percent during the investment period. In this case, you should increase your required rate of return by this expected rate of inflation to about 7 percent [$(1.04 \times 1.03) - 1$]. If you do not increase your required return, the \$104 you receive at the end of the year will represent a real return of about 1 percent, not 4 percent. Because prices have increased by 3 percent during the year, what previously cost \$100 now costs \$103, so you can consume only about 1 percent more at the end of the year [$(\$104/103) - 1$]. If you had required a 7.12 percent nominal return, your real consumption could have increased by 4 percent [$(\$107.12/103) - 1$]. Therefore, an investor's nominal required rate of return on a risk-free investment should be:

$$\text{NRFR} = (1 + \text{RRFR}) \times (1 + \text{Expected Rate of Inflation}) - 1 \qquad \textbf{(76-11)}$$

Rearranging the formula, you can calculate the RRFR of return on an investment as follows:

$$\text{RRFR} = \left[\frac{(1 + \text{NRFR of Return})}{(1 + \text{Rate of Inflation})} \right] - 1 \qquad \textbf{(76-12)}$$

To see how this works, assume that the nominal return on U.S. government T-bills was 9 percent during a given year, when the rate of inflation was 5 percent. In this instance, the RRFR of return on these T-bills was 3.8 percent, as follows:

$$\begin{aligned} \text{RRFR} &= [(1 + 0.09)/(1 + 0.05)] - 1 \\ &= 1.038 - 1 \\ &= 0.038 = 3.8\% \end{aligned}$$

This discussion makes it clear that the nominal rate of interest on a risk-free investment is not a good estimate of the RRFR, because the nominal rate can change dramatically in the short run in reaction to temporary ease or tightness in the capital market or because of changes in the expected rate of inflation. As indicated by the data in Exhibit 76-6, the significant changes in the average yield on T-bills typically were caused by large changes in the rates of inflation.

4.2.3 The Common Effect

All the factors discussed thus far regarding the required rate of return affect all investments equally. Whether the investment is in stocks, bonds, real estate, or machine tools, if the expected rate of inflation increases from 2 percent to 6 percent, the investor's required rate of return for *all* investments should increase by 4 percent. Similarly, if a decline in the expected real growth rate of the economy causes a decline in the RRFR of 1 percent, the required return on all investments should decline by 1 percent.

4.3 Risk Premium

A risk-free investment was defined as one for which the investor is certain of the amount and timing of the expected returns. The returns from most investments do not fit this pattern. An investor typically is not completely certain of the income to be received or when it will be received. Investments can range in uncertainty from basically risk-free securities, such as T-bills, to highly speculative investments, such as the common stock of small companies engaged in high-risk enterprises.

Most investors require higher rates of return on investments if they perceive that there is any uncertainty about the expected rate of return. This increase in the required rate of return over the NRFR is the **risk premium (RP).** Although the required risk premium represents a composite of all uncertainty, it is possible to consider several fundamental sources of uncertainty. In this section, we identify and discuss briefly the major sources of uncertainty, including: (1) business risk, (2) financial risk (leverage), (3) liquidity risk, (4) exchange rate risk, and (5) country (political) risk.

Business risk is the uncertainty of income flows caused by the nature of a firm's business. The less certain the income flows of the firm, the less certain the income flows to the investor. Therefore, the investor will demand a risk premium that is based on the uncertainty caused by the basic business of the firm. As an example, a retail food company would typically experience stable sales and earnings growth over time and would have low business risk compared to a firm in the auto industry, where sales and earnings fluctuate substantially over the business cycle, implying high business risk.

Financial risk is the uncertainty introduced by the method by which the firm finances its investments. If a firm uses only common stock to finance investments, it incurs only business risk. If a firm borrows money to finance investments, it must pay fixed financing charges (in the form of interest to creditors) prior to providing income to the common stockholders, so the uncertainty of returns to the equity investor increases. This increase in uncertainty because of fixed-cost financing is called *financial risk* or *financial leverage* and causes an increase in the stock's risk premium.[5]

Liquidity risk is the uncertainty introduced by the secondary market for an investment.[6] When an investor acquires an asset, he or she expects that the investment will

---

[5] For a discussion of financial leverage, see Eugene F. Brigham, *Fundamentals of Financial Management*, 9th ed. (Hinsdale, Ill.: The Dryden Press, 2001), 232–236.

[6] You will recall from prior courses that the overall capital market is composed of the primary market and the secondary market. Securities are initially sold in the primary market, and all subsequent transactions take place in the secondary market. These concepts are discussed in Chapter 4.

mature (as with a bond) or that it will be salable to someone else. In either case, the investor expects to be able to convert the security into cash and use the proceeds for current consumption or other investments. The more difficult it is to make this conversion, the greater the liquidity risk. An investor must consider two questions when assessing the liquidity risk of an investment: (1) How long will it take to convert the investment into cash? (2) How certain is the price to be received? Similar uncertainty faces an investor who wants to acquire an asset: How long will it take to acquire the asset? How uncertain is the price to be paid?

Uncertainty regarding how fast an investment can be bought or sold, or the existence of uncertainty about its price, increases liquidity risk. A U.S. government Treasury bill has almost no liquidity risk because it can be bought or sold in minutes at a price almost identical to the quoted price. In contrast, examples of illiquid investments include a work of art, an antique, or a parcel of real estate in a remote area. For such investments, it may require a long time to find a buyer and the selling prices could vary substantially from expectations. Investors will increase their required rates of return to compensate for liquidity risk. Liquidity risk can be a significant consideration when investing in foreign securities depending on the country and the liquidity of its stock and bond markets.

Exchange rate risk is the uncertainty of returns to an investor who acquires securities denominated in a currency different from his or her own. The likelihood of incurring this risk is becoming greater as investors buy and sell assets around the world, as opposed to only assets within their own countries. A U.S. investor who buys Japanese stock denominated in yen must consider not only the uncertainty of the return in yen but also any change in the exchange value of the yen relative to the U.S. dollar. That is, in addition to the foreign firm's business and financial risk and the security's liquidity risk, the investor must consider the additional uncertainty of the return on this Japanese stock when it is converted from yen to U.S. dollars.

As an example of exchange rate risk, assume that you buy 100 shares of Mitsubishi Electric at 1,050 yen when the exchange rate is 115 yen to the dollar. The dollar cost of this investment would be about $9.13 per share (1,050/115). A year later you sell the 100 shares at 1,200 yen when the exchange rate is 130 yen to the dollar. When you calculate the Holding Period Yield in yen, you find the stock has increased in value by about 14 percent (1,200/1,050), but this is the HPY for a Japanese investor. A U.S. investor receives a much lower rate of return, because during this period the yen has weakened relative to the dollar by about 13 percent (that is, it requires more yen to buy a dollar—130 versus 115). At the new exchange rate, the stock is worth $9.23 per share (1,200/130). Therefore, the return to you as a U.S. investor would be only about 1 percent ($9.23/$9.13) versus 14 percent for the Japanese investor. The difference in return for the Japanese investor and U.S. investor is caused by the decline in the value of the yen relative to the dollar. Clearly, the exchange rate could have gone in the other direction, the dollar weakening against the yen. In this case, as a U.S. investor, you would have experienced the 14 percent return measured in yen, as well as a gain from the exchange rate change.

The more volatile the exchange rate between two countries, the less certain you would be regarding the exchange rate, the greater the exchange rate risk, and the larger the exchange rate risk premium you would require.[7]

There can also be exchange rate risk for a U.S. firm that is extensively multinational in terms of sales and components (costs). In this case, the firm's foreign earnings can be affected by changes in the exchange rate. As will be discussed, this risk can generally be hedged at a cost.

---

[7] An article that examines the pricing of exchange rate risk in the U.S. market is Philippe Jorion, "The Pricing of Exchange Rate Risk in the Stock Market," *Journal of Financial and Quantitative Analysis* 26, no. 3 (September 1991): 363–376.

Country risk, also called *political risk,* is the uncertainty of returns caused by the possibility of a major change in the political or economic environment of a country. The United States is acknowledged to have the smallest country risk in the world because its political and economic systems are the most stable. Nations with high country risk include Russia, because of the several changes in the government hierarchy and its currency crises during 1998, and Indonesia, where there were student demonstrations, major riots, and fires prior to the resignation of President Suharto in May 1998. In both instances, the stock markets experienced significant declines surrounding these events.[8] Individuals who invest in countries that have unstable political-economic systems must add a country risk premium when determining their required rates of return.

When investing globally (which is emphasized throughout the book), investors must consider these additional uncertainties. How liquid are the secondary markets for stocks and bonds in the country? Are any of the country's securities traded on major stock exchanges in the United States, London, Tokyo, or Germany? What will happen to exchange rates during the investment period? What is the probability of a political or economic change that will adversely affect your rate of return? Exchange rate risk and country risk differ among countries. A good measure of exchange rate risk would be the absolute variability of the exchange rate relative to a composite exchange rate. The analysis of country risk is much more subjective and must be based on the history and current environment of the country.

This discussion of risk components can be considered a security's *fundamental risk* because it deals with the intrinsic factors that should affect a security's standard deviation of returns over time. In subsequent discussion, the standard deviation of returns is referred to as a measure of the security's *total risk,* which considers the individual stock by itself—that is, it is not considered as part of a portfolio.

Risk Premium = *f* (Business Risk, Financial Risk, Liquidity Risk, Exchange Rate Risk, Country Risk)

4.4 Risk Premium and Portfolio Theory

An alternative view of risk has been derived from extensive work in portfolio theory and capital market theory by Markowitz, Sharpe, and others.[9] These theories are dealt with in greater detail in Reading 78 and Reading 79 but their impact on the risk premium should be mentioned briefly at this point. These prior works by Markowitz and Sharpe indicated that investors should use an *external market* measure of risk. Under a specified set of assumptions, all rational, profitmaximizing investors want to hold a completely diversified market portfolio of risky assets, and they borrow or lend to arrive at a risk level that is consistent with their risk preferences. Under these conditions, the relevant risk measure for an individual asset is its *comovement with the market portfolio.* This comovement, which is measured by an asset's covariance with the market portfolio, is referred to as

---

[8] Carlotta Gall, "Moscow Stock Market Falls by 11.8%," *Financial Times,* 19 May 1998, 1; "Russian Contagion Hits Neighbours," *Financial Times,* 29 May 1998, 17; John Thornhill, "Russian Stocks Fall 10% over Lack of Support from IMF," *Financial Times,* 2 June 1998, 1; Robert Chote, "Indonesia Risks Further Unrest as Debt Talks Falter," *Financial Times,* 11 May 1998, 1; Sander Thoenes, "Suharto Cuts Visit as Riots Shake Jakarta," *Financial Times,* 14 May 1998, 12; Sander Thoenes, "Economy Hit as Jakarta Is Paralysed," *Financial Times,* 15 May 1998, 17.

[9] These works include Harry Markowitz, "Portfolio Selection," *Journal of Finance* 7, no. 1 (March 1952): 77–91; Harry Markowitz, *Portfolio Selection—Efficient Diversification of Investments* (New Haven, Conn.: Yale University Press, 1959); and William F. Sharpe, "Capital Asset Prices: A Theory of Market Equilibrium under Conditions of Risk," *Journal of Finance* 19, no. 3 (September 1964): 425–442.

an asset's **systematic risk,** the portion of an individual asset's total variance attributable to the variability of the total market portfolio. In addition, individual assets have variance that is unrelated to the market portfolio (that is, it is nonmarket variance) that is due to the asset's unique features. This nonmarket variance is called *unsystematic risk,* and it is generally considered unimportant because it is eliminated in a large, diversified portfolio. Therefore, under these assumptions, *the risk premium for an individual earning asset is a function of the asset's systematic risk with the aggregate market portfolio of risky assets.* The measure of an asset's systematic risk is referred to as its *beta:*

Risk Premium = f (Systematic Market Risk)

4.5 Fundamental Risk versus Systematic Risk

Some might expect a conflict between the market measure of risk (systematic risk) and the fundamental determinants of risk (business risk, and so on). A number of studies have examined the relationship between the market measure of risk (systematic risk) and accounting variables used to measure the fundamental risk factors, such as business risk, financial risk, and liquidity risk. The authors of these studies have generally concluded that *a significant relationship exists between the market measure of risk and the fundamental measures of risk.*[10] Therefore, the two measures of risk can be complementary. This consistency seems reasonable because, in a properly functioning capital market, the market measure of the risk should reflect the fundamental risk characteristics of the asset. As an example, you would expect a firm that has high business risk and financial risk to have an above average beta. At the same time, as we discuss in Reading 79, it is possible that a firm that has a high level of fundamental risk and a large standard deviation of return on stock can have a lower level of systematic risk because its variability of earnings and stock price is not related to the aggregate economy or the aggregate market. Therefore, one can specify the risk premium for an asset as:

Risk Premium = f (Business Risk, Financial Risk, Liquidity Risk, Exchange Rate Risk, Country Risk)

or

Risk Premium = f (Systematic Market Risk)

4.6 Summary of Required Rate of Return

The overall required rate of return on alternative investments is determined by three variables: (1) the economy's RRFR, which is influenced by the investment opportunities in the economy (that is, the long-run real growth rate); (2) variables that influence the NRFR, which include short-run ease or tightness in the capital market and the expected rate of inflation (notably, these variables, which determine the NRFR, are the same for all investments); and (3) the risk premium on the investment. In turn, this risk premium can be related to fundamental factors, including business risk, financial risk, liquidity risk, exchange rate risk, and country risk, or it can be a function of systematic market risk (beta).

---

[10] A brief review of some of the earlier studies is contained in Donald J. Thompson II, "Sources of Systematic Risk in Common Stocks," *Journal of Business* 49, no. 2 (April 1976): 173–188. There is a further discussion of specific variables in Chapter 10.

4.6.1 Measures and Sources of Risk

In this reading, we have examined both measures and sources of risk arising from an investment. The *measures* of risk for an investment are:

▷ Variance of rates of return

▷ Standard deviation of rates of return

▷ Coefficient of variation of rates of return (standard deviation/means)

▷ Covariance of returns with the market portfolio (beta)

The *sources* of risk are:

▷ Business risk

▷ Financial risk

▷ Liquidity risk

▷ Exchange rate risk

▷ Country risk

5   RELATIONSHIP BETWEEN RISK AND RETURN

Previously, we showed how to measure the risk and rates of return for alternative investments and we discussed what determines the rates of return that investors require. This section discusses the risk-return combinations that might be available at a point in time and illustrates the factors that cause *changes* in these combinations.

Exhibit 76-7 graphs the expected relationship between risk and return. It shows that investors increase their required rates of return as perceived risk (uncertainty) increases. The line that reflects the combination of risk and return available on alternative investments is referred to as the **security market line (SML).** The SML reflects the risk-return combinations available for all risky assets in the capital market at a given time. Investors would select investments that are consistent with their risk preferences; some would consider only low-risk investments, whereas others welcome high-risk investments.

Beginning with an initial SML, three changes can occur. First, individual investments can change positions on the SML because of changes in the perceived risk of the investments. Second, the slope of the SML can change because of a change in the attitudes of investors toward risk; that is, investors can change the returns they require per unit of risk. Third, the SML can experience a parallel shift due to a change in the RRFR or the expected rate of inflation—that is, a change in the NRFR. These three possibilities are discussed in this section.

5.1 Movements along the SML

Investors place alternative investments somewhere along the SML based on their perceptions of the risk of the investment. Obviously, if an investment's risk changes due to a change in one of its risk sources (business risk, and such), it will move along the SML. For example, if a firm increases its financial risk by selling a large bond issue that increases its financial leverage, investors will perceive its common stock as riskier and the stock will move up the SML to a higher risk position. Investors will then require a higher rate of return. As the common stock becomes riskier, it changes its position on the SML. Any change in an asset that affects its fundamental risk factors or its market risk (that is, its beta) will cause the asset to move *along* the SML as shown in Exhibit 76-8. Note that the SML does not change, only the position of assets on the SML.

EXHIBIT 76-7 Relationship Between Risk and Return

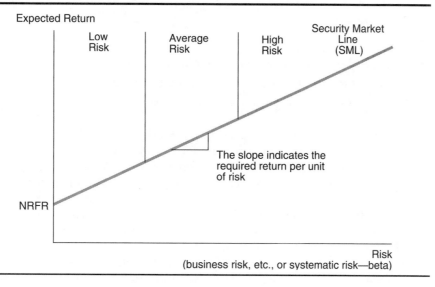

EXHIBIT 76-8 Changes in the Required Rate of Return Due to Movements Along the SML

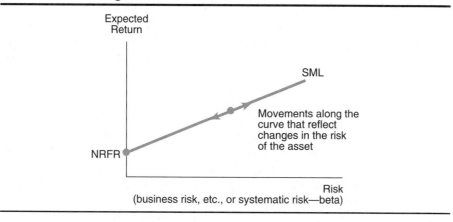

5.2 Changes in the Slope of the SML

The slope of the SML indicates the return per unit of risk required by all investors. Assuming a straight line, it is possible to select any point on the SML and compute a risk premium (RP) for an asset through the equation:

$$RP_i = E(R_i) - \text{NRFR} \qquad\qquad \textbf{(76-13)}$$

where:

RP_i = **risk premium for asset** i

$E(R_i)$ = **the expected return for asset** i

NRFR = **the nominal return on a risk-free asset**

If a point on the SML is identified as the portfolio that contains all the risky assets in the market (referred to as the *market portfolio*), it is possible to compute a market RP as follows:

$$RP_m = E(R_m) - \text{NRFR} \tag{76-14}$$

where:

> RP_m = **the risk premium on the market portfolio**
>
> $E(R_m)$ = **the expected return on the market portfolio**
>
> **NRFR** = **the nominal return on a risk-free asset**

This market RP is *not constant* because the slope of the SML changes over time. Although we do not understand completely what causes these changes in the slope, we do know that there are changes in the *yield* differences between assets with different levels of risk even though the inherent risk differences are relatively constant.

These differences in yields are referred to as **yield spreads,** and these yield spreads change over time. As an example, if the yield on a portfolio of Aaa-rated bonds is 7.50 percent and the yield on a portfolio of Baa-rated bonds is 9.00 percent, we would say that the yield spread is 1.50 percent. This 1.50 percent is referred to as a credit risk premium because the Baa-rated bond is considered to have higher credit risk—that is, greater probability of default. This Baa–Aaa yield spread is *not* constant over time. For an example of changes in a yield spread, note the substantial changes in the yield spreads on Aaa-rated bonds and Baa-rated bonds shown in Exhibit 76-9.

Although the underlying risk factors for the portfolio of bonds in the Aaa-rated bond index and the Baa-rated bond index would probably not change dramatically over time, it is clear from the time-series plot in exhibit 76-9 that the difference in yields (i.e., the yield spread) has experienced changes of more than 100 basis points (1 percent) in a short period of time (for example, see the yield spread increase in 1974 to 1975 and the dramatic yield spread decline in 1983 to 1984). Such a significant change in the yield spread during a period where there is no major change in the risk characteristics of Baa bonds relative to Aaa bonds would imply a change in the market RP. Specifically, although the risk levels of the bonds remain relatively constant, investors have changed the yield spreads they demand to accept this relatively constant difference in risk.

This change in the RP implies a change in the slope of the SML. Such a change is shown in Exhibit 76-10. The exhibit assumes an increase in the market risk premium, which means an increase in the slope of the market line. Such a change in the slope of the SML (the risk premium) will affect the required rate of return for all risky assets. Irrespective of where an investment is on the original SML, its required rate of return will increase, although its individual risk characteristics remain unchanged.

5.3 Changes in Capital Market Conditions or Expected Inflation

The graph in Exhibit 76-11 shows what happens to the SML when there are changes in one of the following factors: (1) expected real growth in the economy, (2) capital market conditions, or (3) the expected rate of inflation. For example, an increase in expected real growth, temporary tightness in the capital market, or an increase in the expected rate of inflation will cause the SML to experience a parallel shift upward. The parallel shift occurs because changes in expected real growth or in capital market conditions or a change in the expected rate of inflation affect all investments, no matter what their levels of risk are.

EXHIBIT 76-9 Plot of Moody's Corporate Bond Yield Spreads (Baa–Aaa): Monthly 1966–2000

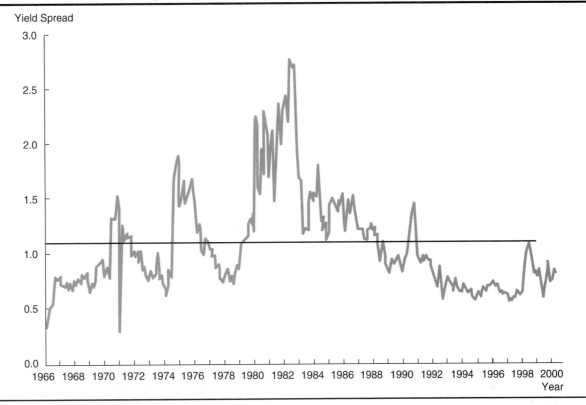

EXHIBIT 76-10 Change in Market Risk Premium

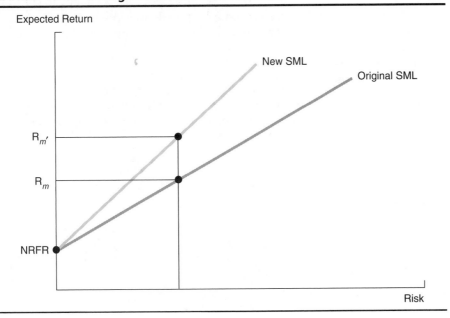

EXHIBIT 76-11 Capital Market Conditions, Expected Inflation, and the Security Market Line

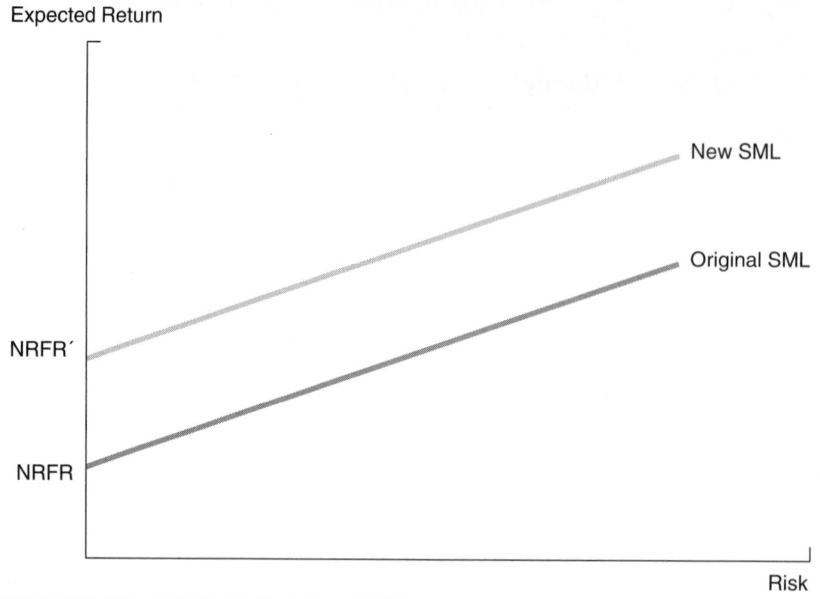

5.4 Summary of Changes in the Required Rate of Return

The relationship between risk and the required rate of return for an investment can change in three ways:

1. A movement *along* the SML demonstrates a change in the risk characteristics of a specific investment, such as a change in its business risk, its financial risk, or its systematic risk (its beta). This change affects only the individual investment.

2. A change in the *slope* of the SML occurs in response to a change in the attitudes of investors toward risk. Such a change demonstrates that investors want either higher or lower rates of return for the same risk. This is also described as a change in the market risk premium ($R_m - $ NRFR). A change in the market risk premium will affect all risky investments.

3. A *shift* in the SML reflects a change in expected real growth, a change in market conditions (such as ease or tightness of money), or a change in the expected rate of inflation. Again, such a change will affect all investments.

THE INTERNET   **6**

Investments Online

There are a great many Internet sites that are set up to assist the beginning or novice investor.

Because they cover the basics, have helpful links to other Internet sites, and sometimes allow users to calculate items of interest (rates of return, the size of an investment necessary to meet a certain goal, and so on), these sites are useful for the experienced investor, too.

▶ **http://www.finpipe.com** The Financial Pipeline is an excellent site for those just starting to learn about investments or who need a quick refresher. A site focused on financial education, it contains information and links on a variety of investment topics such as bonds, stocks, strategy, retirement, and consumer finance.

▶ **http://www.investorguide.com** This is another site offering a plethora of information that is useful to both the novice and seasoned investor. It contains links to pages with market summaries, news research, and much more. It offers users a glossary of investment terms. Basic investment education issues are taught in the "University " section. There are links to personal financial help pages, including sites dealing with buying a home or car, retirement, loans, and insurance. It offers links to a number of calculator functions to help users make financial decisions.

▶ **http://finance.yahoo.com** Yahoo's finance portal is an excellent site for the beginning investor because of the information and data it contains. The site covers a number of investing and personal finance topics and gives visitors access to much financial data and charts.

Here are some other sites that may be of interest:

▶ **http://www.finweb.com** Focuses on electronic publishing, databases, working papers, links to other Web sites.

▶ **http://fisher.osu.edu/fin** Contains links to numerous finance sites.

▶ **http://www.aaii.com** The home page for the American Association of Individual Investors, a group dealing with investor education.

Many representatives of the financial press have Internet sites:

▶ **http://www.wsj.com** *The Wall Street Journal*
▶ **http://www.ft.com** *Financial Times*
▶ **http://www.economist.com** *The Economist* magazine
▶ **http://www.fortune.com** *Fortune* magazine
▶ **http://www.money.cnn.com** *Money* magazine
▶ **http://www.forbes.com** *Forbes* magazine
▶ **http://www.worth.com** *Worth* magazine
▶ **http://www.smartmoney.com** *SmartMoney* magazine
▶ **http://www.barrons.com** *Barron's* newspaper

7

SUMMARY

The purpose of this reading is to provide background that can be used in subsequent readings. To achieve that goal, we covered several topics:

- We discussed why individuals save part of their income and why they decide to invest their savings. We defined *investment* as the current commitment of these savings for a period of time to derive a rate of return that compensates for the time involved, the expected rate of inflation, and the uncertainty.

- We examined ways to quantify historical return and risk to help analyze alternative investment opportunities. We considered two measures of mean return (arithmetic and geometric) and applied these to a historical series for an individual investment and to a portfolio of investments during a period of time.

- We considered the concept of uncertainty and alternative measures of risk (the variance, standard deviation, and a relative measure of risk—the coefficient of variation).

- Before discussing the determinants of the required rate of return for an investment, we noted that the estimation of the required rate of return is complicated because the rates on individual investments change over time, because there is a wide range of rates of return available on alternative investments, and because the differences between required returns on alternative investments (for example, the yield spreads) likewise change over time.

- We examined the specific factors that determine the required rate of return: (1) the real risk-free rate, which is based on the real rate of growth in the economy, (2) the nominal risk-free rate, which is influenced by capital market conditions and the expected rate of inflation, and (3) a risk premium, which is a function of fundamental factors, such as business risk, or the systematic risk of the asset relative to the market portfolio (that is, its beta).

- We discussed the risk-return combinations available on alternative investments at a point in time (illustrated by the SML) and the three factors that can cause changes in this relationship. First, a change in the inherent risk of an investment (that is, its fundamental risk or market risk) will cause a movement along the SML. Second, a change in investors' attitudes toward risk will cause a change in the required return per unit of risk—that is, a change in the market risk premium. Such a change will cause a change in the slope of the SML. Finally, a change in expected real growth, in capital market conditions, or in the expected rate of inflation will cause a parallel shift of the SML.

Based on this understanding of the investment environment, you are prepared to consider the asset allocation decision. This is the subject of Reading 77.

REFERENCES

▶ Fama, Eugene F., and Merton H. Miller. *The Theory of Finance.* New York: Holt, Rinehart and Winston, 1972.

▶ Fisher, Irving. *The Theory of Interest.* New York: Macmillan, 1930; reprinted by Augustus M. Kelley, 1961.

THE ASSET ALLOCATION DECISION*

LEARNING OUTCOMES

The candidate should be able to:

a. describe the steps in the portfolio management process and explain the reasons for a policy statement;

b. explain why investment objectives should be expressed in terms of both risk and return and list the factors that may affect an investor's risk tolerance;

c. describe the return objectives of capital preservation, capital appreciation, current income, and total return and describe the investment constraints of liquidity, time horizon, tax concerns, legal and regulatory factors, and unique needs and preferences;

d. describe the importance of asset allocation, in terms of the percentage of a portfolio's return that can be explained by the target asset allocation and list reasons for the differences in the average asset allocation among citizens of different countries.

Note:
Although this reading addresses the taxation of individual investors from the viewpoint of a U.S. investor, candidates are not expected to know the U.S. tax code. This reading is intended to illustrate the importance of taxation to investors, particularly individual investors.

INTRODUCTION   1

The previous reading informed us that *risk drives return*. Therefore, the practice of investing funds and managing portfolios should focus primarily on managing risk rather than on managing returns.

This reading examines some of the practical implications of risk management in the context of asset allocation. **Asset allocation** is the process of deciding how to distribute an investor's wealth among different countries and asset classes for investment purposes. An **asset class** is comprised of securities that have similar

---

* The authors acknowledge the collaboration of Professor Edgar Norton of Illinois State University on this reading.

Investment Analysis Portfolio Management, by Frank K. Reilly and Keith C. Brown, Copyright © 2003. Reprinted with permission of South-Western, a division of Thomson Learning.

characteristics, attributes, and risk/return relationships. A broad asset class, such as "bonds," can be divided into smaller asset classes, such as Treasury bonds, corporate bonds, and high-yield bonds. We will see that, in the long run, the highest compounded returns will most likely accrue to those investors with larger exposures to risky assets. We will also see that although there are no shortcuts or guarantees to investment success, maintaining a reasonable and disciplined approach to investing will increase the likelihood of investment success over time.

The asset allocation decision is not an isolated choice; rather, it is a component of a portfolio management process. In this reading, we present an overview of the four-step portfolio management process. As we will see, the first step in the process is to develop an investment policy statement, or plan, that will guide all future decisions. Much of an asset allocation strategy depends on the investor's policy statement, which includes the investor's goals or objectives, constraints, and investment guidelines.

What we mean by an "investor" can range from an individual to trustees overseeing a corporation's multibillion-dollar pension fund, a university endowment, or invested premiums for an insurance company. Regardless of who the investor is or how simple or complex the investment needs, he or she should develop a policy statement before making long-term investment decisions. Although most of our examples will be in the context of an individual investor, the concepts we introduce here—investment objectives, constraints, benchmarks, and so on—apply to any investor, individual or institutional. We'll review historical data to show the importance of the asset allocation decision and discuss the need for investor education, an important issue for individuals or companies who offer retirement or savings plans to their employees. The reading concludes by examining asset allocation strategies across national borders to show the effect of market environment and culture on investing patterns; what is appropriate for a U.S.-based investor is not necessarily appropriate for a non-U.S.-based investor.

2 INDIVIDUAL INVESTOR LIFE CYCLE

Financial plans and investment needs are as different as each individual. Investment needs change over a person's life cycle. How individuals structure their financial plan should be related to their age, financial status, future plans, risk aversion characteristics, and needs.

2.1 The Preliminaries

Before embarking on an investment program, we need to make sure other needs are satisfied. No serious investment plan should be started until a potential investor has adequate income to cover living expenses and has a safety net should the unexpected occur.

2.1.1 Insurance

Life insurance should be a component of any financial plan. Life insurance protects loved ones against financial hardship should death occur before our financial goals are met. The death benefit paid by the insurance company can help pay medical bills and funeral expenses and provide cash that family members can use to maintain their lifestyle, retire debt, or invest for future needs (for example, children's education, spouse retirement). Therefore, one of the first steps in developing a financial plan is to purchase adequate life insurance coverage.

Insurance can also serve more immediate purposes, including being a means to meet long-term goals, such as retirement planning. On reaching retirement age, you can receive the cash or surrender value of your life insurance policy and use the proceeds to supplement your retirement lifestyle or for estate planning purposes.

You can choose among several basic life insurance contracts. *Term life insurance* provides only a death benefit; the premium to purchase the insurance changes every renewal period. Term insurance is the least expensive life insurance to purchase, although the premium will rise as you age to reflect the increased probability of death. *Universal* and *variable life policies*, although technically different from each other, are similar in that they each provide both a death benefit and a savings plan to the insured. The premium paid on such policies exceeds the cost to the insurance company of providing the death benefit alone; the excess premium is invested in a number of investment vehicles chosen by the insured. The policy's cash value grows over time, based on the size of the excess premium and on the performance of the underlying investment funds. Insurance companies may restrict the ability to withdraw funds from these policies before the policyholder reaches a certain age.

Insurance coverage also provides protection against other uncertainties. *Health* insurance helps to pay medical bills. *Disability* insurance provides continuing income should you become unable to work. *Automobile and home* (or rental) insurances provide protection against accidents and damage to cars or residences.

Although nobody ever expects to use his or her insurance coverage, a first step in a sound financial plan is to have adequate coverage "just in case." Lack of insurance coverage can ruin the best-planned investment program.

2.1.2 Cash Reserve

Emergencies, job layoffs, and unforeseen expenses happen, and good investment opportunities emerge. It is important to have a cash reserve to help meet these occasions. In addition to providing a safety cushion, a cash reserve reduces the likelihood of being forced to sell investments at inopportune times to cover unexpected expenses. Most experts recommend a cash reserve equal to about six months' living expenses. Calling it a "cash" reserve does not mean the funds should be in cash; rather, the funds should be in investments you can easily convert to cash with little chance of a loss in value. Money market mutual funds and bank accounts are appropriate vehicles for the cash reserve.

Similar to the financial plan, an investor's insurance and cash reserve needs will change over his or her life. We've already mentioned how a retired person may "cash out" a life insurance policy to supplement income. The need for disability insurance declines when a person retires. In contrast, other insurance, such as supplemental Medicare coverage or long-term care insurance, may become more important.

EXHIBIT 77-1 Rise and Fall of Personal Net Worth Over a Lifetime

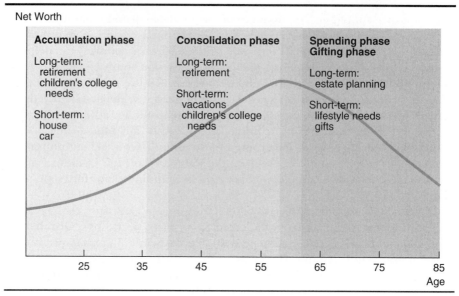

2.2 Life Cycle Net Worth and Investment Strategies

Assuming the basic insurance and cash reserve needs are met, individuals can start a serious investment program with their savings. Because of changes in their net worth and risk tolerance, individuals' investment strategies will change over their lifetime. In the following sections, we review various phases in the investment life cycle. Although each individual's needs and preferences are different, some general traits affect most investors over the life cycle. The four life cycle phases are shown in Exhibit 77-1 (the third and fourth phases are shown as concurrent) and described here.

2.2.1 Accumulation Phase

Individuals in the early-to-middle years of their working careers are in the **accumulation phase.** As the name implies, these individuals are attempting to accumulate assets to satisfy fairly immediate needs (for example, a down payment for a house) or longer-term goals (children's college education, retirement). Typically, their net worth is small, and debt from car loans or their own past college loans may be heavy. As a result of their typically long investment time horizon and their future earning ability, individuals in the accumulation phase are willing to make relatively high-risk investments in the hopes of making above-average nominal returns over time.

2.2.2 Consolidation Phase

Individuals in the **consolidation phase** are typically past the midpoint of their careers, have paid off much or all of their outstanding debts, and perhaps have paid, or have the assets to pay, their children's college bills. Earnings exceed expenses, so the excess can be invested to provide for future retirement or estate planning needs. The typical investment horizon for this phase is still long (20 to 30 years), so moderately high risk investments are attractive. At the same time, because individuals in this phase are concerned about capital preservation, they do not want to take very large risks that may put their current nest egg in jeopardy.

2.2.3 Spending Phase

The **spending phase** typically begins when individuals retire. Living expenses are covered by social security income and income from prior investments, including employer pension plans. Because their earning years have concluded (although some retirees take part-time positions or do consulting work), they seek greater protection of their capital. At the same time, they must balance their desire to preserve the nominal value of their savings with the need to protect themselves against a decline in the *real* value of their savings due to inflation. The average 65-year-old person in the United States has a life expectancy of about 20 years. Thus, although their overall portfolio may be less risky than in the consolidation phase, they still need some risky growth investments, such as common stocks, for inflation (purchasing power) protection.

2.2.4 Gifting Phase

The **gifting phase** is similar to, and may be concurrent with, the spending phase. In this stage, individuals believe they have sufficient income and assets to cover their expenses while maintaining a reserve for uncertainties. Excess assets can be used to provide financial assistance to relatives or friends, to establish charitable trusts, or to fund trusts as an estate planning tool to minimize estate taxes.

2.3 Life Cycle Investment Goals

During the investment life cycle, individuals have a variety of financial goals. **Near-term, high-priority goals** are shorter-term financial objectives that individuals set to fund purchases that are personally important to them, such as accumulating funds to make a house down payment, buy a new car, or take a trip. Parents with teenage children may have a near-term, high priority goal to accumulate funds to help pay college expenses. Because of the emotional importance of these goals and their short time horizon, high-risk investments are not usually considered suitable for achieving them.

    Long-term, high-priority goals typically include some form of financial independence, such as the ability to retire at a certain age. Because of their long-term nature, higher-risk investments can be used to help meet these objectives.

    Lower-priority goals are just that—it might be nice to meet these objectives, but it is not critical. Examples include the ability to purchase a new car every few years, redecorate the home with expensive furnishings, or take a long, luxurious vacation.

    A well-developed policy statement considers these diverse goals over an investor's lifetime. The following sections detail the process for constructing an investment policy, creating a portfolio that is consistent with the policy and the environment, managing the portfolio, and monitoring its performance relative to its goals and objectives over time.

THE PORTFOLIO MANAGEMENT PROCESS   ◣ 3 ◢

The process of managing an investment portfolio never stops. Once the funds are initially invested according to the plan, the real work begins in monitoring and updating the status of the portfolio and the investor's needs.

    The first step in the portfolio management process, as seen in Exhibit 77-2, is for the investor, either alone or with the assistance of an investment advisor, to construct a **policy statement.** The policy statement is a road map; in it, investors specify the types of risks they are willing to take and their investment goals and constraints. All investment decisions are based on the policy statement to ensure they are appropriate for the investor. We examine the process of constructing a policy statement later in this reading. Because investor needs change over time, the policy statement must be periodically reviewed and updated.

EXHIBIT 77-2 The Portfolio Management Process

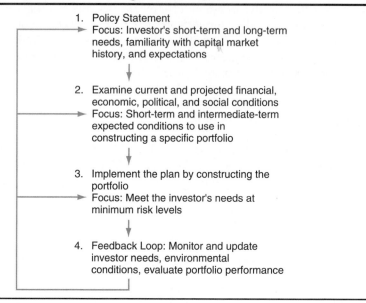

1. Policy Statement
   Focus: Investor's short-term and long-term needs, familiarity with capital market history, and expectations

2. Examine current and projected financial, economic, political, and social conditions
   Focus: Short-term and intermediate-term expected conditions to use in constructing a specific portfolio

3. Implement the plan by constructing the portfolio
   Focus: Meet the investor's needs at minimum risk levels

4. Feedback Loop: Monitor and update investor needs, environmental conditions, evaluate portfolio performance

The process of investing seeks to peer into the future and determine strategies that offer the best possibility of meeting the policy statement guidelines. In the second step of the portfolio management process, the manager should study current financial and economic conditions and forecast future trends. The investor's needs, as reflected in the policy statement, and financial market expectations will jointly determine **investment strategy.** Economies are dynamic; they are affected by numerous industry struggles, politics, and changing demographics and social attitudes. Thus, the portfolio will require constant monitoring and updating to reflect changes in financial market expectations. We examine the process of evaluating and forecasting economic trends in Chapter 12.

The third step of the portfolio management process is to **construct the portfolio.** With the investor's policy statement and financial market forecasts as input, the advisors implement the investment strategy and determine how to allocate available funds across different countries, asset classes, and securities. This involves constructing a portfolio that will minimize the investor's risks while meeting the needs specified in the policy statement. Financial theory frequently assists portfolio construction, as is discussed in Part 2. Some of the practical aspects of selecting investments for inclusion in a portfolio are discussed in Part 4 and Part 5.

The fourth step in the portfolio management process is the **continual monitoring** of the investor's needs and capital market conditions and, when necessary, updating the policy statement. Based upon all of this, the investment strategy is modified accordingly. A component of the monitoring process is to evaluate a portfolio's performance and compare the relative results to the expectations and the requirements listed in the policy statement. The evaluation of portfolio performance is discussed in Chapter 26.

THE NEED FOR A POLICY STATEMENT

As noted in the previous section, a policy statement is a road map that guides the investment process. Constructing a policy statement is an invaluable planning tool that will help the investor understand his or her needs better as well as assist an advisor or portfolio manager in managing a client's funds. While it does not guarantee investment success, a policy statement will provide discipline for the investment process and reduce the possibility of making hasty, inappropriate decisions. There are two important reasons for constructing a policy statement: First, it helps the investor decide on realistic investment goals after learning about the financial markets and the risks of investing. Second, it creates a standard by which to judge the performance of the portfolio manager.

4.1 Understand and Articulate Realistic Investor Goals

When asked about their investment goal, people often say, "to make a lot of money," or some similar response. Such a goal has two drawbacks: First, it may not be appropriate for the investor, and second, it is too open-ended to provide guidance for specific investments and time frames. Such an objective is well suited for someone going to the racetrack or buying lottery tickets, but it is inappropriate for someone investing funds in financial and real assets for the long term.

An important purpose of writing a policy statement is to help investors understand their own needs, objectives, and investment constraints. As part of this, investors need to learn about financial markets and the risks of investing. This background will help prevent them from making inappropriate investment decisions in the future and will increase the possibility that they will satisfy their specific, measurable financial goals.

Thus, the policy statement helps the investor to specify realistic goals and become more informed about the risks and costs of investing. Market values of assets, whether they be stocks, bonds, or real estate, can fluctuate dramatically. For example, during the October 1987 crash, the Dow Jones Industrial Average (DJIA) fell more than 20 percent in one day; in October 1997, the Dow fell "only" 7 percent. A review of market history shows that it is not unusual for asset prices to decline by 10 percent to 20 percent over several months—for example, the months following the market peak in March 2000, and the major decline when the market reopened after September 11, 2001. Investors will typically focus on a single statistic, such as an 11 percent average annual rate of return on stocks, and expect the market to rise 11 percent every year. Such thinking ignores the risk of stock investing. Part of the process of developing a policy statement is for the investor to become familiar with the risks of investing, because we know that a strong positive relationship exists between risk and return.

▷ One expert in the field recommends that investors should think about the following set of questions and explain their answers as part of the process of constructing a policy statement.

1. What are the real risks of an adverse financial outcome, especially in the short run?

2. What probable emotional reactions will I have to an adverse financial outcome?

3. How knowledgeable am I about investments and markets?

4. What other capital or income sources do I have? How important is this particular portfolio to my overall financial position?

5. What, if any, legal restrictions may affect my investment needs?

6. What, if any, unanticipated consequences of interim fluctuations in portfolio value might affect my investment policy?

Adapted from Charles D. Ellis, *Investment Policy: How to Win the Loser's Game* (Homewood, Ill.: Dow Jones–Irwin, 1985), 25–26. Reproduced with permission of The McGraw-Hill Companies.

In summary, constructing a policy statement is mainly the investor's responsibility. It is a process whereby investors articulate their realistic needs and goals and become familiar with financial markets and investing risks. Without this information, investors cannot adequately communicate their needs to the portfolio manager. Without this input from investors, the portfolio manager cannot construct a portfolio that will satisfy clients' needs; the result of bypassing this step will most likely be future aggravation, dissatisfaction, and disappointment.

4.2 Standards for Evaluating Portfolio Performance

The policy statement also assists in judging the performance of the portfolio manager. Performance cannot be judged without an objective standard; the policy statement provides that objective standard. The portfolio's performance should be compared to guidelines specified in the policy statement, not on the portfolio's overall return. For example, if an investor has a low tolerance for risky investments, the portfolio manager should not be fired simply because the portfolio does not perform as well as the risky S&P 500 stock index. Because risk drives returns, the investor's lower-risk investments, as specified in the investor's policy statement, will probably earn lower returns than if all the investor's funds were placed in the stock market.

The policy statement will typically include a **benchmark portfolio,** or comparison standard. The risk of the benchmark, and the assets included in the benchmark, should agree with the client's risk preferences and investment needs. Notably, both the client and the portfolio manager must agree that the benchmark portfolio reflects the risk preferences and appropriate return requirements of the client. In turn, the investment performance of the portfolio manager should be compared to this benchmark portfolio. For example, an investor who specifies low-risk investments in the policy statement should compare the portfolio manager's performance against a low-risk benchmark portfolio. Likewise, an investor seeking high-risk, high-return investments should compare the portfolio's performance against a high-risk benchmark portfolio.

Because it sets an objective performance standard, the policy statement acts as a starting point for periodic portfolio review and client communication with managers. Questions concerning portfolio performance or the manager's faithfulness to the policy can be addressed in the context of the written policy guidelines. Managers should mainly be judged by whether they consistently followed the client's policy guidelines. The portfolio manager who makes unilateral deviations from policy is not working in the best interests of the client. Therefore, even deviations that result in higher portfolio returns can and should be grounds for the manager's dismissal.

Thus, we see the importance of the client constructing the policy statement: The client must first understand his or her own needs before communicating them to the portfolio manager. In turn, the portfolio manager must implement the client's desires by following the investment guidelines. As long as policy is followed, shortfalls in performance should not be a major concern. Remember that the policy statement is designed to impose an investment discipline on the client and portfolio manager. The less knowledgeable they are, the more likely clients are to inappropriately judge the performance of the portfolio manager.

4.3 Other Benefits

A sound policy statement helps to protect the client against a portfolio manager's inappropriate investments or unethical behavior. Without clear, written guidance, some managers may consider investing in high-risk investments, hoping to earn a quick return. Such actions are probably counter to the investor's specified needs and risk preferences. Though legal recourse is a possibility against such action, writing a clear and unambiguous policy statement should reduce the possibility of such inappropriate manager behavior.

Just because one specific manager currently manages your account does not mean that person will always manage your funds. As with other positions, your portfolio manager may be promoted or dismissed or take a better job. Therefore, after a while, your funds may come under the management of an individual you do not know and who does not know you. To prevent costly delays during this transition, you can ensure that the new manager "hits the ground running" with a clearly written policy statement. A policy statement should prevent delays in monitoring and rebalancing your portfolio and will help create a seamless transition from one money manager to another.

To sum up, a clearly written policy statement helps avoid future potential problems. When the client clearly specifies his or her needs and desires, the portfolio manager can more effectively construct an appropriate portfolio. The policy statement provides an objective measure for evaluating portfolio performance, helps guard against ethical lapses by the portfolio manager, and aids in the transition between money managers. Therefore, the first step before beginning any investment program, whether it is for an individual or a multibillion-dollar pension fund, is to construct a policy statement.

▷ An appropriate policy statement should satisfactorily answer the following questions.

1. Is the policy carefully designed to meet the specific needs and objectives of this particular investor? (Cookie-cutter or one-size-fits-all policy statements are generally inappropriate.)

2. Is the policy written so clearly and explicitly that a competent stranger could use it to manage the portfolio in conformance with the client's needs? In case of a manager transition, could the new manager use this policy statement to handle your portfolio in accordance with your needs?

3. Would the client have been able to remain committed to the policies during the capital market experiences of the past 60 to 70 years? That is, does the client fully understand investment risks and the need for a disciplined approach to the investment process?

4. Would the portfolio manager have been able to maintain the policies specified over the same period? (Discipline is a two-way street; we do not want the portfolio manager to change strategies because of a disappointing market.)

5. Would the policy, if implemented, have achieved the client's objectives? (Bottom line: Would the policy have worked to meet the client's needs?)

Adapted from Charles D. Ellis, *Investment Policy: How to Win the Loser's Game* (Homewood, Ill.: Dow Jones–Irwin, 1985), 62. Reproduced with permission of The McGraw-Hill Companies.

5 INPUT TO THE POLICY STATEMENT

Before an investor and advisor can construct a policy statement, they need to have an open and frank exchange of information, ideas, fears, and goals. To build a framework for this information-gathering process, the client and advisor need to discuss the client's investment objectives and constraints. To illustrate this framework, we discuss the investment objectives and constraints that may confront "typical" 25-year-old and 65-year-old investors.

5.1 Investment Objectives

The investor's **objectives** are his or her investment goals expressed in terms of both risk and returns. The relationship between risk and returns requires that goals not be expressed only in terms of returns. Expressing goals only in terms of returns can lead to inappropriate investment practices by the portfolio

EXHIBIT 77-3 Risk Categories and Suggested Asset Allocations for Merrill Lynch Clients

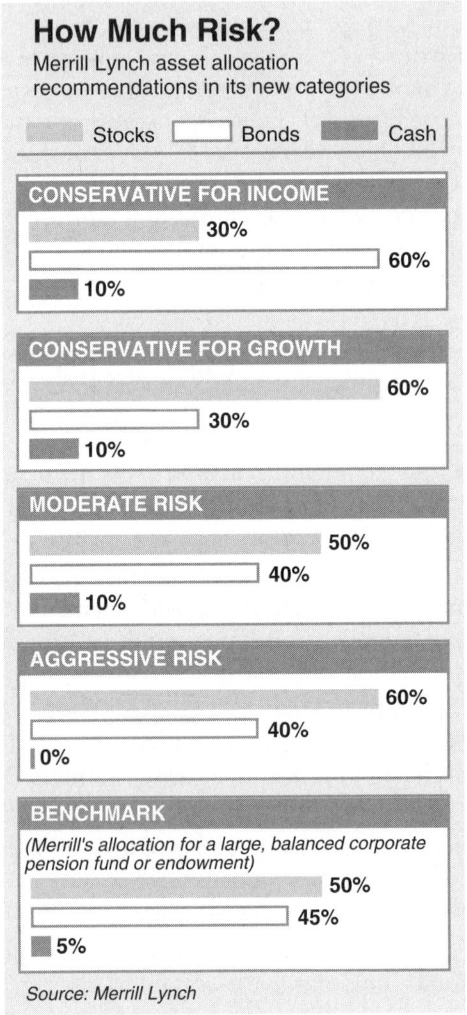

How Much Risk?
Merrill Lynch asset allocation recommendations in its new categories

Stocks   Bonds   Cash

CONSERVATIVE FOR INCOME
30%
60%
10%

CONSERVATIVE FOR GROWTH
60%
30%
10%

MODERATE RISK
50%
40%
10%

AGGRESSIVE RISK
60%
40%
0%

BENCHMARK
(Merrill's allocation for a large, balanced corporate pension fund or endowment)
50%
45%
5%

Source: Merrill Lynch

Source: William Power, "Merrill Lynch to Ask Investors to Pick a Risk Category," *The Wall Street Journal*, 2 July 1990, C1. Reprinted with permission of *The Wall Street Journal*, Dow Jones and Co., Inc. All rights reserved.

manager, such as the use of high-risk investment strategies or account "churning," which involves moving quickly in and out of investments in an attempt to buy low and sell high.

For example, a person may have a stated return goal such as "double my investment in five years." Before such a statement becomes part of the policy statement, the client must become fully informed of investment risks associated with such a goal, including the possibility of loss. *A careful analysis of the client's risk tolerance should precede any discussion of return objectives.* It makes little sense for a person who is risk averse to invest funds in high-risk assets. Investment firms survey clients to gauge their risk tolerance. For example, Merrill Lynch has asked its clients to place themselves in one of the four categories in Exhibit 77-3. Sometimes investment magazines or books contain tests that individuals can take to help them evaluate their risk tolerance (see Exhibit 77-4).

Risk tolerance is more than a function of an individual's psychological makeup; it is affected by other factors, including a person's current insurance coverage and cash reserves. Risk tolerance is also affected by an individual's family situation (for example, marital status and the number and ages of children) and by his or her age. We know that older persons generally have shorter investment time frames within which to make up any losses; they also have years of experience, including living through various market gyrations and "corrections" (a euphemism for downtrends or crashes) that younger people have not experienced or whose effect they do not fully appreciate. Risk tolerance is also influenced by one's current net worth and income expectations. All else being equal, individuals with higher incomes have a greater propensity to undertake risk because their incomes can help cover any shortfall. Likewise, individuals with larger net worths can afford to place some assets in risky investments while the remaining assets provide a cushion against losses.

EXHIBIT 77-4 How Much Risk Is Right for You?

You've heard the expression "no pain, no gain"? In the investment world, the comparable phrase would be "no risk, no reward."

How you feel about risking your money will drive many of your investment decisions. The risk-comfort scale extends from very conservative (you don't want to risk losing a penny regardless of how little your money earns) to very aggressive (you're willing to risk much of your money for the possibility that it will grow tremendously). As you might guess, most investors' tolerance for risk falls somewhere in between.

If you're unsure of what your level of risk tolerance is, this quiz should help.

1. You win $300 in an office football pool. You: (a) spend it on groceries, (b) purchase lottery tickets, (c) put it in a money market account, (d) buy some stock.

2. Two weeks after buying 100 shares of a $20 stock, the price jumps to over $30. You decide to: (a) buy more stock; it's obviously a winner, (b) sell it and take your profits, (c) sell half to recoup some costs and hold the rest, (d) sit tight and wait for it to advance even more.

3. On days when the stock market jumps way up, you: (a) wish you had invested more, (b) call your financial advisor and ask for recommendations, (c) feel glad you're not in the market because it fluctuates too much, (d) pay little attention.

4. You're planning a vacation trip and can either lock in a fixed room-and-meals rate of $150 per day or book standby and pay anywhere from $100 to $300 per day. You: (a) take the fixed-rate deal, (b) talk to people who have been there about the availability of last-minute accommodations, (c) book standby and also arrange vacation insurance because you're leery of the tour operator, (d) take your chances with standby.

EXHIBIT 77-4 How Much Risk Is Right for You? (continued)

5. The owner of your apartment building is converting the units to condominiums. You can buy your unit for $75,000 or an option on a unit for $15,000. (Units have recently sold for close to $100,000, and prices seem to be going up.) For financing, you'll have to borrow the down payment and pay mortgage and condo fees higher than your present rent. You: (a) buy your unit, (b) buy your unit and look for another to buy, (c) sell the option and arrange to rent the unit yourself, (d) sell the option and move out because you think the conversion will attract couples with small children.

6. You have been working three years for a rapidly growing company. As an executive, you are offered the option of buying up to 2% of company stock: 2,000 shares at $10 a share. Although the company is privately owned (its stock does not trade on the open market), its majority owner has made handsome profits selling three other businesses and intends to sell this one eventually. You: (a) purchase all the shares you can and tell the owner you would invest more if allowed, (b) purchase all the shares, (c) purchase half the shares, (d) purchase a small amount of shares.

7. You go to a casino for the first time. You choose to play: (a) quarter slot machines, (b) $5 minimum-bet roulette, (c) dollar slot machine, (d) $25 minimum-bet blackjack.

8. You want to take someone out for a special dinner in a city that's new to you. How do you pick a place? (a) read restaurant reviews in the local newspaper, (b) ask coworkers if they know of a suitable place, (c) call the only other person you know in this city, who eats out a lot but only recently moved there, (d) visit the city sometime before your dinner to check out the restaurants yourself.

9. The expression that best describes your lifestyle is: (a) no guts, no glory, (b) just do it!, (c) look before you leap, (d) all good things come to those who wait.

10. Your attitude toward money is best described as: (a) a dollar saved is a dollar earned, (b) you've got to spend money to make money, (c) cash and carry only, (d) whenever possible, use other people's money.

SCORING SYSTEM: Score your answers this way: (1) a-1, b-4, c-2, d-3 (2) a-4, b-1, c-3, d-2 (3) a-3, b-4, c-2, d-1 (4) a-2, b-3 c-1, d-4 (5) a-3, b-4, c-2, d-1 (6) a-4, b-3, c-2, d-1 (7) a-1, b-3, c-2, d-4 (8) a-2, b-3, c-4, d-1 (9), a-4, b-3, c-2, d-1 (10) a-2, b-3, c-1, d-4.

What your total score indicates.

▷ 10–17: You're not willing to take chances with your money, even though it means you can't make big gains.

▷ 18–25: You're semi-conservative, willing to take a small chance with enough information.

▷ 24–32: You're semi-aggressive, willing to take chances if you think the odds of earning more are in your favor.

▷ 33–40: You're aggressive, looking for every opportunity to make your money grow, even though in some cases the odds may be quite long. You view money as a tool to make more money.

A person's return objective may be stated in terms of an absolute or a relative percentage return, but it may also be stated in terms of a general goal, such as capital preservation, current income, capital appreciation, or total return.

Capital preservation means that investors want to minimize their risk of loss, usually in real terms: They seek to maintain the purchasing power of their investment. In other words, the return needs to be no less than the rate of inflation. Generally, this is a strategy for strongly risk-averse investors or for funds needed in the short-run, such as for next year's tuition payment or a down payment on a house.

Capital appreciation is an appropriate objective when the investors want the portfolio to grow in real terms over time to meet some future need. Under this strategy, growth mainly occurs through capital gains. This is an aggressive strategy for investors willing to take on risk to meet their objective. Generally, longer-term investors seeking to build a retirement or college education fund may have this goal.

When **current income** is the return objective, the investors want the portfolio to concentrate on generating income rather than capital gains. This strategy sometimes suits investors who want to supplement their earnings with income generated by their portfolio to meet their living expenses. Retirees may favor this objective for part of their portfolio to help generate spendable funds.

The objective for the **total return** strategy is similar to that of capital appreciation; namely, the investors want the portfolio to grow over time to meet a future need. Whereas the capital appreciation strategy seeks to do this primarily through capital gains, the total return strategy seeks to increase portfolio value by both capital gains and reinvesting current income. Because the total return strategy has both income and capital gains components, its risk exposure lies between that of the current income and capital appreciation strategies.

5.1.1 Investment Objective: 25-Year-Old

What is an appropriate investment objective for our typical 25-year-old investor? Assume he holds a steady job, is a valued employee, has adequate insurance coverage, and has enough money in the bank to provide a cash reserve. Let's also assume that his current long-term, high-priority investment goal is to build a retirement fund. Depending on his risk preferences, he can select a strategy carrying moderate to high amounts of risk because the income stream from his job will probably grow over time. Further, given his young age and income growth potential, a low-risk strategy, such as capital preservation or current income, is inappropriate for his retirement fund goal; a total return or capital appreciation objective would be most appropriate. Here's a possible objective statement:

> Invest funds in a variety of moderate- to higher-risk investments. The average risk of the equity portfolio should exceed that of a broad stock market index, such as the NYSE stock index. Foreign and domestic equity exposure should range from 80 percent to 95 percent of the total portfolio. Remaining funds should be invested in short- and intermediate-term notes and bonds.

5.1.2 Investment Objective: 65-Year-Old

Assume our typical 65-year-old investor likewise has adequate insurance coverage and a cash reserve. Let's also assume she is retiring this year. This individual will want less risk exposure than the 25-year-old investor, because her earning power from employment will soon be ending; she will not be able to recover any investment losses by saving more out of her paycheck. Depending on her income from social security and a pension plan, she may need some current income from her retirement portfolio to meet living expenses. Given that she can be expected to live an average of another 20 years, she will need protection against inflation. A risk-averse investor will choose a combination of current income and capital preservation strategy; a more risk-tolerant investor will choose a combination of current income and total return in an attempt to have principal growth outpace inflation. Here's an example of such an objective statement:

> Invest in stock and bond investments to meet income needs (from bond income and stock dividends) and to provide for real growth (from equities). Fixed-income securities should comprise 55–65 percent of the total portfolio; of this, 5–15 percent should be invested in short-term securities for extra liquidity and safety. The remaining 35–45 percent of the portfolio should be invested in high-quality stocks whose risk is similar to the S&P 500 index.

More detailed analyses for our 25-year-old and our 65-year-old would make more specific assumptions about the risk tolerance of each, as well as clearly enumerate their investment goals, return objectives, the funds they have to invest at the present, the funds they expect to invest over time, and the benchmark portfolio that will be used to evaluate performance.

5.2 Investment Constraints

In addition to the investment objective that sets limits on risk and return, certain other constraints also affect the investment plan. Investment constraints include liquidity needs, an investment time horizon, tax factors, legal and regulatory constraints, and unique needs and preferences.

5.2.1 Liquidity Needs

An asset is **liquid** if it can be quickly converted to cash at a price close to fair market value. Generally, assets are more liquid if many traders are interested in a fairly standardized product. Treasury bills are a highly liquid security; real estate and venture capital are not.

Investors may have liquidity needs that the investment plan must consider. For example, although an investor may have a primary long-term goal, several near-term goals may require available funds. Wealthy individuals with sizable tax obligations need adequate liquidity to pay their taxes without upsetting their investment plan. Some retirement plans may need funds for shorter-term purposes, such as buying a car or a house or making college tuition payments.

Our typical 25-year-old investor probably has little need for liquidity as he focuses on his long-term retirement fund goal. This constraint may change, however, should he face a period of unemployment or should near-term goals, such as honeymoon expenses or a house down payment, enter the picture. Should any changes occur, the investor needs to revise his policy statement and financial plans accordingly.

Our soon-to-be-retired 65-year-old investor has a greater need for liquidity. Although she may receive regular checks from her pension plan and social security, it is not likely that they will equal her working paycheck. She will want some of her portfolio in liquid securities to meet unexpected expenses or bills.

5.2.2 *Time Horizon*

Time horizon as an investment constraint briefly entered our earlier discussion of near-term and long-term high-priority goals. A close (but not perfect) relationship exists between an investor's time horizon, liquidity needs, and ability to handle risk. Investors with long investment horizons generally require less liquidity and can tolerate greater portfolio risk: less liquidity because the funds are not usually needed for many years; greater risk tolerance because any shortfalls or losses can be overcome by returns earned in subsequent years.

Investors with shorter time horizons generally favor more liquid and less risky investments because losses are harder to overcome during a short time frame.

EXHIBIT 77-5 Individual Marginal Tax Rates, 2001

	Taxable Income	Tax	Percent on Excess
Married Filing Jointly	$ 0	$ 0.00	15%
	45,200	6,780.00	28
	109,250	24,714.00	31
	166,450	42,446.00	36
	297,300	89,552.00	39.6
Single	$ 0	$ 0.00	15%
	27,050	4,057.50	28
	65,550	14,837.50	31
	136,750	36,909.50	36
	297,300	94,707.50	39.6
Head of Household	$ 0	$ 0.00	15%
	36,250	5,437.50	28
	93,600	21,495.50	31
	151,600	39,475.50	36
	297,300	91,927.50	39.6
Married Filing Separately	$ 0	$ 0.00	15%
	22,600	3,390.00	28
	54,625	12,357.00	31
	83,225	21,223.00	36
	148,650	44,776.00	39.6

Because of life expectancies, our 25-year-old investor has a longer investment time horizon than our 65-year-old investor. But, as discussed earlier, this does not mean the 65-year-old should put all her money in short-term CDs; she needs the inflation protection that long-term investments, such as common stock, can provide. Still, because of the differing time horizons, the 25-year-old will probably have a greater proportion of his portfolio in equities, including stocks in growth companies, small firms, or international firms, than the 65-year-old.

5.2.3 Tax Concerns

Investment planning is complicated by the tax code; taxes complicate the situation even more if international investments are part of the portfolio. Taxable income from interest, dividends, or rents is taxable at the investor's marginal tax rate. The marginal tax rate is the proportion of the next one dollar in income paid as taxes. Exhibit 77-5 shows the marginal tax rates for different levels of taxable income. As of 2001, the top federal marginal tax rate was 39.6 percent. Under the provisions of the 2001 tax relief act, the top marginal rate will decline to 35 percent by 2006. State taxes make the tax bite even higher.

Capital gains or losses arise from asset price changes. They are taxed differently than income. Income is taxed when it is received; capital gains or losses are taxed only when the asset is sold and the gain or loss is realized. **Unrealized capital gains** reflect the price appreciation of currently held assets that have *not* been sold; the tax liability on unrealized capital gains can be deferred indefinitely. Capital gains only become taxable after the asset has been sold for a price higher than its cost, or **basis.** If appreciated assets are passed on to an heir upon the investor's death, the basis of the assets is considered to be their value on the date of the holder's death. The heirs can then sell the assets and not pay capital gains tax. Capital gains taxes are paid on **realized capital gains.** Beginning in 2001, gains on assets purchased after January 1, 2001, and held for at least five years will be only 18 percent. For taxpayers in the 15 percent income tax bracket, the capital gains tax rate fell to 8 percent on assets held longer than five years.

Sometimes it is necessary to make a trade-off between taxes and diversification needs. If entrepreneurs concentrate much of their wealth in equity holdings of their firm, or if employees purchase substantial amounts of their employer's stock through payroll deduction plans during their working life, their portfolios may contain a large amount of unrealized capital gains. In addition, the risk position of such a portfolio may be quite high because it is concentrated in a single company. The decision to sell some of the company stock in order to diversify the portfolio's risk by reinvesting the proceeds in other assets must be balanced against the resulting tax liability. To attain the prudent diversification, one should consider making the change over time.

Some find the difference between average and marginal income tax rates confusing. The **marginal tax rate** is the part of each additional dollar in income that is paid as tax. Thus, a married person, filing jointly, with an income of $50,000 will have a marginal tax rate of 28 percent. The 28 percent marginal tax rate should be used to determine after-tax returns on investments.

The **average tax rate** is simply a person's total tax payment divided by his or her total income. It represents the average tax paid on each dollar the person earned. From Exhibit 77-5, a married person, filing jointly, will pay $8,124 in tax on a $50,000 income [$6,780 plus 0.28($50,000 – $45,200)]. His or her average tax rate is $8,124/$50,000 or 16.25 percent.

Note that the average tax rate is a weighted average of the person's marginal tax rates paid on each dollar of income. The first $45,200 of income has a marginal tax rate of 15 percent; the next $4,800 has a 28 percent marginal tax rate:

$$\frac{\$45,200}{\$50,000} \times 0.15 + \frac{\$4,800}{\$50,000} \times .28 = 0.1625, \text{ or the Average Tax Rate of } 16.25\%$$

Another tax factor is that some sources of income are exempt from federal and state taxes. Interest on federal securities, such as Treasury bills, notes, and bonds, is exempt from state taxes. Interest on municipal bonds (bonds issued by a state or other local governing body) are exempt from federal taxes. Further, if the investor purchases municipal bonds issued by a local governing body of the state in which they live, the interest is usually exempt from both state and federal income tax. Thus, high-income individuals have an incentive to purchase municipal bonds to reduce their tax liabilities.

The after-tax return on a taxable investment is:

After-Tax Return = Pre-Tax Return (1 − Marginal Tax Rate)

Thus, the after-tax return on a taxable investment should be compared to that on municipals before deciding which should be purchased by a tax-paying investor. Alternatively, a municipal's equivalent taxable yield can be computed. The equivalent taxable yield is what a taxable bond investment would have to offer to produce the same after-tax return as the municipal. It is given by:

$$\text{Equivalent Taxable Yield} = \frac{\text{Municipal Yield}}{1 - \text{Marginal Tax Rate}}$$

To illustrate, if an investor is in the 28 percent marginal tax bracket, a taxable investment yield of 8 percent has an after-tax yield of 8 percent × (1 − 0.28), or 5.76 percent; an equivalent-risk municipal security offering a yield greater than 5.76 percent offers the investor greater after-tax returns. On the other hand, a municipal bond yielding 6 percent has an equivalent taxable yield of

6%/(1 − 0.28) = 8.33%

To earn more money after taxes, an equivalent-risk taxable investment has to offer a return greater than 8.33 percent.

Other means to reduce tax liabilities are available. Contributions to an individual retirement account (IRA) may qualify as a tax deduction if certain income limits are met. The investment returns of the IRA investment, including any income, are deferred until the funds are withdrawn from the account. Any funds withdrawn from an IRA are taxable as current income, regardless of whether growth in the IRA occurs as a result of capital gains, income, or both. The benefits of deferring taxes can dramatically compound over time. Exhibit 77-6 illustrates how $1,000 invested in an IRA at a tax-deferred rate of 8 percent grows compared to funds invested in a taxable investment that returns (from bond income) 8 percent pre-tax. For an investor in the 28 percent bracket, this taxable investment grows at an after-tax rate of 5.76 percent. After 30 years, the value of the tax-deferred investment is nearly twice that of the taxable investment.

Tax-deductible contributions of up to $2,000 (which is raised, in phases, to $5,000 under the 2001 tax act) can be made to a regular IRA. The Tax Reform Act of 1997 created the Roth IRA. The Roth IRA contribution, although not tax deductible, allows up to $2,000 (to be raised to $5,000) to be invested each year; the returns on this investment will grow on a tax-deferred basis and can be withdrawn, tax-free, if the funds are invested for at least five years and are withdrawn after the investor reaches age 591/2.[1] The Roth IRA is subject to limitations based on the investor's annual income, but the income ceiling is much higher than that for the regular IRA.

For money you intend to invest in some type of IRA, the advantage of the Roth IRA's tax-free withdrawals will outweigh the tax-deduction benefit from the regular IRA—unless you expect your tax rate when the funds are withdrawn to be substantially less than when you initially invest the funds.[2]

Tax questions can puzzle the most astute minds. For example, depending on one's situation, it may be best to hold stock in taxable rather than in tax-deferred accounts, such as IRAs, company retirement plans, and variable annuities, mainly

[1] Earlier tax-free withdrawals are possible if the funds are to be used for educational purposes or first-time home purchases.

[2] For additional insights, see Jonathan Clements, "Jam Today or Jam Tomorrow? Roth IRA Will Show Many Investors It Pays to Wait," *The Wall Street Journal*, 16 September 1997, C1.

EXHIBIT 77-6 Effect of Tax Deferral on Investor Wealth Over Time

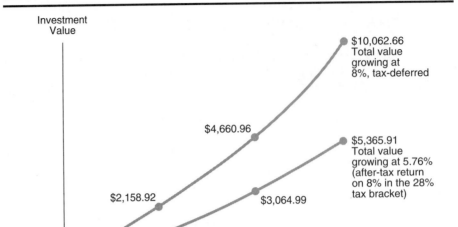

because earnings on such tax-deferred accounts are taxed as ordinary income when the funds are withdrawn. Even if most of the growth in a tax-deferred equity investment arises from capital gains, the withdrawals will be taxed at the higher ordinary income tax rate. Stocks held in taxable accounts will likely have large capital gains tax liability over the years; thus, after the 1997 Tax Reform Act's slashing of realized capital gains tax rates, taxable equity accounts may offer better after-tax return potential than tax-deferred investments. This will not be true in all cases. The point is, any analysis must consider each investor's return, time horizon, and tax assumptions.[3]

Other tax-deferred investments include cash values of life insurance contracts that accumulate tax-free until the funds are withdrawn. Employers may offer employees 401(k) or 403(b) plans, which allow the employee to reduce taxable income by making tax-deferred investments; many times employee contributions are matched by employer donations (up to a specified limit), thus allowing the employees to double their investment with little risk!

Our typical 25-year-old investor probably is in a fairly low tax bracket, so detailed tax planning will not be a major concern, and tax-exempt income, such as that available from municipals, will also not be a concern. Nonetheless, he should still invest as much as possible into tax-deferred plans, such as an IRA or a 401(k). The drawback to such investments, however, is that early withdrawals (before age 59½) are taxable and subject to an additional 10 percent early withdrawal tax. Should the liquidity constraint of these plans be too restrictive, the young investor should probably consider total-return- or capital-appreciation-oriented mutual funds.

Our 65-year-old retiree may face a different situation. If she is in a high tax bracket prior to retiring—and therefore has sought tax-exempt income and tax-deferred investments—her situation may change shortly after retirement. Without large, regular paychecks, the need for tax-deferred investments or tax-exempt income becomes less. Taxable income may now offer higher after-tax yields than tax-exempt municipals due to the investor's lower tax bracket. Should her employer's stock be a large component of her retirement account, careful decisions must be

[3] Terry Sylvester Charron, "Tax Efficient Investing for Tax-Deferred and Taxable Accounts," *Journal of Private Portfolio Management* 2, no. 2 (Fall 1999): 31–37.

made regarding the need to diversify versus the cost of realizing large capital gains (in her lower tax bracket).

5.2.4 Legal and Regulatory Factors

As you might expect, the investment process and financial markets are highly regulated. At times, these legal and regulatory factors constrain the investment strategies of individuals and institutions.

In our discussion about taxes, we mentioned one such constraint: Funds removed from a regular IRA account or 401(k) plan before age 59½ are taxable and subject to an additional 10 percent withdrawal penalty. You may also be familiar with the tag line in many bank CD advertisements—"substantial interest penalty upon early withdrawal." Such regulations may make such investments unattractive for investors with substantial liquidity needs in their portfolios.

Regulations can also constrain the investment choices available to someone in a **fiduciary** role. A fiduciary, or trustee, supervises an investment portfolio of a third party, such as a trust account or discretionary account.[4] The fiduciary must make investment decisions in accordance with the owner's wishes; a properly written policy statement assists this process. In addition, trustees of a trust account must meet the "prudent-man" standard, which means that they must invest and manage the funds as a prudent person would manage his or her own affairs. Notably, the prudent-man standard is based on the composition of the entire portfolio, not each individual asset in the portfolio.[5]

All investors must respect some laws, such as insider trading prohibitions. Insider trading involves the purchase and sale of securities on the basis of important information that is not publicly known. Typically, the people possessing such private or inside information are the firm's managers, who have a fiduciary duty to their shareholders. Security transactions based on access to inside information violate the fiduciary trust the shareholders have placed with management, because the managers seek personal financial gain from their privileged position as agents for the shareholders.

For our typical 25-year-old investor, legal and regulatory matters will be of little concern, with the possible exception of insider trading laws and the penalties associated with early withdrawal of funds from tax-deferred retirement accounts. Should he seek a financial advisor to assist him in constructing a financial plan, the financial advisor would have to obey the regulations pertinent to a client-advisor relationship.

Similar concerns confront our 65-year-old investor. In addition, as a retiree, if she wants to do some estate planning and set up trust accounts, she should seek legal and tax advice to ensure her plans are properly specified and implemented.

5.2.5 Unique Needs and Preferences

This category covers the individual concerns of each investor. Some investors may want to exclude certain investments from their portfolio solely on the basis of personal preferences. For example, they may request that no firms that manufacture or sell tobacco, alcohol, pornography, or environmentally harmful products be included in their portfolio. As of 2001, over 200 mutual funds include at least one social-responsibility criterion.

---

[4] A discretionary account is one in which the fiduciary, many times a financial planner or stockbroker, has the authority to purchase and sell assets in the owner's portfolio without first receiving the owner's approval.

[5] As we will discuss in Reading 78, it is sometimes wise to hold assets that are individually risky in the context of a well-diversified portfolio, even if the investor is strongly risk averse.

Another example of a personal constraint is the time and expertise a person has for managing his or her portfolio. Busy executives may prefer to relax during nonworking hours and let a trusted advisor manage their investments. Retirees, on the other hand, may have the time but believe they lack the expertise to choose and monitor investments, so they may also seek professional advice.

Some of the constraints we previously discussed can also be considered as unique needs and preferences. For example, consider the businessperson with a large portion of his wealth tied up in his firm's stock. Though it may be financially prudent to sell some of the firm's stock and reinvest the proceeds for diversification purposes, it may be hard for the individual to approve such a strategy due to emotional ties to the firm. Further, if the stock holdings are in a private company, it may be difficult to find a buyer except if shares are sold at a discount from their fair market value.

Because each investor is unique, the implications of this final constraint differ for each person; there is no "typical" 25-year-old or 65-year-old investor. Each individual will have to communicate specific goals in a well-constructed policy statement.

Institutional investors (endowments, pension funds, and the like) also need to have investment policy statements. Factors considered by institutional investors when developing policy statements are found in the reading appendix.

5.3 Constructing the Policy Statement

A policy statement allows the investor to determine what factors are personally important for the investor's objectives (risk and return) and constraints (liquidity, time horizon, tax factors, legal and regulatory constraints, and unique needs and preferences). To do without a policy statement is to place the success of the financial plan in jeopardy. In contrast, having a policy statement allows the investor to communicate these needs to the advisor who can do a better job of constructing an investment strategy to satisfy the investor's objectives and constraints.

Surveys show that fewer than 40 percent of employees who participate in their firm's retirement savings plan have a good understanding of the value of diversification, the harmful effect of inflation on one's savings, or the relationship between risk and return. Because of this lack of investment expertise, the market for financial planning services and education is a growth industry.

Participants in employer-sponsored retirement plans have invested an average of 30–40 percent of their retirement funds in their employer's stock. Having so much money invested in one asset violates diversification principles. To put this in context, most mutual funds are limited to having no more than 5 percent of their assets in any one company's stock; a firm's pension plan can invest no more than 10 percent of its funds in the firm's stock. Thus, individuals are unfortunately doing what government regulations prevent many institutional investors from doing.[6] Other studies point out that the average stock allocation in retirement plans is lower than it should be to allow for growth of principal over time.

Studies of retirement plans show that Americans are not saving enough to finance their retirement years and they are not planning sufficiently for what will happen to their savings after they retire.[7] Americans are saving at about one-half the rate needed to finance their retirement. This poor savings rate, coupled with lack of diversification and lack of equity growth potential in their portfolios, can lead to disappointments in one's retirement years.

---

[6] Ellen R. Schultz, "Workers Put Too Much in Their Employer's Stock," *The Wall Street Journal*, 13 September 1996, C1, C25.

[7] Glenn Ruffenach, "Fewer Americans Save for Their Retirement, "*The Wall Street Journal*, 10 May 2001, A2; Jonathan Clements, "Retirement Honing: How Much Should You Have Saved for a Comfortable Life?" *The Wall Street Journal*, 28 January 1997, C1; Jonathan Clements, "Squeezing the Right Amount from a Retirement Stash," *The Wall Street Journal*, 25 February 1997, C1.

THE IMPORTANCE OF ASSET ALLOCATION ◣ 6

A major reason why investors develop policy statements is to determine an overall investment strategy. Though a policy statement does not indicate which specific securities to purchase and when they should be sold, it should provide guidelines as to the asset classes to include and the relative proportions of the investor's funds to invest in each class. How the investor divides funds into different asset classes is the process of asset allocation. Rather than present strict percentages, asset allocation is usually expressed in ranges. This allows the investment manager some freedom, based on his or her reading of capital market trends, to invest toward the upper or lower end of the ranges. For example, suppose a policy statement requires that common stocks be 60 percent to 80 percent of the value of the portfolio and that bonds should be 20 percent to 40 percent of the portfolio's value. If a manager is particularly bullish about stocks, she will increase the allocation of stocks toward the 80 percent upper end of the equity range and decrease bonds toward the 20 percent lower end of the bond range. Should she be more optimistic about bonds, that manager may shift the allocation closer to 40 percent of the funds invested in bonds with the remainder in equities.

A review of historical data and empirical studies provides strong support for the contention that the asset allocation decision is a critical component of the portfolio management process. In general, four decisions are made when constructing an investment strategy.

▷ What asset classes should be considered for investment?

▷ What normal or policy weights should be assigned to each eligible asset class?

▷ What are the allowable allocation ranges based on policy weights?

▷ What specific securities should be purchased for the portfolio?

The asset allocation decision comprises the first two points. How important is the asset allocation decision to an investor? In a word, *very*. Several studies have examined the effect of the normal policy weights on investment performance, using data from both pension funds and mutual funds, from periods of time extending from the early 1970s to the late 1990s.[8] The studies all found similar results: About 90 percent of a fund's returns over time can be explained by its target asset allocation policy. Exhibit 77-7 shows the relationship between returns on the target or policy portfolio allocation and actual returns on a sample mutual fund.

Rather than looking at just one fund and how the target asset allocation determines its returns, some studies have looked at how much the asset allocation policy affects returns on a variety of funds with different target weights. For example, Ibbotson and Kaplan (see Footnote 8) found that, across a sample of funds, about 40 percent of the difference in fund returns is explained by differences in asset allocation policy. And what does asset allocation tell us about the *level* of a particular fund's returns? The studies by Brinson and colleagues and Ibbotson and Kaplan (Footnote 8) answered that question as well. They divided the policy return (what the fund return would have been had it been invested in indexes at the policy weights) by the actual fund return (which includes the effects of varying from the policy weights and security selection). Thus, a fund that was

---

[8] Findings discussed in this section are based on Roger G. Ibbotson and Paul D. Kaplan, "Does Asset Allocation Policy Explain 40, 90, or 100 Percent of Performance?" *Financial Analysts Journal* 56, no. 1 (January–February 2000): 26–33; Gary P. Brinson, Brian D. Singer, and Gilbert L. Beebower, "Determinants of Portfolio Performance II: An Update," *Financial Analysts Journal* 47, no. 3 (May–June 1991): 40–48; Gary P. Brinson, L. Randolph Hood, and Gilbert L. Beebower, "Determinants of Portfolio Performance," *Financial Analysts Journal* 42, no. 4 (July–August 1986): 39–48.

passively invested at the target weights would have a ratio value of 1.0, or 100 percent. A fund managed by someone with skill in market timing (for moving in and out of asset classes) and security selection would have a ratio less than 1.0 (or less than 100 percent); the manager's skill would result in a policy return less than the actual fund return. The studies showed the opposite: The policy return/actual return ratio averaged over 1.0, showing that asset allocation explains slightly more than 100 percent of the level of a fund's returns. Because of market efficiency, fund managers practicing market timing and security selection, on average, have difficulty surpassing passively invested index returns, after taking into account the expenses and fees of investing.

Thus, asset allocation is a very important decision. Across all funds, the asset allocation decision explains an average of 40 percent of the variation in fund returns. For a single fund, asset allocation explains 90 percent of the fund's variation in returns over time and slightly more than 100 percent of the average fund's level of return.

Good investment managers may add some value to portfolio performance, but the major source of investment return—and risk—over time is the asset allocation

EXHIBIT 77-7 Time-Series Regression of Monthly Fund Return Versus Fund Policy Return: One Mutual Fund, April 1988–March 1998

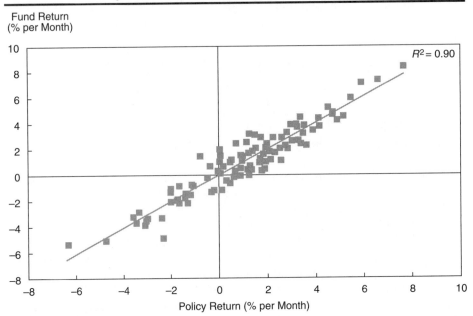

Note: The sample fund's policy allocations among the general asset classes were 52.4 percent U.S. large-cap stocks, 9.8 percent U.S. small-cap stocks, 32 percent non-U.S. stocks, 20.9 percent U.S. bonds, and 13.7 percent cash.

decision. Investors who thought asset allocation was an outmoded concept during the bull market of the late 1990s found they were mistaken in the market declines of 2000–2001.[9] A number of studies have shown that individual investors frequently trade stocks too often—driving up commissions—and sell stocks with gains too early (prior to further price increases), while they hold onto losers too long (as the

---

[9] Ken Brown, "Fund Diversification Dies a Not Very Slow Death," *The Wall Street Journal*, 7 February 2000, R1, R5.

price continues to fall).[10] These results are especially true for men and online traders.[11] The desire to "get rich quick" by trading in the stock market may lead to a few success stories; but, for most investors, implementing a prudent asset allocation strategy and investing over time are a more likely means of investment success. A well-constructed policy statement can go a long way toward ensuring that an appropriate asset allocation decision is implemented and maintained.

EXHIBIT 77-8 The Effect of Taxes and Inflation on Investment Returns, 1926–2001

Compound Annual Returns: 1926–2001	Before taxes and inflation	After taxes	After taxes and inflation
Common Stocks	10.7%	7.9%	4.7%
Long-Term Govt. Bonds	5.3%	3.7%	0.6%
Treasury Bills	3.8%	2.7%	−0.4%
Municipal Bonds (est.)	6.0%	6.0%	2.9%

Legend:
- Common Stocks
- Long-Term Government Bonds
- Treasury Bills
- Municipal Bonds

Note: A 28 percent marginal tax rate was used for income across all years, and we assumed a 20 percent capital gains tax rate with gains realized after 20 years.

Source: Stocks, Bonds, Bills, and Inflation,® 2002 Yearbook, © 2002 Ibbotson Associates, Inc. Based on copyrighted works by Ibbotson and Sinquefield. All rights reserved. Used with permission.

6.1 Real Investment Returns after Taxes and Costs

Exhibit 77-8 provides additional historical perspectives on returns. It indicates how an investment of $1 would have grown over the 1926 to 2001 period and, using fairly conservative assumptions, examines how investment returns are affected by taxes and inflation.

[10] Brad Barber and Terrance Odean, "Trading is Hazardous to Your Wealth: The Common Stock Investment Performance of Individual Investors," *Journal of Finance* 55, no. 2 (April 2000): 773–806; Terrance Odean, "Do Investors Trade Too Much?" *American Economic Review* 89 (December 1999): 1279–1298; Brad Barber and Terrance Odean, "The Courage of Misguided Convictions: The Trading Behavior of Individual Investors, *Financial Analyst Journal* 55, no. 6 (November–December 1999): 41–55; Terrance Odean, "Are Investors Reluctant to Realize Their Losses?" *Journal of Finance* 53, no. 5 (October 1998): 1775–1798.

[11] Brad Barber and Terrance Odean, "Boys Will Be Boys: Gender, Overconfidence, and Common Stock Investment," *Quarterly Journal of Economics* 116, no. 1 (February 2001): 261–292; Brad Barber and Terrance Odean, "Online Investors: Do the Slow Die First?" University of California at Davis working paper.

Focusing first on stocks, funds invested in 1926 in the S&P 500 would have averaged a 10.7 percent annual return by the end of 2001. Unfortunately, this return is unrealistic because if the funds were invested over time, taxes would have to be paid and inflation would erode the real purchasing power of the invested funds.

Except for tax-exempt investors and tax-deferred accounts, annual tax payments reduce investment returns. Incorporating taxes into the analysis lowers the after-tax average annual return of a stock investment to 7.9 percent.

But the major reduction in the value of our investment is caused by inflation. The real aftertax average annual return on a stock over this time frame was only 4.7 percent, which is quite a bit less than our initial unadjusted 10.7 percent return!

EXHIBIT 77-9 Historical Average Annual Returns And Return Variability, 1926–2001

Series	Geometric Mean	Arithmetic Mean	Standard Deviation	Distribution
Large company stocks	10.7%	12.7%	20.2%	
Small company stocks*	12.5	17.3	33.2	
Long-term corporate bonds	5.8	6.1	8.6	
Long-term government bonds	5.3	5.7	9.4	
Intermediate-term government bonds	5.3	5.5	5.7	
U.S. Treasury bills	3.8	3.9	3.2	
Inflation	3.1	3.1	4.4	

*The 1933 Small Company Stock Total Return was 142.9 percent.   —90%   0%   90%

Source: Stocks, Bonds, Bills, and Inflation,® 2002 Yearbook, © Ibbotson Associates, Inc. Based on copyrighted works by Ibbotson and Sinquefield. All rights reserved. Used with permission.

This example shows the long-run impact of taxes and inflation on the real value of a stock portfolio. For bonds and bills, however, the results in Exhibit 77-8 show something even more surprising. After adjusting for taxes, long-term bonds barely maintained their purchasing power; T-bills *lost* value in real terms. One dollar invested in long-term government bonds in 1926 gave the investor an annual average after-tax real return of 0.6 percent. An investment in Treasury bills lost an average of 0.4 percent after taxes and inflation. Municipal bonds, because of the protection they offer from taxes, earned an average annual real return of almost 3 percent during this time.

This historical analysis demonstrates that, for taxable investments, the only way to maintain purchasing power over time when investing in financial assets is to invest in common stocks. An asset allocation decision for a taxable portfolio that does not include a substantial commitment to common stocks makes it difficult for the portfolio to maintain real value over time.[12]

EXHIBIT 77-10 Over Long Time Periods, Equities Offer Higher Returns

Stocks far outperformed Treasury bills during the 34 years through 2001, but stocks often did worse than T-bills when held for shorter periods during those 34 years.

	COMPOUND ANNUAL TOTAL RETURN[a]
S&P 500 stock index	12.1%
Treasury bills	6.6

LENGTH OF HOLDING PERIOD (CALENDAR YEARS)	PERCENTAGE OF PERIODS THAT STOCKS TRAILED BILLS
1	38%
5	21
10	16
20	0

[a] Price change plus reinvested income.

Source: Stocks, Bonds, Bills, and Inflation,® 2002 Yearbook, © Ibbotson Associates, Inc. Based on copyrighted works by Ibbotson and Sinquefield. All rights reserved. Used with permission.

6.2 Returns and Risks of Different Asset Classes

By focusing on returns, we have ignored its partner—risk. Assets with higher long-term returns have these returns to compensate for their risk. Exhibit 77-9 illustrates returns (unadjusted for costs and taxes) for several asset classes over time. As expected, the higher returns available from equities come at the cost of higher risk. This is precisely why investors need a policy statement and why the investor and manager must understand the capital markets and have a disciplined approach to investing. Safe Treasury bills will sometimes outperform equities, and, because of their higher risk, common stocks sometimes lose significant value. These are times when undisciplined and uneducated investors sell their stocks at a loss and vow never to invest in equities again. In contrast, these are times when disciplined investors stick to their investment plan and position their portfolio for the next bull market.[13] By holding on to their stocks and perhaps purchasing more at depressed prices, the equity portion of the portfolio will experience a substantial increase in the future.

The asset allocation decision determines to a great extent both the returns and the volatility of the portfolio. Exhibit 77-9 indicates that stocks are riskier than bonds or T-bills. Exhibit 77-10 and Exhibit 77-11 illustrate the year-by-year volatility of stock

---

[12] Of course other equity-oriented investments, such as venture capital or real estate, may also provide inflation protection after adjusting for portfolio costs and taxes. Future studies of the performance of Treasury inflation-protected securities (TIPs) will likely show their usefulness in protecting investors from inflation as well.

[13] Newton's law of gravity seems to work two ways in financial markets. What goes up must come down; it also appears over time that what goes down may come back up. Contrarian investors and some "value" investors use this concept of reversion to the mean to try to outperform the indexes over time.

returns and show that stocks have sometimes earned returns lower than those of T-bills for extended periods of time. Sticking with an investment policy and riding out the difficult times can earn attractive long-term rates of return.[14]

One popular way to measure risk is to examine the variability of returns over time by computing a standard deviation or variance of annual rates of return for an asset class. This measure, which is contained in Exhibit 77-9, indicates that stocks are risky and T-bills are not. Another intriguing measure of risk is the probability of *not* meeting your investment return objective. From this perspective, based on the results shown in Exhibit 77-10, if the investor has a long time horizon (i.e. approaching 20 years), the risk of equities is small and that of T-bills is large because of their differences in expected returns.

EXHIBIT 77-11　Equity Risk: Long-Term And Short-Term Perspectives, 1940–2001

Historically, the S&P 500 has posted healthy gains . . .
Total returns, by decade, including share price gains and reinvested dividends, in percent

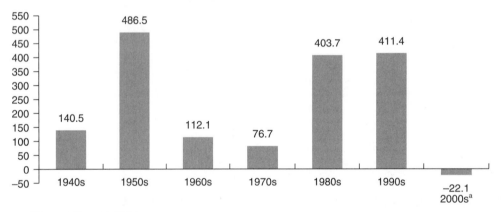

ᵃThrough Dec. 31, 2001.

. . . but getting there can be rough
Annual total returns including share price gains and reinvested dividends, in percent

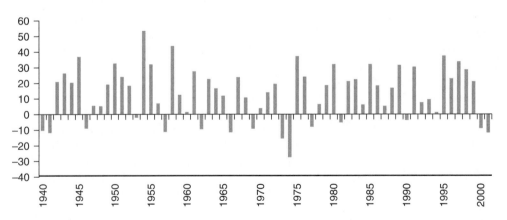

Source: Calculated using data presented in *Stocks, Bonds, Bills, and Inflation,*® *2002 Yearbook,* © Ibbotson Associates, Inc. Based on copyrighted works by Ibbotson and Sinquefield. All rights reserved. Used with permission.

---

[14] The added benefits of diversification—combining different asset classes in the portfolio—may reduce overall portfolio risk without harming potential return. The topic of diversification is discussed in Reading 78.

Focusing solely on return variability as a measure of risk ignores a significant risk for income-oriented investors, such as retirees or endowment funds. "Safe," income-oriented investments, such as Treasury bills or certificates of deposit, suffer from *reinvestment risk*—that is, the risk that interim cash flows or the principal paid at maturity will be reinvested in a lower-yielding security. The year of 1992 was particularly hard on investors in "safe" T-bills, because their T-bill income fell 37 percent from 1991 levels due to lower interest rates. Exhibit 77-12 compares the variability of income payouts from common stocks (measured by the dividends from the S&P 500) and T-bills. Over the 1926 to 2001 time frame, dividend income from stocks rose 59 times compared to 44 times for T-bills. The income from stocks fell only 17 times, while T-bill rollovers resulted in an income loss 32 times. The worst one-year drop in stock income, 39.0 percent in 1932, was not as severe as the largest decline, 76.6 percent, in T-bill income, which occurred in 1940. In addition, the growth rate of income from stocks far outpaced that of inflation and the growth of income from T-bills. During the 1926 through 2001 period, stock dividends rose almost 1,900 percent, inflation rose 886 percent, and T-bill income rose only 70 percent. When one considers the growth in principal that stocks offer, we see that "conservative," income-oriented T-bill investors are in fact exposed to substantial amounts of risk.

EXHIBIT 77-12 Comparison of Income Payouts from Common Stocks and Treasury Bills, 1926–2001

During the past 76 years, stocks have been a more reliable source of income than either bonds or Treasury bills. The following figures presume that each year an investor spent all dividend and interest income kicked off by the securities but left the capital intact.

				1926 TO 2001	
	YEARS WHEN PAYOUT ROSE	YEARS WHEN PAYOUT FELL	WORST ONE-YEAR DROP IN INCOME	CHANGE IN VALUE OF INCOME	CHANGE IN VALUE OF PRINCIPAL
Stocks	59	17	−39%	1,891.8%	4,409.9%
20-Year Treasury bonds	41	35	−15.0	93.1	−13.3
5-Year Treasury bonds	44	32	−36.9	75.5	26.1
Treasury bills	44	32	−76.6	70.1	—

Exhibit data source: Ibbotson Associates, Inc.

Source: "T-Bill Trauma and the Meaning of Risk," *The Wall Street Journal,* 12 February 1993, C1. Reprinted with permission of *The Wall Street Journal.* ©1993 Dow Jones and Co., Inc. All rights reserved. Updated by the authors, using Ibbotson data.

6.3 Asset Allocation Summary

A carefully constructed policy statement determines the types of assets that should be included in a portfolio. The asset allocation decision, not the selection of specific stocks and bonds, determines most of the portfolio's returns over time. Although seemingly risky, investors seeking capital appreciation, income, or even capital preservation over long time periods will do well to include a sizable allocation to the equity portion in their portfolio. As noted in this section, a strategy's risk may depend on the investor's goals and time horizon. At times, investing in T-bills may be a riskier strategy than investing in common stocks due to reinvestment risks and the risk of not meeting long-term investment return goals after considering inflation and taxes.

7   ASSET ALLOCATION AND CULTURAL DIFFERENCES

Thus far, our analysis has focused on U.S. investors. Non-U.S. investors make their asset allocation decisions in much the same manner; but because they face different social, economic, political, and tax environments, their allocation decisions differ from those of U.S. investors. Exhibit 77-13 shows the equity allocations of pension funds in several countries. As shown, the equity allocations vary dramatically from 79 percent in Hong Kong to 37 percent in Japan and only 8 percent in Germany.

National differences can explain much of the divergent portfolio strategies. Of these six nations, the average age of the population is highest in Germany and Japan and lowest in the United States and the United Kingdom, which helps explain the greater use of equities in the latter countries. Government privatization programs

EXHIBIT 77-13   Equity Allocations In Pension Fund Portfolios

COUNTRY	PERCENTAGE IN EQUITIES
Hong Kong	79%
United Kingdom	78
Ireland	68
United States	58
Japan	37
Germany	8

**EXHIBIT 77-14   Asset Allocation And Inflation For Different Countries
Equity Allocation As of December 1997; Average Inflation
Measured Over 1980–1997**

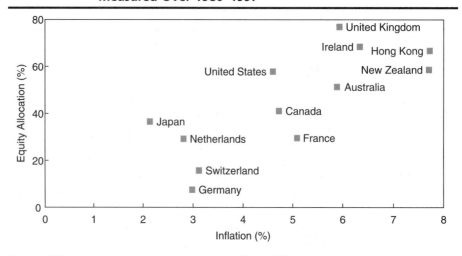

during the 1980s in the United Kingdom encouraged equity ownership among individual and institutional investors. In Germany, regulations prevent insurance firms from having more than 20 percent of their assets in equities. Both Germany and Japan have banking sectors that invest privately in firms and whose officers sit on corporate boards. Since 1960, the cost of living in the United Kingdom has increased at a rate more than 4.5 times that of Germany; this inflationary bias in the U.K. economy favors equities in U.K. asset allocations. Exhibit 77-14 shows the positive relationship between the level of inflation in a country and pension fund allocation to equity in the country. These results indicate that the general economic environment, as well as demographics, has an effect on the asset allocation in a country.

The need to invest in equities for portfolio growth is less in Germany, where workers receive generous state pensions. Germans tend to show a cultural aversion to the stock market: Many Germans are risk averse and consider stock investing a form of gambling. Although this attitude is changing, the German stock market is rather illiquid, with only a handful of stocks accounting for 50 percent of total stock trading volume.[15] New legislation that encourages 401(k)-like plans in Germany may encourage citizens to invest more in equities, but in mid-2001, less than 10 percent of Germans over the age of 14 owned stocks either directly or indirectly.[16]

Other Organization for Economic Cooperation and Development (OECD) countries place regulatory restrictions on institutional investors. For example, pension funds in Austria must have at least 50 percent of their assets in bank deposits or schilling-denominated bonds. Belgium limits pension funds to a minimum 15 percent investment in government bonds. Finland places a 5 percent limit on investments outside its borders by pension funds, and French pension funds must invest a minimum of 34 percent in public debt instruments.[17]

Asset allocation policy and strategy are determined in the context of an investor's objectives and constraints. Among the factors that explain differences in investor behavior across countries, however, are their political and economic environments.

---

[15] Peter Gumbel, "The Hard Sell: Getting Germans to Invest in Stocks," *The Wall Street Journal*, 4 August 1995, p. A2.

[16] Christopher Rhoads, "Germany Is Poised for a Pension Overhaul," *The Wall Street Journal*, 10 May 2001, p. A13.

[17] Daniel Witschi, "European Pension Funds: Turning More Aggressive?" in *Asset Allocation in a Changing World*, edited by Terence E. Burns (Charlottesville, Va., Association for Investment Management and Research, 1998): 72–84; Joel Chernoff, "OECD Eyes Pension Rules," *Pensions and Investments* (December 23, 1996): 2, 34.

8 THE INTERNET

Investments Online

Many inputs go into an investment policy statement as an investor maps out his or her objectives and constraints. Some inputs and helpful information are available in the following websites. Many of the sites mentioned in Reading 76 contain important information and insights about asset allocation decisions, as well.

- **http://www.ssa.gov** Information on a person's expected retirement funds from Social Security can be obtained by using the Social Security Administration's website.
- **http://www.ibbotson.com** Much of the data in this reading's charts and tables came from Ibbotson's published sources. Many professional financial planners use Ibbotson's data and education resources.
- **http://www.mfea.com/ InvestmentStrategies/Calculators/default.asp** This site contains links to calculators on websites of mutual fund families.

Sites with information and sample Monte Carlo simulations for spending plans in retirement include:

- **http://www.financialengines.com, http://www.troweprice.com** (click on investment tools and select the investment strategy planner); **http://www3.troweprice.com/ retincome/RIC/** (for a retirement income calculator), and **http://www.decisioneering.com.**

Many professional organizations have websites for use by their members, those interested in seeking professional finance designations, and those interested in seeking advice from a professional financial adviser. These sites include:

- **http://www.aimr.org** Association for Investment Management and Research home page. AIMR awards the CFA (Chartered Financial Analyst) designation. This site provides information about the CFA designation, AIMR publications, investor education, and various Internet resources.
- **http://www.amercoll.edu** This is the website for The American College, which is the training arm of the insurance industry. The American College offers the CLU and ChFC designations, which are typically earned by insurance professionals.
- **http://www.cfp-board.org** The home page of Certified Financial Planner Board of Standards. Contains links to find a CFP™ mark holder and other information about the financial planning profession.
- **http://www.napfa.org** This is the home page for the National Association of Personal Financial Advisors. This is the trade group for fee-only financial planners. Fee-only planners do not sell products on commission, or, should they recommend a commission-generating product, they pass the commission on to the investor. This site features press releases, finding a fee-only planner in your area, a list of financial resources on the Web and position openings in the financial planning field.
- **http://www.fpanet.org** The Financial Planning Association's website. The site offers features and topics of interest to financial planners including information on earning the CFP designation and receiving the *Journal of Financial Planning.*
- **http://www.asec.org** The home page of the American Saving Education Council.

SUMMARY

9

▶ In this reading, we saw that investors need to prudently manage risk within the context of their investment goals and preferences. Income, spending, and investing behavior will change over a person's lifetime.

▶ We reviewed the importance of developing an investment policy statement before implementing a serious investment plan. By forcing investors to examine their needs, risk tolerance, and familiarity with the capital markets, policy statements help investors correctly identify appropriate objectives and constraints. In addition, the policy statement becomes a standard by which to judge the performance of the portfolio manager.

▶ We also reviewed the importance of the asset allocation decision in determining long-run portfolio investment returns and risks. Because the asset allocation decision follows setting the objectives and constraints, it is clear that the success of the investment program depends on the first step, the construction of the policy statement.

REFERENCES

▷ Bhatia, Sanjiv, ed. *Managing Assets for Individual Investors.* Charlottesville, Va.: Association for Investment Management and Research, 1995.

▷ Burns, Terence E., ed. *Investment Counseling for Private Clients.* Charlottesville, Va.: Association for Investment Management and Research, 1999.

▷ Ellis, Charles D. *Investment Policy: How to Win the Loser's Game.* Homewood, Ill.: Dow Jones–Irwin, 1985.

▷ Miller, Janet T. ed. *Investment Counseling for Private Clients, III.* Charlottesville, Va.: Association for Investment Management and Research, 2001.

▷ Mitchell, Roger S. ed. *Investment Counseling for Private Clients, II.* Charlottesville, Va.: Association for Investment Management and Research, 2000.

▷ Peavy, John. *Cases in Portfolio Management.* Charlottesville, Va.: Association for Investment Management and Research, 1990.

▷ Peavy, John W., ed. *Investment Counsel for Private Clients.* Charlottesville, Va.: Association for Investment Management and Research, 1993.

AN INTRODUCTION TO PORTFOLIO MANAGEMENT

READING

78

LEARNING OUTCOMES

The candidate should be able to:

a. define risk aversion and cite evidence that suggests that individuals are generally risk averse;

b. list the assumptions about individuals' investment behavior of the Markowitz Portfolio Theory;

c. compute expected return for an individual investment and for a portfolio;

d. compute the variance and standard deviation for an individual investment;

e. compute the covariance of rates of return, and show how it is related to the correlation coefficient;

f. list the components of the portfolio standard deviation formula, and explain which component is most important to consider when adding an investment to a portfolio;

g. describe the efficient frontier and explain the implications for incremental returns as an investor assumes more risk;

h. define optimal portfolio and show how each investor may have a different optimal portfolio.

INTRODUCTION   1

One of the major advances in the investment field during the past few decades has been the recognition that the creation of an optimum investment portfolio is not simply a matter of combining a lot of unique individual securities that have desirable risk-return characteristics. Specifically, it has been shown that you must consider the relationship *among* the investments if you are going to build an optimum portfolio that will meet your investment objectives. The recognition of what is important in creating a portfolio was demonstrated in the derivation of portfolio theory.

Investment Analysis Portfolio Management, by Frank K. Reilly and Keith C. Brown, Copyright © 2003. Reprinted with permission of South-Western, a division of Thomson Learning.

This reading explains portfolio theory step by step. It introduces you to the basic portfolio risk formula that you must understand when you are combining different assets. When you understand this formula and its implications, you will increase your understanding of not only why you should diversify your portfolio but also *how* you should diversify. The subsequent readings introduce asset pricing models including capital market theory and multifactor models with an emphasis on determining the appropriate risk measure for individual assets.

2   SOME BACKGROUND ASSUMPTIONS

Before presenting portfolio theory, we need to clarify some general assumptions of the theory. This includes not only what we mean by an *optimum portfolio* but also what we mean by the terms *risk aversion* and *risk*. One basic assumption of portfolio theory is that as an investor you want to maximize the returns from your investments for a given level of risk. To adequately deal with such an assumption, certain ground rules must be laid. First, your portfolio should *include all of your assets and liabilities,* not only your stocks or even your marketable securities but also such items as your car, house, and less-marketable investments, such as coins, stamps, art, antiques, and furniture. The full spectrum of investments must be considered because the returns from all these investments interact, and *this relationship between the returns for assets in the portfolio is important*. Hence, a good portfolio is *not* simply a collection of individually good investments.

2.1 Risk Aversion

Portfolio theory also assumes that investors are basically **risk averse,** meaning that, given a choice between two assets with equal rates of return, they will select the asset with the lower level of risk. Evidence that most investors are risk averse is that they purchase various types of insurance, including life insurance, car insurance, and health insurance. Buying insurance basically involves an outlay of a given amount to guard against an uncertain, possibly larger outlay in the future. When you buy insurance, this implies that you are willing to pay the current known cost of the insurance policy to avoid the uncertainty of a potentially large future cost related to a car accident or a major illness. Further evidence of risk aversion is the difference in promised yield (the required rate of return) for different grades of bonds that supposedly have different degrees of credit risk. Specifically, the promised yield on bonds increases as you go from AAA (the lowest-risk class) to AA to A, and so on—that is, investors require a higher rate of return to accept higher risk.

This does not imply that everybody is risk averse or that investors are completely risk averse regarding all financial commitments. The fact is, not everybody buys insurance for everything. Some people have no insurance against anything, either by choice or because they cannot afford it. In addition, some individuals buy insurance related to some risks such as auto accidents or illness, but they also buy lottery tickets and gamble at race tracks or in casinos, where it is known that the expected returns are negative, which means that participants are willing to pay for the excitement of the risk involved. This combination of risk preference and risk aversion can be explained by an attitude toward risk that depends on the amount of money involved. Friedman and Savage speculate that this is the case for people who like to gamble for small amounts (in lotteries or slot machines) but buy insurance to protect themselves against large potential losses, such as fire or accidents.[1]

While recognizing this diversity of attitudes, our basic assumption is that most investors committing large sums of money to developing an investment portfolio are risk averse. Therefore, we expect a positive relationship between expected return and expected risk. Notably, this is also what we generally find in terms of long-run historical results—that is, there is generally a positive relationship between the rates of return on various assets and their measures of risk as shown in Chapter 3.

2.2 Definition of Risk

Although there is a difference in the specific definitions of *risk* and *uncertainty*, for our purposes and in most financial literature the two terms are used interchangeably. In fact, one way to define risk is the *uncertainty of future outcomes*. An alternative definition might be *the probability of an adverse outcome*. Subsequently, in our discussion of portfolio theory, we will consider several measures of risk that are used when developing the theory.

MARKOWITZ PORTFOLIO THEORY   **3**

In the early 1960s, the investment community talked about risk, but there was no specific measure for the term. To build a portfolio model, however, investors had to quantify their risk variable. The basic portfolio model was developed by Harry Markowitz, who derived the expected rate of return for a portfolio of assets and an expected risk measure.[2] Markowitz showed that the variance of the rate of return was a meaningful measure of portfolio risk under a reasonable set of assumptions, and he derived the formula for computing the variance of a portfolio. This portfolio variance formula indicated the importance of diversifying your investments to reduce the total risk of a portfolio but also showed *how* to effectively diversify. The Markowitz model is based on several assumptions regarding investor behavior:

1. Investors consider each investment alternative as being represented by a probability distribution of expected returns over some holding period.

2. Investors maximize one-period expected utility, and their utility curves demonstrate diminishing marginal utility of wealth.

3. Investors estimate the risk of the portfolio on the basis of the variability of expected returns.

4. Investors base decisions solely on expected return and risk, so their utility curves are a function of expected return and the expected variance (or standard deviation) of returns only.

5. For a given risk level, investors prefer higher returns to lower returns. Similarly, for a given level of expected return, investors prefer less risk to more risk.

---

[1] Milton Friedman and Leonard J. Savage, "The Utility Analysis of Choices Involving Risk," *Journal of Political Economy* 56, no. 3 (August 1948): 279–304.

[2] Harry Markowitz, "Portfolio Selection," *Journal of Finance* 7, no. 1 (March 1952): 77–91; and Harry Markowitz, *Portfolio Selection—Efficient Diversification of Investments* (New York: John Wiley & Sons, 1959).

Under these assumptions, *a single asset or portfolio of assets is considered to be efficient if no other asset or portfolio of assets offers higher expected return with the same (or lower) risk, or lower risk with the same (or higher) expected return.*

3.1 Alternative Measures of Risk

One of the best-known measures of risk is the *variance,* or *standard deviation of expected returns.*[3] It is a statistical measure of the dispersion of returns around the expected value whereby a larger variance or standard deviation indicates greater dispersion. The idea is that the more disperse the expected returns, the greater the uncertainty of future returns.

Another measure of risk is the *range of returns.* It is assumed that a larger range of expected returns, from the lowest to the highest return, means greater uncertainty and risk regarding future expected returns.

Instead of using measures that analyze all deviations from expectations, some observers believe that when you invest you should be concerned only with *returns below expectations,* which means that you only consider deviations below the mean value. A measure that only considers deviations below the mean is the *semivariance.* Extensions of the semivariance measure only computed expected returns *below zero* (that is, negative returns), or returns below some specific asset such as T-bills, the rate of inflation, or a benchmark. These measures of risk implicitly assume that investors want to *minimize the damage* from returns less than some target rate. Assuming that investors would welcome returns above some target rate, the returns above a target return are not considered when measuring risk.

Although there are numerous potential measures of risk, we will use the variance or standard deviation of returns because (1) this measure is somewhat intuitive, (2) it is a correct and widely recognized risk measure, and (3) it has been used in most of the theoretical asset pricing models.

3.2 Expected Rates of Return

The expected rate of return for *an individual investment* is computed as shown in Exhibit 78-1. The expected return for an individual risky asset with the set of potential returns and an assumption of equal probabilities used in the example would be 11 percent.

The expected rate of return for a *portfolio* of investments is simply the weighted average of the expected rates of return for the individual investments in the portfolio. The weights are the proportion of total value for the investment.

The expected rate of return for a hypothetical portfolio with four risky assets is shown in Exhibit 78-2. The expected return for this portfolio of investments would be 11.5 percent. The effect of adding or dropping any investment from the portfolio would be easy to determine because you would use the new weights based on value and the expected returns for each of the investments. This computation of the expected return for the portfolio $[E(R_{port})]$ can be generalized as follows:

$$E(R_{port}) = \sum_{i=1}^{n} W_i E(R_i)$$ (78-1)

[3] We consider the variance and standard deviation as one measure of risk because the standard deviation is the square root of the variance.

where:

W_i = the percent of the portfolio in asset i
$E(R_i)$ = the expected rate of return for asset i

EXHIBIT 78-1 Computation of Expected Return for an Individual Risky Asset

Probability	Possible Rate of Return (Percent)	Expected Return (Percent)
.25	.08	.0200
.25	.10	.0250
.25	.12	.0300
.25	.14	.0350
		$E(R) = .1100$

EXHIBIT 78-2 Computation of the Expected Return for a Portfolio of Risky Asset

Weight (W_i) (Percent of Portfolio)	Expected Security Return $E(R_i)$	Expected Portfolio Return [$W_i \times E(R_i)$]
.20	.10	.0200
.30	.11	.0330
.30	.12	.0360
.20	.13	.0260
		$E(R_{\text{port}}) = .1150$

3.3 Variance (Standard Deviation) of Returns for an Individual Investment

As noted, we will be using the variance or the standard deviation of returns as the measure of risk (recall that the standard deviation is the square root of the variance). Therefore, at this point, we will demonstrate how you would compute the standard deviation of returns for an individual investment. Subsequently, after discussing some other statistical concepts, we will consider the determination of the standard deviation for a *portfolio* of investments.

The variance, or standard deviation, is a measure of the variation of possible rates of return, R_i, from the expected rate of return $[E(R_i)]$ as follows:

$$\text{Variance } (\sigma^2) = \sum_{i=1}^{n} [R_i - E(R_i)]^2 P_i \qquad \textbf{(78-2)}$$

where

P_i **is the probability of the possible rate of return, R_i**

$$\text{Standard Deviation } (\sigma) = \sqrt{\sum_{i=1}^{n} [R_i - E(R_i)]^2 P_i} \qquad \textbf{(78-3)}$$

The computation of the variance and standard deviation of the expected rate of return for the individual risky asset in Exhibit 78-1 is set forth in Exhibit 78-3.

EXHIBIT 78-3   Computation of the Variance of the Expected Rate of Return for an Individual Risky Asset

Possible Rate of Return (R_i)	Expected Return $E(R_i)$	$R_i - E(R_i)$	$[R_i - E(R_i)]^2$	P_i	$(R_i - E(R_i)^2 P_i$
.08	.11	−.03	.0009	.25	.000225
.10	.11	−.01	.0001	.25	.000025
.12	.11	.01	.0001	.25	.000025
.14	.11	.03	.0009	.25	.000225
					.000500

Variance (σ^2) = .00050
Standard Deviation (σ) = .02236

3.4 Variance (Standard Deviation) of Returns for a Portfolio

Two basic concepts in statistics, covariance and correlation, must be understood before we discuss the formula for the variance of the rate of return for a portfolio.

3.4.1 Covariance of Returns

In this section, we discuss what the covariance of returns is intended to measure, give the formula for computing it, and present an example of the computation. **Covariance** is a measure of the degree to which two variables "move together" relative to their individual mean values over time. In portfolio analysis, we usually are concerned with the covariance of *rates of return* rather than prices or some other variable.[4] A positive covariance means that the rates of return for two investments tend to move in the same direction relative to their individual means during the same time period. In contrast, a negative covariance indicates that the rates of return for two investments tend to move in different directions relative to their means during specified time intervals over time. The *magnitude* of the covariance depends on the variances of the individual return series, as well as on the relationship between the series.

---

[4] Returns, of course, can be measured in a variety of ways, depending on the type of asset. You will recall that we defined returns (R_i) in Reading 76 as:

$$R_i = \frac{EV - BV + CF}{BV}$$

where EV is ending value, BV is beginning value, and CF is the cash flow during the period.

Exhibit 78-4 contains the monthly closing prices and dividends for Coca-Cola and Home Depot. You can use these data to compute monthly rates of return

EXHIBIT 78-4 Computation of Monthly Rates of Return: 2001

Date	Coca-Cola			Home Depot		
	Closing Price	Dividend	Rate of Return (%)	Closing Price	Dividend	Rate of Return (%)
Dec-00	60.938			45.688		
Jan-01	58.000		−4.82	48.200		5.50
Feb-01	53.030		−8.57	42.500		−11.83
Mar-01	45.160	0.18	−14.50	43.100	0.04	1.51
Apr-01	46.190		2.28	47.100		9.28
May-01	47.400		2.62	49.290		4.65
Jun-01	45.000	0.18	−4.68	47.240	0.04	−4.08
Jul-01	44.600		−0.89	50.370		6.63
Aug-01	48.670		9.13	45.950	0.04	−8.70
Sep-01	46.850	0.18	−3.37	38.370		−16.50
Oct-01	47.880		2.20	38.230		−0.36
Nov-01	46.960	0.18	−1.55	46.650	0.05	22.16
Dec-01	47.150		0.40	51.010		9.35
			$E(R_{\text{Coca-Cola}}) = -1.81$			$E(R_{\text{Home Depot}}) = 1.47$

for these two stocks during 2001. Exhibit 78-5 and Exhibit 78-6 contain a time-series plot of the monthly rates of return for the two stocks during 2001. Although the rates of return for the two stocks moved together during some months, in other months they moved in opposite directions. The covariance statistic provides an *absolute* measure of how they moved together over time.

For two assets, i and j, the covariance of rates of return is defined as:

$$\text{Cov}_{ij} = E\{[R_i - E(R_i)][R_j - E(R_j)]\} \qquad \textbf{(78-4)}$$

When we apply this formula to the monthly rates of return for Coca-Cola and Home Depot during 2001, it becomes:

$$\frac{1}{12}\sum_{i=1}^{n}[R_i - E(R_i)][R_j - E(R_j)]$$

As can be seen, if the rates of return for one stock are above (below) its mean rate of return during a given period and the returns for the other stock are likewise above (below) its mean rate of return during this same period, then the *product* of these deviations from the mean is positive. If this happens consistently, the covariance of returns between these two stocks will be some large positive value. If, however, the rate of return for one of the securities is above its mean return while the return on the other security is below its mean return, the product will be negative. If this contrary movement happened consistently, the covariance between the rates of return for the two stocks would be a large negative value.

EXHIBIT 78-5 Time Series of Monthly Rates of Return for Coca-Cola: 2001

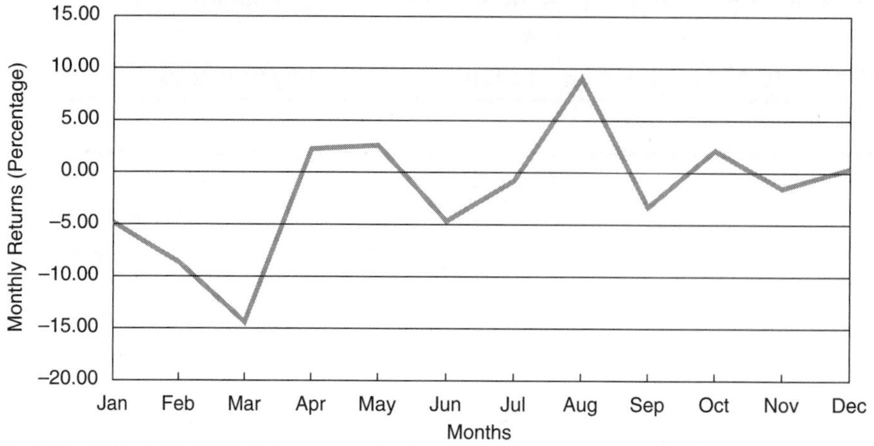

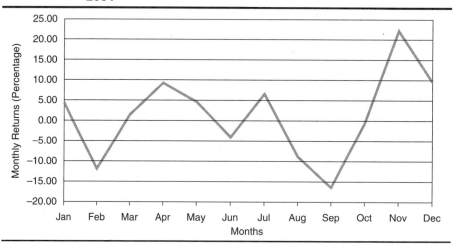

EXHIBIT 78-6 Time Series of Monthly Rates of Return for Home Depot: 2001

Exhibit 78-7 contains the monthly rates of return during 2001 for Coca-Cola and Home Depot as computed in Exhibit 78-4. One might expect the returns for the two stocks to have reasonably low covariance because of the differences in the products of these firms. The expected returns $E(R)$ were the arithmetic mean of the monthly returns:

$$E(R_i) = \frac{1}{12}\sum_{i=1}^{12} R_{it}$$

and

$$E(R_j) = \frac{1}{12}\sum_{j=1}^{12} R_{jt}$$

All figures (except those in the last column) were rounded to the nearest hundredth of 1 percent. As shown in Exhibit 78-4, the average monthly return was −1.81 percent for Coca-Cola and 1.47 percent for Home Depot stock. The results in Exhibit 78-7 show that the covariance between the rates of return for these two stocks was:

$$Cov_{ij} = \frac{1}{12} \times 76.42$$
$$= 6.37$$

EXHIBIT 78-7 Computation of Covariance of Returns for Coca-Cola and Home Depot: 2001

Date	Monthly Return Coca-Cola (R_i)	Home Depot (R_j)	Coca-Cola $R_i - E(R_i)$	Home Depot $R_j - E(R_j)$	Coca-Cola $[R_i - E(R_i)]$ ×	Home Depot $[R_j - E(R_j)]$
Jan-01	−4.82	5.50	−3.01	4.03		−12.13
Feb-01	−8.57	−11.83	−6.76	−13.29		89.81
Mar-01	−14.50	1.51	−12.69	0.04		−0.49
Apr-01	2.28	9.28	4.09	7.81		31.98
May-01	2.62	4.65	4.43	3.18		14.11
Jun-01	−4.68	−4.08	−2.87	−5.54		15.92
Jul-01	−0.89	6.63	0.92	5.16		4.76
Aug-01	9.13	−8.70	10.94	−10.16		−111.16
Sep-01	−3.37	−16.50	−1.56	−17.96		27.97
Oct-01	2.20	−0.36	4.01	−1.83		−7.35
Nov-01	−1.55	22.16	0.27	20.69		5.52
Dec-01	0.40	9.35	2.22	7.88		17.47
	$E(R_i) = -1.81$	$E(R_j) = 1.47$			Sum =	76.42

$$Cov_{ij} = 76.42/12 = 6.37$$

EXHIBIT 78-8 Scatter Plot of Monthly Rates of Return for Coca-Cola and Home Depot: 2001

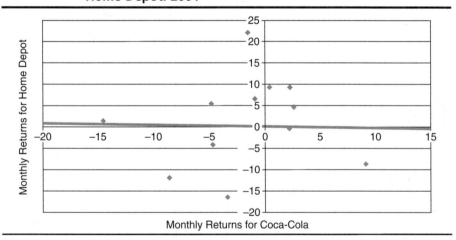

Interpretation of a number such as 6.37 is difficult; is it high or low for covariance? We know the relationship between the two stocks is generally positive, but it is not possible to be more specific. Exhibit 78-8 contains a scatter diagram with paired values of R_{it} and R_{jt} plotted against each other. This plot demonstrates the linear nature and strength of the relationship and shows several instances during 2001 when Coca-Cola experienced negative returns relative to its mean return when Home Depot had positive rates of return relative to its mean.

3.4.2 Covariance and Correlation

Covariance is affected by the variability of the two individual return series. Therefore, a number such as the 6.37 in our example might indicate a weak positive relationship if the two individual series were volatile but would reflect a strong positive relationship if the two series were very stable. Obviously, you want to "standardize" this covariance measure taking into consideration the variability of the two individual return series, as follows:

$$r_{ij} = \frac{\text{Cov}_{ij}}{\sigma_i \sigma_j}$$

(78-5)

where:

r_{ij} = the correlation coefficient of returns
σ_i = the standard deviation of R_{it}
σ_j = the standard deviation of R_{jt}

EXHIBIT 78-9 Computation of Standard Deviation of Returns for Coca-Cola and Home Depot: 2001

Date	Coca-Cola		Home Depot	
	$R_i - E(R_i)$	$[R_i - E(R_i)]^2$	$R_j - E(R_j)$	$[R_j - E(R_j)]^2$
Jan-01	−3.01	9.05	4.03	16.26
Feb-01	−6.76	45.65	−13.29	176.69
Mar-01	−12.69	161.01	0.04	0.00
Apr-01	4.09	16.75	7.81	61.06
May-01	4.43	19.64	3.18	10.13
Jun-01	−2.87	8.24	−5.54	30.74
Jul-01	0.92	0.85	5.16	26.61
Aug-01	10.94	119.64	−10.16	103.28
Sep-01	−1.56	2.42	−17.96	322.67
Oct-01	4.01	16.09	−1.83	3.36
Nov-01	0.27	0.07	20.69	428.01
Dec-01	2.22	4.92	7.88	62.08

	Sum = 404.34		Sum = 1240.90	
	Variance$_j$ = 404.34/12 = 33.69		Variance$_j$ = 240.90/12 = 103.41	
	Standard Deviation$_i$ = $(33.69)^{1/2}$ = 5.80		Standard Deviation$_j$ = $(103.41)^{1/2}$ = 10.17	

Standardizing the covariance by the individual standard deviations yields the **correlation coefficient** (r_{ij}), which can vary only in the range -1 to $+1$. A value of $+1$ would indicate a perfect positive linear relationship between R_i and R_j, meaning the returns for the two stocks move together in a completely linear manner. A value of -1 indicates a perfect negative relationship between the two return series such that when one stock's rate of return is above its mean, the other stock's rate of return will be below its mean by the comparable amount.

To calculate this standardized measure of the relationship, you need to compute the standard deviation for the two individual return series. We already have the values for $R_{it} - E(R_i)$ and $R_{jt} - E(R_j)$ in Exhibit 78-7. We can square each of these values and sum them as shown in Exhibit 78-9 to calculate the variance of each return series.

$$\sigma_i^2 = \frac{1}{12}(404.34) = 33.69$$

and

$$\sigma_j^2 = \frac{1}{12}(1240.90) = 103.41$$

The standard deviation for each series is the square root of the variance for each, as follows:

$$\sigma_i = \sqrt{33.69} = 5.80$$
$$\sigma_j = \sqrt{103.41} = 10.17$$

Thus, based on the covariance between the two series and the individual standard deviations, we can calculate the correlation coefficient between returns for Coca-Cola and Home Depot as

$$r_{ij} = \frac{\text{Cov}_{ij}}{\sigma_i \sigma_j} = \frac{6.37}{(5.80)(10.17)} = \frac{6.37}{58.99} = 0.108$$

Obviously, this formula also implies that

$$\text{Cov}_{ij} = r_{ij}\sigma_i\sigma_j = (.108)(5.80)(10.17) = 6.37$$

as computed in Exhibit 78-7.

As noted, a correlation of $+1.0$ would indicate perfect positive correlation, and a value of -1.0 would mean that the returns moved in a completely opposite direction. A value of zero would mean that the returns had no linear relationship, that is, they were uncorrelated statistically. That does *not* mean that they are independent. The value of $r_{ij} = 0.108$ is quite low. This relatively low correlation is not unusual for stocks in diverse industries (i.e., beverages and building materials). Correlation between stocks of companies *within* some industries approaches 0.85.

3.5 Standard Deviation of a Portfolio

3.5.1 *Portfolio Standard Deviation Formula*

Now that we have discussed the concepts of covariance and correlation, we can consider the formula for computing the standard deviation of returns for a *portfolio* of assets, our measure of risk for a portfolio. As noted, Harry Markowitz derived the formula for computing the standard deviation of a portfolio of assets.[5]

In Exhibit 78-2, we showed that the expected rate of return of the portfolio was the weighted average of the expected returns for the individual assets in the portfolio; the weights were the percentage of value of the portfolio.

One might assume it is possible to derive the standard deviation of the portfolio in the same manner, that is, by computing the weighted average of the standard deviations for the individual assets. This would be a mistake. Markowitz derived the general formula for the standard deviation of a portfolio as follows:[6]

$$\sigma_{\text{port}} = \sqrt{\sum_{i=1}^{n} w_i^2 \sigma_i^2 + \sum_{i=1}^{n} \sum_{\substack{j=1 \\ i \neq j}}^{n} w_i w_j \text{Cov}_{ij}} \qquad (78\text{-}6)$$

where:

σ_{port} = **the standard deviation of the portfolio**

w_i = **the weights of the individual assets in the portfolio, where weights are determined by the proportion of value in the portfolio**

σ_i^2 = **the variance of rates of return for assets i**

Cov_{ij} = **the covariance between the rates of return for assets i and j, where $\text{Cov}_{ij} = r_{ij}\sigma_i\sigma_j$**

This formula indicates that the standard deviation for a portfolio of assets is a function of the weighted average of the individual variances (where the weights are squared), *plus* the weighted covariances between all the assets in the portfolio. The standard deviation for a portfolio of assets encompasses not only the variances of the individual assets but *also* includes the covariances between pairs of individual assets in the portfolio. Further, it can be shown that, in a portfolio with a large number of securities, this formula reduces to the sum of the weighted covariances.

Although most of the subsequent demonstration will consider portfolios with only two assets because it is possible to show the effect in two dimensions, we will demonstrate the computations for a three-asset portfolio. Still, it is important at this point to consider what happens in a large portfolio with many assets. Specifically, what happens to the portfolio's standard deviation when you add a new security to such a portfolio? As shown by the formula, we see two effects. The first is the asset's own variance of returns, and the second is the covariance between the returns of this new asset and the returns of *every other asset that is already in the portfolio*. The relative weight of these numerous covariances is substantially greater than the asset's unique variance; and the more assets in the portfolio, the more this is true. This means that the important factor to consider when adding an investment to a portfolio that contains a number of other investments is *not* the investment's own variance but *its average covariance with all the other investments in the portfolio*.

In the following examples, we will consider the simple case of a two-asset portfolio. We do these relatively simple calculations and provide graphs with two assets to demonstrate the impact of different covariances on the total risk (standard deviation) of the portfolio.

---

[5] Markowitz, *Portfolio Selection*.

[6] For the detailed derivation of this formula, see Markowitz, *Portfolio Selection*.

3.5.2 Demonstration of the Portfolio Standard Deviation Calculation

Because of the assumptions used in developing the Markowitz portfolio model, any asset or portfolio of assets can be described by two characteristics: the expected rate of return and the expected standard deviation of returns. Therefore, the following demonstrations can be applied to two *individual* assets with the indicated return–standard deviation characteristics and correlation coefficients, two *portfolios* of assets, or two *asset classes* with the indicated return–standard deviation characteristics and correlation coefficients.

3.5.2.1 Equal Risk and Return—Changing Correlations

Consider first the case in which both assets have the same expected return and expected standard deviation of return. As an example, let us assume

$$E(R_1) = 0.20$$
$$\sigma_1 = 0.10$$
$$E(R_2) = 0.20$$
$$\sigma_2 = 0.10$$

To show the effect of different covariances, assume different levels of correlation between the two assets. Consider the following examples where the two assets have equal weights in the portfolio ($W_1 = 0.50$; $W_2 = 0.50$). Therefore, the only value that changes in each example is the correlation between the returns for the two assets.

Recall that

$$\text{Cov}_{ij} = r_{ij}\sigma_i\sigma_j$$

Consider the following alternative correlation coefficients and the covariances they yield. The covariance term in the equation will be equal to $r_{1,2}(0.10)(0.10)$ because both standard deviations are 0.10.

A. $r_{1,2} = 1.00$; $\text{Cov}_{1,2} = (1.00)(0.10)(0.10) = 0.010$

B. $r_{1,2} = 0.50$; $\text{Cov}_{1,2} = (0.50)(0.10)(0.10) = 0.005$

C. $r_{1,2} = 0.00$; $\text{Cov}_{1,2} = 0.000(0.10)(0.10) = 0.000$

D. $r_{1,2} = -0.50$; $\text{Cov}_{1,2} = (-0.50)(0.10)(0.10) = -0.005$

E. $r_{1,2} = -1.00$; $\text{Cov}_{1,2} = (-1.00)(0.10)(0.10) = -0.01$

Now let us see what happens to the standard deviation of the portfolio under these five conditions. Recall from Equation 78-6 that

$$\sigma_{\text{port}} = \sqrt{\sum_{i=1}^{n} w_i^2 \sigma_i^2 + \sum_{\substack{i=1}}^{n} \sum_{\substack{j=1 \\ i \neq j}}^{n} w_i w_j \text{Cov}_{ij}}$$

When this general formula is applied to a two-asset portfolio, it is

$$\sigma_{\text{port}} = \sqrt{w_1^2\sigma_1^2 + w_2^2\sigma_2^2 + 2w_1 w_2 r_{1,2}\sigma_1\sigma_2} \tag{78-7}$$

or

$$\sigma_{\text{port}} = \sqrt{w_1^2\sigma_1^2 + w_2^2\sigma_2^2 + 2w_1 w_2 \text{Cov}_{1,2}}$$

Thus, in Case A,

$$\sigma_{\text{port(A)}} = \sqrt{(0.5)^2(0.10)^2 + (0.5)^2(0.10)^2 + 2(0.5)(0.5)(0.01)}$$
$$= \sqrt{(0.25)(0.01) + (0.25)(0.01) + 2(0.25)(0.01)}$$
$$= \sqrt{0.01}$$
$$= 0.10$$

In this case, where the returns for the two assets are perfectly positively correlated ($r_{1,2} = 1.0$), the standard deviation for the portfolio is, in fact, the weighted average of the individual standard deviations. The important point is that we get no real benefit from combining two assets that are perfectly correlated; they are like one asset already because their returns move together.

Now consider Case B, where $r_{1,2}$ equals 0.50:

$$\sigma_{\text{port(B)}} = \sqrt{(0.5)^2(0.10)^2 + (0.5)^2(0.10)^2 + 2(0.5)(0.5)(0.005)}$$
$$= \sqrt{(0.0025) + (0.0025) + 2(0.25)(0.005)}$$
$$= \sqrt{0.0075}$$
$$= 0.0868$$

The only term that changed from Case A is the last term, $\text{Cov}_{1,2}$, which changed from 0.01 to 0.005. As a result, the standard deviation of the portfolio declined by about 13 percent, from 0.10 to 0.0868. Note that *the expected return did not change* because it is simply the weighted average of the individual expected returns; it is equal to 0.20 in both cases.

You should be able to confirm through your own calculations that the standard deviations for Portfolios C and D are as follows:

C. 0.0707

D. 0.05

The final case where the correlation between the two assets is -1.00 indicates the ultimate benefits of diversification:

$$\sigma_{\text{port(E)}} = \sqrt{(0.5)^2(0.10)^2 + (0.5)^2(0.10)^2 + 2(0.5)(0.5)(-0.01)}$$
$$= \sqrt{(0.0050) + (-0.0050)}$$
$$= \sqrt{0}$$
$$= 0$$

Here, the negative covariance term exactly offsets the individual variance terms, leaving an overall standard deviation of the portfolio of zero. *This would be a risk-free portfolio.*

Exhibit 78-10 illustrates a graph of such a pattern. Perfect negative correlation gives a mean combined return for the two securities over time equal to the mean for each of them, so the returns for the portfolio show no variability. Any returns above and below the mean for each of the assets are *completely offset* by the return for the other asset, so there is *no variability* in total returns, that is, *no risk*, for the portfolio. This combination of two assets that are completely negatively correlated provides the maximum benefits of diversification—it completely eliminates risk.

The graph in Exhibit 78-11 shows the difference in the risk-return posture for these five cases. As noted, the only effect of the change in correlation is the change in the standard deviation of this two-asset portfolio. Combining assets that are not perfectly correlated does *not* affect the expected return of the portfolio,

EXHIBIT 78-10 Time Patterns of Returns for Two Assets with Perfect Negative Correlation

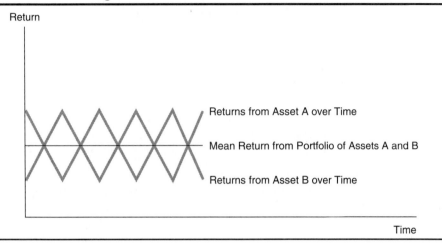

but it *does* reduce the risk of the portfolio (as measured by its standard deviation). When we eventually reach the ultimate combination of perfect negative correlation, risk is eliminated.

EXHIBIT 78-11 Risk-Return Plot for Portfolios with Equal Returns and Standard Deviations but Different Correlations

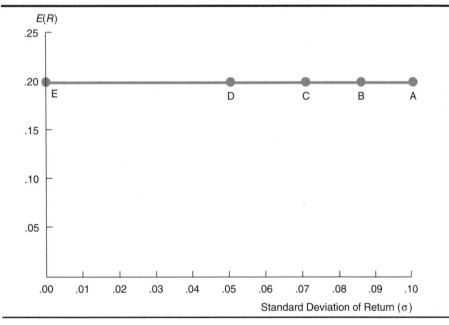

3.5.2.2 *Combining Stocks with Different Returns and Risk*

The previous discussion indicated what happens when only the correlation coefficient (covariance) differs between the assets. We now consider two assets (or portfolios) with different expected rates of return and individual standard deviations.[7] We will show what happens when we vary the correlations between them.

---

[7] As noted, these could be two asset classes. For example, Asset 1 could be low risk–low return bonds and Asset 2 could be higher-return–higher-risk stocks.

We will assume two assets with the following characteristics:

Asset	$E(R_i)$	W_i	σ_i^2	σ_i
1	.10	.50	.0049	.07
2	.20	.50	.0100	.10

The previous set of correlation coefficients gives a different set of covariances because the standard deviations are different. For example, the covariance in Case B where $r_{1,2} = 0.50$ would be $(0.50)(0.07)(0.10) = 0.0035$.

Case	Correlation Coefficient	Covariance $(R_{ij}\sigma_i\sigma_j)$
A	+1.00	.0070
B	+0.50	.0035
C	0.00	.0000
D	−0.50	−.0035
E	−1.00	−.0070

Because we are assuming the same weights in all cases $(0.50 - 0.50)$, the expected return in every instance will be

$$E(R_{\text{port}}) = 0.50(0.10) + 0.50(0.20)$$
$$= 0.15$$

The standard deviation for Case A will be

$$\sigma_{\text{port(A)}} = \sqrt{(0.5)^2(0.07)^2 + (0.5)^2(0.10)^2 + 2(0.5)(0.5)(0.0070)}$$
$$= \sqrt{(0.001225) + (0.0025) + (0.5)(0.0070)}$$
$$= \sqrt{0.007225}$$
$$= 0.085$$

Again, with perfect positive correlation, the standard deviation of the portfolio is the weighted average of the standard deviations of the individual assets:

$$(0.5)(0.07) + (0.5)(0.10) = 0.085$$

As you might envision, changing the weights with perfect positive correlation causes the standard deviation for the portfolio to change in a linear fashion. This is an important point to remember when we discuss the capital asset pricing model (CAPM) in the next reading.

For Cases B, C, D, and E, the standard deviation for the portfolio would be as follows:[8]

$$\sigma_{\text{port(B)}} = \sqrt{(0.001225) + (0.0025) + (0.5)(0.0035)}$$
$$= \sqrt{(0.005475)}$$
$$= 0.07399$$

---

[8] In all the following examples, we will skip some steps because you are now aware that only the last term changes. You are encouraged to work out the individual steps to ensure that you understand the computational procedure.

$$\sigma_{\text{port(C)}} = \sqrt{(0.001225) + (0.0025) + (0.5)(0.00)}$$
$$= 0.0610$$

$$\sigma_{\text{port(D)}} = \sqrt{(0.001225) + (0.0025) + (0.5)(-0.0035)}$$
$$= 0.0444$$

$$\sigma_{\text{port(E)}} = \sqrt{(0.003725) + (0.5)(-0.0070)}$$
$$= 0.015$$

Note that, in this example, with perfect negative correlation the standard deviation of the portfolio is not zero. This is because the different examples have equal weights, but the individual standard deviations are not equal.[9]

Exhibit 78-12 shows the results for the two individual assets and the portfolio of the two assets assuming the correlation coefficients vary as set forth in Cases A through E. As before, the expected return does not change because the proportions are always set at $0.50 - 0.50$, so all the portfolios lie along the horizontal line at the return, $E(R) = 0.15$.

EXHIBIT 78-12 Risk-Return Plot for Portfolios with Different Returns, Standard Deviations, and Correlations

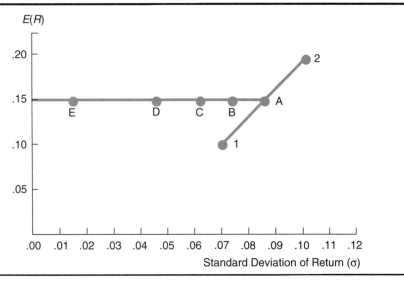

3.5.2.3 Constant Correlation with Changing Weights

If we changed the weights of the two assets while holding the correlation coefficient constant, we would derive a set of combinations that trace an ellipse starting at Asset 2, going through the $0.50 - 0.50$ point, and ending at Asset 1. We can demonstrate this with Case C, in which the correlation coefficient of zero eases the computations. We begin with 100 percent in Asset 2 (Case F) and change the weights as follows, ending with 100 percent in Asset 1 (Case M).

---

[9] The two appendixes to this reading show proofs for equal weights with equal variances and solve for the appropriate weights to get zero standard deviation when standard deviations are not equal.

[10] Again, you are encouraged to fill in the steps we skipped in the computations.

Case	W_1	W_2	$E(R_i)$
F	.00	1.00	.20
G	.20	.80	.18
H	.40	.60	.16
I	.50	.50	.15
J	.60	.40	.14
K	.80	.20	.12
M	1.00	.00	.10

We already know the standard deviation (σ) for Portfolio I. In Cases F, G, H, J, K, and M, the standard deviations would be[10]

$$\sigma_{port(G)} = \sqrt{(0.20)^2(0.07)^2 + (0.80)^2(0.10)^2 + 2(0.20)(0.80)(0.00)}$$

$$= \sqrt{(0.04)(0.0049) + (0.64)(0.01) + (0)}$$

$$= \sqrt{(0.006596)}$$

$$= 0.0812$$

$$\sigma_{port(H)} = \sqrt{(0.40)^2(0.07)^2 + (0.60)^2(0.10)^2 + 2(0.40)(0.60)(0.00)}$$

$$= \sqrt{(0.004384)}$$

$$= 0.0662$$

$$\sigma_{port(J)} = \sqrt{(0.60)^2(0.07)^2 + (0.40)^2(0.10)^2 + 2(0.60)(0.40)(0.00)}$$

$$= \sqrt{(0.003364)}$$

$$= 0.0580$$

$$\sigma_{port(K)} = \sqrt{(0.80)^2(0.07)^2 + (0.20)^2(0.10)^2 + 2(0.80)(0.20)(0.00)}$$

$$= \sqrt{(0.003536)}$$

$$= 0.0595$$

These alternative weights with a constant correlation would yield the following risk-return combinations:

Case	W_1	W_2	$E(R_i)$	σ_{port}
F	0.00	1.00	0.20	0.1000
G	0.20	0.80	0.18	0.0812
H	0.40	0.60	0.16	0.0662
I	0.50	0.50	0.15	0.0610
J	0.60	0.40	0.14	0.0580
K	0.80	0.20	0.12	0.0595
M	1.00	0.00	0.10	0.0700

A graph of these combinations appears in Exhibit 78-13 for the curve with $r_{1,2} = +0.00$. You could derive a complete curve by simply varying the weighting by smaller increments.

A notable result is that with low, zero, or negative correlations, it is possible to derive portfolios that have *lower risk than either single asset*. In our set of examples where $r_{ij} = 0.00$, this occurs in Cases H, I, J, and K. This ability to reduce risk is the essence of diversification. As shown in Exhibit 78-13, assuming the normal risk-return relationship where assets with higher risk (larger standard deviation of returns) provide high rates of return, it is possible for a conservative investor to experience *both* lower risk *and* higher return by diversifying into a higher-risk –higher-return asset assuming the correlation between the two assets is fairly low. As shown in Exhibit 78-13, in the case where it is assumed that the correlation was zero (0.00), the low-risk investor at Point 1 who would receive a return of 10 percent and risk of 7 percent could *increase* his/her return to 14 percent *and* experience a *decline* in risk to 5.8 percent by investing (diversifying) 40 percent of the portfolio in riskier Asset 2. As noted, the benefits of diversification are critically dependent on the correlation between assets; but, even if the correlation is not zero, you still derive some benefit as shown in Exhibit 78-13 when the correlation is 0.50.

EXHIBIT 78-13 Portfolio Risk-Return Plots for Different Weights When
$$r_{i,j} = +1.00; +0.50; 0.00; -0.50; -1.00$$

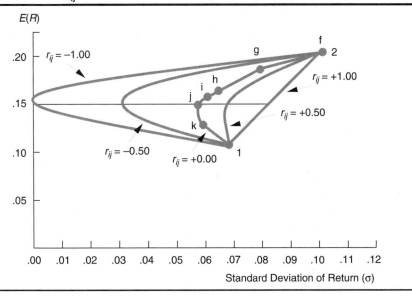

As shown in Exhibit 78-13, the curvature in the graph depends on the correlation between the two assets or portfolios. With $r_{ij} = +1.00$, the combinations lie along a straight line between the two assets. When $r_{ij} = 0.50$, the curve is to the right of our $r_{ij} = 0.00$ curve, while the $r_{ij} = -0.50$ is to the left. Finally, when $r_{ij} = -1.00$, the graph would be two straight lines that would touch at the vertical line (zero risk) with some combination. As discussed in Appendix B of this reading, it is possible to solve for the specified set of weights that would give a portfolio with zero risk. In this case, it is $W_1 = 0.588$ and $W_2 = 0.412$.

3.6 A Three-Asset Portfolio

A demonstration of what occurs with a three-asset class portfolio is useful because it shows the dynamics of the portfolio process when we add additional assets to a portfolio. It also shows the rapid growth in the computations required, which is why we will stop at three assets.

In this example, we will combine three asset classes we have been discussing: stocks, bonds, and cash equivalents.[11] We will assume the following characteristics for these assets:

Asset Classes	$E(R_i)$	σ_i	W_i
Stocks (S)	.12	.20	.60
Bonds (B)	.08	.10	.30
Cash equivalent (C)	.04	.03	.10

The correlations are as follows.

$$r_{S,B} = 0.25; \; r_{S,C} = -0.08; \; r_{B,C} = 0.15$$

Given the weights specified, the $E(R_p)$ is:

$$E(R_p) = (0.60)(0.12) + (0.30)(0.08) + (0.10)(0.04)$$
$$= (0.072 + 0.024 + 0.004) = 0.100 = 10.00\%$$

When we apply the generalized formula to the expected standard deviation of a three-asset class, it is as follows:

$$\sigma_p^2 = [\, W_S^2 \sigma_S^2 + W_B^2 \sigma_B^2 + W_C^2 \sigma_C^2 \,] +$$
$$[\, 2W_S W_B \sigma_S \sigma_B \, r_{S,B} + 2W_S W_C \sigma_S \sigma_C \, r_{S,C} + 2W_B W_C \sigma_B \sigma_C \, r_{B,C} \,]$$

Using the characteristics specified, the standard deviation of this three-asset class portfolio (σ_p) would be:

$$\sigma_p^2 = [(0.6)^2 (0.20)^2 + (0.3) + (0.10)^2 + (0.1)^2 (0.03)^2]$$
$$+ \{[2(0.6)(0.3)(0.20)(0.10)(0.25)]$$
$$+ [(0.6)(0.1)(0.20)(0.03)(-0.08)]$$
$$+ [2(0.3)(0.1)(0.10)(0.03)(0.15)]\}$$
$$= [0.015309] + \{[0.0018] + [-0.0000576 + \{0.000027]\}$$
$$= 0.0170784$$
$$\sigma_p = (0.0170784)^{1/2} = 0.1306 = 13.06\%$$

3.7 Estimation Issues

It is important to keep in mind that the results of this portfolio asset allocation depend on the accuracy of the statistical inputs. In the current instance, this means that for every asset (or asset class) being considered for inclusion in the portfolio, you must estimate its expected returns and standard deviation. In addition, the correlation coefficient among the entire set of assets must also be estimated. The number of correlation estimates can be significant—for example, for a portfolio of 100 securities, the number is 4,950 (that is, $99 + 98 + 97 + \ldots$).
The potential source of error that arises from these approximations is referred to as *estimation risk*.

---

[11] The asset allocation articles regularly contained in *The Wall Street Journal* generally refer to these three asset classes.

It is possible to reduce the number of correlation coefficients that must be estimated by assuming that stock returns can be described by a single index market model as follows:

$$R_i = a_i + b_i R_m + \varepsilon_i \qquad \textbf{(78-8)}$$

where:

> b_i = **the slope coefficient that relates the returns for security i to the returns for the aggregate stock market**
> R_m = **the returns for the aggregate stock market**

If all the securities are similarly related to the market and a slope coefficient (b_i) is derived for each one, it can be shown that the correlation coefficient between two securities i and j is given as:

$$r_{ij} = b_i b_j \frac{\sigma_m^2}{\sigma_i \sigma_j} \qquad \textbf{(78-9)}$$

where:

> σ_m^2 = **the variance of returns for the aggregate stock market**

This reduces the number of estimates from 4,950 to 100—that is, once you have derived a slope estimate (b_i) for each security, the correlation estimates can be computed. Keep in mind that this assumes that the single index market model provides a good estimate of security returns.

3.8 The Efficient Frontier

If we examined different two-asset combinations and derived the curves assuming all the possible weights, we would have a graph like that in Exhibit 78-14. The envelope curve that contains the best of all these possible combinations is referred to as the **efficient frontier.** Specifically, *the efficient frontier represents that set of portfolios that has the maximum rate of return for every given level of risk, or the minimum risk for every level of return.* An example of such a frontier is shown in Exhibit 78-15. Every portfolio that lies on the efficient frontier has either a higher rate of return for equal risk or lower risk for an equal rate of return than some portfolio beneath the frontier. Thus, we would say that Portfolio A in Exhibit 78-15 *dominates* Portfolio C because it has an equal rate of return but substantially less risk. Similarly, Portfolio B dominates Portfolio C because it has equal risk but a higher expected rate of return. Because of the benefits of diversification among imperfectly correlated assets, we would expect the efficient frontier to be made up of *portfolios* of investments rather than individual securities. Two possible exceptions arise at the end points, which represent the asset with the highest return and that asset with the lowest risk.

As an investor, you will target a point along the efficient frontier based on your utility function and your attitude toward risk. No portfolio on the efficient frontier can dominate any other portfolio on the efficient frontier. All of these portfolios have different return and risk measures, with expected rates of return that increase with higher risk.

EXHIBIT 78-14 Numerous Portfolio Combinations of Available Assets

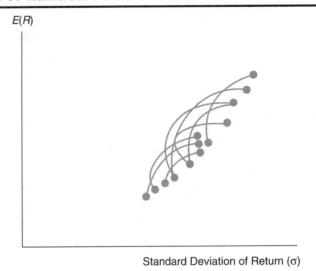

EXHIBIT 78-15 Efficient Frontier for Alternative Portfolios

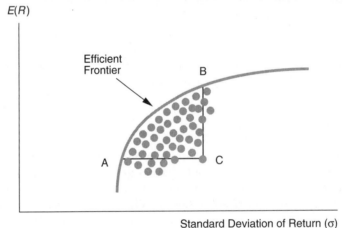

3.9 The Efficient Frontier and Investor Utility

The curve in Exhibit 78-15 shows that the slope of the efficient frontier curve decreases steadily as you move upward. This implies that adding equal increments of risk as you move up the efficient frontier gives you diminishing increments of expected return. To evaluate this slope, we calculate the slope of the efficient frontier as follows:

$$\frac{\Delta E(R_{\text{port}})}{\Delta \sigma_{\text{port}}}$$

(78-10)

An individual investor's utility curves specify the trade-offs he or she is willing to make between expected return and risk. In conjunction with the efficient frontier, these utility curves determine which *particular* portfolio on the efficient frontier best suits an individual investor. Two investors will choose the same portfolio from the efficient set only if their utility curves are identical.

EXHIBIT 78-16 Selecting an Optimal Risky Portfolio on the Efficient Frontier

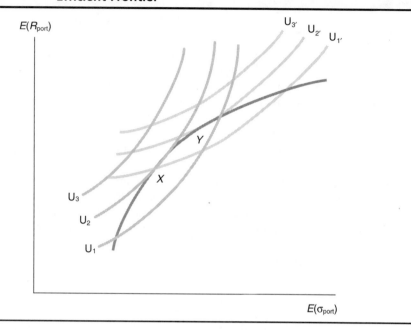

Exhibit 78-16 shows two sets of utility curves along with an efficient frontier of investments. The curves labeled U_1 are for a strongly risk-averse investor (with U_3 U_2 U_1). These utility curves are quite steep, indicating that the investor will not tolerate much additional risk to obtain additional returns. The investor is equally disposed toward any $E(R)$, σ combinations along a specific utility curve, such as U_1.

The curves labeled $U_{1'}$ ($U_{3'}$ $U_{2'}$ $U_{1'}$) characterize a less-risk-averse investor. Such an investor is willing to tolerate a bit more risk to get a higher expected return.

The **optimal portfolio** is the portfolio on the efficient frontier that has the highest utility for a given investor. It lies at *the point of tangency between the efficient frontier and the curve with the highest possible utility*. A conservative investor's highest utility is at point X in Exhibit 78-16, where the curve U_2 just touches the efficient frontier. A less-risk-averse investor's highest utility occurs at point Y, which represents a portfolio with a higher expected return and higher risk than the portfolio at X.

4
THE INTERNET

Investments Online

By seeking to operate on the efficient frontier, portfolio managers try to minimize risk for a certain level of return, or maximize return for a given level of risk. Software programs, called optimizers, are used by portfolio managers to determine the shape of the efficient frontier as well as to determine some of the portfolios that lie on it. Financial planners use information on past returns and manager performance, in addition to optimizers, to make recommendations to their clients. Some interesting websites for money managers include:

▸ **http://www.pionline.com** This is the home page for *Pensions and Investments,* a newspaper for money managers. Items on the home page include links to news of interest to managers and ePIPER performance data on a number of equity, fixed income, real estate, and global portfolios from money manager and pension funds. Contains many links to organizations such as central banks, consultants, and sellers of investment-related products.

▸ **http://www.investmentnews.com** *Investment News* is a sister publication to *Pensions and Investments,* with a focus toward the financial advisor. This site includes information on financial planning, the mutual fund industry, regulation, equity performance, and industry trends.

Software for creating efficient frontiers are available from firms such as

▸ **http://www.ibbotson.com** Ibbotson Associates
▸ **http://www.styleadvisor.com** Zephyr Associates
▸ **http://www.wagner.com** Wagner Associates
▸ **http://www.effisols.com** Efficient Solutions, Inc.

SUMMARY   5

▸ The basic Markowitz portfolio model derived the expected rate of return for a portfolio of assets and a measure of expected risk, which is the standard deviation of the expected rate of return. Markowitz shows that the expected rate of return of a portfolio is the weighted average of the expected return for the individual investments in the portfolio. The standard deviation of a portfolio is a function not only of the standard deviations for the individual investments but *also* of the covariance between the rates of return for all the pairs of assets in the portfolio. In a large portfolio, these covariances are the important factors.

▸ Different weights or amounts of a portfolio held in various assets yield a curve of potential combinations. Correlation coefficients among assets are the critical factor you must consider when selecting investments because you can maintain your rate of return while reducing the risk level of your portfolio by combining assets or portfolios that have low positive or negative correlation.

▸ Assuming numerous assets and a multitude of combination curves, the efficient frontier is the envelope curve that encompasses all of the best combinations. It defines the set of portfolios that has the highest expected return for each given level of risk or the minimum risk for each given level of return. From this set of dominant portfolios, you select the one that lies at the point of tangency between the efficient frontier and your highest utility curve. Because risk-return utility functions differ among investors, your point of tangency and, therefore, your portfolio choice will probably differ from those of other investors.

▸ At this point, we understand that an optimum portfolio is a combination of investments, each having desirable individual risk–return characteristics that also fit together based on their correlations. This deeper understanding of portfolio theory should lead you to reflect back on our earlier discussion of global investing. Because many foreign stock and bond investments provide superior rates of return compared with U.S. securities *and* have low correlations with portfolios of U.S. stocks and bonds as shown in Chapter 3, including these foreign securities in your portfolio will help you to reduce the overall risk of your portfolio while possibly increasing your rate of return.

PROBLEMS

1. The following are the monthly rates of return for Madison Software Corp. and for Kayleigh Electric during a six-month period.

Month	Madison Software	Kayleigh Electric
1	−.04	.07
2	.06	−.02
3	−.07	−.10
4	.12	.15
5	−.02	−.06
6	.05	.02

Compute the following:

A. Expected monthly rate of return $[E(R_i)]$ for each stock

B. Standard deviation of returns for each stock

C. The covariance between the rates of return

D. The correlation coefficient between the rates of return

What level of correlation did you expect? How did your expectations compare with the computed correlation? Would these two stocks offer a good chance for diversification? Why or why not?

2. You are considering two assets with the following characteristics:

$$E(R_1) = .15 \qquad \sigma_1 = .10 \qquad W_1 = .5$$
$$E(R_2) = .20 \qquad \sigma_2 = .20 \qquad W_2 = .5$$

Compute the mean and standard deviation of two portfolios if $r_{1,2} = 0.40$ and -0.60, respectively. Plot the two portfolios on a risk-return graph and briefly explain the results.

3. Given: $E(R_1) = .10$
$$E(R_2) = .15$$
$$\sigma_1 = .03$$
$$\sigma_2 = .05$$

Calculate the expected returns and expected standard deviations of a two-stock portfolio in which Stock 1 has a weight of 60 percent under the following conditions:

A. $r_{1,2} = 1.00$

B. $r_{1,2} = 0.75$

C. $r_{1,2} = 0.25$

D. $r_{1,2} = 0.00$

E. $r_{1,2} = -0.25$

F. $r_{1,2} = -0.75$

G. $r_{1,2} = -1.00$

Calculate the expected returns and expected standard deviations of a two-stock portfolio having a correlation coefficient of 0.70 under the following conditions:

A. $w_1 = 1.00$

B. $w_1 = 0.75$

C. $w_1 = 0.50$

D. $w_1 = 0.25$

E. $w_1 = 0.05$

REFERENCES

▷ Elton, Edwin J., and Martin J. Gruber. *Modern Portfolio Theory and Investment Analysis,* 5th ed. New York: John Wiley & Sons, Inc., 1995.

▷ Farrell, James L., Jr. *Portfolio Management: Theory and Application,* 2d ed. New York: McGraw-Hill, 1997.

▷ Harrington, Diana R. *Modern Portfolio Theory, the Capital Asset Pricing Model, and Arbitrage Pricing Theory: A User's Guide,* 2d ed. Englewood Cliffs, N.J.: Prentice-Hall, 1987.

▷ Maginn, John L., and Donald L. Tuttle, eds. *Managing Investment Portfolios: A Dynamic Process,* 2d ed. Sponsored by The Institute of Chartered Financial Analysts. Boston: Warren, Gorham & Lamont, 1990.

▷ Markowitz, Harry. "Portfolio Selection." *Journal of Finance* 7, no. 1 (March 1952).

▷ Markowitz, Harry. *Portfolio Selection: Efficient Diversification of Investments.* New York: John Wiley & Sons, 1959.

APPENDIX

78A Proof That Minimum Portfolio Variance Occurs with Equal Weights When Securities Have Equal Variance

When $\sigma_1 = \sigma_2$, we have:

$$\sigma_{\text{port}}^2 = w_1^2(\sigma_1)^2 + (1 - w_1)^2(\sigma_1)^2 - 2w_1(1 - w_1)r_{1,2}(\sigma_1)^2$$
$$= (\sigma_1)^2[w_1^2 + 1 - 2w_1 + w_1^2 + 2w_1r_{1,2} - 2w_1^2r_{1,2}]$$
$$= (\sigma_1)^2[2w_1^2 + 1 - 2w_1 + 2w_1r_{1,2} - 2w_1^2r_{1,2}]$$

For this to be a minimum,

$$\frac{\partial(\sigma_{\text{port}}^2)}{\partial w_1} = 0 = (\sigma_1)^2[4w_1 \times 2 + 2r_{1,2} \times 4w_1r_{1,2}]$$

Assuming $(\sigma_1)^2 > 0$,

$$4w_1 - 2 + 2r_{1,2} - 4w_1r_{1,2} = 0$$
$$4w_1(1 - r_{1,2}) - 2(1 - r_{1,2}) = 0$$

from which

$$w_1 \frac{2(1 - r_{1,2})}{4(1 - r_{1,2})} = \frac{1}{2}$$

regardless of $r_{1,2}$. Thus, if $\sigma_1 = \sigma_2$, σ_{port}^2 will *always* be minimized by choosing $w_1 = w_2 = 1/2$, regardless of the value of $r_{1,2}$, except when $r_{1,2} = +1$ (in which case $\sigma_{\text{port}} = \sigma_1 = \sigma_2$. This can be verified by checking the second-order condition

$$\frac{\partial(\sigma_{\text{port}}^2)}{\partial w_1^2} > 0$$

APPENDIX

78B Derivation of Weights That Will Give Zero Variance When Correlation Equals –1.00

$$\sigma^2_{port} = w_1^2(\sigma_1)^2 + (1 - w_1)^2(\sigma_2)^2 - 2w_1(1 - w_1)r_{1,2}(\sigma_1)(\sigma_2)$$
$$= w_1^2(\sigma_1)^2 + (\sigma_2)^2 - 2w_1(\sigma_2) - w_1^2(\sigma_2)^2 + 2w_1 r_{1,2}(\sigma_1)(\sigma_2) - 2w_1^2 r_{1,2}(\sigma_1)(\sigma_2)$$

If $r_{1,2} = 1$, this can be rearranged and expressed as

$$\sigma^2_{port} = w_1^2[(\sigma_1)^2 + 2(\sigma_1)(\sigma_2) + (\sigma_2)^2] - 2w[(\sigma_2)^2 + (\sigma_1)(\sigma_2)] + (\sigma_2)^2$$
$$= w_1^2[(\sigma_1) + (\sigma_2)]^2 - 2w_1(\sigma_2)[(\sigma_1) - (\sigma_2)] + (\sigma_2)^2$$
$$= \{w_1[(\sigma_1) + (\sigma_2)] - (\sigma_2)\}^2$$

We want to find the weight, w_1, which will reduce (σ^2_{port}) to *zero;* therefore,

$$w_1[(\sigma_1) + (\sigma_2)] - (\sigma_2) = 0$$

which yields

$$w_1 = \frac{(\sigma_2)}{(\sigma_1) + (\sigma_2)}, \text{ and } w_2 = 1 - w_1 = \frac{(\sigma_1)}{(\sigma_1) + (\sigma_2)}$$

AN INTRODUCTION TO ASSET PRICING MODELS

LEARNING OUTCOMES

The candidate should be able to:

a. list the assumptions of the capital market theory;

b. explain what happens to the expected return, the standard deviation of returns, and possible risk-return combinations when a risk-free asset is combined with a portfolio of risky assets;

c. identify the market portfolio, and describe the role of the market portfolio in the formation of the capital market line (CML);

d. define systematic and unsystematic risk and explain why an investor should not expect to receive additional return for assuming unsystematic risk;

e. describe the capital asset pricing model, diagram the security market line (SML), and define beta;

f. calculate and interpret, using the SML, the expected return on a security, and evaluate whether the security is undervalued, overvalued, or properly valued;

g. explain how the systematic risk of an asset is estimated using the characteristic line.

INTRODUCTION 1

Following the development of portfolio theory by Markowitz, two major theories have been put forth that derive a model for the valuation of risky assets. In this reading, we introduce one of these two models—that is, the capital asset pricing model (CAPM). The background on the CAPM is important at this point in the book because the risk measure implied by this model is a necessary input for our subsequent discussion on the valuation of risky assets. The presentation concerns capital market theory and the capital asset pricing model that was developed almost concurrently by three individuals. Subsequently, an alternative multifactor asset valuation model was proposed, the arbitrage pricing theory (APT). This has led to the development of numerous other multifactor models that are the subject of the following reading.

Investment Analysis Portfolio Management, by Frank K. Reilly and Keith C. Brown, Copyright © 2003. Reprinted with permission of South-Western, a division of Thomson Learning.

2   CAPITAL MARKET THEORY: AN OVERVIEW

Because capital market theory builds on portfolio theory, this reading begins where the discussion of the Markowitz efficient frontier ended. We assume that you have examined the set of risky assets and derived the aggregate efficient frontier. Further, we assume that you and all other investors want to maximize your utility in terms of risk and return, so you will choose portfolios of risky assets on the efficient frontier at points where your utility maps are tangent to the frontier as shown in Exhibit 78-16. When you make your investment decision in this manner, you are referred to as a *Markowitz efficient investor.*

Capital market theory extends portfolio theory and develops a model for pricing all risky assets. The final product, the **capital asset pricing model (CAPM),** will allow you to determine the required rate of return for any risky asset.

We begin with the background of capital market theory that includes the underlying assumptions of the theory and a discussion of the factors that led to its development following the Markowitz portfolio theory. This includes an analysis of the effect of assuming the existence of a risk-free asset.

Notably, assuming the existence of a risk-free rate has significant implications for the potential return and risk and alternative risk-return combinations. This discussion implies a central portfolio of risky assets on the efficient frontier, which we call the **market portfolio.** We discuss the market portfolio in the third section and what it implies regarding different types of risk.

The fourth section considers which types of risk are relevant to an investor who believes in capital market theory. Having defined a measure of risk, we consider how you determine your required rate of return on an investment. You can then compare this required rate of return to your estimate of the asset's expected rate of return during your investment horizon to determine whether the asset is undervalued or overvalued. The section ends with a demonstration of how to calculate the risk measure implied by capital market theory.

2.1 Background for Capital Market Theory

When dealing with any theory in science, economics, or finance, it is necessary to articulate a set of assumptions that specify how the world is expected to act. This allows the theoretician to concentrate on developing a theory that explains how some facet of the world will respond to changes in the environment. In this section, we consider the main assumptions that underlie the development of capital market theory.

2.1.1 Assumptions of Capital Market Theory

Because capital market theory builds on the Markowitz portfolio model, it requires the same assumptions, along with some additional ones:

1. All investors are Markowitz efficient investors who want to target points on the efficient frontier. The exact location on the efficient frontier and, therefore, the specific portfolio selected will depend on the individual investor's risk-return utility function.

2. Investors can borrow or lend any amount of money at the risk-free rate of return (RFR). Clearly, it is always possible to lend money at the nominal risk-free rate by buying riskfree securities such as government T-bills. It is not always possible to borrow at this riskfree rate, but we will see that assuming a higher borrowing rate does not change the general results.

3. All investors have homogeneous expectations; that is, they estimate identical probability distributions for future rates of return. Again, this assumption can be relaxed. As long as the differences in expectations are not vast, their effects are minor.

4. All investors have the same one-period time horizon such as one month, six months, or one year. The model will be developed for a single hypothetical period, and its results could be affected by a different assumption. A difference in the time horizon would require investors to derive risk measures and risk-free assets that are consistent with their investment horizons.

5. All investments are infinitely divisible, which means that it is possible to buy or sell fractional shares of any asset or portfolio. This assumption allows us to discuss investment alternatives as continuous curves. Changing it would have little impact on the theory.

6. There are no taxes or transaction costs involved in buying or selling assets. This is a reasonable assumption in many instances. Neither pension funds nor religious groups have to pay taxes, and the transaction costs for most financial institutions are less than 1 percent on most financial instruments. Again, relaxing this assumption modifies the results, but it does not change the basic thrust.

7. There is no inflation or any change in interest rates, or inflation is fully anticipated. This is a reasonable initial assumption, and it can be modified.

8. Capital markets are in equilibrium. This means that we begin with all investments properly priced in line with their risk levels.

You may consider some of these assumptions unrealistic and wonder how useful a theory we can derive with these assumptions. In this regard, two points are important. First, as mentioned, relaxing many of these assumptions would have only a minor effect on the model and would not change its main implications or conclusions. Second, a theory should never be judged on the basis of its assumptions but, rather, on how well it explains and helps us predict behavior in the real world. If this theory and the model it implies help us explain the rates of return on a wide variety of risky assets, it is useful, even if some of its assumptions are unrealistic. Such success implies that the questionable assumptions must be unimportant to the ultimate objective of the model, which is to explain asset pricing and rates of return on assets.

2.1.2 Development of Capital Market Theory

The major factor that allowed portfolio theory to develop into capital market theory is the concept of a risk-free asset. Following the development of the Markowitz portfolio model, several authors considered the implications of assuming the existence of a **risk-free asset,** that is, an asset with *zero variance*. As we will show, such an asset would have zero correlation with all other risky assets and would provide the *risk-free rate of return (RFR)*. It would lie on the vertical axis of a portfolio graph.

This assumption allows us to derive a generalized theory of capital asset pricing under conditions of uncertainty from the Markowitz portfolio theory. This achievement is generally attributed to William Sharpe, for which he received the Nobel Prize, but Lintner and Mossin derived similar theories independently.[1] Consequently, you may see references to the Sharpe-Lintner-Mossin (SLM) capital asset pricing model.

---

[1] William F. Sharpe, "Capital Asset Prices: A Theory of Market Equilibrium under Conditions of Risk," *Journal of Finance* 19, no. 3 (September 1964): 425–442; John Lintner, "Security Prices, Risk and Maximal Gains from Diversification," *Journal of Finance* 20, no. 4 (December 1965): 587–615; and J. Mossin, "Equilibrium in a Capital Asset Market," *Econometrica* 34, no. 4 (October 1966): 768–783.

2.2 Risk-Free Asset

As noted, the assumption of a risk-free asset in the economy is critical to asset pricing theory. Therefore, this section explains the meaning of a risk-free asset and shows the effect on the risk and return measures when this risk-free asset is combined with a portfolio on the Markowitz efficient frontier.

We have defined a **risky asset** as one from which future returns are uncertain, and we have measured this uncertainty by the variance, or standard deviation, of expected returns. Because the expected return on a risk-free asset is entirely certain, the standard deviation of its expected return is zero ($\sigma_{RF} = 0$). The rate of return earned on such an asset should be the risk-free rate of return (RFR), which, as we discussed in Reading 76, should equal the expected long-run growth rate of the economy with an adjustment for short-run liquidity. The next sections show what happens when we introduce this risk-free asset into the risky world of the Markowitz portfolio model.

2.2.1 Covariance with a Risk-Free Asset

Recall that the covariance between two sets of returns is

$$\text{Cov}_{ij} = \sum_{i=1}^{n} [R_i - E(R_i)][R_j - E(R_j)]/n \tag{79-1}$$

Because the returns for the risk-free asset are certain, $\sigma_{RF} = 0$, which means that $R_i - E(R_i)$ during all periods. Thus, $R_i - E(R_i)$ will also equal zero, and the product of this expression with any other expression will equal zero. Consequently, the covariance of the risk-free asset with any risky asset or portfolio of assets will always equal zero. Similarly, the correlation between any risky asset i, and the risk-free asset, RF, would be zero because it is equal to

$$r_{RF,i} = \text{Cov}_{RF,i}/\sigma_{RF}\sigma_i$$

2.2.2 Combining a Risk-Free Asset with a Risky Portfolio

What happens to the average rate of return and the standard deviation of returns when you combine a risk-free asset with a portfolio of risky assets such as those that exist on the Markowitz efficient frontier?

2.2.2.1 Expected Return

Like the expected return for a portfolio of two risky assets, the expected rate of return for a portfolio that includes a risk-free asset is the weighted average of the two returns:

$$E(R_{\text{port}}) = w_{RF}(RFR) + (1 - w_{RF})E(R_i)$$

where:

w_{RF} = the proportion of the portfolio invested in the risk-free asset
$E(R_i)$ = the expected rate of return on risky Portfolio i

2.2.2.2 Standard Deviation

Recall from Reading 78 (Equation 78-7) that the expected variance for a two-asset portfolio is

$$\sigma_{\text{port}}^2 = w_1^2\sigma_1^2 + w_2^2\sigma_2^2 + 2w_1w_2r_{1,2}\sigma_1\sigma_2$$

Substituting the risk-free asset for Security 1, and the risky asset portfolio for Security 2, this formula would become

$$\sigma^2_{port} = w^2_{RF}\sigma^2_{RF} + (1 - w_{RF})^2\sigma^2_i + 2w_{RF}(1 - w_{RF})r_{RFi}\sigma_{RF}\sigma_i$$

We know that the variance of the risk-free asset is zero, that is, $\sigma^2_{RF} = 0$. Because the correlation between the risk-free asset and any risky asset, i, is also zero, the factor $r_{RF,i}$ in the preceding equation also equals zero. Therefore, any component of the variance formula that has either of these terms will equal zero. When you make these adjustments, the formula becomes

$$\sigma^2_{port} = (1 - w_{RF})^2\sigma^2_i$$

The standard deviation is

$$\sigma_{port} = \sqrt{(1 - w_{RF})^2\sigma^2_i}$$
$$= (1 - w_{RF})\sigma_i$$

Therefore, the standard deviation of a portfolio that combines the risk-free asset with risky assets is the *linear proportion of the standard deviation of the risky asset portfolio.*

2.2.2.3 The Risk-Return Combination

Because both the expected return *and* the standard deviation of return for such a portfolio are linear combinations, a graph of possible portfolio returns and risks looks like a straight line between the two assets. Exhibit 79-1 shows a graph depicting portfolio possibilities when a risk-free asset is combined with alternative risky portfolios on the Markowitz efficient frontier.

EXHIBIT 79-1 Portfolio Possibilities Combining the Risk-Free Asset and Risky Portfolios on the Efficient Frontier

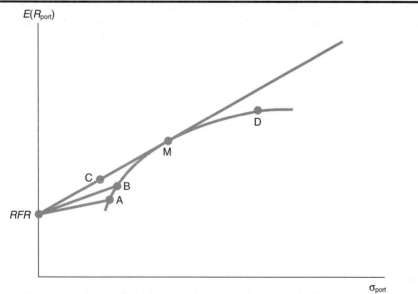

You can attain any point along the straight line *RFR*-A by investing some portion of your portfolio in the risk-free asset w_{RF} and the remainder $(1 - w_{RF})$ in the risky asset portfolio at Point A on the efficient frontier. This set of portfolio possibilities dominates all the risky asset portfolios on the efficient frontier below Point A because some portfolio along Line *RFR*-A has equal variance with a higher rate of return than the portfolio on the original efficient frontier. Likewise, you can attain any point along the Line *RFR*-B by investing in some combination of the risk-free asset and the risky asset portfolio at Point B. Again, these potential combinations dominate all portfolio possibilities on the original efficient frontier below Point B (including Line *RFR*-A).

You can draw further lines from the *RFR* to the efficient frontier at higher and higher points until you reach the point where the line is tangent to the frontier, which occurs in Exhibit 79-1 at Point M. The set of portfolio possibilities along Line *RFR*-M dominates *all* portfolios below Point M. For example, you could attain a risk and return combination between the *RFR* and Point M (Point C) by investing one-half of your portfolio in the risk-free asset (that is, lending money at the *RFR*) and the other half in the risky portfolio at Point M.

2.2.2.4 Risk-Return Possibilities with Leverage

An investor may want to attain a higher expected return than is available at Point M in exchange for accepting higher risk. One alternative would be to invest in one of the risky asset portfolios on the efficient frontier beyond Point M such as the portfolio at Point D. A second alternative is to add *leverage* to the portfolio by *borrowing* money at the risk-free rate and investing the proceeds in the risky asset portfolio at Point M. What effect would this have on the return and risk for your portfolio?

If you borrow an amount equal to 50 percent of your original wealth at the risk-free rate, w_{RF} will not be a positive fraction but, rather, a negative 50 percent ($w_{RF} = -0.50$). The effect on the expected return for your portfolio is:

$$E(R_{port}) = w_{RF}(RFR) + (1 - w_{RF})E(R_M)$$
$$= -0.50(RFR) + [1 - (-0.50)]E(R_M)$$
$$= -0.50(RFR) + 1.50E(R_M)$$

The return will increase in a *linear* fashion along the Line *RFR*-M because the gross return increases by 50 percent, but you must pay interest at the *RFR* on the money borrowed. For example, assume that $E(RFR) = .06$ and $E(R_M) = .12$. The return on your leveraged portfolio would be:

$$E(R_{port}) = -0.50(0.06) + 1.5(0.12)$$
$$= -0.03 + 0.18$$
$$= 0.15$$

The effect on the standard deviation of the leveraged portfolio is similar.

$$\sigma_{port} = (1 - w_{RF})\sigma_M$$
$$= [1 - (-0.50)]\sigma_M = 1.50\sigma_M$$

where:

σ_M = **the standard deviation of the M portfolio**

Therefore, *both return and risk increase in a linear fashion along the original Line RFR-M*, and this extension dominates everything below the line on the original

EXHIBIT 79-2 Derivation of Capital Market Line Assuming Lending or Borrowing at the Risk-Free Rate

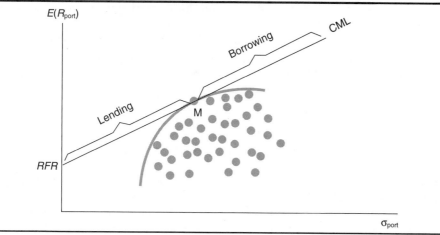

efficient frontier. Thus, you have a new efficient frontier: the straight line from the *RFR* tangent to Point M. This line is referred to as the **capital market line (CML)** and is shown in Exhibit 79-2.

Our discussion of portfolio theory stated that, when two assets are perfectly correlated, the set of portfolio possibilities falls along a straight line. Therefore, because the CML is a straight line, it implies that all the portfolios on the CML are perfectly positively correlated. This positive correlation appeals to our intuition because all these portfolios on the CML combine the risky asset Portfolio M and the risk-free asset. You either invest part of your portfolio in the risk-free asset (i.e., you *lend* at the *RFR*) and the rest in the risky asset Portfolio M, or you *borrow* at the riskfree rate and invest these funds in the risky asset portfolio. In either case, all the variability comes from the risky asset M portfolio. The only difference between the alternative portfolios on the CML is the magnitude of the variability, which is caused by the proportion of the risky asset portfolio in the total portfolio.

2.3 The Market Portfolio

Because Portfolio M lies at the point of tangency, it has the highest portfolio possibility line, and everybody will want to invest in Portfolio M and borrow or lend to be somewhere on the CML. This portfolio must, therefore, include *all risky assets*. If a risky asset were not in this portfolio in which everyone wants to invest, there would be no demand for it and therefore it would have no value.

Because the market is in equilibrium, it is also necessary that all assets are included in this portfolio *in proportion to their market value*. If, for example, an asset accounts for a higher proportion of the M portfolio than its market value justifies, excess demand for this asset will increase its price until its relative market value becomes consistent with its proportion in the M portfolio.

This portfolio that includes all risky assets is referred to as the **market portfolio.** It includes not only U.S. common stocks but *all* risky assets, such as non-U.S. stocks, U.S. and non-U.S. bonds, options, real estate, coins, stamps, art, or antiques. Because the market portfolio contains all risky assets, it is a **completely diversified portfolio,** which means that all the risk unique to individual assets in the portfolio is diversified away. Specifically, the unique risk of any single asset is offset by the unique variability of all the other assets in the portfolio.

This unique (diversifiable) risk is also referred to as **unsystematic risk.** This implies that only **systematic risk,** which is defined as the variability in all risky assets caused by macroeconomic variables, remains in the market portfolio. This systematic risk, measured by the standard deviation of returns of the market portfolio, can change over time if and when there are changes in the macroeconomic variables that affect the valuation of all risky assets.[2] Examples of such macroeconomic variables would be variability of growth in the money supply, interest rate volatility, and variability in such factors as industrial production, corporate earnings, and corporate cash flow.

2.3.1 How to Measure Diversification

As noted earlier, all portfolios on the CML are perfectly positively correlated, which means that all portfolios on the CML are perfectly correlated with the completely diversified market Portfolio M. This implies a measure of complete diversification.[3] Specifically, a completely diversified portfolio would have a correlation with the market portfolio of +1.00. This is logical because complete diversification means the elimination of all the unsystematic or unique risk. Once you have eliminated all unsystematic risk, only systematic risk is left, which cannot be diversified away. Therefore, completely diversified portfolios would correlate perfectly with the market portfolio because it has only systematic risk.

2.3.2 Diversification and the Elimination of Unsystematic Risk

As discussed in Reading 78, the purpose of diversification is to reduce the standard deviation of the total portfolio. This assumes imperfect correlations among securities.[4] Ideally, as you add securities, the average covariance for the portfolio declines. An important question is, about how many securities must be included to arrive at a completely diversified portfolio? To discover the answer, you must observe what happens as you increase the sample size of the portfolio by adding securities that have some positive correlation. The typical correlation among U.S. securities is about 0.5 to 0.6.

One set of studies examined the average standard deviation for numerous portfolios of randomly selected stocks of different sample sizes. Specifically, the authors computed the standard deviation for portfolios of increasing numbers up to 20 stocks. The results indicated a large initial impact wherein the major benefits of diversification were achieved rather quickly. Specifically, about 90 percent of the maximum benefit of diversification was derived from portfolios of 12 to 18 stocks. Exhibit 79-3 shows a graph of the effect.

A subsequent study compared the benefits of lower risk from diversification to the added transaction costs with more securities. It concluded that a well-diversified stock portfolio must include at least 30 stocks for a borrowing investor and 40 stocks for a lending investor.

---

[2] For an analysis of changes in the standard deviation (volatility) of returns for stocks and bonds in the United States, see G. William Schwert, "Why Does Stock Market Volatility Change over Time?" *Journal of Finance* 44, no. 5 (December 1989). 1115–1153; Peter S. Spiro, "The Impact of Interest Rate Changes on Stock Price Volatility," *Journal of Portfolio Management* 16, no. 2 (Winter 1990): 63–68; R. R. Officer, "The Variability of the Market Factor of the New York Stock Exchange," *Journal of Business* 46, no. 3 (July 1973): 434–453; and Frank K. Reilly, David J. Wright, and Kam C. Chan, "Bond Market Volatility Compared to Stock Market Volatility," *Journal of Portfolio Management* 27, no. 1 (Fall 2000): 82–92.

[3] James Lorie, "Diversification: Old and New," *Journal of Portfolio Management* 1, no. 2 (Winter 1975): 25–28.

[4] The discussion in Reading 78 leads one to conclude that securities with negative correlation would be ideal. Although this is true in theory, it is difficult to find such assets in the real world.

EXHIBIT 79-3　Number of Stocks in a Portfolio and the Standard Deviation of Porfolio Return

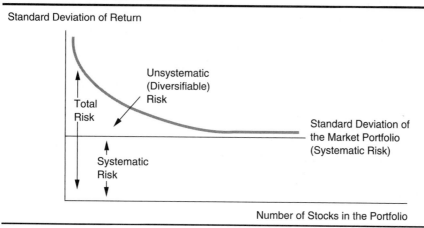

An important point to remember is that, by adding stocks to the portfolio that are not perfectly correlated with stocks in the portfolio, you can reduce the overall standard deviation of the portfolio but you *cannot eliminate variability.* The standard deviation of your portfolio will eventually reach the level of the market portfolio, where you will have diversified away all unsystematic risk, but you still have market or systematic risk. You cannot eliminate the variability and uncertainty of macroeconomic factors that affect all risky assets. At the same time, you will recall from the discussion in Chapter 3 that you can attain a lower level of systematic risk by diversifying globally versus only investing in the United States because some of the systematic risk factors in the U.S. market (such as U.S. monetary policy) are not correlated with systematic risk variables in other countries such as Germany and Japan. As a result, if you diversify globally you eventually get down to a world systematic risk level.

2.3.3　*The CML and the Separation Theorem*

The CML leads all investors to invest in the same risky asset portfolio, the M portfolio. Individual investors should only differ regarding their position on the CML, which depends on their risk preferences.

In turn, how they get to a point on the CML is based on their *financing decisions.* If you are relatively risk averse, you will lend some part of your portfolio at the *RFR* by buying some riskfree securities and investing the remainder in the market portfolio of risky assets. For example, you might invest in the portfolio combination at Point A in Exhibit 79-4. In contrast, if you prefer more risk, you might borrow funds at the *RFR* and invest everything (all of your capital plus what you borrowed) in the market portfolio, building the portfolio at Point B. This financing decision provides more risk but greater returns than the market portfolio. As discussed earlier, because portfolios on the CML dominate other portfolio possibilities, the CML becomes the efficient frontier of portfolios, and investors decide where they want to be along this efficient frontier. Tobin called this division of the investment decision from the financing decision the **separation theorem.**[5] Specifically, to be somewhere on the CML efficient frontier, you initially decide to invest in the market Portfolio M, which means that you will be

---

[5] James Tobin, "Liquidity Preference as Behavior Towards Risk," *Review of Economic Studies* 25, no. 2 (February 1958): 65–85.

EXHIBIT 79-4 Choice of Optimal Portfolio Combinations on the CML

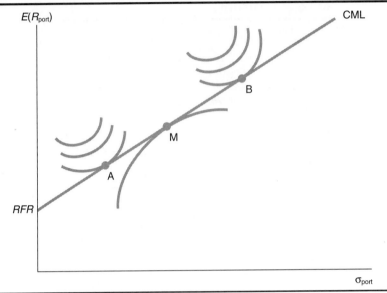

on the CML. This is your *investment* decision. Subsequently, based on your risk preferences, you make a separate *financing* decision either to borrow or to lend to attain your preferred risk position on the CML.

2.3.4 A Risk Measure for the CML

In this section, we show that the relevant risk measure for risky assets is *their covariance with the M portfolio,* which is referred to as their systematic risk. The importance of this covariance is apparent from two points of view.

First, in discussing the Markowitz portfolio model, we noted that the relevant risk to consider when adding a security to a portfolio is *its average covariance with all other assets in the portfolio.* In this reading, we have shown that *the only relevant portfolio is the M portfolio.* Together, these two findings mean that the only important consideration for any individual risky asset is its average covariance with all the risky assets in the M portfolio or, simply, *the asset's covariance with the market portfolio.* This covariance, then, is the relevant risk measure for an individual risky asset.

Second, because all individual risky assets are a part of the M portfolio, one can describe their rates of return in relation to the returns for the M portfolio using the following linear model:

$$R_{it} = a_i + b_i R_{Mt} + \varepsilon \qquad \text{(79-2)}$$

where:

$R_{i,t}$ = **return for asset *i* during period *t***
a_i = **constant term for asset *i***
b_i = **slope coefficient for asset *i***
R_{Mt} = **return for the M portfolio during period *t***
ε = **random error term**

The variance of returns for a risky asset could be described as

$$\begin{aligned}
\text{Var}(R_{it}) &= \text{Var}(a_i + b_i R_{Mt} + \varepsilon) \\
&= \text{Var}(a_i) + \text{Var}(b_i R_{Mt}) + \text{Var}(\varepsilon) \\
&= 0 + \text{Var}(b_i R_{Mt}) + \text{Var}(\varepsilon)
\end{aligned}$$

(79-3)

Note that $\text{Var}(b_i R_{Mt})$ is the variance of return for an asset related to the variance of the market return, or the *systematic variance* or *risk*. Also, $\text{Var}(\varepsilon)$ is the residual variance of return for the individual asset that is not related to the market portfolio. This residual variance is the variability that we have referred to as the unsystematic or *unique risk* or *variance* because it arises from the unique features of the asset. Therefore:

$$\text{Var}(R_{it}) = \text{Systematic Variance} + \text{Unsystematic Variance}$$

(79-4)

We know that a completely diversified portfolio such as the market portfolio has had all the unsystematic variance eliminated. Therefore, the unsystematic variance of an asset is not relevant to investors, because they can and do eliminate it when making an asset part of the market portfolio. Therefore, investors should not expect to receive added returns for assuming this unique risk. Only the systematic variance is relevant because it *cannot* be diversified away, because it is caused by macroeconomic factors that affect all risky assets.

THE CAPITAL ASSET PRICING MODEL: EXPECTED RETURN AND RISK

3

Up to this point, we have considered how investors make their portfolio decisions, including the significant effects of a risk-free asset. The existence of this risk-free asset resulted in the derivation of a capital market line (CML) that became the relevant efficient frontier. Because all investors want to be on the CML, an asset's covariance with the market portfolio of risky assets emerged as the relevant risk measure.

Now that we understand this relevant measure of risk, we can proceed to use it to determine an appropriate expected rate of return on a risky asset. This step takes us into the **capital asset pricing model (CAPM),** which is a model that indicates what should be the expected or required rates of return on risky assets. This transition is important because it helps you to value an asset by providing an appropriate discount rate to use in any valuation model. Alternatively, if you have already estimated the rate of return that you think you will earn on an investment, you can compare this *estimated* rate of return to the *required* rate of return implied by the CAPM and determine whether the asset is undervalued, overvalued, or properly valued.

To accomplish the foregoing, we demonstrate the creation of a security market line (SML) that visually represents the relationship between risk and the expected or the required rate of return on an asset. The equation of this SML, together with estimates for the return on a risk-free asset and on the market portfolio, can generate expected or required rates of return for any asset based on its systematic risk. You compare this required rate of return to the rate of return that you estimate that you will earn on the investment to determine if the investment is undervalued or overvalued. After demonstrating this procedure, we finish the section with a demonstration of how to calculate the systematic risk variable for a risky asset.

3.1 The Security Market Line (SML)

We know that the relevant risk measure for an individual risky asset is its covariance with the market portfolio ($\text{Cov}_{i,M}$). Therefore, we can draw the risk-return relationship as shown in Exhibit 79-5 with the systematic covariance variable ($\text{Cov}_{i,M}$) as the risk measure.

EXHIBIT 79-5 Graph of Security Market Line

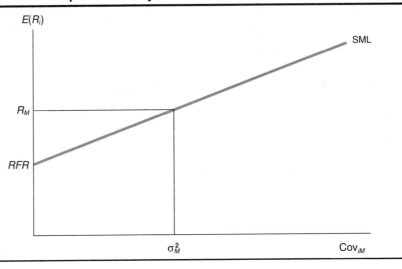

The return for the market portfolio (R_M) should be consistent with its own risk, which is the covariance of the market with itself. If you recall the formula for covariance, you will see that the covariance of any asset with itself is its variance, $\text{Cov}_{i,i} = \sigma_i^2$. In turn, the covariance of the market with itself is the variance of the market rate of return $\text{Cov}_{M,M} = \sigma_M^2$. Therefore, the equation for the risk-return line in Exhibit 79-5 is.

$$E(R_i) = RFR + \frac{R_M - RFR}{\sigma_M^2}(\text{Cov}_{i,M})$$ (79-5)

$$= RFR + \frac{\text{Cov}_{i,M}}{\sigma_M^2}(R_M - RFR)$$

Defining $\text{Cov}_{i,M}/\sigma_M^2$ as beta, (β_i), this equation can be stated:

$$E(Ri) = RFR + \beta_i(R_M - RFR)$$ (79-6)

Beta can be viewed as a *standardized* measure of systematic risk. Specifically, we already know that the covariance of any asset i with the market portfolio (Cov_{iM}) is the relevant risk measure. Beta is a standardized measure of risk because it relates this covariance to the variance of the market portfolio. As a result, the market portfolio has a beta of 1. Therefore, if the β_i for an asset is above 1.0, the asset has higher normalized systematic risk than the market, which means that it is more volatile than the overall market portfolio.

Given this standardized measure of systematic risk, the SML graph can be expressed as shown in Exhibit 79-6. This is the same graph as in Exhibit 79-5, except there is a different measure of risk. Specifically, the graph in Exhibit 79-6 replaces

EXHIBIT 79-6 Graph of SML with Normalized Systematic Risk

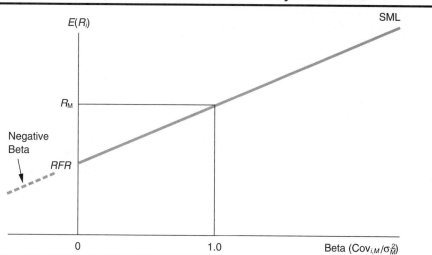

the covariance of an asset's returns with the market portfolio as the risk measure with the standardized measure of systematic risk (beta), which is the covariance of an asset with the market portfolio divided by the variance of the market portfolio.

3.1.1 Determining the Expected Rate of Return for a Risky Asset

The last equation and the graph in Exhibit 79-6 tell us that the expected (required) rate of return for a risky asset is determined by the *RFR* plus a risk premium for the individual asset. In turn, the risk premium is determined by the systematic risk of the asset (β_i), and the prevailing **market risk premium** ($R_M - RFR$). To demonstrate how you would compute the expected or required rates of return, consider the following example stocks assuming you have already computed betas:

Stock	Beta
A	0.70
B	1.00
C	1.15
D	1.40
E	−0.30

Assume that we expect the economy's *RFR* to be 6 percent (0.06) and the return on the market portfolio (R_M) to be 12 percent (0.12). This implies a market risk premium of 6 percent (0.06). With these inputs, the SML equation would yield the following expected (required) rates of return for these five stocks:

$$E(R_i) = RFR + \beta_i (R_M - RFR)$$
$$E(R_A) = 0.06 + 0.70 (0.12 - 0.06)$$
$$= 0.102 = 10.2\%$$
$$E(R_B) = 0.06 + 1.00 (0.12 - 0.06)$$
$$= 0.12 = 12\%$$
$$E(R_C) = 0.06 + 1.15 (0.12 - 0.06)$$
$$= 0.129 = 12.9\%$$

$$E(R_D) = 0.06 + 1.40\ (0.12 - 0.06)$$
$$= 0.144 = 14.4\%$$
$$E(R_E) = 0.06 + (-0.30)\ (0.12 - 0.06)$$
$$= 0.06 - 0.018$$
$$= 0.042 = 4.2\%$$

EXHIBIT 79-7 Price, Dividend, and Rate of Return Estimates

Stock	Current Price (P_t)	Expected Price (P_{t+1})	Expected Dividend (D_{t+1})	Estimated Future Rate of Return (Percent)
A	25	27	0.50	10.0%
B	40	42	0.50	6.2
C	33	39	1.00	21.2
D	64	65	1.10	3.3
E	50	54	—	8.0

As stated, these are the expected (required) rates of return that these stocks should provide based on their systematic risks and the prevailing SML.

Stock A has lower risk than the aggregate market, so you should not expect (require) its return to be as high as the return on the market portfolio of risky assets. You should expect (require) Stock A to return 10.2 percent. Stock B has systematic risk equal to the market's (beta = 1.00), so its required rate of return should likewise be equal to the expected market return (12 percent). Stocks C and D have systematic risk greater than the market's, so they should provide returns consistent with their risk. Finally, Stock E has a *negative* beta (which is quite rare in practice), so its required rate of return, if such a stock could be found, would be below the *RFR*.

In equilibrium, *all* assets and *all* portfolios of assets should plot on the SML. That is, all assets should be priced so that their **estimated rates of return,** which are the actual holding period rates of return that you anticipate, are consistent with their levels of systematic risk. Any security with an estimated rate of return that plots above the SML would be considered under-priced because it implies that you *estimated* you would receive a rate of return on the security that is above its *required* rate of return based on its systematic risk. In contrast, assets with estimated rates of return that plot below the SML would be considered overpriced. This position relative to the SML implies that your estimated rate of return is below what you should require based on the asset's systematic risk.

In an efficient market in equilibrium, you would not expect any assets to plot off the SML because, in equilibrium, all stocks should provide holding period returns that are equal to their required rates of return. Alternatively, a market that is "fairly efficient" but not completely efficient may misprice certain assets because not everyone will be aware of all the relevant information for an asset.

As we discussed in Chapter 6 on the topic of efficient markets, a superior investor has the ability to derive value estimates for assets that are consistently superior to the consensus market evaluation. As a result, such an investor will earn better rates of return than the average investor on a risk-adjusted basis.

3.1.2 Identifying Undervalued and Overvalued Assets

Now that we understand how to compute the rate of return one should expect or require for a specific risky asset using the SML, we can compare this *required* rate of return to the asset's *estimated* rate of return over a specific investment horizon to determine whether it would be an appropriate investment. To make this comparison, you need an independent estimate of the return outlook for the security based on either fundamental or technical analysis techniques, which will be discussed in subsequent readings. Let us continue the example for the five assets discussed in the previous section.

Assume that analysts in a major trust department have been following these five stocks. Based on extensive fundamental analysis, the analysts provide the expected price and dividend estimates contained in Exhibit 79-7. Given these projections, you can compute the estimated rates of return the analysts would anticipate during this holding period.

EXHIBIT 79-8 Comparison of Required Rate of Return to Estimated Rate of Return

Stock	Beta	Required Return $E(R_i)$	Estimated Return	Estimated Return Minus $E(R_i)$	Evaluation
A	0.70	10.2	10.0	−0.2	Properly valued
B	1.00	12.0	6.2	−5.8	Overvalued
C	1.15	12.9	21.2	8.3	Undervalued
D	1.40	14.4	3.3	−11.1	Overvalued
E	−0.30	4.2	8.0	3.8	Undervalued

EXHIBIT 79-9 Plot of Estimated Returns on SML Graph

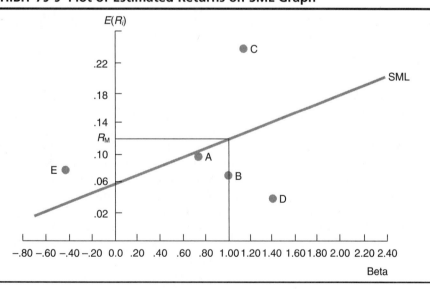

Exhibit 79-8 summarizes the relationship between the required rate of return for each stock based on its systematic risk as computed earlier, and its estimated rate of return (from Exhibit 79-7) based on the current and future prices, and its dividend outlook. This difference between estimated return and expected (required) return is sometimes referred to as a stock's *alpha* or its excess return. This alpha can be positive (the stock is undervalued) or negative (the stock is overvalued). If the alpha is zero, the stock is on the SML and is properly valued in line with its systematic risk.

Plotting these estimated rates of return and stock betas on the SML we specified earlier gives the graph shown in Exhibit 79-9. Stock A is almost exactly on the line, so it is considered properly valued because its estimated rate of return is almost equal to its required rate of return. Stocks B and D are considered overvalued because their estimated rates of return during the coming period are below what an investor should expect (require) for the risk involved. As a result, they plot below the SML. In contrast, Stocks C and E are expected to provide rates of return greater than we would require based on their systematic risk. Therefore, both stocks plot above the SML, indicating that they are undervalued stocks.

Assuming that you trusted your analyst to forecast estimated returns, you would take no action regarding Stock A, but you would buy Stocks C and E and sell Stocks B and D. You might even sell Stocks B and D short if you favored such aggressive tactics.

3.1.3 Calculating Systematic Risk: The Characteristic Line

The systematic risk input for an individual asset is derived from a regression model, referred to as the asset's **characteristic line** with the market portfolio:

$$R_{i,t} = \alpha_i + \beta_i R_{M,t} + \varepsilon \qquad \textbf{(79-7)}$$

where:

> $R_{i,t}$ = **the rate of return for asset i during period t**
> $R_{M,t}$ = **the rate of return for the market portfolio M during period t**
> α_i = **the constant term, or intercept, of the regression, which equals**
> $\overline{R}_i - \beta_i \overline{R}_M$
> β_i = **the systematic risk (beta) of asset i equal to $Cov_{i,M}/\sigma_M^2$**
> ε = **the random error term**

The characteristic line (Equation 79-7) is the regression line of best fit through a scatter plot of rates of return for the individual risky asset and for the market portfolio of risky assets over some designated past period, as shown in Exhibit 79-10.

3.1.3.1 The Impact of the Time Interval

In practice, the number of observations and the time interval used in the regression vary. Value Line Investment Services derives characteristic lines for common stocks using weekly rates of return for the most recent five years (260 weekly observations). Merrill Lynch, Pierce, Fenner & Smith uses monthly rates of return for the most recent five years (60 monthly observations). Because there is no theoretically correct time interval for analysis, we must make a trade-off between enough observations to eliminate the impact of random rates of return and an excessive length of time, such as 15 or 20 years, over which the subject company may have changed dramatically. Remember that what you really want is the *expected* systematic risk for the potential investment. In this analysis, you are analyzing historical data to help you derive a reasonable estimate of the asset's expected systematic risk.

A couple of studies have considered the effect of the time interval used to compute betas (weekly versus monthly). Statman examined the relationship between Value Line (VL) betas and Merrill Lynch (ML) betas and found a relatively weak relationship.[6] Reilly and Wright analyzed the differential effects of

---

[6] Meir Statman, "Betas Compared: Merrill Lynch vs. Value Line," *Journal of Portfolio Management* 7, no. 2 (Winter 1981): 41–44.

return computation, market index, and the time interval and showed that the major cause of the differences in beta was the use of monthly versus weekly return intervals.[7] Also, the interval effect depended on the sizes of the firms. The shorter weekly interval caused a larger beta for large firms and a smaller beta for small

EXHIBIT 79-10 Scatter Plot of Rates of Return

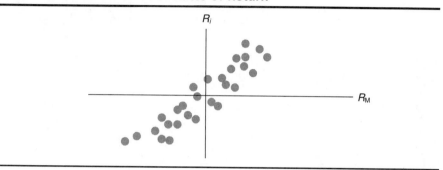

firms. For example, the average beta for the smallest decile of firms using monthly data was 1.682, but the average beta for these small firms using weekly data was only 1.080. The authors concluded that the return time interval makes a difference, and its impact increases as the firm size declines.

3.1.3.2 The Effect of the Market Proxy

Another significant decision when computing an asset's characteristic line is which indicator series to use as a proxy for the market portfolio of all risky assets. Most investigators use the Standard & Poor's 500 Composite Index as a proxy for the market portfolio, because the stocks in this index encompass a large proportion of the total market value of U.S. stocks and it is a value-weighted series, which is consistent with the theoretical market series. Still, this series contains only U.S. stocks, most of them listed on the NYSE.

Previously, it was noted that the market portfolio of all risky assets should include U.S. stocks and bonds, non-U.S. stocks and bonds, real estate, coins, stamps, art, antiques, and any other marketable risky asset from around the world.[8]

3.1.4 Example Computations of a Characteristic Line

The following examples show how you would compute characteristic lines for Coca-Cola based on the monthly rates of return during 2001.[9] Twelve is not enough observations for statistical purposes, but it provides a good example. We demonstrate the computations using two different proxies for the market portfolio.

[7] Frank K. Reilly and David J. Wright, "A Comparison of Published Betas," *Journal of Portfolio Management* 14, no. 3 (Spring 1988): 64–69.

[8] Substantial discussion surrounds the market index used and its impact on the empirical results and usefulness of the CAPM. This concern is discussed further and demonstrated in the subsequent section on computing an asset's characteristic line. The effect of the market proxy is also considered when we discuss the arbitrage pricing theory (APT) in Chapter 9 and in Chapter 26 when we discuss the evaluation of portfolio performance.

[9] These betas are computed using only monthly price changes for Coca-Cola, the S&P 500, and the M-S World Index (dividends are not included). This is done for simplicity but is also based on a study indicating that betas derived with and without dividends are correlated 0.99: William Sharpe and Guy M. Cooper, "Risk-Return Classes of New York Stock Exchange Common Stocks," *Financial Analysts Journal* 28, no. 2 (March–April 1972): 35–43.

EXHIBIT 79-11 Computation of Beta for Coca-Cola with Selected Indexes

Date	INDEX		RETURN			S&P 500 $R_{S\&P} - E(R_{S\&P})$ (1)	M-S World $R_{M-S} - E(R_{M-S})$ (2)	Coca-Cola $R_{KO} - E(R_{RO})$ (3)	(4)[a]	(5)[b]
	S&P 500	M-S World	S&P 500	M-S World	Coca-Cola					
Dec-00	1320.28	1221.253								
Jan-01	1366.01	1244.222	3.46	1.88	-4.82	4.47	3.38	-3.01	-13.44	-10.15
Feb-01	1239.94	1137.879	-9.23	-8.55	-8.57	-8.22	-7.05	-6.76	55.56	47.64
Mar-01	1160.33	1061.262	-6.42	-6.73	-14.50	-5.41	-5.24	-12.69	68.70	66.46
Apr-01	1249.46	1138.087	7.68	7.24	2.28	8.69	8.73	4.09	35.56	35.74
May-01	1255.82	1121.088	0.51	-1.49	2.62	1.51	0.00	4.43	6.71	0.005
Jun-01	1224.38	1084.788	-2.50	-3.24	-4.68	-1.50	-1.74	-2.87	4.30	5.00
Jul-01	1211.23	1069.669	-1.07	-1.39	-0.89	-0.07	0.10	0.92	-0.06	0.09
Aug-01	1133.58	1016.732	-6.41	-4.95	9.13	-5.40	-3.45	10.94	-59.12	-37.77
Sep-01	1040.94	926.023	-8.17	-8.92	-3.37	-7.17	-7.43	-1.56	11.16	11.56
Oct-01	1059.78	943.2	1.81	1.85	2.20	2.82	3.35	4.01	11.29	13.43
Nov-01	1139.45	997.928	7.52	5.80	-1.55	8.52	7.30	0.27	2.27	1.94
Dec-01	1148.08	1003.516	0.76	0.56	0.40	1.76	2.05	2.22	3.91	4.55
Average			-1.01	-1.49	-1.81			Total =	126.85	138.54
Standard Deviation			5.49	5.03	5.80					

$Cov_{KO,S\&P} = 126.85/12 = 10.57$
$Cov_{KO,MS} = 138.54/12 = 11.54$

$Var_{S\&P} = St.Dev._{S\&P}^2 = 5.49^2 = 30.10$
$Var_{MS} = St.Dev._{MS}^2 = 5.03^2 = 25.31$

Correlation coef._{KO,S&P} = 10.57/(5.49 * 5.80) = 0.33

$Beta_{KO,S\&P} = 10.57/30.10 = 0.35$
$Beta_{KO,MS} = 11.54/25.31 = 0.46$

Alpha_{KO,S&P} = -1.81 - (0.35 * -1.01) = -1.46
Alpha_{KO,MS} = -1.81 - (0.46 * -1.49) = -1.13

Correlation coef._{KO,MS} = 11.54/(5.03 * 5.80) = 0.40

[a] ColumnN 4 is equal to Column 1 multiplied by Column 3
[b] Column 5 is equal to Column 2 multiplied by Column 3

First, we use the standard S&P 500 as the market proxy. Second, we use the Morgan Stanley (M-S) World Equity Index as the market proxy. This analysis demonstrates the effect of using a complete global proxy of stocks.

The monthly price changes are computed using the closing prices for the last day of each month. These data for Coca-Cola, the S&P 500, and the M-S World Index are contained in Exhibit 79-11. Exhibit 79-12 contains the scatter plot of the percentage price changes for Coca-Cola and the S&P 500. During this 12-month period, except for August, Coca-Cola had returns that varied positively when compared to the aggregate market returns as proxied by the S&P 500. Still, as a result of the negative August effect, the covariance between Coca-Cola and the S&P 500 series was a fairly small positive value (10.57). The covariance divided by the variance of the S&P 500 market portfolio (30.10) indicates that Coca-Cola's beta relative to the S&P 500 was equal to a relatively low 0.35. This analysis indicates that during this limited time period Coca-Cola was clearly less risky than the aggregate market proxied by the S&P 500. When we draw the computed characteristic line on Exhibit 79-12, the scatter plots are reasonably close to the characteristic line except for two observations, which is consistent with the correlation coefficient of 0.33.

EXHIBIT 79-12 Scatter Plot of Coca-Cola and the S&P 500 with Characteristic Line for Coca-Cola: 2001

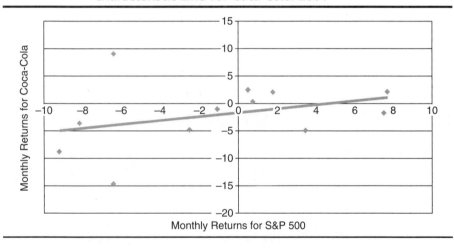

EXHIBIT 79-13 Scatter Plot of Coca-Cola and the M-S World with Characteristic Line for Coca-Cola: 2001

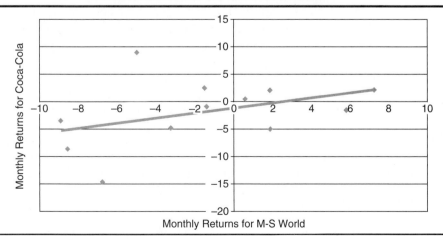

The computation of the characteristic line for Coca-Cola using the M-S World Index as the proxy for the market is contained in Exhibit 79-11, and the scatter plots are in Exhibit 79-13. At this point, it is important to consider what one might expect to be the relationship between the beta relative to the S&P 500 versus the betas with the M-S World Index. This requires a consideration of the two components that go into the computation of beta: (1) the covariance between the stock and the benchmark and (2) the variance of returns for the benchmark series. Notably, there is no obvious answer regarding what will happen for either series because one would expect both components to change. Specifically, the covariance of Coca-Cola with the S&P 500 will probably be higher than the covariance with the global series because you are matching a U.S. stock with a U.S. market index rather than a world index. Thus, one would expect the covariance with the global index to be smaller. At the same time, the variance of returns for the world stock index should also be smaller than the variance for the S&P 500 because it is a more diversified stock portfolio.

Therefore, the direction of change for the beta will depend on the relative change in the two components. Empirically, the beta is typically smaller with the world stock index because the covariance is definitely lower, but the variance is only slighter smaller.[10] The results of this example were not consistent with expectations. The beta of Coca-Cola with the world stock index was larger (0.46 versus 0.35) because the covariance with the global index was unexpectedly larger (11.54 versus 10.57), whereas the variance of the global market proxy was smaller as hypothesized (25.31 versus 30.10). The fact that the betas with the alternative market proxies differed is significant and reflects the potential problem in a global investment environment, which involves selecting the appropriate proxy for the market portfolio.

4   RELAXING THE ASSUMPTIONS

Earlier in the reading, several assumptions were set forth related to the CAPM. In this section, we discuss the impact on the capital market line (CML) and the security market line (SML) when we relax several of these assumptions.

4.1 Differential Borrowing and Lending Rates

One of the first assumptions of the CAPM was that investors could borrow and lend any amount of money at the risk-free rate. It is reasonable to assume that investors can *lend* unlimited amounts at the risk-free rate by buying government securities (e.g., T-bills). In contrast, one may question the ability of investors to borrow unlimited amounts at the T-bill rate because most investors must pay a premium relative to the prime rate when borrowing money. For example, when T-bills are yielding 5 percent, the prime rate will probably be about 7 percent, and most individuals would have to pay about 8 percent to borrow at the bank.

Because of this differential, there will be two different lines going to the Markowitz efficient frontier, as shown in Exhibit 79-14. The segment *RFR–F* indicates the investment opportunities available when an investor combines risk-free assets (i.e., lending at the *RFR*) and Portfolio F on the Markowitz efficient frontier. It is not possible to extend this line any farther if it is assumed that you cannot borrow at this risk-free rate to acquire further units of Portfolio F. If it is

---

[10] For a demonstration of this effect for a large sample that confirms these expectations, see Frank K. Reilly and Rashid A. Akhtar, "The Benchmark Error Problem with Global Capital Markets," *Journal of Portfolio Management* 22, no. 1 (Fall 1995): 33–52.

assumed that you can borrow at R_b, the point of tangency from this rate would be on the curve at Point K. This indicates that you could borrow at R_b and use the proceeds to invest in Portfolio K to extend the CML along the line segment

EXHIBIT 79-14 Investment Alternatives when the Cost of Borrowing is Higher than the Cost of Lending

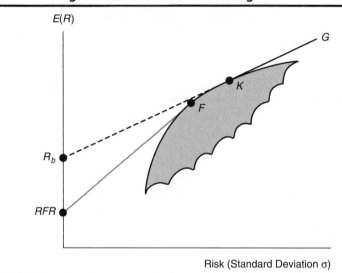

Risk (Standard Deviation σ)

K–G. Therefore, the CML is made up of RFR–F–K–G; that is, a line segment $(RFR$–$F)$, a curve segment $(F$–$K)$, and another line segment $(K$–$G)$. This implies that you can either lend or borrow, but the borrowing portfolios are not as profitable as when it was assumed that you could borrow at the *RFR*. In this instance, because you must pay a borrowing rate that is higher than the *RFR*, your net return is less—that is, the slope of the borrowing line $(K$–$G)$ is below that for *RFR*–*F*.[11]

4.2 Zero-Beta Model

If the market portfolio (M) is mean-variance efficient (i.e., it has the lowest risk for a given level of return among the attainable set of portfolios), an alternative model, derived by Black, does not require a risk-free asset.[12] Specifically, within the set of feasible alternative portfolios, several portfolios exist where the returns are completely uncorrelated with the market portfolio; the beta of these portfolios with the market portfolio is zero. From among the several zero-beta portfolios, you would select the one with minimum variance. Although this portfolio does not have any systematic risk, it does have some unsystematic risk. The availability of this zero-beta portfolio will not affect the CML, but it will allow construction of a linear SML, as shown in Exhibit 79-15. In the model, the intercept is the expected return for the zero-beta portfolio. Similar to the earlier proof in this reading, the combinations of this zero-beta portfolio and the market portfolio will be a linear relationship in return and risk because the covariance between the zero-beta portfolio (R_z) and the market portfolio likewise is similar to the risk-free asset. Assuming the return for the zero-beta portfolio is greater than that

[11] For a detailed discussion, see Michael Brennan, "Capital Market Equilibrium with Divergent Borrowing and Lending Rules," *Journal of Financial and Quantitative Analysis* 4, no. 1 (March 1969): 4–14.

[12] Fischer Black, "Capital Market Equilibrium with Restricted Borrowing," *Journal of Business* 45, no. 3 (July 1972): 444–445.

for a risk-free asset, the slope of the line through the market portfolio would not be as steep; that is, the market risk premium would be smaller. The equation for this zero-beta CAPM line would be

$$E(R_i) = E(R_z) + B_i[E(R_M) - E(R_z)] \tag{79-8}$$

Obviously, the risk premiums for individual assets would be a function of the beta for the individual security and the market risk premium.

$$[E(R_M) - E(R_z)]$$

EXHIBIT 79-15 Security Market Line with a Zero-Beta Portfolio

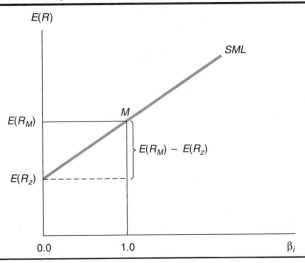

Some of the empirical results discussed in the next section support this model with its higher intercept and flatter slope. Alternatively, several studies have specifically tested this model and had conflicting results. Specifically, studies by Gibbons and Shanken rejected the model, while a study by Stambaugh supported the zero-beta CAPM.[13]

4.3 Transaction Costs

The basic assumption is that there are no transaction costs, so investors will buy or sell mispriced securities until they again plot on the SML. For example, if a stock plots above the SML, it is underpriced so investors should buy it and bid up its price until its estimated return is in line with its risk—that is, until it plots on the SML. With transaction costs, investors will not correct all mispricing because in some instances the cost of buying and selling the mispriced security will offset any potential excess return. Therefore, securities will plot very close to the SML—but not exactly on it. Thus, the SML will be a band of securities, as shown in Exhibit 79-16, rather than a single line. Obviously, the width of the band is a function of the amount of the transaction costs. In a world with a large proportion of trading by institutions at pennies per share and with discount brokers available for individual investors, the band should be quite narrow.

[13] Michael Gibbons, "Multivariate Tests of Financial Models: A New Approach," *Journal of Financial Economics* 10, no. 1 (March 1982): 3–28; Jay Shanken, "Multivariate Tests of the Zero Beta CAPM," *Journal of Financial Economics* 14, no. 3 (September 1985): 327–348; and Robert Stambaugh, "On the Exclusion of Assets from Tests of the Two-Parameter Model: A Sensitivity Analysis," *Journal of Financial Economics* 10, no. 4 (November 1982): 237–268.

EXHIBIT 79-16 Security Market Line with Transaction Costs

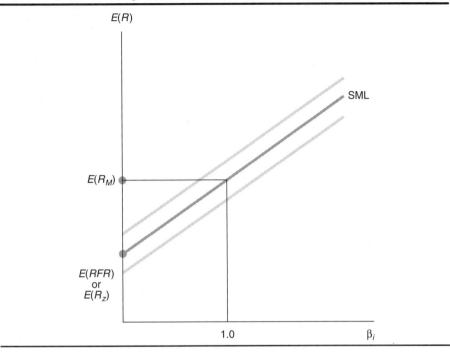

The existence of transaction costs also will affect the extent of diversification by investors. Earlier in the reading, we discussed the relationship between the number of stocks in a portfolio and the variance of the portfolio (see Exhibit 79-3). Initially, the variance declined rapidly, approaching about 90 percent of complete diversification with about 15 to 18 securities. An important question is, How many securities must be added to derive the last 10 percent? Because of transaction costs, at some point the additional cost of diversification would exceed its benefit, especially when considering the costs of monitoring and analyzing the added securities.[14]

4.4 Heterogeneous Expectations and Planning Periods

If all investors had different expectations about risk and return, each would have a unique CML and/or SML, and the composite graph would be a set (band) of lines with a breadth determined by the divergence of expectations. If all investors had similar information and background, the band would be reasonably narrow.

The impact of *planning periods* is similar. Recall that the CAPM is a one-period model, corresponding to the planning period for the individual investor. Thus, if you are using a one-year planning period, your CML and SML could differ from mine, which assumes a one-month planning period.

---

[14] The impact of transaction costs and illiquidity is considered in E. Dimson, "Risk Management When Shares Are Subject to Infrequent Trading," *Journal of Financial Economics* 7, no. 2 (June 1979): 197–226; M. J. Brennan and A. Subramanyam, "Market Microstructure and Asset Pricing on the Compensation for Illiquidity in Stock Returns," *Journal of Financial Economics* 41, no. 3 (July 1996): 341–344.

4.5 Taxes

The rates of return that we normally record and that were used throughout the model were pretax returns. In fact, the actual returns for most investors are affected as follows:

$$E(R_i)(AT) = \frac{(P_e - P_b) \times (1 - T_{cg}) + (Div) \times (1 - T_i)}{P_b}$$

(79-9)

where:

    $(R_i)(AT)$ = **after-tax rate of return**
    P_e = **ending price**
    P_b = **beginning price**
    T_{cg} = **tax on capital gain or loss**
    Div = **dividend paid during period**
    T_i = **tax on ordinary income**

Clearly, tax rates differ between individuals and institutions. For institutions that do not pay taxes, the original pretax model is correctly specified—that is, T_{cg} and T_i take on values of zero. Alternatively, because investors have heavy tax burdens, this could cause major differences in the CML and SML among investors.[15] Several recent studies have examined the effect of the differential taxes on dividends versus capital gains but the evidence is not unanimous.[16]

4   EMPIRICAL TESTS OF THE CAPM

When we discussed the assumptions of capital market theory, we pointed out that a theory should not be judged on the basis of its assumptions, but on *how well it explains the relationships that exist in the real world.* When testing the CAPM, there are two major questions. First, *How stable is the measure of systematic risk (beta)?* Because beta is our principal risk measure, it is important to know whether past betas can be used as estimates of future betas. Also, how do the alternative published estimates of beta compare? Second, *Is there a positive linear relationship as hypothesized between beta and the rate of return on risky assets?* More specifically, how well do returns conform to the following SML equation, discussed earlier as Equation 79-6?

$$E(Ri) = RFR + \beta_i(R_M - RFR)$$

---

[15] For a detailed consideration of this, see Fischer Black and Myron Scholes, "The Effects of Dividend Yield and Dividend Policy on Common Stock Prices and Returns," *Journal of Financial Economics* 1, no. 1 (March 1979): 1–22; and Robert Litzenberger and K. Ramaswamy, "The Effect of Personal Taxes and Dividends on Capital Asset Prices: Theory and Empirical Evidence," *Journal of Financial Economics* 7, no. 2 (June 1979): 163–196.

[16] Edwin Elton, Martin Gruber, and Joel Rentzler, "A Single Examination of the Empirical Relationship between Dividend Yields and Deviations from the CAPM," *Journal of Banking and Finance* 7, no. 1 (March 1983): 135–146; Merton Miller and Myron Scholes, "Dividends and Taxes: Some Empirical Evidence," *Journal of Political Economy* 90, no. 4 (December 1982): 1118–1141; and William Christie, "Dividend Yield and Expected Returns," *Journal of Financial Economics* 28, no. 1 (November–December 1990): 95–125.

Some specific questions might include:

▷ Does the intercept approximate the prevailing *RFR*?
▷ Was the slope of the line positive and was it consistent with the slope implied by the prevailing risk premium ($R_M - RFR$?)

We consider these two major questions in the following section.

4.1 Stability of Beta

Numerous studies have examined the stability of beta and generally concluded that the risk measure was *not* stable for individual stocks but the stability of the beta for *portfolios* of stocks increased dramatically. Further, the larger the portfolio of stocks (e.g., over 50 stocks) and the longer the period (over 26 weeks), the more stable the beta of the portfolio. Also, the betas tended to regress toward the mean. Specifically, high-beta portfolios tended to decline over time toward unity (1.00), whereas low-beta portfolios tended to increase over time toward unity.

Another factor that affects the stability of beta is how many months are used to estimate the original beta and the test beta. Roenfeldt, Griepentrog, and Pflamm (RGP) compared betas derived from 48 months of data to subsequent betas for 12, 24, 36, and 48 months.[17] The 48-month betas were not good for estimating subsequent 12-month betas but were quite good for estimating 24-, 36-, and 48-month betas.

Chen concluded that portfolio betas would be biased if individual betas were unstable, so he suggested a Bayesian approach to estimating these time-varying betas.[18]

Carpenter and Upton considered the influence of the trading volume on beta stability and contended that the predictions of betas were slightly better using the volume-adjusted betas.[19] This impact of volume on beta estimates is related to small-firm effect which noted that the beta for low-volume securities was biased downward as confirmed by Ibbotson, Kaplan, and Peterson.[20]

To summarize, individual betas were generally volatile over time whereas large portfolio betas were stable. Also, it is important to use at least 36 months of data to estimate beta and be conscious of the stock's trading volume and size.

4.2 Comparability of Published Estimates of Beta

In contrast to deriving your own estimate of beta for a stock, you may want to use a published source for speed or convenience, such as Merrill Lynch's *Security Risk Evaluation Report* (published monthly) and the weekly *Value Line Investment Survey*. Both services use the following market model equation:

$$(R_{i,t}) = RFR + \beta_i R_{M,t} + E_t$$

Notably, they differ in the data used. Specifically, Merrill Lynch uses *60 monthly observations* and the S&P 500 as the market proxy, whereas the *Value Line* estimates beta

---

[17] Rodney L. Roenfeldt, Gary L. Griepentrog, and Christopher C. Pflamm, "Further Evidence on the Stationarity of Beta Coefficients," *Journal of Financial and Quantitative Analysis* 13, no. 1 (March 1978): 117–121.

[18] Son-Nan Chen, "Beta Nonstationarity, Portfolio Residual Risk, and Diversification," *Journal of Financial and Quantitative Analysis* 16, no. 1 (March 1981): 95–111.

[19] Michael D. Carpenter and David E. Upton, "Trading Volume and Beta Stability," *Journal of Portfolio Management* 7, no. 2 (Winter 1981): 60–64.

[20] Roger G. Ibbotson, Paul D. Kaplan, and James D. Peterson, "Estimates of Small-Stock Betas Are Much Too Low," *Journal of Portfolio Management* 23, no. 4 (Summer 1997): 104–111.

using *260 weekly observations* and the NYSE composite series as the market proxy. They both use an adjustment process because of the regression tendencies.

Given these relatively minor differences, one would probably expect the published betas to be quite comparable. In fact, Statman found a small but significant difference between the betas for both individual and portfolios of stocks.[21]

Reilly and Wright examined over 1,100 securities for three non-overlapping periods and confirmed the difference in beta found by Statman.[22] They also indicated that the reason for the difference was the alternative time intervals (i.e., weekly versus monthly observations) and the security's market value affected both the size and the direction of the interval effect. Therefore, when estimating beta or using a published source, you must consider the return interval used and the firm's relative size.

5 RELATIONSHIP BETWEEN SYSTEMATIC RISK AND RETURN

The ultimate question regarding the CAPM is whether it is useful in explaining the return on risky assets. Specifically, is there a positive linear relationship between the systematic risk and the rates of return on these risky assets? Sharpe and Cooper found a positive relationship between return and risk, although it was not completely linear.[23]

Douglas examined the relationship, and his results indicated intercepts that were larger than the prevailing risk-free rates and the coefficients for the systematic risk variables were typically not significant.[24]

Because of the statistical problems with individual stocks, Black, Jensen, and Scholes examined the risk and return for portfolios of stocks and found a positive linear relationship between monthly excess return and portfolio beta, although the intercept was higher than the zero value expected.[25] Exhibit 79-17 contains charts from this study, which show that (1) most of the measured SMLs had a positive slope, (2) the slopes change between periods, (3) the intercepts are not zero, and (4) the intercepts likewise change between periods.

5.1 Effect of Skewness on the Relationship

Beyond the analysis of return and beta, several authors also have considered the impact of skewness on expected returns. You will recall from your statistics course that skewness reflects the presence of too many large positive or negative observations in a distribution. A normal distribution is symmetric, which means that balance exists between positive and negative observations. In contrast, positive skewness indicates an abnormal number of large positive price changes.

Investigators considered skewness as a means to possibly explain the prior results wherein the model appeared to underprice low-beta stocks (so investors received returns above expectations) and overprice high-beta stocks (so investors

[21] Meir Statman, "Betas Compared: Merrill Lynch vs. Value Line," *Journal of Portfolio Management* 7, no. 2 (Winter 1981): 41–44.

[22] Frank K. Reilly and David J. Wright, "A Comparison of Published Betas," *Journal of Portfolio Management* 14, no. 3 (Spring 1988): 64–69.

[23] William F. Sharpe and Guy M. Cooper, "Risk-Return Classes of New York Stock Exchange Common Stocks: 1931–1967," *Financial Analysis Journal* 28, no. 2 (March–April 1972): 46–54.

[24] G. W. Douglas, "Risk in the Equity Markets: An Empirical Appraisal of Market Efficiency," *Yale Economic Essays* 9, no. 1 (1969): 3–48.

[25] Fischer Black, Michael Jensen, and Myron Scholes, "The Capital Asset Pricing Model: Some Empirical Tests," in *Studies in the Theory of Capital Markets*, ed. Michael Jensen (New York: Praeger, 1972).

received returns lower than expected). Some early results confirmed these expectations, but also found that high-beta stocks had high-positive skewness, which implied that investors prefer stocks with high-positive skewness that provide an opportunity for very large returns.

Kraus and Litzenberger tested a CAPM with a skewness term and confirmed that investors are willing to pay for positive skewness.[26] They concluded that their three-moment CAPM corrects for the apparent mispricing of high- and low-risk stocks encountered with the standard CAPM. The importance of skewness was supported in studies by Sears and Wei and subsequently by Lim.[27]

EXHIBIT 79-17 Average Excess Monthly Rates of Return Compared to Systematic Risk during Alternative Time Periods

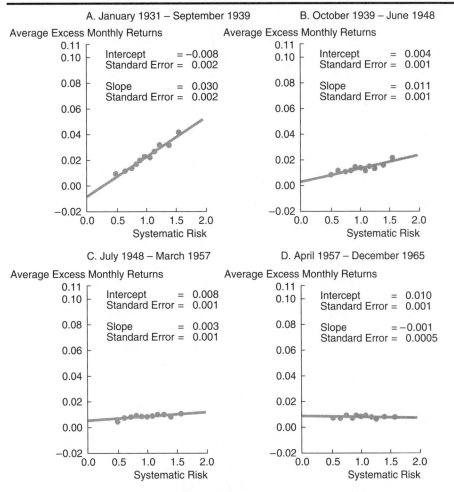

Source: Michael C. Jensen, ed., *Studies in the Theory of Capital Markets* (New York: Praeger Publishers, 1972). 96–97. Reprinted with permission.

[26] Alan Kraus and Robert Litzenberger, "Skewness Preference and the Valuation of Risky Assets," *Journal of Finance* 31, no. 4 (September 1976): 1085–1094.

[27] R. Stephen Sears and John Wei, "The Structure of Skewness Preferences in Asset Pricing Models with Higher Moments," *Financial Review* 23, no. 1 (February 1988): 25–38; and Kian-Guan Lim, "A New Test of the Three-Moment Capital Asset Pricing Model," *Journal of Financial and Quantitative Analysis* 24, no. 2 (June 1989): 205–216.

5.2 Effect of Size, P/E, and Leverage

In the efficient markets hypothesis (EMH) chapter, there was extensive analysis of the size effect (the small-firm anomaly) and the P/E effect. Both of these variables were shown to have an inverse impact on returns after considering the CAPM. These results imply that these variables (size and P/E) are additional risk factors that need to be considered along with beta (similar to the skewness argument). Specifically, expected returns are a positive function of beta, but investors also require higher returns from relatively small firms and for stocks with relatively low P/E ratios.

Bhandari found that financial leverage (measured by the debt/equity ratio) also helps explain the cross section of average returns after both beta and size are considered.[28] This implies a multivariate CAPM with three risk variables: beta, size, and financial leverage.

5.3 Effect of Book-to-Market Value: The Fama-French Study

A study by Fama and French attempted to evaluate the joint roles of market beta, size, E/P, financial leverage, and the book-to-market equity ratio in the cross section of average returns on the NYSE, AMEX, and Nasdaq stocks.[29] While some earlier studies found a significant positive relationship between returns and beta, this study finds that the relationship between beta and the average rate of return disappears during the recent period 1963 to 1990, even when beta is used alone to explain average returns. In contrast, univariate tests between average returns and size, leverage, E/P, and book-to-market equity (BE/ME) indicate that all of these variables are significant and have the expected sign.

In the multivariate tests, the results contained in Exhibit 79-18 show that the negative relationship between size [In (ME)] and average returns is robust to the inclusion of other variables. Further, the positive relation between BE/ME and average returns also persists when the other variables are included. Interestingly, when both of these variables are included, the book-to-market value ratio (BE/ME) has the consistently stronger role in explaining average returns. The joint effect of size and BE/ME is shown in Exhibit 79-18. The top row confirms the positive relationship between return versus the book-to-market ratio—that is, as the book-to-market ratio increases, the returns go from 0.64 to 1.63. The left-hand column shows the negative relationship between return and size—that is, as the size declines, the returns increase from 0.89 to 1.47. Even within a size class, the returns increase with the BE/ME ratio. Similarly, within a BE/ME decile, there is generally a negative relationship for size. Hence, it is not surprising that the single highest average return is in the upper, right-hand corner (1.92), which is the portfolio with the smallest size and highest BE/ME stocks.

The authors conclude that between 1963 and 1990, size and book-to-market equity capture the cross-sectional variation in average stock returns associated with size, E/P, book-to-market equity, and leverage. Moreover, of the two variables, the book-to-market equity ratio appears to subsume E/P and leverage.[30] Following these results, Fama-French suggested the use of a three-factor CAPM model and

---

[28] Laxims Chand Bhandari, "Debt/Equity Ratio and Expected Common Stock Returns: Empirical Evidence," *Journal of Finance* 43, no. 2 (June 1988): 507–528.

[29] Eugene F. Fama and Kenneth French, "The Cross Section of Expected Stock Returns," *Journal of Finance* 47, no. 2 (June 1992): 427–465.

[30] A prior study that documented the importance of the BE/ME ratio was Barr Rosenberg, Kenneth Reid, and Ronald Lanstein, "Persuasive Evidence of Market Inefficiency," *Journal of Portfolio Management* 11, no. 3 (Spring 1985): 9–17.

used this model in a subsequent study to explain a number of the anomalies from prior studies.[31]

EXHIBIT 79-18 Average Slopes (*t*-Statistics) from Month-by-Month Regressions of Stock Returns on β, Size, Book-to-Market Equity, Leverage, and E/P: July 1963 to December 1990

Stocks are assigned the post-ranking β of the size-β portfolio they are in at the end of June of year *t*. BE is the book value of common equity plus balance-sheet deferred taxes, A is total book assets, and E is earnings (income before extraordinary items, plus income-statement deferred taxes, minus preferred dividends). BE, A, and E are for each firm's latest fiscal year ending in calendar year $t-1$. The accounting ratios are measured using market equity ME in December of year $t-1$. Firm size ln(ME) is measured in June of year *t*. In the regressions, these values of the explanatory variables for individual stocks are matched with returns for the CRSP tapes from the University of Chicago for the months from July of year *t* to June of year $t+1$. The gap between the accounting data and the returns ensures that the accounting data are available prior to the returns. If earnings are positive, E(+)/P is the ratio of total earnings to market equity and E/P dummy is 0. If earnings are negative, E(+)/P is 0 and E/P dummy is 1.

The average slope is the time-series average of the monthly regression slopes for July 1963 to December 1990, and the *t*-statistic is the average slope divided by its time-series standard error.

On average, there are 2,267 stocks in the monthly regressions. To avoid giving extreme observations heavy weight in the regressions, the smallest and largest 0.5% of the observations of E(+)/P, BE/ME, A/ME, and A/BE are set equal to the next largest or smallest values of the ratios (the 0.005 and 0.995 fractiles). This has no effect on inferences.

β	ɪɴ(ME)	ɪɴ(BE/ME)	ɪɴ(A/ME)	ɪɴ(A/BE)	E/P Dummy	E(+)/P
0.15						
(0.46)						
	−0.15					
	(−2.58)					
−0.37	−0.17					
(−1.21)	(−3.41)					
		0.50				
		(5.71)	0.50	−0.57		
			(5.69)	(−5.34)		
					0.57	4.72
					(2.28)	(4.57)
	−0.11	0.35				
	(−1.99)	(4.44)				
	−0.11		0.35	−0.50		
	(−2.06)		(4.32)	(−4.56)		
	−0.16				0.06	2.99
	(−3.06)				(0.38)	(3.04)
	−0.13	0.33			−0.14	0.87
	(−2.47)	(4.46)			(−0.90)	(1.23)

---

[31] The three-factor model was suggested in Eugene F. Fama and Kenneth French, "Common Risk Factors in the Returns on Stocks and Bonds," *Journal of Financial Economics* 33, no. 1 (February 1993): 3–56. The model was used in Eugene F. Fama and Kenneth French, "Multifactor Explanations of Asset Pricing Anomalies," *Journal of Finance* 51, no. 1 (March 1996): 55–84.

EXHIBIT 79-18 Average Slopes (*t*-Statistics) from Month-by-Month Regressions of Stock Returns on β, Size, Book-to-Market Equity, Leverage, and E/P: July 1963 to December 1990 (continued)

β	ɪɴ(ME)	ɪɴ(BE/ME)	ɪɴ(A/ME)	ɪɴ(A/BE)	E/P Dummy	E(+)/P
	−0.13		0.32	−0.46	−0.08	1.15
	(−2.47)		(4.28)	(−4.45)	(−0.56)	(1.57)

Source: Eugene F. Fama and Kenneth French, "The Cross Section of Expected Stock Returns," *Journal of Finance* 47, no. 2 (June 1992): 439. Reprinted with permission of Blackwell Publishing.

5.4 Summary of CAPM Risk-Return Empirical Results

Most of the early evidence regarding the relationship between rates of return and systematic risk of portfolios supported the CAPM; there was evidence that the intercepts were generally higher than implied by the *RFR* that prevailed, which is either consistent with a zero-beta model or the existence of higher borrowing rates. In a search for other variables that could explain these unusual returns, additional variables were considered including the third moment of the distribution (skewness). The results indicated that positive skewness and high betas were correlated.

The efficient markets literature provided extensive evidence that size, the P/E ratio, financial leverage, and the book-to-market value ratio have explanatory power regarding returns beyond beta.

The Fama-French study considered most of the variables suggested and concluded that beta was not related to average returns on stocks when included with other variables or when considered alone. Moreover, the two dominant variables were size and the book value to market value ratio.

A subsequent study by Dennis, Perfect, Snow, and Wiles[32] confirmed the Fama-French results and showed that this superiority of the three-factor model prevailed after assuming 1 percent transaction costs and annual rebalancing (the optimal results were derived rebalancing every four years). Alternatively, in contrast to Fama-French who measure beta with monthly returns, Kothari, Shanken, and Sloan (KSS) measured beta with annual returns to avoid trading problems and found substantial compensation for beta risk.[33] They suggested that the Fama-French results may have been periodic to this time frame and might not be significant over a longer period. Pettengill, Dundaram, and Matthur noted that empirical studies typically use realized returns to test the CAPM model when theory specifies expected returns.[34] When the authors adjust for negative market excess returns, they find a consistent and significant relationship between beta and rates of return. When Jagannathan and Wang employed a conditional CAPM that allows for changes in betas and the market risk premium, this model performed well in explaining the cross section of returns.[35] Grundy and Malkiel also contend that beta is a very useful measure of risk during declining markets, which is when it is important.[36]

---

[32] Patrick Dennis, Steven Perfect, Karl Snow, and Kenneth Wiles, "The Effects of Rebalancing on Size and Book-to-Market Ratio Portfolio Returns," *Financial Analysts Journal* 51, no. 3 (May–June 1995): 47–57.

[33] S. P. Kothari, Jay Shanken, and Richard G. Sloan, "Another Look at the Cross Section of Expected Stock Returns," *Journal of Finance* 50, no. 2 (March 1995): 185–224.

[34] Glenn Pettengill, Sridhar Dundaram, and Ike Matthur, "The Conditional Relation between Beta and Returns," *Journal of Financial and Quantitative Analysis* 30, no. 1 (March 1995): 101–115.

[35] Ravi Jagannathan and Zhenyu Wang, "The Conditional CAPM and the Cross Section of Expected Returns," *Journal of Finance* 51, no. 1 (March 1996): 3–53.

[36] Kevin Grundy and Burton Malkiel, "Reports of Beta's Death Have Been Greatly Exaggerated," *Journal of Portfolio Management* 22, no. 3 (Spring 1996): 36–44.

THE MARKET PORTFOLIO: THEORY VERSUS PRACTICE

Throughout our presentation of the CAPM, we noted that the market portfolio included *all* the risky assets in the economy. Further, in equilibrium, the various assets would be included in the portfolio in proportion to their market value. Therefore, this market portfolio should contain not only U.S. stocks and bonds but also real estate, options, art, stamps, coins, foreign stocks and bonds, and so on, with weights equal to their relative market value.

Although this concept of a market portfolio is reasonable in theory, it is difficult—if not impossible—to implement when testing or using the CAPM. The easy part is getting a stock series for the NYSE, the AMEX, and major world stock exchanges, such as Tokyo, London, and Germany. There are stock series for the OTC market, too, but these series generally are incomplete. Also, as noted in Chapter 5, there is a growing number of world stock indexes. There also are some well-regarded U.S. bond series available (e.g., from Lehman Brothers, Merrill Lynch, Ryan Labs, and Salomon Brothers) and several world bond series (e.g., from J. P. Morgan, Salomon Brothers, and Merrill Lynch). Because of the difficulty in deriving series that are available monthly in a timely fashion for the numerous other assets mentioned, most studies have limited themselves to using a stock or bond series alone. In fact, the vast majority of studies have chosen the S&P 500 series or some other NYSE stock series that is obviously limited to only U.S. stocks, which constitutes *less than 20 percent* of a truly global risky asset portfolio (see Exhibit 79-1). At best, it was assumed that the particular series used as a proxy for the market portfolio was highly correlated with the true market portfolio.

Most academicians recognize this potential problem but assume that the deficiency is not serious. Several articles by Roll, however, concluded that, on the contrary, the use of these indexes as a proxy for the market portfolio had very serious implications for tests of the model and especially for using the model when evaluating portfolio performance.[37] Roll referred to it as a **benchmark error** because the

EXHIBIT 79-19 Differential Performance Based on an error in Estimating Systematic Risk

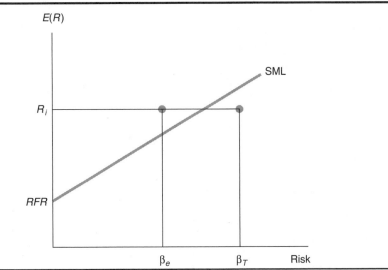

[37] Richard Roll, "A Critique of the Asset Pricing Theory's Tests," *Journal of Financial Economics* 4, no. 4 (March 1977): 129–176; Richard Roll, "Ambiguity When Performance Is Measured by the Securities Market Line," *Journal of Finance* 33. no. 4 (September 1978): 1051–1069; Richard Roll, "Performance Evaluation and Benchmark Error I," *Journal of Portfolio Management* 6, no. 4 (Summer 1980): 5–12; and Richard Roll, "Performance Evaluation and Benchmark Error II," *Journal of Portfolio Management* 7, no. 2 (Winter 1981): 17–22. This discussion draws heavily from these articles.

practice is to compare the performance of a portfolio manager to the return of an unmanaged portfolio of equal risk—that is, the market portfolio adjusted for risk would be the benchmark. Roll's point is that, if the benchmark is mistakenly specified, you cannot measure the performance of a portfolio manager properly. A mistakenly specified market portfolio can have two effects. First, the beta computed for alternative portfolios would be wrong because the market portfolio used to compute the portfolio's systematic risk is inappropriate. Second, the SML derived would be wrong because it goes from the *RFR* through the improperly specified M portfolio. Exhibit 79-19 shows an example where the true portfolio risk (β_T) is underestimated (β_e) possibly because of the proxy market portfolio used in computing the estimated beta. As shown, the portfolio being evaluated may appear to be above

EXHIBIT 79-20 Differential SML Based on Measured Risk-free Asset and Proxy Market Portfolio

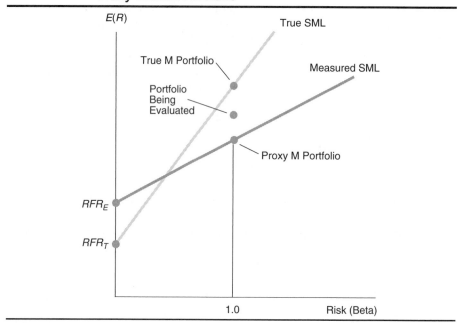

EXHIBIT 79-21 Differential SML Using Market Proxy that is Mean-Variance Efficient

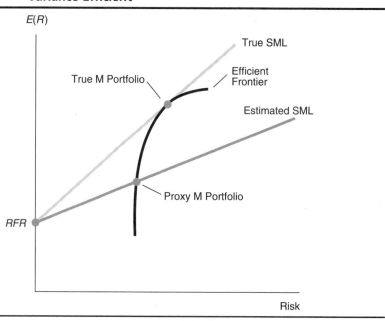

the SML using β_e, which would imply superior management. If, in fact, the true risk (β_T) is greater, the portfolio will shift to the right and be below the SML, which would indicate inferior performance.

Exhibit 79-20 indicates that the intercept and slope will differ if (1) there is an error in selecting a proper risk-free asset and (2) if the market portfolio selected is not the correct mean-variance efficient portfolio. Obviously, it is very possible that under these conditions, a portfolio judged to be superior relative to the first SML (i.e., the portfolio plotted above the measured SML) could be inferior relative to the true SML (i.e., the portfolio would plot below the true SML).

Roll contends that a test of the CAPM requires an analysis of whether the proxy used to represent the market portfolio is mean-variance efficient (on the Markowitz efficient frontier) and whether it is the true optimum market portfolio. Roll showed that if the proxy market portfolio (e.g., the S&P 500 index) is mean-variance efficient, it is mathematically possible to show a linear relationship between returns and betas derived with this portfolio. Unfortunately, this is not a true test of the CAPM because you are not working with the true SML (see Exhibit 79-21).

A demonstration of the impact of the benchmark problem is provided in a study by Reilly and Akhtar.[38] Exhibit 79-22 shows the substantial difference in average beta for the 30 stocks in the DJIA during three alternative periods using three different proxies for the market portfolio: (1) the S&P 500 Index, (2) the Morgan Stanley World Stock Index, and (3) the Brinson Partners Global Security Market Index (GSMI). The GSMI includes not only U.S. and international stocks but also U.S. and international bonds.

EXHIBIT 79-22 Average Beta for the 30 Stocks in the Dow Jones Industrial Average during Alternative Time Periods Using Different Proxies for the Market Portfolios

Time Period	Alternative Market Proxies		
	S&P 500	M-S World	Brinson GSMI
1983–1988			
Average beta	0.820	0.565	1.215
Mean index return	0.014	0.017	0.014
Standard deviation of index returns	0.049	0.043	0.031
1989–1994			
Average beta	0.991	0.581	1.264
Mean index return	0.010	0.004	0.008
Standard deviation of index returns	0.036	0.043	0.026
1983–1994			
Average beta	0.880	0.606	1.223
Mean index return	0.012	0.011	0.011
Standard deviation of index returns	0.043	0.043	0.029

Source: Frank K. Reilly and Rashid A. Akhtar, "The Benchmark Error Problem with Global Capital Markets," *Journal of Portfolio Management* 22, no. 1 (Fall 1995): 33–52.

---

[38] Frank K. Reilly and Rashid A. Akhtar, "The Benchmark Error Problem with Global Capital Markets," *Journal of Portfolio Management* 22, no. 1 (Fall 1995): 33–52.

The results in Exhibit 79-22 are as one would expect because, as we know from earlier in this reading (Equations 79-5 and 79-6), beta is equal to:

$$\text{Beta} = \frac{\text{Cov}_{i,M}}{\sigma_M^2}$$

where:

$\text{Cov}_{i,M}$ = the covariance between asset i and the M portfolio
σ_M^2 = the variance of the M portfolio

As we change from an all-U.S. stock index to a world stock index (M-S World) or a world stock and bond index (GSMI), we would expect the covariance with U.S. stocks to decline. The other component of beta is the standard deviation for the market portfolio. As shown in Exhibit 79-22, typically the M-S World Stock Index has a smaller variance than the S&P 500 because it is more diversified with international stocks. Therefore, while both covariance and market variance decline, the covariance effect dominates, so the beta is smaller with the M-S World Stock Index. In contrast, although the covariance between the U.S. stocks and the GSMI also is lower, the variance of the GSMI market portfolio, which is highly diversified with stocks *and* bonds from around the world, is substantially lower (about 25 to 33 percent). As a result, the beta is substantially larger (about 27 to 48 percent larger) when the Brinson Partners Index is used rather than the S&P 500 Index. Notably, the Brinson Index has a composition of assets that is substantially closer to the "true" M portfolio than either of the other proxies that contain only U.S. stocks or global stocks.

EXHIBIT 79-23 Components of Security Market Lines Using Alternative Market Proxies

	1983–1988			1989–1994			1983–1994		
	R_M	RFR	$(R_M - RFR)$	R_M	RFR	$(R_M - RFR)$	R_M	RFR	$(R_M - RFR)$
S&P 500	18.20	8.31	9.90	13.07	5.71	7.36	15.61	7.01	8.60
Nikkei	26.05	5.35	20.70	−3.62	4.70	−8.32	10.30	5.02	5.28
FAZ	16.36	5.01	11.35	7.97	7.83	0.14	12.09	6.42	5.67
FT AllShare	18.01	10.00	8.01	10.09	10.07	0.02	13.99	10.03	3.95
M-S World	22.64	8.31	14.33	5.18	5.71	−0.52	13.60	7.01	6.60
Brinson GSMI	18.53	8.31	10.22	10.18	5.71	4.48	14.28	7.01	7.28

RFR = risk-free return.

Source: Frank K. Reilly and Rashid Akhtar, "The Benchmark Error Problem with Global Capital Markets," *Journal of Portfolio Management* 22, no. 1 (Fall 1995): 33–52.52

There also was a difference in the SMLs implied by each of the market proxies. Exhibit 79-23 contains the average RFR, the market returns, and the slope of the SML during the three time periods for the three indexes and for market series from Japan (Nikkei), Germany (FAZ), and the United Kingdom (FT All-Share). Clearly, the slopes differ dramatically among the alternative indexes and over time. Needless to say, the benchmark used does make a difference.

Finally, it is necessary to combine the estimate of systematic risk (beta) with the estimated SML to determine the combined effect on the required rate of return for an asset. Exhibit 79-24 shows that during specific time periods the difference between the highest and the lowest expected (required) return ranges from about 4 percent to 7.5 percent, with the highest expected returns when the market proxy was the Brinson GSMI because of the high betas. There were also large differences in the expected (required) returns for individual stocks (i.e., a range of about 4 to 5 percent), which can have a substantial impact on valuation.

EXHIBIT 79-24 The Average Expected Returns for Stocks in the DJIA Based on Different Betas and Security Market Lines Derived with Alternative Benchmarks

Time Period	Mean Expected Rate of Return		
	S&P 500	M-S World	Brinson GSMI
1983–1988	16.41	17.72	20.75
1989–1994	13.00	5.40	11.36

Source: Frank K. Reilly and Rashid A. Akhtar, "The Benchmark Error Problem with Global Capital Markets," *Journal of Portfolio Management* 22, no. 1 (Fall 1995): 33–52.

In summary, an incorrect market proxy will affect both the beta risk measures and the position and slope of the SML that is used to evaluate portfolio performance. In general, the errors will tend to overestimate the performance of portfolio managers because the proxy used for the market portfolio is probably not as efficient as the true market portfolio, so the slope of the SML will be underestimated. Also, the beta measure generally will be underestimated because the true market portfolio will have a lower variance than the typical market proxy due to greater diversification.

Roll's benchmark problems, however, do not invalidate the value of the CAPM as *a normative model of asset pricing;* they only indicate a problem in *measurement* when attempting to test the theory and when using this model for evaluating portfolio performance. Therefore, it is necessary to develop a better market portfolio proxy similar to the Brinson GSMI and/or adjust the portfolio performance measures to reflect this measurement problem.

WHAT IS NEXT?   7

At this point, we have discussed the basic theory of the CAPM, the impact of changing some of its major assumptions, the empirical evidence that does and does not support the theory, and its dependence on a market portfolio of all risky assets. In addition, the model assumes that investors have quadratic utility functions and that the distribution of security prices is normal (symmetrically distributed), with a variance term that can be estimated.

The tests of the CAPM indicated that the beta coefficients for individual securities were not stable, but the portfolio betas generally were stable assuming long enough sample periods and adequate trading volume. There was mixed support for a positive linear relationship between rates of return and systematic risk for portfolios of stock, with some recent evidence indicating the need to consider additional risk variables or a need for different risk proxies. In addition, several papers have criticized the tests of the model and the usefulness of the model in portfolio evaluation because of its dependence on a market portfolio of risky assets that is not currently available.

Consequently, the academic community has considered alternative asset pricing models.

8   THE INTERNET

Investments Online

Asset pricing models show how risk measures or underlying return-generating factors will affect asset returns. Estimates from such models are usually proprietary and are available from providers only by buying their research. Of course, users can always purchase their raw data elsewhere (see some of our earlier Internet discussions) and develop their own estimates of beta and factor sensitivities.

▶ **http://www.valueline.com** The Value Line Investment Survey has been a longtime favorite of investors and many local and college/university libraries subscribe to it. It is a popular source of finding a stock's beta. Value Line Publishing, Inc.'s website contains useful information for the online researcher and student of investments. Its site features investment-related articles, sample pages from the ValueLine Investment Survey, and a product directory that lists the venerable investment survey as well as Value Line's mutual fund, options, and convertibles survey.

▶ **http://www.barra.com** For subscribers, Barra's website offers a gold mine of data and analytical analysis. Links offer information on portfolio management, investment data, market indices, and research. Barra offers its clients data, software, consulting, as well as money management services for equity, fixed income, currency, and other global financial instruments. Barra estimates multiple factor models and their global and single country equity models provide risk analysis on over 25,000 globally traded securities, including predicted and historical beta values. Explore this data to discover its data resources, charts, and graphs.

▶ **http://www.wsharpe.com** William F. Sharpe, the 1990 winner of the Nobel prize in Economics because of his development of the Capital Asset Pricing Model, has a home page on the Internet. Web surfers can read drafts of a sophisticated textbook in progress, some of his published papers, and case studies he has written. Sharpe's site offers monthly returns data on a number of mutual funds, stock indices, and bond indices, and links to other finance sites.

▶ **http://gsb.uchicago.edu/fac/eugene.fama/** The home page of Eugena Fama, whose empirical work first found support . . . and then lack of support . . . for beta as a risk measure.

▶ **http://www.moneychimp.com** This is an informative education site on investments and includes CAPM calculators for estimating a stock's return and a "market simulator" to show the effect of randomness on a portfolio's return over time.

▷ The assumptions of capital market theory expand on those of the Markowitz portfolio model and include consideration of the risk-free rate of return. The correlation and covariance of any asset with a risk-free asset are zero, so that any combination of an asset or portfolio with the risk-free asset generates a linear return and risk function. Therefore, when you combine the risk-free asset with any risky asset on the Markowitz efficient frontier, you derive a set of straight-line portfolio possibilities.

▷ The dominant line is the one that is tangent to the efficient frontier. This dominant line is referred to as the *capital market line* (CML), and all investors should target points along this line depending on their risk preferences.

▷ Because all investors want to invest in the risky portfolio at the point of tangency, this portfolio—referred to as the market portfolio—must contain all risky assets in proportion to their relative market values. Moreover, the investment decision and the financing decision can be separated because, although everyone will want to invest in the market portfolio, investors will make different financing decisions about whether to lend or borrow based on their individual risk preferences.

▷ Given the CML and the dominance of the market portfolio, the relevant risk measure for an individual risky asset is its covariance with the market portfolio, that is, its *systematic risk*. When this covariance is standardized by the covariance for the market portfolio, we derive the well-known beta measure of systematic risk and a security market line (SML) that relates the expected or required rate of return for an asset to its beta. Because all individual securities and portfolios should plot on this SML, you can determine the expected (required) return on a security based on its systematic risk (its beta).

▷ Alternatively, assuming security markets are not always completely efficient, you can identify undervalued and overvalued securities by comparing your estimate of the rate of return to be earned on an investment to its expected (required) rate of return. The systematic risk variable (beta) for an individual risky asset is computed using a regression model that generates an equation referred to as the asset's *characteristic line*.

▷ When we relax several of the major assumptions of the CAPM, the required modifications are reasonably minor and do not change the overall concept of the model. Empirical studies have indicated stable portfolio betas, especially when enough observations were used to derive the betas and there was adequate volume. Although the early tests confirmed the expected relationship between returns and systematic risk (with allowance for the zero-beta model), several subsequent studies indicated that the univariate beta model needed to be supplemented with additional variables that considered skewness, size, P/E, leverage, and the book value/market value ratio. A study by Fama and French contended that during the period 1963 to 1990, beta was not relevant. In their study, the most significant variables were book-to-market value (BE/ME) and size. Subsequent studies both supported their findings and differed with them because some more recent authors have found a significant relationship between beta and rates of return on stocks.

▷ Another problem has been raised by Roll, who contends that it is not possible to empirically derive a true market portfolio, so it is not possible to test the CAPM model properly or to use the model to evaluate portfolio performance. A study by Reilly and Akhtar provided empirical support for this contention by demonstrating significant differences in betas, SMLs, and expected returns with alternative benchmarks.

1. You expect an *RFR* of 10 percent and the market return (R_M) of 14 percent. Compute the expected (required) return for the following stocks, and plot them on an SML graph.

Stock	Beta	$E(R_i)$
U	0.85	
N	1.25	
D	−0.20	

2. *CFA Examination Level II*

An analyst expects a risk-free return of 4.5 percent, a market return of 14.5 percent, and the returns for Stocks A and B that are shown in the following table.

Stock Information		
Stock	Beta	Analyst's Estimated Return
A	1.2	16%
B	0.8	14%

A. Show on the graph provided in the answer book.

   i Where Stock A and B would plot on the security market line (SML) if they were fairly valued using the capital asset pricing model (CAPM)

   ii Where Stock A and B actually plot on the same graph according to the returns estimated by the analyst and shown in the table

B. State whether Stock A and B are undervalued or overvalued if the analyst uses the SML for strategic investment decisions.

REFERENCES

▷ Black, Fischer. "Capital Market Equilibrium with Restricted Borrowing." *Journal of Business* 45, no. 3 (July 1972).

▷ Brinson, Gary P., Jeffrey J. Diermeier, and Gary Schlarbaum. "A Composite Portfolio Benchmark for Pension Plans." *Financial Analysts Journal* 42, no. 2 (March–April 1986).

▷ Campbell, John Y., and John Ammer. "What Moves the Stock and Bond Markets? A Variance Decomposition for Long-Term Asset Returns." *Journal of Finance* 48, no. 1 (March 1993).

▷ Elton, Edwin J., and Martin J. Gruber. *Modern Portfolio Theory and Investment Analysis*, 5th ed. New York: John Wiley & Sons, 1995.

▷ Farrell, James L., Jr. *Portfolio Management Theory and Application*, 2d ed. New York: McGraw-Hill, 1997.

▷ Handa, Puneet, S. P. Kothari, and Charles Wasley. "The Relation between the Return Interval and Betas: Implications of the Size Effect." *Journal of Financial Economics* 23, no. 1 (June 1989).

▷ Hawawini, Gabriel A. "Why Beta Shifts as the Return Interval Changes." *Financial Analysts Journal* 39, no. 3 (May–June 1983).

▷ Reilly, Frank K., and Rashid A. Akhtar. "The Benchmark Error Problem with Global Capital Markets." *Journal of Portfolio Management* 22, no. 1 (Fall 1995).

APPENDICES

SOLUTIONS TO PROBLEMS IN READING 62

1. All other factors constant, the longer the maturity, the greater the price change when interest rates change. So, Bond B is the answer.

2.

Quoted price	Price per $1 par value (rounded)	Par value	Dollar price
96¼	0.9625	$1,000	962.50
102⅞	1.0288	$5,000	5,143.75
109⁹⁄₁₆	1.0956	$10,000	10,956.25
68¹¹⁄₃₂	0.6834	$100,000	68,343.75

3.

	1-year Treasury rate	Coupon rate
First reset date	6.1%	6.4%
Second reset date	6.5%	6.8%
Third reset date	6.9%	7.0%
Fourth reset date	6.8%	7.0%
Fifth reset date	5.7%	6.0%
Sixth reset date	5.0%	5.3%
Seventh reset date	4.1%	4.5%
Eighth reset date	3.9%	4.5%
Ninth reset date	3.2%	4.5%
Tenth reset date	4.4%	4.7%

4. A. This provision is a make-whole redemption provision (also called a yield maintenance premium provision).

   B. A make-whole premium provision provides a formula for determining the redemption price, called the make-whole redemption price. The purpose of the provision is to protect the yield of those investors who purchased the issue at its original offering.

5. For this bond the excerpt tells us that the issue may be redeemed prior to May 1, 1995 but they may not be refunded—that is, they cannot be called using a lower cost of funds than the issue itself. After May 1, 1995, the issue may be redeemed via a refunding. The issue can be called using any source of funds such as a new bond issue with a lower coupon rate than the issue itself.

6. A. While it may be true that the Company can call the issue if rates decline, there is a nonrefunding restriction prior to January 1, 2006. The Company may not refund the issue with a source of funds that costs less than 7.75% until after that date.

B. This is only true if the issuer redeems the issue as permitted by the call schedule. In that case the premium is paid. However, there is a sinking fund provision. If the issuer calls in the particular certificates of the issue held by the investor in order to satisfy the sinking fund provision, the issue is called at par value. So, there is no guarantee that the issue will be paid off at a premium at any time if the issue is called to satisfy the sinking fund provision.

C. It is commonly thought that the presence of a sinking fund provision reduces the risk that the issuer will not have sufficient funds to pay off the amount due at the maturity date. But this must be balanced against the fact that a bondholder might have his or her bonds taken away at par value when the issuer calls a part of the issue to satisfy the sinking fund provision. If the issue is trading above par value, the bondholder only receives par. So, for example, if the issue is trading at 115 and it is called by the Company to satisfy the sinking fund provision, the investor receives par value (100), realizing a loss of 15.

D. As in part C, while it may seem that the right of the issuer to make additional payments beyond the required amount of the sinking fund will reduce the likelihood that the issuer will have insufficient funds to pay off the issue at the maturity date, there is still the potential loss if the issue is called at par. Moreover, the issuer is likely to make additional payments permitted to retire the issue via the sinking fund special call price of 100 when the bond is trading at a premium, because that is when interest rates in the market are less than the coupon rate on the issue.

E. The assistant portfolio manager cannot know for certain how long the bond issue will be outstanding because it can be called per the call schedule. Moreover, because of the sinking fund provision, a portion of their particular bonds might be called to satisfy the sinking fund requirement. (One of the major topics in fixed income analysis is that because of the uncertainty about the cash flow of a bond due to the right to call an issue, sophisticated analytical techniques and valuation models are needed.)

7. The borrowers whose loans are included in the pool can at lower interest rates refinance their loans if interest rates decline below the rate on their loans. Consequently, the security holder cannot rely on the schedule of principal and interest payments of the pool of loans to determine with certainty future cash flow.

8. **A.** An accelerated sinking fund provision grants the issuer the right to redeem more than the minimum amount necessary to satisfy the sinking fund requirement.

B. An accelerated sinking fund provision is an embedded option granted to an issuer because it allows the issuer to retire the issue at par value when interest rates have declined. The issuer can do this even if the issue is nonrefundable or noncallable at that time.

9. When an investor is considering the purchase of a bond, he or she should evaluate any provision granted to the issuer that may affect their expected return over their desired time horizon. Moreover, when a bond is purchased in the secondary market at a price above par value, the concern is that the issue may be paid off prior to the maturity date. The result would be the loss of the premium. So, for example, if an investor believes that a bond is noncallable but the issue has a sinking fund requirement, it is possible that the issue held by an investor can be called at the special redemption price of 100 when the issue is trading at a premium.

10. An investor can purchase a stand alone option on an exchange or in the over-the-counter market. When an investor purchases a bond, there are choices or "options" provided for in the indenture that grants either the bondholder or the issuer the right or option to do something. These choices are commonly referred to as embedded options.

11. A. Institutional investors typically use a repurchase agreement to finance the purchase of a bond.

   B. A term repo is a repurchase agreement where the borrowing is for more than one day; an overnight repo involves borrowing for only one day.

SOLUTIONS TO PRACTICE QUESTIONS

1.

Quoted price	Price per $1 par value (rounded)	Par value	Dollar price
103 1/4	1.0325	$1,000	1,032.50
70 1/8	0.7013	$5,000	3,506.25
87 5/16	0.8731	$10,000	8,731.25
117 3/32	1.1709	$100,000	117,093.75

2.

	6-month Treasury rate	Coupon rate
First reset date	5.5%	6.0%
Second reset date	5.8%	6.3%
Third reset date	6.3%	6.8%
Fourth reset date	6.8%	7.0%
Fifth reset date	7.3%	7.0%
Sixth reset date	6.1%	6.6%

3. A. Inverse floater

    B. Step-up note (or multiple step-up note)

    C. Inflation-linked bond

SOLUTIONS TO PROBLEMS IN READING 63

1. **A.** Below par value since the coupon rate is less than the yield required by the market.

   B. Below par value since the coupon rate is less than the yield required by the market.

   C. Below par value since the coupon rate is less than the yield required by the market.

   D. Above par value since the coupon rate is greater than the yield required by the market.

   E. Par value since the coupon rate is equal to the yield required by the market.

	Issue	Coupon rate	Yield required by the market	Price
A.	A	5¼%	7.25%	Below par
B.	B	6⅝%	7.15%	Below par
C.	C	0%	6.20%	Below par
D.	D	5⅞%	5.00%	Above par
E.	E	4½%	4.50%	Par

2. The price of a callable bond can be expressed as follows:

   price of callable bond = price of option-free bond − price of embedded
   call option

   An increase in interest rates will reduce the price of the option-free bond. However, to partially offset that price decline of the option-free bond, the price of the embedded call option will decrease. This is because as interest rates rise the value of the embedded call option to the issuer is worth less. Since a lower price for the embedded call option is subtracted from the lower price of the option-free bond, the price of the callable bond does not fall as much as that of an option-free bond.

3. **A.** A floating-rate security's exposure to interest rate risk is affected by the time to the next reset date. The shorter the time, the less likely the issue will offer a below-market interest rate until the next reset date. So, a daily reset will not expose the investor of this floater to interest rate risk due to this factor. However, there is interest rate risk which we will see in part B.

   B. The reason there is still interest rate risk with a daily reset floating-rate security is that the margin required by the market may change. And, if there is a cap on the floater, there is cap risk.

4. **A.** While both assistant portfolio managers are correct in that they have identified two features of an issue that will impact interest rate risk, it is the interaction of the two that will affect an issue's interest rate risk. From the information provided in the question, it cannot be determined which has the greater interest rate risk.

   B. You, as the senior portfolio manager, might want to suggest that the two assistant portfolio managers compute the duration of the two issues.

Fixed Income Analysis for the Chartered Financial Analyst® Program, Second Edition, by Frank J. Fabozzi.
Reprinted with permission.

5. The information for computing duration:

   price if yields decline by 30 basis points = 83.50
   price if yields rise by 30 basis points = 80.75
   initial price = 82.00
   change in yield in decimal = 0.0030

   Then,

   $$\text{duration} = \frac{83.50 - 80.75}{2(82.00)(0.0030)} = 5.59$$

6. Since the duration is the approximate percentage price change for a 100 basis point change in interest rates, a bond with a duration of 5 will change by approximately 5% for a 100 basis point change in interest rates. Since the market value of the bond is $8 million, the change in the market value for a 100 basis point change in interest rates is found by multiplying 5% by $8 million. Therefore, the change in market value per 100 basis point change in interest rates is $400,000. To get an estimate of the change in the market value for any other change in interest rates, it is only necessary to scale the change in market value accordingly.

   A. for 100 basis points = $400,000

   B. for 50 basis points = $200,000 (=$400,000/2)

   C. for 25 basis points = $100,000 ($400,000/4)

   D. for 10 basis points = $40,000 ($400,000/10)

7. To calculate duration, the price must be estimated for an increase and decrease (i.e., a rate shock) of the same number of basis points. A valuation model must be employed to obtain the two prices. With an extremely complex bond issue, the valuation models by different analysts can produce substantially different prices when rates are shocked. This will result in differences in estimates of duration.

8. For an individual bond, duration is an estimate of the price sensitivity of a bond to changes in interest rates. A portfolio duration can be estimated from the duration of the individual bond holdings in the portfolio. To use the portfolio's duration as an estimate of interest rate risk it is assumed that when interest rates change, the interest rate for all maturities change by the same number of basis points. That is, it does not consider non-parallel changes of the yield curve.

9. The approach briefly discussed in this reading for doing so is *rate duration*. Specifically, the 5-year rate duration indicates the approximate percentage change in the value of the portfolio if the yield on all maturities are unchanged but the yield for the 5-year maturity changes by 100 basis points.

10. The first form of reinvestment risk is due to the likelihood the proceeds from the called issue will be reinvested at a lower interest rate. The second form of reinvestment risk is the typical risk faced by an investor when purchasing a bond with a coupon. It is necessary to reinvest all the coupon payments at the computed yield in order to realize the yield at the time the bond is purchased.

11. Credit risk includes default risk, credit spread risk, and downgrade risk. While an investor holds a bond in his or her portfolio, if the issuer does not default there is still (1) the risk that credit spreads in the market will increase (credit spread risk) causing the price of the bond to decline and (2) the risk that the issue will be downgraded by the rating agencies causing the price to decline or not perform as well as other issues (downgrade risk).

12. **A.** The probability that a bond rated BBB will be downgraded is equal to the sum of the probabilities of a downgrade to BB, B, CCC or D. From the corresponding cells in the exhibit: 5.70% + 0.70% + 0.16% + 0.20% = 6.76%. Therefore, the probability of a downgrade is 6.76%.

   B. The probability that a bond rated BBB will go into default is the probability that it will fall into the D rating. From the exhibit we see that the probability is 0.20%.

   C. The probability that a bond rated BBB will be upgraded is equal to the sum of the probabilities of an upgrade to AAA, AA, or A. From the corresponding cells in the exhibit: 0.04% + 0.30% + 5.20% = 5.54%. Therefore, the probability of an upgrade is 5.54%.

   D. The probability that a bond rated B will be upgraded to investment grade is the sum of the probabilities that the bond will be rated AAA, AA, A or BBB at the end of the year. (Remember that the first four rating categories are investment grade.) From the exhibit: 0.01% + 0.09% + 0.55% + 0.88% = 1.53%. Therefore, the probability that a bond rated B will be upgraded to investment grade is 1.53%.

   E. The probability that a bond rated A will be downgraded to noninvestment grade is the sum of the probabilities that the bond will be downgraded to below BBB. From the exhibit: 0.37% + 0.02% + 0.02% + 0.05% = 0.46%, therefore, the probability that a bond rated A will be downgraded to noninvestment grade is 0.46%.

   F. The probability that a bond rated AAA will not be downgraded is 93.2%.

13. The market bid-ask spread is the difference between the highest bid price and the lowest ask price. Dealers 3 and 4 have the best bid price (96 15/32). Dealer 2 has the lowest ask price (96 17/32). The market bid-ask spread is therefore 2/32.

14. If this manager's portfolio is marked-to-market, the manager must be concerned with the bid prices provided to mark the position to market. With only one dealer, there is concern that if this dealer decides to discontinue making a market in this issue, bids must be obtained from a different source. Finally, this manager intends to finance the purchase. The lender of the funds (the dealer financing the purchase) will mark the position to market based on the price it determines and this price will reflect the liquidity risk. Consequently, this manager should be concerned with the liquidity risk even if the manager intends to hold the security to the maturity date.

15. **A.** The purchase of a 30-year Treasury exposes the investor to interest rate risk since at the end of one year, the security is a 29-year instrument. Its price at the end of one year depends on what happens to interest rates one year later.

   B. The major difference in risk is with respect to credit risk. Specifically, the AAA issue exposes the investor to credit risk.

   C. There is reinvestment risk for the 1-year zero-coupon Treasury issue because the principal must be reinvested at the end of one year.

   D. The major difference is the quantity of credit risk exposure of both issues. The U.S. corporate bond issue has greater credit risk. (Note that the sovereign issue is dollar denominated so that there is no exchange rate risk.)

   E. The less actively traded issue will have greater liquidity risk.

   F. There are two differences in risk. First, there is the greater credit risk of investing in Italian government bonds relative to U.S. Treasury bonds. Second, investing in the Italian government bonds denominated in lira exposes a U.S. investor to exchange rate risk.

16. Probably the first thing that Ms. Peters should ask is what the investment objectives are of HPLU. Addressing directly the two statements Mr. Steven made, consider the first. Mr. Stevens believes that by buying investment grade bonds the portfolio will not be exposed to a loss of principal. However, all bonds—investment grade and non-investment grade—are exposed to the potential loss of principal if interest rates rise (i.e., interest rate risk) if an issue must be sold prior to its maturity date. If a callable bond is purchased, there can be a loss of principal if the call price is less than the purchase price (i.e., call risk). The issue can also be downgraded (i.e., downgrade risk) or the market can require a higher spread (i.e., credit spread risk), both resulting in a decline in the price of an issue. This will result in a loss of principal if the issue must be sold prior to the maturity date.

    The request that the bond portfolio have 40% in issues that mature within three years will reduce the interest rate risk of the portfolio. However, it will expose the HPLU to reinvestment risk (assuming the investment horizon for HPLU is greater than three years) since when the bonds mature there is the risk that the proceeds received may have to be reinvested at a lower interest rate than the coupon rate of the maturing issues.

17. A. It is reasonable to assume that the municipality will not need to redeem proceeds from the pension fund to make current payments to beneficiaries. Instead, the investment objective is to have the fund grow in order to meet future payments that must be made to retiring employees. Investing in just high investment grade securities that mature in one month or less exposes the pension fund to substantial reinvestment risk. So, while the fund reduces its interest rate risk by investing in such securities, it increases exposure to reinvestment risk. In the case of a pension fund, it would be expected that it can absorb some level of interest rate risk but would not want to be exposed to substantial reinvestment risk. So, this investment strategy may not make sense for the municipality's pension fund.

    B. The opposite is true for the operating fund. The municipality can be expected to need proceeds on a shorter term basis. It should be less willing to expose the operating fund to interest rate risk but willing to sacrifice investment income (i.e., willing to accept reinvestment risk).

18. When the proposed redemption was announced, the securities were treated as short-term investments with a maturity of about six weeks—from the announcement date of January 26th to the redemption date of March 15th. When GECC canceled the proposed redemption issue and set the coupon rate as allowed by the indenture, the price of the issue declined because the new coupon rate was not competitive with market rates for issues with GECC's rating with the same time to the next reset date in three years.

19. A major risk is foreign exchange risk. This is the risk that the Japanese yen will depreciate relative to the British pound when a coupon payment or principal repayment is received. There is still the interest rate risk associated with the Japanese government bond that results from a rise in Japanese interest rates. There is reinvestment risk. There is also credit risk, although this risk is minimal. Sovereign risk is also a minimal concern.

20. Certain events can impair the ability of an issue or issuer to repay its debt obligations. For example, a corporate takeover that increases the issuer's debt can result in a downgrade. Regulatory changes that reduce revenues or increase expenses of a regulated company or a company serving a market that is adversely affected by the regulation will be downgraded if it is viewed by the rating agency that the ability to satisfy obligations has been impaired.

21. This statement about sovereign risk is incomplete. There are actions that can be taken by a foreign government other than a default that can have an adverse impact on a bond's price. These actions can result in an increase in the credit spread risk or an increase in downgrade risk.

SOLUTIONS TO PRACTICE QUESTIONS

1. ► The price for Issue A should be a premium since the coupon rate is greater than the yield required by the market. So, there is no error for Issue A.

   ► The price for Issue B should be a discount since the coupon rate is less than the yield required by the market. So, there is no error for Issue B.

   ► Issue C's coupon rate (0%) is less than the yield required by the market (5%). So, Issue C should be selling at a discount but the reported price is above par value. Hence, the reported price for Issue C is wrong.

   ► Issue D's coupon rate (5.5%) is less than the yield required by the market (5.9%). So, Issue D should be selling at a discount but the reported price is above par value. Hence, the reported price for Issue D is wrong.

   ► The price for Issue E should be par value since the coupon rate is equal to the yield required by the market. So, there is no error for Issue E.

   ► Issue F's coupon rate (4½%) is greater than the yield required by the market (4.0%). So, Issue F should be selling at a premium but the reported price is below par value. Hence, the reported price for Issue F is wrong.

   ► The coupon rate for Issue G and the yield required by the market are equal. So, the price should be par value. Since the reported price is above par value, Issue G's reported price is wrong.

2. Interest rate risk is the exposure of an issue to a change in the yield required by the market or to a change in interest rates. For option-free bonds selling at the same yield, maturity and coupon rate determine the interest rate risk of an issue. Since Issue 3 has both the longest maturity and the lowest coupon, it will have the greatest price sensitivity to changes in interest rates. The issue with the least interest rate risk is Issue 4 since it has the shortest maturity and the highest coupon rate.

3. Issues 5 and 7 have a higher coupon rate and a maturity less than or equal to Issues 4 and 6 and are trading at a higher yield. Thus, Issues 5 and 7 must have less interest rate risk. Issues 4 and 6 have the same maturity and coupon rate. However, Issue 4 is trading at a lower yield relative to issue 6 (7.00% versus 7.20%). Consequently, Issue 4 has the greatest interest rate risk.

4. **A.** If the market wants a higher margin than 120 basis points for similar issues to NotReal.com after issuance, the price will decline because the quoted margin for the issue (120 basis points) is a below-market margin. Even when the coupon rate is reset it will be less than the market required rate for similar issues.

   B. At the time NotReal.com was purchased by an investor, the coupon rate based on the 6-month Treasury rate of 4% was 5.2% (4% plus 120 basis points) considerably below the cap of 8.5%. With the assumed 6-month Treasury rate at 7.0%, the coupon rate is 8.2% (7% plus 120 basis points). Obviously, this is much closer to the cap of 8.5%. While cap risk was present at the time of purchase of this issue, the cap risk was low. With the rise in the 6-month Treasury rate to 7%, cap risk is considerably greater.

5. **A.** In our illustration,

> price if yields decline by 25 basis points = 108.50
> price if yields rise by 25 basis points = 104.00
> initial price = 106.00
> change in yield in decimal = 0.0025

$$\text{duration} = \frac{108.50 - 104.00}{2(106.00)(0.0025)} = 8.49$$

B. For a 100 basis point change and a duration of 8.49, the price will change by approximately 8.49%. For a 50 basis point change it would change by approximately 4.245%. Since the current market value is $10 million, the market value will change by approximately $10 million times 4.245% or $424,500.

6. **A.** The portfolio will change by approximately 5% for a 100 basis point change in interest rates and 2.5% for a 50 basis point change. Since the current market value is $85 million, the portfolio's value will change by approximately 2.5% times $85 million, or $2,125,000.

B. The five bonds in the portfolio have different maturities, ranging from 2 years to 28 years. The assumption when using duration is that if interest rates change, the interest rate for all the maturities changes by the same number of basis points.

C. A 5-year rate duration of 1.5 means that if all other key rates are unchanged but the 5-year rate increases by 100 basis points, the value of the portfolio will change by approximately 1.5%.

SOLUTIONS TO PROBLEMS IN READING 64

1. None of the statements is correct and therefore one must disagree with each statement for the following reasons.

   A. The foreign bond market sector of the Japanese bond market consists of non-Japanese entities that issue bonds in Japan.

   B. All but U.S. government bonds are rated.

   C. The guarantee of semi-government bonds varies from country to country. Some may carry the full faith and credit of the central government while others may have an implied or indirect guarantee.

   D. In the United States, federally related agency securities (with some exceptions) carry the full faith and credit of the U.S. government. Government sponsored enterprises (with some exceptions) have an implied guarantee.

2. The reason for assigning two types of ratings is that historically the default frequency for government issues denominated in a foreign currency is different from that of government issues denominated in the local currency.

3. A. In a single-price auction, all winning bidders are awarded securities at the highest yield bid. In a multiple-price auction, all winning bidders are awarded securities at the yield they bid.

   B. In a tap system, a government issues additional bonds of a previously outstanding bond issue via an auction.

4. A. Since the inflation rate (as measured by the CPI-U) is 3.6%, the semiannual inflation rate for adjusting the principal is 1.8%.

   i. The inflation adjustment to the principal is

   $$\$1,000,000 \times 0.018\% = \$18,000$$

   ii. The inflation-adjusted principal is

   $$\$1,000,000 + \text{the inflation adjustment to the principal}$$
   $$= \$1,000,000 + \$18,000 = \$1,018,000$$

   iii. The coupon payment is equal to

   $$\text{inflation-adjusted principal} \times (\text{real rate}/2)$$
   $$= \$1,018,000 \times (0.032/2) = \$16,288.00$$

   B. Since the inflation rate is 4.0%, the semiannual inflation rate for adjusting the principal is 2.0%.

   i. The inflation adjustment to the principal is

   $$\$1,018,000 \times 0.02\% = \$20,360$$

   ii. The inflation-adjusted principal is

   $$\$1,018,000 + \text{the inflation adjustment to the principal}$$
   $$= \$1,018,000 + \$20,360 = \$1,038,360$$

   iii. The coupon payment is equal to

   $$\text{inflation-adjusted principal} \times (\text{real rate}/2)$$
   $$= \$1,038,360 \times (0.032/2) = \$16,613.76$$

Fixed Income Analysis for the Chartered Financial Analyst® Program, Second Edition, by Frank J. Fabozzi. Reprinted with permission.

5. **A.** The inflation rate selected is the non-seasonally adjusted U.S. City Average All Items Consumer Price Index for All Urban Consumers (denoted CPI-U)

   B. The Treasury has agreed that if the inflation-adjusted principal is less than the initial par value, the par value will be paid at maturity.

   C. When a TIPS issue is purchased between coupon payments, the price paid by the buyer has to be adjusted for the inflation up to the settlement date. That is why the Treasury reports a daily index ratio for an issue.

6. Agency debentures are securities issued by government sponsored enterprises that do not have any specific collateral securing the bond. The ability to pay bondholders depends on the ability of the issuing GSE to generate sufficient cash flow to satisfy the obligation.

7. **A.** Monthly mortgage payment = $1,797.66
   Monthly mortgage rate = 0.00583333 (0.07/12)

Month	Beginning of month mortgage balance	Mortgage payment	Interest	Scheduled principal repayment	End of month mortgage balance
1	200,000.00	1,797.66	1,166.67	630.99	199,369.01
2	199,369.01	1,797.66	1,162.99	634.67	198,734.34
3	198,734.34	1,797.66	1,159.28	638.37	198,095.97
4	198,095.97	1,797.66	1,155.56	642.10	197,453.87
5	197,453.87	1,797.66	1,151.81	645.84	196,808.03
6	196,808.03	1,797.66	1,148.05	649.61	196,158.42

   B. In the last month (month 180), after the final monthly mortgage payment is made, the ending mortgage balance will be zero. That is, the mortgage will be fully paid.

   C. The cash flow is unknown even if the borrower does not default. This is because the borrower has the right to prepay in whole or in part the mortgage balance at any time.

8. **A.** A prepayment is additional principal paid by the borrower in excess of the monthly mortgage payment.

   B. The monthly cash flow of a mortgage-backed security is made up of three elements: (1) net interest (i.e., interest less servicing and other fees), (2) scheduled principal repayments (amortization), and (3) prepayments.

   C. A curtailment is a form of prepayment. Rather than prepaying the entire outstanding mortgage balance, a curtailment is a pay off of only part of the outstanding balance—it shortens (or "curtails") the life of the loan.

9. Prepayment risk is the uncertainty regarding the receipt of cash flows due to prepayments. Because of prepayments the investor does not know when principal payments will be received even if borrowers do not default on their mortgage loan.

10. A. In a mortgage passthrough security, the monthly cash flow from the underlying pool of mortgages is distributed on a pro rata basis to all the certificate holders. In contrast, for a collateralized mortgage obligation, there are rules for the distribution of the interest (net interest) and the principal (scheduled and prepaid) to different tranches.

   B. The rules for the distribution of interest and rules for the distribution of principal to the different tranches in a CMO structure effectively redistributes prepayment risk among the tranches.

11. Two government-sponsored enterprises that issue mortgage-backed securities are Fannie Mae and Freddie Mac.

12. An unlimited tax general obligation bond is a stronger form of a general obligation bond than a limited tax general obligation bond. The former is secured by the issuer's unlimited taxing power. The latter is a limited tax pledge because for such debt there is a statutory limit on tax rates that the issuer may levy to service the debt.

13. A moral obligation bond is a municipal bond that in the case of default of an issuer allows the state where the issuer is located to appropriate funds that are scheduled to be paid to the defaulted issuer and use those funds to meet the defaulted issuer's obligation. This is a nonbinding obligation that depends on the best efforts of the state to appropriate the funds to satisfy the defaulted issuer's obligation.

14. An insured municipal bond is an issue that is backed by an insurance policy written by a commercial insurance company such that the insurer agrees to pay bondholders any principal and/or coupon interest that the municipal issuer fails to pay.

15. A. A prerefunded bond is a municipal bond that may have originally been a general obligation bond or a revenue bond that is effectively refunded by creating a portfolio of Treasury securities that generates a cash flow equal to the debt service payments on the issue.

   B. Regardless of the credit rating of the issue prior to prerefunding, after prerefunding the issue is effectively collateralized by a portfolio of Treasury obligations such that the cash flow of the Treasury portfolio matches the payments on the issue when they are due. Hence, a prerefunded issue has no credit risk if properly structured.

16. A. In a liquidation, all the assets of a corporation will be distributed to the holders of claims and no corporate entity will survive. In a reorganization, a new corporate entity will be created and some security holders will receive in exchange for their claims cash and/or new securities in the new corporation.

   B. The absolute priority principle is that senior creditors are paid in full before junior creditors are paid anything.

   C. The statement is true in a liquidation; however, this is not necessarily the case in a reorganization. In fact, studies suggest that the principle of absolute priority is the exception rather than the rule in a reorganization.

17. A. An unsecured bond is called a debenture. Subordinated debenture bonds are issues that rank after secured debt, after debenture bonds, and often after some general creditors in their claim on assets and earnings.

   B. A negative pledge clause prohibits a corporation from creating or assuming any lien to secure a debt issue at the expense of existing creditors. This is an important provision for unsecured creditors.

18. A. The performance of corporate bonds will depend not only on the default rate, but the recovery rate as well as the spread over Treasury securities.

B. The reason for the discrepancy is that these studies are measuring defaults over different periods. Studies that find that one-third default look at cumulative default rates over a period of time. The 2.15% to 2.4% figure is an annual default rate.

C. The comment is wrong for two reasons. First, studies have found that the recovery rate is about 38% of the trading price at the time of default. Second, studies have found that the higher the level of seniority, the greater the recovery rate.

19. A. A medium-term note and corporate bond differ as to how they are distributed to investors when they are initially sold. For a MTN, an issuer offers securities on a continuous basis via an investment banking firm or a broker/dealer acting as an agent by posting rates daily as to the rate it is willing to pay for specific maturities. In contrast, a corporate bond is issued on a discrete basis—it is issued at a given point in time by an investment banker.

B. An issuer can couple a medium-term note offering with one or more positions in derivative instruments to create an instrument that has a coupon rate customized with respect to risk-return characteristics for an institutional investor. Such medium-term notes are called structured notes.

C. With an index amortizing note (IAN), the coupon rate is fixed and the principal payments are made prior to the stated maturity date based on the prevailing value for some reference interest rate. Specifically, the principal payments decrease when the reference interest rate increases (hence the maturity increases) and increases when the reference interest rate decreases (hence the maturity decreases). The risk faced by the investor is that an IAN will be outstanding for a longer period when interest rates rise, just when the investor would like proceeds to reinvest at a higher interest rate; there is reinvestment risk when interest rates fall because more principal is paid as rates decline, just when the investor would not want to receive principal.

20. A. Since negotiable certificates of deposit issued by U.S. banks typically exceed the federally insured amount of $100,000, there is credit risk for the amount invested in excess of $100,000.

B. LIBOR refers to the London interbank offered rate and it is the interest rate paid on Eurodollar certificates of deposit. "1-month LIBOR" is the interest rate that major international banks are offering to pay to each other on a Eurodollar CD that matures in one month.

21. Investing in bankers acceptances exposes the investor to the risk that neither the borrower nor the accepting bank will be able to pay the principal due at the maturity date; that is, the investor faces credit risk. On the surface, there is liquidity risk because there are few dealers who make a market in bankers acceptances. However, investors typically purchase bankers acceptances with the intent of holding them to maturity. Consequently, in practice, liquidity risk is not a concern to such investors.

22. The advantage is that depending on the quality of the consumer loan portfolio, this BBB rated issuer may be able to issue an asset-backed security with a higher rating than BBB and thereby reduce its borrowing costs, net of the cost of credit enhancement.

23. A special purpose vehicle allows a corporation seeking funds to issue a security backed by collateral such that the security will be rated based on the credit quality of the collateral rather than the entity seeking funds. Effectively, the special purpose vehicle is the owner of the collateral so that the creditors of the entity seeking funds cannot claim the collateral should the entity default.

24. **A.** External credit enhancement includes corporate guarantees, a letter of credit, and bond insurance.

    B. A disadvantage of an external credit enhancement is that it exposes the asset-backed security structure to a credit downgrading should the third-party guarantor be downgraded.

25. **A.** A collateralized debt obligation is a structure backed by a portfolio of one or more fixed income products—corporate bonds, asset-backed securities, mortgage-backed securities, bank loans, and other CDOs. Funds are raised to purchase the assets by the sale of the CDO. An asset manager manages the assets.

    B. The statement is incorrect. When a CDO is issued, the notes are rated. Restrictions are imposed on the asset manager in order to avoid a downgrading of the tranches or the possibility that the trustee must begin paying off the principal to the senior tranches.

    C. The distinction between an arbitrage transaction from a balance sheet transaction is based on the motivation of the sponsor of the CDO. Arbitrage transactions are motivated by the objective to capture the spread between the yield offered on the pool of assets underlying the CDO and the cost of borrowing which is the yield offered to sell the CDO. In balance sheet transactions, typically undertaken by financial institutions such as banks and insurance companies, the motivation is to remove assets from the balance sheet, thereby obtaining capital relief in the form of lower risk-based capital requirements.

26. A bought deal is a form of a bond underwriting. The underwriting firm or group of underwriting firms offers an issuer a firm bid to purchase a specified amount of the bonds with a certain coupon rate and maturity. The issuer is given a short time period to accept or reject the bid. If the bid is accepted, the underwriting firm has bought the deal.

27. In the United States, SEC Rule 144A eliminates the two-year holding period requirement for privately placed securities by permitting large institutions to trade securities acquired in a private placement among themselves without having to register these securities with the SEC. As a result, private placements are classified in two types. The first type are Rule 144A offerings which are underwritten securities. The second type are the traditional private placements which are referred to as non-Rule 144A offerings.

28. The two major types of electronic bond trading systems are the dealer-to-customer systems and exchange systems. The former are further divided into single-dealer systems and multiple-dealer systems. Single-dealer systems are based on a customer dealing with a single, identified dealer over the computer. In multi-dealer systems a customer can select from any of several identified dealers whose bids and offers are provided on a computer screen.

    The second type of electronic system for bonds is the exchange system. In this system, dealer and customer bids and offers are entered into the system on an anonymous basis, and the clearing of the executed trades is done through a common process. Exchange systems can be further divided into continuous trading and call auction systems. Continuous trading permits trading at continuously changing market determined prices throughout the day. Call auctions provide for fixed price auctions at specific times during the day.

SOLUTIONS TO PRACTICE QUESTIONS

1. A. Since the inflation rate (as measured by the CPI-U) is 2.4%, the semiannual inflation rate for adjusting the principal is 1.2%.

   i. The inflation adjustment to the principal is

$$\$10,000 \times 0.012\% = \$120.00$$

   ii. The inflation-adjusted principal is

$$\$10,000 + \text{the inflation adjustment to the principal}$$
$$= \$10,000 + \$120 = \$10,120$$

   iii. The coupon payment is equal to

$$\text{inflation-adjusted principal} \times (\text{real rate}/2)$$
$$= \$10,120 \times (0.038/2) = \$192.28$$

B. Since the inflation rate is 2.8%, the semiannual inflation rate for adjusting the principal is 1.4%.

   i. The inflation adjustment to the principal is

$$\$10,120 \times 0.014\% = \$141.68$$

   ii. The inflation-adjusted principal is

$$\$10,120 + \text{the inflation adjustment to the principal}$$
$$= \$10,120 + \$141.68 = \$10,261.68$$

   iii. The coupon payment is equal to

$$\text{inflation-adjusted principal} \times (\text{real rate}/2)$$
$$= \$10,261.68 \times (0.038/2) = \$194.97$$

2. Monthly mortgage payment = $699.21
Monthly mortgage rate = 0.00625 (0.075/12)

Month	Beginning of Month Mortgage Balance	Mortgage Payment	Interest	Scheduled Principal Repayment	End of Month Mortgage Balance
1	100,000.00	699.21	625.00	74.21	99,925.79
2	99,925.79	699.21	624.54	74.68	99,851.11
3	99,851.11	699.21	624.07	75.15	99,775.96
4	99,775.96	699.21	623.60	75.61	99,700.35
5	99,700.35	699.21	623.13	76.09	99,624.26
6	99,624.26	699.21	622.65	76.56	99,547.70

SOLUTIONS TO PROBLEMS IN READING 65

1. Market participants look at the key indicators watched by the Fed in order to try to predict how the Fed will react to the movement in those indicators.

2. Ms. Peters should inform her client that under one theory of the term structure of interest rates, the pure expectations theory, a downward sloping yield curve does suggest that short-term interest rates in the future will decline. According to the liquidity preference theory a downward sloping yield curve suggests that rates are expected to decline. But it should be noted that the liquidity preference theory does not view a positive yield curve as one where rates may be expected to rise. This is because the yield premium for liquidity can be large enough so that even if expected future rates are expected to decline, the yield curve would be upward sloping. A downward sloping yield curve according to the market segmentation theory cannot be interpreted in terms of the market's expectations regarding future rates.

3. The pure expectations theory asserts that the only factor affecting the shape of the yield curve is expectations about future interest rates. The liquidity preference theory asserts that there are two factors that affect the shape of the yield curve: expectations about future interest rate and a yield premium to compensate for interest rate risk.

4. According to the pure expectations theory, a humped yield curve means that short-term interest rates are expected to rise for a time and then begin to fall.

5. **A.** The data clearly indicate that yield spreads are at their 12-month highs.

   B. A callable agency issue offers a higher yield spread than a noncallable agency issue because of the call risk faced by investors in the former.

   C. For a given maturity, the longer the deferred call period the lower the call risk. Hence, the yield spread for a callable issue is less the longer the deferred call period.

   D. Because yield spreads are not adjusted for call risk, they are referred to as nominal spreads.

   E. The compensation for credit risk, liquidity risk, and call risk are lumped together in the nominal spreads (i.e., yield spreads shown in the second panel). The OAS is an estimate of the yield spread after adjusting for the call (or option) risk. So, the OAS is less than the nominal yield spread.

6. While it is true that a Ginnie Mae mortgage-backed security has no credit risk and that part of the yield spread between a Ginnie Mae mortgage-backed security and a U.S. Treasury security is due to differences in liquidity, the major reason for the yield spread is the prepayment risk of a mortgage-backed security. This risk is ignored in the statement made by the representative of the investment management firm.

7. **A.** Part of the yield spread between a non-Treasury bond with an embedded option and a Treasury security (which is an option-free security) is due to the value of the embedded option. For example, for a callable non-Treasury bond, the yield spread relative to a Treasury security represents compensation for the following: (1) credit risk, (2) liquidity risk, and (3) call risk. When a spread measure includes all three forms of compensation, it is called a "nominal spread." However, investors want to know the yield spread after adjusting for the value of the embedded options (the call option in our illustration).

Fixed Income Analysis for the Chartered Financial Analyst® Program, Second Edition, by Frank J. Fabozzi. Reprinted with permission.

B. The option-adjusted spread seeks to measure the part of the yield spread between a non-Treasury security and a Treasury security once the portion attributed to the call risk is removed. So, the option-adjusted spread is less than the nominal spread. The option-adjusted spread allows an investor to better compare the yield spread on bonds with and without embedded options.

8. A. absolute yield spread = $7.25\% - 6.02\% = 1.23\% = 123$ basis points

   B. relative yield spread $= \dfrac{7.25\% - 6.02\%}{6.02\%} = 0.204 = 20.4\%$

   C. yield ratio $= \dfrac{7.25\%}{6.02\%} = 1.204$

9. A. The percent yield spread is the relative yield spread.

   B. Analysts recognize that historical comparisons of the absolute yield spread for assessing how yield spreads are changing do not take into account the level of yields. For example, a 40 basis point absolute yield spread in a 5% interest rate environment is quite different from a 40 basis point absolute yield spread in a 10% yield environment.

10. Tax-exempt municipal securities offer a lower yield than Treasury securities because of the value of the tax-exempt feature. This feature is more attractive to high tax bracket investors than to low tax bracket investors. A reduction in marginal tax rates makes the tax-exempt feature less attractive to investors. This would require that tax-exempt municipals to offer higher yields compared to yields prior to the reduction.

   Anticipating a reduction in tax rates would affect municipal yields. The extent of this effect would depend on the market's assessment of the probability the proposal would be enacted.

11. A. Because municipals are tax-exempt, their return or yield spread depends on each investor's marginal tax rate. Treasuries are subject to federal income tax so comparing the two yields to calculate a yield spread would be different for various investors.

   B. The AAA rated municipal general obligation yield curve is used because it offers a similar tax-exempt status to compare its yield against when considering other tax-exempt municipal bonds.

12. A. The after-tax yield is

$$0.05 \times (1 - 0.40) = 0.03 = 3\%$$

   B. The taxable-equivalent yield is

$$\dfrac{0.031}{(1 - 0.39)} = 0.0508 = 5.08\%$$

13. A funded investor who borrows short term is interested in the spread above the borrowing cost. Since LIBOR is the global cost of borrowing, a LIBOR yield curve is a more appropriate measure for assessing the potential return than the Treasury yield curve.

14. The swap rate is the sum of the 5-year Treasury yield of 4.4% and the swap spread of 120 basis points. The swap rate is therefore 5.6%.

15. The swap spread is an important spread measure because it is related to credit spreads and therefore can be used in relative value analysis.

16. A. From the Treasury yield curve, the relevant rate is the 2-year rate because the swap has a two year term. The swap rate is 6.8%, computing by adding the 2-year rate of 5.8% and the swap spread of 100 basis points.

B. The annual payment made by the fixed-rate payer of a $10 million notional amount interest rate swap with a swap rate of 6.8% is: $10,000,000 × 0.068 = $680,000. Since the swap specifies quarterly payments, the quarterly payment is $170,000 (= $680,000/4).

C.

If 3-month LIBOR is	Annual dollar amount	Amount of payment
5.00%	$500,000	$125,000
5.50%	550,000	137,500
6.00%	600,000	150,000
6.50%	650,000	162,500
7.00%	700,000	175,000
7.50%	750,000	187,500
8.00%	800,000	200,000
8.50%	850,000	212,500

D. The net payment is equal to the floating-rate payment received by the fixed-rate payer less the fixed-rate payment made by the fixed-rate payer. The quarterly fixed-rate payment is $170,000. In the table below, a negative sign means that the fixed-rate payer must make a payment.

If 3-month LIBOR is	Floating-rate received	Net payment by fixed-rate payer
5.00%	$125,000	−$45,000
5.50%	137,500	−32,500
6.00%	150,000	−20,000
6.50%	162,500	−7,500
7.00%	175,000	5,000
7.50%	187,500	17,500
8.00%	200,000	30,000
8.50%	212,500	42,500

17. A. The risk that the investor faces is that, if 6-month LIBOR falls below 5%, then the return from the floater for the 6-month period (on an annual basis) would be less than the 7% borrowing cost (the fixed coupon rate of 7%). Thus, the investor is exposed to the risk of a decline in 6-month LIBOR. In general terms, the investor is mismatched with respect to assets (which are floating) and liabilities (which are fixed).

B. When there is a mismatch of the assets and liabilities as this investor faces, an interest rate swap can be used to convert a floating-rate asset into a fixed-rate asset or a fixed-rate liability into a floating-rate liability.

C. Note that the payments for the floater, the fixed-rate liability, and the swap are semiannual. Here are the cash flows from the asset, the liability, and the swap:

Cash inflow from the floater	= 6-month LIBOR + 200 basis points
Cash inflow from the swap	= 7.3%
Total cash inflow	= 9.3% + 6-month LIBOR

Cash outflow for the note issued	= 7%
Cash outflow for the swap	= 6-month LIBOR
Total cash outflow	= 7% + 6-month LIBOR

Net cash flow = annual income spread = 2.3% = 230 basis points

SOLUTIONS TO PRACTICE QUESTIONS

1. In the computation, we will treat the Treasury issue as bond B and the corporate issue as bond A.

   A. GE versus Treasury

   $$\text{absolute yield spread} = 4.93\% - 4.18\% = 0.75\% = 75 \text{ basis points}$$

   $$\text{relative yield spread} = \frac{4.93\% - 4.18\%}{4.18\%} = 0.179 = 17.9\%$$

   $$\text{yield ratio} = \frac{4.93\%}{4.18\%} = 1.179$$

   B. Verizon versus Treasury

   $$\text{absolute yield spread} = 5.11\% - 4.18\% = 0.93\% = 93 \text{ basis points}$$

   $$\text{relative yield spread} = \frac{5.11\% - 4.18\%}{4.18\%} = 0.222 = 22.2\%$$

   $$\text{yield ratio} = \frac{5.11\%}{4.18\%} = 1.222$$

2. **A.** Since the call feature is unattractive to an investor because it results in call risk, the callable issues must offer higher yield spreads.

   B. The longer the protection against the issue being called, the lower the call risk. Consequently, the longer the deferred call period, the lower the yield spread.

3. **A.**

   $$\text{after-tax yield for Ms. High} = 0.068(1 - 0.40) = 0.0408 = 4.08\%$$
   $$\text{after-tax yield for Mr. Low} = 0.068(1 - 0.15) = 0.0578 = 5.78\%$$

   B.

   $$\text{taxable equivalent yield for Ms. High} = \frac{0.048}{1 - 0.40} = 0.0800 = 8.00\%$$

   $$\text{taxable equivalent yield for Mr. Low} = \frac{0.048}{1 - 0.15} = 0.0565 = 5.65\%$$

4. The annual income spread locked in is 2% or 200 basis points.

Asset yield	3-month LIBOR	Funding cost	Fixed rate paid in swap	3-month LIBOR rec. in swap	Annual income spread*
8.60%	4.00%	4.60%	6.00%	4.00%	2.00%
8.60%	5.00%	5.60%	6.00%	5.00%	2.00%
8.60%	6.00%	6.60%	6.00%	6.00%	2.00%
8.60%	7.00%	7.60%	6.00%	7.00%	2.00%
8.60%	8.00%	8.60%	6.00%	8.00%	2.00%
8.60%	8.50%	9.10%	6.00%	8.50%	2.00%
8.60%	9.00%	9.60%	6.00%	9.00%	2.00%
8.60%	10.00%	10.60%	6.00%	10.00%	2.00%
8.60%	11.00%	11.60%	6.00%	11.00%	2.00%

* Annual income spread = Asset yield − Funding cost − Fixed rate paid in swap + 3-month LIBOR received in swap

SOLUTIONS TO PROBLEMS IN READING 66

1. The value is $107.6655 as shown below:

Year	Cash flow	PV at 5.6%
1	7.4	7.0076
2	7.4	6.6360
3	7.4	6.2841
4	7.4	5.9508
5	107.4	81.7871
	Total	107.6655

2. The value is $96,326.46 as shown below

Year	Cash flow	PV at 7.8%
1	$23,998.55	$22,262.11
2	23,998.55	20,651.30
3	23,998.55	19,157.05
4	23,998.55	17,770.92
5	23,998.55	16,485.09
	Total	96,326.47

3. A. The present value of the cash flows for the three discount rates is provided below:

Year	Cash flow	PV at 4.5%	Cash flow	PV at 6.2%	Cash flow	PV at 7.3%
1	$6.2	$5.9330	$6.2	$5.8380	$6.2	$5.7782
2	6.2	5.6775	6.2	5.4972	6.2	5.3851
3	6.2	5.4330	6.2	5.1763	6.2	5.0187
4	6.2	5.1991	6.2	4.8741	6.2	4.6773
5	106.2	85.2203	106.2	78.6144	106.2	74.6665
	Total	107.4630	Total	100.0000	Total	95.5258

B. The following relationship holds:

▶ When the coupon rate (6.2%) is greater than the discount rate (4.5%), the bond's value is a premium to par value ($107.4630).

▶ When the coupon rate is equal to the discount rate, the bond's value is par value.

▶ When the coupon rate (6.2%) is less than the discount rate (7.3%), the bond's value is a discount to par value ($95.5258).

4. A basic property of a discount bond is that its price increases as it moves toward maturity assuming that interest rates do not change. Over the one year that the portfolio is being reviewed, while market yields have increased slightly, the bonds selling at a discount at the beginning of the year can increase despite a slight increase in the market yield since the beginning of the year.

5. **A.** The price is $95.9353 as shown below:

Year	Cash flow	PV at 7%
1	5.8	5.4206
2	5.8	5.0659
3	5.8	4.7345
4	105.8	80.7143
Total		$95.9353

B. The price of the 3-year 5.8% coupon bond assuming the yield is unchanged at 7% is $96.8508, as shown below.

Year	Cash flow	PV at 7%
1	5.8	5.4206
2	5.8	5.0659
3	105.8	86.3643
Total		$96.8508

C. The price is $98.9347 as shown below:

Year	Cash flow	PV at 6.2%
1	5.8	5.4614
2	5.8	5.1426
3	105.8	88.3308
Total		$98.9347

D.

Price change attributable to moving to maturity (no change in discount rate)	$0.9155	(96.8508 − 95.9353)
Price change attribute to an increase in the discount rate from 7% to 6.2%	$2.0839	(98.9347 − 96.8508)
Total price change	$2.9994	

6. The value is $94.2148 as shown below:

Year	Discount rate	Cash flow	PV
1	5.90%	5.8	5.4769
2	6.40%	5.8	5.1232
3	6.60%	5.8	4.7880
4	6.90%	5.8	4.4414
5	7.30%	105.8	74.3853
		Total	$94.2148

7. The value is $107.7561 as shown below:

Period	Discount rate	Cash flow	PV at 2.8%
1	0.028	3.7	3.5992
2	0.028	3.7	3.5012
3	0.028	3.7	3.4058
4	0.028	3.7	3.3131
5	0.028	3.7	3.2228
6	0.028	3.7	3.1350
7	0.028	3.7	3.0496
8	0.028	3.7	2.9666
9	0.028	3.7	2.8858
10	0.028	103.7	78.6770
		Total	107.7561

Alternatively, the short-cut formula can be used.

semiannual coupon payment = $3.70
semiannual discount rate   = 2.8%
number of years   = 5

then

$$\$3.70 \times \left[\frac{1 - \dfrac{1}{(1.028)^{5 \times 2}}}{0.028} \right] = \$31.8864$$

To determine the price, the present value of the maturity value must be added to the present value of the coupon payments. The present value of the maturity value is

$$\text{present value of maturity value} = \frac{\$100}{(1.028)^{5 \times 2}} = \$75.8698$$

The price is then $107.7561 ($31.8864 + $75.8698). This agrees with our previous calculation for the price of this bond.

8.

$$\frac{\$1,000,000}{(1.038)^{40}} = \$224,960.29$$

9. A. First, w must be calculated. We know that

Days between settlement date and next coupon payment 115
Days in the coupon period 183

Therefore,

$$w \text{ periods} = \frac{115}{183} = 0.6284$$

Since the discount rate is 5.6%, the semiannual rate is 2.8%. The present value of the cash flows is $108.8676 and is therefore the full price.

Period	Cash flow	PV at 2.8%
1	3.7	3.6363
2	3.7	3.5373
3	3.7	3.4410
4	3.7	3.3472
5	3.7	3.2561
6	3.7	3.1674
7	3.7	3.0811
8	3.7	2.9972
9	3.7	2.9155
10	103.7	79.4885
	Total	108.8676

B. The accrued interest is

AI = semiannual coupon payment $\times$ $(1 - w)$
AI = $3.7 \times (1 - 0.6284) = 1.3749$

C. The clean price is

clean price = full price $-$ accrued interest
$108.8676 - $1.3749 = $107.4927

10. A. The arbitrage-free value was found in Practice Question 9A to be $111.3324.

B. The price based on single discount rate of 5.65% is $111.1395 as shown below:

Period	Years	Cash flow	PV at 2.825%
1	0.5	3.7	3.5983
2	1.0	3.7	3.4995
3	1.5	3.7	3.4033
4	2.0	3.7	3.3098
5	2.5	3.7	3.2189
6	3.0	3.7	3.1305
7	3.5	3.7	3.0445
8	4.0	3.7	2.9608
9	4.5	3.7	2.8795
10	5.0	3.7	2.8004
11	5.5	3.7	2.7234
12	6.0	3.7	2.6486
13	6.5	3.7	2.5758
14	7.0	3.7	2.5051
15	7.5	3.7	2.4362
16	8.0	103.7	66.4048
		Total	111.1395

C. Dealers would buy the 7.4% 8-year issue for $111.1395, strip it, and sell the Treasury strips for $111.3324. The arbitrage profit is $0.1929 ($111.3324 − $111.1395). The table below shows how that arbitrage profit is realized.

Period	Years	Sell for	Buy for	Arbitrage profit
1	0.5	3.6453	3.5983	0.0470
2	1.0	3.5809	3.4995	0.0814
3	1.5	3.5121	3.4033	0.1087
4	2.0	3.4238	3.3098	0.1140
5	2.5	3.3155	3.2189	0.0966
6	3.0	3.2138	3.1305	0.0833
7	3.5	3.1167	3.0445	0.0722
8	4.0	3.0291	2.9608	0.0683
9	4.5	2.9407	2.8795	0.0612
10	5.0	2.8516	2.8004	0.0513
11	5.5	2.7621	2.7234	0.0387
12	6.0	2.6723	2.6486	0.0237
13	6.5	2.5822	2.5758	0.0064
14	7.0	2.5026	2.5051	−0.0024
15	7.5	2.4240	2.4362	−0.0123
16	8.0	65.7597	66.4048	−0.6451
Total		111.3324	111.1395	0.1929

   D. The process of bidding up the price of the 7.4% 8-year Treasury issue by dealers in order to strip it will increase the price until no material arbitrage profit is available—the arbitrage-free value of $111.3324.

11. A. The arbitrage-free value was found in Practice Question 9B to be $89.3155.44.

   B. The price based on a single discount rate of 5.65% is as shown below to be $89.4971.

Period	Years	Cash flow	Present value 2.825%
1	0.5	2	1.9451
2	1.0	2	1.8916
3	1.5	2	1.8396
4	2.0	2	1.7891
5	2.5	2	1.7399
6	3.0	2	1.6921
7	3.5	2	1.6457
8	4.0	2	1.6004
9	4.5	2	1.5565
10	5.0	2	1.5137
11	5.5	2	1.4721
12	6.0	2	1.4317
13	6.5	2	1.3923
14	7.0	2	1.3541
15	7.5	2	1.3169
16	8.0	102	65.3162
		Total	89.4971

   C. The dealer will buy a package of Treasury strips such that the cash flow from the package will replicate the cash flow of a 4% 8-year Treasury issue and sell the overvalued Treasury issue. The cost of buying the package of Treasury strips is $89.3155. The value of selling the Treasury issue or, if reconstituted, the value of the synthetic coupon Treasury created is $89.4971. The arbitrage profit is therefore $0.1816 ($89.4971 − $89.3155).

   D. The process of dealers selling the Treasury issue will drive down its prices until the market price is close to the arbitrage-free value of $89.3154.

SOLUTIONS TO PRACTICE QUESTIONS

1. A. The cash flow per $100 of par value for this security is:

Year	Cash flow
1	$7
2	7
3	7
4	7
5	107

The present value for each cash flow assuming a discount rate of 5% is:

$$\textit{Year 1: present value}_1 = \frac{\$7}{(1.05)^1} = \$6.6667$$

$$\textit{Year 2: present value}_2 = \frac{\$7}{(1.05)^2} = \$6.3492$$

$$\textit{Year 3: present value}_3 = \frac{\$7}{(1.05)^3} = \$6.0469$$

$$\textit{Year 4: present value}_4 = \frac{\$7}{(1.05)^4} = \$5.7589$$

$$\textit{Year 5: present value}_5 = \frac{\$107}{(1.05)^5} = \$83.8373$$

The present value is the sum of the five present values above, $108.6590.

B. The cash flow for this security is $2,309.75 for each year. The present value of each cash flow assuming a discount rate of 6% is:

$$\textit{Year 1: present value}_1 = \frac{\$2,309.75}{(1.06)^1} = \$2,179.0094$$

$$\textit{Year 2: present value}_2 = \frac{\$2,309.75}{(1.06)^2} = \$2,055.6693$$

$$\textit{Year 3: present value}_3 = \frac{\$2,309.75}{(1.06)^3} = \$1,939.3106$$

$$\textit{Year 4: present value}_4 = \frac{\$2,309.75}{(1.06)^4} = \$1,829.5383$$

$$\textit{Year 5: present value}_5 = \frac{\$2,309.75}{(1.06)^5} = \$1,725.9796$$

The present value of the five cash flows is $9,729.5072.

2. The present value for each cash flow assuming a discount rate of 4% is:

$$\textit{Year 1: present value}_1 = \frac{\$7}{(1.04)^1} = \$6.7308$$

$$\textit{Year 2: present value}_2 = \frac{\$7}{(1.04)^2} = \$6.4719$$

$$\textit{Year 3: present value}_3 = \frac{\$7}{(1.04)^3} = \$6.2230$$

$$\textit{Year 4: present value}_4 = \frac{\$7}{(1.04)^4} = \$5.9836$$

$$\textit{Year 5: present value}_5 = \frac{\$107}{(1.04)^5} = \$87.9462$$

The present value is the sum of the five present values above, $113.3555. A 4% discount produced a present value of $113.3555 which is greater than the present value of $108.6590 when the higher discount rate of 5% is used.

3. A. The value of the bond for the three discount rates is provided below:

Year	Present value at 6%	Present value at 7%	Present value at 8%
1	$6.6038	$6.5421	$6.4815
2	6.2300	6.1141	6.0014
3	5.8773	5.7141	5.5568
4	5.5447	5.3403	5.1452
5	79.9566	76.2895	72.8224
	$104.2124	$100.0000	$96.0073

B. The following relationship holds:

▹ When the coupon rate is greater than the discount rate (7% versus 6%), the bond's value is a premium to par value ($104.2124).

▹ When the coupon rate is equal to the discount rate, the bond's value is par value.

▹ When the coupon rate is less than the discount rate (7% versus 8%), the bond's value is a discount to par value ($96.0073).

4. The cash flow per $100 of par value for this security is:

Year	Cash flow
1	$7
2	7
3	7
4	7
5	107

The present value of each cash flow is

$$\textit{Year 1: present value}_1 = \frac{\$7}{(1.035)^1} = \$6.7633$$

$$\textit{Year 2: present value}_2 = \frac{\$7}{(1.039)^2} = \$6.4844$$

$$\textit{Year 3: present value}_3 = \frac{\$7}{(1.042)^3} = \$6.1872$$

$$\textit{Year 4: present value}_4 = \frac{\$7}{(1.045)^4} = \$5.8699$$

$$\textit{Year 5: present value}_5 = \frac{\$107}{(1.050)^5} = \$83.8373$$

The sum of the present values is $109.1421.

5. The semiannual cash flows for the first 9 six-month periods per $100 of par value is $3.50. For the last period, the cash flow is $103.50. The semiannual discount rate is 2.5%. The present value of each cash flow discounted at 2.5% is shown below:

$$\textit{Year 1: present value}_1 = \frac{\$3.5}{(1.025)^1} = \$3.4146$$

$$\textit{Year 2: present value}_2 = \frac{\$3.5}{(1.025)^2} = \$3.3314$$

$$\textit{Year 3: present value}_3 = \frac{\$3.5}{(1.025)^3} = \$3.2501$$

$$\textit{Year 4: present value}_4 = \frac{\$3.5}{(1.025)^4} = \$3.1708$$

$$\textit{Year 5: present value}_5 = \frac{\$3.5}{(1.025)^5} = \$3.0935$$

$$\textit{Year 6: present value}_6 = \frac{\$3.5}{(1.025)^6} = \$3.0180$$

$$\textit{Year 7: present value}_7 = \frac{\$3.5}{(1.025)^7} = \$2.9444$$

$$\textit{Year 8: present value}_8 = \frac{\$3.5}{(1.025)^8} = \$2.8726$$

$$\textit{Year 9: present value}_9 = \frac{\$3.5}{(1.025)^9} = \$2.8025$$

$$\textit{Year 10: present value}_{10} = \frac{\$103.5}{(1.025)^{10}} = \$80.8540$$

The value of this bond is the sum of the present values, $108.7519.

Alternatively, the short-cut formula can be used. The present value of the coupon payments is:

$$\$3.5 \times \left[\frac{1 - \dfrac{1}{(1.025)^{5\times2}}}{0.025} \right] = \$30.6322$$

The present value of the maturity value is

$$\text{present value of maturity} = \frac{\$100}{(1.025)^{5\times2}} = \$78.1198$$

The price is then \$108.7520 (= \$30.6322 + \$78.1198), the same value as computed on the previous page.

6. **A.** The value given the semiannual discount rate i (one-half the annual discount rate) is found by the following formula:

$$\frac{\$1,000}{(1 + i)^{20}}$$

The solutions follow:

Annual discount rate	Semiannual discount rate	Present value
1%	0.5%	905.0629
2%	1.0%	819.5445
3%	1.5%	742.4704
4%	2.0%	672.9713
5%	2.5%	610.2709
6%	3.0%	553.6758
7%	3.5%	502.5659
8%	4.0%	456.3869
9%	4.5%	414.6429
10%	5.0%	376.8895
11%	5.5%	342.7290
12%	6.0%	311.8047
13%	6.5%	283.7970
14%	7.0%	258.4190

B.

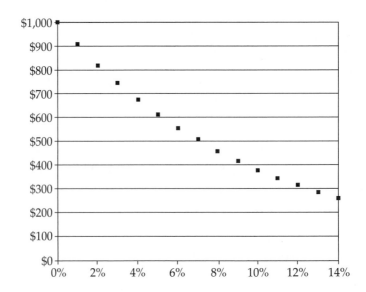

7. First, w must be calculated. We know that

Days between settlement date and next coupon payment	58
Days in the coupon period	183

Therefore,

$$w \text{ periods} = \frac{58}{183} = 0.3169$$

Since the discount rate is 5%, the semiannual rate is 2.5%. The present value of each cash flow is:

$$\textit{Year 1: } \text{present value}_1 = \frac{\$3.5}{(1.025)^{0.3169}} = \$3.4727$$

$$\textit{Year 2: } \text{present value}_2 = \frac{\$3.5}{(1.025)^{1.3169}} = \$3.3880$$

$$\textit{Year 3: } \text{present value}_3 = \frac{\$3.5}{(1.025)^{2.3169}} = \$3.3054$$

$$\textit{Year 4: } \text{present value}_4 = \frac{\$3.5}{(1.025)^{3.3169}} = \$3.2248$$

$$\textit{Year 5: } \text{present value}_5 = \frac{\$3.5}{(1.025)^{4.3169}} = \$3.1461$$

$$\textit{Year 6: } \text{present value}_6 = \frac{\$3.5}{(1.025)^{5.3169}} = \$3.0694$$

$$\textit{Year 7: } \text{present value}_7 = \frac{\$3.5}{(1.025)^{6.3169}} = \$2.9945$$

$$\textit{Year 8: } \text{present value}_8 = \frac{\$3.5}{(1.025)^{7.3169}} = \$2.9215$$

$$\textit{Year 9: } \text{present value}_9 = \frac{\$3.5}{(1.025)^{8.3169}} = \$2.8502$$

$$\textit{Year 10: } \text{present value}_{10} = \frac{\$103.5}{(1.025)^{9.3169}} = \$82.2293$$

The full price for this bond is the sum of the present values, \$110.6019.

8. The value of w is 0.3169 and the coupon interest for the period is \$3.50. Therefore, the accrued interest is:

$$AI = \$3.5 \times (1 - 0.3169) = \$2.3908$$

Since the full price is \$110.6019, the clean price is

$$\text{clean price} = \$110.6019 - \$2.3908 = \$108.2111$$

9. A. The value for the 7.4% coupon 8-year Treasury security is $111.3324 as shown below:

Period	Years	Cash Flow ($)	Spot Rate (%)	Present Value ($)
1	0.5	3.7	3.0000	3.6453
2	1.0	3.7	3.3000	3.5809
3	1.5	3.7	3.5053	3.5121
4	2.0	3.7	3.9164	3.4238
5	2.5	3.7	4.4376	3.3155
6	3.0	3.7	4.7520	3.2138
7	3.5	3.7	4.9622	3.1167
8	4.0	3.7	5.0650	3.0291
9	4.5	3.7	5.1701	2.9407
10	5.0	3.7	5.2772	2.8516
11	5.5	3.7	5.3864	2.7621
12	6.0	3.7	5.4976	2.6723
13	6.5	3.7	5.6108	2.5822
14	7.0	3.7	5.6643	2.5026
15	7.5	3.7	5.7193	2.4240
16	8.0	103.7	5.7755	65.7597
		Total		111.3324

B. The value for the 4% coupon 8-year Treasury security is $89.3155 as shown below:

Period	Years	Cash Flow ($)	Spot Rate (%)	Present Value ($)
1	0.5	2	3.0000	1.9704
2	1.0	2	3.3000	1.9356
3	1.5	2	3.5053	1.8984
4	2.0	2	3.9164	1.8507
5	2.5	2	4.4376	1.7922
6	3.0	2	4.7520	1.7372
7	3.5	2	4.9622	1.6847
8	4.0	2	5.0650	1.6373
9	4.5	2	5.1701	1.5895
10	5.0	2	5.2772	1.5414
11	5.5	2	5.3864	1.4930
12	6.0	2	5.4976	1.4445
13	6.5	2	5.6108	1.3958
14	7.0	2	5.6643	1.3528
15	7.5	2	5.7193	1.3103
16	8.0	102	5.7755	64.6817
			Total	89.3155

SOLUTIONS TO PROBLEMS IN READING 67

1. The three sources are (1) coupon interest, (2) any capital gain (or loss, a reduction in return), and (3) reinvestment income.

2. **A.** The current yield for the bond is

   $$\text{annual coupon payment} = 0.09 \times \$100 = \$9$$

   $$\text{current yield} = \frac{\$9}{\$112} = 0.0804 = 8.04\%$$

   B. The current yield measure only considers coupon interest and ignores any capital gain or loss (a capital loss of $12 for the bond in our example), and reinvestment income.

3. The present value of the cash flows of a 6.5% 20-year semiannual-pay bond using the three discount rates is shown below:

Discount rate (annual BEY)	Semiannual rate (Half annual rate)	Present value of cash flows
7.2%	3.6%	92.64
7.4	3.7	90.68
7.8	3.9	86.94

   Since 3.7% equates the present value of the cash flows to the price of 90.68, 3.7% is the semiannual yield to maturity. Doubling that rate gives a 7.4% yield to maturity on a bond-equivalent basis.

4. This question requires no calculations. (Note that the maturity of each bond is intentionally omitted.) The question tests for an understanding of the relationship between coupon rate, current yield, and yield to maturity for a bond trading at par, a discount, and a premium.

   ▷ Bond A's current yield is incorrect. The current yield should be equal to the coupon rate.

   ▷ Bond B is fine. That is, it has the expected relationship between coupon rate, current yield, and yield to maturity for a bond trading at a premium.

   ▷ Bond C's yield to maturity is incorrect. Since the bond is a premium bond, the yield to maturity should be less than the coupon rate.

   ▷ Bond D is fine. That is, it has the expected relationship between coupon rate, current yield, and yield to maturity for a bond trading at a discount.

   ▷ Bond E is incorrect. Both the current yield and the yield to maturity should be greater than the coupon rate since the bond is trading at a discount.

5. The statement is misleading in that while it is true that the yield to maturity computed on a bond-equivalent basis is flawed, it is not the reason why the yield to maturity is limited. The major reason is that it assumes that the bond is held to maturity and the coupon payments are assumed to be reinvested at the computed yield to maturity.

6. **A.** The total future dollars are found as follows:

   $$\$108.32(1.035)^{10} = \$152.80$$

B. Since the total future dollars are $152.80 and the investment is $108.32, the total interest from the CD is $44.48.

C. The answer is the same as for parts A and B. The total future dollars are $152.80. The total dollar return is the same as the total interest, $44.48.

D. The answer is the same as for part C:

total future dollars = $152.80
total dollar return = $ 44.48

E.

coupon interest   = $ 45.00
capital gain/loss   = −$ 8.32
reinvestment income = $ 7.80
total dollar return   = $ 44.48

F. The percentage of the total dollar return that must be generated from reinvestment income is 17.5% ($7.80/$44.48).

G. The $7.80 reinvestment income must be generated by reinvesting the semiannual coupon payments from the time of receipt to the maturity date at the semiannual yield to maturity, 3.5% in this example. The reinvestment income earned on a given coupon payment of $4.50 if it is invested from the time of receipt in period t to the maturity date (10 periods in our example) at a 3.5% semiannual rate is:

$$\$4.50(1.035)^{10-t} - \$4.50$$

The reinvestment income for each coupon payment is shown below:

Period	Periods reinvested	Coupon payment	Reinvestment income at 3.5%
1	9	$4.5	$1.63
2	8	4.5	1.43
3	7	4.5	1.23
4	6	4.5	1.03
5	5	4.5	0.84
6	4	4.5	0.66
7	3	4.5	0.49
8	2	4.5	0.32
9	1	4.5	0.16
10	0	4.5	0.00
		Total	7.79

The reinvestment income totals $7.79 which differs from $7.80 due to rounding.

7. A. Bond X has no dependence on reinvestment income since it is a zero-coupon bond. So it is either Bond Y or Bond Z. The two bonds have the same maturity. Since they are both selling at the same yield, Bond Z, the one with the higher coupon rate, is more dependent on reinvestment income.

B. As explained in part A, since Bond X is a zero-coupon bond, it has the least dependence (in fact, no dependence) on reinvestment income.

8. The reinvestment risk is that to realize the computed yield, it is necessary to reinvest the interim cash flows (i.e., coupon payments in the case of a nonamortizing security and principal plus coupon payments in the case of an amortizing security) at the computed yield. The interest rate risk comes into play because it is assumed the security will be held to the maturity date. If it is not, the yield no longer applies because there is the risk of having to sell the security below its purchase price.

9. A. The bond-equivalent yield is

$$2[(1.056)^{0.5} - 1] = 0.0552 = 5.52\%$$

B. The annual yield is

$$[(1.028)^2 - 1] = 0.0568 = 5.68\%$$

10. A. The cash flows for this bond to the maturity date are (1) 30 coupon payments of $5 and (2) $100 at the maturity date. The table below shows the present values of the coupon payments and maturity value for the three interest rates in the question:

Annual interest rate (%)	Semiannual interest rate (%)	Present value of 30 payments of $5	Present value of $100 30 periods from now	Present value of cash flows
7.0	3.5	91.9602	35.6278	127.5880
7.4	3.7	89.6986	33.6231	123.3217
7.8	3.9	87.5197	31.7346	119.2543

Since a semiannual interest rate of 3.5% produces a present value equal to the price of the bond ($127.5880), the yield to maturity is 7% on a bond-equivalent basis.

B. The cash flows for this bond up to the first call date are (1) 10 coupon payments of $5 and (2) $105 ten 6-month periods from now. The table below shows the present values of the coupon payments and maturity value for the three interest rates in the question:

Annual interest rate (%)	Semiannual interest rate (%)	Present value of 10 payments of $5	Present value of $105 10 periods from now	Present value of cash flows
4.55	2.275	44.2735	83.8483	128.1218
4.65	2.325	44.1587	83.4395	127.5982
4.85	2.425	43.9304	82.6284	126.5588

Since of the three interest rates in the question, a semiannual interest rate of 2.325% makes the present value of the cash flows closest to the price of $127.5880, the yield to the first call date is 4.65% on a bond-equivalent basis.

C. The cash flows for this bond up to the first par call date are (1) 20 coupon payments of $5 and (2) $100 twenty 6-month periods from now. The table below shows the present values of the coupon payments and maturity value for the three interest rates in the question:

Annual interest rate (%)	Semiannual interest rate (%)	Present value of 20 payments of $5	Present value of $100 20 periods from now	Present value of cash flows
6.25	3.125	73.5349	54.0407	127.5756
6.55	3.275	72.5308	52.4923	125.0231
6.75	3.375	71.8725	51.4860	123.3585

Since of the three interest rates in the question, a semiannual interest rate of 3.125% makes the present value of the cash flows closest to the price of $127.5880, the yield to the first par call date is 6.25% on a bond-equivalent basis.

11. The cash flows to the put date are (1) 8 coupon payments of $2.50 and (2) $100 (the put price) eight 6-month periods from now. The table below shows the present values of the coupon payments and maturity value for the three interest rates in the question:

Annual interest rate (%)	Semiannual interest rate (%)	Present value of 8 payments of $2.5	Present value of $100 8 periods from now	Present value of cash flows
3.38	1.690	18.5609	87.4529	106.0136
3.44	1.720	18.5367	87.2467	105.7834
3.57	1.785	18.4846	86.8020	105.2866

Since of the three interest rates in the question, a semiannual interest rate of 1.785% makes the present value of the cash flows closest to the price of $105.2877, the yield to the put date is 3.57% on a bond-equivalent basis.

12. First, the semiannual effective yield is computed from the monthly yield by compounding it for six months as follows:

$$\text{effective semiannual yield} = (1.0041)^6 - 1 = 0.024854 = 2.4854\%$$

Next, the effective semiannual yield is doubled to get the annual cash flow yield on a bond-equivalent basis. Thus, the cash flow yield on a bond-equivalent basis is 4.97% (2 times 2.4854%).

13. You should agree with Manager B. The cash flow yield, as with any other yield measure such as the yield to maturity or any yield to call date, requires that the investor be able to reinvest any interim cash flows in order to realize the computed yield. A cash flow yield is even more dependent on reinvestment income because the interim cash flows are monthly coupon and principal, rather than simply semiannual coupon for a standard coupon bond. Consequently, the reinvestment risk is greater with an amortizing security.

14. The table on the next page shows the present value using the three discount margins:

5-year floater

current LIBOR   5.00%

quoted margin   30 basis points

				Present value ($) at assumed margin of		
Period	**LIBOR** (annual rate) (%)	**Coupon** rate (%)	**Cash flow** ($)	40 5.400%	50 5.500%	55 5.550%
1	5.00	5.300	2.65	2.5803	2.5791	2.5784
2	5.00	5.300	2.65	2.5125	2.5100	2.5088
3	5.00	5.300	2.65	2.4464	2.4429	2.4411
4	5.00	5.300	2.65	2.3821	2.3775	2.3752
5	5.00	5.300	2.65	2.3195	2.3139	2.3110
6	5.00	5.300	2.65	2.2585	2.2519	2.2486
7	5.00	5.300	2.65	2.1991	2.1917	2.1879
8	5.00	5.300	2.65	2.1413	2.1330	2.1289
9	5.00	5.300	2.65	2.0850	2.0759	2.0714
10	5.00	5.300	102.65	78.6420	78.2601	78.0700
			Total	99.5669	99.1360	98.9214

When a margin of 50 basis points is used, the present value of the cash flows is equal to the price ($99.1360).

15. The discount margin ignores both and hence is a limitation of this measure. The cap is not considered because the reference rate is assumed to be unchanged at the current value for the reference rate. The only way in which the cap is considered is in the special case where the current value for the reference rate is capped and in this case it assumes that the reference rate will not fall below the cap for the life of the floater.

16. A. The yield on a discount basis, d, is

$$(1 - 0.989)\left(\frac{360}{105}\right) = 0.0377 = 3.77\%$$

B. The price of this Treasury bill, p, per $1 dollar of maturity value is:

$$1 - 0.0368 \, (275/360) = 0.971889$$

C. The yield on a discount basis has two major shortcomings. First, it relates the interest return to the maturity or face value rather than the amount invested. Second, it is based on a 360-day year rather than 365-day year as used for Treasury coupon securities.

17. Beyond the 1-year maturity, there are only a few on-the-run Treasury issues available: 2 year, 5 year, and 10 year. For the 30-year maturity, market participants estimate the yield based on the last 30-year Treasury bond that was issued by the U.S. Department of the Treasury. The yield for interim maturities is calculated using an interpolation methodology. The simplest is linear interpolation; however, more elaborate statistical methods can be used.

18. We will use the same notation as in the reading. One-half the annualized spot rate for a 6-month period will be denoted by z_t. We know that the 6-month Treasury bill yield is 4.6% and the 1-year Treasury yield is 5.0%, so

$$z_1 = 4.6\%/2 = 2.3\% \quad \text{and} \quad z_2 = 5.0\%/2 = 2.5\%$$

Now we use the bootstrapping methodology. The 1.5-year Treasury yield from the Treasury yield curve is selling to yield 5.4%. Since the price of the issue is its par value, the coupon rate is 5.4%. So, the cash flow for this issue is:

0.5 year	$0.054 \times \$100 \times 0.5$	$= \$2.70$
1.0 year	$0.054 \times \$100 \times 0.5$	$= \$2.70$
1.5 years	$0.054 \times \$100 \times 0.5 \ + \$100$	$= \$102.70$

The present value of the cash flows is then:

$$\frac{2.7}{(1 + z_1)^1} + \frac{2.7}{(1 + z_2)^2} + \frac{102.7}{(1 + z_3)^3}$$

Substituting the first two spot rates we have:

$$\frac{2.7}{(1.023)^1} + \frac{2.7}{(1.025)^2} + \frac{102.7}{(1 + z_3)^3}$$

The goal is to find z_3. Since the value of this cash flow must be equal to the price of the 1.5-year issue which is par value, we can set the previous equation equal to 100:

$$\frac{2.7}{(1.023)^1} + \frac{2.7}{(1.025)^2} + \frac{102.7}{(1 + z_3)^3} = 100$$

We then solve for z_3 as follows:

$$2.639296 + 2.569899 + \frac{102.7}{(1 + z_3)^3} = 100$$

$$\frac{102.7}{(1 + z_3)^3} = 94.7908$$

$$z_3 = 0.027073 = 2.7073\%$$

Doubling this yield we obtain the bond-equivalent yield of 5.4146%.

The equation for obtaining the 2-year, 2.5-year, and 3-year spot rates are given below.

For the 2-year spot rate, the coupon rate from the Treasury yield curve is 5.8%. So, the present value of the cash flow is:

$$\frac{2.9}{(1 + z_1)^1} + \frac{2.9}{(1 + z_2)^2} + \frac{2.9}{(1 + z_3)^3} + \frac{102.9}{(1 + z_4)^4}$$

Substituting: $z_1 = 2.3\%$ $z_2 = 2.5\%$ $z_3 = 2.7073\%$
and setting the present value equal to the price of the 2-year issue (100), we obtain:

$$\frac{2.9}{(1.023)^1} + \frac{2.9}{(1.025)^2} + \frac{2.9}{(1.027073)^3} + \frac{102.9}{(1 + z_4)^4} = 100$$

Solving the above equation we would find that z_4 is 2.9148%. Therefore, the 2-year spot rate on a bond-equivalent basis is 5.8297%.

For the 2.5-year spot rate, we use the 2.5-year issue from the par yield curve. The yield is 6.4% and therefore the coupon rate is 6.4%. The present value of the cash flow for this issue is then:

$$\frac{3.2}{(1 + z_1)^1} + \frac{3.2}{(1 + z_2)^2} + \frac{3.2}{(1 + z_3)^3} + \frac{3.2}{(1 + z_4)^4} + \frac{103.2}{(1 + z_5)^5}$$

Substituting: $z_1 = 2.3\%$ $z_2 = 2.5\%$ $z_3 = 2.7073\%$ $z_4 = 2.9148\%$
and setting the present value equal to the price of the 2.5-year issue (100), we obtain:

$$\frac{3.2}{(1.023)^1} + \frac{3.2}{(1.025)^2} + \frac{3.2}{(1.027073)^3} + \frac{3.2}{(1.029148)^4} + \frac{103.2}{(1 + z_5)^5} = 100$$

Solving the above equation we would find that z_5 is 3.2333%. Therefore, the 2.5-year spot rate on a bond-equivalent basis is 6.4665%.

For the 3-year spot rate, we use the 3-year issue from the par yield curve. The yield is 7.0% and therefore the coupon rate is 7.0%. The present value of the cash flow for this issue is then:

$$\frac{3.5}{(1 + z_1)^1} + \frac{3.5}{(1 + z_2)^2} + \frac{3.5}{(1 + z_3)^3} + \frac{3.5}{(1 + z_4)^4} + \frac{3.5}{(1 + z_5)^5} + \frac{103.5}{(1 + z_6)^6}$$

Substituting: $z_1 = 2.3\%$ $z_2 = 2.5\%$ $z_3 = 2.7073\%$ $z_4 = 2.9148\%$
$z_5 = 3.2333\%$ and setting the present value equal to the price of the 3-year issue (100), we obtain:

$$\frac{3.5}{(1.023)^1} + \frac{3.5}{(1.025)^2} + \frac{3.5}{(1.027073)^3} + \frac{3.5}{(1.029148)^4} + \frac{3.5}{(1.032333)^5} + \frac{103.5}{(1 + z_6)^6} = 100$$

Solving the above equation we would find that z_6 is 3.5586%. Therefore, the 3-year spot rate on a bond-equivalent basis is 7.1173%.

To summarize the findings for the spot rates:

Period	Year	Annualized spot rate (BEY)	z_t
1	0.5	4.6000%	2.3000%
2	1.0	5.0000	2.5000
3	1.5	5.4146	2.7073
4	2.0	5.8297	2.9148
5	2.5	6.4665	3.2333
6	3.0	7.1173	3.5586

19. To obtain the arbitrage-free value of an 8% coupon 3-year Treasury bond, the cash flows for the bond are discounted at the spot rates in the previous question as shown below:

Period	Annual spot rate (%)	Semiannual spot rate (%)	Cash flow	PV of CF
1	4.6000	2.3000	$4.0	$3.9101
2	5.0000	2.5000	4.0	3.8073
3	5.4146	2.7073	4.0	3.6919
4	5.8297	2.9148	4.0	3.5657
5	6.4665	3.2333	4.0	3.4116
6	7.1173	3.5586	104.0	84.3171
			Total	$102.7037

The arbitrage-free value of this bond is $102.7037.

20. The nominal spread fails to take into consideration (1) the shape of the yield curve (and therefore spot rates) and (2) any option embedded in a bond.

21. The Z-spread relative to the Treasury spot rate curve is the spread that when added to all the Treasury spot rates will produce a present value for the cash flows equal to the market price. The present value using each of the three spreads in the question—80, 90, and 100 basis points—is shown below:

Period	Years to maturity	Spot rate (BEY) (%)	Semiannual spot rate (%)	Cash flow	PV at assumed spread (bp) 80	90	100
1	0.5	5.0	2.50	$3	$2.9155	$2.9140	$2.9126
2	1.0	5.4	2.70	3	2.8223	2.8196	2.8168
3	1.5	5.8	2.90	3	2.7216	2.7176	2.7137
4	2.0	6.4	3.20	3	2.6042	2.5992	2.5942
5	2.5	7.0	3.50	3	2.4777	2.4717	2.4658
6	3.0	7.2	3.60	3	2.3709	2.3641	2.3573
7	3.5	7.4	3.70	3	2.2645	2.2569	2.2493
8	4.0	7.8	3.90	103	73.5466	73.2652	72.9849
				Total	91.7233	91.4083	91.0947

The last three columns in the table show the assumed spread. One-half of the spread is added to the column showing the semiannual spot rate. Then the cash flow is discounted used the semiannual spot rate plus one-half the assumed spread.

As can be seen, when a 90 basis point spread is used, the present value of the cash flow is equal to the price of the non-Treasury issue, $91.4083. Therefore, the Z-spread is 90 basis points.

22. When the yield curve is flat, all the cash flows are discounted at the same rate. Therefore, if Treasury securities are the benchmark, the nominal spread will be equal to the Z-spread. So, in the case of the corporate bond issues where there is no embedded option, using either measure is acceptable. In contrast, for corporate bonds issues in the portfolio with embedded options, the option-adjusted spread is more appropriate than either the nominal spread or the Z-spread regardless of the shape of the yield curve. Consequently, Joan Thomas would have to agree that the option-adjusted spread should be used for the corporate issues with embedded options.

23. **A.** There are several assumptions that are made in valuing bonds with embedded options. One important assumption is interest rate volatility. Because these assumptions differ from dealer to dealer, the OAS values may differ substantially.

   B. The relationship between the OAS, Z-spread, and option cost is as follows:

   $$\text{option cost} = \text{Z-spread} - \text{OAS}$$

   If a bond has no embedded option, then there is no option cost. That is, the option cost is zero. Substituting zero into the above equation, we have

   $$\text{Z-spread} = \text{OAS}$$

   That is, the Z-spread is equal to the OAS. This is the reason why Mr. Tinker observed that for the issues with no embedded options the OAS is the same as the Z-spread.

   C. A negative value for the option cost means that the investor has purchased an option from the issuer. A putable bond is an example of where the investor purchases an option. This explains why Mr. Tinker finds that a negative value for the option cost was reported for the putable bond issues. When there is no embedded option, the option cost is zero and that is why Mr. Tinker finds this value for issues with this characteristic. A positive value for the option cost means that the investor has sold an option to the issuer. This occurs for callable bond issues, as Mr. Tinker observes.

24. **A.** Because the Treasury securities are the benchmark, the OAS reflects a spread to compensate for credit risk and liquidity risk. (Remember that option risk has already been removed.)

   B. Since the benchmark is the issuer's on-the-run yield curve, the spread already reflects credit risk. So, basically the OAS reflects compensation for liquidity risk. (Remember that option risk has already been removed.)

   C. The answer depends on the benchmark interest rates used by the dealer firm. If the benchmark interest rates are Treasury rates, then the OAS is better for the issue that Mr. Dumas is considering. If the benchmark is the issuer's on-the-run yield curve, then the issue that the dealer is offering to Mr. Dumas is more attractive. However, the qualifier is that the answer also depends on the interest rate volatility assumed by the dealer and the interest rate volatility assumed by Mr. Dumas when analyzing the issue using System A and System B. Without knowing the assumed interest rate volatilities, no statement can be made about the relative value of these two issues.

25. We will use these notations in the reading:

   f will denote the forward rate
   t will be the subscript before f and will indicate the length of time that the rate applies
   m will be the subscript after f and will indicate when the forward rate begins

All periods are equal to six months.

The forward rate is then found as follows:

$$_t f_m = \left[\frac{(1 + z_{m+t})^{m+t}}{(1 + z_m)^m} \right]^{1/t} - 1$$

A. For the 6-month forward rate six months from now, $t = 1$ and $m = 1$. Therefore,

$$_1 f_1 = \left[\frac{(1 + z_{1+1})^{1+1}}{(1 + z_1)^1} \right]^{1/1} - 1$$

or

$$_1 f_1 = \left[\frac{(1 + z_2)^2}{(1 + z_1)^1} \right]^1 - 1$$

Since

$$z_1 = 5.0\%/2 = 2.5\% \quad \text{and} \quad z_2 = 5.4\%/2 = 2.7\%$$

then

$$_1 f_1 = \left[\frac{(1.027)^2}{(1.025)^1} \right]^1 - 1 = 0.029004 = 2.9004\%$$

Then the annualized 6-month forward rate six months from now on a bond-equivalent basis is 5.8008%.

B. For the 6-month forward rate one year from now, $t = 1$ and $m = 2$. Therefore,

$$_1 f_2 = \left[\frac{(1 + z_{2+1})^{2+1}}{(1 + z_2)^2} \right]^{1/1} - 1$$

or

$$_1 f_2 = \left[\frac{(1 + z_3)^3}{(1 + z_2)^2} \right]^1 - 1$$

Since

$$z_2 = 5.4\%/2 = 2.7\% \quad \text{and} \quad z_3 = 5.8\%/2 = 2.9\%$$

then

$$_1 f_2 = \left[\frac{(1.029)^3}{(1.027)^2} \right]^1 - 1 = 0.033012 = 3.3012\%$$

Then the annualized 6-month forward rate one year from now on a bond-equivalent basis is 6.6023%.

C. For the 6-month forward rate three years from now, $t = 1$ and $m = 6$. Therefore,

$$_1f_6 = \left[\frac{(1 + z_{6+1})^{6+1}}{(1 + z_6)^6} \right]^{1/1} - 1$$

or

$$_1f_6 = \left[\frac{(1 + z_7)^7}{(1 + z_6)^6} \right]^{1/1} - 1$$

Since

$$z_6 = 7.2\%/2 = 3.6\% \quad \text{and} \quad z_7 = 7.4\%/2 = 3.7\%$$

then

$$_1f_6 = \left[\frac{(1.037)^7}{(1.036)^6} \right]^{1/1} - 1 = 0.04302 = 4.302\%$$

Then the annualized 6-month forward rate three years from now on a bond-equivalent basis is 8.6041%.

D. For the 2-year forward rate one year from now, $t = 4$ and $m = 2$. Therefore,

$$_4f_2 = \left[\frac{(1 + z_{4+2})^{4+2}}{(1 + z_2)^2} \right]^{1/4} - 1$$

or

$$_4f_2 = \left[\frac{(1 + z_6)^6}{(1 + z_2)^2} \right]^{1/4} - 1$$

Since

$$z_2 = 5.4\%/2 = 2.7\% \quad \text{and} \quad z_6 = 7.2\%/2 = 3.6\%$$

then

$$_4f_2 = \left[\frac{(1.036)^6}{(1.027)^2} \right]^{1/4} - 1 = 0.04053 = 4.053\%$$

Then the annualized 2-year forward rate one year from now on a bond-equivalent basis is 8.1059%.

E. For the 1-year forward rate two years from now, $t = 2$ and $m = 4$. Therefore,

$$_2f_4 = \left[\frac{(1 + z_{2+4})^{2+4}}{(1 + z_4)^4} \right]^{1/2} - 1$$

or

$$_2f_4 = \left[\frac{(1 + z_6)^6}{(1 + z_4)^4} \right]^{1/2} - 1$$

Since

$$z_4 = 6.4\%/2 = 3.2\% \quad \text{and} \quad z_6 = 7.2\%/2 = 3.6\%$$

then

$$_2f_4 = \left[\frac{(1.036)^6}{(1.032)^4}\right]^{1/2} - 1 = 0.04405 = 4.405\%$$

Then the annualized 1-year forward rate two years from now on a bond-equivalent basis is 8.810%.

26. The 6-month forward rate six months from now as found in the previous question is 5.8008%. The two alternatives are:

Alternative 1: Invest $X at the 1-year spot rate of 5.4% for one year
Alternative 2: Invest $X today at the 6-month spot rate of 5.0% and reinvest at the end of six months the proceeds at the 6-month forward rate of 5.8008%

For Alternative 1, the amount at the end of one year will be:

$X (1 + 0.054/2)^2 = 1.054729 ($X)

For Alternative 2, the amount at the end of one year will be:

$X (1 + 0.05/2) (1 + 0.058008/2) = 1.054729 ($X)

Thus, the two alternatives produce the same future value if the 6-month forward rate six months from now is 5.8008%.

27. Discounting at spot rates and forward rates will produce the same value for a bond. This is because spot rates are nothing more than packages of short-term forward rates. So, the second sales person's comment is wrong about the superiority of forward rates for valuation compared to spot rates.

28. A. The forward discount factor for period T is computed as follows.

$$\frac{1}{(1 + z_1)(1 + _1f_1)(1 + _1f_2)...(1 + _1f_{T-1})}$$

Therefore,

Period	Annual forward rate (BEY)	Semiannual rate	Forward discount factor
1	4.00%	2.00%	0.980392
2	4.40	2.20	0.959288
3	5.00	2.50	0.935891
4	5.60	2.80	0.910399
5	6.00	3.00	0.883883
6	6.40	3.20	0.856476

B. The value is found by multiplying each cash flow by the forward discount factor for the period as shown below:

Period	Forward discount factor	Cash flow	PV of cash flow
1	0.980392	$4	$3.921569
2	0.959288	4	3.837151
3	0.935891	4	3.743562
4	0.910399	4	3.641598
5	0.883883	4	3.535532
6	0.856476	104	89.073470
		Total	$107.752881

The value of this bond is $107.752881.

SOLUTIONS TO PRACTICE QUESTIONS

1. The cash flow for this bond is 30 payments of $3 plus a maturity value of $100 thirty 6-month periods from now. Below is the present value of the cash flow when discounted at one-half the yields of 7.2%, 7.6%, and 7.8%. The short-cut formula given in Reading 66 was used so the information is provided for the present value of the coupon payments and the present value of the maturity value.

Annual rate (BEY)	7.2%	7.6%	7.8%
Semiannual rate	3.6%	3.8%	3.9%
Present value of:			
Coupon payments	54.49	53.16	52.51
Maturity value	34.61	32.66	31.74
Total present value	89.10	85.82	84.25

Since the semiannual discount rate of 3.9% equates the present value of the cash flows to the price of $84.25, 3.9% is the semiannual yield to maturity. Doubling this yield gives a yield to maturity of 7.8% on a bond equivalent basis.

2. **A.** The total future dollars from an investment of $89.32 if the yield is 7% is:

$$\$89.32 \times (1.035)^{40} = \$353.64$$

Decomposing the total future dollars we see that:

$$
\begin{aligned}
\text{Total future dollars} &= \$353.64 \\
\text{Return of principal} &= \$\ 89.32 \\
\text{Total dollar return} &= \$264.32
\end{aligned}
$$

Without reinvestment income, the dollar return is:

$$
\begin{aligned}
\text{Coupon interest} &= \$120.00 \\
\text{Capital gain} &= \$\ 10.68 \\
\text{Dollar return} &= \$130.68
\end{aligned}
$$

The dollar return shortfall is therefore $133.64 ($264.32 − $130.68). This shortfall is made up if the coupon payments can be reinvested at a yield of 7% (the yield on the bond at the time of purchase). For this bond, the reinvestment income is 51% of the total dollar return needed to produce a yield of 7% ($133.64/$264.32).

   B. There are no coupon payments to reinvest because the coupon rate is 0%. Therefore, no portion of the dollar return of a zero-coupon bond comes from reinvestment income.

3. **A.** The bond-equivalent yield is

$$2[(1.048)^{0.5} - 1] = 4.74\%$$

   B. The annual yield is

$$[(1.024)^2 - 1] = 4.86\%$$

4. A. The cash flows for this bond up to the first call date are (1) 10 coupon payments of $4.50 and (2) $104.50 ten 6-month periods from now. The table below shows the present values of the coupon payments and maturity value for the three interest rates in the question:

Annual interest rate (%)	Semiannual interest rate (%)	Present value of 10 payments of $4.5	Present value of $104.5 10 periods from now	Present value of cash flows
4.4	2.2	40.0019	84.0635	124.0654
4.6	2.3	39.7944	83.2453	123.0397
4.8	2.4	39.5886	82.4360	122.0246

Since a semiannual rate of 2.3% produces a present value for the cash flows of $123.0397 and the price is $123.04, 2.3% is the semiannual yield to call. Doubling this yield gives a 4.6% yield to call on a bond-equivalent basis.

B. The cash flows for this bond up to the first par call date are (1) 16 coupon payments of $4.50 and (2) $100 sixteen 6-month periods from now. The table below shows the present values of the coupon payments and maturity value for the three interest rates in the question:

Annual interest rate (%)	Semiannual interest rate (%)	Present value of 16 payments of $4.5	Present value of $100 16 periods from now	Present value of cash flows
5.41	2.705	57.8211	65.2431	123.0642
5.62	2.810	57.3548	64.1851	121.5399
5.75	2.875	57.0689	63.5393	120.6082

For the three semiannual interest rates used, the one that makes the present value of the cash flows to the first par call date closest to the price of $123.04 is 2.705%. Doubling this yield gives a 5.41% yield to first par call date on a bond-equivalent basis.

5. The discount margin is the margin that when added to LIBOR will make the present value of the cash flows (assuming LIBOR is unchanged over the life of the floater) equal to the price. When the price is 99.8269, it can be seen from Exhibit 67-3 that a margin of 84 basis points makes the present value of the cash flows equal to that price. Thus, if the floater's price is 99.8269, the discount margin is 84 basis points.

6. A. The yield on a discount basis, d, is

$$(1 - 0.9825)\left(\frac{360}{115}\right) = 0.0548 = 5.48\%$$

B. The price of this Treasury bill, p, per $1 dollar of maturity value is:

$$1 - 0.059 \, (162/360) = 0.97345$$

7. From Exhibit 67-4, the coupon rate for the on-the-run issue is 4.4%. Thus, the semiannual coupon payment per $100 of par value is $2.20 (4.4%/2 times $100). The present value of the cash flow is:

$$\frac{2.2}{(1 + z_1)^1} + \frac{2.2}{(1 + z_2)^2} + \frac{2.2}{(1 + z_3)^3} + \frac{2.2}{(1 + z_4)^4} + \frac{102.2}{(1 + z_5)^5}$$

where z_5 is one half of the 2.5-year theoretical spot rate.

Given the other four spot rates, we can write

$$\frac{2.2}{(1.0150)^1} + \frac{2.2}{(1.0165)^2} + \frac{2.2}{(1.017527)^3} + \frac{2.2}{(1.019582)^4} + \frac{102.2}{(1 + z_5)^5} = 100$$

Since the price of the 2.5-year coupon Treasury security is par, the present value must equal par. Therefore,

$$\frac{2.2}{(1.0150)^1} + \frac{2.2}{(1.0165)^2} + \frac{2.2}{(1.017527)^3} + \frac{2.2}{(1.019582)^4} + \frac{102.2}{(1 + z_5)^5} = 100$$

Solving the above equation:

$$2.167488 + 2.129158 + 2.088261 + 2.0355795 + \frac{102.20}{(1 + z_5)^5} = 100$$

$$8.420702 + \frac{102.20}{(1 + z_5)^5} = 100$$

$$\frac{102.20}{(1 + z_5)^5} = 91.5793$$

$$(1 + z_5)^5 = \frac{102.20}{91.5793}$$

$$z_5 = 0.022188 = 2.2188\%$$

Doubling the semiannual yield gives 4.4376% for the 2.5-year spot rate on a bond-equivalent basis. This rate agrees with the rate in Exhibit 67-4.

8. From Exhibit 67-5 it can be seen that if 125 basis points is added to each spot rate, the present value of the cash flow is 105.7165, the assumed price for the non-Treasury issue. Therefore, the Z-spread is 125 basis points.

9. $_1f_{13}$ is found as follows:

$$_1f_{13} = \frac{(1 + z_{14})^{14}}{(1 + z_{13})^{13}} - 1$$

From Exhibit 67-4, the annual spot rates for z_{13} and z_{14} are reported. They are 5.6108% and 5.6643%, respectively. Therefore,

$$z_{13} = 0.056108/2 = 0.028054$$
$$z_{14} = 0.056643/2 = 0.028322$$

Substituting we get

$$_1f_{13} = \frac{(1.028322)^{14}}{(1.028054)^{13}} - 1 = 0.0318 = 3.18\%$$

Doubling this rate gives the annualized rate for $_1f_{13}$ on a bond-equivalent basis of 6.36% reported in Exhibit 67-8.

10. The value is $114.8195 as shown below:

Period	Semiann. forward rate (%)	Forward discount factor	Cash flow	PV of cash flow
1	1.500	0.985222	$5	$4.926108
2	1.800	0.967799	5	4.838996
3	1.958	0.949211	5	4.746055
4	2.577	0.925362	5	4.626810
5	3.268	0.896079	5	4.480396
6	3.166	0.868582	105	91.201111
		Total		$114.819476

11. A. The forward rate sought is $_{12}f_8$. The formula for this forward rate is therefore:

$$_{12}f_8 = \left[\frac{(1 + z_{20})^{20}}{(1 + z_8)^8} \right]^{1/12} - 1$$

The spot rates needed are z_8 (the 4-year spot rate) and z_{20} (the 10-year spot rate). From Exhibit 67-4 we know

z_8 (the 4-year spot rate) = 5.065%/2 = 0.025325
z_{20} (the 10-year spot rate) = 6.2169%/2 = 0.031085

then

$$_{12}f_8 = \left[\frac{(1.031085)^{20}}{(1.025325)^8} \right]^{1/12} - 1 = 0.035943$$

Therefore, $_{12}f_8$ is equal to 3.4943% and doubling this rate gives 6.9885% the forward rate on a bond-equivalent basis.

B. We can verify this result. Investing $100 for 20 periods at the spot rate of 3.1085% will produce the following value:

$100(1.031085)^{20} = \$184.4545$

By investing $100 for 8 periods at 2.5325% and reinvesting the proceeds for 12 periods at the forward rate of 3.4942% gives the same value

$100 \ (1.025325)^8 \ (1.034942)^{12} = \$184.4545$

SOLUTIONS TO PROBLEMS IN READING 68

1. While it is true that a disadvantage of the full valuation approach is that it requires revaluing the bonds in the portfolio, it is not true that the duration/convexity approach does not require a valuation model. A valuation model is required in order to obtain the prices when rates are shocked that are used in the duration and convexity adjustment formulas.

2. The duration/convexity approach does not take into consideration how the yield curve can shift. However, this is not correct for the full valuation approach since yield curve scenarios are part of the full valuation method. In addition, the two bonds may have different prices and coupons thus leading to different percentage price changes for the two bonds.

3. The statement is not correct. While two bonds may have the same duration, they can have different convexities.

4. The problem here is in the definition of price volatility. It can be measured in terms of dollar price change or percentage price change. Smith is correct that there is greater price volatility for bond B because of its higher modified duration—that is, a higher percentage price change. Robertson is correct that bond A has greater price volatility but in terms of dollar price change. Specifically, for a 100 basis point change in rates, bond A will change by $3.60 (4% times 90); for bond B the dollar price change will be $3 (6% times 50) for a 100 basis point rate change.

5. **A.** Mr. Renfro's definition is a temporal definition and it is best not to use such an interpretation. Duration is related to the percentage price change of a bond when interest rates change.

   B. Mr. Renfro's response is correct.

   C. Mr. Renfro's response is correct.

   D. The computation of effective duration requires a valuation model to determine what the new prices will be when interest rates change. These models are based on assumptions. When duration is taken from different sources, there is no consistency of assumptions. While it is true that there is a formula for computing duration once the new prices for the bond are determined from a valuation model when rates are shocked, there is no simple valuation formula for bonds with embedded options.

      Mr. Renfro incorrectly overrode duration measures. It is possible—and it does occur in practice—to have a duration for a bond that is greater than the maturity of the bond. A negative duration does occur for some securities as well. For example, certain mortgage-backed securities have a negative duration. A negative duration of −3, for example, would mean that if interest rates increased by 100 basis points, the price of the bond will increase by approximately 3%. That is, the price of the bond moves in the same direction as the change in rates. In fact, for the types of bonds that have a duration longer than maturity and a negative duration, modified duration is not what the manager would want to use.

   E. The first part of the statement is correct. However, the second part is not true. Two portfolios can have the same duration but perform differently when rates change because they have different convexities. Also, the portfolios may have different yield and coupon characteristics.

6. A negative convexity adjustment simply means that a bond's price appreciation will be less than its price decline for a large change in interest rates

(200 basis points in the question). Whether or not a bond with negative convexity is attractive depends on its price and expectations about future interest rate changes.

7. If one interprets duration as some measure of time, it is difficult to understand why a bond will have a duration greater than its maturity. Duration is the approximate percentage price change of a bond for a 100 basis point change in interest rates. It is possible to have a security with a maturity of 10 years and a duration of 13.

8. Bond ABC exhibits negative convexity—for a 100 basis point change in rates, the gain is less than the loss; Bond XYZ exhibits positive convexity. A high coupon bond will exhibit negative convexity. A low coupon bond will exhibit positive convexity. Therefore, bond ABC is probably the high coupon bond while bond XYZ is probably the low coupon bond.

9. **A.** Modified duration is an inappropriate duration measure for a high coupon callable bond because it fails to recognize that as interest rates change, the expected cash flows will change.

   B. A better measure for a high-coupon callable bond is effective or option-adjusted duration.

10. Because the issue's coupon rate is substantially below the prevailing rate at which the issue can be refunded (500 basis points below), this issue is not likely to be called. Basically, if rates are shocked up and down, the expected cash flows are not likely to change because the coupon rate is so far below the market rate. Thus, modified duration—which assumes that the expected cash flow will not change when rates are changed—will be a good approximation for effective duration.

11. **A.** For a 25 basis point rate shock, the duration formula is:

$$\text{duration} = \frac{V_- - V_+}{2V_0(0.0025)}$$

		5%, 4 year	5%, 25 year	8%, 4 year	8%, 25 year
Initial value	V_0	100.0000	100.0000	110.7552	142.5435
Value at 4.75%	V_-	100.9011	103.6355	111.7138	147.2621
Value at 5.25%	V_+	99.1085	96.5416	109.8066	138.0421
Duration		3.59	14.19	3.44	12.94

B. For a 50 basis point rate shock, the duration formula is:

$$\text{duration} = \frac{V_- - V_+}{2V_0(0.0050)}$$

		5%, 4 year	5%, 25 year	8%, 4 year	8%, 25 year
Initial value	V_0	100.0000	100.0000	110.7552	142.5435
Value at 4.50%	V_-	101.8118	107.4586	112.6826	152.2102
Value at 5.50%	$V+$	98.2264	93.2507	108.8679	133.7465
Duration		3.59	14.21	3.44	12.95

12. For a 25 basis point rate shock, the value for C is:

$$C = \frac{V_+ + V_- - 2V_0}{2V_0(0.0025)^2}$$

		5%, 4 year	5%, 25 year	8%, 4 year	8%, 25 year
Initial value	V_0	100.0000	100.0000	110.7552	142.5435
Value at 4.75%	V_-	100.9011	103.6355	111.7138	147.2621
Value at 5.25%	V_+	99.1085	96.5416	109.8066	138.0421
C		7.68	141.68	7.23	121.89

13. A. For a 10 basis point change:

duration for 8% 4-year bond   = 3.44
duration for 8% 25-year bond = 12.94
$\Delta y* $ = 0.0010

For the 8% 4-year bond: approximate percentage price change for 10 basis point change in yield ($\Delta y* = 0.0010$):

10 basis point increase:
approximate percentage price change $= -3.44 \times (0.0010) \times 100$
$= -0.34\%$

10 basis point decrease:
approximate percentage price change $= -3.44 \times (-0.0010) \times 100$
$= +0.34\%$

For the 8% 25-year bond: approximate percentage price change for 10 basis point change in yield (0.0010):

10 basis point increase:
approximate percentage price change $= -12.94 \times (0.0010) \times 100$
$= -1.29\%$

10 basis point decrease:
approximate percentage price change $= -12.94 \times (-0.0010) \times 100$
$= +1.29\%$

B. For the 4-year bond, the estimated percentage price change using duration is excellent for a 10 basis point change, as shown below:

	Duration estimate	Actual change
10 bp increase	−0.34%	−0.34%
10 bp decrease	+0.34%	+0.35%

For the 25-year bond, the estimated percentage price change using duration is excellent for a 10 basis point change, as shown below:

	Duration estimate	Actual change
10 bp increase	−1.29%	−1.28%
10 bp decrease	+1.29%	+1.31%

14. A. For a 200 basis point change:

$$\begin{aligned}
\text{duration for 8\% 4-year bond} &= 3.44 \\
\text{duration for 8\% 25-year bond} &= 12.94 \\
\Delta y* &= 0.02
\end{aligned}$$

For the 8% 4-year bond: approximate percentage price change for 200 basis point change in yield ($\Delta y* = 0.02$):

200 basis point increase:
$$\begin{aligned}
\text{approximate percentage price change} &= -3.44 \times (0.02) \times 100 \\
&= -6.89\%
\end{aligned}$$

200 basis point decrease:
$$\begin{aligned}
\text{approximate percentage price change} &= -3.44 \times (-0.02) \times 100 \\
&= +6.89\%
\end{aligned}$$

For the 8% 25-year bond: approximate percentage price change for 200 basis point shock:

200 basis point increase:
$$\begin{aligned}
\text{approximate percentage price change} &= -12.94 \times (0.02) \times 100 \\
&= -25.88\%
\end{aligned}$$

200 basis point decrease:
$$\begin{aligned}
\text{approximate percentage price change} &= -12.94 \times (-0.02) \times 100 \\
&= +25.88\%
\end{aligned}$$

B. For the 4-year bond, the estimated percentage price change using duration is very good despite a 200 basis point change, as shown below:

	Duration estimate	Actual change
200 bp increase	−6.88%	−6.61%
200 bp decrease	+6.88%	+7.19%

For the 25-year bond, the estimated percentage price change using duration is poor for a 200 basis point change, as shown below:

	Duration estimate	Actual change
200 bp increase	−25.88%	−21.62%
200 bp decrease	+25.88%	+31.54%

15. A. The convexity adjustment for the two 25-year bonds is:
For the 5% 25-year bond:

$$C = 141.68$$
$$\Delta y* = 0.02$$

convexity adjustment to percentage price change = $141.68 \times (0.02)^2 \times 100 = 5.67\%$

For the 8% 25-year bond:

$$C = 121.89$$

convexity adjustment to percentage price change = $121.89 \times (0.02)^2 \times 100 = 4.88\%$

B. Estimated price change using duration and convexity adjustment.
For the 5% 25 year bond:

$$duration = 14.19$$
$$\Delta y* = 0.02$$

approximate percentage price change based on duration = $-14.19 \times 0.02 \times 100 = -28.38\%$

convexity adjustment = 5.67%

Therefore,

Yield change ($\Delta y*$)	+200 bps
Estimated change using duration	−28.38%
Convexity adjustment	5.67%
Total estimated percentage price change	−22.71%

Yield change ($\Delta y*$)	−200 bps
Estimated change using duration	28.38%
Convexity adjustment	5.67%
Total estimated percentage price change	34.05%

For the 8% 25-year bond:

$$duration = 12.94$$
$$\Delta y* = 0.02$$

approximate percentage price change based on duration = $-12.94 \times 0.02 \times 100 = -25.88\%$

convexity adjustment = 4.88%

Yield change ($\Delta y*$)	+200 bps
Estimated change using duration	−25.88%
Convexity adjustment	4.88%
Total estimated percentage price change	−21.00%

Yield change ($\Delta y*$)	-200 bps
Estimated change using duration	25.88%
Convexity adjustment	4.88%
Total estimated percentage price change	30.76%

C. For a large change in rates of 200 basis points, duration with the convexity adjustment does a pretty good job of estimating the actual percentage price change, as shown below.

	Duration/convexity estimate	Actual change
For 5% 25-year bond		
200 bp increase	-22.71%	-23.46%
200 bp decrease	+34.05%	+35.00%
For 8% 25-year bond		
200 bp increase	-21.00%	-21.62%
200 bp decrease	+30.76%	+31.54%

16. A. The price value of a basis point is

$$\$114.1338 - \$114.0051 = \$0.1287$$

B. Using equation (68-2), the approximate percentage price change for a 1 basis point increase in interest rates (i.e., $\Delta y = 0.0001$), ignoring the negative sign in equation (68-2), is:

$$11.28 \times (0.0001) \times 100 = 0.1128\%$$

Given the initial price of 114.1338, the dollar price change estimated using duration is

$$0.1128\% \times 114.1338 = \$0.1287$$

17. Duration even after adjusting for convexity indicates what the exposure of a bond or bond portfolio will be if interest rates change. However, to capture fully the interest rate exposure, it is necessary to know how volatile interest rates are. For example, in comparing duration of government bonds in different countries, the duration only indicates the sensitivity of the price to changes in interest rates by a given number of basis points. It does not consider the volatility of rates. In a country with little volatility in rates but where the government bonds have a high duration, just looking at duration misleads the investor as to the interest rate risk exposure.

SOLUTIONS TO PRACTICE QUESTIONS

1. **A.** From Exhibit 68-4 we know that

$$V_- \text{ (price at 5.9\% yield)} = 136.1193$$
$$V_+ \text{ (price at 6.1\% yield)} = 133.2472$$

and

$$\Delta y = 0.001$$
$$V_0 = 134.6722$$
$$\text{duration} = \frac{136.1193 - 133.2472}{2(134.6722)(0.001)} = 10.66$$

   Note that this is the same value computed for duration when a 20 basis point rate shock was used. Duration is therefore the same for this bond regardless of whether the yield change used is 20 basis points or 10 basis points.

   B. From Exhibit 68-4 we know that

$$V_- \text{ (price at 5.9\% yield)} = 101.1651$$
$$V_+ \text{ (price at 6.1\% yield)} = 98.8535$$

and

$$\Delta y = 0.001$$
$$V_0 = 100$$
$$\text{duration} = \frac{101.1651 - 98.8535}{2(100)(0.001)} = 11.56$$

2. **A.** The duration for this bond is 11.56. The approximate percentage price change for a 10 basis point increase in interest rates is

$$= -11.56 \times 0.0010 \times 100 = -1.156\%$$

   B. The actual percentage price change from Exhibit 68-6 is -1.15%. Therefore the estimate is good.

   C. The approximate percentage price change for a 10 basis point decrease in interest rates is

$$= -11.56 \times (-0.0010) \times 100 = 1.156\%$$

   D. The actual percentage price change from Exhibit 68-6 is 1.17%. Therefore the estimate is good.

   E. The approximate percentage price change for a 200 basis point increase in interest rates is

$$= -11.56 \times 0.02 \times 100 = -23.12\%$$

   F. The actual percentage price change from Exhibit 68-6 is -19.79%. Therefore duration provides a poor estimate and underestimates the new price.

G. The approximate percentage price change for a 200 basis point decrease in interest rates is

$$= -11.56 \times (-0.02) \times 100 = 23.12\%$$

H. The actual percentage price change from Exhibit 68-6 is 27.36%. Therefore duration provides a poor estimate and underestimates the new price.

3. A. For a rate shock of 10 basis points ($\Delta y = 0.001$)

$$C = \frac{98.8535 + 101.1651 - 2(100)}{2(100)(0.001)^2} = 93.00$$

B.

i. For a 10 basis point increase in interest rates ($\Delta y* = 0.001$)

Estimated change using duration	−1.16%
Convexity adjustment	0.0093%
Total estimated percentage price change	−1.15%
Actual percentage price change	−1.15%

ii. For a 10 basis point decrease in interest rates ($\Delta y* = -0.001$)

Estimated change using duration	1.16%
Convexity adjustment	0.0093%
Total estimated percentage price change	1.17%
Actual percentage price change	1.17%

iii. For a 200 basis point increase in interest rates ($\Delta y* = 0.02$)

Estimated change using duration	−23.12%
Convexity adjustment	3.72%
Total estimated percentage price change	−19.40%
Actual percentage price change	−19.79%

iv. For a 200 basis point decrease in interest rates ($\Delta y* = -0.02$)

Estimated change using duration	23.12%
Convexity adjustment	3.72%
Total estimated percentage price change	26.84%
Actual percent price change	27.36%

SOLUTIONS TO PROBLEMS IN READING 69

1. **B.** A call option is not binding on both parties in the same sense that the other financial instruments are. The call option gives the holder a right but does not impose an obligation.

2. **B.** If the market falls, the buyer of a forward contract could pay more for the index, as determined by the price that was contracted for at the inception of the contract, than the index is worth when the contract matures. Although it is possible that a rise in interest rates could cause the market to fall, this might not always happen and thus is a secondary consideration.

3. **D.** Forward contracts are usually private transactions that do not have an intermediary such as a clearinghouse to guarantee performance by both parties. This type of transaction requires a high degree of credit-worthiness for both parties.

4. **B.** Forward contracts are usually less liquid than futures contracts because they are typically private transactions tailored to suit both parties, unlike futures contracts, which are usually for standardized amounts and are exchange traded.

5. **A.** A swap is most like a series of forward contracts. An example is a swap in which one party makes a set of fixed-rate payments over time in exchange for a set of floating-rate payments based on some notional amount.

6. **C.** Unlike a contingent claim, a forward commitment typically requires no premium to be paid up front. An intuitive way to look at this is to realize that a forward commitment is binding on both parties, so any up-front fees would cancel, while a contingent claim is binding only on the party in the short position. For this, the party in the short position demands (and receives) compensation.

7. **C.** Because the holder of a contingent claim (the party in the long position) has a right but not an obligation, she will only exercise when it is in her best interest to do so and not otherwise. This will happen only when she stands to gain and never when she stands to lose.

8. **A.** The notional principal is the amount of the underlying asset covered by the derivative contract.

9. **A.** The most widely used derivative contracts are written on underlying assets that are financial, such as Treasury instruments and stock indices.

10. **A.** Arbitrage, or the absence of it, is the basis for pricing most derivative contracts. Consequently, it is relatively unusual, although certainly not impossible, for derivative markets to be used to generate arbitrage profits.

11. **B.** One reason derivative markets have flourished is that they have relatively low transaction costs. For example, buying a risk-free Treasury security and a futures contract on the S&P 500 Index to replicate payoffs to the index is cheaper than buying the 500 stocks in the index in their proper proportions to get the same payoff.

12. **C.** In the absence of arbitrage opportunities, an investor bearing no risk should expect to earn the risk-free rate.

13. **C.** The six-month forward price of gold should be $250 \times [1 + (0.10/2)] = 250 \times (1.05) = \$262.50$.

14. **C.** Efficient markets are characterized by the absence, or the rapid elimination, of arbitrage opportunities.

Analysis of Derivatives for the CFA® Program, by Don M. Chance, Copyright © 2003 by Association for Investment Management and Research. Reprinted with permission.

15. C. Stock B should be priced at $24.00 today. To see this, imagine selling 2.4 shares of A short for $24.00, and buying one share of B. Now, in the next period, suppose B is worth $30.00. Then selling B permits you to buy 2.4 shares of A (at $12.50 per share) to return the shares sold short. Alternatively, if B is worth $18.00, selling B permits you to still buy 2.4 shares of A (at $7.50) to return them. The same no-profit situation holds if you sell one share of B and buy 2.4 shares of A. An alternative explanation lies in the fact that in each of the two outcomes, the price of B is 2.4 times the price of A. Thus, the price of B today must be 2.4 times the price of A.

SOLUTIONS TO PROBLEMS IN READING 70

1. A. Discount yield $= 0.0174 = \left(\dfrac{10{,}000 - \text{Price}}{10{,}000}\right)\left(\dfrac{360}{153}\right)$

Price $= \$9{,}926.05$

B. Discount yield $= \left(\dfrac{10{,}000 - 9{,}950}{10{,}000}\right)\left(\dfrac{360}{69}\right) = 0.0261$

2. $\$20{,}000{,}000\,[1 + 0.0435(60/360)] = \$20{,}145{,}000$

3. A. Taking a short position will hedge the interest rate risk for Company A. The gain on the contract will offset the reduced interest rate that can be earned when rates fall.

B. This is a 3×6 FRA.

C. $\$15{,}000{,}000 \left[\dfrac{(0.045 - 0.05)(90/360)}{1 + 0.045(90/360)}\right] = -\$18{,}541.41$

The negative sign indicates a gain to the short position, which Company A holds.

4. A. These instruments are called off-the-run FRAs.

B. $\$20{,}000{,}000 \left[\dfrac{(0.04 - 0.0475)(137/360)}{1 + 0.04(137/360)}\right] = -\$56{,}227.43$

Because the party is long, this amount represents a loss.

5. The contract is settled in cash, so the settlement would be €20,000,000(0.875 − 0.90) = −$500,000. This amount would be paid by Sun Microsystems to the dealer. Sun would convert euros to dollars at the spot rate of $0.90, receiving €20,000,000 × (0.90) = $18,000,000. The net cash receipt is $17,500,000, which results in an effective rate of $0.875.

SOLUTIONS TO PROBLEMS IN READING 71

1. **A.** Parsons would close out his position in April by offsetting his long position with a short position. To do so, he would re-enter the market and offer for sale a June futures contract on the Nasdaq 100 index. When he has a buyer, he has both a long and a short position in the June futures contract on the Nasdaq 100 index. From the point of view of the clearinghouse, he no longer has a position in the contract.

   B. Smith would close out her position in August by offsetting her short position with a long position. To do so, she would re-enter the market and purchase a September futures contract on the S&P 500. She then has both a short and a long position in the September futures contract on the S&P 500. From the point of view of the clearinghouse, she no longer has a position in the contract.

2. The difference between initial and maintenance margin requirements for one gold futures contract is $2,000 - $1,500 = $500. Because one gold futures contract is for 100 troy ounces, the difference between initial and maintenance margin requirements per troy ounce is $500/100, or $5.

   A. Because Evans has a long position, he would receive a maintenance margin call if the price were to *fall* below $320 - $5, or $315 per troy ounce.

   B. Because Tosca has a short position, he would receive a maintenance margin call if the price were to *rise* above $323 + $5, or $328 per troy ounce.

3. *Trader with a long position:* This trader loses if the price falls. The maximum loss would be incurred if the futures price falls to zero, and this loss would be $0.75/lb × 25,000 lbs, or $18,750. Of course, this scenario is only theoretical, not realistic.

   Trader with a short position: This trader loses if the price increases. Because there is no limit on the price increase, there is no theoretical upper limit on the loss that the trader with a short position could incur.

4. **A.** The difference between the initial margin requirement and the maintenance margin requirement is $2. Because the initial futures price was $212, a margin call would be triggered if the price falls below $210.

   B.

Day	Beginning Balance	Funds Deposited	Futures Price	Price Change	Gain/Loss	Ending Balance
0	0	200	212			200
1	200	0	211	−1	−20	180
2	180	0	214	3	60	240
3	240	0	209	−5	−100	140
4	140	60	210	1	20	220
5	220	0	204	−6	−120	100
6	100	100	202	−2	−40	160

On day 0, you deposit $200 because the initial margin requirement is $10 per contract and you go long 20 contracts ($10 per contract times 20 contracts equals $200). At the end of day 3, the balance is down to $140, $20 below the $160 maintenance margin requirement ($8 per contract times 20 contracts). You must deposit enough money to bring the balance up to the initial margin requirement of $200. So, the next day (day 4), you deposit $60. The price change on day 5 causes a gain/loss of $-$120, leaving you with a balance of $100 at the end of day 5. Again, this amount is less than the $160 maintenance margin requirement. You must deposit enough money to bring the balance up to the initial margin requirement of $200. So on day 6, you deposit $100.

C. By the end of day 6, the price is $202, a decrease of $10 from your purchase price of $212. Your loss so far is $10 per contract times 20 contracts, or $200.

    You could also look at your loss so far as follows. You initially deposited $200, followed by margin calls of $60 and $100. Thus, you have deposited a total of $360 so far and have not withdrawn any excess margin. The ending balance, however, is only $160. Thus, the total loss incurred by you so far is $360 − $160, or $200.

5. A.

Day	Beginning Balance	Funds Deposited	Futures Price	Price Change	Gain/Loss	Ending Balance
0	0	2,700.00	96-06			2,700.00
1	2,700.00	0	96-31	25/32	−781.25	1,918.75
2	1,918.75	781.25	97-22	23/32	−718.75	1,981.25
3	1,981.25	718.75	97-18	−4/32	125.00	2,825.00
4	2,825.00	0	97-24	6/32	−187.50	2,637.50
5	2,637.50	0	98-04	12/32	−375.00	2,262.50
6	2,262.50	0	97-31	−5/32	156.25	2,418.75

On day 0, Moore deposits $2,700 because the initial margin requirement is $2,700 per contract and she has gone short one contract. At the end of day 1, the price has increased from 96-06 to 96-31—that is, the price has increased from $96,187.50 to $96,968.75. Because Moore has taken a short position, this increase of $781.25 is an adverse price movement for her, and the balance is down by $781.25 to $1,918.75. Because this amount is less than the $2,000 maintenance margin requirement, she must deposit additional funds to bring her account back to the initial margin requirement of $2,700. So, the next day (day 2), she deposits $781.25. Another adverse price movement takes place on day 2 as the price further increases by $718.75 to $97,687.50. Her ending balance is again below the maintenance margin requirement of $2,000, and she must deposit enough money to bring her account back to the initial margin requirement of $2,700. So, the next day (day 3), she deposits $718.75. Subsequently, even though her balance falls below the initial margin requirement, it does not go below the maintenance margin requirement, and she does not need to deposit any more funds.

B. Moore bought the contract at a futures price of 96-06. By the end of day 6, the price is 97-31, an increase of 1 25/32. Therefore, her loss so far is 1.78125 percent of $100,000, which is $1,781.25.

    You could also look at her loss so far as follows: She initially deposited $2,700, followed by margin calls of $781.25 and $718.75. Thus, she has deposited a total of $4,200 so far, and has not withdrawn any excess margin. Her ending balance is $2,418.75. Thus, the total loss so far is $4,200 − $2,418.75, or $1,781.25.

6. A. Because the IMM index price is 95.23, the annualized LIBOR rate priced into the contract is $100 - 95.23 = 4.77$ percent. With each contract based on $1 million notional principal of 90-day Eurodollars, the actual futures price is $\$1{,}000{,}000[1 - 0.0477(90/360)] = \$988{,}075$.

B. Because the IMM index price is 95.25, the annualized LIBOR rate priced into the contract is $100 - 95.25 = 4.75$ percent. The actual futures price is $\$1{,}000{,}000[1 - 0.0475(90/360)] = \$988{,}125$. So, the change in actual futures price is $\$988{,}125 - \$988{,}075 = \$50$.

You could also compute the change in price directly by noting that the IMM index price increased by 2 basis points. Because each basis point move in the rate moves the actual futures price by $25, the increase in the actual futures price is $2 \times \$25$, or $50.

1. A. $S_T = 579.32$
  i. Call payoff, $X = 450$: $\text{Max}(0, 579.32 - 450) \times 100 = \$12,932$
  ii. Call payoff, $X = 650$: $\text{Max}(0, 579.32 - 650) \times 100 = 0$

  B. $S_T = 579.32$
  i. Put payoff, $X = 450$: $\text{Max}(0, 450 - 579.32) \times 100 = 0$
  ii. Put payoff, $X = 650$: $\text{Max}(0, 650 - 579.32) \times 100 = \$7,068$

2. A. $S_T = \$0.95$
  i. Call payoff, $X = 0.85$: $\text{Max}(0, 0.95 - 0.85) \times 100,000 = \$10,000$
  ii. Call payoff, $X = 1.15$: $\text{Max}(0, 0.95 - 1.15) \times 100,000 = \$0$

  B. $S_T = \$0.95$
  i. Put payoff, $X = 0.85$: $\text{Max}(0, 0.85 - 0.95) \times 100,000 = \$0$
  ii. Put payoff, $X = 1.15$: $\text{Max}(0, 1.15 - 0.95) \times 100,000 = \$20,000$

3. A. $S_T = 0.0653$
  i. Call payoff, $X = 0.05$: $\text{Max}(0, 0.0653 - 0.05) \times (180/360) \times 10,000,000 = \$76,500$
  ii. Call payoff, $X = 0.08$: $\text{Max}(0, 0.0653 - 0.08) \times (180/360) \times 10,000,000 = 0$

  B. $S_T = 0.0653$
  i. Put payoff, $X = 0.05$: $\text{Max}(0, 0.05 - 0.0653) \times (180/360) \times 10,000,000 = 0$
  ii. Put payoff, $X = 0.08$: $\text{Max}(0, 0.08 - 0.0653) \times (180/360) \times 10,000,000 = \$73,500$

4. A. $S_T = \$1.438$
  i. Call payoff, $X = 1.35$: $\text{Max}(0, 1.438 - 1.35) \times 125,000 = \$11,000$
  ii. Call payoff, $X = 1.55$: $\text{Max}(0, 1.438 - 1.55) \times 125,000 = \$0$

  B. $S_T = \$1.438$
  i. Put payoff, $X = 1.35$: $\text{Max}(0, 1.35 - 1.438) \times 125,000 = \$0$
  ii. Put payoff, $X = 1.55$: $\text{Max}(0, 1.55 - 1.438) \times 125,000 = \$14,000$

5. A. $S_T = 1136.76$
  i. Call payoff, $X = 1130$: $\text{Max}(0, 1136.76 - 1130) \times 1,000 = \$6,760$
  ii. Call payoff, $X = 1140$: $\text{Max}(0, 1136.76 - 1140) \times 1,000 = 0$

  B. $S_T = 1136.76$
  i. Put payoff, $X = 1130$: $\text{Max}(0, 1130 - 1136.76) \times 1,000 = 0$
  ii. Put payoff, $X = 1140$: $\text{Max}(0, 1140 - 1136.76) \times 1,000 = \$3,240$

6. A. $S_0 = 1240.89$, $T = 75/365 = 0.2055$, $X = 1225$ or 1255, call options
  i. $X = 1225$
    Maximum value for the call: $c_0 = S_0 = 1240.89$
    Lower bound for the call: $c_0 = \text{Max}[0, 1240.89 - 1225/(1.03)^{0.2055}] = 23.31$
  ii. $X = 1255$
    Maximum value for the call: $c_0 = S_0 = 1240.89$
    Lower bound for the call: $c_0 = \text{Max}[0, 1240.89 - 1255/(1.03)^{0.2055}] = 0$

  B. $S_0 = 1240.89$, $T = 75/365 = 0.2055$, $X = 1225$ or 1255, put options
  i. $X = 1225$
    Maximum value for the put: $p_0 = 1225/(1.03)^{0.2055} = 1217.58$
    Lower bound for the put: $p_0 = \text{Max}[0, 1225/(1.03)^{0.2055} - 1240.89] = 0$
  ii. $X = 1255$
    Maximum value for the put: $p_0 = 1255/(1.03)^{0.2055} = 1247.40$
    Lower bound for the put: $p_0 = \text{Max}[0, 1255/(1.03)^{0.2055} - 1240.89] = 6.51$

7. A. $S_0 = 1.05$, $T = 60/365 = 0.1644$, $X = 0.95$ or 1.10, American-style options

    i. $X = \$0.95$

        Maximum value for the call: $C_0 = S_0 = \$1.05$

        Lower bound for the call: $C_0 = \text{Max}[0, 1.05 - 0.95/(1.055)^{0.1644}] = \$0.11$

        Maximum value for the put: $P_0 = X = \$0.95$

        Lower bound for the put: $P_0 = \text{Max}(0, 0.95 - 1.05) = \$0$

    ii. $X = \$1.10$

        Maximum value for the call: $C_0 = S_0 = \$1.05$

        Lower bound for the call: $C_0 = \text{Max}[0, 1.05 - 1.10/(1.055)^{0.1644}] = \$0$

        Maximum value for the put: $P_0 = X = \$1.10$

        Lower bound for the put: $P_0 = \text{Max}(0, 1.10 - 1.05) = \$0.05$

B. $S_0 = 1.05$, $T = 60/365 = 0.1644$, $X = 0.95$ or 1.10, European-style options

    i. $X = \$0.95$

        Maximum value for the call: $c_0 = S_0 = \$1.05$

        Lower bound for the call: $c_0 = \text{Max}[0, 1.05 - 0.95/(1.055)^{0.1644}] = \$0.11$

        Maximum value for the put: $p_0 = 0.95/(1.055)^{0.1644} = \$0.94$

        Lower bound for the put: $p_0 = \text{Max}[0, 0.95/(1.055)^{0.1644} - 1.05] = \$0$

    ii. $X = \$1.10$

        Maximum value for the call: $c_0 = S_0 = \$1.05$

        Lower bound for the call: $c_0 = \text{Max}[0, 1.05 - 1.10/(1.055)^{0.1644}] = \$0$

        Maximum value for the put: $p_0 = 1.10/(1.055)^{0.1644} = \$1.09$

        Lower bound for the put: $p_0 = \text{Max}[0, 1.10/(1.055)^{0.1644} - 1.05] = \$0.04$

8. We can illustrate put–call parity by showing that for the fiduciary call and the protective put, the current values and values at expiration are the same.

Call price, $c_0 = \$6.64$

Put price, $p_0 = \$2.75$

Exercise price, $X = \$30$

Risk-free rate, $r = 4$ percent

Time to expiration $= 219/365 = 0.6$

Current stock price, $S_0 = \$33.19$

Bond price, $X/(1 + r)^T = 30/(1 + 0.04)^{0.6} = \$29.30$

Transaction	Current Value	Value at Expiration	
		$S_T = 20$	$S_T = 40$
Fiduciary call			
Buy call	6.64	0	$40 - 30 = 10$
Buy bond	29.30	30	30
Total	35.94	30	40
Protective put			
Buy put	2.75	$30 - 20 = 10$	0
Buy stock	33.19	20	40
Total	35.94	30	40

The values in the table above show that the current values and values at expiration for the fiduciary call and the protective put are the same. That is, $c_0 + X/(1 + r)^T = p_0 + S_0$.

SOLUTIONS TO PROBLEMS IN READING 73

1. **A.** The payments at the beginning of the swap are as follows:
   The U.S. company (domestic party) pays the counterparty $100 million.
   The counterparty pays the U.S. company €116.5 million.

   B. The semiannual payments are as follows:
   The U.S. company (domestic party) pays the counterparty
   €116,500,000(0.055)(180/360) = €3,203,750.
   The counterparty pays the U.S. company $100,000,000(0.0675) ×
   (180/360) = $3,375,000.

   C. The payments at the end of the swap are as follows:
   The U.S. company (domestic party) pays the counterparty €116.5 million.
   The counterparty pays the U.S. company $100 million.

2. **A.** The payments at the beginning of the swap are as follows:
   The British company (domestic party) pays the counterparty £75 million.
   The counterparty pays the British company $105 million.

   B. The semiannual payments are as follows:
   The British company (domestic party) pays the counterparty
   $105,000,000(0.06)(180/360) = $3,150,000.
   The counterparty pays the British company £75,000,000(0.05) ×
   (180/360) = £1,875,000.

   C. The payments at the end of the swap are as follows:
   The British company (domestic party) pays the counterparty $105 million.
   The counterparty pays the British company £75 million.

3. The fixed payments are $50,000,000(0.0575)(180/365) = $1,417,808.
   The floating payments are $50,000,000(0.0515)(180/360) = $1,287,500.
   The net payment is $130,308, made by the party paying fixed—that is, the
   dealer pays the company.

4. The fixed payments are €25,000,000(0.055)(90/365) = €339,041.
   The floating payments are €25,000,000(0.05)(90/360) = €312,500.
   The net payment is €26,541, made by the party paying fixed—that is, the
   company pays the dealer.

5. **A.** The small-cap equity payment is $\left(\dfrac{625.60}{689.40} - 1\right)(100,000,000) =$
   $-\$9,254,424.$
   The asset manager owes $9,254,424 to the dealer.

   The large-cap equity payment is $\left(\dfrac{1251.83}{1130.20} - 1\right)(100,000,000) =$
   $10,761,812.
   The asset manager owes this amount to the dealer.
   The overall payment made by the asset manager to the dealer is
   $9,254,424 + $10,761,812 = $20,016,236.

   B. The small-cap equity payment is $\left(\dfrac{703.23}{689.40} - 1\right)(100,000,000) =$
   $2,006,092.
   The dealer owes the asset manager this amount.

   The large-cap equity payment is $\left(\dfrac{1143.56}{1130.20} - 1\right)(100,000,000) =$
   $1,182,092.
   The asset manager owes this amount to the dealer.
   The overall payment made by the dealer to the asset manager is
   $2,006,092 − $1,182,092 = $824,000.

6. A. The small-cap equity payment is $\left(\dfrac{238.41}{234.10} - 1\right)(50,000,000) = \$920,547.$

The asset manager owes the dealer this amount.

The fixed interest payment is $(50,000,000)(0.055)(180/365) = \$1,356,164.$

The dealer owes this amount to the asset manager.

So the dealer pays to the asset manager $\$1,356,164 - \$920,547 = \$435,617.$

B. The small-cap equity payment is $\left(\dfrac{241.27}{234.10} - 1\right)(50,000,000) = \$1,531,397.$

The asset manager owes the dealer this amount.

The fixed interest payment is $(50,000,000)(0.055)(180/365) = \$1,356,164.$

The dealer owes this amount to the asset manager.

So the asset manager pays to the dealer $\$1,531,397 - \$1,356,164 = \$175,233.$

7. A. The large-cap equity payment is $\left(\dfrac{622.54}{578.50} - 1\right)(25,000,000) = \$1,903,198.$

The dealer owes this amount to the asset manager.

The fixed interest payment is $(25,000,000)(0.045)(180/365) = \$554,795.$

The asset manager owes this amount to the dealer.

So the dealer pays to the asset manager $\$1,903,198 - \$554,795 = \$1,348,403.$

B. The large-cap equity payment is $\left(\dfrac{581.35}{578.50} - 1\right)(25,000,000) = \$123,163.$

The dealer owes this amount to the asset manager.

The fixed interest payment is $(25,000,000)(0.045)(180/365) = \$554,795.$

The asset manager owes this amount to the dealer.

So the asset manager pays to the dealer $\$554,795 - \$123,163 = \$431,632.$

SOLUTIONS TO PROBLEMS IN READING 74

1. A. Call buyer

     i. $c_T = \max(0, S_T - X) = \max(0, 55 - 50) = 5$

       $\Pi = c_T - c_0 = 5 - 4 = 1$

     ii. $c_T = \max(0, S_T - X) = \max(0, 51 - 50) = 1$

       $\Pi = c_T - c_0 = 1 - 4 = -3$

     iii. $c_T = \max(0, S_T - X) = \max(0, 48 - 50) = 0$

       $\Pi = c_T - c_0 = 0 - 4 = -4$

  B. Call seller

     i. $\text{Value} = -c_T = -\max(0, S_T - X) = -\max(0, 49 - 50) = 0$

       $\Pi = -c_T + c_0 = -0 + 4 = 4$

     ii. $\text{Value} = -c_T = -\max(0, S_T - X) = -\max(0, 52 - 50) = -2$

       $\Pi = -c_T + c_0 = -2 + 4 = 2$

     iii. $\text{Value} = -c_T = -\max(0, S_T - X) = -\max(0, 55 - 50) = -5$

       $\Pi = -c_T + c_0 = -5 + 4 = -1$

  C. Maximum and minimum

     i. Maximum profit to buyer (loss to seller) $= \infty$

     ii. Maximum loss to buyer (profit to seller) $= c_0 = 4$

  D. $S_T^* = X + c_0 = 50 + 4 = 54$

2. A.   **i.** $c_T = \max(0, S_T - X) = \max(0, 99 - 105) = 0$

       $\Pi = c_T - c_0 = 0 - 7 = -7$

     ii. $c_T = \max(0, S_T - X) = \max(0, 104 - 105) = 0$

       $\Pi = c_T - c_0 = 0 - 7 = -7$

     iii. $c_T = \max(0, S_T - X) = \max(0, 105 - 105) = 0$

       $\Pi = c_T - c_0 = 0 - 7 = -7$

     iv. $c_T = \max(0, S_T - X) = \max(0, 109 - 105) = 4$

       $\Pi = c_T - c_0 = 4 - 7 = -3$

     v. $c_T = \max(0, S_T - X) = \max(0, 112 - 105) = 7$

       $\Pi = c_T - c_0 = 7 - 7 = 0$

     vi. $c_T = \max(0, S_T - X) = \max(0, 115 - 105) = 10$

       $\Pi = c_T - c_0 = 10 - 7 = 3$

  B. $S_T^* = X + c_0 = 105 + 7 = 112$

    Clearly, this result is consistent with our solution above, where the profit is exactly zero in Part A(v), in which the price at expiration is 112.

3. A. Put buyer

     i. $p_T = \max(0, X - S_T) = \max(0, 2100 - 2125) = 0$

       $\Pi = p_T - p_0 = 0 - 106.25 = -106.25$

     ii. $p_T = \max(0, X - S_T) = \max(0, 2100 - 2050) = 50$

       $\Pi = p_T - p_0 = 50 - 106.25 = -56.25$

     iii. $p_T = \max(0, X - S_T) = \max(0, 2100 - 1950) = 150$

       $\Pi = p_T - p_0 = 150 - 106.25 = 43.75$

  B. Put seller

     i. $\text{Value} = -p_T = -\max(0, X - S_T) = -\max(0, 2100 - 1975) = -125$

       $\Pi = -p_T + p_0 = -125 + 106.25 = -18.75$

     ii. $\text{Value} = -p_T = -\max(0, X - S_T) = -\max(0, 2100 - 2150) = 0$

       $\Pi = -p_T + p_0 = -0 + 106.25 = 106.25$

  C. Maximum and minimum

     i. Maximum profit to buyer (loss to seller) $= X - p_0 = 2100 - 106.25 = 1993.75$

     ii. Maximum loss to buyer (profit to seller) $= p_0 = 106.25$

  D. $S_T^* = X - p_0 = 2100 - 106.25 = 1993.75$

4. A.   **i.** $p_T = \max(0, X - S_T) = \max(0, 95 - 100) = 0$
$\Pi = p_T - p_0 = 0 - 5 = -5$
     ii. $p_T = \max(0, X - S_T) = \max(0, 95 - 95) = 0$
$\Pi = p_T - p_0 = 0 - 5 = -5$
     iii. $p_T = \max(0, X - S_T) = \max(0, 95 - 93) = 2$
$\Pi = p_T - p_0 = 2 - 5 = -3$
     iv. $p_T = \max(0, X - S_T) = \max(0, 95 - 90) = 5$
$\Pi = p_T - p_0 = 5 - 5 = 0$
     v. $p_T = \max(0, X - S_T) = \max(0, 95 - 85) = 10$
$\Pi = p_T - p_0 = 10 - 5 = 5$

   B. $S_T^* = X - p_0 = 95 - 5 = 90$
Clearly, this result is consistent with our solution above, where the profit is exactly zero in Part A(iv), in which the price at expiration is 90.

   C.   **i.** Maximum profit (to put buyer) $= X - p_0 = 95 - 5 = 90$.
     ii. This profit would be realized in the unlikely scenario of the price of the underlying falling all the way down to zero.

5. A. This position is commonly called a covered call.

   B.   **i.** $V_T = S_T - \max(0, S_T - X) = 70 - \max(0, 70 - 80) = 70 - 0 = 70$
$\Pi = V_T - V_0 = 70 - (S_0 - c_0) = 70 - (77 - 6) = 70 - 71 = -1$
     ii. $V_T = S_T - \max(0, S_T - X) = 75 - \max(0, 75 - 80) = 75 - 0 = 75$
$\Pi = V_T - V_0 = 75 - (S_0 - c_0) = 75 - (77 - 6) = 4$
     iii. $V_T = S_T - \max(0, S_T - X) = 80 - \max(0, 80 - 80) = 80 - 0 = 80$
$\Pi = V_T - V_0 = 80 - (S_0 - c_0) = 80 - (77 - 6) = 9$
     iv. $V_T = S_T - \max(0, S_T - X) = 85 - \max(0, 85 - 80) = 85 - 5 = 80$
$\Pi = V_T - V_0 = 80 - (S_0 - c_0) = 80 - (77 - 6) = 9$

   C.   **i.** Maximum profit $= X - S_0 + c_0 = 80 - 77 + 6 = 9$
     ii. Maximum loss $= S_0 - c_0 = 77 - 6 = 71$
     iii. The maximum profit would be realized if the expiration price of the underlying is at or above the exercise price of $80.
     iv. The maximum loss would be incurred if the underlying price drops to zero.

   D. $S_T^* = S_0 - c_0 = 77 - 6 = 71$

6. A. This position is commonly called a protective put.

   B.   **i.** $V_T = S_T + \max(0, X - S_T) = 70 + \max(0, 75 - 70) = 70 + 5 = 75$
$\Pi = V_T - V_0 = 75 - (S_0 + p_0) = 75 - (77 + 3) = 75 - 80 = -5$
     ii. $V_T = S_T + \max(0, X - S_T) = 75 + \max(0, 75 - 75) = 75 + 0 = 75$
$\Pi = V_T - V_0 = 75 - (S_0 + p_0) = 75 - (77 + 3) = 75 - 80 = -5$
     iii. $V_T = S_T + \max(0, X - S_T) = 80 + \max(0, 75 - 80) = 80 + 0 = 80$
$\Pi = V_T - V_0 = 80 - (S_0 + p_0) = 80 - (77 + 3) = 80 - 80 = 0$
     iv. $V_T = S_T + \max(0, X - S_T) = 85 + \max(0, 75 - 85) = 85 + 0 = 85$
$\Pi = V_T - V_0 = 85 - (S_0 + p_0) = 85 - (77 + 3) = 85 - 80 = 5$
     v. $V_T = S_T + \max(0, X - S_T) = 90 + \max(0, 75 - 90) = 90 + 0 = 90$
$\Pi = V_T - V_0 = 90 - (S_0 + p_0) = 90 - (77 + 3) = 90 - 80 = 10$

   C.   **i.** Maximum profit $= \infty$
     ii. Maximum loss $= -(X - S_0 - p_0) = -(75 - 77 - 3) = 5$
     iii. The maximum loss would be incurred if the expiration price of the underlying were at or below the exercise price of $75.

   D. $S_T^* = S_0 + p_0 = 77 + 3 = 80$

SOLUTIONS TO PROBLEMS IN READING 75

1. Let us compute the terminal value of $1 invested. The share class with the highest terminal value net of all expenses would be the most appropriate, because all classes are based on the same portfolio and thus have the same portfolio risk characteristics.

   A. Class A. $1 \times (1 - 0.05) = \$0.95$ is the amount available for investment at $t = 0$, after paying the front-end sales charge. Because this amount grows at 9 percent per year, reduced by annual expenses of 0.0125, the terminal value per $1 invested after 1 year is $\$0.95 \times 1.09 \times (1 - 0.0125) = \$1.0226$.

   Class B. Ignoring any deferred sales charge, after 1 year, $1 invested grows to $\$1 \times 1.09 \times (1 - 0.015) = \$1.0737$. According to the table, the deferred sales charge would be 4 percent; therefore, the terminal value is $\$1.0737 \times 0.96 = \$1.0308$.

   Class C. Ignoring any deferred sales charge, after 1 year, $1 invested grows to $\$1 \times 1.09 \times (1 - 0.015) = \$1.0737$. According to the table, the deferred sales charge would be 1 percent; therefore, the terminal value is $\$1.0737 \times 0.99 = \$1.063$.

   Class C is the best.

   B. Class A. The terminal value per $1 invested after three years is $\$0.95 \times 1.09^3 \times (1 - 0.0125)^3 = \$1.1847$.

   Class B. Ignoring any deferred sales charge, after three years, $1 invested grows to $\$1 \times 1.09^3 \times (1 - 0.015)^3 = \$1.2376$. The deferred sales charge would be 2 percent; therefore, the terminal value is $\$1.2376 \times 0.98 = \$1.2128$.

   Class C. There would be no deferred sales charge. Thus, after three years, $1 invested grows to $\$1 \times 1.09^3 \times (1 - 0.015)^3 = \$1.2376$.

   Class C is the best.

   C. Class A. The terminal value per $1 invested after five years is $\$0.95 \times 1.09^5 \times (1 - 0.0125)^5 = \$1.3726$.

   Class B. There would be no deferred sales charge. So, the terminal value per $1 invested after five years is $\$1 \times 1.09^5 \times (1 - 0.015)^5 = \$1.4266$.

   Class C. There would be no deferred sales charge. So, the terminal value per $1 invested after 5 years is $\$1 \times 1.09^5 \times (1 - 0.015)^5 = \$1.4266$.

   Classes B and C are the best.

   D. Class A. The terminal value per $1 invested after 15 years is $\$0.95 \times 1.09^{15} \times (1 - 0.0125)^{15} = \$2.8653$.

   Class B. There would be no deferred sales charge. So, the terminal value per $1 invested after 15 years is $\$1 \times 1.09^{15} \times (1 - 0.015)^6 \times (1 - 0.0125)^9 = \$2.9706$.

   Class C. There would be no deferred sales charge. So, the terminal value per $1 invested after 15 years is $\$1 \times 1.09^{15} \times (1 - 0.015)^{15} = \$2.9036$.

   Class B is the best.

2. Class A performs quite poorly unless the investment horizon is very long. The reason is the high sales charge of 5 percent on purchases. Even though the annual expenses for class A are low, that is not enough to offset the high sales charge on purchases until a very long investment horizon. One could verify that Class A outperforms Class C for an investment horizon of 21 years or more.

   Class B performs worse than Class C at very short-term horizons because of its higher deferred sales charges. However, after its deferred sales charges disappear, the relative performance of Class B starts improving. After six years, Class B shares convert to Class A with its lower annual expenses. At longer horizons, Class B starts to outperform Class C due to its annual expenses, which are lower than that of Class C.

Class C performs well at shorter investment horizons because it has no initial sales charge and it has a low deferred sales charge.

3. The estimated model is

House value in euros = 140,000 + (210 × Living area) + (10,000 × Number of bathrooms) + (15,000 × Fireplace) − (6,000 × Age)

So, the value of the specific house is

140,000 + (210 × 500) + (10,000 × 3) + (15,000 × 1) − (6,000 × 5) = €260,000

4. A. The net operating income for the office building is gross potential rental income minus estimated vacancy and collection costs minus insurance and taxes minus utilities minus repairs and maintenance.

NOI = 350,000 − 0.04 × 350,000 − 26,000 − 18,000 − 23,000 = $269,000

B. The capitalization rate of the first office building recently sold in the area is

NOI/(Transaction price) = 500,000/4,000,000 = 0.125

The capitalization rate of the second office building recently sold in the area is

NOI/(Transaction price) = 225,000/1,600,000 = 0.141

The average of the two capitalization rates is 0.133.

Applying this capitalization rate to the office building under consideration, which has an NOI of $269,000, gives an appraisal value of:

NOI/(Capitalization rate) = 269,000/0.133 = $2,022,556

5. The after-tax cash flow for the property sale year is $126,000 + $710,000 = $836,000. At a cost of equity of 18 percent, the present value of the after-tax cash flows in years 1 through 5 is as follows.

$60,000/1.18 + $75,000/1.18^2 + $91,000/1.18^3 + $108,000/1.18^4 + $836,000/1.18^5 = $581,225

The investment requires equity of 0.15 × $3,000,000 = $450,000. Thus, the NPV = $581,225 − $450,000 = $131,225. The recommendation based on NPV would be to accept the project, because the NPV is positive.

6. A. The amount borrowed is 80 percent of $1.5 million, which is $1.2 million. The first year's interest = 9% of $1.2 million = $108,000. So,

After-tax net income in year 1 = (NOI − Depreciation − Interest) × (1 − Marginal tax rate) = ($170,000 − $37,500 − $108,000) × (1 − 0.30) = $17,150
After-tax cash flow = After-tax net income + Depreciation − Principal repayment

And,

> Principal repayment = Mortgage payment − Interest = \$120,000 − \$108,000 = \$12,000

So,

> After-tax cash flow in year 1 = \$17,150 + \$37,500 − \$12,000 = \$42,650

New NOI in year 2 = 1.04 × \$170,000 = \$176,800. We need to calculate the second year's interest payment on the mortgage balance after the first year's payment. This mortgage balance is the original principal balance minus the first year's principal repayment, or \$1,200,000 − \$12,000 = \$1,188,000. The interest on this balance is \$106,920. So,

> After-tax net income = (\$176,800 − \$37,500 − \$106,920) × (1 − 0.30) = \$22,666
> Principal repayment = \$120,000 − \$106,920 = \$13,080

So,

> After-tax cash flow in year 2 = \$22,666 + \$37,500 − \$13,080 = \$47,086

New NOI in year 3 = 1.04 × \$176,800 = \$183,872. We need to calculate the third year's interest payment on the mortgage balance after the second year's payment. This mortgage balance is the original principal balance minus the first two years' principal repayments, or \$1,200,000 − \$12,000 − \$13,080 = \$1,174,920. The interest on this balance is \$105,743. So,

> After-tax net income = (\$183,872 − \$37,500 − \$105,743) × (1 − 0.30) = \$28,440
> Principal repayment = \$120,000 − \$105,743 = \$14,257

So,

> After-tax cash flow in year 3 = \$28,440 + \$37,500 − \$14,257 = \$51,683

B. Ending book value = Original purchase price − Total depreciation during three years = \$1,500,000 − 3 × \$37,500 = \$1,387,500.

> The net sale price = \$1,720,000 × (1 − 0.065) = \$1,608,200
> Capital gains tax = 0.20 × (\$1,608,200 − \$1,387,500) = \$44,140
> After-tax cash flow from property sale = Net sales price − Outstanding mortgage − Capital gains tax

And,

> Outstanding mortgage = Original mortgage − Three years' worth of principal repayments,

or

> \$1,200,000 − (\$12,000 + \$13,080 + \$14,257) = \$1,160,663

So,

> After-tax cash flow from the property sale = $1,608,200 − $1,160,663 − $44,140 = $403,397

C. The total after-tax cash flow for the property sale year is $51,683 + $403,397 = $455,080. At a cost of equity of 19 percent, the present value of the after-tax cash flows in years 1 through 3 is as follows:

$$\$42,650/1.19 + \$47,086/1.19^2 + \$455,080/1.19^3 = \$339,142$$

The investment requires equity of $0.20 \times \$1,500,000 = \$300,000$. Thus, the NPV = $339,142 − $300,000 = $39,142. The recommendation based on NPV would be to accept the project, because the NPV is positive.

7. No, one would not suggest using real estate appraisal–based indexes in a global portfolio optimization. Real estate appraisal values are a smoothed series. One of the reasons for this smoothness is that the appraisals are done quite infrequently. Another reason is that the appraised values typically show relatively few changes. Due to these two reasons, an appraisal-based index understates volatility. This spuriously low volatility would inflate the attractiveness of real estate.

8. Clearly, the two real estate indexes have very different price behaviors. Their correlation is almost null. As expected, the NAREIT *index* exhibits a strong correlation with U.S. stocks because the REIT share prices are strongly influenced by the stock market. In contrast, the FRC index, which is much less volatile, is not highly correlated with the stock market.

9. A. There are three possibilities.

- Project does not survive until the end of the eighth year
- Project survives and the investor exits with a payoff of $25 million
- Project survives and the investor exits with a payoff of $35 million

There is an 80 percent chance that the project will not survive until the end of the eighth year. That is, there is a 20 percent chance that the project will survive, and the investor will exit the project then. If the project survives, it is equally likely that the payoff at the time of exit will be either $25 million or $35 million.

The project's NPV is the present value of the expected payoffs minus the required initial investment of $1.4 million.

> NPV = $0.8 \times \$0 + 0.2 \times [(0.5 \times \$25$ million $+ 0.5 \times \$35$ million$)/1.2^8] − \$1.4$ million = −$0.004592 million or −$4,592$

B. Because the expected NPV of the project is negative, the project should be rejected.

10. The probability that the venture capital project survives to the end of the first year is $(1 − 0.28)$, 1 minus the probability of failure in the first year; the probability that it survives to the end of the second year is the product of the probability it survives the first year times the probability it survives the second year, or $(1 − 0.28)(1 − 0.25)$. So, the probability that the project survives to end of the sixth year is $(1 − 0.28)(1 − 0.25)(1 − 0.22)(1 − 0.18)(1 − 0.18)(1 − 0.10) = (0.72)(0.75)(0.78)(0.82)(0.82)(0.90) = 0.255$, or 25.5%. The probability that the project fails is $1 − 0.255 = 0.745$, or 74.5%.

The net present value of the project, if it survives to the end of the sixth year and thus earns €60 million, is −€4.5 million + €60 million/1.22^6 = €13.70 million. The net present value of the project if it fails is

−€4.5 million. Thus, the project's expected NPV is a probability-weighted average of these two amounts, or $(0.255)(€13.70$ million$) + (0.745)(−€4.5$ million$) = €141,000$.

Based on the project's positive net present value, VenCap should accept the investment.

11. A. Fee $= 1.5\% + 15\% \times (35\% − 5.5\%) = 1.5\% + 4.425\% = 5.925\%$.

Net return $= 35\% − 5.925\% = 29.1\%$

B. Because the gross return is less than the risk-free rate, the incentive fee is zero. The only fee incurred is the base management fee of 1.5 percent.

Net return $= 5\% − 1.5\% = 3.5\%$

C. Again, the incentive fee is zero.

Net return $= −6\% − 1.5\% = −7.5\%$

12. A. Fixed fee $= 1\%$ of \$2 billion $=$ \$20 million.

If the return is 29 percent, the new value of the fund would be \$2 billion $\times 1.29 =$ \$2.58 billion. This new value would be \$2.58 billion $−$ \$2.1 billion $=$ \$0.48 billion above the high watermark. So, the incentive fee $= 20\% \times$ \$0.48 billion $=$ \$0.096 billion, or \$96 million.

Total fee $=$ \$20 million $+$ \$96 million $=$ \$116 million

B. Fixed fee $= 1\%$ of \$2 billion $=$ \$20 million.

If the return is 4.5 percent, the new value of the fund would be \$2 billion $\times 1.045 =$ \$2.09 billion. Because this new value is below the high watermark of \$2.1 billion, no incentive fee would be earned.

Total fee $=$ \$20 million

C. Fixed fee $= 1\%$ of \$2 billion $=$ \$20 million.
If the return is $−1.8\%$, no incentive fee would be earned.

Total fee $=$ \$20 million

13. Clearly, high watermark provision has the positive implication for the investors that they would have to pay the manager an incentive fee only when they make a profit. Further, the hedge fund manager would need to make up any earlier losses before becoming eligible for the incentive fee payment. However, a negative implication is that the option-like characteristic of the high watermark provision (the incentive fee being zero everywhere below the benchmark and increasing above the benchmark) may induce risk-taking behavior when the fund is below the high watermark. The manager may take more risky positions when the fund is below the high watermark in order to get to above the high watermark and earn an incentive fee. The worst case for the manager is a zero incentive fee, regardless of how far below the benchmark the fund turns out to be. Another negative implication is that the incentive fees, if the fund exceeds the high watermark, are set quite high (typically at 20 percent), which reduces long-run asset growth.

14. A. The Spanish firm will give two of its shares, which are worth €25, for three of the Italian firm's shares, which are worth €24. Thus, the shares of the Italian firm are trading at a discount. The reason for the discount is that there is a possibility that the merger may not go through. If the merger does not go through, the shares of the Italian firm are likely to fall back to the premerger announcement level. An investor currently buying shares of the Italian firm is taking the risk that the merger will indeed occur.

B. The hedge fund will take a hedged position by selling two shares of the Spanish firm short for every three shares of the Italian firm that it buys. So, the hedge fund will buy 250,000 shares of the Italian firm by selling $(2/3) \times 250{,}000 = 166{,}666.67$, that is, 166,667 shares of the Spanish firm. The proceeds from the short sale are $166{,}667 \times €12.50 = €2{,}083{,}338$, which is €83,338 more than the cost of buying the shares of the Italian firm, which is $250{,}000 \times €8 = €2{,}000{,}000$.

C. Because the merger did not go through and the stock price of the Italian firm fell, the hedge fund incurs a substantial loss. The loss is $250{,}000 \times (€8 - €6.10) = €475{,}000$.

15. A. Net return on fund A $= 50\% \times (1 - 0.15) = 42.5\%$

Net return on fund B $= 20\% \times (1 - 0.15) = 17\%$

Net return on fund C $= -10\%$

So, average net return $= (42.5\% + 17\% - 10\%)/3 = 16.5\%$

Average gross return $= (50\% + 20\% - 10\%)/3 = 20\%$

Thus, the average gross return on the three hedge funds is the same as the percentage increase in the stock market index, and the average net return is lower.

B. The publicity campaign launched by Global group illustrates the problem of survivorship bias in performance measure of hedge funds. Although the average gross return on the three hedge funds is the same as the percentage increase in the stock market index, the performance reported by Global group seems much better because it is based on only the funds that survive. That is, the average performance reported by Global group is inflated.

16. The measurement of the performance of the hedge funds suffers from survivorship bias. The 90 hedge funds that the analyst has examined include only those funds that have survived during the last 10 years. Thus, any poorly performing funds that have been discontinued due to low return or high volatility, or both, have been excluded. Accordingly, the average return on hedge funds has been overstated, while the volatility has been understated. Consequently, the Sharpe ratio for the hedge funds has been overstated. Furthermore, the Sharpe ratio may be a misleading measure of risk-adjusted performance for hedge funds because of the optionality in their investment strategies.

17. A. The construction of the index is okay in year 10 but not in the earlier years. By using today's weights in construction of the index in earlier years, the exchange is overweighing those commodities that have become important over the period, and have simultaneously gone up in price.

B. For each year, use the relative economic importance of the commodities in that year as the weights for that year. That is, use year 1 weights for the index calculated in year 1, and so on.

18. A. The expected return on gold, as theoretically derived by the CAPM, is

$$E(R_{gold}) = 7\% + \beta_{gold} \times 4\%$$
$$= 7\% - 0.3\,(4\%) = 5.8\%$$

B. Given its negative beta, gold is likely to perform well when the overall market performs poorly. Thus, our investment in gold is likely to offset some of the loss on the rest of the portfolio. Investors should be willing to accept an overall lower expected return on gold because, in periods of financial distress, gold tends to do well.

SOLUTIONS TO PROBLEMS IN READING 78

1.

Month	Madison(R_i)	Kayleigh Electric(R_j)	$R_i - E(R_i)$	$R_j - E(R_j)$	$[R_i - E(R_i)] \times [R_j - E(R_j)]$
1	−.04	.07	−.057	.06	−.0034
2	.06	−.02	.043	−.03	−.0013
3	−.07	−.10	−.087	−.11	.0096
4	.12	.15	.103	.14	.0144
5	−.02	−.06	−.037	−.07	.0026
6	.05	.02	.033	.01	.0003
Sum	.10	.06			.0222

A. $E(R_i) = .10/6 = .0167 \quad E(R_j) = .06/6 = .01$

B.

$$\sigma_i = \sqrt{.0257/6} = \sqrt{.0043} = .06549$$

$$\sigma_j = \sqrt{.04120/6} = \sqrt{.006867} = .08287$$

C. $COV_{ij} = 1/6(.0222) = .0037$

D.

$$r_{ij} = \frac{.0037}{(.06549)(.08287)}$$

$$= \frac{.0037}{.005427}$$

$$= .682$$

One should have expected a positive correlation between the two stocks, since they tend to move in the same direction(s). Risk can be reduced by combining assets that have low positive or negative correlations, which is not the case for Madison and Kayleigh Electric.

2. $E(R_1) = .15 \qquad E(\sigma_1) = .10 \qquad w_1 = .5$

$E(R_2) = .20 \qquad E(\sigma_2) = .20 \qquad w_2 = .5$

$E(R_{\text{port}}) = .5(.15) + .5(.20) = .175$

If $r_{1,2} = .40$

$$\sigma_p = \sqrt{(.5)^2(.10)^2 + (.5)^2(.20)^2 + 2(.5)(.5)(.10)(.20)(.40)}$$

$$= \sqrt{.0025 + .01 + .004}$$

$$= \sqrt{.0165}$$

$$= 0.12845$$

If $r_{1,2} = -.60$

$$\sigma_p = \sqrt{(.5)^2(.10)^2 + (.5)^2(.20)^2 + 2(.5)(.5)(.10)(.20)(-.60)}$$

$$= \sqrt{.0025 + .01 + (-.006)}$$

$$= \sqrt{.0065}$$

= .08062

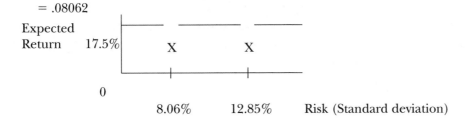

The negative correlation coefficient reduces risk without sacrificing return.

3. For all values of $r_{1,2}$:

$$E(R_{port}) = (.6 \times .10) + (.4 \times .15) = .12$$
$$\sigma_{port} = \sqrt{(.6)^2(.03)^2 + (.4)^2(.05)^2 + 2(.6)(.4)(.03)(.05)(r_{1,2})}$$
$$= \sqrt{.000324 + .0004 + .00072(r_{1,2})}$$
$$= \sqrt{.000724 + .00072(r_{1,2})}$$

A.
$$\sqrt{.000724 + .00072(1.0)} = \sqrt{.001444} = .0380$$

B.
$$\sqrt{.000724 + .00072(.75)} = \sqrt{.001264} = .0356$$

C.
$$\sqrt{.000724 + .00072(.25)} = \sqrt{.000904} = .0301$$

D.
$$\sqrt{.000724 + .00072(.00)} = \sqrt{.000724} = .0269$$

E.
$$\sqrt{.000724 + .00072(-.25)} = \sqrt{.000544} = .0233$$

F.
$$\sqrt{.000724 + .00072(-.7)} = \sqrt{.000184} = .0136$$

G.
$$\sqrt{.000724 + .00072(-1.0)} = \sqrt{.000004} = .0020$$

For all cases, $\rho = 0.70$.

A. $w_1 = 1.00$. Thus $w_2 = 0.00$

$$E(R_{port}) = (1.00)(0.1) + (0.00)(0.15) = 0.1$$
$$\sigma^2 = (1.00)^2(0.03)^2 + (0.00)^2(0.05)^2 + 2(0.70)(1.00)(0.00)(0.03)(0.05)$$
$$= (0.03)^2$$
$$\sigma = 0.03$$

B. $w_1 = 0.75$. Thus $w_2 = 0.25$

$$E(R_{port}) = (0.75)(0.1) + (0.25)(0.15) = 0.1125$$
$$\sigma^2 = (0.75)^2(0.03)^2 + (0.25)^2(0.05)^2 + 2(0.70)(0.75)(0.25)(0.03)(0.05)$$
$$= 0.001056$$
$$\sigma = 0.0325$$

C. $w_1 = 0.50$. Thus $w_2 = 0.50$

$$E(R_{port}) = (0.50)(0.1) + (0.50)(0.15) = 0.125$$
$$\sigma^2 = (0.50)^2(0.03)^2 + (0.50)^2(0.05)^2 + 2(0.70)(0.50)(0.50)(0.03)(0.05)$$
$$= 0.001375$$
$$\sigma = 0.037$$

D. $w_1 = 0.25$. Thus $w_2 = 0.75$

$E(R_{\text{port}}) = (0.25)(0.1) + (0.75)(0.15)$

$\sigma^2 = (0.25)^2(0.03)^2 + (0.75)^2(0.05)^2 + 2(0.70)(0.25)(0.75)(0.03)(0.05)$

$\quad = 0.001856$

$\sigma = 0.0431$

E. $w_1 = 0.05$. Thus $w_2 = 0.95$

$E(R_{\text{port}}) = (0.05)(0.1) + (0.95)(0.15) = 0.1475$

$\sigma^2 = (0.05)^2(0.03)^2 + (0.95)^2(0.05)^2 + 2(0.70)(0.05)(0.95)(0.03)(0.05)$

SOLUTIONS TO PROBLEMS IN READING 79

1. $E(R_i) = RFR + \beta_i(R_M - RFR)$

$= .10 + \beta_i(.14 - .10)$

$= .10 + .04\beta_i$

Stock	Beta	(Required Return) $E(R_i) = .10 + .04\beta_i$
U	85	$.10 + .04(.85) = .10 + .034 = .134$
N	1.25	$.10 + .04(1.25) = .10 + .05 = .150$
D	$-.20$	$.10 + .04(-.20) = .10 - .008 = .092$

2. CFA Examination II (1998)

A. Security Market Line

i. *Fair-value plot.* The following template shows, using the CAPM, the expected return, ER, of Stock A and Stock B on the SML. The points are consistent with the following equations:

ER on stock = Risk-free rate + Beta x (Market return − Risk-free rate)

ER for A = 4.5% + 1.2(14.5% − 4.5%)

$= 16.5\%$

ER for B = 4.5% + 0.8(14.5% − 4.5%)

$= 12.5\%$

ii. *Analyst estimate plot.* Using the analyst's estimates, Stock A plots below the SML and Stock B, above the SML.

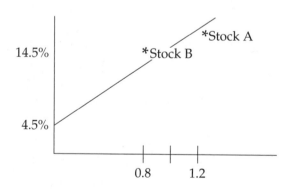

B. Over vs. Undervalue

Stock A is overvalued because it should provide a 16.5% return according to the CAPM whereas the analyst has estimated only a 16.0% return.

Stock B is undervalued because it should provide a 12.5% return according to the CAPM whereas the analyst has estimated a 14% return.

APPENDIX B

ANALYSIS OF DERIVATIVES FOR THE CFA® PROGRAM: EQUATIONS

Reading 70: Forward Markets and Contracts

70-1. Value of Forward Contract at Expiration

$$V_T(0,T) = S_T - F(0,T)$$

70-2. Forward Price

$$F(0,T) = S_0(1 + r)^T$$

70-3. Value of Forward Contract During Its Life

$$V_t(0,T) = S_t - F(0,T)/(1 + r)^{(T-2t)}$$

70-4. Forward Price for Stock Paying Dividends Based on Present Value of Dividends

$$F(0,T) = [S_0 - PV(D,0,T)](1 + r)^T$$

70-5. Forward Price for Stock Paying Dividends Based on Future Value of Dividends

$$F(0,T) = S_0(1 + r)^T - FV(D,0,T)$$

70-6. Forward Price for Stock Paying Continuous Dividends

$$F(0, T) = (S_0 e^{-\delta^c T}) e^{r^c T}$$

70-7. Value of Forward Contract for Stock Paying Discrete Dividends

$$V_t(0,T) = S_t - PV(D,t,T) - F(0,T)/(1 + r)^{(T-t)}$$

70-8. Value of Forward Contract for Stock Paying Continuous Dividends

$$V_t(0,T) = S_t e^{-\delta^c(T-t)} - F(0,T)e^{-r^c(T-t)}$$

70-9. Forward Price for Bond Paying Interest Based on Present Value of Coupons

$$F(0,T) = [B_0^c(T + Y) - PV(CI,0,T)](1 + r)^T$$

70-10. Forward Price for Bond Paying Interest Based on Future Value of Coupons

$$F(0,T) = [B_0^c(T + Y)](1 + r)^T - FV(CI,0,T)$$

70-11. Value of Forward Contract for Bond Paying Interest

$$V_t(0,T) = B_t^c(T + Y) - PV(CI,t,T) - F(0,T)/(1 + r)^{(T-t)}$$

70-12. Payoff of FRA

$$\frac{[L_h(m) - FRA(0,h,m)]\left(\dfrac{m}{360}\right)}{1 + L_h(m)\left(\dfrac{m}{60}\right)}$$

70-13. FRA Rate

$$FRA(0,h,m) = \left[\frac{1 + L_0(h + m)\left(\dfrac{h + m}{360}\right)}{1 + L_0(h)\left(\dfrac{h}{360}\right)} - 1\right]\left(\frac{360}{m}\right)$$

70-14. Value of FRA During Its Life

$$V_g(0,h,m) = \frac{1}{1 + L_g(h - g)\left(\dfrac{h - g}{360}\right)} - \frac{1 + FRA(0,h,m)\left(\dfrac{m}{360}\right)}{1 + L_g(h + m - g)\left(\dfrac{h + m - g}{360}\right)}$$

70-15. Forward Price for Currency Based on Discrete Interest

$$F(0,T) = \left[\frac{S_0}{(1 + r^f)^T}\right](1 + r)^T$$

70-16. Forward Price for Currency Based on Continuous Interest

$$F(0,T) = (S_0 e^{-r^{fc}T}) e^{r^c T}$$

70-17. Value of Forward Contract on Currency Based on Discrete Interest

$$V_t(0, T) = \frac{S_t}{(1 + r^f)^{(T-t)}} - \frac{F(0,T)}{(1 + r)^{(T-t)}}$$

70-18. Value of Forward Contract on Currency Based on Continuous Interest

$$V_t(0,T) = (S_t e^{-r^{fc}(T-t)}) - F(0,T) e^{-r^c (T-t)}$$

Reading 71: Futures Markets and Contracts

71-1. Futures Price at Expiration

$$f_T(T) = S_T$$

71-2. Value of Futures Contract at Initiation Date

$$v_0(T) = 0$$

71-3. Value of Futures Contract During Its Life

$$v_{t+}(T) = f_t(T) - f_{t-1}(T) \text{ } \textit{an instant before the account is marked to market}$$
$$v_{t-}(T) = 0 \text{ } \textit{as soon as the account is marked to market}$$

71-4. Futures Price When Underlying Has No Costs, Benefits, or Cash Flows

$$f_0(T) = S_0(1 + r)^T$$

71-5. Futures Price When Underlying Has Storage Costs

$$f_0(T) = S_0(1 + r)^T + FV(SC,0,T)$$

71-6. Futures Price When Underlying Generates Positive Cash Flows

$$f_0(T) = S_0(1 + r)^T - FV(CF,0,T)$$

71-7. Futures Price When Underlying Generates Costs Minus Benefits

$$f_0(T) = S_0(1 + r)^T + FV(CB,0,T)$$

71-8. Treasury Bill Futures Price

$$f_0(h) = B_0(h + m)[1 + r_0(h)]^{h/365}$$

71-9. Implied Repo Rate for Treasury Bill Futures

$$r_0(h)^* = \left[\frac{f_0(h)^*}{B_0(h + m)}\right]^{365/h} - 1$$

71-10. Discount Rate Implied by Treasury Bill Futures Price

$$r_0^{df}(h) = [1 - f_0(h)]\left(\frac{360}{m}\right)$$

71-11. Treasury Note and Bond Futures Price

$$f_0(T) = B_0^c(T + Y)[1 + r_0(T)]^T - FV(CI,0,T)$$

71-12. Treasury Note and Bond Futures Price Based on Conversion Factor

$$f_0(T) = \frac{B_0^c(T + Y)[1 + r_0(T)]^T - FV(CI,0,T)}{CF(T)}$$

71-13. Stock Index Futures Price Based on Compound Value of Dividends

$$f_0(T) = S_0(1 + r)^T - FV(D,0,T)$$

71-14. Stock Index Futures Price Based on Present Value of Dividends

$$f_0(T) = [S_0 - PV(D,0,T)](1 + r)^T$$

71-15. Stock Index Futures Price Based on Discrete Dividend Yield: Variation 1

$$f_0(T) = \left(\frac{S_0}{(1 + \delta)^T}\right)(1 + r)^T$$

71-16. Stock Index Futures Price Based on Discrete Dividend Yield: Variation 2

$$f_0(T) = S_0(1 - \delta^*)(1 + r)^T$$

71-17. Stock Index Futures Price Based on Continuous Dividends

$$f_0(T) = (S_0 e^{-\delta^c T}) e^{r^c T}$$

71-18. Currency Futures Price Based on Discrete Interest

$$f_0(T) = \left(\frac{S_0}{(1 + r^f)^T}\right)(1 + r)^T$$

71-19. Currency Futures Price Based on Continuous Interest

$$f_0(T) = (S_0 e^{-r^{fc} T}) e^{r^c T}$$

Reading 72: Option Markets and Contracts

72-1. Payoff of Interest Rate Call

$$(\text{Notional Principal})\text{Max}(0, \text{Underlying rate at expiration} -$$
$$\text{Exercise rate})\left(\frac{\text{Days in underlying rate}}{360}\right)$$

72-2. Payoff of Interest Rate Put

$$(\text{Notional Principal})\text{Max}(0, \text{Exercise rate} -$$
$$\text{Underlying rate at expiration})\left(\frac{\text{Days in underlying rate}}{360}\right)$$

72-3. Value at Expiration (Payoff) of European and American Calls

$$c_T = \text{Max}(0, S_T - X)$$
$$C_T = \text{Max}(0, S_T - X)$$

72-4. Value at Expiration (Payoff) of European and American Puts

$$p_T = \text{Max}(0, X - S_T)$$
$$P_T = \text{Max}(0, X - S_T)$$

72-5. Minimum Values of European and American Calls and Puts

$$c_0 \geq 0, \ C_0 \geq 0$$
$$p_0 \geq 0, \ P_0 \geq 0$$

72-6. Maximum Values of European and American Calls

$$c_0 \leq S_0, \ C_0 \leq S_0$$

72-7. Maximum Values of European and American Puts

$$p_0 \leq X/(1 + r)^T, \ P_0 \leq X$$

72-8. Lower Bounds (Intrinsic Values) of American Calls and Puts

$$C_0 \geq \text{Max}(0, S_0 - X)$$
$$P_0 \geq \text{Max}(0, X - S_0)$$

72-9. Lower Bounds of European and American Calls

$$c_0 \geq \text{Max}[0, S_0 - X/(1 + r)^T]$$
$$C_0 \geq \text{Max}[0, S_0 - X/(1 + r)^T]$$

72-10. Lower Bounds of European and American Puts

$$p_0 \geq \text{Max}[0, X/(1 + r)^T - S_0]$$
$$P_0 \geq \text{Max}(0, X - S_0)$$

72-11. Relationship Between Prices of Calls of Different Expirations

$$c_0(T_2) \geq c_0(T_1)$$
$$C_0(T_2) \geq C_0(T_1)$$

72-12. Relationship Between Prices of Puts of Different Expirations

$$p_0(T_2) \text{ can be either greater or less than } p_0(T_1)$$
$$P_0(T_2) \geq P_0(T_1)$$

72-13. Put–Call Parity for European Options

$$c_0 + X/(1 + r)^T = p_0 + S_0$$

72-14. Relationship Between American and European Call and Put Prices

$$C_0 \geq c_0$$
$$P_0 \geq p_0$$

72-15. Hedge Ratio for Binomial Model

$$n = \frac{c^+ - c^-}{S^+ - S^-}$$

72-16. European Call Prices in One-Period Binomial Model

$$c = \frac{\pi c^+ + (1 - \pi)c^-}{1 + r}$$

72-17. Risk-Neutral (Binomial) Probability

$$\pi = \frac{1 + r - d}{u - d}$$

72-18. European Call Prices at Time 1 in Two-Period Binomial Model

$$c^+ = \frac{\pi c^{++} + (1 - \pi)c^{+-}}{1 + r}$$

72-19. European Call Prices at Time 2 in Two-Period Binomial Model

$$c^- = \frac{\pi c^{-+} + (1 - \pi)c^{--}}{1 + r}$$

72-20. Hedge Ratios for Two-Period Binomial Model

$$n = \frac{c^+ - c^-}{S^+ - S^-}$$
$$n^+ = \frac{c^{++} - c^{+-}}{S^{++} - S^{+-}}$$
$$n^- = \frac{c^{-+} - c^{--}}{S^{-+} - S^{--}}$$

72-21. Black–Scholes–Merton Model for Calls and Puts

$$c = S_0 N(d_1) - X e^{-r^c T} N(d_2)$$
$$p = X e^{-r^c T} [1 - N(d_2)] - S_0 [1 - N(d_1)]$$

72-22. d_1 and d_2 in Black–Scholes–Merton Model

$$d_1 = \frac{\ln(S_0 N/X) + [r^c + (\sigma^2/2)]T}{\sigma \sqrt{T}}$$
$$d_2 = d_1 - \sigma \sqrt{T}$$

72-23. Option Delta

$$\text{Delta} = \frac{\text{Change in option price}}{\text{Change in underlying price}}$$

72-24. Payoffs of Options on Futures

$$c_T = \text{Max}[0, f_T(T) - X]$$
$$p_T = \text{Max}[0, X - f_T(T)]$$

72-25. Minimum and Maximum Prices of European and American Options on Futures

$$0 \leq c_0 \leq f_0(T)$$
$$0 \leq C_0 \leq f_0(T)$$
$$0 \leq p_0 \leq X/(1 + r)^T$$
$$0 \leq P_0 \leq X$$

72-26. Lower Bounds of European Options on Futures

$$c_0 \geq \text{Max}\{0, [f_0(T) - X]/(1 + r)^T\}$$
$$p_0 \geq \text{Max}\{0, [X - f_0(T)]/(1 + r)^T\}$$

72-27. Lower Bounds (Intrinsic Values) of American Options on Futures

$$C_0 \geq \text{Max}[0, f_0(T) - X]$$
$$P_0 \geq \text{Max}[0, X - f_0(T)]$$

72-28. Put–Call Parity for Options on Forward Contracts

$$c_0 + [X - F(0,T)]/(1 + r)^T = p_0$$

Reading 73: Swap Markets and Contracts

73-1. Fixed Rate on Interest Rate Swap

$$FS(0, n, m) = \frac{1.0 - B_0(h_n)}{\sum_{j=i}^{n} B_0(h_j)}$$

73-2. Market Value of Equity Swap During Its Life

$$\left(\frac{S_t}{S_0}\right) - B_t(h_n) - FS(0,n,m) \sum_{j=i}^{n} B_t(h_j)$$

73-3. Payoff of Payer Swaption

$$Max[0, FS(0, n, m) - x] \sum_{j=i}^{n} B_0(h_j)$$

73-4. Payoff of Receiver Swaption

$$Max[0, x - FS(0, n, m)] \sum_{j=i}^{n} B_0(h_j)$$

GLOSSARY

Abnormal rate of return   The amount by which a security's return differs from its expected rate of return based on the market's rate of return and the security's relationship with the market.

Absolute advantage   A situation in which a nation, as the result of its previous experience and/or natural endowments, can produce more of a good (with the same amount of resources) than another nation.

Absolute dispersion   The amount of variability present without comparison to any reference point or benchmark.

Absolute frequency   The number of observations in a given interval (for grouped data).

Accelerated method   A method of depreciation that allocates relatively large amounts of the depreciable cost of an asset to earlier years and reduced amounts to later years.

Accounting beta method   A method of estimating a project's beta by running a regression of the company's return on assets against the average return on assets for a large sample of firms.

Accounting estimates   Estimates of items such as the useful lives of assets, warranty costs, and the amount of uncollectible receivables.

Accounting profits   The sales revenues minus the expenses of a firm over a designated time period, usually one year. Accounting profits typically make allowances for changes in the firm's inventories and depreciation of its assets. No allowance is made, however, for the opportunity cost of the equity capital of the firm's owners, or other implicit costs.

Accounting risk   The risk associated with accounting standards that vary from country to country or with any uncertainty about how certain transactions should be recorded.

Accrued interest   (1) Interest earned but not yet due and payable. This is equal to the next coupon to be paid on a bond multiplied by the time elapsed since the last payment date and divided by the total coupon period. Exact conventions differ across bond markets. (2) Interest earned but not yet paid.

Accumulation phase   Phase in the investment life cycle during which individuals in the early-to-middle years of their working career attempt to accumulate assets to satisfy short-term needs and longer-term goals.

Active factor risk   The contribution to active risk squared resulting from the portfolio's different-than-benchmark exposures relative to factors specified in the risk model.

Active return   The return on a portfolio minus the return on the portfolio's benchmark.

Active risk   The standard deviation of active returns.

Active risk squared   The variance of active returns; active risk raised to the second power.

Active specific risk or asset selection risk   The contribution to active risk squared resulting from the portfolio's active weights on individual assets as those weights interact with assets' residual risk.

Activist strategy   Deliberate changes in monetary and fiscal policy in order to inject demand stimulus during a recession and apply restraint during an inflationary boom and thereby, it is hoped, minimize economic instability.

Actuarial rate of return   The discount rate used to find the present value of a defined benefit pension plan's future obligations and thus determine the size of the firm's annual contribution to the plan.

Actuarial yield   The total yield on a bond, obtained by setting the bond's current market value equal to the discounted cash flows promised by the bond. Also called yield to maturity.

Adaptive-expectations hypothesis   The hypothesis that economic decision makers base their future expectations on actual outcomes observed during recent periods. For example, according to this view, the rate of inflation actually experienced during the past two or three years would be the major determinant of the rate of inflation expected for the next year.

Addition   An enlargement to the physical layout of a plant asset.

Addition rule for probabilities   A principle stating that the probability that A or B occurs (both occur) equals the probability that A occurs, plus the probability that B occurs, minus the probability that both A and B occur.

Add-on interest   A procedure for determining the interest on a bond or loan in which the interest is added onto the face value of a contract.

Adjusted beta   Historical beta adjusted to reflect the tendency of beta to be mean reverting.

Adjusted R^2   A measure of goodness-of-fit of a regression that is adjusted for degrees of freedom and hence does not automatically increase when another independent variable is added to a regression.

Administrative lag   The time period after the need for a policy change is recognized but before the policy is actually implemented.

After-tax Cost of Debt, $k_d(1 - T)$ The relevant cost of new debt, taking into account the tax deductibility of interest; used to calculate the WACC.

Agency problem   A potential conflict of interest between the agent (manager) and (1) the outside stockholders or (2) the creditors (debtholders).

Agency trade   A trade in which a broker acts as an agent only, not taking a position on the opposite side of the trade.

Aggregate demand curve   A downward-sloping curve indicating an inverse relationship between the price level and the quantity of domestically produced goods and services that households, business firms, governments, and foreigners (net exports) are willing to purchase during a period.

Aggregate supply curve   A curve indicating the relationship between the nation's price level and quantity of goods supplied by its producers. In the short run, it is probably an upward-sloping curve, but in the long run most economists believe the aggregate supply curve is vertical (or nearly so).

AIMR   The Association for Investment Management and Research (AIMR®) awards the CFA® certification and sets professional standards that must be applied by its members worldwide.

Allocative efficiency   The allocation of resources to the production of goods and services most desired by consumers, at the lowest possible cost.

Alternative hypothesis   The hypothesis accepted when the null hypothesis is rejected.

American Depositary Receipt (ADR)   (1) A certificate of ownership issued by a U.S. bank to promote local trading in a foreign stock. The U.S. bank holds the foreign shares and issues ADRs against them. (2) Certificates of ownership issued by a U.S. bank that represent indirect ownership of a certain number of shares of a specific foreign firm. Shares are held on deposit in a bank in the firm's home country.

American option   (1) An option contract that can be exercised at any time until its expiration date. (2) An option that can be exercised on any day through the expiration day. Also referred to as American-style exercise.

American terms   With reference to U.S. dollar exchange rate quotations, the U.S. dollar price of a unit of another currency.

Amortization   The periodic allocation of the cost of an intangible asset to the periods it benefits.

Amortizing and accreting swaps   A swap in which the notional principal changes according to a formula related to changes in the underlying.

Analysis effect   The difference in performance of a bond portfolio from that of a chosen index due to acquisition of temporarily mispriced issues that then move to their correct prices.

Analysis of variance (ANOVA)   The analysis of the total variability of a dataset (such as observations on the dependent variable in a regression) into components representing different sources of variation; with reference to regression, ANOVA provides the inputs for an F-test of the significance of the regression as a whole.

Annual percentage rate   The cost of borrowing expressed as a yearly rate.

Annuity   A finite set of level sequential cash flows.

Annuity due   An annuity having a first cash flow that is paid immediately.

Anomalies   Security price relationships that appear to contradict a well-regarded hypothesis; in this case, the efficient market hypothesis.

Anticipated change   A change that is foreseen by decision makers in time for them to adjust.

Anticipated inflation   An increase in the general level of prices that was expected by most decision makers.

Appreciation   An increase in the value of the domestic currency relative to foreign currencies. An appreciation increases the purchasing power of the domestic currency for foreign goods.

A priori probability   A probability based on logical analysis rather than on observation or personal judgment.

Arbitrage   (1) The simultaneous purchase of an undervalued asset or portfolio and sale of an overvalued but equivalent asset or portfolio, in order to obtain a riskless profit on the price differential. Taking advantage of a market inefficiency in a risk-free manner. (2) A trading strategy designed to generate a guaranteed profit from a transaction that requires no capital commitment or risk bearing on the part of the trader. A simple example of an arbitrage trade would be the simultaneous purchase and sale of the same security in different markets at different prices. (3) The condition in a financial market in which equivalent assets or combinations of assets sell for two different prices, creating an opportunity to profit at no risk with no commitment of money. In a well-functioning financial market, few arbitrage opportunities are possible. Equivalent to the law of one price. (4) A risk-free operation that earns an expected positive net profit but requires no net investment of money.

Arbitrage approach   A common approach used to value derivative securities, based on an arbitrage strategy involving the underlying securities.

Arbitrage opportunity   An opportunity to conduct an arbitrage; an opportunity to earn an expected positive net profit without risk and with no net investment of money.

Arbitrage portfolio The portfolio that exploits an arbitrage opportunity.

Arbitrage pricing theory (APT) A theory that posits that the expected return to a financial asset can be described by its relationship with several common risk factors. The APT can be contrasted with the single-factor CAPM.

Arithmetic mean (AM) (1) A measure of mean annual rates of return equal to the sum of annual holding period rates of return divided by the number of years. (2) The sum of the observations divided by the number of observations.

Arrears swap A type of interest rate swap in which the floating payment is set at the end of the period and the interest is paid at that same time.

Asian call option A European-style option with a value at maturity equal to the difference between the stock price at maturity and the average stock price during the life of the option, or $0, whichever is greater.

Ask price The price at which a market maker is willing to sell a security (also called offer price).

Asset allocation (1) Dividing of investment funds among several asset classes to achieve diversification. (2) The process of deciding how to distribute an investor's wealth among different asset classes for investment purposes.

Asset class Securities that have similar characteristics, attributes, and risk/return relationships.

Asset impairment Loss of revenue-generating potential of a long-lived asset before the end of its useful life; the difference between an asset's carrying value and its fair value, as measured by the present value of the expected cash flows.

Assets under management (AUM) The total market value of the assets managed by an investment firm.

Asymmetric Information The situation in which managers have different (better) information about firms' prospects than do investors.

At-the-money option An option for which the strike (or exercise) price is close to (at) the current market price of the underlying asset.

Attribution analysis An assessment technique designed to establish whether a manager's performance relative to a benchmark resulted from market timing or security selection skills.

Autocorrelation The correlation of a time series with its own past values.

Autocorrelation test A test of the efficient market hypothesis that compares security price changes over time to check for predictable correlation patterns.

Automatic stabilizers Built-in features that tend automatically to promote a budget deficit during a recession and a budget surplus during an inflationary boom, even without a change in policy.

Automation A production technique that reduces the amount of labor required to produce a good or service. It is beneficial to adopt the new labor-saving technology only if it reduces the cost of production.

Autonomous expenditures Expenditures that do not vary with the level of income. They are determined by factors (such as business expectations and economic policy) that are outside the basic income-expenditure model.

Autoregressive (AR) model A time series regressed on its own past values, in which the independent variable is a lagged value of the dependent variable.

Average fixed cost Total fixed cost divided by the number of units produced. It always declines as output increases.

Average product The total product (output) divided by the number of units of the variable input required to produce that output level.

Average tax rate (ATR) (1) Tax liability divided by taxable income. It is the percentage of income paid in taxes. (2) A person's total tax payment divided by his or her total income.

Average total cost Total cost divided by the number of units produced. It is sometimes called per-unit cost.

Average variable cost The total variable cost divided by the number of units produced.

Back office Settlement and related processes.

Back simulation *See* Historical simulation method.

Backtest A method of testing a quantitative model in which computers are used to examine the composition and returns of portfolios based on historical data to determine if the selected strategy would have worked in the past.

Back-to-back Transactions in which a loan is made in one currency against a loan in another currency.

Backwardated A situation in a futures market where the current contract price is less than the current spot price for the underlying asset.

Backwardation A condition in the futures markets in which the benefits of holding an asset exceed the costs, leaving the futures price less than the spot price.

Balanced budget A situation in which current government revenue from taxes, fees, and other sources is just equal to current government expenditures.

Balanced fund A mutual fund with, generally, a three-part investment objective: (1) to conserve the investor's principal, (2) to pay current income, and (3) to increase both principal and income. The fund aims to achieve this by owning a mixture of bonds, preferred stocks, and common stocks.

Balance of merchandise trade The difference between the value of merchandise exports and the value of merchandise imports for a nation. The balance of merchandise trade is only one component of a nation's total balance of payments. Also called simply balance of trade or net exports.

Balance of payments (1) A summary of all economic transactions between a country and all other countries for a specific time period, usually a year. The balance-of-payments account reflects all payments and liabilities to foreigners (debits) and all payments and obligations received from foreigners (credits). (2) A record of all financial flows crossing the borders of a country during a given time period (a quarter or a year).

Balance of trade *See* Trade balance.

Balance on current account The import-export balance of goods and services, plus net investment income earned abroad, plus net private and government transfers. If the value of the nation's export-type items exceeds (is less than) the value of the nation's import-type items plus net unilateral transfers to foreigners, a current-account surplus (deficit) is present.

Balance on goods and services The exports of goods (merchandise) and services of a nation minus its imports of goods and services.

Balance sheet A financial statement that shows what assets the firm controls at a fixed point in time and how it has financed these assets.

Bank discount basis A quoting convention that annualizes, on a 360-day year, the discount as a percentage of face value.

Bank reserves Vault cash plus deposits of the bank with Federal Reserve banks.

Barriers to entry Obstacles that limit the freedom of potential rivals to enter and compete in an industry or market.

Base case An analysis in which all of the input variables are set at their most likely values.

Basic earnings per share Total earnings divided by the weighted average number of shares actually outstanding during the period.

Basis (1) The difference between the futures (or forward) price of an asset and its spot (or cash) price. The basis can be expressed as a value or as a percentage of the spot price. (2) The difference between the spot price of the underlying asset and the futures contract price at any point in time (e.g., the initial basis at the time of contract origination, the cover basis at the time of contract termination).

Basis of an asset For tax purposes, the cost of an asset.

Basis point One hundredth of 1 percent (0.01%).

Basis point value (BPV) Also called present value of a basis point or price value of a basis point (PVBP), the change in the bond price for a 1 basis point change in yield.

Basis risk (1) The risk that arises from fluctuation in the basis. (2) The residual exposure to the price volatility of an underlying asset that results from a cross hedge transaction.

Basis swap (1) An interest rate swap involving two floating rates. (2) A swap in which both parties pay a floating rate.

Bayes' formula A method for updating probabilities based on new information.

Bearer bond An unregistered bond for which ownership is determined by possession. The holder receives interest payments by clipping coupons attached to the security and sending them to the issuer for payment.

Bearer security A negotiable security. All cash flows paid on the security are remitted to its bearer. No register of ownership is kept by the issuing company.

Bear spread An option strategy that involves selling a put with a lower exercise price and buying a put with a higher exercise price. It can also be executed with calls.

Behavioral finance Involves the analysis of various psychological traits of individuals and how these traits affect how they act as investors, analysts, and portfolio managers.

Benchmark (1) A standard measurement used to evaluate the performance of a portfolio. The benchmark may be some passive index or the aggregate performance on a universe of comparable portfolios (*see* Composite). (2) A comparison portfolio; a point of reference or comparison.

Benchmark bond A bond representative of current market conditions and used for performance comparison.

Benchmark error Situation where an inappropriate or incorrect benchmark is used to compare and assess portfolio returns and management.

Benchmark portfolio A comparison standard of risk and assets included in the policy statement and similar to the investor's risk preference and investment needs, which can be used to evaluate the investment performance of the portfolio manager.

Benchmark value of the multiple In using the method of comparables, the value of a price multiple for the comparison asset; when we have comparison assets (a group), the mean or median value of the multiple for the group of assets.

Bernoulli random variable   A random variable having the outcomes 0 and 1.

Bernoulli trial   An experiment that can produce one of two outcomes.

Best-case scenario   An analysis in which all of the input variables are set at their best reasonably forecasted values.

Beta (β)   (1) A statistical measure of market risk on a portfolio; traditionally used to estimate the elasticity of a stock portfolio's return relative to the market index. (2) A standardized measure of systematic risk based upon an asset's covariance with the market portfolio. (3) A measure of the relationship between the return on a stock portfolio and the return on the market portfolio, which is a portfolio containing all risky assets in the market. (4) A measure of an asset's sensitivity to movements in the market.

Betterment   An improvement that does not add to the physical layout of the plant.

Bid-ask spread   The difference between the quoted ask and the bid prices.

Bid price   The price at which a market maker is willing to buy a security.

Bilateral arbitrage   With reference to currencies, an arbitrage involving two currencies only.

Bill-and-hold basis   Sales on a bill-and-hold basis involve selling products but not delivering those products until a later date.

Binomial model   A model for pricing options in which the underlying price can move to only one of two possible new prices.

Binomial option pricing model   A valuation equation that assumes the price of the underlying asset changes through a series of discrete upward or downward movements.

Binomial random variable   The number of successes in n Bernoulli trials for which the probability of success is constant for all trials and the trials are independent.

Binomial tree   (1) A diagram representing price movements of the underlying in a binomial model. (2) The graphical representation of a model of asset price dynamics in which, at each period, the asset moves up with probability p or down with probability $(1 - p)$.

Bird-in-the-hand theory   MM's name for the theory that a firm's value will be maximized by setting a high dividend payout ratio.

Black market   A market that operates outside the legal system, either by selling illegal goods or by selling goods at illegal prices or terms.

Black-Scholes or Black-Scholes-Merton formula   A standard option pricing formula derived by F. Black and M. Scholes and also by R. Merton.

Block   Orders to buy or sell that are too large for the liquidity ordinarily available in dealer networks or stock exchanges.

Bond   A long-term debt security with contractual obligations regarding interest payments and redemption.

Bond-equivalent basis   A basis for stating an annual yield that annualizes a semiannual yield by doubling it.

Bond-equivalent yield   The yield to maturity on a basis that ignores compounding.

Bond option   An option in which the underlying is a bond; primarily traded in over-the-counter markets.

Bond price volatility   The percentage changes in bond prices over time.

Bond swap   An active bond portfolio management strategy that exchanges one position for another to take advantage of some difference between them.

Book value of equity (or book value)   (1) Shareholders' equity (total assets minus total liabilities) minus the value of preferred stock; common shareholders' equity. (2) The accounting value of a firm.

Book value per share   Book value of equity divided by the number of common shares outstanding.

Bottom-up investing   With respect to investment approaches, a focus on selecting individual securities with whatever allocation of money to asset classes, countries, or industry securities results.

Bourse   A French term often used to refer to a stock market.

Box spread   An option strategy that combines a bull spread and a bear spread having two different exercise prices, which produces a risk-free payoff of the difference in the exercise prices.

Brand name   A registered name that can be used only by its owner to identify a product or service.

Brady bonds   Bonds issued by emerging countries under a debt-reduction plan named after Mr. Brady, former U.S. Secretary of the Treasury.

Break-even exchange rate   The future exchange rate such that the return in two bond markets would be even for a given maturity. Also called implied forward exchange rate.

Breakeven point   The volume of sales at which total costs equal total revenues, causing operating profits (or EBIT) to equal zero.

Break Point (BP)   The dollar value of new capital that can be raised before an increase in the firm's weighted average cost of capital occurs.

Bretton Woods   The site of a 1944 conference that led to the establishment of a semifixed exchange rate system.

Breusch–Pagan test A test for conditional heteroskedasticity in the error term of a regression.

Broker (1) An agent who executes orders to buy or sell securities on behalf of a client in exchange for a commission. (2) *See* Futures commission merchants.

Budget constraint The constraint that separates the bundles of goods that the consumer can purchase from those that cannot be purchased, given a limited income and the prices of the products.

Budget deficit A situation in which total government spending exceeds total government revenue during a specific time period, usually one year.

Budget surplus A situation in which total government spending is less than total government revenue during a time period, usually a year.

Bull floating-rate note A floating-rate note whose coupon increases if interest rates drop; an inverse floater.

Bull spread An option strategy that involves buying a call with a lower exercise price and selling a call with a higher exercise price. It can also be executed with puts.

Business cycle Fluctuations in the general level of economic activity as measured by such variables as the rate of unemployment and changes in real GDP.

Business risk The variability of operating income arising from the characteristics of the firm's industry. Two sources of business risk are sales variability and operating leverage.

Butterfly spread An option strategy that combines two bull or bear spreads and has three exercise prices.

Buy-and-hold strategy A passive portfolio management strategy in which bonds are bought and held to maturity.

Call An option that gives the holder the right to buy an underlying asset from another party at a fixed price over a specific period of time.

Call auction *See* Fixing.

Call market A market in which trading for individual stocks only takes place at specified times. All the bids and asks available at the time are combined and the market administrators specify a single price that will possibly clear the market at that time.

Call option (1) A contract giving the right to buy an asset at a specific price on or before a specified date. (2) Option to buy an asset within a certain period at a specified price called the exercise price.

Call premium Amount above par issuer must pay to bondholder for retiring the bond before its stated maturity.

Call provisions Specifies when and how a firm can issue a call for bonds outstanding prior to their maturity.

Cannibalization Occurs when the introduction of a new product causes sales of existing projects to decline.

Cap (1) A contract on an interest rate, whereby at periodic payment dates, the writer of the cap pays the difference between the market interest rate and a specified cap rate if, and only if, this difference is positive. This is equivalent to a stream of call options on the interest rate. (2) A combination of interest rate call options designed to hedge a borrower against rate increases on a floating-rate loan.

Cap agreement A contract that on each settlement date pays the holder the greater of the difference between the reference rate and the cap rate or zero; it is equivalent to a series of call options on the reference rate.

Capital Man-made resources (such as tools, equipment, and structures) that are used to produce other goods and services. Resources that enhance our ability to produce output in the future.

Capital account (1) The record of transactions with foreigners that involve either (a) the exchange of ownership rights to real or financial assets or (b) the extension of loans. (2) A component of the balance of payments that reflects unrequited (or unilateral) transfers corresponding to capital flows entailing no compensation (in the form of goods, services, or assets). Examples include investment capital given (without future repayment) in favor of poor countries, debt forgiveness, and expropriation losses.

Capital allocation line (CAL) A graph line that describes the combinations of expected return and standard deviation of return available to an investor from combining the optimal portfolio of risky assets with the risk-free asset.

Capital appreciation A return objective in which the investor seeks to increase the portfolio value, primarily through capital gains, over time to meet a future need rather than dividend yield.

Capital asset pricing model (CAPM) (1) An equilibrium theory that relates the expected return of an asset to its market risk (*see* Beta). (2) A theory concerned with deriving the expected or required rates of return on risky assets based on the assets' systematic risk levels. (3) An equation describing the expected return on any asset (or portfolio) as a linear function of its beta.

Capital budgeting The process of planning expenditures on assets whose cash flows are expected to extend beyond one year.

Capital component   One of the types of capital used by firms to make money.

Capital expenditure   An expenditure for the purchase or expansion of a long-term asset, recorded in an asset account.

Capitalism   An economic system based on private ownership of productive resources and allocation of goods according to the signals provided by market prices.

Capital market instruments   Fixed-income or equity investments that trade in the secondary market.

Capital market line (CML)   (1) The line from the intercept point that represents the risk-free rate tangent to the original efficient frontier; it becomes the new efficient frontier since investments on this line dominate all the portfolios on the original Markowitz efficient frontier. (2) A form of the capital allocation line in which investors share identical expectations about the mean returns, variance of returns, and correlations of risky assets.

Capital preservation   A return objective in which the investor seeks to minimize the risk of loss; generally a goal of the risk-averse investor.

Capital rationing   A situation in which a constraint is placed on the total size of the firm's capital budget.

Capital structure   A company's specific mixture of long-term financing.

Caplet   Each component call option in a cap.

Capped swap   A swap in which the floating payments have an upper limit.

Carrying value   The unexpired part of the cost of an asset, not its market value. Also called *book value*.

Cartel   An organization of sellers designed to coordinate supply decisions so that the joint profits of the members will be maximized. A cartel will seek to create a monopoly in the market.

Cash-and-carry arbitrage   An arbitrage strategy with a simultaneous spot purchase and forward sale of an asset. The reverse transaction (borrowing the asset, selling it spot, and buying it forward) is known as a reverse cash and carry, or as a carry-and-cash arbitrage. These arbitrages lead to a relation between spot and forward, or futures, prices of the same asset.

Cash flow additivity principle   The principle that dollar amounts indexed at the same point in time are additive.

Cash flow at risk (CFAR)   A variation of VAR that reflects the risk of a company's cash flow instead of its market value.

Cash price or spot price   The price for immediate purchase of the underlying asset.

Cash settlement   (1) A procedure for settling futures contracts in which the cash difference between the futures price and the spot price is paid instead of physical delivery. (2) A procedure used in certain derivative transactions that specifies that the long and short parties engage in the equivalent cash value of a delivery transaction.

CD equivalent yield   *See* Money market yield.

Central bank   An institution that regulates the banking system and controls the supply of money of a country.

Centralized risk management or companywide risk management   When a company has a single risk management group that monitors and controls all of the risk-taking activities of the organization. Centralization permits economies of scale and allows a company to use some of its risks to offset other risks. *See also* Enterprise risk management.

Central limit theorem   A result in statistics that states that the sample mean computed from large samples of size n from a population with finite variance will follow an approximate normal distribution with a mean equal to the population mean and a variance equal to the population variance divided by n.

Certificates of deposit (CDs)   Instruments issued by banks and S&Ls that require minimum deposits for specified terms and that pay higher rates of interest than deposit accounts.

Ceteris paribus   A Latin term meaning "other things constant," used when the effect of one change is being described, recognizing that if other things changed, they also could affect the result. Economists often describe the effects of one change, knowing that in the real world, other things might change and also exert an effect.

Chain rule of forecasting   A forecasting process in which the next period's value as predicted by the forecasting equation is substituted into the right-hand side of the equation to give a predicted value two periods ahead.

Change in net working capital   The increased current assets resulting from a new project, minus the spontaneous increase in accounts payable and accruals.

Characteristic line   Regression line that indicates the systematic risk of a risky asset.

Cheapest to deliver   A bond in which the amount received for delivering the bond is largest compared with the amount paid in the market for the bond.

Cherry-picking   When a bankrupt company is allowed to enforce contracts that are favorable to it while walking away from contracts that are unfavorable to it.

Choice   The act of selecting among alternatives.

Civilian labor force   The number of persons 16 years of age and over who are either employed or unemployed. In order to be classified as unemployed, one must be looking for a job.

Classical economists   Economists from Adam Smith to the time of Keynes who focused their analyses on economic efficiency and production. With regard to business instability, they thought market prices and wages would decline during a recession quickly enough to bring the economy back to full employment within a short period of time.

Clean price   The price of a bond obtained as the total price of the bond minus accrued interest. Most bonds are traded on the basis of their clean price.

Clearinghouse   (1) An organization that settles and guarantees trades in some financial markets. (2) An entity associated with a futures market that acts as middleman between the contracting parties and guarantees to each party the performance of the other.

Clientele Effect   The tendency of a firm to attract a set of investors who like its dividend policy.

Closed-end fund   An investment company with a fixed number of shares. New shares cannot be issued and the old shares cannot be redeemed. Shares are traded in the marketplace, and their value may differ from the underlying net asset value of the fund.

Closed-end investment company   An investment company that issues only a limited number of shares, which it does not redeem (buy back). Instead, shares of a closed-end fund are traded in securities markets at prices determined by supply and demand.

Closeout netting   Netting the market values of all derivative contracts between two parties to determine one overall value owed by one party to another in the event of bankruptcy.

Coefficient of variation (CV)   (1) A measure of relative variability that indicates risk per unit of return. It is equal to: standard deviation divided by the mean value. When used in investments, it is equal to: standard deviation of returns divided by the expected rate of return. (2) The ratio of a set of observations' standard deviation to the observations' mean value.

Coincident indicators   A set of economic variables whose values reach peaks and troughs at about the same time as the aggregate economy.

Cointegrated   Describes two time series that have a long-term financial or economic relationship such that they do not diverge from each other without bound in the long run.

Collar   (1) A combination of a cap and a floor. (2) An option strategy involving the purchase of a put and sale of a call in which the holder of an asset gains protection below a certain level, the exercise price of the put, and pays for it by giving up gains above a certain level, the exercise price of the call. Collars also can be used to provide protection against rising interest rates on a floating-rate loan by giving up gains from lower interest rates.

Collar agreement   A hedging arrangement where an underlying asset is protected against decreases in value by the simultaneous purchase of a put option and sale of a call option.

Collateral trust bonds   A mortgage bond wherein the assets backing the bond are financial assets like stocks and bonds.

Collateralized mortgage obligation (CMO)   A debt security based on a pool of mortgage loans that provides a relatively stable stream of payments for a relatively predictable term.

Collective decision making   The method of organization that relies on public-sector decision making (voting, political bargaining, lobbying, and so on) to resolve basic issues.

Collusion   Agreement among firms to avoid various competitive practices, particularly price reductions. It may involve either formal agreements or merely tacit recognition that competitive practices will be self-defeating in the long run. Tacit collusion is difficult to detect. In the United States, antitrust laws prohibit collusion and conspiracies to restrain trade.

Combination   A listing in which the order of the listed items does not matter.

Commercial banks   Financial institutions that offer a wide range of services (for example, checking accounts, savings accounts, and extension of loans) to their customers. Commercial banks are owned by stockholders and seek to operate at a profit.

Commercial paper   Unsecured short-term corporate debt that is characterized by a single payment at maturity.

Comparative advantage   The ability to produce a good at a lower opportunity cost than others can produce it. Relative costs determine comparative advantage.

Commission brokers   Employees of a member firm who buy or sell securities for the customers of the firm.

Commodity forward   A contract in which the underlying asset is oil, a precious metal, or some other commodity.

Commodity futures   Futures contracts in which the underlying is a traditional agricultural, metal, or petroleum product.

Commodity option   An option in which the asset underlying the futures is a commodity, such as oil, gold, wheat, or soybeans.

Commodity swap   A swap in which the underlying is a commodity such as oil, gold, or an agricultural product.

Common size statements   (1) Financial statements in which all elements (accounts) are stated as a percentage of a key figure such as revenue for an income statement or total assets for a balance sheet. (2) The normalization of balance sheet and income statement items to allow for more meaningful comparison of different-size firms. Balance sheet items are divided by total assets; income statement items are divided by total sales.

Common stock   An equity investment that represents ownership of a firm, with full participation in its success or failure. The firm's directors must approve dividend payments.

Company fundamental factors   Factors related to the company's internal performance, such as factors relating to earnings growth, earnings variability, earnings momentum, and financial leverage.

Company share-related factors   Valuation measures and other factors related to share price or the trading characteristics of the shares, such as earnings yield, dividend yield, and book-to-market value.

Compensating wage differentials   Wage differences that compensate workers for risk, unpleasant working conditions, and other undesirable non-pecuniary aspects of a job.

Competition as a dynamic process   A term that denotes rivalry or competitiveness between or among parties (for example, producers or input suppliers), each of which seeks to deliver a better deal to buyers when quality, price, and product information are all considered. Competition implies a lack of collusion among sellers.

Competitive bid   An underwriting alternative wherein an issuing entity (governmental body or a corporation) specifies the type of security to be offered (bonds or stocks) and the general characteristics of the issue, and the issuer solicits bids from competing investment banking firms with the understanding that the issuer will accept the highest bid from the bankers.

Competitive environment   The level of intensity of competition among firms in an industry, determined by an examination of five competitive forces.

Competitive price-searcher market   A market where the firms have a downward-sloping demand curve, and entry into and exit from the market are relatively easy.

Competitive strategy   The search by a firm for a favorable competitive position within an industry, which affects evaluation of the industry's prospects.

Complement   With reference to an event S, the event that S does not occur.

Complements   Products that are usually consumed jointly (for example, peanut butter and jelly). They are related such that a decrease in the price of one will cause an increase in demand for the other.

Completely diversified portfolio   A portfolio in which all unsystematic risk has been eliminated by diversification.

Completeness fund   A specialized index used to form the basis of a passive portfolio whose purpose is to provide diversification to a client's total portfolio by excluding those segments in which the client's active managers invest.

Composite   A universe of portfolios with similar investment objectives.

Composite measure   An investment performance statistic that considers both the return and risk associated with a portfolio (e.g., Sharpe measure, Treynor measure, Jensen measure).

Compounding   The process of accumulating interest on interest.

Conditional expected value   (1) Expected value of a variable conditional on some available information set. The expected value changes over time with changes in the information set. (2) The expected value of a stated event given that another event has occurred.

Conditional heteroskedasticity   Heteroskedasticity in the error variance that is correlated with the values of the independent variable(s) in the regression.

Conditional probability   The probability of an event given (conditioned on) another event.

Conditional variance   (1) Variance of a variable conditional on some available information set. (2) The variance of one variable, given the outcome of another.

Confidence interval   A range that has a given probability that it will contain the population parameter it is intended to estimate.

Consistency   A desirable property of estimators; a consistent estimator is one for which the probability of estimates close to the value of the population parameter increases as sample size increases.

Consistent   With reference to estimators, describes an estimator for which the probability of estimates close to the value of the population parameter increases as sample size increases.

Consolidation phase Phase in the investment life cycle during which individuals who are typically past the midpoint of their career have earnings that exceed expenses and invest them for future retirement or estate planning needs.

Constant-cost industry An industry for which factor prices and costs of production remain constant as market output is expanded. Thus, the long-run market supply curve is horizontal.

Constant maturity swap or CMT swap A swap in which the floating rate is the rate on a security known as a constant maturity treasury or CMT security.

Constant maturity treasury or CMT A hypothetical U.S. Treasury note with a constant maturity. A CMT exists for various years in the range of 2 to 10.

Constant returns to scale Unit costs that are constant as the scale of the firm is altered. Neither economies nor diseconomies of scale are present.

Construct the portfolio Given the strategy and economic outlook, what specific stocks and/or bonds will be put into the portfolio at the present time that are consistent with the client's policy statement.

Consumer price index (CPI) (1) An indicator of the general level of prices. It attempts to compare the cost of purchasing the market basket bought by a typical consumer during a specific period with the cost of purchasing the same market basket during an earlier period. (2) A price index defined on a basket of goods consumed.

Consumer surplus The difference between the maximum price consumers are willing to pay and the price they actually pay. It is the net gain derived by the buyers of the good.

Consumption function A fundamental relationship between disposable income and consumption, in which, as disposable income increases, current consumption expenditures rise, but by a smaller amount than the increase in income.

Consumption opportunity constraint The constraint that separates consumption bundles that are attainable from those that are unattainable. In a money income economy, this is usually a budget constraint.

Contango (1) A situation in a futures market where the current contract price is greater than the current spot price for the underlying asset. (2) A condition in the futures markets in which the costs of holding an asset exceed the benefits, leaving the futures price more than the spot price.

Contingent claims Derivatives in which the payoffs occur if a specific event occurs; generally referred to as options.

Contingent deferred sales load A mutual fund that imposes a sales charge when the investor sells or redeems shares. Also referred to as rear-end loads or redemption charges.

Continual monitoring This involves constant evaluation of the economic environment, the policy statement, and the portfolio to ensure that it is consistent with the policy statement. Also involves evaluating performance to determine if changes are required in the portfolio, the strategy, or the policy statement.

Continuing earnings *See* Underlying earnings.

Continuously compounded return The natural logarithm of 1 plus the holding period return, or equivalently, the natural logarithm of the ending price over the beginning price.

Continuous market A market where stocks are priced and traded continuously by an auction process or by dealers when the market is open.

Continuous random variable A random variable for which the range of possible outcomes is the real line (all real numbers between $-\infty$ and $+\infty$) or some subset of the real line.

Continuous time Time thought of as advancing in extremely small increments.

Contract for difference (CFD) A contract between an investor and a broker in which the investor receives (or pays) the difference between the price of the underlying share when the contract is closed and the price when the contract was opened.

Convexity A measure of the change in duration with respect to changes in interest rates.

Contestable market A market in which the costs of entry and exit are low, so a firm risks little by entering. Efficient production and zero economic profits should prevail in a contestable market. A market can be contestable even if capital requirements are high.

Contract price The transaction price specified in a forward or futures contract.

Contrarian An investment strategy that attempts to buy (sell) securities on which the majority of other investors are bearish (bullish).

Convenience yield (1) An adjustment made to the theoretical forward or futures contract delivery price to account for the preference that consumers have for holding spot positions in the underlying asset. (2) The nonmonetary return offered by an asset when the asset is in short supply, often associated with assets with seasonal production processes.

Conversion factors (1) The adjustments made to Treasury bond futures contract terms to allow for the delivery of an instrument other than the standardized underlying asset. (2) An adjustment used to facilitate delivery on bond futures contracts in which any of a number of bonds with different characteristics are eligible for delivery.

Conversion parity price The price at which common stock can be obtained by surrendering the convertible instrument at par value.

Conversion premium The excess of the market value of the convertible security over its equity value if immediately converted into common stock. Typically expressed as a percentage of the equity value.

Conversion ratio The number of shares of common stock for which a convertible security may be exchanged.

Conversion value The value of the convertible security if converted into common stock at the stock's current market price

Convertible bonds A bond with the added feature that the bondholder has the option to turn the bond back to the firm in exchange for a specified number of common shares of the firm.

Convexity A measure of the degree to which a bond's price-yield curve departs from a straight line. This characteristic affects estimates of a bond's price volatility for a given change in yields.

Copyright An exclusive right granted by the federal government to reproduce and sell literary, musical, and other artistic materials and computer programs for a period of the author's life plus 70 years.

Core earnings *See* Underlying earnings.

Core-plus bond portfolio management This is a combination approach to bond portfolio management wherein a significant (core) part of the portfolio (e.g., 70–75 percent) of the portfolio is managed passively in a widely recognized sector of the bond market, such as an aggregate bond index or a U.S. Government/corporate sector. The rest of the portfolio would be actively managed in one or several "plus" sectors that are less efficient than the core component—for example, high-yield bonds, foreign bonds, or emerging market debt.

Corporate, or Within-Firm, risk Risk not considering the effects of stockholders' diversification; it is measured by a project's effect on uncertainty about the firm's future earnings.

Corporation A business firm owned by shareholders who possess ownership rights to the firm's profits, but whose liability is limited to the amount of their investment in the firm.

Correlation A number between −1 and +1 that measures the co-movement (linear association) between two random variables.

Correlation analysis The analysis of the strength of the linear relationship between two data series.

Correlation coefficient A standardized measure of the relationship between two variables that ranges from −1.00 to +1.00.

Cost averaging The periodic investment of a fixed amount of money.

Cost of carry (1) The cost associated with holding some asset, including financing, storage, and insurance costs. Any yield received on the asset is treated as a negative carrying cost. (2) The net amount that would be required to store a commodity or security for future delivery, usually calculated as physical storage costs plus financial capital costs less dividends paid to the underlying asset. (3) The costs of holding an asset.

Cost of carry model A model for pricing futures contracts in which the futures price is determined by adding the cost of carry to the spot price.

Cost of new common equity, k_e The cost of external equity; based on the cost of retained earnings, but increased for flotation costs.

Cost of Preferred Stock, k_{ps} The rate of return investors require on the firm's preferred stock. k_{ps} is calculated as the preferred dividend, D_{ps}, divided by the net issuing price, P_n.

Cost of retained earnings, k_s The rate of return required by stockholders on a firm's common stock.

Countercyclical policy A policy that tends to move the economy in an opposite direction from the forces of the business cycle. Such a policy would stimulate demand during the contraction phase of the business cycle and restrain demand during the expansion phase.

Counterparty A participant to a derivative transaction.

Country risk Uncertainty due to the possibility of major political or economic change in the country where an investment is located. Also called political risk.

Coupon Indicates the interest payment on a debt security. It is the coupon rate times the par value that indicates the interest payments on a debt security.

Coupon reinvestment risk The component of interest rate risk due to the uncertainty of the rate at which coupon payments will be reinvested.

Covariance (1) A measure of the degree to which two variables, such as rates of return for investment assets, move together over time relative to their individual mean returns. (2) A measure of the extent to which the returns on two assets move together. (3) A measure of the co-movement (linear association) between two random variables.

Covariance matrix A matrix or square array whose entries are covariances; also known as a variance–covariance matrix.

Covariance stationary Describes a time series when its expected value and variance are constant and finite in all periods and when its covariance with itself for a fixed number of periods in the past or future is constant and finite in all periods.

Covered call (1) A trading strategy in which a call option is sold as a supplement to a long position in an underlying asset or portfolio of assets. (2) An option strategy involving the holding of an asset and sale of a call on the asset.

Covered interest arbitrage (1) A trading strategy involving borrowing money in one country and lending it to another designed to exploit price deviations from the interest rate parity model. (2) A transaction executed in the foreign exchange market in which a currency is purchased (sold) and a forward contract is sold (purchased) to lock in the exchange rate for future delivery of the currency. This transaction should earn the risk-free rate of the investor's home country.

Covered option An option position that is offset by an equal and opposite position in the underlying security.

Credit Funds acquired by borrowing.

Credit analysis An active bond portfolio management strategy designed to identify bonds that are expected to experience changes in rating. This strategy is critical when investing in high-yield bonds.

Credit derivatives A contract in which one party has the right to claim a payment from another party in the event that a specific credit event occurs over the life of the contract.

Credit risk or default risk The risk of loss due to nonpayment by a counterparty.

Credit spread option An option on the yield spread on a bond.

Credit swap A type of swap transaction used as a credit derivative in which one party makes periodic payments to the other and receives the promise of a payoff if a third party defaults.

Credit unions Financial cooperative organizations of individuals with a common affiliation (such as an employer or a labor union). They accept deposits, including checkable deposits, pay interest (or dividends) on them out of earnings, and channel funds primarily into loans to members.

Credit VAR, Default VAR, or Credit at Risk A variation of VAR that reflects credit risk.

Credit-linked notes Fixed-income securities in which the holder of the security has the right to withhold payment of the full amount due at maturity if a credit event occurs.

Critical value *See* Rejection point.

Cross hedge A trading strategy in which the price volatility of a commodity or security position is hedged with a forward or futures contract based on a different underlying asset or different settlement terms.

Crossover price The price at which the yield to maturity equals the yield to call. Above this price, yield to call is the appropriate yield measure; below this price, yield to maturity is the appropriate yield measure.

Crossover rate The discount rate at which the NPV profiles of two projects cross and, thus, at which the projects' NPVs are equal.

Cross-product netting Netting the market values of all contracts, not just derivatives, between parties.

Cross-rate The exchange rate between two currencies, derived from their exchange rates with a third currency.

Cross-sectional analysis An examination of a firm's performance in comparison to other firms in the industry with similar characteristics to the firm being studied.

Cross-sectional data Observations over individual units at a point in time, as opposed to time-series data.

Cross-sectional return studies Studies wherein investigators look for public information regarding individual stocks that predict the cross-sectional distribution of risk-adjusted returns—e.g., is there an inverse relationship between market-value size of a firm and future risk-adjusted rates of return for its stock?

Crowding-out effect A reduction in private spending as a result of higher interest rates generated by budget deficits that are financed by borrowing in the private loanable funds market.

Cumulative distribution function A function giving the probability that a random variable is less than or equal to a specified value.

Cumulative relative frequency For data grouped into intervals, the fraction of total observations that are less than the value of the upper limit of a stated interval.

Currency board An entity that (a) issues a currency with a fixed designated value relative to a widely accepted currency (for example, the U.S. dollar), (b) promises to continue to redeem the issued currency at the fixed rate, and (c) maintains bonds and other liquid assets denominated in the other currency that provide 100 percent backing for all currency issued.

Currency exposure The sensitivity of the asset return, measured in the investor's domestic currency, to a movement in the exchange rate.

Currency forward   A forward contract in which the underlying is a foreign currency.

Currency option   An option that allows the holder to buy (if a call) or sell (if a put) an underlying currency at a fixed exercise rate, expressed as an exchange rate.

Currency-option bond   A bond in which the coupons and/or the principal may be paid in more than one currency, at the option of the bondholder.

Currency overlay   In currency risk management, the delegation of the management of currency risk in an international portfolio to a currency specialist.

Currency swap   (1) A contract to exchange streams of fixed cash flows denominated in two different currencies. (2) A swap transaction in which the cash flows, which can be either fixed or variable, are denominated in different currencies. (3) A swap in which each party makes interest payments to the other in different currencies.

Current account   (1) The record of all transactions with foreign nations that involve the exchange of merchandise goods and services, current income derived from investments, and unilateral gifts. (2) A component of the balance of payments covering all current transactions that take place in the normal business of the residents of a country, such as exports and imports, services, income, and current transfers.

Current credit risk   The risk associated with the possibility that a payment currently due will not be made.

Current income   A return objective in which the investor seeks to generate income rather than capital gains; generally a goal of an investor who wants to supplement earnings with income to meet living expenses.

Current P/E   *See* Trailing P/E.

Current yield   A bond's yield as measured by its current income (coupon) as a percentage of its market price.

Customer list   A list of customers or subscribers.

Cyclical businesses   Businesses with high sensitivity to business- or industry-cycle influences.

Cyclical change   An economic trend arising from the ups and downs of the business cycle.

Cyclical company   A firm whose earnings rise and fall with general economic activity.

Cyclical stock   A stock with a high beta; its gains typically exceed those of a rising market and its losses typically exceed those of a falling market.

Cyclical unemployment   Unemployment due to recessionary business conditions and inadequate aggregate demand for labor.

Daily settlement   *See* Marking to market.

Data mining   The practice of determining a model by extensive searching through a dataset for statistically significant patterns.

Day trader   A trader holding a position open somewhat longer than a scalper but closing all positions at the end of the day.

Deadweight loss   A loss of gains from trade resulting from the imposition of a tax. It imposes a burden of taxation over and above the burden associated with the transfer of revenues to the government.

Dealer   An agent that buys and sells securities as a principal (for its own account) rather than as a broker for clients. A dealer may function, at different times, as a broker or as a dealer. Sometimes called a market maker.

Debentures   Bonds that promise payments of interest and principal but pledge no specific assets. Holders have first claim on the issuer's income and unpledged assets. Also known as unsecured bonds.

Decentralized risk management   A system that allows individual units within an organization to manage risk. Decentralization results in duplication of effort but has the advantage of having people closer to the risk be more directly involved in its management.

Deciles   Quantiles that divide a distribution into 10 equal parts.

Decision rule   With respect to hypothesis testing, the rule according to which the null hypothesis will be rejected or not rejected; involves the comparison of the test statistic to rejection point(s).

Declaration date   The date on which a firm's directors issue a statement declaring a dividend.

Declining-balance method   An accelerated method of depreciation in which depreciation is computed by applying a fixed rate to the carrying value (the declining balance) of a tangible long-lived asset.

Declining trend channel   The range defined by security prices as they move progressively lower.

Decreasing-cost industry   An industry for which costs of production decline as the industry expands. The market supply is therefore inversely related to price. Such industries are atypical.

Dedication   A portfolio management technique in which the portfolio's cash flows are used to retire a set of liabilities over time.

Dedication with reinvestment   A dedication strategy in which portfolio cash flows may precede their corresponding liabilities. Such cash flows can be reinvested to earn a return until the date the liability is due to be paid.

Deep in the money Options that are far in-the-money.

Deep out of the money Options that are far out-of-the-money.

Default risk The risk that an issuer will be unable to make interest and principal payments on time.

Default risk premium An extra return that compensates investors for the possibility that the borrower will fail to make a promised payment at the contracted time and in the contracted amount.

Defensive company Firms whose future earnings are likely to withstand an economic downturn.

Defensive competitive strategy Positioning the firm so that its capabilities provide the best means to deflect the effect of the competitive forces in the industry.

Defensive stock A stock whose return is not expected to decline as much as that of the overall market during a bear market.

Defined benefit pension plan A pension plan to which the company contributes a certain amount each year and that pays employees an income after they retire. The benefit size is based on factors such as workers' salary and time of employment.

Defined contribution pension plan A pension plan in which worker benefits are determined by the size of employees' contributions to the plan and the returns earned on the fund's investments.

Degree of confidence The probability that a confidence interval includes the unknown population parameter.

Degrees of freedom (df) The number of independent observations used.

Delivery A process used in a deliverable forward contract in which the long pays the agreed-upon price to the short, which in turn delivers the underlying asset to the long.

Delivery option The feature of a futures contract giving the short the right to make decisions about what, when, and where to deliver.

Delta (Δ) (1) Ratio of change in the option price to a small change in the price of the underlying asset. Also equal to the derivative of the option price with respect to the asset price. (2) The change in the price of the option with respect to a one dollar change in the price of the underlying asset; this is the option's hedge ratio, or the number of units of the underlying asset that can be hedged by a single option contract. (3) The relationship between the option price and the underlying price, which reflects the sensitivity of the price of the option to changes in the price of the underlying.

Delta hedge (1) A dynamic hedging strategy using options with continuous adjustment of the number of options used, as a function of the delta of the option. (2) An option strategy in which a position in an asset is converted to a risk-free position with a position in a specific number of options. The number of options per unit of the underlying changes through time, and the position must be revised to maintain the hedge.

Delta-normal method A measure of VAR equivalent to the analytical method but that refers to the use of delta to estimate the option's price sensitivity.

Demand deposits Non-interest-earning checking deposits that can be either withdrawn or made payable on demand to a third party. Like currency, these deposits are widely used as a means of payment.

Demand for money A curve that indicates the relationship between the interest rate and the quantity of money people want to hold. Because higher interest rates increase the opportunity cost of holding money, the quantity demanded of money will be inversely related to the interest rate.

Dependent With reference to events, the property that the probability of one event occurring depends on (is related to) the occurrence of another event.

Dependent variable The variable whose variation about its mean is to be explained by the regression; the left-hand-side variable in a regression equation.

Depletion The exhaustion of a natural resource through mining, cutting, pumping, or other extraction, and the way in which the cost is allocated.

Depository institutions Businesses that accept checking and savings deposits and use a portion of them to extend loans and make investments. Banks, savings and loan associations, and credit unions are examples.

Depreciable cost The cost of an asset less its residual value.

Depreciation (1) A reduction in the value of the domestic currency relative to foreign currencies. A depreciation reduces the purchasing power of the domestic currency for foreign goods. (2) The periodic allocation of the cost of a tangible long-lived asset (other than land and natural resources) over its estimated useful life.

Depression A prolonged and very severe recession.

Derivatives (1) Securities bearing a contractual relation to some underlying asset or rate. Options, futures, forward, and swap contracts, as well as many forms of bonds, are derivative securities.

(2) A financial instrument that offers a return based on the return of some other underlying asset.

Derivatives dealers The commercial and investment banks that make markets in derivatives. Also referred to as market makers.

Derivative security An instrument whose market value ultimately depends upon, or derives from, the value of a more fundamental investment vehicle called the underlying asset or security.

Derived demand The demand for a resource; it stems from the demand for the final good the resource helps to produce.

Descriptive statistics The study of how data can be summarized effectively.

Devaluation Deliberate downward adjustment of a currency against its fixed parity.

Differentiated products Products distinguished from similar products by such characteristics as quality, design, location, and method of promotion.

Diff swaps A swap in which the payments are based on the difference between interest rates in two countries but payments are made in only a single currency.

Diffuse prior The assumption of equal prior probabilities.

Diffusion index An indicator of the number of stocks rising during a specified period of time relative to the number of stocks declining and not changing price.

Diluted earnings per share Total earnings divided by the number of shares that would be outstanding if holders of securities such as executive stock options and convertible bonds exercised their options to obtain common stock.

Direct exchange rate The amount of local or domestic currency required to purchase one unit of foreign currency.

Discount (1) A bond selling at a price below par value due to capital market conditions. (2) To reduce the value of a future payment in allowance for how far away it is in time; to calculate the present value of some future amount. Also, the amount by which an instrument is priced below its face value.

Discounted cash flow (DCF) techniques Methods for ranking investment proposals that employ time value of money concepts.

Discounted payback period The length of time required for an investment's cash flows, discounted at the cost of capital, to cover its cost.

Discounting The procedure used to calculate the present value of future income, which is inversely related to both the interest rate and the amount of time that passes before the funds are received.

Discount interest A procedure for determining the interest on a loan or bond in which the interest is deducted from the face value in advance.

Discount rate The interest rate the Federal Reserve charges banking institutions for borrowing funds.

Discrete random variable A random variable that can take on at most a countable number of possible values.

Discrete time Time thought of as advancing in distinct finite increments.

Discretionary fiscal policy A change in laws or appropriation levels that alters government revenues and/or expenditures.

Discriminant analysis A multivariate classification technique used to discriminate between groups, such as companies that either will or will not become bankrupt during some time frame.

Dispersion The variability around the central tendency.

Disposable income The income available to individuals after personal taxes. It can be either spent on consumption or saved.

Dividend discount model (DDM) A technique for estimating the value of a stock issue as the present value of all future dividends.

Dividend irrelevance theory The theory that a firm's dividend policy has no effect on either its value or its cost of capital.

Dividend reinvestment plan (DRP) A plan that enables a stockholder to automatically reinvest dividends received back into the stock of the paying firm.

Dollar-weighted return The discount rate that sets the present value of a future set of cash flows equal to the investment's current value; also known as the internal rate of return.

Double-declining-balance method An accelerated method of depreciation in which a fixed rate equal to twice the straight-line percentage is applied to the carrying value (the declining balance) of a tangible long-lived asset.

Downtick A price decline in a transaction price compared to the previous transaction price.

Down transition probability The probability that an asset's value moves down in a model of asset price dynamics.

Dual-currency bond A bond with coupons fixed in one currency and principal repayment fixed in another currency.

Dummy variable A type of qualitative variable that takes on a value of 1 if a particular condition is true and 0 if that condition is false.

Dumping The sale of a good by a foreign supplier in another country at a price below that charged by the supplier in its home market.

DuPont system A method of examining ROE by breaking it down into three component parts: (1) profit margin, (2) total asset turnover, and (3) financial leverage.

Duration (1) A measure of an option-free bond's average maturity. Specifically, the weighted average maturity of all future cash flows paid by a security, in which the weights are the present value of these cash flows as a fraction of the bond's price. More importantly, a measure of a bond's price sensitivity to interest rate movements (*see* Modified duration). (2) A measure of the interest rate sensitivity of a bond's market price taking into consideration its coupon and term to maturity. (3) A measure of the size and timing of the cash flows paid by a bond. It quantifies these factors by summarizing them in the form of a single number. For bonds without option features attached, duration is interpreted as a weighted average maturity of the bond.

Duration strategy A portfolio management strategy employed to reduce the interest rate risk of a bond portfolio by matching the modified duration of the portfolio with its investment horizon. For example, if the investment horizon is 10 years, the portfolio manager would construct a portfolio that has a modified duration of 10 years. This strategy is referred to as immunization of the portfolio.

Dutch Book Theorem A result in probability theory stating that inconsistent probabilities create profit opportunities.

Dynamic hedging A strategy in which a position is hedged by making frequent adjustments to the quantity of the instrument used for hedging in relation to the instrument being hedged.

EAFE index A stock index for Europe, Australia, and the Far East published by Morgan Stanley Capital International.

Early stage With reference to venture capital financing, the stage associated with moving into operation and before commercial manufacturing and sales have occurred. Includes the start-up and first stages.

Earned Income Tax Credit A provision of the tax code that provides a credit or rebate to persons with low earnings (income from work activities). The credit is eventually phased out if the recipient's earnings increase.

Earnings at risk (EAR) A variation of VAR that reflects the risk of a company's earnings instead of its market value.

Earnings momentum A strategy in which portfolios are constructed of stocks of firms with rising earnings.

Earnings multiplier Also known as the price/earnings ratio, it is a measure of the relationship between a company's, or the aggregate stock market's, stock prices and earnings. *See also* Price-earnings (P/E) ratio. (I prefer the slash, but can live with either)

Earnings multiplier model A technique for estimating the value of a stock issue as a multiple of its earnings per share.

Earnings surprise A company announcement of earnings that differ from analysts' prevailing expectations. *See also* Unexpected earnings.

Earnings yield Earnings per share divided by price; the reciprocal of the P/E ratio.

Economic efficiency 1) A market meets the criterion of economic efficiency if all the gains from trade have been realized. With well-defined property rights and competition, market equilibrium is efficient. 2) Economizing behavior. When applied to a community, it implies that (1) an activity should be undertaken if the sum of the benefits to the individuals exceeds the sum of their costs and (2) no activity should be undertaken if the costs borne by the individuals exceed the benefits.

Economic exposure The risk associated with changes in the relative attractiveness of products and services offered for sale, arising out of the competitive effects of changes in exchange rates.

Economic profit The difference between the firm's total revenues and its total costs, including both the explicit and implicit cost components.

Economic risk As used in currency risk management, the risk that arises when the foreign currency value of a foreign investment reacts systematically to an exchange rate movement.

Economic regulation Regulation of product price or industrial structure, usually imposed on a specific industry. By and large, the production processes used by the regulated firms are unaffected by this type of regulation.

Economic theory A set of definitions, postulates, and principles assembled in a manner that makes clear the "cause-and-effect" relationships of economic data.

Economic value added (EVA) Internal management performance measure that compares net operating profit to total cost of capital. Indicates how profitable company projects are as a sign of management performance.

Economies of scale Reductions in the firm's per-unit costs that are associated with the use of large plants to produce a large volume of output.

Economizing behavior Choosing with the objective of gaining a specific benefit at the least possible cost. A corollary of economizing behavior implies that, when choosing among items of equal cost, individuals will choose the option that yields the greatest benefit.

Effective annual rate The amount by which a unit of currency will grow in a year with interest on interest included.

Effective annual yield (EAY) An annualized return that accounts for the effect of interest on interest; EAY is computed by compounding 1 plus the holding period yield forward to one year, then subtracting 1.

Effective duration Direct measure of the interest rate sensitivity of a bond (or any financial instrument) based upon price changes derived from a pricing model.

Efficiency A desirable property of estimators; an efficient estimator is the unbiased estimator with the smallest variance among unbiased estimators of the same parameter.

Efficient capital market A market in which security prices rapidly reflect all information about securities.

Efficient frontier (1) The set of all efficient portfolios for various levels of risk. (2) The set of portfolios that has the maximum rate of return for every given level of risk, or the minimum risk for every potential rate of return. (3) The portion of the minimum-variance frontier beginning with the global minimum-variance portfolio and continuing above it; the graph of the set of portfolios offering the maximum expected return for their level of variance of return.

Efficient portfolio (1) A portfolio that provides the best expected return for a given level of risk. (2) A portfolio offering the highest expected return for a given level of risk as measured by variance or standard deviation of return.

Electronic communications networks Order-driven trading systems in which the book of limit orders plays a central role.

Electronic crossing networks Order-driven trading systems in which market orders are anonymously matched at prespecified times at prices determined in the primary market for the system.

Empirical duration Measures directly the interest rate sensitivity of an asset by examining the percentage price change for an asset in response to a change in yield during a specified period of time.

Empirical probability The probability of an event estimated as a relative frequency of occurrence.

Employment discrimination Unequal treatment of persons on the basis of their race, sex, or religion, restricting their employment and earnings opportunities compared to others of similar productivity. Employment discrimination may stem from the prejudices of employers, customers, fellow employees, or all three.

Ending-wealth value The total amount of money derived from investment in a bond until maturity, including principal, coupon payments, and income from reinvestment of coupon payments.

Endogenous growth theory A theory of economic growth that does not assume that the marginal productivity of capital declines as capital is added.

Enhanced derivatives products companies (EDPC) (or special purpose vehicles [SPVs]) A type of subsidiary engaged in derivatives transactions that is separated from the parent company in order to have a higher credit rating than the parent company.

Entrepreneur A profit-seeking decision maker who decides which projects to undertake and how they should be undertaken. A successful entrepreneur's actions will increase the value of resources and expand the size of the economic pie.

Enterprise risk management A form of centralized risk management that typically encompasses the management of a broad variety of risks, including insurance risk.

Equation of exchange $MV = PY$, where M is the money supply, V is the velocity of money, P is the price level, and Y is the output of goods and services produced.

Equilibrium A state of balance between conflicting forces, such as supply and demand, permitting the simultaneous fulfillment of plans by buyers and sellers.

Equipment trust certificates Mortgage bonds that are secured by specific pieces of transportation equipment like boxcars and planes.

Equitizing cash A strategy used to replicate an index. It is also used to take a given amount of cash and turn it into an equity position while maintaining the liquidity provided by the cash.

Equity collar An option-based hedging strategy that protects a stock position from price declines by purchasing a put option that is paid for by the sale of a call option.

Equity forward A contract calling for the purchase of an individual stock, a stock portfolio, or a stock index at a later date at an agreed-upon price.

Equity mutual fund A corporation that pools the funds of investors, including small investors, and uses them to purchase a bundle of stocks.

Equity options Options on individual stocks; also known as stock options.

Equity swap   (1) A swap transaction in which one cash flow is tied to the return to an equity portfolio position, often an index such as the Standard and Poor's 500, while the other is based on a floating-rate index. (2) A swap in which the rate is the return on a stock or stock index.

Equivalent annual annuity (EAA) method   A method which calculates the annual payments a project would provide if it were an annuity. When comparing projects of unequal lives, the one with the higher equivalent annual annuity should be chosen.

Error autocorrelation   The autocorrelation of the error term.

Error term   The portion of the dependent variable that is not explained by the independent variable(s) in the regression.

Escalator clause   A contractual agreement that periodically and automatically adjusts money wage rates upward as the price level rises. They are sometimes referred to as cost-of-living adjustments or COLAs.

Estimate   The particular value calculated from sample observations using an estimator.

Estimated (or fitted) parameters   With reference to regression analysis, the estimated values of the population intercept and population slope coefficient(s) in a regression.

Estimated rate of return   The rate of return an investor anticipates earning from a specific investment over a particular future holding period.

Estimated useful life   The total number of service units expected from a long-term asset.

Estimation   With reference to statistical inference, the subdivision dealing with estimating the value of a population parameter.

Estimator   An estimation formula; the formula used to compute the sample mean and other sample statistics are examples of estimators.

Euribor   Interbank offer rate for short-term deposits in euros. Euribor is determined by an association of European banks.

Euro   The common currency of many European countries.

Eurobond   (1) A bond underwritten by a multinational syndicate of banks and placed mainly in countries other than the country of the issuer; sometimes called an international bond. (2) Bonds denominated in a currency not native to the country in which they are issued.

Eurocurrency market   Interbank market for short-term borrowing and lending in a currency outside of its home country. For example, borrowing and lending of U.S. dollars outside the United States. Thus, it is an offshore market escaping national regulations. This is the largest money market for several major currencies.

Eurodollar   A dollar deposited outside the United States.

Eurodollar market   The U.S. dollar segment of the Eurocurrency market.

European Monetary System   A formal arrangement linking some, but not all, of the currencies of the EU.

European option   (1) An option contract that can only be exercised on its expiration date. (2) An option that can be exercised only at expiration. Also referred to as European-style exercise.

European-style option or European option   An option exercisable only at maturity.

European terms   With reference to U.S. dollar exchange rate quotations, the price of a U.S. dollar in terms of another currency.

European Union (EU)   A formal association of European countries founded by the Treaty of Rome in 1957. Formerly known as the EEC.

European-type option   An option that can be exercised only at expiration.

Event   Any outcome or specified set of outcomes of a random variable.

Event study   Research that examines the reaction of a security's price to a specific company, world event, or news announcement.

Excess burden of taxation   Another term for deadweight loss. It reflects losses that occur when beneficial activities are forgone because they are taxed.

Excess kurtosis   Degree of peakedness (fatness of tails) in excess of the peakedness of the normal distribution.

Exchange clearinghouse   The functional unit attached to a futures exchange that guarantees contract performance, oversees delivery, serves as a bookkeeper, and calculates settlement transactions.

Exchange for physicals (EEP)   A permissible delivery procedure used by futures market participants, in which the long and short arrange a delivery procedure other than the normal procedures stipulated by the futures exchange.

Exchange rate   The price of one unit of foreign currency in terms of the domestic currency. For example, if it takes $1.50 to purchase an English pound, the dollar-pound exchange rate is 1.50.

Exchange rate risk   Uncertainty due to the denomination of an investment in a currency other than that of the investor's own country.

Exchange traded funds (ETFs)   A type of mutual fund traded like other shares on a stock market, having special characteristics particularly related to redemption, and generally designed to closely track the performance of a specified stock market index.

Ex-dividend A synonym for "without dividend." The buyer of a security ex-dividend does not receive the next dividend.

Ex-dividend date The date on which the right to the current dividend no longer accompanies a stock; it is usually four working days prior to the holder-of-record date.

Executive stock option An option to buy stock at a stated price within a specified time period that is granted to an executive as part of his or her compensation package.

Exercise (or exercising the option) The process of using an option to buy or sell the underlying.

Exercise price (or strike price or striking price, or strike) (1) The transaction price specified in an option contract. *See* also Strike price. (2) The fixed price at which an option holder can buy or sell the underlying.

Exercise rate or strike rate The fixed rate at which the holder of an interest rate option can buy or sell the underlying.

Exhaustive Covering or containing all possible outcomes.

Exotic option Designed to have payoffs that differ from those of standard contract options. Three such nonstandard contracts are Asian, lookback, and digital options.

Expansionary fiscal policy An increase in government expenditures and/or a reduction in tax rates such that the expected size of the budget deficit expands.

Expansionary monetary policy A shift in monetary policy designed to stimulate aggregate demand. Bond purchases, creation of additional bank reserves, and an increase in the growth rate of the money supply are generally indicative of a shift to a more expansionary monetary policy.

Expansion project A project that is intended to increase sales.

Expected rate of return The return that analysts' calculations suggest a security should provide, based on the market's rate of return during the period and the security's relationship to the market.

Expected return The rate of return that an investor expects to get on an investment.

Expected value The probability-weighted average of the possible outcomes of a random variable.

Expenditure A payment or obligation to make future payment for an asset or a service.

Expenditure multiplier The ratio of the change in equilibrium output to the independent change in investment, consumption, or government spending that brings about the change.

Numerically, the multiplier is equal to 1 *divided by* (1 − MPCC) when the price level is constant.

Expiration date The date on which a derivative contract expires.

Expiry The expiration date of a derivative security.

Explicit costs Payments by a firm to purchase the services of productive resources.

Exports Goods and services produced domestically but sold to foreigners.

External debt The portion of the national debt owed to foreign investors.

External efficiency When prices reflect all available information about an asset, which implies that prices adjust quickly to new information regarding supply or demand. Also referred to as informational efficiency.

Externalities (1) The side effects, or spillover effects, of an action that influence the well-being of nonconsenting parties. The nonconsenting parties may be either helped (by external benefits) or harmed (by external costs). (2) The effects of a project on cash flows in other parts of the firm.

Extraordinary repairs Repairs that affect the estimated residual value or estimated useful life of an asset thereby increasing its carrying value.

Face value (1) The amount paid on a bond at redemption and traditionally printed on the bond certificate. This face value excludes the final coupon payment. Sometimes referred to as par value. (2) The promised payment at maturity separate from any coupon payment.

Factor A common or underlying element with which several variables are correlated.

Factor risk premium (or factor price) The expected return in excess of the risk-free rate for a portfolio with a sensitivity of 1 to one factor and a sensitivity of 0 to all other factors.

Factor sensitivity (also factor betas or factor loadings) A measure of the response of return to each unit of increase in a factor, holding all other factors constant.

Fair value (1) The price at which an asset or liability would change hands between a willing buyer and a willing seller when the former is not under any compulsion to buy and the latter is not under any compulsion to sell. (2) The theoretical value of a security based on current market conditions. The fair value is the value such that no arbitrage opportunities exist.

Fallacy of composition Erroneous view that what is true for the individual (or the part) will also be true for the group (or the whole).

Federal funds market A loanable funds market in which banks seeking additional reserves borrow short-term (generally for seven days or less) funds from banks with excess reserves. The interest rate in this market is called the federal funds rate.

Federal Reserve System   The central bank of the United States; it carries out banking regulatory policies and is responsible for the conduct of monetary policy.

Fiat money   Money that has neither intrinsic value nor the backing of a commodity with intrinsic value; paper currency is an example.

Fiduciary   A person who supervises or oversees the investment portfolio of a third party, such as in a trust account, and makes investment decisions in accordance with the owner's wishes.

Fiduciary call   A combination of a European call and a risk-free bond that matures on the option expiration day and has a face value equal to the exercise price of the call.

Filter rule   A trading rule that recommends security transactions when price changes exceed a previously determined percentage.

Final market goods and services   Goods and services purchased by their ultimate user.

Financial account   A component of the balance of payments covering investments by residents abroad and investments by nonresidents in the home country. Examples include direct investment made by companies, portfolio investments in equity and bonds, and other investments and liabilities.

Financial futures   Futures contracts in which the underlying is a stock, bond, or currency.

Financial leverage   The extent to which fixed-income securities (debt and preferred stock) are used in a firm's capital structure.

Financial risk   (1) The variability of future income arising from the firm's fixed financing costs, for example, interest payments. The effect of fixed financial costs is to magnify the effect of changes in operating profit on net income or earnings per share. (2) Risk relating to asset prices and other financial variables.

First-differencing   A transformation that subtracts the value of the time series in period $t - 1$ from its value in period t.

First-order serial correlation   Correlation between adjacent observations in a time series.

Fiscal policy   The use of government taxation and expenditure policies for the purpose of achieving macroeconomic goals.

Fixed exchange rate   An exchange rate that is set at a determined amount by government policy.

Fixed exchange rate regime   A system in which the exchange rate between two currencies remains fixed at a preset level, known as official parity.

Fixed-income forward   A forward contract in which the underlying is a bond.

Fixed-income investments   Loans with contractually mandated payment schedules from investors to firms or governments.

Fixing   A method for determining the market price of a security by finding the price that balances buyers and sellers. A fixing takes place periodically each day at defined times. Sometimes called a call auction.

Flat trend channel   The range defined by security prices as they maintain a relatively steady level.

Flexible exchange rates   Exchange rates that are determined by the market forces of supply and demand. They are sometimes called floating exchange rates.

Flexible exchange rate system   A system in which exchange rates are determined by supply and demand.

Flexible portfolio fund   Mutual fund that allows managers to shift assets between stocks, bonds, and cash according to changing market conditions; also known as asset allocation fund.

Floating-rate loan   A loan in which the interest rate is reset at least once after the starting date.

Floating-rate note (FRN)   (1) Bond issued with variable quarterly or semiannual interest rate payments, generally linked to LIBOR. (2) Short- to intermediate-term bonds with regularly scheduled coupon payments linked to a variable interest rate, most often LIBOR.

Floor   (1) A contract on an interest rate, whereby the writer of the floor periodically pays the difference between a specified floor rate and the market interest rate if, and only if, this difference is positive. This is equivalent to a stream of put options on the interest rate. (2) A combination of interest rate put options designed to hedge a lender against lower rates on a floating-rate loan.

Floor agreement   A contract that on each settlement date pays the holder the greater of the difference between the floor rate and the reference rate or zero; it is equivalent to a series of put options on the reference rate.

Floor brokers   Independent members of an exchange who act as brokers for other members.

Floored swap   A swap in which the floating payments have a lower limit.

Floorlet   Each component put option in a floor.

Floor traders or locals   Market makers that buy and sell by quoting a bid and an ask price. They are the primary providers of liquidity to the market.

Flotation Cost, F   The percentage cost of issuing new common stock.

Foreign bond A bond issued by a foreign company on the local market and in the local currency (e.g., Yankee bonds in the United States, Bulldog bonds in the United Kingdom, or Samurai bonds in Japan).

Foreign currency risk premium The expected movement in the (direct) exchange rate minus the interest rate differential (domestic risk-free rate minus foreign risk-free rate).

Foreign exchange The purchase (sale) of a currency against the sale (purchase) of another.

Foreign exchange controls Various forms of government-imposed controls on the purchase (sale) of foreign currencies by residents or on the purchase (sale) of local currency by nonresidents.

Foreign exchange expectation A relation that states that the forward exchange rate, quoted at time 0 for delivery at time 1, is equal to the expected value of the spot exchange rate at time 1. When stated relative to the current spot exchange rate, the relation states that the forward discount (premium) is equal to the expected exchange rate movement.

Foreign exchange market The market in which the currencies of different countries are bought and sold.

Foreign exchange parity A foreign exchange rate of two currencies that is officially fixed by international agreement.

Forex Foreign exchange.

Formative stage With respect to venture capital financing, the seed and early stages.

Forward contract (1) A customized contract to buy (sell) an asset at a specified date and a specified price (forward price). No payment takes place until maturity. (2) An agreement between two counterparties that requires the exchange of a commodity or security at a fixed time in the future at a predetermined price. (3) An agreement between two parties in which one party, the buyer, agrees to buy from the other party, the seller, an underlying asset at a later date for a price established at the start of the contract.

Forward discount or premium Refers to the percentage difference between the forward exchange rate and the spot exchange rate (premium if positive, discount if negative).

Forward P/E *See* Leading P/E.

Forward premium A situation where, from the perspective of the domestic country, the spot exchange rate is larger than the forward exchange rate with a foreign country.

Forward price or forward rate The fixed price or rate at which the transaction scheduled to occur at the expiration of a forward contract will take place. This price is agreed on at the initiation date of the contract.

Forward rate A short-term yield for a future holding period implied by the spot rates of two securities with different maturities.

Forward rate agreement (FRA) (1) An agreement between two parties that will apply to a future notional loan or deposit. (2) A transaction in which two counterparties agree to a single exchange of cash flows based on a fixed and floating rate, respectively. (3) A forward contract calling for one party to make a fixed interest payment and the other to make an interest payment at a rate to be determined at the contract expiration.

Forward swap A forward contract to enter into a swap.

Fourth market Direct trading of securities between owners, usually institutions, without any broker intermediation.

Franchise The right or license to an exclusive territory or market.

Franchise factor A firm's unique competitive advantage that makes it possible for a firm to earn excess returns (rates of return above a firm's cost of capital) on its capital projects. In turn, these excess returns and the franchise factor cause the firm's stock price to have a P/E ratio above its base P/E ratio that is equal to $1/k$.

Franchise value In P/E ratio analysis, the present value of growth opportunities divided by next year's expected earnings.

Free cash flow This cash flow measure equals cash flow from operations minus capital expenditures and debt payments.

Free rider One who receives the benefit of a good without contributing to its costs. Public goods and commodities that generate external benefits offer people the opportunity to become free riders.

Frequency distribution A tabular display of data summarized into a relatively small number of intervals.

Frequency polygon A graph of a frequency distribution obtained by drawing straight lines joining successive points representing the class frequencies.

Frictional unemployment Unemployment due to constant changes in the economy that prevent qualified unemployed workers from being immediately matched up with existing job openings. It results from the scarcity of information and the search activities of both employers and employees for information that will help them make better employment choices.

Fringe benefits Benefits other than normal money wages that are supplied to employees in exchange for their labor services. Higher fringe benefits come at the expense of lower money wages.

Full-costing A method of accounting for the costs of exploring and developing oil and gas resources in which all costs are recorded as assets and depleted over the estimated life of the producing resources.

Full employment The level of employment that results from the efficient use of the labor force after allowance is made for the normal (natural) rate of unemployment due to information cost, dynamic changes, and the structural conditions of the economy. For the United States, full employment is thought to exist when approximately 95 percent of the labor force is employed.

Full price (or dirty price) (1) The total price of a bond, including accrued interest. (2) The price of a security with accrued interest.

Full replication A technique for constructing a passive index portfolio in which all securities in an index are purchased in proportion to their weights in the index.

Fully taxable equivalent yield (FTEY) A yield on a tax-exempt bond that adjusts for its tax benefits to allow comparisons with taxable bonds.

Fundamental beta A beta that is based at least in part on fundamental data for a company.

Fundamental factor models A multifactor model in which the factors are attributes of stocks or companies that are important in explaining cross-sectional differences in stock prices.

Futures commission merchants (FCMs) Individuals or companies that execute futures transactions for other parties off the exchange.

Futures contract (1) A standardized contract to buy (sell) an asset at a specified date and a specified price (futures price). The contract is traded on an organized exchange, and the potential gain/loss is realized each day (marking to market). (2) An agreement that provides for the future exchange of a particular asset at a specified delivery date in exchange for a specified payment at the time of delivery. (3) A variation of a forward contract that has essentially the same basic definition but with some additional features, such as a clearinghouse guarantee against credit losses, a daily settlement of gains and losses, and an organized electronic or floor trading facility.

Futures exchange A legal corporate entity whose shareholders are its members. The members of the exchange have the privilege of executing transactions directly on the exchange.

Future value (FV) The amount to which a payment or series of payments will grow by a stated future date.

Gamma A numerical measure of how sensitive an option's delta is to a change in the underlying.

Game theory Analyzes the strategic choices made by competitors in a conflict situation, such as decisions made by members of an oligopoly.

GDP deflator A price index that reveals the cost during the current period of purchasing the items included in GDP relative to the cost during a base year (currently, 1996). Because the base year is assigned a value of 100, as the GDP deflator takes on values greater than 100, it indicates that prices are higher than during the base year.

General Agreement on Tariffs and Trade (GATT) An organization formed following the Second World War to set the rules for the conduct of international trade and reduce barriers to trade among nations.

Generalized least squares A regression estimation technique that addresses heteroskedasticity of the error term.

Generally accepted accounting principles (GAAP) Accounting principles formulated by the Financial Accounting Standards Board and used to construct financial statements.

General obligation bond (GO) A municipal issue serviced from and guaranteed by the issuer's full taxing authority.

Generic *See* Plain-vanilla.

Geometric mean (GM) (1) The nth root of the product of the annual holding period returns for n years minus 1. (2) A measure of central tendency computed by taking the nth root of the product of n non-negative values.

Gifting phase Phase in the investment life cycle during which individuals use excess assets to financially assist relatives or friends, establish charitable trusts, or construct trusts to minimize estate taxes.

Gilt (or Gilt-edged) A U.K. government bond.

Global Investment Performance Standards™ (GIPS®) A global industry standard for the ethical presentation of investment performance results promulgated by the Association for Investment Management and Research.

Going out of business The sale of a firm's assets and its permanent exit from the market. By going out of business, a firm is able to avoid fixed costs, which would continue during a shutdown.

Gold standard An international monetary system in which the parity of a currency is fixed in terms of its gold content.

Goods and services market A highly aggregated market encompassing the flow of all final-user goods and services. The market counts all items that enter into GDP. Thus, real output in this market is equal to real GDP.

Goodwill The excess of the cost of a group of assets (usually a business) over the fair market value of the assets if purchased individually.

Gray market A forward market for newly issued bonds before the final terms on the bond are set.

Gross domestic product (GDP) (1) The market value of all final goods and services produced within a country during a specific period. (2) Total value of a country's output produced by residents within the country's physical borders.

Gross national product (GNP) (1) The total market value of all final goods and services produced by the citizens of a country. It is equal to GDP minus the net income of foreigners. (2) Total value of a country's output produced by residents both within the country's physical borders and abroad.

Group depreciation The grouping of similar items to calculate depreciation.

Group of Seven (G-7) The seven countries (Canada, France, Germany, Italy, Japan, the United Kingdom, and the United States) that meet periodically to enhance cooperative action on international economic matters. [The Group of Eight (G-8) includes Russia.]

Growth company A company that consistently has the opportunities and ability to invest in projects that provide rates of return that exceed the firm's cost of capital. Because of these investment opportunities, it retains a high proportion of earnings, and its earnings grow faster than those of average firms.

Growth stock A stock issue that generates a higher rate of return than other stocks in the market with similar risk characteristics; usually identified by high P/E or high price-to-book ratios.

Harmonic mean A type of weighted mean computed by averaging the reciprocals of the observations, then taking the reciprocal of that average.

Health and safety regulation Legislation designed to improve the health, safety, and environmental conditions available to workers and/or consumers. The legislation usually mandates production procedures, minimum standards, and/or product characteristics to be met by producers and employers.

Hedge fund A type of investment vehicle often set up as a limited partnership, limited liability corporation, or offshore corporation to be exempt from most governmental regulation.

Hedge ratio (1) The percentage of the position in an asset that is hedged with derivatives. (2) The number of derivative contracts that must be transacted to offset the price volatility of an underlying commodity or security position. (3) The relationship of the quantity of an asset being hedged to the quantity of the derivative used for hedging.

Hedging (1) The process of reducing the uncertainty of the future value of a portfolio by taking positions in various derivatives (e.g., forward and futures contracts). (2) A general strategy usually thought of as reducing, if not eliminating, risk.

Herfindahl index A measure of industry concentration equal to the sum of the squared market shares of the firms in the industry.

Heteroskedasticity The property of having a nonconstant variance; refers to an error term with the property that its variance differs across observations.

Heteroskedasticity-consistent standard errors Standard errors of the estimated parameters of a regression that correct for the presence of heteroskedasticity in the regression's error term.

High-yield bond A bond rated below investment grade. Also referred to as speculative-grade bonds or junk bonds.

Histogram A bar chart of data that have been grouped into a frequency distribution.

Historical method A method of estimating VAR that uses data from the returns of the portfolio over a recent past period and compiles this data in the form of a histogram.

Historical simulation method (or back simulation) (1) Another term for the historical method of estimating VAR. This term is somewhat misleading in that the method involves not a simulation of the past but rather what actually happened in the past, sometimes adjusted to reflect the fact that a different portfolio may have existed in the past than is planned for the future. (2) Simulation involving sampling from a historical data series.

Holder-of-record date If the company lists the stockholder as an owner on this date, then the stockholder receives the dividend.

Holding period return (HPR) (1) The total return from an investment, including all sources of income, for a given period of time. A value of 1.0 indicates no gain or loss. (2) The return that an investor earns during a specified holding period; a synonym for total return.

Holding period yield (HPY) (1) The total return from an investment for a given period of time stated as a percentage. (2) The return that an investor earns during a specified holding period; holding period return with reference to a fixed-income instrument.

Homogenization Creating a contract with standard and generally accepted terms, which makes it more acceptable to a broader group of participants.

Homoskedasticity The property of having a constant variance; refers to an error term that is constant across observations.

Hostile takeover The acquisition of a company over the opposition of its management.

Human capital The value of skills and knowledge possessed by the workforce.

Human resources The abilities, skills, and health of human beings that can contribute to the production of both current and future output. Investment in training and education can increase the supply of human resources.

Hurdle rate The discount rate (cost of capital) which the IRR must exceed if a project is to be accepted.

Hypothesis With reference to statistical inference, a statement about one or more populations.

Hypothesis testing With reference to statistical inference, the subdivision dealing with the testing of hypotheses about one or more populations.

Immunization A bond portfolio management technique of matching modified duration to the investment horizon of the portfolio to eliminate interest rate risk.

Impact lag The time period after a policy change is implemented but before the change begins to exert its primary effects.

Implementation shortfall With respect to execution costs, the difference between the value of the executed portfolio or share position and the value of the same portfolio at the time the trading decision was made.

Implicit costs The opportunity costs associated with a firm's use of resources that it owns. These costs do not involve a direct money payment. Examples include wage income and interest forgone by the owner of a firm who also provides labor services and equity capital to the firm.

Implicit marginal tax rate The amount of additional (marginal) earnings that must be paid explicitly in taxes or implicitly in the form of a reduction in income supplements. Since the marginal tax rate establishes the fraction of an additional dollar earned that an individual is permitted to keep, it is an important determinant of the incentive to work.

Implied forward exchange rate *See* Break-even exchange rate.

Implied repo rate The rate of return from a cash-and-carry transaction implied by the futures price relative to the spot price.

Implied volatility (1) The volatility of an asset that is implicit in the current market price of an option (using a standard Black-Scholes-Merton formula). (2) The standard deviation of changes in the price of the underlying asset that can be inferred from an option's market price in relation to a specific valuation model. (3) The volatility that option traders use to price an option, implied by the price of the option and a particular option-pricing model.

Implied yield A measure of the yield on the underlying bond of a futures contract implied by pricing it as though the underlying will be delivered at the futures expiration.

Import quota A specific limit or maximum quantity (or value) of a good permitted to be imported into a country during a given period.

Imports Goods and services produced by foreigners but purchased by domestic consumers, businesses, and governments.

Income bonds Debentures that stipulate interest payments only if the issuer earns the income to make the payments by specified dates.

Income effect (1) That part of an increase (decrease) in amount consumed that is the result of the consumer's real income (the consumption possibilities available to the consumer) being expanded (contracted) by a reduction (rise) in the price of a good. (2) The known component of the total return for a bond during a period of time if the shape and position of the yield curve did not change.

Income elasticity The percentage change in the quantity of a product demanded divided by the percentage change in consumer income causing the change in quantity demanded. It measures the responsiveness of the demand for a good to a change in income.

Income mobility Movement of individuals and families either up or down income-distribution rankings when comparisons are made at two different points in time. When substantial income mobility is present, one's current position will not be a very good indicator of what one's position will be a few years in the future.

Income statement A financial statement that shows the flow of the firm's sales, expenses, and earnings over a period of time.

Increasing-cost industry An industry for which costs of production rise as output is expanded. Thus, even in the long run, higher market prices will be required to induce the firms to expand the total output in such industries. The long-run market supply curve in such industries will slope upward to the right.

Incremental cash flows The changes or increments to cash flows resulting from a decision or action.

Indenture The legal agreement that lists the obligations of the issuer of a bond to the bondholder, including payment schedules, call provisions, and sinking funds.

Independent   With reference to events, the property that the occurrence of one event does not affect the probability of another event occurring.

Independent and identically distributed (IID)   With respect to random variables, the property of random variables that are independent of each other but follow the identical probability distribution.

Independent projects   Projects whose cash flows are not affected by the acceptance or nonacceptance of other projects.

Independent variable   A variable used to explain the dependent variable in a regression; a right-hand-side variable in a regression equation.

Index amortizing swap   An interest rate swap in which the notional principal is indexed to the level of interest rates and declines with the level of interest rates according to a predefined scheduled. This type of swap is frequently used to hedge securities that are prepaid as interest rates decline, such as mortgage-backed securities.

Indexing   (1) A passive bond portfolio management strategy that seeks to match the composition, and therefore the performance, of a selected market index. (2) An investment strategy in which an investor constructs a portfolio to mirror the performance of a specified index.

Index-linked bond   A bond whose interest rate payments and/or redemption value are contractually linked to some specified index (e.g., a commodity price).

Index of leading indicators   An index of economic variables that historically has tended to turn down prior to the beginning of a recession and turn up prior to the beginning of a business expansion.

Index option   An option in which the underlying is a stock index.

Indifference curve   A curve, convex from below, that separates the consumption bundles that are more preferred by an individual from those that are less preferred. The points on the curve represent combinations of goods that are equally preferred by the individual.

Indirect business taxes   Taxes that increase the business firm's costs of production and, therefore, the prices charged to consumers. Examples would be sales, excise, and property taxes.

Indirect exchange rate   The amount of foreign currency required to purchase one unit of domestic currency.

Industry life cycle analysis   An analysis that focuses on the industry's stage of development.

Inferior good   A good that has a negative income elasticity, so that, as consumer income rises, the demand for that good falls.

Inflation   A continuing rise in the general level of prices of goods and services. The purchasing power of the monetary unit, such as the dollar, declines when inflation is present.

Inflation   The amount by which prices increase over time.

Inflationary premium   A component of the money interest rate that reflects compensation to the lender for the expected decrease, due to inflation, in the purchasing power of the principal and interest during the course of the loan. It is determined by the expected rate of future inflation.

Information   An attribute of a good market that includes providing buyers and sellers with timely, accurate information on the volume and prices of past transactions and on all currently outstanding bids and offers.

Information content (signaling) hypothesis   The theory that investors regard dividend changes as signals of management's earnings forecast.

Information ratio (IR)   (1) The ratio of excess return over the benchmark to tracking error relative to the benchmark. (2) Statistic used to measure a portfolio's average return in excess of a comparison, benchmark portfolio divided by the standard deviation of this excess return. (3) Mean active return divided by active risk.

Informationally efficient market   A more technical term for an efficient capital market that emphasizes the role of information in setting the market price.

Initial margin   The amount that an investor must deposit to open a position in futures and some other derivatives; also used to refer to the initial equity required when a stock is purchased using borrowed money.

Initial margin requirement   The margin requirement on the first day of a transaction as well as on any day in which additional margin funds must be deposited.

Initial public offering (IPO)   A new issue by a firm that has no existing public market.

Innovation   The successful introduction and adoption of a new product or process; the economic application of inventions and marketing techniques.

In-sample forecast errors   The residuals from a fitted time-series model within the sample period used to fit the model.

Instability in the minimum-variance frontier   The characteristic of minimum-variance frontiers that they are sensitive to small changes in inputs.

Insuring   The process of setting a minimum level for the future value of a portfolio by taking positions in various derivatives (e.g., options).

Intangible assets   Long-term assets with no physical substance whose value is based on rights or advantages accruing to the owner.

Intermediate goods   Goods purchased for resale or for use in producing another good or service.

Interest-on-interest   Bond income from reinvestment of coupon payments.

Interest rate   A rate of return that reflects the relationship between differently dated cash flows; a discount rate.

Interest rate anticipation   An active bond portfolio management strategy designed to preserve capital or take advantage of capital gains opportunities by predicting interest rates and their effects on bond prices.

Interest rate call   An option in which the holder has the right to make a known interest payment and receive an unknown interest payment.

Interest rate cap or cap   A series of call options on an interest rate, with each option expiring at the date on which the floating loan rate will be reset, and with each option having the same exercise rate. A cap in general can have an underlying other than an interest rate.

Interest rate collar   (1) The combination of a long position in a cap agreement and a short position in a floor agreement, or vice versa; it is equivalent to a series of range forward positions. (2) A combination of a long cap and a short floor, or a short cap and a long floor. A collar in general can have an underlying other than an interest rate.

Interest rate effect   The return on a bond portfolio caused by changes in the term structure of interest rates during a period that affect both bond prices and reinvestment rates.

Interest rate floor or floor   A series of put options on an interest rate, with each option expiring at the date on which the floating loan rate will be reset, and with each option having the same exercise rate. A floor in general can have an underlying other than the interest rate.

Interest rate forward   *See* Forward rate agreement.

Interest rate option   An option in which the underlying is an interest rate.

Interest rate parity   (1) An arbitrage process that ensures that the forward discount or premium equals the interest rate differential between two currencies. (2) The relationship that must exist in an efficient market between the spot and forward foreign exchange rates between two countries and the interest rates in those countries. (3) A formula that expresses the equivalence or parity of spot and forward rates, after adjusting for differences in the interest rates.

Interest rate put   An option in which the holder has the right to make an unknown interest payment and receive a known interest payment.

Interest rate risk   The uncertainty of returns on an investment due to possible changes in interest rates over time.

Interest rate swap   (1) A contract to exchange streams of fixed-interest-rate for floating-interest-rate cash flows denominated in the same currency. (2) An agreement calling for the periodic exchange of cash flows, one based on an interest rate that remains fixed for the life of the contract and the other that is linked to a variable-rate index. (3) A swap in which the underlying is an interest rate. Can be viewed as a currency swap in which both currencies are the same and can be created as a combination of currency swaps.

Intergenerational data mining   A form of data mining that applies information developed by previous researchers using a dataset to guide current research using the same or a related dataset.

Internal liquidity (solvency) ratios   Financial ratios that measure the ability of the firm to meet future short-term financial obligations.

Internal Rate of Return (IRR)   (1) The discount rate that equates the present value of a future stream of cash flows to the initial investment. (2) The discount rate at which cash outflows of an investment equal cash inflows. (3) The discount rate that makes net present value equal 0; the discount rate that makes the present value of an investment's costs (outflows) equal to the present value of the investment's benefits (inflows).

International CAPM   An equilibrium theory that relates the expected return of an asset to its world market and foreign exchange risks.

International domestic bonds   Bonds issued by a foreign firm, denominated in the firm's native currency, and sold within its own country.

International Fisher relation   The assertion that the interest rate differential between two countries should equal the expected inflation rate differential over the term of the interest rates.

International Monetary Fund (IMF)   An organization set up in 1944 to promote exchange rate stability and to assist member countries facing economic difficulties.

International Securities Market Association (ISMA)   An association formed in 1969 to establish uniform trading procedures in the international bond markets. Formerly named AIBD.

International Swaps and Derivatives Association (ISDA)   An association of swap dealers formed in 1985 to promote uniform practices in the writing, trading, and settlement procedures of swaps and other derivatives.

Interquartile range The difference between the third and first quartiles of a dataset.

Interval With reference to grouped data, a set of values within which an observation falls.

Interval scale A measurement scale that not only ranks data but also gives assurance that the differences between scale values are equal.

In-the-money option (1) An option that has a positive value if exercised immediately. For example, a call when the strike price is below the current price of the underlying asset, or a put when the strike price is above the current price of the underlying asset. (2) An option that has positive intrinsic value. (3) Options that, if exercised, would result in the value received being worth more than the payment required to exercise.

Intrinsic value (1) The value that would be obtained on an option if it were to be exercised immediately. (2) The portion of a call option's total value equal to the greater of either zero or the difference between the current value of the underlying asset and the exercise price; for a put option, intrinsic value is the greater of either zero or the exercise price less the underlying asset price. For a stock, it is the value derived from fundamental analysis of the stock's expected returns or cash flows.

Invention The creation of a new product or process, often facilitated by the knowledge of engineering and scientific relationships.

Inventory investment Changes in the stock of unsold goods and raw materials held during a period.

Inverse floater A floating-rate note or bond in which the coupon is adjusted to move opposite to a benchmark interest rate.

Investment (1) The purchase, construction, or development of capital resources, including both nonhuman capital and human capital (such as better education). Investment expands the availability of capital resources in an economy. The process of investment is sometimes referred to as capital formation. (2) The current commitment of dollars for a period of time in order to derive future payments that will compensate the investor for the time the funds are committed, the expected rate of inflation, and the uncertainty of future payments.

Investment company (1) A firm that issues (sells) shares, and uses the proceeds to invest in various financial instruments or other assets. (2) A firm that sells shares of the company and uses the proceeds to buy portfolios of stock, bonds, or other financial instruments.

Investment decision process Estimation of value for comparison with market price to determine whether or not to invest.

Investment horizon The time period used for planning and forecasting purposes or the future time at which the investor requires the invested funds.

Investment in human capital Expenditures on training, education, skill development, and health designed to increase human capital and the productivity of an individual.

Investment management company A company separate from the investment company that manages the portfolio and performs administrative functions.

Investment Opportunity Schedule (IOS) A graph of the firm's investment opportunities ranked in order of the projects' rates of return.

Investment strategy A decision by a portfolio manager regarding how he or she will manage the portfolio to meet the goals and objectives of the client. This will include either active or passive management and, if active, what style in terms of top-down or bottom-up or fundamental versus technical.

Invisible hand principle The tendency of market prices to direct individuals pursuing their own interests into productive activities that also promote the economic well-being of the society.

IRR The discount rate which forces the PV of a project's inflows to equal the PV of its costs.

IRR rule An investment decision rule that accepts projects or investments for which the IRR is greater than the opportunity cost of capital.

January effect A frequent empirical anomaly where risk-adjusted stock returns in the month of January are significantly larger than those occurring in any other month of the year.

Jensen measure An absolute measure of a portfolio's risk-adjusted performance, computed as the intercept in a regression equation where the excess returns to a manager's portfolio and the market index are, respectively, the dependent and independent variables.

Joint probability The probability of the joint occurrence of stated events.

kth Order autocorrelation The correlation between observations in a time series separated by k periods.

Kurtosis The statistical measure that indicates the peakedness of a distribution.

Labor force participation rate The number of persons in the civilian labor force 16 years of age or over who are either employed or actively seeking employment as a percentage of the total civilian population 16 years of age and over.

Labor union   A collective organization of employees who bargain as a unit with employers.

Laffer curve   A curve illustrating the relationship between the tax rate and tax revenue. Tax revenue will be low for both very high and very low tax rates. Thus, when tax rates are quite high, a reduction in the tax rate can increase tax revenue.

Lagging indicators   A set of economic variables whose values reach peaks and troughs after the aggregate economy.

Later stage   With respect to venture capital financing, the stage after commercial manufacturing and sales have begun. Later-stage financing includes second-stage, third-stage, and mezzanine financing.

Law of comparative advantage   A principle that states that individuals, firms, regions, or nations can gain by specializing in the production of goods that they produce cheaply (that is, at a low opportunity cost) and exchanging those goods for other desired goods for which they are high-opportunity-cost producers.

Law of demand   A principle that states there is an inverse relationship between the price of a good and the amount of it buyers are willing to purchase. As the price of a product increases, other things constant, consumers will purchase less of the product.

Law of diminishing marginal utility   The basic economic principle that, as the consumption of a commodity increases, the marginal utility derived from consuming more of the commodity (per unit of time) will eventually decline.

Law of diminishing returns   The postulate that, as more and more units of a variable resource are combined with a fixed amount of other resources, employment of additional units of the variable resource will eventually increase output only at a decreasing rate. Once diminishing returns are reached, it will take successively larger amounts of the variable factor to expand output by one unit.

Law of one price   The condition in a financial market in which two financial instruments or combinations of financial instruments can sell for only one price. Equivalent to the principle that no arbitrage opportunities are possible.

Law of supply   A principle that states there is a direct relationship between the price of a good and the amount of it offered for sale. As the price of a product increases, other things constant, producers will increase the amount of the product supplied to the market.

Leading indicators   A set of economic variables whose values reach peaks and troughs in advance of the aggregate economy.

Leading P/E (or forward P/E or prospective P/E)   A stock's current price divided by next year's expected earnings.

Lead manager   The bank in charge of organizing a syndicated bank credit or a bond issue.

Leasehold   A right to occupy land or buildings under a long-term rental contract.

Leasehold improvements   Improvements to leased property that become the property of the lessor at the end of the lease.

Legal risk   The risk that the legal system will not enforce a contract in case of dispute or fraud.

Leptokurtic   Describes a distribution that is more peaked than a normal distribution.

Less-developed countries (LDCs)   Low-income countries generally characterized by rapid population growth and an agriculture-household sector that dominates the economy. Sometimes these countries are referred to as developing countries.

Level of significance   The probability of a Type I error in testing a hypothesis.

Leverage   The relation between the value of the asset position and the amount of equity invested.

Leveraged floating-rate note (or leveraged floater)   A floating-rate note or bond in which the coupon is adjusted at a multiple of a benchmark interest rate.

LIBMEAN   The average of LIBID and LIBOR.

License   The right to use a formula, technique, process, or design.

Licensing   A requirement that one obtain permission from the government in order to perform certain business activities or work in various occupations.

Likelihood   The probability of an observation, given a particular set of conditions.

Limit down   A limit move in the futures market in which the price at which a transaction would be made is at or below the lower limit.

Limit move   A condition in the futures markets in which the price at which a transaction would be made is at or beyond the price limits.

Limit order   (1) An order to buy or sell a security at a specific price or better (lower for a buy order and higher for a sell order). (2) An order that lasts for a specified time to buy or sell a security when and if it trades at a specified price.

Limit pricing   Pricing below average cost to deter entry into an industry.

Limit up   A limit move in the futures market in which the price at which a transaction would be made is at or above the upper limit.

Linear association   A straight-line relationship, as opposed to a relationship that cannot be graphed as a straight line.

Linear interpolation The estimation of an unknown value on the basis of two known values that bracket it, using a straight line between the two known values.

Linear regression Regression that models the straight-line relationship between the dependent and independent variable(s).

Linear trend A trend in which the dependent variable changes at a constant rate with time.

Liquid Term used to describe an asset that can be quickly converted to cash at a price close to fair market value.

Liquid asset An asset that can be easily and quickly converted to purchasing power without loss of value.

Liquidity (1) The ability to buy or sell an asset quickly and at a reasonable price. (2) The ability to trade a futures contract, either selling a previously purchased contract or purchasing a previously sold contract.

Liquidity premium A premium added to the equilibrium interest rate on a security if that security cannot be converted to cash on short notice and at close to "fair market value."

Liquidity risk (1) Uncertainty due to the ability to buy or sell an investment in the secondary market. (2) The risk that a financial instrument cannot be purchased or sold without a significant concession in price due to the size of the market.

Loanable funds market A general term used to describe the broad market that coordinates the borrowing and lending decisions of business firms and households. Commercial banks, savings and loan associations, the stock and bond markets, and insurance companies are important financial institutions in this market.

Local currency (foreign currency) exposure The sensitivity of the asset return, measured in the asset's local currency, to a movement in the exchange rate.

Locked limit A condition in the futures markets in which a transaction cannot take place because the price would be beyond the limits.

Logit model A qualitative-dependent-variable multiple regression model based on the logistic probability distribution.

Log-linear model With reference to time-series models, a model in which the growth rate of the time series as a function of time is constant.

Log-log regression model A regression that expresses the dependent and independent variables as natural logarithms.

Logrolling The exchange between politicians of political support on one issue for political support on another issue.

London Interbank Bid (LIBID) The rate quoted to a top-quality lender on the London interbank market.

London InterBank Offer Rate (LIBOR) (1) The rate at which international banks lend on the Eurocurrency market. This is the rate quoted to a top-quality borrower. The most common maturities are one month, three months, and six months. There is a LIBOR for the U.S. dollar and a few other major currencies. LIBOR is determined by the British Banking Association in London. *See* also Euribor. (2) The Eurodollar rate at which London banks lend dollars to other London banks; considered to be the best representative rate on a dollar borrowed by a private, high-quality borrower.

Long The buyer of a derivative contract. Also refers to the position of owning a derivative.

Long hedge (1) A hedge involving the purchase of forward or futures contracts in anticipation of a spot purchase. Also known as anticipatory hedge. (2) A long position in a forward or futures contract used to offset the price volatility of a short position in the underlying asset.

Longitudinal data Observations on characteristic(s) of the same observational unit through time.

Long position The buyer of a commodity or security or, for a forward contract, the counterparty who will be the eventual buyer of the underlying asset.

Long run (in production) (1) A time period long enough to allow the firm to vary all factors of production. (2) A time period of sufficient length to enable decision makers to adjust fully to a market change.

Long-term equity anticipatory securities (LEAPS) Options originally created with expirations of several years.

Long-term, high-priority goal A long-term financial investment goal of personal importance that typically includes achieving financial independence, such as being able to retire at a certain age.

Look-ahead bias A bias caused by using information that was unavailable on the test date.

Loss Deficit of sales revenue relative to the opportunity cost of production. Losses are a penalty imposed on those who misuse resources in lower-valued uses as judged by buyers in the market.

Lower bound The lowest possible value of an option.

Lower-priority goal A financial investment goal of lesser personal importance, such as taking a luxurious vacation or buying a car every few years.

Low-load fund A mutual fund that imposes a moderate front-end sales charge when the investor buys the fund, typically about 3 to 4 percent.

Low-regular-dividend-plus-extras The policy of announcing a low, regular dividend that can be retained no matter what, and then when times are good paying a designated "extra" dividend.

M1 (money supply) The sum of (1) currency in circulation (including coins), (2) checkable deposits maintained in depository institutions, and (3) traveler's checks.

M2 (money supply) Equal to M1 plus (1) savings deposits, (2) time deposits (accounts of less than $100,000) held in depository institutions, and (3) money market mutual fund shares.

Macaulay duration (1) A measure of the time flow of cash from a bond where cash flows are weighted by present values discounted by the yield to maturity. (2) The duration before dividing by $1 + y_b$. The term, named for one of the economists who first derived it, is used to distinguish the calculation from modified duration. *See also* Modified duration.

Macroeconomic factor A factor related to the economy, such as the inflation rate, industrial production, or economic sector membership.

Macroeconomic factor model A multifactor model in which the factors are surprises in macroeconomic variables that significantly explain equity returns.

Macroeconomics The branch of economics that focuses on how human behavior affects outcomes in highly aggregated markets, such as the markets for labor or consumer products.

Maintenance margin (1) The minimum margin that an investor must keep on deposit in a margin account at all times. (2) The required proportion that the investor's equity value must be to the total market value of the stock. If the proportion drops below this percent, the investor will receive a margin call.

Maintenance margin requirement The margin requirement on any day other than the first day of a transaction.

Management and advisory firm A firm that provides a range of services from standard banking transactions (savings accounts, personal loans) to advising individual and institutional investors on structuring their portfolios and managing investment funds.

Management effect A combination of the interest rate anticipation effect, the analysis effect, and the trading effect.

Management fee The compensation an investment company pays to the investment management company for its services. The average annual fee is about 0.5 percent of fund assets.

Margin (1) The percent of cost a buyer pays in cash for a security, borrowing the balance from the broker. This introduces leverage, which increases the risk of the transaction. (2) The amount of money that a trader deposits in a margin account. The term is derived from the stock market practice in which an investor borrows a portion of the money required to purchase a certain amount of stock. In futures markets, there is no borrowing so the margin is more of a down payment or performance bond.

Margin account The collateral posted with the futures exchange clearinghouse by an outside counterparty to insure its eventual performance; the initial margin is the deposit required at contract origination while the maintenance margin is the minimum collateral necessary at all times.

Marginal Term used to describe the effects of a change in the current situation. For example, the marginal cost is the cost of producing an additional unit of a product, given the producer's current facility and production rate.

Marginal benefit The maximum price a consumer would be willing to pay for an additional unit. It is the dollar value of the consumer's marginal utility from the additional unit, and thus falls as consumption increases.

Marginal cost The change in total cost required to produce an additional unit of output.

Marginal Cost of Capital (MCC) The cost of obtaining another dollar of new capital; the weighted average cost of the last dollar of new capital raised.

Marginal Cost of Capital (MCC) Schedule A graph that relates the firm's weighted average cost of each dollar of capital to the total amount of new capital raised.

Marginal probability *See* Unconditional probability.

Marginal product The increase in the total product resulting from a unit increase in the employment of a variable input. Mathematically, it is the ratio of the change in total product to the change in the quantity of the variable input.

Marginal propensity to consume (MPC) Additional current consumption divided by additional current disposable income.

Marginal rate of substitution The change in the consumption level of one good that is just sufficient to offset a unit change in the consumption of another good without causing a shift to another indifference curve. At any point on an indifference curve, it will be equal to the slope of the curve at that point.

Marginal revenue (MR) The incremental change in total revenue derived from the sale of one additional unit of a product.

Marginal revenue product (MRP) The change in the total revenue of a firm that results from the employment of one additional unit of a resource. The marginal revenue product of an input is equal to its marginal product multiplied by the marginal revenue of the good or service produced.

Marginal tax rate (MTR) (1) Additional tax liability divided by additional taxable income. It is the percentage of an extra dollar of income that must be paid in taxes. It is the marginal tax rate that is relevant in personal decision making. (2) The part of each additional dollar in income that is paid as tax.

Marginal utility The additional utility received from the consumption of an additional unit of a good.

Margin call A request by an investor's broker for additional capital for a security bought on margin if the investor's equity value declines below the required maintenance margin.

Margin deposit The amount of cash or securities that must be deposited as guarantee on a futures position. The margin is a returnable deposit.

Marked to market The settlement process used to adjust the margin account of a futures contract for daily changes in the price of the underlying asset.

Market (1) An abstract concept that encompasses the trading arrangements of buyers and sellers that underlie the forces of supply and demand. (2) The means through which buyers and sellers are brought together to aid in the transfer of goods and/or services.

Market impact With reference to execution costs, the difference between the actual execution price and the market price that would have prevailed had the manager not sought to trade the security.

Market maker An institution or individual quoting firm bid and ask prices for a security and standing ready to buy or sell the security at those quoted prices. Also called a dealer.

Market, or Beta, risk That part of a project's risk that cannot be eliminated by diversification; it is measured by the project's beta coefficient.

Market order (1) An order to buy (sell) immediately at the best obtainable price. (2) An order to buy or sell a security immediately at the best price available.

Market portfolio The portfolio that includes all risky assets with relative weights equal to their proportional market values.

Market power The ability of a firm that is not a pure monopolist to earn unusually large profits, indicating that it has some monopoly power. Because the firm has few (or weak) competitors,

it has a degree of freedom from the discipline of vigorous competition.

Market price of risk The slope of the capital market line, indicating the market risk premium for each unit of market risk.

Market risk The risk associated with interest rates, exchange rates, and equity prices.

Market risk premium (1) The amount of return above the risk-free rate that investors expect from the market in general as compensation for systematic risk. (2) The expected excess return on the market over the risk-free rate.

Market value added (MVA) External management performance measure to compare the market value of the company's debt and equity with the total capital invested in the firm.

Market-value-weighted series An indicator series calculated as the total market value of the securities in the sample.

Marking to market (1) Procedure whereby potential profits and losses on a futures position are realized daily. The daily futures price variation is debited (credited) in cash to the loser (winner) at the end of the day. (2) A procedure used primarily in futures markets in which the parties to a contract settle the amount owed daily. Also known as the daily settlement.

Maturity risk premium (MRP) A premium that reflects interest rate risk.

Maturity strategy A portfolio management strategy employed to reduce the interest rate risk of a bond portfolio by matching the maturity of the portfolio with its investment horizon. For example, if the investment horizon is 10 years, the portfolio manager would construct a portfolio that will mature in 10 years.

Mean absolute deviation With reference to a sample, the mean of the absolute values of deviations from the sample mean.

Mean excess return The average rate of return in excess of the risk-free rate.

Mean rates of return The average of an investment's returns over an extended period of time.

Mean reversion The tendency of a time series to fall when its level is above its mean and rise when its level is below its mean; a mean-reverting time series tends to return to its long-term mean.

Means-tested income transfers Transfers that are limited to persons or families with an income below a certain cutoff point. Eligibility is thus dependent on low-income status.

Mean–variance analysis An approach to portfolio analysis using expected means, variances, and covariances of asset returns.

Measure of central tendency A quantitative measure that specifies where data are centered.

Measure of location   A quantitative measure that describes the location or distribution of data; includes not only measures of central tendency but also other measures such as percentiles.

Measurement scales   A scheme of measuring differences. The four types of measurement scales are nominal, ordinal, interval, and ratio.

Median   The value of the middle item of a set of items that has been sorted into ascending or descending order; the 50th percentile.

Medical savings accounts   Special savings accounts that individuals could use for the payment of medical bills or the purchase of a catastrophic (high deductibility) health insurance plan. Unfavorable tax treatment compared to employer-provided health insurance and other regulatory restrictions currently reduce their use.

Medium of exchange   An asset that is used to buy and sell goods or services.

Mesokurtic   Describes a distribution with kurtosis identical to that of the normal distribution.

Method of comparables   An approach to evaluation that involves using a price multiple to evaluate whether an asset is relatively fairly valued, relatively undervalued, or relatively overvalued in relation to a benchmark value of the multiple.

Mezzanine financing   With respect to venture capital financing, capital provided to prepare for the step of going public. Also known as bridge financing.

Microeconomics   The branch of economics that focuses on how human behavior affects the conduct of affairs within narrowly defined units, such as individual households or business firms.

Middleman   A person who buys and sells or who arranges trades. A middleman reduces transaction costs.

Minimum-variance frontier   The graph of the set of portfolios that have minimum variance for their level of expected return.

Minimum-variance hedge ratio   The hedge ratio that is expected to minimize the variance of the rate of return on the hedged portfolio.

Minimum-variance portfolio   The portfolio with the minimum variance for each given level of expected return.

Minimum wage   Legislation requiring that workers be paid at least the stated minimum hourly rate of pay.

Mixed factor models   Factor models that combine features of more than one type of factor model.

Modal interval   With reference to grouped data, the most frequently occurring interval.

Mode   The most frequently occurring value in a set of observations.

Model risk   The use of an inaccurate pricing model for a particular investment, or the improper use of the right model.

Model specification   With reference to regression, the set of variables included in the regression and the regression equation's functional form.

Modified duration   (1) Measure of a bond's price sensitivity to interest rate movements. Equal to the duration of a bond divided by one plus its yield to maturity. (2) A measure of Macaulay duration divided by one plus the bond's periodic yield used to approximate the bond's price volatility. (3) An adjustment of the duration for the level of the yield. Contrast with Macaulay duration.

Modified IRR (MIRR)   The discount rate at which the present value of a project's cost is equal to the present value of its terminal value, where the terminal value is found as the sum of the future values of the cash inflows, compounded at the firm's cost of capital.

Monetarists   A group of economists who believe that (1) monetary instability is the major cause of fluctuations in real GDP and (2) rapid growth of the money supply is the major cause of inflation.

Monetary base   The sum of currency in circulation plus bank reserves (vault cash and reserves with the Fed). It reflects the stock of U.S. securities held by the Fed.

Monetary policy   The deliberate control of the money supply, and, in some cases, credit conditions, for the purpose of achieving macroeconomic goals.

Money interest rate   The percentage of the amount borrowed that must be paid to the lender in addition to the repayment of the principal. It overstates the real cost of borrowing during an inflationary period. When inflation is anticipated, an inflationary premium will be incorporated into this rate. The money interest rate is often referred to as the nominal interest rate.

Money market   (1) The market for short-term debt securities with maturities of less than one year. (2) The market for short-term debt instruments (one-year maturity or less).

Money market mutual funds   (1) Interest-earning accounts offered by brokerage firms that pool depositors' funds and invest them in highly liquid short-term securities. Since these securities can be quickly converted to cash, depositors are permitted to write checks (which reduce their share holdings) against their accounts. (2) A fund that invests in short-term securities sold in the money market. (Large companies, banks, and other institutions also invest their surplus cash in the money market for short periods of time.) In the entire investment spectrum, these are generally the safest, most stable securities available. They include Treasury bills, certificates of deposit of large banks, and commercial paper (short-term IOUs of large corporations).

Money market yield (or CD equivalent yield) A yield on a basis comparable to the quoted yield on an interest-bearing money market instrument that pays interest on a 360-day basis; the annualized holding period yield, assuming a 360-day year.

Moneyness The relationship between the price of the underlying and an option's exercise price.

Money rate of interest The rate of interest in monetary terms that borrowers pay for borrowed funds. During periods when borrowers and lenders expect inflation, the money rate of interest exceeds the real rate of interest.

Money supply The supply of currency, checking account funds, and traveler's checks. These items are counted as money because they are used as the means of payment for purchases.

Money-weighted rate of return The internal rate of return on a portfolio, taking account of all cash flows.

Money-weighted return A rate of return measure corresponding to the internal rate of return; captures a return on average invested capital.

Monopolistic competition Term often used by economists to describe markets characterized by a large number of sellers that supply differentiated products to a market with low barriers to entry. Essentially, it is an alternative term for a competitive price-searcher market.

Monopoly A market structure characterized by (1) a single seller of a well-defined product for which there are no good substitutes and (2) high barriers to the entry of any other firms into the market for that product.

Monte Carlo simulation A risk analysis technique in which probable future events are simulated on a computer, generating estimated rates of return and risk indexes.

Mortgage bonds Bonds that pledge specific assets such as buildings and equipment. The proceeds from the sale of these assets are used to pay off bondholders in case of bankruptcy.

Moving average The continually recalculating average of security prices for a period, often 200 days, to serve as an indication of the general trend of prices and also as a benchmark price.

Multicollinearity A regression assumption violation that occurs when two or more independent variables (or combinations of independent variables) are highly but not perfectly correlated with each other.

Multifactor model An empirical version of the APT where the investor chooses the exact number and identity of the common risk factors used to describe an asset's risk-return relationship. Risk factors are often designated as macroeconomic variables (e.g., inflation, changes in gross domestic product) or microeconomic variables (e.g., security-specific characteristics like firm size or book-to-market ratios).

Multiple IRRs The situation where a project has two or more IRRs.

Multiple linear regression Linear regression involving two or more independent variables.

Multiple linear regression model A linear regression model with two or more independent variables.

Multiple R The correlation between the actual and forecasted values of the dependent variable in a regression.

Multiplication rule for probabilities The rule that the joint probability of events A and B equals the probability of A given B times the probability of B.

Multivariate distribution A probability distribution that specifies the probabilities for a group of related random variables.

Multivariate normal distribution A probability distribution for a group of random variables that is completely defined by the means and variances of the variables plus all the correlations between pairs of the variables.

Mutual fund (1) An open-end investment company. Also called unit trust in the United Kingdom and some other countries. (2) An investment company that pools money from shareholders and invests in a variety of securities, including stocks, bonds, and money market securities. A mutual fund ordinarily stands ready to buy back (redeem) its shares at their current net asset value, which depends on the market value of the fund's portfolio of securities at the time. Mutual funds generally continuously offer new shares to investors.

Mutually exclusive events Events such that only one can occur at a time.

Mutually exclusive projects A set of projects where only one can be accepted.

National Association of Securities Dealers Automated Quotation (Nasdaq) system An electronic system for providing bid-ask quotes on OTC securities.

National debt The sum of the indebtedness of the federal government in the form of outstanding interest-earning bonds. It reflects the cumulative impact of budget deficits and surpluses.

National income   The total income earned by the nationals (citizens) during a period. It is the sum of employee compensation, self-employment income, rents, interest, and corporate profits.

Natural monopoly   A market situation in which the average costs of production continually decline with increased output. Therefore, average costs of production will be lowest when a single, large firm produces the entire output demanded.

Natural rate of unemployment   The long-run average unemployment rate due to frictional and structural conditions of labor markets. This rate is affected both by dynamic change and by public policy. It is sustainable into the future. The current natural rate of unemployment in the United States is thought to be approximately 5 percent.

Near-term, high-priority goal   A short-term financial investment goal of personal importance, such as accumulating funds for making a house down payment or buying a car.

Negative serial correlation   Serial correlation in which a positive error for one observation increases the chance of a negative error for another observation, and vice versa.

Negotiated sales   An underwriting arrangement wherein the sale of a security issue by an issuing entity (governmental body or a corporation) is done using an investment banking firm that maintains an ongoing relationship with the issuer. The characteristics of the security issue are determined by the issuer in consultation with the investment banker.

Neoclassical growth theory   A theory of economic growth that assumes that the marginal productivity of capital declines as more capital is added.

Net asset value   The market value of the assets owned by a fund.

Net asset value (NAV) per share   The market value of an investment company's assets (securities, cash, and any accrued earnings) after deducting liabilities, divided by the number of shares outstanding.

Net exports   Exports minus imports.

Net income of foreigners   The income that foreigners earn by contributing labor and capital resources to the production of goods within the borders of a country minus the income the nationals of the country earn abroad.

Net present value (NPV)   (1) A measure of the excess cash flows expected from an investment proposal. It is equal to the present value of the cash inflows from an investment proposal, discounted at the required rate of return for the investment, minus the present value of the cash outflows required by the investment, also discounted at the investment's required rate of return. If the derived net present value is a positive value (i.e., there is an excess net present value), the investment should be acquired since it will provide a rate of return above its required returns. (2) The present value of an investment's cash inflows (benefits) minus the present value of its cash outflows (costs).

Net present value (NPV) method   A method of ranking investment proposals using the NPV.

Net present value profile   A graph showing the relationship between a project's NPV and the firm's cost of capital.

New classical economists   Economists who believe there are strong forces pushing a market economy toward full employment equilibrium and that macroeconomic policy is an ineffective tool with which to reduce economic instability.

New issue   Common stocks or bonds offered by companies for public sale.

Netting   When parties agree to exchange only the net amount owed from one party to the other.

n Factorial   For a positive integer n, the product of the first n positive integers; 0 factorial equals 1 by definition. n factorial is written as $n!$.

Node   Each value on a binomial tree from which successive moves or outcomes branch.

No-load fund   A mutual fund that sells its shares at net asset value without adding sales charges.

Nominal GDP   GDP expressed at current prices. It is often called money GDP.

Nominal risk-free interest rate   The sum of the real risk-free interest rate and the inflation premium.

Nominal (quoted) risk-free fate, k_{RF}   The rate of interest on a security that is free of all risk; k_{RF} is proxied by the T-bill rate or the T-bond rate. k_{RF} includes an inflation premium.

Nominal scale   A measurement scale that categorizes data but does not rank them.

Nominal values   Values expressed in current dollars.

Nominal yield   A bond's yield as measured by its coupon rate.

Nonactivist strategy   The maintenance of a steady monetary and fiscal policy during all phases of the business cycle. According to this view, adjusting macro policy in response to current cyclical conditions is likely to increase, rather than reduce, instability.

Nondeliverable forwards (NDFs)   Cash-settled forward contracts, used predominantly with respect to foreign exchange forwards.

Nonhuman resources   The durable, nonhuman inputs that can be used to produce both current and future output. Machines, buildings, land, and raw materials are examples. Investment can increase the supply of nonhuman resources.

Economists often use the term physical capital when referring to nonhuman resources.

Nonlinear relation An association or relationship between variables that cannot be graphed as a straight line.

Nonparametric test A test that is not concerned with a parameter, or that makes minimal assumptions about the population from which a sample comes.

Nonpecuniary job characteristics Working conditions, prestige, variety, location, employee freedom and responsibilities, and other nonwage characteristics of a job that influence how employees evaluate the job.

Nonstationarity With reference to a random variable, the property of having characteristics such as mean and variance that are not constant through time.

Normal backwardation The condition in futures markets in which futures prices are lower than expected spot prices.

Normal (business-cycle-adjusted) earnings per share The earnings per share that a business could achieve currently under mid-cyclical conditions.

Normal distribution A continuous, symmetric probability distribution that is completely described by its mean and its variance.

Normal contango The condition in futures markets in which futures prices are higher than expected spot prices.

Normal good A good that has a positive income elasticity, so that, as consumer income rises, demand for that good rises also.

Normal portfolio A specialized or customized benchmark constructed to evaluate a specific manager's investment style or philosophy.

Normal profit rate Zero economic profit, providing just the competitive rate of return on the capital (and labor) of owners. An above-normal profit rate will draw more entry into the market, while a below-normal rate will cause an exit of investors and capital.

Normative economics Judgments about "what ought to be" in economic matters. Normative economic views cannot be proved false, because they are based on value judgments.

North American Free Trade Agreement (NAFTA) A comprehensive trade agreement between the United States, Mexico, and Canada that went into effect in 1994. Tariff barriers will continue to be phased out under the agreement until 2004.

Notes Intermediate-term debt securities with maturities longer than 1 year but less than 10 years.

Notional principal The principal value of a swap transaction, which is not exchanged but is used

as a scale factor to translate interest rate differentials into cash settlement payments.

n-Period moving average The average of the current and immediately prior $n-1$ values of a time series.

NPV rule An investment decision rule that states that an investment should be undertaken if its NPV is positive but not undertaken if its NPV is negative.

Null hypothesis The hypothesis to be tested.

Objective probabilities Probabilities that generally do not vary from person to person; includes a priori and objective probabilities.

Objectives The investor's goals expressed in terms of risk and return and included in the policy statement.

Off-balance sheet asset An item not on the balance sheet that moves to the asset side of the balance sheet when a specified event occurs.

Off-balance sheet liability An item not on the balance sheet that moves to the liability side of balance sheet when a specified event occurs.

Offensive competitive strategy A strategy whereby a firm attempts to use its strengths to affect the competitive forces in the industry and, in so doing, improves the firm's relative position in the industry.

Offer price The price at which a market maker is willing to sell a security (also called ask price).

Official reserves The amount of reserves owned by the central bank of a government in the form of gold, Special Drawing Rights, and foreign cash or marketable securities.

Off-market FRA A contract in which the initial value is intentionally set at a value other than zero and therefore requires a cash payment at the start from one party to the other.

Offsetting A transaction in exchange-listed derivative markets in which a party re-enters the market to close out a position.

Oligopoly A market situation in which a small number of sellers compose the entire industry. It is competition among the few.

One-sided hypothesis test (or one-tailed hypothesis test) A test in which the null hypothesis is rejected only if the evidence indicates that the population parameter is greater than (smaller than) θ_0. The alternative hypothesis also has one side.

Open-end fund An investment company that continuously offers to sell new shares, or redeem them, at prices based on the market value of the assets owned by the fund (net asset value).

Open-end interest The total number of futures or option contracts that have not been closed out by offset or fulfilled delivery.

Open-end investment company The more formal name for a mutual fund, which derives from the fact that it continuously offers new shares to investors and redeems them (buys them back) on demand.

Open market operations The buying and selling of U.S. government securities in the open market by the Federal Reserve.

Operating efficiency ratios Financial ratios intended to indicate how efficiently management is utilizing the firm's assets in terms of dollar sales generated per dollar of assets. Primary examples would be: total asset turnover, fixed asset turnover, or equity turnover.

Operating leverage The use of fixed-production costs in the firm's operating cost structure. The effect of fixed costs is to magnify the effect of a change in sales on operating profits.

Operating profitability ratios Financial ratios intended to indicate how profitable the firm is in terms of the percent of profit generated from sales. Alternative measures would include: operating profit (EBIT)/net sales; pretax profit (EBT)/net sales; and net profit/sales.

Operations risk or operational risk The risk of loss from failures in a company's systems and procedures (for example, due to computer failures or human failures) or events completely outside of the control of organizations (which would include "acts of God" and terrorist actions).

Opportunity cost (1) The highest valued alternative that must be sacrificed as a result of choosing among alternatives. (2) With reference to execution costs, the loss (or gain) incurred as the result of failure or delay in the execution of a trade, or failure to complete a trade in full. (3) The value that investors forgo by choosing a particular course of action; the value of something in its best alternative use.

Opportunity cost of equity capital The implicit rate of return that must be earned by investors to induce them to continue to supply financial capital to the firm.

Opportunity cost of production The total economic cost of producing a good or service. The cost component includes the opportunity cost of all resources, including those owned by the firm. The opportunity cost is equal to the value of the production of other goods sacrificed as the result of producing the good.

Opportunity set The set of assets available for investment.

Optimal dividend policy The dividend policy that strikes a balance between current dividends and future growth and maximizes the firm's stock price.

Optimal portfolio The portfolio on the efficient frontier that has the highest utility for a given investor. It lies at the point of tangency between the efficient frontier and the curve with the investor's highest possible utility.

Optimizer A specialized computer program or a spreadsheet that solves for the portfolio weights that will result in the lowest risk for a specified level of expected return.

Option A financial instrument that gives one party the right, but not the obligation, to buy or sell an underlying asset from or to another party at a fixed price over a specific period of time. Also referred to as contingent claims.

Option-adjusted spread A type of yield spread that considers changes in the term structure and alternative estimates of the volatility of interest rates.

Option contract An agreement that grants the owner the right, but not the obligation, to make a future transaction in an underlying commodity or security at a fixed price and within a predetermined time in the future.

Option premium (or option price or premium) (1) The price of an option. (2) The initial price that the option buyer must pay to the option seller to acquire the contract. (3) The amount of money a buyer pays and seller receives to engage in an option transaction.

Options Clearing Corporation (OCC) A company designed to guarantee, monitor margin accounts, and settle exchange-traded option transactions.

Order-driven market A market without active market makers in which buy-and-sell orders directly confront each other; an auction market.

Ordinal scale A measurement scale that sorts data into categories that are ordered (ranked) with respect to some characteristic.

Ordinary annuity An annuity with a first cash flow that is paid one period from the present.

Ordinary least squares (OLS) An estimation method based on the criterion of minimizing the sum of the squared residuals of a regression.

Orthogonal Uncorrelated; at a right angle.

Other checkable deposits Interest-earning deposits that are also available for checking.

Outcome A possible value of a random variable.

Outliers Small numbers of observations at either extreme (small or large) of a sample.

Out-of-sample forecast errors The differences between actual and predicted value of time series outside the sample period used to fit the model.

Out-of-sample test A test of a strategy or model using a sample outside the time period on which the strategy or model was developed.

Out-of-the-money option   (1) An option that has no value if exercised immediately. For example, a call when the strike price is above the current price of the underlying asset, or a put when the strike price is below the current price of the underlying asset. (2) An option that has no intrinsic value. (3) Options that, if exercised, would require the payment of more money than the value received and therefore would not be currently exercised.

Overfunded plan   A defined benefit pension plan in which the present value of the pension liabilities is less than market value of the plan's assets.

Overnight   A deal from today to the next business day.

Overnight index swap (OIS)   A swap in which the floating rate is the cumulative value of a single unit of currency invested at an overnight rate during the settlement period.

Over-the-counter (OTC)   A market for securities made up of dealers. It is not an organized exchange, and trading usually takes place by telephone or other electronic means.

Overweighted   A condition in which a portfolio, for whatever reason, includes more of a class of securities than the relative market value alone would justify.

Paired comparisons test   A statistical test for differences based on paired observations drawn from samples that are dependent on each other.

Paired observations   Observations that are dependent on each other.

Pairs arbitrage trade   A trade in two closely related stocks involving the short sale of one and the purchase of the other.

Panel data   Observations through time on a single characteristic of multiple observational units.

Parameter   A descriptive measure computed from or used to describe a population of data, conventionally represented by Greek letters.

Parameter instability   The problem or issue of population regression parameters that have changed over time.

Parametric test   Any test (or procedure) concerned with parameters or whose validity depends on assumptions concerning the population generating the sample.

Partial regression coefficients (or partial slope coefficients)   The slope coefficients in a multiple regression.

Partnership   A business firm owned by two or more individuals who possess ownership rights to the firm's profits and are personally liable for the debts of the firm.

Par value   The principal amount repaid at maturity of a bond. Also called face value. *See also* Principal.

Par yield curve   The yield curve drawn for government coupon bonds of different maturities that trade at, or around, par.

Payback period   (1) The length of time required for an investment's net revenues to cover its cost. (2) The time required for the added income from the convertible security relative to the stock to offset the conversion premium.

Payer swaption   A swaption that allows the holder to enter into a swap as the fixed-rate payer and floating-rate receiver.

Payment date   The date on which a firm actually mails dividend checks.

Payment netting   A means of settling payment in which the amount owed by the first party to the second is netted with the amount owed by the second party to the first; only the net difference is paid.

Payoff   The value of an option at expiration.

Peak   The culmination of a bull market when prices stop rising and begin declining.

Peer group comparison   A method of measuring portfolio performance by collecting the returns produced by a representative universe of investors over a specific period of time and displaying them in a simple boxplot format.

Pegged exchange rate regime   A system in which a country's exchange rate in relation to a major currency is set at a target value (the peg) but allowed to fluctuate within a small band around the target.

Pegged exchange-rate system   A commitment to use monetary and fiscal policy to maintain the exchange-rate value of the domestic currency at a fixed rate or within a narrow band relative to another currency (or bundle of currencies).

P/E ratio   *See* Price-earnings ratio.

per capita GDP   Income per person. Increases in income per person are vitally important for the achievement of higher living standards.

Percentiles   Quantiles that divide a distribution into 100 equal parts.

Perfect collinearity   The existence of an exact linear relation between two or more independent variables or combinations of independent variables.

Performance appraisal   (1) The assessment of an investment record for evidence of investment skill. (2) The evaluation of risk-adjusted performance; the evaluation of investment skill.

Performance attribution   The attribution of investment performance to specific investment decisions (such as asset allocation and country weighting).

Performance guarantee   A guarantee from the clearing-house that if one party makes money on a transaction, the clearinghouse ensures it will be paid.

Performance measurement The calculation of returns in a logical and consistent manner.

Performance presentation standards (PPS) A comprehensive set of reporting guidelines created by the Association for Investment Management and Research (AIMR), in an effort to fulfill the call for uniform, accurate, and consistent performance reporting.

Performance shares Stock which is awarded to executives on the basis of the company's performance.

Periodic rate The quoted interest rate per period; the stated annual interest rate divided by the number of compounding periods per year.

Permanent income hypothesis The hypothesis that consumption depends on some measure of long-run expected (permanent) income rather than on current income.

Permutation An ordered listing.

Perpetual bond A bond with no stated maturity.

Perpetuity (1) An investment without any maturity date. It provides returns to its owner indefinitely. (2) A perpetual annuity, or a set of never-ending level sequential cash flows, with the first cash flow occurring one period from now.

Persistent earnings *See* Underlying earnings.

Personal consumption Household spending on consumer goods and services during the current period. Consumption is a flow concept.

Personal income The total income received by domestic households and noncorporate businesses. It is available for consumption, saving, and payment of personal taxes.

Personal trust An amount of money set aside by a grantor and often managed by a third party, the trustee. Often constructed so one party receives income from the trust's investments and another party receives the residual value of the trust after the income beneficiaries' death.

Phillips curve A curve that illustrates the relationship between the rate of change in prices (or money wages) and the rate of unemployment.

Pip The smallest incremental move an exchange rate can make, i.e., the last decimal place in a quote.

Plain-vanilla Refers to a security, especially a bond or a swap, issued with standard features. Sometimes called generic.

Plain vanilla swap An interest rate swap in which one party pays a fixed rate and the other pays a floating rate, with both sets of payments in the same currency.

Platykurtic Describes a distribution that is less peaked than the normal distribution.

Point One percent (1%).

Point estimate A single numerical estimate of an unknown quantity, such as a population parameter.

Policy effect The difference in performance of a bond portfolio from that of a chosen index due to differences in duration, which result from a fund's investment policy.

Policy-ineffectiveness theorem The proposition that any systematic policy will be rendered ineffective once decision makers figure out the policy pattern and adjust their decision making in light of its expected effects. The theorem is a corollary of the theory of rational expectations.

Policy statement A statement in which the investor specifies investment goals, constraints, and risk preferences.

Pooled estimate An estimate of a parameter that involves combining (pooling) observations from two or more samples.

Population All members of a specified group.

Population mean The arithmetic mean value of a population; the arithmetic mean of all the observations or values in the population.

Population standard deviation A measure of dispersion relating to a population in the same unit of measurement as the observations, calculated as the positive square root of the population variance.

Population variance A measure of dispersion relating to a population, calculated as the mean of the squared deviations around the population mean.

Pork-barrel legislation A package of spending projects benefiting local areas at federal expense. The projects typically have costs that exceed benefits, but are intensely desired by the residents of the district getting the benefits without having to pay much of the costs.

Portfolio (1) All the stocks, bonds, or other securities held by an individual or corporation for investment purposes. (2) A group of investments. Ideally, the investments should have different patterns of returns over time.

Portfolio performance attribution The analysis of portfolio performance in terms of the contributions from various sources of risk.

Portfolio possibilities curve A graphical representation of the expected return and risk of all portfolios that can be formed using two assets.

Position trader A trader who typically holds positions open overnight.

Positive economics The scientific study of "what is" among economic relationships.

Positive rate of time preference The desire of consumers for goods now rather than in the future.

Positive serial correlation Serial correlation in which a positive error for one observation increases the chance of a positive error for another observation, and a negative error for one observation increases the chance of a negative error for another observation.

Post-audit A comparison of the actual versus the expected results for a given capital project.

Posterior probability An updated probability that reflects or comes after new information.

Potential credit risk The risk associated with the possibility that a payment due at a later date will not be made.

Potential output The level of output that can be achieved and sustained into the future, given the size of the labor force, expected productivity of labor, and natural rate of unemployment consistent with the efficient operation of the labor market. For periods of time, the actual output may differ from the economy's potential.

Poverty threshold income level The level of money income below which a family is considered to be poor. It differs according to family characteristics (for example, number of family members) and is adjusted when consumer prices change.

Power of a test The probability of correctly rejecting the null—that is, rejecting the null hypothesis when it is false.

Predatory pricing Pricing below average cost to drive competitors out of the industry.

Preferred stock An equity investment that stipulates the dividend payment either as a coupon or a stated dollar amount. The firm's directors may withhold payments.

Pre-investing The strategy of using futures contracts to enter the market without an immediate outlay of cash.

Premium A bond selling at a price above par value due to capital market conditions. *See* also Option premium.

Present (price) value of a basis point (PVBP) The change in the bond price for a 1 basis point change in yield. Also called basis point value (BPV).

Present value (PV) (1) The current worth of future income after it is discounted to reflect the fact that revenues in the future are valued less highly than revenues now. (2) The current worth of a future cash flow. Obtained by discounting the future cash flow at the market-required rate of return. (3) The current (discounted) value of a future cash flow or flows.

Price ceiling A legally established maximum price that sellers may charge for a good or resource.

Price change effect The unknown component of the total return for a bond portfolio during a period of time due to the interest rate effect, sector/quality effect, and residual effect.

Price continuity A feature of a liquid market in which prices change little from one transaction to the next due to the depth of the market.

Price controls Government-mandated prices; they may be either greater or less than the market equilibrium price.

Price discovery A feature of futures markets in which futures prices provide valuable information about the price of the underlying asset.

Price discrimination A practice whereby a seller charges different consumers different prices for the same product or service.

Priced risk Risk that investors require an additional return for bearing.

Price-driven market A market in which dealers (market makers) adjust their quotes continuously to reflect supply and demand; also known as a dealer market.

Price-earnings ratio (P/E ratio) (1) The ratio of the stock market price to the earnings per share. Sometimes called earnings multiplier. (2) The number by which expected earnings per share is multiplied to estimate a stock's value; also called the earnings multiplier.

Price elasticity of demand The percent change in the quantity of a product demanded divided by the percent change in the price causing the change in quantity. Price elasticity of demand indicates the degree of consumer response to variation in price.

Price elasticity of supply The percentage change in quantity supplied, divided by the percentage change in the price causing the change in quantity supplied.

Price floor A legally established minimum price that buyers must pay for a good or resource.

Price limits Limits imposed by a futures exchange on the price change that can occur from one day to the next.

Price momentum A portfolio strategy in which you acquire stocks that have enjoyed above-market stock price increases.

Price multiple The ratio of a stock's market price to some measure of value per share.

Price relative A ratio of an ending price over a beginning price; it is equal to 1 plus the holding period return on the asset.

Price risk The component of interest rate risk due to the uncertainty of the market price of a bond caused by possible changes in market interest rates.

Price searchers Firms that face a downward sloping demand curve for their product. The amount that the firm is able to sell is inversely related to the price that it charges.

Price takers Sellers who must take the market price in order to sell their product. Because each price taker's output is small relative to the total market, price takers can sell all their output at the market price, but they are unable to sell any of their output at a price higher than the market price.

Price-weighted series   An indicator series calculated as an arithmetic average of the current prices of the sampled securities.

Primary market   (1) Market where financial institutions aid in the sale of new securities. (2) The market in which newly issued securities are sold by their issuers, who receive the proceeds.

Principal (par value)   (1) The original value of the debt underlying a bond that is payable at maturity. (2) The amount of funds originally invested in a project or instrument; the face value to be paid at maturity.

Principal-agent problem   The incentive problem arising when the purchaser of services (the principal) lacks full information about the circumstances faced by the seller (the agent) and thus cannot know how well the agent performs the purchased services. The agent may to some extent work toward objectives other than those sought by the principal paying for the service.

Principal trade   A trade through a broker who guarantees full execution at specified discount/premium to the prevailing price.

Prior probabilities   Probabilities reflecting beliefs prior to the arrival of new information.

Private investment   The flow of private sector expenditures on durable assets (fixed investment) plus the addition to inventories (inventory investment) during a period. These expenditures enhance our ability to provide consumer benefits in the future.

Privately held government debt   The portion of the national debt owed to domestic and foreign investors. It does not include bonds held by agencies of the federal government or the Federal Reserve.

Private placement   A new issue sold directly to a small group of investors, usually institutions.

Private property rights   Property rights that are exclusively held by an owner, or group of owners, and that can be transferred to others at the owner's discretion.

Probability   A number between 0 and 1 describing the chance that a stated event will occur.

Probability density function   A function with non-negative values such that probability can be described by areas under the curve graphing the function.

Probability distribution   A distribution that specifies the probabilities of a random variable's possible outcomes.

Probability function   A function that specifies the probability that the random variable takes on a specific value.

Probit model   A qualitative-dependent-variable multiple regression model based on the normal distribution.

Producer surplus   The difference between the minimum supply price and the actual sales price. It measures the net gains to producers and resource suppliers from market trade. It is not the same as profit.

Production opportunities   The returns available within an economy from investments in productive (cash-generating) assets.

Production possibilities curve   A curve that outlines all possible combinations of total output that could be produced, assuming (1) the utilization of a fixed amount of productive resources, (2) full and efficient use of those resources, and (3) a specific state of technical knowledge. The slope of the curve indicates the rate at which one product can be traded off to produce more of the other.

Productivity   The average output produced per worker during a specific time period. It is usually measured in terms of output per hour worked.

Profit   An excess of sales revenue relative to the opportunity cost of production. The cost component includes the opportunity cost of all resources, including those owned by the firm. Therefore, profit accrues only when the value of the good produced is greater than the value of other goods that could have been produced with those same resources.

Progressive tax   A tax in which the average tax rate rises with income. Persons with higher incomes will pay a higher percentage of their income in taxes.

Project cost of capital, k_p   The risk-adjusted cost of capital for an individual project.

Promised yield to call (YTC)   A bond's yield if held until the first available call date, with reinvestment of all coupon payments at the yield-to-call rate.

Promised yield to maturity (YTM)   The most widely used measure of a bond's yield that states the fully compounded rate of return on a bond bought at market price and held to maturity with reinvestment of all coupon payments at the yield to maturity rate.

Property rights   The right to use, control, and obtain the benefits from a good or service.

Proportional tax   A tax in which the average tax rate is the same at all income levels. Everyone pays the same percentage of income in taxes.

Proprietorship   A business firm owned by an individual who possesses the ownership right to the firm's profits and is personally liable for the firm's debts.

Prospective P/E *See* Leading P/E.

Protective put (1) A trading strategy in which a put option is purchased as a supplement to a long position in an underlying asset or portfolio of assets; the most straightforward form of portfolio insurance. (2) An option strategy in which a long position in an asset is combined with a long position in a put.

Pseudo-random numbers Numbers produced by random number generators.

Public bond A long-term, fixed-obligation debt security in a convenient, affordable denomination for sale to individuals and financial institutions.

Public-choice analysis The study of decision making as it affects the formation and operation of collective organizations, such as governments. In general, the principles and methodology of economics are applied to political science topics.

Public goods Jointly consumed goods that are nonexcludable. When consumed by one person, they are also made available to others. National defense, flood control dams, and scientific theories are all public goods.

Purchasing power parity (PPP) A theory stating that the exchange rate between two currencies will exactly reflect the purchasing power of the two currencies.

Pure cash-matched dedicated portfolio A conservative dedicated portfolio management technique aimed at developing a bond portfolio that will provide payments exactly matching the specified liability schedules.

Pure competition A market structure characterized by a large number of small firms producing an identical product in an industry (market area) that permits complete freedom of entry and exit. Also called price-taker markets.

Pure discount instruments Instruments that pay interest as the difference between the amount borrowed and the amount paid back.

Pure factor portfolio A portfolio with sensitivity of 1 to the factor in question and a sensitivity of 0 to all other factors.

Pure play method An approach used for estimating the beta of a project in which a firm (1) identifies several companies whose only business is the project in question, (2) calculates the beta for each firm, and then (3) averages the betas to find an approximation to its own project's beta.

Put An option that gives the holder the right to sell an underlying asset to another party at a fixed price over a specific period of time.

Put-call-forward parity The relationship among puts, calls, and forward contracts.

Put-call parity (1) The theoretical relation between a put and a call option with the same underlying strike price, asset, and expiration. (2) An equation expressing the equivalence (parity) of a portfolio of a call and a bond with a portfolio of a put and the underlying, which leads to the relationship between put and call prices.

Put option (1) A contract giving the right to sell an asset at a specified price, on or before a specified date. (2) Options to sell a firm's common stock within a certain period at a specified price.

Put-call parity The relationship that must exist in an efficient market between the prices for put and call options having the same underlying asset, exercise price, and expiration date.

p-**Value** The smallest level of significance at which the null hypothesis can be rejected; also called the marginal significance level.

Quadratic optimization A technique that relies on historical correlations in order to construct a portfolio that seeks to minimize tracking error with an index.

Qualitative dependent variables Dummy variables used as dependent variables rather than as independent variables.

Quality financial statements Financial statements that most knowledgeable observers (analysts, portfolio managers) would consider conservatively prepared in terms of sales, expenses, earnings, and asset valuations. The results reported would reflect reasonable estimates and indicate what truly happened during the period and the legitimate value of assets and liabilities on the balance sheet.

Quantile (or fractile) A value at or below which a stated fraction of the data lies.

Quantity theory of money A theory that hypothesizes that a change in the money supply will cause a proportional change in the price level because velocity and real output are unaffected by the quantity of money.

Quanto An option in which the foreign exchange risk in the underlying asset has been removed.

Quartiles Quantiles that divide a distribution into four equal parts.

Quintiles Quantiles that divide a distribution into five equal parts.

Random number An observation drawn from a uniform distribution.

Random number generator An algorithm that produces uniformly distributed random numbers between 0 and 1.

Random variable A quantity whose future outcomes are uncertain.

Random walk A time series in which the value of the series in one period is the value of the series in the previous period plus an unpredictable random error.

Random walk theory (1) The theory that current stock prices already reflect known information about the future. Therefore, the future movement of stock prices will be determined by surprise occurrences. This will cause them to change in a random fashion. (2) A theory stating that all current information is reflected in current security prices and that future price movements are random because they are caused by unexpected news.

Range The difference between the maximum and minimum values in a dataset.

Range forward A trading strategy based on a variation of the put-call parity model where, for the same underlying asset but different exercise prices, a call option is purchased and a put option is sold (or vice versa).

Rate anticipation effect The difference in return because of changing the duration of the portfolio during a period as compared with the portfolio's long-term policy duration.

Rate of unemployment The percentage of persons in the labor force who are unemployed. Mathematically, it is equal to number of persons unemployed/number of persons in the labor force × 100.

Rating evaluation Performed by a credit rating agency, such as Moody's or Standard & Poor's, to assign a rating to an issue's investment quality.

Rational-expectations hypothesis The hypothesis that economic decision makers weigh all available evidence, including information concerning the probable effects of current and future economic policy, when they form their expectations about future economic events (such as the probable future inflation rate).

Rational ignorance effect Voter ignorance resulting from the fact that people perceive their individual votes as unlikely to be decisive. Therefore, they rationally have little incentive to seek the information needed to cast an informed vote.

Rationing An allocation of a limited supply of a good or resource to users who would like to have more of it. Various criteria, including charging a price, can be utilized to allocate the limited supply. When price performs the rationing function, the good or resource is allocated to those willing to give up the most "other things" in order to obtain ownership rights.

Ratio scales A measurement scale that has all the characteristics of interval measurement scales as well as a true zero point as the origin.

Ratio spread An option strategy in which a long position in a certain number of options is offset by a short position in a certain number of other options on the same underlying, resulting in a risk-free position.

Real balance effect The increase in wealth generated by an increase in the purchasing power of a constant money supply as the price level decreases. This wealth effect leads to an inverse relationship between price (level) and quantity demanded in the goods and services market.

Real earnings Earnings adjusted for differences in the general level of prices across time periods or geographic areas. When real earnings are equal, the same bundle of goods and services can be purchased with the earnings.

Real estate investment trusts (REITs) Investment funds that hold portfolios of real estate investments.

Real exchange rate The exchange rate adjusted by the inflation differential between the two countries.

Real foreign currency risk The risk that real prices of consumption goods might not be identical in different countries. Also known as real exchange rate risk or purchasing power risk.

Real GDP GDP adjusted for changes in the price level.

Real interest rate (1) The interest rate adjusted for expected inflation; it indicates the real cost to the borrower (and yield to the lender) in terms of goods and services. (2) The interest rate adjusted by the inflation rate of the country.

Real risk-free rate of interest, k* The rate of interest that would exist on default-free U.S. Treasury securities if no inflation was expected.

Realized capital gains Capital gains that result when an appreciated asset is sold; realized capital gains are taxable.

Realized yield The expected compounded yield on a bond that is sold before it matures assuming the reinvestment of all cash flows at an explicit rate. Also called horizon yield for the yield realized during an investment horizon period.

Real options Options embedded in a firm's real assets that give managers valuable decision-making flexibility, such as the right to either undertake or abandon an investment project.

Real rate of interest The money rate of interest minus the expected rate of inflation. The real rate of interest indicates the interest premium, in terms of real goods and services, that one must pay for earlier availability.

Real risk-free rate (RRFR) The basic interest rate with no accommodation for inflation or uncertainty. The pure time value of money.

Real values Values that have been adjusted for the effects of inflation.

Receiver swaption A swaption that allows the holder to enter into a swap as the fixed-rate receiver and floating-rate payer.

Recession A downturn in economic activity characterized by declining real GDP and rising unemployment. In an effort to be more precise, many economists define a recession as two consecutive quarters in which there is a decline in real GDP.

Recognition lag The time period after a policy change is needed from a stabilization standpoint but before the need is recognized by policymakers.

Refunding issue Bonds that provide funds to prematurely retire another bond issue. These bonds can be either a junior or senior issue.

Registered bond A bond for which ownership is registered with the issuer. The holder receives interest payments by check directly from the issuer.

Regime With reference to a time series, the underlying model generating the times series.

Registered competitive market makers (RCMMs) Members of an exchange who are allowed to use their memberships to buy or sell for their own account within the specific trading obligations set down by the exchange.

Registered traders Members of the stock exchange who are allowed to use their memberships to buy and sell for their own account, which means they save commissions on their trading but they provide liquidity to the market, and they abide by exchange regulations on how they can trade.

Regression coefficients The intercept and slope coefficient(s) of a regression.

Regressive tax A tax in which the average tax rate falls with income. Persons with higher incomes will pay a lower percentage of their income in taxes.

Regulatory risk The risk associated with the uncertainty of how derivative transactions will be regulated or with changes in regulations.

Reinvestment rate assumption The assumption that cash flows from a project can be reinvested (1) at the cost of capital, if using the NPV method, or (2) at the internal rate of return, if using the IRR method.

Reinvestment rate risk The risk that a decline in interest rates will lead to lower income when bonds mature and funds are reinvested.

Rejection point (or critical value) A value against which a computed test statistic is compared to decide whether to reject or not reject the null hypothesis.

Relative dispersion The amount of dispersion relative to a reference value or benchmark.

Relative frequency With reference to an interval of grouped data, the number of observations in the interval divided by the total number of observations in the sample.

Relative-strength (RS) ratio The ratio of a stock price or an industry index value to a market indicator series, indicating the stock's or the industry's performance relative to the overall market.

Relevant cash flows The specific cash flows that should be considered in a capital budgeting decision.

Rent seeking Actions by individuals and interest groups designed to restructure public policy in a manner that will either directly or indirectly redistribute more income to themselves.

Repeat-purchase item An item purchased often by the same buyer.

Replacement analysis An analysis involving the decision of whether or not to replace an existing asset with a new asset.

Replacement chain (common life) approach A method of comparing projects of unequal lives which assumes that each project can be repeated as many times as necessary to reach a common life span; the NPVs over this life span are then compared, and the project with the higher common life NPV is chosen.

Replacement rate The share of previous earnings replaced by unemployment benefits.

Replacement value The market value of a swap.

Required rate of return The return that compensates investors for their time, the expected rate of inflation, and the uncertainty of the return.

Reserve borrowing capacity The ability to borrow money at a reasonable cost when good investment opportunities arise. Firms often use less debt than specified by the MM optimal capital structure to ensure that they can obtain debt capital later if they need to.

Residual autocorrelations The sample autocorrelations of the residuals.

Residual claimants Individuals who personally receive the excess, if any, of revenues over costs. Residual claimants gain if the firm's costs are reduced or revenues increased.

Residual Dividend Model A model in which the dividend paid is set equal to the actual earnings minus the amount of retained earnings necessary to finance the firm's optimal capital budget.

Residual effect The return on a bond portfolio after taking account of the three prior factors—yield to maturity, interest rate effect, and sector/quality effect.

Resistance level A price at which a technician would expect a substantial increase in the supply of a stock to reverse a rising trend.

Resource An input used to produce economic goods. Land, labor, skills, natural resources, and capital are examples. Throughout history, people have struggled to transform available, but limited, resources into things they would like to have—economic goods.

Resource market 1) A highly aggregated market encompassing all resources (labor, physical capital, land, and entrepreneurship) that contribute to the production of current out-put. The labor market forms the largest component of this market. 2) Markets in which business firms demand factors of production (for example, labor, capital, and natural resources) from household suppliers. The resources are then used to produce goods and services. This market is sometimes called factor markets or input markets.

Resource mobility The ease with which factors of production are able to move among alternative uses. Resources that can easily be transferred to a different use or location are said to be highly mobile. Resources with few alternative uses are immobile.

Restrictive fiscal policy A reduction in government expenditures and/or an increase in tax rates such that the expected size of the budget deficit declines (or the budget surplus increases).

Restrictive monetary policy A shift in monetary policy designed to reduce aggregate demand and place downward pressure on the general level of prices (or the rate of inflation). Bond sales by the Fed, a decline in bank reserves, and a reduction in the growth rate of the money supply are generally indicative of a restrictive monetary policy.

Return prediction studies Studies wherein investigations attempt to predict the time series of future rates of return using public information. An example would be predicting above-average returns for the stock market based on the aggregate dividend yield—e.g., high dividend yield indicates above average future market returns.

Revenue bond A bond that is serviced by the income generated from specific revenue-producing projects of the municipality.

Rho The sensitivity of the option price to the risk-free rate.

Ricardian equivalence The view that a tax reduction financed with government debt will exert no impact on current consumption and aggregate demand because people will fully recognize the higher future taxes implied by the additional debt.

Right-to-work laws Laws that prohibit the union shop, the requirement that employees must join a union as a condition of employment. Each state has the option to adopt (or reject) right-to-work legislation.

Rising trend channel The range defined by security prices as they move progressively higher.

Risk The uncertainty that an investment will earn its expected rate of return.

Risk allocation The decomposition of the risk of a portfolio into the various risk exposures taken by a manager.

Risk-adjusted discount rate The discount rate that applies to a particular risky stream of income; the riskier the project's income stream, the higher the discount rate.

Risk aversion Describes the fact that investors want to minimize risk for the same level of expected return. To take more risk, they require compensation by a risk premium.

Risk budgeting (1) In a portfolio management context, the setting of risk limits for individual managers. (2) The establishment of objectives for individuals, groups, or divisions of an organization that takes into account the allocation of an acceptable level of risk.

Risk-free asset An asset with returns that exhibit zero variance.

Risk governance The setting of overall policies and standards in risk management.

Risk management The process of identifying the level of risk an entity wants, measuring the level of risk the entity currently has, taking actions that bring the actual level of risk to the desired level of risk, and monitoring the new actual level of risk so that it continues to be aligned with the desired level of risk.

Risk-neutral probabilities Weights that are used to compute a binomial option price. They are the probabilities that would apply if a risk-neutral investor valued an option.

Risk-neutral valuation The process by which options and other derivatives are priced by treating investors as though they were risk neutral.

Risk premium (1) The difference between the expected return on an asset and the risk-free interest rate. (2) The increase over the nominal risk-free rate that investors demand as compensation for an investment's uncertainty. (3) The expected return on an investment minus the risk-free rate.

Risky asset An asset with uncertain future returns.

Robust The quality of being relatively unaffected by a violation of assumptions.

Robust standard errors Standard errors of the estimated parameters of a regression that correct for the presence of heteroskedasticity in the regression's error term.

Root mean squared error (RMSE)   The square root of the average squared forecast error; used to compare the out-of-sample forecasting performance of forecasting models.

Roy's safety first criterion   A criterion asserting that the optimal portfolio is the one that minimizes the probability that portfolio return falls below a threshold level.

RS ratio   *See* Relative-strength ratio.

Rule of 70   If a variable grows at a rate of x percent per year, $70/x$ will approximate the number of years required for the variable to double.

Rule of 72   The principle that the approximate number of years necessary for an investment to double is 72 divided by the stated interest rate.

Runs test   A test of the weak-form efficient market hypothesis that checks for trends that persist longer in terms of positive or negative price changes than one would expect for a random series.

Safety-first rules   Rules for portfolio selection that focus on the risk that portfolio value will fall below some minimum acceptable level over some time horizon.

Samaritan's dilemma   General assistance to those with low incomes reduces the opportunity cost of choices that lead to poverty. Thus, there is a conflict between providing income transfers to the poor and discouragement of behavior that increases the incidence of poverty.

Sample   A subset of a population.

Sample excess kurtosis   A sample measure of the degree of a distribution's peakedness in excess of the normal distribution's peakedness.

Sample kurtosis   A sample measure of the degree of a distribution's peakedness.

Sample mean   The sum of the sample observations, divided by the sample size.

Sample selection bias   Bias introduced by systematically excluding some members of the population according to a particular attribute—for example, the bias introduced when data availability leads to certain observations being excluded from the analysis.

Sample skewness   A sample measure of degree of asymmetry of a distribution.

Sample standard deviation   The positive square root of the sample variance.

Sample statistic or statistic   A quantity computed from or used to describe a sample.

Sample variance   A sample measure of the degree of dispersion of a distribution, calculated by dividing the sum of the squared deviations from the sample mean by the sample size (n) minus 1.

Sampling   (1) A technique for constructing a passive index portfolio in which the portfolio manager buys a representative sample of stocks that comprise the benchmark index. (2) The process of obtaining a sample.

Sampling distribution   The distribution of all distinct possible values that a statistic can assume when computed from samples of the same size randomly drawn from the same population.

Sampling error   The difference between the observed value of a statistic and the quantity it is intended to estimate.

Sampling plan   The set of rules used to select a sample.

Sandwich spread   An option strategy that is equivalent to a short butterfly spread.

Saving   The portion of after-tax income that is not spent on consumption. Saving is a "flow" concept.

Savings and loan associations   Financial institutions that accept deposits in exchange for shares that pay dividends. Historically, these funds have been channeled into residential mortgage loans. Under banking legislation adopted in 1980, S&Ls are permitted to offer a broad range of services similar to those of commercial banks.

Say's Law   The view that production creates its own demand. Demand will always be sufficient to purchase the goods produced because the income payments to the resource suppliers will equal the value of the goods produced.

Scalper   A trader who offers to buy or sell futures contracts, holding the position for only a brief period of time. Scalpers attempt to profit by buying at the bid price and selling at the higher ask price.

Scarcity   Fundamental concept of economics that indicates that there is less of a good freely available from nature than people would like.

Scatter plot   A two-dimensional plot of pairs of observations on two data series.

Scenario analysis   A risk management technique involving the examination of the performance of a portfolio under specified situations. Closely related to stress testing.

Scientific thinking   Development of a theory from basic postulates and the testing of the implications of that theory as to their consistency with events in the real world. Good theories are consistent with and help explain real-world events. Theories that are inconsistent with the real world are invalid and must be rejected.

Seasoned equity issues   New equity shares offered by firms that already have stock outstanding.

Seats   Memberships in a derivatives exchange.

Secondary effects   Consequences of an economic change that are not immediately identifiable but are felt only with the passage of time.

Secondary market (1) Market where financial institutions aid in the buying and selling of existing securities. (2) The market in which outstanding securities are bought and sold by owners other than the issuers.

Sector/quality effect The return on a bond portfolio caused by changing yield spreads between bonds in different sectors and with different quality ratings.

Sector rotation strategy An active strategy that involves purchasing stocks in specific industries or stocks with specific characteristics (low P/E, growth, value) that are anticipated to rise in value more than the overall market.

Secured (senior) bond A bond backed by a legal claim on specified assets of the issuer.

Security market indicator series An index created as a statistical measure of the performance of an entire market or segment of a market based on a sample of securities from the market or segment of a market.

Security market line (SML) (1) The line that reflects the combination of risk and return of alternative investments. In CAPM risk is measured by systematic risk (beta). (2) The graph of the capital asset pricing model.

Seed stage With reference to venture capital financing, the stage associated with product development and market research.

Semideviation The positive square root of semivariance (sometimes called semistandard deviation).

Semilogarithmic Describes a scale constructed so that equal intervals on the vertical scale represent equal rates of change, and equal intervals on the horizontal scale represent equal amounts of change.

Semistrong-form efficient market hypothesis The belief that security prices fully reflect all publicly available information, including information from security transactions and company, economic, and political news.

Semivariance The average squared deviation below the mean.

Sensitivity analysis A risk analysis technique in which key variables are changed one at a time and the resulting changes in the NPV and IRR are observed.

Separation theorem The proposition that the investment decision, which involves investing in the market portfolio on the capital market line, is separate from the financing decision, which targets a specific point on the CML based on the investor's risk preference.

Serially correlated With reference to regression errors, errors that are correlated across observations.

Serial obligation bond A bond issue that has a series of maturity dates.

Settlement date or payment date The date on which the parties to a swap make payments.

Settlement period The time between settlement dates.

Settlement price (1) The official closing price of a futures contract set by the clearinghouse at the end of the day and used for marking to market. (2) The price determined by the exchange clearinghouse with which futures contract margin accounts are marked to market. (3) The official price, designated by the clearinghouse, from which daily gains and losses will be determined and marked to market.

Settlement risk When settling a contract, the risk that one party could be in the process of paying the counterparty while the counterparty is declaring bankruptcy.

Severance pay Pay by an employer to an employee upon the termination of employment with the firm.

Shareholders' equity Total assets minus total liabilities.

Sharpe ratio (1) The ratio of mean excess return (return minus the risk-free rate) to standard deviation of returns (or excess returns). (2) The average return in excess of the risk-free rate divided by the standard deviation of return; a measure of the average excess return earned per unit of standard deviation of return.

Shirking Working at less than a normal rate of productivity, thus reducing output. Shirking is more likely when workers are not monitored, so that the cost of lower output falls on others.

Short The seller of a derivative contract. Also refers to the position of being short a derivative.

Shortage A condition in which the amount of a good offered for sale by producers is less than the amount demanded by buyers at the existing price. An increase in price would eliminate the shortage.

Shortfall risk The risk that portfolio value will fall below some minimum acceptable level over some time horizon.

Short hedge (1) A hedge involving the sale of forward or futures contracts to cover the risk of a long position in the spot market. (2) A short position in a forward or futures contract used to offset the price volatility of a long position in the underlying asset.

Short run (in production) A time period so short that a firm is unable to vary some of its factors of production. The firm's plant size typically cannot be altered in the short run.

Short sale (1) The sale of a security not owned by the seller at the time of trade. (2) The sale of borrowed securities with the intention of repurchasing them later at a lower price and earning the difference.

Shortsightedness effect Misallocation of resources that results because public-sector action is biased (1) in favor of proposals yielding clearly defined current benefits in exchange for difficult-to-identify future costs and (2) against proposals with clearly identifiable current costs but yielding less concrete and less obvious future benefits.

Shutdown A temporary halt in the operation of a business firm. Because the firm anticipates returning to the market in the future, it does not sell its assets and go out of business. The firm's variable cost is eliminated by the shutdown, but its fixed costs continue.

Signal An action taken by a firm's management which provides clues to investors about how management views the firm's prospects.

Simple interest The interest earned each period on the original investment; interest calculated on the principal only.

Simple random sample A subset of a larger population created in such a way that each element of the population has an equal probability of being selected to the subset.

Simulation trial A complete pass through the steps of a simulation.

Single-payment loan A loan in which the borrower receives a sum of money at the start and pays back the entire amount with interest in a single payment at maturity.

Sinking fund (1) Bond provision that requires the bond to be paid off progressively rather than in full at maturity. (2) Bond provision that requires the issuer to redeem some or all of the bond systematically over the term of the bond rather than in full at maturity.

Skewed Not symmetrical.

Skewness A quantitative measure of skew (lack of symmetry); a synonym of skew.

Small-firm effect A frequent empirical anomaly where risk-adjusted stock returns for companies with low market capitalization (i.e., share price multiplied by number of outstanding shares) are significantly larger than those generated by high market capitalization firms.

Socialism A system of economic organization in which (1) the ownership and control of the basic means of production rest with the state, and (2) resource allocation is determined by centralized planning rather than by market forces.

Soft dollars A form of compensation to a money manager generated when the manager commits the investor to paying higher brokerage fees in exchange for the manager receiving additional services (e.g., stock research) from the broker.

Sovereign risk The risk that a government may default on its debt.

Spearman rank correlation coefficient A measure of correlation applied to ranked data.

Special Drawing Right (SDR) An artificial official reserve asset held on the books of the IMF.

Special-interest issue An issue that generates substantial individual benefits to a small minority while imposing a small individual cost on many other voters. In total, the net cost to the majority might either exceed or fall short of the net benefits to the special-interest group.

Specialist The major market maker on U.S. stock exchanges who acts as a broker or dealer to ensure the liquidity and smooth functions of the secondary stock market.

Special purpose vehicles (SPVs) *See* Enhanced derivatives products companies (EDPC).

Speculative company A firm with a great degree of business and/or financial risk, with commensurate high earnings potential.

Speculative stock A stock that appears to be highly overpriced compared to its reasonable valuation.

Spending phase Phase in the investment life cycle during which individuals' earning years end as they retire. They pay for expenses with income from social security and returns from prior investments and invest to protect against inflation.

Spot price Current market price of an asset. Also called cash price.

Spot rate The required yield for a cash flow to be received at some specific date in the future—for example, the spot rate for a flow to be received in one year, for a cash flow in two years, and so on.

Spread (1) Difference between the ask and the bid quotations. Also refers to a mark-up paid by a given borrower over the market interest rate paid by a top-quality borrower. (2) A trading strategy where long and short positions in two call (or two put) option contracts having the same underlying asset but different exercise prices or expiration dates are combined to create a customized return distribution. (3) An option strategy involving the purchase of one option and sale of another option that is identical to the first in all respects except either exercise price or expiration.

Spurious correlation A correlation that misleadingly points towards associations between variables.

Stand-alone risk The risk an asset would have if it were a firm's only asset and if investors only owned one stock. It is measured by the variability of the asset's expected returns.

Standard deviation (1) A measure of variability equal to the square root of the variance. (2) The positive square root of the variance; a measure of dispersion in the same units as the original data.

Standardized beta With reference to fundamental factor models, the value of the attribute for an asset minus the average value of the attribute across all stocks, divided by the standard deviation of the attribute across all stocks.

Standardizing A transformation that involves subtracting the mean and dividing the result by the standard deviation.

Standard normal distribution (or unit normal distribution) The normal density with mean (μ) equal to 0 and standard deviation (σ) equal to 1.

Stated annual interest rate or quoted interest rate A quoted interest rate that does not account for compounding within the year.

Statement of cash flows A financial statement that shows the effects on the firm's cash flow of income flows and changes in its balance sheet.

Static yield spread Yield spreads that consider a spread over the total term structure.

Statistic A quantity computed from or used to describe a sample of data.

Statistical factor models A multifactor model in which statistical methods are applied to a set of historical returns to determine portfolios that best explain either historical return covariances or variances.

Statistical inference Making forecasts, estimates, or judgments about a larger group from a smaller group actually observed; using a sample statistic to infer the value of an unknown population parameter.

Statistically significant A result indicating that the null hypothesis can be rejected; with reference to an estimated regression coefficient, frequently understood to mean a result indicating that the corresponding population regression coefficient is different from 0.

Statistics The science of describing, analyzing, and drawing conclusions from data; also, a collection of numerical data.

Stock dividend A dividend paid in the form of additional shares rather than in cash.

Stock index arbitrage A trading strategy involving a long position in a stock portfolio and a short position in a stock index futures contract (or vice versa) designed to exploit a mispricing in the futures contract relative to the underlying index.

Stock options The option to buy a specified number of shares of the firm's stock at a designated price. The designated price is generally set so that the options will be quite valuable if the firm's shares increase in price, but of little value if their price falls. Thus, when used to compensate top managers, stock options provide a strong incentive to follow policies that will increase the value of the firm.

Stock repurchase A transaction in which a firm buys back shares of its own stock, thereby decreasing shares outstanding, increasing EPS, and, often, increasing the stock price.

Stock split An action taken by a firm to increase the number of shares outstanding, such as doubling the number of shares outstanding by giving each stockholder two new shares for each one formerly held.

Storage costs or carrying costs The costs of holding an asset, generally a function of the physical characteristics of the underlying asset.

Store of value An asset that will allow people to transfer purchasing power from one period to the next.

Straddle (1) A trading strategy requiring the simultaneous purchase of a call option and a put option having the same exercise price, underlying asset, and expiration date. Variations of this theme include strips, straps, strangles, and chooser options. (2) An option strategy involving the purchase of a put and a call with the same exercise price. A straddle is based on the expectation of high volatility of the underlying.

Straight bond Refers to a plain-vanilla bond with fixed coupon payments and without any optional clauses.

Strangle A variation of a straddle in which the put and call have different exercise prices.

Strap An option strategy involving the purchase of two calls and one put.

Strategic asset allocation The allocation to the major investment asset classes that is determined to be appropriate, given the investor's long-run investment objectives and constraints.

Strategic Business Plan A long-run plan which outlines in broad terms the firm's basic strategy for the next 5 to 10 years.

Stratified random sampling A procedure by which a population is divided into subpopulations (strata) based on one or more classification criteria. Simple random samples are then drawn from each stratum in sizes proportional to the relative size of each stratum in the population. These samples are then pooled.

Stress testing A risk management technique in which the risk manager examines the performance of the portfolio under market conditions involving high risk and usually high correlations across markets. Closely related to scenario analysis.

Stress testing/scenario analysis A set of techniques for estimating losses in extremely unfavorable combinations of events or scenarios.

Strike An action of unionized employees in which they (a) discontinue working for the employer and (b) take steps to prevent other potential workers from offering their services to the employer.

Strike price Price at which an option can be exercised (same as exercise price).

Strip An option strategy involving the purchase of two puts and one call.

Strong-form efficient market hypothesis The belief that security prices fully reflect all information from both public and private sources.

Structural change Economic trend occurring when the economy is undergoing a major change in organization or in how it functions.

Structural unemployment Unemployment due to the structural characteristics of the economy that make it difficult for job seekers to find employment and for employers to hire workers. Although job openings are available, they generally require skills that differ from those of the unemployed workers.

Structured note (1) A bond or note issued with some unusual, often option-like, clause. (2) A bond with an embedded derivative designed to create a payoff distribution that satisfies the needs of a specific investor clientele. (3) A variation of a floating-rate note that has some type of unusual characteristic such as a leverage factor or in which the rate moves opposite to interest rates.

Style analysis An attempt to explain the variability in the observed returns to a security portfolio in terms of the movements in the returns to a series of benchmark portfolios designed to capture the essence of a particular security characteristic such as size, value, and growth.

Style grid A graph used to classify and display the investment style that best defines the nature of a security portfolio.

Subjective probability A probability drawing on personal or subjective judgment.

Subordinate (junior) bonds Debentures that, in case of default, entitle holders to claims on the issuer's assets only after the claims of holders of senior debentures and mortgage bonds are satisfied.

Substitutes Products that serve similar purposes. They are related such that an increase in the price of one will cause an increase in demand for the other (for example, hamburgers and tacos, butter and margarine, Chevrolets and Fords).

Substitution effect That part of an increase (decrease) in amount consumed that is the result of a good being cheaper (more expensive) in relation to other goods because of a reduction (increase) in price.

Sunk cost A cash outlay that has already been incurred and which cannot be recovered regardless of whether the project is accepted or rejected.

Supply shock An unexpected event that temporarily either increases or decreases aggregate supply.

Supply-side economists Modern economists who believe that changes in marginal tax rates exert important effects on aggregate supply.

Support level A price at which a technician would expect a substantial increase in price and volume for a stock to reverse a declining trend that was due to profit taking.

Surplus A condition in which the amount of a good offered for sale by producers is greater than the amount that buyers will purchase at the existing price. A decline in price would eliminate the surplus.

Surprise The actual value of a variable minus its predicted (or expected) value.

Survivorship bias The bias resulting from a test design that fails to account for companies that have gone bankrupt, merged, or are otherwise no longer reported in a database.

Sustainable growth rate A measure of how fast a firm can grow using internal equity and debt financing and a constant capital structure. Equal to retention rate × ROE.

Swap (1) A contract whereby two parties agree to a periodic exchange of cash flows. In certain types of swaps, only the net difference between the amounts owed is exchanged on each payment date. (2) An agreement between two parties to exchange a series of future cash flows.

Swap spread (1) A measure of the risk premium for an interest rate swap, calculated as the difference between the agreement's fixed rate and the yield on a Treasury bond with the same maturity. (2) The difference between the fixed rate on an interest rate swap and the rate on a Treasury note with equivalent maturity; it reflects the general level of credit risk in the market.

Swaption (1) An option to enter into a swap contract at a later date. (2) An option to enter into a swap.

SWOT analysis An examination of a firm's Strength, Weaknesses, Opportunities, and Threats. This analysis helps an analyst evaluate a firm's strategies to exploit its competitive advantages or defend against its weaknesses.

Symmetric information The situation in which investors and managers have identical information about firms' prospects.

Synthetic call The combination of puts, the underlying, and risk-free bonds that replicates a call option.

Synthetic forward contract   The combination of the underlying, puts, calls, and risk-free bonds that replicates a forward contract.

Synthetic index fund   An index fund position created by combining risk-free bonds and futures on the desired index.

Synthetic put   The combination of calls, the underlying, and risk-free bonds that replicates a put option.

Systematic factors   Factors that affect the average returns of a large number of different assets.

Systematic risk   The variability of returns that is due to macroeconomic factors that affect all risky assets. Because it affects all risky assets, it cannot be eliminated by diversification.

Systematic sampling   A procedure of selecting every kth member until reaching a sample of the desired size. The sample that results from this procedure should be approximately random.

Tactical asset allocation   (1) Short-term adjustments to the long-term asset allocation to reflect views on the current relative attractiveness of asset classes. (2) An investment strategy that adjusts the investor's mix of stocks and bonds by increasing the allocation to the asset class that is relatively undervalued.

Tangible book value per share   Common shareholders' equity minus intangible assets from the balance sheet, divided by the number of shares outstanding.

Tap   Procedure by which a borrower can keep issuing additional amounts of an old bond at its current market value. This procedure is used for bond issues, notably by the British and French governments, as well as for some short-term debt instruments.

Target capital structure   The mix of debt, preferred stock, and common equity with which the firm plans to raise capital.

Target (optimal) Capital Structure   The percentages of debt, preferred stock, and common equity that will maximize the firm's stock price.

Target payout ratio   The percentage of net income paid out as cash dividends.

Target semideviation   The positive square root of target semivariance.

Target semivariance   The average squared deviation below a target value.

Tariff   A tax levied on goods imported into a country.

Tax base   The level or quantity of the economic activity that is taxed (e.g., gallons of gasoline sold per week). Because they make the activity less attractive, higher tax rates reduce the level of the tax base.

Tax incidence   The manner in which the burden of a tax is distributed among economic units (consumers, producers, employees, employers, and so on). The actual tax burden does not always fall on those who are statutorily assigned to pay the tax.

Tax rate   The per-unit amount of the tax or the percentage rate at which the economic activity is taxed.

Tax risk   The uncertainty associated with tax laws.

t-Distribution   A symmetrical distribution defined by a single parameter, degrees of freedom, that is largely used to make inferences concerning the mean of a normal distribution whose variance is unknown.

Team production   A process of production wherein employees work together under the supervision of the owner or the owner's representative.

Technical analysis   (1) A forecasting method for asset prices based solely on information about past prices. (2) Estimation of future security price movements based on past price and volume movements.

Technological advancement   The introduction of new techniques or methods that enable production of a greater output per unit of input.

Tenor   The original time to maturity on a swap.

Term bond   A bond that has a single maturity date.

Terminal price multiple   The price multiple for a stock assumed to hold at a stated future time.

Termination date   The date of the final payment on a swap; also, the swap's expiration date.

Term structure   *See* Yield curve.

Term structure of interest rates   The relationship between term to maturity and yield to maturity for a sample of comparable bonds at a given time. Popularly known as the yield curve.

Term to maturity   Specifies the date or the number of years before a bond matures or expires.

Test statistic   A quantity, calculated based on a sample, whose value is the basis for deciding whether or not to reject the null hypothesis.

Theta   The rate at which an option's time value decays.

Third market   Over-the-counter trading of securities listed on an exchange.

Tick   The minimum price movement for the asset underlying a forward or futures contract; for Treasury bonds, one tick equals 1/32 of 1 percent of par value.

Time-period bias   The possibility that when we use a time-series sample, our statistical conclusion may be sensitive to the starting and ending dates of the sample.

Time preferences for consumption   The preferences of consumers for current consumption as opposed to savings for future consumption.

Time premium   The difference between an option's total market value and its intrinsic value.

Time-series analysis   An examination of a firm's performance data over a period of time.

Time-series data   Observations of a variable over time.

Time to expiration   The time remaining in the life of a derivative, typically expressed in years.

Time value decay   The loss in the value of an option resulting from movement of the option price toward its payoff value as the expiration day approaches.

Time value of money   The principles governing equivalence relationships between cash flows with different dates.

Time value or speculative value   The difference between the market price of the option and its intrinsic value, determined by the uncertainty of the underlying over the remaining life of the option.

Time-weighted rate of return   The compound rate of growth of one unit of currency invested in a portfolio during a stated measurement period; a measure of investment performance that is not sensitive to the timing and amount of withdrawals or additions to the portfolio.

Time-weighted return   (1) A rate of return measure that captures the rate of return per unit of currency initially invested. (2) The geometric average of (one plus) the holding period yields to an investment portfolio.

Times-interest-earned (TIE) ratio   A ratio that measures the firm's ability to meet its annual interest obligations, calculated by dividing earnings before interest and taxes by interest charges.   TIE = EBIT/I.

Tombstone (or Tumbstone)   Advertisement that states the borrower's name, gives the conditions of an issue, and lists the various banks taking part in the issue.

Top-down   With respect to investment approaches, the allocation of money first to categories such as asset classes, countries, or industry followed by the selection of individual securities within category.

Total cost   The costs, both explicit and implicit, of all the resources used by the firm. Total cost includes an imputed normal rate of return for the firm's equity capital.

Total fixed cost   The sum of the costs that do not vary with output. They will be incurred as long as a firm continues in business and the assets have alternative uses.

Total probability rule for expected value   A rule explaining the expected value of a random variable in terms of expected values of the random variable conditional on mutually exclusive and exhaustive scenarios.

Total product   The total output of a good that is associated with alternative utilization rates of a variable input.

Total return   A return objective in which the investor wants to increase the portfolio value to meet a future need by both capital gains and current income investment.

Total return swap   A swap in which one party agrees to pay the total return on a security. Often used as a credit derivative, in which the underlying is a bond.

Total variable cost   The sum of those costs that rise as output increases. Examples of variable costs are wages paid to workers and payments for raw materials.

Tournament pay   A form of compensation where the top performer (or performers) receives much higher rewards than other competitors, even if the others perform at only a slightly lower level.

Tracking error   (1) The standard deviation of the difference in returns between an active investment portfolio and its benchmark portfolio; also called tracking error volatility. (2) The condition in which the performance of a portfolio does not match the performance of an index that serves as the portfolio's benchmark. (3) A synonym for tracking risk and active risk; also, the total return on a portfolio (gross of fees) minus the total return on a benchmark.

Tracking portfolio   A portfolio having factor sensitivities that are matched to those of a benchmark or other portfolio.

Tracking risk   The standard deviation of the differences between a portfolio's returns and its benchmark's returns; a synonym of active risk.

Trade balance   The balance of a country's exports and imports; part of the current account.

Trade deficit   The situation when a country's imports of goods and services are greater than its exports.

Trade surplus   The situation when a country's exports of goods and services are greater than its imports.

Trading effect   The difference in performance of a bond portfolio from that of a chosen index due to short-run changes in the composition of the portfolio.

Trading rule   A formula for deciding on current transactions based on historical data.

Trading turnover   The percentage of outstanding shares traded during a period of time.

Trailing P/E (or current P/E)   A stock's current market price divided by the most recent four quarters of earnings per share.

Tranche   Refers to a portion of an issue that is designed for a specific category of investors. French for "slice."

Transaction accounts   Accounts, including demand deposits and interest-earning checkable deposits, against which the account holder is permitted to transfer funds for the purpose of making payment to a third party.

Transaction costs   (1) The time, effort, and other resources needed to search out, negotiate, and consummate an exchange. (2) The cost of executing a trade. Low costs characterize an operationally efficient market.

Transaction exposure   The risk associated with a foreign exchange rate on a specific business transaction such as a purchase or sale.

Translation exposure   The risk associated with the conversion of foreign financial statements into domestic currency.

Translation risk   Risk arising from the translation of the value of an asset or flow from a foreign currency to the domestic currency.

Treasury bill   A negotiable U.S. government security with a maturity of less than one year that pays no periodic interest but yields the difference between its par value and its discounted purchase price.

Treasury bond   A U.S. government security with a maturity of more than 10 years that pays interest periodically.

Treasury note   A U.S. government security with maturities of 1 to 10 years that pays interest periodically.

Tree diagram   A diagram with branches emanating from nodes representing either mutually exclusive chance events or mutually exclusive decisions.

Trend   A long-term pattern of movement in a particular direction.

Treynor measure   A relative measure of a portfolio's benefit-to-risk ratio, calculated as its average return in excess of the risk-free rate divided by its beta coefficient.

Triangular arbitrage   With respect to currencies, an arbitrage involving three currencies only.

Trimmed mean   A mean computed after excluding a stated small percentage of the lowest and highest observations.

Trough   The culmination of a bear market at which prices stop declining and begin rising.

t-Test   A hypothesis test using a statistic (t-statistic) that follows a t-distribution.

12b-1 plan   A fee charged by some funds, named after the SEC rule that permits it. Such fees pay for distribution costs, such as advertising, or for brokers' commissions. The fund's prospectus details any 12b-1 charges that apply.

Two-sided hypothesis test (or two-tailed hypothesis test)   A test in which the null hypothesis is rejected in favor of the alternative hypothesis if the evidence indicates that the population parameter is either smaller or larger than a hypothesized value.

Type I error   The error of rejecting a true null hypothesis.

Type II error   The error of not rejecting a false null hypothesis.

Unanticipated change   A change that decision makers could not reasonably foresee. Thus, choices made prior to the event did not take the event into account.

Unanticipated inflation   An increase in the general level of prices that was not expected by most decision makers.

Unbiasedness   Lack of bias. A desirable property of estimators, an unbiased estimator is one whose expected value (the mean of its sampling distribution) equals the parameter it is intended to estimate.

Unconditional heteroskedasticity   Heteroskedasticity of the error term that is not correlated with the values of the independent variable(s) in the regression.

Unconditional probability (or marginal probability)   The probability of an event not conditioned on another event.

Uncovered interest rate parity   The assertion that expected currency depreciation should offset the interest differential between two countries over the term of the interest rate.

Underfunded plan   A defined benefit pension plan in which the present value of the fund's liabilities to employees exceeds the value of the fund's assets.

Underground economy   Unreported barter and cash transactions that take place outside recorded market channels. Some are otherwise legal activities undertaken to evade taxes. Others involve illegal activities, such as trafficking in drugs and prostitution.

Underlying   (1) Refers to a security on which a derivative contract is written. (2) An asset that trades in a market in which buyers and sellers meet, decide on a price, and the seller then delivers the asset to the buyer and receives payment. The underlying is the asset or other derivative on which a particular derivative is based. The market for the underlying is also referred to as the spot market.

Underweighted   A condition in which a portfolio, for whatever reason, includes less of a class of securities that the relative market value alone would justify.

Underlying earnings (or persistent earnings or continuing earnings or core earnings) Earnings excluding nonrecurring components.

Unemployed The term used to describe a person not currently employed who is either (1) actively seeking employment or (2) waiting to begin or return to a job.

Unexpected earnings (earnings surprise) The difference between reported earnings per share and expected earnings per share.

Unitary hedge ratio A hedge ratio equal to 1.

Unit normal distribution *See* Standard normal distribution.

Unit of account The units of measurement used by people to post prices and keep track of revenues and costs.

Unit root A time series that is not covariance stationary is said to have a unit root.

Univariate distribution A distribution that specifies the probabilities for a single random variable.

Unrealized capital gains Capital gains that reflect the price appreciation of currently held unsold assets; taxes on unrealized capital gains can be deferred indefinitely.

Unsecured bonds Bonds that promise payments of interest and principal but pledge no specific assets. Holders have first claim on the issuer's income and unpledged assets. Also known as debentures.

Unsystematic risk Risk that is unique to an asset, derived from its particular characteristics. It can be eliminated in a diversified portfolio.

Unweighted index An indicator series affected equally by the performance of each security in the sample regardless of price or market value. Also referred to as an equal-weighted series.

Unwind The negotiated termination of a forward or futures position before contract maturity.

Uptick An incremental movement upward in a transaction price over the previous transaction price.

Uptick-downtick ratio A ratio of the number of uptick block transactions (indicating buyers) to the number of downtick block transactions (indicating sellers of blocks). An indicator of institutional investor sentiment.

Up transition probability The probability that an asset's value moves up.

User charges Payments that users (consumers) are required to make if they want to receive certain services provided by the government.

Utility The subjective benefit or satisfaction a person expects from a choice or course of action.

Valuation The process of determining the value of an asset or service.

Valuation analysis An active bond portfolio management strategy designed to capitalize on expected price increases in temporarily undervalued issues.

Valuation process Part of the investment decision process in which you estimate the value of a security.

Value The amount for which one can sell something, or the amount one must pay to acquire something.

Value at risk (VaR) (1) A money measure of the minimum loss that is expected over a given period of time with a given probability. (2) A probability-based measure of loss potential for a company, a fund, a portfolio, a transaction, or a strategy over a specified period of time. (3) A money measure of the minimum value of losses expected during a specified time period at a given level of probability.

Value chain The set of transformations to move from raw material to product or service delivery.

Value of marginal product (VMP) The marginal product of a resource multiplied by the selling price of the product it helps to produce. For a price taker firm, marginal revenue product *(MRP)* will be equal to the value marginal product *(VMP)*.

Value stocks Stocks that appear to be undervalued for reasons besides earnings growth potential. These stocks are usually identified based on high dividend yields, low P/E ratios, or low price-to-book ratios.

Variable-rate note A debt security for which the interest rate changes to follow some specified short-term rate, for example, the T-bill rate; see floating rate note.

Variance (1) A measure of variability equal to the sum of the squares of a return's deviation from the mean, divided by the total number of returns. (2) The expected value (the probability-weighted average) of squared deviations from a random variable's expected value.

Variation margin Profits or losses on open positions in futures and option contracts that are paid or collected daily.

Vega The relationship between option price and volatility.

Volatility (1) A measure of the uncertainty about the future price of an asset. Typically measured by the standard deviation of returns on the asset. (2) As used in option pricing, the standard deviation of the continuously compounded returns on the underlying asset.

Warrant An instrument that allows the holder to purchase a specified number of shares of the firm's common stock from the firm at a specified price for a given period of time.

Weak-form efficient market hypothesis The belief that security prices fully reflect all security market information.

Weighted mean An average in which each observation is weighted by an index of its relative importance.

Weighted-average cost of capital A weighted average of the after-tax required rates of return on a company's common stock, preferred stock, and long-term debt, where the weights are the fraction of each source of financing in the company's target capital structure.

White-corrected standard errors A synonym for robust standard errors.

Wholesale Price Index (WPI) A price index defined on a basket of goods produced.

Winsorized mean A mean computed after assigning a stated percent of the lowest values equal to one specified low value, and a stated percent of the highest values equal to one specified high value.

Withholding tax A tax levied by the country of source on income paid.

Working capital management The management of a company's short-term assets (such as inventory) and short-term liabilities (such as money owed to suppliers).

World Bank A supranational organization of several institutions designed to assist developing countries. The International Bank for Reconstruction and Development (IBRD) and the International Finance Corporation (IFC) are the more important members of the World Bank group.

World Trade Organization (WTO) The new name given to GATT in 1994; it is currently responsible for monitoring and enforcing the multilateral trade agreements among the 133 member countries.

Worst-case scenario An analysis in which all of the input variables are set at their worst reasonably forecasted values.

Write-down A reduction in the value of an asset as stated in the balance sheet.

Writer of an option A term used for the person or institution selling an option and therefore granting the right to exercise it to the buyer of the option.

Yankee bonds Bonds sold in the United States and denominated in U.S. dollars but issued by a foreign firm or government.

Yield The promised rate of return on an investment under certain assumptions.

Yield beta A measure of the sensitivity of a bond's yield to a general measure of bond yields in the market that is used to refine the hedge ratio.

Yield curve A curve showing the relationship between yield (interest rate) and maturity for a set of similar securities. For example, the yield curve can be drawn for U.S. Treasuries or for LIBOR. Typically, different yield curves are drawn for zero-coupon bonds (zero-coupon yield curve) and for coupon bonds quoted at par (par yield curve).

Yield illusion The erroneous expectation that a bond will provide its stated yield to maturity without recognizing the implicit reinvestment assumption related to coupon payments.

Yield spread (1) The difference between the promised yields of alternative bond issues or market segments at a given time relative to yields on treasury issues of equal maturity. (2) The difference between the yield on a bond and the yield on a default-free security, usually a government note, of the same maturity. The yield spread is primarily determined by the market's perception of the credit risk on the bond.

Yield to maturity The total yield on a bond obtained by equating the bond's current market value to the discounted cash flows promised by the bond. Also called actuarial yield.

Yield to worst Given a bond with multiple potential maturity dates and prices due to embedded call options, the practice is to calculate a yield to maturity for each of the call dates and prices and select the lowest yield (the most conservative possible yield) as yield to worst.

Zero-cost collar A transaction in which a position in the underlying is protected by buying a put and selling a call with the premium from the sale of the call offsetting the premium from the purchase of the put. It can also be used to protect a floating-rate borrower against interest rate increases with the premium on a long cap offsetting the premium on a short floor.

Zero-coupon bond (1) A bond paying no coupons until final redemption. Such bonds trade at a discount to their face value so that the price differential (face value minus market price) ultimately provides a return to the investor commensurate with current interest rates. (2) A bond that pays its par value at maturity but no periodic interest payments. Its yield is determined by the difference between its par value and its discounted purchase price. Also called original issue discount (OID) bonds.